GLAM SOCCER!

(A Story of the Colourful Years of
English Football League clubs, 1967-1976.)

Written by Malcolm Stark

Cover Photograph: Roker Park (November 1975) by V. J. Iley

GLAM SOCCER! Logo and book cover design by Jonathan Young

First published by Dog Ear Publishing
4010 W. 86th Street, Ste H
Indianapolis, IN 46268
www.dogearpublishing.net

ISBN: 978-1-4575-2645-9

This book is printed on acid-free paper.

Printed in the United States of America

With very special thanks and love to Nessie.

CONTENTS

INTRODUCTION

IN 1967, ENGLISH FOOTBALL was as strong as it would ever be. England were freshly crowned World Cup Winners, and Manchester United were on the way to their first European Cup triumph, beating Benfica at Wembley in May 1968. The English First Division also saw a terrific four-way battle between favourites Manchester United, Bill Shankly's former Champions Liverpool, Don Revie's mighty Leeds United, and also Manchester City's wondrous counter-attacking style of fluent football, with the brilliant Bell and Oakes, calm and classy, controlling play, pumping fast and slow, slow and fast, commanding the flow and the rhythm of the game like two conductors.

As those four gigantic warships fought their imperial battle, though, a surging underwater turbulence was breaking waves, into swirling currents, tide rips and bubbling maelstroms, and a Deep and Colourful coral reef began to form beneath the wash, sprouting and springing into life.

Football was moving away from the monochrome memories of the Fifties and early Sixties. Pathe News had departed, and proper legends like Lofthouse, Matthews, Milburn, Finney, Haynes and Blanchflower had all thrown their boots into their garden sheds. Their brylcreemed hairstyles, in black and white, were now growing, long and wild, and a new era was dawning, of Match of the Day on Saturday nights, and on **Colour Television,** and also The Big Match on ITV, on Sunday afternoons.

Weekly, glossy magazines, like **SHOOT!** And **GOAL,** portrayed flamboyant superstar players like George Best, Stan Bowles, Tony Currie, Alan Hudson, Peter Osgood, Charlie George and Kevin Keegan, on crisp, sharp, colour poster-sized photos, with trendy long hair, posters destined for the bedroom walls of Girls, as well as Boys.

This story doesn't attempt to argue that the football played between 1967 and 1976, the **GLAM SOCCER!** era, was any better than it was during the 2012-13 season.

Sometimes it was, but sometimes it wasn't. Sure enough, neither of the epic FA Cup Finals between Chelsea and Leeds United, nor the absolutely fabulous romance of Sunderland beating Leeds three years later, has yet to be equalled in any subsequent Cup Final. The mighty six-team title race of 1971-72, and then the unpredictable twelve horse chase of 1974-75, has been succeeded by mostly two-horse races involving only the richest of modern Premier League clubs.

Also, although the England national team were removed as World Champions by the brilliance of Brazil, and also overtaken in Europe by the emerging greatness of both West Germany and Holland, and eventually even by Poland, English club sides were enjoying an almost unprecedented period of dominance in European tournaments, equalled by only one other European country, before or since.

English teams reached the Final of a European tournament for eighteen consecutive seasons, from 1965 until 1982, but during those Glam Soccer year, 1967 to 1976, ten different English clubs had reached European Finals. Only eleven different English teams have reached European Finals during the thirty-seven years since 1976.

Nevertheless, this story doesn't attempt to argue that football now is any worse than during the Glam Soccer years, particularly due to the influence of World Class international talent on the English Premier League, since the early Nineties.

Since 1976, of course, there have been many teams equal to the greatest teams of the *Glam Soccer* era, Leeds United, Liverpool, Derby County, Arsenal, Manchester City, Everton and Manchester United, and all the rest; Chelsea's 2005 team that conceded only fifteen Premier League goals; Manchester United's treble winners; Arsenal's *Invincibles;* Everton's magnificent near treble winners of 1985; Liverpool's mighty conquerors of the Eighties; Manchester City's superstars of 2011-12; Jack Walker's Blackburn Rovers; and Newcastle United's wonderful entertainers from 1994; they were teams that all compared very favourably with the very best of English from 1967 to 1976.

Football at the very highest level in England, though, since 1976, has unfortunately become an increasingly exclusive club.

Twenty teams were genuine title contenders during those ten years between 1967 and 1976. When I say genuine title contenders, I'm suggesting teams that were less than six points behind the First Division leaders -accounting for games in hand- at any time from late February onwards.

During the twenty-one years since the Premier League was founded, only ten clubs have been similarly genuine title contenders, and in the thirteen years since 2000, it's been only six clubs.

And those title races during the Glam Soccer era were also often all-inclusive, extending the full length and breadth of the country, north, east, south, west and middle.

A list of the hundred greatest players from the Glam Soccer years, compared with the hundred best players from the first ten years of the Premier League, 1992 to 2001, provides some obvious, but interesting differences. There is no such definitive list, of course, but I'd argue that eighty per cent of each list would be carved in stone.

The first, and the clearest, difference is that the list of players from 1967 to 1976 consists entirely of British Isles born players, with just a handful from Commonwealth countries. But in the more recent list, half of them are overseas players.

This book doesn't attempt to argue for or against, criticize or praise the influence of foreign players in the modern game. However, while we've enjoyed some marvellous talent in the Premier League, and some of the greatest players that World Soccer has ever seen, the depth of talent of Home Nations players, in various positions, has worn very, very thin in comparison.

Until 1978, the Department of Employment had adopted coldly restrictive rules on the granting of work permits for Football League clubs, and while teams in continental Europe had pulled the very best players out of Germany, Holland, Sweden and Denmark, as well as South America, English football found itself in a period of Splendid Isolation.

Furthermore, while the probable hundred best players from the Premier League years had represented about twenty teams, scattered across six major regions of England, with maybe Norwich and Swindon being isolated exceptions, the hundred greatest players from 1967-76 had played for well over thirty teams, that covered the length, width, top, bottom, heart, lungs, left, right and centre of the whole country; except for Cornwall and Kent, of course.

The Glam Soccer era, between 1967 and 1976, was the last great era of truly British football, when English clubs dominated continental football, and Italian, German, Turkish, Greek and Spanish teams had to cheat to try and beat us, and sometimes, by cheating, they actually did beat us.

It was while we were returning from a holiday in Shropshire, a couple of Summers ago, driving back through the wonderful cider farms amongst the rolling green Herefordshire hills, and with the Malvern Hills in the distance, that the vast scope of English football during the Seventies really grabbed me.

This book wasn't intending to include any freak, **_flash in the pan_**, shock FA Cup fairy-tale stories, but I decided to have a good look at the Hereford United story.

After I then realised that Hereford had to be included, the true significance and the fundamental point of this book hit me hard.

It simply attempts to celebrate that glorious decade of English football, across a decade of Glam Rock, flower power, prog rock, soul, funk and disco, folk and punk.

I settled on the years 1967 to 1976 because I wanted to select a period of time, that appeared less than ten years, and didn't want to start in 1966, because that meant focussing on England's World Cup triumph, a huge story in itself, that extended back into the early Sixties, and it would've carried me further away from the Glam Rock years.

1967 was a great start, as it was the year when Manchester United won the League title, and then set about their glorious European Cup campaign.

1976 was also a good finish, as Liverpool were halfway into their 1976-77 European Cup winning season, and about to become the real Giants of Europe. Two mighty bookends.

Everything else just fell into place. 1967 to 1976 was the perfect period to present English League football at its most colourful, and at the forefront of English Pop culture.

From Ride a White Swan to Bohemian Rhapsody, Pop Culture in England between those years was mostly dominated by Glam Rock.

The airwaves were saturated with exaggerated guitar chords and riffs, the great stomping of silver platform boots, and glittered faces.

While in the Sixties, some players grew their fringes long to resemble the Beatles or the Stones, most players looked like young lawyers. From the very start of the early Seventies, many players properly grew their hair long, with sideburns and beards, and they looked as good as all the pop and rock superstars on Top of the Pops or the Old Grey Whistle Test.

Some were even better looking than Pan's People!

It was the Glam Soccer era, as much as they were the Glam Rock years.

This book attempts to celebrate a Decade of English football, when uniquely, the Whole of England was involved in a golden spell. From the Lake District to the Norfolk Broads; from the Fog, and the Grime, on the Tyne to the Frolicking Yachts down on the bright Solent; from the North Yorkshire Moors, through Derbyshire's Beautiful Peaks, and down to the Malvern and Mendip Hills; from the Dark, Satanic Mill Towns of Lancashire to the water Mills of Constable's Stour Valley; from Smoke Blackened Black Country towns and the Potteries to the Sunny Seaside Resorts of Blackpool and Bournemouth; and from Stainless Steel to Jellied Eels.

There were, during those ten years, at least thirty teams that developed into especially great teams in the long histories of their clubs, teams most fondly remembered by their fans as legends.

In a golden awakening of the English game, attendances had also surged again by 1971. As well as the arrival of Colour Television, making the game appear more… well, colourful, there was a resurgence of football in popular culture.

You just couldn't escape the game. Petrol stations gave away coins, metal photo discs, and white plastic busts of players, with each gallon of petrol sold; jars of strawberry jam had the friendly faces of footballers on their lids; and players advertised beers and cars on billboard posters in cities all over the country. There was something for everyone.

You just couldn't escape the game.

Nineteen different English club sides won at least one major trophy between 1967 and 1976. That is like all but one of the current Premier League clubs winning a major trophy during the next ten years. It's just not going to happen, is it?

To put this fully into context, only eleven different teams won major trophies in the ten seasons following 1976, and more recently, during the eleven seasons between 1996 and 2007, only eight different English teams won a major trophy. Beneath the top four elite of United, Arsenal, Chelsea and Liverpool, English clubs were starving. Football was never so competitive in English league football, in the history of the game, as during those colourful Glam Soccer years.

English Seventeen Football League clubs, nearly a fifth of all league clubs, had also recorded their all-time record home attendances between 1967 and 1975. And this was an era of declining interest in the game, if you chose to listen to some analysts.

Of course, not all of the clubs had their greatest ever teams, in their history, during the Glam Soccer years. For some of these clubs, their teams from those years were rated as low as second-best, At That Time, during their hundred years' history.

You could say, well that's all well and good, but was English football really *that* great during its years of ***Splendid Isolation***, while the rest of Europe were paying record cash amounts for World class Superstars? Well, English clubs filled sixteen of the forty available places in European Finals between 1967 and 1976; that equates to forty per cent of European Finals' places being filled by English club sides during those ten years.

Only during the Nineties, when Italian clubs jam-packed with all of the World's best players filled twenty-five places in European Finals, has any country surpassed the feat of English clubs in European competitions during those Glam Soccer years.

Yes, English clubs were bloody great internationally, as well as in their own First Division.

Over half of the clubs celebrated in this book did undoubtedly field the very greatest football teams in their history, never since bettered, during those Glam Soccer years.

There are no other decades, or similar periods, throughout the entire history of English league football that can proudly boast that fact.

That is well worth celebrating.

A TALE OF TWO UNITEDS, Part One

I N 1968, MANCHESTER UNITED AND LEEDS UNITED both won major European trophies.

In late May, Manchester United had beaten Benfica 4-1 at Wembley to win the European Cup; becoming the first English club team to ever become Champions of Europe.

Then, during August and September, Leeds United beat Ferencvaros, 1-0 on aggregate, to win the Inter Cities Fairs Cup, only their second-ever major trophy.

Manchester United *were* the best team in Europe, but they'd lost their grip on the League title by just two points, to neighbours Manchester City. Leeds United, on the other hand, were a rising force, having finished fourth in the First Division in 1968, after being runners-up in 1965 and 1966.

With an average age of 24.18 years, their young, Fairs Cup winning team looked like they were on the verge of erupting into a dominant force in English and European football, just as Manchester United had done, led by their superstar trio of Best, Charlton and Law.

Manchester United's European Cup winning team had an average age of 25.64 years, only a year and a half older than Leeds United's young, developing side, and seven of them were still under twenty-six years old, but with Everton, Arsenal and Derby County also strongly improving, whilst Liverpool's ageing team was declining, Manchester United still looked forward to a fierce defence of their status as England's greatest club, with the Seventies just around the corner.

However, while Leeds United's team stuck together strongly, just like a family, over the next half-decade, becoming the dominant force they'd envisaged themselves, only two of Manchester United's European Cup winning team were still playing at Old Trafford, just five years after their Wembley win.

Tony Dunne had moved to Bolton Wanderers, while John Aston had joined Luton Town. David Sadler had also dropped into Second Division football, joining his old team-mates Nobby Stiles and Bobby Charlton at Preston North End, while Denis Law had been released by Tommy Docherty, to join neighbours City.

George Best had retired, been suspended, sacked, and then retired again. Paddy Crerand, Bill Foulkes and Shay Brennan had all legitimately retired. Only Brian Kidd and Alex Stepney remained at Manchester United five seasons after their finest hour.

At the time of George Best's second retirement, just after the Festive period of 1973, Manchester United were bottom of Division One, while, contrastingly, Leeds United were leading the table by nine points, and still unbeaten, having lost only Gary Sprake to Birmingham City, and also Jack Charlton to retirement, from their Fairs Cup winning team. How the hell did they end up there?

Why did these two great United teams, united by greatness, destined to duel, head to head, neck and neck, at the top of the table, at the dawn of the decade, divide so diabolically?

Furthermore, could Leeds United continue their conquest, and how could Manchester United ever hope to rebound from the shame of relegation?

In 1968, Manchester United had the greatest team in all of Europe. They owned the trophies to prove it, and they also boasted the best player in the World.

They had won the First Division title for the second time in two seasons, just a year earlier, and only nine years after losing Duncan Edwards, Roger Byrne, Tommy Taylor, Eddie Colman, David Pegg, Billy Whelan, Mark Jones and Geoff Bent, eight members of their team amongst twenty-three fatalities, following the Munich-Reim air crash.

Apart from making up most of Manchester United's team, England had also lost nearly half of their team for the 1958 World Cup Finals. Manchester United just got by over the next four years, after the football world had united around them.

In 1962, manager Matt Busby CBE, who had himself been close to death after the crash, paid Torino a British record transfer fee of £110,000 for Denis Law.

Slim built; Law was fiercely competitive, multi-skilled, dynamic and driven, with a vast range of goal-scoring methods. Like Jimmy Greaves, he had hated the heavily defensive style of football played in Italy.

Busby also paid Celtic £50,000 for their Scottish international midfield half-back Paddy Crerand, during February 1963. Crerand joined Law, and the remaining survivors from Munich, Bobby Charlton and Bill Foulkes, plus Irish youngster John Giles, as Manchester United won the FA Cup in 1963, beating Leicester City 3-1, although Manchester-born left half Nobby Stiles had been left out of their Cup Final team, having originally joined as a fifteen year old, six years earlier.

Johnny Giles was their midfield ball-winner and playmaker during that Final, but three months later, Matt Busby CBE, made the biggest mistake of his career by selling him to Leeds United in August 1963.

Don Revie had effectively stolen Giles for just £32,000.

"...I HAVE FOUND A GENIUS, STOP..."

After watching his Belfast junior side Boysland lose at home to Cregagh Boys, suffering humiliation and demolition by a much younger and a much smaller boy than any in his own team, Bob Bishop, Manchester United's chief scout in Northern Ireland, sent a telegram message to Matt Busby CBE.

"I have found a genius." It was reputed to have said. George Best was immediately signed up, and he made his debut for Manchester United, as a seventeen year old, in September 1963. Bestie was a genetically unique talent in British football, with two twinkling feet, perfect balance, a cold eye for goal opportunities, and a surprisingly huge leap for a lad with such a small frame.

He had everything, in fact.

Matt Busby said that Best was the very best attacking player in his team. He was their best centre forward. But Busby believed he was also their best left winger, their best right winger, their best wing half, their best centre half, their best right back, and also Manchester United's best left back.

The Best, Law and Charlton forward line propelled Manchester United to a close second place behind Champions Liverpool in 1963-64. Denis Law had scored a massive total of forty-five goals from just forty-one league and cup matches, including thirty First Division goals, and at the end of 1964, he became the first British player to ever be voted European Footballer of the Year.

Then in 1964-65, Law scored thirty-nine goals from just fifty-two matches, as Manchester United won the Football League Championship trophy, just beating Leeds United on goal average.

Best and Charlton had also combined for thirty-two goals, while David Herd scored twenty and John Connelly fifteen.

Leeds United had led the table with one week remaining, by a single point, but they could only draw 3-3 away at Birmingham City, so Manchester United beat Arsenal 3-1 to become English Champions for the first time in eight years.

That was also the last time, though, that five players from the same team hit double figures in First Division goals scored. Manchester United battled past Djurgaarden of Sweden, Borussia Dortmund, Everton, and then Racing Strasbourg to reach the Fairs Cup Semi-finals. Back in the Second round, they'd thrashed Borussia Dortmund, European Cup Semi-finalists during the previous season, by an aggregate score of Ten goals to One, after winning 6-1 away at the Stadion Rote Erde.

After drawing 3-3 on aggregate with Ferencvaros, of Hungary, in the last four, they were beaten 2-1 in a play-off match in Budapest, on 16th June 1965, when all the players had really needed, and also deserved, a Summer Holiday.

Manchester United, though, were playing the most stylish and dynamic football in the World, and then they routinely reached the European Cup Quarter-finals, in 1966.

Following their narrow 3-2 home win over Benfica, the European Champions from both 1961 and 1962, and also runners-up a year earlier, few had expected United to maintain their one-goal advantage in the second leg, away at the Stadium of Light.

Eusebio was the newly crowned European Footballer of the Year, and possibly the best player in the World in 1966, but that game was remembered as The Best Match.

George Best ran the Benfica defence all over the place, inspired rather than intimidated by the fiery 90,000 crowd, and gladdened that so many were there to see him play. The nineteen year old scored twice inside the first twelve minutes, twisting and turning three Portuguese defenders inside out for his second, as the stadium had fallen totally silent, open-mouthed in shock.

Eventually, Benfica lost 1-5 at home to Manchester United, and 3-8 on aggregate.

It was the most devastating display in the European Cup by any team since Real Madrid had beaten Eintracht Frankfurt 7-3 back in 1960.

It then took the cynical, cruel and suffocating tactics of Partizan Belgrade to defeat them 2-1 in the Semi-finals." Partizan weren't what you'd call a gentlemanly team," Paddy Crerand remembered.

"I mean, we could look after ourselves, but they kicked lumps out of us."

During 1966-67, Manchester United made the most of an unbelievable collapse by runaway leaders Tottenham, back in October and November, and they led the table thereafter. On Saturday 6th May 1967, they hammered West Ham, with Moore, Peters and Hurst, 6-1 away from home and with over 38,000 packed inside Upton Park, to secure their title. Denis Law had scored twice, while George Best, Bobby Charlton, Paddy Crerand and Bill Foulkes all completed the scoring.

A week later, over 61,000 gave United a spine-tingling ovation for their last game of the season, a goalless draw against Stoke City, at Old Trafford. They finished the season four points ahead of Nottingham Forest, and also a bitterly disappointed Tottenham Hotspur, who'd had high hopes of their second League and Cup double until the last few weeks of the season.

On Saturday 11th November 1967, George Best scored two cracking goals at Anfield, in their 2-1 over former leaders Liverpool. The second was a Champagne moment, and one to remember on Remembrance weekend.

Best collected a short diagonal pass from Brian Kidd, while closely marked by Ron Yeats, and twenty-five yards from goal. He turned 180 degrees, and just flicked the ball around the outside of Yeats as he skipped inside. He then met the ball, with the outside of his right boot, and sent it spinning like a cannonball, away from Tommy Lawrence's dive, and crashing into the top right corner of the Liverpool net.

After a few seconds of shocked silence, Anfield exploded into warm applause.

First, one Liverpool supporter had raised his arms and applauded George Best, on the Kop, and then his neighbours followed. The applause then spread across the whole Kop, and very quickly, the ladies and gents in the seats also all rose, and cheered the genius that they'd just witnessed. Eventually, the whole of the 54,515 Anfield crowd was cheering Manchester United's Superstar.

Best had back-heeled, side-stepped, and also outpaced and overpowered Yeats, Smith, Hughes and Lawler throughout the match, but more important than his two goals, was his influence, and his incision into Liverpool's previous invincibility, that had incited that Anfield crowd.

In spite of the fact that Manchester United went to the top of the table because of the win, footballing genius had been acclaimed by the Liverpool supporters.

By January, Manchester United had a three point lead over Liverpool, a lead they maintained a month later, with Leeds United then in second place, although they'd played one game more than Matt Busby's team. By the end of February, Leeds United had improved slightly, still in second place and still three points behind Manchester United, but both teams had played twenty-nine games.

On Saturday 2nd March 1968, Leeds United had beaten Arsenal 1-0 in the League Cup Final, at Wembley Stadium, to win the first major trophy in their history.

Leeds United had the nucleus of a team that had already played together for over five years. Billy Bremner had joined Leeds United straight from school, in 1958, after playing for Scotland schoolboys against England. After Johnny Giles then arrived at Elland Road during the late summer of 1963, Bremner and Giles formed one of the greatest midfield partnerships in footballing history.

Jack Charlton had been a first team regular since the mid-Fifties. Six feet tall, but with a thin, sloping frame that loomed menacingly over centre-forwards, he appeared to be much taller, he was the older brother of Manchester United's Bobby.

Jack, however, had a more direct and devilish style than his more elegantly and elaborately skilled younger brother. As opposed to Bobby's warm and friendly appearance, making him a hero to many football supporters who didn't even follow Manchester United, Jack had a rat-like scowl and fiercely cold eyes that made him an anti-hero and a feared fiend of a figure, both in his own half, and also in opposing penalty areas at corner kicks.

Norman Hunter was Charlton's partner in crime, or in defence, if you prefer. Hunter had joined Leeds United back in 1961, and he was an equally tough tackler, both in the air, but more particularly on the ground.

"In those days, we never got booked for the first tackle," Hunter admitted, so he made sure the first one was the one that hurt. Norman Hunter could play a bit, though, as illustrated when he moved to Bristol City in 1976, becoming a bit of a playmaker for the Robins. At Leeds, however, he was just driven to win the ball and give it, as soon as possible, to Bremner, Giles or Eddie Gray.

Norman Hunter was at his most unbeatable and impenetrable, though, alongside Jack Charlton; two fearsome, ferocious peaks at the back in white, and impossible to beat by anyone, when they were at their best.

Paul Reaney had also joined Leeds United in 1961, and Fulham-born, he was the only Southerner in their team. An incredibly quick right back, and equally quick in the tackle, Reaney had an intelligent defensive brain, anticipating dangers often missed by team-mates, but he knew some dirty tricks, too.

He was quick, though, an extraordinarily active full back, both in overlapping the midfield, and supporting the attackers, but more importantly in sweeping behind his central defence many times, executing timely challenges inside his own area, as well as clearing the ball off his line.

Gary Sprake became Leeds United's regular goalkeeper during 1963-64, having originally made his debut in 1962. Sprake was an outstanding keeper on his day, which was most of the time, but he became more well-known and remembered for the rare, odd howlers he made.

While Manchester United were battling with Liverpool for the First Division title in 1964, Leeds had won the Second Division title, with their top class defence only allowing thirty-four goals in forty-two matches, and losing just three times.

Terry Cooper made his debut for Leeds United in April 1964, in their 3-0 win at Swansea, to guarantee promotion back to the First Division. Born in Castleford, Cooper had been a left winger with Wolves Juniors, but after he was released from Molineux, Leeds United immediately signed him.

He was reverted to left back, and by the start of the 1964-65 season, the classic Leeds United back four of Reaney, Charlton, Hunter and Cooper was born.

In 1968, at twenty-three years old, Terry Cooper had scored the only goal of the League Cup Final against Arsenal. It was at that very game, at Wembley, when Norman Hunter earned his famous nickname, after a banner was held up by the Leeds United fans proclaiming,

"NORMAN BITES YER LEG!"

The 1968 League Cup Final was a tight game, though, and a game with no real pattern. However, Jack Charlton's tactic of standing right in front of the opposing team's goalkeeper, at Leeds United's corners, a tactic hated by the opposition, had worked wonders. He stood right in front of Jim Furnell, as Eddie Gray swung over a great, out-swinging cross. Furnell was unable to get anywhere near the ball, and so Cooper fired home the winner, standing directly on the penalty spot. The ball flew high into the Arsenal goal, beating Terry Neill's terrific airborne dive, in a superb attempt to head the ball over his bar.

That was the first major honour in Leeds United's history, but then they had a tough Fairs Cup Quarter-final first leg match, away at Rangers, three and a half weeks later, on Tuesday 26th March.

Sixty Thousand growling, glowering Glaswegians filled the great terraces of Ibrox Park, gloating and boasting of John Greig, Ronnie McKinnon, David Provan, Sandy Jardine, Willie Johnston, Willie Henderson and Alex Ferguson.

Thirty-three times Champions of Scotland, Rangers had been, the Royal Standard bearers; and facing the young English pretenders, who'd won absolutely fuck all.

Leeds United had, however, arrived at Ibrox with no pretences, and with Reaney, Charlton, Hunter and Cooper water-tight at the back and with Bremner and Giles, their midfield enforcers, Rangers lacked the guile and grace to break the deadlock.

After a frantic and frustrating goalless draw, Rangers travelled to Elland Road a fortnight later, with over 50,000 piled onto the banks of the West Yorkshire terraces.

A Peter Lorimer cracker, and then Johnny Giles' coolly-taken penalty-kick had ensured Leeds United's progress into the Semi-finals, while they'd also kept their thirty-second clean sheet of the season.

After drawing 1-1 away at Dundee (Paul Madeley), with 30,000 inside Dens Park, in the Semi-finals, Leeds United secured their second major Cup Final of the year, winning 2-1 on aggregate after Eddie Gray curled in the only goal of the game at Elland Road, on Wednesday 1st May.

Manchester United played the highest quality, greatest ever Manchester derby match in their history, on Wednesday 27th March 1968, at Old Trafford.

Over 62,000 watched the reigning Champions and current First Division leaders take on the hopeful, title pretenders of Manchester City.

City had their very own Sky Blue answer to Best, Law and Charlton, though, with Bell, Lee and Summerbee. They also had Mike Doyle and Alan Oakes to match Stiles and Crerand. City fought back after a very early, dynamic George Best goal, making the best out of a rare Tony Book mistake, to win 3-1. Manchester City won six of their final nine matches, while losing just twice, to win the title by two points.

After losing the First Division title to their City neighbours, Manchester United had the consolation of a European Cup Semi-final against the giants of Real Madrid.

Three weeks later, on Wednesday 15th May, United achieved a thrilling 3-3 draw at the Bernabau Stadium, having been losing 3-1 with just eighteen minutes remaining.

Beneath a sky high, spectacular crowd of 125,000, David Sadler and Bill Foulkes turned the game around, giving United the aggregate lead after they'd been looking certain for elimination. Sadler glanced in a header to make it 3-2, and then with twelve minutes to go, George Best turned it on. Paddy Crerand took a throw-in on the right, just inside the Madrid half, and Best took the ball past Sanchis, then teased Zoco, before skipping past him, and reaching the bye-line.

Best looked up, and he was surprised to see Foulkes advancing from defence. He crossed the ball over to the far post, and Bill Foulkes calmly side-footed the ball home.

United held onto a great 4-3 Semi-final aggregate win, watched by a combined attendance of nearly 190,000, and they celebrated wildly in Spain, before facing Benfica a fortnight later, in the European Cup Final at Wembley Stadium.

Matt Busby, CBE, was without his star centre forward, Denis Law, though, who'd been ruled out following a knee operation, after suffering an injury during their league title-losing 6-3 defeat away at West Bromwich Albion, at the end of April.

Manchester United finished two points behind Manchester City, though, after losing their hold on the League Championship trophy.

George Best had scored twenty-eight goals in 41 First Division matches, and he was voted Footballer of the Year.

Manchester United also scored eighty-nine goals during 1967-68, the highest-scoring team in the First Division, and only one First Division or Premier League team has scored more than 89 goals since 1968.

Scoring goals, though, was not United's problem. The trouble was that Manchester City, who'd scored 86 goals themselves, had conceded just over a goal per game, 43 in total. Manchester United had conceded 55 goals, which was good for league winning teams from the Fifties or early Sixties, but football had entered a new era, with dominant defences on top.

Over the next three to four years, Arsenal, Leeds United, Derby, Liverpool, Everton and Manchester City all developed classic back fours that turned great defence into an art form.

Manchester United's lack of a dominant defence made life very difficult for them over the next twenty-five years.

Even so, 92,225 almost filled Wembley Stadium, as Benfica arrived from Portugal. Eusebio was the best player of the World Cup Finals, two years before, and the greatest Portuguese footballer in history, having arrived in Lisbon in 1961. He was born in Mozambique, and played for Lourenco Marques, a nursery team for Sporting Lisbon, Benfica's hated city rivals. He arrived in Lisbon, aged just nineteen, but was virtually kidnapped, straight off the plane by Benfica officials, in the very same way that Clough and Taylor used to sniff out a legend, then hidden away, until Sporting had forgotten him and lost interest.

Eusebio, as a Benfica player, was voted as European Footballer of the Year in 1965, and then top scored at the 1966 World Cup Finals, with nine goals from just six games. He also won the European Golden Boot in 1968, after scoring forty-two goals, and made Benfica wonderfully worthy opponents for Matt Busby CBE, and Manchester United.

Benfica, though, were more worried about the threat of George Best, who'd destroyed them inside their *Cathedral*, the Stadium of Light, two years before, and had scored fifty-seven league and cup goals over the previous three seasons, a hell of an achievement for a creative player who wasn't an outright striker.

They were correct to worry.

After a tight, tactical first half, of which the one real highlight was Eusebio thudding the ball against Alex Stepney's crossbar from twenty-five yards, the European Cup Final was finally struck alight during the second half. Nine minutes after the break, captain Bobby Charlton headed in David Sadler's cross.

MANCHESTER UNITED		BENFICA
Alex Stepney	1	Jose Henrique
Shay Brennan	2	Adolfo Calisto
Tony Dunne	3	Humberto Fernandes
Paddy Crerand	4	Jacinto Santos
Bill Foulkes	5	Fernando Cruz
Nobby Stiles	6	Jaime Graca
George Best	7	Mario Caluna (C)
Brian Kidd	8	Jose Augusto
Bobby Charlton (C)	9	Jose Torres
David Sadler	10	Eusebio
John Aston	11	Antonio Simoes

United successfully defended their lead, right into the dying minutes, but Jaime Graca hit a dramatic late equalizer for Benfica, firing in from close range, past Stepney, after Jose Torres had headed the ball into his path.

Moments later, Eusebio was sent clear, straight through to United's goal area, running quickly between Foulkes and Dunne, as United's defence tired. Eusebio fired a thunderous shot, from just outside the area, but Stepney saved instinctively, not the best save ever, in the history of football, but a great save, nevertheless.

Eusebio then displayed one of the classiest moments of sportsmanship, applauding Stepney, hand-clapping him and attempting to shake his hand, after the ball had gone clear. Stepney just watched the ball, intently, as it went fully clear, before accepting Eusebio's pat on his back with grace, waving back at the great man with respectful appreciation, but gesturing that the game was still on.

In extra-time, Manchester United regained their composure, and their superiority; George Best scored a glorious goal, running clear onto Sadler's flick-on, side-stepping keeper Henrique and rolling the ball into the empty net, with his left foot.

On his nineteenth birthday, Brian Kidd netted with a header, from another John Aston cross, after Henrique had parried his initial headed shot. John Aston's adventurous and energetic wing performances had taken much of the pressure off United's back four, and driven pressure upon pressure onto the Portuguese defence.

Brian Kidd's goal from Aston's cross settled the nerves, before Bobby Charlton fired United to a brilliant, if flattering, 4-1 win, firing in Kidd's low cross from the right side of the Benfica area.

With Brian Kidd having played, and scored, on his nineteenth birthday, and with the match being played on a bright Spring evening, as it always is; it seemed, that Spring evening, late on a Wednesday, that a fresh Spring was blossoming at Manchester United. Bobby Charlton lifted the huge trophy and paraded it with his beloved team, around Wembley Stadium, under the floodlights, as Spring was heading for Summer.

In fact, Manchester United were entering an Autumn.

Leeds United hosted the Hungarian Champions Ferencvaros for the first leg of the Inter Cities Fairs Cup Final, on Wednesday 7th August 1968. Because of the match being played just three days before the start of the new season, and also shown live on television, only 25,000 die-hard fans had turned up at Elland Road.

LEEDS UNITED		FERENCVAROS
Gary Sprake	1	Geczi
Paul Reaney	2	Novak
Terry Cooper	3	Pancsics
Billy Bremner	4	Havasi
Jack Charlton	5	Szucs
Norman Hunter	6	Juhasz
Peter Lorimer	7	Szoke
Paul Madeley	8	Varga
Mick Jones	9	Albert
Johnny Giles	10	Rakosi
Eddie Gray	11	Fenyvesi

Leeds United won a tentative, nervous match 1-0 after Mick Jones scrambled in a goal from Lorimer's corner kick. Jack Charlton had again stood right in front of keeper Geczi, and he'd flicked the ball on for Jones to attack. The Hungarians protested that Charlton had fouled their keeper, but no foul was given, and it was no less than Leeds United deserved, as Ferencvaros had stuck nine men behind the ball all game.

Florian Albert was the European Footballer of the Year in 1967, and also the inspiration of Hungary's 3-1 win over Brazil in the 1966 World Cup Finals, at Old Trafford, but he rarely got a touch, so defensive were his team's tactics.

A massive, hostile 76,000 crowd packed the Nepstadion in Budapest for the second leg, and they whistled, hissed and booed every Leeds United touch, just over a month later, on Wednesday 11th September.

Gary Sprake made several World Class reflex saves from the great Albert and Rakosi, but his defence, superbly protected by both Bremner and Madeley in midfield, had also produced a hard-fought rear-guard performance.

That goalless draw won Leeds United their second major trophy in just over six months, after forty-nine years of barrenness.

At the start of 1968-69, Leeds United went unbeaten through their first nine matches, winning seven of them. Their only serious competition for the title came from Liverpool, and they meant business. During their five matches from the start of September until early October, Liverpool won every match, while conceding no goals at all, yet scoring eighteen.

On Saturday 5th October, Liverpool led Leeds United on goal average, with both teams tied on eighteen points from eleven matches. A month later, after a 5-1 thrashing by Burnley, at Turf Moor, Leeds United were a point behind the Reds, but they did have a game in hand.

By December 1968, Liverpool had extended their lead over Leeds United, at the top of Division One to four points.

DIVISION ONE LEADERS, 7TH DECEMBER 1968

	P	W	D	L	F	A	PTS
Liverpool	23	16	4	3	43	13	36
LEEDS UNITED	21	13	6	2	31	17	32

On 21st December, Leeds United ran riot against Burnley, winning 6-1 with all of their front six scoring, except for O'Grady. Peter Lorimer had smashed a brace, and Bremner, Gray, Giles and Jones scored the remainder in a sparkling performance.

Leeds United were now just three points behind Liverpool, but still with two games in hand.

They were then only a couple of points behind Liverpool by the beginning of February, having played one of their games in hand, top scorer Mick Jones' goal earning a 1-0 away win over QPR, at Loftus Road.

Leeds United then launched a blitz attack on Liverpool's lead, winning seven games in a row up until Saturday 8th March, and furthermore, they allowed no goals against them, in six matches, from the middle of January until the beginning of March.

In contrast, Liverpool had seen their season begin to fall apart. They only gained three points from the middle of January until the middle of March. They had, admittedly, played only three Division One games during that period, due to FA Cup participation, but Leicester City had knocked them out of the Fifth round of that competition, after a replay.

Leeds United led Liverpool by seven points, in mid-March, in a reversal of fortunes, but they'd played two extra games.

By Saturday 5th April, Liverpool had closed the gap on the leaders to five points, but they now only had one game in hand. Both teams went tit for tat during April, winning exactly the same amount of points from their first four matches of the month. On Tuesday night, 22nd April 1969, this was the position at the top of Division One:

	P	W	D	L	F	A	PTS
LEEDS UNITED	40	26	12	2	65	26	64
Liverpool	39	25	9	5	62	21	59

On Bank Holiday Monday, 28th April 1969, Anfield hosted the Summit Meeting between Liverpool and Leeds United. Liverpool needed to win to keep alive their chances of winning the Championship. If they did win, and then Leeds United failed to beat Nottingham Forest, two days later, on the last day of April, then Liverpool would have to win both of their remaining away games, at reigning Champions Manchester City, and also at Newcastle, in May, to win the league.

LIVERPOOL		LEEDS UNITED
Tommy Lawrence	1	Gary Sprake
Chris Lawler	2	Paul Reaney
Geoff Strong	3	Terry Cooper
Tommy Smith	4	Billy Bremner
Ron Yeats	5	Jack Charlton
Emlyn Hughes	6	Norman Hunter
Ian Callaghan	7	Mike O'Grady
Bobby Graham	8	Paul Madeley
Alun Evans	9	Mick Jones
Ian St John	10	Johnny Giles
Peter Thompson	11	Eddie Gray

Liverpool were without their World Cup hero Roger Hunt, who'd been missing since suffering an injury at Stoke City on Easter Monday. In front of 53,570, the second largest crowd of the season at Anfield, Liverpool went at Leeds United very hard, spurred on by a fanatical and partisan Kop, which roared loudly with laughter every time the ball went close to Gary Sprake's hands.

"I let my heart fall into Careless Hands," they'd sang. *"Careless hands broke my heart in two,"* after Sprake threw the ball back into his own goal at Anfield back in December 67, in the snow.

That night, though, Gary Sprake was excellent, absolutely faultless.

Don Revie, though, was missing Peter Lorimer, and Leeds United really had to dig in deep to earn the point they needed. At the final whistle, their hard work had won them the League Championship trophy for the very first time, and amidst ecstatic scenes on the Anfield pitch, one of the most extraordinary moments of English football history then occurred.

Revie ordered his team to go and salute the Kop, the Kop that had so loudly abused and mocked them throughout the match. So Leeds United went to salute the Kop.

Some in the Kop began to applaud their bitter rivals.

The applause grew louder and louder, and wider and wider, and in unprecedented scenes, Anfield was chanting, "*Champions! Champions! Champions!*" towards their rivals who'd won the title at their own home.

Bill Shankly also went to visit the away team's changing room, despite his bitter disappointment, to warmly congratulate Leeds United. He said, close to tears, "there were two sets of Champions in a great game tonight, and a third set of Champions emerged at the finish, when the wonderful Liverpool fans showed the World what wonderful supporters they are."

Mick Jones was the Champions' top goal scorer, with fourteen goals from forty matches. Also, Peter Lorimer, Johnny Giles and Mike O'Grady had all combined to contribute twenty-five goals from midfield, but it was their classic, legendary back four of Reaney, Charlton, Hunter and Cooper, with the excellent Sprake behind them, that was the key to their title-winning season.

Between the five of them, they missed just nine First Division matches during the season, and eight of those were missed by Terry Cooper in December, when the more than capable Paul Madeley deputised. Leeds United kept twenty-four clean sheets from their 42 matches, and they'd conceded just 26 goals.

From their final seventeen First Division matches, after the middle of January, Leeds United had conceded only five goals.

In spite of this, their first ever title triumph, Don Revie strived for better. He knew that having only one quality striker wasn't going to be sufficient, as English football moved into the 4-4-2 future of the Seventies. He subsequently paid a British record transfer fee of £165,000 for the supreme, and the most sought-after, centre-forward in England, during the Summer of 1969.

Allan Clarke had scored thirty-two First Division goals for Fulham and Leicester City, over the two previous seasons 1967-69, and he'd been voted Man of the Match after the 1969 FA Cup Final, despite Leicester's 0-1 defeat against Manchester City.

Tall, over six feet tall, and commanding, Allan Clarke was good in the air, with an alert footballing brain, and he could clear 100 yards in just over ten seconds, but with a deceptive turn of pace, and a change of direction that challenged the best defenders in England. His athleticism allowed him to turn effortlessly in enclosed spaces, and fire ferocious shots, with either foot. He was a character who truly cared about his team. In modern day terms, Allan Clarke was like a Robin Van Persie, a Fernando Torres, or a David Villa.

Despite the huge fee that he cost, £165,000 was a real bargain for one of the very greatest ever Leeds United footballers.

While Leeds United were moving forward, building on their success, hitting the accelerator towards the Seventies, with their new striker, Allan Clarke, *Sniffer,* and his sprinting pace of a hundred yards in 10.2 seconds; Manchester United had yanked up their handbrake, on a hill, and within three years, they were rolling backwards.

They just couldn't engage any forward gear.

Bill Foulkes, their oldest survivor from the Munich tragedy, played the first two matches of 1969-70, before he'd been displaced by Ian Ure, a £62,500 signing from Arsenal. Ure played only 47 league games at Old Trafford, before retiring in 1973, when he was only 33. He'd been displaced by Steve James in 1971.

More significantly though, Sir Matt Busby had retired from football management, in June 1969, after one thousand, one hundred and twenty league and cup matches in his twenty-four seasons as Manchester United boss. His team won five hundred and sixty-five matches; most managers don't even last five hundred matches. Manchester United lost just 292 games, giving Sir Matt a sixty-six per cent winning ratio. Only 263 of his matches ended in draws.

He returned on 26th December 1970, as effectively a caretaker manager, steering the club clear of relegation problems, after Wilf McGuiness's sacking.

After his retirement, Sir Matt Busby had become a member of the Manchester United board, as a director, until he was made club president in 1982.

Sir Matt Busby died, aged 84, twelve years later, on 20th January 1994, after losing a five year battle with blood cancer. At Manchester United's first match after his death, a Premier League game at home to Everton; a loan piper led both teams out onto the pitch, playing *"A Scottish Soldier."* One minute's silence was perfectly observed, before kick-off, by the whole of the 44,750 crowd at Old Trafford. In Munich, Lisbon and Madrid, and all across Europe, one minutes' silences were also observed, where he remained fondly remembered.

At Blackburn Rovers, however, many Leeds United supporters ruined their minute's silence, prior to their 2-1 defeat, chanting the name of Don Revie throughout the sixty seconds. Half of that Leeds United team had pleaded to their fans to be silent, but they failed.

Sir Matt Busby was buried in Southern Cemetery, in Chorlton-cum-Hardy, on Thursday 27th January 1994, next to his wife Joan, who'd died five years before. Thousands had lined the streets to watch the funeral procession.

In 1993, Warwick Road North, which leads to Old Trafford, was renamed Sir Matt Busby Way. A bronze statue of Sir Matt was also unveiled outside of the East Stand of Old Trafford, in 1996.

Allan Clarke scored in his first competitive match for Leeds United, nodding a through ball over Pat Jennings, in a 3-1 win over Tottenham on Saturday 9th August.

However, by the end of August, their grip on the title was slipping. Leeds United did not have a disastrous start to the season, going unbeaten through their first six matches, but they won only twice. Everton, on the other hand, won five out of their first six games, and then, on Saturday 30th August, they beat Leeds United 3-2 at Goodison Park. Nearly 52,000 saw Jimmy Husband and Joe Royle the Toffees 2-0 up at half-time, and Royle hit his second of the game, after Bremner and Clarke scored for Leeds, to secure two crucial points for Everton.

By Saturday 8th October, Everton held a seven point lead over Leeds United, having gained twenty-four points from their first fourteen matches. It was a lead that Leeds United weren't able to overcome, and Everton went on to win the 1970 League Championship in a glorious fashion, and with a devastating style of football. Four of their players, Alan Ball, Brian Labone, Keith Newton and Tommy Wright, all played for England at the World Cup Finals in Mexico.

Leeds United still battled away, in second place, winning forty points from their last thirty matches, but finished nine points behind Everton. Allan Clarke and Mick Jones scored a combined total of fifty-two league and cup goals, becoming the most devastating attacking double act in English football.

In their first ever European Cup campaign, Leeds United did not disappoint.

First, they hammered Lyn Oslo, the Champions of Norway, 16-0, before easily disposing of their Fairs Cup Final opponents, Ferencvaros, in November.

The Hungarians, now without the great Florian Albert, had lost 3-0 at Elland Road. Then, with just 5,400 attending the away leg, Mick Jones scored twice, and Peter Lorimer hammered a third, to complete an aggregate win of 6-0.

In the Quarter-finals, they were handed a relatively easy draw, considering the quality of the remaining teams, against Standard Liege. Peter Lorimer scored away in Belgium, and then, Johnny Giles fired in a second half penalty kick at Elland Road, to secure a hard-fought 2-0 aggregate win.

The might of Glasgow Celtic awaited Leeds United in the Semi-finals.

In the FA Cup, Leeds United had also made good progress, beating Swansea 2-1 in the Third round, before hammering non-league side Sutton United 6-0 away, in front of a record crowd of 14,000 at the Borough Sports Ground. Allan Clarke scored four, and Peter Lorimer smashed in two, as Leeds United fielded their best eleven against their Isthmian League opposition.

Johnny Giles and Allan Clarke both scored first half goals to beat Mansfield Town in the Fifth round, and then, Twenty-seven and a half thousand filled Swindon Town's County Ground for the visit of the League Champions, on Saturday 21st February. Leeds United won 2-0, after Allan Clarke's brilliant brace bagged the re-battle of Bosworth Field, against Manchester United, in the Semi-finals.

The FA Cup Semi-final between Manchester United and Leeds United was not a classic.

It was an Epic.

Manchester United's European Cup winning vintage was just beginning to turn, but like a beautiful Beaujolais, it was flowering brilliantly with strawberry, blackcurrant, biscuit, Danish buns, and Best.

Leeds United, on the other hand, were a young, maturing Sauvignon Blanc from New Zealand, spine-quivering and sharp and rude, with smoke from burnt wood, gooseberries, and Bremner.

The Semi-final, watched by a packed 55,000 at Hillsborough, on 14th March, ended goalless after a tough match, the first Battle of the Roses.

Nine days later, Villa Park hosted the replay, with 62,500 filling its vast banks. Paul Madeley replaced the slightly injured Norman Hunter, and he man-marked Bobby Charlton, while Paul Reaney was appointed to take good care of George Best.

George Best said of Paul Reaney, "he was among the toughest players I played against. He was at you the whole ninety minutes, using every dodgy trick in the book." George Best was something special, the first World Superstar of British football, possibly, but Reaney's defensive quality was equal, yet again. The replay ended goalless, again, after extra-time.

A second replay was needed, and the War of the Roses moved to Lancashire, Manchester United's home turf, and to Burnden Park, the home of Bolton Wanderers. 56,000 absolutely jam-packed, solidly and tightly, the ground on that Thursday afternoon of 26th March 1970.

I went to Burnden Park a few times in the early Eighties, supporting a truly awful Newcastle team at the old Railway End, and there were fewer than 20,000 there, but it seemed pretty full then.

To imagine 56,000 inside Burnden Park during the 1970's is almost unbelievable.

MANCHESTER UNITED		LEEDS UNITED
Alex Stepney	1	Gary Sprake
Paul Edwards	2	Paul Reaney
Tony Dunne	3	Terry Cooper
Paddy Crerand	4	Billy Bremner
David Sadler	5	Jack Charlton
Nobby Stiles	6	Paul Madeley
Willie Morgan	7	Peter Lorimer
Carlo Sartori	8	Allan Clarke
Bobby Charlton	9	Mick Jones
Brian Kidd	10	Johnny Giles
George Best	11	Eddie Gray
Denis Law	12	Mick Bates
(rep. Sartori)		

Manchester United still had eight survivors from their European Cup Final win, two years earlier, plus the small menacing matter of Denis Law to come on from the bench. Leeds United, though, were a tighter unit, and more of a team in 1970.

Manchester had the boutique superstar George Best, the most talented player on the pitch, by some distance, but Leeds relied on their five foot four, and five foot five inches midfield partnership of Billy Bremner and Johnny Giles, the best in the world.

Paddy Crerand was the driving force behind Manchester's spectacular successes, and Nobby Stiles was their enforcer, as ultra-competitive as ever, but Bremner and Giles were just a bit better. To have one player of mediocrity, a weak link, over a marathon battle against a team of Leeds United's calibre, was costly. To be honest, though, Manchester United had two or three.

The pressure eventually told on Manchester, as midfield general Billy Bremner unleashed a vicious half-volley from the edge of the area, despite attracting close attention from David Sadler.

In a superb celebration of the goal that sent Leeds United to Wembley, Allan Clarke lifted his captain above his head, and then, he and Mick Jones chaired Bremner away, as the rest of their team-mates ran to join in.

173,500 had watched the greatest FA Cup Semi-final of all time.

Six days later, though, on Wednesday 1st April, Leeds United were understandably jaded during their European Cup Semi-final first leg tie at home to Celtic. Celtic were the wrong team to be jaded against, though. They'd easily retained their Scottish League Championship trophy, with a twelve point advantage over Rangers, and they still had seven players who'd won the European Cup Final, three years before.

Celtic still had McNeill, Murdoch, Gemmell, Lennox, Auld and Wallace, but most importantly of all, they had one of the greatest, fastest, trickiest and most skilful wingers in the World, ever: the magnificent and the greatest ever, Jimmy Johnstone.

Johnstone created George Connelly's goal in the very first minute of the first half, a goal that stunned Elland Road's 45,505 crowd. Celtic's defence, as equally tough and uncompromising as Leeds Uniteds', held on despite heavy home pressure for a crucial away win.

On the following night, Thursday 2nd April, Paul Reaney's season, and also his World Cup dreams, was ended after he broke his leg during Leeds United's 2-2 draw away at West Ham United.

GOAL IN A MILLION

Despite that disappointing set-back, Eddie Gray had been influenced by some of Johnstone's tricks and flicks. On the following Saturday, two days later, Leeds United recovered some form and confidence with a 2-1 win over Burnley. Eddie Gray scored both of their goals, but it was the second that hit the headlines; Goal in a Million, the back pages proclaimed.

Gray linked up with Mick Bates in midfield, then played a one-two with Albert Johanneson, and then Lorimer smashed a shot in from the edge of the area, which Peter Mellor parried. Gray charged down the Burnley clearance, and from the left corner flag, he back heeled and side stepped his way past Mick Docherty, Arthur Bellamy, Colin Waldron and John Angus, all the way on a long weaving, balletic run into the penalty area.

He then fired, right-footed, the ball inside Mellor's near post.

The goal was voted as the greatest ever goal, the *Goal in a Million*, in Leeds United's history, in a 2010 online poll.

A fortnight after their defeat at home to Celtic, Leeds United travelled up to Glasgow for the second leg of their European Cup Semi-final.

CELTIC		LEEDS UNITED
Evan Williams	1	Gary Sprake
David Hay	2	Paul Madeley
Tommy Gemmell	3	Terry Cooper
Bobby Murdoch	4	Billy Bremner
Billy McNeill	5	Jack Charlton
Jim Brogan	6	Norman Hunter
Jimmy Johnstone	7	Peter Lorimer
George Connelly	8	Allan Clarke
John Hughes	9	Mick Jones
Bertie Auld	10	Johnny Giles
Bobby Lennox	11	Eddie Gray

A staggeringly huge 136,505 crowd was wedged tight inside the gigantic Hampden Park.

It was a record attendance for the European Cup that still stands today, and it's also the greatest-ever crowd between two British club sides.

It was a dangerous, but wonderful night for Celtic's home supporters, and many had to escape from the terraces, to avoid being crushed.

Early on, and from out of the mud, Billy Bremner buried a thirty yard right-footed rocket, high into the far left corner of the Celtic goal, to cancel their first leg deficit.

Even when John Hughes equalised soon after, benefitting from another Gary Sprake howler, Leeds United still needed only one goal to reach the European Cup Final in Milan.

But Celtic's very own midfield general, Bobby Murdoch, scored from yet another dangerous pass from Jimmy Johnstone, after Johnstone had danced around Terry Cooper.

Bill Shankly was a visitor at Hampden Park, that night, and he'd proclaimed Leeds United as the very best. Shankly, who knew his football teams, said, "Chelsea could win the FA Cup, but they're not in the same class as Leeds United. The best team this country has seen, for a long, long time, might win nothing. The whole world has come down on them.

Celtic were healthy and strong. Leeds were not, they had too many games."

It was no consolation, at the end of the 1969-70 season, for Billy Bremner, that he was voted FWA Footballer of the Year, with 95% of the vote, a record to this day. Billy Bremner and Paul Reaney had each played 110 league and cup matches over those two seasons, 1968-1970, while Norman Hunter had played only 106 matches.

Leeds United had a good season in 1969-70, losing only ten of their sixty-two league and cup matches, but Everton were worthy Champions. They had won twenty-nine of their First Division games, more than any other team in the history of the First Division or the Premier League, apart from Tottenham back in 1961.

The pain of winning nothing, after so much effort and quality offered, made Leeds United even more determined for supreme success in the Seventies.

Manchester United's future, over the following four years, was full of frolics and fizz, of flair and flash, and falls and failures.

They faced a multiple exodus of European Cup winning stars, managerial instability, and miserable relegation struggles.

KIPPAX CLASS

COLIN BELL WAS SIGNED BY MANCHESTER CITY in March 1966, for just £45,000 from Bury. At only nineteen, he'd become the youngest captain in the Football League, while at Gigg Lane. Bell then played the final eleven league games of 1965-66 at Maine Road, helping City win the Second Division Championship title, and he became the inspiration, the pass-master, and the beating heart of City's greatest ever team.

By 1967, though, City were a lower half of the table First Division team, who'd won only twelve games during their first season back in the top flight. They'd won the First Division Trophy only once previously, thirty years previously in fact, back in 1936-37, and a single FA Cup Final win over Birmingham, back in 1956, had been their only major honour since the turbulent Thirties.

City had ended that 1966-67 season on thirty-nine points, a full ten points above the relegation zone, but over twenty points behind their neighbours, and Champions Manchester United. Hopes of a First Division title weren't really that high on the Maine Road crowd's minds in August 1967, especially as their team started with two defeats, one win and a draw. Only 22,002 had watched their 4-2 home win over Southampton (Colin Bell 2, Neil Young 2), on Wednesday 30th August.

Neil Young, their elegant, six-foot tall forward from Fallowfield in Manchester, had joined City as an apprentice in 1961. With a devastatingly hard left footed strike, and a hugely intense look on his face, he was probably the greatest English forward of the Sixties to have never won an England cap.

Their win over Southampton sparked a run of five wins from five games through to mid-September, though, and lifted City up to the heady heights of second place, just behind Bill Shankly's Liverpool on goal average.

One week later, City lost 1-0 at Arsenal and dropped a place. Reigning Champions Manchester United had overtaken them into second place after beating Spurs 3-1.

62,942 bulged the walls of Maine Road, on Saturday 30th September 1967, for a top of the First Division table clash between the two Manchester football giants, for the first time in nearly Sixty Years, and one of only two such games in over a Century.

MANCHESTER CITY		MANCHESTER UNITED
Ken Mulhearn	1	Alex Stepney
Tony Book	2	Tony Dunne
Glyn Pardoe	3	Francis Burns
Mike Doyle	4	Paddy Crerand
George Heslop	5	Bill Foulkes
Alan Oakes	6	Nobby Stiles
Stan Bowles	7	George Best
Colin Bell	8	David Sadler
Mike Summerbee	9	Bobby Charlton
Neil Young	10	Denis Law
Tony Coleman	11	Brian Kid

Harry Dowd, City's first choice goalkeeper, had dislocated his finger during the week before the game, and Ken Mulhearn, who'd signed from Stockport County, only nine days before, as cover, was making his City debut.

Also, nineteen year old Stan Bowles was making only his second league start, and in such an important game, and United's experience gave them a vital advantage. Two Bobby Charlton goals won the game for United, while Colin Bell's goal was only a mere consolation for City's 63,000 fans.

That 2-1 defeat rattled City, and they also lost 1-0 away at lowly Sunderland a week later.

Joe Mercer responded by paying Bolton Wanderers £60,000 for their top scorer Francis Lee. A real livewire, Lee had scored 92 goals in just 139 league games for Bolton, and he was seen by Mercer as the "final piece of their jigsaw."

Lee made his City debut during their 2-0 home win over Wolves on 14th October (Doyle, Young).

Francis Lee scored his first-ever City goal one week later in their 4-2 away win at bottom club Fulham (Summerbee 2, Lee, Young), and City were back in the League Championship race, behind both Liverpool and Manchester United.

Manchester City won ten points from their next six games prior to Christmas Day, but they then lost twice, in successive games, to West Brom, on Boxing Day and then on Saturday 30th December, with Jeff Astle (2) and Tony Brown (2) doing the damage.

A massive crowd of nearly Forty Thousand were inside The City Ground, Nottingham Forest, and City regained some form against the previous seasons' surprise First Division runners-up. Tony Coleman's penalty kick and then goals from Mike Summerbee and Neil Young won the match 3-0.

Coleman, their Liverpool-born blond-haired winger, should really have relished scoring that penalty kick, as it was the last Manchester City penalty to be taken by a player other than Francis Lee for more than five seasons.

Tony Coleman had won the Fourth Division Championship trophy back in 1966 with Doncaster Rovers. He then signed for Manchester City during March 1967, but after he'd left Belle Vue, Rovers struggled and they were immediately relegated back to Division Four.

Manchester City then won eleven points out of their next six matches, including two 1-0 wins over both Sunderland and Burnley, with Lee scoring in both games.

Francis Lee had scored fourteen goals in his first twenty Division One games with City, and his Speed, Strength and Tenacity, allied with Neil Young's Tall, Elegant Power, had a huge impact on City's assault on the 1968 title race.

In the space of just four days, in late March 1968, Manchester City played two crucial crunch matches. Firstly, on 23rd March, they visited Elland Road.

A colossal match-up between two real powerhouse teams, and watched by a huge 51,818 home crowd, eventually swung Leeds United's way.

Even without playmaker Eddie Gray, the Yorkshire team ground out a 2-0 win after a trademark Jack Charlton header, and a sweet strike by Johnny Giles.

LEEDS UNITED		MANCHESTER CITY
Gary Sprake	1	Ken Mulhearn
Paul Reaney	2	Tony Book
Terry Cooper	3	Glyn Pardoe
Billy Bremner	4	Mike Doyle
Jack Charlton	5	George Heslop
Norman Hunter	6	Alan Oakes
Jimmy Greenhoff	7	Francis Lee
Peter Lorimer	8	Colin Bell
Mick Jones	9	Mike Summerbee
Johnny Giles	10	Neil Young
Terry Hibbitt	11	Tony Coleman
Paul Madeley	12	David Connor

On that very same day, Manchester United had smashed Nottingham Forest 3-0, though, in front of Sixty-one thousand, nine hundred and seventy-eight fans, to join Leeds United at the summit of Division One with forty-five points apiece.

Manchester City and Liverpool both followed on forty-three points.

Their defeat at Elland Road meant that another defeat, away at Manchester United on the following Wednesday night, 27th March, would rule City out of the title race.

62,243 had tightly squeezed into Old Trafford's massive stadium for a match that created Legends Forever. Joe Mercer and Malcolm Allison had kept faith with the same eleven that lost away at Elland Road, just four days earlier, but United had John Fitzpatrick in their forward line, in place of Brian Kidd. Matt Busby fielded an otherwise full strength side, though, with Best, Charlton, Law, Stiles and Crerand.

George Best scored after just 38 seconds, making the very most out of Tony Book's rare mistake, but here was a much meatier City team than the one which had been so out-muscled and completely mastered by United, back in September.

Colin Bell equalised, before George Heslop and Francis Lee completed their 3-1 comeback win. John Aston replaced David Herd to worry Tony Book, with some decent runs and dangerous crosses, but City's hardened back four held on for an historic and totally-deserved win.

Manchester City rose back up to second place, after that tremendous away win.

However, their 1-0 defeat at Leicester City ten days later again lost them momentum, especially with both Leeds and Liverpool winning.

City then played two games at Maine Road in two days, hosting Chelsea on Good Friday, winning 1-0 before 47,132 (Doyle). On the following Saturday, 13th April, West Ham United visited City. The Sky Blues won 3-0 (Young 2, Doyle).

Manchester City's defence kept sixteen clean sheets during 1967-68, superbly organised by both Mike Doyle and George Heslop.

Heslop, who'd scored City's second goal at Old Trafford, had arrived from Everton prior to the 1965-66 season. He was a key member of their Second Division Championship winning team, and then missed only one of City's 1967-68 First Division games, their 6-0 home win over Leicester City on Saturday 11th November (Lee 2, Young 2, Doyle, and Oakes).

Following their 3-0 win over West Ham, though, City took just one point from their two away games at Chelsea and Wolves.

The First Division table, on Saturday 20th April, did not fill City fans with much optimism that the title race was still really on, even if they didn't mind part of it.

FIRST DIVISION LEADERS, 20TH APRIL 1968

	PL	W	D	L	F	A	PTS
Manchester United	39	23	8	8	79	47	54
Leeds United	38	22	9	7	65	29	53
MANCHESTER CITY	38	22	6	10	76	39	50
Liverpool	37	19	10	8	57	34	48
Everton	37	21	5	11	58	35	47

Manchester City had to not only win all of their four remaining games, but they also had to hope for more than just one miracle elsewhere, having gained just five points from their last five games.

Firstly, on the following Tuesday, Peter Dobing scored a St George's Day hat-trick for Stoke City as they beat Leeds United 3-2. A couple of nights later, Usher's own goal then gifted City a scrappy late-season 1-0 home win over lowly Sheffield Wednesday.

Liverpool offered no miracles at all on Saturday 27th April. Instead they really applied the pressure with their 4-1 hammering of already-relegated Fulham.

On Bank Holiday Monday, though, West Brom offered miracle number two.

Albion had hammered Manchester United 6-3, aided by Jeff Astle's hat-trick.

Oh, and yes, miracle number three? Liverpool were also held to a 1-1 draw by Spurs at Anfield, while Manchester City had beaten Everton 2-0 (Book, Coleman), effectively eliminating the Toffees from that title race.

Suddenly, Manchester City were actually favourites in the title race.

	PLAYED	POINTS
MANCHESTER CITY	40	54
Manchester United	40	54
Leeds United	39	53
Liverpool	39	51

On the following Saturday, 4th May, Liverpool defeated Leeds 2-1 at Elland Road.

Both teams were virtually eliminated from the race, though, after both Manchester clubs had won. As George Best scored a hat-trick during Manchester United's 6-0 hammering of Newcastle, City's thrilling 3-1 away win over Tottenham Hotspur (Bell 2, Summerbee), with 51,242 inside White Hart Lane, had turned the First Division title into a two horse race.

Due to the afore-mentioned performances of City's defence, and also City's prolific strike force, having scored eighty-two goals, City had a goal difference of over 2.00, whilst United's goal average had slipped to 1.66. That advantage which City had gained over United meant, therefore, that City only had to win at Newcastle on the final Saturday of the season to secure the League title.

On Saturday 11th May 1968, Manchester City visited St James's Park for their historic title decider.

NEWCASTLE UNITED		MANCHESTER CITY
Iam McFaul	1	Ken Mulhearn
David Craig	2	Tony Book
Frank Clark	3	Glyn Pardoe
Bobby Moncur	4	Mike Doyle
John McNamee	5	George Heslop
Jim Iley	6	Alan Oakes
Jackie Sinclair	7	Francis Lee
Jim Scott	8	Colin Bell
Wyn Davies	9	Mike Summerbee
Pop Robson	10	Neil Young
Tommy Robson	11	Tony Coleman

During the opening quarter of an hour, Newcastle had settled down much better than City, though, so much was at stake for the Sky Blues, and Wyn Davies, the *Mighty Wyn*, had a chance to open the scoring, but he shot wildly over the bar.

Then after fourteen minutes, City struck. John McNamee and Mike Summerbee were enjoying a vigorous battle, and after another epic tussle, Summerbee came off worse, but he was awarded a free-kick by the referee. Doyle floated his right-sided free-kick low to Bell inside the area. Bell laid off for the onrushing Doyle to spank a hard cross along the ground, dangerously, for Summerbee to deftly flick over McFaul at the near post. Just one minute later, though, good work by Jackie Sinclair had set up Bryan 'Pop' Robson inside City's area with only Mulhearn to beat.

Robson buried the ball high into the net. Newcastle should have then taken the lead when Book cleared Wyn Davies's looping header off the line from Jim Iley's free-kick.

It was City who went 2-1 up, though, after thirty-three minutes, when Bell and Oakes combined to set up Young on the edge of the area. Without even touching the ball, Young spun around, and then he shot, on the turn, left-footed, with superb technique and sublime timing.

The ball flew past the Iam McFaul into the top corner of the net.

Almost immediately, Newcastle attacked again. Heslop tried to run the ball too far out of defence, but he was dispossessed, and Iley's long ball was controlled by Sinclair, who turned and half-volleyed over Mulhearn, just inside City's penalty area.

This was a peculiar atmosphere, unique almost, for a top flight English Division One game, as every time either Newcastle or City scored, the crowd noise sounded exactly the same as a home goal, with both sets of fans in exuberant form. It was a carnival atmosphere, with 20,000 City fans amongst the 46,492 crowd. It was assumed there were many more than that inside the ground, though. It felt like a classic FA Cup Final match, as the first half ended 2-2.

Just three minutes into the second half, Summerbee fed Colin Bell from the right, and the midfield maestro tricked and twisted his way into the area, turning Tommy Robson inside out, and then he finally shot.

McFaul saved, but he turned the ball away to his right. Neil Young raced in and blasted the loose ball into the far side of the goal for a 3-2 lead to City.

Soon after, Colin Bell collected a pass in midfield, from around thirty-five yards out. He instantly controlled the ball, then swivelled slightly, under pressure from Scott, before deftly flicking the ball with the outside of his right boot, between the two Newcastle centre-backs, and sublimely releasing the late-rushing Francis Lee, inside the United penalty area.

It was the most elegant display of skill of the entire match, grace under pressure, skill that transcended time, and it preceded *Cruyff, Ardiles, Beardsley, Redondo, Pirlo, Iniesta, Xavi, and Fabregas.* But it was on a muddy, bumpy North-eastern pitch, and he was surrounded by tough tackling old-school British defenders, McNamee and Moncur. It was wonderful skill that released Francis Lee on goal, and Lee finished clinically, first time past McFaul.

As a whole season's work was crowned by that one great, great moment, almost the entire Manchester City team just ran in to join Francis Lee inside Newcastle United's Gallowgate End to celebrate, ecstatically.

McNamee headed in Pop Robson's cross with just a few minutes remaining, but City easily played out the rest of the match to win 4-3 and secure their second ever Football League First Division Championship trophy.

The fans, who'd been celebrating each team's goals together at both ends of the ground, finally poured onto the pitch to embrace both teams.

Some City players were chaired off the pitch, and there was not a hint of trouble. City were Champions of England, but Newcastle's fans also celebrated.

It was a day never to be forgotten for those lucky enough to have been there.

Colin Bell said that 90,000 City fans must have told him they were at St James's Park that day, back in May 1968.

Captain Tony Book lifted the trophy three days later at Maine Road, as Bury, having just won promotion to the Second Division, played a celebration match. Book had started his career at Bath City and he'd played 399 games for the non-league club, before moving to Plymouth Argyle in 1964. He played 81 games for the Pilgrims, before signing for Manchester City, at the age of thirty-one.

Not only did he sign for City, though, he was made their team captain. And not only was he made their team captain, Book became City's most successful captain, having played most of his career outside of the Football League, and arriving at Maine Road well into his thirties.

One great thing about this City team, was that the goals were shared amongst all their four top scorers. All four of them had hit the teens in their goal-scoring totals, a feat never since repeated.

Neil Young was City's top scorer with nineteen league goals from forty games. Francis Lee had scored sixteen from just thirty-one games, while Colin Bell and Mike Summerbee scored fourteen each. Tony Book was City's only ever-present in their Championship winning season.

Manchester City started poorly in the defence of their title in 1968-69, winning only six points from their first nine games, and they'd lost four times. They'd badly missed Tony Book, however, through injury until the New Year. By the time Tottenham Hotspur had arrived at Maine Road on 12th October, City were well out of the title race having won just four of their opening eighteen league and cup matches.

George Heslop, though, had been displaced by a local nineteen year-old centre half.

Tommy Booth, Manchester-born, was excellent in the air, but he was equally comfortable with the ball at his feet. Also, Harry Dowd had returned to fitness and he'd replaced Ken Mulhearn in goal. City beat Spurs 4-0 (Lee 2 (1 pen), Coleman, Connor), but they'd lost too much momentum and were forced to settle for a mid-table First Division position, the year after they were Champions.

City had also been knocked out of the European Cup, in the First round, by Turkish side Fenerbahce, 2-1 on aggregate. City had taken a 0-0 first leg home draw to Turkey for their away second leg.

Amidst an intimidating atmosphere, on a terrible pitch, and against hostile opponents, City played well and Tony Coleman had even given them the lead, but Fenerbahce equalised, and then they scored a devastating late winner, after poor Ken Mulhearn had dropped a cross, under heavy pressure from a Turkish forward.

On Saturday 4th January 1969, Francis Lee's penalty was sufficient to knock Luton Town out of the FA Cup Third round, at Maine Road. An epic Fourth round tie against Newcastle United followed, but a replay was needed, the two games were watched by a combined attendance of 118,838.

The first match, at Newcastle on 25th January, in front of a deafening 57,994 St James's Park crowd, and with Tony Book having settled back into City's defence, after over four months out of action, City battled out a 0-0 draw.

On the following Wednesday night, 29th January, 60,844 bulged the Maine Road barriers, and they were elated as future Carlisle legend Bobby Owen and Neil Young both scored to win the tie 2-0.

The Fifth round draw sent City on a short trip up to Blackburn Rovers, but they won 4-1 (Coleman 2, Lee 2) in front of a massive 42,315 Ewood Park crowd.

A home crowd of just 48,872 then watched their Sixth round match against Spurs.

MANCHESTER CITY		TOTTENHAM HOTSPUR
Harry Dowd	1	Pat Jennings
Tony Book	2	Phil Beal
Glyn Pardoe	3	Cyril Knowles
Mike Doyle	4	Alan Mullery
Tommy Booth	5	Mike England
Alan Oakes	6	Peter Collins
Mike Summerbee	7	Neil Johnson
Colin Bell	8	Jimmy Greaves
Francis Lee	9	Alan Gilzean
Neil Young	10	Terry Venables
Tony Coleman	11	Jimmy Pearce

Spurs were without the cup-tied Roger Morgan, their £100,000 signing from QPR, but they'd come with a definite game plan to pressure and also subdue City, to take the reigning Champions back to White Hart Lane.

They almost succeeded.
Only seconds before full-time, Francis Lee conjured up a cracking, classic winning goal. He'd cut in from the right, and then curled a rocket beyond Pat Jennings.
Tottenham were visibly gutted.

On Saturday 22nd March, Villa Park, a muddy Villa Park, a very muddy Villa Park, hosted the Semi-final between City and Everton.

Everton had been doing very well in the league, unlike City, and they had two fluent goal scoring forwards in Joe Royle and Jimmy Husband, who'd ended up scoring forty-eight league and cup goals between them during 1968-69.

Everton's water-tight defence had also conceded only one goal in their four FA Cup matches prior to the Semi-finals.

A tight, tense and tough match, between two truly tenacious teams, was won through yet another last-minute decider. Neil Young's corner was clipped back by Summerbee, to Tommy Booth inside the area, and Booth slammed the ball up into the roof of the net, right under the masses of City fans filling the Holte End. Almost immediately, the final whistle sounded, and City were ecstatic.

Leicester City had beaten the FA Cup holders West Brom up at Hillsborough, and they met the Sky Blues at Wembley Stadium on Saturday 26th April.

Manchester City, however, played in red and black stripes against Leicester. Malcolm Allison had introduced that kit as the team's away colours, intending City to become as great and as famous as the current European Champions AC Milan.

MANCHESTER CITY		LEICESTER CITY
Harry Dowd	1	Peter Shilton
Tony Book	2	Peter Rodrigues
Glyn Pardoe	3	David Nish
Mike Doyle	4	Bobby Roberts
Tommy Booth	5	Alan Woollett
Alan Oakes	6	Graham Cross
Mike Summerbee	7	Rodney Fern
Colin Bell	8	Dave Gibson
Francis Lee	9	Andy Lochhead
Neil Young	10	Allan Clarke
Tony Coleman	11	Len Glover
David Connor	12	Malcolm Manley

City had the better of the early chances, with Tony Coleman blasting over from six yards after Summerbee's right sided pass across the six yard box being their best chance. Then, Allan Clarke cut inside from the left, and he shot on the run, just inside the area, but Harry Dowd flew and turned the ball behind, stinging his fingers, at the top right corner of his goal.

From Dave Gibson's resultant corner, Clarke flicked on for Rodney Fern to shoot wide from eight yards out.

Peter Rodrigues then missed from inside the six yard box, following Gibson's cross.

After 24 minutes, and against the run of play, Manchester City broke, and they won a throw-in halfway inside Leicester's half. Francis Lee's throw towards the right side of the penalty area was seized upon by Mike Summerbee, under pressure from Alan Woollett. Woollett squeezed Summerbee to the bye line, but then Summerbee wriggled free, and he pulled the ball back to Neil Young, free in space, just to the right of the penalty spot. Young's left footed shot beat the diving Shilton, and two covering defenders on the goal-line, smashing the ball high into the goal net.

Allan Clarke had had a magnificent match for Leicester, his last game for the Foxes, and he was voted Man of the Match by the football writers. He'd also secured himself a British record transfer fee to new Champions Leeds United during the summer of 69, while Man landed on the Moon.

It had been a wonderful FA Cup triumph for Manchester City. Over their seven matches in the competition, 410,170 people had paid to watch them, at an average crowd of 58,596 per match, surely some sort of a post-war record?

Manchester City gave up their League Championship trophy by finishing down in thirteenth place. They'd conceded far more goals than a year before, and they hadn't scored as many. Neil Young and Colin Bell were equal top scorers on fourteen goals, while Francis Lee had scored just twelve from thirty-seven games.

Manchester City again failed to compete for the League Championship, during 1969-70, finishing down in tenth place with only 43 points.

Just two games into that season, though, Harry Dowd was replaced as regular goalkeeper by the young, Manchester-born Joe Corrigan.

At six feet, four and a half inches tall, Corrigan had been signed straight from school, and he was one of the tallest keepers in the Football League, throughout his career. His physical dominance, agility, and confidence in the air earned him an England under-23 cap before the end of the year.

Unfortunately, Tony Coleman had played just five league games for City during 1969-70 before he joined Sheffield Wednesday, after playing 83 league games and scoring twelve goals, during his two and a half years at Maine Road.

Coleman's place in their team was taken by Ian Bowyer, another product of City's youth system. On Wednesday 17th September, City travelled to Spain for the First round of their European Cup Winners' Cup campaign. Drawn against Athletic Bilbao, City battled superbly before 40,000 hostile and partisan Basques. They drew 3-3, after coming back from 3-1 down (Young, Pardoe, and an Echevarria own goal).

Two weeks later, on Wednesday 1st October, 49,665 swelled Maine Road under the floodlights, for a great European night. Alan Oakes, Colin Bell and Ian Bowyer all scored to give City a fantastic 3-0 win and a 6-3 aggregate victory, to slightly dim their nightmares of Fenerbahce.

Having already seen off Southport 3-0 in the Second round of the Football League Cup, and then Liverpool (an ageing Liverpool side) 3-2 in the Third round, City then faced Everton in the Fourth round, on 14th October. The same eleven that had hammered Bilbao, Corrigan, Book, Pardoe, Doyle, Booth, Oakes, Summerbee, Bell, Lee, Young and Bowyer, won 2-0 (Bell, Lee pen), with 45,643 inside Maine Road.

Manchester City then beat QPR 3-0 in the Quarter-finals (Bell 2, Summerbee), and they were drawn against Manchester United in the Semi-finals.

City had beaten Lierse SK of Belgium 8-0 (Lee 4, Bell 3, Summerbee), on aggregate in their Cup Winners' Cup Second round tie, during November, before, on Wednesday 3rd December, City hosted United in their League Cup Semi-final first leg match.

55,799 again swelled Maine Road to bursting point, as Colin Bell and Francis Lee's penalty kick gave City a narrow 2-1 advantage over United (Bobby Charlton).

63,418 filled Old Trafford, two weeks later, on December 17th 1969.

MANCHESTER UNITED		MANCHESTER CITY
Alex Stepney	1	Joe Corrigan
Paul Edwards	2	Tony Book
Tony Dunne	3	Glyn Pardoe
Nobby Stiles	4	Mike Doyle
Ian Ure	5	Tommy Booth
David Sadler	6	Alan Oakes
Willie Morgan	7	Mike Summerbee
Paddy Crerand	8	David Connor
Bobby Charlton	9	Francis Lee
Denis Law	10	Neil Young
George Best	11	Ian Bowyer

Despite missing Colin Bell, City launched an early attack, as they never intended to sit on their narrow lead. Summerbee crossed from the right for Young to shoot from the left, on the run, but Ure magnificently cleared off the line. Stepney was unable to grab the loose ball, however, and Bowyer pounced to fire in from six yards, past Ure who was still guarding the goal-line, for a 3-1 aggregate lead.

Bobby Charlton then won the ball inside the centre-circle, and he fed Crerand in midfield. Pat Crerand laid the ball off for right-back Paul Edwards, who fired high into Corrigan's goal from the edge of the area. That simple, slick move illustrated the ease with which United could break, but they then scored a magnificent second half goal to level the aggregate scores.

George Best received the ball from Ure, five yards inside his own half, and with space ahead of him, he ran with the ball, being vigorously chased and challenged by Bowyer, ten yards inside the City half. His run was so strong, though, Bowyer just couldn't get a tackle in, and only nibbled at Best's heels. Booth came across with a strong challenge just outside the area, but Best rode it well, recovered, and then drove in a cracking eighteen yard shot, which Stepney could only palm into Denis Law's path, who couldn't miss from three yards.

Cue the famous three man goal celebration of Charlton, Law and Best, embracing each other, arms aloft. It had been a truly great red Ferrari of a goal, owned by Law, but it had been engineered, shaped, coloured and driven by Best.

Heading towards extra-time, only eight minutes before the end of the game, Willie Morgan obstructed Bowyer just outside United's penalty area, and the ref awarded an indirect free-kick.

Maybe Francis Lee noticed something that nobody else did, or maybe he hadn't seen the referee's arm aloft, because he drove in a fierce shot, straight at goal. Stepney dived and saved, parrying the ball to Summerbee, who was first to the rebound. At the ball, Summerbee drove the shot into the inviting, empty net for City's big party. As fairy-tales go, you couldn't make it up. It had made Cinderella seem far-fetched.

Maybe Stepney saw something that nobody else did, or maybe he just hadn't seen the referee's arm aloft? Did he think there'd been a slight deflection?

If he had just left it, a goal kick would have been given.

Anyway, it was a mistake that cost his team possibly their place at Wembley, and Summerbee, Lee, Young and Bowyer all celebrated wildly right under the Stretford End.

West Bromwich Albion had beaten Carlisle United 4-2, on aggregate, in the other Semi-final, and they met City at Wembley, on Saturday 7th March.

MANCHESTER CITY		WEST BROMWICH ALBION
Joe Corrigan	1	John Osborne
Tony Book	2	Doug Fraser
Arthur Mann	3	Ray Wilson
Mike Doyle	4	Tony Brown
Tommy Booth	5	John Talbut
Alan Oakes	6	John Kaye
George Heslop	7	Len Cantello
Colin Bell	8	Colin Suggett
Mike Summerbee	9	Jeff Astle
Francis Lee	10	Asa Hartford
Glyn Pardoe	11	Bobby Hope
Ian Bowyer	12	Dick Krzywicki
(rep. Summerbee)		(rep. Hartford)

On a muddy, muddy *Ypres* of a field, due to the **Horse of the Year Show** having been held at Wembley Stadium during the week, West Brom took an early lead.

Left-back Wilson's high cross was met by both Corrigan and Astle jumping together, but Astle's head had crucially beaten Corrigan's touch and Albion were 1-0 up.

City then laid siege to Albion's goalmouth. Francis Lee was thwarted by John Osborne's sharp save; Glyn Pardoe shot just wide; and Osborne also saved Alan Oakes' long range drive.

Mike Summerbee's season was ended by a hairline fracture of his right leg, but still *he limped on, wounded, boots heavy like meat, he cursed through sludge, sucked down into the mud, hobbled back into the bottomless mud.*

Glyn Pardoe's right-sided corner was flicked on by the hobbling Summerbee, and Bell's header was volleyed in by Mike Doyle.

Into extra-time, Summerbee was eventually replaced by Ian Bowyer. With the day darkening and the mud worsening, Francis Lee crossed from the right for Colin Bell to flick on with his head, and from six yards out, Glyn Pardoe steered the ball past John Osborne into the empty net.

Glyn Pardoe's dramatic late winner triggered on-field elation, both on the bench and on the Wembley terraces. Joe Mercer jumped as high as an Olympic long jumper at the final whistle. Their thirty-five year old captain Tony Book then lifted his third major trophy in less than two years, and only six years after he'd been playing Southern League football.

Eleven days after their Wembley triumph, Manchester City hosted Academica Coimbra of Portugal in their European Cup Winners' Cup Quarter-final second leg match. After their 0-0 draw in the first leg, Tony Towers came off the substitute's bench to replace Heslop, and he bundled home a late winner to secure Manchester City's first-ever European competition Semi-final place.

Tony Towers went on to play 122 First Division games for City between 1969 and March 1974, when he signed for Sunderland in a player exchange deal that brought Dennis Tueart to Maine Road, and he eventually represented England as a Sunderland player, but Wednesday 18th March was *his* night.

On April Fools' Day, City lost 1-0 away at Schalke 04, in front of 35,000 in Gelsenkirchen.

Two weeks later, though, a packed Maine Road witnessed City's rampant, imperious performance, and the sublime demolition of their West German opponents in the second leg, on Wednesday 15th April 1970.

Francis Lee and Alan Oakes both combined to set up Mike Doyle inside Schalke's penalty area for the first, before Colin Bell cut inside from the right and clipped in a good ball for Oakes to set up Neil Young for their 2-0 lead.

Neil Young's left-footed shot had scuffed the far post before going in.

Alan Oakes was always going forward, and then he provided his third assist of the match, after setting up Young with a defence-splitting pass.

Neil Young drove his first time shot, left-footed, high into Schalke's goal.

Five minutes into the second half, Bell played the ball along the edge of the Schalke area, to Doyle, whose diagonal pass invited the clinical Francis Lee to drive the ball to the right of the German keeper, 4-0.

MANCHESTER CITY		SCHALKE 04
Joe Corrigan	1	Nigbur
Tony Book	2	Slomiany
Glyn Pardoe	3	Becher
Mike Doyle	4	Ruessmann
Tommy Booth	5	Fichtel
Alan Oakes	6	Wittkamp
Tony Towers	7	Libuda
Colin Bell	8	Neuser
Mike Summerbee	9	Pohlscmidt
Francis Lee	10	Erlhoff
Neil Young	11	Van Haaren
Frank Carrodus	12	

Glyn Pardoe then played the ball out wide left to Young, whose powerful cross was flicked by Bell into the far corner of the goal. Schalke did score a late consolation, but it had been a devastating display by City, one of the Best Ever by an English team in Europe, slaughtering Schalke, a good West German team, 5-1.

Inspired by West German international winger and club legend "Stan" Reinhard Libuda, nicknamed *Stan* over in Germany because of his quick, Stanley Matthews dribbling skills, Schalke finished runners-up in the Bundesliga, behind Bayern Munich, just two years later.

The European Cup Winners' Cup Final was played in Vienna, against the Polish team Gornik Zabrze. Gornik had qualified for the Final after drawing 2-2 at home against AS Roma in the Semifinal first leg, and then drawing 1-1 away in Rome.

In subsequent seasons following 1969-70, away goals counted double, and then penalty kicks further decided which team progressed in European ties.

Under those rules, City would have been playing AS Roma in Vienna.

However, this Semi-final went to a replay, which was also drawn, and then Gornik actually reached the Final on the toss of a coin.

The match was watched by less than 8,000 fans, most of whom were City supporters. Polish fans were mostly absent due to Eastern Bloc travel restrictions to the West, and the dreadful weather had also kept many locals away from the game. As the teams entered the pitch, the heavens opened wide, and flooded the open stadium.

Gornik were a decent side that had already defeated Rangers, and included not only Jerzy Gorgon, a powerful, six foot two inches tall, blond defender who played for Poland in both the 1974 and 1978 World Cup Finals tournaments, but also Wlodzimierz Lubanski, Poland's star player who went on to harass and embarrass Bobby Moore during their 2-0 World Cup win over England, in June 1973, in Chorzow.

Manchester City opened the scoring twelve minutes into the Final. Francis Lee teased and tormented his marker Olek, before working free from two further pursuers into space. He fired in a long range shot from outside of the area, that the Polish keeper Kostka could only parry, and Neil Young scored on the rebound, before jubilantly turning away, with his arm aloft.

And, two minutes before half-time, Young was then fouled inside the Gornik area. Francis Lee powered home his penalty kick, through the keeper's legs, in the driving rain.

Halfway into the second half, Gornik scored what was a consolation, when captain Oslizlo scored from inside the area after clever work by Lubanski.

City hung on grimly in the awful conditions, on the waterlogged pitch, *lashed with rain,* with the ball splashing through, and then stopping dead, in puddles. Players' boots were saturated on exhausted legs, but never mind, Tony Book lifted the Cup Winners' Cup in the rain, *guttering down in waterfalls,* like the four major Trophies that City had won in just over two years.

Manchester City started 1970-71 quite well, winning six games and earning fourteen points from their first eight games, including a great 1-0 away win at reigning Champions Everton on 29th August. Colin Bell, now nicknamed Nijinsky after the magnificent 2000 Guineas and Epsom Derby winning race horse, had scored the goal. They fell behind leaders Leeds and Arsenal in October, but were still deep in the race for a UEFA Cup place when City visited Old Trafford on 12th December.

City won 4-1 (Doyle, Lee hat-trick), but the game was marred by a terrible injury to left-back Glyn Pardoe, after a poor tackle by George Best.

Pardoe would not return to first team football for nearly two years, by which time his left-back place had been taken by Willie Donachie, and he was never the same player again. The tackle also disturbed George Best, himself, and was seen as one of the reasons for his descent into darker ways, and his eventual demise.

Glyn Pardoe played his 304th and final league game away at Leicester City in March 1975, having played only forty games for City in the previous four and a half seasons. He'd made his City debut in 1962 as a sixteen year old in an 8-1 defeat by Wolves.

Pardoe missed only ten league and cup games during Manchester City's golden years of 1967-70, and he was undoubtedly their greatest left-back.

After the New Year of 1971, City were also missing Bell, Oakes and Summerbee, as well as Pardoe, for much of the remainder of the season, and they subsequently won only one of their final nineteen First Division games.

Only 18,000 watched a City reserve side draw 2-2 at home with Liverpool on Monday 26th April, as City ended up down in eleventh place.

An underlying cause of City's refrain from glory was the sublime partnership between manager Joe Mercer and coach Malcolm Allison which began to disintegrate after 1970. A takeover battle for Manchester City caused a rift that reflected Caesar, Brutus and Mark Antony. Bitterness, ambition, betrayal and recriminations eventually caused a permanent split between Mercer and Allison.

It was believed that Joe Mercer had privately agreed to eventually step aside and allow Allison to become City manager, but then he decided to carry on in 1970. Mercer saw their partnership as the big reason City had been so successful. He needed Allison as much as Allison needed him. They balanced the other, perfectly.

Allison saw things very differently, and he was furious at Mercer's change of heart. He helped engineer a boardroom takeover by a rival group led by Peter Swales, who had promised him he would become manager when they were successful.

Joe Mercer continued to support the incumbent board, headed by Albert Alexander, with whom he enjoyed a great relationship. That board was actually on the verge of sacking Malcolm Allison, but Mercer had then threatened to quit if Allison was sacked, so Allison stayed.

Albert Alexander's son, Eric, took over as chairman, as an interim choice, and the battles continued to rage, as the board was totally split over their support of Allison.

The takeover eventually succeeded, though, and in October 1971, Joe Mercer discovered that his car parking space had been removed, and his office was now occupied by Malcolm Allison. Joe Mercer had been relieved of his position, and moved upstairs into a GM role.

On Tuesday 18th January 1972, Neil Young was sold to Preston North End, along with David Connor, for a combined fee of £90,000. Connor, a great man-marker who'd crucially kept Alan Ball quiet during their 1969 FA Cup Semi-final win, was a utility player of fine quality, but he found the utility badge difficult to lose, and could never command a regular place in City's first eleven.

He still played over 140 league matches for City, in nearly ten years at Maine Road.

Neil Young was a real City legend, though, as influential as Bell, Lee and Summerbee, during their 'Glory years' successes. The intense-faced six-footer, with his devastating left foot, had played 334 league games at City, and scored 86 goals.

But it was his forty-nine goals in all competitions between 1967 and 1970 for which he would be most remembered, loved and celebrated by City fans.

He went on to play sixty-eight league games at Deepdale, scoring eighteen Second Division goals, before he moved to Fourth Division Rochdale, where he retired from football during the 1974-75 season.

Neil Young died on Thursday 3rd February 2011, aged sixty-six years old, having been diagnosed with terminal cancer only a few weeks earlier.

Manchester City issued a special commemorative red and black scarf, celebrating Neil Young's FA Cup winning goal, with all proceeds going to Cancer Research.

With City back on top of the First Division, in March 1972, Allison then paid QPR a club record transfer fee of £200,000 for Rodney Marsh. Joe Mercer had advised Allison not to start Marsh straight away, but to hold him back until the following season, and to use him mainly as a substitute. Most of the City players had even noticed that Marsh was a little overweight when he first arrived, and Joe Mercer also advised Allison to work on Marsh's fitness.

Malcolm Allison ignored all of Mercer's advice and he started Rodney Marsh in all but two of City's nine remaining league games. They lost two games at the beginning of April, with Marsh starting, at home to Stoke and also away at Southampton, and they ultimately lost their lead at the top of Division One.

On 12th June 1972, Joe Mercer resigned, becoming Coventry City's new manager three days later. One of his first activities at Highfield Road was to buy Tommy Hutchison from Blackpool.

If Allison had bought Tommy Hutchison, instead of Marsh, City would probably have won the title in April 1972

Mercer became England's caretaker manager in 1974, after Sir Alf Ramsey was sacked. He won three and drew three of his seven very entertaining games in charge, and he gave international debuts to Frank Worthington, Keith Weller and Alec Lindsay.

Joe Mercer died on Thursday 9th August 1990, on his 76th birthday, after he'd been suffering from Alzheimer's disease. Joe Mercer Way now leads Twenty-first Century Manchester City fans to the City of Manchester/Etihad Stadium.

Malcolm Allison, despite his desperation for years to become manager, seemed all at sea after Mercer was forced out. Under his management, City won only eleven of 35 First Division games during 1972-73, were knocked out of the FA Cup by Sunderland, in the Fifth round, and by Bury in the League Cup Third round.

After City had earned just a single point from six league games in March, Allison left Maine Road to become Crystal Palace's manager on 30th March 1973.

Big-mouthed, and larger than life in his fedora hat and sheepskin coat, the flamboyant Champagne-drinking, Cuban cigar-puffing Malcolm Allison was among the finest, deepest-thinking and most innovative football coaches English football has ever known. As City manager, though, he was underwhelming.

Allison then suffered successive relegations with Crystal Palace. However, he did change their old-fashioned pin-striped strip to the striking red and blue stripes still worn today, and he also changed their nickname from the Glaziers to the Eagles.

He also almost made history, by nearly taking a Third Division team to an FA Cup Final, managing Palace to wins, all away from home, over Leeds United, Chelsea and Sunderland, en route to the 1976 Semi-finals.

However, he resigned in May 1976 having failed to achieve promotion back to Division Two, and after Palace had been a long way clear at the top of the Third Division, back in December 1975.

It had indeed been a Bohemian Rhapsody of a season for Crystal Palace, but it ended with Malcolm Allison leaving Selhurst Park.

"No, baby, can't do this to me baby. Got to get out, just got to get right out of here."

Malcolm Allison did return to Manchester City at the end of the Seventies, as manager, but it was another experiment that didn't work, resulting in City dropping down to the bottom of the First Division, before John Bond arrived and lifted City back up the table, as well as taking them back to Wembley.

On Thursday 10th September 2009, Malcolm Allison was inducted into Manchester City's Hall of Fame, along with Joe Mercer and all of City's players that had won the League Championship trophy, the FA Cup, League Cup and European Cup Winners' Cup between 1968 and 1970.

Malcolm Allison died aged eighty-three, on Thursday 14th October 2010.

Malcolm Allison was replaced as City's manager by Johnny Hart, who remained as their manager for six months, and he even signed Denis Law on a free transfer just before the start of 1973-74, but he was forced to retire after a pancreatic attack.

Johnny Hart's permanent replacement, Ron Saunders, was unpopular with many senior players, particularly Summerbee, Doyle and Lee, but he took City to the 1974 League Cup Final, where they lost to Wolves. Saunders had also signed Dennis Tueart from Sunderland, in the exchange deal that sent Tony Towers up to Roker Park.

However, after an awful April in 1974, during which City did not win in six games and dropped into a relegation battle, Ron Saunders was sacked as manager.

Tony Book was then given the manager's job on a permanent basis, having been caretaker manager after Johnny Hart retired.

City's legendary captain had played 244 First Division games, having signed as a thirty-one year old, a remarkable achievement.

Book's first victory as City manager was their 1-0 away win over Manchester United, thanks to Denis Law's back heeled goal. Law did not celebrate the goal with his teammates, as he thought he had relegated his old team. He was wrong. Birmingham had won anyway, so United were down, even if they'd won. Denis Law retired after the 1974 World Cup Finals, having played during Scotland's 2-0 win over Zaire.

He was City's second highest scorer during 1973-74, with nine goals from 22 games.

City's top scorer Francis Lee was fed up, though, and he signed for Derby County on Wednesday 14th August 1974, for £100,000. Joe Mercer's *"final piece of the jigsaw"* had scored just ten goals in 29 games during 1973-74, and he then became Dave Mackay's *"final piece..."*, as Derby launched another League Championship assault. Lee scored twelve goals from 34 games, in 1974-75, as part of Derby's fluent-scoring attack.

Lee's strength and tenacity made him an all-time legend at Maine Road, as a player, after he'd scored 112 First Division goals in 248 league games with City.

He went on to score 25 goals in 62 First Division games while at Derby.

The day before, on 13th August, Tony Book had paid a club record transfer fee of £250,000 to West Bromwich Albion for their creative midfielder Asa Hartford.

Hartford's British record £170,000 transfer to Leeds United, back in November 1971, had been scratched due to Leeds' infamous, and totally inaccurate, *hole in the heart* medical report.

With a fresh mixture of old and new, Manchester City returned to winning ways during 1974-75, with Bell, Marsh, Hartford, Tueart and Summerbee playing some scintillating football.

In the season when anyone could have won the league, City sat on top of the First Division on Saturday 23rd November 1974, for the first time in nearly three years. Three months later, City were still only three points behind the league leaders Stoke.

However, despite the arrival of £200,000 striker Joe Royle from Everton on Monday 23rd December, City fell away at the Melling Road in early March, and they ended up in eighth place, but only seven points behind Francis Lee's Derby County.

Colin Bell enjoyed the new way of City's adventurous football, becoming their top scorer with fifteen First Division goals. Dennis Tueart had scored fourteen, while Rodney Marsh also hit nine, and once again, City fans felt the thirst for silverware.

On June 13th 1975, Mike Summerbee was freed to join Jimmy Adamson's Burnley. *Buzzer* had played 357 league games for Manchester City, scoring 46 goals, but he'd provided goals for many other scorers. A true City hero, he'd been denied a dream move to Leeds United over a year earlier, after chairman Peter Swales had raised the asking price at the last minute.

Summerbee's move to Burnley was not successful. Star player Leighton James was sold to Derby County in December 1975, while midfield architect Doug Collins was injured for most of the season.

Burnley were relegated, after finishing second from bottom in the First Division. Summerbee left for Blackpool, soon after, before his career wound down at Stockport County, playing in an Argentina 78 Adidas World Cup team kit.

Mike Summerbee then went on to play with Bobby Moore, Pele, Osvaldo Ardiles, Sylvester Stallone and Michael Caine, in John Huston's Escape to Victory.

In June 1975, Tony Book strengthened City's defence by signing Sunderland's England international centre-back Dave Watson for £175,000. And on 9th September, Watson scored his first City goal to cancel out Ted McDougall's goal as they drew 1-1 with Norwich City, away at Carrow Road, in the League Cup Second round.

A week later, McDougall scored twice to equalise goals by Joe Royle and a Dennis Tueart penalty in the replay at Maine Road.

Only 6,238 attended the second replay at Stamford Bridge on 29th September.

World Cup winner Martin Peters scored for Norwich in the first half, but Dennis Tueart's hat-trick, including two penalty kicks, plus further goals for Royle, Doyle and also Butler's own goal, completed their emphatic 6-1 hammering of the Canaries.

In the Third round, City hosted Brian Clough's Nottingham Forest, a team already including six players who'd eventually become European Cup winners. City won 2-1 (Royle, Bell), though, with former City hero Ian Bowyer scoring Forest's goal.

Then, on Wednesday 12th November, 50,182 packed into Maine Road for their Fourth round clash with newly-promoted First Division title contenders Manchester United, a game Colin Bell would never forget, as much as he'd like to.

Dennis Tueart opened the scoring for City after just one minute, amidst a tremendous atmosphere, and then with Tommy Docherty's young United side rattled, City pushed on for a second.

Colin Bell, while turning inside Martin Buchan, then suffered a terrible, horrible injury to his right leg, following Buchan's poor tackle. Bell, at that time, was City's leading goal-scorer with six First Division goals, as they sat just below the UEFA Cup places.

MANCHESTER CITY		MANCHESTER UNITED
Joe Corrigan	1	Paddy Roche
Kenny Clements	2	Chris Nicholl
Willie Donachie	3	Stewart Houston
Mike Doyle	4	Tommy Jackson
Dave Watson	5	Brian Greenhoff
Alan Oakes	6	Martin Buchan
Peter Barnes	7	Steve Coppell
Colin Bell	8	Sammy McIlroy
Joe Royle	9	Stuart Pearson
Asa Hartford	10	Lou Macari
Dennis Tueart	11	Gerry Daly
Tommy Booth	12	David McCreery

Colin Bell did not properly return to first team football, until over two years later, as a substitute against Newcastle United on Boxing Day 1977.

He was never the same player again, though, and Bell's England career was also over, after just 48 international matches.

City went on to beat United 4-0 (Tueart 2, Hartford, Royle), but Colin Bell's injury greatly soured their victory. Nobody, though, had foreseen the seriousness or the consequences of Bell's injury at the time.

Their 4-2 home win over giant-killing Quarter-finalists Mansfield Town (Royle, Oakes, Tueart, Hartford), secured a straightforward passage to the last four.

City were then drawn against Jack Charlton's Middlesbrough in the Semi-finals.

Boro were a defensively brilliant, counter-attacking team in 1975-76, and they'd kept fourteen clean sheets, up to then, from their twenty-six First Division games.

John Hickton gave Middlesbrough a 1-0 first leg win, on Tuesday 13th January, with a massive 35,000 crowd inside Ayresome Park. Middlesbrough had conceded only one single goal during their five previous League Cup matches as they travelled down to Maine Road for the second leg, eight days later, with their one goal lead.

Boro had to replace former European Cup winner Bobby Murdoch with Tony McAndrew, though, and they suffered a little without Murdoch's experience.

City took full advantage. Gerard Keegan, Alan Oakes, Peter Barnes and Joe Royle scored two in each half for their easy 4-0 win, and a 4-1 aggregate victory.

Newcastle had beaten Spurs 3-2 in the other Semi-final, and they met City in the League Cup Final at Wembley Stadium on Saturday 28th February.

City struck early on.

After only eleven minutes, Hartford swung in a free-kick from right of centre, thirty yards out. Doyle leapt to beat Howard in the air, and his knock-down wasn't well dealt with by Keeley, so Peter Barnes pounced to hook in from six yards.

With Tommy Booth playing freely in Colin Bell's position, alongside Oakes, and the equally adventurous Cassidy and Craig in United's midfield, the game opened up into a bright, absorbing clash, with superb skills and many chances.

MANCHESTER CITY		NEWCASTLE UNITED
Joe Corrigan	1	Mike Mahoney
Gerard Keegan	2	Irving Nattrass
Willie Donachie	3	Alan Kennedy
Mike Doyle	4	Stuart Barrowclough
Dave Watson	5	Glen Keeley
Alan Oakes	6	Pat Howard
Peter Barnes	7	Micky Burns
Tommy Booth	8	Tommy Cassidy
Joe Royle	9	Malcolm MacDonald
Asa Hartford	10	Alan Gowling
Dennis Tueart	11	Tommy Craig

Booth beautifully teed up Oakes on the edge of the area, but Alan Oakes shot just wide of Mahoney's goal.

Newcastle United's equaliser, ten minutes before half-time, was brilliant. Alan Gowling steered home MacDonald's cross, after a lovely five-man passing move.

Donachie's long left-sided free-kick was then well-collected by Tueart inside the area, but Mike Mahoney pulled off a good, clean save at Tueart's feet.

Then, Dennis Tueart's flying header from Donachie's left wing cross went just a yard over, and the teams went in level at half-time.

Just a minute into the second half, though, Donachie crossed for Booth, inside the area. Tommy Booth headed back inside, and on the penalty spot, with his back to the goal, Dennis Tueart performed the most perfect, wonderful overhead bicycle kick ever seen for a 2-1 lead.

Tueart's goal was voted as the greatest moment in the League Cup's history by 20,000 fans on the Football League website in 2011.

Mahoney then saved well from Joe Royle, after Barnes' excellent left-footed cross. Royle chipped over Mahoney from twenty yards, but his goal was ruled out after an arguable offside decision.

Newcastle responded well before the end. Burns turned inside the six yard box and shot just an inch or two wide of the far post, with Corrigan beaten.

Corrigan was also forced to make a great save from Gowling's shot, but City withstood Newcastle's late pressure, and captain Mike Doyle lifted the League Cup.

City's fans were delirious, after seeing a bright, entertaining mixture of the new and the old win a Cup at Wembley again, having waited six years.

With a UEFA Cup place secure, City took their foot off the gas in the First Division for the remaining two months, and they finished in eighth place. Dennis Tueart was their top scorer, with twenty-four goals in all competitions, while Joe Royle had also scored eighteen, and Asa Hartford twelve goals.

Rodney Marsh had moved to Tampa Bay Rowdies in the NASL, back in January 1976, before he returned to England to guest-star for Second Division Fulham during 1976-77. The gifted, but inconsistent and maverick Marsh is generally credited for City losing the League Championship in 1972, but that's not entirely true.

Malcolm Allison should have developed Marsh into a City first team player more gradually than he did, but he also lost Joe Corrigan for seven of their last eight league games. Rodney Marsh's different, more individual style of play to City's fluent, quick-passing game was certainly a cause of them losing their grip on that title, but not the only cause.

Marsh played 116 First Division games for Manchester City, scoring 36 goals. He was City's top scorer in 1972-73 with nineteen goals in all competitions, from 46 games.

After a brief and underwhelming spell at Fulham, he returned to Tampa Bay in 1977 and he played in the NASL for two years. The football and lifestyle suited him perfectly, as Rodney Marsh scored 41 goals in 87 NASL games.

After a club record 565 league appearances for Manchester City, Alan Oakes moved to Third Division Chester City in July 1976, as their player-manager. An unsung hero, he was so described; and tipped for an international future, he was always on the fringe of England's team for many seasons.

Oakey didn't bother; he just got on with his job with City quietly, and determinedly. His performance against Schalke 04 in 1970 was World Class, and he was a key player, a major force, in Manchester City's greatest ever team.

Oakes played 211 times for Chester, and his total of 776 Football League matches is the seventh-most in history. His record of 669 league and cup games for Manchester City is likely to stand forever.

With Colin Bell still out, on 1st July 1976, Tony Book signed Brian Kidd from Arsenal for a bargain £100,000 fee. The former Manchester United forward and European Cup winner had scored thirty goals during the previous two seasons at Highbury.

Also local youngster Paul Power had taken Alan Oakes' place in midfield. With Peter Barnes, and their diminutive midfield creator Gary Owen, from St Helens, finding regular starting places in City's team, they resembled a team of the future again, and bulging with quality.

The new-look, *Umbro-striped* Manchester City hosted West Ham United on Saturday October 2nd 1976, while sitting nicely in fourth place, and only one point behind leaders Liverpool.

City moved up to second place, level on points with Liverpool, watched by a Maine Road crowd of just 37,795. City were missing Paul Power, but Gary Owen gave them a 1-0 half-time lead, before a second half goal-fest resulted in a 4-2 win (Owen, Tueart 2, Hartford).

MANCHESTER CITY		WEST HAM UNITED
Joe Corrigan	1	Mervyn Day
Kenny Clements	2	Keith Coleman
Willie Donachie	3	Kevin Lock
Mike Doyle	4	Billy Bonds
Dave Watson	5	Bill Green
Gary Owen	6	Tommy Taylor
Peter Barnes	7	Mick McGiven
Brian Kidd	8	Graham Paddon
Joe Royle	9	Alan Taylor
Asa Hartford	10	Trevor Brooking
Dennis Tueart	11	Billy Jennings

Back in Europe, in the UEFA Cup, it had taken Juventus, and their Italian international all-stars of Zoff, Tardelli, Gentile, Morini and Boninsegna, to literally scrape past City, 2-1 on aggregate.

Free-scoring City were once again excellent at the back, scoring sixty goals but conceding only thirty-four goals in 42 games, as they finished 1976-77 in second place, and only one point behind the mighty European Champions Liverpool.

They'd also kept twenty-two clean sheets.

Brian Kidd was their top scorer with 21 goals from 39 games, and Dennis Tueart had scored 18 from 38. Joe Royle also chipped in with nine in all competitions.

Back in the high life again, Tony Book had brought them to where they had been back in 1968 and 1972, but he'd brought them back brilliantly.

Mike Doyle moved to Stoke City in 1978, after 448 league games with Manchester City over thirteen seasons. Voted City's hardest ever player in the club's official magazine, Doyle was an accurate passer, strong in possession, and famed for his great long distance throw-ins.

Stoke City paid £50,000 for Doyle, and he then played over 100 games at the Victoria Ground, helping them back up to the First Division, before he retired. Mike Doyle played five times for England, having made his debut in their 2-1 win over Wales on March 24th 1976, in Wrexham, partnering Phil Thompson in central defence.

Only two other players, Alan Oakes and Joe Corrigan, played more games for City than Doyle. Mike Doyle died, aged only sixty-four, on Monday 27th June 2011, while being treated for liver failure.

Dave Watson was made City's club captain in 1978, after Mike Doyle left, before he himself left City, via Werder Bremen, for Southampton, in 1979.

He had played 146 First Division games for City in four seasons, and eventually played a career total of 65 games for England, including all of their matches during the 1980 European Championship Finals.

Dennis Tueart left for the NASL in 1978, to play for New York Cosmos, after 140 league games for City in four seasons. He returned to Maine Road for the 1979-80 season, though, and continued to play for City until they were relegated, on the final day of the 1982-83 season.

Tueart earned six England caps, while at Maine Road, scoring two goals, and he later became a director at the club, before finally standing down in 2007, ending his thirty-three year association with Manchester City.

Asa Hartford played 185 First Division games with City, before signing for Brian Clough's European Champions Nottingham Forest in 1979, for £500,000. However, he played only three games for Forest before moving on to Everton. He returned to Maine Road in 1981, after which he played a further 75 league games.

Hartford played fifty times for Scotland, including both of the 1978 and 1982 World Cup Finals tournaments. He moved to Norwich City in 1984, and won a second League Cup winners' medal in 1985, having created the winning goal against Sunderland in the Final...

... not a bad career for a player who Leeds wouldn't buy due to his *hole in the heart.*

Tommy Booth moved to Preston North End in 1981, after 382 First Division games for Manchester City in thirteen seasons. He was City's substitute in the 1981 FA Cup Final against Tottenham Hotspur, having played in midfield during their Semi-final victory over that great UEFA Cup winning Ipswich Town team at Villa Park. Preston paid just £30,000 for Tommy Booth, and he then played 84 league games for the North Enders.

Joe Corrigan was still City's goalkeeper during that 1981 FA Cup Final. The six foot four and a half inches giant goalkeeper played 476 league games for Manchester City, and 592 games in all competitions, the second most of any City player, ever.

Along with legends Bert Trautmann and Frank Swift, Joe Corrigan is one of City's three greatest ever goalkeepers.

Colin Bell's career was not ended by that Martin Buchan tackle in November 1975, but his career as a key player in City's team was ended. At the time of his eventual retirement in 1979, at thirty-three years old, he'd played only thirty-one league games during the previous four seasons.

Colin Bell played a total of 394 First Division games for his club, scoring 117 goals.

He was the greatest ever player in Manchester City's history.

This was confirmed, as if there were any doubt, by a 2009 Times Online report of the fifty greatest City players that placed Bell securely at Number One.

There were eight members of that 1968-70 team in the top sixteen, with Glyn Pardoe at 22, and Tony Book at a ridiculously high 36. Heslop, Coleman, Mulhearn and Dowd were the only City regulars from 1968-70 who missed out on the top fifty.

I would go even further. Colin Bell was the best all-round English midfield football player, in my lifetime.

In the history of English football, those great City teams of 1968-70 compares favourably with the greatest teams of all time.

With an all-English eleven and most were from the North-west, they'd competed with, and proved equal to the likes of Manchester United, the European Champions, Liverpool, and the near-perfection of Leeds United. I'm not over-hyperboling, if such a verb even existed, when I suggest how exciting it would be to see, on the eve of the 2011 Champions League Final, as I write, a European Cup Final between that 1970 Manchester City team and Pep Guardiola's Barcelona side.

How good would it be to see Bell and Oakes' midfield craft against Xavi and Iniesta, or Summerbee and Coleman's dynamic wing plays supplying Lee's devilish runs, or Neil Young's power? So satisfying it'd be to see City's quick, strong defence, with Doyle and Booth, holding Messi and Villa. Only in your imagination can such match-ups occur, and it's probably true that Barca would no doubt just about win, but *that* City team did merit *that* level of occasion, denied to them by a fierce combination of a high level of competition in the First Division, and their own infuriating, managerial and boardroom infighting.

I do wonder, for all the millions and millions of pounds in the world, if City will ever again have a team to even equal Tony Book's team from 1974-77, let alone Joe Mercer and Malcolm Allison's great team from those Glory years of 1967-72.

The Man City team that won 6-1 at Old Trafford, and then won probably the most dramatic League Championship title of all time, after beating QPR 3-2, *"Balotelli, Aguerooooooo!"*, on Sunday 13th May 2012, came very close.

But they'll never, ever have the same legendary or beloved status at Manchester City.

SKY BLUE HEAVEN

I N 1962, THE CONSECRATION and opening of the new Coventry Cathedral took place. Graham Sutherland's magnificent tapestry, **Christ in Glory,** the largest in the world, was unveiled, and Benjamin Britten's 20th Century masterpiece, **War Requiem,** was premiered at Coventry Cathedral.

Twenty-two years after enduring the longest single air raid ever suffered by any British city, the skies were blue once again for the city. The West Tower, the third tallest spire in England, behind Salisbury and Norwich, and the outer walls were all that survived of the Gothic cathedral. A new open-front porch attached the Gothic ruins to the new 20th century cathedral, and the space between the West Tower and the Gothic walls was left open to the sky.

It was a sky blue future for the city.

The same year, new Coventry City manager Jimmy Hill, a visionary, a spin doctor, an inspiration, changed the team's home colours to sky blue. The match day programme was re-branded as The Sky Blue. In the redevelopment of Highfield Road, two new stands were built sky blue. Even trains in the city were going to be sky blue, and Jimmy Hill wrote the team anthem **The Sky Blue Song**, adapted from the tune of the **Eton Boating Song**. Hill felt it gave his team an advantage.

Coventry City had not worn sky blue for over forty years, but like their unique cathedral, they were embracing the future, and Sky Blue was its colour.

Then to properly link the twin re-births between the church and the football club, Dr Cuthbert Bardsley, Bishop of Coventry, was appointed Coventry City's club President in June 1965.

Back in the summer of 1962, Coventry City were a lowly Third Division team. They had spent a few years either side of the War in Division Two, but for the remainder of the previous forty years, they'd languished in the Third and Fourth Divisions. By 1963, Jimmy Hill had propelled Coventry up to fourth in Division Three, and he then paid Nelson F.C. just fifty pounds for wing half Ernie Machin.

During the following year, Hill splashed out a world record transfer fee for a goalkeeper, by paying Crystal Palace £35,000 for Bill Glazier. He also bought left footed playmaker Dave Clements from Wolves, and took Coventry up to Division Two, for the first time in twelve years, as Champions of the Third Division.

Coventry settled into Second Division mid-table in 1965, but then they finished third, just a single point behind promoted Southampton.

Jimmy Hill then shocked home supporters by selling their best player and club legend George Hudson to Northampton Town for £28,500. Hudson had scored sixty-two league goals from just 113 games in three seasons at Coventry.

City fans had even called Pele the **black George Hudson,** he was so good.

Ball-playing inside forward Ian Gibson was then bought from Middlesbrough for a club record transfer fee of £57,000. The Dumfries and Galloway man supported City's Coventry-born centre forward Bobby Gould and also youngster John Tudor in attack during 1966-67.

Coventry City attracted their record home crowd, 51,455, against the Second Division leaders Wolves on Saturday 29th April 1967, at Highfield Road.

51,455 was the official attendance, anyway. Those present were sure there were more than 55,000 at the game, and some had even suspected sixty thousand. The Swan Lane terraces, City's Spion Kop, were swelled to overspill. Supporters sat on the pitch side, just inches behind the touch-line. They were stood on the roof of Coventry's commentary box, and had even climbed the flood-light pylons.

Coventry beat Wolves 3-1 (Machin, Gibson, Rees) and eventually won the Second Division Championship. Jimmy Hill took great delight in the fact that sixty of City's 74 league goals had been scored by players who'd cost a total of less than £1550.

After taking Coventry up to the First Division, Jimmy Hill wanted a ten year contract, but he was offered only five years. So, on the eve of the 1967-68 season, he officially resigned, and was immediately replaced by Noel Cantwell.

Cantwell, captain of Manchester United's FA Cup winning team, had just retired after helping United to win the First Division Championship. Hill had spent the summer helping the club to search for a suitable replacement, and Noel Cantwell, who had also been Chairman of the PFA, was the correct choice.

The season started disastrously, though. After their opening day defeat at Burnley, City's captain and inspirational centre-half George Curtis suffered a terrible leg break, during their second game at Nottingham Forest, which put him out of action until September 1968.

Ernie Machin was subsequently appointed captain of City.

Coventry won just two of their first twenty games, during a difficult first half of their first season in the First Division. Thanks to Bill Glazier's superb performances, however, they drew eight times, earning valuable points, from what would've been defeats with a lesser goalkeeper.

Willie Carr, a Glaswegian, red-headed youth team graduate, made his Coventry debut in their 2-1 home win over Southampton on Tuesday 5th September (Tudor, Rees). It was Coventry's first ever win in the First Division.

On Saturday 16th December, City gave their 28,560 home fans an early Christmas present, after beating Burnley 5-1 (Gould 3, Rees, Machin). However, hat-trick hero Bobby Gould would only play five more games for Coventry, before Arsenal bought him for £90,000 at the end of January 1968.

Bobby Gould had scored 40 league goals in just 82 games for Coventry City. However, somewhat annoyingly, Gould never stayed at any club for much more than one season, thereafter, despite boasting a First Division goal per game ratio of better than one in three.

Neil Martin was Gould's immediate replacement. Noel Cantwell paid Sunderland a club record transfer fee of £90,000 for the dark-haired, intense-looking, six-footer from Alloa, Clackmannanshire.

47,111, Coventry's largest crowd of the season filled Highfield Road on Saturday 16th March 1968, as they hosted league leaders Manchester United. And they desperately needed points to haul themselves out of the bottom two.

Ernie Hunt, a new club record £65,000 signing from Everton, and Chris Cattlin, an elegant left back, signed from Huddersfield Town, were both making their City debuts.

Ernie Hunt had actually been Wolverhampton Wanderers' top scorer the previous season, as Wolves finished second behind the Sky Blues. Everton manager Harry Catterick then signed Hunt, due to his goal scoring prowess, but he'd failed to settle at Goodison Park.

COVENTRY CITY		MANCHESTER UNITED
Bill Glazier	1	Alex Stepney
Dietmar Bruck	2	Shay Brennan
Chris Cattlin	3	Francis Burns
Ernie Machin	4	Paddy Crerand
Maurice Setters	5	David Sadler
Dave Clements	6	Nobby Stiles
Ernie Hannigan	7	George Best
Ernie Hunt	8	Brian Kidd
Neil Martin	9	Bobby Charlton
John Tudor	10	John Fitzpatrick
Willie Carr	11	David Herd
	12	John Aston

Willie Carr nutmegged Bobby Charlton, twice, to set up Ernie Machin, and Coventry won 2-0 (Machin, Setters), sending Sky Blue fans buzzing back to their homes.

Right back Dietmar Bruck was however about to be replaced as City's regular number 2, by a lad from Warwickshire, Mick Coop. Bruck could play on either the right or left side, though, and he remained at Highfield Road until 1970, when Charlton Athletic paid £15,000 for their veteran.

Born in Danzig, during Wartime, whilst the Polish city was in German territory, Bruck was a German national, but his family emigrated. In England, he was then raised in Coventry from childhood, and attended the very same Coventry school that Gabby Logan went to during the late Seventies, while her father Terry Yorath was at Coventry City. Bruck had made his Coventry debut back in 1961, and he was City's regular full-back for most of the Sixties, playing 182 league games at Coventry. He still lives in Coventry, and occasionally organises Fun Days at the Ricoh Arena.

Two goalless draws away at West Ham and Southampton, at the end of the season, were enough to maintain their top flight status by just one point, over second bottom club Sheffield United.

Neil Martin's eight goals in his fifteen games were a crucial factor in their survival. Coventry City's average home attendance of 34,705, though, had placed the club firmly in the Top Ten best supported teams in England.

1968-69 was similar to their First Division debut season. They won ten games, but lost twenty-one, and they again finished only one point above relegated Leicester. Once again, Ian Gibson, their creative outlet in attack, had missed the majority of the second half of the season.

Coventry had again attracted average home crowds of over 33,223, and they remained in the top ten of First Division average crowds. They'd even attracted home crowds of between 8,000 and 10,000, occasionally, just to watch their reserves play in the Football Combination.

For the 1969-70 season, Leicester-born six-footer Jeff Blockley was promoted to City's team, partnering the great George Curtis in their centre of defence. After an opening day goalless draw away at Sunderland, Coventry hosted West Bromwich Albion on a Tuesday night for their first home match.

36,905 watched redheaded Willie Carr fire a hat-trick, as their awesome front five of Trevor Gould, Ian Gibson, Neil Martin, Carr and Dave Clements tore Albion's rugged defence apart.

In contrast, West Brom's excellent forward line of Tony Brown, Colin Suggett, Jeff Astle and Bobby Hope were kept very quiet by Coop, Curtis, Blockley and Cattlin.

By Saturday 30th August, Coventry had won three and drawn two of their opening six First Division matches, as their old rivals from Wolverhampton visited Highfield Road. 38,336 watched the Sky Blues continue their great start to the season.

COVENTRY CITY		WOLVERHAMPTON WANDERERS
Bill Glazier	1	Phil Parkes
Mick Coop	2	Les Wilson
Chris Cattlin	3	Derek Parkin
Ernie Machin	4	Mike Bailey
George Curtis	5	John Holsgrove
Jeff Blockley	6	Frank Munro
Ernie Hunt	7	Jim McCalliog
Ian Gibson	8	Peter Knowles
Neil Martin	9	Derek Dougan
Willie Carr	10	Hugh Curran
Dave Clements	11	John Farrington

A team as near to the ultimate Coventry City eleven, as you could ever find, almost a perfect team, won a great game against a good Wolves team, but who'd been badly missing their brilliant left winger Dave Wagstaffe since the opening day of the season.

Gentleman's barber Ernie Hunt slotted home the game's only goal, after running onto Machin's perfect through pass, as City's 1-0 win lifted them up to third place in the First Division, just behind Everton and Liverpool.

September brought a tough run of matches, though, and only three points were gained from five games, before Ernie Hunt scored the winner in their 1-0 win at Arsenal, in early October. Then, in front of almost 40,000 supporters, away at newly-promoted Derby County, Coventry won 3-1 (Martin, Blockley, McFarland own goal), and they'd pulled themselves right back into the race for an unlikely European place.

Coventry then went on a winless run of six league matches up to late November, which had again dropped the Sky Blues right back down to mid-table.

In the midst of that barren run, they lost 1-2 at home to Manchester United, on Saturday 8th November, when George Curtis, *The Ironman*, played his 486th and final league game for Coventry City. Second Division Aston Villa paid the Sky Blues just £20,000 for their greatest ever centre-half and captain.

Noel Cantwell had simultaneously paid Dunfermline Athletic £40,000 for Roy Barry, who immediately became Coventry's new captain, tightening the defence and inspiring their attack.

Barry, a relatively short centre-half, at just five feet and nine inches tall, had starred for the Pars, when they'd won the Scottish Cup Final, against Hearts, back in 1968.

Thereafter, from November 20th until February 11th 1970, Coventry City achieved a fantastic run of eight First Division wins from nine matches, one of the greatest periods in their history. They beat Newcastle United 1-0 (Ernie Hunt), on Thursday 20th November, before hosting Tottenham Hotspur on Saturday 6th December.

COVENTRY CITY		TOTTENHAM HOTSPUR
Bill Glazier	1	Pat Jennings
Mick Coop	2	Tony Want
Dave Clements	3	Cyril Knowles
Ernie Machin	4	Alan Mullery
Roy Barry	5	Mike England
Jeff Blockley	6	John Pratt
Ernie Hunt	7	Neil Johnson
Willie Carr	8	Jimmy Greaves
Neil Martin	9	Alan Gilzean
John O'Rourke	10	Martin Chivers
Ian Gibson	11	Steve Perryman

28,372 watched their classic, rollercoaster 3-2 home win (Machin, O'Rourke, Gibson), before sweeping Crystal Palace aside 3-0 (Hunt, Joicey 2), and before beating Ipswich Town 3-1 at home on Boxing Day, (Hunt, Harper own goal, Martin penalty). Dennis Mortimer had made his league debut for Coventry during that home win over Ipswich, coming on as substitute for Ian Gibson.

On Saturday 10th January, Coventry hammered Manchester City's star-studded front five of Summerbee, Bell, Lee, Bowles and Bowyer, by 3-0. Neil Martin's header, and then John O'Rourke's brace, had secured the two points, to lift City up to ninth place.

A week later, Leeds beat Coventry 3-1 at Elland Road, after a couple of goals from Allan Clarke, and Jack Charlton's header. That was the only blemish, though, in Coventry's great run, but they immediately returned to winning ways, 1-0 away at Sheffield Wednesday, after John O'Rourke had scored the only goal at Hillsborough.

30,935 then watched Dennis Mortimer's first home start for Coventry, as they beat Arsenal 2-0 (O'Rourke, Martin), on Saturday 31st January, with both Ernie Machin and Ian Gibson again out injured. Coventry's eighth and final win of that tremendous run came away at Upton Park, as Neil Martin's two goals secured their 2-1 away win over West Ham United, with Moore, Peters, Hurst, Brooking, Bonds and Best.

After two seasons of just making up the numbers in Division One, Coventry had finally arrived, rising up to fourth place, twelve points behind leaders Leeds United, but with three games in hand.

Ten days later, league leaders Everton hosted an injury-riddled Coventry, who nevertheless battled for a great goalless draw in front of a huge 45,934 Goodison Park crowd. Coventry were perched near to the pinnacle, the very peak of their Football League history at this time, and with three games in hand on the leaders. Never again were they ever so high up in the league, and at such a late stage of the season.

	PL	W	D	L	F	A	PTS
Leeds United	33	18	13	2	71	32	49
Everton	32	21	6	5	54	28	48
Chelsea	30	14	11	5	51	34	39
COVENTRY CITY	30	15	7	8	41	29	37
Derby County	33	15	7	11	44	32	37

On Saturday 28th February, 37,448 Sky Blues fans packed Highfield Road for Coventry's home game against third-placed Chelsea. However, it shouldn't have been under-estimated how good their opposition was on that day. Chelsea had a spectacular front five of Cooke, Hudson, Osgood, Baldwin and Houseman, and they hammered the below-strength Sky Blues 3-0, with a devastating display of quality attacking.

Coventry then lost at home to Liverpool, and they drew with Sheffield Wednesday, but Ian Gibson returned for the match with Tottenham on Saturday 21st March, even though Hunt, Machin and Clements were still out. Martin Peters was making his debut for Spurs, after a £200,000 British record transfer move from West Ham United.

Gibson's return to the team was inspirational, though, and future Aylesbury United manager Trevor Gould had played the game of his life out on the right wing, as goals from Martin and O'Rourke, City's big man/smaller man double act again proving effective, had beaten their star-studded opponents 2-1.

Coventry's 2-1 away win at White Hart Lane was followed by three 1-1 draws against Sunderland, Burnley and Manchester United. That final draw, away at Old Trafford, took place on 30th March, the afternoon of Easter Monday.

On the following night, Tuesday 31st March, the heavily influential Ernie Hunt had returned to Coventry's team, as well as both Ian Gibson and Willie Carr, and they thrashed Southampton 4-0 (Joicey 2, O'Rourke, Martin).

Coventry City's rollercoaster season continued on the following Saturday, though, with their 0-3 home defeat to Stoke City. Qualification for the Fairs Cup was virtually secured, however, on Tuesday 7th April, as John O'Rourke scored a sparkling hat-trick during their 4-1 hammering of Nottingham Forest.

Three days later, on Friday 10th April, the night before the 1970 FA Cup Final, Coventry made the short trip up to Wolverhampton needing a win to guarantee European competition at Highfield Road for the following season. Due to the match being on a Friday night, the crowd was small for a derby match, with just 23,395 inside Molineux, but most of them were Sky Blues supporters that night.

Coventry didn't disappoint them.

Hunt, Clements, Carr, Martin, Gibson and O'Rourke were electric and inventive in possession, as the brilliantly and joyously side-burned Brian Joicey scored their vital goal for City's 1-0 away win.

Neil Martin had top scored for the Sky Blues during 1969-70 with fourteen league goals from 40 games. John O'Rourke also scored eleven from just 20 games, while Ernie Hunt had scored nine. Coventry City's back four, often the weak link during their early years in First Division football, had kept fifteen clean sheets.

Player of the season, though, had to be David Clements, who'd worked hard through injuries, playing 33 First Division games, and starting at left-back, right-half, left-half, right wing and left wing, fully embodying the new idea of Total Football.

At the end of their finest ever league season, Coventry finally finished sixth, having been overtaken during the final few weeks of March and April by both Derby and Liverpool, but they'd continued to attract average home crowds of more than 33,000.

In August 1970, Noel Cantwell paid Liverpool £30,000 for defender Geoff Strong. An FA Cup winner in 1965, Strong had also played 31 games for Liverpool two seasons earlier, when the Reds finished runners-up behind Leeds United.

However, Ian Gibson was very surprisingly sold to Cardiff City for £35,000 after ninety-three league games for Coventry, over four seasons.

Cardiff, chasing promotion to the First Division themselves, had signed Gibson to support their two star strikers John Toshack and Brian Clark. A dynamic and tireless inspiration, Ian Gibson was very greatly missed by Coventry. He went on to play ninety league games for Cardiff, also, and he was selected in many Bluebirds' fans' all-time Cardiff City teams in an online debate set up on the BBC Radio 606 website in 2010. A greatly respected player at both clubs, he retired through injury shortly after joining AFC Bournemouth in 1974.

On Wednesday 30th September, Coventry eliminated Trakia Plovdiv of Bulgaria in their Fairs Cup First round tie, 6-1 on aggregate, after winning their second leg home match 2-0 (Joicey, Blockley).

Three days later, on Saturday, 3rd October 1970, Coventry hosted the reigning Champions Everton, and 28,563 witnessed the Sky Blues scoring one of the most famous goals in English football history.

Coventry were 2-1 up late in the game, with just ten minutes to go, Martin and Hunt having scored for the Sky Blues. It was a tight match, poised to go either way, when Everton conceded a free-kick just outside their penalty area.

In a four man wall, substitute Sandy Brown, Howard Kendall, John Hurst and Roger Kenyon all fidgeted nervously, in their yellow and royal blue away kit.

Keith Newton was tightly marking the troublesome John O'Rourke, alongside.

COVENTRY CITY		EVERTON
Bill Glazier	1	Andy Rankin
Mick Coop	2	Tommy Wright
Dietmar Bruck	3	Keith Newton
Dave Clements	4	Howard Kendall
Jeff Blockley	5	Roger Kenyon
Geoff Strong	6	Colin Harvey
Ernie Hunt	7	Alan Whittle
Willie Carr	8	Alan Ball
Neil Martin	9	Joe Royle
John O'Rourke	10	John Hurst
Brian Alderson	11	Johnny Morrissey

The ball rose fully ten feet into the air, then Hunt stepped forward, strode forward, and volleyed the ball off the laces of his right boot, full force, with both of his legs off the ground as he struck the ball. O'Rourke peeled away from his marker, shifting Newton from his defensive spot by just a few inches. The ball slammed through where Newton's head would have been, and it flew, rising, past the diving Rankin, and smashing into the far right corner of the Everton goal.

It was voted *Goal of the Month* for October 1970, on BBC TV's Match of the Day, and it also won BBC's *Goal of the Season* award in 1970-71.

What made the goal even more impressive was that Ernie Hunt was not quite ready when Carr flicked it up. With the Everton wall still fidgeting about nervously, he was waiting to see where it would finally place itself.

Like the Cruyff turn, Dennis Tueart's overhead kick, and Beckham's goal from the halfway line, in years and generations to come, that goal was iconic. It was symbolic of the inventive football and entertainment that Coventry introduced to the First Division in their first four years.

School playgrounds and playing fields all over the country played host to many attempts to copy that goal, almost always unsuccessfully.

John Sillett, Jimmy Hill's first ever signing for Coventry, and a future City manager, said that Hill had made the team practice about fifty inventive free-kicks time and again, and that particular free-kick was possibly number 49 in their repertoire.

Willie Carr says, even now, never a week goes by without someone mentioning the goal to him... but he didn't even score the goal.

On November 3rd 1970, Coventry City hosted Bayern Munich at Highfield Road in the Fairs Cup Second round, second leg. Bayern Munich brought an immense West German all-star team to Coventry, including Franz Beckenbauer, Gerd Muller, Sepp Maier and Uli Hoeness, possibly among the most illustrious opponents ever to play at Highfield Road.

Dennis Mortimer was, by now, a regular first team player. The young Mortimer, with his rebellious looks and long dark hair, shoulder length, the first properly long-haired player at Coventry, resembling James Taylor in the 1970 road movie *Two Lane Backtop,* would play against Bayern Munich in Europe again.

COVENTRY CITY		BAYERN MUNICH
Bill Glazier	1	Maier
Mick Coop	2	Hansen
Wilf Smith	3	Koppenhofer
Dennis Mortimer	4	Beckenbauer
Jeff Blockley	5	Pumm
Brian Hill	6	Hoeness
Ernie Hunt	7	Zobel
Willie Carr	8	Roth
Neil Martin	9	Muller
John O'Rourke	10	Mrosko
Dave Clements	11	Brenninger
Brian Joicey	SUB	Schneider

City's double act of Martin and O'Rourke secured a great 2-1 win.

A really great win it was, over the legendary West German superstars. Unfortunately, Bayern Munich's 6-1 thrashing of Coventry in the first leg, just a fortnight earlier, had given them a 7-3 aggregate win, as brilliant as Real Madrid's thrashing of Eintracht Frankfurt in 1960, to put it into context.

Coventry City would never again play in European club competitions.

Neil Martin was the third player of that great 1970 Coventry City team to leave Highfield Road. In February 1971, Nottingham Forest paid £66,000 for his services, after he'd scored forty First Division goals in 106 games.

Martin was seriously dangerous in the air, thriving with smaller, more skilful forwards like Gibson, Carr, Hunt, O'Rourke and John Tudor, and he also formed a good attacking partnership with Duncan McKenzie at Nottingham Forest.

Forest considered themselves very unlucky not to reach the FA Cup Semi-finals in 1974, after a riot-affected match at St James's Park had undone all the hard work by both Neil Martin and Duncan McKenzie against Newcastle, helping the Reds to a 3-1 lead with a quarter of an hour remaining, during their Sixth round match.

Coventry finished 1970-71 in mid-table, a huge advance from their relegation struggles during their first two seasons in Division One, but a long way short of the sixth place they achieved the previous season.

Also, City's average home attendance had dropped to an underwhelming 26,047.

On August 27th, only one game into 1971-72, Sheffield Wednesday paid Coventry £100,000 for both Dave Clements and Brian Joicey.

Clements, one of the greatest players to play for Coventry, simply used Wednesday as a stepping stone before he joined title challengers Everton two seasons later.

David Clements had played 229 league games for the Sky Blues.

Coventry only won nine matches in the First Division in 1971-72, and despite finishing eight points above the relegation zone, they ended up down in eighteenth place. Attendances continued to drop, slightly, to an average of 24,505, the sixth lowest in the First Division, and over 10,000 fewer than just four years earlier.

1972-73 saw the further disintegration of Coventry's great 1970 team. Ernie Hunt had played their first seven games, but then no more. He was amazingly loaned out to Doncaster Rovers, then struggling in the Fourth Division, in January 1973.

Hunt played at Doncaster for two months, and then four further games for City in 1973 after returning to Coventry, before he finally joined Bristol City in December 1973. He played a dozen league games at Ashton Gate, before eventually dropping down to non-league football, but he'd played in the Robins' famous FA Cup Fifth round away win over First Division leaders Leeds United in February 1974.

Ernie Hunt played 142 First Division matches, and scored 45 goals for Coventry City.

On 4th October, Jeff Blockley was sold to Arsenal for a club record transfer fee of £200,000. Blockley had played 144 games at centre-half for Coventry. Two days after he signed for Arsenal, Blockley was included in Alf Ramsey's England squad, and he made his international debut in their match against Yugoslavia at Wembley Stadium.

In December 1972, the great Ernie Machin joined Plymouth Argyle. He'd played 257 league games for Coventry, having joined for just fifty pounds nine years earlier, but he'd have played nearly 400 if it wasn't for his persistent knee injuries.

Ernie Machin never wasted a pass. He was a great passer and he passed with craft and subtlety. Machin was never a quick player, but he had a sharp eye and a great sense of timing, scoring 32 league goals for the Sky Blues.

During 1973-74, he formed an attacking partnership with Paul Mariner, as Plymouth reached the League Cup Semi-finals. Machin played 42 league games for the Pilgrims, and he became as fondly remembered at Home Park as he was at Highfield Road.

Having suffered from ill health for several years, Ernie Machin, Coventry's Warwickshire-born, bright-haired and blue-eyed Sky Blue captain, died on Sunday 22nd July 2012, aged only sixty-eight.

Jim Brown, Coventry City's official historian, wrote in his obituary of Machin, "the epithet Legend is a word used too often about mediocre players in the hyperbole-driven media; however, Ernie Machin was a true Coventry City legend."

On October 11th 1972, Coventry City's new manager Joe Mercer had paid a club record transfer fee of £140,000 to Blackpool for midfielder Tommy Hutchison, while he'd also paid £140,000 to Rangers for their striker Colin Stein.

Hutchison would become regarded as the greatest player of Coventry City's thirty-four year stay in the top flight of English league football. He played over 300 First Division matches for Coventry between 1972 and 1980, when he signed for John Bond's Manchester City.

Despite the great Tommy Hutchison's presence, however, Coventry were fading, on-field. During 1972-73, they finished only five points above the relegation zone, after winning just thirteen games.

Willie Carr was injured for most of 1973-74, an injury that had ruined his big money move to Wolverhampton Wanderers. He did eventually join Wolves, in March 1975, for £100,000, after playing 245 league matches for Coventry, and scoring 32 goals, but creating countless other goals. Coventry ended 1973-74 just two points above the relegation zone, and home crowds now averaged just over 23,000.

The great Bill Glazier played his 346th and final league game for Coventry away at Wolves on Saturday 7th December 1974. Bill Glazier was, and always will be, the greatest goalkeeper in the Sky Blues' history.

After Dennis Mortimer had joined Aston Villa for £175,000 in December 1975, after 190 First Division games for Coventry, only Mick Coop and Chris Cattlin remained by the mid-seventies from their great 1969-70 teams.

Chris Cattlin retired at the end of 1975-76, having played 217 league games at Coventry. On Saturday 13th March 1976, however, only 13,938 had turned up to watch Coventry City draw 1-1 with Arsenal at Highfield Road.

Mick Coop played on until 1981, when he retired after a club record 485 First Division matches at Highfield Road. A great defender, with good crossing ability, he then coached City's 1987 F.A. Youth Cup winning team.

Coventry ended their 1975-76 First Division season in mid-table, well clear of relegation, but well short of any European adventures. They'd scored only forty-seven goals in 42 games, while conceding fifty-seven.

Coventry City had drawn either 0-0 or 1-1 on fourteen occasions, and their average home crowd remained just above 19,000, now the second-worst in the First Division.

The safe, unspectacular football Coventry were playing in the mid-Seventies was a complete contrast to their progressive, and refreshing, more *funky* type of football from the late Sixties and very early Seventies.

Their style had endeared them to football supporters all over the land, and many football supporters actually adopted Coventry as their favourite second team.

Heavens, back in 1965, Coventry City had been the first Football League club to stage a closed-circuit live television match at Highfield Road, while the Sky Blues played away at Cardiff City. Over 10,000 had attended the live televised match at their ground, watching those big screens.

Now, only 13,000 were bothering to attend an actual First Division match at home to the mighty Arsenal.

By 1976, Coventry had become a team that wasn't exactly disliked by the average supporter, but they were much easier to ignore. Apart from Tommy Hutchison, and maybe David Cross, Mick Coop and John Craven, many neutrals couldn't name another Sky Blues player.

The teams built by Jimmy Hill, and then developed by Noel Cantwell were the foundation stones upon which over three decades of top flight football emerged.

However, their 1969-70 teams, easily their best of the Glam Soccer period, should have transformed into a perfect and impenetrable team, a grand and impressive fortress, with Gothic flourishes, a magnificent and glorious Cathedral, reflecting St Michael's in Coventry.

Instead, Coventry City had emerged in 1976 as a very nice suburban semi-detached house, with a few award-winning rose bushes in their front garden.

If football could be related to music, which it easily can, then Coventry can be well compared to the more successful, trophy-winning teams of the era.

If Manchester United, Leeds, Liverpool, Derby County, Tottenham, Manchester City and Arsenal were the million sellers, the chart-topping Led Zeppelin, Rolling Stones, Pink Floyd, The Who or Beatles' albums, then Coventry City's exciting, diverse, developing team of 1967-70, were more your King Crimson, your Van Der Graaf Generator or even your Blackfoot Sue, of Association Football.

They produced the inventive, the progressive, the odd, and the refreshing, for your more discerning type of football lover.

Coventry would go on and have better days ahead, and they even experienced a surprise, magical trophy-winning success at the 1987 FA Cup Final. They also embraced multi-racial football before most other teams, but their days would never be so euphoric, so fever pitched, so fearless and unpredictable, such a Rolls Royce ride, such a rollercoaster ride, so delirious and delightful as those Sky Blue days, and their greatest teams between 1967 and 1970.

They made the skies blue.

TANGERINE DREAM
(Oh I Do Like To Be Beside the Seaside)

IN 1954, JIMMY ARMFIELD JOINED A GREAT BLACKPOOL team, just a year after their classic 1953 FA Cup Final win, the ***Matthews Final,*** when Stan Mortensen scored a hat-trick. Mortensen, Stanley Matthews, Bill Perry, Ernie Taylor, Allan Brown, Jackie Mudie, George Farm and Harry Johnston were all Blackpool legends during the very greatest period of their club's history.

Armfield's own international pedigree grew to become top class, though, winning 43 England caps, fifteen times as captain, and he was voted the best right back at the 1962 World Cup Finals in Chile.

He was also a non-playing member of their victorious 1966 squad, after George Cohen had replaced the thirty year old Armfield before the tournament.

However, by the end of the Sixties, having captained Blackpool for nearly a decade, Armfield led a new fresh young team of Tangerine talents, with a young, dynamic and talented midfield, an energetic Blackpool team that displayed an exciting type of colourful football.

Tony Green was just five feet seven inches tall and very slightly built, but he played 121 league games in Tangerine. He would have played many more, but he'd missed seventeen months at the very end of the Sixties, due to an Achilles tendon injury, and by the start of the Seventies he was wanted by many top First Division clubs.

A Glaswegian, Green didn't score prolifically, but he was a classy and clever provider of goals, of close control, clean passing, and long range shooting, and he created many goals in an era when assists were not officially counted.

Alan Suddick had joined Blackpool back in December 1966 from Newcastle United.

He'd been the golden boy of the Magpies' return to First Division football in 1965. Many believed he had the talent of George Best, and if he had been at the right club, he might have been as successful, but Newcastle were not the right club in those times.

His £60,000 transfer fee was a Blackpool club record.

A practical joker, Suddick had famously pulled down the shorts of a Bury defender lined up in a defensive wall at the Gallowgate End in 1964. His elaborate ball skills, superb passing and famous banana free kicks made him one of Blackpool's greatest and most loved players, and half of their wonderful midfield partnership alongside Tony Green.

Stan Mortensen then paid Alloa Athletic just £10,000, in February 1968, for their brilliant twenty-year-old ball-playing winger, Tommy Hutchison, to fill the left side of their midfield.

During 1967-68, boosted by Hutchison's impressive performances, Blackpool won eight of their final nine Second Division games, to finish level on points with second-placed QPR. However, QPR won promotion by the very, very smallest of goal averages.

At the end of the following season, though, Blackpool finished a little further down the table, and the great man Stan Mortensen, was sacked as their manager and replaced by Les Shannon.

Les Shannon then signed Micky Burns from top amateur team Skelmersdale United during the summer of 1969. The Skem had reached the 1967 Amateur Cup Final at Wembley, with a twenty year-old Burns in their team, and they drew 0-0 with Enfield in front of a 75,000 crowd. A teacher by profession, Micky Burns was a quick and tricky front player, but he played mostly out on the right wing, becoming Blackpool's top goal-scorer in three of his five seasons at Bloomfield Road.

Fred Pickering had also been signed by Les Shannon, from Birmingham City, for 1969-70. Pickering was a proven, prolific goal-scorer, having scored 56 First Division goals for Everton in just ninety-seven games between 1963 and 1967.

Overall, prior to joining Blackpool, Pickering had scored 142 league goals from 294 games for Blackburn, Everton and Birmingham. He was a £30,000 bargain.

Pickering was most famous as being one of the very few players to have scored a hat-trick for England on his international debut, their 10-0 away win over USA in New York on 27th May 1964. However, he only played twice more for England, despite scoring in both games, their 4-3 win over Northern Ireland in October 1964, and also a 2-2 draw with Belgium during the same month.

With Johnny Byrne (eight goals from 11 games), and also Roger Hunt challenging for a place alongside Jimmy Greaves in England's attack at the 1966 World Cup, the competition was fierce, and Pickering just missed out.

John Craven had begun his career at Blackpool back in 1965, and he'd played mainly in defence, at left-back or left-half, but Les Shannon moved him permanently into midfield, as a direct response to Tony Green's serious injury, back in April 1969.

Thereafter, Jimmy Armfield's Blackpool blasted off on their great 1969-70 promotion campaign, fired by their ferocious front five of Burns, Craven, Pickering, Suddick and Hutchison, and backed up by their steady defence of Armfield, Welsh international centre-half Glyn James, Terry Alcock and Dave Hatton.

On Saturday 13th April 1970, Blackpool hammered Lancashire rivals Preston North End 3-0, in front of a huge away crowd of 34,000, Deepdale's largest of the season by a long way.

Fred Pickering's majestic hat-trick had assured their promotion back to the First Division, in second place behind Champions Huddersfield Town.

Fred Pickering was their top scorer with seventeen goals from 35 Second Division matches, while John Craven had hit ten from 39. Alan Suddick had played in all 42 league games, while Hutchison missed only one league game. Jimmy Armfield, their veteran, had also started forty league games, but Blackpool's 1970-71 First Division season would be his last season as a player.

Blackpool started life in Division One very, very poorly, only winning twice during their first twenty games, and they'd earned just eight points. Les Shannon left the club just two months into the season, and Bob Stokoe was appointed Blackpool's new manager. But the Tangerines were all but relegated by Christmas.

However, buoyed by Tony Green's return to action, after 17 months out, as well as appearances from both Alan Suddick and Fred Pickering, whose unfortunate seasons had also been injury-ravaged, Blackpool went on a five match unbeaten run over Christmas and the New Year. It was a festive awakening, with a Tangerine glow.

Bob Stokoe brought in Tony Coleman, Manchester City's former winger, for the remainder of the season, and he played seventeen First Division games for Blackpool.

Away at Anfield, after the New Year, 42,939 had watched Blackpool battle to a 2-2 draw with Liverpool (Pickering, Burns). An attacking Blackpool side, playing in away colours of all white, with tangerine cuffs and trims, Taylor, Armfield, Mowbray, Kemp, James, Hatton, Burns, Green, Pickering, Craven and Coleman really went at Liverpool. Stokoe even sent on substitute Alan Suddick for Hatton during the second half, so keen he was to attack. That Anfield draw was Blackpool's best result of their season, and a week later, the same team hosted Manchester City at Bloomfield Road.

BLACKPOOL		MANCHESTER CITY
Alan Taylor	1	Joe Corrigan
Jimmy Armfield	2	Tony Book
Henry Mowbray	3	Arthur Mann
Fred Kemp	4	Mike Doyle
Glyn James	5	Tommy Booth
Dave Hatton	6	Alan Oakes
Micky Burns	7	Mike Summerbee
Tony Green	8	Colin Bell
Fred Pickering	9	Francis Lee
John Craven	10	Neil Young
Tony Coleman	11	Derek Jeffries

29,356, Bloomfield Road's second largest crowd of the season, watched a wonderful 3-3 draw. Coleman received a warm reception from his former Sky Blue fans, while Green and Burns proved themselves equal to both Bell and Summerbee on the day, and Pickering and Craven were a real handful for City's excellent central defensive partnership of Booth and Doyle.

John Craven scored, and Pickering blasted in a brace, to match Summerbee's two goals, and another from Bell.

The good times did not last, though. That awakening was a wonderful, but false dawn.

Fred Pickering was again injured against Coventry during early February, and he missed all of their final fourteen games.

In spite of Neil Ramsbottom, Terry Alcock, Dave Hatton, Fred Kemp, Glyn James, Peter Suddaby, Micky Burns, Tony Green, John Craven, Alan Suddick and Tommy Hutchison earning a 1-1 draw away at UEFA Cup qualifiers Southampton, in late March, Blackpool had won just once in their last seventeen games, and gained only nine points.

Bob Stokoe had realised that a huge problem was their lack of a regular, top quality goalkeeper. He looked hard to find one, from somewhere.

He went to Workington Town, of all places, for his solution. John Burridge was signed on loan until the end of the season, and he made his First Division debut with a clean sheet on 24th April in their goalless draw at Everton.

John Burridge played three games for Blackpool at the end of the 1970-71 season, conceding just two goals, and Blackpool were unbeaten in the First Division with him between the sticks.

Blackpool went down in rock bottom place, but on the final game of the season, John Burridge was in goal for Jimmy Armfield's 567th and final league game for Blackpool, at home to Manchester United.

29,857, Bloomfield Road's largest crowd of the season, said their fond goodbyes to Jimmy Armfield, one of English football's greatest ever players.

They were also saying farewell to the First Division, though, as Blackpool drew 1-1, after Tony Green had cancelled out Denis Law's goal. It was a real shame that Blackpool couldn't exhibit their true potential during 1970-71, with their three best players, Suddick, Green, and Pickering out for such long periods. Those three players missed a combined total of sixty-seven league starts, and you have to consider that it might have been different if they'd been fully fit. It wasn't exactly a tragedy, but it was a real damn shame. Also, John Burridge arrived just too late in the season...

It is an interesting thing that John Burridge was playing his third game for Blackpool during Jimmy Armfield's last match. With Armfield being Blackpool's last survivor from their great Fifties' side, Burridge went on to play for Newcastle United nineteen years later, behind a sixteen year old Steve Watson. Steve Watson then retired from league football, himself, nineteen years later, in 2009, aged thirty-five, while he was Sheffield Wednesday's oldest player.

Just one year later, in 2010, Blackpool returned to the top flight of English league football for the first time in thirty-nine years: *six degrees of separation,* indeed.

After Jimmy Armfield's exit from Bloomfield Road, manager Bob Stokoe appointed John Craven as Blackpool's captain, as well as permanently signing John Burridge, after he'd paid just £10,000 to Workington Town.

On Saturday 12th June 1971, John Craven's first game as captain was Blackpool's Anglo-Italian Cup Final. Alan Suddick masterminded their away victory over Bologna, though, playing some delightful one-twos with the lively Tony Green around Bologna's tight defence, while John Burridge was absolutely excellent in goal.

John Craven headed in Tony Green's cross, but the game ended 1-1 after ninety minutes. Micky Burns, though, their top scorer during 1970-71 with ten First Division goals, ran onto Alan Suddick's measured pass from the right of the penalty area, in extra-time, and he drove in their winner.

Under Bob Stokoe, Blackpool had won their first Silverware for eighteen years.

The following season, back in Division Two, Blackpool had started brightly, leading the promotion race, after winning four out of their first five games.

Welsh international centre-half Glyn James was converted to centre-forward in John Craven's absence, as well as the departure of Fred Pickering, and he'd scored six from five games. However, an awful September and October destroyed their promotion hopes. Blackpool won only once in ten games, and they'd taken just four points.

Furthermore, Tony Green, Blackpool's jewel, was sold to Newcastle United for £140,000, on 28th October 1971. The deal did include centre-forward Keith Dyson arriving at Blackpool from St James's Park, after he'd become surplus to requirements at Newcastle, since Malcolm MacDonald's arrival.

Tony Green only played 33 First Division matches for Newcastle. On September 2nd 1972, at Crystal Palace, Green's career was ended after a tackle by Mel Blyth. After months and months of surgery, Tony Green was forced to retire in 1974, aged just 27.

It's a testament to his skill, and his brilliant influence on that entertaining Newcastle team, that over forty years later, Tony Green is still held up as an idol on Tyneside, despite such a short stay.

He was a real treasure, and one of ten players from the Sixties and Seventies to be placed in the Official Blackpool Supporters Association Hall of Fame.

After retirement, Tony Green returned to the Fylde coast to become a PE teacher.

Blackpool ended up in sixth position in Division Two at the end of the 1971/72 season. Micky Burns was again their top scorer with a decent total of 17 goals from 39 league matches, while Keith Dyson had also fitted in well to score twelve from 28 games.

Alan Suddick, while missing only one league game, had also scored ten goals.

During 1972-73, Blackpool were pretty much the same again, ending up seventh, but only four points behind third placed Aston Villa. Burnley and QPR were a long way clear, though, in the two promotion places, fifteen points clear above the Seasiders.

Alan Suddick had played in all 42 league matches and he was their joint top scorer with ten goals, alongside Alan Ainscow. Keith Dyson did well yet again, scoring nine from twenty-five during an injury-affected season.

Blackpool's biggest loss of the season, though, was their sale of Tommy Hutchison to Coventry City, for a club record transfer fee of £145,000.

Tommy Hutchison had played 166 league games for Blackpool between 1967 and 1972. At Coventry, he went onto win seventeen caps for Scotland, scoring one goal, and he also became part of their 1974 World Cup Squad, playing against both Zaire and Yugoslavia.

He also joined Alan Suddick, John Burridge, Micky Burns, Tony Green and Jimmy Armfield from Blackpool's 1970-71 Division One team in the OBSA Hall of Fame. Over the following eight seasons, the £145,000 that Coventry's manager Joe Mercer had paid for him looked a real bargain. Hutchison missed only one game during his first three seasons at Highfield Road, and he eventually played a total of 314 First Division games for the Sky Blues, while scoring 24 goals. In 1973, Hutchison was reunited with his old teammate John Craven at Coventry.

Craven then spent three seasons at Highfield Road, after playing 163 league games for Blackpool, anchoring their midfield unselfishly, while playing another eighty-nine First Division games.

John Craven died in the United States on Saturday 14th December 1996, aged just forty-nine.

Blackpool manager Bob Stokoe left for Sunderland, in November 1972. The Seasiders' rhythm had been jolted, the loss of Hutchison had appeared to affect Micky Burns' offensive impact, and 1972-73 was not a Golden Mile for Blackpool.

For the start of 1973-74, their new manager Harry Potts had recruited veteran Welsh striker Wyn Davies from Manchester United.

It was not a success. Davies played only 17 games and scored three goals.

Micky Burns once again led the goal scoring charts, with fourteen goals from 42 games, but a brand new club legend had made his league debut on Wednesday 12th September 1973.

Mickey Walsh had an inconsistent first season with Blackpool, scoring only three league goals from sixteen starts, but he'd eventually build up a goal-scoring pace through the mid-Seventies like an Inter-City express starting off for Euston Station.

Keith Dyson again did just about all right, with seven goals from 26 games, but defender Terry Alcock was their surprise turn of the Show, hitting twelve goals, and all from open play, in forty-one league games.

Despite lacking a headline-making top class centre-forward, yet again, Blackpool ended 1973-74 in fifth place in Division Two, and only two points behind Carlisle in third place.

This was the first ever season when three teams were promoted to Division One. They'd scored only 57 goals, 13 less than two seasons earlier, but their central defensive partnership of Glyn James and Peter Suddaby, in front of John Burridge, had conceded only 40 goals from 42 games, their best defensive record of the decade, so far.

The summer of 1974 saw another departure; that of top scorer Micky Burns to Newcastle United for a new club record transfer fee of £170,000.

Burns had scored 53 goals in 179 league games during his five seasons at Blackpool. However, his goals return was just not good enough for an attacking player. He'd scored only six goals from 39 games during 1972-73, and he also frustrated many home fans with an often far too individualistic and unpredictable playing style.

It's got to be remembered, though, that Blackpool never played with a fully fit, dynamic centre-forward *in the Fred Pickering mould*, after 1971.

Also, the disintegration of the Tangerines' classic midfield through the early Seventies, with no replacements bought, had helped no-one at Blackpool.

Those statistic negatives regarding Micky Burns' attacking style simply failed to sour the delightful tangerine memories of an excellent period of Blackpool football club's history, when Burns, Green, Suddick and Hutchison had all provided some of the most magical midfield moments in Blackpool's post-War history.

Their new kid on the Blackpool rock, Mickey Walsh, had scored a sensational goal during their 3-2 win over Sunderland at Bloomfield Road, on Saturday 1st February. Chesting down a long ball inside the centre circle, Walsh dragged the ball through the mud, tracked by both Moncur and Guthrie.

He then halted, with his back to the goal, just outside the right side of the penalty box, and with seemingly nowhere to go, except for playing a straight square pass into the onrushing Alan Ainscow, or a limp lay-off back to a midfield player, Walsh instead switched inside.

Then, from out of the mud, he belted a rocket between his two markers, which flew in off the flying Jim Montgomery's left-hand post.

Barry Davies was ecstatic in his commentary on Match of the Day.

"Davies is on the far side, Ainscow is coming square. That's the ball... That's a good try... What a goal! *OH, WHAT A GOAL!!!*"

It was voted as BBC TV's Goal of the Season for 1974-75.

That 1974-75 season saw Blackpool finish seventh again, only eight points behind Norwich City in the third promotion place. Walsh had taken Micky Burns' place in the team and he was top scorer with twelve goals from 35 games, but nobody else was scoring. Alan Suddick had had his season ended through injury back in September and he played only five league games.

No other Blackpool player scored more than five league goals.

Without Burns, Suddick, Green and Hutchison, Blackpool's midfield now looked a little empty.

For John Burridge, it was particularly galling to watch from his goal, and see his team fail to score enough goals to mount a real promotion campaign.

During that 1974-75 season, John Burridge had kept 20, twenty, clean sheets from his 38 games. Blackpool had conceded only 33 goals in their 42 Second Division games, but they scored only 38 goals, and had hit just seven away from home.

With only Mickey Walsh just hitting double figures, Blackpool had played thirteen goalless draws.

On Monday 23rd September 1975, Burridge finally left Bloomfield Road for Villa Park for a £100,000 transfer fee. Ron Saunders' Aston Villa needed defensive assurance, having just won promotion back into Division One.

Burridge had played 134 league matches for Blackpool over four and a bit seasons, and he'd kept fifty clean sheets. During his time at the Seasiders, Blackpool had finished sixth, seventh, fifth and seventh in the Second Division, without any renowned strikers. John Burridge was that defensive assurance Aston Villa needed to become of one the top First Division teams during the late Seventies.

Mickey Walsh increased his goal tally again in 1975-76, scoring seventeen from 41 games, but with Alan Suddick ageing and fading, Blackpool then became a mid-table Second Division team.

Walsh then hit twenty-six goals during 1976-77, leading a top quality Blackpool forward line for the first time in the Seventies, with former Birmingham City legend Bob Hatton also scoring ten from 39 games. Blackpool only finished only one point behind third-placed Nottingham Forest. But this was no more a golden Blackpool team. They were then relegated to the Third Division, just a year after finishing one point behind the future First Division and European Champions.

Alan Suddick joined Stoke City in December 1976, but he played only nine league games at The Victoria Ground, and he couldn't help prevent them from being relegated to Division Two. He'd played 309 league games for Blackpool, scoring 64 goals. One of football's innovators, his Newcastle United captain Bobby Moncur had said that Suddick had as much natural ability as George Best, and he played just as effortlessly.

Alan Suddick died on Monday 16th March 2009, aged only sixty-four, following a short battle with cancer that had resulted in both of his legs being amputated below the knees, after he'd contracted gangrene. He was a special type of footballer and his passing was much mourned by all football fans, not just the thousands of fans at both Bloomfield Road and St James's Park.

Following Blackpool's relegation to the Third Division for the first time in their history, Mickey Walsh left Bloomfield Road, having scored seventy-two goals in only one hundred and seventy-two league starts, and after two unhappy stays with Everton and QPR, he signed for FC Porto in 1980.

Walsh remained with Porto for six years, playing 85 league games, often used as an impact substitute, and he scored 42 goals. He played in their 1984 European Cup Winners' Cup Final 2-1 defeat to Juventus, and then helped Porto to two Portuguese Liga titles, in 1985 and in 1986.

Mickey Walsh left Porto for Salgueiros during the summer of 1986, but then in the balmy warmth of the following spring, Porto won a magnificent European Cup Final, in Vienna, against mighty Bayern Munich. The Chorley-born Blackpool legend can claim an assist in *THAT* great triumph.

Z-STARS: A STORY OF THE BLUES

IN 1970, DAVID BOWIE RELEASED The Man Who Sold the World; T-Rex and Marc Bolan recorded Ride a White Swan. And Slade sung The Shape of Things to Come.

These were the first sounds of the Glam Rock era, and the shape of things to come.

Everton, looking like absolutely nothing to do with Glam Rock, with their sensible haircuts or Merseybeat mop-tops, were the emphatic Champions of England. They had beaten off a strong challenge from Leeds United, and had beaten every other team in the First Division, at least once, during that season.

Not since 1956 had any team won the title by nine points or more, and Everton had a potential seven players that should have gone to the World Cup Finals in Mexico, as England players.

Everton were brilliant, but they were not the Shape of Things to Come, as expected.

They slowly, but definitely, fell apart during the immediate years following 1970. Everton spent all of their next three seasons in the bottom half of Division One, and they didn't battle for the First Division title for another five years.

Many cynical observers pointed at Everton's collapse after 1970, claiming it detracted from their true quality; that they didn't have staying power; that they were a freak of occurrences, a one season wonder.

This wasn't true. It was, in fact, very false.

To qualify how good Everton really were, in 1970, just as you did for Leeds United after 1964, you needed to turn Everton's record upside down. You had to judge their record during the ten years prior to 1970, under Harry Catterick's management.

Harry Catterick had led Everton to a great First Division Championship success back in 1963, superbly out-duelling Bill Nicholson's Tottenham to the finishing line.

That brilliant Spurs team had scored a second-best ever First Division total of one hundred and eleven goals, courtesy of Jimmy Greaves, Cliff Jones, John White and Les Allen, and spurred on by their magnificent wing-half partnership of Danny Blanchflower and Dave Mackay, possibly the finest-ever wing half, or midfield, partnership in English football history.

Everton, though, with their tight defence, imperiously marshalled by both Brian Labone and Jimmy Gabriel, had conceded only forty-two goals, against the sixty-two that had been hit past Bill Brown. Despite having scored twenty-seven fewer goals than Tottenham, Everton had clearly demonstrated how important defence was to become in English League football.

Brian Labone had made his debut for Everton back in March 1958, when he was just eighteen, and by the time Harry Catterick had arrived at Goodison Park, three years later, Labone was a regular in their team.

Liverpool-born, and an Everton fan, Labone missed just two out of 42 First Division matches during their title winning 1962-63 season. Standing majestically tall, at six feet and one inch, Labone was a commanding centre-half, well-assured on the ground as well as powerful and decisive in the air.

Brian Labone made his England debut in October 1962, during their 3-1 away win against Northern Ireland, in Belfast, and he retained his place, a month later, when England hammered Wales 4-0 at Wembley.

In February 1963, though, France thrashed England 5-2 in Paris. Not since Hungary's 7-1 hammering of England, nine years earlier, had England been so soundly beaten, and Alf Ramsey dropped Labone, as well as Chelsea's Bobby Tambling.

Harry Catterick's first activity in the transfer market, after becoming Everton's manager, was to pay Blackpool £27,000 for their eighteen year old goalkeeper, Gordon West, in March 1962. That was a British record transfer fee for a goalkeeper, at the time, but West was born to keep goal.

Gordon West became Everton's regular keeper during the following season, keeping seventeen clean sheets from thirty-eight matches, as Everton became Champions for the first time since 1939.

Johnny Morrissey had been a key player in helping Liverpool to return to the First Division, as Second Division Champions, scoring six goals in thirty-six league matches. It is very tough, particularly when you consider their more recent history, to think of Liverpool as standard Second Division fodder for eight full seasons, but it did happen; and Morrissey's energetic displays on the left wing were an huge influence in the resurgence of his home town club.

On 30th August 1962, though, Harry Catterick paid just £10,000 for Morrissey. The transfer was agreed by the Liverpool board, but Bill Shankly was furious that he'd not been consulted. He warned his bosses that if they did it again, he be telling them to take their money, and fuck off.

They never made the same mistake again.

They were lucky he was so easy going.

Johnny Morrissey, just twenty-two, made thirteen straight appearances on the left wing for title chasing Everton, and he even scored a hat-trick during their 4-2 home win over West Brom, in the autumn. He lost his place to Ray Veall, though, after suffering an injury in early November. Morrissey played fifteen more league games that season, as Everton won the league by six clear points.

Colin Harvey, also Liverpool-born, was Catterick's next recruit, from Everton's juniors. He made his Everton debut, aged only eighteen, as Everton visited Inter Milan for their European Cup First round, second leg match. Everton had been held to a goalless draw at Goodison Park by Internazionale, the masters of Catenaccio, with legends like Mazzola, Suarez, Burgnich and Facchetti gracing their team.

In the volatile, white-hot atmosphere of the San Siro, in the Autumn of 1963, Inter Milan won 1-0; after Jair had scored, and then went on to beat Real Madrid, Puskas, Di Stefano, Gento, and all, in the Final. Colin Harvey had deputised brilliantly for Jimmy Gabriel, but he made only two more First Division appearances for Everton that season. He became a first team regular in 1964, though.

Colin Harvey was not unlike Martin Peters, running from box to box, intelligently and inspired, quick and clean in the tackle; but quick-thinking and clever, dangerous and dynamic, deep inside his opponents' half.

Also joining Everton in 1964, was left-back Ray Wilson. Wilson had signed from Huddersfield Town, after playing 272 league games at Leeds Road, of which 266 had been Second Division matches.

Yet, Ray Wilson had already played thirty games at left-back for England, including all four of their matches in the 1962 Chile World Cup Finals, as a Second Division defender.

Harry Catterick paid Huddersfield £50,000 for Wilson, who was twenty-nine years old by the time he joined Everton, but after just two games, he was injured and ruled out for nearly four months.

That season, 1964-65, was a huge disappointment for Ray Wilson, and by the time he returned for his third game in an Everton shirt, and only his ninth First Division match, he'd turned thirty.

Tommy Wright had been an Everton youth team player, joining straight from school, as a much-acclaimed and talented inside forward. However, he never looked like he'd make the grade at First Division level, until a series of injuries forced him to fill in at full back, and then he excelled.

By the middle of 1964-65, at just twenty years old, Wright was a first team regular in the team, at right back, but he'd also used his attacking instincts to great effect, finding attackers with perfect crosses and clever passing.

As Ray Wilson returned from injury, he and Tommy Wright became one of the finest full back partnerships of the whole decade, and Everton then reached the 1966 FA Cup Final. Gordon West, Tommy Wright, Ray Wilson, Brian Labone and Colin Harvey all played in that Final, on Saturday 14th May, against Sheffield Wednesday.

Johnny Morrissey missed out, as he was still battling Derek Temple for a left wing place.

Temple wore Morrissey's number eleven shirt, and he scored Everton's winning goal, coming back to win 3-2, after going 0-2 down after fifty seven minutes.

That comeback win was one of the greatest ever Wembley Finals, but Everton were disappointed at finishing down in mid-table, in Division One, their lowest league finish of the Sixties.

Even so, Ray Wilson had been selected by Alf Ramsey for England's World Cup squad, at thirty-one years old. Just as he did four years earlier, Wilson played in all of England's games, all six of them, and he was Everton's only representative in their World Cup winning team.

Harry Catterick responded by paying a British record transfer fee of £110,000, on Monday 15th August, for Blackpool's Alan Ball.

Alan Ball was widely regarded as the man of the match, during England's 4-2 extra-time win over West Germany, just a couple of weeks earlier. He'd crossed the ball from the right wing for Geoff Hurst's disputed third goal for England, and generally, and quite literally, he ran his socks off.

He played both central, and wide, in Alf's much-celebrated **Wingless Wonders,** and it was down to the energy, and talent, of Alan Ball, that made the system work.

Alan Ball was Everton's leading goal-scorer in 1966-67, hitting eighteen league and cup goals, as Everton rose to sixth place in the First Division.

In March 1967, Catterick paid Preston North End £80,000 for their star midfield player, Howard Kendall. Kendall had become the youngest ever player in an FA Cup Final, for Preston, as they lost the 1964 Final to West Ham.

The Lancashire Evening Post had acclaimed, in spite of North End's defeat, *"Preston lost the Cup, but discovered a star: 17 year old Kendall."*

MALCOLM STARK

Bill Shankly was also desperate to sign Kendall. Liverpool had watched him over the two years following the 1964 Cup Final, and in October 1966, they entered an official bid for him, but were told that he wasn't for sale.

Liverpool asked just to be kept informed if the Preston board changed their mind.

Howard Kendall, upon hearing of Liverpool's bid for him, submitted a transfer request, which was refused by Preston. Kendall was desperate to play First Division football, though, and Liverpool, the reigning Champions, were as good a side as he could join, with North End languishing in deep mid-table in the Second Division.

The Preston fans, who'd already seen several of their players leave, and often just disappear into Liverpool's reserves, were fed up of being Liverpool's nursery club. They were, after all, the club that gave Tom Finney to the football world.

Home crowds at Deepdale even took to shouting "*STAY AWAY SHANKLY!*", their defiant cry to Liverpool. This was ironic as Shankly had been such a club legend during his 296 league games for Preston, inspiring them to promotion to Division One in 1934, as well as their FA Cup Final victory over Huddersfield in 1938.

In 1998, the Spion Kop End at Deepdale, the end of the hard-core Preston fans, was redeveloped, and renamed The Bill Shankly Stand.

Bill Shankly was frustrated, and even distraught, at Everton's signing of Howard Kendall. It was a major blow to his hopes of keeping Liverpool at the top of English football as the Sixties came to an end. "All we asked Preston," He retorted, "was to be kept informed."

Preston didn't give us a chance."

Shankly had to almost completely re-build his team, after 1970, as Everton had overtaken them.

Also becoming first team regulars at Everton, during 1966-67, were John Hurst, Jimmy Husband and Joe Royle.

Joe Royle had made his debut for Everton, back in January 1966, aged only sixteen, against Blackpool. He became the youngest ever Everton first team player, a long-time record that was broken thirty-six years later, by Wayne Rooney. Liverpool-born, Royle played in four of Everton's last seven games of 1966-67, and he scored twice in their 3-1 win over Cup finalists Chelsea, still aged only eighteen.

Joe Royle was, like Wayne Rooney, a big lad for a teenager, at six feet and one inch tall, and weighing twelve and a half stone, but he quickly became regarded as one of the best young centre forwards in football. He was good with both of his feet, as well as his head.

John Hurst had scored their third goal during that 3-1 win over Chelsea. Born in Blackpool, Hurst arrived at Everton as a fourteen year old who'd played as a centre forward for England schoolboys. Harry Catterick developed him into a defensive wing half, though, and when he was eighteen, he helped Everton win the 1965 FA Youth Cup. Hurst also made his First Division debut that year, before becoming a regular in December 1966, starting in all of Everton's remaining twenty-seven league and cup matches. He mostly wore the shirt numbers of inside forward positions, **8** or **10**, though, despite Harry Catterick playing John Hurst mostly as a central defender.

Hurst scored his first Everton goal during their 2-2 draw away at Leicester City, on Saturday 4th March 1967, just one month after his twentieth birthday. A week later, he marked Roger Hunt out of the game, as with 64,851 absolutely Jam-packed inside Goodison Park, Everton beat Liverpool 1-0 in the FA Cup Fifth round.

Jimmy Husband had first played for Everton, in 1965, during their Inter Cities Fairs Cup match against Ujpest Dozsa, at just seventeen years old, but he had to wait until January 1967, before he became an Everton regular.

Aged only nineteen, Jimmy Husband scored four goals in five games, through January and February, and Everton won four out of five games. He scored the fourth goal in their 4-1 home win over Sheffield United; the second goal in their 2-0 win over Leeds; the second goal in their 3-0 thrashing of Newcastle, away at St James's Park; before finally, on 25th February, he scored Everton's opening goal in their 4-0 win over World Cup winning West Ham.

A Star was born, among a Team of Stars.

A dangerous winger, with a terrifying turn of speed, and an explosive shot at goal, Husband also scored twice during Everton's 3-1 win over Wolves, on 21st February, in their FA Cup Fourth round replay, with over 60,000 inside Goodison Park.

Despite the efforts and influence of both Hurst and Husband, Nottingham Forest overcame Everton with a 3-2 victory, in the 1967 FA Cup Quarter-finals, after nearly 48,000 had packed their tight City Ground.

Everton rose up to sixth in Division One, finishing twelve points behind Champions Manchester United. United had lost just six of their forty-two games, but none at all at Old Trafford.

Z-CARS!

With Best, Law and Charlton firing at their very best, they were the team to beat in 1967. The Football League revealed the most exciting of all opening day fixtures for 1967-68, with Everton hosting the rampant Champions Manchester United, who'd not lost in twenty league games, an unbeaten run that went way back to Boxing Day 1966.

With 61,452 squashed inside Goodison Park, Harry Catterick played Alex Young in attack, his veteran, thirty year-old forward, instead of their free-scoring teenager, Jimmy Husband. Alex Young had scored seventy-one Scottish First Division goals for Hearts, winning the title twice, back in 1958 and 1960, before he joined Everton in November 1960, in a £60,000 deal. Young had scored twenty-two league goals as Everton won the title in 1962-63, and Catterick just felt that Young would just offer more muscle up front against the highly-fancied Champions, offering stronger support for the young Joe Royle.

Harry Catterick's decision to play Young was perfect, as Everton outplayed Manchester United all over the field, for the entire match.

On a warm afternoon, Saturday 19th August, the Goodison Park loudspeakers played the *Z-Cars* theme tune, recorded by Johnny Keating, from the BBC TV drama series set in Kirby, to welcome both teams onto the pitch.

Everton were the first team to play a team anthem, Z-Cars!, as both teams entered the pitch, and then, they set upon the Champions, right from the start.

After thirteen minutes, Labone fired a fierce forward pass up for Royle to head back into Ball's path. Ball ran at Dunne, before he laid the ball out wide to the right of the United area. Morrissey crossed to just beyond the far post, where the predatory Royle sneaked in and slipped the ball back inside, past the hands of Stepney, and Alan Ball slid in to finish from inside the six yard box.

EVERTON		MANCHESTER UNITED
Gordon West	1	Alex Stepney
Tommy Wright	2	Shay Brennan
Ray Wilson	3	Tony Dunne
Howard Kendall	4	Paddy Crerand
Brian Labone	5	Bill Foulkes
Colin Harvey	6	Nobby Stiles
Alex Young	7	George Best
Alan Ball	8	Denis Law
Joe Royle	9	Bobby Charlton
John Hurst	10	Brian Kidd
Johnny Morrissey	11	John Aston
Sandy Brown	12	David Sadler

Everton were like marauding bees, attacking United's players in packs of twos and threes. Wright, Harvey, Ball and Kendall were biting into the Champions with sharp, stinging tackles, while the young Royle buzzed around United's defence like a huge, dangerous wasp.

United just couldn't get out of their own half, so fierce was Everton's high pressure game. Stepney had to save well from Royle, Young, and Johnny Morrissey, who was darting down the left one minute, and then down the right, the next.

Any individual attempt by George Best, to run the ball into Everton's danger area, was quickly seized upon and stopped by the packs of defenders swarming over him. Denis Law was stifled, battling away with Ball, Harvey and Kendall in midfield.

Early in the second half, Harvey's left wing cross was headed just over Stepney's bar by Ball, and then Royle volleyed just inches wide of the United left post, after Ball had robbed his England teammate Stiles, before crossing from the right. Morrissey then glanced his header, from Harvey's left wing cross, just wide of Stepney's far post, while being tightly marked by Brennan.

Every time Best or Crerand got the chance to make something happen, Everton just pounced on them as soon as they had a half chance of getting the ball.

Kendall struck a twenty-five yard rocket that deflected in off Royle, but Stepney dived well to save the ball. Alan Ball then robbed Denis Law, but he shot just a whisker wide of Stepney's right post.

Then, out of nowhere, George Best drove a brilliant, swerving, twenty yard shot, with his right foot, that swung away from Gordon West, towards the near right corner of the Everton goal, but West flung himself high to turn the ball just round his post.

West then rose again to grab Best's corner kick out of the air, and he immediately sent Everton away on another attack. Royle ran brilliantly from the halfway line, beating Brennan, before running on, and dribbling past Foulkes. He shot from the edge of United's area, but Stepney managed to get his arms to it, and then he dived onto the ball, gratefully.

Alex Young chipped just over, from twenty yards, before Gordon West launched a huge drop kick. Royle flicked the ball on to Morrissey. Morrissey pushed the ball back to Ball, who sprayed the ball wide left to Harvey. Harvey ran into the area, and chipped the ball over Stepney, onto the far right post. Stepney and Stiles both clambered to clear the ball away, but Ball had continued his run, and he simply dinked it back, through both of them, the ball rolling into the far side of the United net.

Despite all of Everton's pressure and superiority, it was only 2-0. With twenty-five minutes to play, though, Alex Young collected a left wing cross from Ray Wilson, and he wriggled past Dunne and Foulkes inside the United area, then blasted an unstoppable drive past Stepney, into the top right corner of the United goal.

"NINE-NINE-ONE"

"Oh, it's great stuff by Everton!" commentator Kenneth Wolstenholme proclaimed.

Alan Ball, their man of the match, by miles, dived onto Young's shoulders, in delight.

"Manchester United are playing 4-3-3," Wolstenholme reminded us.

"But they must think that Everton are playing *9-9-1*," he continued. "They get everybody back in defence, and then everybody swarms up in attack."

After John Hurst was adjudged to have fouled Stiles, twenty yards out, Law teed the free-kick up for Charlton, and Bobby belted the ball towards the top left corner of Everton's goal. Gordon West, though, threw himself again to tip the ball around the angle.

West was desperate to keep a clean sheet against this United side.

With just four minutes left, though, Bobby Charlton scuffed an eighteen yard shot with his left foot, which squeezed past Tommy Wright, and just inside West's dive at his near post.

All of Goodison Park, including the reigning Champions' several thousand away supporters, who'd all been shouting *"UNITED! UNITED!" very loudly*, just a little while earlier, was completely and utterly silent.

It had been an outstanding performance, and 3-1 totally flattered Manchester United. Everton should have scored five or six, but it could have been eight or more, so dominant they were.

On this form, Alan Ball was the best and most valuable player in the First Division, if not Europe. On the following Wednesday, though, away at Tottenham, Ball limped off as they were held to a 1-1 draw by the previous season's Cup winners. Alan Ball missed Everton's next two matches, away at Sunderland, and at home to Spurs.

Ball was much missed. Everton lost 1-0 in both matches.

Then, just as Ball returned, they lost Johnny Morrissey for most of September. Morrissey missed five games in total, and as a result, Everton were down in fifteenth position, in late September, after nine games, having lost five times.

They were only six points below leaders Liverpool, but just a single point above Sheffield United, down in the relegation zone.

Despite looking like Champions in August, it was clear, by Christmas that Everton weren't going to be Champions. A home crowd of just 38,000 watched their 3-0 win over Sunderland on Saturday 23rd December, with Ball, Husband and Royle scoring.

In the FA Cup, though, Everton made steady, if unspectacular progress. Joe Royle scored to secure their 1-0 away win at Southport, in the Third round, with nearly 19,000 filling Haig Avenue.

25,000 then packed Carlisle United's Brunton Park ground, in the Fourth round, on Saturday 17th February, but Everton won 2-0. Jimmy Husband and Joe Royle scored a goal in each half, in Cumbria, sending the Toffeemen into the last sixteen.

It was a Merseyside derby match in the Fifth round, on Saturday 9th March.

62,634 packed Goodison Park for Everton's home draw against Second Division Tranmere Rovers. Johnny Morrissey and Joe Royle both scored to win the game 2-0, and then, one week later,

Alan Ball hit four goals during their 6-2 away thrashing of West Bromwich Albion, at The Hawthorns, with Morrissey and Royle also scoring.

On Saturday 30th March 30th, 43,519 jammed into Filbert Street for Leicester City's FA Cup Quarter-final match against The Blues. The huge crowd was less than four thousand below Leicester's record crowd, set way back in the Twenties.

Teenage full back David Nish scored for Leicester, but Jimmy Husband's brace, and then Howard Kendall gave the Blues a 3-1 away win, to reach the Semi-finals.

By Easter Monday, 15th April 1968, Everton had won eleven out of their last thirteen First Division games, and fifteen wins from seventeen, in all competitions.

They'd pulled themselves up to fifth position in the league, only eight points behind leaders Manchester United, but with three games in hand. (Everton were a good outside bet to win the League and Cup double.)

On the following evening, they were held to a goalless draw by Sheffield Wednesday, but then they beat Chelsea 2-1 on Saturday 20th April, after goals from John Hurst and Howard Kendall had secured a scrappy win, with their following week's FA Cup Semi-final match against Leeds United clearly high in their minds.

FIRST DIVISION LEADERS, 16th APRIL 1968

	PL	W	D	L	F	A	PTS
Manchester United	39	23	8	6	79	47	54
Leeds United	38	22	9	7	65	29	53
Manchester City	38	22	6	10	76	39	50
Liverpool	37	19	10	8	57	34	48
EVERTON	37	21	5	11	58	35	47

On the following Monday, though, Ian Storey-Moore hammered the final nails into the coffin of Everton's title hopes, just as he'd done in the FA Cup one year earlier, scoring the only goal in Nottingham Forest's 1-0 home win over Everton.

Old Trafford hosted their FA Cup Semi-final on Saturday 27th April, with 63,000, the fourth-biggest crowd of the season, packing the ground for a tight, tense game between Leeds and Everton.

Everton, fearless, with nothing to lose, had played with more fluency and potency, despite being without the suspended Alan Ball, against Leeds United, who still had a great chance of winning the Double.

Again without Alan Ball for their fifth successive match, Everton had already dropped points against Nottingham Forest and Sheffield Wednesday without him, games they'd have expected to win, but Tommy Jackson had done a good job protecting his back four, while Kendall and Harvey cancelled out the threat of Bremner and Giles.

LEEDS UNITED		EVERTON
Gary Sprake	1	Gordon West
Paul Reaney	2	Tommy Wright
Terry Cooper	3	Ray Wilson
Billy Bremner	4	Tommy Jackson
Jack Charlton	5	Brian Labone
Norman Hunter	6	Colin Harvey
Peter Lorimer	7	Jimmy Husband
Paul Madeley	8	Roger Kenyon
Mick Jones	9	Joe Royle
Johnny Giles	10	Howard Kendall
Eddie Gray	11	Johnny Morrissey
Jimmy Greenhoff	12	Alex Young

Everton made the very best with what they had, unlike Don Revie, who probably ought to have started with the skilful Greenhoff.

Just before half-time, Joe Royle stood in front of Gary Sprake, who was preparing to drop kick the ball away. Royle prevented Sprake from kicking the ball away with his stronger right foot, and forced him to kick, weakly, with his left.

It was a deliberate tactical play that Harry Catterick had instructed Royle and Husband to use during the game.

The ball went straight to Husband, who shot straight at goal. Jack Charlton sprinted back and prevented the ball from going in, with his hand.

Johnny Morrissey drove home his penalty kick, sweetly, and so Everton led 1-0 at half-time, a lead they fought very hard to protect throughout the second half, keeping their eighteenth clean sheet of the season. Everton were off to Wembley, again.

Everton ended their league season by hammering Stoke City 3-0, and Fulham 5-1, either side of their 1-1 draw at West Ham, and they finished up in fifth place, just six points behind Champions Manchester City. They conceded only forty league goals, their best-ever defensive record up to then, while they'd scored sixty-seven.

Alan Ball, despite missing eight games, was Everton's top goal scorer for the second successive season, hitting twenty First Division goals. Joe Royle had scored sixteen from thirty-three, while Jimmy Husband, Johnny Morrissey, Howard Kendall, Alex Young and John Hurst shared thirty-five league and cup goals.

On Saturday 18th May, red-hot favourites Everton faced West Bromwich Albion, who'd beaten Birmingham City in their Semi-final at Villa Park, in the 1968 FA Cup Final.

They wasted goal opportunity, though, time after time, with Albion's goalkeeper John Osborne absolutely brilliant, and without any doubt, the man of the match.

Osborne leapt to grab cross after cross from both Morrissey and Husband, and then saved superbly from Alan Ball, while John Hurst missed an open goal, late on, with a close-range header.

Centre back John Talbut succeeded in keeping Joe Royle quiet, for most of the game, as Royle was deprived of a clear shot on goal, but full backs Fraser and Williams pushed the laws of the game beyond the pale, at times, fouling Morrissey and Husband nearly every time they were beaten, which was many, many times.

Jeff Astle's excellent left-footed strike on the rebound, after Labone had blocked his first, right-footed shot, just two minutes into extra-time, won the Cup for Albion.

It was a victory for hard work and resolve over football.

At the start of the 1968-69 season, Ray Wilson suffered a twisted knee, and he missed all but four starts of the season. The tall, and slightly balding Sandy Brown, from Grangemouth, replaced England's World Cup winner at left back.

Everton started off with two wins and two defeats, but from Monday 19th August until Saturday 16th November, they went on a sixteen match unbeaten run, climaxing in a superb 4-0 romp over QPR, at Goodison Park. In front of just 43,552, Colin Harvey, Jimmy Husband, Johnny Morrissey and Joe Royle scored the goals that lifted Everton up to joint first place in Division One, tied with Liverpool.

DIVISION ONE LEADERS, 16TH NOVEMBER 1968

	Pl	W	D	L	F	A	PTS
Liverpool	19	12	4	3	37	13	28
EVERTON	19	11	6	2	40	16	28
Leeds United	18	11	5	2	26	15	27
Arsenal	18	9	7	2	22	11	25
West Ham	19	8	7	4	38	21	23

Leeds United then beat Everton 2-1, at Elland Road, although they followed that disappointment by hammering Leicester City 7-1.

On Saturday 7th December, though, Everton lost 3-1 away at Arsenal.

Everton then went on another unbeaten run of nine games, winning five out of seven up to Wednesday 1st February, that kept them very close behind leaders Leeds United.

They were still only three points behind after twenty-nine games.

Everton did not play another league game in February, though, while Leeds United carried on playing, and they also carried on winning. Leeds beat Ipswich, Chelsea, Nottingham Forest and Southampton before the start of March, amassing an enormous points lead over Everton. Although Everton had games in hand, the points gap piled the pressure onto Everton, by the time they finally did play another league game.

On Saturday 8th March, Everton played their first Division One match for over five weeks, away at Tottenham, and they were held to a 1-1 draw.

Joe Royle scored his twentieth league goal of the season, but on that same day, Leeds hammered Stoke 5-1, opening up a twelve point lead over Everton, albeit having played four more games.

Everton were unable to close that gap, and they finished the season in third position, ten points behind Leeds United, English League Champions for the first time ever. They'd conceded a new low of just thirty-six goals, though, whilst scoring seventy-seven goals.

Once again, though, it was in the FA Cup, where Everton's hopes of silverware lay. John Hurst and Joe Royle had both scored, on Saturday 4th January, during their 2-1 Third round win over Ipswich Town, before the same two players netted yet again, as Coventry City were beaten 2-0 at Goodison Park, three weeks later.

In the Fifth round, Bristol Rovers arrived on Merseyside, with their ten thousand raucous Pirates' fans amongst the huge 55,000 Goodison Park crowd.

The Third Division side fought hard, making Everton beat ten men behind the ball, every time they attacked. Joe Royle's header, though, from Morrissey's corner, had put the title chasers safely into the Sixth round.

On Saturday 1st March, as Leeds United were gleefully romping away with the league title, Everton visited Manchester United, with 63,464 filling Old Trafford for their Quarter-final clash.

Everton's defence of Wright, Labone, Hurst and Sandy Brown coped brilliantly against United's star-studded forward line of Best, Law, Charlton and Kidd, and they were well protected by Tommy Jackson, again deputising for Kendall, against the marauding runs of Crerand or Stiles.

Joe Royle chipped over Alex Stepney, after turning Bill Foulkes, just inside the United area, and the ball curled sharply inside the far right post.

Everton hung on for their 1-0 win, for a Semi-final visit to Villa Park, against the reigning League Champions, Manchester City.

City were well out of the race to defend their title, down in fourteenth position, with fifteen less points than Everton had gained, and with relegation-bound Leicester City playing West Brom in the other Semi-final, Everton were once again short-priced favourites to win the Cup.

Even better, Howard Kendall was back, after nearly two months out, with an ankle injury, and with the expected exception of Ray Wilson, Everton were at full strength, fielding the team that had romped to the top of the First Division by early November.

EVERTON		MANCHESTER CITY
Gordon West	1	Harry Dowd
Tommy Wright	2	Tony Book
Sandy Brown	3	Glyn Pardoe
Howard Kendall	4	Mike Doyle
Brian Labone	5	Tommy Booth
Colin Harvey	6	Alan Oakes
Jimmy Husband	7	Mike Summerbee
Alan Ball	8	Colin Bell
Joe Royle	9	Francis Lee
John Hurst	10	Neil Young
Johnny Morrissey	11	David Connor
Tommy Jackson	12	Bobby Owen (unused)
(rep Kendall)		

City were missing their skilful winger Tony Coleman, but after just over half an hour into the match, Howard Kendall also hobbled off, following a recurrence of his ankle injury, and he missed the remainder of Everton's season.

Both sides, though, were perfectly matched. Alan Ball and Colin Harvey were tracked, and traced, over every inch of the pitch, by the classy midfield duo of Bell and Oakes.

It was an epic Semi-final with nothing to separate either team.

"Everton were like us," Colin Bell said. "They could play, and believed in their own ability from one to eleven."

With 63,025 fans roaring Everton on, the game remained goalless until the very last minute, when Neil Young, City's big striker, their target man at corner kicks, went over to take a corner from the left.

Young swung the ball in, and with Everton under heavy pressure and struggling to clear, Tommy Booth poked in from close range, right in front of the vast bank of City fans on the North Stand.

City went on to beat Leicester in the Final, on the Wembley mud, and Everton were left with a third successive unsuccessful, nearly season. They'd launched a serious assault on the title race, however, for the second time since back in '63.

Furthermore, having lost only one of their last ten league games of 1968-69, Everton were on a high, entering the 1970 World Cup season.

THE CHAMPIONSHIP-WINNING SEASON

Everton won 1-0 on the opening day, Saturday 9th August, beating Arsenal 1-0, away at Highbury. John Hurst's second half goal secured the points, but once again, Howard Kendall had had to be substituted, and he missed their following six league matches.

On the following Wednesday night, away at Manchester United, Hurst headed in his second goal in two games. He gave Everton a 1-0 half-time lead, in front of a hostile 60,000 Old Trafford crowd, and then Alan Ball made it 2-0, halfway into the second half. United were in a transitional phase after Sir Matt Busby's retirement, but it was still a great triumph.

A huge 50,700 crowd filled Goodison for Everton's first home game of the season, on the second Saturday, for the visit of Crystal Palace. Mel Blyth equalised Johnny Morrissey's first half goal, and then Palace played a dogged defensive game, as they could always do, blocking every shot and cross.

Roger Hynd was very harshly adjudged to have hand-balled, though, late in the second half, and Joe Royle fired home his penalty kick, for a hard-fought two points.

On Tuesday 19th August, Everton completed their double over Manchester United, hammering them 3-0 at Goodison Park, in front of 53,185. Alan Ball, Johnny Morrissey and Joe Royle all scored to send Everton up to the top of Division One.

On the following Saturday, Everton travelled up the A57, to Manchester City, wearing their away kit of yellow and blue, and they stormed into City's sky blue, from the very start. Joe Corrigan saved brilliantly from both Joe Royle and Alan Ball, before Johnny Morrissey eventually put Everton 1-0 up at the break.

Alan Ball had fed Joe Royle on the right of the City penalty area, and then galloped in, looking for the return pass. Royle, though, delivered a beautiful cross beyond Book, Booth and Pardoe, over to the far left edge of the six yard box, and Morrissey dashed in to head Everton into a half-time lead, right in front of goal.

Cup holders City came back, though, and during the second half, Tony Book's right wing cross was headed in by the leaping Ian Bowyer, a future European Cup winner, from twelve yards out, and the 43,678 Maine Road crowd went wild.

On Tuesday 26th August, Everton scraped past bottom club Sheffield Wednesday, at Goodison. Ball and Royle scored in each half, giving them a 2-1 win, and keeping Everton two points clear of second-placed Liverpool.

Four days later, Leeds United visited Everton, and a crowd of nearly 52,000 packed Goodison Park for the battle between the best two teams in the First Division. Leeds were at full strength, but Howard Kendall was missing for a sixth successive match for Everton.

Don Revie had paid his hosts great respect though, by playing Paul Madeley in midfield, in place of Peter Lorimer, to guard against Alan Ball's marauding runs and to provide proper defensive cover.

EVERTON		LEEDS UNITED
Gordon West	1	Gary Sprake
Tommy Wright	2	Paul Reaney
Sandy Brown	3	Terry Cooper
Tommy Jackson	4	Billy Bremner
Brian Labone	5	Jack Charlton
Colin Harvey	6	Norman Hunter
Jimmy Husband	7	Paul Madeley
Alan Ball	8	Johnny Giles
Joe Royle	9	Mick Jones
John Hurst	10	Allan Clarke
Johnny Morrissey	11	Eddie Gray
Frank D'Arcy	12	Peter Lorimer (rep. Gray)

Leeds had been boosted by the addition of Allan Clarke, their £165,000 summer signing, who'd scored sixteen goals for Leicester City during the previous season.

Clarke and Mick Jones became the deadliest and most-feared forward line in English football, and they'd already scored four goals between them, from their opening six matches.

Everton, though, had absolutely no fears, and they set upon Leeds United with their blitz-style of all-attacking and all-defending football. Alan Ball teed up Jimmy Husband on the edge of the Leeds United area, and Husband's sublime first touch took him past Hunter. Husband toe-poked the ball at Sprake with his second touch, a shot that Sprake should have saved; but instead he fumbled the ball over his goal-line.

Johnny Morrissey then crossed from the left, for Joe Royle to head against the Leeds bar, from six yards, before he headed in the rebound from close range.

Everton went in 2-0 up at half-time, but they didn't sit on their lead, and very quickly after the break, Brian Labone started yet another Everton attack, dispossessing Clarke and passing square to Hurst. John Hurst then beat both Allan Clarke and Johnny Giles inside the centre circle, and he ran fifteen yards, before feeding Husband on the edge of the Leeds area.

Husband squared the ball for Royle, who chipped over Sprake into the far right corner of the goal, a peach of a goal for a three goal lead.

Bremner headed in from Johnny Giles' corner, and then sub Lorimer headed Terry Cooper's cross into Clarke, to score from close range, very late on. Everton held on, though, for a great victory against the Champions, but that 3-2 score-line certainly flattered Leeds. It was also a rare Goodison Park appearance on Match of the Day.

Action footage of Everton's 1969-70 team is rare, because Harry Catterick was always unwilling to allow the BBC television cameras into Goodison Park. He didn't want rival managers watching his team from their comfy armchairs.

He actually resented the idea.

Everton's 3-2 win over Leeds United, and their later home defeat to Liverpool, were the only games out of twenty-one to show the English Champions, at their home ground, on television, during their title-winning season.

Everton's sixth win of the season put them firmly in command, though, at the top of the First Division, and just as Howard Kendall returned to full training.

FIRST DIVISION LEADERS, 30TH AUGUST 1969

	Pl	W	D	L	F	A	PTS
EVERTON	7	6	1	0	14	5	13
Liverpool	7	5	2	0	18	8	12
Derby County	7	3	4	0	8	3	10
Coventry City	7	4	2	1	7	4	10
Wolves	7	4	2	1	12	8	10
Spurs	7	4	1	2	13	8	9

Kendall scored on his Everton comeback, away at Derby, but goals from The Rams' prolific attacking duo, Hector and O'Hare, inflicted a first defeat of the season on Everton, with nearly 38,000 packed inside The Baseball Ground.

One week later, on Saturday 13th September, over 49,000 were inside Goodison to enjoy Everton's return to winning ways, as Ball, Kendall and Harvey totally overran Martin Peters, Bobby Moore and Trevor Brooking.

Colin Harvey's more subtle qualities were often overshadowed by those of Ball and Kendall. But he was defensively quicker than any in the league, a fine tackler, and fit enough to run all day, from box to box.

While Howard Kendall was "a magnificent passer of the ball," as Harvey remembers, "he could play it short or sweep it long," Ball was the innovator. Alan Ball's runs from nowhere literally pulled opposing defences apart, and his sublime control and perfect first touch tore them to pieces, but it was Colin Harvey's sharpness, on and off the ball, his competitive spirit and whole-hearted dedication as an Evertonian, which was crucial to their midfield triumvirate.

"At that time, if you won the midfield, then you won your games," Howard Kendall suggested, and he was right that season, as no teams could ever contain Ball, Kendall and Harvey at their best.

Everton beat West Ham 2-0, after second half goals by Ball and Husband; as their resounding pounding of the Hammers finally demolished their opponents' resolve.

That win launched a ten game unbeaten league run up to the middle of November, and with Everton winning nine of them.

Newcastle, Ipswich, Southampton and Sunderland were all thrashed by an aggregate score of 12-4, with Palace battling to a goalless draw at Selhurst Park, at the beginning of October.

On Saturday 18th October, Stoke City visited Everton, with 48,684 inside Goodison, for a real thriller, and a game that presented Everton, more than most, as true Champions of the highest quality.

EVERTON		STOKE CITY
Gordon West	1	George Farmer
Tommy Wright	2	John Marsh
Sandy Brown	3	Mike Pejic
Howard Kendall	4	Jimmy Greenhoff
Brian Labone	5	Denis Smith
Colin Harvey	6	Alan Bloor
Jimmy Husband	7	Terry Conroy
Alan Ball	8	Peter Dobing
Joe Royle	9	John Ritchie
John Hurst	10	George Eastham
Johnny Morrissey	11	Harry Burrows

Stoke City's keeper, George Farmer, who was deputising for the injured Gordon Banks, was injured himself, early on, after an aerial clash with Royle, and he had to be replaced in goal by Denis Smith. Stoke subsequently missed Smith's commitment and influence in their back four, and Everton fully capitalised.

Although Everton were leading by just 2-1 at half-time, after Morrissey and Royle had both scored, they then ran riot in the second half. Morrissey and Royle each added another goal to their tallies, while Royle then converted his third penalty kick in four games, and Jimmy Husband and Alan Ball completed their 7-2 rout.

Stoke's captain, Peter Dobing, had hit a late consolation, but in spite of their weakened team, due to goalkeeping injuries, they were still a formidable eleven to have been so comprehensively drubbed; one of the best-ever Stoke City teams, in fact.

While Everton's midfield had won the battles, and the territory for the team, they'd have been less worthwhile if they'd had inconsistent and wasteful wingers to feed the ball out to.

Morrissey and Husband had scored three of the goals that had hammered Stoke 7-2, and 1969-70 was their most productive season.

Johnny Morrissey had already displayed his brilliance during that historic win over Manchester United, on the opening day of the 67-68 season, attacking aggressively down either wing, at will, and he'd built on it since.

With Joe Royle's aerial dominance, and clever reading of the early pass, as well as Alan Ball's marauding runs, Morrissey rarely went two games without creating a goal.

Jimmy Husband, however, was a real jewel in the finding, and a serious offensive threat that provided perfect weight to Everton's attack. Having scored twenty goals, nineteen in the First Division, during 1968-69, Husband was particularly targeted by opposing defences, thereafter.

Husband's goal tally during Everton's title-winning season was consequently half of that from the previous season, but the heavy attention given to him by defenders had provided space for not only Ball, Kendall and Harvey in the middle, but also Morrissey out on the left wing.

Johnny Morrissey had his best ever season, as a result, in front of goal.

With Morrissey and Husband giving perfect balance to the team, on the wings, First Division goals ran freely for Everton, throughout the team. Every outfield position, apart from left-back, scored at least one league goal during 1969-70.

Joe Royle scored their winner away at Coventry City, on Saturday 25th October.

A huge crowd of 37,865 had filled Highfield Road, with the Sky Blues up in sixth place, prior to the match, and enjoying the best season in their history.

A week later, Tommy Wright re-discovered his original inside forward instincts to score his second league goal for Everton, belting in a ferocious drive from the right, to beat Nottingham Forest 1-0.

FIRST DIVISION LEADERS, 1ST NOVEMBER 1969

	Pl	W	D	L	F	A	PTS
EVERTON	18	15	2	1	40	15	32
Leeds United	17	8	8	1	32	16	24
Liverpool	18	9	6	3	34	22	24
Derby County	18	9	5	4	28	13	23
Wolves	18	7	8	3	27	22	22
Man City	17	8	5	4	27	17	21

On Saturday 8th November, though, West Brom continued their bogey team record over Everton, when they ended Everton's unbeaten run, after winning 2-0 at The Hawthorns. Jeff Astle and Dick Krzywicki scored a goal in each half, while Leeds had smashed Ipswich Town 4-0 to trail Everton by just six points, and with a game in hand.

Everton suffered a lean month from November, through to early December, taking just three points from four games, while Leeds had gained ten points from six, lifting themselves to just a point behind the leaders.

Alan Whittle was a bright-blonde haired, Liverpool-born, nineteen year old, who'd made his Everton debut two years earlier, but he'd made only ten starts during the previous two seasons. He was a lightning quick, dynamically paced forward, though, and went straight into their team in December, replacing the injured Jimmy Husband.

Everton were thrashed 3-0 by Liverpool on his first start of the season, with over 57,000 inside Goodison Park, in front of the BBC-TV cameras.

A week later, though, on Saturday 13th December, Everton corrected their slide, with a 1-0 away win at West Ham United.

Bobby Moore misplaced a pass that was intended for Martin Peters, in the middle of the pitch, and Alan Whittle pounced on the ball, a few yards inside his own area. Whittle pushed the ball around the outside of Alan Stephenson, and then he galloped away, inside of the defender.

Frank Lampard chased him, the lightning fast nineteen year old, but Whittle's thirty yard run, in the mud, gave the left back no chance of catching him. He placed the ball past Bobby Ferguson, *Fester,* from just inside the West Ham penalty area.

On the following Monday, Harry Catterick paid £80,000 to Third Division Blackburn Rovers, for their twenty-eight year old Manchester-born full back, Keith Newton.

Keith Newton was a white-haired, very distinguished looking player, strong in the tackle, and as fast as most wingers. He was a great passer and crosser of the ball, who'd already made eighteen appearances for England, including all of their 1968 European Championship matches, in Italy. He made his first appearance for the league leaders on Saturday 20th December, as Brian Clough's Derby visited Everton.

Derby County provided a stiff test for the out of sorts Merseysiders, feeling the pressure of Leeds United on their backs, and with their tight back four of Webster, McFarland, Mackay and Robson, they presented an almost impenetrable brick wall that Everton struggled to break through.

Late on, in the second half, though, Alan Ball threaded a through-ball to Joe Royle, on the right of the penalty area. Ball dashed forward, meeting the return ball perfectly, a yard quicker than the ageing Dave Mackay, before he blasted his shot past Green.

The trouble was, while Everton were scraping results, Leeds just kept winning, and in some style. Leeds United had won seven of their eight league and cup games, from the middle of December to the middle of January, and they actually overtook Everton at the top of the league.

On Saturday 27th December, in front of a 47,000 Elland Road crowd, Leeds United had won the match of the season against Everton. Mick Jones scored twice during the first half, before Alan Whittle pulled a goal back, after half-time, but Leeds hung on for one of their greatest league wins of that decade.

One month later, Everton were held to a goalless draw by Newcastle, at Goodison Park. Leeds also drew 2-2, away at Manchester United, in front of over 60,000. Goals from Mick Jones and Billy Bremner ensured Leeds stayed at the top of Division One.

	Pl	W	D	L	F	A	PTS
Leeds United	30	17	11	2	64	29	45
EVERTON	29	20	4	5	51	26	44
Chelsea	28	13	10	5	46	31	36
Liverpool	27	13	9	5	49	30	35

Everton fought back, as January moved into February. Joe Royle's goal secured a battling 1-0 win over fifth-placed Wolves on Saturday 31st January, to return to the top, but Leeds bit back with a 5-1 thrashing of West Brom. Everton then drew three games on the trot, 2-2 at home to Arsenal, on St Valentine's Day; 0-0 at home to Coventry, a week later; and finally, 1-1 away at Nottingham Forest, on the final day of February.

Leeds had beaten Crystal Palace 2-0 on that final day of Winter, to go two points clear of Everton, with just eight games to play. For all observers, it looked as if the pressure had finally told, and the courageous Evertonians' hopes had collapsed as the hardier, more powerful, and more experienced, but less graceful Leeds team had had the title in their hands, once again, as the season ran downhill towards April.

Everton had a stronger, tougher spine than that. They were fighters, and they continued to fight back. After their 2-1 away win at Burnley, on the first Saturday in March, Everton returned to the top of the table four days later, following their great 1-0 away win at Tottenham. Alan Whittle had scored his sixth goal of the season, running clear of Ray Evans during the first half, before beating Pat Jennings, but it was Everton's defence, keeping their sixteenth clean sheet of the season, that had controlled the game, and set them right back on track for the title.

Brian Labone, in particular, was the tall, elegant Evertonian warhorse who led from the back. At thirty years old, by then, Labone's experience and his ability to inspire by calm example was the most crucial factor, by some way, in Everton's resurgence.

He'd also returned to Sir Alf Ramsey's England team for their 3-1 win over Belgium, away in Brussels, along with teammates Tommy Wright and Alan Ball.

Brian Labone had moved ahead of Jack Charlton in the international pecking order, because although both players were equally commanding, Labone was a better passer, and more composed with the ball at his feet.

Labone's captaincy had steered his club around the corner.

On the following Saturday, Everton played Spurs for the second time in three days, and they won 3-2. Alan Whittle, and then an Alan Ball penalty kick, had given them a 2-1 half-time lead, in front of 51,533 at Goodison, before top scorer Joe Royle secured both points late in the match.

With just six points to play, Everton led by three points, although Leeds did have a game in hand.

A raucous atmosphere, from a 54,496 crowd, then welcomed Everton to Anfield on Saturday 21st March, with Liverpool's ageing team from the days of *A Hard Day's Night* attempting to do the double over their younger neighbours, the young pretenders.

Alan Whittle, in again for Jimmy Husband, and Joe Royle scored a goal in each half, as Everton won 2-0, but Leeds had also won, 2-1 away at Wolves.

	Pl	W	D	L	F	A	PTS
EVERTON	37	25	7	5	63	32	57
Leeds United	36	20	14	2	75	33	54
Chelsea	35	17	13	5	58	36	47
Derby County	37	19	7	11	55	34	45
Liverpool	36	16	11	9	57	39	43

Everton's accomplished demolition of their neighbours, amidst a ferocious Anfield atmosphere, had an effect on Leeds United's morale, though, as well as Leeds' on-going FA Cup Semi-final against Manchester United, which went to two epic replays, and also their forthcoming European Cup Semi-final versus Celtic.

On the following Saturday, the pressure finally told, and it was Leeds United who collapsed, completely and comprehensively.

In front of the hugest crowd of the season, at Goodison, Everton smashed third-placed Chelsea to pieces. 57,828 roared and screamed as Howard Kendall, Alan Ball and Joe Royle all scored to put Everton 3-0 up at half-time.

On the old *ABCDEFGHIJKLM* scoreboards, Leeds were drawing 0-0 at home to Southampton, but it was only a matter of time before Revie's lucky, flashy whites scraped their two points against lowly opposition. Royle smashed in his second of the match, after the break, before Alan Whittle then fired in Everton's fifth goal.

Osgood and Dempsey hit late consolations for Chelsea, as they prepared for their FA Cup Final against either Manchester United or Leeds.

Leeds! Of course, what happened to Leeds? If the Everton fans were partying as good as anyone could party, with nearly 58,000 stuffed tightly against each other, and with the Final Scores coming through on their Transistor radios, things really then took off at ten to five.

Jack Charlton and Terry Yorath had both scored at Elland Road, in the second half, but into their own goals. A Ron Davies penalty kick had sealed the 3-1 away win for Southampton.

Everton now had a five point lead at the top, although Leeds still had that one game in hand.

As if things couldn't get any better, they actually did. On the following Monday, Easter Monday, Alan Whittle's first half strike secured a 1-0 away win at Stoke City, with over 33,000 inside The Victoria Ground, ten thousand of whom were Everton supporters.

Again, they could not believe their ears, when the BBC's Sports Report broadcast the stunning news that Derby County had thrashed Leeds United 4-1 at The Baseball Ground.

Don Revie had actually fielded an entire reserve eleven against Derby, to rest his first team players in preparation for their home match against Celtic, two days later.

He'd given up on the title race, and Brian Clough never forgot that.

That meant that an Everton win, at home to West Bromwich Albion, on Wednesday 1st April, would secure the title. With a seven point lead, however, and with Leeds only having four more games, and having apparently given up, it was highly improbable that Everton couldn't win it. The pressure was off, and so Everton showed their total class against the team that had deprived them of the FA Cup, two years earlier.

Roger Kenyon, who had made his league debut for Everton back in November 1967, replaced captain Labone, who was out with a knock, and Sandy Brown had also returned to left back, in place of the injured Keith Newton. Newton had restored a measure of stability to Everton's defence, when the wheels had looked like they might be falling off, but Sandy Brown, a fierce Scotsman, was also an Evertonian at heart, and he fought for every cause for the club.

EVERTON		WEST BROMWICH ALBION
Gordon West	1	John Osborne
Tommy Wright	2	Lyndon Hughes
Sandy Brown	3	Ray Wilson
Howard Kendall	4	Doug Fraser
Roger Kenyon	5	Alistair Robertson
Colin Harvey	6	Alan Merrick
Alan Whittle	7	Len Cantello
Alan Ball	8	Colin Suggett
Joe Royle	9	Jeff Astle
John Hurst	10	Tony Brown
Johnny Morrissey	11	Bobby Hope

Alan Whittle, with an impressive record of five goals from Everton's last five games, was keeping Jimmy Husband out of the team, on form. Whittle scored a first half goal, from the edge of the area, to give Everton a 1-0 half-time lead. He'd also set an Everton club record of scoring in six consecutive First Division matches.

Colin Harvey then smashed home a fantastic twenty-five yard rocket to complete Everton's 2-0 win, after the break.

58,523, Goodison Park's biggest crowd of the season, went wild in celebration.

It was one of those nights few Evertonians forgot; those that went to the game, went straight from work, on foot, to the pub, and then straight to Goodison; even those that didn't go, but just went to the pub, and listened on the radio, then met those that went afterwards.

"WE ARE THE CHAMPIONS! WE ARE THE CHAMPIONS! WE ARE THE CHAMPIONS!"

Everton's players completed a lap of honour under the floodlights, on that wonderful April Fools' Night.

On Saturday 4th April, Johnny Morrissey scored his ninth First Division goal of the season, as Everton won 1-0 away at Sheffield Wednesday, and Leeds United's season then totally fell apart, after they could only draw with West Ham, and then lost to Man City and also away at Ipswich.

Leeds finished nine points behind the new Football League Champions, Everton Football Club, a gap that belied the true closeness of that title race.

Everton had kept twenty-one First Division clean sheets and they won twenty-nine matches, during 1969-70. Only Tottenham's double-winning team of 1961 have won more league matches, in the history of the First Division, or the Premier League.

Everton had also beaten every other team in Division One, on at least one occasion, and they'd conceded only thirty-four goals, while scoring seventy-two.

West, Wright, Hurst and Royle were all ever-presents, while Morrissey missed only one game. Joe Royle had his greatest season, scoring twenty-three First Division goals, sitting in joint-second place in the league goal-scoring table along with Peter Osgood, just behind England's top scorer Jeff Astle.

Alan Whittle, whose six in six were so valuable at the back end of the season, had scored eleven; Alan Ball hit ten, Johnny Morrissey nine, Jimmy Husband six, John Hurst five, Howard Kendall four, and Colin Harvey three.

For the 1970 World Cup Finals, Sir Alf Ramsay picked eight Everton players in his initial pool of forty players. Colin Harvey and Howard Kendall did not make the final squad, though, which perplexed most Everton supporters.

How could you not select the midfield that had won the league so convincingly?

Sir Alf always went with continuity, though, and he preferred Alan Mullery, Colin Bell and Nobby Stiles. Gordon West was offered a place, as third-choice keeper, behind Gordon Banks and Peter Bonetti, but he declined, choosing to watch the World Cup at home with his family instead.

Joe Royle was also one of six players who went home, despite making the final twenty-eight.

Sir Alf instead picked Geoff Hurst, Francis Lee, Allan Clarke, Jeff Astle and Peter Osgood as his five forwards.

Brian Labone was chosen as Bobby Moore's partner in defence for all but their 1-0 win over Czechoslovakia. Keith Newton also started three out of their four games, and he provided two great crosses for both of England's goals, scored by Mullery and Peters, as England tore West Germany apart during the first hour of their Quarter-final match, leading 2-0.

Alan Ball played in all four of England's matches, but he was left puzzled when Sir Alf replaced Bobby Charlton with Colin Bell, and then, more confusingly, Martin Peters with Norman Hunter, as West Germany came back to win 3-2, while both Newton and Terry Cooper were hobbling for the majority of the extra-time period.

Keith Newton had been kicked hard during their opening win over Romania, and he was replaced by teammate Tommy Wright, who also started as right back during their epic 1-0 defeat against Brazil. He'd also spent some time on the ground, receiving treatment after suffering another foul by Schultz, just moments before Hunter replaced Peters.

Most people believed that Sir Alf's substitutions had cost England their chance of going on to defend their title against Italy, in the Semi-finals. England had the game won, and the change of their shape, as well as his inability to address any physical weaknesses, merely benefitted the resurgent Germans. Even the players knew it; they blamed themselves for throwing away a winning position on the pitch, but the substitutions that Sir Alf made had just made it tougher for them.

If anyone needed replacing, it was the two full backs, who'd ran themselves to exhaustion in the Leon heat, and it was into those wide areas which both Grabowski and Schnellinger were beginning to exploit.

Sir Alf refused to admit his error, to anyone, not the press, not the television presenters, nobody. Over a decade later, though, he did admit to Martin Peters that he had made two mistakes, and England would have won, had he not made them.

Even so, England's defence, made up mostly of Everton players, had done superbly, conceding just a single goal in three and three-quarter games, until West Germany scored two goals during those last twenty minutes of that Quarter-final.

Alan Ball and Alan Mullery had also been superb in midfield, with Ball hitting the Brazilian crossbar, with ten minutes to go in their 1-0 defeat, in Guadalajara.

On Sunday 8th August, less than two months after England's World Cup defeat, Labone, Ball, Newton and Wright were all back in action, in the FA Charity Shield.

Stamford Bridge hosted the match between Cup winners Chelsea, and Champions Everton, and a decent crowd of 43,547 attended what was effectively a home game for Chelsea.

In the first half, the white-booted Alan Ball collected the ball, deep inside his own area, and he exchanged passes with Colin Harvey, inside the centre circle. Ball then scampered off to halfway inside Chelsea's half, and after a great thirty yard run, he played the ball wide to Alan Whittle, out on the left. Whittle cut inside David Webb, and unleashed a fierce drive up into the top left corner of Bonetti's goal.

Ten minutes into the second half, after dreadful defensive mistakes by both Webb and Hollins, Joe Royle ran onto the ball on the left side of the Chelsea area, and crossed to the far post for Howard Kendall, in yards of space, to simply nod in for a two-nil lead.

Ian Hutchinson flicked in a consolation, from Keith Weller's left wing cross, with only ten minutes remaining, but Everton held on, continuing their dominance of English football. Everton were playing with the confidence and class of a team well-prepared to dominate the game in Europe, as well as in England.

But no, their 1970-71 season was a comparative disaster.

Everton lost three of their opening six matches, winning none of them, but they'd lost Brian Labone to injury after just three games. Labone played in only thirteen of their remaining thirty-nine matches, and Jimmy Husband also started only fourteen league matches throughout that season.

A slight recovery, winning four on the trot during September, lifted them up to eighth place at the end of that month, before their poor form again returned. Everton eventually won only seven of their opening twenty-four matches, up to the New Year, and they were well out of the race for UEFA Cup places, by January 1971.

In the European Cup, though, Everton had made good progress. They knocked out Icelandic club Keflavik in the First round, in September, winning 9-2 on aggregate.

Joe Royle had scored four, Alan Ball three, and Kendall and Whittle one apiece.

In the Second round, they were drawn against Borussia Moenchengladbach, who boasted Berti Vogts, who'd started in four of West Germany's World Cup matches in Mexico, as well as three other future European and World-conquering West German stars, Gunter Netzer, Jupp Heynckes, and goalkeeper Wolfgang Kleff.

In Germany, on 21st October, the tall, fair-haired Vogts gave Moenchengladbach a half-time lead, but Howard Kendall fired a vital equaliser, from the edge of the area.

For the second leg, at Goodison, two weeks later, on Wednesday 4th November, 42,744 witnessed a dynamic, heroic, and ultimately, historic European Cup match; a prototype for dozens of dramatic European and World competition matches for decades to come.

Everton attacked from the very start, throughout the match, and until the final whistle. They actually took the lead with their first shot at goal, even if it may not have been, technically, a shot.

In the first minute, Johnny Morrissey swerved in a wonderful cross-shot from thirty yards out, from wide on the left, which Royle appeared to attack. Keeper Kleff had appeared to have covered Royle's header, but the ball just sailed between both men, and it curled just inside the far right post.

Delighted, Everton players all mobbed Morrissey.

Royle's shot from Morrissey's corner was then cleared off Borussia's goal-line by Mueller, and Kleff then dived to save Ball's header from Morrissey's left-sided cross.

Herbert Laumen, Borussia's top goal-scorer as they'd won the Bundesliga, during the previous season, headed Gunter Netzer's free-kick straight at Gordon West, ten minutes before half-time. West couldn't hold on, though, and Laumen bounced up to fire in from the rebound. The scores were level on the night, and on aggregate.

Kleff then tipped Royle's header, from Alan Ball's corner kick, over his crossbar, before just moments later, Ball again crossed from the right, and Royle's header from only six yards out was again tipped over the bar, by the flying Kleff.

Joe Royle then fiercely headed just over the crossbar, from Keith Newton's cross.

Into the second half, Royle blasted over, from six yards out, after Tommy Wright had crossed from the right, and then he clipped Kleff's crossbar with a cracking drive from outside the area, after Ball had virtually ran through Borussia's entire midfield.

Kleff then cleared Kendall's goal-bound drive off his line, with his knees, and he also saved bravely at Whittle's feet, inside his six yard box.

Borussia had just one shot on goal during the entire second half, Koppel's eighteen yard blast being well saved by West. In a fever-pitch Goodison atmosphere, Everton's frenzied offensive pressure never weakened. Morrissey actually thought he'd won the tie, in extra-time, as he headed towards an empty net, but Kleff jumped fully ten feet off the ground, to tip the ball out, unbelievably, from beneath his bar.

Kleff then saved Morrissey's ten yard shot, during the second period of extra-time, before he punched away Ball's angled drive on the rebound. Kleff then punched away Joe Royle's bicycle kick, from the edge of the area, and that was it.

The match was ended, and it was to be decided by a penalty kick shootout, the first ever European Cup penalty shootout.

Joe Royle's penalty kick was saved, low to his right, by Wolfgang Kleff.

Kleff had been Man of the Match by miles.

Sielhoff put Borussia 1-0 up, before Alan Ball fired decisively, low into the bottom right corner.

Laumen then missed the goal completely, firing wide of Everton's left post, having sent West the wrong way.

Johnny Morrissey powered his kick high up into the far right corner of Kleff's goal, giving Everton a 2-1 lead, but Jupp Heynckes, after taking a massive run-up, fired a missile right up into the right stanchion of West's goal. That was an un-saveable penalty.

Howard Kendall put Everton 3-2 up, before Koppel equalised again, for Borussia.

Substitute Sandy Brown fired the ball high to Kleff's right, before, finally, full back Mueller's shot was brilliantly saved by West, diving to his right, in the mud.

You could hear the resultant cheers and screams on the Wirral. Why Borussia's captain Gunter Netzer hadn't taken a penalty, one of the all-time greatest German playmakers and set-piece takers, it's not certain. Maybe the Goodison noise just got to him, but it was one of the most wonderful nights in European competition, for English football.

In the FA Cup, Jimmy Husband scored twice, as Everton defeated Blackburn 2-0 at Goodison Park, before they hammered Middlesbrough 3-0, three weeks later, in the Fourth round. Henry Newton, who'd signed from Nottingham Forest, en route to Derby County, had scored their first, in front of 54,827, the biggest crowd of the day, and Colin Harvey and Joe Royle completed their rout.

David Johnson, a nineteen year-old Liverpool-born striker, then scored the only goal of the game to beat Derby County 1-0, with 53,490 inside Goodison. Johnson was eventually on his way to Liverpool, via Ipswich, in a £200,000 transfer, six years later.

Another 53,000 home crowd watched Everton smash the FA Cup giant-killers of that year, in the Quarter-finals. Colchester United who'd beaten league leaders Leeds United 3-2, back in the

Fifth round, were smashed 5-0. Howard Kendall scored twice, and Joe Royle, Jimmy Husband and Alan Ball had hit the others, sending Everton to Old Trafford, to face Liverpool in a Semi-final classic.

With almost the whole of Merseyside in Manchester on that Saturday, 27th March, 62,144 totally filled United's vast stadium, and the noise from the Blue half was deafening after Alan Ball had shot them into a 1-0 lead. Liverpool came back, though, with goals from both Alun Evans and Brian Hall, to break Everton's hearts.

That isn't idle rhetoric, it did literally break their hearts.

In the European Cup Quarter-finals, Everton blitzed Panathinaikos' penalty area, at Goodison Park, on Tuesday 9th March, but they could only beat some excellent goalkeeping from Oikonomopoulos with David Johnson's solitary second half strike.

Then, Antoniadis fired in a late goal to give the Greeks a totally undeserved draw.

On the Tuesday night before the second leg, played on Wednesday 24th March, the Greek hotel where Everton's team were staying was swarmed with Panathinaikos supporters, in cars, on motorbikes, beeping horns, screaming and blaring sirens, and all night long, determined to keep the English awake. That was the reality of European football on the continent, in certain places, and nothing could be done about it.

Only 25,000 attended the match, but it was a highly hostile and hateful crowd that spat at the Everton players as they took throw-ins and corner kicks. One of the Greek players actually stabbed John Hurst, in his eyes, with both of his out-stretched fingers. It was very cynical, and all behind the back of the referee; cowardly, in fact.

The goalless draw that Everton achieved, and it was an achievement, in such a vitriolic venue, was not enough to keep them in the competition, and, just like Derby County a year later, and also Leeds United, twice during the next four years, Everton could feel themselves cheated out of a competition that did not ensure fair play.

Everton finished the 1970-71 season in fifteenth position, only ten points above relegated Burnley, but nearly Thirty Points below Arsenal, the new Champions.

Joe Royle had had a decent season, though, scoring 23 league and cup goals, but no other player hit double figures in goals scored, not even Alan Ball, who'd scored only two First Division goals, in thirty-nine games. That was also Alan Ball's last full season for Everton, as Harry Catterick decided to cash in on his underperforming superstar, midway into the following season.

Brian Labone broke down, yet again, with an Achilles tendon injury, after only four games of the 1971-72 season, and he was finally forced to retire, after 530 league and cup matches, including 451 First Division matches.

Labone had only been booked twice during all of those games, despite being a thoroughly competitive, winning centre-half, and playing against some of football's roughest, toughest and fastest strikers of all time, Ron Davies, Wyn Davies, Roger Hunt, Francis Lee, Mick Jones, Allan Clarke, Denis Law and Jimmy Greaves.

He was one of the very greatest Everton players of all time, and probably their greatest ever defender. When he retired, he was just twelve games short of Ted Sagar's all-time First Division appearances record for Everton.

After a night out with his great friend, Gordon West, at the Winslow Hotel in Walton, Brian Labone collapsed in the street, close to his home in Sefton, and he died, aged only sixty-six, on Monday 24th April 2006.

Keith Newton was dropped by Harry Catterick, in October 1971, after 50 First Division matches for Everton, because he was reluctant to kick the ball long, out of defence, every time, as he'd been instructed, preferring instead to play the ball out, with their triangular passing movements. It was the first sign that Harry Catterick was beginning to lose control of the footballing principles that had made the team great.

Newton moved to Burnley, on a free transfer, during the Summer of 1972, and he became a key player in helping the Clarets back up into the First Division elite.

Two months later, Alan Ball was sold to Arsenal, for a club record transfer fee of £220,000, just because it was the right price for Harry Catterick.

Ball had scored sixty-six First Division goals for Everton, in 208 games, and he'd been their greatest post-war player. Alan Ball wasn't desperate to leave Everton, but because Mr Catterick had agreed the sale, he moved because he wasn't wanted. He was never the same player again, as he'd been during those four years between 1966 and 1970, at Everton, and in truth, Everton were never the same team again. It took years before they truly became a dominant force in English football, once again.

Again, Everton finished the 1971-72 season down in fifteenth place, having won just nine of their forty-two league games, and they won only three of their five cup matches. Only David Johnson had hit double figures, in goals scored, but he wasn't even guaranteed a first team place, whence his subsequent move to Ipswich, and then Johnny Morrissey eventually left Goodison Park, for the Third Division depths of Oldham Athletic, after scoring 42 First Division goals in 258 games.

The glory days for Everton were well and truly waning. Transition was the word of those days, and those Days were long and dark amidst the Power Cuts. Howard Kendall was named as Everton's captain after Ball had left, and on Monday 8th May 1972, Everton paid Stoke £125,000 for their midfield battler Mike Bernard, who'd helped the Potters win the League Cup, and missed only six league games during 1971-72.

In 1972-73, Everton were even worse than before, finishing seventeenth in the First Division, and only seven points above the relegation zone. They won only one of their three cup games. Again, Joe Royle was their top-scorer, but with just seven league goals, joint top scorer, tied with John Connolly and Joe Harper. Crowds were also down, with an average of just 34,000 half-filling their iconic, historic Goodison Park.

On 14th April 1973, Tommy Wright played his 308th and final First Division match for Everton, hobbling off for the third time inside six months, as they lost 4-2 away at Wolves. Wright, Everton's greatest-ever right back, due to his consistent passing, pinpoint crossing, and calm and stylish defending, was forced to retire during the following season, having failed to recover from his recurrent knee injuries.

Two days prior to this, Harry Catterick, who'd suffered a heart attack back in 1972, was moved upstairs by Everton's board, and he became their new general manager, after twelve years as first team manager. Catterick had become the most successful manager in the club's history, winning two League Titles and also an FA Cup, as well as losing in another, and two third-placed finishes in Division One.

However, his great, great team was falling apart, and the club needed a new, younger man to build a new Everton team for the future.

On 28th May, Billy Bingham, Everton's outside right during their 1962-63 League Championship winning team, was appointed as the new first team manager, having previously been in charge of the Greek national football team.

Gordon West had also retired from football, having played just four games during that 1972-73 season, after he'd been displaced as first choice keeper by Dave Lawson.

West had played 335 First Division games for Everton, and he didn't concede a single goal in seven FA Cup matches, against Sunderland, Coventry, Bedford Town, Manchester City and Manchester United, en route to their 1966 Cup Final triumph.

He did return to football, in the mid-Seventies, with Tranmere Rovers, but West played only seventeen more league games, and he made his final league appearance in November 1978.

Gordon West was very close friends with Brian Labone, and *Labbie's* death had hit him hard.

On Sunday 10th June 2012, One of the two greatest goalkeepers in Everton's long history, Gordon West died, aged sixty-nine, after he lost his battle with cancer.

In November 1973, Jimmy Husband was sold to Luton Town, Second Division promotion chasers, for just £80,000. Husband had scored 44 goals in 165 First Division matches for Everton, but since 1970, he'd never had as important an impact in their team, as he had during the late Sixties, when he was completely unplayable at his best.

Joe Royle missed nearly three months of action during 1973-74, through injury, so Billy Bingham needed a new striker. He paid a club record £350,000 transfer fee to Birmingham City for Bob Latchford, who'd fired sixty-eight league goals in 158 starts, and as part of the complex transfer package, he sent Howard Kendall to Birmingham.

Effectively, Bob Latchford cost £350,000, and Kendall's price was £180,000, while Archie Styles was given to Birmingham City on a free transfer, so Everton had officially paid £170,000, plus two players... £170,000 plus two players.

Plus two players? Howard Kendall was certainly the most important character in the history of Everton Football Club. He won that 1970 League Championship trophy as a player, but then, after he returned to Goodison Park as Everton's manager in 1981, with Colin Harvey as his assistant, Everton won two further league titles, an FA Cup Final, and the European Cup Winners' Cup, while his Everton team also reached three other Wembley Finals, under his six year reign, up until 1987.

Howard Kendall played over 230 First Division matches for Everton, scoring twenty-one goals, and his drive and rhythm, at the bottom of the engine room that had driven Everton to the 1970 title, was delightful to watch. Mild-mannered and of a superb temperament, his perfect patience, in possession, had led him to be repeatedly fouled by opponents, far less patient than him, yet he rarely remonstrated with referees.

Despite losing several of their stars, Everton had a surprisingly decent season in 1973-74, with no consistent team fielded at any time, and they sat as high as fourth, just after Christmas, while they'd been as high as second at the end of October.

Bob Latchford scored seven goals in thirteen matches, at the end of the season, but Everton fell just two points short of UEFA Cup qualification, finishing in seventh place. Billy Bingham's second-most significant signing, of the 1973-74 season, was paying £80,000 to Sheffield Wednesday for Dave Clements, who'd been Coventry City's most consistent player when they'd qualified for the Fairs Cup back in 1970.

Dave Clements was a stockier, and less athletic-looking Howard Kendall type of player. His good build enabled him to ensure he was never, ever knocked off the ball, and his solid possession and clever passing were big reasons for Everton's resurgence.

Clements was a decent tackler too, and like Mike Summerbee, he liked to attack full backs, before they got to him.

If I were writing this book on the years of 1970-74, rather than 1967 to 1976, then it's highly unlikely Everton would have an entire chapter about them.

A club in perpetual transition, and effective stagnation, is never very exciting to remember, nor even to write about, but then in 1974-75, they suddenly became very good again.

They should have won the league title, more so than Liverpool, Stoke and Ipswich, who could also very easily have won the title, with a bit more consistency.

In September 1974, having played in all of Everton's opening four matches, winning two and drawing two, Colin Harvey was the last of *Los Tres Magnificos, the Holy Trinity, Ball, Kendall and Harvey*, to leave Everton.

Billy Bingham sold Harvey to Second Division side Sheffield Wednesday, for just £70,000, after he'd played 321 First Division games for Everton.

Colin Harvey played thirty league games for The Owls in 1974-75, but their lack of a goal-scorer meant that he was unable to prevent Wednesday from slipping down to Division Three. He played his 45th and last game for Wednesday in November 1975, during their 3-0 defeat at home to Port Vale, before he retired from football.

At his best, Colin Harvey was like a race horse, speeding in from nowhere, cleanly winning tackles. His goal against West Brom, in April 1970, was one of the very greatest goals ever seen at Goodison Park. At his best, he was better than Bobby Moore, but you didn't hear it here, right. (Actually, he was better than Bobby Moore most of the time, but some people just never get the credit.)

To replace Harvey in Everton's team, Billy Bingham broke the bank, and he paid £300,000 to Burnley, in straight cash, for their brilliant, elegant, and intelligent midfield creator, Martin Dobson.

Dobson had been the jewel of Burnley's beautifully balanced midfield that had made the Clarets the only realistic pursuers of Leeds United, for much of 1973-74.

Now, playing alongside the roundly respected, and roundly built Dave Clements, Everton had a midfield that was certainly comparable to, though never as good as, their 1970 engine room.

Roger Kenyon, who'd replaced Brian Labone, now captained the team, and he partnered John Hurst in central defence, and with Mike Bernard converted to right back, and Steve Seargeant, a rugged, bearded Scouser, at left back, Everton kept fifteen clean sheets during the 1974-75 season, and they conceded just forty-two goals.

Bob Latchford scored seventeen goals from thirty-six First Division games, but the £200,000 sale of Joe Royle to Manchester City, on Christmas Eve in 1974, probably cost Everton the league title.

Joe Royle had scored 102 First Division goals in just 229 starts for Everton, and he never enjoyed the same degree of prolificacy, thereafter, becoming more of a support striker, a holding forward player, using his strength and his ability to make space for others. He won a League Cup winners' medal with City, in February 1976, but his greatest days, after leaving Everton, were as a manager.

Royle led Oldham Athletic into the First Division, and in 1992, Oldham became inaugural members of the FA Premier League, under his management, while also reaching two FA Cup Semi-finals, as well as a League Cup Final.

Joe Royle then returned to Everton, as manager, in November 1994. They were rooted at the bottom of the Premier League, but in his first game in charge, Everton beat Liverpool 2-0, with nearly 40,000 inside Goodison Park. Royle easily succeeded in keeping them up, but he also led them to an 1-0 FA Cup Final win over Manchester United. That win, in the 1995 Cup Final, remains Everton's last major honour, to date.

He resigned in March 1997, fed up of working on financial scraps, and seeing Everton fall into the shadows of North-west giants Manchester United and Liverpool.

Royle's departure, as a player, from Everton in 1974, had left John Hurst as the only survivor from their 1970 Championship winning team.

Everton won their first three games of 1975, to return to the top of Division One, and they then led the league for all but one week until late March, when they lost 3-0 away at bottom club Carlisle United.

Eleven days later, on Wednesday 9th April, they lost 2-1 away at second-bottom Luton Town.

Everton had had the title fixed hard in their grasping hands before those two defeats, and despite winning away at Newcastle, their misery was compounded when Sheffield United, chasing a UEFA Cup place, came and won 3-2 at Goodison Park.

Tony Currie struck the Blades' winning goal, late in the second half, after Everton had been 2-0 up at half-time.

Everton finished up in fourth position, just three points below Champions Derby County. £200,000 had probably cost Everton the title, as they surely wouldn't have lost it if they'd just kept Joe Royle?

Still, the crowds had returned to Goodison Park, with their average home attendance of 40,020, the third highest in the Football League, and Everton's highest since 1971.

Once again, Everton were at least competing at the top, if not playing the sensational football that had 60,000 overfilling their ground during the last three to four years of the Sixties, up until 1970.

Bob Latchford was their new hero. And in 1977-78, he was the First Division's top goal-scorer, hitting thirty goals from thirty-nine games, before going on to score a total of 106 goals in 235 First Division games, while winning twelve England caps.

Everton finished in third place, that season, nine points behind Nottingham Forest.

Despite their League Cup Final appearance in 1977, though, Everton had never really fulfilled the potential they'd promised during 1974-75, and it wasn't until the Kendall/Harvey era of the Eighties, when Real Success returned to Goodison Park.

John Hurst came on as a substitute during Everton's 3-1 win over Middlesbrough, on Monday 19th April 1976, replacing Bryan Hamilton, with only 18,000 inside Goodison Park. That was John Hurst's 349th and final First Division appearance for Everton.

Hurst was the often forgotten, unsung hero of Everton's 1970 Championship season, but he was so dependable alongside Brian Labone, just as he was, alongside Roger Kenyon, five years later.

He was the last of that 1970 team, their greatest ever side, to leave Goodison Park.

Harry Catterick, the architect of that side, was an Evertonian to his core, and he died at Goodison Park, after watching Howard Kendall's great Everton team beat Ipswich Town in the FA Cup Quarter-finals, on Saturday 9th March 1985.

He was only sixty-five.

Harry Catterick's team, the Champions of 1970, have often been decried as not being that good, because of their immediate decline into mediocrity, and also their subsequent break-up. It was even claimed that his team was not as good as Howard Kendall's 1985 Champions and European Cup Winners' Cup winners.

Kendall's team really should have won the treble in 1984-85, and they were a great team, one of the very greatest of all English club teams since the Seventies. But were they better than Harry Catterick's Everton? Nobody can tell. It *is* impossible to judge, but to point at the decline of the 1970 team as a failure of the team is ridiculous.

Aside from the fact that Howard Kendall's two-time Champions also declined sharply into mediocrity after 1987, from which they've never really recovered, the 1970 team was nearing the end of its cycle.

Harry Catterick's 1970 Champions were the crème de la crème of an Everton team that finished first on two occasions, but they'd had six top four finishes in the eight years up to their 1970 title triumph. They also won one FA Cup, and in their other Cup Final, they totally outplayed West Brom, despite losing 1-0.

They were irresistible at their best, and the most innovative football team of the Glam Soccer era. They were quite probably, the best of all Everton's post-war teams, that won forty, and lost only seven, out of sixty-four league games, from November 1968 up to April 1970.

Everton's average home attendance was 49,531 during 1969-70, the very last time that Goodison Park enjoyed crowds of fifty thousand, or anywhere near 50,000.

Everton's fans felt their team was an international side. *SEND OUR TEAM TO MEXICO*, they'd chanted from all four sides of Goodison Park, during their April Fools' Day title-winning victory over West Brom. Their fluent style of play, both going forwards and coming backwards, was unique, and though many teams have attempted to borrow the style, notably Manchester United under Tommy Docherty, Ipswich under Bobby Robson, Newcastle under Kevin Keegan, and then Reading under Steve Coppell, all proper entertainers, none of them have enjoyed much success.

Just as Brazil presented their Samba rhythm of football in 1970, Holland introduced Total Football in 1974, and Spain beat the World with total possession tiki-taka football in 2010, Everton's World Cup Finals were played during 1969-70, when they produced a unique style of play, unprecedented, inimitable and unequalled.

The School of Science had arrived.

Everton faded, sure, but Brazil did not continue their unique style into the rest of the Seventies, and Holland were more of a functional team by 1978.

That Everton team introduced a footballing style that was the first of its kind, a complete attack-attack-attack when they had the ball, and then absolute defence when they didn't. Kenneth Wolstenholme had put it perfectly when he commented that it was as if they played a *9-9-1* formation.

For three successive seasons, Everton swamped and blitzed, outplayed and outclassed the reigning Champions, great Champions, home or away.

Manchester United, Manchester City, and Leeds United, all at their very best, were simply slaughtered by Harry Catterick's Everton, the greatest Everton of all time.

THE BIG RED MACHINE

IN FEBRUARY 1970, THE Quarter-final draw for the FA Cup had pitched four of the biggest First Division teams away to Second Division opposition.

Tricky though all the ties were, they almost entirely followed all expectations.

Manchester United drew 1-1 at Middlesbrough, in front of a sell-out 40,000 Ayresome Park crowd, before going through 2-1 back at Old Trafford. Leeds United went through 2-0 away at Swindon Town, after Allan Clarke's two second half goals had killed the hopes of the huge 27,500 County Ground crowd.

Peter Osgood's hat-trick helped Chelsea win a 4-2 classic away at West London rivals QPR, with a club record 33,572 crowd filling Loftus Road.

Watford's near club record 34,047 crowd had also filled Vicarage Road in Hertfordshire, on Saturday 21st February 1970, for the visit of Bill Shankly's mighty Liverpool.

Shankly had already began rejuvenating his Liverpool side, having sold World Cup winner Roger Hunt to Bolton Wanderers, back in December, for just £30,000.

Hunt had scored a club record 245 league goals from only 401 games for Liverpool, but in his last match at Anfield, the warning signs were already there for Shankly.

On Saturday 13th December 1969, Manchester United had visited Liverpool, and they ran riot in the second half, winning 4-1 and shocking the biggest crowd of the day, with nearly 48,000 packed inside Anfield.

For their Quarter-final match at Watford, Liverpool were missing both Tommy Smith and Peter Thompson, but they still fielded a star-studded team that should have been able to overcome the lowliest of the four Second Division teams left in the Cup.

WATFORD		LIVERPOOL
Mike Walker	1	Tommy Lawrence
Duncan Welbourne	2	Chris Lawler
John Williams	3	Peter Wall
Ron Lugg	4	Geoff Strong
Walter Lees	5	Ron Yeats
Tom Walley	6	Emlyn Hughes
Stewart Scullion	7	Ian Callaghan
Terry Garbett	8	Ian Ross
Barry Endean	9	Alun Evans
Mike Packer	10	Ian St John
Brian Owen	11	Bobby Graham

Liverpool, *the finest team in England since the War*, could find no reply, though, to Barry Endean's second half header, after Ron Lugg had weaved up the right wing.

Indeed, they were comfortably, very, comfortably held off by Watford's hardworking back eight.

In the Semi-finals, Watford were soundly hammered 5-1 by Chelsea, but Bill Shankly already knew he'd have to find fresh talent, and very quickly, losing his Sixties' legends and building a brand new Big Red Machine for the Seventies.

Liverpool had been a great team during the Merseybeat/Beatles years, following their Second Division Championship title in 1962, *Love Me Do.*

They had won the First Division Championship twice, in 1964, *A Hard Day's Night,* and then again in 1966, *Tomorrow Never Knows.* Liverpool had also beaten Leeds United 2-1 in a classic 1965 FA Cup Final, *Ticket To Ride.*

However, they'd failed to achieve European success, losing 4-3 to Inter Milan in the 1965 European Cup Semi-finals, *Help!*

Then Ajax hammered them in the First round, two years later, *Hello Goodbye.*

They'd narrowly lost to Borussia Dortmund in the 1966 European Cup Winners' Cup Final, though, at Hampden Park, *Here, There And Everywhere.*

Even as recently as November 1969, *The End,* they'd actually been turfed out of the Fairs Cup by Portuguese middle weights Vitoria Setubal, but that Watford defeat was the final straw, for Bill Shankly, by 1970. *Let It Be,* he certainly wasn't doing.

Bill Shankly's ambition to build Liverpool up and up and up into a bastion of invincibility had drawn flat as the Beatles broke up. The Reds had conquered England, twice, but they'd been nearly men, at best, in Europe.

His changes began immediately.

For Derby County's visit to Anfield on 28th February, just a week after Liverpool's FA Cup exit, Ray Clemence replaced Tommy Lawrence in goal. Clemence, their twenty-one year old reserve team keeper, had played nearly fifty league matches for Scunthorpe, as a teenager, when Shankly paid just £18,000 for him back in June 1967.

Tommy Lawrence had played 305 league matches for Liverpool, and he'd been a virtual ever-present for the Reds throughout the Sixties. He was picked to play only one more match by Shankly, though, over a year later, in their penultimate game of the 1970-71 season, away at Manchester City.

Ian St John had also started his final Liverpool match in that defeat at Vicarage Road. Saint had played 335 league games for Liverpool, scoring 95 goals. He left Anfield at the end of the season, though, to become a football coach in South Africa during the Summer of 1970. He went on to manage Portsmouth in the mid-Seventies, before finally teaming up with Jimmy Greaves, in the early Eighties, for an amusing review of contemporary football issues on ITV's *World of Sport* programme.

In March 1970, Larry Lloyd made his Liverpool debut, having signed from Bristol Rovers, for £50,000, back in April 1969. The twenty-one year old Bristolian had played forty-three Third Division matches for his hometown club, and he played eight games in central defence, for Liverpool, at the end of the 1969-70 season.

A giant of a man, six feet and two inches tall, brilliant in the air and a fierce tackler, with a menacing pair of eyes, Larry Lloyd took over from Ron Yeats as Liverpool's dominant centre half.

Ron Yeats reverted to left back for the remainder of the season, and he also played a dozen more games, at left back, during the following 1970-71 season.

Big Ron Yeats, all fourteen and a half stone of him, left Liverpool during the Summer of 1971. Exceptionally tough and physical, Yeats had played 359 league matches for Bill Shankly throughout the Sixties, but he gained only two Scotland caps, so equally dominant were Dave Mackay, Billy McNeill and Ron McKinnon at that time.

Because of the fresher strength struck into their defence, Liverpool improved at the end of 1969-70, gaining ten points from their last eight First Division matches.

They rose to fifth in the table, although they were still fifteen points behind Champions Everton.

Apart from Bobby Graham, though, their forward line had struggled to score. Of the eleven goals that they scored in their last eight matches, more than half of them were scored by defenders. Right back Chris Lawler was Liverpool's second top goal-scorer in 1970, with ten goals.

A mediocre first month of the following season forced Bill Shankly to strengthen his team even further. With Liverpool out of the First Division title race, yet safe from relegation worries, Shankly found time and space to develop his team without the pressures of needing to win games.

On Saturday 12th September, away at Newcastle, he finally filled the "problem" left back position that he'd always struggled to fill since the departure of Gerry Byrne.

Alec Lindsay had signed for Liverpool, from his hometown club Bury, back in March 1969. Lindsay played over one hundred and twenty games for the Shakers, commanding his back four, whilst still only a teenager for most of 1967-68, when Bury gained promotion to Division Two.

Lindsay played at left back against Newcastle, and Liverpool kept a clean sheet, drawing 0-0.

A fortnight later, on Saturday 26th September, Liverpool University science graduate Brian Hall made his league debut in midfield, due to Ian Callaghan's cartilage injury. He remained in the team for most of the rest of the season, though, starting in all but three of Liverpool's last fifty-one league and cup games of 1970-71.

On Saturday 10th October, a second University graduate made his First Division debut for Liverpool. Steve Heighway had left Warwick University with a degree (BA) in economics, but while at University, he'd been recruited by Roy Rees, manager of Skelmersdale United.

Dublin-born, Heighway had made his international debut for the Republic of Ireland while he was still playing non-league football with Skelmersdale. A two-footed left winger, Heighway also remained in the Liverpool team for most of the rest of that season. Brian Hall and Steve Heighway were jovially nicknamed **Little Bamber and Big Bamber**, because of their University degrees, by their Liverpool teammates.

Bill Shankly still needed a proven goal scorer, though, so he then paid a club record £110,000 transfer fee to Cardiff City, on 11th November 1970, for their Welsh international striker John Toshack.

Having scored seventy-four Second Division goals for the Bluebirds, from only 159 games, John Toshack scored his first Liverpool goal just ten days later.

Liverpool had beaten Everton 3-2, on Saturday 21st November, in front of 53,777, their largest league crowd of the season. Steve Heighway and Chris Lawler scored their other goals in a loudly-celebrated win, but by Christmas, Liverpool were a long, long way behind the top two, Leeds United and Arsenal.

In the Inter Cities Fairs Cup, though, Liverpool had squeezed past Ferencvaros in the First round, and they then beat Dinamo Bucharest, 4-1 on aggregate.

In the Third round, they were drawn against Hibernian, played in December 1970.

Hibs were a great side in the Seventies, driven by their brilliant playmaker Pat Stanton, and guarded by a gritty defence of Blackley, Brownlie, Schaedler and Black.

Alex Cropley, Arthur Duncan and Arthur Graham were notable names in their forward line, highly-skilled and sought-after by English First Division clubs, and over 30,000 filled Easter Road on Wednesday 9th December, for a pre-Christmas cracker.

John Toshack's late, long range shot, though, laid low the European lights on Leith. Then, three days before Christmas, goals at Anfield from Steve Heighway and reserve forward Phil Boersma completed their 3-0 aggregate win.

Liverpool looked forward to a Spring Quarter-final tie against Bayern Munich, after the dark winter months of January and February had passed.

In the FA Cup Third round, 45,500 watched the might of Liverpool defeat Fourth Division Aldershot 1-0, on Saturday 2nd January. Liverpool-born forward John McLaughlin scored the only goal, after meeting Ian Callaghan's perfect through-ball.

Callaghan had just returned to the team after injury had kept him out of action since September, and due to the wings now being occupied by Steve Heighway and Peter Thompson, Bill Shankly had moved him into a central midfield position.

Three weeks later, Swansea City were more easily disposed of.

Cardiff-born Toshack fired Liverpool ahead in the first half, and then in the second half, Ian St John came on as a substitute for Callaghan for an emotional farewell to Anfield. Saint scored Liverpool's second, before their rampaging right back Chris Lawler completed a 3-0 rout.

Chris Lawler also scored their Fifth round winner, at home to Southampton, running onto a John Toshack lay-off, sneaking around Denis Hollywood, before blasting past Eric Martin. Southampton had come with a packed bank of five players all protecting their back four, and they were frustrated after conceding such a late goal.

On Saturday 6th March, Liverpool played the first of five scintillating Cup games within twenty-one days, watched by a combined attendance of almost 242,000 fans.

First, in the FA Cup Quarter-finals, Tottenham succeeded where Southampton had failed, and they held Liverpool to a goalless draw at Anfield, watched by Liverpool's biggest home crowd of the season, 54,731.

Alun Evans had been signed by Bill Shankly back in September 1968, from Wolves, for a club record fee of £100,000. A golden haired, blue-eyed pin-up teenager, Evans had run rings around Ron Yeats back in November 1967, and he'd then enjoyed a dynamic start to his Liverpool career, scoring five goals in his first seven games.

Thereafter, though, Alun Evans had underwhelmed and disappointed. The weight of expectation wore down such a young prospect, *the first ever £100,000 teenager,* being labelled the new Tony Hateley, the new Roger Hunt, and even the blonde George Best.

It had all appeared to overload him, and he scored only five goals during his next forty-three First Division matches.

Alun Evans started the 1970-71 season stronger again, and he scored eight goals in twelve, but then a broken glass attack by a yob in a Wolverhampton nightclub had left him facially scarred.

Evans was mentally affected, and he didn't play again, for four months, after a succession of injuries, but he'd replaced John McLaughlin during that goalless draw against Spurs.

ALUN EVANS' MATCH

Three days later, on Tuesday 9th March, Liverpool hosted Bayern Munich in their European Fairs Cup Fourth round tie. Bayern arrived with all of their West German World Cup stars, Maier, Beckenbauer, Breitner, Hoeness, and Gerd Muller.

Alun Evans was selected to start, and in front of a 45,616 home crowd, he had his best ever game in a Liverpool shirt. He evaded the tough Koppenhofer after half an hour, and then fired past the great Sepp Maier to give Liverpool a 1-0 half-time lead.

He flicked in a second, four minutes into the second half, before completing both his hat-trick, and Liverpool's 3-0 win, just over a quarter-hour before the end.

Alun Evans was wildly applauded off the pitch by the packed Kop, after the match.

On Monday 15th March, 56,283 overcrowded White Hart Lane, as the gates were locked an hour before kick-off, for Liverpool's FA Cup replay at Spurs. Steve Heighway scored the only goal of the game, a right-footed shot from close range.

Nine nights later, only 23,000 bothered to go to the Grunwalder Stadion for the second leg of Liverpool's Fairs Cup Quarter-final against Bayern Munich, although half of the 23,000 were from Merseyside.

So superior was Liverpool's advantage, Shankly had started Scottish utility player Ian Ross, for the first time since November. Ross responded by scoring their crucial second half goal that secured their first European Semi-final place for five seasons.

Liverpool drew 1-1, and they won 4-1 on aggregate, but they were then drawn against fierce rivals Leeds United in the last four.

Three days later, on Saturday 27th March 1971, Merseyside totally invaded Manchester as 62,144 Liverpool and Everton fans packed Old Trafford, for the Reds' FA Cup Semi-final against the reigning League Champions.

EVERTON		LIVERPOOL
Andy Rankin	1	Ray Clemence
Tommy Wright	2	Chris Lawler
Keith Newton	3	Alec Lindsay
Howard Kendall	4	Tommy Smith
Brian Labone	5	Larry Lloyd
Colin Harvey	6	Emlyn Hughes
Alan Whittle	7	Ian Callaghan
Alan Ball	8	Alun Evans
Joe Royle	9	Steve Heighway
John Hurst	10	John Toshack
Johnny Morrissey	11	Brian Hall
Sandy Brown	12	Peter Thompson

After eleven minutes, Colin Harvey's long throw-in, down the left wing, was met by the head of Joe Royle, on the edge of the Liverpool penalty area. Royle headed back to Johnny Morrissey, who crossed for Alan Whittle at the near post. Whittle flicked the ball on to the far post, where Alan Ball volleyed in from a tight angle, past Emlyn Hughes, for a brilliantly-crafted team goal by Everton.

Every Everton player had been absolutely, tightly marked by a Liverpool player, but it had been perfect one-touch football. Everton went wild with the wide, massed Blue half of Old Trafford. Everton comfortably held their deserved lead until a quarter of an hour after half-time, by which time the hobbling Labone had been replaced by Brown.

A long, high ball was cleared up the Liverpool left, and Steve Heighway out-muscled Tommy Wright, before flicking the ball past Sandy Brown's desperate challenge, over to Alun Evans, who'd escaped the attentions of both Hurst and Kendall.

Amidst the ferocious pace of the Liverpool break, Evans took one touch, and from just inside the Everton area, he slipped the ball under Rankin's dive for a dramatic equaliser, and right under the Liverpool fans in the Stretford End.

The whole Liverpool team ran to hug Evans. It was the greatest moment of his career.

With just about twenty minutes to go, Heighway threw to Evans on the edge of the Everton area. Alun Evans, tracked by Tommy Wright, teased and turned the full back, before he let fly a towering reverse ball from the corner flag, over to the far post.

Andy Rankin came to claim the cross, but Toshack climbed to challenge, crunching the Everton keeper, and the ball crept loose for Brian Hall to karate-kick the ball into the net for a Classic comeback win.

Everton were absolutely broken and inconsolable.

The European Fairs Cup Semi-final was a much tighter and colder affair. On Wednesday 14th April, nearly 53,000 watched Liverpool and Leeds kick lumps out of each other, but sadly for the Kop, there were no Careless Hands that night, as Sprake had a cracking match. A late strike from the best player on the pitch, Billy Bremner, was the difference between the two teams.

A fortnight later, at Elland Road, over 40,000 watched Leeds battle and scrap for a crucial goalless draw, to reach the Fairs Cup Final, 1-0 on aggregate.

For Liverpool, another fifth place finish, in Division One, was disappointing, especially as they'd conceded only twenty-four goals in forty-two matches, and also kept twenty-two clean sheets.

Their midfield and attack had been irregular all season, though, having an adverse effect on the form of John Toshack. Toshack had scored just five goals during his first season at Anfield, while Alun Evans was top scorer with fifteen league and cup goals.

Saturday 8th May 1971 was a boiling hot, sunny afternoon, as Liverpool faced the newly-crowned First Division Champions Arsenal in the FA Cup Final.

Both teams attacked from the start of the match, though, but these were the two best defensive teams in England, having kept a combined 47 First Division clean sheets, and conceding only 53 goals in 84 matches.

Therefore, as busy and willing as each team were in their attacks, a combination of defensive dominance and the burning heat kept real goal chances few and far between.

Two minutes into extra-time, though, substitute Peter Thompson, who'd replaced Alun Evans, set up Steve Heighway for Liverpool's goal; and that looked like it for Arsenal. Bob Wilson then saved sharply from Toshack, soon after, as Liverpool fully imposed their apparent advantage.

But then, a soft and confusing goal by either Eddie Kelly or George Graham, four minutes before the break, took the stuffing out of Liverpool, before Charlie George's great goal, followed by that famous celebration, had eventually secured Arsenal's first League and Cup double success.

Liverpool were shattered, probably too shattered in the heat to be inconsolable.
In any case, Shankly was still working on his regeneration of Liverpool.

Although Shankly's Liverpool team had changed almost entirely from just a few years earlier, it was still incomplete. Shankly knew he had a defence as good as Leeds United's, and also Arsenal's, as well as one of the very best goalkeepers in England, and his midfield, enforced by both Hughes and Callaghan, was beginning to work and create attractive football, but they'd lacked goals, and particularly, an attacking double act that would be feared in every English football ground.

A week prior to the FA Cup Final, on Saturday 1st May 1971, Kevin Keegan had sat on a dust-bin, in the car park outside Anfield, waiting to get in. He'd scored ten goals for Scunthorpe United during 1970-71, and he had also been made their captain, at just twenty years old, when Bob Paisley and Joe Fagan went to see him.

They only watched him for twenty minutes, before both deciding that he'd be good for Liverpool.

Bill Shankly knew that Ipswich were also keen to sign Keegan, so he didn't risk waiting for the Summer. He paid a bargain price of £35,000, but only because Scunthorpe were Fourth Division strugglers. Keegan even travelled with the Liverpool squad to the FA Cup Final.

Signed as a midfield player, primarily to replace the ageing Ian Callaghan, Kevin Keegan was subsequently asked to play up front, due to his hardworking ethos and attacking instincts, never giving up any lost cause, never letting opposing defenders relax for a single second, for Liverpool's first game of 1971-72.

Against Nottingham Forest, in front of an Anfield crowd of nearly 51,000, twenty times the size of crowd that Keegan had last played before, when beating Workington Town 4-0, he scored Liverpool's first goal of that season.

Keegan had mishit Peter Thompson's pull-back, but the ball bounced luckily past Forest's keeper Barron, and into the corner of the net. That sort of good fortune complemented Keegan's excellent work rate throughout his career.

In an era when George Best's career and popularity was starting to go off the rails, Kevin Keegan became the new pin-up idol in both **SHOOT!** and *Jackie,* the top selling teenage girls' magazine. Tommy Smith buried a penalty kick past Jim Barron, and Emlyn Hughes scored their third as Liverpool beat Forest 3-1.

Kevin Keegan's arrival had spelt the end of Alun Evans' Liverpool career. After nearly four years at Anfield, Evans eventually joined Aston Villa in June 1972, having scored twenty-one First Division goals from seventy-seven games.

He was Aston Villa's unused substitute in their 1975 League Cup Final win over Norwich City, and then he moved to Walsall prior to Villa's promotion back to Division One during that season. Alun Evans never again played First Division football, after leaving Liverpool, but he'd always have that Bayern Munich game, and their Semi-final win over Everton, to very proudly remember.

Liverpool started the season without Brian Hall, however, and by the time Hall had returned to the team, in September, they were without Tommy Smith. By the time the Iron Man returned in late October, Liverpool had then lost both John Toshack and Alec Lindsay. John Toshack missed a total of ten successive league and cup matches, from November until the end of January, and when he returned, Brian Hall was again out of action, for yet another month.

During that time, Liverpool were drawn at home to Leeds United in the FA Cup Fourth round. On Saturday 5th February, 56,300 overfilled Anfield's ground capacity by nearly two thousand, with thousands more locked out.

Ian Ross was in for Brian Hall, while for Leeds, Mick Bates was in for Eddie Gray and Paul Madeley was in for Jack Charlton. Other than that, both teams were at their fullest strength. It was a titanic battle between the two major powers of English football, at the very top of their game, but Liverpool could not unlock Leeds United's classy defence.

The game ended goalless.

Four days later, on Wednesday 9th February, Eddie Gray and Jack Charlton were both back for Leeds, while Bobby Graham had replaced Toshack.

A Partisan, hostile 46,000 crowd packed the vast terraces of Elland Road. Fans had climbed on top of the old South Stand, and they'd also sat on the roof of the Old Peacock pub, on Elland Road, with their pints of beer, and with a diabolical view of the game.

Under strength, and the underdogs, Liverpool finally capitulated to a class display by Allan Clarke. Clarke first fired Leeds ahead 1-0, but then he scored one of his best ever goals. *Sniffer* picked up the ball in midfield, before running past Hughes, and at full pace, at both Lloyd and Lindsay. He then fired past Clemence from twenty yards out. Elland Road bounced and bellowed, and the noise reverberated all across Beeston.

Liverpool were beaten, and still six points behind leaders Manchester City. They were fifth in Division One, with the might of Leeds, Derby County and reigning Champions Arsenal between them and the leaders. With just twelve games to go, Liverpool could count themselves out of the title race, fighting only for a UEFA Cup place.

On Saturday 4th March 1972, less than two years after their humiliating loss to Watford, Bill Shankly's transformation of Liverpool was complete.

From their Merseybeat stars of the Sixties to the mighty Big Red Machine of the Seventies, Liverpool hosted Everton, and Shankly fielded this team for the very first time: Ray Clemence, Chris Lawler, Alec Lindsay, Tommy Smith, Larry Lloyd, Emlyn Hughes, Kevin Keegan, Brian Hall, Steve Heighway, John Toshack and Ian Callaghan.

It was a momentous occasion, and nearly 54,000 filled Anfield, as Liverpool took the lead in the very first minute, through Tommy Wright's own goal. Scottish full back John McLaughlin then scored a second own goal, for Liverpool, after half-time, before Chris Lawler smashed in a third, and then, with just three minutes remaining, the incomparable Emlyn Hughes ghosted in from deep to clip Keegan's centre beyond Gordon West to send the packed house home delirious.

With that 4-0 win over Everton, Liverpool rose above Arsenal up to fourth place, but they still remained six points behind Manchester City's free-scoring leaders.

Only Lawler, Smith, Hughes and Callaghan had survived the post-Watford cull.

Peter Thompson was still in their squad, but he'd played his final match for Liverpool against Wolves back in late January. Thompson remained at Anfield, recovering from a serious knee injury, during which time nobody had wanted to buy him, and Bill Shankly never even wanted to see injured players hanging around, so he didn't want him.

It was a very miserable time for Thompson, after all his great days with Liverpool and England. He eventually signed for Bolton Wanderers nearly two years later, in November 1973, after playing 317 First division games for Liverpool, and scoring forty-two goals.

Faster than Stanley Matthews or Tom Finney, and so fast he could catch pigeons, Peter Thompson was the fastest player in England. He'd played sixteen times for England, as a Liverpool player.

Back in May 1964, the Wizard of the Wing had impressed Pele so much during Brazil's 5-1 win over England, the great man positively insisted that he swapped shirts with Peter Thompson.

Captain Bobby Moore enforced his seniority, though, and ensured that it was he who changed his shirt with Pele, instead. Liverpool eventually played Bolton Wanderers at Burnden Park, five years later, in 1978, in Peter Thompson's Testimonial match.

That classic Liverpool team from Saturday 4th March 1972 played on and on, and they remained unchanged until the end of 1971-72, winning eight, and drawing one, of their next nine games.

On Bank Holiday Monday, 1st May 1972, Liverpool travelled to third placed Derby County, having not conceded any goals in any of their First Division away matches, for more than nine hours.

A massive capacity crowd of nearly 40,000 had packed the moderately-built Baseball Ground, for the Clash of the Season. The top of the First Division saw Manchester City top with 57 points, but having played all of their 42 matches, and out of the title race.

Liverpool were second, with 56 points from 40 games, while Derby County were third with 56 points from 41 games, but behind Liverpool on goal average.

Fourth placed Leeds United had the easiest run-in, though, with 55 points from 40 games.

The title was now Liverpool's to lose.

Derby County, though, had an equally tough defence as Liverpool and Leeds, having kept 22 clean sheets from 41 matches, and they kept their twenty-third clean sheet against Liverpool.

John McGovern's second half strike sent Derby County up to the top of the First Division, for the first time since the War.

On Monday 8th May, Liverpool visited Highbury to face deposed League Champions and FA Cup Final losers Arsenal, needing a win to secure the title, but while also hoping that Leeds failed to win at Wolves. Arsenal were weakened, without either Bob Wilson, Bob McNab or Charlie George, and John Toshack did score for Liverpool, but the goal was ruled out due to an disputed off-side decision.

Liverpool eventually finished third, behind Derby and Leeds, but with only one point separating the top four clubs. Even so, Bill Shankly was a classy manager, and he warmly congratulated Derby County, acclaiming them as the best team his Liverpool had faced that season.

Liverpool's watertight defence had kept thirteen clean sheets from their nineteen First Division matches after the New Year, while Keegan and Toshack had combined for a total of twenty-two league goals. In support, Steve Heighway, Emlyn Hughes, Tommy Smith and Chris Lawler also scored twenty-four goals between them.

Liverpool's momentum, that picked up pace after Shankly had fielded his best eleven for the first time, didn't slow during August 1972. They beat both Manchester clubs at Anfield, both of them 2-0 wins (Hall, Callaghan, Toshack and Heighway all scoring).

Against Manchester City, Liverpool had been particularly brilliant.

In the first half, Keegan's flicked header had allowed Heighway to escape from Book. Heighway then skipped Booth's scything challenge, before flicking the ball past Doyle towards Brian Hall. Hall scored with a cool finish, from just inside City's area.

Liverpool's second goal, though, was a team classic. After a period of sustained City pressure during the second half, with City's travelling fans in loud voice, acclaiming their beloved striker, *The Mighty Wyn!*, Larry Lloyd headed his clearance wide left over to Lindsay.

Alec Lindsay played the ball back inside to Keegan. Kevin Keegan ran to the centre circle, then passed to Lawler, wide right. Chris Lawler fed John Toshack, inside City's half, and the big Welshman advanced to City's area, laying the ball back to Hall. Brian Hall took one touch, and then shot at City's near post, which Joe Corrigan managed to parry, but only to Ian Callaghan, who calmly placed the ball inside Corrigan's far post.

It was a great move, running through seven players, and it cut totally through City's sharp defence. They then beat two London clubs, Chelsea and West Ham, to top the First Division table with nine points from five games.

A pair of defeats, however, away at Leicester City and also Champions Derby County saw Liverpool slip down to sixth place by the start of September, but they were still only two points behind unbeaten leaders Arsenal.

While School was Out, Bill Shankly had spent the Summer of 72, negotiating a club record transfer fee of £150,000 for Huddersfield striker Frank Worthington, before he called the deal off after medical tests had revealed high blood pressure. Frank Worthington's career stats proved it would never have been a problem for Liverpool, but Shankly couldn't risk a club record fee on a player who'd failed a medical test.

So instead, Bill Shankly paid recently-relegated Nottingham Forest £110,000 for their Scottish international midfield player, Peter Cormack. The skilful, Edinburgh-born, Cormack had scored fifteen goals in seventy-three First Division games, becoming Forest's second-highest goalscorer over the previous two seasons.

Peter Cormack effectively took Brian Hall's place in their team, from September onwards, after Hall's lengthy injury. He scored his first goal for Liverpool during their 4-2 win over Wolves on Saturday 9th September, and then his second goal a fortnight later, Liverpool's fourth goal in their 5-0 hammering of Sheffield United.

Boersma, Lindsay, Heighway and Keegan had scored the other goals, lifting the Reds back up to the top of Division One.

On Tuesday 12th September, Liverpool hosted a strong Eintracht Frankfurt side in the first leg of their UEFA Cup First round match. Eintracht were captained by West German legend Jurgen Grabowski, and with winger Bernd Holzenbein, they were a surprisingly tough opposition for a First round tie.

Goals from Kevin Keegan and Emlyn Hughes, though, secured their great 2-0 win.

A fortnight later, Liverpool held Frankfurt to a goalless draw in front of a disappointing German home crowd of just 18,000. Nevertheless, it was a great victory over a useful side that would probably have punished Liverpool during previous European campaigns. Eintracht were actually the toughest opposition to visit Anfield in the UEFA Cup, until the Semi-finals. The Reds then despatched AEK Athens 6-1, Dynamo Berlin 3-1, and finally Dynamo Dresden 3-0, en route to the last four.

Peter Cormack had headed in the only goal of the game, from Heighway's perfect left wing cross, on 7th October, to beat Everton 1-0. Nearly 56,000 had again squeezed into Anfield, well above capacity, and the Kop went absolutely wild.

Larry Lloyd then made Football History, on Thursday 9th November. He became the first player to ever be cleared of an on-field offence, by an FA disciplinary committee, due to Television Evidence.

Amersham referee Gordon Kew had sent Lloyd off for chopping and then kicking Manchester City forward Wyn Davies, on the opening day of the season, and although the television replays showed the committee that he wasn't free from blame, the sending off was regarded as sufficient punishment, and his three match suspension was not imposed.

Following their 2-0 defeat away at Old Trafford, after George Best had set up both of Manchester United's goals, scored by Wyn Davies and Ted MacDougall, on Saturday 11th November, Liverpool then went unbeaten up to late January, winning seven of their next ten matches.

On 30th December 1972, at home to Crystal Palace, the last game of a significant year for Liverpool, and with nearly 51,000 inside Anfield, Peter Cormack headed his eighth goal of the season past Palace keeper John Jackson, from Alec Lindsay's effortless long pass, for their 1-0 win.

As 1973 arrived, the most successful year of Liverpool's history, they held a three point lead over Arsenal, and with a game in hand. Kevin Keegan's goal secured a 1-0 win over West Ham, one week later, on Saturday 6th January, five days after the UK finally joined the EEC, but they could then only draw at home to Derby County. Roger Davies's goal for the reigning Champions had cancelled out John Toshack's header.

Liverpool then lost 2-1 away at Wolves on Saturday 27th January, after John Richards had scored a late, late winner, his eighteenth of the season, and the wheels had threatened to come off the Reds' Championship express.

On Saturday 10th February, Arsenal then visited Anfield, and the Gunners' superlative performance, in the mud, literally tore Liverpool apart.

Alan Ball's penalty kick, and then a brilliant solo goal by John Radford gave Arsenal a 2-0 away win to overtake Liverpool at the top of the league.

One week later, Liverpool were then held to a 1-1 draw away at Manchester City, as Tommy Smith was sent off, while Arsenal had beaten Leicester City 1-0. Arsenal were two points clear of Liverpool, at the top of the First Division, with Leeds also very dangerously on their shoulders.

	PL	PTS
Arsenal	31	44
LIVERPOOL	30	42
Leeds United	29	40

On Saturday 3rd March, Liverpool walked over to a jam-packed, 54,269 filled Goodison Park. As the darkness descended in the second half, and with Everton holding them to an unwelcome stalemate, Ian Callaghan received a Brian Hall pass, and he waited, and waited, before dinking a delightful ball between both Hurst and Darracott, for the late-running Hughes to meet right on the edge of the Everton area.

Despite keeper Dave Lawson charging out and diving at his laces, Emlyn Hughes side-stepped, then coolly placed the ball into the empty net.

With the clock ticking down, Lindsay lofted a long, looping cross for Keegan to head back to Hughes inside the Everton area. Hughes volleyed home his second of the match for a 2-0 away win.

Emlyn Hughes then went off on a delighted run around the touchline. *"Yes! You bastard!"* He cried, with delight, in his high-pitched tone. *"You fucking bastard! Yes!"* And Liverpool returned to the top of the table.

	PL	PTS
LIVERPOOL	32	46
Arsenal	33	46

However, while Manchester City had knocked Liverpool out of the FA Cup, in the Fourth round, both Arsenal and Leeds had reached the Semi-finals, which then detracted from their title hopes. Liverpool won three in a row, following their Goodison Park victory, beating Southampton, Stoke City and then Norwich City, before drawing at home to UEFA Cup Semi-final opponents

Tottenham on Saturday 31st March. Leeds United, however, had taken only four points from their next four matches, while Arsenal took six.

At the beginning of April, Liverpool held a one point lead over Arsenal, and with a game in hand, but with only six games remaining.

Leeds United, barring a biblical flood, were out of the title race.

On Tuesday 10th April, Anfield hosted the first leg of the UEFA Cup Semi-final between Liverpool and holders Tottenham Hotspur.

It was the draw which neither club wanted. Borussia Moenchengladbach and Twente Enschede, the other two teams in the Semi-finals, were, with respect, seen as easier opposition. An all-English Semi-final produced a rivalry that was fiercer anyway, but for Liverpool, the tournament favourites, facing the Cup holders was an unneeded extra barrier in their struggle to win both the league and their first European trophy.

Liverpool were only missing John Toshack, while Spurs were at full strength, but it was surprising that only 42,000 had attended Anfield for such an important match.

LIVERPOOL		TOTTENHAM HOTSPUR
Ray Clemence	1	Pat Jennings
Chris Lawler	2	Joe Kinnear
Alec Lindsay	3	Cyril Knowles
Tommy Smith	4	Ralph Coates
Larry Lloyd	5	Mike England
Emlyn Hughes	6	Phil Beal
Kevin Keegan	7	Alan Gilzean
Peter Cormack	8	Steve Perryman
Brian Hall	9	Martin Chivers
Steve Heighway	10	Martin Peters
Ian Callaghan	11	John Pratt

Peter Cormack, usually 100% accurate with his headers, headed just over Pat Jennings' crossbar in the twentieth minute, but midway through the first half, Alec Lindsay scored for Liverpool. As the Reds piled on the pressure, Steve Heighway shot at goal, but Jennings parried, and Lindsay, running in late, fired home from the rebound.

Spurs, in an all-white strip, then counter-attacked. Martin Chivers drove a left-footed shot just wide of Clemence's post, and then Chivers and Gilzean combined to set up Coates inside the Liverpool area, but the classy Ralph Coates missed the target.

Heighway then flashed a fierce shot from distance, that Jennings saved with his finger-tips, and the ball just glanced his crossbar. Jennings also tipped Tommy Smith's smart free-kick just over his bar.

Brian Hall had actually hit the crossbar, just before half-time, but the ball ballooned over and away to safety. Ralph Coates sent Chivers clear in the second half, but as the England striker set himself up for a shot, Clemence dived and saved at Big Chiv's feet.

Liverpool held on, after that, for a 1-0 win that really flattered Spurs.

Back in the First Division, Liverpool beat Coventry City 2-1 away at Highfield Road, and then after Heighway was fouled by Roger Minton, Kevin Keegan scored from the penalty spot to beat West Brom 1-0 at home.

On Saturday 21st April, over 37,000 packed the three sides of St James's Park, while United's new East Stand was being built, for the visit of the Champions-elect.

Terry Hibbitt and Jimmy Smith were in electric form, though, for Newcastle, and Malcolm MacDonald gave Larry Lloyd a particularly tough time. John Tudor made the most of their tremendous service and his freedom of space, given MacDonald's ebullient performance. Tudor consequently scored twice, one in each half.

Kevin Keegan replied for Liverpool, but the Reds lost 2-1 and they'd failed to win the title in the North East. They then needed to beat their old rivals Leeds United on Bank Holiday Monday, St George's Day 1973.

	PL	PTS	GOAL AVG.
LIVERPOOL	40	57	1.67
Arsenal	39	54	1.53
Leeds United	38	51	1.70

If Liverpool won, and Arsenal also lost at Southampton, then Shankly's team were English Champions for the first time in seven years. However, if Leeds won, then they would become favourites for a League and Cup double, with their Wembley Final against Second Division Sunderland to look forward to.

LIVERPOOL		LEEDS UNITED
Ray Clemence	1	David Harvey
Chris Lawler	2	Paul Reaney
Phil Thompson	3	Trevor Cherry
Tommy Smith	4	Billy Bremner
Larry Lloyd	5	Roy Ellam
Emlyn Hughes	6	Norman Hunter
Kevin Keegan	7	Peter Lorimer
Peter Cormack	8	Allan Clarke
Brian Hall	9	Joe Jordan
Steve Heighway	10	Terry Yorath
Ian Callaghan	11	Paul Madeley

For the fifth time during the 1972-73 season, Liverpool's 55,000 capacity was well exceeded, with nearly fifty-six thousand packed into Anfield on a warm, late April afternoon.

With Leeds ridiculously under-strength, without Jones, Giles, Gray, Charlton and McQueen, Liverpool literally attacked Leeds' penalty area with the ferocity of a wasp attack on a sweet picnic, and they never, ever let up.

Former Huddersfield defender, the veteran Roy Ellam was swarmed by the relentless pressure of the buzzing Liverpool players, and after the break, their pressure bore fruit.

Phil Thompson won the ball, 30 yards from goal, then he passed to Lawler, attacking the edge of the Leeds area. Lawler back-heeled to Keegan, who nodded down to Cormack. Peter Cormack drove home his half-volleyed shot just inside Harvey's left post.

Then, Emlyn Hughes crossed from the left wing. Cormack collected, inside the penalty area, but closely guarded by Reaney. He escaped to the bye-line, and hit a snap-shot from a narrow angle.

Harvey got his hands to the ball, and he should have caught it, but due to a mix-up between him and Ellam, Keegan sneaked in and fired the loose ball into the empty net.

Two nights after that 2-0 win over Leeds, that left them one point short of winning the title, after Arsenal had drawn 2-2 at Southampton, Liverpool visited White Hart Lane, for the second leg match of their UEFA Cup Semi-final against Spurs.

A raucous, abusive 47,000 North London crowd filled all the terraces, desperate for Tottenham to defend their title as Cup holders.

Tottenham captain Martin Peters gave Spurs a 1-0 lead, curling his eighteen yard shot past Ray Clemence's dive. The scores were tied on aggregate, but the game remained on a knife-edge.

Steve Heighway scored that vital away goal, taking a flick-on from Peter Cormack, evading Mike England, and then drilling the ball, first time, from the edge of the area, past Pat Jennings. Tottenham now had to score two more goals to progress to the Final.

Martin Chivers took a throw-in, and he threw it very long, for Peters to run onto, unmarked, before he slotted the ball beneath Clemence's dive.

The whole place went crazy. With the aggregate scores tied, and the White Hart Lane atmosphere at white-hot decibel levels, Liverpool's defence was heroic against Tottenham's ferocious attack of Chivers, Peters, Gilzean, Perryman and Coates.

Bill Shankly felt as much admiration for Tottenham, after the match, as he did for his own victorious team. "For both teams to give that sort of performance at this stage of the season, after more than sixty games, was unbelievable," he raved.

Liverpool drew 0-0 at home to Leicester City, on the last Saturday of the season, and in front of their biggest league crowd of the season, 56,202. It was their fourth tough game inside seven days, but that one point was all they needed. Liverpool were the new First Division Champions, finishing three points ahead of Arsenal.

John Toshack and Kevin Keegan were joint top scorers, sharing twenty-six league goals, but Cormack, Hughes, Heighway and Phil Boersma had also contributed a combined total of 28 goals towards Liverpool's Championship success.

Joe Mercer had acclaimed Keegan and Toshack as the finest attacking combination since John Charles and Omar Sivori at Juventus during the late Fifties.

On Thursday 10th May, Liverpool hosted Borussia Moenchengladbach in the first leg of the UEFA Cup Final. There were only 41,000 at Anfield, though, mainly due to Liverpool's UEFA obligation to reserve a large portion of the stadium for the away fans, which was far from filled. The Kop was filled to capacity, though, and it was at that end in the first half where Liverpool scored their first two crucial goals.

Brian Hall had played in all fifteen of Liverpool's last fifteen league and cup matches of the season, helping them back to the top of the league, after Arsenal had briefly overhauled the Reds, and also past both Dresden and Tottenham to this very Final.

Hall was devastated, therefore, to be told by Shankly that John Toshack was taking his place in the team for the Final.

Toshack had not played since early March, but the telepathic partnership that he'd formed with Keegan was the reason Shankly had to be so ruthless.

LIVERPOOL		BORUSSIA MOENCHENGLADBACH
Ray Clemence	1	Wolfgang Kleff
Chris Lawler	2	Heinz Michalik
Alec Lindsay	3	Gunter Netzer
Tommy Smith (c)	4	Rainer Bonhof
Larry Lloyd	5	Berti Vogts (c)
Emlyn Hughes	6	Herbert Wimmer
Kevin Keegan	7	Dietmar Danner
Peter Cormack	8	Christian Kulik
John Toshack	9	Henning Jensen
Steve Heighway	10	Bernd Rupp
Ian Callaghan	11	Jupp Heynckes
Brian Hall	12	Allan Simonsen (rep. Rupp)

Borussia had a good side, the fourth German team to face Liverpool in the UEFA Cup that season, but they were certainly the best. They contained four stars of the West Germany squad that would win the World Cup a year later, plus Henning Jensen was one of Denmark's all-time footballing greats. Also, coming on off their bench was the future European Footballer of the Year, Allan Simonsen.

Chris Lawler sent over a looping right wing cross, early in the first half. John Toshack, on the edge of the six yard box, leapt above his marker and he nodded the ball back inside to Keegan, who flew and sent his superb header past Kleff.

Then, after Borussia had failed to clear Tommy Smith's long ball, Hughes headed back into the German area. Toshack again nodded down to Keegan, who buried his low shot past the hapless Kleff, under the noses of the Kop.

In the second half, Keegan's left-sided corner-kick was powered in at the far post by the head of an unmarked Larry Lloyd, for a fully deserved 3-0 lead.

Late on, though, Steve Heighway came in to challenge Dietmar Danner. The two players' shoulders collided, and the German attacker collapsed in the area.

Austrian referee Linemayr harshly ruled that it was a foul by the distraught University graduate, and he awarded a penalty kick to Borussia.

Jupp Heynckes, with over one hundred Bundesliga goals to his credit, took the spot-kick, hitting it low and hard to the left post.

Clemence had dived to his right, though, and extended his arm, pushing the ball, hard, and away to safety. It was a brilliant penalty save, but also a crucial one.

In the second leg, Heynckes scored twice, but Liverpool hung on for a 2-0 defeat, winning the UEFA Cup 3-2 on aggregate.

Had Clemence not saved that penalty, they'd have lost on away goals.

Liverpool became the first English team ever to win the First Division Championship and also a European trophy in the same season.

In just over three years, Bill Shankly had brilliantly re-built a Liverpool team that now looked set to dominate English football for years to come, and also become more consistent and commanding conquerors of Europe.

He had done it, though, without ever buying any player from another First Division club. Ray Clemence had come from Scunthorpe, as had Kevin Keegan; Alec Lindsay came from Bury, Larry

Lloyd from Bristol Rovers, John Toshack from Cardiff, and Heighway and Hall straight from University, although Heighway had been starring for Skelmersdale. Peter Cormack came from Nottingham Forest, who had just been relegated to Division Two, and Phil Thompson, who'd played a dozen games covering Tommy Smith, was a Liverpool youth team graduate.

Lindsay, Lloyd, Keegan, Cormack, Hall, Heighway and Toshack had all cost combined total fees of just £372,000, less than the amount Brian Clough and Peter Taylor had paid to take both Colin Todd and David Nish to Derby County.

Six members of that 1972-73 team, Clemence, Smith, Hughes, Keegan, Heighway and Callaghan, were in Liverpool's team away in Rome, four years later, winning the 1977 European Cup Final.

Liverpool were without John Toshack for over half of the 1973-74 season, due to his recurrent thigh condition, and they spent the whole of that season chasing Leeds United. Leeds had made an unprecedented great start to the season, leading by nine points at Christmas, after winning sixteen of their first twenty-two league matches, and remaining unbeaten.

Liverpool were not so much chasing Leeds United, more like tracking them with a compass and a map.

One bright light for the future, though, was the form of their nineteen year-old Liverpool-born defender Phil Thompson. He'd played a dozen games during the previous season, covering Tommy Smith, but he began 1973-74 in a similar role, covering for both Smith and Alec Lindsay for their first seven matches.

In November, though, the Liverpool-born teenager made Liverpool's number four shirt his own. After Tommy Smith had returned from injury, he moved over to right back, replacing the injured Chris Lawler.

Chris Lawler's career as Liverpool's regular right back was over.

The Silent Knight, or *The Ghost,* as The Kop had nicknamed him, Lawler played only a few games during the following 1974-75 season, but in central defence, with Tommy Smith still preferred at right back.

Chris Lawler played 406 First Division games for Liverpool, before he joined Portsmouth in October 1975, who were managed by his former teammate Ian St John.

Lawler's forty-one First Division goals make him the highest scoring defender in Liverpool's history. He only missed three league games between 1965 and 1972.

In most fans' eyes, Lawler was the greatest right back in Liverpool's history. He'd earned four England caps, all during 1971, and he even scored on his international debut, against Malta, on Friday 12th May. If it hadn't been for Sir Alf Ramsay picking Keith Newton, Paul Madeley, Peter Storey and Colin Todd at right back for England, in Paul Reaney's absence, who weren't even their club's first-choice right backs, then Lawler would have, *and should,* have won many more England caps.

He could also have been one of England's greatest-ever right backs.

Chris Lawler played thirty-six games alongside Eoin Hand and Paul Went in Portsmouth's defence, and behind George Graham, Chris Kamara and Peter Marinello, but they were unable to prevent Pompey from dropping into Division Three in 1976. They finished at the bottom of the Second Division, such was the quality that year.

On Tuesday 8th January 1974, Steve Heighway and Peter Cormack both scored to beat Doncaster Rovers 2-0 in an FA Cup Third round replay away at Belle Vue.

22,499, nine times Doncaster's average home crowd, were silenced as a full strength Liverpool ruthlessly defeated Rovers, after Bill Shankly had fielded some reserves in the original tie at Anfield.

Their Fourth round match away at First Division-bound Carlisle United, at the end of January, was far more straight-forward. Liverpool again won 2-0, after goals from Phil Boersma and a fit-again John Toshack.

In the Fifth round, an under-strength Liverpool, again without Toshack, but also missing their wing creator Steve Heighway faced Ipswich Town, third-placed in the First Division, on Saturday 17th February. The 45,340 Anfield crowd had anticipated and feared an upset, but Liverpool comfortably won, again by 2-0, after Brian Hall and Kevin Keegan scored in each half.

The Quarter-final draw on the following Monday produced the FA Cup tie of the round, of the decade, even?

Bristol City or Leeds United will play… Liverpool.

Leeds United v Liverpool; it was a potential nightmare for Liverpool. Leeds had been held to a 1-1 draw by the Robins at Ashton Gate on Saturday, but, still unbeaten in the First Division, after twenty-nine games, they fully expected to clinically dispatch their mid-table Second Division opposition, back at Elland Road, on Tuesday 20th February.

Don Gillies had other ideas. A Leeds United reserve team had lost at Ipswich, in the League Cup, back in October, but their 0-1 home defeat to Bristol City, with a full strength team, was their first domestic loss of the season that really mattered.

What followed for Leeds was the real nightmare. They sailed into a 2-0 lead at Stoke City on the following Saturday, but then lost 3-2. They then drew 1-1 at home to Leicester City, and also to Newcastle. However, they did beat Manchester City 1-0 in early March, to heal the rift.

Liverpool, on the other hand, took five points from the next three games following their win over Ipswich, and on Saturday 9th March, they visited Ashton Gate. In front of nearly 38,000, Bristol City's biggest crowd since the Thirties, Thompson, Lindsay, Heighway, Cormack and Keegan produced a wonderful passing movement to set Toshack up inside the area. John Toshack's second half goal killed their dreams, and sent Liverpool into the FA Cup Semi-finals.

On the following Saturday, Liverpool hosted Leeds United in what was the Match of the Season. *"LIVERPOOL can stop LEEDS says RAY CLEMENCE,"* the front page cover of *GOAL* magazine proclaimed. "It's the crunch of 1974… the game of the season. LIVERPOOL versus LEEDS… Virtually at stake is the League Championship," Tony Stenson's article continued.

Liverpool were still eight points behind Leeds, but with two games in hand. Over 56,000 again over-filled Anfield on Saturday 16th March, with two of the greatest ever English club teams going head to head for possibly the greatest ever First Division title.

LIVERPOOL		LEEDS UNITED
Ray Clemence	1	David Harvey
Tommy Smith	2	Paul Reaney
Alec Lindsay	3	Trevor Cherry
Phil Thompson	4	Billy Bremner
Peter Cormack	5	Gordon McQueen
Emlyn Hughes	6	Norman Hunter
Kevin Keegan	7	Peter Lorimer
Brian Hall	8	Allan Clarke
Steve Heighway	9	Joe Jordan
John Toshack	10	Terry Yorath
Ian Callaghan	11	Paul Madeley

It was a scrappy match, in the end. Far from a festival of football, defences were on top, and Steve Heighway scored a predatory goal for Liverpool, chasing Alec Lindsay's long ball out of defence, and he skipped in between McQueen and Harvey to put the Reds 1-0 up.

Don Revie sent on his top scorer, Mick Jones, from the bench, but Leeds just couldn't find an opening against one of the strongest ever Liverpool defences.

After their defeat at Anfield, Leeds fell apart at home to Burnley, losing 1-4 at Elland Road, but then they also lost 3-1 at West Ham. Clyde Best, Pop Robson and Trevor Brooking had seemingly hammered the nails into Leeds' Championship coffin.

At the beginning of April, Liverpool were the hot favourites for the First Division title, and for their first ever League and Cup double. They'd been held to a 0-0 draw during their FA Cup Semi-final match against Leicester City, at Old Trafford. Peter Shilton had a superb match in the Leicester goal.

At the top of the First Division, Liverpool were still on for the double:

	PL	PTS	G. Avg.
Leeds United	36	52	2.00
LIVERPOOL	33	46	1.87
Derby County	36	42	1.36

Liverpool easily defeated Leicester City 3-1 in their FA Cup replay at Villa Park. Brian Hall, Kevin Keegan and John Toshack all scored against Peter Shilton, wearing his all-white Admiral goalkeeper's strip, to secure a Cup Final battle with Newcastle United's Black and White army at Wembley.

On Saturday 6th April, Liverpool beat high-risers QPR 2-1, at Anfield, but Leeds also hammered third-placed Derby County 2-0, after goals from both Lorimer and Bremner.

Leeds United's surprising win had appeared to take the stuffing out of Liverpool, as they lost their next game away at Sheffield United. Terry Nicholl scored his first-ever, and only, league goal for the Blades. Leeds drew 1-1 at Coventry, therefore increasing their lead at the top of the league by one significant point.

Liverpool drew 1-1 away at Manchester City (Peter Cormack), on Good Friday, and then, a day later, they travelled to Suffolk and held Ipswich to yet another one-all draw. Emlyn Hughes had equalised Trevor Whymark's first half goal.

On the following Tuesday, Liverpool's third league match inside five days, Brian Hall scored twice, and Phil Boersma and Kevin Keegan the others in their 4-0 win over League Cup Finalists Manchester City.

The First Division still promised an exciting title race.

	PL	PTS
Leeds United	39	56
LIVERPOOL	38	54
Derby County	40	46

Leeds United though, in the key and major match of their title run-in, then won 2-0 away at Bramall Lane. Two goals from World Cup-bound Peter Lorimer helped beat Sheffield United. That Leeds win at Sheffield re-energized Leeds' form, and they then won at home to Ipswich, and also away at QPR on the last day of the season, to secure their second First Division Championship.

Liverpool lost hope following Leeds' late resurgence, and they finished five points behind the Champions, having taken only three points from their final four matches.

Even so, if Liverpool had taken all eight points from their final four matches, they would still have lost the league on goal average.

Newcastle United arrived at Wembley on May 4th 1974, after weeks of newspaper and television hype, with reputed tabloid newspaper boasts from ***Supermac/Supermouth!,*** Malcolm Mac-Donald, about how many goals he'd put past Liverpool.

For days and days, Bill Shankly's team talks consisted of him just walking into Liverpool's training ground changing room, pinning Supermac's latest tabloid newspaper headlines onto the wall, and saying, "there you go, boys."

LIVERPOOL		NEWCASTLE UNITED
Ray Clemence	1	Iam McFaul
Tommy Smith	2	Frank Clark
Alec Lindsay	3	Alan Kennedy
Phil Thompson	4	Terry McDermott
Peter Cormack	5	Pat Howard
Emlyn Hughes	6	Bobby Moncur
Kevin Keegan	7	Jimmy Smith
Brian Hall	8	Tommy Cassidy
Steve Heighway	9	Malcolm MacDonald
John Toshack	10	John Tudor
Ian Callaghan	11	Terry Hibbitt
Chris Lawler	12	Tommy Gibb (rep. Smith)

On that warm afternoon, Supermac only got two touches of the ball with his feet, and John Tudor only got one, as Emlyn Hughes, Phil Thompson and Tommy Smith literally owned the ground that MacDonald and Tudor walked on.

Liverpool spanked Newcastle, and the 3-0 score-line totally flattered the Magpies, and embarrassed their fans, though it didn't silence them.

The first half was like shadow boxing. Liverpool merely used the ball to their advantage, better in possession, with Newcastle unable to impose themselves on the match.

Newcastle went in at half-time level, but having played poorly. Such was Liverpool's dominance without scoring, Tommy Smith said to Bobby Moncur, "you've won this one Bob."

But it had been the calm before the storm, as Liverpool had simply and cleverly sapped the life out of Newcastle. Alec Lindsay scored the first goal of the game. After fifty-one minutes, Lindsay intercepted a pass by Jimmy Smith, and he made a strong overlapping run up the left wing, hitting the ball into Keegan, to the right of the United area, before smashing the return ball past McFaul.

The referee, though, Gordon Kew of Amersham, disallowed the goal for offside. Replays showed, though, that Lindsay was not offside. Although he was just about level when the ball was played back to him, which would have been offside then, it had been played to him by the boot of Bobby Moncur.

Newcastle had benefited from the decision, and could count themselves lucky, but the decision just fired Liverpool into a higher gear.

Liverpool swarmed forward. Shanks' Army penned Newcastle inside their penalty area. Heighway threw to Tommy Smith, who crossed from the right. Hall dived underneath the cross, and deftly flicked the ball on to Keegan, whose right-footed shot, from just inside the area, buried the ball into the top right corner of McFaul's goal.

Steve Heighway took Toshack's flick-on from Clemence's long goal-kick, just outside Newcastle's area, then he ran across Moncur, and from inside the area, he fired home, driving the ball inside the far left post.

Liverpool celebrated; on the pitch, on the bench, and all around Wembley.

Liverpool's third was the best goal. Tommy Smith was the toughest tackler in the game, just about, and one of the hardest men in the history of football. He showed, though, late on, that he could also be Colin Bell, at the very best of times.

Keegan sprayed the ball left to right, and Smith just flicked the ball forward to Lindsay, with the outside of his right boot. Lindsay passed the ball on, down the right wing, for Smith to run onto. Smith played a one-two with Heighway, bamboozling Alan Kennedy, and then he carried the ball into the area, before crossing into the six yard box. Tommy Smith's cross went through a throng of players, but Keegan, unmarked at the back post, stuck his leg out and diverted the ball into Newcastle's net.

"Keegan's second, Liverpool's third, and Newcastle were undressed," Barry Davies's excellent commentary proclaimed.

"They were absolutely stripped naked."

On July 12th 1974, after paying a club record transfer fee of £200,000 to Arsenal for Ray Kennedy, the whole of the football world was shocked when Bill Shankly suddenly announced his retirement from football.

Bill Shankly had been manager of Liverpool since December 1959, but he'd claimed he was feeling the strain of top class football.

Nobody believed him, and no-one ever found out the real reason why he just left Liverpool, having forked out a record fee on a great footballer of title-winning pedigree.

Nobody will ever really know. They can only guess.

Bill Shankly had done a magnificent job re-building his great club. From a collection of lesser known players, coming into Anfield from far and wide, from all over the back of beyond and way, way off the football map, Shankly had formed a team, and a good team too, a great team, in fact.

Actually, they were amongst the Greatest of all Teams.

He could be ruthless too, having offloaded legends like St John, Hunt, Yeats, Lawrence, and Peter Thompson, without batting an eyelid. He'd coldly told Brian Hall that he was dropped for the 1973 UEFA Cup Final, and then he dropped Phil Boersma from his squad on the day of the 1974 FA Cup Final, after Boersma had believed all week that he would be Liverpool's substitute. All his decisions, though, were done for the best for Liverpool Football Club, and were never, ever, personal.

If Bill Shankly's retirement had shocked the world, then the news of his death, just seven years later, on Tuesday 29th September 1981, was a much greater shock. Only sixty-eight years old, it had been thought that he was indestructible. It was said he died of a broken heart.

They built a pair of wrought-iron gates at Anfield called the Shankly Gates, and the Kop End, **His Kop,** was eventually renamed the Shankly Kop End.

Bill Shankly's replacement as Liverpool manager was Bob Paisley, Shankly's right hand man.

Bob Paisley had originally signed for Liverpool back in May 1939, having just won the FA Amateur Cup with Bishop Auckland.

An El Alamein veteran of World War II, Paisley's first task was to deal with the shocking situation that had occurred with Billy Bremner and Kevin Keegan. No, not the little punch-up during that hot Saturday afternoon at Wembley, during the Charity Shield on 10th August, but that shocking decision by an FA Disciplinary Committee, chaired by Mr Vernon Stokes, to suspend both players for eleven matches each.

Despite that set-back, Liverpool started 1974-75 well, winning five of their opening six games, and they topped the table in early September. There were four or five very good teams in Division One that season; Stoke, Ipswich, Everton and Manchester City, in particular, were strongly tipped as possible Champions. Leeds United were in disarray after Don Revie's departure, as well as the absence of Bremner, so Liverpool looked the red hot favourites for the title, after their red hot start.

On 20th August 1974, Bob Paisley sold his first player as Liverpool manager.

Larry Lloyd had suffered a leg injury in their 1-0 win over Norwich City, back on Saturday 2nd February, and he'd missed the remaining fifteen games of their season. Coventry City manager Gordon Milne was delighted to pay £240,000 for Lloyd, as Phil Thompson had cemented his place in Liverpool's centre of defence.

Larry Lloyd, at six feet, two inches tall, and twelve and a half stone in weight, had given every ounce of himself to Liverpool's cause, during his 150 First Division games under Bill Shankly, but he became hidden amongst the mediocrity, effectively, after being sent to Coventry.

Coventry City had good players in the mid-Seventies like Tommy Hutchison, Willie Carr, Dennis Mortimer and David Cross.

Carr and Mortimer both left halfway into Lloyd's first season at Highfield Road, though, and the Sky Blues then settled into a passionless existence in lower mid-table.

Lloyd missed three quarters of the 1975-76 season, due to injury, and by October 1976, he was rotting in Coventry's reserves.

Brian Clough came to his rescue, paying a bargain price of just £60,000 to warmly welcome Larry Lloyd into his promotion-chasing Nottingham Forest team.

At twenty-eight years old, the signing of Larry Lloyd had reflected Clough and Taylor's signing of Dave Mackay for Derby County, eight years earlier, except it was even more successful.

Lloyd won his second First Division Championship winners' medal in 1977-78, with Forest, but then he also won two European Cup Finals, in both 1979 and 1980.

After 148 First Division matches for Cloughie, Larry Lloyd left Forest in 1981, to become Wigan Athletic's player-manager.

Liverpool badly missed Larry Lloyd, after Phil Thompson was injured in September 1974.

They went six games without a win, and dropped behind the league leaders.

They did return to the top of the table again, on three or four times during the season, but they couldn't hold on.

Liverpool drew, or lost, twenty-two matches, in total; far too many to be Champions.

They finished the 1974-75 season as runners-up, two points behind the surprise Champions, Derby County, managed by Dave Mackay. Bob Paisley blamed himself for their failure, claiming he'd felt like an apprentice riding in the Epsom Derby.

However, on Saturday 8th March 1975, he fielded the following team during Liverpool's unspectacular 1-1 away draw at Burnley: Clemence, Smith, Neal, Thompson, McDermott, Hughes, Keegan, Hall, Heighway, Ray Kennedy and Callaghan.

In that fairly nondescript match, Bob Paisley had fielded, for the very first time, nine of the eleven players that won the European Cup in Rome, two years later, in May 1977.

Terry McDermott had signed from Newcastle United, on 13th November 1974, for £175,000. The Kirby-born midfield schemer had played 53 First Division matches for the Magpies, and he'd been their key midfield player, alongside Terry Hibbitt and Tommy Cassidy, during Newcastle's epic run to the Cup Final.

Phil Neal was Bob Paisley's first ever signing for Liverpool, joining from Northampton Town for £60,000, one month earlier, on 11th October.

Full back Neal, who could easily play either side of defence, had started over 200 league and cup games for the Cobblers, and he permanently displaced Alec Lindsay, at left back, before the season was done.

On Saturday 26th April 1975, Liverpool-born Jimmy Case, the tenth member of Bob Paisley's 1977 European Champions, then made his Liverpool debut during their 3-1 home win against QPR.

Overall, although the 1974-75 season was an exciting title race, and the closest in history, it was a severely disappointing season for Liverpool, but one that laid fresh, strong foundations, around the brilliance built by Shankly, for future European dominance, as well as in England.

After receiving a football lesson from QPR on the opening day of the 1975-76 season, with Gerry Francis scoring BBC TV's Goal of the Season in their 2-0 win, Liverpool continued inconsistently, and they were down in seventh place by mid-September.

They chased both QPR, and a youthful, resurgent Manchester United, until a week before Christmas, when John Toshack, and Phil Neal's penalty kick, helped beat leaders QPR 2-0 at Anfield, and Liverpool took over as First Division leaders.

An injury to Peter Cormack, at the end of 1975, had seen Ray Kennedy replace him in Liverpool's midfield. Kennedy had been playing second fiddle to the lead strings of Toshack and Keegan in Liverpool's attack, and for once, Toshack was enjoying a mostly injury-free season.

Bob Paisley's decision to revert Ray Kennedy into a midfield player reinvigorated his football career.

Peter Cormack, unfortunately, was not so fortunate. After returning from injury, later in 1976, he couldn't displace Ray Kennedy from Liverpool's midfield, and so, after playing 125 First Division matches, and scoring twenty-one goals for the Reds, Cormack signed for fellow First Division club Bristol City in November 1976, for just £50,000.

His first season with Liverpool was his best, their title winning season of 1972-73, when he'd headed many crucial goals during 1-0 wins, and he also kept Brian Hall out of the team for their UEFA Cup Final triumph.

On Saturday 31st January 1976, Liverpool travelled down to Upton Park in East London, to face sixth-placed West Ham United.

WEST HAM UNITED   LIVERPOOL

Mervyn Day	1	Ray Clemence
John McDowell	2	Tommy Smith
Frank Lampard	3	Phil Neal
Pat Holland	4	Phil Thompson
Tommy Taylor	5	Ray Kennedy
Keith Coleman	6	Emlyn Hughes
Alan Taylor	7	Kevin Keegan
Graham Paddon	8	Jimmy Case
Billy Jennings	9	Steve Heighway
Trevor Brooking	10	John Toshack
Yilmaz Orhan	11	Ian Callaghan

It was Liverpool's greatest performance of the season, against a team that went on to reach the European Cup Winners' Cup Final, outplaying the greatest-ever Anderlecht team for much of that match. They badly missed their midfield enforcer Billy Bonds, though, while John Toshack was in World Class, superlative form, scoring a hat-trick, and also setting up Keegan's goal during their 4-0 away thrashing.

A fortnight later, Keegan and Toshack both scored again in Liverpool's 2-0 win over old foes Leeds United. "Old" foes Leeds certainly were, as well, with seven of their eleven survivors from their Sixties team.

Liverpool returned to the top of the First Division.

In the UEFA Cup, Liverpool had just squeezed past Hibernian, Pat Stanton's Hibernian, 3-2 in the First round.

They then hammered Real Sociedad 9-1, before thrashing Polish side Slask Wroclaw 5-1, in the Third round.

Liverpool met Dynamo Dresden, just as they'd done three years earlier, in the Quarter-finals, in March, while they embarked on a five match winning run in the First Division, in a tight, neck and neck battle with QPR. Liverpool defeated Dresden 2-1 on aggregate, and were then drawn against the best team in the tournament, Barcelona!

Against Cruyff and Neeskens, and beneath an 80,000 crowd of baneful Catalans, John Toshack latched onto Keegan's flick, and he fired Liverpool into a 1-0 lead at the Campo Nuevo.

Only 55,104 packed into Anfield for the second leg match, and Phil Thompson's strong header powered Liverpool into their second UEFA Cup Final, winning 2-1 on aggregate.
"THOMMO! THOMMO! THOMMO!"

Then, on Saturday 17th April. QPR lost 3-2 at Norwich City, handing the title advantage back to Liverpool. That was QPR's only defeat during their final fifteen matches, and they'd won thirteen of those matches.

It still concerns Rangers' fans, today, that if they'd only drawn the Norwich game 2-2, instead of chasing the win, they'd have won the title. That is very harsh on themselves. To ask yourselves to go from January until the very end of April, and not lose a league game, while dropping only two points out of the thirty available, then to just pip your big city rivals to the title on goal difference?

That was putting themselves under so much pressure in each successive game. Something really had to give, eventually.

QPR were, and possibly still are, the best ever team to have failed to win the title. Tottenham in the late-Sixties, Ipswich Town in both 75 and 81, and also Newcastle United in the mid-Nineties would've run them close, but QPR probably just scraped it.

Liverpool, however, were just the slightest bit better in 1976, though not by much, and it was tough to see the difference, because QPR were *so* good that season.

John Toshack and Kevin Keegan had shared twenty-eight First Division goals, while David Fairclough was their third top scorer with seven, after making nine appearances from the substitute's bench, earning him the nickname *Supersub.*

Liverpool's crack back four had kept twenty-two clean sheets, and they conceded only thirty-one First Division goals from 42 games.

56,000 again filled Anfield, as Bruges raced into a 2-0 half-time lead in the UEFA Cup Final, first leg. The majestic Belgians, Van Der Eychen, Lambert, Van Gool, Cools and Leekens, en route to a Golden Era of Belgian football, for both club and country, had shocked all inside Anfield.

Paisley's side had a higher gear, though, and they raised the tempo in the second half. Liverpool stunned the Belgians; Ray Kennedy and Jimmy Case levelled the scores, before Kevin Keegan's late penalty kick gave them a slender 3-2 advantage.

In Bruges, a week later, Kevin Keegan's first half goal settled Liverpool's nerves. They controlled the game, and subdued the expectant 32,000 Belgian home supporters. The 1-1 score draw just won Liverpool their second European trophy in three years.

It's been suggested that Liverpool played more effective football during 1976, than the attractive and colourful football they'd played in 1972-73, with their two rampaging full backs.

In 1976, their full backs, Tommy Smith and Phil Neal were there to defend, just defend. It was effective football that was necessary, though, by the mid-Seventies, particularly to win in Europe.

After the delightful entertainment displayed by Ajax during the early Seventies, Bayern Munich had won three European Cups in a row, in the mid-Seventies, playing dour, oppressive, effective football.

One Anfield legend who didn't fit into this effective football was Brian Hall. He moved to Plymouth Argyle in the hot Summer of 1976, after playing 222 league and cup games at Anfield. *Little Bamber* played thirty-five European matches for Liverpool, but he will always be best remembered for his dramatic winning goal in the 1971 FA Cup Semi-final.

Brian Hall is now the Community Liaison Manager at Anfield.

Liverpool, under Bob Paisley, won three European Cups over the following five years, and they also won a total ten First Division titles in the fifteen years between 1976 and 1990, but it was Bill Shankly's re-building of Liverpool, after 1970, that had laid the foundations for that success to begin and continue.

Otherwise, Liverpool might have become just like Tottenham Hotspur or Leeds United, whose teams burnt out after the early Seventies, to mediocrity or worse.

The timing was that precise, and perfect.

After their 1977 European Cup Final 3-1 win over Borussia Moenchengladbach, in Rome, Liverpool said goodbye to two of their all-time greats.

Kevin Keegan joined European Cup Winners' Cup winners SV Hamburg, in July, for half a million pounds. Keegan had scored one hundred league and cup goals in his six seasons with Liverpool, and he was voted as runner-up in the 1977 European Footballer of the Year awards, so influential was his role in helping Liverpool to their first ever European Cup success.

Keegan's appetite for success helped Hamburg win the Bundesliga title in 1979, and they also reached the 1980 European Cup Final, in Madrid, where despite being hot favourites to win the Cup, Nottingham Forest won 1-0.

Kevin Keegan was twice awarded the European Footballer of the Year title, in 1978 and 1979, the only British footballer to win the award on two occasions, as a result of his talismanic presence in that greatest Hamburg team of all time.

He returned to England in 1980, joining Lawrie McMenemy's star-studded Southampton, before moving to Newcastle United two years later.

King Kev was worshipped by the sell-out Gallowgate crowds, and he inspired Newcastle's return to Division One in 1984.

Kevin Keegan played sixty-three games for England, scoring 21 goals, between 1972 and 1982. He missed a great chance to head England into the Spain 1982 World Cup Semi-finals, against Spain, during his very last match for his country.

Alec Lindsay was an unused substitute in Rome, as Liverpool became European Champions, and he joined Stoke City during August 1977. He'd played 168 First Division matches for Liverpool, and although subsequent Liverpool left backs won more honours than him, many Liverpool fans felt that Alec Lindsay was their most skilful left back. He could play a fifty yard pass, accurately, onto the chest of Kevin Keegan, but he made it look so effortless.

Brian Hall, the Master of Science, put it perfectly when he said, "he had such a lovely sweet movement when he kicked a ball," praising Lindsay.

"He could kick it three quarters the length of the pitch and make it look so easy."

Alec Lindsay scored a penalty on his Second Division debut with Stoke, but they lost 2-1 at Mansfield Town. Stoke were in a financial mess, and they were falling apart.

Only Marsh, Smith and Conroy had survived from their League Cup Final win, just five years earlier. After only twenty league games, and with the Potters down in the bottom half of Division Two, Alec Lindsay eventually retired from league football.

He played with Oakland Stompers in the NASL, during the Summer of 1978, before finishing his football career.

John Toshack only played three First Division matches for Liverpool, during the 1977-78 season. He left Anfield, for Swansea City, in February 1978, after scoring ninety-six league goals for Liverpool in 246 matches.

As Swansea's player-manager, Toshack led them out of Division Four, in April 1978. By 1981, he'd built a team that had gained promotion yet again, and then again, up to the First Division.

John Toshack's Swansea City actually topped the Division One table on Christmas Day 1981.

For a friendly match against Switzerland, on Wednesday 7th September 1977, Ron Greenwood, the new England manager, had tried an experiment for the future of English football. He picked six Liverpool players, Clemence, Neal, McDermott, Hughes, Kennedy and Callaghan, as well as their former attacker Keegan, in a Liverpool-based England team.

Bob Paisley was delighted, but he felt that Greenwood should have gone for all or nothing. It was no good picking a Liverpool midfield, but leaving out Jimmy Case, who did all the legwork and ball-winning for playmakers Callaghan and McDermott. Greenwood had picked both Trevor Francis and Mike Channon up front, meaning Keegan had to do more unnecessary midfield work.

So, the whole idea of utilising Liverpool's attacking system was entirely nullified.

Ian Callaghan, at thirty-five years old, was shattered and eventually replaced by Ray Wilkins. England were held to a 0-0 draw, and the experiment was never used again.

Ian Callaghan retired in 1978, after 848 league and cup games for Liverpool, and scoring sixty-nine goals, but creating six times as many. Awarded both an MBE and the Football Writer's Footballer of the Year award in 1974, Callaghan holds the record number of appearances for Liverpool, a record that's never likely to be broken.

The quiet, classy midfielder was booked only once in his career, and despite being written off several times, Callaghan kept on, switching from the wing to a central, creative midfield role during the early Seventies.

In June 2009, Ian Callaghan was finally presented with his FIFA World Cup winners' medal by Prime Minister Gordon Brown, having been a squad player in 1966. He played in their 2-0 group stage win over France, but wasn't selected again, and that 0-0 draw with Switzerland was his next game for England, over eleven years later.

Liverpool's defensive legend Tommy Smith had also retired in 1978, having played 467 First Division matches, and scoring 48 goals. The goal he'd scored in the 1977 European Cup Final, a mighty header from Keegan's corner, was his very last for the club.

Tommy Smith's twenty-five yard bullet, that zipped low and hard, and smashed in off the post, had set Liverpool on the way to a 2-1 home win over reigning Champions Man United, back on New Year's Day 1966. That win had lifted the Reds to the top of the First Division for the first time that season, a lead they wouldn't ever give up.

Awarded the MBE in 1978, for services to football, Tommy Smith was also included in the Daily Mail's top ten list of the Greatest Hard Men in football, in January 2009.

He was voted at number seven, behind Dave Mackay, Roy Keane, Ron Harris, Billy Bremner, Stuart Pearce and Graeme Souness. It should have been a seven-way dead heat for first place, because Tommy Smith was as hard as all of them.

Emlyn Hughes captained Liverpool to a second European Cup triumph in 1978, beating FC Bruges 1-0, at Wembley. In 1978-79, however, even he lost his place in their team, to Scottish centre back Alan Hansen.

I'll say this. For all of Liverpool's key players between 1967 and 1976, Clemence, Lawler, Smith, Lloyd, Heighway, Keegan and Toshack, they'd have been half as successful without Emlyn Hughes' absolute energy and enthusiasm.

Ian Callaghan was comparable in his influence, but he never rivalled Hughes' work-rate.

After playing 474 First Division matches during his twelve years at Anfield, Crazy Horse moved to Wolves in 1979. He won the tenth major honour of his career, the following year, captaining Wolves to their 1980 League Cup Final win over Nottingham Forest.

Hughes won 62 England caps, but he never played in a World Cup Finals tournament. He was in their squad for the 1980 European Championships, but he didn't play.

After leaving Wolves, his career wound down as Rotherham United's player-manager, lifting the Merry Millers as high as seventh in the Second Division in 1982. Between 1982 and 1987, Emlyn Hughes was a team captain, opposite Bill Beaumont, in the BBC TV sports quiz show, A Question Of Sport.

Emlyn Hughes died, aged only fifty-seven, on Tuesday 9th November 2004.

After Emlyn Hughes' departure, Phil Thompson took over as Liverpool's team captain, and he captained them to their third European Cup Final win, in five seasons, the greatest moment of his career, after they'd beaten Real Madrid in Paris, in 1981. Afterwards, *Thommo* lost the captaincy to Graeme Souness, but he continued to play in central defence until 1983, when he won the fourteenth major honour of his career, as Liverpool romped to their sixth League Championship title in eight years.

From 1998, until 2004, Thompson was Gerard Houllier's assistant manager at Liverpool, as they won the UEFA Cup, FA Cup, and Football League Cup, before Rafa Benitez took charge, Phil Thompson is now an enthusiastic pundit on Sky Sports News, opposite Jeff Stelling.

Steve Heighway played in Liverpool's 1981 League Cup Final win over West Ham United, winning the eleventh major honour of his career, but he failed to make their European Cup Final team against Real Madrid, in Paris.

Big Bamber played a total of 444 league and cup games for Liverpool, scoring seventy-six goals.

The brilliantly exciting and energetic, moustached, two-footed forward player became Director of Liverpool's Academy of Football, as Liverpool won three FA Youth Cup Finals in 1996, 2006 and 2007.

Steve Heighway's 1996 FA Youth Cup Final team was particularly memorable, as Liverpool's youth team had included Michael Owen, Jamie Carragher and also David Thompson. They beat a West Ham United side that starred both Rio Ferdinand and Frank Lampard. Steven Gerrard signed for Liverpool during the following season.

Ray Clemence was the last of Shankly's team to leave Liverpool, joining Tottenham during the Summer of 1981, for a fee of £300,000.

Between September 1972 and March 1978, Clemence had played 336 consecutive matches, without missing a single game.

He'd also kept a total of 335 clean sheets in 650 matches for Liverpool.

During his eleven years as Liverpool's regular starting goalkeeper, Ray Clemence had missed only six league and cup matches.

The greatest goalkeeper in their history, Clemence was awarded the MBE in 1987, and is third behind only Ian Callaghan and Jamie Carragher in total appearances for Liverpool. Ray Clemence also won sixty-one caps with England, before falling behind Peter Shilton in Bobby Robson's team in the Eighties.

Clemence won the FA Cup with Spurs in 1982, his thirteenth major honour in football, making him the most successful goalkeeper in English football history.

After his retirement in 1988, he had amassed a huge total of 710 First Division appearances, 470 with Liverpool, and 240 with Spurs.

Between 1996 and 2007, he was goalkeeping coach for the England national team, until former Roma keeper Franco Tancredi was appointed by Fabio Capello.

ONE HUNDRED PLAYERS THAT SHOOK THE KOP?

On Liverpool FC's official website, a poll was run in 2006, and voted for by over 110,000 Liverpool supporters, before being published on Sunday 8th October; One Hundred Players That Shook The Kop.

All of the players from the classic Liverpool teams of 1971-76 are in the list, but the list is flawed. It has clearly been voted for by a mostly younger audience.

Kevin Keegan is in at number eight, Emlyn Hughes at ten, and Ray Clemence at eleven. Ian Callaghan is also in the top twenty, at number fifteen, three places above David Fairclough in eighteenth place.

Eighteenth, for heaven's sake? Fairclough didn't even play 100 games.

Tommy Smith is in at 25th position, one behind Luis Garcia, at 24. It gets even worse.

Ray Kennedy, Phil Thompson, Steve Heighway and Phil Neal all make the top thirty. John Toshack is in at 34, but Chris Lawler, Liverpool's greatest ever full back, fails to make the top fifty, down at number fifty-one.

Brian Hall makes it in at 75, and Alec Lindsay is in at 85. Both players are rated below Jari Litmanen, Steve Finnan, Rob Jones and Stephane Henchoz. It is, frankly, a load of rubbish, a pile of shit, and you do wonder if Liverpool fans deserved such a magnificent team in their magnificent history, so easily they are forgotten.

As good as Jamie Carragher is, and he is *very* good, even he would be embarrassed to be up there at number seven, with Tommy Smith not even in the top twenty.

THE BIG RED MACHINE.

The Cincinnati Reds are a Major League Baseball team who won back-to-back World Series, back in 1975 and 1976, the years when Liverpool became really dominant in English football. Driven by a fierce offensive line-up of Pete Rose, Joe Morgan, George Foster, Ken Griffey, Tony Perez and Dave Concepcion, they became the most feared line-up in 1970s baseball.

They were called *The Big Red Machine* by writers, and the name stuck.

The Big Red Machine became as much a part of baseball folklore as the Black Sox, the Bronx Bombers, and the Miracle Mets.

The Cincinnati Reds didn't even wear Red, though. They wore white uniforms, with red trims, and red baseball caps or batting helmets, and with **CINCINNATI** emblazoned across their chests in Red.

It was still more white than red, though.

Liverpool wore a completely Ferrari red strip, with simple white rounded collar and cuffs. They were also more successful than the Cincinnati Reds, with their brilliant back-to-back World Series wins during the mid-Seventies, before waiting for a solitary Championship in 1990, but nothing since.

Liverpool's achievements, under Shankly and Paisley, stand loud and proudly above that.

I suppose the Cincinnati Reds achievements stand more on a par with Nottingham Forest's.

Liverpool were, and are, the real Big Red Machine.

Whilst Manchester United were the best team in England in 1967, and Leeds were the best English team between 1968 and 1974, Liverpool emerged as the dominant force in football for nearly two decades, thanks to Bill Shankly's foresight.

Shankly's 1973 team was the very best of them all, bought for nothing, and brought from nowhere, but World dominating.

THE DEEP NORTH, Part One

The Fellowship Of The Withering

THE NORTH-EAST OF ENGLAND, the Deep North, has always been a hot bed of foot-balling talent. It always will be, and things were no different in 1967, with on average, nearly one player born in the North-east playing for each First Division club.

There were twenty-one players playing regular First Division football, during 1967, who were born in the region, including some of the real cream of English football.

You could have put a very good First Division team together, made up entirely of North-east-erners, that would have battled strongly for the title...

1	Jim Montgomery
2	Joe Kirkup
3	Frank Clark
4	Howard Kendall
5	Jack Charlton
6	Norman Hunter
7	George Armstrong
8	Colin Bell
9	Bobby Charlton
10	Pop Robson
11	Jimmy Husband

With a choice of substitutes of George Heslop, Colin Todd, Colin Suggett, Ralph Coates and Alan Suddick, it would have been some squad.

The three biggest clubs within that region, though, were very much withering, sleeping giants.

They had huge, fanatical support, but as clubs, they had gone far too long, collectively, with-out success, or even a sniff of success.

By 1967, Newcastle United had gone twelve years without winning a major honour, the FA Cup back in 1955, and then they'd even spent four years in Division Two during the early Sixties. They finished the 1966-67 season in twentieth position in Division One, just four points above rel-egated Aston Villa, despite attracting home crowds regularly above 40,000, and an average crowd of over 32,000.

Sunderland won just three more points than Newcastle, up in the heights of seventeenth place. Roker Park had attracted crowds of nearly 33,000 in 1966-67, but Sunderland hadn't won a major honour for thirty years, the FA Cup back in 1937.

They'd also lost a record run of fifty-seven successive seasons in Division One, when they were relegated in 1958.

They spent six seasons in the Second Division, before then returning to top flight football in 1964, as runners-up behind Leeds United.

Middlesbrough were the third big team in the North-east, the Deep North.

A great town, built on coal exports and pig iron production, it's skyline was dominated by the giant, iconic Transporter Bridge, standing 225 feet high and 850 feet long, and seen from miles around.

"Boro" were a club famous for Wilf Mannion, George Camsell and Brian Clough. They were also a club that hadn't played First Division football since 1954, but it had got even worse than that.

In 1966, the very year that Ayresome Park had staged World Cup Finals games between the Soviet Union, North Korea, Italy and Chile, Middlesbrough suffered the ignominy of becoming a Third Division club, for the first time in their history, having finished second bottom of the Second Division.

Boro were promoted immediately, though, back up to Division Two as distant runners-up to the 1967 League Cup-winning thoroughbreds of QPR, and just a single point above Watford.

John O'Rourke was their top scorer, with twenty-seven goals, during their promotion season, while Arthur Horsfield had hit twenty-two. John Hickton joined Middlesbrough, though, back in the Summer of 1966, having scored twenty-one First Division goals for Sheffield Wednesday, from just fifty-three games.

Born in Chesterfield, on the edge of Derbyshire's Peak District, and just below the mass of the Sheffield conurbation, it was a surprise when Hickton left The Owls, for Boro. For whatever reasons he had, and despite scoring only fifteen goals in his first season at Ayresome Park, John Hickton became a Middlesbrough club legend.

An example of the passion that remains in the North-east, right to this day, was evident during that 1966-67 season. 57,643 had packed St James's Park to suffer Newcastle's 0-3 home defeat to Sunderland, on Saturday 29th October 1966.

Then, four months later, 50,442 filled Roker Park for Sunderland's home match against Newcastle.

Nineteen year old Bobby Kerr scored twice, and George Mulhall the other, as the Wearside club again won 3-0, on Saturday 4th March. Bobby Kerr had joined Sunderland straight from school, during the early Sixties, and he'd even scored on his league debut, their 1-0 win over Manchester City, on New Year's Eve 1966, with only 29,000 inside Roker Park. Kerr went on to score seven league and cup goals during his next ten games, including that hammering of their fiercest rivals.

One week after their 3-0 win over Newcastle, however, Sunderland hosted Don Revie's Leeds United, in the FA Cup Fifth round, on Saturday 11th March 1967, with a massive 55,763 crowd packed tightly inside Roker Park.

That huge crowd fell deadly silent, though, as Bobby Kerr broke his leg after a collision with Norman Hunter, as both players had gone in for a fifty-fifty ball.

John O'Hare scored to earn Sunderland a 1-1 draw, with Jack Charlton heading Leeds United's goal. Kerr suffered a re-break of the same leg during a comeback reserve team match at Ashington, and he never played regularly again until November 1968.

He was very lucky his sickening double leg-break hadn't cost him his career.

57,892 over-filled Elland Road, four days after Bobby Kerr's leg break, Leeds United's **Record Home attendance,** for the replay. A crush barrier collapsed under the sheer weight of the mass of supporters, though, and more than thirty people were rushed to hospital in ambulances. In an era of ageing, crumbling football grounds regularly having their capacities pushed by the demands of huge crowds, Leeds were an unlucky exception to the generally warm safety of packed terraces.

Given the subsequent disasters on crumbling terraces, and the emphasis of public order over that of public safety, by police forces in later years, Leeds had certainly been very lucky.

I'd like to refer again to Sunderland's 3-0 home win over Newcastle, back on 4th March, and it's clear that on paper, that day, Sunderland had had the more impressive line-up: Montgomery, Irwin, Harvey, Todd, Kinnell, Baxter, Kerr, O'Hare, Martin, Herd and Mulhall. Colin Todd and John O'Hare would re-join Brian Clough, rejected as a potential manager of Sunderland back in 1965, after he'd previously worked at Roker Park as their youth team coach. And Neil Martin also went on to fire the goals that took Coventry City into Europe, in 1970, for the only time in their history.

The big name in Sunderland's team, though, was Jim Baxter, one of the greatest ever Scottish footballers. Baxter had signed for Sunderland, in May 1965, at twenty-seven years old, still in his prime, for £72,500, a record fee ever received by a Scottish club.

The former Rangers star had however become heavily dependent on drink, downing up to three bottles of Bacardi a day, but he was just so good a player, he'd just turned up for games, after getting up still falling-down drunk from the late night before, and he was voted Man of the Match every time, just as he was during Sunderland's 3-0 win over Newcastle. Having experienced many Rangers-Celtic matches, a Tyne-Wear derby games was just a walk in Victoria Park for him.

Jim Baxter played ten games for Scotland, as a Sunderland player, but the most famous of those, by far, was Scotland's European Championship qualifier, away at Wembley Stadium, on Saturday 15th April 1967, against the still unbeaten World Champions, England.

In front of a massive 99,063 crowd, Scotland won the match 3-2, giving themselves a great chance of qualification, which they subsequently blew, after Denis Law, Bobby Lennox and Jim McCalliog had all scored. The Scots then declared themselves as the new World Champions.

Sunderland's Jim Baxter had a hell of a game. At one point, he famously just juggled the ball, along the touchline, while waiting for his teammates to regain their shape.

It was like watching Brazil.

Jim Baxter had also pre-arranged, with Billy Bremner, that he'd play a fifty-fifty ball for Bremner to contest with Alan Ball, who neither of them liked, just so Bremner could hit Ball like a train, leaving the England midfield star totally flattened.

Newcastle's team, though, during that 3-0 hammering away at Roker Park, had the greater future: Gordon Marshall, David Craig, Frank Clark, Dave Elliott, John McNamee, Bobby Moncur, Pop Robson, Ron McGarry, Wyn Davies, Dave Hilley and Tommy Robson.

Their eleven had contained nearly half of the team that won a major trophy, just over two years later. It was, however, Ron McGarry's last-ever match for Newcastle. McGarry had been United's top scorer as United had won the Second Division Championship, back in 1965, with sixteen goals.

He was replaced, firstly, by Peter Noble, Sunderland-born, and who'd later face Newcastle in a dramatic FA Cup Semi-final, and then at the start of the 67-68 season, by Albert Bennett.

Bennett was a Durham-born, six foot tall, leggy, and deftly-skilled inside forward, who'd joined Newcastle from Rotherham, in July 1965, for £27,500.

Jim Scott had also signed from Hibernian, for £40,000, during that Summer of Love, and his typically, unlovely, gritty Scottish drive and ball skills, either on the wing or in midfield, were a huge reason for Newcastle's success towards the end of the Sixties.

Newcastle's formidable attacking partnership, though, after 1967-68, was their little and large duo of Pop Robson and Wyn Davies. Robson, at just five foot eight, had scored on his debut against Charlton, aged only eighteen, back in September 1964.

He scored seven important goals during Newcastle's Second Division title winning 1964-65 season, to help them back up to the First Division.

He was then Newcastle's top scorer, with only ten league goals as they just avoided relegation to the Second Division in 1966-67, but during the following season, his partnership with big Wyn Davies began to bring real success.

Davies, at six feet and one inch tall, was a huge, powerful menace for opposing defenders and goalkeepers. Very agile and skilful, despite his great build, Wyn Davies was a real hyper-active livewire in opposing penalty areas, both in the air, and on the ground, and he never gave his opponents even half a second with the ball.

Wyn Davies, and his superb Welsh international teammate, Ron Davies of Southampton, who'd scored thirty-seven First Division goals during 1966-67, had already played a combined twenty-four games for Wales, prior to the 1967-68 season.

They were nicknamed the **Welsh Air Force,** due to their aerial dominance.

Sunderland, despite their apparent superiority over Newcastle during 1966-67, were going through tough times. In spite of Jim Baxter's performances on the pitch, driving Sunderland to just enough victories to achieve safety, but nothing else, his off-the-pitch behaviour had created a huge rift in Sunderland's changing room.

Discipline had disappeared, and Sunderland's full back Len Ashurst, who would later manage the club, taking them to the 1985 Football League Cup Final, had suggested, "it doesn't take much to upset the very fine balance of a dressing room, but Baxter's arrival wrecked Sunderland's."

Jim Baxter's love affair with Bacardi had also introduced a new culture of drinking into Sunderland FC. There were often two sides of the changing room: Scots and drinkers on one side, and the rest over on the opposite side.

On Saturday 2nd December 1967, Jim Baxter played his ninety-eighth and final First Division game for Sunderland, as they lost 3-2 at home to Chelsea.

He was then sold to Nottingham Forest for a club record transfer fee of £100,000.

On Boxing Day 1967, a massive crowd of 59,579 filled the mighty St James's Park, for the visit of Sunderland, who'd won just six of their opening twenty-one league games, while losing ten times. Newcastle, in contrast, were in strong form, having lost just once in their previous nine matches.

Ian Porterfield was making his First Division debut for Sunderland, though, having just signed from Raith Rovers, for £38,000, after playing 117 league games at Starks Park.

He'd helped Raith to second place in the Scottish Second Division, and back into the top flight of Scottish football for the first time in nearly twenty years, alongside Celtic and Rangers. Porterfield, Dunfermline-born, was a tall, elegant, modern midfield playmaker, with a calm nature and a quick mind.

He proved himself to be invaluable to Sunderland over the following eight years.

NEWCASTLE UNITED		SUNDERLAND
Gordon Marshall	1	Jim Montgomery
Ollie Burton	2	Cecil Irwin
Frank Clark	3	Len Ashurst
Dave Elliott	4	Colin Todd
John McNamee	5	Charlie Hurley
Bobby Moncur	6	Ian Porterfield
Jim Scott	7	Jim Stuckey
Albert Bennett	8	Colin Suggett
Wyn Davies	9	Neil Martin
Jim Iley	10	Ralph Brown
Pop Robson	11	George Mulhall

Colin Suggett, Sunderland's Washington-born attacking midfield player, who'd started just five games during the previous season, was one of only two ever-presents for the Rokerites in 1967-68, along with Colin Todd. He had come in for John O'Hare, who'd left to become Kevin Hector's support striker at Derby County.

Nevertheless, while Sunderland's superiority had been clear, during 1966-67, Newcastle now had the greater cohesion. They also had a more acute understanding than their Wearside rivals, and goals from both Bennett and Davies secured a 2-1 win.

Only four days later, the two teams met again, in the return match at Roker Park, but a crowd of just 46,000 saw Newcastle battle to a 3-3 draw, after two dynamic penalty kicks by Ollie Burton, and a terrific, towering header from John McNamee.

Colin Suggett had scored his eighth and ninth league goals of the season, with Jim Stuckey adding a third for Sunderland, but the paper over the cracks was beginning to fray and rip at Roker Park.

Sunderland won only a quarter of their First Division games during 1967-68, and they finished down in fifteenth position, only five points above relegated Sheffield United, and four points below Newcastle. Worse was to follow for them, though.

Ollie Burton had made his Newcastle debut, back in August 1963, against Derby County, at twenty-one years of age. Chepstow-born, ginger-haired, and bespectacled off the pitch, Burton was a fine, sharply-focussed defender who could capably play anywhere along the back four.

Big John McNamee, who thudded in United's third goal in that 3-3 draw, was a six foot tall, thirteen and a half stone road-block.

"A big gorilla," as Mike Summerbee affectionately remembered him, McNamee was a burly, cast iron defender, renowned for his no-nonsense roughness.

His heading ability at corners added massive weight to United's attacking threat, just as it had done at Roker Park.

A month after their 2-1 win over Sunderland, Newcastle welcomed Carlisle United to St James's Park, in the Third round of the FA Cup. Another huge crowd of nearly 57,000, possibly the largest crowd to ever watch Carlisle play, witnessed a shock, as Ollie Burton had a penalty saved by Alan Ross, and Tom Murray fired the Cumbrians into the Fourth round.

No matter, Newcastle strode on and they won two of their three games during February 1968, taking five points. On Saturday 24th February, they were up in fifth place, after thirty matches, and only three points below third-placed Liverpool.

Just eight points behind the reigning Champions and league leaders, Manchester United, Newcastle collapsed thereafter. They won only one of their last twelve matches, and lost seven, including all of their final five games.

Newcastle United ended up in tenth place, twelve points below a Fairs Cup qualifying position, and seventeen points behind the new Champions, Manchester City.

City had even won the league with a sensational 4-3 win away at St James's Park, on the last day of the season. So, Newcastle's European dream was over.

Indeed it was, except, no it wasn't.

As the Fairs Cup was open only to one team per city, Chelsea had secured London's spot in the tournament, after finishing in sixth place, with Manchester United, Liverpool and Leeds claiming the three top places. Everton, up in fifth place, wouldn't be playing European football at all, unless they won the FA Cup Final against West Brom, who'd finished in eighth place, two above Newcastle. Tottenham, in seventh position, and Arsenal, ninth, would definitely not be playing in Europe in 1968-69.

So, what happened next? West Brom shocked Everton to win the FA Cup Final, against all odds, and then, on Wednesday 29th May 1968, Manchester United defeated Benfica 4-1 to lift the European Cup. Manchester United subsequently qualified for the 1968-69 European Cup, as holders, alongside the Champions Manchester City.

You knock out Manchester United, Everton, Spurs, West Brom, who had qualified for the Cup Winners' Cup, and then Arsenal, and suddenly, Newcastle were up in fifth place, in Fairs Cup calculations. If Everton had beaten West Brom, as expected, and as deserved, then Everton would have been playing in the Cup Winners' Cup, and West Brom would have qualified for the Fairs Cup.

Thank heavens for those fouling, *dirty* West Brom full backs!!!

Middlesbrough? They finished down in sixth position in Division Two, twelve points behind second-placed QPR. John Hickton was their top scorer, with twenty-nine league and cup goals from fifty games. Only one other Boro player, John O'Rourke, had hit double figures, in goals, but he'd left for Ipswich Town, for £20,000, during February 1968. O'Rourke then fired twelve goals in just fifteen games, for Ipswich, helping the Suffolk club win the Second Division Championship, ahead of QPR.

Frank Spraggon, a home produced player who'd made his league debut during Boro's promotion-winning season of 1966-67, from Division Three, playing only one game, finally became a regular in their defence in October 1967. Born in Wickham, Spraggon played a total of thirty-nine league and cup games during 1967-68.

Frank Spraggon became the first piece of the jigsaw, of what became one of the finest, and tightest, defences of the following Decade.

For Sunderland, Billy Hughes, a stocky, powerfully-built Scot from Coatbridge, had played only eleven league games over the previous two seasons. He became a regular during 1968-69, though, at the age of just nineteen..

Other significant debutants, during that season, were Dennis Tueart, who'd played in their goalless draw at home to Sheffield Wednesday, on Boxing Day 1968, and Ritchie Pitt, who first played on 4th March 1969, as Sunderland lost 3-1 at Coventry City.

Alan Brown, the Sunderland manager, was greatly interested in developing youth at Roker Park. He knew all the youth team players by their first names, and he took an active interest in each of their development. Alan Brown also oversaw the building of a new training complex, and a gymnasium, with four training pitches, at Washington, and he began a youth revolution at Sunderland, drawing heavily from their youth team that won the FA Youth Cup during 1968-69.

Paddy Lowrey was another Sunderland youth team player who'd graduated to the first team, after scoring a hat-trick against West Brom in their 6-0 second leg victory at Roker Park.

It was Ryhope-born Pitt, and the Geordie Tueart, though, who'd made most of an impact in Sunderland's first team during the latter part of their disappointing 1968-69 season. Bobby Kerr had returned to regular action at the end of November, and he played in twelve of their next fifteen games, scoring just one goal, before being injured again, in the middle of March, and he missed yet another month of action.

Crowds had deteriorated as Sunderland won only three of their final eighteen league games, slumping from mid-table, right down to nineteenth place by the middle of April. Dennis Tueart had scored his first Sunderland goal in one of those three victories, their 4-1 home win over Stoke City, watched by only 16,092, in early March.

By Saturday 12th April, Sunderland's team had begun to develop a more futuristic look, though, as they travelled away to FA Cup Finalists Manchester City. This was the last of the six matches that Bobby Kerr missed, but Ritchie Pitt and Dennis Tueart were starting together for only the second time.

MANCHESTER CITY		SUNDERLAND
Harry Dowd	1	Jim Montgomery
Tony Book	2	Martin Harvey
Glyn Pardoe	3	Len Ashurst
Mike Doyle	4	Brian Heslop
George Heslop	5	Ritchie Pitt
Alan Oakes	6	Colin Todd
Mike Summerbee	7	Gordon Harvey
Colin Bell	8	Ian Porterfield
Francis Lee	9	Paddy Lowrey
Neil Young	10	Colin Suggett
Tony Coleman	11	Dennis Tueart
Bobby Owen	12	Billy Hughes
(rep. Coleman)		(rep. Lowrey)

The game was a damp squib for Sunderland, as City won a dour match 1-0, after Neil Young scored, watched by a poor Maine Road crowd of 22,842.

In the later stages, though, Billy Hughes had replaced the ineffective Lowrey, and at that moment, Sunderland had fielded five members of a much more illustrious team, still to come, for the very first time.

Bobby Kerr returned to their team, for their last three matches, and he scored in all three, helping Sunderland to a 2-0 home win over Wolves, and also a 2-1 away win at Burnley.

Those wins ensured their First Division survival, at least.

Newcastle United finished in ninth position in Division One, during 1968-69, winning nineteen of their forty-two matches, but they made only slight progress in both of the domestic Cups.

It was, however, in their first ever season in European football, in the Inter-Cities Fairs Cup, into which they had totally *fluked* qualification, that Newcastle made the headlines.

In the First round, Newcastle were drawn against Feyenoord of Rotterdam, a team en route to a Dutch league and cup double, winning their ninth Dutch league title in 1969. They also boasted several members of Holland's national team, including Wim Van Hanegem, Rinus Israel and Henk Wery.

On Wednesday 11th September 1968, 46,348 flocked to St James's Park, to feel the experience of United's entrance into proper European competition.

Newcastle's players hadn't really felt the importance of the Fairs Cup; they'd thought it was just like the Anglo-Italian Cup, or other lesser European novelty cups. The fact that the United fans had turned up, en masse, to roar them on, had put them right.

Also, the fact that Newcastle had fluked their participation in the tournament, through that series of unlikely events, in those two subsequent Wembley Cup Finals, despite finishing below the more fashionable London teams, Spurs and Arsenal, had meant that the national, London-based tabloids were hostile to Newcastle's participation.

It had been widely predicted that Newcastle United would be an embarrassment to English football, especially after they'd been drawn against Feyenoord.

Only twice did St James's Park attract a higher attendance, in First Division matches (against both Sunderland and Manchester United, *obviously*) than the 46,000 who'd turned up for that Feyenoord game, but that was their lowest crowd for that Fairs Cup competition during 1968-69.

Feyenoord would win the European Cup, during the following season, in 1969-70, so they were certainly no European middleweights, but Newcastle pounded their defence all evening.

Davies flicked on for Pop Robson, just outside the Dutch area, and then Robson played the ball wide to Geoff Allen, out on the left wing. Allen fired a low cross for Jim Scott to simply side-foot past Graafland.

Pop Robson shot in from close range, and then Wyn Davies rose above Van Duivenbode to head powerfully home, before Tommy Gibb made it 4-0 to United.

Feyenoord won their home leg, six days later, by 2-0, but Newcastle had advanced, 4-2 on aggregate. They then met Sporting Lisbon, the 1964 European Cup Winners' Cup winners, in the Second round. Jim Scott scored to earn a good 1-1 away draw, with a tiny crowd of just 9,000 attending the vast Estadio Jose Alvalade, which actually had a 52,000 capacity.

Fifty-three thousand, seven hundred and forty-seven packed St James's Park, three weeks later, on Wednesday 20th November, and after just ten minutes, Tommy Gibb lofted a ball up to Wyn Davies, who nodded on for Pop Robson to run onto. Robson did not run onto the ball, though.

He jumped, fully three feet into the air, and volleyed in a stunning right footed shot, from just inside Sporting's area.

The whole place just went wild. It was a move worked many times on the United training pitch, but it "worked like a dream," admitted Robson.

If it had been scored by a Brazilian, or George Best, then that goal would have been shown all around the world on television.

Sadly, television had not yet caught onto the fever of Newcastle's European adventure.

Newcastle's defence, brilliantly marshalled by Bobby Moncur and Ollie Burton, had kept the necessary clean sheet to secure their aggregate 2-1 win.

On New Year's Day 1969, in the year that Man landed on the Moon, Newcastle first landed in northern Spain, to face Real Zaragoza, the 1964 Fairs Cup winners, and then Fairs Cup runners-up, two years later.

Another poor Iberian Peninsula crowd of just 15,000 watched the slightly superior Spaniards totally outplay Newcastle. However, under the vast, and multi-layered La Romareda Stadium, Wyn Davies and Pop Robson forced two crucial away goals.

United had escaped with a 3-2 defeat. Wyn Davies, with his physical presence and aerial dominance, had caused Real's defence problems all night, and if it wasn't for the Mighty Wyn, Newcastle would definitely not have reached the Quarter-finals.

Two weeks later, Tommy Gibb and Pop Robson both scored first half goals, and Newcastle hung on for their 2-1 win, going through on the away goals rule.

January 1969 was an epic month for Newcastle. They hammered Reading 4-0, in the FA Cup Third round, on Saturday 4th January, with over 41,000 inside St James's Park.

In the Fourth round, three weeks later, a massive 57,994 home crowd watched Newcastle hold the reigning league Champions Manchester City 0-0. Then on the following Wednesday, 29th January, 60,844 filled Maine Road, as Bobby Owen and Neil Young both scored to send City forwards, towards lifting the Cup at the Final.

In March, Newcastle faced another Portuguese team, Vitoria Setubal, in the Fairs Cup Quarter-finals. On the evening of Wednesday 12th March, though, during the city rush hour, a huge Arctic blizzard covered the centre of Newcastle with three inches of snow, including the St James's Park pitch, by the time Newcastle kicked off.

Most of the Portuguese players had never even seen snow before, and they came out to play, in the freezing cold, with stockings over their legs, and also their hands and arms. Vitoria, who'd admirably eliminated both Fiorentina and Lyon, were clearly affected by the icy blizzard that continued throughout the evening.

57,662 had packed into St James's Park, with their Brown Ale breath warming the freezing air, and Newcastle hammered Setubal 5-1. Pop Robson scored two, and Wyn Davies, Alan Foggon and Tommy Gibb hit the rest. A fortnight later, Wyn Davies fired his fourth goal of the tournament, and he secured a place in the Semi-finals, as Vitoria won 3-1, in the warmth of their home surroundings, but they lost 6-4 on aggregate.

There was a six week wait until the Semi-finals, during which time, Joe Harvey had bought the Danish international midfield player Preben Arentoft, for just £18,000, from Scottish First Division side Morton.

Preben Arentoft, known to players, fans and friends as **Benny**, had played just four games for Denmark, prior to joining Morton in 1965, but due to strict Danish rules of only amateur players being allowed to play for the National team, he didn't play again for Denmark. He was a skilful, steady midfield worker, the **Jan Molby**, or **Thomas Gravesen**, if you like, of his day.

He made his debut in Newcastle's 1-0 win, away at Spurs, on Wednesday 2nd April, and with Arentoft in the team, Newcastle won eight, but lost only two of their last fourteen league and cup games of the season.

76,083 packed out Ibrox Park, an all-time record crowd for the Fairs Cup, on Wednesday 14th May, as Glasgow Rangers faced Newcastle, in their Semi-final. Iam McFaul saved Andy Penman's penalty, though, and McFaul, Moncur and McNamee were all outstanding in withstanding constant pressure from Rangers' physical attacks.

59,303, Newcastle's biggest crowd of their last-ever Cup-winning season, filled St James's Park, seven days later, for their second leg match.

Jim Scott put Newcastle 1-0 up, but just one goal by Rangers would have put them into the Final.

The game was an epic battle, with Ollie Burton superb against the ferociously competitive Colin Stein, and John Greig also equal to Wyn Davies in the air.

With just about fifteen minutes remaining, Jackie Sinclair volleyed Newcastle 2-0 up, from inside the penalty area, right in front of the Leazes End, to send Newcastle wild with excitement.

The Rangers fans, who'd totally packed the Gallowgate End, on the opposite end of the ground, then began to launch beer bottles and beer cans onto the pitch. Ollie Burton then saw the hell break loose, and he shouted at his keeper, McFaul, *"RUN!"*

McFaul then glanced over his shoulder, towards the invasion, and off he sprinted, straightaway. Referee John Gow, from Wales, took both teams off the pitch, as the police battled to contain the Rangers' fans.

John Lawrence, the Rangers chairman, visited Newcastle's changing room, and actually conceded the match, so ashamed of the trouble he was, as were all of the Rangers' team.

The referee, though, had insisted that the game must be finished.

After seventeen minutes of delay, and with a full line of police, with dogs and horses, defending the pitch from the Gallowgate End, the game was played to a finish, without any incident or initiative, before both teams galloped off the pitch at the final whistle.

"We would have arrested two thousand fans, if we'd enough men (tonight)," a police spokesman had said after the match. The day after the match, club staff cleared the Gallowgate End, and a full lorry load of beer bottles was taken away.

If Newcastle had chosen to cash in on the empties, they could probably have recouped half of the amount they'd laid out for Preben Arentoft.

Anyway, Newcastle faced Ujpest Dozsa in the Final, after the Hungarian club had thrashed Goztepe Izmir, of Turkey, 8-1 in their Semi-final.

More significantly, though, they had defeated Leeds United, the new English Champions 3-0, back in the Quarter-finals. Don Revie had acclaimed Ujpest Dozsa as "the greatest team in Europe."

Six of their players had helped Hungary reach the Quarter-finals of the 1968 European Championships, before losing 3-2 on aggregate to the Soviet Union.

On the Thursday night of 29th May, another huge crowd of mostly home supporters, 59,234, again filled St James's Park for the first leg of the Fairs Cup Final.

Team captain Bobby Moncur, who'd made his Newcastle debut over six years earlier, had never scored a goal in a competitive match for United.

Newcastle had been all over the Hungarians, throughout the first half, as both Davies and Robson worried the Ujpest defence with their superb movement, presence and understanding. They spearheaded a United attack that ran fluently down either wing, with great supply from the Scottish wing pair of Jim Scott and Jackie Sinclair, as Gibb and Arentoft held the middle, picking their passes, and sustaining the pressure.

After sixty-three minutes, Tommy Gibb's floated free-kick, from 25 yards out, was chested down by the mighty Wyn Davies, and he shot from close range, but Szentimihalyi, diving bravely at his feet, pulled off a strong leg save.

Captain Bobby Moncur ran in, though, and swung his left foot around the ball, squeezing it just inside Ujpest's left post. Eight minutes later, Moncur then went on a wonderful run, from the halfway line, playing two one-twos, first with Arentoft, and then with Pop Robson, before driving a strong, low, left-footed shot, from the edge of the area, past the Szentimihalyi's dive, and the ball bounced in off the far right upright.

The Newcastle captain had waited over six years to score for Newcastle, and now he'd scored twice inside ten minutes in a major Cup Final.

Six minutes before the end, Jim Scott went on a superb run from the right wing, playing another wonderful one-two with Arentoft, before lifting the ball over the onrushing Szentimihalyi, from six yards out.

Wyn Davies fractured his cheekbone, on the back of Bobby Moncur's head, going for the same ball as Moncur, inside the Ujpest area, as Moncur went for his hat-trick.

Davies, however, played on heroically, when lesser players would have required an operation and an immediate six week absence from football, but Wyn played on for the Newcastle United cause, until Cup success was achieved.

UJPEST DOZSA		NEWCASTLE UNITED
Antai Szentimihalyi	1	Iam McFaul
Beno Kaposta	2	David Craig
Emo Solymosi	3	Frank Clark
Istvan Bankuti	4	Tommy Gibb
Emo Nosko	5	Ollie Burton
Ede Dunai	6	Bobby Moncur
Luszio Fazekas	7	Jim Scott
Janos Gorocs	8	Pop Robson
Ferenc Bene	9	Wyn Davies
Antai Dunai	10	Preben Arentoft
Zandor Zambo	11	Jackie Sinclair
	12	Alan Foggon (rep. Scott)

Thirteen days later, on Wednesday 11th June, almost in the middle of Summer, Newcastle travelled to Budapest, for the final match of their season.

The Fairs Cup had not only expanded their season beyond early May, but the name of Newcastle United, famous across all of England during the Fifties, was now well-known all across Europe, for the very first time. The Inter-Cities Fairs Cup had extended the name of Newcastle United from the Arctic Circle down to the Mediterranean coast.

It was a hot and sweaty June night in Budapest and for the first time in the Final, Ujpest Dozsa, totally unchanged from the first leg, finally began to play just like the "greatest team in Europe."

The great Ferenc Bene, who'd helped lead Hungary to the World Cup Quarter-finals back in 1962, and then again in 1966, drove home an angled shot from the right of Iam McFaul's goal, after Frank Clark's initial block of Antai Dunai's effort had deflected the ball nicely into his path.

Antai Dunai then collected a loose pass from Jackie Sinclair, on halfway, and he sent Gorocs running free, down the left, at the United area. Janos Gorocs beat both Arentoft and David Craig, before he fired past McFaul, at his near post. Newcastle, who were also unchanged from the first leg, were completely rattled.

"It could have been four or five-nil at half-time. We got well hammered in the first half," Moncur admitted. The sweat was literally dripping from Newcastle's players onto the changing room floor, totally shattered and stunned by the Hungarian onslaught. They'd not even got over the halfway line during the first half.

"What's the fucking matter?" Joe Harvey asked, when he strolled nonchalantly through the door, as his demoralised team looked up to him, looking for inspiration. "All you've got to do is go and score a goal, and these foreigners will collapse like a pack of cards," he told them.

Sure enough, in the very first minute of the second half, Newcastle forced a corner. Jackie Sinclair's left-sided corner was half-cleared away, but Sinclair got the ball back.

His second cross was superb, straight to Bobby Moncur, in the clear. Moncur volleyed, left-footed, and the ball flew high into the roof of the Ujpest net.

Jim Scott then fired the ball from outside of the Hungarian area, but Nosko got a foot to it. The ball ballooned up, and over the heads of the Ujpest defence, and down into space, onto the penalty spot. Ben Arentoft met the ball perfectly, and he volleyed it, first time and left-footed, high beyond the Szentimihalyi's dive, into the top right corner, for his third Newcastle goal.

Wyn Davies then leapt and headed the ball on for substitute Alan Foggon to run onto, from forty yards out, with Kaposta pestering him all the way.

Foggon rode a clip from behind by Ede Dunai, before he then shot from just inside the Hungarian area. Szentimihalyi dived low, and he palmed the shot up and over, as the ball came down and hit the crossbar, but Foggon had ran on, still with Kaposta in hot pursuit, and he smashed the ball high into the roof of the net.

All ten of Newcastle's jubilant outfield players ran to celebrate with Foggon. They'd won 3-2, in one of the most amazing turnarounds, and won the Fairs Cup, 6-2 on aggregate. It was their first major trophy for fourteen years, but it would also be their last for how many more decades?

The Hungarian fans, who'd been fairly hostile at the start of the match, were unanimously warm in their applause of the victorious Newcastle United players, as hat-trick hero Bobby Moncur lifted the Cup, presented by Sir Stanley Rous.

Middlesbrough finished the 1968-69 season in fourth place in the Second Division, seven points behind second-placed Crystal Palace. They'd kept sixteen clean sheets, but only John Hickton hit double figures in goals scored, though both David Mills and Willie Maddren had made their Middlesbrough debuts towards the end of that season.

Both players were local teenagers, who had developed through Boro's youth team. David Mills was from Robin Hood's Bay, near Whitby, but he'd lived in nearby Thornaby for most of his life. A young, fair-haired, highly skilful front runner, he would have to wait a couple more seasons, before he played more regularly for Boro, with Hickton and Middlesbrough-born Joe Laidlaw both filling the forward positions.

Willie Maddren, though, born in Billingham, played ten successive games towards the end of the 1969-70 season, with tremendous success, as Middlesbrough launched the most unlikely of promotion charges, after a poor start to their season.

By October 8th 1969, Middlesbrough had lost seven of their opening fourteen matches, while winning just four times, and they were down in sixteenth place, only three points above bottom-placed Aston Villa.

Boro had scored only eleven goals, and having conceded twenty-one, their goal average was 0.52, the absolute worst in the Second Division.

As a result, only 14,000 had forced themselves out of their homes to reluctantly attend Ayresome Park, on Saturday 11th October, when John Hickton scored twice, and Hugh McIlmoyle scored two more, as Middlesbrough hammered Bolton 4-0. That win was the first of six wins from their next seven matches, and they'd drawn the other, to rise to seventh place by the end of November, just five points below a promotion place.

By the middle of February, Middlesbrough had continued their steady form, winning four, drawing two and losing two of their previous eight games, since December. They were only three points below the promotion zone, and with games in hand too.

Their 2-1 defeat at mid-table Bolton, though, on February 11th, was the second of those defeats, and Boro's performance didn't inspire confidence that they were a team capable of promotion. It was a game they shouldn't have lost, never mind that World Cup winning forward Roger Hunt scored for Bolton, in his fifth match for Wanderers, since signing from Liverpool. It was a game that Middlesbrough should have won.

So, on Saturday 28th February, manager Stan Anderson selected Willie Maddren to play in central defence, alongside Frank Spraggon, in place of Bill Gates, and although Boro were held to a 1-1 draw by Preston, in front of over 25,000 at Ayresome Park, they played with style and confidence at the back, against a good quality attack that boasted Archie Gemmill, Clive Clark and Ricky Heppolette.

On the following Tuesday, Middlesbrough won 2-0 away at Charlton Athletic, after John Hickton and Joe Laidlaw had scored a goal in each half, and Maddren and Spraggon were imperious again. Laidlaw and Hickton again scored a goal apiece, on 7th March, during Boro's 2-1 home win over Portsmouth.

Middlesbrough were now only two points behind second placed Sheffield United.

A 2-0 defeat away at Norwich was a serious blemish on Boro's promotion charge, but then their goalless draw at Birmingham City, on the middle Saturday in March, was of little help either.

As disappointing as these dropped points were, they had been, in reality, Middlesbrough's games in hand on Sheffield United, and so effectively free points in gaining ground on the Blades.

On Tuesday 17th March, over 25,000 packed into Ayresome Park, for the visit of high-scoring, second-placed Sheffield United. The Blades' line-up shone brightly with their dazzling, sharp, attacking talent. Tony Currie, Alan Woodward, Geoff Salmons, Colin Addison and Gil Reece really went at Boro, but Maddren and Spraggon were both the dominant figures of the match, yet again.

Keeper Bill Whigham made a superb save from Woodward, diving high to his left, late in the first half, before John Hickton then struck his twentieth goal of the season, after half-time, and Boro rose to third in the table.

DIVISION TWO LEADERS, 17TH MARCH 1970

	PL	W	D	L	F	A	PTS
Huddersfield Town	35	20	9	6	54	21	49
Sheffield United	35	19	5	11	63	31	43
MIDDLESBROUGH	35	17	8	10	44	36	42
Blackpool	33	16	10	7	46	38	42
Swindon Town	33	14	13	6	45	34	41
Cardiff City	34	15	10	9	53	35	40
QPR	35	17	6	12	59	48	40

A disappointing goalless home draw to Norwich then dropped Boro back to fifth, although it was their fourth clean sheet in six games. As loud as the 24,514 Ayresome Park crowd roared, Norwich City's defensive partnership of Dave Stringer and Duncan Forbes were totally equal to the dominance of Maddren and Spraggon, and neither Hickton nor Laidlaw ever got a proper kick in front of Kevin Keelan's goal.

Never mind, on Good Friday, 22,486 packed Watford's Vicarage Road, half of which had travelled down the A1 from the North-east, and Middlesbrough won a 3-2 thriller over the FA Cup Semi-finalists. John Hickton scored twice, once in each half, and Eric McMordie had smashed in the other, but how the hell did lowly Watford score two against such a tight defence? Frank Spraggon was missing, and the big South Shields lad, Mike Allen, had partnered Maddren in defence.

It was a great win, though, and for the first time, Boro were in the promotion zone.

DIVISION TWO LEADERS, 27TH MARCH 1970

	PL	W	D	L	F	A	PTS
Huddersfield	37	21	10	6	57	32	52
'BORO	37	18	9	10	47	38	45
Cardiff City	37	17	10.	10	57	37	44
Blackpool	35	17	10	8	48	40	44
Sheffield Utd	36	19	5	12	64	33	43
Swindon Town	35	14	15	6	49	38	43

Away at Hull City, on the following day, Saturday 28th March, fatigue got the better of Willie Maddren, who was still only nineteen, and he suffered a knock to his knee.

He had to be replaced by Stan Webb, and with Frank Spraggon still missing, Boro's central defensive partnership of Allen and Webb couldn't contain Hull's legendary strike-force of Ken Wagstaff and Chris Chilton, with over 300 league goals between them at that time. Wagstaff hit two, and Chilton the other, during Hull's 3-2 win.

Middlesbrough had spent less than twenty-four hours in the top two, dropping four places, down to sixth place, one point behind Blackpool, who'd played two less games.

Nevertheless, Middlesbrough never gave up, and 27,519 packed Ayresome Park, their biggest home crowd of the season, for the visit of virtually-promoted Huddersfield Town, on Tuesday 31st March.

Willie Maddren returned for that must-win match, and John Hickton scored his twenty-third goal of the season, but from the penalty spot, Steve Smith scored a first half leveller, to earn a 1-1 draw, and certain promotion for Huddersfield.

That dropped point made it improbable for Boro to go up, sitting three points behind Blackpool, with just three games to play, but having played one game more than the Tangerines. Only 13,829 subsequently turned up for their 2-1 home win over Cardiff, which ruled The Bluebirds out of the promotion race. In the end, Boro stumbled to a fourth place finish, but only three points behind second-placed Blackpool.

John Hickton, one of only two ever-presents, had scored twenty-eight league and cup goals, while Joe Laidlaw chipped in with twelve.

While Middlesbrough's late, dramatic surge had crashed into rocks before the end of the season, both Newcastle and Sunderland had equally dramatic, or traumatic, seasons that went right to the very last day of 1969-70.

Sunderland had begun the season very, very poorly. They failed to score in any of their first four matches, and lost seven of their first ten games, hitting the First Division basement with a huge bang, a start from which they found it very difficult to recover.

They finally won their first match six weeks into the season, beating Nottingham Forest 2-1 on Saturday 20th September, but with only 16,044 inside Roker Park. Dennis Tueart, and Gordon Harris's penalty-kick, had given Sunderland a hard-earned two points. This victory was followed, a week later, by an unlikely away win at Spurs, Greaves, Gilzean, Mullery, Perryman and all. Mike England's rare own goal, during the first half, presented Sunderland with a gift, but they still remained bottom.

This was the one golden period for Sunderland, though, of the entirety of 1969-70, between late September and the start of November.

During that Golden October, Sunderland lost only twice in eight games, while drawing four times, but they still remained bottom.

Newcastle started the season as Newcastle often started seasons. They lost one, they won one; they won one, they lost one; they drew a couple, and then they won one.

Then, they lost a couple, before they beat Dundee United 2-1 away, at Tannardice Park, in front of a 21,000 full house. Wyn Davies had recovered from his fractured cheekbone to score two second half headers, giving Newcastle a firm foot into the Second round of their Fairs Cup, that they were defending.

Newcastle's average home crowd was 42,150, over the first five games of the season, following on from the euphoria of their Fairs Cup success during the Summer. Sunderland's average crowd, during that same period, was only 17,730.

At the start of October, Keith Dyson gave them a 1-0 win over Dundee United, to put Newcastle into the Second round of the Fairs Cup, after their 3-1 aggregate win. Alan Foggon then scored their winning goal at home to Liverpool, ten days later, with nearly 44,000 inside St James's Park, but then they lost at Spurs, and also at home to Chelsea, before Wyn Davies scored the only goal during their 1-0 away win at Burnley.

On Saturday 8th November, bottom club Sunderland visited Newcastle United, and 55,420 filled St James's Park, for what was the last time that Sunderland visited Newcastle in a competitive capacity for several seasons.

NEWCASTLE UNITED		SUNDERLAND
Iam McFaul	1	Jim Montgomery
David Craig	2	Cecil Irwin
Frank Clark	3	Len Ashurst
Tommy Gibb	4	Colin Todd
Ollie Burton	5	Brian Heslop
Bobby Moncur	6	Mick McGiven
Pop Robson	7	Gordon Harris
Keith Dyson	8	Billy Hughes
Wyn Davies	9	Joe Baker
Preben Arentoft	10	Bobby Kerr
Jackie Sinclair	11	Dennis Tueart

Newcastle cleanly took care of Sunderland. Keith Dyson gave the Magpies a 1-0 half-time lead, and after the break, Newcastle turned on the style, keeping possession better, and opening up Sunderland's defence with ease, and at their leisure.

Wyn Davies fired United two up, and then, Dyson added another, completing a 3-0 hammering of their neighbours.

Sunderland then lost 3-0, again, away at Derby County, and also 2-0 away at Leeds, on Wednesday 19th November. They were firmly rooted at the bottom of Division One, with just eleven points from twenty-one matches, and a diabolical goal average of 0.32. They were absolutely dreadful.

But due to the appalling form of both Sheffield Wednesday and Crystal Palace, immediately above them, Sunderland were still, *unbelievably,* only one point from safety. Their 2-2 draw with Southampton, on Saturday 22nd November, lifted them above Wednesday, up into twenty-first place, in front of a home crowd of just 15,385.

Sunderland were greatly missing Colin Suggett, who'd been sold to West Brom, back in the Summer, for a club record transfer fee of £100,000. Suggett was the glue that had held the young Sunderland team together, and manager Alan Brown found it difficult to replace his Washington-born, lightning-quick attacking midfielder.

Ian Porterfield was also left out of their team for the whole season, though, having had a huge falling-out with Brown, over his pre-season training methods, but there was nobody else to fill that hole.

Wolves then defeated Sunderland 1-0 at the end of November, in the drabbest, dullest affair you could possibly imagine, before one week later, Sunderland actually beat Ipswich Town 2-1, for only their third win in twenty-four games.

Goals from Gordon Harris and Bobby Park, either side of half-time, but in front of just 12,739, Roker Park's lowest crowd of the season, had lifted them to within a point of Crystal Palace in twentieth position.

Two weeks later, a slightly larger crowd of 15,205 was scattered around Roker Park, to see Sunderland surrender to Stoke City, losing 0-3, before they also lost 2-0 on Boxing Day, away at Sheffield Wednesday.

The Owls could at least attract a crowd for a relegation clash, with 35,126 inside Hillsborough, and they moved back above Sunderland, but only one single point was separating the bottom four clubs.

Sunderland then lifted themselves out of the bottom two for the first time, following their 1-1 home draw with Manchester United, and also a 2-1 win over Tottenham.

Billy Hughes and Gordon Harris, with a penalty kick, had scored in each half, for their great win over Greaves, Gilzean and Chivers, on Saturday 17th January, but in front of another tiny Roker Park crowd of just 13,993.

Five successive defeats followed, though, and by late March, they'd sunk back to the bottom of the table, four points adrift of safety, and with only six games left to play.

In the Fairs Cup Second round, Newcastle had drawn 0-0 away at Porto, on Tuesday 18th November, at the Antas Stadium. They'd been ordered, by Joe Harvey, to present a professional, tight defensive unit, and his team perfectly obliged.

Jim Scott scored United's one, crucial goal eight days later, on Wednesday 26th November, with almost 45,000 inside St James's Park. Ben Arentoft had weaved between two Porto defenders, on a frosty pitch, and in freezing conditions, then he laid the ball off for Scott to bury the ball past Rui, from the edge of the six yard box.

Between the end of November and Boxing Day, Newcastle won twice in the league, and they lost once and drew once, as well as drawing 0-0 at home to Southampton, on Wednesday 17th December, in the Fairs Cup Third round.

On Boxing Day, second-placed Leeds United arrived at St James's Park, with the reigning Champions still fighting a tight battle with Everton, in the First Division title race, and they'd also just knocked Ferencvaros out of the European Cup, 6-0 on aggregate, to reach the Quarter-finals.

54,527, as many as possible, given the ground restrictions, had filled St James's Park, for probably their best performance of the season, as Newcastle's fans sung in the second half, there was *"Only One United!"*

Wyn Davies headed in Arentoft's cross, and then Robson buried Davies's knock-down, as the Magpies went in 2-0 up at half-time. Ollie Burton, who'd proved himself as unafraid as any, in the First Division, to put his head in where it really hurt for Newcastle's cause, was then flattened in an aerial challenge with Mick Jones.

The Leeds man was absolutely innocent of any wrong-doing, but Burton was left semi-conscious, and he was helped off the pitch, and replaced by big John McNamee.

NEWCASTLE UNITED		LEEDS UNITED
Iam McFaul	1	Gary Sprake
David Craig	2	Paul Reaney
Frank Clark	3	Terry Cooper
Tommy Gibb	4	Billy Bremner
Ollie Burton	5	Jack Charlton
Bobby Moncur	6	Norman Hunter
Pop Robson	7	Peter Lorimer
Keith Dyson	8	Johnny Giles
Wyn Davies	9	Mick Jones
Preben Arentoft	10	Allan Clarke
David Ford	11	Paul Madeley
John McNamee	12	Mick Bates

It was almost as if Joe Harvey had expected a bruising battle at the back, against Leeds, and he fortunately had a tough defender on his bench, rather than a slim attacker. Johnny Giles rifled in an eighteen yard rocket, but Newcastle's defence hung on for their superb 2-1 win, and they rose up to twelfth in the table.

Mike Channon put Southampton 1-0 up, at The Dell, in their Fairs Cup Third round, second leg match with Newcastle, on Wednesday 14th January, and Ron Davies should have made it two, but he crashed his volley against Iam McFaul's crossbar, before Frank Clark then cleared Bobby Stokes' drive off the goal-line.

Jimmy Smith delicately chipped the ball, from the left wing, with just six minutes remaining, and Wyn Davies nodded the ball down for Pop Robson to smash the ball in, from close range. It was classic Newcastle United.

Jimmy Smith had joined Newcastle, from Aberdeen, during the Summer, for £100,000. *"Unable to command a regular first team place"*, would be *Jinky's* epitaph on his Newcastle United tombstone, but when he was good, he **was** World Class.

Jimmy Smith played in only half of Newcastle's First Division matches, during that 1969-70 season, despite his high price-tag, because of his lazy appearance and inconsistency, not to mention his frequent, niggling, minor injuries.

"I always knew in the first ten minutes of a match, whether I was going to have a good game," Jimmy Smith admitted. "If it looked like I wasn't, then I just wouldn't bother."

After their 1-1 draw with Southampton that sent Newcastle United into the Fairs Cup Quarter-finals, again, on the away goals rule, they also drew with Wolves, Everton and Crystal Palace. Their goalless home draw with Palace frustrated the 35,440 St James's Park crowd, but it did send Sunderland back into the bottom two.

On Wednesday 11th February, Newcastle defeated Southampton 2-1 at home (Jimmy Smith and Wyn Davies), to rise up to ninth in Division One.

They then took four points from their next four matches, ahead of their Fairs Cup Quarter-final tie with Anderlecht.

Away in Brussels, on Wednesday 11th March, Newcastle struggled to contain an Anderlecht team that boasted the Belgian national captain, Paul Van Himst, who'd later star with Pele, in John Huston's *Escape To Victory.*

Newcastle lost player after player, to injury, during the match, as they defended superbly to lose only 2-0, preventing the score-line from becoming an absolutely insurmountable defeat.

John McNamee and Jimmy Smith had both limped off, and the badly-struggling Bobby Moncur was sent up front, while Wyn Davies covered brilliantly in defence, and alongside Ollie Burton, they kept out Van Himst.

Back at St James's Park, a week later, United set upon Anderlecht in the most ferocious manner. Alan Foggon came in for the unreliable Smith, and after just four minutes, Davies leapt highest for the ball, pulling two defenders with him, but the Mighty Wyn intentionally missed the ball, allowing Pop Robson to head it in, over at the far post, and free of any markers. Just over a quarter of an hour later, Tommy Gibb threaded a wonderful through-ball to Robson, who drove his unstoppable shot past Trappeniers, from the edge of the area.

The scores were level, on aggregate, but Newcastle continued their dominance, with Foggon's pace particularly troubling the Belgian defence.

Roared on by a huge 60,000 crowd, Newcastle were thwarted, time after time, by some heroic, last-ditch Belgian defending. The game looked to be heading for extra-time, but Keith Dyson then fired Newcastle 3-0 up, with only four minutes remaining. Dyson had got the decisive touch, bundling the ball home after a frantic goalmouth scramble, with Anderlecht unable to clear, but United prevented from getting a shot in.

It was a graceless, un-elegant goal, but it was thoroughly dramatic, and all of St James's Park went mad, celebrating their second successive European Semi-final.

The most sensational climax to a European match then took a most devastating turn for the worse. Almost immediately afterwards, with the crowd's noise still heard all over the city, Ollie Burton cleared the ball into the back over an Anderlecht midfield player, and it bounced, ballooned up and back into the path of Nordahl.

The Swedish international forward, who went on to play in the Mexico World Cup Finals, advanced and fired his low, angled shot beyond Iam McFaul's dive, into the Newcastle goal.

The contrast from the glorious noise, to the sheer, stunned silence that immediately followed, was chilling. Men and children were in tears.

Not for the first, or last time, it was the most glorious defeat for Newcastle, who would have played Inter Milan in the Semi-finals, but instead they went out on the away goals rule.

On the following Saturday, a small crowd of 28,227 die-hards watched Newcastle beat Stoke 3-1, after Pop Robson scored two, one from the penalty spot, and Wyn Davies hit their other, as they rose up into sixth place, above Coventry City.

THE ONE HUNDREDTH TYNE-WEAR LEAGUE MATCH

Sunderland hosted Newcastle United, on Good Friday, 27th March 1970, in the historic one hundredth league game between those two fierce rivals, and with nearly 52,000 packing their ground, Roker Park finally attracted a crowd.

Jimmy Smith gave United a first half lead, with a beautiful, dipping chip from the edge of the Sunderland area. With their young attack of Kerr, Hughes and Tueart attacking Newcastle's penalty box like wasps on a country park dustbin, however, Sunderland levelled before the end, through Bobby Park.

Their deserved point, though loudly celebrated by home fans, had left Sunderland still three points below safety, and with only four games to play.

Twenty-four hours later, Sunderland hosted high-flying Derby County, in a must-win home match, but the same eleven that had fought so bravely, just the day before, for a good point against their fierce rivals, must have felt a little flattened when they ran out at Roker Park, to be welcomed by a small crowd of just 18,818.

It was a drop of over 33,000 fans from the Newcastle United game.

Former England international Gordon Harris fired Sunderland into a 1-0 lead, but John McGovern levelled the scores before the break.

Defences reigned supreme during the second half, but the draw did Sunderland no favours, leaving them still three points below Crystal Palace, with just three to play.

Sunderland were presented with a gift, though, on the following Saturday. They travelled to Maine Road to face a Manchester City side without Bell, Lee and Summerbee, who'd been rested for their European Cup Winners' Cup Semi-final, second leg match against Schalke 04.

Dennis Tueart fired a great second half winner, to leave Sunderland level on points with Palace, with one game in hand, and two to play. Unfortunately, though, City also paid that same favour to Crystal Palace, as they travelled to Selhurst Park just two days later, again without their three superstars, and Palace also won 1-0.

Sunderland needed three points from their last two matches, in order to assure survival. On Wednesday 8th April, Everton, the new First Division Champions, arrived on Wearside, and their first choice eleven held Sunderland's young team to a goalless draw, before the Roker roar of 29,000 fans.

Their task was simple, therefore: Sunderland simply had to beat Liverpool, in their final match, to stay up.

After their Fairs Cup exit, and their draw away at Roker Park, Newcastle United drew at Forest on 28th March, but then they lost at home to Burnley on Easter Monday.

In front of their superb 42,550 home crowd, though, on the following Saturday, Newcastle hammered Manchester United 5-1. Pop Robson smashed home a hat-trick, including two penalty kicks given away by United's plodding defence, while Wyn Davies and Jimmy Smith completed their scoring against the former European Champions, who were without Best, Law and Kidd.

It reignited Newcastle's European dreams.

When Coventry City visited St James's Park, however, those dreams had dimmed. As another sensationally eventful, brilliantly entertaining, but inevitably inconsistent season was coming to an end, Newcastle had slipped out of the top five, and they couldn't qualify for the Fairs Cup again.

Only 32,840 watched Newcastle slaughter Coventry City, who'd qualified for Europe, by four goals to nil. Pop Robson, Keith Dyson, Tommy Gibb and Alan Foggon all scored to bring a victorious end to a season of the greatest highs and the most chilling lows, but ultimately, unrewarded; or so it seemed.

Derby County were barred from European competitions, for one season though, for financial irregularities, and so, with third-placed Chelsea having won the FA Cup, Newcastle United, way down in seventh place, had once again qualified for the Fairs Cup for the third successive season.

Iam McFaul, Tommy Gibb and Pop Robson were all ever-presents for Newcastle, and Pop Robson was their top scorer with twenty-four league and cup goals during the 1969-70 season. Wyn Davies and Keith Dyson had also shared twenty-three goals.

Newcastle United's average home crowd was 37,162, while Sunderland's was just 21,790, but their average attendance had only pipped above 20,000 due to their crucial last home game against Liverpool, on Wednesday 15th April, when 33,007 had packed Roker Park's terraces.

SUNDERLAND		LIVERPOOL
Jim Montgomery	1	Ray Clemence
Cecil Irwin	2	Chris Lawler
Martin Harvey	3	Ron Yeats
Colin Todd	4	Tommy Smith
Ritchie Pitt	5	Larry Lloyd
Mick McGiven	6	Emlyn Hughes
Bobby Park	7	Ian Callaghan
Bobby Kerr	8	Doug Livermore
Billy Hughes	9	Alun Evans
Gordon Harris	10	Bobby Graham
Dennis Tueart	11	Peter Thompson

Liverpool had already qualified for the Fairs Cup, so they had nothing to play for, and Bill Shankly even fielded a young, weakened team. Alan Brown should have been able to field his strongest eleven, win the match, and secure First Division football.

It was a scandalous decision not to play Ian Porterfield at any point during that season, purely to illustrate who was in charge of the club. In the end, it proved costly.

Although Shankly had fielded a weakened forward line, his defence was not weak, and certainly not inexperienced, and try as they might, Sunderland couldn't break through Liverpool's tough back line. After half-time, Chris Lawler, the best attacking right back in England, stormed in to put Liverpool 1-0 up.

It was a lead that Liverpool wouldn't ever relinquish, and they condemned Sunderland to Second Division football for only the second time in their eighty year Football League history.

It was a terrible end to an awful season. Mick McGiven was their only ever-present, and he was also Sunderland's second-top scorer with just four goals. The 33,000 crowd applauded their Sunderland team off the field, but they too were culpable in their team's downfall.

Sunderland were never much adrift of safety, so to only attract crowds of 12,000 and 13,000 for First Division matches, when over 50,000 and 40,000 had flocked to their big games, and when they had a team packed with young talent like Todd, Kerr, Hughes and Tueart, was a disgrace, no more, no less.

So, while Newcastle again looked forward to visiting the likes of either Inter Milan or Bayern Munich, during 1970-71, both Sunderland and Middlesbrough had the pleasure of facing each other once again, while also searching out those old AA road maps for the best routes to Luton, Orient, Oxford and Watford.

But, football was entering the sensational Seventies, and the noisy Glam Rock era. *Far beyond the pale horizon,* things were about to change for all three North-east teams.

THE GREATEST CUP FINAL OF ALL

I T WAS ONLY AS RECENTLY as 1967, when Chelsea reached their first FA Cup Final, when they faced Tottenham Hotspur in the first ever all-London Cup Final.

It was also their first ever Wembley Final in their sixty-two year history.

Chelsea had been Champions of the First Division, back in 1955, but that was their first major honour. They then won the League Cup, ten years later, beating Leicester City in a two-legged Final, two years prior to the League Cup Final being deemed worthy of a Wembley Stadium occasion.

It was Tommy Docherty's Chelsea that reached the 1967 FA Cup Final, beating Huddersfield, Brighton, Sheffield United and Sheffield Wednesday, before they met Leeds United at Villa Park, in the Semi-finals. Three minutes before half-time, Charlie Cooke went off on a run from halfway, pursued by Billy Bremner, who was "snapping at his heels," Tommy Docherty remembered.

"Bremner had two or three lunges, but on each occasion Charlie evaded him and carried on with the ball bouncing on the toe of his boot."

Cooke danced away from a final Bremner tackle, before floating the ball into the Leeds box. Tony Hateley launched into the air, like a Harrier, high above his marker, Paul Madeley, and he hung there, before meeting the ball, full-blooded, and burying it past Sprake. The Chelsea fans packed into the huge Holte End exploded into a sea storm of blue and white.

Charlie Cooke, who created that goal with his magical run, pursued by one of the best tacklers, one of the best players, in the history of football, was from St Monans, in the Firth of Forth. He'd played for both Aberdeen and Dundee between 1960 and 1966, while making his Scotland international debut back in 1965, against Wales.

He joined Chelsea in April 1966, for a club record £72,000 transfer fee, having scored thirty-seven goals from 169 Scottish First Division matches for the Dons and Blues.

Cooke replaced Terry Venables in Chelsea's team, and a month later, Venables was sold to Tottenham Hotspur for £80,000, having played more than 200 First Division games at Stamford Bridge.

One year later, Venables was in the Spurs team that faced Chelsea in that Cockney Cup Final. Besides Venables, Spurs boasted an all-star line-up of Greaves, Gilzean, Mullery, Mackay, England, Knowles and Jennings. Chelsea's star Peter Osgood was out, badly injured, for the Final, just as he'd been for the Semi-final.

Peter Osgood, born in Windsor, Berkshire, brought a Royal swagger, and an arrogant air to Chelsea, when he joined, making his debut as a seventeen year old, during their 2-0 League Cup win over Workington, back in 1964.

At six feet and one inch tall, and with a huge presence, Osgood was nicknamed *The Wizard of Os,* and he became as popular at Stamford Bridge as any player in Chelsea's history, but he was also booed by fans of most other teams, which he always loved.

Peter Osgood was disappointingly not included in Alf Ramsey's World Cup Finals squad in 1966, but then, during October 1966, an awful challenge from Blackpool's Emlyn Hughes had broken his leg. Ossie was ruled out for the rest of that season.

Badly missing Peter Osgood, Chelsea were a huge disappointment on the day of the FA Cup Final, playing way, way, way below their best form.

Jimmy Robertson gave Spurs a half-time lead, firing in after Ron Harris had deflected Mullery's left-sided shot into his path, from ten yards out. Then, in the second half, Frank Saul turned on a sixpence, inside the Chelsea area, and fired past Peter Bonetti.

John Hollins hit a shot into the post of Tottenham's goal, and then Jennings could only tip a swerving twenty yard shot from John Boyle into the feet of Bobby Tambling.

Tambling's goal gave Chelsea some slight hope, but Spurs held on as the Blues poured forward, late in the game.

For all their first half dominance and chances, Tottenham definitely deserved the Cup.

Tommy Docherty then resigned as Chelsea manager, on Friday 6th October, after early season defeats to Newcastle (1-5) and Southampton (2-6), as well as home draws with Fulham, Stoke and Coventry, that left Chelsea near to the bottom of the table.

On the day after Docherty had quit, Leeds United hammered Chelsea 7-0 at Elland Road. Dave Sexton, who'd been Docherty's former assistant at Chelsea, but had left back in 1965 to become Orient's manager, was then appointed their new manager.

Dave Sexton signed David Webb from Southampton, during February 1968, his first significant signing for the club. He also began to play Peter Houseman more regularly, after John Boyle, a member of Chelsea's defeated Cup Final team, had been injured.

Battersea-born Peter Houseman had signed for Chelsea in 1963, as a seventeen year old, but he'd played only forty-one First Division games during his first three full seasons, down at the Bridge.

Chelsea enjoyed a revival after Christmas 1967, winning eleven of their eighteen league and cup games. 53,049 filled Stamford Bridge for the visit of fierce rivals Tottenham Hotspur, on Saturday 13th April 1968. Eddie McCreadie was back at left back for Chelsea, having been suspended for their defeat away at Manchester City.

Glaswegian McCreadie had joined Chelsea back in 1962, from East Stirlingshire, for just £5,000, to add fight and steel to Chelsea's promotion push back up to the First Division, behind Division Two Champions Stoke City.

McCreadie would become best remembered, at Stamford Bridge, for his winning goal during the first leg of their 1965 League Cup Final victory. He'd dribbled eighty yards, through almost the whole Leicester City team, before calmly sliding the ball beyond the dive of England keeper Gordon Banks, for their 3-2 home win.

He was most importantly, though, a decent, dependable, and knowledgeable full back in Chelsea's back line, one of their greatest-ever defenders, and Eddie McCreadie had also played at left back during Scotland's famous 3-2 win over England, at Wembley, in their European Championship qualifier back in April 1967.

Against a tour de force Spurs team, with Mackay, Greaves, Jones and Venables complementing the cream of Spurs' great early Seventies' stars, Chelsea were unstoppable, with the passion of a 53,000 home crowd roaring them on.

CHELSEA		TOTTENHAM HOTSPUR
Peter Bonetti	1	Pat Jennings
Ron Harris	2	Phil Beal
Eddie McCreadie	3	Cyril Knowles
John Hollins	4	Alan Mullery
David Webb	5	Mike England
Marvin Hinton	6	Dave Mackay
Charlie Cooke	7	Alan Gilzean
Tommy Baldwin	8	Jimmy Greaves
Peter Osgood	9	Martin Chivers
Alan Birchenall	10	Terry Venables
Peter Houseman	11	Cliff Jones

Tommy Baldwin gave Chelsea an early lead, turning in Charlie Cooke's pass. The Gateshead-born twenty-two year old forward had joined in 1966, as a make-weight in the part exchange deal that sent George Graham from Stamford Bridge to Highbury.

He then went on to score sixteen First Division goals for Chelsea, during 1966-67.

Peter Houseman then repaid Dave Sexton's faith, by dispossessing Phil Beal, and then driving in a shot from the edge of the Tottenham area, which rifled the ball inside Pat Jennings' near post, for a great 2-0 win.

Tommy Baldwin and Peter Osgood shared eight league goals, as Chelsea won six of their last eight matches, to end up in sixth place, only ten points behind Champions Manchester City, and the top team in London, despite their poor start to the season.

Ian Hutchinson had been turned down, as a teenager, by Nottingham Forest, so he signed for non-league Burton Albion instead, close to his home town of Derby.

He scored nineteen goals in just forty-nine games for The Brewers, and attracted attention from Chelsea. Dave Sexton paid £5,000 for him, in July 1968, and Forest's stupid great loss was Chelsea's greater gain, as he became famed, and hated, for his competitive physical presence.

Hutchinson had an aggressive aerial dominance, with his effective heading abilities, but he became really famous for his very, very long throw-ins.

On his league debut for Chelsea, on Saturday 5th October 1968, Ian Hutchinson, still only twenty years old, had launched across a series of hugely long throw-ins that actually reached the opposite sides of the opposition's penalty area.

They totally confused the 32,000 Stamford Bridge crowd, unfamiliar to such an *avant-garde* tactic, but more importantly, they completely unsettled Ipswich Town's defence, and the vastly experienced Billy Baxter accidentally diverted a long throw past his own keeper.

A half-hour earlier, John Hollins had given Chelsea the lead, but Birchenall scored late on, to secure their 3-1 win and lift Chelsea up to fifth in the First Division.

John Hollins joined as an apprentice in 1961, before signing professionally prior to the 1963-64 season. He made his Chelsea debut, aged only seventeen, in September 1963, during their League Cup defeat at Swindon Town. He secured a regular first team place though, as Chelsea enjoyed their first season back in the First Division, achieving a top five place for the first time since winning the league, nine years earlier.

John Hollins, at only five feet, and seven and three-quarter inches tall, had a superb centre of gravity; he was not only sublimely balanced but also wonderfully calm. He eventually became widely regarded as a top-rated holding midfield player, although he was originally a wing half.

Some wing halves became centre backs during the modern era of 4-4-2, or 4-3-3 formations, at the end of the Sixties, but many became midfield players, a brand new football term. Hollins was somewhere in between, like Bremner or Mullery, who protected the defence, but he could hold onto the ball, rarely giving it away cheaply.

He could also run with it, though, easing past opponents, just like Bremner and Mullery. Better at closing down opponents, narrowing angles, and preventing forward passes, John Hollins didn't need to steam in, making aggressive tackles, giving away unnecessary free-kicks or collecting needless bookings.

After Chelsea's 3-1 win over Ipswich, they lost just nine of their next twenty-six games, during which time, Dave Sexton paid £70,000 for centre-half John Dempsey, in the middle of January 1969. Dempsey had played 149 league matches for Fulham, who were on their way down to Division Three.

Dempsey was a local lad, born in Hampstead, just a couple of miles north of Chelsea, but he'd already played half a dozen games for the Republic of Ireland, due to his parents' birthplaces. Still only twenty-two, Dempsey's debut for Chelsea was horrible, though, as both Ron Davies and Mike Channon took him and Dave Webb apart at The Dell. Southampton hammered Chelsea 5-0, on Saturday 1st February.

Nevertheless, that disaster apart, Chelsea enjoyed a great run into the spring of 69, reaching the FA Cup Quarter-finals, but they lost at home to the holders West Brom. With Chelsea in fifth place in Division One, a heaving, thronging mass of 60,436 packed Stamford Bridge to welcome Manchester United on 15th March.

It was the third-last sixty thousand crowd to ever squash onto the vast, crumbling Stamford Bridge terraces. With the cream of British football among the visiting team, Best, Charlton, Law, Stiles, Crerand and Kidd, it was United's centre-half Steve James who opened the scoring, before goals from Webb, Hutchinson and Bobby Tambling gave Chelsea a great win under an electric atmosphere.

Late on, Willie Morgan was impeded by Eddie McCreadie, but Denis Law's penalty kick was too little, too late. Chelsea held on for their 3-2 win.

Their great finish, at the end of that 1968-69 season, had sent them well clear into fifth place, five points above sixth-placed Spurs. Chelsea's defensive statistics were not as impressive as Leeds, Arsenal, Liverpool or Everton, who'd all conceded less than a goal per game, but they were still decent.

Chelsea's goal scoring record was second only to Everton, though, and they enjoyed their best goal average since 1964, when they finished in a close third place behind Manchester United and Leeds.

Bobby Tambling and Tommy Baldwin had combined for thirty-three First Division goals, while Ossie and Alan Birchenall contributed twenty-one goals between them.

Although Ian Hutchinson was the find of their season, scoring six goals in just fourteen starts, at just twenty years old, Chelsea's stability was provided by their four regular defenders. Goalkeeper Peter Bonetti, captain Ron Harris, David Webb and Eddie McCreadie had missed just seven out of a total 216 league and cup games, between them. Webb had been ever-present and was voted Chelsea's Player of the Year, while Bonetti missed only one out of their fifty-four matches.

Peter Bonetti had made his debut back in 1960, as an eighteen year old, and by the end of 1968-69, he'd already played 347 First Division games for Chelsea, at just twenty-seven years old.

Due to his safe handling from crosses, his good positional sense, and his graceful style of movement, Bonetti became known as **The Cat.**

His one-armed throw was among the very first, of all modern goalkeepers, and he could reach the opposite half of the pitch. He won his fifth international cap for England during their 1-0 win over Holland, in Amsterdam, on 5th November 1969.

Ron Harris played in Chelsea's 1961 FA Youth Cup Final victory over Everton, alongside Terry Venables, and he was promoted to the first team during 1961-62, making his debut against Sheffield Wednesday, aged seventeen.

Harris was appointed as captain of Chelsea in January 1966, aged only twenty-one.

At just five feet and eight inches tall, he was one of the smallest players to play in central defence, but his uncompromising, aggressive, clever, and totally focussed mentality, not to mention his rough tackling, more than made up for his lack of height.

He'd earned the nickname **Chopper,** and became renowned as one of the hardest defenders to ever play in the First Division.

In 1967, Ron Harris led Chelsea out against Spurs, in the FA Cup Final, becoming the youngest ever Cup Final captain, at just twenty-two, but David Nish, of Leicester City, broke that record just two years later.

Chopper was a real London boy, though, from Hackney, and he became best friends with Ossie.

"Just remembering the strokes Ossie used to pull," Chopper told Jim White of the Daily Telegraph, in 2010, "you wouldn't believe it, what that lad got up to.

You could never ever do that now," he laughed.

Ossie had the season of his career, during 1969-70, which was possibly also the very season when Chelsea had their best ever team. Peter Osgood was Chelsea's top goal scorer, in their unstoppable attacking double act with Ian Hutchinson.

That season had, however, started really quite poorly. By 20th September, Chelsea had won only two of their opening eleven First Division matches, and they lay in a lowly position, down in thirteenth place, just five points above the relegation places.

One bright light, though, a new star, *a speck of blue up in the sky* for Chelsea, had made his league debut in that 5-0 spanking by Southampton, back in February.

He'd captained Chelsea's youth team in 1968-69, and then started four of Chelsea's first eleven games of the new season. In one of those games, against Burnley on Wednesday 17th September, Chelsea won 2-0. In the other three games during which he started, Chelsea did not lose.

In the match immediately following Chelsea's win over Burnley, they travelled to Leeds, and Dave Sexton left him out. Leeds United won, through goals from Giles and Lorimer, and Sexton realised he couldn't leave him out of the team.

He could not do without Alan Hudson.

Alan Hudson was a supremely skilled, brilliantly creative midfield player, who'd joined his home town team as an apprentice, in 1966. Chelsea-born and bred, and one of six Londoners in their regular 1969-70 team, he inspired Chelsea to a thirty-one match run, between late September and late March, during which they lost only three games, and they scored seventy-four goals, but conceded only thirty-one.

This was one of the greatest footballing periods, if not the greatest period, of Chelsea's history, and it began with a 2-2 draw against Derby County, with Houseman and Hollins both scoring.

Alan Hudson was an electric talent; colourful, imaginative, incisive, and very tough to tackle. He could read a game and pass the ball as well as anybody of his time, as well as anybody in the World.

The Alan Hudson "drag-back" became his famed, iconic action. He'd show the ball to an opponent, asking for a tackle, before dragging the ball back, and then forward again, before gliding past his marker.

It was a move that was impossible to stop without giving away a free-kick.

On Saturday 6th December, Chelsea went to Old Trafford, not for the last time during that 1969-70 season, and in front of 50,000, Alan Hudson outplayed George Best, as Chelsea won 2-0, thanks to the mighty Ian Hutchinson's first half brace.

Chelsea then defeated Man City 3-1, before outplaying Southampton in another 3-1 win, on Boxing Day. Hutchinson scored two more, and Webb headed in their other goal, to take revenge on the Saints for eleven months earlier.

With a club record 49,498 crowd packed inside Selhurst Park, fourth-placed Chelsea visited Crystal Palace on the day after Boxing Day, Saturday 27th December.

Yes, Selhurst Park was indeed once a great, vast ground, not the bland, Meccano-built stadium it is now, with a Supermarket in place of where the mighty, two-tiered Whitehorse Lane End used to be.

Chelsea fielded their very best-ever eleven against Palace; Peter Bonetti, David Webb, Eddie McCreadie, John Hollins, John Dempsey, Ron Harris, Charlie Cooke, Alan Hudson, Peter Osgood, Ian Hutchinson, Peter Houseman, and substitute Tommy Baldwin. Chelsea's best ever starting eleven, playing at full pelt, were in their very best form, in front of the first of two Club Record Crowds to watch them, that season.

With the scores at 1-1 at half-time, Chelsea romped home after the break.

Ossie fired a magnificent four goals, and Peter Houseman scored another, in their 5-1 win that lifted Chelsea above Liverpool, up to third place, and only seven points behind leaders Everton.

The Blues continued to win, four from their next six, and by the end of February, the title race was between the top three teams, with Chelsea nine points behind the leaders, Everton and Leeds, but with two games in hand.

In the FA Cup, Chelsea hammered Birmingham City 3-0 in the Third round (Osgood, Hutchinson 2), but they were then held to a 2-2 draw by Burnley, at Stamford Bridge. Martin Dobson's brace had cancelled out goals by both Hollins and Osgood.

32,000 packed Turf Moor, for the replay on Tuesday 27th January, and Burnley were winning 1-0, thanks to Ralph Coates' first half blast, when Peter Houseman collected the ball, deep inside his own half.

Houseman went on a superb, individual, dribbling run through Burnley's midfield, hurdling and side-stepping challenges by O'Neil, Dobson and Merrington, before he smashed a shot, from the edge of Burnley's penalty area, into the top corner of Peter Mellor's goal. Houseman then crossed for Tommy Baldwin to poke Chelsea 2-1 up.

Houseman then also fired in Chelsea's third goal, sending them into the last sixteen.

Tommy Baldwin, Chelsea's top goal scorer from 1966-67, was reduced to substitute and covering appearances by 1969-70. On this occasion, though, against Burnley, he'd replaced the suspended Peter Osgood.

He was the best substitute in the First Division at the start of the Seventies.

In the Fifth round, another huge crowd of nearly fifty thousand, 48,479, had filled Selhurst Park, as Chelsea again thrashed Crystal Palace, on Saturday 7th February. Osgood, Dempsey, Houseman and Hutchinson fired them to a 4-1 away win, and into the last eight.

33,572 then packed Loftus Road, in the Quarter-finals, on Saturday 21st February, QPR's all-time club record home crowd for their match with Chelsea. Osgood smashed in a very arrogant hat-trick, and Webb scored another, as Chelsea breezed past their West London neighbours and into the Semi-finals with a 4-2 away win.

After their 3-0 win away at Coventry, at the end of February, with Baldwin, Webb and Hudson all scoring, Chelsea were held to a 1-1 draw by Nottingham Forest, before beating Stoke City 1-0 (Charlie Cooke), on Tuesday 17th March.

Four days later, 55,200 packed into White Hart Lane for their FA Cup Semi-final against Watford, who'd shocked Liverpool in the Quarter-finals. Terry Garbett gave Chelsea a shock in the first half, but David Webb's header made it 1-1 at the break.

Peter Houseman then crossed from the left for Osgood to head Chelsea ahead, before then scoring twice himself, the second after another great run around two Watford defenders, and then finally, Hutchinson made it 5-1.

A massive crowd of 61,479, a crushed and crowded mass squeezed into Stamford Bridge for the visit of Manchester United, a week later. This was a transitional United, though; they still had Best, Charlton, Law, Stiles and Crerand, but they also had Morgan, Sartori, Burns and Paul Edwards.

Eddie McCreadie was missing for one of only four games of that season, here, so Chopper Harris moved over to left back, and Marvin Hinton returned to the centre of Chelsea's defence, for his twenty-fourth game of the season.

Marvin Hinton was born in Norwood, near to the Crystal Palace BBC radio mast, and he'd played 131 league games for Charlton Athletic, before signing for Chelsea back in 1963. He was thirty years old by 1970, though, and after the arrivals of both David Webb and John Dempsey, he'd become more of a squad player, having missed just ten out of a possible 126 First Division matches, between 1964 and 1967.

Hinton had even been a member of Alf Ramsey's provisional forty man squad for the 1966 World Cup Finals, but he didn't make the final twenty-two.

Alan Hudson, in a two-man midfield, alongside John Hollins, once again ran the show, as Chelsea's fluent 4-2-4 formation swamped United's discordant, dysfunctional team. Their two wide players, Charlie Cooke and Peter Houseman, had Francis Burns and Paul Edwards chasing them all afternoon.

Ian Hutchinson headed in their first, and then he volleyed Osgood's knock-down past Stepney for a 2-0 half-time lead. Chelsea pressed not so hard in the second half, preserving their energies, but Ossie's great shot from ten yards was brilliantly turned aside by Stepney.

Willie Morgan pounced on some ponderous defending to make the score 2-1, a result that really flattered United, because in truth they'd been totally thrashed again.

Four days later, Hutchinson and Osgood both scored again, and Alan Hudson chipped in a third, during their 3-1 win over Sheffield Wednesday, and Chelsea were in strong pursuit of second-placed Leeds, with just six games to play.

	PL	W	D	L	F	A	PTS
Everton	37	25	7	5	62	32	57
Leeds United	36	20	14	2	75	33	54
CHELSEA	36	18	13	5	61	37	49
Derby County	37	19	7	11	55	34	45
Liverpool	37	17	11	9	59	39	45
Newcastle Utd	37	15	11,	11	45	30	41
Coventry City	35	16	9	10	47	38	41

A master-class footballing performance from the supreme Champions-to-be Everton, on Saturday 28th March, then buried any slight hopes Chelsea had of winning a League and Cup double. Joe Royle scored twice, while Howard Kendall, Alan Ball and Alan Whittle had also netted in Everton's 5-2 hammering of Chelsea's wonder boys.

At The Hawthorns on the following Monday, Easter Monday, it was a black day in the Black Country. One hour into the game, Alan Hudson, playing his thirty-third consecutive league and cup game, while still only eighteen years old, jumped up for a harmless-looking ball.

As Hudson landed, he went over on his ankle, and he felt like it had been half-severed inside. The pain was absolutely excruciating. It was a major injury that ruled him out of Chelsea's FA Cup Final against Leeds, a fortnight later, as well as strong contention for England's 1970 World Cup squad.

Even though Alan Hudson did return to action, just five months later, during August 1970, he was never the same player again. "I was not going to recover from this one ever," admitted Hudson. "Nowadays, surgery is done arthroscopically and you get back much sooner. More importantly, you recover... I never did."

Albion had beaten Chelsea 3-1, through goals from Tony Brown (2), and Jeff Astle, the First Division's leading scorer, with Ian Hutchinson scoring his fifteenth league goal of the season, in reply.

With the title race over, and now, only second place to fight for, Chelsea prepared for the FA Cup Final, on Saturday 11th April.

THE GREATEST CUP FINAL OF ALL

Chelsea versus Leeds was a dynamic clash of superb styles. It was the boys from the Kings Road, in Savile Row suits, and designer shirts, against the Northern bite and grit of Leeds, in plaid suits from *Man at Burton.* Chelsea came from the Champagne swigging club lifestyle of Swinging London, while Leeds got together for carpet bowls and bingo nights, under Don Revie's fatherly organisation.

More importantly, the two teams had genuinely disliked each other, despite respecting each other's achievements.

Ian Hutchinson and Jack Charlton just disliked each other.

CHELSEA		LEEDS UNITED
Peter Bonetti	1	Gary Sprake
David Webb	2	Paul Madeley
Eddie McCreadie	3	Terry Cooper
John Hollins	4	Billy Bremner
John Dempsey	5	Jack Charlton
Ron Harris	6	Norman Hunter
Tommy Baldwin	7	Peter Lorimer
Peter Houseman	8	Allan Clarke
Peter Osgood	9	Mick Jones
Ian Hutchinson	10	Johnny Giles
Charlie Cooke	11	Eddie Gray
Marvin Hinton	12	Mick Bates

Tommy Baldwin came in for Alan Hudson; that was the one obvious decision for Dave Sexton. Other than that, it was the same great team that had hammered Palace, during the Festive period.

On another disgraceful, patched up Wembley pitch, after another *Horse of the Year Show* held during the week, forty-seven year old grandfather Eric Jennings, from Stourbridge in Worcestershire, was refereeing his last ever competitive match.

Bonetti caught a good long cross from Lorimer, on the right, and he threw the ball, long, up to Osgood, near halfway, but Charlton dispossessed him, and then he was immediately hacked down by Osgood, smirking.

Charlton was certainly not smirking. He was livid, and said a few words towards Osgood, all beginning with *F* and *B*.

Cooper's free-kick was headed back to Madeley, who crossed for Clarke, six yards out. Sniffer's header was caught by Bonetti. Clarke was offside anyway, but Bonetti wasn't to know.

Madeley put in a good tackle on Cooke, thirty-five yards out, then he played a sweet diagonal ball inside to Lorimer, free of McCreadie.

Peter Lorimer's eighteen yard blast was tipped over the bar by Bonetti.

Bonetti then leapt five feet into the air to clutch Eddie Gray's right sided corner.

Cooke and Hollins combined down the Chelsea left, setting up Houseman in space, but tracked by Charlton. Houseman's left wing cross was superbly headed behind by a diving Madeley, with Baldwin set to shoot past Sprake. It was beautiful defensive work by the calm and composed Paul Madeley.

Dempsey, under pressure from Jones inside his own six yard box, flicked Lorimer's long, left-sided cross behind for another Leeds United corner. Eddie Gray's kick was headed goalwards by Jack Charlton's towering leap. Both Harris and McCreadie, on the goal line, swung a kick at the ball, but it just rolled beneath them, and over the line.

1-0 up and on the attack again, Leeds drove the ball towards the right of Chelsea's area, and Madeley's cross for Allan Clarke, six yards out, was headed clear by the leaping Webb. Houseman and Hollins then calmly carried the ball out of their own area. Hutchinson, just inside his own half, played a lovely reverse pass back to the galloping Hollins, now on the left wing.

Hollins played a short pass to Cooke, five yards further forward. Cooke was held up by Hunter, so he passed simply back to Hollins, about thirty yards out. Hollins crossed diagonally towards Hutchinson on the right corner of Leeds' six yard box, and Hutch's header down to Osgood was hit, first time, by Ossie, twelve yards out, past the sprawling Sprake, but Charlton turned and stretched, and just cleared the shot off his goal line, and away to safety, via Hunter.

It was a superb, sublime nine man move by Chelsea, from a goal line clearance in their own six yard box, to a superb goal line clearance off out of the Leeds goal, in just thirty seconds, and with Leeds having eight men behind the ball, fully in shape. After a dominant Leeds start, Chelsea were now getting back into the game, and we had a Cup Final on our hands.

Osgood found Cooke, on the edge of the Leeds area. Cooke outwitted Madeley, before firing over the bar from twelve yards.

Four minutes before half-time, Charlton slid through the back of Osgood, just inside his own half, retribution for his own earlier pain. From the free-kick, Harris played a simple ball to Eddie McCreadie. McCreadie lofted a right-footed ball up to Hutchinson, on the edge of the Leeds area. Hutchinson flicked it back to Houseman, pursued by Bremner, but Peter Houseman's swerving, left-footed shot, from twenty-five yards out, crept under Gary Sprake's dive, at his left post.

Just as with Leeds United's goal, the ball just rolled over the line.

Houseman stood still, with one arm aloft, and he was subsequently mobbed by all of his team-mates, as Mick Jones just fell to his knees in despair, and Sprake pulled his shorts up tightly around his green jersey, to hide inside.

John Hollins then hacked down Eddie Gray, right on the stroke of the half-time whistle.

As Chelsea began the second half, on the attack, Cooper dispossessed Baldwin inside his own area, and he sprinted away like Nijinsky, before lofting a long pass up to Jones, on halfway. John Dempsey just flattened the Leeds striker. Mick Jones had enjoyed ten minutes rest from Dempsey's close attentions, but here it was, back again.

Osgood played in Hutchinson, on the edge of the Leeds area, and Hutch ran at Cooper, until, just as he was about to shoot, Sprake flew out to the edge of his six yard box and smothered the ball, but it ran loose again. Hutchinson regained possession, as Madeley, Charlton and Cooper all guarded their goal line. He played the ball back to Houseman, on the edge of the Leeds area. House-man hurdled Bremner's diving tackle, then found Hutchinson again, eight yards out, but again Sprake smothered Hutchinson's shot, although he was once again unable to land on the ball.

Osgood darted in, and he shot at goal, from six yards out, but Hunter cleared the ball off his line. Eddie Gray finally ran the ball to safety, out of his area, before he was fouled by Hutchinson.

Again, Chelsea had created the most wonderful and sustained period of attacking pressure, but Leeds' defence had survived.

Baldwin flicked Houseman's right wing cross, deftly, past Charlton, but Sprake got his right hand to the ball, on his goal line, and he fell gratefully on the ball.

As Clarke and Baldwin battled for the ball, Harris slid in late on Bremner, and Bremner throt-tled Chopper's neck with both hands, and pushed him away. The two captains, and the two hard-est men on the pitch, got into a tangle, not the first and nowhere near the last of what was turning into the tastiest of all Cup Finals.

Referee Mr Jennings just signalled play on, so Clarke and Giles combined to set up Gray, on the edge of Chelsea's box. Eddie Gray side stepped Webb, and he cracked the ball onto Bonetti's crossbar, with the ball rebounding back to the edge of the area, so fierce was Gray's shot. Harris calmly headed the ball back into Bonetti's arms.

Time after time, Eddie Gray had totally roasted Webb, leaving him behind, behind, and on his behind, on the appalling surface, with his silky skills, quick feet and wonderful control. After the match, Gray was unsurprisingly given the Man of the Match award.

Bremner picked up play, just inside Chelsea's half, and then, as Houseman closed him down, thirty yards out, he lofted a ball down the right wing for Giles to chase.

Johnny Giles crossed for the flying Clarke to head the ball against the foot of Bonetti's right post, from eight yards out. The ball bounced through the mud, and Mick Jones hammered the ball back in, from ten yards, off the far post, and into the net.

With just over five minutes left, Leeds had surely won the Cup?

Leeds United had kept twenty-two clean sheets during 1969-70. All they had to do was keep Chelsea out for six more minutes. They didn't even last two.

A couple of minutes later, with the match fading away, Bremner and Clarke took the ball into Chelsea's half, again, when they might have been better just keeping possession and awaiting an opening, but Bremner sent Madeley off down the right wing. Houseman tackled Madeley, and the ball rolled out to McCreadie, who passed forward to Cooke, with Leeds still well forward, as Chelsea counter-attacked.

Hollins, Harris, Osgood and Houseman worked the ball to thirty yards from the Leeds United goal, and Jack Charlton, under pressure, was forced to obstruct Osgood.

Charlie Cooke took a short free-kick, out wide on the Chelsea left, to John Hollins. Hollins curled in a cross for Hutchinson, six yards out, and Hutch flicked the ball past Sprake, and inside the near post.

Chelsea's players went wild, as Leeds sank to the mud.

On a Wembley pitch that more resembled Southport's beach, as the game went into extra-time, Hutchinson flicked McCreadie's long ball down for Dempsey to fire just over Sprake's bar.

Madeley ran the ball out of defence, and he passed out to Clarke, wide right. Allan Clarke carried play ten yards into Chelsea's half, and then played a wonderful pass across to the brilliant Gray, on the opposite flank. Eddie Gray ran at substitute Marvin Hinton, on for Ron Harris, and he beat him. Gray crossed from the bye-line, and Clarke smashed a volley goalwards, but David Webb's Kung Fu kick, on his own goal-line, had saved a certain goal, brilliantly deflecting the ball over for a corner kick.

Gray crossed for Lorimer to head back into the path of Clarke, who shot against the crossbar, from just twelve yards out.

That was the third time in the match, that Leeds had hit the woodwork.

Cooke ran loose, in the second period of extra-time, and he beat Charlton, before playing out to Houseman, wide left. Houseman's deep cross was headed just inches wide by Osgood, while closely marked by Terry Cooper, who then went down on the bye-line, suffering from cramp in his right leg.

Peter Osgood returned to help out his England teammate, and he received a grateful pat on his back from another England colleague, Hunter, for his honest efforts.

Lorimer freed Madeley on the right of Chelsea's penalty area. Madeley dummied, and then beat McCreadie, before crossing for Jones at the far post. Jones jumped above both Hollins and Dempsey, to head at goal, but Bonetti leapt like a Cat, and he grabbed the ball from just under his crossbar.

From their own penalty area, under attack from Terry Cooper, Chelsea then launched another seven man counter attack of slick passing and intelligent running.

Cooke and McCreadie dispossessed Cooper, and Cooke ran away with the ball. Baldwin, on halfway, played to Hollins, into the Leeds half, to Hutchinson, running down the left at the Leeds penalty area. Hutchinson crossed for Baldwin on the right side of the area. Baldwin centred for Peter Houseman to fire, left-footed, but Sprake dived to make a good two-handed save, turning the ball around his left-hand post.

Warm handshakes between both teams, and then a joint lap of honour followed the match, after a brilliant Cup Final, preceding what became one of the fiercest and most fiery games in English football history.

For the first time since 1912, the FA Cup Final went to a replay.

Eighteen days later, after Leeds had been narrowly beaten by Celtic, in the European Cup Semi-finals, a massive crowd totally filled Old Trafford.

62,078 filled Old Trafford to its absolute capacity for the first FA Cup Final to be decided away from Wembley, since Wembley Stadium became home to the FA Cup Final back in 1923.

The television audience that night, Wednesday 29th April 1970, was 28.49 million.

It is still the sixth most watched television programme in British television history.

It was also the largest global TV audience for a football match between two club sides, and that record still stands today. In an age of Sky TV and multi-channel high-definition televisions, that World record will never be beaten, almost certainly.

For the replay, Don Revie replaced the injured, and erratic Gary Sprake with his twenty-two year old Leeds-born goalkeeper, David Harvey. Dave Sexton also switched Ron Harris over to right back, while pairing David Webb with John Dempsey in central defence, so Chopper could hopefully contain Eddie Gray's electric talents more effectively.

LEEDS UNITED		CHELSEA
David Harvey	1	Peter Bonetti
Paul Madeley	2	Ron Harris
Terry Cooper	3	Eddie McCreadie
Billy Bremner	4	John Hollins
Jack Charlton	5	John Dempsey
Norman Hunter	6	David Webb
Peter Lorimer	7	Tommy Baldwin
Allan Clarke	8	Charlie Cooke
Mick Jones	9	Peter Osgood
Johnny Giles	10	Ian Hutchinson
Eddie Gray	11	Peter Houseman
Mick Bates	12	Marvin Hinton

For the 7.30 pm kick-off, Chelsea slightly moderated their kit, noticeable only on colour TV sets, playing in yellow socks, as opposed to white at Wembley, and yellow numbers on the backs of their Blue shirts, and yellow stripes on their Blue shorts, as opposed to white at Wembley. Mr Jennings, the Worcestershire grandfather, again took charge of the game, enjoying an unexpected extra match, before retiring.

With the magnificent Old Trafford ground so full of passionate supporters of either team, and with far fewer FA dignitaries watching as neutrals, the atmosphere was terrific, electric, and the roar that met both teams was a special sound to hear.

Also, with a tighter, more compact pitch, there was more of a First Division match feel about the game, for both sides, with no hiding place. Straight from kick-off, Lorimer galloped up the right, and he beat McCreadie, playing a hard one-two with Clarke, but somehow, his rocket shot ricocheted off Bonetti, onto Dempsey, and back into Bonetti's arms.

Eddie Gray launched himself into action, and he cut away from the left wing, running through the middle, and just as he was about to send Allan Clarke free, he was scythed down by an unapologetic Webb.

Bonetti rose high above Mick Jones to grab Johnny Giles' free-kick. Charlie Cooke then cut down Bremner, while in possession. Bremner just lay on the green turf, playing the fifty-fourth match of his season, before taking the free-kick himself.

After eight minutes, Chelsea threatened seriously for the first time, after forcing Cooper to give away a throw-in by the right wing corner flag. Hutchinson launched a huge throw over to the Leeds far post, but David Harvey leapt and secured an assured first touch, grabbing the ball with both hands, above Tommy Baldwin's challenge.

Johnny Giles upended Osgood, sending Chelsea's star rolling on the dry mud in the Old Trafford centre circle. Osgood got up, said nothing, and simply advanced to await Dempsey's free-kick. Ossie jumped to head the long, long ball, but Madeley gave him a slight bump in his back, sending him to ground again. Peter Osgood bounced back up, gesturing at Mr Jennings, who'd actually awarded a goal kick to Leeds.

Brian Moore gave a slight mention to Osgood's penalty appeal.

Mr Jennings gave his nose a blow, and a wipe, in response to Ossie's somewhat justified penalty appeal. The grandkids back home didn't want to see any snot.

David Webb chopped Clarke by the left side corner flag, after the ball had gone, but again, no free-kick was awarded by Mr Jennings.

Even the minor tackles were taking their toll on bones and muscles, as the match was played at a pace more suited to today's Premier League matches.

Harris got a bite out of Jones; Baldwin got a bite out of Cooper; and Harris, Cooke and Hutchinson all got a bite out of Eddie Gray.

To illustrate the sheer quality on display during this scintillating Cup Final, nearly one third of Sir Alf Ramsey's 1970 World Cup squad was formed of players from these two teams: Bonetti, Cooper, Charlton, Hunter, Osgood and Clarke.

Considering there were six Scots, two Irishmen and one Welshmen playing, and also, Paul Madeley eventually pulled out of Ramsey's initial forty man squad, the quality was of an unprecedented high standard.

Osgood obstructed Gray for a foul that *was* given by Mr Jennings, just to the left of the Chelsea penalty area, and forty yards from goal. Johnny Giles' free-kick was lofted high to the penalty spot, and Bonetti climbed high to claim the ball, but Jack Charlton was definitely impeded, blocked, obstructed, and forced to the ground by Hutchinson, who'd made no play for the ball, only for the player. Again, no foul was awarded by Eric Jennings, much to Big Jack's vociferous annoyance.

Giles then winded Harris, out on the Chelsea right, another foul that was given. A scrappy, scruffy scramble of play followed, as the late Spring sun sunk behind the Old Trafford Main Stand,

---

and shadows lengthened over the pitch. Then, after 24 minutes, Eddie Gray took on Harris, beating Chopper's challenge, and he crossed for Jones to flick goalwards, from six yards out, only for Bonetti to save brilliantly at his near post.

Webb made a superb defensive tackle on Clarke, inside the Chelsea area, that Bonetti again cleared up. John Dempsey then played a bad ball back in, from the left back position, towards Bonetti, and Lorimer intercepted to steal the ball from out of Bonetti's hands. Lorimer fired goalwards, but McCreadie rescued the situation, and he cleared to the halfway line.

Boos rang out over Old Trafford, twenty-two years before the back-pass was outlawed, as Terry Cooper passed back to Harvey, having missed an initial high ball. David Harvey's long drop-kick was misjudged by Dempsey, and Lorimer's first touch then beat McCreadie. Lorimer's good cross to Clarke and Jones, was clasped by Peter Bonetti, though, at his near post.

" Don Revie must be delighted with the way his Leeds defenders are playing at the moment, a really good, solid unit," Brian Moore suggested, just prior to Bremner feeding Clarke on the edge of the area. Clarke turned Webb, before shooting just wide of Bonetti's right post.

Allan Clarke side-stepped Webb's scything challenge, just inside his own half, and then he hurdled Cooke, before gliding past Dempsey inside Chelsea's half, on full gallop. Clarke slipped the ball forward to Mick Jones, who ran to the edge of the penalty area, between both Hollins and McCreadie, and then he fired past Bonetti, from twelve yards out, into the top left corner of Chelsea's goal.

It was a superlative goal, created and scored by the best strike partnership in England.

Ron Harris took away Eddie Gray's left leg, three minutes before half-time, and the Leeds left winger needed treatment, while Harris pleaded his case to Allan Clarke.

Hutchinson then went in late on Gray, who stamped on Hutch's calf in reply, so Hutch grabbed Gray's midriff and spun him round, to Gray's protestations.

It all went on behind Mr Jennings' back, so it just wasn't seen.

Peter Bonetti, heavily bandaged on his left knee, caught a snap shot from Mick Jones, who'd beaten Dempsey on the right side of Chelsea's area.

Then, Osgood beat Cooper, but he was dispossessed by Jack Charlton. Osgood then slid in behind Charlton, putting the ball out for a throw-in, but he tapped Big Jack's ankles as he did so. Charlton got back up and shoulder charged Osgood, with his fists showing.

"The referee surely is going to take some action here," Brian Moore incredulously queried. Mr Jennings, though, was in a "very lenient frame of mind."

He booked no players, but he did award a free-kick to Leeds.

Ian Hutchinson was taken down by Bremner's scything foul, but he had a good kick at the ankles of the Scottish international captain, in reply.

Eddie Gray fired just a few inches over Bonetti's bar, from thirty yards, as Leeds piled on the pressure. Hutchinson slung Bremner over as he cleared, from the edge of the Leeds area, and Bremner chopped back at Hutchinson's calves. Giles went in hard on Webb. Bremner took out Osgood, after the ball had been played, on halfway. Hutchinson ran in, and flattened Bremner, with Osgood still lying on the ground.

This was war!

Referee Eric Jennings booked Ian Hutchinson for his retaliation on Bremner, the first and the only booking, of one of the most physically bruising Cup Finals.

Chasing a long ball out of the Leeds defence, Eddie McCreadie wonderfully hooked the ball back over his left shoulder to safety. It was top drawer defending.

He had Mick Jones galloping behind him, awaiting any slight mistake for a chance to put Leeds United two-nil up.

Hunter won the ball, cleanly, off Charlie Cooke, so Cooke chopped him down in return, conceding a free-kick.

Hunter didn't really mind, though. It just meant more precious seconds used up.

Time was beginning to run out for Chelsea, but equally, Leeds were unable to take control of the ball.

Tommy Baldwin miscontrolled Bonetti's throw-out, though, and Cooper pounced, then dribbled in, shooting from fifteen yards. Bonetti turned the shot just around his right post for a Leeds corner. Peter Lorimer's corner swung over Bonetti's bar, but Charlton sunk to the turf, after a bang on his thigh from Webb, as the ball flew in.

As Don Revie lit a huge cigar on the Leeds United bench, Bonetti launched a long goal-kick. Osgood, Hutchinson, Cooke and Harris set up the immaculate Hollins for a strong shot from twenty yards. The ball flew narrowly wide of Harvey's post.

John Hollins then set up Osgood, inside the Leeds half. Osgood passed short to Hutchinson, and Cooke took over on a diagonal run, before lobbing the ball, from thirty yards out, over the Leeds defence, and into the area, where Osgood, having stolen five yards of space from Charlton, sent his diving header past David Harvey.

With only twelve minutes remaining, Chelsea were level.

With parity restored, the tackles again flew in, thick and fast. Baldwin hacked down a furious Hunter, who glared at his fellow Geordie with his right fist clenched.

Harris then headed Jones' header, from Gray's corner, off his own goal-line.

Eddie McCreadie, in attempting to clear Cooper's left wing cross, flew in, head high and two-footed, onto Billy Bremner's skull, inside Chelsea's area, with only seven minutes left.

Amazingly, Mr Jennings waved play on, while McCreadie tried to tend to the grounded Bremner, lying in absolute agony. Bonetti tentatively gestured McCreadie back towards play, as Chelsea piled forward in counter-attack. Osgood laid the ball off to Hutchinson, on the right side of the Leeds United area. Hutch shot the ball hard, but just wide, into Harvey's side netting, while Bremner was still clutching his face, on the ground inside Chelsea's penalty area.

After he'd got back up, following a couple of minutes of treatment, Bremner was again hacked down from behind, by Ian Hutchinson.

Bremner lost his temper at this point, and he went to both the referee and to Hutch, demanding some justice, besides a cheap free-kick. Hutchinson responded with a hand-yap-yapping gesture right in Bremner's face, implying that the Leeds captain was talking too much.

Billy Bremner certainly hadn't been talking too much during this match.

"You could just get the feeling," Brian Moore suggested, "that this game is one that could just teeter over the edge."

From that Leeds free-kick, Lorimer fired just over the bar, from twenty yards.

Then, Giles lobbed forward to Bremner, who gathered the ball, but was pushed in the back by Webb, and he fell over Hollins' knee, inside the Chelsea penalty area. Bremner got back up, astonished that his team had received no penalty kick, but he just got straight on with the game.

Eddie Gray fired just over Bonetti's bar, from twenty yards out, just before the final whistle, and yet again, extra-time was needed.

Chelsea had now fully caught up with the quality of Leeds, and they were squeezing the life out of Leeds United's game, and indeed, their season.

They were taking their time over every set-piece, and key players like Gray and Clarke and Lorimer were so shattered, that Hunter and Madeley were coming up in attack; an increase in numbers, but a decrease in quality.

The balance of the game had shifted. Giles had had a quiet game, and Bremner was still dazed by McCreadie's Kung Fu kick to his skull.

Terry Cooper was fouled by Baldwin, unnecessarily, and Johnny Giles' free-kick, from twenty yards out, was headed back to Lorimer, who half-volleyed from the edge of the area, into the grateful hands of Peter Bonetti.

Bonetti bounced the ball on the turf, before finally catching it.

Hunter went down with cramp, as did Osgood. Charlton rubbed his injured thigh, from Osgood's challenge in the second half. The game slowed down, and it almost stopped.

Eddie McCreadie sat on the ball out on the left touchline, chatting cheerfully to the linesman. Leeds United appeared to switch off, with just one minute of the first period of extra-time to play.

McCreadie's throw up-field was headed out by Paul Madeley. Ian Hutchinson threw in again, but Jack Charlton headed out for another Chelsea throw-in, this time level with the edge of Leeds United's penalty area.

Hutchinson then launched one of his long ones. Charlton jumped with Osgood, but he misjudged his header, and flicked on for David Webb, jumping above Eddie Gray, over at the far post, to head in beyond Harvey. Chelsea's fans exploded with delight in the Stretford End, singing their hearts out with their blue and white woollen scarves aloft.

Marvin Hinton came on as substitute, again, but for Osgood this time, with just eight minutes left, as Chelsea attempted, and succeeded in flattening the game. The game had been totally squeezed out of Leeds United. Leeds' efforts on goal became more and more desperate as the game, and their long, ill-fated season, wore out.

At the final whistle, Chelsea's players jumped and hugged each other. Allan Clarke, again the loser in his second successive Cup Final, went to shake hands and congratulate every Chelsea defender. Jack Charlton stormed off the pitch, fuming at the injustice, and to underline Ian Hutchinson's name in his **black book.**

Peter Osgood exchanged shirts with Billy Bremner, and he was then refused a winner's medal by an FA official, because he was wearing a Leeds shirt, before John Hollins pointed out who *he* was.

Chelsea ran to the Blue and white Stretford End with their FA Cup, in front of their delirious supporters, and then they also applauded the Leeds United fans in front of the Clock End.

Reviewing the match on video, twenty-seven years later, back in 1997, David Elleray, a former Premier League referee and Harrow school teacher, suggested that there should have been six red cards shown, and twenty yellow cards, during the replay at Old Trafford, alone.

It was, quite certainly, the most personal battle of all FA Cup Finals, and the greatest of them all. Other, higher scoring Cup Finals have been acclaimed as greater, by sensationalists, but they just weren't. The 1970 FA Cup Final, played in the same year as the greatest ever World Cup

Finals tournament, was played between the two greatest teams in the history of both Chelsea and Leeds United, and both teams had really went for it, playing to the very, very tops of their ability.

It was a game you could not take your eyes off the telly for even a minute.

There was no other Final quite like it.

Chelsea finished 1969-70 in third place, in the First Division, just two points behind runners-up Leeds United. They'd won more games, and lost fewer matches than Chelsea's team that had won the First Division title back in 1955, and they'd gained three more points also.

It was the most exciting season in Chelsea's history, and the future was bright for Chelsea's young team. The only way was up… or down?

In 1970-71, Chelsea finished in sixth place in the First Division, but only a point behind third placed Tottenham. Alan Hudson started only thirty-three league games, but he was never as fully fit as he'd been prior to his ankle injury. Therefore, Chelsea weren't the offensive force they were in 1970. They scored only fifty-two goals, eighteen fewer than they'd scored the previous season. However, they conceded only 42 goals, the first time they'd ever conceded just a goal a game, or less, in their entire club history.

Keith Weller was their top scorer, with thirteen goals, but he was going to be off to Leicester, just a couple of games into the 1971-72 season. John Hollins had scored nine league and cup goals, while Hutchinson and Osgood scored just ten First Division goals between them, much fewer than the sixteen goals and twenty-three goals they'd each respectively scored, during the 1969-70 season.

In the 1970-71 European Cup Winners' Cup competition, though, it was a different story to their underwhelming domestic achievements. First, during September, Chelsea had overcame Aris Salonika, 6-2 on aggregate. Ian Hutchinson had secured a 1-1 draw in front of 50,000 whistling and jeering Greeks, before they won 5-1 back at Stamford Bridge. Hollins scored two, as did Hutchinson, while Marvin Hinton headed in a fifth.

Tommy Baldwin's first half strike secured their 1-0 win away at CSKA Sofia, on Wednesday 21st October, before David Webb completed their victory in early November. Their 2-0 aggregate victory sent Chelsea into the Quarter-finals.

On Wednesday 10th March 1971, 23,000 were packed inside Bruges' tiny cramped Albert Dyserynckstadion, screaming a deafening din, and the Belgian side went at Chelsea like tigers.

Rob Rensenbrink was among Bruges' stars, but it was their record goal-scorer, Raoul Lambert, who'd headed in past John Phillips, from Johnny Thio's corner kick.

Rensenbrink then fired in from Thio's next corner. The ball hit Marmenout, full in the face, and the ball was deflected past Phillips, deputising for Peter Bonetti.

Bruges couldn't add to their 2-0 half-time lead, but even so, Chelsea really had a mountain to climb, back in London.

45,558 watched a real classic European Quarter-final at the Bridge, a fortnight later. Their forty-five thousand fans sounded more like a sixty or seventy thousand crowd.

The real hard-core of Chelsea supporters were out that night, in full numbers and in full voice, and just as the Bruges fans had lifted their team in Belgium, Bruges wilted as the sheer noise came down in waves, from the back of the Shed, and across all the Stands.

Early on, Peter Houseman gave Chelsea the lead, and then, Peter Osgood, who was finally back from a nine week suspension for receiving too many bookings, fired in a shot at the far post.

Alan Hudson then cut the ball back, from the bye-line, for Ossie, who was out to make up for lost time, lost time imposed on him by the FA who seemed intent on making an example of a high profile star.

Osgood smashed the ball home, and Chelsea were ahead in the tie, but still they never let up.

Charlie Cooke played to Osgood, to Hudson, back to Cooke, and in for Baldwin, in space inside the Bruges penalty area. It was superb, crisp, one touch interplay, but the timing of Baldwin's run was sublime. He finished the move off, clinically, and Chelsea went into the Semi-finals, 4-2 on aggregate. Bruges were a broken team.

The Semi-final was not a classic. Manchester City, the European Cup Winners' Cup holders, were missing Corrigan, Bell, Summerbee, Oakes, Pardoe and Doyle, and on Wednesday 28th April, an own goal at Maine Road gave Chelsea a 1-0 away win, a fortnight after Derek Smethurst had won the first leg match, by the same score, down at the Bridge.

Ten thousand fans had followed Chelsea up to Manchester for that second leg match, but their London-bound Inter-City trains were bombarded with bricks and boulders, as they left Piccadilly Station, afterwards.

Chelsea faced the mighty Real Madrid, who'd just beaten PSV Eindhoven, in the Final.

42,000 filled the Karaiskakis Stadium in Athens, for another Cup Final battle royal, on Wednesday 19th May 1971, this time with the absolute giants of European football, six times European Cup winners, and eight times Finalists since 1956.

Furthermore, they still boasted a player who'd played in all of those Finals.

Francisco Gento had scored their winning goal against AC Milan in 1958, and he'd also scored against Fiorentina the previous year, but by 1971, he was 37 years old.

In the place of Puskas, Di Stefano and Kopa alongside him, though, he had Gregorio Benito, Ignacio Zoco, and Pirri, the architect of Spain's national midfield.

Pirri was, at twenty-six years old, in the very peak of his career.

For Chelsea, Eddie McCreadie was out, so Chopper Harris had moved over to left back, and their veteran forward John Boyle came in at right back.

Keith Weller had also replaced the injured Ian Hutchinson.

After 56 minutes, Peter Osgood fired Chelsea ahead, with a fine left footed strike, from just inside the area, but Real came back at them.

Inspired by the masterly Pirri, Real pinned Chelsea down with their tremendous pressure, their high-percentage possession football, but only twenty seconds remained when Zoco pounced on Dempsey's mistake, in front of his own goal, and he drove the ball in from three yards.

Peter Osgood fought his way to a Hudson free-kick, but he was so tightly marked by Benito's vicious tactics, he couldn't find a free angle to beat Borja.

The Final ended 1-1, after extra-time, so a replay was held, at the same stadium, two nights later, on Friday 21st May.

Chelsea's fans, now kicked out of their hotels after their travel packages had expired, had pooled together their remaining funds, and they slept on Greek beaches, just so they could stay in Athens until Friday. Of the much smaller 20,000 crowd at the replay, half of them were hungry and dirty, unshaven Chelsea fans.

The Paraguayan star, Fleitas, who'd replaced the ageing Gento, two nights before, and been superb in inspiring Real's response, kept his place in their starting line-up. Gento had dropped to the Real substitutes' bench. For Chelsea, Tommy Baldwin came in for the injured John Hollins. Otherwise, they were a settled side.

Chelsea were far and above the better team for the whole of the first half. Pirri, who had been the man of the match on the Wednesday night, controlling play, and keeping Chelsea prisoners inside their own third, for the last hour of the match, was subdued.

His teammates were also mostly jaded, but Fleitas and Zoco were the exceptions.

REAL MADRID		CHELSEA
Jose Luis Borja	1	Peter Bonetti
Jose Luis	2	John Boyle
Fernando Zunzunegui	3	Ron Harris
Pirri	4	Charlie Cooke
Gregorio Benito	5	John Dempsey
Ignacio Zoco	6	David Webb
Sebastian Fleitas	7	Keith Weller
Amancio Amaro	8	Tommy Baldwin
Ramon Grosso	9	Peter Osgood
Manuel Velazquez	10	Alan Hudson
Manuel Bueno	11	Peter Houseman

After thirty-three minutes, Webb's shot on the break was tipped the bar, by Borja. Then, Cooke's left-wing corner kick was volleyed in by John Dempsey, after the keeper had punched out his initial header on goal.

Six minutes later, from the halfway line, Ron Harris played forward to Tommy Baldwin *in the hole.* Baldwin ran at a quartet of white shirted Madrid players, to the edge of the Real penalty area, before laying off to Osgood, twenty yards out.

Ossie fired a beautiful shot, first time, from the edge of the *D*, past Borja's dive.

The ball squeezed just inside Madrid's right post.

In the second half, with a quarter of an hour remaining, Fleitas beat Boyle, and he ran at the Chelsea area, before firing home from twenty yards out, right-footed, past Bonetti at his near post. Fleitas then crossed from the right, but Ignacio Zoco's header was caught by the flying Peter Bonetti, diving to his left.

Chelsea became the eighth English club side to win a European trophy. No other country has had such a vast dominance in European club competitions than England. Between 1967 and 1976, eight English clubs won ten European club competitions.

No other country even gets close to this record.

Defending their Cup Winners' Cup, in September 1971, Chelsea hammered Jeunesse Hautcharage, of Luxembourg, 21-0 on aggregate, an all-time record score in European competition.

Chelsea won 8-0 in Luxembourg, and then 13-0 at Stamford Bridge, before 27,621, a World Record crowd for a 13-0 victory. Peter Osgood had scored eight goals over the two legs, but Tommy Baldwin also hit four, and Peter Houseman three.

Hollins and Webb scored two each, while Hudson and Harris completed the scoring.

In the Second round, though, Chelsea were stunned by Swedish side Atvidaberg. They had drawn 0-0 away in Scandinavia, but despite absolutely battering Atvidaberg back at the Bridge, the Swedes went in goalless at half-time.

Only fifteen seconds into the second half, though, Alan Hudson fired Chelsea ahead, curling in a beautiful shot from the edge of the penalty area.

Chelsea were then awarded a penalty-kick, but John Hollins, usually so safe from the spot, missed the target. At 2-0, the tie would have been won.

That penalty miss proved costly, as shortly afterwards, Atvidaberg's star player, and Swedish international forward, Roland Sandberg ran onto a through ball, that beat Chelsea's entire back four, and he rammed the ball past Peter Bonetti. Despite heavy pressure burying them inside their own penalty area, the Swedes defended desperately and they battled through to the end with a score draw, scraping through to the Quarter-finals on the away goals rule.

In the League Cup, Chelsea enjoyed a longer run. They won 2-0 away at Plymouth Argyle (Houseman, Hollins), in the Second round, before goals from Baldwin and Osgood helped them scrape past Nottingham Forest 2-1, after a replay in mid-October.

Having been held to a 1-1 home draw by Bolton Wanderers, in late October, Chelsea then hammered the Trotters 6-0 away, with just under 30,000 packed inside Burnden Park, to reach the Fifth round. Tommy Baldwin's hat-trick destroyed Bolton, with Charlie Cooke and John Hollins also scoring, before Hollins added a late penalty kick.

After a tough start in Division One, winning only three of their opening thirteen games, Chelsea improved from late October, through to the end of November. They won five out of six games, while drawing the other, including a 1-0 win over Tottenham, with 52,581 inside the Bridge, after Charlie Cooke had scored late on.

By Saturday 27th November, Chelsea were up to ninth position, but only four points behind third-placed Derby County, and a UEFA Cup place.

Chelsea had beaten Norwich City 1-0, in the League Cup Quarter-finals, in front of a massive Carrow Road crowd of nearly 36,000. Peter Osgood finished a wonderful move that had ran through Cooke, Hudson and Houseman.

At the start of the season, Chelsea had paid Bristol City £100,000 for their attacking marauder, Chris Garland. Garland had scored thirty-one league goals, in 143 games, for his home town club, and he was purchased as a bustling, physical presence, but also as cover for Ian Hutchinson, who didn't play any football at all between February 1971 and November 1972.

On Wednesday 22nd December, Chelsea hosted their League Cup Semi-final, first leg match against the Cup holders, Tottenham. Peter Osgood fired Chelsea 1-0 up, just before the break, but early in the second half, Terry Naylor equalised, and then, less than a minute later, Martin Chivers stormed through, and he put Spurs 2-1 up, with his twenty-fourth goal of the season.

This was the game, though, when Chris Garland became a real Chelsea player, hitting the crossbar in the first half, and he'd generally terrorised Cyril Knowles all through the game. Charlie Cooke came on as a substitute, for Baldwin, and Chelsea were reinvigorated. Cooke found Houseman out wide, in yards of space, and Peter Houseman crossed beautifully for Garland to thump his header home, past Jennings.

With time running out, Naylor handled inside his area, and John Hollins scored from the penalty spot, giving Chelsea a crucial advantage, after such a tight, bruising battle. David Webb was given five stitches on his blooded eyebrow afterwards, and Ossie had also been knocked about by Mike England all night.

Nearly 53,000 packed White Hart Lane on Wednesday 5th January 1972, for a titanic tussle between two of the greatest teams ever fielded in the modern history of both Chelsea and Tottenham Hotspur.

TOTTENHAM HOTSPUR		CHELSEA
Pat Jennings	1	Peter Bonetti
Ray Evans	2	Paddy Mulligan
Cyril Knowles	3	Ron Harris
John Pratt	4	John Hollins
Mike England	5	John Dempsey
Phil Beal	6	David Webb
Ralph Coates	7	Charlie Cooke
Steve Perryman	8	Chris Garland
Martin Chivers	9	Peter Osgood
Martin Peters	10	Alan Hudson
Alan Gilzean	11	Peter Houseman
Jimmy Pearce	12	Tommy Baldwin

Chelsea had withstood total pressure on their goalmouth, for most of the first half, but they'd survived, only just. Disaster struck, though, as they switched off in injury time.

Coates crossed from the left for Peters to flick on, and Chivers flew in at the far post, to fire in from just about two yards out.

Early in the second half, though, Chelsea had much more of the ball, and Chris Garland cut inside Knowles, from the right, and he bulleted a shot into the top of Pat Jennings' goal. The power of Garland's shot had given Jennings no chance.

Charlie Cooke started to find time to pick his passes, time for composure and the sublime control and acute vision, for which he was famed. He freed Osgood, again tightly marked by England, all night long, but Ossie couldn't get the best purchase on the ball, and Jennings gratefully gathered.

Then, Spurs went ahead again. Martin Chivers hurled a long throw into Chelsea's penalty area. Alan Hudson was back defending, pointing at his teammates, and where they should stand, but Chivers' ball flew onto the top part of his arm.

With the forty-odd thousand home fans thronged into the Shelf, all baying for a penalty, the referee gave the easy decision.

It was a very, very harsh decision.

Martin Peters, though, drilled in his penalty kick.

With the game approaching full-time, and then extra-time, Mike England, who'd been bullying and bullied by Osgood, all through the night, was perhaps harshly adjudged to have fouled Ossie, over by the left side corner.

Alan Hudson took the free-kick, low, driving it into the box. The ball took a sharp deflection, though, and it bounced in off Pat Jennings' far post.

Chelsea supporters went wild. Tottenham-Chelsea games are among the bitterest rivalries in football, and Chelsea fans smashed up Seven Sisters tube station, and also a pub near to White Hart Lane, that night, for their troubles.

They'd felt that Chelsea were the top dogs in their home city, and they were probably right, but they wanted to leave the evidence behind. Sadly, that side of football, a darker side, became more and more evident during the **Glam Soccer** era.

So, Glam Soccer amidst the glitter and sparkle of Glam Rock? What do you do? You make a fucking hit record, that's what you do. And, if you're going to do it, you might as well make the best football record ever.

For the 1972 League Cup Final, against Stoke City, probably the best ever Stoke side, Chelsea FC's players recorded a single. **Blue Is The Colour** became one of the greatest ever selling football songs, and it was, very probably, the best of them all. All of the players sung on it; Ossie, Hudson, Charlie, Chopper, Johnny, Eddie, Marvin, Webby.

"Blue is the colour, football is the game," it went. "We're all together, and winning is our aim. So cheer us on through the sun and rain, 'cos Chelsea! Chelsea is our name."

It was really quite a catchy song.

There were various other big-selling records at that time. England's 1970 World Cup song went to number one, beating The Moody Blues' **Question** into second place, but **Back Home** was fairly pedestrian. Arsenal's **Good Old Arsenal,** after their Double-winning season, was simply boring.

Leeds United had a great song released, for their 1972 FA Cup Final match, called **Leeds, Leeds, Leeds (Marching On Together),** which is still played, and sung en masse, by Elland Road home crowds, both before, during and after matches, to this very day.

Blue Is The Colour, though, was the cream of the crop, with a great hook, and passionately sung by the players, especially Ossie, Hudson, Charlie and Chopper, who really thrived at being Pop Stars, and going on Top of the Pops. On 11th March 1972, the song made number five in the UK singles charts. It doesn't sound that great these days, where if you go straight in at number two, you're regarded as a fading flop, but just look at the quality of that top six?

1. Nilsson – Without You
2. Don McLean – American Pie
3. Chicory Tip – Son Of My Father
4. New Seekers – Beg, Steal or Borrow
5. Chelsea FC – Blue Is The Colour
6. Michael Jackson – Got To Be There

The top four were all million sellers, and the top three were classics, all-time classics, occasionally covered by present day superstars, but never improved upon. Number four was the UK entry into the Eurovision Song Contest, and that really mattered back then.

Got To Be There was Michael Jackson's debut solo single, and purists argue that this was one of his best ever songs. It lost to Chelsea.

Incidentally, Chelsea lost to Stoke City, by 2-1, who were superb on the day of the League Cup Final.

On a couple of occasions during 1971-72, Chelsea could've been found on the outer limits of the Greatest Ever Title Race, in February, and then again in April, but eventually, they burnt out during their last half-dozen games, taking just four points out of twelve, and they ended up down in twelfth position, but only ten points behind Champions Derby County.

Peter Osgood scored thirty-two competitive goals in 1971-72, and John Hollins also had his best ever season, offensively, with eighteen goals, five of them from the penalty spot. Hollins was also Chelsea's only ever-present player in the First Division.

Sadly, during the following 1972-73 season, the spirit of that 1970 team began to break up.

Into the team came a beefier, more physical, less footballing future with Steve Kember, Micky Droy and Ian Britton. Alan Hudson played in just over half of Chelsea's First Division matches;

Peter Houseman played in less than half of their games; and Ian Hutchinson returned at the end of November, but he lasted only three matches.

On Friday 29th September, though, Dave Sexton got rid of Charlie Cooke, one of the finest ball-players to have ever worn a Chelsea shirt.

He was sold to fellow First Division London club Crystal Palace, for £85,000.

Charlie Cooke had played 212 First Division matches in his six and a half years at the Bridge, scoring only fifteen goals, but setting up over a hundred.

Also joining Cooke at Selhurst Park was full back Paddy Mulligan, who'd joined for £75,000. Charlie Cooke and Paddy Mulligan were a part of Palace's mad mass recruitment of players, that had also brought in Alan Whittle from Everton, Don Rogers from Swindon, and Derek Possee from Millwall.

Overall, Palace manager Bert Head spent over £600,000 in just three months, in an attempt to achieve First Division survival. In spite of four excellent results, though, from their five games in the weeks before and after Christmas 1972, including a superb 5-0 hammering of Manchester United, Palace did not survive, and they were relegated after losing away at Norwich, finishing the season just two points behind the Canaries.

Chelsea started the season wonderfully, beating the mighty Leeds United 4-0, at home, with Osgood and Cooke scoring two crackers, before Chris Garland brought about an ecstatic pitch invasion by the Chelsea crowd, at the Shed End, after firing two late goals past Peter Lorimer, Leeds' emergency keeper, after Harvey had been injured.

The massive Stamford Bridge crowd of 51,102 was even more impressive, because the East side of the ground was total rubble, awaiting the construction of the huge, three-tiered, new East Stand. The Shed End, at the South, was so full, the kids were allowed to sit on the pitch side of the goal, and it was they who invaded the pitch, not just after Garland's two late goals, but also at the final whistle.

Chelsea were reported, and as a result, such liberal policies were outlawed. Chelsea did not draw another crowd above 44,000 that season.

In the League Cup, Chelsea beat Southend, and then Champions Derby County, after a replay. They then pushed aside Bury and Notts County, before being defeated by the Norfolk ascendancy of Norwich City, in the Semi-finals.

In the FA Cup, Chelsea beat Brighton, Ipswich and Sheffield Wednesday, before losing away to Arsenal, after a replay, in the Quarter-finals. However, during the first game, at the Bridge, which was drawn 2-2, Peter Osgood scored a goal that won the BBC TV Goal of the Season award.

Gary Locke crossed from the right. Osgood flicked on, just outside the Arsenal area. Kember teed the ball up, under close attention from Ray Kennedy, and Osgood then smashed a left-footed volley high into the top corner of Bob Wilson's goal.

Commentator David Coleman was overwhelmed. "And only players like Osgood take goals like that! You don't blame goalkeepers, you congratulate the scorer."

Peter Osgood was again Chelsea's top scorer, during 1972-73, with seventeen league and cup goals, as his team dropped to a lowly mid-table position, finishing down in twelfth place, seven points behind any kind of European action. John Hollins was again their only ever-present, for the second successive season.

1973-74 was a nightmare, of all nightmares, for Chelsea fans. They said goodbye to both Alan Hudson and Peter Osgood, sold by Sexton to Stoke City and Southampton, respectively, and also to Peter Bonetti, who'd retired from football. John Hollins was again ever-present, for the third successive season, but in emergency situations, he also had to cover at right back, left back, and also centre back, on several occasions.

Only 8,171 fans turned up for their home game against UEFA Cup hopefuls Burnley, on Wednesday 13th March. Kember, Houseman, and Ian Hutchinson, who'd at least played ten matches during the season, all scored during their 3-0 win over the Clarets, that ultimately secured Chelsea's survival in Division One.

The following season, 1974-75, was not so kind. Chelsea lost at home to First Division new-comers Carlisle United, on the opening Saturday. They won just two of their first eleven league matches, losing five times.

Dave Sexton was finally sacked as manager of Chelsea, on Thursday 3rd October. He'd fallen out with Peter Osgood, Alan Hudson, and Tommy Baldwin, leading to the departures of both Ossie and Hudson. He had gone with his heart, for a less-footballing future for the club, and they'd ended up in the relegation zone, from which they were just one point clear, at the end of 73-74.

A few days later, Dave Sexton took over as manager of QPR, and he managed their greatest-ever team to second place in Division One, but eventually, his limitations emerged there too, and though he led Manchester United to a Division One runners-up position, in 1980, he was sacked a year later, and was never seen in First Division football again.

David Webb had been signed by the previous QPR manager, Gordon Jago, at the end of May 1974, for £100,000. Webb played 230 First Division games for Chelsea, scoring twenty-one goals. At QPR, he formed a great central defensive partnership with Frank McLintock, and a year later, he was joined at Loftus Road by John Hollins, as QPR launched a proper title campaign in 1975-76.

Tommy Baldwin left Chelsea in November 1974, on loan to Millwall, before joining Tommy Docherty's Manchester United, also on loan, during January 1975.

He played two games for the Doc, who'd originally signed him for Chelsea, back in 1966, but neither he nor United scored in either of those games, and his 1974-75 season was over.

Tommy Baldwin had his contact cancelled by Chelsea, during the 1975-76 season, after he'd scored seventy-four goals in only 184 First Division matches for the club.

In the middle of April 1975, Eddie McCreadie, who'd played the last of his 332 league matches for Chelsea on Saturday 20th December 1973, against Newcastle United, returned as first team manager.

He replaced Ron Suart, who'd been their interim manager for six months.

McCreadie's first decision was to drop John Hollins from their vital relegation clash away at Tottenham Hotspur. The two teams were a complete mess from the classic sides that had met back in January 1972, but Spurs had a vital twelfth man that proved crucial; their 51,064 White Hart Lane crowd.

That was the fifth largest First Division attendance of 1974-75.

TOTTENHAM HOTSPUR		CHELSEA
Pat Jennings	1	John Phillips
Joe Kinnear	2	Gary Locke
Cyril Knowles	3	John Sparrow
Phil Beal	4	Ian Britton
Keith Osgood	5	Micky Droy
Terry Naylor	6	Ron Harris
Alfie Conn	7	Steve Kember
Steve Perryman	8	Ray Wilkins
Chris Jones	9	Ted Maybank
John Duncan	10	Ian Hutchinson
Jimmy Neighbour	11	Charlie Cooke

Charlie Cooke had re-joined Chelsea, back in January 1974, for just £17,000, after Palace had dropped to the bottom of Division Two, despite regularly drawing crowds of over twenty thousand. Cooke played forty-four league games at Selhurst Park, but Malcolm Allison had felt that the future was brighter with young talents like Peter Taylor and Dave Swindlehurst, so he cut his losses.

Perryman and Conn both scored second half goals to condemn Chelsea to relegation back to Division Two. John Hollins, insulted at being dropped, demanded a transfer, and he left Stamford Bridge in June 1975, to join his old boss Dave Sexton at QPR, for a fee of £80,000.

Hollins had played 592 league and cup matches, in nearly twelve years at the Bridge, scoring sixty-nine goals. Hollins eventually left QPR for Arsenal in 1979, but then he returned to Chelsea in 1983, and helped his team to promotion back to the First Division, along with both Sheffield Wednesday and Newcastle, playing behind a new Chelsea generation, that included Pat Nevin, Kerry Dixon and David Speedie.

John Hollins was awarded the MBE, in 1981, for services to football.

After finishing well behind Sunderland, Bristol City and West Brom, in 1976, Eddie McCreadie's Chelsea eventually gained promotion back to Division One in 1976-77, along with Wolves, and future League and European Champions Nottingham Forest.

McCreadie had even persuaded Peter Bonetti to return to football at the start of that season, and The Cat played in the majority of his team's games, keeping ten clean sheets, and helping Chelsea to the Second Division runners-up spot, with his new teammates at Stamford Bridge, Ray Wilkins, Steve Finnieston, Steve Wicks and Tommy Langley.

Peter Bonetti continued to play a further 105 league matches for Chelsea, before he played his six-hundredth and last league game in May 1979, their 1-1 draw with Arsenal. Bonetti had played a total of 729 league and cup games for Chelsea, and he'd kept over 200 clean sheets. He conceded just one goal, or less, in over 65% of his Chelsea games.

Only Ron Harris played more games for Chelsea, than Peter Bonetti.

Ron Harris played a club record 795 league and cup matches for Chelsea, before he left for Brentford in 1980, after nearly twenty years at Stamford Bridge. He'd been captain of Chelsea for nearly ten years, before the teenager Ray Wilkins was appointed captain by Eddie McCreadie. Chopper was hard, but fair and dignified.

His fouls were rarely personal, but merely for the cause, and in the call of duty for his team. He had had to administer *a reducer* on Eddie Gray during the 1970 Cup Final replay, or Chelsea would otherwise have lost.

Chopper Harris now conducts Legends Tours at Stamford Bridge.

Eddie McCreadie, dignified, honest and passionate, could not have the piss taken out of him, for all he'd done for Chelsea, and after taking the club back up to the First Division in 1976-77, he asked for a company car, but the club refused, so he resigned at the start of July 1977.

The Chelsea Board then changed their minds and agreed to his request, after his resignation had been submitted, but McCreadie was a proud man and he decided to stay with his original decision. Eddie McCreadie had played a total of 410 league and cup matches for Chelsea, while also making twenty-three appearances for Scotland.

Peter Houseman had signed for Oxford United, after Chelsea's relegation, during the Summer of 1975. He played 269 First Division matches for Chelsea, and with six FA Cup goals in 1970, he was their top scorer as they won the Greatest Cup Final of all.

Eddie McCreadie, though, wanted to try out younger players such as Bill Garner and John Sparrow, and at the age of just twenty-nine, Houseman was offloaded to fellow Second Division team Oxford United.

On Sunday 20th March 1977, Peter Houseman and his wife, were driving home to their home in Witney, on the A40, with two married friends, after he'd been playing in a charity football match in Oxfordshire.

They were all killed, though, when their car crashed.

It was a real tragedy that had also left behind two sets of orphaned children.

Peter Houseman was only thirty-one years old.

After playing only eighteen games during Chelsea's first season back in Division Two, in 1975-76, and having scored four goals, Ian Hutchinson's contract was cancelled after just 144 league and cup games, a career totally ruined by injuries after 1971, or else he'd have easily played well over 400 games, and scored 150 goals.

He'd scored fifty-eight goals during his eight years at Stamford Bridge.

After being previously banned, and booted out of Stamford Bridge, by chairman Ken Bates, Ian Hutchinson returned to Chelsea during the late Nineties, as their Commercial Manager, but he died on Thursday 19th September 2002, having suffered a lengthy illness, aged only fifty-four.

John Dempsey played his 165th and final First Division match for Chelsea, on Boxing Day 1975, in a 3-2 home defeat to Charlton Athletic, and his contract was finally cancelled, over two years later, in March 1978.

In 1978, Dempsey joined Philadelphia Fury, of the NASL, alongside Peter Osgood, Alan Ball, Frank Worthington, Johnny Giles and Colin Waldron. He was even voted Defender of the Year in 1979, beating Franz Beckenbauer into second place, as the Fury reached the Semi-finals of the American Conference.

Dempsey played for the Fury for three years, making 81 NASL appearances.

After retirement, John Dempsey worked with people with learning disabilities at Edgware's Broadfields Resource Centre. He has no doubts as to where that 1970 team stands, in the history of Chelsea Football Club.

"I think I was part of the best Chelsea team, ever," he suggested.

"We used to relish the physical away trips on cold winter nights, but the current side doesn't fancy it. In 1970, we were getting £60 or £80 per week, and the average man was getting £30."

Alan Hudson had played 145 First Division games for Chelsea, when he signed for Stoke City on Saturday 12th January 1974, for a club record fee of £240,000.

While Chelsea went into decline after he'd left, Hudson's career thrived. He played eighteen First Division matches for Stoke in the second half of the 1973-74 season, and Stoke lost only twice, while winning nine times, and they rose from the bottom half of the table to fifth position, and to a UEFA Cup place.

The following season was even better, and Stoke City led the First Division for several weeks, and even as late as early March. Playing in an adventurous, attacking midfield, alongside both Jimmy Greenhoff and Geoff Salmons, passing the ball around just like Hudson, Holins and Cooke, with the great Geoff Hurst as their Ossie up front, Stoke played a little like that Chelsea side of 1970. Stoke City could, and should, have been Champions, but they dropped vital points late in the season.

Alan Hudson was given his first full international cap, as a Stoke City player, in March 1975, when England beat West Germany 2-0, at Wembley Stadium. The manager of the World Champions, Helmut Schoen, was hugely and particularly impressed by Hudson.

Schoen said of Alan Hudson, who was still only twenty-three at the time, "finally England have a World Class player."

Colin Bell and Malcolm MacDonald had scored both of England's goals.

A month later, Hudson kept his place, as England hammered Cyprus 5-0, in their European Championship home qualifier, with Supermac scoring all five of England's goals. On 11th May 1975, Hudson was again selected for their away match against Cyprus, in Limassol, and England won again, by 1-0, giving them a great start to the campaign, with seven points from four games, but Hudson was then dropped for England's Home International matches.

Against Scotland, Gerry Francis had Hudson's shirt, and he scored twice in England's 5-1 win, in their brand new Admiral strip.

Alan Hudson was never picked by Don Revie again. In 1974-75, he was selected by the PFA for their First Division Team of the Year, amongst a superb midfield with Colin Bell, Billy Bonds and Leighton James. One year later, he was again selected, along with Kevin Keegan, Don Masson and Dennis Tueart.

After 105 First Division games for Stoke, he signed for Arsenal in 1976, and he finally played in his first FA Cup Final in 1978, but Arsenal lost 1-0 to Ipswich Town.

After his retirement, Alan Hudson returned to the Potteries, where he was much loved, and he worked on Signal Radio as a match expert analyst, as well as writing for the Stoke Evening Sentinel.

A car crashed into him, in December 1997, and nearly killed him.

Hudson spent two months in a coma, and the accident left him with a hole in his bladder, so that he needed a bag. He'd also totally lost all feeling in his right leg.

Alan Hudson then appeared in Nick Love's 2004 film, *The Football Factory,* about football violence between Chelsea and Millwall fans, appearing as himself, as did his old mate Peter Osgood.

To this very day, kids and adults on fields all over the country, and all over the world, practise that *Alan Hudson drag back,* without even knowing who perfected the move.

Football's like that, though; no credit is ever given.

Peter Osgood was the King of Stamford Bridge. He left Chelsea in March 1974. He'd even been humiliated into training with the reserves. One day, Dave Sexton had felt he might need Ossie, and so he sent his trainer to ask him if he'd come to train with the first team, so he could have a look.

Osgood told him to fuck off. The rift between Sexton and Ossie was permanent.

Peter Osgood had been knocked about too much, and he refused to be treated like a young junior player.

After scoring 148 goals from 369 league and cup games for Chelsea, Osgood moved to Southampton, who were fighting for their First Division lives, in March 1974. Chelsea received a new club record transfer fee of £275,000, smashing the amount they'd received for Alan Hudson, just two months before.

Unlike Hudson's career away from Chelsea, though, Ossie's career didn't rise so wonderfully. He scored just one goal in ten games, at the end of Southampton's season, and the Saints went down.

Ossie and Mike Channon scored thirty-two Second Division goals between them, though, during the following season, but no other player hit more than five goals, and Southampton fell a long way behind the promotion chasers.

In 1976, though, Osgood helped Southampton to the FA Cup Final. It was a real veterans' team, with Osgood, Jim McCalliog, Jim Steele, Peter Rodrigues and Mel Blyth. Unlike Hudson, Ossie actually won something after he'd left Chelsea, when Bobby Stokes fired a great, late winner against the red hot favourites Manchester United, on a red hot afternoon, to give Osgood his second FA Cup winners' medal.

Peter Osgood, having been banned by Ken Bates from Stamford Bridge during the 80's and 90's, along with many of his fellow Chelsea teammates, was welcomed back in 2003, by Roman Abramovich. He became a very popular hospitality host on match days at Stamford Bridge, charming fans with his humour, confidence, and his likeability.

It was awful that he should ever have been away. Peter Osgood was badly missed at the Bridge. Ken Bates was not, after he finally left.

Peter Osgood died on Wednesday 1st March 2006. He'd been a pall-bearer at a family funeral in Windsor, but he collapsed, himself, during the ceremony, and died of a heart attack.

He was only fifty-nine years old.

A bronze statue of Peter Osgood was unveiled, outside Stamford Bridge's West Stand, on Saturday 2nd October 2010. His ashes were buried under the penalty spot, at the Shed End, on Chelsea's pitch.

Peter Osgood was, and always will be, the King of Stamford Bridge.

It is difficult, and unfair, to compare the title winning Chelsea teams of 2005-2010, under the managements of Jose Mourinho and Carlo Ancelotti. The more recent Chelsea line-up was bought after the vast financial investment of Russian multi-billionaire Roman Abramovich, propelling the team up into the elite, not only of English football, but of European football, too.

Dave Sexton's team of 1969-72 was almost entirely home grown, and most of them were Londoners. They had little financial backing, compared to the likes of Leeds, Arsenal, Spurs, Derby and Manchester City, yet they still pushed hard, punching well above their weight, in both title races and Cup competitions.

They also played a better class of football.

Every penalty kick scored by Frank Lampard or Didier Drogba, at Stamford Bridge, was taken directly above the presence of the King of Stamford Bridge. Before and after every home match, **Blue Is The Colour** is blasted out of the Stamford Bridge speakers, and sung along to, and danced to, by the Chelsea supporters.

If you took the spine out of Chelsea's 2012 Champions League winners, Cech, Terry, Cole, Lampard and Drogba, and you added Harris, Dempsey, Hollins, Hudson, Cooke, Osgood and Hutchinson, from 1970, you'd have almost the perfect football team.

When Chelsea became European Champions at the Allianz Arena, in Munich, on Saturday 19th May 2012, Cech, Terry, Cole, Lampard and Drogba all sang along with the 1972 League Cup Finalists, while **Blue Is The Colour** was played wonderfully loud over Bayern Munich's PA system.

Two teams, forty years apart, beautifully united in song; a fantasy football team reigning over all.

The 2012 vintage of Chelsea FC won games, not just for themselves, and not just for their supporters, but they also win for Chelsea, *that* Chelsea team from 1969-72, who put a smile on the face of football, and were excellent against the most supreme competition in English football history, for such small rewards, in terms of money or awards. But they won the hearts of most football fans.

More importantly, though, Chelsea won the War that was the 1970 FA Cup Final, the Greatest Cup Final of all.

THE MAVERICKNESS OF KING GEORGE

BACK IN 1968, ARSENAL WERE a run of the mill, middle of the table, First Division side.

On Saturday 2nd March, though, having beaten Huddersfield 6-3 on aggregate in the Semi-finals, they faced Leeds United in the League Cup Final, their first Wembley Final for sixteen years.

Terry Cooper's disputed goal won the game for a distinctly better Leeds side.

Arsenal were certainly sleeping giants, having overslept for nearly two decades.

They'd hammered fierce rivals Tottenham 4-0, back on Saturday 16th September 1967, the highlight of their season, with a massive crowd of nearly 63,000 packed inside their majestic Art Deco home ground, Roaring at them to Wake Up.

By the end of the season, though, they had dropped to ninth place, closer to the relegation zone, in points gained, than they were to Champions Manchester City, and only 11,000 bothered to turn up for their scrappy 3-2 win over Sheffield Wednesday, at the end of April.

Nobody in N5 was bothering to set the alarm clocks for the following season.

Bob Wilson permanently replaced Jim Furnell in goal, at the start of the 1968-69 season, however, and his assured performances behind their hardened defence of Peter Storey, Bob McNab and Peter Simpson, with either Terry Neill or Ian Ure alongside Simpson in the middle, drove Arsenal to a Fairs Cup qualifying position, finishing in fourth place.

That was their highest First Division finish since the Fifties.

Arsenal had conceded only 27 goals from their 42 league games, and they'd also kept twenty clean sheets. They weren't so fluent at scoring, though, with John Radford top scoring on fifteen goals.

On Boxing Day 1968, with 62,300 filling Highbury, the third largest First Division crowd of the entire season, Arsenal beat the reigning European Champions Manchester United 3-0, after Radford, George Armstrong and David Court had all scored.

Another League Cup Final defeat against Third Division minnows Swindon Town, on Saturday 15th March, hit them really hard. They'd already overcome a tough Tottenham team over two physical legs in the Semi-final, winning 2-1 on aggregate, before Christmas.

A combined attendance of over 111,000 had watching those two brutal, bruising matches, at both Highbury and White Hart Lane.

To face Swindon Town in the Final felt a lot easier to Arsenal's weary players, who'd expected that it would be their Cup that year, but Swindon Town won 3-1 after extra-time.

That defeat, though, drove a deep determination and desire into Arsenal's team, ashamed of their show, of their shoddy lack of achievement, and assuring that it shouldn't ever happen again.

It shook them.

Finally, *finally*, IT WOKE THEM UP!

On November 8th 1969, Arsenal were spluttering towards a 0-0 draw at home to newly-promoted Derby County, well into the second half of their First Division match, with nearly fifty thousand swelling the banks of Highbury. Charlie George then replaced Terry Neill, for only his ninth appearance for Arsenal, after a decidedly indistinctive start to his career.

A tall player, at five feet and eleven inches, and with an arrogant air of aloofness and attitude about his appearance, Charlie George turned that particular match around.

An Islington Schools XI graduate, he scored Arsenal's first goal, and performed with such a lively enthusiasm behind John Radford and George Graham, neither McGovern nor Mackay could contain him. Jon Sammels scored twice, and George Armstrong hit the other as they thrashed the high-flying Rams 4-0.

An Arsenal fan who'd regularly stood on the North Bank as a boy, a new star was born. Charlie George was their only local lad in an Arsenal team full of Scots, Geordies, Yorkshiremen, and East Anglians, and he became their long-haired, *Maverick* Superstar as the Seventies arrived, but Arsenal's 1969-70 First Division campaign also fizzled out to yet another mid-table disappointment.

In the Inter-Cities Fairs Cup, though, Arsenal reached the Semi-finals, having beaten Glentoran, Sporting Lisbon, Rouen, and then Dinamo Bacau, of Romania, en route.

On Wednesday 8th April 1970, Ajax of Amsterdam, European Cup Finalists just a year earlier, arrived at Highbury for the first leg of their Semi-final.

Frank McLintock had dropped back into central defence, from midfield, back in December. He'd been a good quality midfield player, Mostly, but also prone to the odd comical mistake, which often cost Arsenal points.

This was a *Eureka!* moment for manager Bertie Mee and coach Don Howe.

As a central defensive partnership, McLintock and Simpson were among the very strongest of their era, or of any other era.

Also, Peter Marinello had been bought for £100,000, from Hibernian. It had been intended by Bertie Mee, at some point anyway, that Marinello would replace George Armstrong on the right side of midfield, and he started that match against Ajax.

Ajax were brim-full of talent, with Rudi Krol, Wim Suurbier, Gerry Muhren, Piet Keizer, Barry Hulshoff, and a young, twenty-two year old Johan Cruyff in their team.

Within three years, Cruyff became regarded as the best player in the World.

The prodigious Charlie George was the best player in this match, though, scoring twice, once in each half, as the ineffective Marinello was replaced by George Armstrong, who then set up Jon Sammels for Arsenal's third goal. Armstrong would keep his place in the team for their second leg game in Amsterdam, and for the Final.

A week later, Gerry Muhren scored for Ajax, at their Olympic Stadium, but Arsenal's 3-0 first leg win was a sufficient advantage, as an heroic defensive performance repelled a high-pressure, high-possession Ajax attack, time and time again.

Arsenal had succeeded in reaching their third Cup Final in three seasons.

On Wednesday 22nd April 1970, just one week after knocking out Ajax, Arsenal travelled to Brussels for the first leg of their Fairs Cup Final, against RSC Anderlecht.

Inspired and directed by the great Paul Van Himst, Anderlecht's Johan Devrindt and Jan Mulder, their Dutch international striker, had both scored before the half-hour mark. Then, twenty minutes into the second half, Mulder then struck his second goal to give Anderlecht an unbeatable 3-0 lead.

Arsenal were rattled, strangled, and facing a real massacre, but then, out of nowhere, Ray Kennedy scored what had appeared to be a mere consolation goal, late in the game.

Anderlecht had methodically picked Arsenal apart.

The 3-0 score-line had totally flattered Arsenal, to be honest, prior to Kennedy's goal.

That was, however, an invaluable goal. While Arsenal weren't exactly celebrating their 3-1 defeat, as they flew back to England, there was still some hope.

Anderlecht had already conceded three goals during their away legs of that season's Fairs Cup competition on three previous occasions, against Coleraine, Dunfermline and also Newcastle United. All Arsenal needed was to match this and also keep a clean sheet.

51,612 packed Highbury six days later, on Tuesday 28th April, for their Fairs Cup Final, second leg match.

ARSENAL		ANDERLECHT
Bob Wilson	1	Trappeniers
Peter Storey	2	Heylens
Bob McNab	3	Martens
Eddie Kelly	4	Nordahl
Frank McLintock	5	Velkeneers
Peter Simpson	6	Kialunda
George Armstrong	7	Desanghere
Jon Sammels	8	Devrindt
John Radford	9	Mulder
Charlie George	10	Van Himst
George Graham	11	Puis

Arsenal's desire and determination for achievement, deeply driven into them, deeply hurt into them after their Wembley defeat against Swindon Town, tore into Anderlecht from the very start, and they were within winning reach of the Belgians early on, after a stunning, long range goal by youth team graduate Eddie Kelly.

George Armstrong played an out-swinging corner kick from the left, which McLintock collected and controlled. He played the ball back to Kelly, twenty-five yards out, in the awful, sticky mud. Eddie Kelly beat the Swede Nordahl, who'd lost his footing, and then he hammered a right-footed shot, from outside of the crowded penalty area, just inside the left hand post of Anderlecht's goal.

Later on, into the second half, with only a quarter of an hour to go, and with Anderlecht still 3-2 ahead on aggregate, George Graham got the better of Nordahl, in midfield, and then passed wide to Bob McNab, on the green, green grass of the left wing.

From near the left bye-line, McNab floated a beautiful cross to the far post, which Radford attacked with a giant leap and headed the ball back across goal, and inside Trappeniers' right hand post on the bounce.

The whole Arsenal team celebrated under the rocking North Bank.

One minute later, Charlie George lofted a high one to the far side of the Anderlecht penalty area. Jon Sammels didn't jump as high as the giant Belgian defender, Velkeneers, but he'd jumped far more accurately. Sammels won the header and put the ball onto a plate for himself to strike it low along the mud, past Trappeniers, and inside the far post.

Arsenal held on to their 3-0 lead, and that was the First time any Team had Come back from Three Goals Down in any European Final, to win the Cup. Liverpool repeated the feat thirty-five years later.

At the beginning of their 1970-71 season, Northern Ireland international full-back Pat Rice finally became Arsenal's regular right back.

He'd actually played more games for his country than his club, prior to this season.

This tactical decision by both Bertie Mee and Don Howe had allowed them to release the hard tackling and cold-eyed Peter Storey into midfield, to unleash his damage.

Peter Storey admitted that he'd respectfully intended to smack his opponents early, and hard, just so they'd feel as if they'd been in a car crash, or had hit a brick wall.

Even Johnny Giles claimed that Storey was the hardest player that he'd ever faced.

Peter Storey could also play, though, and just like Arsenal's re-invention of Frank McLintock as a centre half, the moving of Storey to his new midfield space, in front of both McLintock and Simpson, was an inspired change that transformed their future.

For their first game of the new season, on Saturday 15th August 1970, nearly 50,000 filled Goodison Park, and witnessed Arsenal come back twice, against the defending Champions, to draw 2-2 with Everton. Goals from Charlie George and George Graham secured a good away point, but Charlie George had broken his ankle while scoring his goal, and he was unfortunately ruled out until the following February.

Even so, Frank McLintock uttered a huge understatement by claiming that this Arsenal team was the very best, during his six years at Highbury.

At that point, though, nobody guessed just how good this Arsenal team really was.

As well as Charlie George, Arsenal had also missed Peter Simpson for the first three months of the season. The blonde John Roberts, a Welsh international signing from Northampton Town, filled in alongside McLintock during Simpson's absence.

Ray Kennedy, a young and enthusiastic twenty year old centre forward from County Durham, had taken Charlie George's position in Arsenal's team. He'd been rejected at Port Vale, and in fact, Sir Stanley Matthews had even told him that he wasn't good enough to be a professional footballer.

So, at sixteen years old, Kennedy took the Greatest's advice, and he returned home quietly to County Durham. He went to work in a sweet factory, but continued playing for local amateur side New Hartley Juniors.

Luckily, he was miraculously spotted by a Scout, and then he signed for Arsenal in 1968.

Arsenal drew 0-0 at West Ham, and then they hammered Manchester United 4-0, in their opening home match of the season.

John Radford's hat-trick and George Graham had won the match, with a 54,117 Highbury crowd watching their demolition of Best, Charlton, Law, Stiles and Crerand.

Still, nobody was expecting Arsenal to challenge for the title, not even their own fans.

On Tuesday 25th August, only 34,000 attended their home match against Huddersfield Town, but Ray Kennedy scored his first goal of the season as Arsenal won 1-0. They lost 2-1 away at FA Cup winners Chelsea, followed by a goalless draw at home to leaders Leeds United, but Arsenal were down in sixth place, after five games.

Three wins in a row then propelled Arsenal up to second place, as they beat Tottenham 2-0 (Armstrong 2), Burnley 2-1 (Radford, Kennedy), and finally West Brom 6-2 (Graham 2, Kennedy 2, Armstrong, own goal), during September 1970.

Also, in the First round of the Fairs Cup, Arsenal had beaten Lazio 2-0, winning 4-2 on aggregate. However, on Saturday 26th September, rampant Stoke City were on fire, as they hammered Arsenal 5-0 at the Victoria Ground, and all the while, Leeds just kept pulling away, taking sixteen points from their first ten matches.

Arsenal regained some form on the following Monday night, beating Ipswich Town 4-0 in their League Cup Second round replay, having already drawn 0-0 at Portman Road. Ray Kennedy then hit a great hat-trick in Arsenal's 4-0 win over Nottingham Forest, at the beginning of October, with George Armstrong scoring the other.

That win over Forest launched a superb three months for Arsenal, during which they dropped just three points from fourteen matches.

By New Year's Eve 1970, Arsenal were only three points behind Leeds, having played a game less, and the two clubs were way, way ahead of third-placed Spurs.

On Tuesday 6th October, Arsenal won 1-0 away at Luton Town, in the League Cup Third round, with George Graham scoring the winner. Graham also scored on the following Saturday, away at Newcastle, but Pop Robson equalised to deprive Arsenal of both points. Emphatic 4-0 victories over Everton, and then Coventry City by 3-1, sent Arsenal up to second in the league, before a Hallowe'en treat at Highbury, against a tricky Derby County side.

Early on, from Bob Wilson's throw-out to McNab on the left, Arsenal swept swiftly through Derby's swamped midfield. McNab, Graham, Radford and Kennedy all combined sweetly to release George Armstrong, galloping in dangerously from the left wing. Roy McFarland slid in to tackle Armstrong, but he unwittingly played in the late-running, and unmarked Eddie Kelly on the edge of the penalty area. Kelly then smashed the ball home past Les Green.

Arsenal's second goal, in the second half, was classic Arsenal.

Bob McNab threw in to George Graham, and Graham launched a right-footed mortar-bomb into Derby's area, for John Radford to leap above McFarland and head the ball over Green, and into the net for a 2-0 win.

George Armstrong had been in electric form throughout, absolutely unplayable when he was at his very best, crossing from both the left and the right, and with both feet. Awarded the Man of the Match award on ITV's *The Big Match*, he'd been absolutely impossible to defend against by Derby's top quality back four.

Ray Kennedy and Peter Storey's penalty kick helped Arsenal to a 2-0 home win over Sturm Graz, in the Fairs Cup Second round, winning 2-1 on aggregate.

On Saturday 7th November, John Radford's second half goal secured Arsenal's hard fought 1-0 away win at Bloomfield Road, against an entertaining, but beleaguered and bottom-placed Blackpool.

Crystal Palace then visited Highbury twice inside five days. On Monday 9th November, in their League Cup Fourth round replay, after Palace and Arsenal had drawn 0-0 at Selhurst Park a fortnight earlier, 45,000 were stunned as Arsenal lost 0-2 at home to the struggling Glaziers.

On the following Saturday, though, and back in the First Division, Palace struck again. Their top scorer Alan Birchenall equalised John Radford's first half goal, to earn a 1-1 away draw.

Even so, Arsenal responded to those disappointments by welcoming Peter Simpson back to action, and then winning 1-0 away at Ipswich.

George Armstrong had scored, securing their first win in two weeks. Bill Shankly's regenerated Liverpool side then visited Highbury, on Saturday 28th November.

ARSENAL		LIVERPOOL
Bob Wilson	1	Ray Clemence
Pat Rice	2	Chris Lawler
Bob McNab	3	Alec Lindsay
Eddie Kelly	4	Tommy Smith
Frank McLintock	5	Larry Lloyd
Peter Simpson	6	Emlyn Hughes
George Armstrong	7	Brian Hall
Peter Storey	8	John Toshack
John Radford	9	Steve Heighway
Ray Kennedy	10	John McLaughlin
Jon Sammels	11	Ian Ross
George Graham	12	Phil Boersma

Early in the first half, Peter Storey drove his dynamic shot through Liverpool's crowded penalty area, that was deflected just a foot wide of the left post for an Arsenal corner. From Armstrong's left-sided corner kick, Sammels volleyed, first time, from the right side of the area. Ray Clemence just managed to save low at his knees.

Into the second half, McLintock's loose pass, inside the centre circle mud, was intercepted by Heighway on the halfway line, and he raced clear, chased by Rice. Bob Wilson, though, came out to save bravely at Heighway's feet, inside his own area.

Jon Sammels, an experienced skilful attacker with a powerful shot, and also a really elegant player, but often barracked by the Highbury crowd for an apparent lack of effort, was starting only his second First Division game of the season He'd started thirty-six league games during 1969-70, but their team restructuring, which had moved Peter Storey forward into midfield, and also brought Ray Kennedy in as a replacement for the injured Charlie George, had greatly reduced his first team chances.

Sammels had played only fourteen league games for Arsenal during 1970-71, and he was eventually sold to Leicester City for £100,000 during July 1971, after he'd played over 200 First Division games at Highbury.

Twenty-five yards from the Liverpool goal, Jon Sammels tackled Ian Ross superbly, and he then played a one-two with substitute George Graham, before lofting a diagonal pass into the Liverpool area, which Graham volleyed, left-footed, through Clemence's arms for an unstoppable goal.

Late on, George Armstrong launched a long ball from the halfway line, that was chested down by Graham, twenty yards out, into the penalty area. Clemence came out to save at Ray Kennedy's feet, but Kennedy kept his head well enough to keep the ball alive, and he prevented it from being cleared away from the six yard box.

John Radford darted in like a missile, and he hammered home his shot.

That great 2-0 win, which highlighted Arsenal as the only team able to challenge Leeds United for the title, was followed by a 2-0 away win at Manchester City, on Saturday 5th December, with Armstrong and Radford both scoring.

In December 1970, Arsenal reached the Fairs Cup Quarter-finals, after they'd easily beaten Beveren, winning 4-0 at Highbury (Graham, Kennedy 2, Sammels), and then drawing 0-0 away at Beveren's tiny, but tightly packed, 14,000 filled Belgian ground.

Their 2-1 win over Wolves, was followed up by a 3-1 drubbing of Manchester United, away at Old Trafford, a week before Christmas. Frank McLintock, George Graham and Ray Kennedy all scored, and all of them were headed goals.

Southampton, going well and heading for a UEFA Cup place, then held Arsenal 0-0 at Highbury, as the Gunners sat just three points behind Leeds, with one game in hand.

A boisterous 14,500 crowd filled The Huish, on Wednesday 6th January 1971, as Southern League side Yeovil Town hosted Arsenal in the FA Cup Third round.

They were shattered, though, as John Radford scored two goals, and Ray Kennedy their other, during Arsenal's imperious 3-0 victory. On the following Saturday, George Graham and Ray Kennedy both scored in the Gunners' 2-0 win over West Ham United, at Highbury.

Furthermore, Leeds United had surprisingly lost 1-2 at home to Tottenham's brilliant performance. Martin Chivers had scored both of Spurs' goals, and Arsenal were then suddenly only one single point behind Leeds, but they'd played a game less.

Unfortunately, subsequent defeats at Huddersfield Town, and then Liverpool, in the latter half of January, had coincided with Leeds United's victories over both West Ham and Manchester City.

So Arsenal dropped back to five points behind the red-hot First Division favourites.

Then, on Monday 1st February, Charlie George returned, after five and a half months out. And he scored, during Arsenal's 3-2 home win over Portsmouth in their FA Cup Fourth round replay, having originally drawn 1-1 away, in front of nearly 40,000, at Fratton Park. Just in time, as Arsenal's season had begun showing cracks, their tall, long-haired Maverick had returned. On Saturday 6th February, John Radford's late goal earned Arsenal a 1-0 home win over Manchester City, their first league win for a month. Charlie George then scored both of Arsenal's goals, at Maine Road, on Wednesday 17th February, as Arsenal won a tough away FA Cup Fifth round match, 2-1, against Manchester City.

Charlie George then scored Arsenal's third goal in their 3-2 home win over Ipswich, although Town had come back from 3-0 down, inspired by Colin Viljoen.

Leeds United just continued winning, though, beating Wolves 3-0 (Madeley, Clarke, Giles), at the very same time as **The Who** recorded *Live at Leeds*.

Derby County then defeated Arsenal 2-0 at The Baseball Ground, at the end of February, however, while Leeds went on to win three times in February.

As March arrived, Leeds United led the First Division by seven points.

FIRST DIVISION LEADERS, 27TH FEBRUARY 1971

	PL	W	D	L	F	A	PTS
Leeds United	31	21	7	3	55	22	49
ARSENAL	29	18	6	5	51	25	42
Chelsea	31	14	11	6	41	33	39
Wolves	30	16	6	8	49	44	38
Liverpool	30	11	13	6	29	17	35
Tottenham	28	12	9	7	41	27	33
Southampton	30	12	9	9	39	32	33

On Tuesday 2nd March, Arsenal won 3-0 away at Wolves Radford, Armstrong, Kennedy), and on the following Saturday, with 42,000 filling Filbert Street, Arsenal held Leicester City to a goalless away draw in the FA Cup Quarter-finals.

One week later, on Saturday 13th March, 35,000 packed into Selhurst Park, as Bob Wilson, Pat Rice, Bob McNab, Peter Storey, Frank McLintock, Peter Simpson, George Armstrong, George Graham, John Radford, Ray Kennedy and Charlie George visited Crystal Palace.

In their away strip of yellow and royal blue, Arsenal had fielded that classic eleven for the very first time. Arsenal weathered a heavy period of Crystal Palace pressure throughout the first half. Birchenall, Tambling, Sewell and Jim Scott all created sustained assaults of attack after attack, hitting the woodwork twice, and having another shot cleared off the line.

Eventually, though, Arsenal got the ball back, and they were ruthless. Frank McLintock collected a Palace clearance on the halfway line, and he launched a rocket of a ball, thirty yards forward for the leaping George Graham to cushion a header across Jackson's goal, and in off the far post.

Late in the second half, George Graham crossed for McLintock to head on for Radford. Radford headed back for substitute Jon Sammels to drive home a decisive deflected second goal, his only goal of the season, in his last ever match for Arsenal.

That 2-0 win at Crystal Palace was even more valuable, as bottom club Blackpool had fought back to draw 1-1 at home with Leeds United. Arsenal were six points behind Leeds, but still with two games in hand.

57,443, Highbury's biggest crowd of the season, up to then, went into a frenzy as the King, Charlie George, scored his fourth FA Cup goal of the season, heading in George Armstrong's corner, to beat Leicester City 1-0, on Monday 15th March, in their Sixth round replay.

Peter Storey then scored their only goal of the game, on the following Saturday, as Arsenal beat Blackpool 1-0, to stay just six points behind Leeds United.

FC Cologne then drew 2-2 with Arsenal in the Quarter-finals of the Fairs Cup, over the two legs, but the Germans reached the Semi-finals on the away goals rule.

On Saturday 27th March, in their FA Cup Semi-final at Hillsborough, Arsenal were absolutely hammered by Stoke City for over an hour of the game, and they trailed 2-0, but it really should have been three or four, before Peter Storey had the game of his life. First, he scored with a brilliant long range screamer, and then equalised with the very last kick of the match, calmly placing his penalty kick beyond Peter Shilton, after John Mahoney had handled on the line.

On that same day, two goals by Peter Houseman, and another from Peter Osgood, had helped Chelsea beat Leeds United 3-1, with more than 58,000 swarmed inside Stamford Bridge. Arsenal then had three games in hand on the league leaders.

On the last day of March, Arsenal supporters packed Villa Park's huge Holte End, for their FA Cup Semi-final replay against Stoke.

62,500 filled the stadium, and during the first half, George Armstrong's right-footed, outswinging, right sided corner was buried by George Graham's header at the far post.

Then, during the second half, Armstrong set up John Radford on the left wing, with a sweet reverse pass. Radford crossed low from the bye-line, and Ray Kennedy then stabbed home from close range, amidst the broken Stoke City defence, for a 2-0 win.

Stoke were totally shattered, completely different to the vibrant side that had outplayed Arsenal for most of the first game, appearing physically and emotionally spent. Arsenal had their Wembley Final booked, though, their fourth Final in four years. Now they just needed to win their First Division games, and put some pressure on Leeds United.

A huge 62,037 crowd totally filled Highbury under roasting hot Saturday afternoon sunshine on the 3rd of April 1971, as fans climbed up onto the North Bank roof, for some fresh air and a better view of their home match against Chelsea.

After a tight, goalless first half, Ray Kennedy opened the scoring, finishing left-footed, after Charlie George had cleverly dummied George Armstrong's square pass.

Kennedy then scored his second before the end, hammering home inside the area, after a dazzling run and deft chip by Charlie George had played him in, for a 2-0 win.

Leeds United had also won, though, hammering Burnley 4-0, with the sensational Allan Clarke scoring all four of their goals.

But on Tuesday 6th April, Arsenal won the first of their three games in hand.

Ray Kennedy fired them to a 1-0 home win over Coventry City, during the second half.

Then, on the following Saturday, Arsenal chipped further away at Leeds United's lead, beating Southampton 2-1 away at The Dell.

John Radford and Frank McLintock had scored in each half, to stun a hostile 30,000 home crowd, roaring Saints back into Europe.

Leeds United had been held to a 1-1 draw away at Newcastle United. The Magpies' recent signing, John Tudor, had equalised Peter Lorimer's earlier strike, and now Leeds led by only three points, having played two more games.

The City Ground's largest crowd of the season, 40,727, saw Arsenal move within two points of Leeds, three days later, as Kennedy, McLintock and George all scored to secure a 3-0 win away at Nottingham Forest.

Arsenal still had those two games in hand, though, after Leeds had been held to a goalless draw by lowly Huddersfield, at Leeds Road on the previous night.

On Saturday 17th April, one of the most notorious moments in the history of English league football occurred, and on the very day when Leeds United threw away their lead at the top of the league. West Bromwich Albion won 2-1 at Elland Road, through goals from Tony Brown and Jeff Astle, but Leeds also handicapped themselves against winning the title the following season, too.

There were scenes of riot and disorder on the pitch, following Astle's goal, which Leeds' players were sure was offside, and they harassed Ray Tinkler, the referee. Unfortunately, fans also attempted to confront him, and were restrained by the police.

Leeds United were subsequently ordered to play their first four home games of the following season away from Elland Road, as a result of the troubles.

Down at Arsenal, at home to Newcastle United, Charlie George picked up a ball from Peter Storey, late in the second half. On the edge of the penalty area, he strode past Barrowclough, before smashing home a great, left-footed winner, from just inside the area. It was a crucial winner that sent Arsenal up to the top of Division One, on goal average, for the first time since the early Fifties.

On the following Tuesday, Arsenal won 1-0 against Burnley, and also relegated the Clarets, following Charlie George's twenty-sixth minute penalty kick.

Arsenal's nine match league-winning run then came to an end, four days later, as they were held to a 2-2 draw away at West Brom. Leeds United, however, had won their first league game for three weeks, beating Southampton 3-0 away.

On Bank Holiday Monday, 26th April, Elland Road hosted the Summit Meeting between Leeds United and Arsenal. Both sides were at full strength, except for Leeds, who were missing Peter Lorimer for three games, due to injury. Mick Bates played in his place, while Paul Reaney was also injured, but Paul Madeley was nearly as good.

A 48,350 crowd, not Elland Road's largest attendance of 1970-71, oddly enough, watched a tactical first half, during which neither team created any serious attempts on goal. Arsenal were content to simply absorb Leeds' fruitless attacks, time after time.

Eddie Gray's creativity was strangled by a massed double-ranked defence. Neither Clarke nor Jones ever found space, while Storey versus Bremner was a classic duel.

As time ticked on towards stoppage time, Paul Madeley and Billy Bremner combined to release Jack Charlton, their World Cup winner, running apparently four or five yards in an offside position. Big Jack shot past Wilson, as McLintock and Simpson both stood, with arms aloft, appealing for an offside flag. The ball hit a post, but the tall, long-legged Charlton stabbed the rebound home, just beating Bob McNab to the ball.

Referee Norman Burtenshaw, from Norfolk, allowed the goal to stand, and Arsenal loudly protested, long and hard and angrily. Charlie George was booked after he'd drop-kicked the ball, through frustration, into the ecstatic Leeds United home fans, who'd momentarily forgotten West Brom's goal of nine days earlier.

They'd remember it again, of course, and would refuse to forget it for another forty-odd years.

The game ended, shortly afterwards, and Leeds returned to the top of Division One, by just a single point, but having played one game more.

Television replays, shown afterwards, had suggested that McNab had very probably played Charlton just onside, and the Arsenal players, who'd protested so bitterly towards Mr Burtenshaw, agreed that he'd been correct.

To their discredit, though, most of the Leeds players still blame Ray Tinkler for their home defeat to West Brom.

That, for all their wonderful, World Class football, still stands as one of the main reasons why many fans still resent Don Revie's Leeds, and probably always will.

They lost to West Brom, when at best, they might have scraped a point, but who do they blame for their dropped points away at rock bottom Blackpool, and the other mediocre teams?

Who do Leeds blame for their home defeats to both Spurs and Liverpool?

To blame the pantomime villain Tinkler is the much easier option.

On the final Saturday of the season, Leeds beat Nottingham Forest 2-0 (Bremner, Lorimer), while Arsenal scraped a 1-0 win over Stoke City at Highbury. Eddie Kelly came on as a substitute for Peter Storey, to force home a late winner, sending their 55,000 home crowd absolutely wild with mad joy.

Not that it had really mattered; if Arsenal had only drawn 0-0 with Stoke, a win away at Tottenham would still win them the Championship, on goal average.

Eddie Kelly's goal only meant that Arsenal could actually draw 0-0, and still win the league, but no team ever plays for a goalless draw.

An official crowd of 51,992 were packed into White Hart Lane for the title decider on May Bank Holiday Monday, 3rd May 1971. Police estimates, though, had suggested that as many as Fifty Thousand were locked out of the ground that night.

Referee Kevin Howley was officiating his very last game, prior to his retirement, but due to the swelling of the crowds down Tottenham High Road, he'd had to abandon his car on the street, and walk a mile to the ground, as indeed had several players.

TOTTENHAM HOTSPUR		ARSENAL
Pat Jennings	1	Bob Wilson
Joe Kinnear	2	Pat Rice
Cyril Knowles	3	Bob McNab
Alan Mullery	4	Eddie Kelly
Peter Collins	5	Frank McLintock
Phil Beal	6	Peter Simpson
Alan Gilzean	7	George Armstrong
Steve Perryman	8	George Graham
Martin Chivers	9	John Radford
Martin Peters	10	Ray Kennedy
Jimmy Neighbour	11	Charlie George

Spurs had created the clearer chances on the night, though, amidst the racket; McLintock and Simpson both had an uncomfortable night against their lively and powerful attacking partnership of Chivers and Gilzean. Martin Peters had also fizzed about dangerously, alongside the unhurried class of Mullery.

Peters volleyed onto the top of Arsenal's crossbar, after half an hour, and then Mullery and Gilzean combined to release Peters just inside the penalty area, but Bob Wilson was at his sharpest, turning Peters' shot around his post.

Alan Gilzean should have then turned in a cross that zipped across the face of Arsenal's goal, but he just couldn't make contact.

George Armstrong was at his usual ubiquitous self, and he eventually created Arsenal's vital chance, just three minutes before the end. Tottenham's defence, greatly missing the commanding Mike England's presence, were guilty of some disastrous decision making inside their own area, allowing John Radford a shot at their near post.

Pat Jennings saved brilliantly, though, punching the ball out wide to his right, and outside of his penalty area, as Spurs regrouped. Armstrong met the ball, in mid left field, and he crossed, left-footed. Ray Kennedy flung himself up and headed Arsenal to almost their first title since 1953, in his first full season as a professional footballer.

Arsenal then defended desperately for the long, final three minutes of that long season. Tottenham Hotspur, neither the team, nor their fans had wanted Arsenal to win that League title. Spurs fans had even worn Leeds United scarves at the match, and they **ROARED** Tottenham forward for the equaliser that would give the title to Leeds.

Jimmy Neighbour sent one final corner into a packed Arsenal penalty box, but Bob Wilson sprung like a buck and he grabbed the ball, before Mr Howley's whistle blew.

Arsenal became the first team to win the First Division title on eight occasions.

Thousands invaded the pitch; they totally filled the pitch, in fact. It was a totally jubilant occasion, though, and Tottenham Hotspur, as a club, and as supporters, displayed absolute class. Bill Nicholson supplied a box of Champagne for Arsenal's changing room, while Frank McLintock was chaired off the pitch by a fan with a Leeds United scarf tied around his neck.

On the following Saturday, 8th May, with the long, long Monday celebrations over, and the many Tuesday hangovers well-recovered from, Arsenal arrived at Wembley Stadium to face Liverpool in the FA Cup Final.

It was a boiling hot day, at the very beginning of the long Hot Pants summer, with temperatures up in the high nineties'.

The red hot heat affected both teams, and the first ninety minutes weren't filled with classic attacking football. Peter Storey welcomed Steve Heighway, very much, to his first visit to Wembley Stadium, while McLintock and Simpson subdued Liverpool's attacking threat of Toshack and Evans, and in truth, neither Clemence nor Wilson had much to do, during the ninety minutes.

ARSENAL LIVERPOOL

Bob Wilson	1	Ray Clemence
Pat Rice	2	Chris Lawler
Bob McNab	3	Alec Lindsay
Peter Storey	4	Tommy Smith
Frank McLintock	5	Larry Lloyd
Peter Simpson	6	Emlyn Hughes
George Armstrong	7	Ian Callaghan
George Graham	8	Alun Evans
John Radford	9	Steve Heighway
Ray Kennedy	10	John Toshack
Charlie George	11	Brian Hall
Eddie Kelly	12	Peter Thompson

Both teams were shattered, as the match went into extra-time.

But then, the fireworks started. In the first minute of extra-time, the classy Peter Thompson, who'd replaced the ineffective Evans, found Steve Heighway in yards of space, out on the left side of Liverpool's midfield. Heighway descended on Arsenal's penalty area, tracked by Pat Rice, and chased by Armstrong.

Heighway beat both players with a single touch, before he drove his left-footed shot past Wilson at his near post. It was a terrible goal to concede, but McLintock, running off his reserve energy tank, wouldn't allow his team to give up.

Kennedy passed to Radford in midfield, thirty yards out, and Radford hooked the ball up over his own head, with his back to the Liverpool goal, and into the penalty area. Neither Smith, nor Lloyd, marking Eddie Kelly, could clear the ball, and with the subtlest of flicks, Kelly, who'd come on for Storey in the second half, just rolled the ball past Clemence.

George Graham ran over the ball as it rolled in, though, and he actually claimed the goal, but it was Eddie Kelly's equaliser.

John Radford then collected a McLintock's forward header, and he set up Charlie George on the eighteen yard line. George took one touch, and then drove the ball high into Ray Clemence's goal, just inside the left post of the Liverpool goal.

Charlie George then lay on his back with his arms aloft, just lying there, waiting for his teammates to come and pick him up. He was the King of Highbury!

It was one of the most famous goal celebrations, and an iconic moment in football history.

Tommy Smith, one of football's hardest men, was the complete gentleman, warmly shaking the hand of every Arsenal player, the referee and both linesmen.

Arsenal's achievement was truly immense. They had turned around a massive, almost insurmountable lead by one of the greatest of all football teams.

Arsenal had won twenty-nine First Division games, during 1970-71, while Leeds United won twenty-seven. Their combined total of fifty-six top flight wins by the top two teams remains an all-time record in English football, although it was equalled by the equally dominant Manchester City and Manchester United during 2011-12.

In eighty-three years of English league football, only eight teams had won more games than Leeds United's 27 wins in 1970-71. Unfortunately for them, one of those teams was this Arsenal team. In the forty-two years since 1971, a further nine teams have won more than 27 top flight matches during a single season.

During 1970-71, Arsenal had kept an All-time record Thirty-seven Clean Sheets in league and cup matches, including Twenty-five in the First Division. They'd won the league with a family attitude of all for one, and one for all, fighting together from the first kick of the season, to the very, very last.

Their team spirit was indeed their strength, a spirit that kept them going through the tough winter months, when aches and bruises and knocks were simply ignored, and Leeds United's advantage just grew and grew. Arsenal just kept going, kept chasing, when other teams, lesser teams, would have folded.

The nucleus of Arsenal's team, Bob Wilson, Pat Rice, Bob McNab, Peter Storey, Frank McLintock, George Armstrong, George Graham, John Radford and Ray Kennedy missed only twelve matches, between them all, out of a total of 378 league games; Wilson, McLintock and Armstrong were all ever-presents.

Peter Simpson had missed their first seventeen games of the season, but he played in all of their remaining twenty-five games, alongside McLintock, and Charlie George missed most of the season, from August to February, but he scored five FA Cup goals in only six games, after his return.

He'd also scored vital match-winning goals in three games during April.

Ray Kennedy, rated as not good enough for either Port Vale or professional football, was the English Champions' top goal-scorer, with twenty-six league and cup goals, at just nineteen years of age.

John Radford had also hit twenty-one, with George Graham on fourteen, while Charlie George completed a quartet of Arsenal players to reach double figures, by firing in ten goals.

George Armstrong, who'd created a third of Arsenal's total goals, also contributed eight himself.

Arsenal's success, though, was mainly down to the dual managerial partnership of Bertie Mee, their man-manager, and Don Howe, their master tactician. Just as Man City had thrived under their Joe Mercer and Malcolm Allison dream team, yet floundered when half of their partnership had seen himself as the King; the same fate awaited Arsenal, when one half of their partnership strived for success on his own.

Less than two months after 250,000 had lined all the roads from Highbury to Islington, on the Sunday after the FA Cup Final, Don Howe left Arsenal.

The tactical genius and the footballing brains of the Mee/Howe partnership had been lured away by West Bromwich Albion to become their manager.

Bertie Mee greatly missed his right hand man. Arsenal also greatly missed Don Howe, but mostly, they greatly missed Charlie George and Bob McNab for over half of the following season.

By late November 1971, Arsenal had lost half of their First Division matches, and they were way behind in the title race. They were out of the race to defend their title. However, eight points were gained from their next five games, prior to Christmas, pulling them much closer to the leaders.

Then, on 22nd December, Bertie Mee signed World Cup winner Alan Ball from Everton, for a club record £200,000 transfer fee. Inspired by this, Arsenal then went on a superb run through to the end of February, winning eleven points from seven games, to get right back into the meat of the First Division Championship race, along with Manchester City, Leeds, Derby and Liverpool.

FIRST DIVISION LEADERS, 19TH FEBRUARY 1972

	PL	W	D	L	F	A	PTS
Man City	30	16	9	5	59	34	41
Leeds United	29	16	7	6	44	22	39
Derby County	29	15	8	6	50	28	38
ARSENAL	29	16	5	8	44	27	37
Liverpool	30	15	7	8	40	27	37
Wolves	30	13	10	7	50	42	36
Tottenham	29	13	9	7	45	31	35
Man United	29	14	7	8	52	43	35

March was a horrible month, though. Arsenal lost three out of four of their First Division matches, including a 3-0 thrashing by Leeds United at Elland Road, and they fell eleven points behind leaders Manchester City, and out of the title race, for good.

On Wednesday 22nd March, Arsenal played the second leg of their European Cup Quarter-final match against Ajax of Amsterdam.

Having easily dumped Stromsgodset of Norway (7-1), and then Grasshoppers of Zurich (6-0) out of the first two rounds, Arsenal had been drawn against the reigning European Champions and the strongest opposition that remained in the last eight.

They'd only lost 2-1 in the first leg, away in Amsterdam, as a massive, hostile 65,000 crowd filled the Olympic Stadium, and Dutch boos greeted every Arsenal touch.

Ray Kennedy had given Arsenal a surprise early lead, but Gerrie Muhren equalised before half-time. Then, with only fifteen minutes remaining, Ajax were awarded a very arguable penalty kick, but Muhren converted it for a slender advantage to take to Highbury.

56,145 packed Highbury for the second leg, with Ajax playing in an away kit of white shirts and blue shorts. They'd also introduced the now commonly-used system of squad numbers to an English football ground.

Arie Haan wore 15, Blankenburg 12, and Johan Cruyff wore his famous number 14 shirt.

Peter Marinello came back into the team for the injured John Radford, and young Sammy Nelson was also playing in place of Bob McNab, who'd suffered a bad knee injury in early January. Early on, Blankenburg made a terrible error on the edge of his own area, giving possession to Marinello, who advanced into the box, but from ten yards out, he totally fucked up his chance, and Heinz Stuy was able to gather the ball.

Then, Cruyff ran from his own penalty area, through the entire Arsenal team, leaving Frank McLintock chasing his heels, but his low shot from twenty yards out was gathered by the diving Bob Wilson. Some of Cruyff's turns and moves, throughout the game, were among the most dazzling ever seen at Highbury.

After fourteen minutes, though, disaster struck. Rudi Krol advanced into the Arsenal half, and he lofted a forward pass up towards the Arsenal penalty box. The back-pedalling George Graham, under pressure from Arie Haan, got his head to the ball on the edge of his own area, but he got his direction completely wrong.

The ball ballooned up over Bob Wilson and bounced over his goal-line. Ajax led 3-1 on aggregate.

Charlie George's low pass from the left was shot just wide of the far post by McLintock, from inside the area. Arsenal were dearly missing John Radford's aerial presence, especially inside the Ajax penalty area, from their many crosses and set-pieces. Marinello was never a strong aerial player, and far too often, good attacks came to nothing. George Armstrong, though, had managed to head a decent half-chance into Stuy's arms. Charlie George's good right-sided cross into the six yard box, was then cushion headed just wide by the heavily-marked George Graham.

Time was running out, and Arsenal were looking more and more desperate and disconsolate, as their trademark aerial dominance in attack was diminished by total Dutch aerial dominance over Peter Marinello.

Even so, Arsenal's sustained pressure resulted in another Ajax defensive error, on the edge of their own area. The ball was swung in from the right. Graham headed back inside, and Charlie George volleyed first time, from just inside the penalty area. His shot flashed just wide of the left post.

Charlie George looked up at the dark London skies, and he almost cried.

Ajax held on for a great 3-1 aggregate win. For all of their European Cup Final wins, this was one of the very best wins of their Golden, Total Football era.

They went on to beat Benfica in the Semi-finals, and then Inter Milan 2-0 in the Final in Rotterdam, retaining their title as European Champions, but it was Arsenal who were the best team that they'd faced in 1972, and that match should've been the Final.

Arsenal, at their best, would have had a great chance of overturning Ajax's slim advantage, but that match proved just how valuable John Radford was to Arsenal's balance of attack. With recent signing Alan Ball unable to play due to UEFA's rules, Peter Marinello entered a level of football that he clearly was just not good enough for.

Bertie Mee made two major mistakes as Arsenal's manager. His first mistake was forking out a club record transfer fee for a player who'd played just 45 games for Hibs, and had scored only five goals.

Joe Jordan had gone to Leeds United from Morton, during the same year, for a third of the price.

Peter Marinello was eventually freed to join Second Division Portsmouth in July 1973, after starting just 38 league games during three and a half years at Highbury.

He was a victim of the hype that had heralded his arrival in English First Division football, hype for which Marinello could not be blamed, but he rode the rollercoaster gleefully, with his modelling career, as well as guest appearances on *Top of the Pops*, but he just forgot about the football.

It's never pleasurable to see the personal life of a young, naïve player descend into turmoil, but that's what happened. Peter Marinello will always be remembered as the "next George Best" that never was. *Mama told you not to come*, some opposing fans used to sing at him as he struggled, but he did eventually do okay at Portsmouth, as well as up at Motherwell, in the Scottish Premier League, during the late Seventies.

Out of the European Cup, and also out of the Championship race, Arsenal at least had their FA Cup to play for. They'd visited Swindon Town on Saturday 15th January, with a club record 32,000 crowd filling The County Ground to its capacity, providing Arsenal with the chance to banish their nightmare of 1969.

Thirty-seven year old Dave Mackay was now Swindon's player-manager, and he marshalled their defence that day. The cameras were there. An FA Cup upset was widely predicted, and Swindon had their chances.

Alan Ball, though, had showed his class, after setting up George Armstrong for the first, and then dampening the Wiltshire fervour by scoring his first goal for Arsenal as they won 2-0.

Arsenal then set off along the Great Western Railway again, in the Fourth round, visiting Reading on Saturday 5th February.

Another huge 25,756 crowd filled Elm Park, bringing record receipts of £17,500 to the Berkshire club. Stuart Morgan's own goal, and then a rare Pat Rice goal had scraped Arsenal through, though, with their 2-1 away win.

They were then drawn away at Derby County in the Fifth round, a tie that took three matches to decide the winner, and that was watched by nearly 143,000 supporters over the three games.

39,662 then filled The Baseball Ground, Derby's largest crowd of the season in the very year that they ended up as League Champions, to watch a thrilling match in the mud. Charlie George put Arsenal 1-0 up at half-time, but John O'Hare was fouled inside the Arsenal area at the start of the second half, and Alan Hinton buried his penalty kick past Bob Wilson.

Charlie George fired Arsenal ahead again, ten minutes before the end, but Alan Durban headed home Hector's cross in the 89th minute to force a replay.

On the following Tuesday, 29th February, the match had to be played in the afternoon, due to power cuts preventing Arsenal from using their floodlights. It was startling then, that 63,077 had over-filled Highbury, their largest crowd of the Decade, but thousands were also locked out.

Touts were collecting twenty times the face value of tickets, outside the Stadium.

Colin Todd and Roy McFarland were never really troubled by Arsenal's attack throughout two hours of goalless football. Arsenal had one scare when Armstrong's careless tackle on John O'Hare, inside his own area, went unpunished, but Derby had had a very strong case for a penalty kick.

DERBY COUNTY   ARSENAL

Colin Boulton	1	Bob Wilson
Ron Webster	2	Pat Rice
John Robson	3	Sammy Nelson
Alan Durban	4	Peter Storey
Roy McFarland	5	Frank McLintock
Colin Todd	6	Peter Simpson
John McGovern	7	George Armstrong
Archie Gemmill	8	Alan Ball
John O'Hare	9	Charlie George
Kevin Hector	10	Ray Kennedy
Alan Hinton	11	George Graham

The second replay, held two weeks later due to Arsenal's European Cup match away in Amsterdam, was played at Filbert Street in Leicester, on Monday 13th March.

This game attracted Filbert Street's biggest attendance for three years, 40,000, as another massive crowd watched the 1971 English Champions play the future 1972 Champions, on a Monday afternoon.

It was inevitable, perhaps, with those two great teams so finely balanced and evenly matched, that just one mistake would settle the tie.

After only four minutes, John McGovern attempted a back pass, having just tackled Charlie George. The ball hit Colin Todd, though, and it deflected straight to the feet of Ray Kennedy, who took one touch, then he buried the ball past Boulton.

Arsenal's tight defensive unit then simply closed out the match over the following 85 minutes.

Derby County had to be content with their League Championship trophy.

Arsenal travelled to Orient five days later, and another huge 31,678 crowd, three times Orient's average home attendance, had filled Brisbane Road. Having faced McGovern, Gemmill and O'Hare in the previous round, Arsenal faced another future European Champion in the Quarter-finals. Ian Bowyer had just joined Orient from Man City.

In his white boots, though, Alan Ball scored early in the second half to send Arsenal into the Semi-finals, where they were then drawn, yet again, against Stoke City.

Stoke had just won their first major trophy in 109 years, beating Chelsea in the League Cup Final a month earlier.

56,576 bulged Villa Park's walls again, and early on, George Armstrong picked up a poor defensive clearance, from about twenty-five yards out. He killed the ball with a single touch, before smashing the ball past Gordon Banks.

Arsenal were then well able again to close down the game, to kill it off, just as they'd previously done against Derby County back at Filbert Street.

The trouble was, Bob Wilson had torn a cartilage which finished his season.

With only Ray Kennedy on the bench, though, Bertie Mee decided to keep Wilson on the field, hobbling about on one leg. A straightforward cross by Terry Conroy, with only fifteen minutes remaining, would have ordinarily been eaten up by Wilson. Unfortunately, Peter Simpson, trying too hard to look after his injured keeper, attempted to head the ball away. The confusion between keeper and centre half resulted in the ball ballooning off Simpson's head, and back into their goal.

Arsenal immediately changed things. Stoke were heading for victory, with the Gunners' defence in total disarray. Ray Kennedy replaced Wilson, and John Radford went in goal for the last quarter-hour. Stoke City piled on the pressure, but John Radford was faultless, *heroic* even, in goal.

The game ended one-one, and yet another replay between Arsenal and Stoke was required.

For once, an ordinary-sized crowd of just 39,000 attended Goodison Park on the following Wednesday, 19th April 1972. Geoff Barnett replaced Bob Wilson for the remainder of the season, and he'd also continue in goal for half of the following season.

Jimmy Greenhoff's penalty kick was equalised by Charlie George's penalty-kick for Arsenal, and then, late on, George broke from what looked like to be a clear offside position.

He played in John Radford, who won the tie with a simple finish past Banks. It was a controversial and contentious finish to a colourful and competitive encounter, that had left Stoke City completely and bitterly gutted.

Arsenal finished that season in fifth place in Division One, five points behind the supreme top four of Derby, Leeds, Liverpool and Manchester City, but one point ahead of Tottenham.

There were no repeats of the defensive records set during the previous season. Ray Kennedy top scored yet again, but with only twelve league goals. No other player hit double figures, though, with Radford, Graham and George all scoring only twenty-three between them.

Arsenal and Leeds United met at Wembley Stadium, on Saturday 6th May, for the Centenary Year FA Cup Final. They had been by far the best two teams in England, twelve months earlier, and apart from Geoff Barnett on for Wilson, and Paul Madeley at left back for Leeds, in place of Terry Cooper, both teams were at full strength.

John Radford and Charlie George were the chosen front two for Arsenal, with top scorer Ray Kennedy named as their substitute.

Arsenal had chances early on, particularly when Alan Ball volleyed Armstrong's corner sharply at David Harvey's goal. Paul Reaney got his body in the way, on the goal line, however, and he cleared the ball away.

In the 53rd minute, though, Leeds struck their one crucial goal. Mick Jones just beat McNab down the right side of the penalty area, and he crossed for Allan Clarke to send a diving header past Barnett. Geoff Barnett had had a great game, saving well from Lorimer's drive, and then from Jones' short range effort.

Late on, Charlie George swivelled, just inside the Leeds penalty area, and smashed the ball against the crossbar. He just looked skywards in despair.

Leeds United had won the Cup, and deservedly so. McLintock and Simpson had an uncomfortable afternoon against Clarke and Jones, who'd rarely looked better together. Also, Bremner kept Storey quiet, while Radford received no change from the powerful Charlton and Hunter, and he was replaced by Kennedy during the second half.

Alan Ball had his best season in an Arsenal shirt, the following season, when despite missing Charlie George, again, for half of the season, and with Peter Simpson and Frank McLintock both missing fifteen games each, Arsenal enjoyed another great title race. They began 1972-73 unbeaten from their first seven matches, winning four times to lead the First Division at the start of September.

They dropped back to sixth place, though, after losing away at Newcastle and Norwich.

However, led by the midfield presence of Alan Ball, and the bite of Peter Storey, Arsenal kept up with Liverpool and Leeds right up to Christmas, winning two out of every three games, and also picking up the odd point too.

Arsenal had lost just five of their twenty-six league matches, prior to the New Year.

George Graham had, however, become surplus to requirements in November.

The arrival of Alan Ball had weakened Graham's importance in Arsenal's midfield, and with Radford and Kennedy regulars in attack, Bertie Mee sold George Graham to Manchester United for £120,000 on Boxing Day 1972.

George Graham never enjoyed the same success as a player, after he left Arsenal.

He did help to lift Manchester United off the bottom of the table, using his experience in midfield to steer Tommy Docherty's side to safety, finishing seven points above the relegation zone. 1973-74, though, was a disaster for Graham, as United again rocketed to the bottom of the table, and by March 1974, George Graham had been replaced by Jim McCalliog.

George Graham made just one appearance, as a substitute, during United's first nineteen games of 1974-75, as they ran away with the Second Division title.

In November 1974, Tommy Docherty sent him to Portsmouth, in an exchange deal for Ron Davies.

At Fratton Park, Graham was reunited with his old teammate, Peter Marinello, but the South Coast was a cold place for George Graham, as they finished the season sixth from bottom in Division Two, just five points above relegated Millwall.

Graham was appointed Portsmouth's captain, for the 1975-76 season, but in spite of the fact that Chris Kamara made his league debut alongside George Graham, during October 1975, and played twenty-four matches for Pompey that season, Portsmouth were in the bottom three all season, and they were relegated in bottom place.

In November 1976, his old Chelsea teammate Terry Venables rescued him from his nightmare at Portsmouth, who were by then bottom of the Third Division, signing him up for Crystal Palace. George Graham missed just five of the Eagles' last twenty-eight games, as Palace rose from mid-table to third place, by May, and they won promotion back to Division Two. As Venables lifted Palace up to the fringe of the Second Division promotion race, George Graham became a coach at Selhurst Park, under Venables, following his retirement from playing in 1978.

Venables and Graham took Crystal Palace back into the First Division in 1979, and created what became known as the **Team of the Eighties.** It was a nickname that didn't hold much substance, though, and in 1980, both men left for QPR, taking the Hoops to Wembley in 1982, facing Spurs in the FA Cup Final. With QPR heading for promotion back to the First Division in 1982-83, though, George Graham left Loftus Road in December 1982, to become manager of Third Division Millwall. He lifted the Lions away from the relegation zone, and in May 1985, led them to promotion back up to Division Two, as runners-up behind Champions Bradford City.

After Millwall had finished in a decent mid-table position in 1985-86, Graham returned to Highbury in May 1986, replacing his old coach Don Howe as Arsenal's new manager.

George Graham had been the first of that great 1971 Arsenal team to leave Highbury, but he was to have, above all of any of them, the greatest impact on the club's future...

Arsenal continued their good form into 1973, and on Saturday 10th February, they visited the league leaders Liverpool, while just one point behind in second place, and with a big 49,898 crowd packed inside Anfield.

After a scrappy first half, played on a scrappy pitch, McNab released a long ball up to Kennedy on the left wing, where some actual grass remained. Ray Kennedy then played a lovely ball across to Armstrong, attacking the right of the Liverpool area. While attempting to take the ball around the outside of Lindsay, Armstrong was clipped in the mud. It was easy to tell by his reaction, that clipping Armstrong was not Alec Lindsay's intention, but the mud had affected the accuracy of his challenge.

Alan Ball coolly placed his penalty kick to Ray Clemence's left.

Then, Eddie Kelly, just outside his own area, launched a long ball out of the Anfield mud, right footed up to John Radford in the centre circle, but still inside his own half.

Radford turned Tommy Smith brilliantly, clipping away clear, but with Larry Lloyd blocking his way, ten yards inside the Liverpool half. Ray Kennedy ran free behind Lloyd, from right to left, and Radford then played the ball forward, running to the right side of Lloyd, who'd expected a pass to the offside Kennedy.

Radford ran on, away from Lloyd, and he raced towards goal. Clemence came "haring out like a loony," so Radford touched the ball past him, and then from eighteen yards out, he rolled the ball through the mud, into the goal, under the still, packed Kop.

Arsenal went top of the league, for the first time since early September, having played one game more than Liverpool. On the following Saturday, though, they beat Leicester City 1-0, unconvincingly, at Highbury, after Malcolm Manley's own goal had given them both points, while Liverpool had been held to a 1-1 draw away at Manchester City.

	PL	W	D	L	F	A	PTS
ARSENAL	31	18	8	5	43	27	44
Liverpool	30	17	8	5	53	32	42
Leeds United	29	16	8	5	51	30	40
Ipswich Town	29	14	10	5	43	29	38
Derby County	31	14	6	11	40	43	34
Newcastle Utd	30	12	9,	9	48	39	33
West Ham Utd	30	12	8	10	51	40	32

On Wednesday 28th February, West Bromwich Albion, the bottom club, surprisingly, and ironically, beat Arsenal 1-0. Two years after breaking clear of Leeds' weak offside trap, to set up Jeff Astle and hand the title advantage to Arsenal, Tony Brown scored his eleventh goal of the season, handing the title advantage back to Liverpool.

Liverpool returned to the top of the league after beating Ipswich 2-1, and they stayed there.

Liverpool lost just twice in their last eleven matches, while winning seven times, to lead the league until the end of the season. Arsenal, in contrast, fell apart after late March, winning only one of their final seven league and cup games, but they lost three times, including their 6-1 hammering away at third-placed Leeds United on the final day of their season.

In the FA Cup Quarter-finals, Peter Osgood had given Chelsea the lead, after scoring BBC TV's *Goal of the Season*, volleying the ball beyond Bob Wilson's dive, into the top right corner. Alan Ball headed Arsenal level, from Armstrong's left wing corner kick, before Charlie George fired them into a 2-1 lead, after Ray Kennedy had chased McLintock's long ball, taking the ball away from Bonetti, and then playing it back into the six yard box for George.

John Hollins ran onto a Chris Garland's flick-on, just before half-time, and he blasted in from close range, past Wilson, to equalise.

Amazingly, after such an exciting first half, and with Stamford Bridge filled to capacity, there were no further goals during the second half.

Arsenal won their replay, in front of 62,642, Highbury's second biggest crowd of the Seventies, after Alan Ball scored his thirteenth goal of the season from the penalty spot, his sixth penalty-kick, and then Ray Kennedy clipped in their winning goal from close range, after Houseman had levelled for Chelsea.

Having beaten Chelsea 2-1 in their FA Cup replay, Arsenal had looked good for another League and Cup double, on Tuesday 20th March.

They were just two points behind Liverpool, with eight games remaining, and four points ahead of third-placed Leeds.

Arsenal's reward was a Semi-final match at Hillsborough, against Second Division nobodies Sunderland. Arsenal fans must have looked at Sunderland's line-up of Montgomery, Malone, Guthrie, Horswill, Watson, Pitt, Kerr, Hughes, Halom, Porterfield and Tueart, and probably wondered, "who are this bunch of fucking gorillas?"

Sunderland were the hairiest team that Arsenal ever faced, but they became the most famous FA Cup winners in the long, long history of the competition.

Anyway, that was it. Sunderland shocked Arsenal 2-1, on Saturday 7th April, with two devastating goals from Vic Halom and Billy Hughes, while Jim Montgomery made half a dozen international class saves from Ball, Armstrong, George and Radford.

Arsenal finished 1972-73 just three points behind Champions Liverpool.

John Radford was their top scorer, with nineteen league and cup goals, as they'd come so close, again, in 1972-73. Alan Ball had also hit fourteen goals, while Charlie George and Ray Kennedy both scored eleven.

Bob McNab, injury-affected throughout the previous season, his absence badly affecting Arsenal's title defence, had been their only ever-present player.

So, that was indeed it. Arsenal then began selling off their Crown Jewels, and they replaced them with plastic baubles from a lucky bag, with all due respect.

The next player to follow George Graham out of the door, was captain Frank McLintock, during the Summer of 1973, after playing 314 First Division games for Arsenal. He'd fallen behind Jeff Blockley in the defensive pecking order at Highbury.

An outstanding reader of the game, and an outstanding leader too, McLintock had roared at his down-hearted teammates, when Arsenal had gone 1-0 down to Liverpool, in extra-time, during that 1971 FA Cup Final. He won the FWA Footballer of the Year award, during Arsenal's 1971 double-winning season, and then he was awarded the MBE in 1972, for services to football.

Nicknamed *True Grit*, McLintock showed that very quality after he moved to Loftus Road, at thirty-three years of age, and he captained QPR to a close-run First Division title race during 1975-76, when they lost the Championship by just a single point, while Arsenal struggled.

Bertie Mee later considered his selling of McLintock to QPR as the biggest professional mistake of his career. Frank McLintock played 127 First Division games for QPR, until his retirement in 1977, when he returned to his first club, Leicester City, as manager.

That was a decision he regretted ever since. Leicester were relegated in bottom place, and McLintock resigned at the end of the season.

McLintock played 611 First Division matches, throughout his eighteen year career. He never played a single match outside of Division One. He is now, mostly, a voice on the media, for Sky Sports and *talksport* radio. Frank McLintock remains a true gentleman, honest and dignified, and the second-greatest captain in Arsenal's post-war history, behind Tony Adams, but his Highbury career had been cut short too soon.

Bob Wilson retired at the end of the 1973-74 season, at thirty-one years of age, having played just 234 First Division matches for Arsenal. Robert Primrose Wilson would have played many more games, but during his first five years at Highbury, he was an understudy to Jim Furnell.

Chesterfield-born to a Scottish schoolmaster, Wilson played twice for Scotland, while Tommy Docherty was caretaker manager in 1971. He played in all sixty-four of Arsenal's league and cup matches in 1970-71, and was voted the club's Player of the Season, despite his captain winning the Football Writers' Footballer of the Year award.

Bob Wilson stayed on at Highbury, as goalkeeping coach, whilst simultaneously presenting *Football Focus* on BBC TV's Grandstand sports programme, and he worked with Pat Jennings, after the Tottenham keeper had moved to Highbury in 1977.

Wilson declares Pat Jennings as the best goalkeeper he'd ever seen.

In 1985, Bob Wilson and Emlyn Hughes were both persuaded out of retirement to play for the fictional football team Melchester Rovers, in the comic Roy of the Rovers, along with both Spandau Ballet's Martin Kemp and Steve Norman. Wilson, Hughes, Kemp and Norman all helped Rovers to win the Milk Cup Final, at Wembley.

Ray Kennedy scored fifty-three First Division goals in just 156 games for Arsenal, before he was sold to Liverpool, for a club record transfer fee of £180,000, in July 1974. He was Bill Shankly's last-ever purchase for Liverpool, and the player who'd actually won the title for Leeds, having scored the only goal in Arsenal's 1-0 win over Liverpool, back in April.

Rejected by Sir Stanley Matthews, at Port Vale, Ray Kennedy proved that in football, even the very Greatest of all can also be the most Wrongest.

Kennedy played 275 First Division games for Liverpool, scoring fifty-one goals, and he won three European Cups and five First Division Championship winners' medals, while at Anfield. He also played seventeen times for England, including two appearances at the 1980 European Championships' Finals, in Milan and Turin.

He moved to Swansea City in January 1982, who were managed by his former teammate John Toshack. Toshack publicly criticized Kennedy's seemingly lethargic performances, though, calling him "lazy."

Ray Kennedy was greatly hurt and offended by Toshack's public criticisms. It eventually transpired he'd been suffering the early stages of Parkinson's Disease, whilst still playing First Division football for Swansea. He was forced to retire in 1984, at the age of thirty-two, and although he was awarded a testimonial match by Liverpool in 1991, he was forced to sell all his medals in 1993.

The *Ray of Hope* appeal was jointly set up, between both Liverpool and Arsenal fans, under the Parkinson's Disease Society banner, to assist with Kennedy's domestic, financial and medical needs.

Jimmy Greaves described Ray Kennedy as the "Player of the Seventies", and he was certainly the most successful player of that decade, winning eight major trophies, and eleven in total, throughout his career.

Bob McNab was a left back who never really stood out, but when he wasn't playing, you noticed his absence, whether you were an Arsenal player or fan, and you really missed him. Signed from his hometown club, Huddersfield Town, back in October 1966, McNab was a good one-touch player, with an intelligent defensive brain. He saw everything and reacted to everything, and he could run all day.

McNab was a big celebrity, with a charming, cheerful personality, also. He was on ITV's panel for their live coverage of the Mexico World Cup Finals in 1970, and he also guest-starred as "Bob", a ringer for the bus depot football team, kitted out in full Arsenal colours, in a 1973 On The Buses episode, entitled *The Football Match.*

After McNab was injured by Blakey's training routine, the episode descended into absolute, sexist farce, and the opposition to Stan Butler's Luxton Bus Company team was provided by an all-ladies team. It was all tight-fitted tops, and bouncing boobs, without Bob's respectable presence.

Bob McNab played a total of 365 league and cup games for Arsenal, before he was sold to Wolves in 1975. He played just thirteen games for Wolves, of which they won only twice, before he was seriously injured, and had to retire at the age of thirty-two.

He played four times for England, during 1969, but he wasn't selected in Sir Alf Ramsey's final World Cup squad, whence his appearance as a panellist Back Home in the ITV studios, for their live colour television coverage.

Charlie George was also sold, during July 1975, to Derby County, the Champions of England, after Arsenal had fallen to worse than mediocre in Division One.

Dave Mackay paid just £90,000 for George, Arsenal's maverick, who'd scored only thirty-one First Division goals in 133 games. His contribution to Arsenal, though, during their great period in the early Seventies, was far greater than that.

Charlie George brought a swagger to Arsenal. Slightly built, prodigious, ill-disciplined, and with a rebellious streak to his demeanour, he was Arsenal's long-haired superstar, with a cynical scowl here, and a look of disdain there… arrogant, aloof and attitudinal.

Charlie could have been England's George Best, but he suffered a broken ankle in 1970, and then various other injuries and inconsistencies had affected him after 1971, when he was their King.

He was voted Derby County's Player of the Season in 1976, having scored a brilliant hat-trick during their 4-1 European Cup win over Real Madrid, on Wednesday 22nd October 1975, with 35,000 inside The Baseball Ground. Charlie George scored twenty-four goals for Derby County during 1975-76, his best ever goal tally, as the Rams reached the FA Cup Semi-finals, and they also finished fourth in another very strong First Division.

He was then awarded his first *and only* England cap on 8th September 1976, for their 1-1 draw with the Republic of Ireland. George eventually left Derby County in March 1979, after 106 First Division matches, moving to Southampton. His first game for the Saints was an FA Cup Quarter-final replay away at his beloved Highbury, in front of nearly 45,000. Alan Sunderland scored a goal in each half for Arsenal, though, en route to their famous 3-2 win over Manchester United at Wembley.

Charlie George remains at Highbury to this day, except now it's the Emirates Stadium, where the King of Highbury provides guided tours to 21st Century Arsenal fans, around his new home.

John Radford left Arsenal, for West Ham United, in December 1976. He made his 481st and final appearance as a substitute for Frank Stapleton, during Arsenal's 2-0 home win over Stoke City, on Saturday 16th October.

A powerful and effective forward, Radford was crucial in creating space for his attacking partners, pulling defenders away from danger areas, whence the fact that goals during Arsenal's golden spell were so spread out amongst their whole team.

"I wasn't an out and out goal scorer," John Radford claimed. "If you look through the records, you'll find a lot of the lads who played alongside me, did finish top scorer, so I believe I had a lot more than just scoring goals."

Even so, Radford still scored one hundred and forty-nine goals for Arsenal, and he will be most remembered for creating both goals during their 2-1 comeback win over Liverpool in the 1971 FA Cup Final.

Peter Storey moved to Fulham, for just £10,000, in March 1977, after having first fallen out with Bertie Mee, and then failing to make an impression on their new manager, his old teammate Terry Neill.

Cold eyes, Peter Storey's hard-tackling and general tough play placed him at number twenty-six on The Times' list of the Fifty Greatest Hard Men, in 2007.

Peter Storey could play football too, though, and having played half of his career at full back, he finally found his special place in Arsenal's midfield, just in front of McLintock and Simpson, as Arsenal made a date with Greatness. Storey played over five hundred league and cup games for Arsenal, including 391 First Division matches.

Alan Ball had left Arsenal in December 1976, having scored fifty-two goals in 217 league and cup games, when he joined Southampton for a £60,000 fee. He'd rarely had the same effect on Arsenal's team, though, as he'd had at Everton, where he pretty much ran the show, all over the field.

Arsenal were a ready-made, family type of team, very close-knit, when he joined, and he was a bit of a Superstar in a team that had no superstars.

It was tough for Ball to justify his massive price tag, but although Arsenal won nothing after his arrival, he certainly justified his club record fee, through his performances, particularly during the 1972-73 season.

By the time Alan Ball left Arsenal, at thirty-one, there was a new Superstar, Supermac, at Highbury. Malcolm MacDonald had joined for a new club and British record transfer fee of £333,333.33, but young guns like Liam Brady, Frank Stapleton and David O'Leary were also emerging for the future.

After his retirement, Alan Ball managed Stoke City, Exeter City, Southampton and Manchester City. Particularly though, he'd managed Portsmouth, and he lifted Pompey back up to the First Division in 1987, as runners-up to Derby County in Division Two.

Under his management, and assisted by both Graham Paddon and Peter Osgood, Portsmouth won ninety-four out of 222 league games, as they enjoyed top flight football for the first time in twenty-eight years, back in the high life again.

Alan Ball died of a heart attack, while attempting to put out a fire in his back garden, on Wednesday 25th April 2007, after a bonfire he'd extinguished had suddenly reignited, and then spread to his garden fence. He was only sixty-two, but his life was celebrated at every football ground in England, over the following weekend.

George Armstrong, amazingly, never played for England. He remains one of the most accomplished players to have failed to win a full international cap. Sir Alf Ramsey didn't like to use wingers, ever, and Armstrong, at just five feet and six inches tall, was one of the most talented and industrious wingers in the First Division.

By 1970-71, he was, quite simply, far and away, the very best in England.

Selfless, courageous and perfectly balanced, *Geordie* could attack from either wing, crossing accurately and precisely from both sides. It was estimated that Armstrong had a hand in over half of Arsenal's total goals during that 1970-71 season.

After playing 621 league and cup games for Arsenal, including 500 First Division appearances, and also scoring sixty-eight goals, Geordie left Arsenal during September 1977, joining his old teammate Frank McLintock, Leicester City's new manager.

Leicester had paid just £15,000 for George Armstrong, who joined former Arsenal teammates Eddie Kelly, Jon Sammels and Jeff Blockley in City's team.

Armstrong struggled for fitness, though, after arriving at Filbert Street. He started just fourteen league matches, as Leicester finished the season in bottom place. He then joined Stockport for the 1978-79 season, playing alongside another of the greatest English wingers, Mike Summerbee, and they both wore County's famous Argentina 1978 World Cup Adidas strip, for that season.

George Armstrong remains third on Arsenal's all-time appearances list, behind only David O'Leary and Tony Adams, and he returned to Arsenal in 1990, as their new reserve team coach.

On Wednesday 1st November 2000, Geordie Armstrong collapsed and died of a brain haemorrhage, aged only fifty-six, at Arsenal's training ground in Hertfordshire.

Like George Armstrong, Peter Simpson never played for England, either, despite being one of the most respected and dominant centre halves in the First Division. Considering how good he was for Arsenal, and seeing lesser talents given caps by Sir Alf, it's fair to say that he was unfortunate not to have had half of an England career.

There were certainly some great central defenders in England, at that time... Moore, McFarland, Todd, Labone, Hunter, Charlton and Lloyd, for example.

But there were some names you saw in some England teams, where you had to wonder, how could Peter Simpson not get in?

He is possibly the best defender to never win an England cap.

Peter Simpson's central defensive partnership with Frank McLintock was among the greatest of all time. After 369 First Division games for Arsenal, his contract was cancelled during April 1978, and at thirty-three years old, he moved to play for New England Tea Men, in the NASL, where he finished his career.

Peter Simpson's total of 477 league and cup games places him in tenth position on Arsenal's all-time appearances list.

Pat Rice was the last of that great 1971 team to leave Highbury, leaving first as a player back in 1980, and then finally leaving as Arsenal's assistant manager in 2012.

Rice was almost ever-present at right back, for ten years, after Peter Storey had moved into midfield. He played 528 league and cup games for Arsenal, winning two FA Cup Finals, and he lifted the Cup as Arsenal's captain in 1979, as well as that brilliant 1970-71 League Championship title.

He played forty-nine times for Northern Ireland, and at the time of his international retirement, he was the eighth most-capped Ulsterman. Rice moved to Watford in 1980, after starting the 1980 European Cup Winners' Cup Final, in Brussels, where Arsenal lost to Valencia on penalty kicks, after extra-time.

Pat Rice was appointed as Watford's captain by Graham Taylor, and he led the Hornets up to First Division football, for the first time, in 1982. He played over one hundred league games at Vicarage Road, before his retirement in 1984, when he returned to Highbury to become Arsenal's youth team coach.

In 1996, Arsene Wenger appointed Pat Rice as his assistant at Arsenal, a post he held for sixteen years, before he eventually, and finally, left Arsenal in May 2012.

After arriving back at Arsenal, as their new manager, George Graham began to re-build their team, attempting to assemble a side that was as great as their 1971 team.

He'd inherited an already well-blooded nucleus of young players with John Lukic, Paul Davis, David Rocastle, Niall Quinn and Tony Adams, plus David O'Leary, their old veteran from Bertie Mee's last Arsenal side.

George Graham then gave the Arsenal captaincy to Adams, their twenty-one year old centre half, and he also gave Arsenal debuts to youth team players, Paul Merson, Michael Thomas and Kevin Campbell. Pat Rice had done very well.

Over the next two years, he bought seven new players for moderate sums of cash.

Lee Dixon had arrived from Stoke; Nigel Winterburn came from Wimbledon; Steve Bould from Stoke; Perry Groves from Colchester; Brian Marwood from Sheffield United; Kevin Richardson from Everton; and Alan Smith from Leicester City.

The whole lot had cost less than three million pounds, but George Graham moulded a team of understated greatness, that brought an emotionally-charged First Division Championship trophy back to Arsenal at the very end of the 1988-89 season, only three years after his arrival.

The blueprint that Graham had used to develop his Arsenal team was not dissimilar to the team built by Bertie Mee and Don Howe.

At the back, there was the tough central defensive partnership of a tough, Gaelic veteran, and a no-nonsense English stopper, David O'Leary and Tony Adams, in place of McLintock and Simpson.

Their two adventurous, but defensively safe full backs, Dixon and Winterburn, were both similar in style to Rice and McNab. For George Armstrong, you read David Rocastle, and for their local superstar Charlie George, there was Paul Merson.

You had Alan Smith and Michael Thomas, instead of John Radford and Ray Kennedy, and for Storey and George Graham himself, he'd introduced the enforcers Paul Davis and Kevin Richardson.

George Graham then paid a club record transfer fee of £1.3 million to QPR for goalkeeper David Seaman, and he also paid a million pounds to Cremonese, for their Swedish international winger, Anders Limpar, introducing foreign talent to Highbury for the very first time.

Two years later, Arsenal won the title again, losing just once in thirty-eight matches, and conceding only eighteen goals, whilst scoring seventy-four. Two years after that record-breaking achievement, Arsenal won both the League Cup, and the FA Cup.

Then in 1994, George Graham led Arsenal to their first European trophy for twenty-four years. Alan Smith hooked in the winner during their European Cup Winners' Cup Final 1-0 win over Parma, in Copenhagen.

George Graham was sacked by Arsenal in 1995, after he'd been found to have accepted a bung of nearly half a million pounds from a Norwegian agent during previous signings of players, two and a half years earlier.

Just like their 1971 team, George Graham's 1989 and 1991 Champions had no Stars, but a team built on team spirit. Also, apart from Tony Adams, and latterly David Seaman, none of his two title-winning teams had any prolonged England international careers, just like Arsenal's 1971 team, of whom only Pat Rice had an international career with Northern Ireland, while Peter Storey and Ray Kennedy had shared about thirty England caps between the two of them.

George Graham had built teams based on the same principles of discipline and teamwork as the very team he'd played in.

That 1971 Arsenal team differed from the Leeds Uniteds, the Manchester Uniteds, the Liverpools, and the Tottenhams of their day, all filled with international superstars.

That Arsenal team was a team with no Stars. They just fought for each other, and to the very best of their games.

The sum of the team was much greater than the sum of each of their individual parts.

Arsenal were not unlike Don Revie's Leeds United, in some ways, in that they had a strong family feel within their club, that lifted their game above the consistent standards of other First Division teams, that boasted supposedly better players.

However, Leeds had a divisive attitude, an arrogant attitude towards other teams, an often dirty approach to opposing teams, that aroused a disdainful reaction from other teams, as well as their fans, towards Leeds United, that lasted for generations.

At Arsenal, though, there was a definite warmth to their team spirit.

There was nothing very prickly about them. Simpson and McLintock were hard, but fair, and McNab and Rice weren't prone to too many of Paul Reaney's "tricks up his sleeve" tactics that he'd often adopted against more skilful opponents.

Peter Storey was a rough, tough tackler, who did hurt opponents, but like Reaney, it was never personal, unlike Charlton, Hunter, Bremner and Giles, on occasions.

And neither George Armstrong, Ray Kennedy nor Charlie George ever went to ground as often as Peter Lorimer or Billy Bremner did, just to gain free-kicks or penalties.

That 1970-71 Arsenal team, despite never repeating their success, was no less of a great side; they were a truly great team like Everton, the year before, or Derby County, a year later.

Just like those teams, they were almost a perfect team.

Arsenal's 2004 *Invincibles* team may possibly have surpassed Bertie Mee and Don Howe's 1971 Double winners, with its international World Class collection of legendary, foreign Superstars, absolutely the antithesis of King Charlie George's Arsenal team.

They may well have done, but not by much at all.

A WHITER SHADE OF PAIN

1961

BILL NICHOLSON'S TOTTENHAM HOTSPUR looked set to dominate English football, throughout the Sixties, after they'd famously won the first League and FA Cup Double of the 20th Century, in 1960-61. Spurs had finished eight points clear of runners-up Sheffield Wednesday, scoring an all-time record 115 goals, while conceding just fifty, and they'd also won a record thirty-one First Division matches, never since equalled.

Unfortunately, age was catching up with Tottenham. Danny Blanchflower, their captain and superstar, the heart and soul of Everything Good, not just about Spurs, but also about Football, was well into his mid-thirties by 1961.

After his retirement in 1964, most of that 1961 Spurs team, who were also either over thirty, or pushing thirty, soon followed Danny Blanchflower out of White Hart Lane.

Bill Brown was replaced by Pat Jennings during the Summer of 1964.

In 1966, the Arbroath-born goalkeeper moved to Northampton Town, after playing 222 First Division games for Spurs. Top scorer Bobby Smith, their big beer-barrel chested centre forward who'd hit 176 league goals in just 271 games, also left during 1964. He joined Brighton and Hove Albion, at the age of thirty-one, where he finished his career, scoring nineteen goals, and helping the Seagulls win the Fourth Division title in 1965. Les Allen, Bobby Smith's attacking partner, and the youngest member of their 1961 team, had scored fifty-five goals in 128 league games, before he joined QPR in 1965, at twenty-seven years old. Allen formed a prolific strike partnership with Rodney Marsh, at Loftus Road, and he helped the team to victory over West Brom in 1967, in the first League Cup Final played at Wembley Stadium, while also scoring sixteen league goals as the Hoops won the Third Division title.

A year later, with Rangers back in the Second Division for the first time in fifteen years, Allen played as more of a support striker, at thirty years old, and he scored only six goals from twenty-four starts, but he'd provided essential experience as QPR gained promotion to the First Division for the first time in their history.

In Division One, QPR and Les Allen both struggled, and the Hoops went back down in bottom position, thirteen points adrift of safety. Allen had started just fourteen league games, but his final match, significantly, as a thirty-one year old, was at home to Tottenham Hotspur, on Saturday 15th February 1969.

In front of a near record Loftus Road crowd of over 30,000, Les Allen set up Frank Clarke's goal in their 1-1 home draw.

Tottenham's away fans gave him a loud and warm ovation, at the end of his career.

Terry Dyson, Tottenham's five foot and three inches tall left winger, also left White Hart Lane during 1965, joining Fulham at thirty years old. Dyson played rarely over the next three years, though, due to a series of knee injuries, and he came on as a substitute in just one game during his last two seasons at Craven Cottage.

He moved to Colchester United in 1968, where at the age of thirty-four, he started forty league matches on the left wing, as the U's finished up in sixth place, only four points below promotion. Terry Dyson retired from professional football, at thirty-five, and he joined Southern League side Guildford City.

Maurice Norman, **Big Mo,** was a complete physical contrast to Terry Dyson. Signed for £28,000 from Norwich, his home city team, back in 1955, Norman was "big in build and big in heart," according to Jimmy Greaves.

"I played with more skilful centre halves than Mo", Greavsie had added, "but none stronger."

Their rock at centre half, and also a useful presence at corners, Maurice Norman was a colossus in Spurs' defence during their Double-winning season, but a double fracture of his tibia and fibula ended Big Mo's football career, when he was only thirty, in November 1965.

Maurice Norman played 357 First Division games during his ten years at Tottenham, and only England, Mabbutt, Campbell and King have surpassed his standards.

John White was one of the youngest players of Tottenham's Double winning team, aged only twenty-four when he'd collected his FA Cup and League Championship winner's medals. Known as **The Ghost,** due to his unique ability to glide from deep positions, White went unnoticed, effortlessly and smoothly, into clear scoring opportunities.

Working just in front of Blanchflower and Dave Mackay, White was an immaculate passer, who could glide the ball with ease and pinpoint precision, who created many goals for Smith, Allen and Cliff Jones. White had signed from Falkirk, for £20,000 back in October 1959.

"The final piece in the jigsaw", Mackay had described him.

John White was also a talented golfer, with a handicap of just fourteen, but during the Summer of 1964, when he was practising his game at Crews Hill Golf Club, in Enfield, he'd sheltered under a tree during a thunderstorm.

That tree was struck by lightning, and John White was killed, at the age of only twenty-seven, on 21st July 1964. He left behind his wife Sandra, a twenty-two year old widow, and also their two young kids, Mandy and Rob.

John White had played twenty-two games for Scotland, as well as 183 First Division matches for Spurs, and he'd scored his only international goal, just eight months before his death, in a 2-1 win over Wales, at Hampden Park. With Bill Brown in goal, and Dave Mackay at right half, John White was one of three Tottenham players to represent Scotland on 20th November 1963, two days before the shot that rang out across the World. Also playing for Scotland in that win over the Welsh, were Billy McNeill, Jim Baxter, Denis Law and Alan Gilzean.

John White was the **David Beckham** of his day, but a much better footballer.

Of all the players from Tottenham's Double-winning team, John White was the toughest for Bill Nicholson to replace, and it took nearly six years for him to find a player who was even comparable.

By the mid-Sixties, therefore, Bill Nicholson was forced to re-build his great Tottenham Hotspur team, amidst a changing football world, with new super-teams, built on great defences, now rising to the top of English and European football.

By the start of the 1966-67 season, only Cliff Jones and Dave Mackay had survived from their 1961 team, and by then, both players were thirty-one years old.

Cliff Jones was considered the finest winger in the World, when Tottenham had won the Double. He'd joined Spurs back in 1958, after playing in all five of Wales' World Cup Finals matches over in Sweden. Jones also scored forty-seven goals in 168 games for his home town team Swansea Town, during the Fifties, before he moved to White Hart Lane, at just twenty-three years of age.

"He had a terrific sense of timing," Jimmy Greaves said of Jones. "He was so fast we used to say that if he played in his overcoat, it wouldn't make any difference. He'd still fly past his full back."

Cliff Jones was only five feet, and nine inches tall, but he was a fearless header of the ball, and headed many of his forty-seven total goals for Tottenham, diving in where the boots were flying.

"Cliff was one of the bravest little men I ever saw," Alan Mullery also wrote.

"The ball would be in the net and Cliff would be on the ground with a cut eye."

Dave Mackay, Edinburgh-born, and as tough and rugged as Arthur's Seat, was one half of probably the greatest-ever wing-half partnership, alongside Belfast's Danny Blanchflower.

In modern, midfield terms, it's tough to think of a partnership that stands above Blanchflower and Mackay. Leeds had Bremner and Giles; Everton had their trio of Ball, Harvey and Kendall; Manchester City had Bell and Oakes; United had Roy Keane and Paul Scholes; Arsenal had Vieira and Gilberto Silva; while Barcelona have Iniesta and Xavi.

Were any of them really better than Blanchflower and Mackay? It's very arguable.

Mackay had begun his professional career with Hearts, playing 135 Scottish League games at Tynecastle, before he joined Tottenham in March 1959.

Bill Nicholson then paid £32,000 for the twenty-four year old left half. "Dave Mackay had everything," Jimmy Greaves stated, without any hyperbole.

"Power, skill, drive, strength, stamina, and above all, infectious enthusiasm," Greavsie continued, "he tore into opponents, and he tore them apart."

By 1966-67, Dave Mackay had been reverted to a centre half, though, alongside Mike England, in their modern 4-4-2 or 4-3-3 formation. Just as he and Blanchflower had been among the finest-ever wing-half partnerships, Mackay and Mike England became the greatest, and the hardest, central defensive partnership in Tottenham's history.

Mike England, born in Holywell, was a tall and commanding, tough and uncompromising centre half, who'd joined Spurs in August 1966, for a fee of £95,000, after playing 165 First Division matches for Blackburn Rovers.

A six feet and two inches tall giant of a man, dark haired and heavily browed, and lantern-jawed, the Welsh international was brilliant in the air, but also excellent with the ball at his feet.

Calm and comfortable in possession, Mike England had made his Wales debut in April 1962, at just twenty years of age, in their 4-0 win over Northern Ireland.

So dominant was England in international football, he became Wales' youngest-ever captain, only two years later, also against Northern Ireland, a record that stood for nearly forty-seven years.

Mike England was the second "final piece in the jigsaw," following the completion of Bill Nicholson's re-building of Tottenham, in just two short years, between 1964 and 1966.

Probably the first piece of that jigsaw was Bill Nicholson's signing of Jimmy Greaves back in November 1961, his first new signing for Tottenham following their Double winning season.

Jimmy Greaves had scored 124 First Division goals for Chelsea, in only 157 games, between 1957 and 1961. He was the top goal-scorer in the First Division, at the age of just nineteen, when he'd hit thirty-two league goals during 1958-59, and then he set a club record of forty-one First Division goals in 1960-61, the season Spurs won the Double.

Chelsea had finished down in twelfth place, despite scoring Ninety-Eight goals. They had conceded double the fifty goals that Spurs had conceded, though, and Greavsie knew he wouldn't be winning things there.

He felt as if he was "constantly bailing water out of a sinking ship."

AC Milan's manager, Giuseppe Viani, paid £80,000 for Greaves in April 1961, and he scored nine Serie A goals in just twelve games for Milan, during an unhappy five months at the San Siro.

Jimmy Greaves was, in fact, desperately unhappy in Italy.

The culture didn't suit him, and neither did their style of football.

Milan adopted the *Catenaccio* system, a dour, colourless football, peppered with cynicism, niggling fouls and spite that bordered on the vicious. Greavsie unhappily remembered, "it was a type of football I was not used to, but I dealt with it and continued to score goals."

Catenaccio was a very heavily defensive system, based on formations like 1-4-3-2, or 1-4-4-1, where defenders would not cross the halfway line, and teams used a sweeper to defend the "scoring space." Attacks were broken down before a forward could even smell the ball, and matches resulted in tactical stalemates, with games being won 1-0, due to rare counter-attacks, or breakaways, otherwise it was 0-0.

There were lengthy periods throughout every game, when Greavsie never saw the ball at all.

It's a tribute to his tremendous talent that he'd score nine goals in less than half an Italian league season, and it should also be remembered that he was only twenty-one, while he was in Milan.

Tottenham manager Bill Nicholson went to visit Jimmy and his wife Irene, to sign him for Spurs. Greavsie was delighted at the chance to return to London, and especially to White Hart Lane, home of the best team in England. Spurs offered £90,000, giving Milan a £10,000 profit on their short-term investment, but then, Chelsea also entered into the negotiations, and they started a bidding war.

Returning to Chelsea had no appeal for Greaves; it would have just meant a return to the problems he'd been so eager to escape from.

Bill Nicholson, though, was determined to get his forward, and, after the bids had reached £96,500, he finally offered £99,999, a World record transfer fee involving an English footballer.

AC Milan immediately accepted that offer.

Mr Nicholson had refused to offer £100,000, because he was worried that the pressure of having a £100,000 price tag around his neck might affect Greavsie's form. It was a worry dismissed by Jimmy Greaves.

Neither price tags, nor transfer fees, ever affected how Greavsie played his football.

On Saturday 8th October 1966, Tottenham were the early leaders of the First Division, having won eight of their first eleven games, and with Jimmy Greaves and Alan Gilzean proving to be the best attacking partnership in English football, after sharing fourteen league goals.

Greaves and Gilzean had both scored during Spurs' 2-1 win over Manchester United, back on Saturday 10th September, with over 56,000 packed into White Hart Lane.

Alan Gilzean had scored 113 Scottish league goals for Dundee, from only 134 matches, and his goals had fired Dundee to their first and only Scottish League title, during the 1961-62 season.

Sublimely skilled but also dominant in the air, Gilzean became renowned as an International Class forward player due to his performances in the 1962-63 European Cup competition.

He scored nine European Cup goals, including hat-tricks against both FC Cologne and Sporting Lisbon, as Dundee reached the Semi-finals.

Hold on for one second! Dundee in the Semi-finals of the UEFA Champions League?
Next thing you'll hear is that they beat AC Milan!

Dundee actually lost 5-2, on aggregate, to AC Milan, in those European Cup Semi-finals, but Alan Gilzean had scored the only goal of the game, on Wednesday 1st May, during Dundee's famous 1-0 victory over the Serie A Champions, with 40,000 packed inside Dens Park.

One of the most skilful forwards to ever come out of Scotland, Alan Gilzean eventually joined Spurs in December 1964, for a fee of £72,500. Sunderland had also wanted Gilzean, and they'd actually offered him more money, but Gilzean wanted to go to Tottenham.

Totally unselfish and commanding in the air, Gilzean was the perfect partner for Greavsie, especially with his excellent, guided, glancing headers.

They combined for thirty-one First Division goals in their first full season together, during 1965-66.

"I enjoyed a great understanding with Gilly. We had an almost telepathic understanding," Greavsie admitted. "I don't think I was ever happier than when playing with him at my side."

However, as the Autumn leaves continued to fall, and subsequently decay on the ground, so did Tottenham's title hopes. For no explicable reason, other than a run of the poorest of forms, Spurs began to lose games. And they continued to lose games.

First, on Saturday 15th October, bottom club Blackpool, who hadn't won a single game, came and won 3-1 at White Hart Lane. Spurs were missing both Pat Jennings and Alan Gilzean, but the defeat had totally stunned their 36,000 home crowd.

Both Jennings and Gilzean were back, eleven days later, for their game at Chelsea, but Jimmy Robertson was now missing, and Tommy Baldwin's brace, and another from record goal-scorer, Bobby Tambling, had given the Blues an excellent 3-0 win, with 54,000 inside Stamford Bridge.

Jimmy Robertson, born in Cardonald, a suburb of Glasgow, had played fifty-four Scottish League games for St Mirren, before he signed for Tottenham in 1964, at nineteen years old.

Baby faced, and only five feet and eight inches tall, Robertson had cost Bill Nicholson just £25,000, a bargain buy for the former Scotland Amateur International player, caps won while he was at his first club Cowdenbeath.

Jimmy Robertson was a direct and dangerously speedy winger, though, and he could play either on the right or the left, providing countless accurate crosses and passes for both Greaves and Gilzean, over the next four seasons.

Robertson returned for Tottenham's home match against Aston Villa, struggling to escape relegation, on Saturday 29th October, but this time, Cliff Jones was missing.

Again though, Tottenham, unbelievably, fired more blanks.

Lew Chatterley scored the only goal of the game, in Villa's shock 1-0 away win. Spurs dropped to sixth place, four points behind new leaders Chelsea, but they were back to full strength, as they visited bottom club Blackpool on November the Fifth.

Fireworks went missing again, and despite two goals from Alan Gilzean, his first goals for a month, Jimmy Armfield's Blackpool battled hard for a 2-2 draw.

57,127, Spurs' biggest home league crowd of that season, then filled the Lane for the visit of lowly West Ham United, with their World Cup winning trio of Moore, Peters and Hurst. Jimmy Greaves scored his first goal, from the penalty spot, for five weeks, and for six matches, the longest barren spell of his Tottenham career, while Gilzean and Terry Venables also both scored in a thrilling match. Brabrook, Byrne, Hurst and Sissons had all netted for the Hammers, though, for a great 4-3 away win. West Ham had the most prolific attack, but also the leakiest defence in the First Division.

By the time David Ford scored the only goal of the game in Sheffield Wednesday's 1-0 win over a full strength Spurs side, on Saturday 19th November, Tottenham had dropped to tenth place, and six points below leaders Chelsea.

They'd taken just one point from six games, and apart from their tough visit to Stamford Bridge, all of those games were not only winnable, but games they'd have expected to win.

Tottenham returned to some sort of form, as November turned into December, winning three, but also losing two, of their next six games.

By Bank Holiday Tuesday, 27th December, Spurs were still down in ninth place, and now seven points behind the new league leaders Manchester United. They'd lost nine of their opening twenty-three matches, in spite of a brilliant start to the season.

Over the next four months, though, Tottenham Hotspur played some of the best football they'd ever displayed, not just during the Sixties, but throughout their history.

Their lowest home crowd of the season, 27,948, dragged themselves reluctantly to White Hart Lane, on New Year's Eve, for the visit of Newcastle United. Jimmy Greaves fired in two goals, and Dave Mackay and Terry Venables completed the scoring in their 4-0 Cull of the Magpies.

Terry Venables had joined Tottenham in May 1966, after playing over 200 First Division games for Chelsea. Venables was "a wonderful player and a very popular figure" at Chelsea, but Blues boss Tommy Docherty had also believed that Venables was taking a greater interest in the tactical and technical elements of the game, and occasionally, although unintentionally, he'd undermined his position as manager, Docherty had felt.

On the field, too, Docherty had felt that the influence Venables had on his Chelsea team was so strong that they couldn't mount an attack without Venables conducting the play. As a result, teams came to close down Venables, so Chelsea couldn't play.

Docherty placed Venables on the transfer list, and Bill Nicholson offered £70,000.

Docherty told Nicholson that he thought Venables was worth £80,000, so Nicholson immediately agreed, and the deal was done.

It was implied that Bill Nicholson might have seen Terry Venables as the new John White, but that was a huge standard to live up to, and as skilful and hardworking Venables was, in a Tottenham shirt, he always fell slightly short of those high standards that were expected of him. As a result, Venables had a rough deal at Spurs, particularly with the fans, who regarded him as a luxury player.

Even so, during his first full season, Terry Venables missed only one out of fifty-one league and cup matches, and he was a key part of Tottenham's attacking play during their resurgence in the first four months of 1967.

Spurs followed up their thrashing of Newcastle United, by winning 2-0 away at Arsenal, on Saturday 7th January, in front of a Highbury crowd of just under fifty thousand.

Jimmy Robertson and Alan Gilzean scored their goals, but Gilzean limped off before the end, and he also missed Spurs' next match, away at leaders Manchester United, one week later.

57,365 were packed into an electric Old Trafford, but Tottenham were offered some hope when Denis Law was also ruled out, through injury. Law had already scored fifteen First Division goals in just twenty-one games that season, and United struggled without their top scorer.

MANCHESTER UNITED		TOTTENHAM HOTSPUR
Alex Stepney	1	Pat Jennings
Tony Dunne	2	Phil Beal
Bobby Noble	3	Cyril Knowles
Paddy Crerand	4	Alan Mullery
Bill Foulkes	5	Mike England
David Sadler	6	Dave Mackay
George Best	7	Jimmy Robertson
Jim Ryan	8	Jimmy Greaves
Bobby Charlton	9	Frank Saul
David Herd	10	Terry Venables
John Aston	11	Keith Weller

With Cliff Jones absent since early December, twenty year old Keith Weller made only his sixth league start for Spurs. The Islington-born midfield creator eventually moved onto Millwall and Chelsea, before becoming possibly Leicester City's greatest ever player during the Seventies.

Tottenham had also not conceded a single goal during their previous three matches mainly due to the stability of their back four, but particularly because of the pure brilliance of Pat Jennings.

Pat Jennings had made his senior debut for Newry, in Northern Ireland, aged just sixteen, before he joined Watford in May 1963, as an eighteen year old. After playing forty-eight consecutive league games for the Brewers, his performances attracted scouts from Tottenham, and in June 1964, Bill Nicholson paid £27,000 for Jennings.

Cyril Knowles had also joined in 1964, after playing thirty-nine Second Division matches for Middlesbrough. From Fitzwilliam in West Yorkshire, Knowles had made his league debut for Boro back in April 1963, away at Derby County, aged only eighteen, just as Pat Jennings had been.

"He was a hard man and all good sides need a hard man, a player who can win the ball," Bill Nicholson admitted, when he paid £45,000 for the teenager in May 1964. Cyril Knowles was certainly a tough tackling left back, but he also loved to overlap the midfield, providing superb support in attack, and he became famed for his pinpoint left wing crosses.

Very tall for a full back, Knowles was actually as tall as Mike England. He was also as "cool as a cucumber, under pressure. He never seemed to panic and always played within himself," his future Spurs teammate Martin Chivers appraised Cyril Knowles' superior skills for a full back.

"He was happy to dribble the ball along his own goal-line, rather than just kick it clear."

Against United, though, Spurs sorely missed Alan Gilzean.

If Tottenham had beaten Manchester United, they might have won the league, but United, in fairness, also greatly missed Denis Law, their European Footballer of the Year from only two seasons before.

With George Best and Bobby Charlton always dangerous, though, from thirty yards out, John Aston bustling down the left wing, and Paddy Crerand enjoying a royal battle with Alan Mullery, United were still classy and lively First Division leaders.

Tottenham, though, had much the better of the game. Phil Beal, unhurried and calm on the ball, was mostly untroubled by John Aston all afternoon, and he was more of an attacking threat than Aston, in truth. Blonde-haired and twenty-two years old, Beal tackled tidily, and he distributed the ball with soft feet to Mackay, Mullery and Venables, and as a result, Spurs' possession rate was far better than United's.

Jimmy Robertson gave Bobby Noble, United's twenty-one year old full back from Reddish, in Cheshire, a torrid afternoon. Robertson screamed in cross after cross for both Greavsie and Frank Saul. Saul hit the post, while Greaves fiercely glanced a header towards the top right corner of United's goal, from Robertson's cross, but Stepney flew high to tip the ball behind his angle for a corner kick.

Dave Mackay thundered a header from Keith Weller's corner towards the inside corner of Stepney's left post, but John Aston, on the goal-line, deflected the ball behind for another corner.

Tottenham were in scintillating form, but despite attack after attack, they were thwarted by desperate, last-ditch defending by the home team, the league leaders.

It was, therefore, a real shock when David Herd got in between Terry Venables and Mike England, during the dying moments of the game, and he fired a low shot past Jennings for a 1-0 United win.

That was Tottenham's one and only league and cup defeat during their final twenty-seven matches of that 1966-67 season. One week later, Cliff Jones returned to the team and he headed the second, decisive goal during their 2-0 win over Burnley. Greavsie had scored the opener, in front of their 42,000 home crowd.

On the final Saturday of January, Spurs were drawn away at Millwall in the FA Cup Third round. With a capacity crowd of over 41,000 inside The Den, verbally abusing every Tottenham player, very loudly, but particularly Jimmy Greaves, calling him an England reject, a failure, etc, and all sorts of insults coloured with plenty of *C* and *F* words. Occasional fights also broke out between home and away fans in the Ilderton Road End and the North Stand, but Spurs battled hard for a goalless draw.

Tottenham's biggest home crowd of the season, 58,189, completely overran and overfilled White Hart Lane's capacity, on the following Wednesday 1st February.

Again, though, Millwall battled like lions, with Eamon Dunphy putting himself about, menacingly, against both Mullery and Mackay.

Dunphy didn't give a fuck who he clashed with in these big games, just as long as he clashed with them. Players like Dunphy, as well as Harry Cripps, Billy Neill, Derek Possee and the great Barry Kitchener, were a big reason why Millwall punched well above their weight for eight seasons, between 1966 and 1974, competing in many Second Division promotion battles.

Millwall finished above many more star-studded and illustrious Second Division teams, during every season, with Bryan King often voted the best goalkeeper in the Division, by the PFA, but Eamon Dunphy was their heart and soul in the middle of the field.

Alan Gilzean curled his well-placed shot past Leslie in Millwall's goal, finally breaking down their opponents' resolve, near the end of a battering and bruising battle.

Greavsie then scored in their 1-1 away draw at second-placed Nottingham Forest, the surprise team of the season, with nearly 42,000 filling the City Ground.

Cliff Jones then scored twice, on Saturday 11th February, during their 4-2 win over Fulham, for whom legends of different eras, Johnny Haynes and Allan Clarke, had both scored. Bobby Robson, George Cohen, John Dempsey, Les Barrett, Jimmy Conway and Steve Earle also played in a good Fulham team that afternoon, but goals from both Greaves and Gilzean completed Spurs' victory.

Another huge crowd of just under 58,000 again squeezed into the Lane, a week later, for the visit of another Second Division team, Portsmouth, in the FA Cup Fourth round.

After struggling to break through Portsmouth's rugged defence during the first half, Cyril Knowles' free-kick was met by Alan Gilzean's dynamic diving header, just seven minutes after the break. Then, Jimmy Robertson and Jimmy Greaves exchanged a couple of crisp one-two's, cutting straight through Pompey's tiring defence, before setting up Gilzean for a cool finish, just inside the penalty area.

With twenty minutes left, Gilzean returned the favour, threading a killer pass past the Pompey back four, who were holding a high line, into the path of his strike partner.

Greaves sprinted clear, before cutting the ball past Albert Milkins' dive. The ball just squeezed inside the near right post of the Portsmouth goal.

Jimmy Robertson's goal scraped a tired 1-1 home draw with Manchester City, after four tough, exhausting matches within that opening fortnight of February, but with Jimmy Greaves and Cliff Jones both missing. That was the first of three successive league draws, with their 3-3 draw away at Aston Villa, and a 1-1 draw at home to Chelsea sandwiching their 2-0 win over Bristol City, in the Fifth round of the FA Cup.

Jimmy Greaves had scored both goals to put Spurs into the Quarter-finals, and then he hit the only goal of their away game at Everton, on Wednesday 22nd March, with over 50,000 inside Goodison Park. Jimmy Robertson's goal was then enough to beat Leicester 1-0 on the following Saturday, away at Filbert Street, and finally at the end of March, Mullery and Gilzean both scored during their 2-0 home win over Everton.

On Saturday 1st April, Jimmy Greaves then scored twice during Spurs 2-1 win over the reigning Champions Liverpool, with more than 53,000 inside White Hart Lane.

Greavsie's first goal was scored direct from a right wing corner kick. He fired over an inswinger, and Alan Gilzean feigned to attack the ball at the near post, as it just squeezed between Gerry Byrne and Tommy Lawrence on the goal-line.

Left foot, right foot, with his head, from either the right wing, or the left wing, or even straight from a corner kick, it really didn't matter how Greaves scored his goals. He was simply the best centre-forward in the World.

"Jimmy Greaves could be out of the game for eighty minutes," Alan Mullery said of his teammate, "and then he'd score two in the last ten."

Alan Mullery had played 199 league games for Fulham, between 1958 and 1964, after becoming a first team regular at seventeen years old, as they gained promotion back to the First Division during 1958-59.

Bill Nicholson then paid £72,000 for Mullery, in March 1964, and eight months later, Mullery was making his England debut in their 1-1 draw with Holland, in Amsterdam.

Mullery was the driving force behind Tottenham, hard in the tackle, but he could also blast tremendous shots at goal from long range distances. With Jennings in goal, the mighty Mackay and England at the back, Mullery their general in midfield, and Greaves and Gilzean up front, Spurs had the strongest spine in English football, in 1967.

Tottenham travelled to St Andrews, on Saturday 8th April, to face Birmingham City in the FA Cup Quarter-finals. Birmingham were their fourth Second Division opposition in the competition, but it was a big First Division crowd that coldly welcomed Spurs, with 51,467 packed into the ground.

Trevor Hockey tracked the influential Mullery all over the St Andrews pitch. Defences were on top, and Birmingham hung on for a goalless draw, earning a financially lucrative replay away at White Hart Lane on the following Wednesday.

Over 52,000 watched an entirely different type of match, to the dull and defensive display at Birmingham. Tottenham simply swept Blues aside, winning 6-0, with Jimmy Greaves and Terry Venables both scoring two apiece, and Alan Gilzean and Frank Saul completed their scoring.

Spurs beat Sheffield Wednesday 2-1 at White Hart Lane, and Alan Gilzean then scored to beat Southampton 1-0 away, with a crowd of over 30,000 inside The Dell.

More importantly, though, Tottenham's defence of Joe Kinnear, Mike England, Dave Mackay and Cyril Knowles had kept out Ron Davies and Martin Chivers, the most prolific strike-force in the First Division. Ron Davies had scored thirty-nine goals, so far that season, but both he and Chivers eventually scored over sixty combined league and cup goals, during 1966-67.

Joe Kinnear had moved from his home city of Dublin, as a sixteen year old, during the early Sixties, to St Albans City of the Isthmian League. He then moved to Tottenham Hotspur as a junior, in 1963, after starring in St Albans' defence.

Kinnear eventually made his Spurs debut in 1966, aged only nineteen, but then he regained his place two weeks into 1966-67, before he was replaced by Phil Beal after their 4-3 away win at Fulham.

He'd returned in March 1967, though, following Beal's season-ending injury, suffered during their 1-1 draw at home to Manchester City. Of those sixteen league and cup games in which Kinnear played, over the final three months of the 1966-67 season, Spurs conceded only five goals, while scoring twenty-seven.

With a game in hand, Tottenham were six points behind leaders Manchester United, who'd just drawn 0-0 at Sunderland, with four games to play. It was a tall order for Tottenham to catch United, but they'd played themselves back into the race.

FIRST DIVISION LEADERS, 22ND APRIL 1967

	PL	W	D	L	F	A	PTS
Man United	39	22	11	6	75	43	55
Nottm Forest	39	21	10	8	58	37	52
TOTTENHAM	38	21	7	10	66	48	49
Leeds Utd	37	19	10	8	54	37	48
Liverpool	38	18	12	8	61	42	48
Chelsea	40	15	13	12	63	57	43

Spurs had to beat both Sunderland and Sheffield United at White Hart Lane, but they also needed wins away at West Ham, and at Liverpool. And United had to fail to take more than a single point at home to nearly-relegated Aston Villa or Stoke City, as well as their away game at West Ham.

On Saturday 29th April, United beat Villa 3-1, eliminating Spurs from the title race. Spurs could still catch United's points total, but the 0.40 goal average difference couldn't be made up with just four games left.

On that very same day, Hillsborough hosted the FA Cup Semi-final between Tottenham and second-placed Nottingham Forest. Despite playing Second Division teams all the way up to the last four, Spurs had attracted an average crowd of nearly 53,000 for all of their FA Cup matches.

Nottingham Forest's surprising success was built on their goals scored by both Ian Storey-Moore and Joe Baker, but they also had some good quality talent in Alan Hinton, Terry Hennessey and Frank Wignall, future League Champions at Derby County, as well as Henry Newton, John Barnwell, and Bob McKinley, the holder of Forest's all-time League appearances record.

Ian Storey-Moore and Joe Baker scored forty-three combined League and Cup goals during 1966-67, firing Nottingham Forest towards their best-ever season in the First Division… up to then.

Joe Baker had had an eventful career. Born in Liverpool, he'd scored 102 Scottish League goals for Hibernian in just 117 games, between 1957 and 1961. At just eighteen years old, he was the Scottish League's top goal-scorer back in 1958-59, and then he repeated the feat one year later. Alan Gilzean had also been top scorer in the Scottish League on two occasions, though, in 1962 and 1964.

In 1961, Baker joined the small exodus of British talent to Italy, along with both Jimmy Greaves and Denis Law. Torino had paid £75,000 for the twenty year old, but Baker's stay, just like Greavsie's time in Italy, was an unhappy one. It was almost tragic, though, as he was involved in a car crash, and subsequently kept alive on a drip.

After his recovery, though, Arsenal paid £70,000 for Baker in 1962, and he scored ninety-three First Division goals in just 144 games while at Highbury, until he moved to Nottingham Forest during the Summer of 1966, for just £65,000.

Sadly, for Forest, Joe Baker had been injured as they'd beaten Everton 3-2, in the Quarter-finals, and he didn't return to action before the end of the season.

In his absence, the Reds struggled to trouble Spurs' defence.

Jimmy Greaves fired a long range rocket shot, after half an hour, sending the ball spinning in off Grummitt's left post, from well outside the penalty area.

Frank Saul then burst through, onto Mullery's through-ball, and he put Spurs 2-0 up, with twenty-five minutes to play, but Forest never gave up. Terry Hennessey fired in from close range, with only ten minutes remaining, and Forest threatened to equalise soon after, but Cliff Jones brilliantly blocked Frank Wignall's shot.

Mike England marked Moore effectively, so much so that Forest's twenty-four goal striker didn't get one shot on target. Tottenham pushed forward for a third goal towards full-time, with Peter Grummitt making three superb saves from Gilzean, Saul and Greaves, but their 2-1 win set up the first all-London FA Cup Final, after Chelsea had beaten Leeds 1-0 at Villa Park.

Tottenham ended the season well, beating Sunderland, West Ham and Sheffield United, and also drawing 0-0 away at Liverpool. They finished level on points with second placed Forest, and only four points behind Manchester United.

Spurs had won thirteen, and lost only one, of their last nineteen league games, taking thirty-one out of a possible thirty-eight points.

The problem was, that as they'd hit Championship-winning form, scoring thirty-two goals, and conceding just eleven, Manchester United never collapsed. United won nine, and lost none, of their last nineteen games, gaining twenty-eight points.

Tottenham lost the title, after their silly season back in October and November, when they gained just one point out of a possible twelve, ten of which were easily winnable points. If they'd just underperformed and won five points from those six games, they'd have been Champions, but then the Manchester United of Best, Charlton, Law, Stiles and Crerand would never have been Champions. Ifs and buts, swings and roundabouts, there was nothing else between those two teams, except four points.

It was, however, the best chance that most of that Tottenham team had of winning the League Championship, and the pain of coming so close, and knowing they could blame nobody but themselves, was tough to take.

In the FA Cup Final, on Saturday 20th May, Spurs and Chelsea played a lively, end to end match to finish the season, with Tottenham having the better of possession, but Chelsea were always dangerous on the counter attack.

TOTTENHAM HOTSPUR		CHELSEA
Pat Jennings	1	Peter Bonetti
Joe Kinnear	2	Allan Harris
Cyril Knowles	3	Eddie McCreadie
Alan Mullery	4	John Hollins
Mike England	5	Marvin Hinton
Dave Mackay	6	Ron Harris
Jimmy Robertson	7	Charlie Cooke
Jimmy Greaves	8	Tommy Baldwin
Alan Gilzean	9	Tony Hateley
Terry Venables	10	Bobby Tambling
Frank Saul	11	John Boyle
Cliff Jones	12	Joe Kirkup

Alan Mullery did not misplace a pass all day, though, and five minutes before the break, he fired a long range shot, low along the ground, which Bonetti managed to stop, but he couldn't hold it, and from just inside the area, Jimmy Robertson caught the loose ball and he drove it sharply into the net.

Like Mullery and Robertson, Alan Gilzean was also superb, troubling the hardworking Ron Harris and Marvin Hinton at every attack. Halfway into the second half, Gilzean was being double-marked, as Dave Mackay flung a long throw-in towards Jimmy Robertson, who flicked on for the Canvey Island-born Frank Saul to turn and volley the ball beyond Bonetti, from ten yards out.

John Boyle crossed for Bobby Tambling to score a late consolation goal, as Spurs held on for a 2-1 win, and captain Dave Mackay lifted the Cup, after a bitter-sweet season, when Tottenham could have won the Double, a **BETTER** Double, for the second time, but they didn't.

Wearing an all-white kit, for the benefit of black and white television viewers- *that 1967 Final was the last Final not to have been broadcast on Colour Television*- Tottenham's triumph masked their pain, on that day, that they'd experienced in failing to catch United, their heart-wrenching pain, despite having such a great season; a Whiter Shade of Pain.

Tottenham Hotspur had been just four points away from winning the Double, four points behind the same team that became the 1968 European Champions, the first English team to do so. It *would* have been a better double.

In 1960-61, the English game was still in a slump following the Munich air disaster, and the demise of those great Fifties legends, Milburn, Lofthouse, Finney, Matthews, etc. It was the shallow water era of First Division football, where good teams could win the league, like Burnley and Ipswich, that were not necessarily great teams, although they did have some great players. During 1960-61, there were no other real top quality First Division teams, besides Tottenham.

In 1966-67, besides Champions Manchester United, Tottenham had Don Revie's young Leeds United team of Bremner, Giles, Gray, Lorimer, Charlton, Hunter, Reaney and Cooper. Everton had their all-action midfield of Ball, Harvey, Kendall, Morrissey and Husband; and Liverpool boasted their 1966 title-winning attack of Hunt, St John, Callaghan and Thompson. Manchester City, Arsenal and Chelsea were also developing their teams that were to dominate in Europe, as well as in England, over the next five or six seasons, and of course West Ham had their World Cup winning trio of players.

In 1966-67, the First Division was a strong league, possibly not as strong as it would become in 1971-72, when most of those teams, as well as Derby County, were hitting their peaks, but it was as strong as any other, all the way down.

In any case, Manchester United and Tottenham Hotspur, in 1967, were as good as any teams, any teams at all, that had played either First Division or Premier League football, since then.

Spurs and United met in the Charity Shield, on Saturday 12th August, with over 54,000 inside Old Trafford. Other than 1974, for its non-footballing content, Charity Shields aren't referred to here, but for its footballing content, and its competitive spirit, the 1967 Charity Shield was a classic match, and the best Charity Shield of all time.

Two great teams, both at full strength, went at each other, with some of the finest attacking football ever seen at Old Trafford.

Jimmy Robertson stretched to connect with Jimmy Greaves' low cross, cut back from the left side of the United area, and he steered the ball, left footed, past Stepney from six yards out, but then Tottenham went 2-0 up with one of the most famous ever televised goals.

Pat Jennings launched a huge, long drop kick from his penalty area, and the ball bounced just outside United's area. It was left alone by Bill Foulkes, under pressure from the menacing Greaves. The ball then ballooned up, over the leap of keeper Alex Stepney, caught in no-man's land, before it dropped to bounce again, inside the six yard box, and then nestled in the back of the United net.

Bobby Charlton pulled a goal back, after he collected a short pass from Crerand, before blasting the ball high into the top of Jennings' goal, from twenty yards out.

Then, Denis Law and Brian Kidd combined in an electric counter attack, down the United left wing, from their own penalty area. Kidd played the ball inside for Bobby Charlton to fire, first time, again from well over twenty yards out, past the flying Pat Jennings, high into the Tottenham net.

"Oh! That was a goal good enough to win the League, the Cup, the Charity Shield, the World Cup, and even the Grand National," Kenneth Wolstenholme enthused.

Into the second half, Frank Saul put Spurs 3-2 up, heading in Alan Gilzean's left wing cross, the ball bouncing into United's goal off Alex Stepney's left post.

Bobby Charlton, Man of the Match by some distance, again hit another twenty-five yard thunderbolt of a shot, but which Jennings managed to save this time. He couldn't hold onto it, though, and Denis Law pounced to smash home the ball on the rebound.

So how good exactly was that 1967 Spurs side? How would you compare it to the 1961 Double winning team? I don't really like comparisons of teams from different footballing eras, but people will make them anyway, and would suggest that the '61 side won both the title and the Cup, whereas their '67 side could only win the Cup, therefore their '61 side was better. So I'll offer a counter-argument.

Sure, the 1967 team didn't have Danny Blanchflower, John White, or Bobby Smith, and neither did it have Cliff Jones at his very best, nor Maurice Norman or Les Allen.

On the other hand, that 1961 team was missing Jimmy Greaves and Alan Gilzean. They had no Mike England, nor Pat Jennings. Cyril Knowles, Spurs greatest ever left back, was not there in 1961. Alan Mullery, the greatest holding midfield player in the history of the club, also arrived at White Hart Lane after 1961, while Dave Mackay, one of the best players from the Double-winning team, was still a key player during 1967, and Cliff Jones, although no longer a top draw winger, was a big influence in their 1967 successes.

It will be asked, then, how can a team that didn't win the league be a better team than one that did win the league? Well, the Leeds United team that finished second behind Everton, in 1970, and behind Arsenal, in 1971, was clearly a better team, with Allan Clarke included, than their 1969 team that did win the title. Also, QPR's team that finished second behind Liverpool in 1976, were a much better team than the Derby County team that had won the title a year earlier.

Spurs began the 1967-68 season with a 3-2 win away at Leicester, with 32,552 inside Filbert Street, before drawing 1-1 at home to Everton. Alan Gilzean's goal scraped a point against the Toffees, who'd outclassed Manchester United on the opening day.

THE DECLINE

On Saturday 26th August, nearly 56,000 packed into the Lane for the visit of West Ham United. Jimmy Greaves, who'd scored twenty-five First Division goals during the previous season, scored twice, while Cliff Jones, Alan Mullery and Frank Saul also netted second half goals during their 5-1 win, that was slightly soured after Dave Mackay was carried off injured.

Mackay missed Tottenham's following thirteen matches, and although Spurs went top of the league after their 1-0 away win at Everton, in front of nearly 58,000, on Tuesday 29th August, they won only four of those thirteen games played without Dave Mackay.

By early November, when Mackay finally returned to action, Tottenham had dropped back to sixth place, but then they also lost Mike England for three months, and by Christmas, they were even further back in tenth position and way behind the title race.

Only 36,000 turned up for their 2-2 home draw with relegation-bound Fulham, despite Cliff Jones scoring twice.

In the European Cup Winners' Cup, Spurs had beaten Hajduk Split 6-3, on aggregate, before they went out after their 4-4 aggregate draw with Olympique Lyonnaise, during *The Beatles' All You Need Is Love* December of 67, losing on the away goals rule.

Jimmy Greaves had felt that team spirit, the team spirit that had driven Spurs to such a good season during 1966-67, was now missing.

"The domestic season of 1967-68 was one of the unhappiest I ever experienced in football. Most worrying of all," Greavsie admitted, "I realised my appetite for football was not the same... I actually contemplated retiring."

Their slump in form and the lack of motivation throughout the team hadn't escaped Bill Nicholson's attention, either. In the middle of darkest January, he paid a club record transfer fee of £125,000 to Southampton for Martin Chivers, who'd scored twenty-seven First Division goals in just sixty-five games at The Dell.

Chivers was a tall, powerful forward, nearly six feet and two inches tall, who'd scored a total of ninety-six league goals for his home town club, displaying speed, control, and a strong tactical brain, as his thirty Second Division goals had helped the Saints gain promotion to the First Division in 1966, for the first time in their history.

"Martin had everything," Norman Hunter wrote of Chivers, or **Big Chiv,** as he'd become. "He had pace, great touch; good in the air, very quick; the only thing he lacked was aggression."

Big Chiv scored his first goal for Spurs on his debut, a 2-1 win away at Sheffield Wednesday, on 17th January 1968, Spurs' first league win at Hillsborough since before the War. Bill Nicholson paired Chivers and Greaves up front, whilst dropping Alan Gilzean to a more creative midfield role, attacking from deeper positions.

In the FA Cup Third round, Spurs flew up to Manchester, to face United at Old Trafford. Before a massive crowd of sixty-three and a half thousand, Chivers weaved between both John Fitzpatrick and Francis Burns, before driving his left-footed shot past Alex Stepney.

George Best equalised, and then Bobby Charlton gave United the lead during the second half, but two minutes before the end, Big Chiv immediately repaid his fee. Alan Gilzean flicked on Cliff Jones' corner kick, and Martin Chivers smashed the ball into the roof of the net.

Over 57,000 packed into White Hart Lane for the replay, on Wednesday 31st January, and a solitary goal by Jimmy Robertson secured a hard-fought 1-0 win. Spurs then beat Preston 3-1 in the Fourth round, in front of over 47,000.

Jimmy Greaves scored twice, and Martin Chivers hit his fifth goal for Tottenham.

Liverpool beat Spurs 2-1, though, after a Fifth round replay.

Roger Hunt and Tommy Smith scored at Anfield, cancelling out Cliff Jones' goal, but an average crowd of more than 55,000 had watched each of Tottenham's five FA Cup ties. If it hadn't been for Martin Chivers, though, that was a Cup run that wouldn't have lasted more than one match.

His huge transfer fee was indeed repaid.

With Chivers providing a huge boost to Tottenham's attack, their form improved from March onwards, and they eventually finished up in seventh place, eleven points behind Champions Manchester City. Spurs had scored as many goals as they'd scored in 1967, seventy league goals, but they'd conceded fifty-nine goals in forty-two games.

Dave Mackay, at thirty-two years old, had declared himself to be knackered, and he asked for a move back to his home town club, Hearts, as their new player-manager.

Brian Clough and Peter Taylor, though, hi-jacked that move, and they snapped up Mackay for just £10,000 during the Summer of 1968. Mackay played sweeper at Derby County, alongside Roy McFarland, and the two led Derby from the back, back to the First Division, as they became the best central defensive partnership in English football, just as Mackay and England had been at Spurs.

"Dave Mackay was the best player, the best player by far, that I ever played with in the same team," claimed Roy McFarland. "And I played with a lot of great players in my twenty-eight games for England."

Dave Mackay had played 318 First Division matches for Spurs, scoring fifty-one goals, in more than nine years at White Hart Lane.

Jimmy Greaves was even more glowing in his praise of Mackay. "Dave Mackay is to my mind, the greatest player ever to have worn a Tottenham shirt," Greavsie suggested. "He was a mighty player, ferocious in the tackle but always very fair."

Jimmy Greaves endured his worst full season during 1967-68, having scored only twenty-three league goals, and six in the Cups, failing to hit thirty goals. Martin Chivers scored ten league and cup goals in twenty-three games, after arriving in January, but Cliff Jones, at thirty-three years old, was Tottenham's second highest scorer, with just fourteen league and cup goals.

His fitness, though, was becoming an issue, and during the first two months of the 1968-69 season, Cliff Jones was more out of the team than he was it.

In October 1968, after playing 318 First Division games for Spurs, and scoring 135 goals in his ten years at the Lane, Cliff Jones was sold to Fulham, to end his legendary professional football career. He made twenty-five league appearances for Fulham, but he couldn't help prevent them getting relegated to the Third Division in April 1969.

He was then transferred to non-league Kings Lynn, at the age of thirty-four.

Dave Mackay's permanent replacement in Spurs' central defence was Phil Beal.

By August 1968, at just twenty-three years old, Phil Beal had already played over one hundred league games for Tottenham, covering either Joe Kinnear, Mike England or Dave Mackay in their defence.

The blonde, mild-mannered ball-playing defender, from Godstone in Surrey, had lacked Mackay's aggression and leadership qualities, as well as his immense skill, but Beal was cool, composed and sure in all of his Tottenham performances.

Phil Beal would never have pulled Billy Bremner off the ground by the scruff of his Leeds shirt, as Mackay famously did. Instead, he was Tottenham's tactical equivalent of West Ham's Bobby Moore. Beal was clean and consistent, a good tackler, and a tidy distributor of the ball. While his partnership, in defence, with Mike England was not as superior as England's partnership with Mackay, Beal's classy performances and his natural ability to make time for himself, allied to England's aerial dominance and game-winning groundwork, had helped form a rich and highly rated defensive partnership during the early Seventies.

It didn't start off so well. Spurs won just three of their opening nine games of the 1968-69 season, despite Greaves, Chivers and Gilzean scoring fourteen goals between them, and they were seven points behind leaders Arsenal on Saturday 21st September, before their home game against Nottingham Forest.

Spurs won 2-1, but disaster struck with half an hour remaining.

Martin Chivers had been working to build up his physique, to deal with the heavily muddied White Hart Lane pitch, in comparison with his old, drier pitch at Southampton, working with weights, and doing extra physical exercises after training, as well as being given cortisone injections to build up his muscles.

After playing an innocuous square ball to Terry Venables, Big Chiv suddenly collapsed onto the ground. Players ran over, and tried to pull him up, despite Chivers' pleas that his knee had gone. Club physiotherapist Cecil Poynton, who'd played over one hundred and fifty games for Tottenham, way back in the Twenties and Thirties, asked him to slowly bend his leg.

As Chivers bent his leg, his left knee cap began to ride right up his thigh. Some Tottenham players were physically sick, at the sight of Chivers' injury.

He was stretchered off, and also ruled out of football for twelve months, due to his snapped tendon, after he'd been given cortisone injections into his patella tendon during the pre-season. During his long period away from playing football, his Dad also died, aged only fifty-nine, just before Christmas 1968. After Martin Chivers returned to football in October 1969, he'd always thought about his Dad, whenever he played for Spurs, or for England at Wembley.

Regarding Big Chiv's mild-mannered nature, Bill Nicholson was often eager to try and pull some aggressive reaction out of him. Mr Nicholson had always felt that Chivers would be a better player if he had more aggression. But, that simply wasn't Martin Chivers' style of game. He just wanted to keep his eye on the ball, beat his defender, and then score. It was as simple as that.

For as long as Bill Nicholson remained as Tottenham manager, though, he disagreed with Martin Chivers about his non-aggressive style. At one point, Nicholson was even reproached by captain Alan Mullery, after Chivers had received another ear-bashing, following a Tottenham win.

"In the end I got sick of it," Mullery said, remembering Nicholson's rants at Chivers.

"Hey Bill," Mullery called out. "Chiv's just won us the game," to a general murmur of agreement from all around Tottenham's changing room.

Martin Chivers became one of the best-loved players in the Spurs team, by fans and his teammates, even if his manager had seemed constantly exasperated by his laid-back manner.

During Chivers' absence in 1968-69, Jimmy Greaves had another great season, at twenty-nine years old, becoming the First Division's top goal-scorer for the sixth time in his career, hitting twenty-seven goals, as well as nine in the Cup competitions.

One of his best goals of the season, though, and indeed one of the best goals of his entire career, was scored during Tottenham's 3-2 win over Leicester City on Saturday 5th October 1968. Greavsie scored a hat-trick that day, but it was his second goal that was a candidate for Goal of the Decade. He turned Malcolm Manley, thirty yards from goal, before spinning quickly and sprinting away, losing his close marker in an instant.

He then outran Mike Stringfellow, and also breezed past Graham Cross's tackle, twenty-five yards out, while running diagonally, from left to right.

Greaves ran clear into City's area, with three Leicester players snapping at his heels, but no matter; with a lethal combination of speed and close ball control, he just accelerated, and flew past Peter Shilton's dive, on the edge of the six yard box, then he slid the ball back in towards goal, as Willie Bell came in to challenge from the left.

Kenneth Wolstenholme was so overcome with excitement, amazement and admiration, he struggled to speak for a moment.

"Changing direction so well... oh, beautiful football... What a great goal!" he'd exclaimed.

It was such a great goal, that even the great Wolstenholme couldn't do it justice. They should have recruited one of those wild South American commentators, just for when Jimmy Greaves got the ball, to truly illuminate his genius.

Apart from Greavsie, no other Spurs player hit double figures in goals scored. Alan Gilzean was flicked about from wide midfield to centre forward, and back and forth, back and forth, and the instability didn't suit him. Tottenham finished the season in sixth place, but a massive twenty-two points behind Leeds, the new Champions.

During June 1969, Terry Venables was sold to QPR for £70,000, after playing 115 First Division games for Spurs. Venables remained at Loftus Road for four years, holding Rangers' young midfield together, and he also played thirty-seven games during their 1972-73 promotion season.

Venables played one more full season in the First Division, with QPR, before he moved to Crystal Palace in September 1974, where he was eventually appointed player-manager in 1976, before he was finally appointed their full-time boss.

He led Palace out of Division Three in 1977, and back into the First Division, as Second Division Champions, two years later. Terry Venables moved back to QPR in 1980, and he took the Hoops to their only FA Cup Final appearance, so far, when his old team Tottenham won with a penalty kick, after a replay in 1982. In 1983, his young and dynamic QPR team then ran away with the Second Division title, but he shocked the football world a year later, by becoming Barcelona's first team coach.

Terry Venables was the first Englishman to manage a top European club, and he led Barca to their first La Liga title for eleven years, during 1984-85. Barcelona then reached the 1986 European Cup Final, a tournament somewhat devalued due to the enforced absence of Everton, after UEFA had banned all English clubs from European competitions for five years, following the Heysel Stadium tragedy. They lost to a spirited Steaua Bucharest side, though, that included Marius Lacatus and Gavril Balint.

Venables was sacked by Barcelona in 1987, after Dundee United had knocked them out of the UEFA Cup, so he returned to England, to manage Tottenham Hotspur.

He then built a gifted and talented side that included Hoddle and Waddle, Lineker and Gascoigne, but suffered from similar inconsistencies, that had affected Spurs' chances of Real Glory when he was a player at White Hart Lane.

Spurs never seriously challenged for any First Division title under his management, despite finishing third in 1990. Tottenham did reach the 1991 FA Cup Final, though, where they won 2-1 after a lively match against Nottingham Forest.

That was Terry Venables' only major honour as a manager in English football.

Although Steve Perryman had made his debut during September 1969, as a seventeen year old, 1969-70 was a fairly miserable season for Spurs fans.

Tottenham lost sixteen games in the First Division, but they'd also conceded more goals than they scored, for the first time in eleven years.

On Saturday 18th October, only 33,000 turned up at the Lane, to see tenth-placed Tottenham beat Newcastle United 2-1. Jimmy Greaves scored both goals, though, but his winning goal was another Greavsie Classic.

Greaves ran from the halfway line, with Ollie Burton in pursuit. He stepped outside of Burton's challenge on the edge of the Newcastle area, while in full flow, and then he darted back inside the box, leaping over McFaul's dive, before flicking the ball past Burton's desperate goal-line clearance.

Things were flat at White Hart Lane. By the beginning of February 1970, no Tottenham player had reached double figures in First Division goals scored.

On Saturday 10th January, Jimmy Greaves fired in his two hundred and fifty-seventh and final goal for Spurs, during their 2-1 home win over Derby County.

But after their 2-1 defeat at Sunderland, a week later, Greaves was dropped from the team, and he began scoring for Tottenham's reserves, helping them to the top of the Football Combination. He was determined to fight his way back into Spurs' first team.

Then on transfer deadline day, March 16th 1970, Bill Nicholson agreed to pay a British record transfer fee of £200,000 for West Ham United's Martin Peters.

Mr Nicholson then called Greaves into his office to tell him that he was letting him go to West Ham, as a makeweight, a £90,000 makeweight, in the deal.

Jimmy Greaves had eighteen months left on his contract, but he was so upset, and so furious with his boss, that he just agreed to go, there and then. He certainly didn't have to go.

He could have stayed and carried on fighting for his place in an improved Spurs team, with a World Cup winner amongst them, but off he went to West Ham.

From that day, until today, and even until tomorrow, Jimmy Greaves regretted not insisting upon staying at White Hart Lane.

Although Greavsie scored twice on his debut, in the Hammers' 5-1 win away at Manchester City, he'd struggled in a struggling West Ham team, deep in miserable transition between their World Cup-winning *Academy of Football* and their 1975 FA Cup-winning *Bearded Bar-room Brawlers.*

He scored only thirteen league goals in thirty-six games for West Ham, before he finally retired, disillusioned with football, at the end of 1970-71.

Jimmy Greaves was quite simply, and unarguably, the greatest-ever English-born centre-forward. Nobody was better.

He was the First Division's top goal-scorer for a record six seasons, twice with Chelsea, and four times with Spurs. Greavsie had scored 357 First Division goals, in just 516 games, but he also scored 44 goals for England, in fifty-seven international matches. He'd scored a hundred First Division goals by the time he was twenty-one. He scored a total of 412 league and cup goals in fourteen seasons, but by far, he was most remembered, and best loved, as a Tottenham player.

His close control and sheer pace; his athleticism, swagger, and relentless drive, allied to his superb timing, had made him absolutely impossible to mark out of games, when he was on his game, which was most of the time.

Furthermore, despite defences taking his legs from beneath him, or attempting to take his legs away, or being nobbled, elbowed, bruised and battered, throughout his career, Greavsie missed only twenty-seven out of a possible 442 First Division games, between 1958 and 1969, missing an average of just two games per season.

Bill Nicholson saw only a future with Martin Chivers and Alan Gilzean up front for Tottenham, though, and by bringing in Martin Peters, alongside Mullery in midfield, he finally went some way to replacing the late John White, six years after his death.

THE REVIVAL

Just as John White was known as *The Ghost,* Peters was also famed for his box to box displays, timing his runs just the same as White, ghosting in behind defences, and scoring "impossible goals", as Sir Alf Ramsey had claimed.

Despite the loss of Greavsie, Spurs had gained a real World Class midfield talent, at the peak of his career, at just twenty-six years old. Martin Peters steadied the ship, slightly, as he, Alan Mullery and Steve Perryman formed a tight and flexible midfield unit, with Roger Morgan, their £100,000 signing from QPR, lively out on the wing.

Tottenham hammered Nottingham Forest 4-1, on 27th March, and Roger Morgan hit the best form of his career, speeding past full backs, cutting inside at full pace, firing shots away, and winning midfield headers.

On this form, which was infrequent during 1969-70, Tottenham were unbeatable. Alan Mullery set up Alan Gilzean for the first, before Martin Chivers headed Morgan's left wing cross past Dave Hollins. Morgan then fired a blast from fifteen yards, which Hollins saved, but couldn't hold, and Chivers chipped in from the rebound.

Alan Gilzean glanced in the fourth, with his head, from Martin Peters' free-kick, and Tottenham ended that season in eleventh place, twenty-three points behind Everton, the First Division Champions. It had been another season to forget for Spurs.

Tottenham started slowly during 1970-71, winning only two of their opening seven matches, and a small crowd of just 19,894 had bothered to attend their 3-0 win over Blackpool. Alan Mullery converted a penalty kick, and his England teammate Martin Peters scored twice in a straightforward victory over the bottom placed Tangerines.

Then Spurs won eight of their next ten league games, moving right up to second in the table, just two points behind Leeds United, and they'd also eased past Swansea City, Sheffield United and West Brom, to reach the League Cup Quarter-finals.

Martin Chivers fired a superb hat-trick on 18th November, during their 4-1 thrashing of Coventry City, hitting all three goals high into the top corner of Bill Glazier's net, and also lifting Spurs into the last four.

In the league, though, Tottenham didn't win again in their next five games, between late November and the New Year, and they dropped down to fourth place. Spurs did beat Bristol City, though, in the Semi-finals of the League Cup in December, winning 3-1 on aggregate, to face Third Division Aston Villa, in the Final.

One man who'd continued to take the brunt of Bill Nicholson's frustrations, when the going was tough, as well as when the going was good, was Martin Chivers. In one game against Stoke City, on Saturday 24th October, Chivers had shoulder-barged the mighty Denis Smith off the ball, then he ran from halfway, before firing an unstoppable blast past Gordon Banks, the best goalkeeper in the World, and then he scored a second goal before half-time, giving Spurs an unassailable 3-0 lead.

But Bill still tore into him in the changing room, before Alan Mullery again stood up for him.

On Saturday 9th January, Spurs visited Leeds United, the mighty Leeds, who were running away with the title, three points ahead of second-placed Arsenal. Leeds had not lost in sixteen league games, winning ten of them, and a big 44,000 crowd had packed into Elland Road, expecting a fourth successive win. Mike England was ruled out of action for the rest of the season, though, after suffering an injury late in their goalless home draw with Wolves, while Phil Beal was suspended.

Their makeshift central defensive pairing of Peter Collins and Terry Naylor was not expected to hold Allan Clarke and Mick Jones, the most dangerous attacking partnership in England.

Leeds were subsequently all over Spurs for most of the match, and Pat Jennings was truly great, keeping out shot after shot, at times defying the laws of physical gravity, as he liked to do. Martin Chivers scored twice, though, earning Spurs an amazing 2-1 win away at the league leaders, but he got no praise.

Instead, he was just told by his own manager that he should give back his win bonus to the fans, as he hadn't earned it.

For the Spurs fans, though, the ones who paid to watch their team, it was totally different.

They loved Big Chiv. By the time the reigning Champions Everton arrived at White Hart Lane, on Saturday 30th January 1971, they were calling for him to be picked for England.

TOTTENHAM HOTSPUR		EVERTON
Pat Jennings	1	Andy Rankin
Joe Kinnear	2	Tommy Wright
Cyril Knowles	3	Henry Newton
Alan Mullery	4	Howard Kendall
Peter Collins	5	Brian Labone
Phil Beal	6	Colin Harvey
Alan Gilzean	7	Jimmy Husband
Steve Perryman	8	Alan Ball
Martin Chivers	9	Joe Royle
Martin Peters	10	John Hurst
Jimmy Neighbour	11	Johnny Morrissey
Jimmy Pearce	12	Roger Kenyon (rep. Labone)

Steve Perryman had made his debut during the previous season, and he'd played in half of Tottenham's games, but by the 1970-71 season, at nineteen years old, he was a first team regular. Ealing-born, he became one of the most respected midfield players of his era, through his tenacious battling and ball winning ability, combined with his refined and constructive attacking skills. Perryman was, as well as Martin Peters and Martin Chivers, one of only three ever-present players for Spurs during 1970-71.

Alan Gilzean headed down Phil Beal's cross, for Jimmy Neighbour to fire goalwards, but Rankin managed to turn the ball around his right hand post.

Everton counter-attacked, with Joe Royle heading Tommy Wright's cross into Alan Ball's path, inside the Tottenham box. Pat Jennings dived to brilliantly save Ball's first time strike, though, from just six yards out.

"Oooh! A magnificent save by Jennings," Brian Moore exclaimed!

"Ball looks amazed by it, as well he might!"

Martin Peters took a free-kick, from thirty yards out, after Chivers was fouled.

He floated the ball into the Everton area, and Martin Chivers swooped to beat his marker, Roger Kenyon, and he headed the ball high into the top left corner of Rankin's goal. It was his fifteenth goal in eighteen games.

"Chivers for England! Chivers for England!" the 42,000 home fans shouted loudly.

Husband then set up Colin Harvey, twenty yards out, but Jennings again pulled off another good save, turning Harvey's sharp drive behind for a corner.

Just before half-time, though, Howard Kendall crossed for Joe Royle to leap and head Everton level, giving Jennings no chance at all.

After the break, Martin Peters headed Alan Mullery's right-sided corner kick back into the box, where Alan Gilzean swivelled and turned the ball beyond Rankin's desperate dive.

Cyril Knowles then floated a long pass up to Chivers, whose beautifully weighted lay-off fell perfectly for Peters to hammer the ball beyond Rankin, from thirty yards out. The ball swung away, though, and passed just wide of the left post, but Spurs hung on to beat the Champions 2-1.

Despite beating Villa 2-0 in the League Cup Final, on Saturday 27th February, with Martin Chivers scoring twice, their season disintegrated after February. Spurs had qualified for the UEFA Cup, following their Wembley win, but they then won only seven of their final seventeen league games.

They'd battled past Sheffield Wednesday, Carlisle United (with 24,500 Cumbrians inside Brunton Park), and Nottingham Forest, to reach the FA Cup Quarter-finals, where they faced an away trip to Liverpool.

Spurs battled for a goalless draw at Liverpool, on Saturday 6th March, with nearly 55,000 inside Anfield. Ten days later, though, with 56,283 packed into White Hart Lane, their biggest crowd of the season, Steve Heighway scored the game's only goal.

Tottenham lost their last home game of the season, on the Monday night of 3rd May, against Arsenal, with 52,000 packed inside White Hart Lane, and with fifty thousand locked outside of their ground, filling the North London streets

So heavy was the congestion out in the streets, that traffic had stood still for miles around, and referee Kevin Howley, as well as Alan Mullery and Phil Beal, both travelling up from Surrey, all had to abandon their cars and walk to the ground.

Fired up by an impassioned crowd, Tottenham Hotspur did their best to deprive Arsenal of the title, but Ray Kennedy headed in a late goal, after a dramatic goalmouth scramble, to give Arsenal the lead. Spurs piled forward in numbers, trying to grab an equaliser that would have deprived Arsenal of the title, but the defence that had already kept thirty-six clean sheets that season, hung on for another to win 1-0.

Two nights later, Martin Peters scored as Spurs beat Stoke City at the Victoria Ground, a win that lifted Tottenham up three places, above Wolves, Liverpool and Chelsea, up into third position, their highest finish since 1967.

They'd finished thirteen points behind Arsenal, but it was a much better season than in 1970, and defensively, it had been their best-ever, having only conceded thirty-three goals in forty-two matches. Only 18,000 fans had attended their penultimate home game of the season, though, against Huddersfield Town.

They were scoring goals again, though, in contrast to the bleak season before. Martin Chivers scored twenty-nine goals, while Martin Peters and Alan Gilzean had scored a combined thirty-two league and cup goals.

On the very same day that Spurs had beaten Stoke to finish in third place, Bill Nicholson paid £190,000 for Burnley's midfield architect Ralph Coates. Coates had played 215 league games for the Clarets, and he'd been selected twice for England by Sir Alf Ramsey.

He was not a flying winger in the Cliff Jones or Jimmy Robertson style, but he was a slower player, and more creative with the ball.

Still only twenty-five, but looking closer to forty with his balding head and swept-over hair-style, and having the appearance of being overweight, Ralph Coates was a hard-working grafter, who dug in behind Cyril Knowles, when Knowles flew past him.

The £190,000 paid for Coates was a British record cash fee, at that time, but it provided Spurs with the missing piece of their jigsaw, in Tottenham's revival, after their late Sixties decline.

The following season, Tottenham lost just two of their opening twelve league matches, but they hadn't exactly set the league alight, by drawing five of them, when Nottingham Forest came to White Hart Lane on Saturday 23rd October 1971.

A moderate crowd of just under 36,000 enjoyed Spurs' most rampant attacking performance of the season. Ralph Coates had been ruled out for six weeks, following a knee injury, but Jimmy Neighbour took his place out on the left wing.

Alan Gilzean nodded down Cyril Knowles' cross, and Martin Peters fired beneath Eric Hulme's body, from close range. Jimmy Neighbour then set Peters free down the left, with a clever reverse pass, and Peters' cross was headed in dynamically by the diving Chivers, from just six yards out.

Bob *Sammy* Chapman was very harshly adjudged to have fouled Gilzean, just inside his own area, but Martin Peters slotted the ball just inside the right post, from the spot.

Martin Chivers galloped onto a Phil Beal's long ball, but he hit the far post, from just inside the Forest box, near the end of the first half. Alan Mullery then made it four, though, after he scored the goal of the match, carrying the ball from the left corner flag, beating Barry Lyons' challenge, and then stepping outside Liam O'Kane's tackle on the edge of the Forest area, before he curled the ball past Hulme, into the far corner of the goal.

Cyril Knowles then carried the ball over halfway, and from forty yards out, he crossed for substitute Jimmy Pearce to blast the ball past Hulme at the far post. With ten minutes remaining, Knowles' free-kick was first headed by Martin Peters, and then by Martin Chivers, into Jimmy Pearce's path.

Pearce fired his second goal of the game, high into Forest's goal, for a six-nil lead.

Ian Storey-Moore then danced around the outside of Knowles, and he lofted the ball across the face of goal, for Richardson to head in a consolation, on the goal-line, with the last kick of the game.

Tottenham's 6-1 win lifted them up to fifth in Division One, six points behind leaders Manchester United, but with a game in hand. Defeats at Stoke and Manchester United, however, had dropped Spurs from the main title-chasing clubs, and by late January, having won just four games in fourteen, since their thrashing of Forest, they had dropped to eighth position. They'd only lost five games, though, and remained just seven points behind the leaders Leeds United, on 22nd January. In the League Cup, Tottenham had beaten West Brom, Torquay United, Preston North End, after a replay, and then Blackpool, to reach the Semi-finals for the second successive season.

Tottenham were drawn against Keflavik in the First round of the inaugural UEFA Cup. In a match set amongst the Moon-like landscape of south-west Iceland, Spurs won 6-1 away, on Tuesday 14th September, in front of a noisy 5,000 crowd of Icelanders, braving an icy, gale force storm.

Alan Gilzean hit a hat-trick, in Tottenham's first European match for nearly four years, while Ralph Coates scored his first goal for the club, and Alan Mullery also volleyed in two goals.

Gilzean scored two more goals, a fortnight later, while Martin Chivers fired another hat-trick, as Spurs won the second leg 9-0, in front of 23,818 die-hard home fans.

On Wednesday 20th October, Tottenham travelled to Nantes, and they scraped a goalless draw, in front of a sell-out 18,000 crowd. Their back four of Kinnear, England, Beal and Knowles helped Pat Jennings keep the French out, but ten days later, Alan Mullery, who'd cleaned up so much danger in front of them, went off, suffering from a pelvic strain, during their 2-0 defeat away at Stoke.

Mullery remained out of action for over four months.

Martin Peters scored on Tuesday 2nd November, to secure their 1-0 aggregate win over Nantes, and setting up a Third round tie against Rapid Bucharest in December.

Martin Peters scored his tenth goal of the season, striking the ball high into the net, after Gilzean had flicked on Chivers' long throw-in, on Wednesday 8th December. Martin Chivers hit two more, during Tottenham's 3-0 win over a tame-looking Romanian outfit, with nearly 31,000 inside White Hart Lane.

In the second leg, a week later, and just ten days before Christmas, Rapid Bucharest were not offering gifts, but instead had appeared to declare War.

Pop, Boc, Dinu and Codrea, particularly, just kicked lumps out of the Spurs stars all night. Tottenham won 2-0, after goals from substitute Jimmy Pearce, and Martin Chivers, but Alan Gilzean and Steve Perryman both went off injured, and there was a bizarre late penalty incident.

Spurs were awarded a penalty-kick following another foul suffered by Big Chiv.

Martin Peters placed the ball on the spot, but he was alarmed to see Raducanu, the Rapid goalkeeper, dashing off his line like a nutcase, with his fists flailing, straight at him. As the mad Romanian goalkeeper was only about six yards away from Peters, the England star kicked the ball away, towards goal, and it ran past the post. Spurs were then shocked to see the referee declare the kick taken, and he awarded a goal kick.

After the match, eight Tottenham players were lying everywhere, injured, in their treatment room, before they staggered onto the team coach, and returned home.

Bucharest had refused to hand over the film of the match, their team's behaviour was so bad. "If this is European football," Bill Nicholson responded, "we're better off out of it. I haven't seen a dirtier game in thirty years."

One week later, on the Wednesday before Christmas, Tottenham went to Chelsea, for the first leg of their League Cup Semi-final, without Alan Gilzean, Steve Perryman and Peter Collins, still bruised and bandaged after the Battle of Bucharest.

Chelsea won 3-2, with 43,330 packed inside Stamford Bridge while their massive, three tiered East Stand was still under construction.

A fortnight later, a wall of noise welcomed Chelsea to White Hart Lane, with nearly 53,000 fans roaring Spurs to a 2-1 lead, after goals from both Chivers and Peters, with extra-time awaiting. With only a minute or two remaining, though, Mike England unnecessarily fouled Peter Osgood, near the right corner flag.

Alan Hudson miss-hit his low free-kick, and Cyril Knowles went to clear it, but the direction of the ball caught him out, and he missed his kick. The ball continued and it beat a stunned Pat Jennings, who'd believed the danger was dealt with, and he couldn't react in time.

Chelsea won 5-4 on aggregate, thanks to that freak goal, and they awaited the winner of the Stoke v West Ham Semi-final.

In the FA Cup, Tottenham beat Carlisle United, after a replay, and then Rotherham United, before they met Everton in the Fifth round.

On Saturday 26th February 1972, Gilzean and Peters both scored in front of a Goodison Park crowd of over 50,000, reaching the Quarter-finals with a 2-0 win, their nineteenth clean sheet of the season.

Back in the First Division, Spurs had gone five games without a win, over the Christmas and New Year period, drawing three of them, but then they won three successive games, from the end of January to late February, to keep them, *only just,* on the edge of a very exciting title race.

Martin Chivers scored, as they beat Leeds 1-0 at the Lane, in front of nearly 47,000, and a fortnight later, Martin Peters secured their 1-0 away win at Nottingham Forest. Then, on Saturday 19th February, Chivers scored a goal in each half, as Spurs beat League Cup Finalists Stoke City 2-0.

	PL	W	D	L	F	A	PTS
Manchester City	29	16	9	4	59	31	41
Leeds United	29	16	7	6	44	22	39
Derby County	29	15	8	6	50	28	38
Arsenal	29	16	5	8	44	27	37
TOTTENHAM	29	13	9	7	45	31	35
Liverpool	29	14	7	8	37	27	35
Manchester Utd	29	14	7	8	52	43	35
Wolves	29	13	9	7	48	40	35

Spurs could not sustain the winning run they needed to catch the leaders, though, while they were also battling on two other fronts, in the FA Cup and the UEFA Cup. And although they finished the season well, winning six and losing only three, of their final thirteen games, they couldn't gain ground on either City, Leeds or Derby.

On Saturday 18th March, Tottenham visited Leeds United, favourites for the First Division title, in the FA Cup Quarter-finals. Surprisingly, Alan Mullery had returned from his period of absence at the start of March, declaring himself fit, but Bill Nicholson had continued to play John Pratt and Philip Holder in his position.

Just like Jimmy Greaves, two years earlier, Mullery had been dropped to the reserves, and he played against Swansea reserves, and then Swindon Town reserves, before he was totally excluded from Tottenham's squad that travelled to Arad, for their UEFA Cup Quarter-final tie.

Alan Mullery confronted Mr Nicholson, and told him that he wasn't happy with the situation. He was the club captain, but he felt like an outcast, after all the great service he'd given Spurs. He asked if he could go on loan to his old club Fulham, managed by his old teammate Bill Dodgin.

Without emotion, Bill Nicholson said "okay," and the phone call was made, and then the door was shut. Alan Mullery, captain of Tottenham Hotspur, with his club still in the title race, and also in both the FA Cup and UEFA Cup Quarter-finals, was off to play Second Division football with Fulham.

It was unbelievable.

At Elland Road, in front of 44,000, Allan Clarke and Jack Charlton had both scored to give Leeds United a 2-1 win, and a place in the FA Cup Semi-finals against Second Division Birmingham City.

John Pratt, Mullery's replacement in midfield, had scored Tottenham's consolation.

On Tuesday 7th March, Spurs had returned to Romania, to face UT Arad, in the first leg of the UEFA Cup Quarter-finals. Arad, up in the north of the country, close to Timisoara, and near the Hungarian border, were a more cultured and accomplished footballing team than Rapid Bucharest, and they gave Tottenham an excellent game.

20,000 filled their tiny stadium, while the town folk had removed slates from the roofs of their houses, just so they could watch international stars like Martin Peters, Martin Chivers and Pat Jennings.

Roger Morgan, playing only his seventh game of the season, scored his first goal since September 1970, and then Mike England thudded in a header for a 2-0 win.

Arad did well, a fortnight later, holding their own against Spurs, in the second leg, drawing 1-1 in front of a 30,000 crowd at the Lane. Domide had replied to Gilzean's header, but Tottenham went through to the Semi-finals, 3-1 on aggregate.

On Wednesday 5th April, Tottenham hosted AC Milan for the first leg match in the Semi-finals, their fourth game in six days, having already beaten Coventry 1-0 on Good Friday, before losing 2-0 away at West Ham on Easter Saturday, and then losing 2-1 away at Ipswich Town on Bank Holiday Monday, 3rd April 1972.

It wouldn't happen today.

Even worse, Bill Nicholson was suffering a midfield crisis at Tottenham. John Pratt, Phil Beal, and Philip Holder were all inured, as well as Jimmy Neighbour and Roger Morgan out on the wings.

An *SOS* was sent out to London SW6, asking Fulham to release Alan Mullery from his loan spell, to return to White Hart Lane, and to captain Spurs in his comeback game, in Tottenham's European Semi-final against the former European Champions, having been left to rot away in Division Two.

It was comic-book stuff, a fairy-tale story, that you couldn't make up.

A 42,064 crowd, subjected to UEFA restrictions, had packed White Hart Lane for Tottenham's biggest game in nearly five years. AC Milan had brought a strong team, including Gianni Rivera, European Footballer of the Year in 1969, who'd joined Milan back in 1960, for £130,000.

TOTTENHAM HOTSPUR		AC MILAN
Pat Jennings	1	Fabio Cudicini
Joe Kinnear	2	Giuseppe Sabadini
Cyril Knowles	3	Giulio Zignoli
Ralph Coates	4	Angelo Anquilletti
Mike England	5	Karl-Heinz Schnellinger
Terry Naylor	6	Roberto Rosato
Alan Gilzean	7	Riccardo Sogliano
Steve Perryman	8	Romeo Benetti
Martin Chivers	9	Alberto Bigon
Martin Peters	10	Gianni Rivera
Alan Mullery	11	Lino Golin
Jimmy Neighbour	SUB	Vinanzo Zazzaro

Rivera had helped Milan win the European Cup in 1963, and again in 1969, and he'd also played in all of Italy's last three World Cup Finals tournaments.

Roberto Rosato had also played in Milan's 1969 European Cup Final victory, and had played in both of Italy's 1968 European Championship Final winning team, and their 1970 World Cup Final losing team. Also in their team was the West German legend, thirty-four year old Karl-Heinz Schnellinger, a veteran of four World Cup tournaments, and nicknamed *Volkswagen,* for the consistency of his high quality of play in their defence.

AC Milan, excellently marshalled by Schnellinger, had conceded less than a goal per game, during their previous eight UEFA Cup matches, and kept four clean sheets.

Steve Perryman gave Spurs the lead with a cracking goal. It was a delightful move that had led to his strike, though, with Knowles crossing deep from the left. Gilzean leapt up to knock the ball down, and Chivers then laid the ball back neatly for Perryman to fire a bullet from the edge of the area.

Then, in the sixty-fifth minute, Alan Mullery's corner kick was headed clear to Steve Perryman, thirty yards out. Perryman half-volleyed an unstoppable shot into the top right corner of Cudicini's goal. Home spirits sunk, though, when Benetti got the better of a tiring Mike England, late on, right on the edge of Spurs' penalty area, to pull a good goal back for Milan.

While 2-0 had looked a good lead to defend, 2-1 was very vulnerable.

A fortnight later, en route to the gigantic San Siro stadium, filled with nearly 65,000 Italians, bottles were thrown at the Tottenham team coach, and then a mob of thugs tried to turn their coach on its side, when it had got stuck in traffic. It was a very worrying situation, even more so given that they'd been given a police escort, and there seemed to be little order, or any proper protection.

"Italian hooligans made us even more determined to go out and get a result, if anything," Alan Mullery insisted. Firecrackers were thrown at Spurs players as they'd walked around the pitch before kick-off, and for the first quarter-hour, the noise was immense, unlike any First Division atmosphere; just constant and incessant chanting, whistling, and firecrackers exploding.

Martin Chivers played a square ball to Alan Mullery, and Mullery crashed one of his famous long range shots, from twenty-five yards out, past Cudicini, and into the Milan net.

Chivers ran and picked the ball out of the back of the net, and the whole stadium was silent. "You could have heard a pin drop," Big Chiv recalled with enjoyment.

Twenty-five minutes into the second half, Spurs gave away a penalty kick, and Gianni Rivera scored from the spot. It was all hands to the pump, for the last twenty minutes, which seemed to last an eternity, as Spurs fought to protect their slender lead.

Phil Beal, who'd already been booked, then fouled Benetti, but after all the pushing and shoving and finger-pointing that followed, the referee was confused and he booked Steve Perryman, instead of Beal. Perryman took the hit for his team, and with eleven men, Spurs held out for a truly magnificent 3-2 aggregate win.

Tottenham's players and staff then had to stand in the centre circle for twenty minutes after the final whistle, as bottles, coins, darts and those predictable firecrackers were thrown onto the pitch by the Milan fans, before police and the Italian Army cleared the stadium.

For the UEFA Cup Final, all the wives and girlfriends of all the Tottenham players had been promised fully paid travel and hotel expenses at their away destination.

They **weren't** expecting to receive a return ticket to Wolverhampton railway station.

Wolves had also enjoyed a superb UEFA Cup run, beating the mighty Juventus in the Quarter-finals, and then Ferencvaros in the Semis, but it was an anti-climax for both English teams to play a fellow First Division team in the Final.

On Wednesday 3rd May, with over 38,000 packed inside Molineux, Martin Chivers had the game of his career, as Tottenham totally took control of the tie.

Big Chiv hit the angle of Phil Parkes' goal, after just five minutes, but the first half was even as both teams found their feet. Danny Hegan then fired a superb shot from the halfway line, though, which Jennings had to fling himself to, fully in mid-air, and he just managed to palm the ball over his bar.

WHY ALWAYS ME?

At half-time, Martin Chivers received another verbal tirade from both Bill Nicholson and coach Eddie Baily, for his lacklustre performance.

"Am I the only fucking player in this team?" Chivers shouted back. "Why is it just me again?" Then he went and spent the whole of the remainder of the half-time interval hidden in the Molineux toilets. As Martin Chivers returned to the pitch, after the buzzer went, his teammate Phil Beal went up to him and said, "come on big fella, we know what you can do. Now show *them* what you can do," pointing over at their manager and coaches.

Twenty minutes into the second half, Chivers won a free-kick, about forty yards out, and Mike England took it. Big Chiv rose in front of John McAlle and he headed Spurs into the lead. Shortly afterwards, Chivers had another good chance, from Martin Peters' free-kick, but he headed over on that occasion.

Jim McCalliog, Wolves' captain in the absence of the injured Mike Bailey, equalised from the edge of the box, and then Derek Dougan screwed his shot just wide of Jennings' far post. Substitute Pratt then deflected Dave Wagstaffe's cross just past his own post. Wolves had Spurs on the rack.

A moment of true footballing magic and brilliance then tilted the balance of the tie towards Tottenham Hotspur. Cyril Knowles played a long forward pass up to Martin Chivers, forty yards out. Chivers played a one-two with Perryman, and then he went on a run, from left to right, for ten to fifteen yards, before firing the ball, right footed, from thirty yards out. His shot screamed past Phil Parkes' dive, bulging the net, under the huge, packed South Bank, filled with Tottenham fans.

It was, without doubt, the best goal of Martin Chivers' career, and it gave Spurs a crucial 2-1 lead to defend at home, a fortnight later. Tottenham had won their final league match of the season, in between, beating Arsenal 2-1 away, with Mullery and Coates both scoring in front of over 42,000 inside Highbury.

Tottenham finished the season in sixth place, their best season since 1967, one point below Arsenal in fifth, but only seven points behind Champions Derby County.

Spurs had also kept twenty-five league and cup clean sheets.

Martin Chivers had the season of his life, scoring forty league and cup goals, while Martin Peters and Alan Gilzean had shared thirty-eight goals. White Hart Lane was also attracting big crowds again, averaging home attendances of nearly 39,000.

It was Tottenham's best team since 1967 that started their UEFA Cup Final second leg match, on Wednesday 17th May 1972, with 53,000 filling the Lane.

TOTTENHAM HOTSPUR		WOLVERHAMPTON WANDERERS
Pat Jennings	1	Phil Parkes
Joe Kinnear	2	Bernard Shaw
Cyril Knowles	3	Gerald Taylor
Alan Mullery	4	Danny Hegan
Mike England	5	Frank Munro
Phil Beal	6	John McAlle
Alan Gilzean	7	Jim McCalliog
Steve Perryman	8	Kenny Hibbitt
Martin Chivers	9	John Richards
Martin Peters	10	Derek Dougan
Ralph Coates	11	Dave Wagstaffe

SUBSTITUTES

Tottenham	Wolverhampton
Ray Evans	Mike Bailey (rep. Hibbitt)
Terry Naylor	Rod Arnold
John Pratt	Derek Parkin
Jimmy Pearce	Steve Daley
Barry Daines	Hugh Curran (rep. Dougan)

Alan Mullery flew in and met Martin Peters' free-kick with a diving header that gave Parkes no chance. He collided with the keeper just after his head had sent the ball in, and he lay still on the ground for a long while, before being treated with Epsom salts and getting up groggily.

Dave Wagstaffe placed a wonderful left-footed shot past Pat Jennings, from well outside the area, but Spurs held on to lift their first European silverware for nine years.

The whole team completed a joyous lap of honour, with their medals and the Cup, before captain Alan Mullery, caught up in the occasion, and possibly still under the influence of salts, went on a solo lap of honour, while still holding the UEFA Cup.

Tottenham continued their form of the last few months of 1971-72 into the following season. They won seven of their opening eleven matches, playing mostly with the same eleven players that had won the UEFA Cup, and they were flying high in second place on 23rd September, level on points with leaders Liverpool.

They had lost just four of their previous twenty-six league and cup matches.

Spurs were missing Alan Mullery, though, who'd been allowed to leave White Hart Lane, for Fulham, without even a thank you or a goodbye, before the beginning of the season. The message from Bill Nicholson was basically, "fine then, go!" when Mullery had told his manager he needed to play more first team games.

Captaining his team to victory in the UEFA Cup Final, over Wolves, was Alan Mullery's last game for Spurs. His lap of honour around the ground, while he carried the UEFA Cup, was actually his farewell to the Tottenham fans.

Alan Mullery had played 312 First Division matches for Tottenham, during his eight years at the club, and he also made thirty-five appearances for England as a Spurs player. He played in all four of England's World Cup Finals matches in Mexico, and was seen by most commentators as an improvement on Nobby Stiles, in that protective midfield role.

He was faultless in all of his England displays, apart from when he became the first England player to be sent off, in the 1968 European Championship Semi-finals, against Yugoslavia.

Mullery had reacted to a dreadful challenge by Dobrivoje Trivic, by booting his opponent in the balls. He just lost his temper, but in those days, it seemed that some continental teams could simply stamp all over English teams and receive no punishment from referees.

Nobby Stiles, who'd been in a few wars with foreign agitators himself, and whose place in the team Mullery had taken, ran over to accompany him back to their changing room.

After leading Fulham to the FA Cup Final in 1975, he retired in 1976, and then succeeded Peter Taylor as manager of Brighton and Hove Albion.

Mullery lifted Brighton up from the Third Division, and then into Division One in 1979.

To this day, that was the only time that the Seagulls were promoted into top flight football during their history.

Spurs were missing Alan Mullery, but they also lost both Joe Kinnear and Phil Beal during their 1-0 home defeat to Chelsea, on 21st October, with both players ruled out of action for three and a half months. Despite a superb four goal haul by Martin Peters, in their 4-1 away win at bottom club Manchester United, Tottenham won only one of their next seven games, and by the Festive period, they'd dropped down to ninth place.

Tottenham beat three Second Division teams, Huddersfield, Middlesbrough and Millwall, en route to the League Cup Quarter-finals. The League Cup had no longer seemed to excite Tottenham's fans, though, as their average home attendances for these matches was only around 22,000.

They then met Liverpool in the Fifth round, and nearly 49,000 crammed into Anfield, as Martin Peters scored a second half goal to earn a replay, after Emlyn Hughes had scored for the Reds. Both teams were also going well in the UEFA Cup, and in fact, they were the only English teams left in the tournament, after Manchester City and Stoke had been knocked out in the First round.

It was because of both teams' involvement in the Third round of the UEFA Cup, that their League Cup tie was played on a Monday night, so the replay was hastily arranged for just two nights later, on Wednesday 6th December.

Marin Peters smashed a first half brace past Clemence, and John Pratt added a third to kill the game off with a 3-0 half-time lead. Ian Callaghan curled in a consolation after the break, but Spurs went on to beat Wolves in the Semi-finals, winning 4-3 on aggregate over two legs.

Tottenham had begun the defence of their UEFA Cup by hammering Nordic opposition, just as they'd done one year earlier. Martin Chivers scored five, Gilzean and Coates hit two apiece, and Peters, Pratt and Pearce also scored in Spurs' 12-3 aggregate win over Lyn Oslo, of Norway.

In October, Spurs then hammered Olympiakos 4-0 at White Hart Lane, going through 4-1 on aggregate, after the Greeks had won 1-0 in front of their partisan 40,000 home crowd. Again, the idiots had been driving around outside Tottenham's hotel all night long, blasting their horns, and setting off fireworks to stop them sleeping.

They then beat Red Star Belgrade 2-0 at home, at the end of November, but with another disappointing crowd of under 24,000 inside White Hart Lane. Martin Chivers scored his thirteenth goal of the season, while Alan Gilzean scored his sixth.

Alan Gilzean was thirty-four, by then, and he was looking it too. For the first time, age was catching up with the great man. He scored the lowest First Division goals tally of his career during 1972-73, hitting just five in thirty-five games.

In Belgrade, in mid-December, and in front of 75,000 irrational Serbs, lighting bonfires all around their vast terraced stadium, Spurs held on for a 1-0 defeat, after Cyril Knowles had marked the legendary Dragan Djazic out of the game.

Spurs scored less than a goal a game in their eleven league matches, though, between the start of November and the end of January 1973. By the time that they'd lost 3-2 at Manchester City, on 10th February, with Chivers scoring twice, they were down in the bottom half of the table.

The trouble was, Spurs **WERE** missing Alan Mullery, just as they had missed Jimmy Greaves, immediately after 1970. John Pratt, who'd taken Mullery's place in midfield, was a good London lad, who lived and breathed Tottenham Hotspur, and he ran all day, battling and grappling and tackling for the ball. He knew he wasn't as good as Peters and Perryman and Coates, and of course, Alan Mullery, but he put in the work rate to make up for it. The trouble was, he lacked Mullery's vision, Mullery's finesse, Mullery's composure, Mullery's innovation, and Mullery's class.

Little by little, Spurs were fading as a First Division force, and even worse, they were being allowed to fade by a manager who had openly admitted that he didn't enjoy the modern game.

Bill Nicholson didn't even enjoy football anymore, yet he'd allowed Greavsie and Mullery, who did love modern football and Spurs, to both leave without even looking up from his desk.

Nevertheless, Tottenham had another Wembley Final to look forward to, the League Cup Final, on Saturday 3rd March, against First Division newcomers Norwich City. *The Cockerel Chorus* released a single entitled *Nice One, Cyril*, in honour of left back Cyril Knowles, which reached no. 14 in the UK singles charts, during March 1973.

"Nice one, Cyril; nice one, son. Nice one, Cyril, let's have another one!"

The Final was a flat affair. Norwich City, significantly inferior to Tottenham, in terms of quality, had come to stifle Spurs, not to startle them. They were managed by their hardened, dour tactician, Ron Saunders, whose football religion was in the belief of fitness over finesse. Norwich had a very talented pair of midfielders in Graham Paddon and Doug Livermore, who just ran around all day stopping both Peters and Perryman from playing, while their legendary central defensive partnership of Duncan Forbes and Dave Stringer had kept on top of Chivers and Gilzean.

Late in the match, though, Tottenham created a breakthrough. Martin Chivers took a throw-in from the left, for Gilzean to flick on at the near post. The ball fell to Ralph Coates, on the edge of the Norwich area, and Coates belted the ball into the bottom left-hand corner of Kevin Keelan's net.

It was the best goal, and the best moment of Ralph Coates' career at Spurs. Until that moment, the jury had been mostly undecided, regarding his huge price tag, and he'd often been in and out of matches. Previously seen as a talented luxury player, that winning goal made him a Spurs legend, and he could relax a bit afterwards.

On Wednesday 7th March 1973, in the UEFA Cup Quarter-finals, Spurs beat Vitoria Setubal 1-0 at White Hart Lane. Full back Ray Evans scored his first ever goal for Tottenham, running onto a long throw from Martin Chivers, and firing past Joaquin Torres.

A fortnight later, though, with over 30,000 filling the Estadio do Bonfim, Spurs were heading out of the tournament, after both Campora and Jose Torres, Vitoria's giant, six foot five inch Portuguese international striker, had given them a 2-0 lead, with just ten minutes remaining.

Spurs won a free-kick, though, just outside the penalty area, and Martin Chivers blasted a brilliant shot through the wall, and into the roof of the Vitoria net, putting Tottenham through on the away goals rule.

They were then drawn against English opposition, Liverpool, in the Semi-finals, while the two weaker teams, Borussia Moenchengladbach and FC Twente met in the other Semi.

It was cruel luck for one of the English clubs, as it probably might have been another all-English European Final, had Tottenham and Liverpool both avoided each other.

After a supremely competitive, and high-quality Semi-final, Spurs drew 2-2 on aggregate, after losing 1-0 at Anfield, before Martin Peters scored twice at the Lane, in front of 47,000, but their 2-1 home win was insufficient. Liverpool went through on the away goals rule, and also won the Cup.

For the second successive year, Spurs' last home competitive game of the season was against Wolves. Back in 1972, it had been the second leg match of the UEFA Cup Final, but in 1973 it was a meaningless league game, although not for Wolves, who needed just one point to qualify for the 1973-74 UEFA Cup. While 53,000 had filled White Hart Lane back in May 1972, there were only 16,942 inside their ground on Monday 30th April 1973. Alan Sunderland gave Wolves a 1-0 half-time lead, but Ralph Coates and Peter Collins hit back after the break. John Richards' thirty-third goal of the season then earned Wolves their 2-2 draw and sent them into Europe.

Martin Chivers enjoyed another excellent season, having become an England regular alongside Allan Clarke and Mike Channon. He'd scored thirty-three league and cup goals for Tottenham, and another four for England.

Martin Peters also scored twenty-four goals for Spurs during 1972-73, and he captained England on Wednesday 17th October 1973, with Chivers playing in attack, as they needed to beat Poland, at Wembley, to qualify for the 1974 World Cup Finals.

Despite England pounding away at the Polish goal, Poland hung on for a 1-1 draw.

It was the worst night, the worst moment, in the careers of both Peters and Chivers, but it was also Martin Chivers' last ever game in an England shirt.

Tottenham were also having a disappointing season, having won just four of their opening fourteen matches, and by 3rd November, they were down in fifteenth place, thirteen points behind the leaders, but just three points above the relegation zone.

After Leicester City hammered them 3-0 at the beginning of December, Spurs had dropped to sixteenth position, and only fourteen thousand attended their next home game, a 2-1 win over Stoke City. That slightly relieved their relegation worries, but they had also lost Cyril Knowles for five months, following a bad knee injury.

Of course, while all these struggles were going on, Spurs were fighting to regain *their* UEFA Cup, and they were doing quite well. They hammered Grasshoppers of Zurich 9-2 in the First round, before then beating Aberdeen 5-2, on aggregate, in the Autumn.

During December, only 20,000 attended White Hart Lane to see Tottenham hammer Dynamo Tbilisi 5-1. Chivers and Peters both scored two apiece, but Spurs went into the Quarter-finals, 6-2 on aggregate.

In the league, Spurs lost three of their four games prior to Christmas, and on Boxing Day, they'd dropped to sixth from bottom, only four points clear of the relegation places, while all three of the teams directly below them had a game in hand.

Tottenham then went on a nine match unbeaten run up to the end of February, however, lifting themselves up to twelfth place, nine points clear of relegation worries. Amazingly, they were also only three points below a UEFA Cup qualifying place.

The high point of that run was their 4-2 home win over Birmingham City, with Martin Chivers scoring a hat-trick, but in front of only 14,000 Spurs fans.

Tottenham beat Wolfgang Overath's FC Koln 5-1 on aggregate, during March 1974, to reach their third successive UEFA Cup Semi-final. They then beat Lokomotiv Leipzig, both home and away, in April, winning 4-1 on aggregate.

They were less consistent in the league, though, than they'd been in Europe, where they had won eight, and lost none of their ten matches. Spurs won just four of their final thirteen First Division games, and they finished the season in mid-table.

They'd also conceded more goals than they scored, though, and their league total of forty-five goals was their lowest tally since 1913. Also, their average home crowd of just 26,000 was their lowest since the Thirties. Only twice did they attract crowds of more than forty thousand, and most of their crowds were less than half that figure.

On Tuesday 21st May 1974, though, 46,281 filled the Lane for the first leg of Spurs' UEFA Cup Final against Feyenoord. Captain Rinus Israel, Wim Van Hanegem, and Wim Jansen were all survivors from the Rotterdam team that had won the European Cup, four years earlier, and Bill Nicholson warned his players that Feyenoord would be the best team they'd face that season.

Feyenoord were indeed their toughest test, but the Final wouldn't be best remembered for the football played by either Tottenham or Feyenoord.

TOTTENHAM HOTSPUR		FEYENOORD
Pat Jennings	1	Eddy Treijtel
Ray Evans	2	Wim Rijsbergen
Terry Naylor	3	Joop van Daele
John Pratt	4	Rinus Israel
Mike England	5	Harry Vos
Phil Beal	6	Theo de Jong
Chris McGrath	7	Wim Jansen
Steve Perryman	8	Wim Van Hanegem
Martin Chivers	9	Peter Ressel
Martin Peters	10	Lex Schoemaker
Ralph Coates	11	Jorgen Kristensen

Spurs had a lucky break when van Daele's unfortunate own goal added to Mike England's earlier headed goal, giving them a 2-0 lead over the Dutch side, in the pouring rain.

Feyenoord were always the more comfortable side, though, and the majestic Wim Van Hanegem fired a superb 25 yard free-kick curling beyond Pat Jennings' dive, before, with only four minutes remaining, Theo de Jong flicked in an equaliser.

One player who played no part in either of Tottenham's UEFA Cup Final matches was Alan Gilzean. He was thirty-five, and by 1974, he'd been replaced in the team by the misfiring Chris McGrath. Gilzean started only five of Tottenham's twenty-five matches after the New Year.

Alan Gilzean enjoyed two great partnerships during his nine and a half years at White Hart Lane, firstly with Greavsie, and then with Big Chiv.

"Gilly and I developed a real partnership," Martin Chivers admitted.

"I had to anticipate his flick-ons which he managed brilliantly off that shiny bonce. He had such a deft touch and so I always strived to get on the end of it."

On Saturday 11th May 1974, Alan Gilzean played his 439th and final league and cup match for Tottenham, away at Newcastle United, who'd just lost the FA Cup Final.

Tottenham won 2-0, after Gilzean had set up Martin Chivers' twenty-third goal of the season, and then he sealed the win by scoring his 133rd league and cup goal for Spurs.

Gilly retired after the 1973-74 season, but he was awarded a testimonial match in November 1974, with Red Star Belgrade agreeing to play Tottenham Hotspur at White Hart Lane.

If the Tottenham support could be criticized for their disappointingly inconsistent support of their team throughout the season, then their behaviour was appalling at the second leg match of the UEFA Cup Final. They were disgraceful en route to Rotterdam, in Rotterdam, and also on the way home. There were several other instances of mass misbehaviour by English football fans, during the early Seventies, and particularly in 1974, but the crowd disturbance and total violence by Spurs fans, at the second leg of the UEFA Cup Final, was by some distance the worst of all.

In the days prior to the actual match, hundreds of drunken thugs caused chaos and damage on the Ferries to Holland. On Wednesday 29th May, Feyenoord's massive three-tiered stadium was filled to its 63,000 capacity. The 5,000 Tottenham fans were given the middle tier at one end of the stadium, and when Wim Rijsbergen opened the scoring, just before half-time, they began to throw bottles, and seats that they'd smashed up, down onto the Dutch fans below them.

After appeals from club officials, pleading with their fans to stop, had been ignored, Bill Nicholson then stepped out onto the pitch. Unable to give a half-time team talk, Bill pleaded with them, the fans of the football club that he'd loved for forty years, from the centre circle.

"You hooligans are a disgrace to Tottenham Hotspur and England," he told them. "Will you listen? It is a game of football, not a war."

Even Martin Peters tried to wave down the rioters, but he was told to f*** off as well.

Fans then charged out of the exits to fight with police and gangs of Feyenoord supporters outside the stadium. As if it mattered, Peter Ressel, who later also won a European Cup Winners' Cup winners' medal with Anderlecht, then scored a second goal, seven minutes before the end, giving Feyenoord a 4-2 aggregate win.

In all their years in European football, Tottenham Hotspur had never been in any trouble, and over the previous three seasons in the UEFA Cup, not one single Spurs fan had been arrested, either home or away. The trouble at Feyenoord was inexplicable.

Seats were set on fire, as the rioting continued after the final whistle, while the trophy was presented to Rinus Israel, before the Feyenoord team and all the UEFA officials hurried off the pitch. Two hundred people had ended up in hospital.

Bill Nicholson was devastated. Tottenham Hotspur sent a heartfelt letter of apology to Feyenoord, and to the Rotterdam police. They were fined a small sum of cash, and ordered to play their next two European home matches at least 200 miles away from White Hart Lane.

It was generally felt, by all, that Spurs had got off very lightly, and it was probably the attempts of the staff, players, and particularly Bill Nicholson, to calm their rioting supporters, and the shame they felt and subsequently showed for the disgraceful incidents that had resulted in such leniency.

On 15th July 1974, Bill Nicholson attempted to replace Alan Gilzean by paying Rangers £150,000 for their heavily afro-haired and side-burned Alfie Conn.

The Kirkcaldy-born striker had scored only twenty-one Scottish League goals in ninety-four appearances, but he'd also been injured since scoring in their 5-1 win against St Johnstone, back in December 1973, and he wouldn't be fit enough to play again until the New Year.

Alfie Conn was Bill Nicholson's first significant new signing for three years, and although he enjoyed a famous start to his Spurs career, firing a first half hat-trick during their 5-2 away win at Newcastle on Saturday 11th January 1975, Conn was in and out of the team over the following three seasons.

He made only 35 league starts for Tottenham, scoring six goals, before he returned to Scotland at the end of March 1977, joining Celtic on the cheap.

It was an odd decision for Bill Nicholson to pay such a sizeable sum for a forward with such an underwhelming record, not to mention one with a long-term injury. On the very same day, Arsenal signed Brian Kidd from Manchester United for just £110,000. Now, there was a player with loads of class, who'd have been much better for Spurs. Kidd scored fifty-one First Division goals in just 116 games, over the next three seasons, yet he cost forty thousand less.

So Tottenham started that 1974-75 season without Gilzean, without Conn, and without even Martin Chivers. Big Chiv had scored one hundred and twenty-five league and cup goals for Spurs over the previous four seasons, proving himself to be right up there with Allan Clarke, Supermac and Mike Channon, as one of the premium strikers in England, but he became locked in a dispute with his manager, regarding the terms of his new contract. Chivers felt he should be paid a fair wage, and given financial security, at the age of twenty-nine.

Bill Nicholson disagreed and he placed Chivers in the reserves, just as he'd done with both Greavsie and Mullery. Spurs subsequently lost 1-0 at home to Ipswich, 1-0 away at Manchester City, and then 1-0 away at First Division newcomers Carlisle United. That third result had put Carlisle top of the First Division, but Tottenham were bottom of the league. Martin Chivers was recalled for their match at home to Manchester City, on Wednesday 28th August, but Spurs lost 2-1, despite Martin Peters scoring.

On the following day, Bill Nicholson resigned.

He cited a "lack of respect" from "some of the players" for his decision, but in truth, it was an accumulation of reasons. Most importantly, though, it was time for him to leave. Bill Nicholson had not enjoyed the game, since some way into the Sixties, as teams became more defensive, or tactically efficient, and Spurs couldn't walk over teams as they'd done back in 1961.

He never loved his 1967 side, or his 1972 side, as much as he'd loved his *Glory, Glory Days* Spurs' team from 'Sixty-one.

He'd let Jimmy Greaves go too easily, but particularly, he'd also let Alan Mullery leave far too willingly. Mullery had proved he'd much more to give, and all he wanted from Bill Nicholson was a sign that he was wanted. He was refused that, even.

During the six years before he resigned, Bill Nicholson spent money on just three players: Martin Peters, Roger Morgan and Ralph Coates. However, by paying a sizeable sum of money on a mediocre, injured player, just before he left, he did his successor Terry Neill no favours at all, and the club took four years, in truth, to properly recover.

In October 1974, Terry Neill did exactly what Bill Nicholson had done ten years previously. He went to Dundee and he paid £125,000 for John Duncan, a decent striker who'd scored sixty-two Scottish First Division goals in only 121 starts.

Duncan was Tottenham's top scorer in 1974-75, with twelve goals from twenty-eight games, goals that were crucial in helping Spurs survive on the very last day of the season, by just a single point.

On 13th March 1975, though, Norwich City manager John Bond had paid Spurs a bargain price of just £50,000 for their captain Martin Peters. A tour de force during Tottenham's UEFA Cup adventures between 1971 and 1974, scoring twelve goals in thirty-four European matches, from midfield, Martin Peters had missed the presence of Bill Nicholson since his resignation.

Peters had scored forty-six First Division goals in 189 games for Spurs, and he'd produced dozens of dynamic performances, combining brilliantly with both Big Chiv and Alan Gilzean, creating many goals with his pinpoint corners and free-kicks, as well as forging a superb midfield triumvirate with both Mullery and Perryman.

Mike England was also replaced at centre back, at the beginning of March 1975, by Keith Osgood. At thirty-three years old, England moved to Cardiff City after the end of the season, having played three hundred First Division matches for Spurs. He'd also played forty-four games for Wales, and in his country's capital city, Mike England played forty games for the Bluebirds during 1975-76.

He helped Cardiff keep nineteen clean sheets as they gained promotion back to the Second Division, as runners-up behind Hereford United, before he then retired from football. He played over five hundred league games, 465 of them in the First Division. Mike England was one of the greatest centre halves in Football League history.

Martin Chivers couldn't have been more correct when he suggested, "Mike England was the best centre half of his time and Spurs, even to this day, have failed to find a better man."

Phil Beal, Mike England's regular partner in central defence since 1968, had also left White Hart Lane during the Summer of 75. Phil Beal was Spurs' underrated player from their great 1971-72 team, tidy, reliable and versatile.

He effected a near-perfect partnership with his tougher and harder Welsh teammate. Beal and England were comparable, in style, to England's World Cup partnership of Jack Charlton and Bobby Moore.

Phil Beal could tackle gracefully, and also beat a man. He never panicked, was tactically alert, and he could play the telling pass; while England just defended with all of his six foot two inch frame, heart and soul. Rugged, square-jawed and sharp-witted, Mike England was a winner.

Since Spurs first adopted the four man defensive system during the Sixties, the central defensive partnership of Dave Mackay and Mike England was far and away their best. Their partnership of England and Beal, though, was as good as any since, including Mabbutt and Campbell, and also King and Dawson.

Phil Beal was awarded a testimonial match against Bayern Munich, at White Hart Lane, in December 1973. Sadly, after leaving Tottenham, he suffered several regular injuries and made only ten league appearances for Brighton and Hove Albion over the following two seasons.

He was forced to retire in March 1977, at thirty-two years of age, when his contract was cancelled.

Joe Kinnear had also joined Brighton in 1975, after making 196 league appearances for Spurs in nine years. He too was more out of Peter Taylor's team than in it, though, making only fifteen starts for the Seagulls, and of those games he started, they won only four. In August 1976, his contract was cancelled by Brighton's new manager, and Kinnear's old teammate, Alan Mullery.

While Phil Beal was understanding and cool upon hearing the news that he was being released, Joe Kinnear was angry and he accused Mullery of betraying their friendship. Kinnear refused to talk to Mullery for years afterwards, but they did eventually make up, and settled their differences, once Kinnear had become a manager, himself.

Joe Kinnear managed Wimbledon in the Premier League for over seven years, from January 1992 until June 1999, and he realised that tough decisions have to sometimes be made, and you have to upset people, for the good of the club.

Kinnear did a lot of good things for Wimbledon. Nicknamed *The Crazy Gang,* Wimbledon became a much feared, and much respected Premier League team, under Kinnear's management. He transformed Wimbledon from the long ball team they were, during their early days in Division One, back in the Eighties, and with the likes of Oyvind Leonhardsen, Robbie Earle,

Marcus Gayle, Warren Barton and Alan Kimble, they played some proper, colourful football, with leading scorers Dean Holdsworth and Efan Ekoku both benefitting from some regular high-quality service.

Joe Kinnear won one hundred and thirty of the 364 league and cup games of which he was in charge of Wimbledon, losing just 125, and in 1994, he was awarded the Manager of the Year trophy, by the League Managers' Association.

Cyril Knowles played just ten games of the 1975-76 season, before a recurrent knee injury, first suffered two years earlier, forced his retirement at thirty-one years of age.

His last match for Spurs was their 2-2 draw with Everton, on Wednesday 10th December 1975, in front of just 18,638 home fans at White Hart Lane.

Knowles played more games for Tottenham than any other outfield player, between 1967 and 1976. Only Pat Jennings played more games than Knowles, during the Glam Soccer years. He played 507 league and cup games for Spurs, creating many goals with his lightning quick overlapping runs and his terrific left-footed crosses.

"He was a cheerful fellow, always bubbling with the sheer joy of life," Pat Jennings said of his teammate, whose name had made the pop charts, and was sung regularly from the East Stand terraces, even after Cyril Knowles' retirement.

"Nice one Cyril, nice one Son. Nice one, Cyril, let's have another One!"

After his retirement, Cyril returned to his native West Yorkshire, where he became a Yorkshire based scout for Spurs, a role that led to him becoming a manager, for Darlington, Torquay United and Hartlepool.

Cyril Knowles led Hartlepool to promotion to Division Three, for only the second time in their history, during the 1990-91 season. He died on August 30th 1991, after losing his battle with brain cancer; he was just forty-seven years old.

In 1995, Hartlepool United rebuilt their Clarence Road main stand, and they renamed it as The Cyril Knowles Stand, an all-seated stand that holds a capacity of 1,599 supporters.

Jimmy Neighbour was rarely a first choice player, during Tottenham Hotspur's Cup winning period of 1971-73, but he was still a crowd favourite, due to his hard work, his dependable displays and his excellent left wing crosses. A spontaneous, instinctive winger, he'd also often fill in behind Knowles, when Cyril had bombed forward.

Spurs fans were saddened to see Neighbour, who'd never had a bad game for the club, leave White Hart Lane after 119 First Division matches for Tottenham.

He was sold to Norwich City for £75,000, in September 1976, at the same time that new Spurs manager Keith Burkinshaw had paid £200,000 to Crystal Palace for England winger Peter Taylor.

At Norwich, Jimmy Neighbour completed an attractive, exciting midfield, alongside Martin Peters, Graham Paddon and Colin Suggett.

Martin Chivers scored one hundred and seventy-four league and cup goals for Tottenham, in just 355 games. His club record of twenty-two goals in European football, and twenty-three goals in the League Cup, are unlikely to ever be broken.

He moved to Servette in 1976, where he scored thirty-six goals in 64 Swiss League games. Chivers was the third highest goal-scorer in the Swiss League in 1976-77, but the following season, he was the league's top goal-scorer. Servette were just pipped at the post by Basel, for the title, but they did beat Grasshoppers in the Swiss Cup Final, giving Big Chiv the fourth major honour of his career.

It certainly hadn't made up for England failing to qualify for the 1974 World Cup, but he was presented with the Foreigner of the Year award by the Swiss PFA.

Martin Chivers was one of the most talented and enigmatic centre forwards of the early Seventies, and indeed, of any era. He showed promise with Southampton in the Sixties, and then briefly, with Spurs, before the lengthy break due to his knee injury, but it was after 1970 when he became an internationally renowned, and feared, centre forward. He was feared for his talent and ability, because for a great, big man, he wouldn't hurt or upset anyone.

It was sometimes noted that Chivers was tall, languid and lazy, because he looked moody and lazy. Chivers hated the "lazy" reputation, because in his heart, within his unaggressive and passive nature, he did the absolute best for his team.

He was the Chris Waddle, or the Dimitar Berbatov of his time, and Chivers was neither slow, lazy nor languid. Tottenham's assistant manager Eddie Baily said that Martin "gave you the impression he was slow, and yet, he was the fastest player at the club over sixty yards."

Martin Chivers was Tottenham's Superstar player of the Glam Soccer era. There hasn't been a better English centre forward since Big Chiv; not Lineker, not Shearer, not Wrightie, not Fowler, nor Rooney. They all might have been as good as him, but none were better.

Chivers also possessed one of the longest throws in football, measured at one hundred and thirty feet, and he regularly notched what are now called "assists", with many goals scored from his gigantic, deep throws from the touchline, often reaching the far post.

Steve Perryman, his club captain for the last two years of his Tottenham career, admitted when imagining Chivers playing in the modern Premier League game, "people always ask me, *HOW WOULD MARTIN CHIVERS GET ON IN TODAY'S GAME?* I think if Martin had played today, he would have been the absolute bollocks.

To a certain degree, I think Martin was a player out of his era. Today he would have got what he was worth."

Steve Perryman, himself, became Spurs' club captain in 1974, at just twenty-three years old, and he became rated as one of the most complete footballers of the Seventies and Eighties. He lifted two FA Cups as captain of Tottenham, and in 1982, he won the Footballer of the Year award. He captained Spurs to the 1983-84 UEFA Cup Final, but he was suspended for their Cup-winning second leg victory over Anderlecht.

Perryman played an all-time club record 854 league and cup games for Spurs, including 655 First Division matches, which is also a record. He is the only player in the history of the club to have won six major honours with Tottenham Hotspur.

Steve Perryman will always be best remembered, though, for his two sensational long range goals against AC Milan, that swung their UEFA Cup Semi-final to Spurs' advantage.

Perryman eventually left Spurs in 1986, the same year that he was awarded an MBE for services to football, when he joined fellow Division One club Oxford United, as a thirty-five year old.

Pat Jennings played 591 league and cup matches for Spurs, before he was sold to Arsenal, after Tottenham were relegated at the end of the 1976-77 season. He had lifted the PFA Player of the Year award in 1976, after his performances in goal had lifted Spurs away from the relegation zone, after Christmas, and into a top half of the table position by April.

After one particular, virtuoso performance in goal, when Spurs beat Wolves 2-1 in November 1976, Mike Bailey, the captain of Wolves, had declared, "all I know, and everyone at Wolverhampton Wanderers agrees, is that he is the best goalkeeper in the World."

After Tottenham were relegated in 1977, several First Division clubs were after Jennings, but Arsenal, Spurs' deadliest rivals, had also expressed a desire to sign him. On the very day when Tottenham's players were leaving for a pre-season tour, Pat Jennings had gone into White Hart Lane, still unsure as to where he was heading, to say farewell to his teammates.

As he walked back out into the car park, all of the Tottenham Hotspur directors totally blanked, not even making eye contact, so Jennings thought, "*SOD IT!*"

He went down the road to sign for Arsenal. "It was like Christmas for Arsenal," Bob Wilson said about the deal, which was finalised on 17th August 1977, and "the craziest thing that Tottenham ever did," he added.

Bob Wilson was Pat Jennings' goalkeeping coach at Highbury, a role he found odd, as Jennings was "a far greater goalkeeper" than he ever was. Of all the great goalkeepers he'd ever seen, Banks, Schmeichel, Seaman, Shilton, etc, Bob Wilson placed Jennings above them all.

Pat Jennings had the hugest hands in football, and he was famed for making one handed catches from crosses. As well as all that, he had supreme fitness, agility and athleticism, and a driven determination to do his job every day, as best as he could.

He played a further 327 league and cup games for Arsenal, up to 1985, and accumulated a total of seven hundred and nine First Division appearances for both Spurs and Arsenal. He holds the unique honour of being about the only player to be regarded as a legend at both North London clubs.

Pat Jennings was, frankly and honestly, one of the very greatest two or three keepers to have ever played in the English First Division or Premier League, and if nothing else, the fact that Bill Nicholson's Spurs teams, after 1966, had Jennings in goal, made them as good as their 1961 Double-winning team, before you even reflected on the talents of Greaves, Gilzean, Peters, Mullery, England, Perryman and Knowles.

Bill Nicholson seemed to be so in love with his 1961 team, with Blanchflower, White, Smith, Jones and Mackay, that by the time Liverpool, Manchester United, Leeds and Everton had caught up, he'd fallen out of love with the modern game, and its defensive structures. He seemed more in love with Bobby Smith than Big Chiv, that's for certain.

The game is a great game, though, and it's there to be won, no matter how it's played.

Effectively, though certainly not intentionally, Bill Nicholson had neglected Spurs. He loved them so much, that he just couldn't let go, despite him disliking modern football, until it was too late.

That Spurs team, with its great spine of Jennings, England, Mullery, Peters, Greaves, Chivers and Gilzean could, and *should* have been Champions quite easily; maybe even possibly European Champions, during those early 70s.

It's very hard to imagine either Brian Clough or Bobby Robson allowing Greavsie to leave, just as they'd brought in Martin Peters, or letting the great Alan Mullery, just after he'd led Tottenham to UEFA Cup victories over Milan and Wolves, go away and fester in Second Division football.

And as for trying to get rid of Martin Chivers, for an injured Rangers support striker, that's not even a realistic suggestion.

It is certainly possible that if Cloughie or Bobby had been given the job at the Lane, between 1967 and 1968, then Spurs might have been closer to the biggest prize, the First Division title, than they were under Bill, which was six points away at best.

Those Tottenham teams were great teams, as good as Derby, Everton, Arsenal, Liverpool and Manchester City, with spirit, great balance and real international class. They were just a blade's width away, and it can only be down to the responsibility of their most celebrated manager, that they failed to enjoy proper success.

A TALE OF TWO UNITEDS, Part Two

AFTER LOSING TO CHELSEA in the 1970 FA Cup Final, four Leeds United players represented England at the World Cup Finals, in Mexico. Terry Cooper was voted as the best left back of the tournament, having played in all four of England's matches. Jack Charlton deputised for Brian Labone in their crucial 1-0 win over Czechoslovakia, his last ever match for England.

Allan Clarke made his international debut during that win, scoring the only goal of the game, confidently firing the ball to Viktor's left, from the penalty spot, after Kuna had handled inside his own area.

And Norman Hunter went on as a substitute during their Quarter-final match against West Germany, replacing Martin Peters, the best box to box midfielder in Europe, as England held a 2-1 lead. No, I don't get that last one, either.

Both full backs were suffering from knocks, and they were shattered by extra-time, so England returned back home, after their 3-2 defeat.

Still, Leeds United returned to First Division football on Saturday 15th August 1970, fully recharged, physically refreshed, and with their appetite returned. With Paul Madeley in for Paul Reaney, who was still recovering from his broken leg, they visited Manchester United for their first match of the season.

Manchester United had parted company with their second European Cup Final hero, midway through the previous season. Shay Brennan had made his final appearance during their 4-1 win away at Liverpool, back in December 1969, a match which had also been Roger Hunt's final match for Liverpool. Brennan had been a dependable and consistent full back, and fast enough to also play on the wing. He'd made his Manchester United debut against Sheffield United in February 1958, Roger Byrne's replacement in their first match following the Munich tragedy.

After 355 First Division matches at Old Trafford, Shay Brennan retired from English league football in 1970, and moved to Ireland, where he became player-manager of Waterford United for four years.

Shay Brennan died after collapsing from a heart attack, on Friday 9th June 2000, while playing golf near to his beloved Tramore home, in County Waterford. He was the first member of Manchester United's European Cup winning team to pass away, and George Best, who'd remained a close friend of Brennan's, was grief-stricken.

A massive opening day crowd of 59,365 packed into Old Trafford on a hot August afternoon, as the two great rival clubs went at each other.

MANCHESTER UNITED		LEEDS UNITED
Alex Stepney	1	Gary Sprake
Paul Edwards	2	Paul Madeley
Tony Dunne	3	Terry Cooper
Paddy Crerand	4	Billy Bremner
Ian Ure	5	Jack Charlton
David Sadler	6	Norman Hunter
John Fitzpatrick	7	Peter Lorimer
Nobby Stiles	8	Allan Clarke
Bobby Charlton	9	Mick Jones
Brian Kidd	10	Johnny Giles
George Best	11	Eddie Gray

Leeds United struck decisively in the first half. Allan Clarke ran from the left wing, at Crerand, who blocked his run into the area, so Clarke sprayed the ball across the eighteen yard line, to Lorimer, who was marked by Sadler. Peter Lorimer scooped a cross, with the inside of his right boot, over to the far left side of the six yard box, where the late running Mick Jones buried a booming bullet header past Stepney, across goal and into the far top corner of the net.

"That was a picture book goal by Mick Jones," proclaimed Brian Moore.

Despite Manchester United attacking more after half-time, George Best could not create an opening, while they also continued to miss Denis Law, who'd started only ten league matches the previous season, a huge factor in their lowly finish of eighth place.

After their opening day win away at Old Trafford, Leeds United won six of their first seven matches, picking up thirteen points, and conceding only two goals. During this spell, on Saturday 22nd August, reigning Champions Everton had scored those two goals in the first half at Elland Road.

46,718 then roared Leeds United to a spectacular comeback from two goals down, winning 3-2. Their inspirational General, Billy Bremner, had hit two, and his midfield Major, Johnny Giles, stroked home the other.

Leeds United went unbeaten through October, November, and then December. Paul Reaney had returned from his horrific leg break at the end of November, at which point Paul Madeley moved over to replace Eddie Gray, who was ruled out for over four months, due to an ankle injury.

On Saturday 5th December, Leeds United visited Liverpool, with a massive 51,357 crowd inside Anfield. After a goalless first half, with two dominant top class defences, Liverpool's Lawler, Smith, Lloyd and Lindsay, and Leeds United's Reaney, Charlton, Hunter and Cooper, completely in command.

Two titanic, towering headers, in the second half, secured a point apiece for each team. Terry Cooper swept a sharp cross into the area, and Paul Madeley rose high above Alec Lindsay to power Leeds United ahead.

Liverpool, however, were a developing side of impressive strength, and from Tommy Smith's free-kick, just outside the Leeds United area, John Toshack beat Jack Charlton in the air, to head over Sprake, and inside the far post.

After that hard-fought 1-1 draw, Leeds United took a maximum four points from their two Festive matches. Jack Charlton headed them to a 1-0 win at Everton on Saturday 19th December, and then two Johnny Giles penalty kicks, and Allan Clarke's classy clipper outclassed Newcastle United 3-0, on Boxing Day, at Elland Road.

By the New Year, Leeds United held a three point lead over Arsenal. Those two clubs had been so dominant, though, they were both eight points clear of third-placed Tottenham. Leeds United had conceded only fifteen goals in their twenty-four First Division matches prior to the New Year, and they'd kept fifteen clean sheets.

Manchester United, in contrast, had not enjoyed the first five months of 1970-71. They'd lost both their driving force Pat Crerand, and their goalkeeper Alex Stepney, back in August, both to injury, and neither player returned until the New Year. They had consequently lost nine of their opening twenty-three matches, winning only five. They certainly weren't in relegation trouble, as Blackpool and Burnley had suffered such poor starts to the season, but with only nineteen points from twenty-three matches, Manchester United were struggling deep in the bottom half of the table.

Following their thrilling, Boxing Day 4-4 draw away at Derby County, after coming back from 0-2 down to lead 3-2, before then going 3-4 down, Manchester United were down in eighteenth place, seven points above the relegation places, but twenty points behind Leeds United.

Brian Kidd, a George Best header, and Denis Law's brace, while playing his first game for a couple of months, had earned them a great point, after one of the very best matches of the Seventies, but Wilf McGuinness was sacked as manager, after only a season and a half in charge.

The state of apparent emergency that loomed over Old Trafford in the dark midwinter gloom forced director Sir Matt Busby to agree to manage Manchester United again until the end of the 1970-71 season.

It was almost as if Spring had arrived in darkest January. Manchester United won four of their next five matches, with young Alan Gowling hitting four during their 5-1 demolition of seventh placed Southampton, on 20th February. They then lost narrowly away at Everton, after World Cup right back Tommy Wright's first half drive earned a 1-0 win for the reigning Champions, but then, Manchester United continued to win three from their next four games, rising to ninth in the table by Saturday 20th March.

Manchester United had gained fifteen points from just ten games, since Sir Matt returned, scoring twenty goals, a run of form that was just a point worse than Leeds United's excellent runaway start to the season.

The feel-good factor involved all at Old Trafford. Over those ten matches, Alan Gowling had scored five goals, George Best four, John Aston and Willie Morgan three, while Denis Law and Brian Kidd scored two apiece. Just by simply returning to the manager's dugout, Sir Matt Busby had once again turned Manchester United into a goal scoring machine.

During their 2-1 win over third-placed Tottenham Hotspur on Saturday 6th February, the long-haired George Best scored one of his best ever goals. Pat Crerand sent a free-kick into the penalty area, and Tottenham centre-back Peter Collins met the ball under his own crossbar, but he ballooned his header up into the air.

Alan Gowling challenged for the second ball, and he flicked it back to Best, twelve yards out.

With full back Ray Evans quickly closing in for the challenge, and with three defenders on the goal-line, Jennings, Beal and Collins, Best simply scooped the ball up and over their heads, but it dropped just under the bar, with none of the three men on the line able to do anything about it.

"Beautiful!" commentator Barry Davies screamed, "absolutely beautiful!"

"You didn't know there were so many different ways of scoring, did you?" Bestie said of that goal, afterwards.

George Best, in this form, was "balletic and yet at the same time aggressive, warming to the heart and yet clinically cold in his application," Barry Davies emphasized his love of Manchester United's greatest ever player.

"He combined grace with courage, and pace with unbelievable balance."

Best's dynamic form was a huge factor in their resurrection, as well as the return of the influential Pat Crerand. Manchester United were only four points behind a UEFA Cup qualifying place.

However, as Spring arrived, Manchester United lost three out of four matches in early April, and their European dream died. Their 2-1 defeat away at Coventry City, on Tuesday 13th April, after Best had given Manchester United a 1-0 half-time lead, was also Nobby Stiles' last match for the club.

The feel-good factor that had lifted all inside Old Trafford hadn't involved Stiles.

He'd developed into one of the first holding midfield players in English football, having been an expendable left half during the early Sixties, due to his hard tackling, competitive style of play, and simple use of distribution.

Only five feet and six inches tall, and becoming bald in his very early twenties, Stiles was also severely short-sighted, having to wear strong contact lenses during matches, and thick-rimmed glasses off the pitch. He became invaluable to both Manchester United and England, playing in all six of their matches at the 1966 World Cup Finals.

Nobby Stiles was transferred to Middlesbrough for just £20,000, only five years after helping England win the World Cup, at the end of that season, having played 312 First Division matches for Manchester United. He'd also played twenty-eight matches for England, as a Manchester United player, between 1965 and 1970.

Stiles played 57 Second Division matches for Middlesbrough, before joining former teammate Bobby Charlton, OBE, at Preston North End in 1973. Charlton had been appointed player-manager at Deepdale, and he also recruited further former teammates David Sadler and Francis Burns, as well as his ex-rival centre forward at City, Neil Young. It was an attempt to lift the Lilywhites back up into the First Division, with players of proven First Division quality.

It failed. Preston were relegated to Division Three in April 1974, and Nobby Stiles had had his contract cancelled after just 27 matches, one month earlier.

In 2000, Nobby Stiles was awarded the MBE by the Queen, as well as Alan Ball, Roger Hunt, George Cohen and Ray Wilson, after The Sun newspaper had campaigned for all members of England's 1966 World Cup winning team to be awarded for their services to football, and to their country.

Then, in June 2010, Stiles suffered a stroke, and then in October of that year, he sold both his World Cup winners' medal and his European Cup winners' medal, as well as various England and Manchester United shirts, caps and mementos, for a total of £424,000, so he could look after his family.

Manchester United paid £209,000 for the two medals, and they placed them in their club museum. Nobby Stiles still lives in Manchester, with his wife Kay.

A Martin Chivers master class ran the Leeds United defence ragged, with Peters, Mullery, Perryman and Gilzean playing the ball freely through and around the jaded home midfield, for the rampant Chivers to run free at Sprake for two goals during Tottenham's surprise 2-1 away win at Elland Road, on Saturday 9th January.

Leeds United immediately returned to winning ways, though, and they won six of their next seven matches. On Saturday 6th March 1971, Leeds held a seven point lead over Arsenal at the top of Division One, with only ten games to play. To emphasize the lead that they had over Arsenal, under the contemporary three-points-for-a-win system, Leeds United would have been ten points clear, and with a far superior goal difference.

In the last-ever Inter-Cities Fairs Cup, before it became known as the UEFA Cup, from 1971 onwards, Leeds United had hammered Sarpsborg of Norway, in the First round, back in September. Dynamo Dresden, though, had provided much tougher opposition in October. Peter Lorimer's explosive strike at Elland Road gave them a very slight advantage to take to East Germany.

Dundee-born Lorimer had signed for Leeds United nine years earlier, back in 1962, making his first team debut in September of that year, while still aged only fifteen. He was the youngest ever player in the club's history. Peter Lorimer played rarely for the first team, during the next two seasons, but he became a regular during 1965-66, when he scored nineteen First Division goals, at just nineteen years old, becoming Leeds United's top scorer with his famous hard shots from outside of the penalty area.

That Dynamo Dresden team included two key members of the East German team that eventually qualified for the 1974 World Cup Finals, particularly their curly-haired top scorer Hans-Jurgen Kreische, but Mick Jones' first half strike at the Sportvereinigung Dynamo secured Leeds United's progress into the Third Round, despite losing 2-1. They went through 2-2, on the away goals rule.

In the Third round, on Wednesday 2nd December, Leeds United hammered Sparta Prague 6-0 (Clarke, own goal, Bremner, Gray 2, Charlton), and then won 3-2 away in Czechoslovakia, a week later, to complete their 9-2 aggregate win.

Then in the Quarter-finals, during March, Peter Lorimer's scorcher helped Leeds United squeeze past Vitoria Setubal, 3-2 on aggregate, to reach the last four.

Colchester United had knocked Leeds United out of the FA Cup Fifth round, though, on Saturday 13th February. With 16,000 filling the U's tiny Layer Road ground, Gary Sprake flapped at a couple of crosses in the first half, and the veteran Ray Crawford, their former England centre-forward and First Division title winner with Ipswich, scored twice to help Colchester win 3-2.

Leeds United then suffered a sticky patch on the heavy, boggy pitches of March. They were held to a 1-1 draw away at bottom club Blackpool, before scrambling and scraping themselves a 2-1 win at home to lowly Crystal Palace.

Then, on Saturday 27th March, at Stamford Bridge, against their old rivals Chelsea, Peter Houseman's brace and a half-volley by Peter Osgood secured a 3-1 home win.

Leeds United were rocking unsteadily, while Arsenal had just won two on the trot.

A week later, though, Allan Clarke smashed in all four goals as Leeds United buried relegation-bound Burnley 4-0 to steady their nerves. Arthur Hopcraft wrote in the Observer, "Allan Clarke accepts possibilities and alternatives with exceptional speed, and yet has such control that he never looks hurried when he exploits them."

As Arsenal went on winning, Leeds United could only draw 1-1 up at Newcastle United on Saturday 10th April, and then 0-0 away at Huddersfield Town on Easter Monday. These were games that Leeds would normally have expected to win.

Two nights later, on Wednesday 14th April, nearly 53,000 filled Anfield for the Fairs Cup Semi-final, first leg match between Liverpool and Leeds United.

Billy Bremner's second half headed goal stunned the Liverpool fans, though, and gave Leeds United an advantage that they would not allow to slip away.

Their lead over Arsenal was slipping away, however, and as lowly West Bromwich Albion visited Elland Road on Saturday 17th April, Arsenal were then only two points behind, having won seven consecutive First Division matches.

A Leeds United win over West Brom would kill off the Gunners' hopes.

39,145 packed into Selhurst Park, on 17th April 1971, as George Best scored twice, and Denis Law hit a hat-trick in Manchester United's thrilling 5-3 win over Crystal Palace, after they were losing 2-1 at half-time. Just as they'd done against Arsenal, a month earlier, Palace had attacked Sir Matt's team with joie de vivre, verve and vigour.

Alan Birchenall, Jim Scott, Steve Kember and Bobby Tambling had played superbly, forcing Best, Law and Charlton to produce their very best to win a classic.

At the end of the season, a George Best double, of goals, not the drink, and Bobby Charlton sent Manchester United into a 3-0 half-time lead over neighbours Manchester City, at Maine Road. A young City team, however, led from the front by Francis Lee, with nothing to play for but their futures, came storming back after the break, and it took Denis Law's great goal from three yards out to secure the two points in a 4-3 win.

Manchester United finished up in a creditable eighth position, after their dreadful first half of the season, but more importantly, they'd finished above their City rivals, thanks to that last day victory.

They might have been in decline, but it was an entertaining decline for Manchester United.

During 1970-71, the Red Devils played in five or six absolute classic matches, richly coloured with unforgettable goals.

George Best had scored eighteen First Division goals, and he was once again their leading goalscorer, with Denis Law having scored fifteen in only 28 matches. Brian Kidd, Alan Gowling and Bobby Charlton all contributed twenty-one goals between them, while Charlton, at the age of thirty-three, had played in all of Manchester United's fifty league and cup matches.

Sir Matt Busby would not stay on as manager, though, after the end of the season. Their 4-3 win at Maine Road, on Wednesday 5th May 1971, was his final match as a football manager. He was replaced by Frank O'Farrell, who had just led Leicester City to the Second Division title, and a return to Division One after two seasons away from top flight football.

Pat Crerand had been sent off, after an incident with Blackpool's John Craven, during their penultimate match of the season, a 1-1 draw away at Bloomfield Road.

He was subsequently suspended for the start of the 1971-72 season, and so O'Farrell played Alan Gowling in his place. The Alan Gowling experiment worked, and Paddy Crerand never regained his place in the team, especially after Manchester United's storming start, winning fourteen, and losing just two, of their opening twenty games.

He retired in 1972, after 304 First Division matches for the club.

Crerand won only sixteen caps for Scotland, but it should be noted that he was competing against both Billy Bremner and Bobby Murdoch, for his place in the national team, not to forget Dave Mackay and Frank McLintock. Scotland were a very good international team back in the late Sixties, beating World Champions England, at Wembley in 1967, in a European Championship qualifying match, and running West Germany really close for a place at the 1970 World Cup Finals, in the toughest of all the eight European qualifying groups.

Paddy Crerand is currently a football correspondent on Sky TV, talksport radio, and MUTV. He was, as well as both Bryan Robson and Roy Keane, the greatest midfield General in Manchester United's history.

West Brom were certainly a beatable team, and a team that Leeds United certainly expected to beat. They did, however, possess the First Division's leading goal-scorer of 1970-71. Tony Brown had, so far, scored twenty-six goals from 38 matches, and Jeff Astle had also been the First Division's top scorer, during the previous season, with twenty-five from thirty-four matches.

Leeds United, though, were forced to start the match without the injured Peter Lorimer, but then they also lost Paul Madeley on the very morning of the match, after he'd fallen ill at the Craiglands Hotel, where the team had been preparing for the game.

That was the only game that Madeley missed all season.

Paul Madeley had made his first team debut back in January 1964, playing at centre half during Leeds United's 1-0 win over Manchester City. The most versatile player at the club, and in England, Madeley played in every outfield position, during his first four years at Leeds United.

Paul Madeley wasn't ever going to displace any of Leeds United's ten first choice outfield players, when they were at full strength, so excellent was their quality, but he was no substitute, as Allan Clarke acclaimed. During Leeds United's greatest seven seasons between 1968-75, Madeley was their most prolific player with 367 league and cup starts, at an average of 52 games per season.

He was no utility player, either, and so genuinely great and his ability and reliability to play anywhere at the highest level, Paul Madeley was the most played player for many of Leeds United's seasons. During 1970-71, only Norman Hunter had played more games than Madeley, and they really missed his teamwork value at home to West Brom.

Leeds United were not at their best. Eddie Gray was playing his first game since early December, after a recurrence of his ankle injury, and he was rusty. During the two previous seasons, his performances on the left wing had been so fleet footed, quick witted and sweetly skilled, Don Revie famously said of Gray, "when he plays on snow, he doesn't leave any footprints."

(Sportsmail Top Fifty Managerial Quotes of All Time, # seventeen, May 2010; Daily Mail Online.)

Eddie Gray had started only fifteen of Leeds United's first thirty-eight games of 1970-71, though, and he was not *twinkle-toes* on the seventeenth of April. He was not playing on snow, but looking fairly awkward, plodding around on the heavy mud…

LEEDS UNITED		WEST BROMWICH ALBION
Gary Sprake	1	Jim Cumbes
Paul Reaney	2	Lyndon Hughes
Terry Cooper	3	Alan Merrick
Mick Bates	4	Graham Lovett
Jack Charlton	5	John Wile
Norman Hunter	6	Tony Kaye
Billy Bremner	7	Colin Suggett
Allan Clarke	8	Tony Brown
Mick Jones	9	Jeff Astle
Johnny Giles	10	Bobby Hope
Eddie Gray	11	Asa Hartford

The nerves spread right through the team, and Jack Charlton played a careless square ball inside to Astle on the halfway line. Jeff Astle sprayed the ball, left footed, over to Colin Suggett on the right wing. Suggett's beautifully weighted inside pass was collected by Tony Brown, and **Bomber** hammered the ball past Sprake from the edge of the area.

Leeds United's classic defence had been cut clean through, and just like a warm knife through soft butter, by Astle, Suggett and Brown.

West Brom led 1-0 at half-time, but in the second half, a controversial incident occurred, that still sparks red-hot heated debates over forty years later.

As Leeds United attempted another attack to equalise, from the halfway line, Tony Brown intercepted Norman Hunter's pass, which was a little panicky, and he pushed the ball back over the halfway line. Colin Suggett had been slow to come back from West Brom's previous attack, and he was still deep inside the Leeds United half, but at least ten to fifteen yards away from the ball.

The linesman, Bill Troupe, on the near side, raised his flag, but seeing that Suggett had not received the ball, and not at all attempting any forward run to meet the ball, referee Ray Tinkler waved play on.

Tony Brown, having ran onto his own through-ball, past Leeds United's static defence, stopped for a quick moment, but seeing the referee's arm gestures, he then ran on. The majority of the home defence had just stopped, except for Paul Reaney, who chased from right back.

Once inside the Leeds United area, Brown played the ball across Sprake's body, and Jeff Astle, looking very much offside, had come in from out of the picture, to score a sitter.

All hell then broke loose. Leeds United's players surrounded the referee, and supporters invaded the pitch, many of them middle-aged men, wearing suits and ties. They were dragged away by policemen, as they'd was realised that the referee had actually allowed the goal to stand.

"Leeds United are going mad, and they've every right to go mad," yelled the BBC TV commentator, Barry Davies. After some sort of calm had descended, Leeds United pulled a goal back, thanks to Allan Clarke's close range smash, but West Brom, even before then, had had chances to increase their lead.

After Ray Tinkler blew the whistle on a devastating 1-2 home defeat, he became hated, almost forever, by Leeds United fans and players alike. Tinkler needed a police escort away from the ground, and he never again refereed at Elland Road.

"My linesman raised his flag straight away, but I waved him on," Mr Tinkler said of the incident. "The ball never went anywhere near Suggett."

"In those days when you were offside you were offside," said Norman Hunter, whose bad pass had allowed the chance. "There were no ifs or buts about it."

"He saw my signal," Mr Tinkler said of his linesman, "but the problem was he didn't move. He should have lowered his flag and tried to keep up with play."

"You work so hard to achieve things, and to miss out because of a decision like that was scandalous," Paul Madeley said, after watching the match on television.

"Suggett was plain offside and the goal hung on that. We all stopped running," Billy Bremner admitted. "But the match just got away from us."

"Because he (the linesman) didn't move," Mr Tinkler concluded, "several Leeds players wrongly assumed that play had stopped. Of course the roof fell in."

"By far the worst part of the incident was when Brown squared the ball across Gary Sprake for Astle to tap in," Allan Clarke remembered. "Astle had to be offside because our only defender, Paul Reaney, was still chasing back and is clearly behind him when he scored. Astle couldn't have been onside."

BBC TV's Barry Davies had given a disgraceful example of commentary, thick with ignorance, when he screamed, "Leeds have every right to go mad." He'd even suggested that Tinkler was guilty of a "non-decision", by allowing the goal to stand.

The Laws of the Game, as published at that time, back in 1970, stated under **LAW ELEVEN: OFFSIDE...** "A player in an off-side position shall not be penalised unless, in the opinion of the Referee, he is interfering with the play or with an opponent, or is seeking to gain an advantage by being in an off-side position."

In the opinion of the Referee, therefore, Colin Suggett was not interfering with play, and nor was he seeking to gain an (obvious) advantage. Suggett was, quite correctly, not penalised.

Players of England international quality should have known this, and *offside certainly didn't mean offside, no ifs or buts.* The Laws were even published in a great little handbook, *Association Football Know the Game*, published by E.P. Publishing Co. Ltd, in collaboration with the Football Association, priced 4 shillings (20p), in 1970. Norman Hunter could have easily bought a copy.

With reference to Allan Clarke's point, you've just got to look at the very first sentence of Law Eleven. "A player is off-side if he is nearer his opponent's goal-line than the ball at the moment the ball is played."

Even though Jeff Astle was undoubtedly in front of Paul Reaney, when Tony Brown squared the ball, he'd come in from out of the picture, and possibly from behind Brown, and from behind the ball, although TV replays are not conclusive. But the linesman was stood like a statue, thirty yards behind play with his flag still up, so Astle could not have ever been ruled offside. Ray Tinkler was just too far behind play to give a definitive decision, so he allowed advantage to the attacking side.

I feel the linesman fancied himself as a bit of an Elland Road hero, and he hung Tinkler out to dry. But he did neither Leeds United, nor the game, any favours at all by ignoring the ref's signals, and not being in position when Brown played that crucial pass.

It is pointless, and counter-productive, to continue to argue and believe that Leeds United lost the League Championship in 1971, just because Ray Tinkler made a "dodgy decision." His decision to allow play to continue was absolutely and completely 100% correct in accordance with the laws of Association Football, although nobody would have bothered if he'd blown his whistle.

Nine days later, on Monday 26th April, Leeds United beat Arsenal 1-0, after a Jack Charlton goal, that was angrily protested against by the Arsenal team, who were certain, as were the crowd, that Charlton had been offside.

Afterwards, however, Arsenal had seen television replays, and their players admitted that Bob McNab had appeared to have been playing Big Jack just onside, and the goal was good.

Four decades later, great Leeds United players still protest, and criticize Ray Tinkler's decision. Whole chapters in players' autobiographies are entitled, "Tinkler's Blunder", "Dodgy Decisions", and "Ref Trouble". That Leeds United team were the classiest team on the pitch of almost all other English club sides, on most days, but they lose a little bit of that class, off the pitch, by constantly and consistently blaming a referee for their failure to win the 1970-71 Championship.

Leeds United had drawn with Blackpool, Huddersfield and Newcastle, back in March and April, after they still had a seven point lead. They'd significantly underperformed, but no mention of those matches ever appear in any memoirs. They should have won at least **ONE** of those matches.

Leeds United's players also give little credit to Arsenal, who'd won ten successive First Division matches, from the start of March to late April, while also reaching the FA Cup Final, and they kept 37 clean sheets in league and cup games during 1970-71.

Arsenal finished one point ahead of Leeds United, having won 29 First Division matches, a total bettered only by Tottenham's 1961 team, and they also beat Liverpool in the FA Cup Final, on Saturday 8th May.

Anyway, having drawn 0-0 with Liverpool in their Fairs Cup Semi-final, second leg match, with over 40,000 inside Elland Road, Leeds United went on to meet Juventus in the Final. 58,555 filled the Stadio Communale, in Turin, on Friday 28th May 1971, two days after the original first leg tie had been postponed due to heavy rain and a waterlogged pitch.

Juventus fielded an all-star line-up, including seven players with World Cup Finals experience, while Leeds United were again without Eddie Gray.

JUVENTUS		LEEDS UNITED
Massimo Piloni	1	Gary Sprake
Luciano Spinosi	2	Paul Reaney
Sandro Salvadore	3	Terry Cooper
Gianpetro Marchetti	4	Billy Bremner
Giuseppe Furino	5	Jack Charlton
Francesco Morini	6	Norman Hunter
Helmut Haller	7	Peter Lorimer
Fabio Capello	8	Allan Clarke
Franco Causio	9	Mick Jones
Petro Anastasi	10	Johnny Giles
Roberto Bettega	11	Paul Madeley

Leeds United were under relentless pressure at times, and twice came back from going behind, through "courage, enlightened football and determination," Barry Foster wrote in the Yorkshire Post.

Juventus led 1-0 at half-time, after Bettega's 27th minute goal, but just after the break, Paul Madeley's twenty-five yard shot caught out Piloni, in the Juve goal. Then, future England manager Fabio Capello again gave Juventus the lead, eight minutes later, but Mick Bates came on as a late substitute for Jones, and he volleyed home, with his first touch, thirteen minutes before full-time.

Leeds United provided a master class in defensive football for the final quarter-hour, as Juve failed to break through their lines.

In the second leg, a week later, on Thursday 3rd June, Piloni was replaced by Tancredi in Juventus' goal, but Allan Clarke fired Leeds United ahead, from the edge of the area, after just twelve minutes.

Pietro Anastasi, though, who'd cost a World Record transfer fee of £440,000, when moving from Varese to Juventus, back in 1968, equalised eight minutes later.

With 42,483 inside Elland Road, Leeds United again played superbly to defend their away goals advantage, while Clarke and Jones made life very difficult for Juve's defence, with their bustling activity and attacking strength.

Winning their second European trophy, inside three years, was Some Consolation for the First Division's runners-up.

In gaining 64 points, or 91 points if it were three points for a win, Leeds United were officially the best ever team to finish as League Runners-up, and the twelve point gap between the second and third placed teams, Leeds and Spurs, was also an all-time record. It came as no consolation at all to Leeds United, but for the second successive season, they were beaten by a team that had played to the very highest of levels, yet couldn't ever repeat, or even get close to those levels, while Leeds United played consistently to a very high standard throughout the late Sixties, and early Seventies.

A consequence of those Elland Road crowd disturbances on 17th April, following Jeff Astle's goal, was that Leeds United were ordered to play their first four First Division home matches of 1971-72, away from Elland Road.

On Saturday 21st August, they were held to a 0-0 draw by Wolves, at Leeds Road, Huddersfield, watched by just 20,686. That was Leeds United's lowest *Home crowd* for nearly six years, until Wednesday 23rd March 1977, and then four days later, on the Wednesday night of 25th August, they hosted Tottenham Hotspur, at Hull City's Boothferry Park.

Over 25,000 made the journey across from West Yorkshire, but again, Leeds were held to a 1-1 home draw by Spurs. Billy Bremner had equalised late on, after Alan Gilzean's first half goal. It would have been normal to expect Leeds United to have won at least one of these matches, at the start of the season, at that time, and at Elland Road. It was those dropped points that eventually and crucially proved costly.

Manchester United hosted Leeds United, at Old Trafford, on Saturday 30th October 1971, while they were sitting on top of Division One, with twenty-three points from fourteen matches, four points clear of second-placed Derby County, and six points above Leeds, who trailed back in sixth position.

53,960 watched the biggest game between the two Uniteds, since that 1970 FA Cup Semi-final epic trilogy.

Joe Jordan, a young forward signed for only £15,000 from Scottish League side Morton, back in October 1970, was starting only his second game for Leeds United, with both Mick Jones and Allan Clarke missing. A huge six-footer, Jordan was powerful in the air, climbing above defenders with ease, and he gave Manchester United's defence a tough time, going in where it very much hurt.

MANCHESTER UNITED		LEEDS UNITED
Alex Stepney	1	Gary Sprake
Tom O'Neil	2	Paul Reaney
Tony Dunne	3	Terry Cooper
Alan Gowling	4	Billy Bremner
Steve James	5	Jack Charlton
David Sadler	6	Norman Hunter
Willie Morgan	7	Peter Lorimer
Brian Kidd	8	Eddie Gray
Bobby Charlton	9	Joe Jordan
Denis Law	10	Johnny Giles
George Best	11	Paul Madeley
Carlo Sartori	12	Rod Belfitt
(rep. Kidd)	(rep. Jordan)	

Peter Lorimer was allowed time to fire in their winner, from just inside the area, during the first half, and Leeds United's defence hung on for a crucial 1-0 win, inflicting only Manchester United's second defeat of the season, from nineteen games.

Despite this setback, Manchester United set off on yet another eight match unbeaten league run, before the New Year.

The first post-Busby Babe, and a future Manchester United club legend, made his league debut during their next match, away at Manchester City, on Saturday 6th November, and with a capacity crowd of 63,366 packed inside Maine Road.

Sammy McIlroy was only seventeen years old, when he'd joined the club straight from school, and from East Belfast, drawing inevitable, and unwanted comparisons with George Best. McIlroy scored United's opening goal, giving them a half-time lead, and Brian Kidd and Alan Gowling then added second half goals, but Lee, Bell and Summerbee all replied for City in another classic 3-3 draw.

The Red Devils then beat Spurs 3-1, Leicester 3-2, Southampton 5-2, then finally Nottingham Forest 3-2, and Manchester United were romping away with the First Division title, by the beginning of December. With thirty-two points from twenty matches, they held a five point lead over Derby, Manchester City and Leeds United.

Manchester United had scored 46 goals, and those goals had been shared evenly amongst their wide forward line. Best had scored fourteen, Law ten, Kidd eight, Charlton and Gowling both five apiece, while McIlroy had scored three from his first four games. United then drew their final three First Division matches of the year, to lead the league by three points on New Years' Day, as they visited West Ham United.

Through the calendar year of 1971, Manchester United had gained fifty-nine points from their forty-two First Division matches, just one point less than their League Championship winning total back in 1966-67.

Then the roof fell in on Frank O'Farrell's title dreams.

Pop Robson, Clyde Best and Geoff Hurst all scored, delighting Upton Park's packed crowd of over 41,000, and West Ham hammered Manchester United 3-0.

The Red Devils went on to lose all seven of their first league matches of 1972, and they were also beaten by Preston North End in the FA Cup Fourth round.

On Saturday 19th February, over 45,000 gave a warm Elland Road welcome to Manchester United, just one week after Leeds United had overtaken the Christmas Day runaway First Division leaders.

LEEDS UNITED		MANCHESTER UNITED
Gary Sprake	1	Alex Stepney
Paul Madeley	2	Tom O'Neil
Terry Cooper	3	Tony Dunne
Billy Bremner	4	Francis Burns
Jack Charlton	5	Steve James
Norman Hunter	6	David Sadler
Peter Lorimer	7	Willie Morgan
Allan Clarke	8	Brian Kidd
Mick Jones	9	Bobby Charlton
Johnny Giles	10	Alan Gowling
Eddie Gray	11	George Best
Mick Bates	12	Sammy McIlroy

Jack Charlton gave warm welcome to Brian Kidd, who had to go off. Norman Hunter gave a warm welcome to Alan Gowling. Billy Bremner gave a warm welcome to Willie Morgan. And Johnny Giles gave a warm welcome to Francis Burns.

Basically, in spite of the false hope that they'd given their fans, following their dream first half of the season, Manchester United were a mess. And Leeds United were the one team who could best expose the extent of that mess. Although Manchester United had lost their first seven First Division matches of 1972, they'd never been hammered, not properly taken apart, until this particular match.

Leeds United literally annihilated their opponents.

They won 5-1, but it could have been Seven, Eight, Nine, or even Ten. Mick Jones hit a magnificent hat-trick, while Clarke and Lorimer had also helped themselves to a goal apiece, after some desperate defending by Manchester United. A fortnight later, though, Leeds United did score seven, beating Southampton 7-0, and then they also went and beat Forest 6-1, later on in March.

One major reason why Leeds United were playing catch-up after Christmas 1971, was the absence of Mick Jones during those first three months of the season.

Jones, who'd terrorized Manchester United's defence back in late November, had missed all but three of Leeds' first seventeen matches, prior to mid-November.

During his absence, Rod Belfitt and Joe Jordan had shared his number nine shirt, but they'd scored a combined total of just one goal in fourteen games.

Leeds United lost five of the fourteen games they were forced to play without Jones.

Mick Jones was the last player to join Leeds United's great team of 1967-69.

Aged only twenty-two, he had scored sixty-three First Division goals for Sheffield United in four years, but he'd scored a superb twenty-one in forty league matches during 1965-66. So, in September 1967, Don Revie paid a club record transfer fee of £100,000 for Jones. Blades manager John Harris had predicted that it was the biggest mistake his club would ever make.

He was probably right.

Born in Worksop, Nottinghamshire, Mick Jones scored only eight league goals during his first season at Elland Road, but he was their top scorer, with eighteen goals during Leeds' title-winning 1968-69 season. It was however, the arrival of Allan Clarke during the Summer of 69, that ignited the greatest attacking partnership in English football.

At their best, Allan Clarke and Mick Jones were unstoppable.

A fortnight following Manchester United's 5-1 thrashing away at Elland Road, Martin Buchan made his debut in their defence during their 2-0 defeat at Tottenham, on Saturday 4th March. Buchan was Frank O'Farrell's first signing for the club, after he paid Aberdeen a club record transfer fee of £130,000 for the Aberdonian, who could also cover in midfield, as well as anywhere along their back four.

Upon his arrival at Old Trafford, he immediately became Manchester United's best defender by some distance. Buchan's calm play helped stabilise their position in the table, and they kept three clean sheets from their next four matches.

On Saturday 11th March, Ian Storey-Moore made his Manchester United debut, after the most controversial transfer of the Seventies.

On Friday 3rd March, Derby County announced that they had agreed a club record transfer fee to sign Moore from Nottingham Forest, and on the following Saturday, Brian Clough paraded Moore before the Baseball Ground crowd, prior to their First Division match against Wolves.

Nottingham Forest, however, then claimed on that very same day that Moore was still their player, and the deal had not yet been fully completed.

Manchester United's Frank O'Farrell suddenly, and simultaneously, announced that he was confident of signing the England forward.

To Brian Clough's absolute SHOCK, and FURY!, two days later, Manchester United went and paid a new club record transfer fee of £200,000 for Ian Storey-Moore, on Monday 6th March 1972.

Ian Moore, as he was more regularly known, had been Forest's top scorer in the First Division for the previous three seasons, and he'd scored 105 league goals in 233 matches at The City Ground. Moore scored three goals during his first four matches for Manchester United, helping them beat Huddersfield Town 2-0, Crystal Palace 4-0, and then Coventry City 3-2.

Their resurgence in form did not last, though, and Manchester United lost four of their final eight matches, while they'd won only two. They'd beaten Southampton 3-2 (Best (pen), Moore, Kidd), and also Stoke City 3-0 (Charlton, Moore, Best (pen)), but Manchester United again ended up in eighth place, ten points behind the new First Division Champions.

Leeds United could, and should, have been the First Division Champions in 1971-72, but they finished just one point short of the title, down in Second Place, yet again.

In the FA Cup, however, they'd hammered Bristol Rovers 4-1, at Elland Road, back in the Third round. Johnny Giles scored two, one from the penalty spot, and Peter Lorimer smashed in the other two.

In the Fourth round, they overcame a tough, new-look Liverpool team, following a replay at Elland Road, on 8th February. Allan Clarke fired in a great double during Leeds United's 2-0 win, after their goalless draw at Anfield. A combined crowd of over 102,000 had watched those two matches.

Giles scored twice, again, with 50,000 filling Ninian Park, in the Fifth round, as Leeds United won 2-0 away at Cardiff City.

Saturday 18th March 1972 was a momentous day, as Leeds United wore their famous stocking tags for the very first time, at home to Tottenham Hotspur in the FA Cup Quarter-finals. Leeds United were becoming a prototype for Premier League clubs twenty years into the future. They also wore their names on the backs of their Admiral tracksuit tops during pre-match warm-ups, and the stocking tags just provided an extra touch of class.

Don Revie simply believed that if you feel classier than your opposition, then you'll play classier.

Gary Sprake, however, completely misjudged John Pratt's forty yard free-kick, allowing the ball to go through his arms and into his net. Even Don Revie, who'd been Fiercely defensive of Sprake, was now Tiring of his occasional calamitous errors.

Gary Sprake became known, throughout his career, as a brilliant goalkeeper, athletic and confident, but prone to errors and howlers. Sprake had mostly performed perfectly at Anfield, since his *Careless Hands* own goal back in December 67, but his performances at Colchester, Derby County, and now at home to Spurs, had persuaded Revie to replace him with his younger, and better concentrated Leeds-born keeper David Harvey, by early April.

David Harvey was qualified to play for Scotland, due to his parents' birthplaces, and he made his international debut for their World Cup qualifier at home to Denmark, on November 15th 1972. Scotland won 2-0.

Having dropped to the Leeds United reserves for eighteen months, Gary Sprake was eventually sold to Birmingham City in October 1973. Blues manager Fred Goodwin paid a then British record £100,000 transfer fee for a goalkeeper, after Sprake had kept over two hundred clean sheets in 504 league and cup matches for Leeds United.

Injuries and form affected Sprake at Birmingham, though. There was no hiding place behind Birmingham City's leaking back four, as there could sometimes be behind Leeds United's mighty defence.

Over the next two seasons, Sprake played just sixteen matches, before permanently losing his place, to Dave Latchford, and his contract was cancelled in 1975.

Allan Clarke hooked home an equaliser on the stroke of half-time, as Leeds United began to press the Spurs defence, more and more, inside their own third. Tottenham struggled to get out of their own half, and late in the second half, Johnny Giles' free-kick was headed in by the frightening figure of Jack Charlton in full flight.

The 44,000 Elland Road crowd were ecstatic. They could actually taste a league and cup Double success. This Leeds United team was certainly good enough. Graeme Garvey called that 2-1 comeback win over Spurs, "Leeds United's Best ever performance."

With David Harvey in goal, Leeds United swept to a straightforward 3-0 win over Second Division promotion hopefuls Birmingham City, at Hillsborough. Blues had boasted a free-scoring attack of Bob Latchford, Trevor Francis, Bob Hatton and Alan Campbell, but they had a mostly-Second Division defence, and Mick Jones, Allan Clarke, Johnny Giles, Eddie Gray, Peter Lorimer and Billy Bremner outclassed them.

Beneath a massed bank of Leeds fans on the Spion Kop end, Jones scored twice, and Lorimer thundered in another, as Leeds United reached Wembley for the third time in five years. Prior to 1965, Leeds United had never played at Wembley Stadium. Terry Cooper, though, had broken his leg at Stoke City, on Saturday 8th April, and he remained out of action for two years.

Once Trevor Cherry had arrived at Elland Road, Cooper, the best-ever left back in Leeds United's history, never returned to their left back position, on a regular basis.

The best left back at the Mexico World Cup Finals, Terry Cooper, fully moustached, was sold to Jack Charlton's Middlesbrough in February 1975. He'd played over 240 First Division matches for Leeds United, helping the team to six major Cup Finals, of which they won three, but also five times as First Division runners-up.

On Saturday 6th May, Leeds United met Arsenal, the FA Cup holders, at the 1972 FA Cup Final, the Centenary Final, at Wembley Stadium.

LEEDS UNITED		ARSENAL
David Harvey	1	Geoff Barnett
Paul Reaney	2	Pat Rice
Paul Madeley	3	Bob McNab
Billy Bremner	4	Peter Storey
Jack Charlton	5	Frank McLintock
Norman Hunter	6	Peter Simpson
Peter Lorimer	7	George Armstrong
Allan Clarke	8	Alan Ball
Mick Jones	9	Charlie George
Johnny Giles	10	John Radford
Eddie Gray	11	George Graham
Mick Bates	12	Ray Kennedy (rep. Radford)

From George Armstrong's left-sided corner, during the first half, Alan Ball volleyed the ball, right-footed, hard and low, towards goal, from the edge of the Leeds United area. Paul Reaney slid across and just kept the ball out, on his goal line, at Harvey's right hand post.

Peter Lorimer then brought out a sharp save from Barnett, with a low-hit rocket from 25 yards out. Allan Clarke headed the ball onto Barnett's crossbar, from Eddie Gray's looping cross, and it bounced fortunately away for Pat Rice to clear.

Into the second half, Lorimer fed Mick Jones out wide on the right. Jones carried the ball to the edge of the Arsenal area, and then he took on McNab, before managing to squeeze a cross over to the far side of the six yard box, where Clarke leapt and headed the ball back across Barnett's body and into the goal.

Late on, Charlie George hooked Alan Ball's through ball onto Harvey's bar, from just inside the penalty area. George looked disbelievingly at the sky, with his head in his hands. As time ran out, into injury-time, Mick Jones took on and then beat McLintock inside Arsenal's penalty area, but Barnett came out and fell on the ball, and Jones collapsed as Barnett's legs followed through in his momentum.

Mick Jones just lay on the Wembley bye-line, writhing in agony, as referee David Smith, from Stonehouse in Gloucestershire, blew the final whistle.

Jack Charlton, two days short of his thirty-seventh birthday, had won his first FA Cup winners' medal.

After Leeds United's players had climbed the steps to lift their FA Cup, and then descended again with the trophy, for their lap of honour, Norman Hunter returned to help Mick Jones up the Wembley steps, with his dislocated left elbow taped and bandaged onto his body, to collect his winners' medal.

The two players slowly climbed the steps to great and spontaneous applause from the whole crowd, and congratulations from the Queen.

Clarke and Jones were the best double act in Europe on their day, and this was one of their days, having constantly harassed Arsenal's defence, running at and around McLintock, Simpson, McNab and Rice, all day long.

The loss of Mick Jones had badly affected Leeds United's chances of victory, though, as they played their title-deciding match at Molineux, on the following Monday.

Frank Munro and Derek Dougan both scored to beat a jaded Leeds United 2-1.

For the second successive season, they'd lost the title by just a single point.

After an awful start to 1972-73, during which Manchester United had failed to win any of their first nine matches, and gained just four points, lying deep in a relegation battle, Frank O'Farrell splashed the cash, once again, to try and sort things.

On 14th September, he paid £65,000 to neighbours Man City for their thirty year old striker Wyn Davies. The Welsh international forward had scored nearly fifty First Division goals for both Newcastle United and City, but he was on the decline and more of a supporting forward by then.

A fortnight later, O'Farrell further strengthened his attack, after paying Bournemouth £200,000 for their highly sought-after striker Ted MacDougall.

MacDougall had scored 103 league and cup goals from just 116 matches, over the previous two and a bit seasons at Dean Court.

On Saturday 28th October, Manchester United hosted Tottenham Hotspur, with 52,497 packed inside Old Trafford to watch their new-look attacking team take on high-flying Spurs, but their attacking experiment was doomed to fail.

Manchester United were simply top heavy with forwards, and they lacked the presence of the ball-winning midfield authority of either Stiles or Crerand. They'd become a mess, and Spurs, spearheaded by an inspired Martin Peters, simply picked them off and sped to a 3-0 half-time lead.

Peters poked past Stepney, after Chivers had flicked on a Cyril Knowles long pass, and then he finished, left-footed, from inside the area, after Coates had squared the ball to him. He completed his hat-trick, before half-time, sliding in at the far post, and firing high into the net after Chivers had pulled the ball back across goal from the United bye-line.

MANCHESTER UNITED		TOTTENHAM HOTSPUR
Alex Stepney	1	Pat Jennings
Willie Watson	2	Ray Evans
Tony Dunne	3	Cyril Knowles
Denis Law	4	John Pratt
David Sadler	5	Mike England
Martin Buchan	6	Mike Dillon
Willie Morgan	7	Jimmy Pearce
Ted MacDougall	8	Steve Perryman
Wyn Davies	9	Martin Chivers
George Best	10	Martin Peters
Bobby Charlton	11	Ralph Coates
	12	Jimmy Neighbour (rep. Coates)

In the second half, Peters completed a "perfect hat-trick", after he'd headed in Jimmy Neighbour's left-wing cross. His four goals had included two right-footed strikes, a neat left-footer, and a header.

Bobby Charlton's goal was of no consolation to Manchester United.

Frank O'Farrell had found George Best very difficult to understand. The absence of Sir Matt Busby, his father figure, had hit Best hard as Manchester United declined in 1972, a decline that burnt him up inside.

He just went outside to get absolutely slaughtered, and returned home only when daylight was returning.

Manchester United's 2-1 win over Southampton, at the end of November, with both Davies and MacDougall scoring, was George Best's last game of the 1972-73 season. He missed training the following week, was suspended by the club, and then finally transfer-listed by O'Farrell.

Bottom-placed Crystal Palace hammered Manchester United 5-0, at Selhurst Park, on Saturday 16th December, and United dropped back into the bottom two.

Frank O'Farrell was sacked three days later.

Tommy Docherty, Scotland's international team manager, was at the Palace game, just to have a look at their young left-back Tony Taylor. Sir Matt Busby tracked him down and asked Docherty if he might fancy the job as Manchester United boss.

Tommy Docherty was appointed as Manchester United's new manager, on Friday 22nd December. As Scotland's manager, Docherty had won seven, and drawn two, of his twelve games in charge, and he'd sent the Scots well on their way to qualification for the 1974 World Cup Finals with wins, both home and away, over Denmark.

It didn't take long for Docherty to get rid of Ted MacDougall and Wyn Davies. Davies started his last match on Boxing Day, in their 3-1 defeat at Derby, and he was transferred to Blackpool at the end of the season. MacDougall made his final appearance during their 4-1 defeat at Ipswich on Saturday 17th February, and he was sold to West Ham United for £150,000, seven days later.

European Cup-winning full back Tony Dunne also made his final appearance for Manchester United during their Boxing Day defeat away at Derby County.

Tony Dunne had played 415 First Division matches, at Old Trafford, but he joined Bolton Wanderers in the Summer of 1973, after his contract was cancelled.

Tommy Docherty had wasted no time in bringing in new, hungrier players.

By mid-January, he had signed four players, all of them Scottish internationals, and all of whom he knew well as their former national manager.

On 27th December, he paid Arsenal £120,000 for their title-winning midfield grafter George Graham. Graham had scored sixty goals in 219 First Division matches for Arsenal, and he immediately took Paddy Crerand's number four shirt.

On the following day, Docherty signed Partick Thistle's Scottish international full back Alex Forsyth, for £100,000.

Then, on January 11th 1973, Shrewsbury Town sold their Scottish under-23 international centre-back Jim Holton, for £80,000, to Manchester United. Holton made his full international debut, four months later, against Wales.

A week later, Docherty paid an equal club record transfer fee of £200,000 for Lou Macari, who joined from Scottish Champions Celtic. Macari had scored twenty-seven Scottish League goals in just fifty-one matches at Celtic Park.

Tommy Docherty's new signings inspired Manchester United to gain twenty points from their final seventeen matches of 1972-73. It was uninspiring, mid-table stuff, but it did help lift them up to eighteenth position by the end of the season, seven points above relegated Crystal Palace.

Denis Law had endured an awful, injury-affected season, and he was freed by Tommy Docherty at the end of the season, to Law's great disappointment and personal distress. Having scored 171 First Division goals in 305 matches, after eleven years at Old Trafford, he was jobless.

However, a chance meeting with Manchester City manager Johnny Hart, at the Footballer of the Year awards dinner, on Friday 4th May 1973, led to him signing for Manchester City for the following season.

Also departing Old Trafford, in April 1973, was their all-time legend Bobby Charlton. After playing more than 600 First Division matches for Manchester United, and scoring 198 goals, Bobby Charlton had retired at the age of thirty-five.

Bobby Charlton's total of 249 goals in 758 league and cup games, remain a club record by some comfortable distance. His 106 England caps were also an international record, at the time of his international retirement in 1970.

44,184 packed out the vast, crumbling terraces of Stamford Bridge, on the final day of that 1972-73 season, and both Chelsea and Manchester United gave Charlton a guard of honour as he entered the pitch, while he was also rapturously applauded by all sides of the ground.

Peter Osgood's second half goal won the match 1-0 for Chelsea, bundling the ball home, a fluke, scuffed goal and he was bit embarrassed. Ali Goodman remembered him on his knees and shrugging his shoulders. But at the end, Bobby just shook hands with the opposition's players, as usual, and he left the pitch for the changing room, as if it were any ordinary match.

Six days later, Bobby Charlton was appointed as player-manager of Preston North End. He also recruited former teammates Nobby Stiles, as his player-coach, and David Sadler as his defensive coach.

David Sadler was the ninth member of their European Cup winning team to leave Old Trafford, when he joined Preston in November 1973, after playing 270 First Division matches for United, having seen Jim Holton and Martin Buchan secure the central defensive places under the Doc.

Bobby Charlton played 38 league games for Preston North End, over the following two seasons, but he couldn't prevent them from relegation to Division Three in 1974, He resigned in 1975, in protest at the club selling defender John Bird to Newcastle United, over his head.

He became a director at Manchester United in 1984, and Sir Bobby Charlton was then knighted by the Queen in 1994.

Leeds United had started steadily in 1972-73, fighting it out for second and third place with Arsenal, from September through to December. On 23rd December 1972, they travelled to Old Trafford to play Manchester United. It was Tommy Docherty's first game in charge of Manchester United, who were second bottom of the First Division, while Leeds United were in third place, and only two points behind leaders Liverpool, with Arsenal sandwiched in between them both.

MANCHESTER UNITED		LEEDS UNITED
Alex Stepney	1	David Harvey
Tom O'Neil	2	Paul Reaney
Tony Dunne	3	Trevor Cherry
Denis Law	4	Terry Yorath
David Sadler	5	Jack Charlton
Martin Buchan	6	Paul Madeley
Willie Morgan	7	Peter Lorimer
Ted MacDougall	8	Allan Clarke
Bobby Charlton	9	Mick Jones
Wyn Davies	10	Johnny Giles
Ian Moore	11	Mick Bates
Brian Kidd	12	

Trevor Cherry had signed from Huddersfield Town, back in June, for £100,000, having played over 180 league matches in the Terriers' defence. He'd been a key player during their Second Division Championship winning season in 1970.

Leeds United were missing the suspended Billy Bremner and Norman Hunter, while Eddie Gray had again been injured against Sheffield United in November, and he missed most of the rest of the season.

Ian Moore's perfectly placed pass presented Ted MacDougall with a great chance before halftime, and Manchester United went in 1-0 up at the break.

Two minutes before the end of the match, a great win over their great rivals would have seemed the greatest of Christmas presents for Manchester United, but the slightest lapse in communication, and concentration, between O'Neil and Sadler, gave Allan Clarke a chance which he couldn't waste. He advanced past them both, before carefully and clinically beating Stepney.

This 1-1 draw was the last time that Bobby Charlton and Jack Charlton ever faced each other, as opponents. "United" by the fiercest of rivalries, these two great teams had become, they had been United, also, over the past two decades by the greatest of brethren.

Jack Charlton started only two further First Division matches before the end of the season, and he wasn't selected for Leeds United's FA Cup Final team to face Sunderland, although he did play in their 1-0 Semi-final win over Wolves.

He played 629 league matches for Leeds United, and 773 in all competitions, a club record unlikely to ever be beaten, after twenty years at Elland Road.

Big Jack will always be remembered as one of the toughest, hard-nosed, no-nonsense centre halves in Football League history, setting defensive standards which few have ever equalled, and nobody has ever beaten, *ever.*

Charlton was appointed as manager of Middlesbrough, on his thirty-eighth birthday, in May 1973, and he built a team that not only won the Second Division title in 1974, but also became one of the toughest teams to beat in the First Division between 1974 and 1976. He moved to Sheffield Wednesday, and then to Newcastle United during the Eighties, before moving into international management in 1986, becoming manager of the Republic of Ireland.

Jack Charlton made the very most of ancestry laws, and Ireland enjoyed the happiest football days of their lives, qualifying for two World Cup Finals tournaments, in 1990 and 1994, and also the 1988 European Championships.

After Ireland were beaten by Holland, in a play-off match for Euro 96, Big Jack retired after nearly ten years in charge of the best-ever Republic of Ireland team. He was awarded the OBE in 1974, and given the Freedom of the city of Dublin in 1994.

In the European Cup Winners' Cup, Leeds United battled past Ankaragucu, of Turkey, and then Carl Zeiss Jena, of East Germany, before they hammered Rapid Bucharest 8-1 in the Quarter-finals.

Allan Clarke's clinical left-footed strike, from just inside the penalty area, in the first leg of Leeds United's Semi-final against Hajduk Split, gave them a 1-0 lead to take to Yugoslavia. However, Dzoni had been hacking away at Clarke all game, without any punishment from the referee, and five minutes after he'd scored, Allan Clarke had his legs taken away in yet another crude challenge. He lost his temper, on this occasion, for a brief moment, and he booted his opponent between the legs...

Allan Clarke's sending off meant that he'd miss both the second leg, and the Final, if Leeds were successful. Leeds United drew 0-0 in Yugoslavia, to win 1-0 on aggregate, but a late booking for the perplexed Billy Bremner meant that both Bremner and Clarke would miss the Final in Salonika, as well as Giles, Cooper, and Eddie Gray.

Before the Final, Leeds United hammered Arsenal 6-1 and finished in third position in Division One, seven points behind Champions Liverpool, the first time in five years they'd finished outside the top two. Allan Clarke was their top scorer with eighteen league goals, twenty-six in total, and Lorimer and Jones had combined to score thirty-nine goals between them.

Leeds United had also been shocked by Sunderland's 1-0 win in the FA Cup Final, at Wembley, before they faced AC Milan in the European Cup Winners' Cup Final, in Salonika, on Wednesday 16th May 1973.

Leeds United were severely under-strength, without their midfield engine room, or their top striker. But it was, however, the performance of the referee, Christos Michas, that will forever irritate not only Leeds United supporters and players, but true football supporters from all over the World.

AC MILAN		LEEDS UNITED
Vecchi	1	David Harvey
Sabadini	2	Paul Reaney (Captain)
Zignoli	3	Trevor Cherry
Anquilletti	4	Mick Bates
Turone	5	Terry Yorath
Rosato	6	Norman Hunter
Sogliano	7	Peter Lorimer
Benetti	8	Joe Jordan
Bigon	9	Mick Jones
Rivera	10	Frank Gray
Chiarugi	11	Paul Madeley
Dolci	12	Gordon McQueen

Christos Michas' bias towards the Italian side was transparent and outrageous. He turned down three penalty appeals for Leeds United, that were at least strong, but at worst, blatant fouls by Milan. He'd also allowed Italian fouls to go unchecked throughout the game, but then he sent off Norman Hunter, when the big man had retaliated after suffering just one foul too many.

Leeds United had had no protection, at all, but they had their pride.

Unlike Ray Tinkler's infuriating decision, against West Brom, with his technically correct interpretation of the laws of the game, within the actual laws of the game, the performance of Christos Michas was an absolute disgrace.

To this day, there are still attempts, albeit futile, at the European Parliament, to reverse the result of that Final, a dirty, hollow 1-0 win for the Italians.

Unlike Mr Tinkler, who continued to referee for several seasons following that Leeds versus West Brom match, and he even became chairman of the FA Referees' Association during the late Seventies, Michas was investigated and suspended over bribery allegations, and he never officiated in a professional match again.

AC Milan were booed, barracked and cat-called by the Greek fans, as they did their dirty lap of dishonour with the Cup. Leeds United, as under-strength as they were, and captained with great dignity by Paul Reaney, gave everything they had against a distinguished AC Milan team.

Distinguished Milan certainly were, but their display was shameful on that night, and only a hollow heart could feel pride at such a triumph.

Leeds United, however, having won just two trophies in the past four seasons, while finishing second on six occasions, were on the brink of doing something truly great.

In the early stages of transition, things were finally about to go just right for Leeds United.

In their latter stages of transition, things were about to go very wrong for Manchester United during 1973-74, a season of extreme and contrasting fortunes for the two Uniteds. Eventually, though, both teams ended up wondering who had really risen, and who'd fallen.

One thing was certain. You just couldn't take your eyes off either of them.

IT'S POTTERY TIME!

O N SATURDAY 4TH MARCH 1972, Chelsea walked out of the Wembley Stadium tunnel, with Stoke City to their left, for the 1972 Football League Cup Final.

Stoke City were the second oldest football league club in the world, at 109 years old.

97,852 were inside Wembley, the largest crowd to have ever watched Stoke City, and the largest crowd that will ever watch Stoke City.

CHELSEA		STOKE CITY
Peter Bonetti	1	Gordon Banks
Paddy Mulligan	2	John Marsh
Ron Harris	3	Mike Pejic
John Hollins	4	Mike Bernard
John Dempsey	5	Denis Smith
David Webb	6	Alan Bloor
Charlie Cooke	7	Terry Conroy
Chris Garland	8	Jimmy Greenhoff
Peter Osgood	9	John Ritchie
Alan Hudson	10	Peter Dobing
Peter Houseman	11	George Eastham
Tommy Baldwin	12	John Mahoney

Chelsea were led out by their manager Dave Sexton, who had led Chelsea to an FA Cup triumph two seasons earlier, and a European Cup Winners' Cup triumph during the previous season. Stoke City had won absolutely no trophies at all during their 109 year history, even with Stanley Matthews and all at The Victoria Ground, not one single trophy won, but they were led out by Tony Waddington.

Tony Waddington had arrived at the Victoria Ground, nearly twelve years earlier, during June 1960, having been appointed as manager of Stoke at just thirty-five years old. Tony Waddington had a double mission. Firstly, he needed to bring back the crowds to the Stoke End and the Boothen End and the Butler Street Stand, as they'd had dropped to average crowds of under 10,000. Secondly, he had to keep Stoke in the Second Division, to stop them dropping into the Third Division.

Stoke had avoided the drop by just five points back in 1959-60.

Waddington helped them through another relegation battle during 1960-61, as Stoke just avoided relegation down to Division Three by three points. He brought Stanley Matthews back to the Victoria Ground, though, and by 1963, after two years of improvement, Stoke City had won the Second Division Championship trophy, beating Chelsea by one point.

Sir Stanley Matthews continued to play First Division football for Stoke until 1965, when he was fifty. But by then, Waddington had the new backbone of a good team he could really build upon, particularly Alan Bloor, Eric Skeels, Mike Bernard, Peter Dobing and John Ritchie.

In 1966, Waddington paid Arsenal just £35,000 for George Eastham. At twenty-nine years old, Eastham was dainty, delicate and diminutive. Bandy-legged also, he could've often been knocked off the ball by tougher players, and sometimes he was found ineffective on mud-ridden pitches.

Eastham was a quick-thinking and imaginative player, though, with a delightful ability and colourful range of passing, and he could unlock a defence in an instant.

Among the most creative inside forwards in England, Eastham was most famous for going on strike in 1960, when he was at Newcastle United, after the Newcastle board had refused to sell him. In October 1960, Newcastle finally sold him to Arsenal for £47,000, but he continued to fight Newcastle, and at the High Court in 1963, he won his claim for unpaid wages and bonuses. That historic case resulted in fairer terms for players, and the "annulment of an unreasonable restraint of trade", but Eastham was unkindly treated by St James's Park crowds, following the national annulment.

Following the National Anthem, which was sung loudly by the Wembley crowd, but by none of the players, as it always used to be, there was the presentations of the teams to not only Len Shipman of the Football League, but also the UEFA President, Gustav Wiederkehr of Switzerland.

Then the captains of Chelsea and Stoke City met at the centre spot, for the coin toss.

An ordinary blue Chelsea pennant was presented by Ron Harris, Chelsea's captain, to Peter Dobing, while a beautiful framed Wedgwood china plate was presented to Harris by Dobing.

Stoke was the headquarters of the Wedgwood bone china company, up in the Potteries.

As the coin was tossed, Ron Harris, to his absolute credit, looked embarrassed.

Chelsea kicked off, and signalled an attacking and exciting Final, as, right from the kick-off, Hollins shot straight at goal, from fifty yards out, wide and comfortably collected by Gordon Banks.

After five minutes, Peter Dobing sent a long throw-in over from the left, and Denis Smith created havoc inside the six yard box as he jumped for the ball with Bonetti. Bonetti only managed to punch weakly away as he landed on the turf.

Eastham played the ball back in, and although Greenhoff's flick was blocked by Dempsey, as Harris also stopped Smith's scuffed shot, Terry Conroy lunged and nodded the loose ball, bobbing about in there, into the far corner of the goal, left empty by the desperate Chelsea defence, way, way out of position.

It was Stoke City's first ever goal at Wembley. Conroy was mobbed by all of his team-mates, amidst the Stoke noise. Charlie Cooke responded by hitting a fierce twenty yard drive, well saved by Gordon Banks, the World's best goalkeeper.

The World's best goalkeeper, Gordon Banks, was bought by Tony Waddington in April 1967, when he paid £55,000 to Leicester City, smashing the World Record fee for a goalkeeper. A couple of weeks earlier, just £10,000 was paid to Northern Irish club Glentoran for Terry Conroy, their red-headed, lightening quick winger.

After yet another season of struggling at the lower end of the First Division, Mike Pejic, Denis Smith, John Marsh and John Mahoney were all also brought up through Stoke City's youth system.

Jimmy Greenhoff, a lively blond striker who'd played over a hundred games for Don Revie's Leeds United, had previously won the League Cup in March 1968, playing in their 1-0 win over Arsenal.

Greenhoff had been Leeds' second top scorer in 1967-68, with 18 goals in 56 league and cup games, but Revie had sold him to Birmingham City in August 1968, after the emergence of Mick Jones as Leeds' main striker.

Jimmy Greenhoff then scored 14 goals in 32 league games at St Andrews.

Tony Waddington smashed Stoke's record transfer fee by signing Greenhoff from Birmingham, for £100,000, during August 1969. In his first season at The Victoria Ground, Greenhoff played mainly in support of Stoke's quick winger Harry Burrows and centre-forward John Ritchie. Those three players combined for a total of 37 First Division goals, as Stoke finished up in ninth position. Arsenal, who'd finished five points below Stoke, had won the Fairs Cup, though, and they qualified for the following season's Inter-City Fairs Cup in Stoke's place.

Stoke City were an unlucky team.

Then, Stoke City were a lucky team. Garland was sent clear by Hollins' long ball, and he ran a yard clear of defender Eric Bloor. Just outside his own penalty area, with only Gordon Banks behind him, Bloor went and hacked Garland down from behind. Referee Norman Burtenshaw of Great Yarmouth awarded a free-kick and he also booked Bloor. The punishment would have been worse today.

John Hollins hit his free-kick just wide of Banks' right hand post.

Soon after, Chris Garland was again sent clear down the right wing by Charlie Cooke's well-weighted ball, but he was scythed down again, this time by Mike Pejic.

Pejic was also booked by Mr Burtenshaw.

Moments later, Peter Osgood was then lucky not to be booked for a crude slice of Greenhoff's legs, equally as bad as Pejic's foul. Greenhoff's shoulder was badly injured as he'd collapsed awkwardly on the bumpy turf.

Hardman Ron Harris stepped in between the cocky Osgood and the fiery Conroy, and he managed to cheerfully cool tempers a little.

Gordon Banks then dived low, on the bumpy ground, to grab Garland's shot on the turn from ten yards out. Without playing particularly well, Chelsea were certainly the better side.

Stoke City were certainly a better side, as the Seventies began, than they had been during the Sixties. They were no longer relegation fighting fodder. Also, the Victoria Ground was attracting average crowds of 20,000, while Stoke were playing stylish and fluent passing football.

This was evident on September 26th 1970, when league title chasers Arsenal visited the Victoria Ground, with only George and Simpson missing from their classic team.

Stoke City thrashed Arsenal 5-0 (Ritchie 2, Bloor, Conroy, Greenhoff), but their inability to grind out winning results had badly affected their challenge for a UEFA Cup place, as they drew ten of their twenty-four matches before New Year 1971.

On Saturday 2nd January, Stoke narrowly beat Millwall 2-1 (Ritchie, Greenhoff) at home, in the FA Cup Third Round. They were rewarded with a home tie against fellow First Division side Huddersfield Town, that included both Frank Worthington and Trevor Cherry. Worthington had scored nineteen goals during Huddersfield's 1970 Second Division Championship season.

A huge crowd of 34,231 sensed a happening as they'd packed into the Victoria Ground on Saturday 23rd January. Goals from Greenhoff, Conroy and Burrows could only force a 3-3 draw, though, with Worthington scoring for the Terriers.

40,363 nearly filled Leeds Road for the replay, three days later, that ended 0-0 after extra-time. Their second replay at Old Trafford, on Monday 8th February, was attended by 39,302 and finally won 1-0 by Stoke City (Jimmy Greenhoff).

36,809 again swelled the Victoria Ground for their Fifth round home match against Ipswich Town. A tight game between two very good defensive teams ended 0-0, but three days later, on Tuesday 16th February, Denis Smith's headed goal won the replay 1-0 away at Portman Road.

Stoke then played a classic Quarter-final clash on Saturday 6th March, away at Hull City, a great Hull team who were strongly fancied for promotion to the First Division.

41,452 literally filled Boothferry Park to capacity, and the game was an excellent exhibition of enterprising football, as Hull attacked fiercely from the very start with Ken Wagstaff, Chris Chilton, Malcolm Lord, Roger De Vries, Terry Neill and Frank Banks squeezing Stoke City back into their own third of the pitch.

Hull City opened the scoring when Wagstaff turned two defenders, before finishing inside the penalty area. Then, from Frank Banks' long ball, Ken Wagstaff ran clear into the area, before hammering his shot past Gordon Banks for a well-deserved 2-0 lead.

Wagstaff then made space for another shot from the edge of the area, but he fired wide, when his hat-trick had looked much more likely. Stoke were on the rack, amidst all the mayhem, and the highly intense North Yorkshire atmosphere, but suddenly, Jackie Marsh sent Terry Conroy running free, and the sheer pace, energy and body swerve of the Irish wizard took him around McKechnie, and he fired just inside the near post with a lovely right footed finish, just before half-time.

Just before half-time, at Wembley, Banks saved Osgood's diving header on his own goal-line from Hollins' free-kick. Peter Osgood then got involved in a shoving match against Denis Smith, grounding the Stoke centre half, and leaving him in need of medical treatment.

Denis Smith has actually been placed in the Guinness Book of Records as the most injured man in professional football, suffering nearly twenty broken bones, and over one hundred stitches in his legs, feet, toes, arms, hands and face during his fifteen years as a footballer.

"What's your name?" asked referee Norman Burtenshaw, booking Osgood.

"Peter Osgood," replied Chelsea's star player, with a typical Ossie smile.

In the last seconds of the first half, in the 48th minute, in fact, Stoke could not hold onto the ball outside of their own area, and Cooke lofted a cross into Stoke City's box, which Osgood collected but could not connect with.

However, he was given a second chance thanks to Webb's superb harassment inside the area, and while still lying on the pitch, Osgood twisted and he drove the ball, while still lying on his side, between Smith and Marsh, and beyond Banks, into the net, for his first ever goal at Wembley.

With the scores surprisingly level at half-time, Tommy Baldwin replaced the injured Mulligan for Chelsea, as the teams emerged for the second half.

For the second half, more heavy and sustained Hull pressure followed in and around the Stoke City area, but the home crowd were shocked, late in the match.

Very, very late on, and out of nowhere, and totally against the run of play, John Ritchie poached two late goals; first, a shot from inside the area after McKechnie had punched poorly at Marsh's free-kick, and then a last-ditch free header at the far post from Terry Conroy's right wing cross, giving McKechnie no chance, to steal the win.

Hull City had had two or three excellent opportunities to go 3-1 up and kill Stoke's hopes, but on the heavy pitch, they found Gordon Banks and his hardworking defence just too good or just too lucky to beat during that second half.

Stoke were in the last four of the FA Cup for only the second time in their long one hundred and eight year club history, and for the first time since 1899.

At Hillsborough, on Saturday 27th March, Stoke City faced Arsenal in their FA Cup Semi-final. This was **THE** classic Double-chasing Arsenal side, and 55,000 had filled the ground, with the Gunners' fans massed up on the huge Spion Kop End.

All of the goals were scored over at the opposite West Stand end, however, and Stoke actually opened the scoring early on, shocking the Cup favourites, when Denis Smith, up for Harry Burrows' right-sided corner kick, had smacked a sharply-hit shot on the turn, just inside the Arsenal six yard box, from a tight angle.

Then, disaster struck for Arsenal.

John Ritchie stole Charlie George's awful back pass and he rounded Bob Wilson, before simply passing the ball into the empty net for a 2-0 half-time lead.

Soon into the second half, John Mahoney was sent clear by Jimmy Greenhoff's superb through-ball, running between two markers, but Bob Wilson was alert, and he advanced to dive at Mahoney's feet, just as the 3-0 trigger was being pulled, saving Arsenal's humiliation.

Storey volleyed in, from outside the area, pulling one back, but totally against the run of play.

Jimmy Greenhoff then showed the best piece of skill of the whole match, picking up a defensive clearance following an Arsenal corner, inside his own half, with his back to goal, and marked by two defenders. He wriggled clear of both McNab and Simpson on the halfway line and he raced clear.

His pace was startling, but so was Wilson's focus and reaction, with Greenhoff running one on one. Wilson came out to the edge of his area, forcing Greenhoff into an early shot, which was lifted over the diving Wilson, but it also flew just over the bar, beneath the Arsenal fans.

With 30 seconds of injury-time left, Arsenal had desperately piled forward for George Armstrong's right-sided corner. Frank McLintock headed firmly goalwards, but John Mahoney on the post cleared the ball away.

Penalty! Pat Partridge had seen a handball and he awarded a penalty-kick. Mahoney was inconsolable. Peter Storey was calm, though, against the World's best goalkeeper, and he just stroked the ball in past the shattered Gordon Banks.

With the very last kick of the match, Arsenal had levelled the scores at 2-2.

Four days later, on Wednesday 31st March, another massive 62,500 crowd again filled another huge ground, Villa Park, to capacity.

Stoke were a force spent, though, and Arsenal won the replay 2-0.

A total attendance of 361,289 had watched Stoke City's nine games during their great FA Cup run, at an average of 40,143 per game. Waddington had clearly succeeded in the second part of his initial mission as Stoke's manager…

Tony Waddington had pulled the crowds back to Stoke City.

Dave Sexton had pulled Osgood back to midfield. He'd also dropped Hollins into central defence, and then moved Webb over to right back, after Tommy Baldwin's entrance. Just minutes into the second half, Baldwin hit a shot that deflected off Denis Smith, and ran just wide of goal, out for a corner kick, following a fluent passing exchange between both Cooke and Hudson.

From Cooke's corner, Dempsey sent his header over Banks' crossbar.

George Eastham, the legend, hadn't had a great game. His old legs had regularly been caught in possession by the younger terriers, Hudson, Cooke and Garland. His stylish scheming and thoughtful passing had been afforded little time by the speed of the game on the heavy Wembley turf.

With just over a quarter-hour left, though, captain Dobing swept the ball out of midfield to Conroy, wide on the left. Conroy beat Webb, and he crossed from the edge of the area. John Ritchie headed down, and Greenhoff swivelled and volleyed sharply. Bonetti made a good save, but George Eastham pounced and he poked in the loose ball from the rebound.

30,000 Stoke fans went potty, massed behind Chelsea's goal, erupting into the most ferocious frenzy of noise, the likes of which had never been heard before during a Stoke City match.

Chelsea's fluent passing moves and quick breaks that had troubled Stoke so much during the first half, were now clearly affected by their second half re-shuffle, but also by Stoke City's greater defensive resolve in the second half.

With Osgood finding less freedom of space in which to torment the Stoke back line, Chelsea really went for it, anyway, throughout the last fifteen minutes.

Dempsey crossed incomprehensibly wide over to the right wing, when sent clear on goal by Ron Harris's through ball. Cooke then blocked team-mate Hudson's shot on the edge of the area, and Baldwin only just failed to connect with Dempsey's forward header to divert it past Banks.

Stoke defended grimly, stopping shot after shot. Osgood, Webb, Hudson, Garland and Baldwin were all thwarted by sharp saves, tackles, blocks, and toe-ins from Stoke's back eleven, while Chelsea assistant manager Ron Suart nervously smoked his cigarette alongside Dave Sexton.

Jimmy Greenhoff, with his face contorted in agony, after suffering knock after hard knock to his injured shoulder from Osgood's first half foul, went off with only five minutes remaining, replaced by Welsh international John Mahoney, to loud cries of "Greenhoff, Greenhoff, Greenhoff!" from the Stoke End of Wembley, acclaiming their match-winner and heroic ace.

The Stoke End of Southport's Haig Avenue acclaimed their match-winner and heroic ace, on Wednesday September 8th 1971, in the League Cup Second round. The huge 10,223 crowd had dwarfed Southport's average home attendance of 3,254.

Jimmy Greenhoff scored Stoke's winning goal to secure their 2-1 away win. They then despatched Oxford United in the Third round, after a replay, before their tremendous Fourth round match on Tuesday 26th October.

Stoke City drew 1-1 away at Manchester United, after Alan Gowling and John Ritchie both scored in front of a 47,062 Old Trafford crowd, before they also drew the replay 0-0 back at the Victoria Ground, in front of another massive 40,829 crowd, and with Sammy McIlroy starting his second ever match for United.

A week later, again at the Victoria Ground, 42,223 squeezed in for the second replay, and Peter Dobing and John Ritchie both scored to eventually overcome United 2-1.

In the Fifth round, Bristol Rovers' Eastville was completely filled to its outer walls, with a huge 33,624 crowd watching Stoke knock Rovers out of the Quarter-finals. Greenhoff, Smith, Bernard and Conroy all scored in a 4-2 win, sending a rampant Stoke City through to their second successive major Semi-final.

It was an epic Semi-final, as well, played against a dynamic West Ham United side, watched by a total of 170,665 fans over four matches. Stoke lost 1-2 at home, firstly, to Geoff Hurst's penalty kick and also Clyde Best's rocket, before they then won 1-0 away at Upton Park. John Ritchie had scored Stoke's vital leveller.

The away goals rule didn't count in the League Cup, back then, so a replay was played at Hillsborough. 46,196 watched a tight 0-0 draw on Wednesday 5th January 1972.

STOKE CITY		WEST HAM UNITED
Gordon Banks	1	Bobby Ferguson
John Marsh	2	John McDowell
Mike Pejic	3	Frank Lampard
Mike Bernard	4	Billy Bonds
Denis Smith	5	Tommy Taylor
Alan Bloor	6	Bobby Moore
Terry Conroy	7	Harry Redknapp
Jimmy Greenhoff	8	Clyde Best
John Ritchie	9	Geoff Hurst
Peter Dobing	10	Trevor Brooking
George Eastham	11	Pop Robson
John Mahoney	12	Peter Eustace

Three weeks later, on 26th January, Old Trafford hosted their Semi-final second replay, and 49,247 made the long trip up from the Potteries and East London.

An enthralling game, between two attacking sides of real strength, resulted in a five goal thriller. Early on, though, Hammers goalkeeper Ferguson suffered a nasty collision with Terry Conroy, and he was replaced in goal by Bobby Moore. West Ham played the rest of the first half with only ten men, then after just half an hour, referee Pat Partridge awarded a penalty to Stoke City, but Moore saved from Mike Bernard.

He couldn't hold onto the ball, though, and Bernard scored from the rebound.

West Ham emerged after half-time with a heavily bandaged Bobby Ferguson back in goal, but back to a full team, and they took the lead through goals from both Bonds and Brooking.

However, with their goalkeeper's vision badly affected, West Ham were punished by late goals from Dobing and Conroy. It was a classic Semi-final.

Stoke withstood a late battery from The Hammers, and Tommy Taylor's late header from Robson's corner was well saved by Banks.

Peter Osgood's header from Cooke's corner was well saved by Banks, and then Conroy won a corner at the other end for Stoke, after some great left wing running. Conroy's corner was headed in at the far post by Ritchie, but Houseman cleared off the line.

Mike Bernard then played an uncharacteristic awful back pass that Garland caught hold of, but Banks came out to block the shot on the edge of his area, crucially. Chris Garland lay, his face in the goalmouth mud, in disbelief.

Banks was fouled as the Chelsea corner flew in. He cleared with the free-kick, and then the final whistle blew.

Few teams have celebrated so joyously after a Cup Final triumph as Stoke City did that afternoon, dancing delightfully with the Cup as they applauded the Stoke fans applauding them. George Eastham, at 35 years and 161 days old, became the oldest ever Wembley winner. The team who'd brought their beautiful Wedgwood plate and its lovely design to Wembley, left with a major Cup, for the first time in 109 years.

As good as that Chelsea team were, and as much loved as they were, it was easy to feel as happy as Greenhoff, Banks, Smith and Conroy were, jigging genially, with unassuming euphoria, brilliantly bouncing.

Stoke City also reached the FA Cup Semi-finals in 1972, for the second successive season, and their third successive major Semi-final. After beating Chesterfield 2-1 in the Third round (Conroy,

Dobing), Tranmere were then knocked out after a Fourth round replay at the Victoria Ground, by 2-0 (Bernard, Greenhoff penalty).

Their 4-1 win over Hull in the Fifth round (Greenhoff 2, Conroy, Ritchie), then led to another sparkling Cup-tie against Manchester United in the Quarter-finals.

Jimmy Greenhoff's goal at Old Trafford earned Stoke a replay after George Best had scored United's goal, during their 1-1 draw.

49,097 really filled the Victoria Ground on Wednesday 22nd March 1972, just 2,283 below Stoke City's record home attendance, set against Arsenal back in 1937, back in the days when kids were ordered into the grounds on the shoulders of an adult, just to pack more in.

Goals by George Best, again, and then Denis Smith took the game into extra-time, and the squashed crowd went potty when Conroy scored Stoke City's winner, well into stoppage time. Arsenal, with Alan Ball now in their midfield, beat Stoke 2-1 in their Semi-final replay at Old Trafford, after drawing 1-1 at Villa Park. Stoke had been missing livewire Terry Conroy, though, with the dependable utility player Eric Skeels taking his place.

Eric Skeels was a Stoke City legend, despite having never had a regular position in their great years. A player in the mould of Nobby Stiles, he could play, and he could pass, but he was a workhorse who left nothing behind in the changing room whenever he played for Stoke. He could cover any of Marsh, Bloor, Smith or Pejic across their back line, as well as in midfield.

In 1969-70, he'd started thirty-four First Division games in five different positions in the team. Skeels holds the Stoke City club record of 507 football league games from 1960-76, and he played a total of nearly 600 competitive games in all competitions.

In May 1972, Everton paid Stoke £130,000 for their midfield star Mike Bernard. Bernard had played 136 First Division games for Stoke. Stoke City's League Cup glory, FA Cup run, and developing footballing elegance had raised Stoke's average home attendance to more than twenty-four thousand during 1971-72.

So in June 1972, Tony Waddington paid West Ham United £80,000 for their 1966 World Cup winner and hat-trick hero Geoff Hurst. Hurst had scored 180 goals in 410 league games for the Hammers, but he was still only thirty years old.

Stoke began the following season well, beating Crystal Palace 2-0 at home (Smith, Ritchie), but then they failed to win any of their next eight league matches.

On Wednesday 13th September 1972, Stoke City entertained 1.FC Kaiserslautern, in their first ever game in European competition. Only 22,182 had sadly watched their UEFA Cup First round first leg match at the Victoria Ground.

Even so, second half goals by Conroy, Hurst and Ritchie gave Stoke what appeared to have been a safe 3-1 lead, to defend a fortnight later.

At the Fritz-Walter-Stadion, though, without Banks, Ritchie or Mahoney, Stoke fell apart, and Kaiserslautern stormed to a 4-0 win, beating the Potters 5-3 on aggregate.

Their 5-1 hammering of Manchester City, Colin Bell, Francis Lee and Rodney Marsh, on Saturday 23rd September, broke their winless First Division sequence, after Jimmy Greenhoff had scored a hat-trick, with Conroy and Hurst completing the scoring. Despite this win, Stoke entered October still inside the First Division's bottom three.

During October, Stoke lost twice and won twice, including a 1-0 win over Leicester on the 28th, Geoff Hurst scoring their winner to lift Stoke out of the relegation zone.

However, on Sunday 22nd October 1972, the day after they'd lost 2-1 away at league leaders Liverpool, Gordon Banks lost control of his car, and he ended up in a ditch. As a result of the accident he lost the sight in his right eye.

After 487 First Division games for both Leicester and Stoke City, and also 73 games for England, Gordon Banks' playing career was over. He'd won the Football Writers' Footballer of the Year award in 1972, and the International Federation of Football History and Statistics eventually voted Banks as the second best goalkeeper of the 20th Century, behind Lev Yashin.

John Farmer, who had been Stoke City's goalkeeper for the two seasons prior to Banks' arrival in 1967, replaced Banks in goal, and he kept his place in their team until November 1974. Farmer had remained loyal to Stoke over the five seasons when Gordon Banks was first choice keeper, turning down several moves to other clubs where he would have been first choice. He went on to play 163 First Division games for Stoke City, and helped them to once again qualify for Europe, in April 1974.

Also in October 1972, during their 1-0 win over Leicester, club captain Peter Dobing had played his last game for Stoke. He was serving a nine week suspension, when he broke his leg, early in 1973, and was forced to retire at the age of thirty-four.

Peter Dobing had played 307 league games for Stoke City since 1963, scoring 79 goals. Including his time at Blackburn Rovers and Manchester City, prior to joining Stoke, he'd played 568 Football League games, and fifteen seasons in the top flight of English football.

There were no glorious Cup runs in 1973, nor no push for UEFA Cup qualification in the league. It was a battle against relegation all the way, with all hands on deck for the cause. Skeels, Jimmy Robertson and Sean Haslegrave were invaluable squad players, though, as Stoke struggled to keep their heads above rising water all season.

A good end to the season, winning six out of their last eight games, had finally lifted Stoke City to safety.

1973-74 initially brought no reprieve for Stoke. They won none of their opening eight games, and then only seven out of twenty-eight league matches. Stoke were down in seventeenth place on Saturday 16th February 1974, after drawing 0-0 away at Sheffield United.

Among their seven wins was a 2-0 home win over West Ham on 29th September 1973. That was George Eastham's 194th and final First Division match for Stoke.

Eastham's arrival in 1966 had begun the Potteries' renaissance, and their pass master and midfield marshal was thirty-seven years and six days old, when he'd played his last game. He was awarded an OBE in 1974, following his retirement.

George Eastham had played 525 league games for Newcastle, Arsenal and Stoke City, all of them First Division games.

Then, on January 12th 1974, Tony Waddington signed Alan Hudson from Chelsea for £240,000, smashing their club record fee. Hudson, Stamford Bridge's playmaker, had played 145 games at Chelsea, creating loads of goals, but scoring only ten.

On Saturday 23rd February, Stoke then hosted Leeds United in the First Division.

Leeds had been unbeaten during their first twenty-nine Division One matches, and they led the league by nine clear points.

39,598 attended what would be a pivotal performance for Stoke City.

Stoke were under-strength, without either Greenhoff, Conroy or Bloor, as indeed were Leeds United, minus Jones, Reaney, Eddie Gray or McQueen, but Leeds still sailed into a 2-0 first half lead, on a sunny afternoon. Billy Bremner and Allan Clarke had set them up nicely for their 20th league win of the season.

Stoke then turned on the style, over-running the Champions-elect in all areas of the pitch, with Mike Pejic pulling one back, before Alan Hudson scored his first ever goal in Stoke colours, equalising, just before half-time.

STOKE CITY		LEEDS UNITED
John Farmer	1	David Harvey
John Marsh	2	Terry Yorath
Mike Pejic	3	Trevor Cherry
Alan Dodd	4	Billy Bremner
Denis Smith	5	Roy Ellam
Eric Skeels	6	Norman Hunter
Jimmy Robertson	7	Peter Lorimer
John Ritchie	8	Allan Clarke
Geoff Hurst	9	Joe Jordan
Alan Hudson	10	Johnny Giles
John Mahoney	11	Paul Madeley

Stoke took advantage of Johnny Giles' absence, replaced by sub Terry Cooper due to injury, and then Denis Smith headed in a second half winning goal that fired up Stoke's sensational end of the season while, for a while, Leeds could not buy a win.

During the early part of 1974, Chelsea's Peter Osgood had been quoted as criticizing John Ritchie's style of play, allegedly stating that the big man could only score with his head.

John Ritchie, who'd always respected Osgood, like most football fans during the Seventies, was greatly hurt by those comments.

So, on March 16th 1974, Southampton visited the Victoria Ground, with their brand new £275,000 signing Peter Osgood, who was making his Saints' debut. Geoff Hurst gave Stoke the lead, but Alan Dodd's own goal had sent the teams in level at half-time.

The great John Ritchie rose to the occasion during the second half, though, showing the full gamut of his skills at exactly the right time. He first finished off Jimmy Greenhoff's through-ball, firing past Martin inside the Southampton area.

Then, Ritchie collected a Jimmy Robertson cross with his right foot, and he lobbed the ball over the nearest defender, onto his left foot without moving more than a couple of yards. The defender turned to recover, but Ritchie then lobbed it back over the defender's head again back onto his right foot, with which he shot, from the edge of the area, firing the ball high up into Martin's goal net.

Even that cracking strike was then bettered, as Ritchie beat two defenders, before dribbling around Eric Martin. He then stopped the ball on the goal-line. John Ritchie stopped by the ball, knelt down and then nodded the ball over the line for the most brilliant hat-trick. That 4-1 win sent Stoke up to mid-table in the First Division, and Peter Osgood had experienced first-hand, the great goal scoring talent of John Ritchie.

Stoke then repeated their end of season heroics from 1973, winning six of their last eight games, and drawing the other two, gaining fourteen points out of a possible sixteen.

They lifted themselves above Burnley on the very last day of the season, finishing in fifth place, and qualifying for the 1974-75 UEFA Cup.

John Ritchie was their top scorer with fourteen goals from twenty-six games as Stoke achieved their second-highest ever First Division finish. Geoff Hurst also scored twelve from thirty-five, and Jimmy Greenhoff nine from thirty-nine. Alan Hudson had scored three crucial goals during his eighteen games, including their winner as they won 1-0 away at his former club Chelsea, during Stoke's penultimate match.

John Farmer, and his defence of Marsh, Pejic, Smith, Bloor, Dodd and Skeels, had kept seven clean sheets from their last nine games, while conceding only two goals.

Tony Waddington had seen the signing of Hudson as the final piece of his jigsaw that would help Stoke City finally enjoy a proper League title challenge, and that now looked a realistic ambition.

On 9th July, Waddington even further strengthened his team by signing Sheffield United's creative winger Geoff Salmons for £200,000. Apart from Tony Currie, Salmons was regarded as the best player at Bramall Lane, and he'd played 180 league games for the Blades in six seasons.

Unfortunately, just as they'd been for the previous season, they remained without Terry Conroy for most of 1974-75, and then on Saturday 24th September, with Stoke City up in the First Division's top five, disaster really struck.

Stoke were playing away at league leaders Ipswich Town, when all-time club record goal scorer John Ritchie suffered a double leg fracture, which ended his career.

John Ritchie had played 269 First Division games in his two spells at Stoke, scoring 135 goals, and 171 in all competitions. He had been sold to Sheffield Wednesday in 1966 for a club record fee of £70,000, and then bought back for his second spell three years later for a bargain £25,000. Ritchie also still holds the club record for goals scored in the League Cup, eighteen of them.

He then ran a pottery business in Stoke, after his retirement.

John Ritchie died on Friday 23rd February 2007, aged sixty-five. A bronze bust of Ritchie was unveiled behind the Boothen End of the Britannia Stadium a year later by manager Tony Pulis, the second greatest manager in Stoke City's history.

On 18th September, Stoke City had hosted three-times European Champions Ajax of Amsterdam in the UEFA Cup First round first leg.

37,398 watched Stoke, in their second ever European adventure, take on players who'd graced the World Cup Finals during the Summer with their Total Football, Johnny Rep, Arie Haan, Rudi Krol and Piet Keizer.

Ajax took Stoke apart during the first half, but they led by just one goal, after Krol had given Ajax the lead. Stoke calmed down in the second half, and equalised late on through Denis Smith.

Two weeks later, Stoke totally dominated Ajax in Holland.

Marsh, Smith, Dodd and Pejic were barely troubled, and Hurst, Greenhoff, Hudson and Conroy all went close to winning the tie for Stoke, but they couldn't beat the goalkeeping brilliance of Piet Schrivers.

After a magnificent performance of which English fans could feel proud, Stoke City sadly went out on the away goals rule.

On November 21st 1974, Tony Waddington then signed England's brilliant goalkeeper Peter Shilton, from Leicester City, for £350,000, a new world record transfer fee for a goalkeeper. Shilton had played 286 league games for Leicester, and also twenty games for England, at that time.

Stoke led the First Division several times during the 1974-75 season, and they even beat the mighty Liverpool 2-0 on Saturday 31st March.

Conroy had scored both goals, with 45,594 swelling the Victoria Ground.

However, the massive loss of Ritchie proved too much of a loss during their run-in. Although Conroy had returned to score ten goals in just five matches throughout March, they'd lacked any top class attacking support for Jimmy Greenhoff, their top scorer with 14 goals from 39 games. Geoff Salmons also scored eight goals from 42 games, his best-ever season, while the ageing Geoff Hurst had scored eight from 31.

Stoke could not win any of their final three games, and they didn't score either, finishing just four points behind the Champions, down in fifth place again. They'd averaged crowds of over 27,000 at the Victoria Ground, though, and were the thirteenth most watched team in England, ahead of Derby, Ipswich and Wolves.

Peter Shilton had kept eleven clean sheets during his twenty-five league matches, and he made the PFA Awards First Division team of the year, along with Alan Hudson, but their failure to win the League Championship after the most open title race of all time had hit Stoke City hard.

Geoff Hurst was sold to West Bromwich Albion for just £20,000 in August 1975, after scoring 30 league goals in 103 starts for Stoke City.

He played only ten games for West Brom, though, before leaving English league football altogether, to finish his career with a season at Seattle Sounders in the NASL.

1975-76 was a mediocre season for Stoke. They were held to a 0-0 home draw by Second Division Sunderland, in the FA Cup Fifth round, with 41,176, their biggest crowd of the season, filling The Victoria Ground.

Sunderland won the replay 2-1, with nearly 50,000 inside Roker Park.

That was Stoke City's highlight of the 1975-76 season.

During 1976, the roof blew off the Butler Street Stand during a fierce gale. Repairs to the stand were expensive due to engineering technicalities, as the foundations of the corner of the stand were embedded deep into the bed of the River Trent, just yards behind the corners of the Butler Street and Boothen End stands.

Stoke City were subsequently forced to sell players to pay for the repairs.

In November 1976, Jimmy Greenhoff joined Manchester United for a bargain price of £100,000. Greenhoff had scored 76 First Division goals for Stoke in 274 games over seven seasons. He then scored Manchester United's winning goal in the 1977 FA Cup Final, and played nearly 100 First Division games for United over the following four seasons. His career fizzled out with Crewe, Port Vale and Rochdale into the Eighties, but Greenhoff had played a total of 465 First Division matches at Leeds, Stoke and Manchester United. He was undoubtedly Stoke City's talisman, though, the jewel in their crown between 1969 and 1976.

Then, on 14th December, Arsenal bought Alan Hudson for £200,000. Hudson had played 105 league matches at Stoke between 1974 and 1976.

He eventually settled back in the Stoke area after his retirement.

Finally, on 11th March 1977, Mike Pejic was sold to Everton for £140,000.

The greatest left-back in their history had played 274 First Division matches for Stoke City. The former England defender, from Chesterton, Staffordshire, had actually been dropped by England's caretaker manager Joe Mercer, during the Summer of 1974, "because he didn't smile enough."

Pejic played three seasons with Everton, before eventually retiring, after a career total of 360 First Division games.

That was the final straw for Tony Waddington, the longest serving manager in the First Division. He resigned on 22nd March 1977, disillusioned at seeing his masterpiece being broken up, firstly through injury, and then due to financial troubles. It was a sad day for all at Stoke City, and also the whole world of sport, in general.

He was, and always will be, the greatest manager in Stoke City's history, but there is still no statue of Tony Waddington at the Britannia Stadium.

Tony Waddington died, aged sixty-nine, on Friday 21st January 1994.

John Mahoney left for Middlesbrough during the Summer of 1977, following Stoke City's relegation, after playing 270 league games at The Victoria Ground.

The midfield anchor had also played 51 games for Wales, and he went on to help Swansea City into the First Division in 1981.

Peter Shilton also left in 1977 for Brian Clough's Nottingham Forest, for another huge fee of £250,000. Shilton had played a total of 110 league games for Stoke, and despite them being relegated in second bottom position, Shilton had kept fourteen clean sheets, while Stoke conceded just one more goal than fourth-placed Aston Villa.

Without either Greenhoff, Ritchie, Hudson or Hurst, though, Stoke had failed to score in twenty-four of their forty-two league matches.

During 1977-78, Shilton conceded only eighteen goals in 37 First Division matches, as Forest won the League Championship, and Peter Shilton won the PFA Player of the Year award.

Alan Bloor, Stoke's regular defensive rock alongside Denis Smith, also left The Victoria Ground during the following 1977-78 season, after playing 388 league games.

Bluto remained in the Potteries, though, playing for, and then managing Port Vale for one single season, before he retired from football to manage a carpet shop in Longton, Stoke-on-Trent.

Terry Conroy, their irresistible, yet inconsistent Irish winger, left in 1979 after 271 league games, although he'd scored only 49 goals. In sharp contrast to this very poor ratio, *White Legs* had scored thirteen vital goals in just 21 games during Stoke City's best-ever league season, 1974-75.

He played one season at Crewe, before changing for Waterford and Limerick, where he terminated his career.

John Marsh also left in 1979, after 355 league games for Stoke City in twelve years. *Jackie* is in eighth place on the club's all-time appearances list.

Alan Dodd left in 1982, after ten years at Stoke. The 1974-75 season was his best, though, when he missed only three First Division games, keeping Alan Bloor out of central defence, while also helping Stoke keep sixteen clean sheets in the process.

He then ousted John Marsh from the right back spot, playing a total of 356 league games for Stoke, before moving to Wolves.

Denis Smith was the backbone of Stoke City, and also the most broken-boned player in professional football. Norman Hunter once laughed off comments about his own Hard Man reputation, and he referred his interviewer to Smith.

"If you think I'm hard, go and look at that nutter down Stoke," Hunter suggested.

Denis Smith finally left The Victoria Ground for York City in 1982, having played 407 league matches in fourteen seasons.

He was the King of the Potteries, and a genuine Stoke-on-Trent legend.

Born in the Potteries, just like John Marsh, Alan Bloor, Alan Dodd and also Mike Pejic, Denis Smith had put success on the field for Stoke City ahead of concerns for his own personal safety, time after time, every time. "I was committed," he admitted. "I wanted to go and win the ball. At times I was perhaps foolish as far as injuring myself, but in the end I wanted to win."

After playing, Denis Smith managed seven clubs, but particularly York, Sunderland, Oxford and Wrexham. Between 1982 and 2007, he managed Football League teams for a total of 1,155 league matches, but he never, ever managed Stoke City, despite being offered the job more than once.

"It's very difficult being a massive Stoke fan, and then going back to manage the team you've always supported," Denis Smith said of his decisions to never manage Stoke City.

"If I'd come to Stoke and got the sack, that would've hurt me a great, great deal."

There has never been another Stoke City team like Tony Waddington's Stoke City team between 1967 and 1976. There was never one like it before, and, despite that brilliant 5-0 FA Cup Semi-final win over Bolton Wanderers in 2011, and their subsequent FA Cup Final defeat against Roberto Mancini's Manchester City, at Wembley Stadium, there has never been one like it since.

There probably won't ever be another Stoke City team like it.

CLOUGHIE: MAN OF THE SEVENTIES

I N 1972, DERBY COUNTY BECAME the best team in English football.

Their best ever team was crowned as Football League Division One Champions, in May, having beaten both Leeds United and Liverpool, with almost 40,000 packed inside their beautiful Baseball Ground.

Derby County had been Second Division relegation strugglers, though, sitting just a few points above relegated Rotherham, back in May 1968, only four years before, with only 15,000 and 16,000 die-hard hopefuls scattered sparsely around the Baseball Ground at their home defeats to Cardiff, Preston and Hull City.

To have entirely re-built a team, lifting them up from foot of the Second Division, and into one of the classiest teams in one of the most fiercely competitive and high calibre First Divisions in football history, and inside only four seasons, was nothing less than miraculous.

That miracle took a man with a strong belief in the pure way that he felt the game must be played, and a man with the vision that Bill Shankly and Sir Matt Busby had both had up at Liverpool and Manchester United.

That man was Brian Clough, and he had a belief, and a faith, in four fundamental factors in the foundations of his football team. Oh, and he also had a flaming good right hand man, too, to steer him away from mistakes, to support him and reassure him, when doubts ever arose, and to fully share his faith, his belief and his vision.

That man was Peter Taylor, and Brian Clough and Peter Taylor became the best management double act in the history of English football.

Their belief, their faith, focussed on four fundamental footballing factors: ***Harmony, Integrity, Unity and Solidarity.*** Those four wonderful qualities formed the foundations of their Derby County, and all of Cloughie's subsequent teams, and they effectuated their vision: Victory!

The four factors of Harmony, Integrity, Unity and Solidarity would result in ***Victory!***

It was that simple. That was Clough and Taylor's belief and vision, their wonderful approach to football, that was rewarded by the most miraculous four year rise in English football history, but they actually went and did it twice.

Clough was a motor mouth, opinionated and self-assured, with a talent for enraging, but also enlightening and inspiring those to whom he spoke, or spoke about.

"The voice of Brian Clough has been likened to the sound of rending calico," Peter Taylor had said of Cloughie's knack of equally riling and refining, of inspiring both revulsion and revelry, "but it can also be as rousing as a bugle call and change people's lives, as it did mine in the Autumn of 1965."

In October 1965, Brian Clough was appointed as manager of Hartlepools United, who were stuck right at the bottom of the Fourth Division, but he persuaded his former Middlesbrough team-mate Peter Taylor to join him. Taylor, seven years older than Clough, had already entered the world of football management, ahead of Clough, and he lead Burton Albion to their first major non-league honour, after winning the Southern League Cup in 1964.

Interestingly, forty years later, Brian Clough's own son Nigel was also managing Burton Albion, and he led them to almost certain promotion to the Football League, winning their second major non-league honour, the Conference title, before he, himself, then became Derby County manager.

Brian Clough had been the most prolific goal-scorer in the history of the Football League, hitting 197 goals in only 213 Second Division games for Middlesbrough between 1955 and 1961, when Peter Taylor was Boro's goalkeeper.

Clough then joined Sunderland in 1961, for £42,000, a record transfer fee outside of the First Division, and he continued to score fluently. He scored 53 goals in just 58 Second Division matches, while at Roker Park, before tearing cruciate ligaments in his right knee in a collision with the shoulder of Bury's goalkeeper, Chris Harker.

The injury ended Brian Clough's career, as although he attempted a comeback in 1964, two years later, after Sunderland had been promoted back to Division One, he was not the same player. He played just three more matches, before being forced to retire, at the age of twenty-nine.

Brian Clough had scored a total of 251 goals in 274 league matches. At 0.916 goals per match, he was the most prolific striker ever, and he'd scored the fastest two hundred goals in Football League history, a record that will never be broken.

Unfortunately, to Clough's total disdain, neither Middlesbrough's ambition, nor their defence did not match his own excellence. *Goals That Counted For Nothing*, he wrote, lamenting the failure of his home-town team to gain promotion to Division One, being held to 6-6 score draws, and subsequently resulted in his own failure to gain more than just two England caps in October 1959, alongside Bobby Charlton and Jimmy Greaves.

Brian used this disappointment to positive effect, though, as a manager, as he and Peter Taylor built his teams from the back, in the future.

In 1965, at thirty years old, Brian Clough became the youngest manager in the Football League.

"The old Fourth Division had just been blessed with genius," Clough said. "I'm kidding, honest," he insisted, "but I'm not far wide of the mark." He persuaded Peter Taylor to join him from Burton Albion, and a football partnership, a friendship, both professional and personal, was born, and it would remain unbreakable and unbeatable, for nearly thirty years.

John McGovern was a fifteen year old Grammar School boy, on trial at Hartlepools, when Clough and Taylor first arrived, and the players all lined up to meet their new manager, on the training ground. As they moved down the line, saying their hello's, McGovern was seen to have longer hair than the rest of the team, because he'd wanted to be Mick Jagger.

When Clough finally got to McGovern, at the very end of the line, he told him: "Stand up straight.

Get your shoulders back.

Get your hair cut.

You LOOK LIKE A GIRL!"

Clough and Taylor signed John McGovern, though, and they lifted Hartlepools to the safety of seventh-bottom position, by the end of their first season, and free of the re-election zone. Brian Clough went on to sign John McGovern on three further occasions, during his managerial career.

During their second season, Clough and Taylor had lifted Hartlepools to the edge of the promotion race, finishing in eighth place. It wasn't good enough for chairman Ernie Ord, though.

Hartlepools hadn't finished in the top half of the Fourth Division since 1957, but Ernie Ord gave Clough and Taylor the sack anyway.

"That horrible little bugger," as Clough described him, could not understand the good that he and Taylor had done for Pools. They had not only given the team a winning record, but they'd raised the media profile of the club, and they'd even painted and repaired the leaking roofs at Victoria Road, themselves, physically.

The season after Clough and Taylor were sacked, in 1967-68, Hartlepools, the team that *they* had built, achieved promotion for the first time in the club's forty-seven year Football League history.

Brian Clough developed a healthy dislike and distaste for Football League chairmen, after that episode, which served him well throughout his career. Cloughie's old friend, Len Shackleton, though, another Sunderland legend, *the very greatest of Sunderland legends*, had telephoned Derby County during the Summer of 1967. Len set Brian up for a meeting with Mr Sam Longson, the Derby County chairman.

Brian told Mr Longson that he would manage his club, but he would be bringing Peter Taylor with him, as his assistant.

On joining Derby County, at the start of the 1967-68 season, Clough and Taylor hadn't yet arrived at their five words that symbolised their belief and vision.

In 1967, their words weren't *Harmony, Integrity, Unity, Solidarity and Victory.*

Derby were a mess, having just struggled to avoid relegation to Division Three. Their words, in 1967, becoming Clough and Taylor's war cry, were *Observe! Expose! Replace!*

Only four players, Colin Boulton, Ron Webster, Alan Durban and Kevin Hector, were good enough to survive the cull and become first team regulars. Defender Peter Daniel and midfielder Jim Walker were also retained, but they became squad players.

Colin Boulton was a police cadet in his native Cheltenham, when Derby County signed him as a goalkeeper in 1964. He kept goal rarely before the arrival of Clough and Taylor, though, and he also kept goal rarely, in fact, after their arrival also, but he must have shown them something that they liked, because they kept him on, as a reserve, for over three years, before he finally became the club's regular number one.

Ron Webster, Belper-born, had been at Derby for nine years, when Clough and Taylor arrived, but he'd been the team's regular right back for six seasons.

Alan Durban had joined Derby County from Cardiff City, for £10,000, in June 1962, and he'd also made his Welsh international debut against Brazil, that same month, in June 1962. Famed for his long range shooting, he was converted into a dependable midfield engine, having previously played at inside forward.

Kevin Hector had scored 44 Fourth Division goals for Bradford Park Avenue, during the 1965-66 season, and he signed for Derby County in September 1966, for £40,000, having scored over one hundred goals for the West Yorkshire club. Hector scored sixteen Second Division goals during his first season at The Baseball Ground, and his goals were a major reason for Derby's survival.

Immediately upon his arrival at Derby County, Brian Clough returned to his old club Sunderland, and he paid £21,000 for their centre-forward John O'Hare.

O'Hare had scored fourteen First Division goals in just over a season at Roker Park, and he also scored in his first match for Derby, a 3-2 win over Charlton Athletic, with Hector and an own goal completing their narrow victory.

There were, though, only 19,000 scattered around The Baseball Ground.

Roy McFarland was also signed from Tranmere Rovers, for a bargain fee of £24,000, in August 1967. Clough and Taylor had arrived at McFarland's family home, after midnight, and asked his Dad to get him out of bed. McFarland was asleep, and asked if he could sleep on a move to Derby, but Clough couldn't risk that. He knew either Liverpool or Everton might persuade him away from Tranmere, so he and Taylor succeeded in getting him to sign there and then, with the helpful encouragement of McFarland's father.

On a roll, Derby won seven of their opening nine Second Division matches, topping the table on Wednesday 27th September, after their 4-1 hammering of Rotherham United, with their Hector and O'Hare partnership combining to score fourteen goals.

Alan Hinton had just had a superb season with Nottingham Forest, helping them to a runners-up place in the First Division, just four points behind Champions Manchester United, and ahead of Tottenham Hotspur on goal average.

A fast and direct winger, Hinton had scored a total of twenty-four goals in 112 First Division matches, at The City Ground, and on Friday 26th September, he joined Derby for just £30,000. With his big curly blonde hair, and his striking white boots, for which he became famed, Alan Hinton became labelled as **Gladys** by fans.

"What COLOUR'S your fucking HANDBAG, Gladys?" They used to sing at him.

Derby's form surprisingly dipped, disappointingly, after October, as Derby failed to win fourteen of their next sixteen matches, and they gained just nine points.

After their 4-0 defeat to Ipswich Town, on Saturday 14th October, Brian Clough sacked a tea lady who'd laughed about it. Disharmony, nor disunity, were no longer tolerated at The Baseball Ground. John O'Hare fired a hat-trick, however, as Derby beat Hartlepools in the League Cup, before scraping past Birmingham, Lincoln and the might of Darlington, to reach the Semi-finals of the League Cup, where they faced Don Revie's Leeds.

32,000 packed into The Baseball Ground, on Wednesday 17th January 1968, but Johnny Giles' penalty kick dampened Derby's Wembley dreams. One month later, Derby fought hard, and actually scored twice at Elland Road, through Kevin Hector and Arthur Stewart, but Eddie Gray and Rod Belfitt's brace finished them off, as Leeds United won 4-2 on aggregate, before beating Arsenal in the Final.

Peter Taylor had been invited to watch a seventeen year old defender, John Robson, playing for a youth team in Birtley, County Durham, during the winter of 1967-68, but he'd been warned that Robson was going for a trial at nearby Newcastle United the following week.

Impressed with Robson, Peter Taylor and Brian Clough bent the rules, by arranging a transfer on the Sunday after they'd watched him. It was forbidden to sign players on the Sabbath, so they arranged with John Robson's family and the secretary of his youth club, that Robson would sign a contract with Derby, and they sent a donation to both his family and the youth club.

With Webster, McFarland, Durban, Hinton, Hector, O'Hare, and now Robson in Derby's team, by April 1968, they limped out the remainder of the 1967-68 season, safe from relegation. On the last day of the season at The Baseball Ground, a crowd of just 20,000 watched their 1-3 home defeat by Blackpool, as they finished down in eighteenth place.

That crowd could never have foreseen the euphoric rise of their team over the next four seasons.

For the beginning of the following season, Clough and Taylor were greatly concerned at the lack of a natural leader to steer their team. Peter Taylor had an idea, a suggestion for Clough.

He knew of a grizzled, fearless Scottish veteran defender, who'd been a key player in one of the greatest post-war First Division teams, winning both the First Division title, and the FA Cup, *twice,* but who was on the verge of leaving English football, altogether.

Dave Mackay was about to join Hearts, as their player manager, but he then received a surprise visit from Brian Clough, at White Hart Lane.

Taylor had the eyes and ears, and he persuaded Clough that Mackay was the man they needed, really needed, but Cloughie had *the stomach and the balls.*

It took just two hours of persuasion from Cloughie, two hours of talk about the team whom Mackay'd never played against, nor even heard of, but the team which he was about to transform.

Derby County signed Dave Mackay for a nominal fee of £5,000 from Tottenham Hotspur.

As the fee was so cheap, they were able to pay Mackay £250 a week, plus bonuses that actually made him a better paid player than either George Best, Denis Law or even Bobby Moore.

Over three years, Mackay cost a total of just over £50,000, and both Clough and Taylor saw the signing of Mackay as the best day's work they ever did.

Dave Mackay went straight into the Derby County team as their sweeper, with Roy McFarland playing either behind or ahead of him at centre half, and with Webster and Robson on either flank.

The 1968-69 season started just the same as the previous season had ended, though… not very well. Derby failed to win any of their first five games, and they gained only three points.

Their 2-0 victory over Oxford United, though, on Saturday 31st August, was a turning point.

The team was starting to play with *harmony, integrity, unity* and *solidarity.* Roy McFarland and John O'Hare scored both goals to win the match, with a clean sheet, and igniting a nineteen match league and cup run, during which Derby lost only twice, that took them to the top of Division Two, and also to the League Cup Quarter-finals, for the second successive season. They won twelve of those nineteen matches, gaining twenty points, and keeping twelve clean sheets.

Over 34,000 packed The Baseball Ground for the penultimate match of this run, against lowly Birmingham City, on Saturday 26th October 1968.

Birmingham City were missing former England striker Fred Pickering, through suspension, and a second half goal by club record signing Willie Carlin, who'd joined from Sheffield United in August, for £63,000, secured the points. Derby were in third place, but only one point behind the leaders Middlesbrough.

DERBY COUNTY		BIRMINGHAM CITY
Les Green	1	Jim Herriot
Ron Webster	2	Ray Martin
John Robson	3	Winston Foster
Alan Durban	4	Malcolm Page
Roy McFarland	5	David Robinson
Dave Mackay	6	Malcolm Beard
Jim Walker	7	Trevor Hockey
Willie Carlin	8	Jimmy Greenhoff
John O'Hare	9	Geoff Vowden
Kevin Hector	10	Johnny Vincent
Alan Hinton	11	Phil Summerhill
Richie Barker	12	Bert Murray

Richie Barker, who'd played under Taylor at Burton Albion, and the Brewers' record goal scorer with 157 goals, replaced Hinton late on. Barker scored twelve league goals in 38 matches at Derby County, before he moved to Notts County in 1969. He went on to manage Stoke City, in the First Division, for two and a half seasons during the Eighties, between August 1981 and December 1983.

Clough and Taylor had also signed John McGovern for a bargain price of £7,000, at the end of September, from their old club Hartlepool United.

McGovern had played over seventy matches at Victoria Road, and he'd been an inspiration in Hartlepools' promotion to Division Three, six months earlier.

John McGovern made his Derby County debut on Saturday 9th November, in their 2-1 home win over Charlton Athletic, with O'Hare and Hector scoring. That win lifted Derby up to second in the table, just one point behind Millwall.

Derby hammered local rivals Chesterfield 3-0, in the League Cup First round, and then Alan Hinton had an amazing night, scoring four goals, including two penalties, during their 5-1 spanking of Stockport County, on Wednesday 4th September.

In the Third round, County's new back four kept a clean sheet at Stamford Bridge, against Chelsea's ferocious forward line of Peter Osgood, Charlie Cooke, Alan Birchenall and Tommy Baldwin. In the replay, on Wednesday 2nd October, with over 34,000 inside The Baseball Ground, Mackay, Durban and Hector all scored to secure a 3-1 win over their First Division top five opponents.

A fortnight later, Derby County travelled to Everton, with nearly 45,000 inside Goodison Park. But Yet Again, their defence kept a clean sheet against a Top Class attack of Joe Royle, Alan Ball, Jimmy Husband and Johnny Morrissey.

Over 34,000 again filled The Baseball Ground on Wednesday 23rd October, for the replay, as Kevin Hector's eighth goal of the season secured a tight, hard-fought 1-0 home victory.

In the Quarter-finals, on Wednesday 30th October, another sell-out crowd of 35,000 again filled the ground, for the visit of Third Division Swindon Town. Derby were missing Alan Hinton, though, due to a calf strain, and they were unable to break through Swindon's disciplined defence, and one week later, on Bonfire Night, Don Rogers' firework of a goal, a rocket from the edge of the penalty area, sent the 26,000 County Ground crowd sparkling into celebration.

Don Rogers and Peter Noble were a tremendous attacking partnership during that 1968-69 season, scoring fifty league and cup goals between them, and helping Swindon gain promotion to Division Two for only the second time in their forty-nine year Football League history.

In the Semi-finals, Swindon Town then beat Burnley 6-5, over three matches, and Noble's classy performance persuaded Burnley's Jimmy Adamson to continue watching him, and the Clarets eventually paid Swindon £50,000 for him during the early Seventies.

In the League Cup Final, Rogers' brilliant brace won Swindon Town their first, and so far only, major trophy after a 3-1 victory over a disappointing Arsenal team.

Derby finally led the Second Division after their 2-1 away win at second-placed Crystal Palace (McFarland, Carlin), on Saturday 30th November, and between the end of November and the middle of March, Derby County lost only twice out of sixteen Second Division matches, and they easily maintained their lead at the top of the table.

Then, in a marvellous and masterly display of majesty, the Rams won all nine of their final league games of 1968-69, finishing seven points above runners-up Crystal Palace, who were themselves six points clear of third-placed Charlton Athletic.

Derby were promoted back to the First Division, for the first time in sixteen years, on Saturday 5th April, following their 5-1 home win over Bolton Wanderers (McFarland, O'Hare, Hector, Carlin, Wignall), with four games remaining.

Kevin Hector and John O'Hare had scored thirty goals between them, but Derby were a team with no star attackers, no superstars, defending as a team, and attacking as a team, and Alan Hinton, Alan Durban, Roy McFarland and Willie Carlin also contributed a combined total of thirty-seven league and cup goals.

Derby County scored sixty-five goals during their Second Division Championship campaign, but they conceded only thirty-two. Brian Clough's super defence had kept twenty-three clean sheets.

Cloughie's reward for his team was to make no changes for their opening game of the 1969-70 season, on Saturday 9th August, at home to Burnley. A 29,459 crowd had welcomed First Division football back to The Baseball Ground, but Burnley's defence, well marshalled by Colin Waldron, hung on for a goalless draw. Three days later, though, on a Tuesday night, Roy McFarland scored the Rams' first goal in the First Division, during their 1-0 win away at Ipswich Town.

COVENTRY CITY		DERBY COUNTY
Bill Glazier	1	Les Green
Mick Coop	2	Ron Webster
Chris Cattlin	3	John Robson
Brian Hill	4	Alan Durban
George Curtis	5	Roy McFarland
Jeff Blockley	6	Dave Mackay
Trevor Gould	7	John McGovern
Ian Gibson	8	Willie Carlin
Neil Martin	9	John O'Hare
Willie Carr	10	Kevin Hector
Dave Clements	11	Alan Hinton

Nearly forty thousand packed into Coventry City's Highfield Road, on the second Saturday of the season, in a battle between two of the footballing purists of English football: Brian Clough's Derby against Noel Cantwell's Sky Blues, who were themselves enjoying the finest Football League season of their eighty-six year history.

While Derby County were at full strength, Coventry were missing their *Two Ernies,* Hunt and Machin, through injury, and while the tall Neil Martin scored with a great, towering header, from Dave Clements' cross; Roy McFarland made up for his slip, with a crucial equaliser, heading in Alan Durban's corner. It was a delightful game, though, between two young teams of great adventure, energy, discipline and quality, both in the ascendancy, and no player from either team was booked.

As one-all draws went, it was a Minor Classic.

"Discipline was crucial," Brian Clough wrote. "Without discipline you have no team. The rules are the rules. They might be good or they might be bad, but the rules enable us to have a game. My players learned to understand that referees were doing their best, and honestly."

Derby County went unbeaten, over their first ten matches, beating both Everton and Southampton at The Baseball Ground, and winning away at Ipswich, West Brom and Newcastle. On the morning of Saturday 20th September, they were in second place in Division One, behind leaders Everton.

37,728 had packed into their ground on Saturday 6th September, as O'Hare and Hector both scored to beat the league leaders 2-1, but when Bill Nicholson's Tottenham Hotspur arrived two weeks later, a Club Record Attendance of 41,826 overfilled The Baseball Ground, with ten thousand disappointed fans locked outside, as Derby enjoyed their greatest ever Saturday.

DERBY COUNTY		TOTTENHAM HOTSPUR
Les Green	1	Pat Jennings
Ron Webster	2	Phil Beal
John Robson	3	Cyril Knowles
Alan Durban	4	Alan Mullery
Roy McFarland	5	Mike England
Dave Mackay	6	Peter Collins
John McGovern	7	Jimmy Pearce
Willie Carlin	8	Jimmy Greaves
John O'Hare	9	Alan Gilzean
Kevin Hector	10	John Pratt
Alan Hinton	11	Roger Morgan
Frank Wignall	12	Tony Want
(rep. Durban)	(rep. Morgan)	

Mackay was facing his old team, watching for the lightening quick breaks of both Greaves and Gilzean, and matching them, break after break. Durban, Hector and Carlin fired Derby into a 3-0 half-time lead, and then Durban scored his second before being replaced by Frank Wignall.

Frank Wignall had joined in January 1969, from Wolverhampton Wanderers, for a fee of just £20,000. He'd scored fifteen First Division goals, in only thirty-two matches for Wolves, but prior to that, he had played twice for England, beside Roger Hunt and Jimmy Greaves, in late 1964, scoring twice. Wignall had scored forty-seven goals for Nottingham Forest, in four years, helping them to second place in the First Division, back in 1967.

John O'Hare completed the scoring, for a tremendous 5-0 rout of Spurs, as the packed Baseball Ground, and all of Derbyshire, was bouncing, from Thorpe Cloud to Winnats Pass, from

Chatsworth House to the Kinder Edge, and up and down The Heights of Abraham, all night long, and all around the beautiful Peak District.

Everton also won 3-0, away at Ipswich, though, to deny Derby County top spot. Everton, with nineteen points from eleven matches, had a goal average of 2.75.

With one point less in second place, Derby's goal average was an incredible 4.75, having scored twenty-five goals, but they'd conceded only six.

Alan Warboys brought Derby back down to earth on Saturday 27th September, as he scored the only goal of the game during Sheffield Wednesday's shock 1-0 win, with over 45,000 inside Hillsborough.

Kevin Hector and a Fitzpatrick own goal, in either half, helped Derby beat Manchester United 2-0, at the start of October, with 40,000 again packed into The Baseball Ground. But Everton just kept on winning, and on Wednesday 8th October, Coventry effectively ended Derby's Championship dreams for 1970, beating them 3-1.

Neil Martin, Jeff Blockley and a Roy McFarland own goal did the damage in front of another huge Baseball Ground crowd of 39,880.

A four game run without a win ended on Saturday 1st November, when Derby smashed Bill Shankly's Liverpool 4-0, in front of 40,993. McGovern, O'Hare, and Kevin Hector's two goals destroyed Liverpool's great defence of Lawler, Smith, Yeats and Strong.

By Wednesday 19th November, though, Derby were down to fifth in the league, eight points behind Everton, but now also trailing reigning Champions Leeds, Liverpool and Manchester City.

Then, by late November, The Rams had dropped to seventh place, below both Chelsea and Coventry City, but then they won 1-0 at Crystal Palace at the start of December, with Hector scoring, to return to the top five, where they remained.

County lost just one of their remaining twenty-one Division One matches, and eventually finished fourth behind Everton, Leeds and Chelsea, to qualify for the Fairs Cup competition in 1970-71, after beating Wolves 2-0 (Wignall, Hennessey), on Saturday 4th April.

Terry Hennessey had arrived from Nottingham Forest, for a club record transfer fee of £110,000, at the beginning of February. Regarded as one of the very best defensive wing halves in English football, throughout the Sixties, and capped over thirty times by Wales, Hennessey had gone straight into Derby's team against Chelsea on Wednesday 11th February. His Welsh international teammate, Alan Durban, and Kevin Hector both scored to earn a 2-2 with the form team of the second half of the 1970 season, and one of the best ever Chelsea teams, after Alan Hudson and Peter Osgood had given the Blues a 2-0 lead, early in the first half.

Tall and balding, Terry Hennessey had played nearly 340 First Division matches for both Forest and Birmingham, and his aerial presence at corner kicks and free-kicks added punch to Derby's attack.

"A classy Welsh international, and an unflappable sweeper," Peter Taylor described Hennessey. "We saw him as the eventual replacement for Dave Mackay."

He'd set up Hector's equaliser against Chelsea, with a flicked header.

Kevin Hector and John O'Hare scored thirty-two league and cup goals between them, but they were well-supported by Durban, Hinton, Carlin and McFarland, who'd scored thirty-seven combined goals.

Derby County, after conceding just six goals during their first eleven First Division matches, had allowed only 37 goals from 42 matches in their first season back in Division One, the second best defensive record behind Champions Everton.

Derby's average attendance of nearly 36,000 was also the sixth highest in the whole Football League, during 1969-70, as a truly spontaneous, fever pitch furore for the club had swept all over Derbyshire.

The future for Derby was brighter than ever in their history, though never again would they fill their ground with such crowds, or with such regularity.

On the Wednesday following their win over Wolves, though, Derby County faced a joint FA and Football League Commission, after the club was charged with administrative and financial errors. The Commission found Derby guilty of eight charges, and fined the club £10,000, but more significantly, they expelled them from all European competitions in 1970-71.

That expulsion, which punished the players for administrative failures by the club's board, had simply increased the sense of bitterness between Brian Clough and the directors. The team and supporters were all devastated to suffer such a substantial blow, after a successful and magical first season back in the high life again.

Derby County unsuccessfully attempted to consolidate their top five position the following season. More importantly, though, Clough and Taylor further developed their plans for the club to prepare for a greater achievement than European qualification.

On the opening day of the 1970-71 season, Derby's half-time 1-0 lead, away at Chelsea, provided by John O'Hare's goal, was overturned by Ian Hutchison's second half brace, but they then won three games in a row, to go fourth in the table.

A draw away at lowly Huddersfield was then followed by home defeats to both Coventry and Newcastle United, though, before Mike Channon and Ron Davies both scored two goals each, as Southampton hammered Derby 4-0 at The Dell, on Saturday 12th September.

Things were going very badly. Terry Hennessey was admitted into hospital for a cartilage operation, and he missed most of the rest of the season. Brian Clough didn't waste any time, though, strengthening his midfield resources.

Archie Gemmill had played over one hundred league matches for Preston North End, over the three previous seasons, having arrived in England in 1967 from his home town Scottish club, St Mirren. Only five feet and five inches tall, Gemmill's tremendous work rate, natural ball skills and enthusiasm more than made up for his lack of height.

Everton, though, were also particularly interested in signing him, and they'd laid a superior offer onto the table. There were definite benefits for Gemmill signing for Everton. They were the reigning Champions, and moving to Goodison Park meant they wouldn't have to move home, away from the Lancashire coast.

Also, Archie Gemmill's wife Betty, six months pregnant with their son Scott (who also went on to play under Clough in the 1990's), really couldn't stand Brian Clough.

Again, Clough had break from the mould, and in classic Clough and Taylor style, they both travelled to Gemmill's home, and Cloughie poked his smiling face around the wall of Betty Gemmill's kitchen.

"I believe you hate me," he joked. The ice was immediately broken.

Clough enthused about the natural beauty of Derbyshire's Peak District, Bakewell, Dovedale, Matlock, the Blue John Caverns, and the Dark Peaks. Clough actually got into Gemmill's head, as a player, talking about Gemmill's future with Scotland, cups, league titles, European football, and also a guaranteed first team place, of which Gemmill certainly couldn't be assured at Everton.

"I believed him," Gemmill admitted. "No…., more than that, I believed *in* him."

Archie Gemmill signed for Derby County, in a £60,000 deal, and he made his debut away at West Bromwich Albion on Saturday 26th September.

Three weeks later, Peter Taylor introduced Willie Carlin to Leicester City manager Frank O'Farrell, and he broke Carlin's heart, by balancing the books and selling him for £40,000. Carlin had scored fourteen goals in 89 league matches for Derby, and he never forgave Taylor for his decision to sell him. Derby won only three of their eighteen First Division matches from late September to Christmas.

On Boxing Day 1970, though, 34,068 snuggled into a freezing cold, snowy Baseball Ground for the visit of Manchester United. The match turned out to be not only one of the games of the season, but one of the Games of the Decade, in fact.

Dave Mackay's cracking, driving, direct free-kick, from just outside the area, gave Derby the lead, and then, Frank Wignall doubled their lead, firing home from close range, after Jimmy Rimmer had saved Roy McFarland's shot from ten yards out.

Into the second half, Denis Law pulled one back for United, flicking a great header, from Willie Morgan's right wing cross, past Les Green. Then, Bobby Charlton's right sided corner was touched in, on the goal-line, by the bearded poacher George Best.

Bobby Charlton then took another corner, from the left side, as United piled on the pressure, to save their manager Wilf McGuiness's job, and Denis Law powered in another super header.

Archie Gemmill's through ball was met by Kevin Hector, whose decisive finish again levelled the scores. Gemmill then ran onto Hector's through ball, and he squeezed his clipped shot just inside Rimmer's near post.

Then, with time running out, Charlton's right wing corner was headed in by the leaping Brian Kidd.

That sensational 4-4 score-line couldn't save Wilf McGuinness's job, though.

He was sacked three days later, but it was also Les Green's last game in goal for Derby County.

On Saturday 2nd January 1971, Colin Boulton was chosen to play in Derby's 2-1 win away at Chester City, in the FA Cup Third round, having played only twenty-five league games, for The Rams, in seven years.

Colin Boulton kept his place for their home game against Wolves, a week later, back in the First Division. Over the next five years, he missed just two out of 209 First Division matches, as well as collecting two Football League Championship medals. He eventually played 272 league matches for Derby County, 247 of them First Division games.

1970-71 was going to be Dave Mackay's last season for Derby County, though, and Brian Clough knew he needed a central defensive replacement.

He made the decision, without even telling his chairman until the deal was done, to sign Sunderland's Colin Todd, who he regarded as "the best technical player in England."

Only five feet and nine inches tall, Colin Todd had played over 190 league matches for Sunderland, and his consistently sound performances were a feature of their rich style of play. At Derby County, his partnership with Roy McFarland, at the heart of their defence, was to become the finest in English football.

On May 1st 1971, Dave Mackay played his last game for Derby County, before moving to Swindon Town as player-manager. He did return to The Baseball Ground two and a half years later, as manager, and he led The Rams to their second First Division title in 1974-75, after bringing in Francis Lee, Bruce Rioch, Henry Newton and Rod Thomas.

At thirty-six years old, Mackay had played in all 42 of Derby's First Division matches during 1970-71, one of only three ever-presents, along with Hector and O'Hare.

He'd played a total of 122 league games for Derby County, in his three great years at The Baseball Ground. Mackay had been invaluable in developing their young team into a confident force of fluent, forward-moving, fundamental football.

Roy McFarland considered Mackay to be the best player he ever played with, for either Derby or England, but he was ready to be as effective and inspirational a captain as Mackay had been.

Derby County finished 1970-71 in a very mediocre position of tenth place. Not only had their goals scored total dropped, and their goals conceded risen, but average crowds at The Baseball Ground had also dropped by over five thousand, to just 30,878.

John O'Hare was Derby's top scorer, with thirteen First Division goals, while Hector and Hinton provided a combined total of twenty-one goals, in support. Their defence had still kept fifteen clean sheets, though, despite being a little leakier than in their first season back in the top flight.

With Terry Hennessey back to full fitness, but now providing cover for central defence and midfield, Derby started 1971-72 excellently, going unbeaten in their first twelve league matches, winning five of them.

The twelfth of those matches was their home game against Spurs, on Saturday 9th October 1971, with 35,774 rammed inside The Baseball Ground.

DERBY COUNTY		TOTTENHAM HOTSPUR
Colin Boulton	1	Pat Jennings
Ron Webster	2	Ray Evans
John Robson	3	Cyril Knowles
Colin Todd	4	Alan Mullery
Roy McFarland	5	Peter Collins
John McGovern	6	Phil Beal
Archie Gemmill	7	Alan Gilzean
Alan Durban	8	Steve Perryman
John O'Hare	9	Martin Chivers
Kevin Hector	10	Martin Peters
Alan Hinton	11	Jimmy Pearce
Frank Wignall	12	John Pratt

Derby were only one point behind leaders Manchester United, but Spurs were also enjoying a strong start to the season, just four points behind the Rams, but with a game in hand.

Spurs were missing their defensive rock, Mike England, through suspension, but for Derby, this was the very first match, with Terry Hennessey still missing through injury, when their classic Championship-winning eleven had played together.

After a goalless first half, Chivers and Pearce both scored for Spurs, but Derby's central defensive duo of Todd and McFarland levelled the match. Tottenham had an immense forward line, supported and supplied by Mullery, Peters and Perryman, while their talented left winger Pearce was always dangerous, and that 2-2 draw, given their come-back, was a great result for Derby.

Crucially, Derby County won ten of their final fourteen matches, after February, losing only twice, and they won the title by one point after Leeds had lost against Wolves at Molineux, just two days after they'd beaten Arsenal in the FA Cup Final, and without their top scorer Mick Jones.

Colin Boulton and Kevin Hector played in all 42 of Derby's Championship winning First Division matches, but six of their players had started forty, or more games.

Furthermore, out of a possible 420 league games, Boulton, Webster, Robson, McFarland, Todd, McGovern, Gemmill, O'Hare, Hector and Hinton had missed a combined total of only twenty-two games, throughout the season.

Alan Durban, Derby's oldest player at thirty years old, had started thirty-one games.

Derby's regular defence of Boulton, Webster, McFarland, Todd and Robson missed a total of just eleven matches, suffering no suspensions, and they kept twenty-three clean sheets, while allowing only thirty-three First Division goals.

Their quick and clinical attack force of Hinton, Hector and O'Hare had scored a combined forty First Division goals.

Harmony, Integrity, Unity and Solidarity, those great words, had truly imbedded themselves into Derby County, and been rewarded, justly, with Victory.

Brian Clough and Peter Taylor's belief and vision had made dreams real.

Derby County missed Ron Webster for three months, at the start of the 1972-73 season, and they lost eight of their sixteen matches, sitting in a lowly sixteenth place, on Saturday 7th October.

They'd also missed Alan Durban for most of the season. Durban, thirty-one years old by then, was in and out, but mostly he was out, and he started just eleven games during 1972-73, before moving to Shrewsbury Town in September 1973, for £12,000.

Alan Durban had played 346 league matches for Derby, in eleven years, scoring ninety-one goals. He eventually became Shrewsbury's player-manager in 1974, before taking over as manager of First Division Sunderland, between 1981 and 1984. He'd also played 27 matches for Wales, and he was the second member of Derby County's Championship winning team to leave The Baseball Ground.

John Robson was the first title-winning player to leave Derby County. **Robbo** had left for Aston Villa, for £90,000, back in December 1972, after Clough and Taylor had bought left back David Nish from Leicester City. Robson went on to play 144 league matches for Villa, missing only one match during 1974-75, as they won promotion back to the First Division. He also won two League Cup winner's medals, after Villa beat Norwich in 1975, and then Everton in 1977.

At the age of just twenty-seven, however, Robson was forced to retire from football after developing Multiple Sclerosis, during the 1977-78 season.

John Robson died, aged only fifty-three, on Wednesday 12th May 2004.

David Nish had joined Derby County for a British record transfer fee of £225,000, back on Friday 25th August 1972. Nish had become the youngest ever captain in a Wembley Cup Final, when Leicester played Manchester City in 1969, and he'd played 228 league matches for Leicester City, before his twenty-fifth birthday.

The cultured and stylish full back went on to start 184 First Division matches for Derby, winning a League Championship medal in 1975, before leaving for Tulsa Roughnecks, in the NASL, along with both Colin Boulton and Roger Davies, in 1979.

Another signing that Clough had made, for their 1972-73 season, was Roger Davies, a six feet and four inches tall giant of a striker. Elegantly skilled, as well as very tall, Davies had arrived at The Baseball Ground from Worcester City, in a £15,000 cash deal, a British record transfer fee paid to a non-league club.

In the European Cup, Derby achieved more success than they did in the First Division. McFarland and Gemmill scored in their 2-0 home win over Zeljeznicar Sarajevo in the First round, before winning the away leg 2-1, beneath 60,000 hostile Bosnian Yugoslavs, with their firecrackers and bonfires.

Hinton and O'Hare had both scored to complete a 4-1 aggregate win.

A tougher task awaited Derby in the Second round, as former European Champions Benfica visited The Baseball Ground. 38,100 fans filled the ground, and they celebrated a night to remember.

Alan Hinton's left wing cross was headed down, into the net, by Roy McFarland, and Kevin Hector then volleyed Derby into a 2-0 lead, after McFarland had headed on Hinton's right sided corner kick. Hector then flicked on for John McGovern to fire Derby into a 3-0 half-time. Peter Daniel was playing in place of the injured Webster, and the Derby back four kept Eusebio at bay in the second half.

Colin Boulton was magnificent at the Stadium of Light in Lisbon. 75,000 jeered and whistled every Derby touch, roaring on their red shirted national Champions, but Eusebio, Vitor Baptista, Simoes and Artur Jorge all failed to beat the former Cheltenham police cadet. Only Ajax, and now Derby County had stopped Eusebio scoring in the last twelve seasons of European football.

In the FA Cup Third round, on Saturday 13th January, Roger Davies scored his third goal for Derby, as they won 1-0 away at Peterborough United, with a big crowd of over 22,000 inside London Road. Next, though, Derby had an epic Fourth round tie with Tottenham Hotspur.

At The Baseball Ground, on Saturday 3rd February, with only thirteen minutes remaining, Martin Chivers scored to put one of Tottenham's feet into the Fifth round.

Spurs' back four of Kinnear, England, Beal and Knowles had been barely troubled all afternoon, and Roger Davies had not had a good game, but Cloughie, despite having warmed up substitute Tony Parry on several occasions, kept faith in him. With five minutes left, Davies toe-poked home from the edge of the area to earn Derby a replay at White Hart Lane.

Three days later, on the Wednesday night of 7th February, nearly 53,000 packed White Hart Lane to bursting point for the visit of the reigning Champions, who'd risen to fifth in the First Division, by then, behind Liverpool, Leeds, Arsenal and Ipswich Town. That replay between Spurs and Derby was one of the very best matches of the Seventies.

Spurs were also enjoying a good run in Europe. As UEFA Cup holders, they had knocked out Red Star Belgrade, 2-1 on aggregate, back in December. In December, though, they'd also reached the League Cup Final, after beating Wolves 4-3 on aggregate, and England teammates Martin Chivers and Martin Peters had scored a combined forty-one league and cup goals, before the end of January.

After twenty minutes, Chivers fired home Cyril Knowles' low cross, after the full back had broken free down the left wing.

Derby County then piled on the pressure, hitting the bar from Kevin Hector's shot, and McGovern, Davies and Gemmill all went close to equalising, but Spurs actually doubled their lead just after half-time, when Alan Gilzean headed against Colin Boulton's bar, from Chivers' long throw, but he beat the keeper to the rebound, and nodded Tottenham 2-0 up.

Hector halved Tottenham's lead with a lobbed shot that just dipped under Pat Jennings' bar, but Tottenham then went 3-1 up after John O'Hare was harshly judged to have handled the ball. Mike England hammered home their penalty kick.

With just over ten minutes left, Brian Clough replaced Terry Hennessey with the more attacking Alan Durban, and almost immediately, the Tottenham defence lost their focus and failed to clear.

Roger Davies fired through the thickly crowded penalty area, before with just five minutes remaining, John O'Hare crossed, and Roger Davies volleyed home, high into the roof of the Spurs net.

Derby County were in the ascendency as the game went into extra-time.

After a goalless first period, amidst an electric atmosphere, Roger Davies lifted his six feet and four inch frame, high above his marker Mike England, and he met Kevin Hector's corner perfectly, heading home his hat-trick just as the second period began.

Spurs chased the game, but a long ball out of the Derby defence was chased by Hector, beating Tottenham's offside trap. As Jennings rushed out, Hector placed the ball beyond him, and completed one of the greatest FA Cup comebacks since the Matthews and Mortensen 1953 Final, winning 5-3 after being 3-1 down with just ten minutes remaining.

If there was one game when Roger Davies became a true County player, that was it.

In the Fifth round, at home to QPR, 38,100 packed the walls of The Baseball Ground, as Kevin Hector hit a first half hat-trick, and Roger Davies then added another, as a devastating display of attacking football destroyed the Second Division high flyers. Derby took their foot off the accelerator in the second half, and QPR pulled a couple of goals back, but Derby reached the Quarter-finals, following their 4-2 win.

Gordon Jago, the QPR manager who was, himself, building a super team at Loftus Road, had said that Derby had attacked with a quality and "the sort of football we have never met before. We came up to play the best team in the country."

In the European Cup Quarter-finals, Derby travelled to Czechoslovakia, on Wednesday 7th March, for their first leg match at Spartak Trnava.

Horvath gave Spartak a 1-0 win, but a good defensive performance, as well as two or three crucial saves by Colin Boulton, provided a good opportunity for the Rams to reach the Semi-finals, a fortnight later.

In the FA Cup Quarter-finals, Derby were drawn at home against their nemesis. 38,350, the largest crowd of the season, filled The Baseball Ground for the visit of Leeds United, on Saturday 17th March. While Leeds were at full strength, Derby were still missing Alan Hinton, out due to a groin injury, since mid- February.

It was a tight, high quality match, but Leeds played a perfect game, and Peter Lorimer's blast, while Allan Clarke was in an offside position, but not interfering with play, was all they needed to advance to the Semi-finals.

Four days later, Alan Hinton returned to the Derby line-up for the second leg of their European Cup Quarter-final tie against Spartak Trnava. Archie Gemmill worked the ball out of the busy midfield traffic, on the heavy Derby mud, and he played it out wide right, to John McGovern on the grass. McGovern's low cross was fired home sharply by Kevin Hector, to level the tie. Hector also volleyed home Alan Hinton's left wing cross, from outside of the box, to put Derby 2-1 up. As Spartak attacked in numbers, knowing one goal would put them through, on away goals, Derby defended desperately and determinedly, as they could do, and did just enough to hold on.

Three weeks later, on Wednesday 11th April, 72,000 packed out the Communale Stadium in Turin, for Derby County's European Cup Semi-final, first leg, match away at Juventus. Derby were again without Alan Hinton, and Derby-born Steve Powell took his place.

Steve Powell had made his debut for County in October 1971, just one month after his sixteenth birthday, in their Texaco Cup tie at home to Stoke City. Powell played only occasionally during Derby's two League Championship winning seasons, in 1972 and 1975, but he did play for Derby until 1985, by which time he'd played 420 league and cup games for the club, placing him in the top ten of most appearances in Derby County's history. Powell was also voted as Derby's Player of the Year in 1979.

JUVENTUS		DERBY COUNTY
Dino Zoff	1	Colin Boulton
Luciano Spinosi	2	Ron Webster
Gianpetro Marchetti	3	David Nish
Giuseppe Furini	4	Alan Durban
Francesco Morini	5	Roy McFarland
Sandro Salvadore	6	Colin Todd
Franco Causio	7	John McGovern
Antonello Cuccureddu	8	Archie Gemmill
Pietro Anastasi	9	John O'Hare
Fabio Capello	10	Kevin Hector
Jose Altafini	11	Steve Powell
Helmut Haller	SUB	Peter Daniel

Juventus started with seven members of Italy's World Cup Finals' teams from either 1970 or 1974, but Derby competed well in front of a coldly and brutally hostile crowd. Jose Altafini, though, who'd scored nearly 200 Serie A goals in less than 400 games, opened the scoring for Juve in the twenty-eighth minute.

With Roger Davies missing for Derby, due to a slight groin strain, John O'Hare returned to his old role as centre-forward, partnering Kevin Hector, and he had one of his best ever games, against their strongest ever opponents.

Two minutes later, O'Hare received the ball from Hector, on the edge of the area, and he measured a beautifully balanced wall pass back to Hector, who side-stepped two Italian defenders and finished classily past Dino Zoff, one of the three best goalkeepers of the Twentieth Century.

It was the first ever goal scored by any English club away in Italy, in the European Cup.

With the score still 1-1, at half-time, the fireworks truly started. As the teams went into their changing rooms, Peter Taylor spotted the Juventus substitute, Haller, going back into the West German referee's room. Helmut Haller had been seen in the referee's room for a good half hour before the match. Both referee Gunther Schulenberg, and Haller, who'd played and scored for West Germany during their 1966 World Cup Final defeat against England, were laughing and joking.

Peter Taylor was enraged, and he caught up with them and asked them, "I speak German, gentlemen. Do you mind if I listen, too?" Helmut Haller jabbed Taylor in his ribs, bending him double, then called out to officials and police, who shoved the Derby assistant manager against a wall, and demanded to see his passport. Taylor had thought he'd be arrested, and miss the second half, but John Charles, the former Juventus and Leeds United legend, who'd travelled to Turin as an adviser to the English Champions, then stepped in.

John Charles used his presence and his prestige to influence the Italian police, and he remained very calm, while also telling Taylor not to surrender his passport. Taylor was released, but the game had already taken a very sinister turn away from Derby's control of the game.

Archie Gemmill had been booked, for nothing except trying to keep the ball in play on the bye line, while Roy McFarland was also booked for jumping for a high ball, that resulted in an accidental clash of heads with Cuccureddu.

Those two bookings meant that Gemmill and McFarland, the only two Derby players with bookings to their names, were both suspended for the second leg.

John McGovern insisted, "this referee was giving every decision to the Italians. I was almost brought to tears by the decisions being made."

He emphasised "the last time I had cried was when I was eleven, and I lost my dad. We'd been cheated in front of all the UEFA officials, the television cameras, the crowd."

Derby County's players had been conditioned to say "yes, no, and thank you" to referees, and so, no complaint was ever made to the referee, on the pitch, but the decisions were heavily favouring the Italians. Derby County, the fairest of all First Division clubs, had over forty free-kicks given against them, mostly unfairly, while Juventus were penalised on less than ten occasions. With just 24 minutes remaining, the German sub Haller set up Causio for a 2-1 lead. Then, in the eighty-third minute, Altafini made the score 3-1.

Jose Altafini, one of Italian football's all-time legends, became a commentator on Italian television, after retiring, and his voice became popular in England, through his internationally famous catchphrase "*GOLACCIOOOOOO!*", after it was used on Channel 4's *Football Italia*, during the Nineties.

Altafini was not the villain, though. That was Haller, for whatever he did during that half-time interval. Even if he did do nothing, he shouldn't have been in the referee's changing room, and to get himself off the hook by trying to get Taylor arrested was just dirty.

After the game, Brian Clough was absolutely livid. He remained absolutely livid for the rest of his life, and he came out with his infamous rant at the awaiting Italian press gang.

"I will not talk to any cheating Italian bastards," he told them. "No cheating bastards do I talk to."

Even so, Derby County's away goal gave them a good chance, a fortnight later, on Wednesday 25th April, at their packed Baseball Ground. With over 35,000 inside and welcoming Roger Davies back to Derby's team, Cloughie had a headache as to how he'd replace his captain and also his classiest midfielder. John O'Hare moved back into Archie Gemmill's position, while Peter Daniel directly replaced Roy McFarland. Alan Hinton had also returned to the left wing spot, and the fresh-faced Steve Powell, who'd been very impressive in Turin, replaced Alan Durban in midfield.

With the scores still 0-0, at half-time, despite Derby being entirely on top, and Juventus defending like demons, after Clough had ordered the pitch to be well and truly watered, it seemed only a matter of time before The Rams created a breakthrough.

They waited until just eleven minutes, after half-time. Kevin Hector was tripped up by Luciano Spinosi, inside the Juve area, but Alan Hinton, normally lethal from the penalty spot, dragged his kick well wide of Dino Zoff's goal.

Six minutes after that penalty miss, Roger Davies was sent off for a head butt on Morini, and the tie was then over for Derby. Juventus went on to lose to Johan Cruyff's Ajax in the European Cup Final, while Derby won their last three First Division matches to finish seventh, just one point behind European qualification.

1972-73 had ended up as a disappointment for the defending Champions, but injuries had blasted huge gaps into the first team throughout the season. Only Boulton, Nish, McFarland, Todd, McGovern and Hector had been regular starters right through the season.

On Sunday 5th August 1973, Brian Clough had his famous back page headline published in the Sunday Express, stating that Leeds United should be relegated for their poor on-field behaviour.

This had soured relations between Cloughie and chairman Sam Longson even further, while director Jack Kirkland was also constantly hounding and harassing Peter Taylor.

And although Derby enjoyed a decent start to 1973-74, gaining fifteen points from their first twelve matches, and having beaten Manchester United away, on Saturday 13th October, to go third in the table, just two points behind second-placed Burnley, relations had slipped to such a bitterly uncomfortable point that Clough and Taylor offered their resignations. Club officials had urged them to stay and fight, but their resignations were accepted by the majority of the board.

They were both ordered out of the club, with neither a thank you nor a handshake offered.
"It was the biggest professional mistake of my career," Clough regretted.
"We should have stayed, and ridden the storm… If we'd stayed at Derby, they would have been the Manchester United of the present day."

Clough and Taylor had certainly left Derby County in a very great state. They were among the top three clubs in England, and the board had been left with £250,000 in the bank.

Sure, they'd spent money on players, but during their ninety First Division matches at the Baseball Ground, since they'd been promoted from Division Two, Derby had attracted an average home crowd of over 32,000, double their average attendances before Clough and Taylor took over.

Over that period, only Manchester United, Liverpool, Everton, Leeds United, Arsenal, Tottenham, Manchester City and Chelsea had attracted higher attendances. They were all clubs in huge cities, though, with immense grounds, each with the capacity to hold up to 60,000. Derby County were a provincial club, who had never lived near these heights before. They'd been Division One runners-up back in 1930, and again in 1936, and they won the first FA Cup Final after the War, but they had regularly attracted their biggest ever crowds during the reign of Clough and Taylor.

Roy McFarland, their captain, their League Championship winning captain, handed a letter to Sam Longson, signed by the entire first team squad, asking for the reinstatement of Clough and Taylor.

After their letter had received no word of reply, McFarland had led his team, rampaging through The Baseball Ground offices, bitter that they'd been brushed off, banging their fists on the boardroom door. The board were believed to have been hiding behind the bolted door.

McFarland and the rest of the team staged a sit-in protest at the ground, on Tuesday 23rd October, after it was announced by the club that they had appointed former captain Dave Mackay as the new manager. The players were professionals, though, and despite them reputed to have threatened not to play at West Ham on the following Saturday, they played, and earned a decent goalless draw, as Mackay praised his new team for their professionalism.

Roy McFarland was one of several players who would never play under Clough or Taylor, ever again. He played a total of 434 league games for Derby County, between 1967 and 1981.

The second player to have been signed by Clough and Taylor, Roy McFarland was the greatest captain in Derby's history.

McFarland also became the most capped player in their history, in Rome, on Wednesday 17th November 1976, having earned his 28th England cap as England lost 2-0 to Italy in a World Cup qualifier. His season-long injury between 1974 and 1975, though, at the very start of Don Revie's reign as England manager, had ruined his chances of playing over fifty matches for his country.

Colin Todd, McFarland's partner in defence, played his twenty-seventh, and final, international match in May 1977, as England beat Northern Ireland 2-1 in Belfast. In Todd and McFarland's combined 58 matches for England, though, they played as central defensive partners on just three occasions, a ridiculous statistic, considering they were the First Division's best defensive partnership for five years after 1971.

On the first occasion, on Saturday 11th May 1974, England beat Wales 2-0 in Cardiff. Four days later, England beat Northern Ireland 1-0 at Wembley Stadium, again with both McFarland and Todd at the back, but McFarland suffered his awful injury during that match, and he was ruled out of football for eleven months, just as Todd and McFarland had looked set to be right at the heart of England's 1976 European Championships' campaign.

The third time occurred in Bratislava, eighteen months later, on October 30th 1975, when Czechoslovakia won 2-1, to effectively ruin England's qualification chances. The damage was done, though, not in Bratislava, but at Wembley eleven months earlier, when Revie selected a confusing team that could only draw 0-0 with Portugal.

Colin Todd played 293 First Division matches for Derby County, between 1971 and 1978, winning the PFA Player of the Season award in 1974-75, after The Rams won their second First Division Championship title. He joined Everton in 1978, for one season, before playing for Birmingham City for three years.

In August 1982, Todd re-joined Brian Clough, at Nottingham Forest, when he was thirty-three years old, and he played 34 matches during 1982-83, including nine clean sheets, as Forest qualified for the UEFA Cup. He played only two games during the following season, however, and retired after over 640 Football League games.

Todd's defensive partnership with McFarland was easily the greatest in Derby County's history, and remains among the very best in the history of the First Division, or the Premier League.

Ron Webster played his 455th and final league match for Derby County on Saturday 10th September 1977, coming on as a substitute for Leighton James, during their 1-1 draw away at Chelsea.

At thirty-four years old, Webster retired from league football, having played for his local team for his entire career. Ron Webster is second-placed, behind only Kevin Hector, on the Football League appearances list for The Rams.

In May 2010, Webster was voted as Derby's greatest ever right back on County's official website. In an all-time eleven, Webster was joined by Boulton, Nish, McFarland, Durban, Gemmill, Hinton and Hector. Controversially, Igor Stimac was voted into the eleven, ahead of Todd, but I suppose they couldn't just put the whole of Clough and Taylor's team in?

Kevin Hector's total of 486 league matches for Derby County is an all-time record. He finally left in 1978, after twelve years at The Baseball Ground, having scored 147 goals in 430 league matches. After messing about in the NASL for three years, for Vancouver, where he scored fifteen goals in 1979, as the Whitecaps won the NASL Championship for the first and only time, he then returned to Derby County in 1980. The Rams had been relegated to the Second Division by then, but Hector played a further 56 league games for the club, scoring just eight goals, before retiring in 1982.

Alan Hinton, "the best two-footed crosser" that Peter Taylor ever saw, scored sixty-three goals in his 253 league matches for Derby, between 1967 and 1975, before he played for two seasons in the NASL, during 1977 and 1978. He was offered the job of managing Tulsa Roughnecks in 1979, and he brought Boulton, Nish and Davies from his old League Championship winning team to Oklahoma!, as well as Sheffield United's Alan Woodward.

From 1980, Alan Hinton managed Seattle Sounders for three seasons, and then finally settled at home in Washington State, where he became widely known as *Mr Soccer*. Still white haired, he now broadcasts as a local radio expert soccer analyst, on Seattle Sounders matches in the MLS.

Roger Davies scored twelve goals in 39 matches, as Derby County won the First Division title in 1974-75, under Dave Mackay. He left Derby in August 1976, for Belgian League side Club Bruges, and scored twenty-one goals from just 34 games, as Bruges won the Belgian league and cup double.

Davies also won the Belgian Player of the Year award, in 1977, and he scored four goals in four European Cup matches, during the Autumn of 77, helping Bruges into the Quarter-finals, en route to a Wembley Final, against Liverpool in May.

He returned to England in December 1977, though, having been signed by Frank McLintock to boost Leicester City's hopes of avoiding relegation from Division One. Roger Davies and Leicester were unsuccessful, though. He scored only six goals in twenty-six league matches at Filbert Street.

Recruited by Alan Hinton at Tulsa Roughnecks in 1979, he followed Hinton to Seattle, during the following Summer. Roger Davies scored twenty-five goals for Seattle Sounders, in 1980, in only 29 matches. His great height and superior skills outclassed most defences, and he was voted as the *MVP* of the NASL that year. Davies played in Seattle for three seasons, and he scored a total of forty goals from eighty-seven games, during his four years in North America.

Roger Davies is still celebrated as a cult hero in Derby, and he now commentates on their matches at Pride Park, on local radio.

In spite of the players' revolt at The Baseball Ground, and the angry demonstrations of Derby's fans, as well as the buzz that had lifted Clough's popularity way above that of the Derby County board, Peter Taylor knew that they could not go back.

The Story of the Damned United

On Thursday 1st November 1973, Clough and Taylor accepted an offer from Brighton and Hove Albion's chairman, Mike Bamber, to become joint managers at The Goldstone Ground. They need never go hungry, again.

For Clough, life in Brighton was a complete paradox.

Mike Bamber was "the pleasantest and finest chairman," that he ever worked for.

Brighton and Hove Albion, though, were about the worst football team that he ever managed.

They were lingering just above the relegation zone of the Third Division at the time of Clough and Taylor's arrival, and crowds immediately rose significantly at The Goldstone Ground.

16,000 watched their 0-0 draw with York City, on their first Saturday in charge, but within three days, at the end of November, the degree of difficulty facing them became very apparent. Brighton and Hove Albion Football Club suffered the worst two consecutive results, in their entire history.

On Wednesday 28th November, having battled for a home goalless draw in their FA Cup First round match on the previous Saturday, non-league side Walton and Hersham then hammered Brighton 4-0 away, in the replay at the Goldstone Ground.

Then, on the following Saturday, on the first day of December, nearly 11,000 watched Bristol Rovers, Alan Warboys, Bruce Bannister and all, thrash Brighton 8-2, again at the Goldstone, and also with ITV's *The Big Match* cameras present.

Clough and Taylor brought in four new players, a goalkeeper, a left back, a defensive midfield player, and also a right back. And in the New Year, results did improve.

In February and March, Brighton went six games unbeaten, winning four in a row, including a wonderful 2-1 home win over Hereford United, in front of 17,000, on Saturday 10th March.

At the end of the season, Brighton finished eight clear points above the relegation zone. But for Clough and Taylor, they would surely have been doomed.

After Leeds United had won a magnificent second First Division Championship trophy, finishing fourteen points above Dave Mackay's third-placed Derby County, Don Revie was appointed as the new England manager on Thursday 4th July 1974.

Sixteen days later, Brian Clough left Brighton, after he'd been offered the job as Leeds United manager. He had asked Taylor to go with him, but Taylor was loyal to Mike Bamber, and he refused to betray that loyalty.

Less than twelve months after his highly-publicised headline statement, that Leeds should be relegated for the behaviour of their players, Brian Clough was manager of those same players.

During the Summer of 2008, while queuing up in HMV, in Norwich, I found myself standing next to a meshed display stall filled with dozens of copies of the same paperback book. It was on offer at £2.99, so I picked it up, and flicked through the pages, as I recognized the blanked out faces of Billy Bremner, David Harvey and Paul Reaney on the cover, being led out at Wembley by Brian Clough, all with glum faces.

Waiting to pay for the new Sigur Ros CD, I found something compelling about the style of David Peace's The Damned Utd, so I bought it there and then.

Once home, I read it inside four nights, and then I read it again. Afterwards, I bought and read the autobiographies of Allan Clarke, Norman Hunter and Paul Madeley.

The book, The Damned Utd, sent me on a rollercoaster journey over the next two years, buying football programmes, magazines, and also Topps and A & BC football cards, from the early Seventies, re-living my childhood.

I would not be writing this, now, if I hadn't read The Damned Utd.

It's a **"*fiction based on works of fact*"**, and though many of the discussions that took place in the book may not have been real, they may well have took place. It basically chronicled the 44 days during which Clough was Leeds United manager, segued between the rise of him from the end of his playing career, through Hartlepool, and to Derby County, and heavily features his dislike of Don Revie which grew and grew.

It's a great book, possibly one of the greatest ever written on the theme of football, but I'm aware that some despised it, notably Brian Clough's family, and Johnny Giles.

I can accept that, and understand it, but as the book did not leave me, personally, feeling any less about the main characters in the story, and instead it mostly enhanced my views of them, I cannot accept or understand how the book, however provocative, can be despised.

The film, however, the film **The Damned United**, that was released a year after I'd bought the book, and to which I had been very much looking forward to seeing, was an entirely different matter.

I will discuss the film, but first let's concentrate on the facts of Brian Clough's short time in charge of Leeds. On Tuesday 6th August 1974, he paid a club record fee of £250,000 to Nottingham Forest for their striker Duncan McKenzie. McKenzie had scored twenty-eight league and cup goals for Forest, in 1973-74, helping them to the brink of the FA Cup Semi-finals, before some Newcastle fans invaded the possibility.

Four days later, Leeds met Liverpool in the Charity Shield, at Wembley, and after being hacked several times, mainly by Johnny Giles, Kevin Keegan turned round and thumped Billy Bremner.

The two players were sent off for fighting, but as both Keegan and Bremner left the pitch, they pulled off their shirts and threw them to the turf.

On 17th August, the first Saturday of the season, Stoke City hammered the reigning Champions 3-0 at The Victoria Ground. Clough reacted to this, two days later, by signing both John O'Hare and John McGovern from his old club Derby County, for a combined total of just £125,000.

John O'Hare had scored sixty-five goals in 248 matches for Derby, but he'd dropped behind Kevin Hector, Roger Davies and Francis Lee at The Baseball Ground. Brian Clough's first signing at Derby had become his second signing at Leeds.

John McGovern, who'd been Clough's first signing as a manager, had played 190 league matches at Derby, but likewise, he had lost his place in Dave Mackay's team to Bruce Rioch and Steve Powell.

On Wednesday 21st August, QPR beat Leeds 1-0 at Elland Road, after Gerry Francis' early goal, but then, on the second Saturday of the season, Birmingham City were the visitors to Elland Road, on the only good day of Brian Clough's time at Leeds.

This was a match that Leeds could not, and did not fail to win. This was Brian Clough's Leeds United, minus the dropped Duncan McKenzie, and they ran the show from the start.

Gallagher's clearance hit the referee, and Sbragia, City's eighteen year old debutant, was too slow to get to the ball before Allan Clarke. The England striker was just too quick for Sbragia, and he fired a classy finish, from just outside the area, past Latchford.

LEEDS UNITED		BIRMINGHAM CITY
David Harvey	1	Dave Latchford
Paul Reaney	2	Malcolm Page
Trevor Cherry	3	Archie Styles
John McGovern	4	Howard Kendall
Gordon McQueen	5	Joe Gallagher
Norman Hunter	6	Ricky Sbragia
Peter Lorimer	7	Alan Campbell
Allan Clarke	8	Trevor Francis
John O'Hare	9	Kenny Burns
Johnny Giles	10	Bob Hatton
Paul Madeley	11	Gordon Taylor

The two new signings had decent starts, but especially O'Hare, who put himself about among the Blues defence, playing well alongside Lorimer and Clarke.

Four days later, Billy Bremner and Kevin Keegan were both suspended, by an FA Disciplinary Committee, until the end of September, for their dismissals at Wembley. Bremner was effectively out for eleven matches, and he never played under Clough again.

It didn't get any better. After drawing 1-1 away at QPR, on the evening before that fateful FA Committee hearing, with Terry Yorath scoring Leeds' second goal of the season, they then lost 2-1 at Manchester City, on Saturday 31st August. Leeds United, the reigning Champions, were fourth from bottom of the First Division, and only a point above the relegation zone.

On the fourth Saturday of the season, Leeds were held to a 1-1 draw, at Elland Road, by lowly Luton Town. It was probably the worst moment of John McGovern's career.

He was booed and jeered by the home fans, and he never played again for Leeds United.

John McGovern said of his experience at Leeds United, in response to suggestions that players had frozen him out, that there was "never any hostility from the players to (himself), John O'Hare or Duncan McKenzie, but there was a cold, icy atmosphere at the club."

Three days later, Clough left McKenzie, O'Hare and McGovern out of his line-up, in Leeds' League Cup Second round match away at Huddersfield. He played Mick Bates in Bremner's position, and his Leeds United team finally had a familiar Don Revie look about it.

Peter Lorimer scored to earn a 1-1 draw against the team that was bottom of the Third Division.

On Friday 13th September 1974, Leeds United announced that they had sacked Brian Clough. "I think it's a very sad day for Leeds and for football," Clough told the press afterwards.

On that Friday night, Yorkshire TV broadcast an interview with Clough, on their acclaimed Calendar programme, but they surprised him at the last minute, by placing a chair next to him, and then presenter Austin Mitchell accompanied Don Revie to that chair.

In an electric live studio discussion, the clear dislike that each man had for the other made for scintillating and compelling viewing. Austin Mitchell, obviously favouring his beloved Mr Revie, finally asked Clough, "who's going to touch you with a barge pole, now?"

Don Revie smirked. Clough loved that question, though. Almost every team in the land, he replied, pointing to his record.

He said everyone could see that Leeds United had not given him a chance to do his job, in just 44 days.

In all fairness, Leeds United should have had a longer game plan. It obviously wouldn't have worked like a dream, straight off, and they should have had a contingency plan for a period of bad form at the start of Clough's period in charge.

They didn't.

Don Revie was a failure as an England manager, becoming renowned for rejecting skill, flair and innovation, and preferring work rate, instead.

He picked a series of jumbled teams, sometimes picking four centre-backs in his back four, and England failed to qualify for the Quarter-final stages of the 1976 European Championships.

By the time he finally departed, for the Middle East in 1977, he'd left it virtually impossible for his successor, Ron Greenwood, to get England to the 1978 World Cup Finals in Argentina.

Brian Clough had a more successful future.

Don Revie had been the most successful manager in Leeds United's history, building a team, just as Clough had done at Derby, that would probably never be bettered.

"I hate Revie and Bremner, for what they did," Vanessa told me, on Sunday 5th April 2009, when we were driving away from watching The Damned United at High Wycombe.

"I never knew they were such shits," she added.

I almost stopped the car, but just replied "don't take everything that film showed as real."

The book had never made me feel like that. I found it appalling that the film visually portrayed certain key characters in a deliberately bad light, sometimes bending over backwards to do so, even changing history, with the primary intention of prejudicing the viewer against those characters.

That isn't something that came out of David Peace's novel.

There are at least as many historical errors, or made up scenes, in the film, The Damned United, to allow an average of more than one for every minute of the film.

There are, of course, several minor mistakes, like wrong numbers on players' backs during matches, and others where players are mentioned after matches that they hadn't even played in.

Most of the more glaring errors can be easily forgiven, such as Clough parading O'Hare, McGovern and Mackay as new signings for Derby County, at the same time, when all three players were signed at different times over a fourteen month period.

They just allow for a smoother narrative. It's understandable that film makers can't get bogged down in ensuring every scene shown was chronologically correct, and little matters like Allan Clarke scoring in their 1968 FA Cup tie against Derby, when he didn't join Leeds until eighteen months later, have to be overlooked.

However, there are two or three moments during the film that I found highly objectionable, and mainly concerning the portrayal of Billy Bremner. The first view of Bremner, during the film, is of him smoking, smoking while on the Leeds United training ground.

I'm aware that more players smoked cigarettes in the Seventies, and they probably did have smoking breaks, but the film shows only Bremner smoking, amongst Hunter, Giles and the rest.

I feel that it instantly influenced the viewer in a negative way towards Bremner, and it's possible that this was one of the film's intentions.

If you think I'm being a little harsh, just a little later on, Billy Bremner's character is shown scratching his testicles during the National Anthem, prior to the 1974 Charity Shield.

"What upset me was that it portrayed as if Billy was a trouble maker," said Allan Clarke, of his former captain, "which couldn't be further from the truth. It was absolute rubbish, that. That upset me, that did."

The whole premise of the film is the aversion that Brian Clough develops towards Don Revie, after Revie had reputedly ignored Clough after their FA Cup Third round tie at The Baseball Ground. Clough had had the pitch prepared beautifully for the visit of Leeds, re-painted the doors, polished the corridors and the away team's changing room. He even produced a pair of cut crystal glasses and a vintage bottle of Bordeaux, just for the visit of Mr Revie.

He did all this, but he was then blanked by the Leeds manager, before, during and after the match.

That match was played at Elland Road, though, and not at Derby County. It was a slur on the character of Brian Clough, anyway, that the reason he'd disliked Revie so much, as stated in the film, is because of this supposed snub, even if it had happened.

Brian Clough was a stronger character than that, to have experienced, as he was on the up, many moments where he wasn't recognised.

The book details several incidents that add to Cloughie's professional disdain of Revie, including his fielding of a Leeds reserve side against Derby, back in 1970, ahead of their European Cup Semi-final against Celtic.

The film illustrates just that one example, when the pride of Clough was hurt by the arrogance of Revie, plus one other, very false incident.

The most offensive error from the film, though, was included, I can only assume and suggest, for the solitary purpose of prejudicing viewers against Leeds United.

With Leeds United the visitors to The Baseball Ground, just four days before Derby's European Cup Semi-final first leg match in Turin, against Juventus, Sam Longson made the effort to complain to Clough, who was planning to field a full strength team against Leeds. He asked Clough to "manage his resources."

In the film, Clough refused Longson's request, and he fielded his best available first eleven. Leeds United, the dirty bastards, went hell for leather, in the mud and torrential rain, flying two-footed into tackles, hacking down every Derby player.

Stretcher bearers carried heavily bleeding players off the field, after some horrific and vitriolic challenges by Leeds United.

Then, to rub salt into wounds, of which there were many, Billy Bremner went over, smiling, smirking even, at Clough and Taylor, shaking their hands and wishing them good luck in Europe.

"You bloody fool!" Longson yelled at Clough, after the match, with the Derby County changing room and corridor resembling a First World War Red Cross tent.

After losing 3-1 to Juventus in midweek, Clough blamed "the brutality of Leeds United," but commended his players, as his "reserve team" had just played the Italian Champions, due to his long injury list.

It was a total fabrication.

Leeds United won 3-2 away at Derby County on Saturday 3rd March 1973, five and a half weeks before the Juventus match. Derby had suffered no injuries in that match, and no substitutions had been made. Of the team that faced Leeds, only David Nish was missing from Derby's line-up against Leicester, a week later. Derby had no match on Saturday 7th April, the day of the FA Cup Semi-finals, on the Saturday before their match in Turin, and apart from Alan Hinton, out since February, and Roger Davies with his slight groin problem, Derby played Juventus with a full-strength team.

On the Saturday before their crucial European Cup Semi-final second leg tie, in their 1-1 draw at home to West Ham, Clough did indeed field a weakened side, resting Boulton, Webster and Durban, while giving Moseley, Parry and Daniel rare starts.

Derby County's exit from the European Cup had nothing to do with Leeds United, but 100% more to do with a chat between one West German to another West German in an out of bounds changing room, before the match, back in Turin.

On a positive note, the performances of Jim Broadbent, Timothy Spall and Colm Meaney as Longson, Taylor and Revie were top class, and as Brian Clough, Michael Sheen might have pulled off one of the finest portrayals of his increasingly illustrious acting career.

His Yorkshire TV debate with Meaney as Revie, at the end of the film, was truly gripping, and should have been longer. *The Damned United* could, and should have been a great football film, up there with the very greatest of all sports movies, but the imbalanced way in which it illustrates certain people, and manipulating the truth in doing so, damns it as an experience for me.

My main worry is that, in forty years' time, when Michael Sheen will be Sir Michael Sheen, the high quality of the performances of the four lead cast members will have propelled the film to classic status. The airbrushing of all the positive points of Leeds United, and Billy Bremner in particular, out of the film, providing a simple good guys and bad guys story, will be disregarded as irrelevant.

I believe the story, and Billy Bremner's side in the story, deserved better.

It is a good piece of entertainment, but it isn't *Eight Men Out* or *Remember The Titans*, when it really could have been.

Tom Hooper scrapes a seven out of ten from me.

After United….. Reunited

Brian Clough was out of work for less than four months. Due to his generous financial settlement from Leeds United after his sacking, he could afford a good four months, and a Happy Christmas, away from football, at home with his wife and family.

But on Friday 3rd January 1975, Nottingham Forest sacked Allan Brown.

After selling Duncan McKenzie to Brian Clough's Leeds, Brown had brought a quarter of a million pounds into the club, and after their near miss in April 1974, Forest had high hopes of a Second Division promotion battle, especially after his team had knocked out Manchester City and Newcastle, almost, during a great FA Cup run.

Those high hopes had fallen flat. Forest had floundered, and found themselves flailing about and foraging in mid-table in the Second Division.

On Monday 6th January 1975, Brian Clough was appointed as the new manager of Nottingham Forest. His immediate task was to prepare his new team for an FA Cup Third round replay against Tottenham, at White Hart Lane, the scene of one of his greatest ever victories, Derby's 5-3 win over Spurs back in 1973.

Forest had been held to a 1-1 draw at The City Ground, on the day after Brown was sacked, just as Peter Taylor's Brighton had lost at home to non-league Leatherhead.

Former Coventry City star Neil Martin scored the first goal of Clough's reign as Forest's manager, with a towering header, as they shocked Spurs, winning 1-0 away.

There was no repeat of Nottingham Forest's romantic Cup run of 1974, though. Fulham, en route to Wembley, knocked them out of the FA Cup in the Fourth round, after three replays.

On Wednesday 19th February, Clough ended the Elland Road nightmares of both John McGovern and John O'Hare, paying £60,000 to Jimmy Armfield for them. O'Hare was Clough's first signing as Derby County manager, and Cloughie had now also signed McGovern for the fourth time.

When Clough arrived at The City Ground, Ian Bowyer, John Robertson, Martin O'Neill, Viv Anderson and Tony Woodcock were already in Nottingham Forest's squad, although Woodcock was a young reserve. He'd also managed to talk both Robertson and O'Neill into staying, as both players were on the transfer list.

While Dave Mackay's Derby County won a brilliant, comeback First Division title, and Peter Taylor's Brighton avoided relegation to the Fourth Division, by just four points, Brian Clough's Nottingham Forest finished 1974-75 in sixteenth position in Division Two, three places lower than when Allan Brown was sacked.

Neil Martin was their top scorer, with twelve league and cup goals, from thirty-four matches. At thirty-four years old, Neil Martin joined Peter Taylor's Brighton during the Summer of 75, and he scored eight goals in thirteen league matches.

At the same time, Frank Clark was released by the new manager of Newcastle United, Gordon Lee.

Frank Clark had played nearly five hundred matches for Newcastle, and on the verge of retiring, at the age of only thirty-one, having been effectively sacked by the club he loved. Brian Clough envisaged another Dave Mackay opportunity, and he snapped up the veteran full back for free.

Clark responded by playing in all 42 of Forest's Second Division matches during 1975-76, as they finished in eighth place, seven points behind promoted West Brom, then managed by Johnny Giles.

Dave Mackay's Derby County had finished fourth in Division One, the Rams' fifth top four First Division finish in seven years. Derby had experienced a dramatic European Cup experience.

Francis Lee's brace had helped Derby to a 3-1 aggregate win over Slovan Bratislava, of Czechoslo-vakia, in the First round. But they were then drawn against Real Madrid, in the Second round.

Nearly 35,000 had packed The Baseball Ground for the visit of the six times European Cham-pions, back in October, as Charlie George's hat-trick, and David Nish's thirty yard strike, gave Derby a sensational, historic 4-1 win over Real, Breitner, Netzer, Pirri, Amancio, etc.

Two weeks later, 120,000 magnificently filled the Bernabau, for the second leg, but Derby were on course for victory at half-time, despite Roberto Martinez's early goal. McFarland, Todd, Thomas and Nish looked capable of guiding Derby to their greatest ever victory.

Martinez, however, made the score 2-0, six minutes into the second half, before Santillana's towering header then put Real ahead in the tie. Charlie George scored to put Derby 5-4 up on aggre-gate, though, with half an hour remaining, but Pirri's late penalty kick sent the match into extra-time.

In extra-time, Santillana broke Derby's hearts with his close range shot, giving Real a 5-1 win on the night, and going through 6-5 on aggregate.

Back at Brighton and Hove Albion, Peter Taylor's team were second in the Third Division, behind Hereford United, at the start of April. Sammy Morgan's two goals on Saturday 24th Febru-ary, had secured a great 2-0 home win over Malcolm Allison's Crystal Palace, and in front of a mas-sive 33,300 Goldstone Ground crowd, to lift them up to second place.

That crowd was the largest at the Goldstone for seventeen years, and Taylor's Brighton looked definitely destined for promotion going into Spring.

Their 3-1 defeat away at Millwall on Good Friday, in front of 23,000, The Den's biggest crowd of the season, was followed by draws against Aldershot, Gillingham and Sheffield Wednesday, though, and Brighton's promotion hopes were ruined.

Disillusioned and despondent after finishing in fourth place, three points behind Millwall, Taylor resigned in July 1976. Mike Bamber had been the most understanding, patient, honest, and genuinely football-minded chairman either he or Clough ever worked for. It had become clear, though, that over two years since they'd parted, Clough and Taylor were at their best when working together.

Taylor had left Brighton with Peter Ward, Brian Horton, Peter O'Sullivan and Andy Rollings in Brighton's first team. Three years later, under the management of Alan Mullery MBE, those four players made up 36% of Brighton's team that gained promotion to the First Division.

Just five and a half years after appointing Clough and Taylor, Mike Bamber had finally achieved his dream of bringing Division One football down to East Sussex, for the very first time.

On 17th July 1976, Peter Taylor joined up with his friend Brian Clough, as assistant manager at Nottingham Forest. Their re-union didn't happen quite as shown at the ridiculous end of The Damned United.

Cloughie did NOT get down on his knees to beg. *"Shall I tell you about my life?"*

Sorry Tom Hooper, I'm dropping your film to a six out of ten. It had taken nearly two full sea-sons, after he'd been sacked by Leeds, before Brian Clough was finally re-united with Peter Taylor, "the goods in the back of the shop, to Cloughie's shop window."

Just one month into the 1976/77 season, Clough and Taylor paid Birmingham City £42,000 for Peter Withe, a six foot and three inches tall, bearded, brave, bustling centre-forward. Taylor had

---

already fancied Withe, when he was still at Brighton, but Birmingham City suddenly bid £10,000 more than Taylor had offered, and at the very last minute, so Withe left Wolves for St Andrews.

Peter Withe was a forward who loved a regular supply of crosses, and Forest had John Robertson and Martin O'Neill, two of the most accurate crossers in the country. He went on to score sixteen goals from thirty-three starts during Forest's 1976-77 promotion season, and he was also their top scorer as Nottingham Forest won the First Division title, during the following season.

As well as Peter Withe, Clough and Taylor also recruited another beast, one of the very best in the air, at the start of October 1976. Larry Lloyd had won the league title, and also the UEFA Cup, with Liverpool back in 1973, but he was rotting in Coventry City's reserves by 1976. Lloyd joined Forest, for a one month loan period, before he returned to Coventry back in November. During his loan spell at The City Ground, Forest had hammered Sheffield United 6-1, and Burnley 5-2.

On Wednesday 1st December, Clough and Taylor paid a bargain price of only £55,000 to Coventry for Larry Lloyd, an offer that the Sky Blues couldn't wait to accept.

On Saturday 4th December 1976, with just over 16,000 scattered around The City Ground, third-placed Forest welcomed Bristol Rovers to Nottingham.

NOTTINGHAM FOREST		BRISTOL ROVERS
John Middleton	1	Jim Eadie
Viv Anderson	2	Phil Bater
Frank Clark	3	Lindsay Parsons
John McGovern	4	David Williams
Larry Lloyd	5	Stuart Taylor
Ian Bowyer	6	Peter Aitken
Martin O'Neill	7	Ken Stephens
John O'Hare	8	Gordon Fearnley
Peter Withe	9	Alan Warboys
Tony Woodcock	10	Bruce Bannister
John Robertson	11	Dave Staniforth

Bannister and Warboys brought back the very worst of memories for both Clough and Taylor, having scored seven of Rovers' goals during their 8-2 away win over Brighton, three years earlier, but Nottingham Forest fielded nine players who would later win European Cup winners' medals.

Forest won 4-2, with John Robertson scoring twice, including a penalty kick, and Tony Woodcock and Peter Withe completed the scoring.

Only Kenny Burns, Peter Shilton, Trevor Francis and Archie Gemmill were left to join the club *who had the whole world in their hands* in both 1978 and 1979.

Archie Gemmill joined on 23rd September 1977, for a fee of £100,000, after Forest had gained promotion back to Division One. He had played 261 First Division matches for Derby County, and also earned twenty-one Scottish caps.

He played a further 58 league games, under Clough and Taylor, before leaving after being left out of their 1979 European Cup Final team that beat Malmo 1-0.

Archie Gemmill scored one of the most famous goals of all time, as a Forest player, during the 1978 World Cup Finals. He danced around the Dutch defence, before placing the ball past Jongbloed, from just inside the area, to put Scotland 3-1 up against Holland, in Mendoza.

Gemmill's goal was voted the fifth greatest World Cup goal of all time, by CBC Sports in 2006.

The goal was also acclaimed in Danny Boyle's 1996 film Trainspotting, when Renton, played by Ewan McGregor, had sensational, climactic sex with Diane (Kelly MacDonald), and then excitedly exclaimed, "*Christ, I haven't felt that good since Archie Gemmill scored against Holland in 1978!*"

Gemmill moved to Birmingham City in 1979, but he returned to Derby County, under Peter Taylor's management, after they'd been relegated back to Division Two. He retired in 1984, having played nearly six hundred Football League matches.

John O'Hare was never as influential for Forest as he was at Derby, once they were back in the First Division. Voted as the Rams' Player of the Year in 1969-70, after Derby's glorious first season back in Division One, the older O'Hare was only occasionally selected after Forest's return to top flight football, and he was an unused substitute during their 1979 European Cup Final 1-0 win over Malmo, in Munich.

However, a year later, he was rewarded for his loyalty and his versatility, by replacing Gary Mills in the second half of the 1980 European Cup Final in Madrid, as Forest beat Hamburg 1-0.

John O'Hare scored fourteen goals for Nottingham Forest, from one hundred and one league games, before he retired from league football in 1980, after five years at the City Ground, to join Midland League club Belper Town.

Brian Clough and Peter Taylor succeeded in doing at Forest what they might have succeeded in doing at Derby County, by winning not just the league title, but the League Cup twice, and then twice becoming European Champions.

Under John McGovern's captaincy, and in front of Peter Shilton's goalkeeping excellence, Forest kept twenty-five clean sheets during 1977-78, conceding only 24 goals, but scoring 69, with the greatest goal average/goal difference, and the largest points advantage, since Everton's title winning season of 1969-70.

John McGovern, having been booed, snubbed and rejected at Elland Road, lifted the European Cup twice as Forest's captain, as well as three other major domestic trophies, winning as many major honours as Billy Bremner won during his career.

It could be said about Leeds United, as well as at Derby County, if only, if only, if only...?

Peter Taylor retired as assistant manager at Nottingham Forest in May 1982, but he returned to management six months later, though, and at Derby County of all places.

Derby were then a Second Division club, but also struggling to avoid relegation to the Third Division, just as they were when Clough and Taylor first arrived at The Baseball Ground.

Clough was vexed that his great friend had returned to the club he'd always loved, always admitting that the happiest days of his career were at Derby. He never succeeded in losing his love for that club, from which they'd both walked away in October 1973, on the back of his own initiative and instinct, but the knife that wielded the fatal cut between them, was slammed down onto the butcher's table, severing their friendship, by Taylor's next move.

Then, in May 1983, Peter Taylor signed John Robertson, who'd missed only eight games as Forest had secured a UEFA Cup qualifying place, while Brian Clough was away on holiday.

Clough took the transfer as a personal insult, and he responded by throwing some deeply derisory and destructive personal insults towards Taylor, in the tabloid newspapers.

Afterwards, and thereafter, the two men never spoke, or even shook hands, ever again. Brian Clough gladly downed a double whisky to celebrate Taylor's Derby getting relegated to Division Three in May 1984.

After Peter Taylor had died on Thursday 4th October 1990, aged only sixty-two, Cloughie's destructive comments became self-destructive. Because he'd never said sorry to his great friend, before the death of his friend, Cloughie's comments bit deeply into himself, forever afterwards.

Clough was left desolate and guilt-ridden, deeply regretting the manner of the end of their friendship, and that he'd not been brave enough to make it up with Taylor, during those seven very short years.

Nevertheless, with the help of his youth team and reserve team coach, Archie Gemmill, Cloughie had built a third generation of stars at Nottingham Forest by 1990.

Gemmill had left Forest after a bitter row with Clough, having been left out of their team to face Malmo in 1979, but he and his wife Betty, who'd also hated Clough prior to meeting him, back in 1970, both became close and very fond friends of Brian.

Archie Gemmill had brought through a range of outstanding talent like Steve Stone, his own son Scot Gemmill, Ian Woan, Lee Glover, Mark Crossley, but most significantly of all, Roy Keane.

Brian Clough had already developed a good young team with Stuart Pearce, Des Walker, Steve Chettle, Steve Hodge, Gary Charles, Garry Parker, Gary Crosby, Nigel Jemson, and the best of all, his own youngest son, Nigel Clough.

With Crossley, Keane, Woan and Glover immediately added to their first team, Clough's Forest reached the Final of the one trophy in which he'd always failed to achieve success: the FA Cup.

During the 1991 FA Cup Final, Cloughie's Forest were the better team, but they lost to Terry Venables' Spurs, thanks to an own goal, after extra-time.

Tottenham should have played most of the match with just ten men, though, following two outrageous, over the top challenges by Paul Gascoigne. *Gazza,* rather than being deservedly sent off, was instead carried off on a stretcher with a serious, self-inflicted, long-term injury, due to the fierce impact of his own challenge, after his second lunge on Gary Charles.

Two years later, Brian Clough retired from football management, after he'd failed to prevent Forest from relegation out of the inaugural Premier League.

During the mid-Nineties, Nottingham Forest's *Executive Stand,* built in 1980 from the proceeds of their European glories, was renamed *The Brian Clough Stand.*

Cloughie was reported to have wished that it had been renamed *The Brian Clough And Peter Taylor Stand.*

Brian Clough died, aged sixty-nine, on Monday 20th September 2004.

As a manager, Cloughie had taken charge of One Thousand, three hundred and nineteen league matches, winning 594, and losing as many as 385.

Less than a year after his death, in August 2005, the A52 main road between Nottingham and Derby was renamed The Brian Clough Way.

In November of the same year, a statue of Brian Clough was erected and unveiled on the corner of King Street and Queen Street, in Nottingham. It was the first time a statue of a football figure was unveiled in a city centre, and not outside of a football ground.

In August 2010, a statue of both Brian Clough and Peter Taylor holding the Football League First Division trophy was opened outside Pride Park, in Derby.

Named **Unity Plaza,** it pointed the direction and the distance in miles, just like a trig point, to various other football grounds, significant to the history of Derby County and the lives of Brian Clough and Peter Taylor. Brass plaques point you to the location of The Baseball Ground, only one mile away, and to Wembley Stadium, scene of Derby's 1946 FA Cup Final win. Likewise, Juventus and Real Madrid are both there, as are Liverpool, Manchester United, Manchester City, Arsenal, and the Millennium Stadium in Cardiff. Sunderland's Roker Park, and Middlesbrough's Ayresome Park are there, as is Hartlepool's Victoria Road.

Of course, The City Ground, just fourteen miles away, home of Derby County's great local rivals, Nottingham Forest, is also there.

One ground blatantly missing, though, is Leeds United's Elland Road. It's just not there. It has been ignored. Derby County might as well have included it, as Leeds were very much a dark, inverted inspiration to Clough's bright theory of Harmony, Integrity, Unity and Solidarity. The Spirit of Cloughie very much needed the presence of Peter Taylor, but the omission of Leeds United, always his nemesis, from the statue, wasn't necessary.

Cloughie's teams won more titles and trophies than Don Revie's Leeds United, anyhow; harmony, integrity, unity, solidarity....

VICTORY!

1971-72: THE GREATEST EVER TITLE RACE

AFTER THE TWO HORSE RACE of 1970-71, when Arsenal's sublime counter-attacking outfit, built on strong defensive unity and offensive dominance, had caught the mighty Leeds United napping at the line, with both teams twelve points clear, six good wins clear, of third-placed Spurs, there was little to suggest that we could expect anything than another two horse race in Division One as the *Hot Pants* Summer of '71 had burnt into August.

Everton, the runaway Champions of 1970, had faded badly, while Liverpool were still in transition between their Merseybeat Sixties' stars and Shankly's new Team of the Seventies.

Manchester United had plenty of talent, and plenty of goals, but they lacked any defensive consistency, since they'd become European Champions, and they failed to qualify for any type of European football during the following three seasons.

Manchester City, Football League Champions only three years earlier, had suffered disappointing First Division campaigns since, in spite of having one of the best defences in the game, one of the best balanced midfields, and also Francis Lee, potentially the best striker in England.

Tottenham Hotspur boasted the best goalkeeper in English football, and a defence, well-marshalled by Mike England, that had kept 26 clean sheets during 1970-71, and a star-studded midfield, with England legends Martin Peters and Alan Mullery. They had newly acquired a winger, Ralph Coates, also an England international, and in Martin Chivers and Alan Gilzean, Spurs had one of the very best strike partnerships in their history.

In spite of all that quality, it did look, as the season began on Saturday 14th August 1971, as if it would be just another season where Leeds United would be fighting it out with Arsenal, high above all the rest, at the top of the table.

It wasn't.

It was a huge shock to all, when the early runaway leaders were none of the above, but a team promoted from Division Two, in second position, that started the season with a refreshing attack, attack, attack mentality, and a twenty-one year old star player, who'd become one of the greatest players, not only of the Glam Soccer era, but in the history of English football.

Tony Currie had Done Magic in sparking Sheffield United's sparkling promotion season, scoring nine goals, but being the architect of most of the twenty-nine goals scored by both Alan Woodward and Billy Dearden. The Blades had fought off a strong challenge from Cardiff City, Bob Hatton's Carlisle United, and Ken Wagstaff and Chris Chilton's Hull City, to finish second behind Champions Leicester City, following an eleven game unbeaten run at the end of the 1970-71 season.

That unbeaten league run by The Blades was extended to twenty-one, as they romped to nine wins and two draws, at the start of their 1971-72 First Division campaign.

On the opening Saturday, Sheffield United entertained Southampton at Bramall Lane. The Saints had finished the previous season in seventh place, and qualified for the UEFA Cup, with Mike Channon and Terry Paine, as well as their greatest-ever central defensive partnership, John McGrath and Jimmy Gabriel, in their eleven.

They also had the notorious "reducer", Brian O'Neil, to kill the power of the Currie.

No matter, Alan Woodward converted a penalty kick, following a Hollywood foul on Geoff Salmons, and then, in the heavy rain, Salmons stabbed in a second, slicing the Blades into an irretrievable 2-0 half-time lead. John Flynn then fired in from close range, following Stewart Scullion's corner-kick, and United won 3-1, their first game back in Division One.

Leeds United had been ordered to play their first four home matches of the season away from Elland Road, by the Football League, after the pitch invasion during their crucial home 1-2 defeat to West Brom, back on Saturday 17th April. They did beat Manchester City, at Maine Road, on the opening Saturday, however, after Peter Lorimer's second half hot-shot.

The reigning Champions Arsenal had also won, beating Chelsea 3-0 (McLintock, Kennedy, Radford), with nearly 50,000 inside Highbury. Then, on the following Tuesday, Leeds United visited Bramall Lane, to face the First Division's new boys and Yorkshire rivals Sheffield United.

A huge crowd of 40,725 filled every inch of terracing in the old ground, with over fifteen thousand Leeds invaders expecting a straightforward victory, just as they'd done against West Brom, four months before.

SHEFFIELD UNITED		LEEDS UNITED
John Hope	1	Gary Sprake
Len Badger	2	Paul Reaney
Ted Hemsley	3	Paul Madeley
John Flynn	4	Billy Bremner
Eddie Colquhoun	5	Jack Charlton
Trevor Hockey	6	Norman Hunter
Alan Woodward	7	Peter Lorimer
Geoff Salmons	8	Allan Clarke
Billy Dearden	9	Rod Belfitt
Tony Currie	10	Johnny Giles
Stewart Scullion	11	Mick Bates

Leeds were still missing Eddie Gray, not fully fit for nearly a year, and also Mick Jones, but Sheffield United were superb, launching an all-out attack on Leeds United's full-strength defence. Playing with intelligence and style, the Blades stunned the First Division title favourites.

After a goalless first half, Tony Currie started to pull the strings, running with the ball, past his better-known opponents, and passing intelligently. Defender John Flynn headed them into a 1-0 lead, out-witting Jack Charlton at Alan Woodward's right-wing corner kick. Billy Dearden then doubled their advantage, converting Scullion's left wing cross, from a narrow angle. A late header from captain Colquhoun turned the win into a great 3-0 thrashing.

On the second Saturday of the season, Alan Woodward, Sheffield United's top scorer from the previous season, fired a second half winner away at Everton, to send them up to the top of the First Division.

West Bromwich Albion also started like a train on full steam. Tony Brown had scored twenty-eight First Division goals, ending up as England's leading scorer of the 1970-71 season, and he hit goals in all three of Albion's opening matches, their 1-0 wins away at West Ham, and 2-0 at home to Everton, and their 1-1 draw against Coventry City. Derby County, Manchester United, Spurs, Arsenal, Ipswich and Liverpool were all close behind.

FIRST DIVISION LEADERS, SATURDAY 21ST AUGUST 1971

	PL	W	D	L	F	A	PTS
Sheffield United	3	3	0	0	7	1	6
West Brom	3	2	1	0	4	1	5
Derby County	3	2	1	0	6	2	5
Manchester Utd	3	2	1	0	8	5	5
Ipswich Town	3	1	2	0	3	1	4
Tottenham	3	1	2	0	6	3	4
Arsenal	3	2	0	1	5	3	4
Liverpool	3	2	0	1	8	6	4

On Monday 23rd August, Tony Brown scored his fourth goal in four games, but George Best replied with two goals, and Alan Gowling also scored, as Manchester United won 3-1 at home, at Stoke City's Victoria Ground. Albion dropped to fifth place, and in spite of Brown scoring seventeen First Division goals in 1971-72, West Brom fell away badly, with Jeff Astle missing half of the season, and they finished up down in sixteenth place.

Manchester United had also been ordered to play their first two home games of the season away from Old Trafford, after an idiot had thrown a knife onto their pitch during the previous season.

Crucially, at Huddersfield Town's Leeds Road, Wolves had held Leeds to a goalless draw, after a mediocre crowd of just 20,686 attended their opening home match, but then, Tottenham drew away 1-1 with Leeds at Hull City's Boothferry Park. Billy Bremner had equalised Alan Gilzean's first half goal. Those dropped points, from two games which Leeds would have expected to have won at least once, had they been played at Elland Road, proved costly.

On Tuesday 24th August, Sheffield United sprung a real shock, winning 1-0 away at Arsenal. Badger, Hemsley, Dearden and Salmons worked a lovely move into the Arsenal penalty area, and Alan Woodward's shot was blocked by Bob Wilson. Stewart Scullion, though, a bargain £30,000 Summer purchase from Watford, stunned the 45,000 Highbury crowd with a cracking volley from the edge of the area.

Percy M. Young wrote, "a kind of feverish brilliance attended the play of United while so much depended on the wayward talents of Tony Currie- a histrionic player with mannerisms characteristic of what one day will be termed *'the Best era.'*"

The comparisons of Tony Currie with George Best were not so ridiculous. Currie was simply among the most gifted midfield players of the Seventies, if not the most talented English footballer of that decade. Only Hoddle, Gascoigne, Beckham, Scholes, Lampard and Gerrard can only really compare with Currie, since 1971.

Manchester City had paid Newcastle United £60,000 for Wyn Davies back in August. **Wyn the Leap**, or the **Mighty Wyn,** had had a disappointing season in front of goal, during the previous season, and Newcastle boss Joe Harvey had brought in Malcolm MacDonald to replace him, but in the air, Davies was still the very best in the game.

On the last Saturday in August, eighth-placed Spurs visited Maine Road, for a game that launched Manchester City's Championship challenge, in front of just 33,683 disillusioned home fans.

MANCHESTER CITY		TOTTENHAM HOTSPUR
Joe Corrigan	1	Pat Jennings
Derek Jeffries	2	Joe Kinnear
David Connor	3	Tony Want
Mike Doyle	4	Alan Mullery
Tommy Booth	5	Mike England
Colin Bell	6	Terry Naylor
Mike Summerbee	7	Ralph Coates
George Heslop	8	Steve Perryman
Wyn Davies	9	Martin Chivers
Francis Lee	10	Martin Peters
Ian Mellor	11	Alan Gilzean

Doyle's long throw into the Spurs six yard box was partially cleared by both England and Kinnear, back to Mike Doyle's feet. Doyle skimmed a cross back into the area, where Davies leapt and flicked on for Bell to bury a right-footed volley past Jennings into the roof of the net.

Joe Kinnear and Alan Mullery were dispossessed by City's reserve left-back Dave Connor, and the ball fell nicely for Ian Mellor to launch it up the left wing. Mike Summerbee sprinted onto it, and then teased and twisted Perryman so much, the Spurs midfield worker lost his footing inside the area. Pat Jennings had no chance after Summerbee placed a close-range, right-footed swerver past him, just inside his far post.

Colin Bell then fed Summerbee on the right wing, who advanced with a couple of touches, then crossed into the Tottenham penalty area, where the Mighty Wyn, closely marked by his Welsh international captain Mike England, jumped away from his man, and simply guided the ball with a cushioned header just away from the clambering Jennings, and in off his left post.

England's poor clearance from the edge of his area was collected by right back Jeffries, who laid the ball off for Lee to turn and fire in a fabulous fourth goal, from twenty yards out.

Without Tony Book, Alan Oakes, Neil Young or Tony Towers, City had turned on the style, hammering a much-fancied, nearly full-strength Tottenham, at a canter.

City had been without Colin Bell for their first four matches, and they'd won just one game, but he was back, now. On that same day, Sheffield United were held to a 0-0 draw by fifth-placed West Brom, at Bramall Lane.

Manchester United, despite George Best's first half strike, were also held to a 1-1 draw away at Molineux. Bernard Shaw, Wolves' tiny Sheffield-born full back, had scored a late equaliser to thrill their huge 46,000 Black Country crowd.

Despite their setback against West Brom, the Blades enjoyed September as much as they'd enjoyed August. They beat Nottingham Forest 3-2 (Dearden, Scullion, Currie), on Saturday 4th September, and then they drew 2-2 at home to Spurs on the following Saturday. Goals in each half by Billy Dearden and Stewart Scullion were cancelled out by a Tottenham team that was back to full strength. Knowles and Beal had both returned, while Martin Peters and Alan Gilzean scored.

Alan Woodward's second half finish, from Tony Currie's pass, finished off Leicester City at Filbert Street, on Saturday 18th September, before another giant crowd of over 40,000 filled Bramall Lane's vast banks, on the final Saturday of September, for the visit of European Cup Winners' Cup winners Chelsea.

Up against the sheer class of Osgood, Hudson and Hollins, Tony Currie was the Star of the Show, spraying pin-point seventy yard cross-field passes with both of his feet, and his shirt worn rakishly outside his shorts.

A natural born pin-up, Currie blew kisses to his home crowd, while beating Peter Houseman down the John Street side of the pitch.

Stewart Scullion fired a first half volley to send Blades three points clear at the top of Division One. Derby County had been plugging away, in third or fourth place, and were still unbeaten up to then. After drawing four of their first six matches, they won 2-0 away at Everton, on Saturday 4th September, with over 41,000 inside Goodison Park. Kevin Hector and Frank Wignall had both scored their fourth goals of the season, before a week later, with 32,545 packed into The Baseball Ground, Derby hammered Stoke City 4-0 (O'Hare, Todd, Hinton, Gemmill). The Rams then drew against Chelsea and West Brom to sit in third place at the end of September.

Leeds had played their last two "home" games away from Elland Road at the beginning of September, hammering Newcastle 5-1 at Hillsborough, and then beating Crystal Palace 2-0, on Saturday 4th September, at Leeds Road, Huddersfield. On the second Saturday of the month, though, they lost 2-0 away at Arsenal.

George Graham headed past Sprake, before a hard-hit penalty kick by Peter Storey had lifted Arsenal back into the title race, in front of a Highbury crowd of over 51,000.

Winger Ian Mellor had scored in Manchester City's 1-0 home win over Liverpool, on Wednesday 1st September, and then, after drawing 0-0 away at Leicester, goals from Colin Bell and Francis Lee beat Newcastle United 2-1.

City's 2-2 draw away at Nottingham Forest was followed by a 3-0 home win against Southampton. Superstars Francis Lee and Colin Bell both scored first half goals, before Wyn Davies headed his fourth goal in ten games, lifting City up to fourth in the First Division.

Manchester United beat Ipswich Town 1-0 at home, before hammering Crystal Palace 3-1, away, with more than 44,000 packed into Selhurst Park.

George Best then scored a brilliant hat-trick in their 4-2 win over West Ham, on Saturday 18th September. His third goal, though, was a Best classic. He called for a quick, short corner-kick from John Fitzpatrick, but then he took full responsibility.

Bestie weaved towards the Hammers' penalty area, turning John McDowell inside out, not just once, but twice. He then side-stepped Bobby Moore, before blasting his shot past Bobby Ferguson, from just inside the area.

At the end of September, United visited Liverpool, and with 55,634 overfilling Anfield, in the game of the day, Liverpool stormed to a 2-0 half-time lead. Bobby Graham obliviously scored a lucky, deflected goal, after Ian Callaghan's tentative long-range daisy-cutter had hit him and deflected past Stepney. Brian Hall doubled their lead, but then George Best, in top form, inspired a second half come-back.

Best beat Alec Lindsay and crossed for Denis Law to finish sharply, after a perfectly-timed run. He then side-heeled a delightful pass to Bobby Charlton, on the left side of the Liverpool area, completely surprising the entire Liverpool defence.

Charlton buried his shot past Ray Clemence, for a decent 2-2 draw.

As October arrived, Manchester United were second-placed, three points behind Sheffield United, but there were only five points between the second and ninth placed teams.

FIRST DIVISION LEADERS, 25TH SEPTEMBER 1971

	PL	W	D	L	F	A	PTS
Sheffield United	10	8	2	0	18	6	18
Manchester Utd	10	6	3	1	22	13	15
Derby County	10	4	6	0	17	7	14
Manchester City	10	5	3	2	19	8	13
Leeds United	10	5	2	3	13	9	12
Wolves	10	4	4	2	14	12,	12
Liverpool	10	5	1	4	15	14	11
Arsenal	9	5	0	4	12	7	10
Tottenham	9	3	4	2	14	11	10

Manchester United hosted Sheffield United on Saturday 2nd October, in the Match of the Season, up to then. 51,735 packed Old Trafford for their top of the table clash, and they witnessed one of George Best's greatest ever goals.

After a tight, goalless first half, Blades lost their left-back Ted Hemsley due to an ankle injury. As good as Currie, Woodward, Salmons, Dearden and Scullion had been in attack in their shock rise to the top, Hemsley had been superb in defence, alongside captain Colquhoun, John Flynn and Len Badger, and it was that left-sided area of Sheffield United's defence that George Best targeted.

The supremely confident Best collected the ball, forty yards out, and He ran, diagonally, from left to right, towards the Blades' penalty area, with six Blades' defenders protecting their six yard box.

Best fired in a shot from a narrow angle, past the crowd of players, towards the far post. The ball just hit the target, inside John Hope's right hand post.

Brian Kidd then received a pass, wide left, from Alan Gowling, and he crossed for the diving Gowling to head Manchester United to a 2-0 win.

Sheffield United had played the same starting eleven for the first two months of the season, and that had been the secret of their success. They had a great attempt at European qualification three years later, but this eleven was the best they ever had. Once they began to miss Dearden, Woodward and Scullion through injury, though, results began to go against them.

In December, John Flynn was ruled out for the rest of the season, but then they lost their midfield dynamo, the bearded Trevor Hockey, two months later. Sheffield United lost 2-3 at home to Stoke City on Saturday 9th October.

John Ritchie, Denis Smith and Terry Conroy had all scored to lift Stoke up to ninth.

Manchester United continued their rampant form, though, winning 3-0 away at Huddersfield Town. Goals from Best, Law and Charlton ensured that United replaced the Blades at the top of the league, and Sheffield United's glorious two month First Division title challenge had come to an end.

On Saturday 16th October, George Best scored early in the second half in United's 1-0 win over Derby, as the Rams' twelve match unbeaten run was also finished. Brian Kidd and Alan Gowling had also both headed against Colin Boulton's bar, so County were lucky their defeat wasn't heavier.

Arsenal had begun the season without their maverick talisman Charlie George, but the long haired wonder kid then returned for their 4-2 win over Newcastle United, on Saturday 9th October.

George Graham, Eddie Kelly, Ray Kennedy and George Armstrong all scored, benefitting from the return of the King.

Ray Kennedy's brace then helped Arsenal beat Chelsea 2-1 at Stamford Bridge, one week later, and the Gunners had won four straight First Division games, lifting them right back into the defence of their title, only five points behind the leaders with a game in hand.

FIRST DIVISION LEADERS, 16TH OCTOBER 1971

	PL	W	D	L	F	A	PTS
Manchester Utd	13	9	3	1	28	13	21
Sheffield United	13	8	2	3	22	14	18
Manchester City	13	7	3	3	22	11	17
Derby County	13	5	7	1	20	10	17
Arsenal	12	8	0	4	19	10	16
Tottenham	12	5	5	2	22	15	15
Leeds United	13	6	3	4	17	12	15
Liverpool	13	6	3	4	18	16	15
Stoke City	13	6	3	4	15	15	15

Spurs were also putting pressure on the leaders, having beaten Ipswich 2-1, and then Wolves 4-1, in October. Alan Gilzean and Martin Chivers had shared fifteen First Division goals during their opening twelve games, with Martin Peters chipping in with six.

Tottenham then thrashed Nottingham Forest 6-1 at White Hart Lane, on Saturday 23rd October. Martin Peters and Jimmy Pearce scored two apiece, in front of nearly 36,000, while Martin Chivers hammered one in from just inside the Forest area.

The best goal of the game, though, by far, was Alan Mullery's excellent thirty-five yard volley, after the Forest defence had worked hard to clear a sustained Spurs attack. Tottenham lifted themselves up to fifth in the Division, just two points behind second-placed Derby.

A week later, Manchester United lost only their second game of the season, 1-0 at home to Leeds United. Peter Lorimer's early rocket fired Leeds into the top five, following their poor start, having waited until late September before they could finally play at Elland Road.

Johnny Giles had squared a quick free-kick to Lorimer, thirty-five yards out, and his speculative, swerving right-footed shot sneaked under Stepney's body, as he attempted to save. Lorimer's goal had stunned the 54,000 Old Trafford crowd.

"The sort of mistake no goalkeeper would ever want to make," Barry Davies sympathized, fatuously. "Poor Alex Stepney!"

It was only a momentary blip, though, as Man United drew a 3-3 cracker away at Maine Road. Sammy McIlroy clipped in his first ever league goal, with Kidd and Gowling also scoring to earn a draw, while Lee, Bell and Summerbee had all scored for Manchester City.

United then beat Spurs 3-1 (McIlroy, Law 2), Leicester City 3-2 (Kidd, Law 2), and finally, Southampton away, by 5-2. George Best's hat-trick had given him seventeen league and cup goals for the season, but the win also lifted United three points clear of neighbours City at the top of Division One, by the end of November.

Manchester City had been cruising gently, losing only twice in eighteen games, since their opening day defeat at home to Leeds. After that 3-3 draw with United, they won 2-1 away at in-form Arsenal, and then hammered West Ham, 2-0 at Upton Park. Francis Lee fired his fourteenth goal of the season (and his fifth penalty kick), while the mighty Wyn Davies scored his fifth goal in Sky Blue.

After a sustained, over-physical tussle between Davies and Tommy Taylor, the two big men both guilty of shirt-pulling and shoving, Taylor was adjudged to have fouled the Welsh legend, just inside the West Ham penalty area.

Francis Lee then blasted his penalty kick high up into the top right corner of Ferguson's goal. The ball actually pin-balled off the inner stanchion, and then across to the opposite side of the goal frame, so fierce was Lee's shot.

Then, Mike Doyle dispossessed Taylor inside the centre circle, and he freed Wyn Davies, who ran clear from halfway, under pursuit from McDowell. Davies slid the ball just beneath Ferguson's dive. A week later, on Saturday 27th November, City smashed Coventry City 4-0, with Francis Lee and Colin Bell scoring two apiece.

For the first time since 1968, United and City were the top two teams in Division One.

Chelsea, the European Cup Winners' Cup holders, had also hit form, winning all four of their league matches during November 1971.

Charlie Cooke and Peter Osgood both scored to secure a 2-0 home win over Nottingham Forest, on Saturday 6th November. After an inglorious start to the season, there were only 26,000 inside Stamford Bridge. Ossie then scored the winning goal in their 1-0 win away at Stoke, before they won 3-2 at Crystal Palace, with over 34,000 packed into Selhurst Park. Tommy Baldwin, Alan Hudson and Ossie all scored in a vibrant performance. Then, on the final Saturday of the month, Charlie Cooke's goal secured their 1-0 home win over Spurs.

52,581, double their crowd three weeks earlier, had packed into the Bridge for that win which lifted Chelsea up to ninth place. They then held Newcastle United to a goalless draw away at St James's Park, on Saturday 4th December, with nearly 38,000 packed into a three-quarters built ground, due to United's new East Stand being constructed.

That point Chelsea moved to within five points of second-placed Derby.

League leaders Manchester United had won their fourth successive game on that first Saturday in December. Denis Law and Brian Kidd gave them a 2-1 lead at home to Nottingham Forest. Peter Cormack and Martin O'Neill both scored for Forest, either side of the break, but Kidd's second goal of the game, and his eighth of the season, won the game 3-2, giving United a five point lead at the top of Division One.

Derby County moved up to second with their superb 3-1 win over Manchester City. Kevin Hector was fouled by Mellor inside the City area, and Alan Hinton fired his penalty kick just inside the left side post, giving Corrigan no chance. Hinton had a magnificent game on the Baseball Ground mud, crossing deep from the left, for a flying Ron Webster to drill his header past Corrigan for a 2-0 lead, and then he beat Tony Book to cross for Alan Durban to head Derby three-up.

A second half penalty kick scored by Francis Lee, his eighteenth goal of the season, was no consolation for City.

	PL	W	D	L	F	A	PTS
Manchester Utd	20	14	4	2	46	24	32
Derby County	20	10	7	3	35	16	27
Manchester City	20	11	5	4	37	20	27
Leeds United	20	12	3	5	30	17	27
Sheffield United	20	11	3	6	36	26	25
Liverpool	20	10	5	5	27	20	25
Tottenham	20	9	6	5	37	25	24
Arsenal	20	10	2	8	29	25	22
Chelsea	20	8	6	6	27	24	22

Under today's three points for a win system, Manchester United would have held a seven point lead over Leeds United, but following this apparent title-winning position, they fell apart, literally.

United's team spirit evaporated. "Players were just doing their own things," Bobby Charlton sadly admitted. "There was no team cohesion, or confidence."

They won none of their next eleven games, up to mid-March, and scored only six goals, conceding twenty-one, to drop out of the top six.

On Tuesday 21st December, Arsenal paid Everton £220,000 for Alan Ball, their World Cup winning midfield schemer, and the best player of Everton's title-winning team two years earlier. It was a British record transfer fee, and a desperate attempt by Bertie Mee to revive Arsenal's stuttering defence of their title. They had again lost Charlie George to injury back in November, but they were now also without Peter Storey, until March.

Nevertheless, Arsenal were in the midst of a twelve game unbeaten run, and on Boxing Day, George Graham's first half strike earned a 1-1 away draw with Nottingham Forest, at The City Ground.

On Boxing Day, Monday 27th December 1971, these were the Final Scores, and match attendances:

CHELSEA	2-0	IPSWICH TOWN	43,896
EVERTON	2-2	HUDDERSFIELD	41,088
LEEDS UNITED	3-0	DERBY COUNTY	44,214
LEICESTER CITY	1-2	WOLVES 37,966	
MANCHESTER UNITED	2-2	COVENTRY CITY	52,117
NEWCASTLE UNITED	1-2	SHEFFIELD UNITED	52,900
NOTTINGHAM FOREST	1-1	ARSENAL	42,750
SOUTHAMPTON	1-0	CRYSTAL PALACE	28,310
STOKE CITY	1-3	MANCHESTER CITY	43,007
TOTTENHAM HOTSPUR	0-1	WEST HAM	52,888
WEST BROMWICH ALBION	1-0	LIVERPOOL	43,804

It was an amazing day in the history of English football. For the first time since folk wore flat caps and ridiculous rosettes, and grinned like George Formby into Pathe News film cameras, eleven First Division matches all played on the same day had attracted an average crowd of 43,903.

It was a record not since equalled, and nor will it ever be, given present attendance restrictions at most modern stadiums, and is even more impressive, given that Arsenal, Liverpool and Manchester City were all away from home.

Also, with Birmingham City attracting 40,793, for their Second Division home win over Cardiff, and Norwich City beating Charlton, with 31,041 filling Carrow Road, and both teams headed for promotion to Division One, the future of the First Division did look bright on that day.

On New Year's Day 1972, Leeds United wasted no time in continuing their ascent to the top, beating under-achievers Liverpool 2-0, away from home. Allan Clarke and Mick Jones, the best attacking partnership in English football, bar none, had both scored to silence a massive Anfield crowd of 53,847.

Ipswich Town came to Elland Road a week later, and they battled for a 2-2 draw, before Leeds finally went top after Allan Clarke's first half strike at home to Sheffield United, on Saturday 22nd January.

For the first time in three months, Manchester United, who'd looked like clear Champions as the Advent calendars were being opened, were not the leaders of Division One.

FIRST DIVISION LEADERS, 22ND JANUARY 1972

	PL	W	D	L	F	A	PTS
Leeds United	26	15	6	5	39	20	36
Manchester City	26	14	8	4	50	26	36
Manchester Utd	26	14	7	5	50	34	35
Derby County	26	13	8	5	45	26	34
Sheffield United	26	13	6	7	45	34	32
Wolves	26	12	8	6	45	35	32
Arsenal	26	13	5	8	36	27	31
Spurs	26	10	9	7	41	31	29
Chelsea	26	10	9	7	33	28	29
Liverpool	26	11	7	8	30	26	29

You'll notice Liverpool, down in tenth place, and seemingly out of the title race? Well, they **had** been without their huge, powerful centre-back Larry Lloyd since early November, but they'd also missed striker John Toshack for the same length of time.

Both players returned for Liverpool's next match, though, at home to Crystal Palace, on Saturday 29th January. Anfield's lowest league crowd of the season by some distance, 39,538, witnessed the birth of a resurrection for Liverpool Football Club.

From that day onwards, Liverpool would first challenge, and then overcome Leeds United's title as the greatest football team in England, but they even went on to succeed where Leeds did not... domination of European football.

It all started with that innocuous looking match against struggling Palace.

Free-scoring full-back Chris Lawler scored twice, while Ian Callaghan and Kevin Keegan both fired second half goals to complete a 4-1 thrashing. In Liverpool's starting eleven, that day, were seven players who went on to win at least one European Cup winners' medal.

That victory was their first win within an unbeaten run of fifteen matches, including thirteen wins, that eventually propelled Liverpool to the propeller front of the First Division title race from the absolute tail.

LIVERPOOL		CRYSTAL PALACE
Ray Clemence	1	John Jackson
Chris Lawler	2	David Payne
Alec Lindsay	3	Peter Wall
Tommy Smith	4	Bobby Kellard
Larry Lloyd	5	John McCormick
Emlyn Hughes	6	Mel Blyth
Kevin Keegan	7	John Craven
Ian Ross	8	Gerry Queen
Steve Heighway	9	Willie Wallace
John Toshack	10	Bobby Tambling
Ian Callaghan	11	Tony Taylor

Also, on Saturday 29th January, Charlie George returned to Arsenal's starting line-up, and he scored twice in their 5-0 win over Sheffield United, away at Bramall Lane. George Graham, Peter Simpson and Ray Kennedy also scored in the third of six successive league and cup wins that fired the Gunners right back up into the meat of the title race.

On Saturday 12th February, Arsenal beat fellow title contenders Derby County 2-0, at Highbury. Charlie George scored with a fantastic, flying, diving header from George Armstrong's left-wing cross, in front of a home crowd of over 52,000, and then he buried his penalty kick past Colin Boulton. A week later, the King scored his fifth goal in three starts since returning, during Arsenal's 1-0 away win at Ipswich.

That day, Saturday 19th February, saw a much more impressive performance, though. In front of an Elland Road crowd of 45,399, Leeds United faced the fading force of Manchester United. Throughout the first half, Leeds had Man Utd penned inside their own half, but Alex Stepney made four great saves from Lorimer, Gray and Clarke, while Tony Dunne also slid in to block a certain goal by Mick Jones.

After fifty minutes, though, Manchester United ran out of luck. Stepney pushed Eddie Gray's ferocious shot from Clarke's cross onto his post, but Jones buried the rebound. Five minutes later, Peter Lorimer beat Tom O'Neil and he crossed for Jones to shoot, but Allan Clarke flicked the ball into the net, just as Stepney dived to save Jones' shot. Francis Burns netted after Leeds were unable to clear Bobby Charlton's free-kick, but then Billy Bremner teased and turned and then beat Dunne out on the Leeds United right, and he crossed superbly for Jones to head in at the far post.

Eddie Gray beat Bobby Charlton, to the right of the Reds' penalty area, and he dashed to the bye-line, before cutting the ball back for Lorimer. Peter Lorimer fired in a sharp shot-cum-cross, for Jones to score from close range. Stepney had covered Lorimer's shot, but he was beaten by Jones' intervention. Clarke then dispossessed Morgan. He weaved and wound through Sadler and Steve James, but he was tackled, by Stepney's dive, ten yards out, just as he was about to shoot and score.

Lorimer fired high into Stepney's net, from six yards out, after Mick Jones had crossed, for a 5-1 thrashing of the former European Champions. Eddie Gray was superb, playing his best game since the 1970 FA Cup Final; Bremner and Giles were World Class, while Clarke, Jones and Lorimer were far too skilful and lively for Manchester United's back four.

Derby County had won 4-0 against local rivals Nottingham Forest, who were missing their star player Ian Storey-Moore, through goals from Alan Hinton (2), John O'Hare and Kevin Hector.

Manchester City held a two point lead over Leeds, Derby, Arsenal and Liverpool, on Saturday 26th February, with only four points separating those five great teams, but the Sky Blues were about to embark on a four game winning streak that made them almost impossible to catch.

	PL	W	D	L	F	A	PTS
Manchester City	30	16	9	5	59	34	41
Leeds United	29	16	7	6	44	22	39
Derby County	29	15	8	6	50	28	38
Arsenal	29	16	5	8	44	27	37
Liverpool	30	15	7	8	40	27	37
Wolves	30	13	10	7	50	42	36

After a great run, giving themselves an excellent chance to retain their title, Arsenal then lost away, twice, 2-0 at Manchester City and also 2-0 at Newcastle United, during early March, to rule them out of the title race.

Manchester City were rampant, though. Their classy *Nijinsky,* Colin Bell, had scored twice during their 2-1 win over West Brom, on St David's Day, and then Francis Lee also scored twice (one pen) during that 2-0 win over Arsenal. A week later, City won 2-1 away at Everton, on Saturday 11th March, thanks to a Tommy Wright own goal, and defender Freddie Hill's first goal of the season.

In this form, if City's stars couldn't score, then anyone would.

On Wednesday 8th March, though, Malcolm Allison, City's manager paid a club record transfer fee of £200,000 to QPR for their top goal-scorer Rodney Marsh. Marsh had scored 106 league goals for Rangers, in just 211 games, and he made his City debut at home to Chelsea, ten days later.

Malcolm Allison saw Marsh as the flair City needed, the final piece of his jigsaw in securing the First Division title. What he didn't see, though, but what he admitted afterwards, was how unfit Marsh was upon his arrival at Maine Road. Joe Mercer, City's Director of Football, and the previous manager, had advised Allison to use Marsh only as a substitute until the end of the season, to sharpen him up for 1972-73.

Allison intended to do things his way, though, and just ignored Mercer's advice. He put Rodney Marsh straight into City's team, replacing the effective and hard-working Tony Towers.

53,322 had packed Maine Road as the golden-haired new star of Manchester ran out, with his arms aloft, to loud acclaim. The fans weren't to know how unfit, or ill-fitting, Marsh was for their well-oiled sky blue machine.

Tommy Booth was back, after limping off at home to West Brom, at the start of the month, while Chelsea, who'd lost against Stoke City in the League Cup Final only a fortnight earlier, were missing the mighty Ron Harris, through suspension.

Eddie McCreadie had also played just half a dozen games all season, and he would remain out of action for another six weeks.

Booth scored early on, with a shot from just inside Chelsea's area, giving City a 1-0 half-time lead. Chelsea, with their golden trio of Osgood, Hudson and Cooke, fired forward, directed by the influential Hollins. Even when they did break City's stiff line of Book, Booth, Doyle and Donachie, though, Charlie Cooke's shot from the edge of the area was turned aside by Corrigan.

MANCHESTER CITY		CHELSEA
Joe Corrigan	1	Peter Bonetti
Tony Book	2	Paddy Mulligan
Willie Donachie	3	John Boyle
Mike Doyle	4	John Hollins
Tommy Booth	5	John Dempsey
Alan Oakes	6	David Webb
Mike Summerbee	7	Charlie Cooke
Colin Bell	8	Chris Garland
Wyn Davies	9	Peter Osgood
Francis Lee	10	Alan Hudson
Rodney Marsh	11	Peter Houseman
Tony Towers	12	Steve Kember
(rep. Marsh)		(rep. Houseman)

Peter Houseman was helped off, and out for five weeks, to finish off Chelsea's fading title hopes, while the maverick Marsh was hauled off, and replaced by Tony Towers to protect their victory, increasing City's lead at the top of the table to five points.

In spite of that five point lead, Leeds, Liverpool and Derby County were all in red hot form, and had played less matches than City.

The most famous, and most celebrated footballing moment of the season occurred during the match between Leeds United and Southampton, on Saturday 4th March. Leeds were in good form, having lost once in their last sixteen league and cup games since early November, while winning ten of them.

Southampton, though, were no mugs. They'd finished in seventh place in 1970-71, only six points behind third-placed Spurs, and had again qualified for the UEFA Cup. They also had the *Incredible Tackling Man*, Brian O'Neil, back in their side. It was O'Neil's first appearance since 13th November, following a cartilage operation, but a record nine week suspension had also lengthened his absence.

Brian O'Neil's last starting appearance was, ironically, during Southampton's 2-1 win over Leeds United, after which Leeds had started their great run. This match was also Mick Jones' 300th league game for Leeds, but a modest crowd of just 34,275 attended Elland Road.

From the very start, Steele, O'Neil, Davies, Gabriel and McCarthy were in the faces of Jones, Bremner, Gray, Clarke and Lorimer, sharp at their feet.

Channon, set up by Ron Davies, had shot wide from twenty yards, and then, Jimmy Gabriel, Southampton's classiest ever centre half, brought out a good save from Gary Sprake, following Terry Paine's corner-kick.

In the 38th minute, though, Bremner, Jones and Gray combined in a sweet passing move to set up Allan Clarke, who fired Leeds ahead from a narrow angle, to the left of Martin's goal. Then, just four minutes before half-time, Eddie Gray played a sublime ball through to Peter Lorimer, with a reverse left-footed pass, and Lorimer beat Fry for pace, before firing a power-packed rocket low past Eric Martin's dive.

LEEDS UNITED		SOUTHAMPTON
Gary Sprake	1	Eric Martin
Paul Reaney	2	Bob McCarthy
Paul Madeley	3	Roger Fry
Billy Bremner	4	Bobby Stokes
Jack Charlton	5	Jimmy Gabriel
Norman Hunter	6	Jim Steele
Peter Lorimer	7	Terry Paine
Allan Clarke	8	Mike Channon
Mick Jones	9	Ron Davies
Johnny Giles	10	Brian O'Neil
Eddie Gray	11	Tommy Jenkins
Mick Bates	12	Tony Byrne (rep. Paine)

As the second half wore on, despite continued pressure from a determined and dogged Southampton back eight, Leeds United's possession play became more accomplished, less rushed, and they played with greater patience.

Clarke, Lorimer, Jones, Giles, Bremner and Gray were happy to play the ball along the line of the Saints' area, just waiting for gaps to appear.

With only Davies and Channon there as a forward release valve, any chances of a break for Southampton, while tackles flew in from both Steele and O'Neil, were smothered by the defensive majesty of Reaney, Charlton, Hunter and Madeley.

Channon and Davies were swamped, in mud, as well as against an impregnable wall. Terry Paine's clever and well-guided aerial balls were held up and misdirected by the Wuthering, high, winter winds.

After an hour, Clarke took a wonderful pass by Giles, and he easily side-stepped Gabriel's tackle, before firing past Martin, from inside the area. Four minutes later, Lorimer danced into the Saints' area, and shot from fifteen yards. McCarthy attempted to clear the ball away, but the ferocity of Lorimer's rocket blast only diverted the ball into the middle of his goal.

Roger Fry played a loose pass, as Southampton's spirits dimmed, and Lorimer charged into the penalty area, firing past Martin for a 5-0 lead. The more defensive Tony Byrne had replaced Terry Paine, playing his 717th competitive game for Southampton, to try and stem the flow of possession and goals for Leeds.

Jack Charlton headed in Norman Hunter's left-wing cross, as the defence backed up their attack, after 73 minutes. Leeds' confidence was sky-high, while Southampton's, for all they continued to battle, was rock-bottom.

Johnny Giles ball-juggled on the halfway line, then passed wide to Madeley, who played a one-two with Eddie Gray, before Stokes attempted to steal the ball. Gray challenged, though, and beat Stokes' tackle, then he crossed from the left for Lorimer to head back inside, for Mick Jones to finish from six yards.

With Leeds United now 7-0 up, having broken down the stiff resistance of a good Southampton side, they decided to keep possession for the last five minutes.

What followed was an imperious display of majestic mastery of keeping the ball, and intelligent passing, with nonchalant back-heels and inside step flicks.

Mick Jones won the ball just inside the Southampton half, and passed back to Norman Hunter. Hunter passed to Madeley, who passed forward to Allan Clarke. Clarke switched inside for

Bremner, who played a one-two with Giles. Billy Bremner then exhibited some great ball-juggling and back-heeled to Lorimer out on the left.

Bremner received the ball again and played to Clarke, who laid off for Giles, and the ball came home again to Bremner. Bremner sprayed out wide right to Paul Reaney, who rode two tackles, and passed long, across the field, out to Giles, wide left.

Barry Davies' joy was completely clear in his commentary. "Every man-jack of this Leeds side is now turning it on," he cried.

"Oh look at that! It's almost cruel."

Giles passed to Clarke, back to Giles, to Bremner, to Giles, and to Lorimer. Peter Lorimer moved right again, playing in Reaney, who played the ball back home to Hunter. Hunter passed forwards to Bremner, to Giles, to Clarke, back to Bremner, and to Paul Madeley.

Madeley lost the ball, but regained possession immediately, with a typically classy tackle, and he played wide to Giles. Giles played back to Reaney, a nicely weighted high ball touched first time by Reaney, to Hunter, who pushed the ball up to Lorimer.

Lorimer passed to Bremner, to Giles. Johnny Giles back-heeled to Allan Clarke, who rode a tackle from Bobby Stokes, who then hacked at the tall, classy England striker, but Clarke continued, in possession, no complaints, despite Stokes' ugly foul, but the final whistle finished his run.

It had been a thrilling thirty-odd pass move, recorded on film, that captured the true footballing excellence and dominance of that Leeds United team.

Leeds went on to enjoy a great March, reaching the FA Cup Semi-finals, while killing Nottingham Forest 6-1, back in the league, as well as beating Arsenal 3-0 and then Coventry City 1-0, after that thrashing of Southampton.

Arsenal suffered a dreadful March. Despite knocking Derby out of the Cup, in the Fifth round, they lost three times in the league, in successive games. City had beaten them on 4th March, and then they lost 2-0 away at Newcastle, and 3-0 at Elland Road.

Arsenal were out of the title race, having never managed to regain their consistent form from the previous season. They suffered too many losing runs, inflicting irreparable damage to their chances. Arsenal's destructive, defensive dominance was no longer dreaded. They'd missed both Peter Simpson and Peter Storey for much of the season, but significantly, they also badly missed their unsung and under-rated left-back Bob McNab for over half of the season. McNab's defensive nous and tactical sharpness was a huge factor in the thirty-seven clean sheets that Arsenal had kept during 1970-71.

A week later, Manchester City were held to a 0-0 draw, away at Newcastle United. It was only the second game of a twenty-seven match run, in which City failed to score. They had lost 3-0 at Liverpool on Saturday 26th February, when they had greatly missed Colin Bell.

Now, City were missing Joe Corrigan, for all seven matches up to their last game of the season. Corrigan's absence resulted in an imbalance in the City defence, with the less experienced and less commanding Ron Healey taking his place in goal, but it was one man, Rodney Marsh, whether fairly or unfairly, who took the blame for City's subsequent collapse.

	PL	W	D	L	F	A	PTS
Manchester City	34	20	9	5	66	36	49
Derby County	32	18	8	6	56	29	44
Leeds United	31	18	7	6	52	22	43
Liverpool	33	17	8	8	49	27	42
Wolves	33	15	10	8	55	45	40
Spurs	32	14	10	8	48	33	38
Manchester Utd	32	15	8	9	54	45	38
Arsenal	31	16	5	10	44	31	37

"Everything we worked on was based on a one-touch or two-touch basis," Colin Bell explained. "Unfortunately, Rodney (would) take three or four unnecessary touches."

Mike Summerbee added, "our football that season was a quick, attacking game. When Rodney came into the side, it was a problem because he wasn't passing the ball to players where they were used to receiving it."

"Marshy would reach the line with a half-yard advantage," Colin Bell continued, "but then (he'd) check back to beat his opponent for a second time. We'd be running into the box, coming out and then going back in again."

"Losing the title that season was not solely down to him," Summerbee suggested, "but his arrival definitely disrupted the performances of what had been a settled team. We should have been Champions that year."

"We all ended up looking foolish," concluded Bell.

Tony Towers had been the player who Marsh had displaced. A good, local lad, Towers was a strong, stable number eleven who'd fulfilled the position left vacant after the departure of Tony Coleman. It was a position that both Joe Mercer and Malcolm Allison had struggled to fill.

Tony Towers knew he wasn't the best player in City's front six, but he knew who he was.

During Towers' eleven match run on the left wing, from Christmas to mid-March, City won seven matches, and scored twenty-three goals. They had risen from second place and four points behind, to top of the table and five points clear, during Tony Towers' golden period in City's number eleven shirt. Never mind, City lost 2-1 to Stoke City, at home, on April Fools' Day, with Marsh on the left wing, and three days later, they lost 2-0 to Southampton, at The Dell.

On Saturday 1st April, second-placed Leeds United visited third-placed Derby County, with both teams just one point below Manchester City. 39,450 filled every square foot of the Baseball Ground terraces for the match of the season, so far.

Leeds were missing their centre forward Mick Jones, and their forward line was subsequently subdued, but Derby were without their dynamic, white-booted, top scoring left-midfielder Alan Hinton, who'd hit fifteen goals in thirty-three games.

It was from the left side, though, that Derby's first half goal was created. Alan Durban crossed for John O'Hare to head home, at Sprake's near post. Then, after the break, Kevin Hector ran a long, long way, from his own penalty area, before firing a pass into O'Hare, inside the Leeds penalty area. Sprake managed to parry O'Hare's poked shot, but the ball hit Norman Hunter and rebounded back into his own goal.

DERBY COUNTY		LEEDS UNITED
Colin Boulton	1	Gary Sprake
Ron Webster	2	Paul Reaney
John Robson	3	Terry Cooper
Alan Durban	4	Billy Bremner
Roy McFarland	5	Jack Charlton
Colin Todd	6	Norman Hunter
John McGovern	7	Peter Lorimer
Archie Gemmill	8	Allan Clarke
John O'Hare	9	Paul Madeley
Kevin Hector	10	Johnny Giles
Jim Walker	11	Eddie Gray

Two days later, though, on Easter Monday, all that hard work was undone at St James's Park, as Tommy Cassidy's goal gave Newcastle United a 1-0 win over Derby.

Liverpool were the real form team in the First Division, but they still had a lot to do. They had taken nine points from their five matches in March, and then beaten West Brom 2-0 (Tommy Smith and Chris Lawler), at Anfield. On Easter Monday, they also smashed Manchester United 3-0, away at Old Trafford, with Lawler, Toshack and Hughes all scoring in front of 54,000 disillusioned supporters.

On Saturday 8th April, Liverpool beat Coventry 3-1 (Keegan, Smith (pen), Toshack), in front of a rampant Anfield crowd of nearly 51,000, to rise above Manchester City, and into third place. Only two points separated the top four First Division teams.

FIRST DIVISION LEADERS, 8TH APRIL 1972

	PL	W	D	L	F	A	PTS
Derby County	39	22	10	7	65	31	54
Leeds United	38	22	9	7	69	28	53
Liverpool	38	22	8	8	60	29	52
Manchester City	38	21	10	7	70	41	52
Arsenal	36	19	6	11	50	35	44

Manchester City ended their season decently enough, gaining five points from four games, but it wasn't enough.

They won 3-1 away at Manchester United, after two more goals from Francis Lee and also Rodney Marsh's third goal for the club rubbing salt into the Old Trafford wounds.

A recall to the starting eleven for Tony Towers, away at Coventry, had proved beneficial, as he scored his third of the season to earn a 1-1 draw. Mike Summerbee could only score a consolation, though, as Ipswich had beaten City 2-1 at Portman Road, on 18th April.

That defeat in Suffolk destroyed City's hopes of winning their second First Division title in four years, but they finally turned on the style at Maine Road against leaders Derby County, four days later, in front of 55,000 home fans.

Rodney Marsh outpaced Roy McFarland, and cracked the ball past Boulton, from the right, and then Francis Lee fired his penalty kick high into the top left corner of the Derby goal, after Terry Hennessey had scythed into Marsh on the left side of the penalty area.

Manchester City had finished their season by topping the table, but Derby, Leeds and Liverpool all had games to play, and City couldn't win the league.

While Derby had won 3-0, at home to Huddersfield, on Saturday 15th April, Leeds United lost 1-0, four days later, away at Newcastle, four days later, after a stunning Malcolm MacDonald swerver, but Liverpool were still on fire. They beat West Ham United 2-0 (Toshack, Heighway), away at Upton Park, and then one week later, on Saturday 22nd April, they hosted Bobby Robson's Ipswich Town, with 54,316 filling the mighty Anfield, for their final home game of the season.

This was a classic Liverpool line-up, almost perfect, probably their greatest-ever team, up to then. They were to sail away with the First Division title the following season, as well as winning their first ever European trophy, the UEFA Cup.

LIVERPOOL		IPSWICH TOWN
Ray Clemence	1	David Best
Chris Lawler	2	Mick Mills
Alec Lindsay	3	Colin Harper
Tommy Smith	4	Peter Morris
Larry Lloyd	5	Allan Hunter
Emlyn Hughes	6	Derek Jefferson
Kevin Keegan	7	Jimmy Robertson
Brian Hall	8	Colin Viljoen
Steve Heighway	9	Rod Belfitt
John Toshack	10	Trevor Whymark
Ian Callaghan	11	Mick Lambert
John McLaughlin	12	Bryan Hamilton (rep. Lambert)

John Toshack linked with Kevin Keegan to score twice, either side of half-time, for a clinical 2-0 win, lifting Liverpool up to just a single point behind the leaders, with two games to play. Liverpool had conceded just three goals in their last fourteen First Division games, but they'd scored thirty-four, a Goal Average of 11.33!

Leeds had taken revenge on West Brom, after their 2-1 win at Elland Road had deprived them of the title in 1971, by beating them 1-0 away at The Hawthorns. Johnny Giles' second half penalty kick kept the pressure on those teams above them.

There were still only two points separating the top four. Manchester City had completed their season in first place, but they couldn't win the league. With Liverpool set to visit Derby, the title was theirs to lose.

FIRST DIVISION LEADERS, 22ND APRIL 1972

	PL	W	D	L	F	A	PTS
Manchester City	42	23	11	8	77	45	57
Liverpool	40	24	8	8	64	29	56
Derby County	41	23	10	8	68	33	56
Leeds United	40	23	9	8	70	29	55

On Monday 1st May, Leeds United hosted Chelsea, and Derby County hosted Liverpool, who'd gained 27 points from their last fourteen matches.

46,565 packed Elland Road, and goals from Billy Bremner and Mick Jones, one in each half, secured an efficient enough 2-0 win over Chelsea, who finished the season in seventh place.

At The Baseball Ground, though, 39,420 literally filled the place, in *THE* Match of the Season. Brian Clough's team were only missing right-back Ron Webster, injured nine days earlier in their defeat at Maine Road. Sixteen year old Derby-born lad Steve Powell made only his second league start for The Rams, while Liverpool were at full strength.

DERBY COUNTY		LIVERPOOL
Colin Boulton	1	Ray Clemence
Steve Powell	2	Chris Lawler
John Robson	3	Alec Lindsay
Alan Durban	4	Tommy Smith
Roy McFarland	5	Larry Lloyd
Colin Todd	6	Emlyn Hughes
John McGovern	7	Kevin Keegan
Archie Gemmill	8	Brian Hall
John O'Hare	9	Steve Heighway
Kevin Hector	10	John Toshack
Alan Hinton	11	Ian Callaghan
Jim Walker	12	John McLaughlin

Derby's defence was imperious and impressive, allowing few chances to Liverpool's classy attacking eight. Liverpool had a strong claim for a penalty kick, when Kevin Keegan was felled by Colin Boulton's strong challenge, but referee Clive Thomas waved play on.

Young Steve Powell was brilliant in place of Webster, Derby's greatest ever full back. At one point, Powell flicked the ball up over Emlyn Hughes, and then he rounded the England player, before passing to Alan Durban.

Halfway through the second half, John McGovern collected a Liverpool clearance, and from just outside the area, he hit a fine swerving shot past the dive of Ray Clemence. It was a classic goal, at the exact right time of the season, and fans went wild all over Derbyshire. Derby's 1-0 win sent them to the top of the table, at the end of their season, but it looked very unlikely that they, the good guys, with the fewest bookings in the league, could actually hold onto top spot, and win the title.

FIRST DIVISION LEADERS, 1ST MAY 1972

	PL	W	D	L	F	A	PTS
Derby County	42	24	10	8	69	33	58
Leeds United	41	24	9	8	72	29	57
Manchester City	42	23	11	8	77	45	57
Liverpool	41	24	8	9	64	30	56

Leeds United had a winnable game away at Wolves, on the following Monday, but only two days after their FA Cup Final against the Cup holders, Arsenal.

On that same day, Liverpool also had to visit fifth-placed Arsenal, and could win the league only if they won, and Leeds lost. Leeds United would win the league if they simply avoided defeat at Molineux.

Leeds losing away at Wolves was unlikely. Wolves had lost all of their last four league games at home, to Leicester, Chelsea, West Brom and Sheffield United. Furthermore, they hadn't won at Molineux since Saturday 12th February.

In their FA Cup Final, Leeds were far superior to Arsenal, outplaying the holders, and only allowed a couple of chances. Reaney cleared a long range Alan Ball shot off the line, and Charlie George smashed the ball onto David Harvey's crossbar, late on.

Allan Clarke headed in Mick Jones' right sided cross, in the second half, and the first half of Leeds United's potential league and cup Double had been won.

Mick Jones, though, had suffered an awful shoulder injury, going in for an innocent looking challenge with Geoff Barnett, deep into stoppage time.

Having been physically helped up the steps, by Norman Hunter, to warm applause from all supporters all over Wembley, Mick Jones' 1971-72 season was sadly over.

It was a ridiculous decision for the FA to order Leeds to play their most crucial game of the season just two days after the Cup Final. Arsenal had, after all, been allowed to play their final match of the season, at home to Spurs, on the Thursday after the Final, so why couldn't Leeds have also done so?

Anyway, at Highbury, on Monday 8th May, Liverpool were held to a goalless draw by outgoing Champions Arsenal. John Toshack appeared to have scored a potential title-winning goal in the 88th minute, but referee Roger Kirkpatrick disallowed it, amidst loud protests from Liverpool's players, and the vast mass of Merseyside fans in the Clock End. Bill Shankly admitted afterwards, however, that Tosh was just in an offside position when Emlyn Hughes had passed to him.

In any case, it was still a long shot for Liverpool to win the title, after their defeat away at Derby. They'd still needed Leeds to lose, and considering their league position on Saturday 22nd January, it would have been a sporting miracle, had they actually won the title.

Liverpool had started their season too late, but their time was to come.

In spite of Leeds United's annoyance at the FA's order, they travelled up to Wolverhampton on the Monday after winning the Cup at Wembley, intending, and expecting, to win the Double.

After *their* defeat at Derby, and then Gary Sprake's subsequent mistake at home to Huddersfield, on Wednesday 5th April, Don Revie had finally decided to drop Sprake.

Revie had been fiercely loyal towards his inconsistent and constantly under-fire keeper, but he'd brought the Leeds-born David Harvey into the team for their last five league games, as well as their FA Cup Semi-final and Final victories.

Harvey was a more highly-rated keeper than the incident-prone Sprake. He went on to play for Scotland, due to parental grounds, and he kept goal as Scotland qualified for the 1974 World Cup Finals. It was possibly the best-ever Scotland team, of which David Harvey was a member.

Sprake played just one more First Division game for Leeds before he was sold to Birmingham City, seventeen months later, after playing 381 league matches at Elland Road. Inconsistent he might have been, but there weren't that many bad matches during his nine years with Leeds United.

Wolves played the same team that played in their first leg match of the UEFA Cup Final, against Spurs, five nights earlier. Wolves might well have lost their last four home league games, but they **HAD** beaten the mighty Juventus, in the UEFA Cup Quarter-finals.

A massive 53,379 crowd filled the huge, mountainous South and North Banks at Molineux, Wolves' biggest home attendance for over six years. To suggest that this match didn't matter to Wolves was well wide of the mark, and with Leeds not fully fit, and a little knackered, what had seemed a straightforward two points suddenly seemed a little harder.

Even harder to take were numerous rumours of bribery, offered to Wolves players, prior to the match. It seems hard to digest that Leeds United, fresh from their Cup Final success, with Mick Jones ruled out of action for months, that on Sunday or Monday, Leeds officials or management could have made contact with Wolves players, with offers of cash to reward their "lack of effort", on that Monday night.

The great Derek Dougan killed off any rumours of a "deal " between Leeds and Wolves. He suggested that any idea of a financial deal to fall over and die, against Leeds, would have to have become known about by him and his attacking partner, John Richards. They'd scored twenty-nine combined First Division goals that season, up to then, so if they hadn't heard about it, how could such a deal have been made?

"Nobody tapped us up," Dougan insisted, "and the game was played absolutely fair and square."

There were thousands locked out of Molineux, that Monday night. There were also the usual dozens of fans climbing the floodlight pylons to get a better view, and two hundred Leeds United supporters actually broke into the Polytechnic building overlooking the ground, to secure a rooftop view of a part of the pitch.

Wolves were playing for confidence, though, as well as pride, with their UEFA Cup Final second leg match at White Hart Lane just nine days away, and they set off sharply against the drained Leeds team.

WOLVERHAMPTON WANDERERS		LEEDS UNITED
Phil Parkes	1	David Harvey
Bernard Shaw	2	Paul Reaney
Gerald Taylor	3	Paul Madeley
Danny Hegan	4	Billy Bremner
Frank Munro	5	Jack Charlton
John McAlle	6	Norman Hunter
Jim McCalliog	7	Peter Lorimer
Kenny Hibbitt	8	Allan Clarke
John Richards	9	Mick Bates
Derek Dougan	10	Johnny Giles
David Wagstaffe	11	Eddie Gray

Allan Clarke and the innovative Eddie Gray both wore heavy strapping around their thighs, and they were clearly less than half-fit for a match of this importance.

Mick Bates, who'd sat on the bench for all four hours of the 1970 FA Cup Final, was picked to play in Mick Jones' place ahead of Terry Yorath, and as a result, Leeds United's attack was weakened.

Just before half-time, Frank Munro forced the ball in from close range, after Leeds had struggled to clear Kenny Hibbitt's corner. They looked half-asleep.

Just over twenty minutes into the second half, John Richards collected the ball, in a central position. He glanced both ways, and then squeezed a wonderful through-ball into the path of Derek Dougan, beating the Leeds offside trap.

The Doog slid his shot just beyond Harvey's dive.

Captain Billy Bremner, who'd been brilliant and an inspiration all night, fired in past Parkes, immediately after, and he was mobbed by all his Leeds teammates.

With just over twenty minutes of the 1972 title race to go, Leeds needed just one goal to win the Championship. The match momentum had swung, and after one brief Wolves barrage on Harvey's goal area, Leeds took full control.

Leeds United forgot all their aches and their pains and their excuses, as Bremner had been telling them to do all evening, and they began to command the match, just as they were used to.

The Wolves crowd, though, was beside itself, overjoyed at the thought that they might deny Leeds their deserved title. Wolves were spurred on by their spine-tingling home support, and while lesser First Division teams would have folded, They, led by both Munro and McCalliog, were determined to win.

Lorimer crossed, from the right. The ball hit Shaw on his arm. Penalty! Leeds players all appealed! Referee John Gow, however, ruled that it was accidental, and he waved play on. Allan Clarke was replaced by the young Terry Yorath, and Leeds United's attacking power was even further reduced.

The 53,000 Black Country crowd roared loudly as Leeds' title hopes ended, yet again.

Outside of Leeds, the rest of England celebrated. Brian Clough's Derby County were on holiday in the Scilly Isles and Majorca when they won the title. They had won the Football League Championship with their unspectacular, but attractive football, based on fair play and a refusal to confront the referee over any controversial decisions.

Football was the loser, but football was the winner. Bill Shankly, whose Liverpool had timed their run just too late, but whose greatest times would be recorded over the following twelve months, praised Derby County as "the best team we have played this season."

Leeds United, despite their disappointing start to the season, had dropped just two points from their seventeen home games played at Elland Road, after playing their first four home games away from home. They should have won the league, but you could pick the bones out of their season, if you liked. They should have got a point at Newcastle, or at Spurs, and they should have won at both Leicester and West Ham.

Don Revie admitted, though, that "all of us at Leeds are pleased that Derby have won the title."

In the end, just one point, *just one point*, had separated the top four teams in the First Division; the tightest ever finish in the history of the Football League, and it has yet to be tightened, tighter.

FIRST DIVISION LEADERS, MONDAY 8TH MAY 1972

	PL	W	D	L	F	A	PTS
Derby County	42	24	10	8	69	33	58
Leeds United	42	24	9	9	73	31	57
Liverpool	42	24	9	9	64	30	57
Manchester City	42	23	11	8	77	45	57
Arsenal	41	22	8	11	58	38	52
Spurs	41	18	13	10	61	42	49
Chelsea	42	18	12	12	58	49	48

Manchester City could have won the title, and should have, but they imploded.

Liverpool shouldn't have won the title, but they nearly did. Thanks, however, to the firm foundations finally laid during 1971-72, by Bill Shankly, Liverpool did win eleven of the next eighteen First Division titles.

Leeds United should have won the title, and they ***should*** have won it.

Whilst the best team possibly didn't win it, the fairest team did, the team with the best defence, and a very classy front six. Derby kept twenty-nine league and cup clean sheets during 1971-72, and they suffered only two suspensions throughout the season.

Alan Hinton, Kevin Hector and John O'Hare scored a combined forty-five goals for the superb Champions, while Alan Durban also hit double figures with his spectacular long range shooting.

Goals were in good supply, comparatively, in 1972, in an apparent age of defensive dominance. Francis Lee was the First Division's leading scorer with 33 goals, thirteen of which were penalties. Martin Chivers, though, was the country's top goal-scorer, from open play, with 25 league goals, and forty-one in all major competitions.

Peter Lorimer scored 28 league and cup goals, while George Best, Malcolm MacDonald and Peter Osgood all scored 26 league goals apiece. For tenth-placed Sheffield United, Alan Woodward and Billy Dearden had combined for thirty-seven goals, during a vintage season for the club.

Not only was 1971-72 the greatest Championship battle in the history of English league football, with the high quality of talent shining deep into lower mid-table, but it was also the greatest ever First Division (or Premier League) in the history of English football.

Of all the twenty-two teams in Division One, only Ipswich Town, with a top crowd of 29,229, had failed to attract a crowd of over thirty thousand.

Seventeen First Division teams attracted crowds of more than 40,000! Nine teams drew crowds of more than 50,000, and the average First Division crowd, of all the games played, of all twenty-two teams, at 462 First Division football matches, was 31,351.

Those crowds have never returned to English football, in such vast numbers, since 1971-72, the Greatest Ever Title Race.

SUNNY DAYS AND EUROPEAN NIGHTS
ON THE SOLENT

I N 1966, SOUTHAMPTON WON promotion to the First Division, for the first time in their eighty-one year history, after finishing second behind Second Division Champions Manchester City.

Southampton-born centre-forward Martin Chivers was their top scorer with thirty league goals. A gentle giant of a striker, with elegant ball skills, Chivers had also enjoyed great service from both wings, with John Sydenham on the left and Terry Paine on the right.

Southampton had scored 85 Division Two goals during 1965-66, due to their quick breaking football and accurate crossing. Terry Paine, from Winchester, only a few miles up the M3, was then rewarded with a place in England's squad for the 1966 World Cup Finals. Paine played in England's 2-0 win over Mexico, but he wasn't picked again by Alf Ramsey, as the *Wingless Wonders* went on to win the World Cup.

Terry Paine finally collected his FIFA World Cup Winner's medal, forty-three years later, at Number Ten Downing Street.

Southampton manager Ted Bates then strengthened his attack, in preparation for Division One, by signing Welsh international centre forward Ron Davies from Norwich City. The lantern-jawed Davies, from Holywell on the Dee Estuary, cost Southampton a club record transfer fee of £55,000, having scored fifty-eight goals in only 113 Second Division matches for the Canaries.

Ron Davies finished the 1966-67 season as the First Division's leading scorer, with a sensational total of thirty-seven goals from 41 matches. Martin Chivers had also chipped in with fourteen goals, giving the Saints' front two a combined tally of over fifty goals during their first season in Division One.

Only four other First Division teams scored more than the 74 goals that Southampton had scored, but despite the arrival of David Webb from Orient, in March 1966, their defence was not so sharp. Webb was one of only two defenders of First Division pedigree in Southampton's back line, and Ted Bates spent money on improving their defence, over the next season and a half.

Not a single team in Division One, though, had conceded more than Southampton's 92 goals against. But due to their fluent goal-scoring, Southampton had finished their first top flight season up in nineteenth place, five points above the relegation zone.

Southampton's manager, Ted Bates, knew that he had to reinforce his defence to lift his Hampshire team. Eric Martin had been signed from Dunfermline Athletic during March 1967, and the Perth-born goalkeeper settled into the Saints' defence for the next seven seasons.

Hugh Fisher, another Scot, had also signed from Blackpool during March 1967, for only £30,000. The tireless Glaswegian holding midfielder provided plenty of forceful protection to the Saints' defence.

In July 1967, though, Jimmy Gabriel signed from Everton for £42,500. Gabriel had played 256 First Division games for Everton, and he brought valuable experience.

He'd won the First Division title with Everton, back in 1963, and also the FA Cup, three years later. However, when Everton paid £85,000 to Preston North End for Howard Kendall, during the summer of 1967, Gabriel finally agreed to leave Everton, having always previously refused a move away from Goodison.

Martin Chivers then joined Tottenham Hotspur in January 1968. Spurs manager Bill Nicholson had broken the British record transfer fee, paying Southampton £125,000 for Chivers who'd scored 97 league goals in just 174 games for his home town club.

One month later, John McGrath then joined Southampton from Newcastle United, for just £30,000. McGrath, who'd played 170 league games for Newcastle, was a tough, big man; both rough and clumsy but built like a brick barn.

John McGrath wasn't a dirty player, but he had a good habit of taking both man and ball in the tackle, and hard! Just what the doctor had ordered for Southampton.

Also during that same month, February 1968, Joe Kirkup had signed from Chelsea, in a player swap deal that saw David Webb move to the Stamford Bridge club.

Kirkup had only played fifty-three First Division matches for Chelsea, but prior to that, he'd played 165 games for West Ham United, and he was the Hammers' right back when they beat 1860 Munich in the 1965 European Cup Winners' Cup Final.

David Webb had played 75 league games in nearly two seasons at The Dell, and then during 1968-69, his first full season at Stamford Bridge, he was voted as Chelsea's Player of the Season.

Ron Davies was again the First Division's leading scorer, during 1967-68, with twenty-eight goals from 40 games, sharing the prize with George Best, but Bestie had played 41 games.

Southampton still finished down in sixteenth place, just five points above the drop. They'd scored sixty-six goals, but they still conceded very heavily, eighty-three goals.

Only bottom-placed Fulham had conceded more First Division goals.

Southampton's highlight of that season was their 2-2 home draw with the First Division leaders and European Cup Semi-finalists Manchester United on Saturday 13th April 1968. Ron Davies and Terry Paine both scored in front of a club record attendance of 30,079.

Of that eleven who drew with United, Martin, Kirkup, Fisher, McGrath, Gabriel, Hollywood, Paine, Channon and Davies were all players for the future. Frank Saul was eventually transferred to QPR in 1970, and Jimmy Melia became Aldershot manager after retiring in the autumn of 1968.

Southampton's left-back, on that day, was the splendidly named Dennis Hollywood, or to give him his full name, amongst the greatest of all full names, Dennis Fallen Hollywood. A golden-haired, strong tackling, attacking full-back from Govan, Glasgow. Hollywood played on for the Saints until retiring at the end of the 1971-72 season, when Francis Burns arrived from Manchester United for one season.

During the 1968-69 season, their newly structured defence settled into a unit. Martin, Kirkup, McGrath, Gabriel and Hollywood, and with Fisher on protection duties, learnt two new words for Southampton's First Division dictionary: Clean Sheet.

Southampton kept fifteen clean sheets that season, as they chased a European Fairs Cup qualifying place.

On Easter Monday 1969, an eighteen year old Bobby Stokes had made his league debut at home to Burnley, replacing the injured Mike Channon, as Saints needed a win. The Portsmouth-born attacking midfield player then scored twice as Southampton thrashed Burnley 5-1, with Paine, Davies and Judd scoring their other goals.

Stokes ended the season with three goals from his first four games, helping Southampton finish in seventh position, and qualifying for the Inter-Cities Fairs Cup.

Ron Davies was again their top scorer, during 1968-69, with twenty First Division goals from 38 games, but John McGrath had really made a difference at the back, forming an excellent defensive partnership with Jimmy Gabriel. McGrath started all 42 league games, as well as Terry Paine, and Southampton also set a post-war defensive record after conceding only forty-eight league goals.

On 16th August 1969, Southampton visited Old Trafford in the First Division, without Channon, Martin or Kirkup. 49,936 home fans had expected very few problems for Manchester United when Francis Burns' free-kick was flicked on by Brian Kidd, and then Willie Morgan volleyed home from six yards, for a 1-0 lead.

Southampton equalised though, after John Sydenham's right-footed, in-swinging cross from the left was headed in by Ron Davies, almost on the goal-line.

Davies then swept the ball out to Paine, in right midfield. Terry Paine found Sydenham with a superb cross-field pass. Sydenham's long left wing cross beyond the far post was attacked by Davies, whose towering header was adjudged to have beaten Jimmy Rimmer on the goal-line, despite the keeper attempting to claw the ball out.

Into the second half, Sydenham then notched a hat-trick of assists. He weaved in from the left wing, teasing Shay Brennan, before crossing from the bye line, just on the edge of the penalty area. Ron Davies launched himself, fully five feet into the air, and way above his marker, at the far post, with the force of his header giving Rimmer no hope, to complete his hat-trick of headed goals.

With Southampton 3-1 up, the blond-haired Jimmy Gabriel played the ball out of defence, and then arched a through-ball on for Davies to chase with lone defender Brennan. Ron Davies easily out-muscled Brennan, and slotted the ball under Rimmer, from just inside the penalty area.

A wonderful performance by Ron Davies was acknowledged by Sir Matt Busby, United's former manager, now their director and GM, who praised him as the very best centre forward in Europe.

On Wednesday 17th September, Southampton flew to Norway, for their first ever European competition match against Rosenborgs of Trondheim.

Rosenborgs, who were managed by Coventry City's former legend George Curtis, won 1-0. Two weeks later, though, back at The Dell, goals from both Ron Davies and Terry Paine won the tie for Southampton, 2-1 on aggregate.

An under strength Manchester United visited Southampton a week later, on Wednesday 8th October. United were missing Law, Stiles and Crerand, but the home team were without Davies in their line-up.

31,044 bulged their 30,000 ground capacity, Southampton's biggest-ever home crowd, geared up for a legendary win to grace the occasion. The Dell, John Bugden remembered, was "a tight little ground but could it rock when full? The night games were even better."

United killed their hopes, though. George Best gave United the lead in the first half, and then Francis Burns and Brian Kidd both netted late on for their 3-0 away thrashing of the Saints.

On Wednesday 5th November, Southampton visited Vitoria Guimares of Portugal, and they battled for a superb 3-3 draw. Their big three, Channon, Davies and Paine all scored, levelling goals from Mendes, twice, and also Pinto's penalty kick.

A week later, Southampton hammered Guimares 5-1, in front of only 21,414, after an own goal, Ron Davies's brace, Jimmy Gabriel and Mike Channon had given Southampton an 8-4 aggregate win.

The 1969 Fairs Cup winners and Cup holders, Newcastle United, hosted Southampton for the Third round first leg on Wednesday 17th December, in what was seen as the battle of the *Welsh Air Force*, with Ron Davies up against the mighty *Wyn the leap* Davies. Southampton's back four did superbly well, though, at a fervent St James's Park, keeping a clean sheet, but they managed to only draw 0-0.

In between their two European matches against Newcastle, Ted Bates had forked out £55,000 for left winger Tom Jenkins. Jenkins had been playing non-league football for Margate, starting 76 games for them until July 1969, when Reading paid just £500 for him. So, only five months after he'd been playing Southern League football, Jenkins had been signed by a First Division club for a record fee.

25,182 packed into The Dell on Wednesday 14th January 1970, for their Fairs Cup second leg match, with Southampton needing any sort of win...

SOUTHAMPTON		NEWCASTLE UNITED
Eric Martin	1	Iam McFaul
Joe Kirkup	2	David Craig
Brendan Byrne	3	Frank Clark
Hugh Fisher	4	Tommy Gibb
Jimmy Gabriel	5	Bobby Moncur
David Walker	6	John McNamee
Tom Jenkins	7	Pop Robson
Mike Channon	8	Jimmy Smith
Ron Davies	9	Wyn Davies
Terry Paine	10	David Young
John Sydenham	11	David Ford
Bobby Stokes	12	Ron Guthrie
(rep. Sydenham)		

Southampton, without their leader John McGrath, who'd been injured during the first leg up at Newcastle, took the lead when the blue eyed winger Jenkins set up Channon right on the edge of the penalty area, just before half-time.

Bryan 'Pop' Robson volleyed Newcastle level, though, during the second half.

Southampton pressed and pressed for the winner, lifted by a deafening roar from their home fans, an electric atmosphere under the floodlights.

"The Dell was a tight little ground but could it rock when full? The night games were even better."

The dynamic and direct Bobby Stokes came on for Sydenham, playing his final game for Southampton, but Newcastle hung on, going through 1-1, on the away goals rule.

John Sydenham left Southampton in March 1970, joining his old team-mate Jimmy Melia, Aldershot's new manager, to finish his career at The Recreation Ground. Sydenham, who'd arrived at The Dell as a teenager, back in 1957, had made 343 league appearances, scoring 36 goals, but creating over a hundred. Man of the Match during their 4-1 win at Old Trafford just seven months earlier, he was one of the greatest wingers to ever play for Southampton. The balance he provided to the team during the Sixties, with Terry Paine on the opposite wing was precious and perfect.

Southampton finished the season just above the relegation zone, once again. Missing Davies, Kirkup, Hollywood and Stokes for much of the 1969-70 season, their strength in depth wasn't sufficient to sustain another successful Division One campaign.

During the Summer of 1970, Ted Bates bought Brian O'Neil from Burnley, for £80,000. O'Neil was regularly celebrated in the alternative football paper, *FOUL,* for his, *ahem,* firm tackling.

FOUL called both Brian O'Neil and Joe Kirkup "the Hearts of Oak".

Manchester City's Colin Bell even commented on O'Neil, "I think they just bought him to kick people." The hard-tackling, determined player soon became a real cult hero at Southampton, after giving them a bit more steel.

During 1970-71, Southampton enjoyed yet another competitive Division One campaign, with O'Neil and Fisher commanding their midfield, in front of a balanced back four of Kirkup, Gabriel, McGrath and Hollywood. Terry Paine and Tom Jenkins were regular suppliers of good crosses from the wings, and Mike Channon and Ron Davies regularly connected, scoring thirty-five goals between them, from 82 league games.

Tom Jenkins had scored a superb goal on 31st August 1970, voted BBC TV's Goal of the Month, securing Southampton a 1-1 draw away at West Ham, after he dribbled past three defenders, and left the World class Bobby Moore sitting on his backside. Then he fired past Peter Grotier to give Saints a first half lead.

However, it was one of only four goals Jenkins scored in 84 First Division matches at Southampton.

Southampton again qualified for Europe on April 17th 1971, after winning 1-0 away at Wolverhampton Wanderers, with Channon scoring their important, solitary goal.

Southampton's classic line-up of Martin, Kirkup, Hollywood, Fisher, McGrath, Gabriel, Paine, Channon, Davies, O'Neil and Jenkins had provided great balance which Southampton enjoyed throughout the season, and they finished seventh again.

As well as Mike Channon, Brian O'Neil, Hugh Fisher and Joe Kirkup also played in all 42 of Southampton's First Division games. The Saints also kept eighteen clean sheets that season, setting a new post-war defensive record of just forty-four goals conceded, and they crowned their success in style, hammering Crystal Palace 6-0 on the Solent, on the very last day of the season. Goals from Gabriel, Harfield, Davies, O'Neil and Mike Channon's brace delighted their home crowd.

The opening game of 1971-72 finally welcomed the return of Bobby Stokes from injury. At twenty-one years old by then, Stokes became a first team regular, thereafter, starting thirty-seven games during 1971-72.

Southampton had been given a tough, tough UEFA Cup First round draw against Athletic Bilbao, in September 1971. 21,600 fans, not a huge Dell crowd, but decent enough for a First round match in a brand new Cup competition, turned up to watch Martin, Kirkup, Hollywood, Fisher, McGrath, Gabriel, Paine, Channon, Stokes, O'Neil and Jenkins take on the pride of the Basques.

Jenkins and Channon both scored to put Southampton 2-0 up, but Arieta gave the Basque club a valuable away goal. Ron Davies came on as a substitute for Stokes, but he couldn't restore his team's two goal advantage. A fortnight later, late at night in the Biscay province, amidst a fierce and hostile atmosphere, and with a massive 45,000 crowd whistling and jeering Saints' every touch, Bilbao won 2-0 to advance, 3-2 on aggregate.

Once again, the season that had followed a terrific season on the Solent was a poor one. Southampton lost 8-0 at Everton, 7-0 at Leeds, and also 2-5 at home to a fading Manchester United. However, they won just enough games, here and there, to finish six points above the relegation places.

Jim Steele had signed for Southampton in January 1972, after manager Ted Bates had equalled their club record transfer fee, by paying Dundee £80,000 for the Edinburgh-born centre-back. Nicknamed *Ironsides,* Jim Steele started their final sixteen First Division games of the season in midfield, after Hugh Fisher had broken his leg when he'd collided with Arsenal goalkeeper Bob Wilson, on Saturday 2nd October 1971.

Mike Channon was Southampton's top scorer in 1971-72 with just fourteen goals, while the ageing Ron Davies also contributed eleven goals from twenty-seven games, and the rejuvenated Bobby Stokes had scored seven goals from midfield.

1972-73 was a mediocre season, following Jimmy Gabriel's move to Bournemouth during July 1972, after 191 First Division matches with Southampton, and scoring twenty-six goals in his five seasons at The Dell.

The great man had played 447 First Division matches in total at both Everton and Southampton. Jim Steele took Gabriel's place in central defence, but before September was done, John McGrath had also played his 167th and final game for Southampton.

The two men, probably the greatest central defensive partnership in Southampton's history, had been so vital in their First Division successes, but their departures left a huge gap to fill, for many seasons thereafter.

Paul Bennett, a Southampton-born youth team graduate, had replaced McGrath in their team. Bennett and Steele did reasonably well in their thirty games' central defensive partnership during 1972-73, as Saints lost only nine games.

However, Southampton had also won only eight games.

In November 1972, Tom Jenkins moved to Swindon Town after 84 league games at The Dell. Scorer of that superb, individualistic goal against West Ham, Jenkins was often too individualistic, dribbling into cul-de-sacs, rather than seeing the simple, early ball, that had frustrated both supporters and teammates, and Bobby Stokes became a better left midfield attacker.

On the last day of March, in 1973, Ron Davies came on as a substitute for Bobby Stokes, for his 240th and final league match for Southampton.

He was sold to Portsmouth for just £45,000 in April 1973, having scored 134 First Division goals for the Saints.

At his very best, Ron Davies certainly was the very best centre-forward, the most frightening and unstoppable centre-forward, in Europe. Davies scored 13 goals in his first full season at Fratton Park, to take his career league goals total clear above 270.

Mike Channon remained Southampton's top scorer with sixteen goals from forty games, during 1972-73, but Ron Davies, one of Southampton's three or four greatest ever players, was still second-placed with nine from only twenty-four games.

Paul Gilchrist, a £30,000 signing from Doncaster Rovers in March 1972, had also scored six goals from 22 appearances. Those stats suggested, though, that Southampton could be starved of goals, if Channon struggled the following season.

Mike Channon certainly didn't struggle during 1973-74, but apart from his goals, the rest of Southampton's entire squad scored only 26 goals in 42 games.

Joe Kirkup played his 169th and final First Division game for Southampton, on Wednesday 12th September, as they lost 2-0 away at Norwich City.

Kirkup had moved over to left back during the previous season, following Southampton-born Bob McCarthy's introduction at right back.

On Sunday 18th November, Southampton were safely in the First Division's top ten, after Mike Channon had scored nine goals during their opening sixteen matches.

On that very day, though, Lawrie McMenemy became their new manager, after Ted Bates had decided to stand down, and become the club's Chief Executive.

Ted Bates had first joined Southampton 46 years earlier, back in 1937, and he'd been their manager since 1955. Bates had lifted them up from the lower reaches of Division Three, as Third Division Champions in 1960, and then into the high life of Division One, where he'd kept them, and where they were now spending their eighth season.

SOUTHAMPTON		IPSWICH TOWN
Eric Martin	1	David Best
Bob McCarthy	2	Geoff Hammond
Steve Mills	3	Mick Mills
Hugh Fisher	4	Peter Morris
Paul Bennett	5	Allan Hunter
Jim Steele	6	Kevin Beattie
Terry Paine	7	Bryan Hamilton
Mike Channon	8	Colin Viljoen
Paul Gilchrist	9	David Johnson
Brian O'Neil	10	Trevor Whymark
Bobby Stokes	11	Clive Woods

Southampton were an established top flight force in July 1973, when Ted Bates had welcomed Lawrie McMenemy as his number two at The Dell. He saw McMenemy as the right man for the future of the Saints. By November, though, Nottingham Forest were declaring a firm interest in appointing McMenemy as their new manager, so Southampton were forced to reshuffle their pack to secure McMenemy's services.

Ted Bates made way for the young McMenemy for the good of Southampton.

On Saturday 15th December 1973, eighth-placed Southampton hosted Ipswich Town, who were also fighting for a UEFA Cup place with the Saints.

A small crowd of just 14,863 half-filled The Dell, as Mike Channon's second half penalty kick, and then Paul Gilchrist's late goal, gave Southampton a hard-earned 2-0 win, lifting the Saints up to fifth in the league, above both Newcastle and Derby.

	PL	W	D	L	F	A	PTS
Leeds United	20	14	6	0	39	11	34
Liverpool	20	11	5	4	25	16	27
Burnley	19	10	6	3	27	17	26
Everton	20	8	7	5	23	19	23
SOUTHAMPTON	20	8	7	5	26	25	23
Newcastle Utd	19	9	4	6	28	21	22
Derby County	20	8	6	6	22	20	22
Coventry City	21	9	4	8	23	25	22
QPR	20	6	9	5	30	26	21
Leicester City	20	7	7	6	24	21	21
Ipswich Town	19	8	5	6	29	30	21

Southampton did not win again in their next seven league games, though, and they were back down in mid-table by the time they finally beat Newcastle 3-1 at The Dell (Peach, Channon, Fisher), on Tuesday 5th February.

David Peach had signed from Gillingham for £50,000, on Monday 14th January. The twenty-two year old full back had played 187 league games for The Gills. Peach was the first of four new players to make their Saints' debuts, within just two months, that formed one third of a future, legendary Southampton team.

Nick Holmes, another Southampton-born youth team player, had made his debut in central defence during Southampton's 1-0 defeat at Arsenal, on Saturday 2nd March. Ian Turner then joined from Grimsby Town on Wednesday 6th March, as cover for goalkeeper Eric Martin.

Finally, on that very same day, Lawrie McMenemy smashed the club's record transfer fee, paying £275,000 for Chelsea and England legend Peter Osgood.

Amidst all this mass recruitment, though, Southampton had stopped scoring and started slipping. During the eleven matches following their 3-1 win over Newcastle, Mike Channon scored only two goals, and Bobby Stokes also scored only two goals, but no other Saints player scored a single goal in any of those eleven matches.

They'd even been dumped out of the FA Cup, beaten 0-1 at home by Wrexham, in the Fifth round, with nearly 25,000 inside The Dell.

By the time they hosted second-bottom Manchester United, on Saturday 20th April, Southampton had dropped right down to nineteenth position, just one place above the relegation zone.

30,789 filled The Dell on a desperately vital Saturday afternoon. Southampton had to beat United, a result that would relegate the former European Champions, and keep their heads above Birmingham City, who scored fluently, but had a colander defence.

Jim McCalliog hammered a penalty kick past Eric Martin for the resurgent Red Devils before the break, his fourth goal in three games since he'd joined United.

Mike Channon then clipped in a second half equaliser, but the Saints' otherwise light-scoring attack couldn't find any way past United's tight Scottish defence, that conceded only 48 First Division goals, despite their eventual relegation.

Southampton remained in nineteenth place, though, because Birmingham had only managed to draw at Newcastle, but during midweek, Burnley hammered Southampton 4-0, while Birmingham also spanked QPR 4-0, and Saints suddenly sunk into the bottom three.

On 27th April, the final Saturday of the season, Southampton finally found their goal touch, slaughtering Everton 3-0, but those goals scored by Peter Osgood, Mike Channon and Brian O'Neil were too little, too late, because Birmingham City had also beaten bottom club Norwich 2-1 to survive.

Southampton had pulled off a unique achievement, having been in a UEFA Cup qualifying place one week before Christmas, prior to then being relegated in April, never done before or since by any other club.

Mike Channon was Southampton's top scorer, and indeed, the First Division's top goal-scorer, with twenty-one goals. Bobby Stokes was their next highest scorer, though, with only seven. As it was Birmingham's inability to keep goals out that almost saw them down, it was inevitably Southampton's difficulty in scoring goals that had resulted in their relegation.

Terry Paine had played in forty-one league games during their relegation season, but he missed the final game against Everton through injury. In June, Paine moved to Hereford United on a free transfer, to become their player-coach.

Terry Paine holds a club record of 713 Football League matches for Southampton, while scoring 160 goals. He remains one of Southampton's greatest three players in their history. Paine went on to play 110 games for Hereford United, before finally retiring in 1977, following the Bulls' relegation from Division Two.

1974-75 was a dreadful season. Southampton began terribly, winning only once in their first eight games, and they dropped into the Second Division relegation zone.

There were a few small bright points from this catastrophe, however. Their one win was at home to their fierce local rivals Portsmouth, and Peter Osgood was finally starting to feel comfortable in his new surroundings.

Ossie had scored both goals during their 2-1 win in front of a 19,361 crowd.

Ian Turner was also beginning to take over from Eric Martin as their regular goalkeeper, and Mel Blyth had joined from Crystal Palace on Saturday 14th September for £60,000. Blyth had played over 200 league games for Palace, most of them First Division games, and he was well experienced and hardened, just as McGrath and Gabriel were when they both joined during the 1967-68 season.

Due to their Channon/Osgood double act, Southampton pulled themselves well clear of relegation troubles, but they rarely threatened the top half of the table.

They settled in and around thirteenth place after the New Year.

Manchester United were running away with the Second Division title, and in February, while they were busy eyeing up Steve Coppell, a young winger from Tranmere Rovers, Tommy Docherty sold Jim McCalliog to Southampton for a bargain price of £40,000. McCalliog had scored *the* goal that had all but relegated the Saints, ten months earlier, but he brought invaluable midfield experience.

He'd scored 62 goals from his 351 Football League matches, most of them in the First Division, and he also captained Wolves in the 1972 UEFA Cup Final.

Southampton ended up nine points above the relegation zone, but twelve points below the promotion places. Mike Channon and Peter Osgood had scored thirty-two league goals between them, but no other player scored more than five.

Brian O'Neil had also played the last of his 149 league games for Southampton, against Nottingham Forest, back in October.

He was sold to Huddersfield Town a week later, for only £40,000, but he couldn't help prevent the Terriers from being relegated to the Fourth Division.

Brian O'Neil became a race horse owner after he retired, and he continued his firm friendship with Mick Channon, an acclaimed and successful trainer after he eventually stopped playing football.

In July 1975, Channon, Southampton's captain, was concerned about his England future, while playing for a club languishing in the lower half of the Second Division. So he handed in a written transfer request. Lawrie McMenemy persuaded Channon to stay, but his request meant that he'd also reluctantly relinquished his captaincy.

Peter Rodrigues had joined Southampton during the Summer of 1975, after his contract at Sheffield Wednesday had expired. A veteran of 385 league games with both Cardiff and Leicester City, as well as the Owls, Rodrigues took over as Southampton's new captain shortly after his arrival.

With a sharper, and more experienced defence of Rodrigues, Steele, Blyth and Peach, Southampton enjoyed a more successful start to the 1975-76 season, winning five of their opening eight league games.

They then went on a five-match winning run during December to sit just behind Sunderland, Bolton Wanderers and Bristol City, in fourth place. Their finest performance of this run was on Boxing Day 1975, when the Saints had hammered Bristol Rovers 3-0 at The Dell, with Holmes, Stokes and Channon all scoring.

Then, on Saturday 3rd January 1976, Southampton hosted Aston Villa, in the FA Cup Third round, with a promotion battle more on their minds than any Wembley dreams. Their largest home crowd of the season, 24,138, packed The Dell as David Peach swung in a wonderful cross, and Channon laid the ball on for High Fisher to thrash the ball past Burridge, his first goal since 1974, to equalize Andy Gray's very early header.

Four days later, 44,623 strolled into Villa Park, expecting a routine home win for the First Division team, and a straightforward passage into Round four.

Saints took the lead, though, after half an hour, when McCalliog set himself up for a great finish from the edge of the area, firing his fierce shot beyond John Burridge's dive. Villa then equalised just before half-time, though, after Ray Graydon had made the most of a poor back pass by Peach.

The game finished 1-1 and it went into extra-time. During the first period, Peach's in-swinging corner kick was knocked away back to McCalliog, who hammered the ball through a crowd of players, giving the unsighted Burridge no chance.

Southampton then beat Blackpool 3-1 in the Fourth round, with Channon scoring twice and Bobby Stokes the other, but all three goals had come from David Peach passes; a left-wing cross, a free-kick and a corner kick.

David Peach was Southampton's left-back, but he'd previously played in midfield at Gillingham, and he had a supremely cultured left foot. He became one of the best attacking full backs in English football during the mid-late Seventies.

He also became Southampton's regular penalty taker, later on in 1976.

Bobby Stokes scored again in the Fifth round, at The Hawthorns, as Southampton drew 1-1 away at fellow Second Division side West Brom. Their 27,614 home crowd, the largest of the season at The Dell, could be heard in the middle of The Solent, on Tuesday 17th February.

Mike Channon's hat-trick put Saints into the FA Cup Quarter-finals for the first time since 1963. He fired in his first goal after just fifty-two seconds, as Southampton won the replay 4-0, with Paul Gilchrist scoring their other goal.

In the midst of all this eventfulness, though, Southampton had slipped down to sixth place, behind both Notts County and West Brom, in the Second Division promotion race. They'd only taken five points from four games since the New Year, but two quick wins over Orient and Fulham then lifted them back up to fifth by the end of February.

League consistency was again a problem for Saints, though, and successive defeats to bottom-placed York City, and also Luton Town, dropped them down well below the promotion places by the time they visited Bradford, on Saturday 6th March.

Fourth Division Bradford City had battled past Isthmian League team Tooting and Mitcham United, and also First Division Norwich City, en route to the Sixth round, but due to their disgraceful, extortionate pricing structure to try and make big money from the match, only 14,000 attended Valley Parade, seven thousand less than the crowd that had watched their Fourth round win over Tooting.

It was the lowest ever crowd for an FA Cup Quarter-final match.

Jim McCalliog illustrated his international pedigree by winning the game with a decisive, delightful, dipping volley from twenty yards out, and Southampton's experienced, well-drilled defence easily contained Bradford's Fourth Division attack.

The home fans, who had stoned and bricked the travelling coaches from Tooting, back in the Fourth round, then resorted to the old chants, *"you're gonna get your fucking heads kicked in!"*

Bradford had actually increased the volume of their home support with hidden microphones, placed in the home sides of the ground, during their 3-1 win over Tooting and Mitcham.

For once, it was very pleasing that there was no FA Cup shock here.

Southampton were drawn against Third Division Crystal Palace, who'd just shocked the Second Division leaders Sunderland, away at Roker Park. 52,810 packed the vast terraces of Stamford Bridge, on Saturday 3rd April 1976, for their Semi-final. Palace had also already knocked out both Leeds United and Chelsea, and Southampton seemed to be their easiest draw of the lot. Many hoped Palace would go all the way to Wembley, and become the first ever Third Division team to reach the FA Cup Final.

Palace manager Malcolm Allison had even predicted, in the tabloids, that his team would not only beat Southampton, but also win the Cup. With the exciting talents of Peter Taylor, Dave Swindlehurst, Alan Whittle and Nicky Chatterton, many neutrals also believed in the Palace dream.

A young Kenny Sansom didn't play at Stamford Bridge, although he'd made his debut a month earlier, and he then started all but one of their remaining league games after the Semi-final. For Southampton, Hugh Fisher had suffered a pelvic strain during the week before the Semi-final, and he was replaced in midfield by Paul Gilchrist.

Also, Jim Steele returned to partner Mel Blyth in central defence.

Paul Bennett had deputised for Jim Steele in their Quarter-final away win over Bradford, with *Ironsides* missing for three weeks due to having mumps.

McMenemy chose his very best eleven, though, in spite of Bennett's assured performances, and during the Summer, Paul Bennett was sold to Reading for just £8,000, having played 106 league games for Saints.

Paul Gilchrist, though, had found a second chance under Lawrie McMenemy. He'd never really sustained a good run in the first team, since signing four years earlier, unable to break through the brick walls of Fisher and O'Neil, and then Fisher and McCalliog, in central midfield. He'd often filled in as an attacking partner for Mike Channon, but once Ossie arrived, that position disappeared, and he lived on scraps.

Gilchrist had started only four of their final 26 league games during the previous season, and he'd started only nine of their first 31 games of 1975-76.

Injuries, firstly to Nick Holmes, and then Hugh Fisher, had allowed Paul Gilchrist a good run in midfield for the remaining eleven, or so, games of that season.

After a tight, tactical first half, Gilchrist opened the scoring after 73 minutes.

He played a one-two with Osgood, after Channon had won the ball in midfield, and then, with a brilliant first time shot, he sent the ball whizzing past Palace keeper Paul Hammond, from thirty yards out.

Five minutes later, with Crystal Palace pressing for a goal, the ball broke away swiftly. Mike Channon ran onto a long ball, and then, just inside the Palace area, he was brought down by Jim Cannon.

David Peach took their penalty kick. He'd scored nineteen successive penalties for Gillingham, between Saturday 8th November 1969 and Saturday 17th November 1973, but this was his first for Southampton. Peach drove the ball confidently past Hammond, and he became the Saints' regular penalty taker from then on.

Manchester United won the other Semi-final against Derby County, also by 2-0, and they still had an strong outside chance of a League and Cup Double.

Most pundits had believed that that Derby v United match at Hillsborough should have been the Final, and that the Cup Final to be was going to be a non-match.

United were red hot, hot favourites.

Back in the Second Division, fifth-placed Southampton kept chasing the top three, but fourth-placed West Bromwich Albion also kept winning. Defeats to both Plymouth and Bristol Rovers, in successive days on Good Friday and Easter Saturday, had ended Saints' promotion hopes for yet another year.

If it **weren't** for the Cup Final, that might have been curtains for McMenemy, after failing to achieve promotion back to Division One for two successive seasons, but there **was** the FA Cup Final and we'll never know.

Southampton won their final two league games to end up in sixth place, only four points behind promoted West Brom.

It must be noted, given Southampton's disappointments, that all of the teams promoted to Division One in both 1975 and 1976, Manchester United, Aston Villa, Norwich City, Sunderland, Bristol City and West Brom, were of a high, high quality.

Mike Channon was again top scorer with twenty-four league and cup goals, but Bobby Stokes, Jim McCalliog and Nick Holmes had all also hit double figures.

On the morning of the FA Cup Final, on a very hot Saturday 1st May, Southampton were 7-1 at the bookmakers, to win the Cup. They were even less fancied than Sunderland had been, against the mighty Leeds United, three years earlier.

MANCHESTER UNITED		SOUTHAMPTON
Alex Stepney	1	Ian Turner
Alex Forsyth	2	Peter Rodrigues
Stewart Houston	3	David Peach
Gerry Daly	4	Nick Holmes
Brian Greenhoff	5	Mel Blyth
Martin Buchan	6	Jim Steele
Steve Coppell	7	Paul Gilchrist
Sammy McIlroy	8	Mike Channon
Stuart Pearson	9	Peter Osgood
Lou Macari	10	Jim McCalliog
Gordon Hill	11	Bobby Stokes
David McCreery	12	Hugh Fisher

Seven to one in a two horse race? They were truly ridiculous odds.

On a hot and energy sapping afternoon in north London, both teams went for victory, straight from Clive Thomas's whistle.

In the very first minute, Steve Coppell dribbled into the Saints area from the right wing, and fired away a clear, left-footed shot on goal, which was too hot for Turner to catch, but the ball was beaten down just beyond the reach of Macari's left boot, and Mel Blyth cleared.

Gordon Hill came straight back, taking a pass from Houston, and he attacked Rodrigues, before driving a low cross into the box. Pearson fired in a first time shot, on the turn, and Turner could again only parry the ball, but he managed to push the ball away from Sammy McIlroy, attacking the rebound.

Stuart Pearson played Hill through on goal, one on one with the keeper, with a wonderful lofted pass. Again, though, Ian Turner came out and saved right on the edge of his area.

Then, Southampton came into the Final. Jim McCalliog played Mike Channon in with a World Class forty yard pass, but Alex Stepney saved Channon's first time shot with his left boot.

Channon and his teammates, most of them much older and more experienced than United's young whizz-kids, realised the pace of the game was far too fast for the heat, and they started to slow things down.

Early in the second half, Gordon Hill's in-swinging corner, from the right, was flicked on by Pearson at the near post, and McIlroy crept in, though, unmarked at the far post, but he headed up against the crossbar, with Rodrigues beaten on the line.

Mike Channon collected a lay-off from McCalliog, and ran at Houston and Greenhoff along the edge of the United area, making space for himself, then he fired, left footed, from eighteen yards, just over the left angle of Stepney's goal.

With just seven minutes remaining, Paul Gilchrist flicked on a goal kick on the halfway line, and Channon hooked the ball square, inside to McCalliog, on the edge of the centre circle. Jim McCalliog lofted a pass, with the instep of his right foot, forward to Bobby Stokes, twenty yards out.

Stokes looked offside to some, but also as if he may have been played onside by Martin Buchan, just out of the TV shot. Television replays are totally inconclusive, but Stokes wasn't flagged offside. He brought the ball under control with a delightful back heel, and then he guided the ball from the edge of the area, across Stepney's diving body, and just inside the far right post.

Seven minutes later, "the longest seven minutes of Lawrie McMenemy's life", the final whistle was blown, and Southampton had won the FA Cup, the greatest day of their entire history. Peter

Rodrigues became the only Southampton captain to ever lift a major trophy. It certainly wasn't the greatest Saints team of all time, not as good as either of their 1969 or 1971 teams that had qualified for Europe because of their First Division quality, but they'd given Southampton the greatest day in their history.

250,000 Sotonians then welcomed them back, as they went on an open-topped bus tour of the city with the Cup, and on the Monday night, they played QPR in their long arranged Mike Channon Testimonial match. A near record 29,500 crowd filled The Dell, as Bobby Stokes scored twice and Peter Osgood the third in their 3-2 win.

In September 1976, Southampton knocked Olympique de Marseille out of the European Cup Winners' Cup First round, 5-2 on aggregate, with Channon, Peach and Osgood all scoring. Then, in October, they thrashed Northern Ireland side Carrick Rangers, 9-3 on aggregate.

In the Quarter-finals in March 1977, mighty Anderlecht, the European Cup Winners' Cup holders, with Francois van der Elst, Rob Rensenbrink, Arie Haan and Jean Thissen, could only just scrape past Southampton, 3-2 on aggregate.

Hugh Fisher, Peter Rodrigues, Jim Steele, Jim McCalliog, Paul Gilchrist and Mel Blyth, all FA Cup winners, had all left Southampton before the end of that season.

Hugh Fisher had been on the bench during both the Semi-final and the Cup Final, coming on for Stokes in the dying minutes.

Fisher had played 302 league games, 366 in all competitions, in his ten years at The Dell. He'd played his last game for the Saints back in November 1976, as Alan Ball signed from Arsenal, and Fisher dropped into the Southampton Reserves.

He moved to Fourth Division Southport, as their player-manager, in March 1977, and then played sixty league games for The Sandgrounders, but he couldn't prevent them from dropping out of the Football League in 1978.

Peter Rodrigues retired in late 1976, after persistent knee troubles. He had captained Southampton for fifty-nine Second Division games, and also played a total of over 440 career league matches, plus forty international games for Wales.

Ironsides Jim Steele left Southampton, in April 1977, after 161 league games at The Dell, to play for four years in the NASL. He is now the landlord of The Black Bear pub, in Moreton-in-Marsh, in Gloucestershire.

Jim McCalliog, the architect of that Cup-winning goal, had played 72 games in over two seasons at The Dell, but he also left for a stint in the NASL, in 1977, before retiring after a very brief period at Lincoln City, one year later.

McCalliog had played more than 400 Football League games.

Paul Gilchrist played over a hundred league games for Southampton, but he was never a first team regular place during his five years at The Dell.

However, when his chance came, he completely rose to the occasion, smashing in that brilliant goal against Palace, at Stamford Bridge, and he was also England manager Don Revie's Man of the Match after the 1976 FA Cup Final. He moved to Portsmouth in March 1977, for an unhappy fifteen months at Fratton Park.

Mel Blyth had played 105 league games for Southampton, between 1974 and 1977, before he was replaced by Chris Nicholl. The thirty-three year old left for Millwall, before ending his career three years later, after 430 career league appearances.

Peter Osgood had played 126 league games for Southampton, before he left during November 1977. After the obligatory spell in the NASL, with Philadelphia, to earn some proper dosh, he returned to his beloved Chelsea in December 1978, where he played just a few games before retiring the following year.

Bobby Stokes left Southampton during the Summer of 1977, joining his home town club Portsmouth on a free transfer, having only made eight league starts during the season after His Goal had won Saints the FA Cup.

His time at Fratton Park was unhappy, though, making just 24 appearances and scoring only twice, as Pompey struggled at the bottom of Division Three.

Bobby Stokes ended his playing career, happily playing for Washington Dips, in the NASL, where he was re-united with Eric Martin and Jim Steele. But then in 1980, he had the pleasure of playing alongside the World's best footballer, Johan Cruyff.

Bobby Stokes died, aged only forty-four, on Tuesday 30th May 1995, having contracted bronchial pneumonia. On that exact same day, though, Ted Bates, his first boss, and the greatest manager in Southampton's history, had also died.

After Southampton had moved to St Mary's Stadium in August 2001, a luxury block of flats was built on the former site of The Dell, and it was called Stokes Court.

After Southampton had failed to gain promotion for a third successive season, Mike Channon finally left the club he loved on 28th July 1977, joining Manchester City for £300,000.

Channon had scored 155 league goals from 388 starts for Saints, but his times at Maine Road were not as good as he'd hoped, and in spite of a fourth-placed finish during his first season, he scored only twelve league goals from thirty-three games. City also struggled in his second season, and although Channon was equal top scorer with eleven league goals, they'd slumped to the bottom half of the table.

Channon returned to The Dell in 1979, and he played a further 119 First Division games for Southampton, more as a support striker, just as Ron Davies had been during the latter years of his career.

Mike Channon moved to Norwich City in 1982, playing eighty-eight league matches for the Canaries, and he helped them win the League Cup Final in 1985.

He was also inducted into Norwich City's Hall of Fame in 2002.

Mike Channon played forty-six games for England, and he'd scored twenty-one international goals. After football, though, he totally re-invented himself as Mick Channon, one of the most respected racehorse trainers in England.

One huge highlight of Mick Channon's career in horse racing was when Zafeen won the St James's Palace Stakes at Royal Ascot, on Tuesday 17th June 2003.

One of four executive hospitality suites at St Mary's Stadium was named after Mick Channon.

The other three were named after Terry Paine, Bobby Stokes and Matthew Le Tissier.

Mike Channon was arguably the greatest player in Southampton's history.

David Peach captained Southampton back into the First Division in 1978, just one single point behind Second Division Champions Bolton Wanderers, but then he also helped Saints reach their second Wembley Final, the 1979 League Cup Final against Nottingham Forest.

He actually scored the first goal of the match, but Forest came back to win 3-2. Peach and Nick Holmes were the only survivors from their 1976 team, and to this day, they remain the only Southampton players to have played in two Wembley Finals.

On Saturday 18th August 1979, David Peach scored his thirty-third league goal for Southampton, smashing his penalty kick past Manchester United's Gary Bailey, and he subsequently became the greatest scoring full back in Football League history, with sixty-three goals in total.

Then in March 1980, Swindon Town paid a club record transfer fee of £150,000 for the twenty-nine year old Peach. He had played 224 league games for Southampton, scoring 34 goals, and he was also voted their Player of the Season back in 1975-76.

David Peach retired in 1983, after playing just one season with Orient, where he'd also become the first player to have played at every Football League ground.

So in 1980, Nick Holmes had become the sole survivor from their 1976 Cup Final team, as well as becoming club captain following David Peach's departure.

He played his final match for Southampton against Tottenham in February 1987.

Nick Holmes had played 444 league games for the Saints, and 543 matches in all competitions, captaining the team to a First Division runners-up place in 1984.

Only Terry Paine and Mike Channon have played more games for Southampton than Nick Holmes.

If it was an amazing feat for Lawrie McMenemy to build a team that won the FA Cup, it was positively miraculous that, just over a year later, he'd replaced all but two of that famous team, and he'd built a team that was finally good enough to achieve promotion back to Division One.

With the money he gained from the sale of Channon, he'd bought Alan Ball from Arsenal, and also Ted MacDougall and Phil Boyer from Norwich, and off they went.

Wells, Andruszewski, Peach, Williams, Nicholl, Pickering, Ball, Boyer, MacDougall, Holmes and Funnell lost only seven Second Division games during 1977-78, as the Saints returned to First Division football, four years after their relegation.

Back in Division One, McMenemy led Southampton to fourteenth place in 1979, but also to their second Wembley appearance in the League Cup Final. They then finished eighth in 1980, but rose to sixth place in 1981, their best-ever league finish.

In 1982, they ended up in seventh-place, but then dropped down to twelfth in 1983.

In 1984, though, Southampton enjoyed their best-ever season, reaching the FA Cup Semi-finals, but losing in extra-time to eventual winners Everton, while they ended up as runners-up behind Champions Liverpool in the First Division.

Southampton finally finished in fifth place in 1985, qualifying for Europe once again, a place that then disappeared following the Heysel Stadium tragedy, and Lawrie McMenemy suddenly left The Dell, aged only forty-eight, during June 1985.

In a move that shocked, and confused, the whole world of football, he was then appointed as the new manager of Second Division Sunderland, less than one week later.

McMenemy left Roker Park two years later though, in 1987, after Sunderland were in grave danger of relegation down to the Third Division.

The most successful manager in Southampton's history, Lawrie McMenemy is now a director at the club. He is also, perhaps, an example for modern day football club owners who hire and fire managers, like a child in a sweet shop, after just a couple of defeats, and even if their team are as far down as second place in the Premier League.

Lawrie McMenemy took Southampton down in 1974, after they'd been sitting happily in a UEFA Cup qualifying place during December. He failed to gain promotion in 1975, and also failed to gain promotion in 1976, although he did win the Cup.

They then failed, very, very miserably, to gain promotion in 1977.

In today's game, at any point during those three and a half years, McMenemy and Southampton would have parted company "by mutual consent."

But no, he was listened to, and also believed, and given time to build. Although Southampton had enjoyed their greatest ever decade between 1967 and 1976, they were rewarded for their faith, and their patience, with their most successful ever period in top flight football between 1978 and 1985.

Between them, Ted Bates and Lawrie McMenemy provided Southampton Football Club with their greatest ever ten years, during the Glam Soccer years.

They gave Southampton their biggest ever crowds, and their first ever adventures into European football, for which they qualified on three different occasions.

They'd also brought colour and glamour back to South Coast football, a long time missing since the days of Jimmy Dickinson, and, for the very first time, they put Southampton, and the Solent, onto England's football map.

CIDER WITH RONNIE

I N 1966, HEREFORD UNITED WERE a decent enough Southern League club, which had nearly won the Southern League Championship back in 1951, but they didn't, and instead they'd won just three Southern League Cups during the Fifties.

They got by on a week-to-week basis, with just two to three thousand die-hard fans scattered round Edgar Street. Hereford United just got by in the Southern League.

In 1966, though, John Charles joined Hereford United.

"Hang on, John Charles? What, **THE** John Charles, the greatest-ever Welsh footballer?" Yes, **THAT** John Charles, the only player to have ever been the top goal scorer in the First Division, for Leeds United, and also in Italy's Serie A, for Juventus.

The very same John Charles who reverted to centre-half in Turin, and was equally World Class, before joining a run-of-the-mill Southern League club, at the age of 34?

It was surely a publicity stunt? Of all the players celebrated in this book, Dave Mackay, Billy Bremner, George Best, Johnny Giles, Jimmy Greaves and Colin Bell would be right up there with John Charles, but he wouldn't be topped by any of them.

It wasn't actually a publicity stunt, John Charles joining Hereford, but it **was** a move by Hereford's manager Bob Dennison to boost home attendances, as well as giving the Welsh legend a chance to continue playing competitive football.

It was a genius move by Mr Dennison, and the impact was felt immediately. John Charles scored thirty-seven goals from only fifty-one competitive matches during that 1966-67 season.

Then, in December 1967, Charles replaced Bob Dennison as Hereford manager, becoming their player-manager. Over the following four years, as well as treating Southern League crowds to his skills, and nobody anywhere ever booed him, John Charles also transformed Hereford United into a real non-league force.

In 1969, winger Dudley Tyler was signed by Charles, after he'd been spotted playing parks football in the Swindon local leagues, and a year later, Colin Addison joined Hereford United from Sheffield United. Addison had been one of Bertie Mee's first signings at Arsenal back in 1966, having scored sixty-two goals in 160 First Division matches for Nottingham Forest.

He certainly seemed a bit too good for Southern League football, but who could ever say "no" to the Gentle Giant?

In September 1970, John Charles signed the former Doncaster Rovers goalkeeper Fred Potter, from Burton Albion. Potter, who'd been the Brewers' Player of the Season in 1969-70, played sixty league and cup games for Hereford during 1970-71.

In 1971, John Charles continued to recruit more new players at Edgar Street.

Ken Mallender had played nearly 130 First Division matches for Sheffield United, until 1968, when he signed for Norwich City, for £40,000, where he became the Canaries' captain. Mallender played forty-six Second Division games at Carrow Road, before he also signed for Hereford.

In January 1971, Ricky George signed for John Charles' Hereford United, from his hometown club Barnet, and then, during the Summer of 71, striker Billy Meadows, one of Ricky George's close friends, also joined Hereford, from Barnet.

Tony Gough had spent all of the Sixties playing for West Country non-league teams, Trowbridge, Frome Town and Bath City, before he moved to Swindon Town in 1970, his big break into league football.

However, playing for Swindon against Sunderland on Saturday 3rd April 1971, Gough was stretchered off the Roker Park pitch with a knee injury.

At the age of thirty-one, and only 26 league games, it appeared to be the end of his Football League career, before it had even started. During the Summer of 1971, John Charles also signed Gough, and he immediately appointed him as Hereford's captain.

Finally, in July 1971, John Charles paid just £5,000 to Newport County for their midfield artist Ronnie Radford. Radford had played sixty-six league games for Newport, and he'd been voted their Player of the Season in 1970.

Ronnie Radford had only decided to join Hereford because Edgar Street was closer to his Cheltenham carpentry business than he was over in South Wales.

Then, suddenly, after all that fierce recruitment, during October 1971, just before Hereford's FA Cup Fourth Qualifying round match at home to Cheltenham Town, John Charles left Hereford United to become player-manager over at Merthyr Tydfil.

John Charles, CBE, had played 173 Southern League matches for The Bulls, and he'd scored eighty goals. It certainly hadn't been a publicity stunt.

For all of his great moments at Leeds and Juventus, the work he'd done at Hereford had possibly been better than all of them, considering what was to follow.

Colin Addison was immediately appointed as their player-manager, and on Saturday 6th November, a massive non-league crowd, 6,441, watched Hereford easily beat Cheltenham 3-0, to reach the FA Cup First round.

Two weeks later, Hereford made the long journey to North Norfolk and they scraped a goalless draw at King's Lynn. Nearly 8,000 packed into Edgar Street for the replay, as captain Tony Gough scored the game's only goal to set up a Second round home game against Fourth Division strugglers Northampton Town. It was an epic tie.

With another tremendous crowd of 9,519 inside Edgar Street, Addison's men thought they'd blown their chance, on Saturday 11th December, as the combatant Cobblers came and clattered Radford, and closed the door on Tyler and Meadows.

Three days later, following that stalemate, Northampton's biggest crowd of the season, more than 9,000, filled their County Ground, and Hereford brilliantly battled for a 2-2 draw, after extra-time, Dudley Tyler and steelworker Brian Owen scored to earn a lucrative second replay.

West Bromwich Albion's First Division ground, The Hawthorns, hosted the second replay, but it looked like the grand surroundings had got the better of The Bulls, as they trailed Northampton 1-0 with the game approaching injury-time.

The 8,331 crowd, though, many of them Black Country locals supporting Hereford, were ecstatic after Ken Mallender had hammered home a dramatic late equaliser from twenty yards out.

"The ball came to me, so I just hit it, and it happened to go in," Mallender admitted afterwards, presumably to Monty Python's Eric Idle.

Then, even further into injury-time, Dudley Tyler hit an unbelievable winner to earn Hereford United a Third round away trip to Newcastle United, the First Division giants Newcastle United.

On Monday 24th January, nine days after the initial round of Third round matches, due to an atrocious spell of winter weather hitting the North-east, 39,000 totally filled the three-sided St James's Park for the visit of Hereford United.

It was eight years since Newcastle had last entertained non-league opposition in the FA Cup, but Bedford Town had beaten them back then, 2-1 at St James's Park.

After only seventeen seconds, Brian Owen gave Hereford a shock lead, firing a perfect, right-footed strike, from outside the area, high into the top corner of McFaul's goal.

Supermac equalised from the penalty spot, his eighteenth goal of the season, and then John Tudor also scored to put the Magpies 2-1 up.

Only two minutes later, though, though, a phenomenal thirty yard shot by Colin Addison had levelled the scores at 2-2, and the game was still only twenty minutes old. After that, though, Hereford defended brilliantly, more like a Second Division club than a Southern League team, to force a replay.

Hereford United had a resilience and quality that was unlike any other non-league team. They were still, however, a non-league team, and they were filled with amateur footballers. Centre-back Mike McLaughlin had a job in Newport, and needed to travel straight back to Wales, immediately after the match, on the supporters' train.

The replay was scheduled for Wednesday 26th January, two nights later, but it was postponed on four separate occasions, due to diabolical Herefordshire weather.

Newcastle United's players spent most of the next ten days in a Worcester hotel, fighting boredom, and shopping for underwear in Marks and Spencer, as they'd only packed enough for two days.

Newcastle's only football activity, during those ten days, had been a 0-0 draw away at Huddersfield Town, on Saturday 29th January.

A week later, on Saturday 5th February 1972, on the same day as all of the other Fourth round ties were played, their Third round replay with Hereford was finally played, on an awful, mud-drenched pitch.

16,100 over-filled Edgar Street beyond bursting point. Hereford's chairman had authorised extra tickets to be printed after the initial allowance was sold out. The actual number of fans at the game was generally known to be more than 16,000.

Fans sat in the branches of trees around the ground, and stood up in the floodlight pylons to watch the game, so packed was the ground.

HEREFORD UNITED		NEWCASTLE UNITED
Fred Potter	1	Ian McFaul
Roger Griffiths	2	David Craig
Ken Mallender	3	Frank Clark
Alan Jones	4	Irving Nattrass
Mick McLaughlin	5	Pat Howard
Colin Addison	6	Bobby Moncur
Tony Gough	7	Viv Busby
Dudley Tyler	8	Tony Green
Billy Meadows	9	Malcolm MacDonald
Brian Owen	10	John Tudor
Ronnie Radford	11	Terry Hibbitt
Ricky George	12	Alex Reid

Also, for the very first time, the BBC TV cameras were at Edgar Street, as the match was also the main match on Match of the Day that night, watched by more than fourteen million viewers.

In an all-red away strip, Newcastle attacked Hereford straight from the start.

From Hibbitt's left-sided free-kick, MacDonald beat McLaughlin in the air, on the edge of the six yard box, and the ball dropped to Pat Howard. Howard took a touch, but then as he shot, Potter dived bravely at his feet. The ball ricocheted back off Howard, and then out for a goal kick.

From Hereford's resultant goal kick, Hibbitt played the ball back up to the edge of the Hereford area, and McLaughlin's hurried clearance ballooned off Tudor's head and bounced back off Potter's crossbar. Hibbitt immediately smacked the rebound back onto the crossbar, before the ball was eventually scrambled clear to safety.

"That was quite remarkable," remarked John Motson.

The stunned, and still-grounded John Tudor couldn't believe it either.

At the start of the second half, Dudley Tyler went off on a superb run, through the mud, beating both Hibbitt and Clark, and then Green and Howard, to the edge of the Newcastle area. Hereford then worked the ball out to Gough out on the left, and his cross was collected by Tyler, just inside the area, who volleyed, left-footed, towards the near post.

McFaul just managed to clamber across and push the ball wide for a corner.

The crowd noise was absolutely rampant. From Tyler's right-sided corner, Mallender headed against the angle, and then Alan Jones' shot, on the rebound, flashed just wide of McFaul's right post.

Potter saved MacDonald's bullet header brilliantly, following Hibbitt's corner, and then, from Hibbitt's sublime through-ball, MacDonald darted past McLaughlin, and beat the dive of the onrushing Potter, but from eight yards, he blasted over the bar.

Supermac held his head in front of the cheering, roaring home fans.

The classy and composed Tony Green then broke out of the midfield mud, and he fed Viv Busby out wide on the right. Busby's cross was smashed in by MacDonald's header, leaping high above Roger Griffiths at the far post. MacDonald punched the air, howling loud-mouthed roars of relief and celebration, with great dark sideburns covering his cheeks.

"That's it!" John Motson claimed, having decided the contest was now over.

Newcastle's players all came to hug Supermac. With just eight minutes left, the First Division side looked to be through to the Fourth round.

Colin Addison signalled for the attacking Ricky George to replace Griffiths. Roger Griffiths had astonishingly broken his leg after a collision with Fred Potter during the first half, but he'd actually played on heroically through the pain, for seventy minutes.

The Hereford-born full-back had also been their first ever substitute back in 1966, and he played over 250 games for The Bulls.

Roger Griffiths died after a heart attack, aged only sixty-two, on Wednesday 19th July 2006.

Ricky George almost immediately made an impact on the game, in the eighty-sixth minute. He collected the ball from David Craig's poor control, and then turned Tony Green, before passing to Mallender, five yards behind him. Ken Mallender sent in a diagonal cross which was flicked on by the mighty Billy Meadows.

Newcastle's Pat Howard, weakly and insufficiently, half-cleared the ball away, and Ronnie Radford won the ball well, inside the centre circle, against the John Tudor's firm challenge, and he passed forward to Brian Owen, twenty yards out.

Owen returned the ball straight back to him, bobbling on the well-ploughed battlefield of a pitch. The ball hit a divot and bounced slightly, for Radford to thunder a classic hotshot strike, from thirty yards, straight and high, into the top corner of McFaul's goal.

On Match of the Day, the young John Motson was overwhelmed and overjoyed. "Radford. Now Tudor's gone down for Newcastle. Radford, again…. Oh, what a goal! **WHAT A GOAL!** Radford the scorer, **Ronnie Radford!**"

A joyous and spontaneous pitch invasion of fans erupted from out of the Edgar Street stands, to celebrate with Radford, running around with his arms aloft. Never was there such a vast display of Seventies' green Parkas seen in one location at any one time.

That goal was voted as BBC TV's Goal of the Season in 1971-72.

Hereford withstood late Newcastle pressure to force the match into extra-time.

Two minutes before the end of the first period, Radford and Tyler combined, just outside the Newcastle area, to free Ricky George inside the box, and in space. George turned and drilled the ball past Moncur and Green, beating McFaul's dive at the near post. The ball crept into the far corner of the Newcastle goal, and triggered yet another jubilant, scarf-waving mass invasion of green Parkas onto the pitch, with a few Hereford bobbies smiling, as they restored order.

Newcastle were stunned, and they couldn't force an equaliser during the fifteen minute second period. The final whistle signalled a third, celebratory, pitch invasion by all 16,000 inside Edgar Street.

Ronnie Radford's thunderbolt goal was voted at number 97 in the 100 Greatest Sporting Moments, broadcast on Channel 4 in 2002.

There were only five other footballing moments from the years between 1967 and 1976 among those One Hundred Moments.

That goal, which was replayed during the opening theme tune and titles of BBC's Match of the Day, for years afterwards, is also replayed every January, as the FA Cup Third round takes place.

It is one of the most famous FA Cup moments of all time.

In the Fourth round, Hereford hosted another First Division club, a star-studded West Ham United, on Wednesday 9th February, and another sell-out crowd of 15,000 had filled Edgar Street.

Ricky George had a great chance to put Hereford through to the Fifth round, but he missed what was described as a sitter, and West Ham hung on for a 0-0 draw, despite Tyler absolutely terrorizing McDowell down the left, and earned a replay back at Upton Park.

HEREFORD UNITED		WEST HAM UNITED
Fred Potter	1	Bobby Ferguson
Tony Gough	2	John McDowell
Ken Mallender	3	Frank Lampard
Alan Jones	4	Billy Bonds
Mick McLaughlin	5	Tommy Taylor
Colin Addison	6	Bobby Moore
Ricky George	7	Harry Redknapp
Dudley Tyler	8	Clyde Best
Billy Meadows	9	Geoff Hurst
Brian Owen	10	Trevor Brooking
Ronnie Radford	11	Pop Robson

42,271 filled Upton Park for the replay, at 2.15 pm on the following Monday, St Valentine's Day, due to the government power cuts. The crowd was just one thousand fewer than West Ham's all-time record crowd, but it *was* their biggest crowd of the season, even bigger than their League Cup Semi-final second leg match against Stoke City, and bigger than the 41,892 who'd watched their 3-0 win over Manchester United on New Year's Day. Thousands were also locked out, and hundreds of fans spilled out onto the roof of the Priory Court high rise flats overlooking the North Bank.

It was the Third Largest Attendance in Upton Park's history. Many were absolutely sure that the crowd was much bigger than 42,000, but knew that West Ham couldn't admit that their biggest ever crowd was for a game against a non-League club at a quarter past two on a Monday afternoon, in the middle of February.

Anyway, despite Billy Meadows beating Bobby Moore in the air to score for Hereford, World Cup Final hat-trick hero Geoff Hurst hit yet another hat-trick to win the match 3-1 for the Hammers, and he ended Hereford's wonderful adventure.

Hereford United received a standing ovation as they did a lap of honour at Upton Park. This had been their tenth FA Cup game of the season.

Hereford played a total of seventy-nine league and cup matches during 1971-72, due to all of the various league cup competitions and regional knockout tournaments that Southern League sides are committed to.

It was mostly due to this schedule, as well as their heroic FA Cup run, that Hereford finished as runners-up to Chelmsford City in the Southern League Premier Division.

Never mind, thanks to their huge crowds and impressive performances in the FA Cup, they were elected into the Football League in place of Barrow.

It was a no-brainer.

Fred Potter had kept an incredible thirty-eight clean sheets, and he was voted Hereford's Player of the Season, while Ken Mallender also started an unbelievable seventy-two of Hereford's league and cup matches during 1971-72.

Captain Tony Gough was transferred down to Torquay United during the Summer of 72, after Hereford had been elected to the league. He played just two matches, however, in front of goalkeeper Mike Mahoney and alongside Mike Trebilcock, before returning to non-league football in Somerset, Gloucestershire and Wiltshire.

Also, Ricky George and top scorer Billy Meadows both returned to Barnet during that Summer of 1972, while *School was Out.* In spite of his winning goal against Newcastle, George had been in and out of Hereford's team all season, and he played over thirty games less than regulars Mallender, Jones, Tyler, Meadows and Radford.

Barnet was his hometown team, and he could dine out on his FA Cup goal, for the rest of his life.

Billy Meadows became player-manager at Barnet, and in 1977, he brought another half-decent striker, Jimmy Greaves, to Underhill.

Greaves, who'd previously played for such teams as Chelsea, Tottenham, Milan and England, also became a Barnet hero, but behind both Meadows and George, after scoring twenty-five goals.

Jimmy Greaves was voted as Barnet's Player of the Season, though, in 1977-78.

West Ham United signed Hereford winger Dudley Tyler during the Summer of 1972, for a fee of £25,000, a record transfer fee for a non-league footballer. Tyler started twenty-one of West Ham's first thirty-two First Division matches during 1972-73, and the Hammers did well with him in their team, flying high in seventh place for much of the season. He only scored one goal, though, as they thrashed Leicester City 5-2, on Saturday 19th August, beating Peter Shilton.

By 1973, though, the arrival of record signing Ted MacDougall at Upton Park had forced a team reshuffle, and Tyler's chances became more limited. He did regain his place in September 1973, but West Ham struggled at the bottom of the First Division, and Tyler was dropped again, after just eight games.

Graham Paddon arrived from Norwich City, in December 1973, and when Pat Holland eventually took the right midfield role, Dudley Tyler was sold back to Hereford, for just £13,000. He'd played a total of 29 First Division matches at West Ham, scoring just that one goal.

After their 1-0 defeat away at Colchester United, on Saturday 12th August 1972, Hereford United, the first and, so far, only Herefordshire club to be elected to the Football League, entertained Reading on the following Saturday.

8,839 provided a raucous, cider-induced Edgar Street atmosphere, and Fred Potter kept his first Football League clean sheet, while Ken Wallace, Colin Addison and Ivan Hollett all scored during their 3-0 home win.

Ivan Hollett, a big Andy Williams fan, had played over 350 Football League games, mainly at Chesterfield and Mansfield, but also at Crewe and Cambridge, and he'd scored 137 league goals.

He had originally signed back in March 1972, providing an influential injection of experience to Hereford's chase for the Southern League Championship, but he was getting on.

Hollett scored just two goals in eleven Fourth Division games for Hereford, before he was forced to retire in January 1973.

Hereford had a poor start to life in the Fourth Division. They won only two of their first fourteen games, gaining just nine points, and were down in twenty-first place by the middle of October. After the introduction of goalkeeper David Icke, though, and also Eric Redrobe, who had scored 55 league goals at Southport in 186 games, Hereford lost only four out of their final thirty-two games, winning twenty-one of them, to finish as Fourth Division runners-up.

Fred Potter had played his final game of the season in goal during Hereford's 1-0 win over Bury, back on Saturday 9th December. An aggravation of a knee injury kept him out of action for the remainder of the season, and David Icke took over in goal, keeping eighteen clean sheets from his 37 games.

Brian Owen, one of the heroes of their win over Newcastle, was Hereford's top scorer with eleven goals from 31, while Eric Redrobe hit nine from 26. Hereford's team for their final game of the season, a 1-0 home win over Crewe Alexandra, with 12,616 again packed into Edgar Street, had still contained Mallender, McLaughlin, Billy Tucker, Owen and Radford from their Southern League days. Colin Addison had suffered a back injury against Hartlepool in October, though, and he never played again. Alan Jones was also injured for most of the final three months, but Ken Mallender had played in 45 out of 46 Fourth Division matches, and he was voted Hereford United's Player of the Season.

Hereford United's average crowd of nearly 9,000 was not only the biggest average crowd in Division Four, but also only six Third Division clubs had boasted higher average crowds. Hereford United had also attracted bigger average crowds than four Second Division clubs, Huddersfield Town, Watford, Bristol Rovers and Charlton Athletic, during 1972-73.

At the beginning of the 1973-74 season, Fred Potter suffered a broken leg against Grimsby Town, and he was forced to retire. David Icke had also been suffering from arthritis in his knees, though, so Tommy Hughes took over in goal.

Fred Potter had played a total of 131 matches for Hereford, and he'd kept sixty-two clean sheets. He was voted as their Hereford United's goalkeeper in their all-time greatest ever team, by Vital Bulls, the Hereford fans' website.

During 1973-74, Hereford dallied with a relegation scrap in Division Three, but they won just enough games to stay up, especially after mid-March, when they went on a nine match unbeaten run, gaining thirteen points.

The Bulls finished in eighteenth place, eight points above the bottom four.

Ken Mallender played his final game for Hereford United on Tuesday 26th February, in their 1-1 draw away at Rochdale, after 144 games at Edgar Street. He played for Miami Toros in the NASL, in 1974, before finally retiring.

Brian Owen also had his contract cancelled in March 1974, after playing his final game away at Bournemouth on Saturday 2nd March. Owen had scored thirteen Football League goals in 57 matches, but it was his influence and energetic persistence in that famous Southern League team for which he'd be most fondly remembered.

Dudley Tyler had returned to Edgar Street from West Ham in early December, and he played twenty-one games before suffering an injury during Hereford's 3-0 home win over Southport, on Saturday 30th March.

Mike McLaughlin, an unsung hero in their 1972 Cup run, played 43 Third Division matches during 1973-74, in their centre of defence, and he was voted Hereford's Player of the Season.

By December 1973, Ronnie Radford had been converted into a full back, playing twenty games in defence, before he played his final game for Hereford United on Easter Monday, 15th April, at home to local rivals Shrewsbury Town.

Ronnie Radford had played sixty-one Football League matches, scoring six goals for The Bulls. At thirty years old, Radford joined Southern League Worcester City in 1974-75, as their player-manager, for just one season, but he was unable to lift The Royals back up to the Premier Division, and the great man retired from football.

During the Summer of 1974, Colin Addison left his job as manager of Hereford United. He'd suffered a broken leg back in March, and so was forced to give up his player-manager role, and concentrate on management. He didn't feel ready for it.

Addison had played only twenty-three Football League games for Hereford during their first two seasons as a league club, but he'd amassed a career total of 391 league games. It was, however, his seventy matches as player-manager back in 1971-72, and his sensational screamer at St James's Park, as well as taking Hereford straight up to Division Three in their first Football League season, for which he'll always be remembered as an all-time club legend.

Just down the road from Hereford United's ground, on Edgar Street, just across the road, is a newly-built housing development, named after him: Addison Court.

Colin Addison didn't return to full-time football management for another five years, when, after being Ron Atkinson's assistant at West Brom, he was appointed as manager of First Division Derby County, during July 1979.

Addison's replacement at Edgar Street was Bristol City's coach, John Sillett. Sillett immediately strengthened Hereford by signing Irish international defender Tony Byrne, from Southampton, as well as the Saints' legend Terry Paine, who'd just been released by Lawrie McMenemy.

In August 1974, though, just before the start of the season, Sillett paid just £15,000 to Lincoln City for their striker Dixie McNeil, who'd scored fifty-three goals in only 96 games at Sincil Bank.

McNeil scored fifteen goals from just 22 games, prior to December, with Hereford sitting comfortably in the top half of the table, and Sillett then further strengthened his attack by signing John Galley from Nottingham Forest.

Mike McLaughlin played his final match for Hereford on Saturday 8th March 1975, during their 1-5 home defeat to Plymouth Argyle, in front of an Edgar Street crowd of 9,296. At the end of their second season in Division Three, the Bulls finished twelfth, a decent position, with the prolific Dixie McNeil having scored thirty-one goals from 44 matches.

Terry Paine, Hereford's former England player, also played forty league matches, as he and Dudley Tyler had forged a good balance of creativity from wide midfield, that evoked Paine's earlier wing partnership with John Sydenham down at The Dell.

In August 1975, John Sillett signed Plymouth Argyle's legendary midfield attacker Steve Davey, the final piece of his jigsaw to lift Hereford United to their highest ever Football League placing.

Steve Davey had played over two hundred league games in over ten years at Home Park, and by October, after his goals had won successive games against both Chester and Wrexham, the Bulls were in second place.

Hereford won nine out of thirteen games, between November 1975 and the start of February 1976, while losing only three times, and by Tuesday 7th February, they had even overhauled long-time leaders Crystal Palace, to top the Third Division.

On Wednesday 14th April, a massive crowd of 35,549 packed Ninian Park, as Hereford visited Cardiff City, needing two points to be assured of promotion.

Cardiff won 2-0, though, and Hereford then drew 0-0 at Walsall on the following Saturday.

So, on Bank Holiday Monday, 19th April 1976, Hereford hosted local rivals Shrewsbury Town, needing just a single point to guarantee their promotion to the Second Division.

12,314 packed into Edgar Street, evoking memories of 1972, as the Shrews were themselves also still in the race for the third promotion place, and had former First Division Champions Alan Durban and Ken Mulhearn in their line-up.

HEREFORD UNITED		SHREWSBURY TOWN
Kevin Charlton	1	Ken Mulhearn
Steve Emery	2	John King
Steve Ritchie	3	Carlton Leonard
Billy Tucker	4	Alan Durban
John Galley	5	Colin Griffin
Jimmy Lindsay	6	Graham Turner
Terry Paine	7	Sam Irvine
Dudley Tyler	8	Ian Atkins
Steve Davey	9	Mick Kearney
Dixie McNeil	10	Chic Bates
Roy Carter	11	Nigel O'Loughlin
Eric Redrobe	12	Steve Hayes

Carter, Davey and McNeil all scored to secure a famous and much-celebrated 3-1 home win, and it was even better that Southern League survivors Tucker and Tyler were still in Hereford's team.

Dudley Tyler played thirty-four league games in 1975-76, and he scored five very valuable goals, including the winner in their 3-2 win over Rotherham that secured the Division Three Championship trophy.

However, he played in only six Second Division matches during the following season, and Tyler was released after 102 league games for United, since returning from West Ham.

Billy Tucker was not at Edgar Street for their FA Cup wins over King's Lynn, Northampton or Newcastle in 1972, but he did come on as a substitute, for Ken Mallender, during Hereford's away defeat at Upton Park, and was instantly influential in their Southern League promotion campaign, and ultimately, their entry into the Football League.

Billy Tucker was the very last survivor from their non-league days when he played his final game for Hereford United in their 4-2 defeat away at Millwall, on Saturday 30th October 1976. It was the end of a fever-pitch era, as Tucker was transferred to Bury in December, having played 137 Football League matches for the Bulls.

Dixie McNeil scored thirty-four goals in 40 Third Division matches, during Hereford's title-winning season, enjoying great service from Tyler, Steve Davey and Terry Paine.

Hereford United's average crowd had dipped slightly from the euphoric levels of their first league seasons, but at 8,273, they still boasted the fifth-best average home attendance of the bottom two Divisions.

Life in the Second Division started brilliantly for Hereford. Dixie McNeil could not be stopped, as he scored six goals during their first four matches, and Hereford United were fighting for promotion up to the First Division, just two points behind the leaders, on Saturday 14th September.

SECOND DIVISION LEADERS, 14TH SEPTEMBER 1976

	PL	W	D	L	F	A	PTS
Blackpool	5	4	0	1	12	5	8
Bolton Wanderers	5	4	0	1	12	5	8
Oldham Athletic	5	3	2	0	9	4	8
Wolves	5	2	3	0	8	3	7
Chelsea	5	3	1	1	7	7	7
HEREFORD UTD	5	2	2	1	10	7	6
Hull City	5	2	1	2	9	8	5
Sheffield United	5	1	3	1	7	6	5

After that high point, however, things went pear-shaped for the cider city, and Hereford lost eleven of their following fifteen games up to the New Year, dropping down to the bottom of the Division Two apple barrel.

And there they stayed until the end of the season.

Terry Paine left Hereford at the end of the season, having played 111 league games for the Bulls, retiring after a Football League record career total of Eight Hundred and Twenty-four matches.

During the Summer of 1977, Dixie McNeil moved to Wrexham, after scoring an incredible eighty-five goals from just 129 league matches, and Hereford spiralled back down to the Fourth Division. They suffered a series of financial troubles, as home attendances dropped right down to two or three thousand during the dark, grey Eighties, and they were eventually relegated back to non-league football in 1997.

In 2006, though, they rose like a Phoenix from the flames, again, and finished as runners-up behind Accrington Stanley in the Conference. Managed by former Shrewsbury Town player Graham Turner, Hereford defeated Halifax Town 3-2 in the Play-off Final at Leicester City's Walker's Stadium.

Travelling back home, through the rolling Herefordshire hills, and past the wonderful Perry and Cider orchards and farms, I knew that Hereford United team needed to be remembered, and remembered as more than just another story in the FA Cup book of Romances.

Unique as they are, having their own chapter, despite never being a First Division club at any point, their story should really be an epic Hollywood fairy-tale movie, with Ben Affleck as John Charles, and with Matt Damon as Ronnie Radford.

"The team would die for each other," Ronnie Radford said of that 1972 team, but that team was supported by one of the greatest, most enthusiastic and infectious army of fans in English football history. It was that army of supporters, as much as their team, that was highly influential in the decision by most clubs to elect Hereford into the Football League, despite them never having won a League title. Without their fans, it would have been unlikely for Hereford United to have been elected in 1972.

There was a drive. There was a force. There was an organic energy at Hereford United between 1971 and 1976. Maybe it was something in the local cider, but they became an inspired club, an inspiration that fired the fans into a frenzy, and warmed the hearts of all supporters. Well over 42,000 watched them on a bright, crisp February Monday afternoon, at West Ham United, with thousands locked out.

Hereford became a happening. Everyone had loved it, everyone except Newcastle, more than any other giant-killing, when they'd beaten Newcastle United.

In Hereford United's euphoric rise from non-league football obscurity, while ranked below Weymouth, Yeovil Town, Bedford Town, Bath City, Chelmsford and even Tooting and Mitcham, up to the Second Division in just four years, it would be unfair on all of their other great players, but it is Ronnie Radford who most football fans remember when the Bulls are mentioned.

His goal is one of the most celebrated, and most replayed goals in the history of the FA Cup, in the history of football in fact.

There it is in the 100 Greatest Sporting Moments, just beneath Arthur Ashe's 1975 Wimbledon win.

Radford remains very modest about that goal, preferring instead to highlight the two goals scored by Owen and Addison up at St James's Park, and he attributes Hereford United's team spirit to their famous comeback win over one of the finest ever Newcastle United sides, as much more important than his goal.

It was one of the Goals of the Century, though, and Radford's influence, within Hereford's team, over the following seasons, had helped them first achieve, and then also consolidate their Third Division status.

A West Yorkshire man, Ronnie Radford will always be a real Herefordshire legend... Right up there with the Mappa Mundi, John Charles, Mott the Hoople, Colin Addison, Ellie Goulding, Terry Paine and Dixie McNeil.

And I raise my pint glass of pump-drawn Henry Weston's' Old Rosie cloudy scrumpy to Ronnie, and to Hereford United.

Wonderful stuff!

OUT OF THE BLUE

I N 1971-72, BIRMINGHAM CITY SAILED AWAY, back into the high life of the First Division, from where they'd been relegated seven years earlier. Blues had never been a glamour club, nor even a glamorous team, and in the ten years during which they were last in the First Division, between 1955 and 1965, they'd finished in the top half of the table only twice.

ELDORADO

In 1972, however, Birmingham City boasted a forward line that was ready made for top flight, international football. With Alan Campbell and Gordon Taylor both galloping down the wings like Wild West Heroes, though, providing crosses for their prolific forwards Bob Latchford, Bob Hatton and Trevor Francis, the Blues were brimming with rugged, Glam Rock glamour.

Birmingham City set sail for the Lands of Gold with a style resembling the ELO; all thick, long, dark hair, big, BIG beards, and *Jason King* moustaches.

Despite their frontline flourishes and flamboyances, however, Birmingham had not, in fact, sailed back up to the top flight; their defensive deficiencies had almost destroyed their survival at an early stage.

Neither was the team ready made. Bob Hatton was the ignition that fired their flight towards the top of Division Two, but he'd only been signed six months earlier. Blues were down in eighth place when manager Freddie Goodwin had paid Carlisle United £80,000 for Hatton, back on Wednesday 27th October 1971.

City had won only six of their first twenty-two league matches before Christmas, and they lay down low in seventh position in Division Two. They'd drawn twelve matches, though, and actually lay only six points below the promotion places.

Bob Hatton had scored only twice during his first eight games for Blues, while Trevor Francis had scored only four goals. Things weren't going great. The bearded Bob Latchford was the only player firing, having scored fourteen goals.

Bob Latchford had scored twice on his Blues debut, on Friday 21st March 1969, aged just eighteen. He headed two goals during Birmingham's 3-1 win over Preston, in front of only 22,020 home fans at St Andrews. Birmingham-born, and a Blue through and through, Latchford was strong and burly, but very young, and he struggled at first, scoring only three goals in fourteen games, over his first two seasons.

During 1970-71, though, Bob Latchford became City's regular number nine, just as Alan Campbell and Gordon Taylor became regulars on the wings in October and December 1970, respectively. Bob Latchford subsequently scored nine league goals in twenty-five games prior to his twentieth birthday.

Alan Campbell, born in Arbroath, had signed from Charlton Athletic, aged only twenty-two, on Thursday 15th October 1970, for £70,000. He'd played 198 Second Division matches for the Valiants, scoring twenty-eight goals. With his growing black hair, Campbell struggled early on, but when the blonde-haired Gordon Taylor arrived, a couple of months later, providing a great mono-chrome look to the Blues wings, the double barrelled ammunition from their flanks was fully loaded.

Gordon Taylor was older, at twenty-five years old, and he'd played over two hundred and fifty league games for Bolton Wanderers, since the early Sixties, but he cost Fred Goodwin just £18,000. Goodwin had been appointed as Birmingham City manager at the end of May 1970, two months after Stan Cullis's retirement.

A tall, stooping figure, Goodwin was a serious, deep-thinking man who'd learnt his trade under both Sir Matt Busby and Don Revie. Goodwin had even been recommended to Birmingham by Revie, and the great Leeds United manager's word had proven vital.

Fred Goodwin introduced some slightly leftfield off-field match preparations for the team, including yoga and dance. These innovations, used more commonly nowadays, had produced slightly ineffective results of matches, but it provoked a positive response from the players, and inad-vertently, their team spirit improved.

OUT OF THE BLUE

What Goodwin did brilliantly, was to nurture, and then introduce his youngest stars into reg-ular first team action at the exact right time. Trevor Francis had made his league debut on Saturday 12th September 1970, aged just sixteen, and blasted in a goal in Birmingham's 1-1 draw at home to Oxford United, in front of 22,346.

FRANCIS IS THE HERO!, and *TEENAGE ACE KEEPS BLUES BUBBLING!,* the news-papers had acclaimed him as the *BOY WONDER,* and even Goodwin said of Francis, that he was "the best prospect since George Best. For Trevor, though, it has to be different."

Goodwin was referring, of course, to the growing rumours of Best's nightclub lifestyle, which was beginning to affect the consistency of his football.

It was on Saturday 13th February 1971, though, when Francis and Latchford both scored in the same match, for the first time, during their 3-3 away draw with Sheffield Wednesday, at Hills-borough. A tiny crowd of 13,000 witnessed the occasion.

One week after that goal-scoring double act was born, though, and with *the Boy Wonder* still only sixteen, Trevor Francis scored all four of Birmingham's goals, two in each half, during their 4-0 win over Bolton. It was the way he just left his markers standing, by hurtling through the space on either side of them, with his incredible speed, close control, and quickness on the turn.

He was impossible to hold, and irresistible to watch.

Out of the Blue, a star was born. Between the beginning of February, and the end of March 1971, Trevor Francis had scored twelve Second Division goals from just eight games, yet he was only sixteen. He was the greatest teenage prospect since Duncan Edwards, Jimmy Greaves, and George Best.

Anyway, after winning just six league games before Christmas, during their 1971-72 season, Birmingham hosted Cardiff City on Boxing Day. Blues were just six points behind second-placed

Millwall, and certainly not out of any promotion race, but it was still a huge surprise when a massive crowd of 40,793 filled St Andrews.

Gary Pendrey, Bob Hatton and Trevor Francis all scored in their 3-0 thrashing, and Birmingham then won thirteen of their next eighteen league and cup games, scoring thirty-six goals, to reach the FA Cup Semi-finals and rise to fourth in Division Two.

Blues' front three, Francis, Latchford and Hatton, had combined to score twenty-nine of those goals. City had beaten beat Port Vale, Ipswich Town and Portsmouth in the Cup, before they were drawn at home to First Division Huddersfield Town, in the Quarter-finals.

A heaving, capacity crowd of 52,500 had filled St Andrews, on Saturday 10th March. Every inch of the Tilton Road End, the Cattell Road Side, the City End, and the St Andrew's Street grandstand was totally packed, for the penultimate match at which more than fifty thousand attended a Birmingham City home game.

Malcolm Page, Bob Latchford and Bob Hatton secured Birmingham's fourth FA Cup Semi-final place in sixteen years, after their 3-1 victory.

Dave Latchford was the goalkeeper in that historic, and one of the most celebrated of all of Blues' wins over the last forty years. Birmingham's regular keeper, though, for the majority of the second half of the season, for their promotion push, was Paul Cooper, a seventeen year old local boy from Brierley Hill.

Cooper kept seven clean sheets in twelve games, and conceded just four goals in his final eleven games, but he inexplicably lost his place in the team, after Birmingham had suffered a poor start to their First Division campaign, in August 1972.

Paul Cooper played just five First Division games for Birmingham, over the next two seasons, and he was loaned out to fellow First Division rivals Ipswich Town, before permanently joining the Suffolk team, becoming their greatest-ever goalkeeper.

HOLD ON TIGHT

Birmingham City continued their rise, during March 1972. Bob Hatton scored twice, as they beat both Luton Town and Oxford United 1-0. After a goalless draw away at Cardiff, 45,181 again packed St Andrews, on Tuesday 4th April, and Latchford and Francis both scored to beat Blackpool 2-1. Blues rose to third in the table, three points behind second placed Millwall, but with a game in hand.

In their FA Cup Semi-final at Hillsborough, Mick Jones scored twice, and Peter Lorimer completed the scoring, as Leeds United's master-class of Harvey, Reaney, Madeley, Bremner, Charlton, Hunter, Lorimer, Clarke, Jones, Giles and Gray hammered hapless Birmingham 3-0.

Draws against both Fulham and Middlesbrough were followed by a 2-0 win over Hull City, in Birmingham's final home match of the season. Another massive crowd of over forty thousand had again filled St Andrews, as Alan Campbell's penalty kick, and a late Trevor Francis strike, from outside the penalty area, sealed the points.

Bob Hatton and Trevor Francis both scored to secure a 2-1 win away at Sheffield Wednesday, on the final Saturday of the season. With just one game remaining, and with Birmingham only one point behind Millwall, who'd played all of their 42 games, Blues needed just a draw away at Orient on the following Tuesday for promotion.

33,383 filled Brisbane Road, on Tuesday 2nd May, three times Orient's average crowd, with over 20,000 of them Blues supporters. Birmingham's back four were brilliant, led by the giant Roger

Hynd, and they held on tight, after Bob Latchford's second half rocket gave them a 1-0 win. They finished as runners-up, just a point behind Norwich City. Their fluent, five man attack was greatly expected to enhance the attacking quality of an increasingly defensive nature of First Division football, and Birmingham's promotion was celebrated in full colour on the front cover of SHOOT!

Birmingham's top scorer was Bob Latchford, with 27 goals, but Bob Hatton and Trevor Francis had also combined for thirty-one league and cup goals.

Central defender, and team leader, Roger Hynd, who'd actually been Fred Goodwin's first signing, back in July 1970, had played in all of Birmingham's forty-two league matches. Hynd, who played for Rangers in the 1967 European Cup Winner's Cup Final, was as influential as the front five players during their promotion charge after Christmas. In their final seventeen games, after Saturday 8th January, Birmingham had conceded only six goals, and they kept twelve clean sheets.

Roger Hynd's solid all-round displays won him the Player of the Season award, at St Andrews.

Pre-season hopes that Birmingham would illuminate Division One, with their progressive attacking play, floundered just a little during the first three months of the season. Blues won only three of their first eighteen league matches, losing nine, and they were also eliminated from the League Cup by Blackpool.

After mid-November, though, they started to find their groove. Bob Latchford's brace helped beat Stoke 2-1, at the Victoria Ground, on Saturday 18th November, and Birmingham then thrashed Norwich City 4-1, at St Andrews.

Then, they led 3-1 at Liverpool, during the first half, on Saturday 2nd December.

Gordon Taylor, Bobby Hope and Bob Latchford had all scored to stun the 45,000 Anfield crowd, before Cormack pulled another goal back for the league leaders before the break, but Birmingham went in 3-2 up at half-time. Latchford's goal that had put Blues 3-1 up brought warm applause from the Anfield crowd.

Roger Hynd sent forward a long pass, which Latchford met and he flicked inside to Hatton. Hatton returned the ball back to Latchford, twenty-five yards out, and he headed it back to Hatton. Hatton then delivered a perfectly-weighted diagonal pass into the area, which Latchford collected and belted past Clemence.

It was a wonderful, sublime piece of interplay, a couple of delightful one-two's, that had totally wiped Hughes, Storton and Lloyd out of the picture. After the break, though, Shankly's Liverpool came out firing live rounds, and Alec Lindsay and John Toshack both scored late in the game, following sustained Scouse pressure.

That late Liverpool comeback 4-3 win triggered another brief slump in confidence, and during December and January, they lost four out of seven, dropping to second-bottom place by late January. Brilliantly, though, they lost only twice out of their final fifteen matches, winning ten of them, and scoring twenty-two goals.

STRANGE MAGIC

The game that sparked their great revival was a superb win over reigning Champions Derby County, on Saturday 10th February. Bearded Bob Latchford buried the ball beyond Boulton, giving Blues a half-time lead, but then in the second half, Gordon Taylor won the ball on the halfway line. The golden-haired winger ran from halfway, sprinting up the left, whizzing past Ron Webster, as if Derby's greatest ever right back wasn't even there. Taylor crossed from the left side of the penalty area, and Trevor Francis fired, right-footed, beyond Colin Boulton at the far post. Birmingham held on comfortably, in front of 38,000, for a great 2-0 home win over the Champions.

That was great, but the real highlight of their winning run was on Saturday 7th April, when the league leaders Liverpool visited, with 48,114 packed into St Andrews, climbing the floodlights.

BIRMINGHAM CITY		LIVERPOOL
Dave Latchford	1	Ray Clemence
Ray Martin	2	Chris Lawler
Gary Pendrey	3	Alec Lindsay
Malcolm Page	4	Tommy Smith
Roger Hynd	5	Larry Lloyd
John Roberts	6	Emlyn Hughes
Alan Campbell	7	Kevin Keegan
Trevor Francis	8	Peter Cormack
Bob Latchford	9	Steve Heighway
Bob Hatton	10	Brian Hall
Gordon Taylor	11	Ian Callaghan

Bob Latchford scored his nineteenth league and cup goal of the season, flicking in Alan Campbell's cross, to give Blues a 1-0 half-time lead. Bob Hatton then doubled their lead, after the break, and despite Tommy Smith's late, scrambled goal, Birmingham City held on for one of the greatest league wins of their history.

More importantly, those two points lifted them seven points clear of the relegation zone, and virtually secured their top flight survival, with just five games left.

In any case, Birmingham beat Leicester 1-0 away (Campbell); Stoke City 3-1 at home (Page, Francis and Hatton); West Brom 3-2 at home (Latchford, Hynd and Burns); and then, finally, they eased past a virtual Leeds United reserve team that only had the FA Cup Final to look forward to. Trevor Francis and Kenny Burns had both scored during that 2-1 win, on Monday 30th April.

Kenny Burns' goal was his third of the season, from just nine games. The nineteen year old Glaswegian had made his debut during the previous season, but he'd been unable to break into Birmingham's regular attack, and he made just sixteen league starts during his first two seasons at St Andrews. After August 1973, though, he began to start more regularly, replacing Stan Harland in the centre of Birmingham's defence.

In the end, Birmingham finished in a respectable tenth position at the end of their first season back in the First Division, finishing twelve points clear of the relegation places, but just six points below a UEFA Cup qualifying position. In the minefields of muddy First Division pitches, Birmingham weren't the goal machine they'd been, when winning promotion back in '72.

Bob Hatton and Trevor Francis had only managed thirteen league goals between them, but Bob Latchford was a prolific revelation. Latchford had scored nineteen First Division goals, all from open play, and he was England's fourth highest goal-scorer, profiting greatly from the craft and cleverness, the strange magic of Francis, Hatton, Taylor and Campbell.

Roger Hynd missed just two games, and his back four, with Dave Latchford behind them, kept seven clean sheets during their final fifteen matches, after the start of February, conceding only ten goals.

A NEW WORLD RECORD

More importantly, Birmingham's average crowd at St Andrews, during 1972-73, was 36,663, the fourth highest crowd in England, bettered only by Manchester United, Liverpool and Arsenal. Amazingly, their fans had outnumbered those at Leeds United, Everton, Tottenham and Newcastle.

These had been Blues' best two seasons, since the middle of the Fifties, before anyone had even heard of Telstar or Elvis. Moreover, they'd mostly done it with charm, and with a smile on their faces. Things looked very bright for Birmingham.

1973-74 was a complete **paradox** of a season for Birmingham City. They retained their place in the top five supported clubs in England, with an average home crowd of over 33,000, and they also scored as many First Division goals as second-placed Liverpool.

There were more goals scored in games involving Birmingham, than any other First Division team, except for Ipswich.

On the other hand, though, Birmingham had fought a relegation battle all season, and looked doomed at the start of December. They only achieved safety on the final Saturday of the season, and only Southampton had conceded more goals than Blues.

To start off with, they'd made an awful start, in direct contrast to their superb finish to 1972-73, winning none of their first ten league games, up to mid-October. They drew only three of those games, but against three of the best teams in Division One, Derby County, Liverpool and QPR.

A Trevor Francis penalty kick, and a Kenny Burns header had provided them with their first league win, on Saturday 13th October, over fierce rivals Wolves, but then, Birmingham earned just two points from their next five games up to late November.

On the Friday night of 23rd November, Birmingham were rock bottom, and three points from safety, having scored only fourteen goals from sixteen games. Their top scorer Bob Hatton had scored four of them.

FIRST DIVISION BOTTOM FIVE, FRIDAY 23RD NOVEMBER 1973

	PL	W	D	L	F	A	PTS
Man United	16	4	4	8	15	20	12
Wolves	16	3	4	9	15	26	10
Norwich City	16	2	6	8	12	25	10
West Ham United	16	1	7	8	14	25	9
BIRMINGHAM	16	1	5	10	14	33	7

Bob Latchford fired an emotionally charged hat-trick against Leicester City, on Saturday 24th November, during their 3-0 home win, before Kenny Burns, deputising for Alan Campbell, hit the winner in their 1-0 win over Newcastle.

In mid-December, Burns scored another two, and Bob Hatton hit his fifth of the season, as Birmingham beat West Ham United 3-1.

Over Christmas, they lost to high-flying Ipswich, but then they beat Coventry to lift themselves, temporarily, out of the relegation zone, before drawing 1-1 with runaway leaders Leeds United, on Saturday 29th December.

With 50,451 filling St Andrews, Bob Latchford had given Blues a 1-0 half-time lead, but Joe Jordan equalised, boosting his chances of a World Cup call-up.

Birmingham earned only three points from their next six league matches, though, scoring just six goals, to drop right back into the relegation zone by 22nd February.

They were one point above both Manchester United and Norwich, but six points adrift of fourth bottom West Ham, who they would never catch. Fortunately for Blues, though, another team were suffering a collapse far worse than Birmingham's.

Just over a week earlier, Birmingham weakened their survival hopes even further, by accepting a £350,000 bid from Everton for top scorer Bob Latchford. Everton's Howard Kendall and Archie Styles were the makeweights in the deal, after Freddie Goodwin had made it clear that he wasn't prepared to accept only cash for Latchford.

Bob Latchford had been an all-time hero at Birmingham, scoring sixty-eight goals in 158 games, including twenty-nine First Division goals in just over a season and a half. At just 23 years old, though, the best years were still to come for Bob Latchford.

The £350,000 that Birmingham received for Latchford was a new World Record transfer fee for an English player, but with them in a deeply dangerous hole, down in the First Division drop zone, hopes were dimmed, and Manchester United were about to launch a massive march for survival, making matters even more difficult.

Tommy Docherty's United lost only twice during their twelve games between Saturday 16th February and St George's Day, winning five of them, but Fred Goodwin had had a plan, and Birmingham City matched them , point for point.

After Bob Latchford's departure from his home city team, Goodwin converted Kenny Burns to centre-forward, and Burns didn't disappoint. He scored the first goal in Birmingham's 2-0 away win at Southampton, on 23rd March, and then, he smashed a hat-trick in their 3-3 draw at eighth-placed Leicester City, on Saturday 6th April.

Birmingham drew with Stoke, they drew with Burnley, and then they drew at Newcastle, with Campbell, Francis and Hatton scoring four between them, to sit just a single point below fourth-bottom placed Southampton, who'd dropped down from a UEFA Cup qualifying place, just a week before Christmas.

WILD WEST HERO

On Wednesday 23rd April, St George's Day, 39,160 filled the St Andrews terraces, as Blues hosted seventh-placed QPR, chasing a UEFA Cup place. They had to win.

BIRMINGHAM CITY		QUEENS PARK RANGERS
Dave Latchford	1	Phil Parkes
Ray Martin	2	Tony Hazell
Gary Pendrey	3	Ian Gillard
Howard Kendall	4	Terry Venables
Roger Hynd	5	Terry Mancini
John Roberts	6	Ian Evans
Alan Campbell	7	Dave Thomas
Trevor Francis	8	Gerry Francis
Kenny Burns	9	Martyn Busby
Bob Hatton	10	Stan Bowles
Gordon Taylor	11	Don Givens
Joe Gallagher	12	Mick Leach

There was actually little for Blues fans to worry about. Howard Kendall totally bossed Terry Venables, and the fast-paced, possession football of the long haired Wild West Heroes, Campbell, Francis, Burns, Hatton and Taylor wreaked havoc on the Rangers penalty area, like the **Hole in the Wall Gang** rampaging into town, giving Mancini and Hazell, particularly, a nightmare of a day.

Gordon Taylor's long range effort, and Trevor Francis' clipped shot, from fifteen yards out, gave Birmingham a 2-0 half-time lead, before Francis fired his second of the match. Howard Kendall also scored his first for the club giving Blues a 4-0 win, lifting them out of the relegation zone, by just a single point, and with one game remaining.

On the final Saturday of the season, Birmingham hosted already-relegated Norwich City, needing just one point to ensure their First Division survival, having a much superior goal average to third-bottom Southampton. The 44,000 St Andrews crowd were stunned, though, when the bearded Dave Stringer headed in Colin Suggett's free-kick, early on. The Canaries were by far the better team in the early stages, not allowing the Hole in the Wall Gang a moment on the ball.

Against the run of play, however, Bob Hatton squeezed home a shot from ten yards, and then from Gordon Taylor's right wing cross, Kenny Burns leapt highest and he thumped his header past the helpless Kevin Keelan.

Bob Hatton was City's top scorer with twenty league and cup goals, but he, Kenny Burns and Trevor Francis had scored a combined forty goals between them.

Birmingham scored fifty-two First Division goals in 1973-74, the same amount as second-placed Liverpool, but they'd conceded sixty-four goals, more than any other club except Southampton.

Blues made another obligatory awful start to a First Division season, during August 1974, losing at home to Middlesbrough and Leicester, and also away at Leeds. That defeat at Elland Road was Leeds United's only win under Brian Clough. After five games, Birmingham were second bottom of Division One, on the last day of August.

Joe Gallagher's header secured a 1-0 away win at QPR, on Saturday 7th September, and then a week later, Bob Hatton and Trevor Francis, with two penalties, helped Birmingham beat Derby County 3-2, at St Andrews.

Defeats to Carlisle, West Ham and Coventry dropped them back into relegation troubles by early October, but four wins from their next five matches, over Luton, Leeds, Newcastle and Chelsea, lifted them well away from the bottom three. On Saturday 16th November 1974, the league leaders Manchester City visited St Andrews.

BIRMINGHAM CITY		MANCHESTER CITY
Dave Latchford	1	Keith MacRae
Ray Martin	2	Geoff Hammond
Archie Styles	3	Willie Donachie
Howard Kendall	4	Mike Doyle
Joe Gallagher	5	Colin Barrett
Malcolm Page	6	Alan Oakes
Alan Campbell	7	Mike Summerbee
Gordon Taylor	8	Colin Bell
Kenny Burns	9	Rodney Marsh
Bob Hatton	10	Phil Henson
Jimmy Calderwood	11	Dennis Tueart

Blues tore through the red and black striped former league Champions in a wonderful display of attacking football, and defensive excellence against a team of greater attacking quality, on paper.

Kendall, Hatton and Burns gave Birmingham a 3-0 half–time lead, in front of 35,143, as the darkening skies danced to the noise and songs, the colours of the city lights and club floodlights mixed with the smoke from fags, and the steam from urine rolling down the Tilton Road End. Football really was like this once. It was the most wonderful day of 1974 for Birmingham City.

Hatton even added a fourth before the end.

That 4-0 win, followed by a goalless draw at Spurs, lifted Blues up to ninth in the First Division, only four points behind the leaders, and just two points behind a UEFA Cup place. The only time since the Fifties that Birmingham have been in an actual title race at any point of any season, it was a golden moment in the club's modern-day, Colour Television period.

FIRST DIVISION LEADERS, 23RD NOVEMBER 1974

	PL	W	D	L	F	A	PTS
Man City	19	10	4	5	25	23	24
Liverpool	18	10	3	5	24	13	23
Ipswich Town	19	10	2	7	25	14	22
Everton	18	5	12	1	23	18	22
Derby County	19	8	6	5	32	27	22
West Ham	19	8	5	6	35	28	21
Stoke City	18	7	7	4	31	25	21
Sheffield United	18	8	5	5	27	29	21
BIRMINGHAM	19	8	4	7	30	25	20

TURN TO STONE

"I am certainly proud of what we have achieved but not satisfied, however," Freddie Goodwin said of his team's ascent towards the top of Division One. "Not satisfied however, because I will **never** be satisfied until we have won the First Division Championship."

But of course it was the Birmingham City way, that because of their defensive fragility and inconsistency, they obviously just couldn't sustain their ascent.

By late December, they'd fallen back into the high teens, where they remained.

In the FA Cup, Birmingham battled past Luton Town, in the Third round.

A boisterous 17,543 Kenilworth Road crowd was silenced by Howard Kendall's great strike from the edge of the penalty area, during the second half.

Three weeks later, on Saturday 25th January, Birmingham travelled to Chelsea in the Fourth round, but they were without Trevor Francis, Bob Hatton and Alan Campbell. A hostile Stamford Bridge crowd of over 35,000 extended a rude welcome to Blues, wearing their distinctive red and white striped away kit.

Fortunately, this was a Chelsea side with John Phillips, David Hay, Gary Locke, Steve Kember and John Sissons. Gone were the Chelsea boys of Hudson, Osgood, Hutchinson, Bonetti and Webb. Charlie Cooke and John Dempsey were both missing.

Kenny Burns' energy made the most of a lack of cohesion and consistency in Chelsea's central defence, turned to stone, burying the ball past Phillips, on the break.

Birmingham held on for a good 1-0 away win, and they were rewarded with a Fifth round tie at home to Third Division Walsall.

On Saturday 15th February, Walsall travelled the full four miles down the M6 motorway to Birmingham, and they took ten thousand fans with them.

43,841, the biggest crowd of the round, packed St Andrews, as Bob Hatton fired Blues 1-0 up before half-time. Hatton collected Kendall's perfect through-ball, and with composure, control and quality, he finished classily past Ireland's keeper Mick Kearns. Kenny Burns thumped home a second goal after the break, and despite Brian Taylor's goal for the Saddlers, Birmingham held on for a 2-1 win.

In the Quarter-finals, they were drawn at home, again, to Middlesbrough.

Boro were the First Division's newcomers, back in the top flight again after a twenty-one year absence. Jack Charlton had developed an effective, dangerous side, built on firm defence, and quick counter-attacks, with good passing players, Bobby Murdoch, David Armstrong and Graeme Souness, feeding their swift front runners Foggon, Mills and Hickton. The Oxford United chairman, Bob Kearsey had accused Boro of being a "non-football" team, but they certainly weren't that. They were a great team of their style, and they'd been second in the First Division over Christmas and the New Year, behind Ipswich Town. Alan Foggon, David Mills and John Hickton had scored a combined total of twenty-six goals up to then.

This was the best team to ever represent Middlesbrough.

SHOWDOWN

BIRMINGHAM CITY		MIDDLESBROUGH
Dave Latchford	1	Jim Platt
Malcolm Page	2	John Craggs
Steve Bryant	3	Frank Spraggon
Howard Kendall	4	Graeme Souness
Joe Gallagher	5	Stuart Boam
Kenny Burns	6	Willie Maddren
Paul Hendrie	7	Bobby Murdoch
Gordon Taylor	8	John Hickton
John Roberts	9	David Mills
Bob Hatton	10	Alan Foggon
Gary Emmanuel	11	David Armstrong
Alan Campbell	12	Alan Willey

It was the biggest crowd of the season at St Andrews, 47,260, although still a few thousand below capacity. Middlesbrough never sold out Ayresome Park, though, and they'd failed to fill their away end. Anyway, Blues were roared into the Semi-finals.

Against the defensive proficiency of Craggs, Boam, Maddren and Spraggon, it was always going to be a hard game, especially without the prolonged absence of Trevor Francis, and with Boro's midfield combination of Souness and Murdoch against both Kendall and Burns, it would always be dangerous.

Boro would have a chance. That was certain. Dave Latchford did brilliantly, though, diving low to his right to palm David Mills' swivel shot around his post.

Birmingham fought very well against Boro's first-choice eleven, with Hendrie and Emmanuel having not yet started a combined total of ten matches, but they also fought, really fought, every bit of the way, with their Scottish and Welsh pride and courage.

It took the best bit of skill, from one of the best players on the pitch, amongst the likes of Bobby Murdoch and Howard Kendall, but Bob Hatton found an opening during the first half. Hatton fired beyond Platt, planting the ball inside the far post, from outside the area; a wonderful goal, in the context of how tight the match was, to send Birmingham City into the last four.

In Monday's draw, Birmingham might have been drawn against the in-form West Ham United, or the title-chasing Ipswich Town, or even European Cup hopefuls Leeds United. The Sixth round tie between Leeds and Ipswich wouldn't be settled, though, for another four games, a fortnight into the future, and anyway, Birmingham were drawn against the "soft" opposition of Second Division Fulham.

Most purists would have preferred West Ham versus Ipswich, after they'd ground out a win over Leeds, to have been the Wembley Final, and the Birmingham v Fulham Semi-final showdown was seen, by most, as second billing.

55,000 packed Hillsborough as Fulham attempted to contain Birmingham's famous five of Campbell, Francis, Burns, Hatton and Taylor, wearing their red and black striped away kit, the same colours they'd worn as when they'd defeated the mighty Everton at Goodison Park.

CAN'T GET IT OUT OF MY HEAD

BIRMINGHAM CITY		FULHAM
Dave Latchford	1	Peter Mellor
Malcolm Page	2	John Fraser
Gary Pendrey	3	Les Strong
Howard Kendall	4	Alan Mullery
Joe Gallagher	5	John Lacy
John Roberts	6	Bobby Moore
Alan Campbell	7	John Mitchell
Trevor Francis	8	Jimmy Conway
Kenny Burns	9	Viv Busby
Bob Hatton	10	Alan Slough
Gordon Taylor	11	Les Barrett

It was a one-sided first half, with Fulham completely dominant, running the game; both Mullery and Slough completely controlled the midfield, and both Les Barrett and Viv Busby ran Birmingham's defence ragged. Dave Latchford had dived to make three excellent saves, from Mitchell, Busby and Barrett, but Fulham continued to boss the game. Joe Gallagher just couldn't hold the lightening quick pace of Barrett.

Les Barrett, who'd not played First Division football since the late Sixties, and had even played in the Third Division for two years, until 1971, flew past Joe Gallagher, time and time again. The young Gallagher had never even heard of Barrett, and he just couldn't get that out of his head, as Barrett kept coming back to beat him again and again.

Into the second half, with Fulham attacking the West Stand, filled with their own fans, Alan Slough out-muscled Gallagher for the ball, just outside the Birmingham area, and he fed John Mitchell, further outside, on the right. Mitchell was playing his first game of Fulham's FA Cup run, and he'd started just five league games up to then, but with one touch, he flicked the ball up with his left foot, and on the full volley, he smashed the ball into the top left corner of Latchford's goal, from thirty yards. Mitchell, having scored the goal of his career, then jumped, arms aloft, with his teammates, into the ecstatic Fulham fans, behind the goal.

Birmingham then scored an equaliser they really didn't deserve. Malcolm Page's long pass was collected by Joe Gallagher, inside the Fulham area. Gallagher, who'd had an absolute nightmare, swivelled to just beat the close attentions of Slough and Lacy, and he finished low inside Mellor's far post, from six yards out.

The replay was at Maine Road, on the following Wednesday, 9th April, and over thirty-five thousand fans travelled up the M1 and M6 motorways, filling the terraces, but the influential Alan Campbell was replaced by youngster Paul Hendrie.

This time, though, it was Birmingham City who were completely all over Fulham.

Peter Mellor played the game of his life, having a real Tomaszewski match, stopping shots from Hatton, Francis, Burns, Kendall, Gallagher and Taylor, with absolutely every part of his body.

Paul Hendrie was also very unlucky when he was appeared to have been fouled inside the Fulham area, but no penalty kick was awarded.

Late on, into the night game, late into extra-time, late into injury-time of extra-time, Alan Slough launched a long right-wing cross into the Birmingham City area.

John Dowie nodded down to the six yard box, as Gallagher and Latchford both went for the ball, but John Mitchell stole in and he caught a ricochet off Latchford's face from his initial effort, and just he kneed the rebound bouncing towards goal.

It was a diabolically bouncing ball from Mitchell's half-hit shot, that could have gone anywhere, but the ball comically bounced in over the line, deceiving desperate lunges from both Latchford and the shattered Gallagher.

The Fulham fans had felt it was they who'd sucked that oddly bouncing ball over the goal-line, as the remaining seconds of the game ticked away.

As purple patches go, Fulham's purple patch had not been quite as purple as other, more illustrious clubs' purple patches, but the second half of that 1974-75 season had Fulham's fans tickled pink with delight.

The uncontrolled elation experienced by those fifteen thousand bouncing Fulham fans at Maine Road, late, very, very late, on that April midweek night, was an unbelievable experience, the heights of which few fans ever feel in a lifetime.

Despite their severe disappointment, Birmingham took three points from their last four games, to finish down in seventeenth place, but well clear of the relegation zone.

Bob Hatton and Trevor Francis shared twenty-nine goals, while, as a deputy striker, Kenny Burns had bustled his way to ten league and cup goals.

For the fourth successive season, City had averaged league crowds of over 30,000. Their average home attendance of 30,854 was the seventh highest average crowd in English football, with only the two Manchester clubs, the two Merseyside clubs, and Leeds and Newcastle attracting more fans.

1975-76 brought some major changes to Birmingham City, but not their perpetual struggle against the drop to Division Two. After a 3-3 draw away at Leicester City (Hatton, Kendall 2), the Blues lost 0-2 at home to Tommy Docherty's young, energetic Manchester United, on Tuesday 19th August.

Defeats away at Everton, and then at home to Middlesbrough followed, and by late August, Birmingham were second bottom in the First Division.

TELEPHONE LINE

On Thursday 28th August, Freddie Goodwin paid Newcastle United £100,000 for their creative left-winger Terry Hibbitt, who'd been marginalised at St James's Park following the arrival of the more functional Tommy Craig. Peter Withe was also signed from Wolves, to fill Bob Latchford's place as Blues' bearded centre-forward, while allowing Kenny Burns to return to the back four again.

Defeats kept coming, though. Despite Bob Hatton scoring twice, Birmingham lost 4-2 away at Ipswich on Saturday 30th August, and then they were held to a 1-1 draw at home by QPR, after Howard Kendall had given them a half-time lead.

Two second half goals by the great Willie Carr, on Saturday 13th September, helped Wolves beat Blues, up at Molineux, and Birmingham City were in dire straits, second from bottom, and only one point above Sheffield United, who'd earned only a single point from seven matches.

Five days later, Birmingham City sacked Freddie Goodwin, after nearly five and a half years in charge of the club. Despite their dreadful start, it was a big shock, but the board behaved in a disgraceful manner in sacking Goodwin.

A telephone call had summoned him to the boardroom, along with his coach Willie Bell, and he was told there and then that he was being replaced by his coach.

Fred Goodwin was dignified as he left St Andrews, insisting that he'd had absolutely "no regrets about (his) years at Birmingham, and had always given 100% and had faith in (his) methods." He also acknowledged that the bad start to the season had put the board under pressure to make a decision.

When exactly had Birmingham not suffered a "bad start to the season"?

A High Court judge, though, ruled that Goodwin had been unfairly dismissed, and that the sacking had "been done in a particularly nasty way, summoned before his employers like a schoolboy sent for by his headmaster."

Thirty-eight year old Willie Bell, from Renfrewshire, had played over two hundred league games for Leeds United back in the early Sixties, during Don Revie's revolution, and he'd played at left back during their 1965 FA Cup Final defeat against Liverpool. He was initially appointed as caretaker manager of Birmingham.

A couple of days later, on Saturday 20th September, the Blues Came Alive, playing more for their old boss, most probably though, than their new one, and they slaughtered Burnley 4-0. Campbell, Withe, Kendall and Francis all scored, before, on the following Tuesday, nearly 32,000 filled St Andrews for the visit of Newcastle.

Peter Withe drove home two dynamic diving headers in the first half, and then Trevor Francis converted a penalty kick, giving Birmingham a 3-1 half-time lead.

City won 3-2, and they rose to seventeenth place.

After their 2-1 defeat at Aston Villa, with nearly 54,000 filling Villa Park, Hatton and Francis again combined to give City a 2-0 win over bottom club Sheffield United on the first Saturday in October. A week later, on Saturday 11th October, Birmingham travelled to Anfield, and Willie Bell dropped both Howard Kendall and Terry Hibbitt.

It was the first time in his career, that Kendall had ever been dropped for a match, and as an ex-Evertonian, it was difficult to take, being forced to just sit, numbly, in the Liverpool stands, as his old rivals won 3-1.

On the following Monday, Willie Bell was finally appointed as the new manager of Birmingham City, though, and the fun, fondly remembered days at St Andrews were coming quickly to a close.

By Saturday 29th November 1975, they were back in second bottom position, having won just one game out of seven, since Bell's full-time appointment.

Three wins from four matches during December, though, had lifted them up to nineteenth place, two points above both Burnley and Wolves, which was where they remained for the remainder of the season.

ALL OVER THE WORLD

On Monday 4th March 1976, Alan Campbell was transferred to Third Division promotion contenders Cardiff City, after playing 175 league games for Birmingham. Cardiff won seven and lost only one of their final fourteen matches, with Alan Campbell in their team, and they finished second in Division Three, behind Champions Hereford United. When Campbell arrived at Ninian Park, they were fifth.

Campbell played a total of 167 league games at Cardiff, over the following four seasons, as the Bluebirds established themselves as a Second Division force again. He retired during the 1981-82 season, after playing 571 Football League matches, 104 of them in the First Division with Birmingham City.

Alan Campbell is now a regular Crown Green Bowls player, with the Baldwin Bowling Club, in Hall Green, Birmingham, the self-proclaimed best Bowls Club in Great Britain.

A week later, Willie Bell also sent Gordon Taylor packing. The thirty-one year old had played one hundred and sixty-six league games for Birmingham, when he was transferred to Second Division club Blackburn Rovers.

Gordon Taylor became the gruff-voiced Chief Executive of the PFA, after retiring from football, and he was awarded an OBE in 2008. He also gained an economics degree, and was appointed vice-president of England's 2018 World Cup bid, going all over the world with David Beckham, John Barnes and Fabio Capello, before Sepp Blatter's FIFA fixed it for Russia to host the 2018 Finals.

On 31st July 1976, the great Bob Hatton was off-loaded, surplus to Willie Bell's requirements, through the back door to Blackpool. He'd been dropped for Birmingham's last five matches of the season, anyway, and he never even had the chance to properly say goodbye.

A reunion wasn't too far away, though, when Blackpool were drawn at home, in the Second round of the League Cup, to Birmingham City. Hatton's second half goal for the Tangerines, on Wednesday 31st August, won the game 2-1, and he was gladly able to say farewell to the five thousand travelling Blues fans, who'd come to cheer their great man as much as for the match.

Bob Hatton scored fifty-eight league goals in 175 games for Birmingham City, and his famed, drooping moustache made him a folk hero forever for all Blues fans. He finally retired in 1983, aged thirty-six, having scored 215 Football League goals.

Trevor Francis had now become the top striker at Birmingham, their only remaining jewel. All his old teammates, Hatton, Latchford, Campbell, Taylor and Hynd had gone, and the good days at St Andrew's were now old. Francis scored sixty-four First Division goals over the three seasons between 1975 and 1978, and he also became an England regular under Don Revie, and then Ron Greenwood, earning twelve caps, as a Birmingham City player, between February 1977 and May 1978.

Francis and Kenny Burns scored a combined total of forty First Division goals during 1976-77, becoming the most prolific attacking partnership in English football, but off the field, Trevor and Kenny weren't on speaking terms at all.

They had properly fallen out after Burns had reputedly gone in very hard on Francis in a training routine, under the management of Freddie Goodwin. Trevor felt that Kenny was pushing the authority of Freddie on a daily basis, and that he was untouchable, quite aside from the pain he'd felt for quite a while, after that tackle.

DON'T WALK AWAY

Brian Clough and Peter Taylor paid Birmingham £150,000 to bring Kenny Burns to newly-promoted Nottingham Forest, on Saturday 17th July 1977. In their own inimitable manner, though, Clough and Taylor were not impressed by Burns being fifth highest in the First Division goal-scoring table in 1976-77, and they immediately started playing Burns back in central defence.

With Peter Shilton behind him, Kenny Burns helped Forest keep 24 clean sheets in his 41 First Division games during the 1977-78 season, winning both First Division Championship, and League Cup winners' medals, as well as the Football Writers' Footballer of the Year award.

As the late Seventies' freezing cold set into the West Midlands, and the Winter of Discontent reared its ugly head, average crowds at St Andrews shrank from well over 30,000 between 1971 and 1975, to 28,000 in 1976 and 1977, then below 24,000 in 1978, before finally, as relegation back to Division Two was inescapable, less than 20,000 were watching Birmingham home games during their dreaded 1978-79 season.

By 1978, Birmingham were a complete mess of a team. Despite the heroically loyal Joe Gallagher and Gary Pendrey defending as bravely as they always did, conceding as many goals as they did in 1973, Blues were scoring fifteen fewer, and second bottom in the table from the Autumn of 1978 until May.

Only 12,000 had watched their 3-1 home win over QPR on Tuesday 6th March 1979.

Just under a month earlier, Trevor Francis did walk away from his beloved club, when he became English football's first-ever one million pound footballer.

Brian Clough paid that significant fee for the Golden Boy, and Trevor Francis played nineteen First Division games for Forest, over the final three months of 1978-79, scoring six goals, and he was rewarded with a place in their team for the European Cup Final, against Malmo.

Trevor Francis only started in Munich because Brian Clough had chosen to drop the fit-again Archie Gemmill, who'd been injured since early April, but he scored Forest's winning goal, turning in John Robertson's left-wing cross, just as he'd done many times before, from Gordon Taylor's crosses.

Trevor Francis had scored 119 league goals for Birmingham City, from 280 matches, before leaving St Andrews at the age of twenty-four. He was a special player who managed to combine electrifying pace, close control and a presence on the pitch. Eventually he totalled 392 First Division appearances for Birmingham, Forest, Manchester City, QPR and Sheffield Wednesday. He'd also made eighty-nine Serie A appearances for Sampdoria and Atalanta, between 1983 and 1987, as well as eighteen Scottish Premier League games for Rangers in 1987-88.

When he finally retired in 1993, at the age of thirty-nine, Trevor Francis had played 499 top flight games in England, Italy and Scotland. He'd also played fifty-two games for England, and started all five of their matches during the 1982 World Cup Finals, scoring two goals, against Czechoslovakia and Kuwait.

Trevor Francis was one of the greatest ever English footballers, and most probably, the greatest player in Birmingham City's history. Well-behaved, an outstanding footballer and an ambassador, he was a "sensational, phenomenal talent," according to Brian Clough. Despite this, he won only one trophy throughout his career, the Coppa Italia in 1985. Alongside Graeme Souness, Gianluca Vialli and also Roberto Mancini, he helped Sampdoria beat AC Milan 3-1 in the Final.

On Friday 10th May 1996, Trevor Francis was appointed manager of Birmingham City, at the age of 42. He led the Blues to three successive Championship play-off defeats, against Watford in 1999, Barnsley in 2000, and then Preston North End in 2001. In 2001, Francis had also led Birmingham to their first Wembley Final since 1956, the League Cup Final. They drew 1-1 with Liverpool, though, after extra-time, and Blues lost 5-4 on penalties.

Trevor Francis left Birmingham City on Monday 15th October 2001, after six and a half years as their manager. Birmingham had won 139 out of 290 games, of which Francis was in charge, and they lost only 81. Francis had a massive 47.9 winning percentage, the best for a permanent manager since Harry Storer back in the Forties.

On Monday 12th May 2002, the team that he had left behind finally beat Norwich City in the Premier League Play-off Final, on penalty kicks, to return to the top flight of English football for the first time in fifteen years.

MR BLUE SKY

It was often rumoured that Jeff Lynne wrote *Mr Blue Sky* for Trevor Francis, and indeed, Blues fans even adopted the anthem for their Golden Boy, singing the song loudly on the Tilton Road End; magical days!

That song is still sung today, as it's played out of the St Andrew's loudspeakers, before and after games, but the rumours were not true. It wasn't written for Trevor Francis.

Jeff Lynne is a huge Blues fan, though, and also a great friend of Trevor's. It was a friendship that went all the way back to when Trevor was a fifteen year old youth team player at St Andrews, and Jeff had just joined The Move, which eventually morphed into ELO, as Birmingham strode into the First Division, Out of the Blue.

Jeff was a passionate Blues fan, even calling one of his songs on that best-selling album *Birmingham Blues*. Trevor also loved The Move, and he became a massive fan of ELO, too. It was a perfect friendship.

Jeff Lynne said of Trevor Francis, "he's always striving to be better. One thing you sense with him, that you sense with very, very few players- it's like a sigh of relief when he gets the ball. You sense something's going to happen. All the crowd used to shout: Give it the kid! Give it the kid! You'd suddenly see Trevor shoot off on one of those runs."

"He had a spell of doing these solo efforts," Jeff Lynne continued, "you'd see him dive into about a hundred and fifty defenders by the corner flag and there would be a horde of people around him, and he'd come out the other end, still with the ball bobbling around his feet. It used to draw gasps."

Nobody could have put it better than that, the great Jeff Lynne remembering the true greatness of Trevor Francis.

There was no more exciting team than Birmingham City, at their very best, with Campbell, Francis, Latchford, Hatton and Taylor in full flow. Having said that, there was no worse team than City at their worst, as they sometimes were, but there was always, *always*, a speck of blue, a bright blue light to hold on tight to.

That's why nearly 35,000 always filled St Andrews, week in and week out, to watch a team mostly battling relegation, but in a thoroughly attacking and entertaining way.

Birmingham City were, for three or four years, one of the best-supported teams in England, for all the right reasons. In contrast to the present day, when teams like Birmingham need to play a tightly tectonic 4-5-1 type of game, squeezing the life out of football, to have any chance of survival in the Premier League, That Great Blues team under Freddie Goodwin glowed brightly, from the grim Midlands, as a gleaming irresistible Blue beacon, lighting up English football.

ASCENT FROM THE BROADS

B Y 1969, NORWICH CITY HAD been a lower league team for all of their forty-nine year Football League history. After the War, despite finishing in second position in Division Three (South) on two occasions, Norwich were trapped by the Football League's tight, almost suffocating rules, where only the Champions of a Twenty-four Team Division gained promotion to the Second Division.

They were indeed the dark ages of the lower reaches of the Football League.

Once the two separate Divisions Three (North) and (South) were combined, however, to create the new Divisions Three and Four in 1958, it took Norwich only two seasons to finally achieve promotion to Division Two, as runners-up behind Third Division Champions Southampton in 1960.

Under the old Division Three (South) system, they'd have stayed down, yet again.

Norwich City finished fourth in Division Two in 1961, their highest-ever league finish, but they then settled, thereafter, back into the mid-table comfort of Second Division life, for the remainder of the Sixties.

Kevin Keelan joined Norwich City from Wrexham, for a fee of just £6,500, back in August 1963. At just twenty-two years old, his first game in goal for the Canaries was their 3-1 away defeat, at Cardiff City.

Two years later, in 1965, Dave Stringer made his debut for Norwich. The blonde haired, right-footed defender was locally-born and raised in Great Yarmouth, and with Kevin Keelan, very un-locally born, over in Calcutta, they became two of the best-loved players in Norwich City's history.

Kenny Foggo had played 129 First Division matches for West Brom, when he joined the Canaries in September 1967. The twenty-three year old Scottish winger, from Perth, was a quick, two-footed forward, who could attack down either flank.

"KEEP YOUR VOICE DOWN TO A ROAR!"

Almost exactly a year later, in September 1968, Duncan Forbes, another Scot, had arrived at Carrow Road, having travelled up the A140 from Colchester United.

Forbes had played 270 league games for the U's, since joining from East of Scotland League side Musselburgh Athletic back in 1962.

Costing just £10,000, Forbes was a vociferous and aggressive player, who instilled an inspired and positive leadership in the Canaries' defence. He became a cult hero at Norwich for his famous phrase, *"keep your voice down to a roar!"*

In May 1969, though, following another mid-table Second Division "failure", Norwich City sacked manager Lol Morgan, who'd signed Duncan Forbes.

Ron Saunders was appointed as Norwich City's new boss. Only thirty-six years old, Saunders had scored 145 league goals, from just 236 games, for Portsmouth, between 1958 and 1964.

Ron Saunders was dour-faced, and uncompromising in his approach to management, with a strict, hard-edged, military method of training. His bunny hop and piggy back training routines up the rugged, steep slopes of Mousehold Heath, in the north-east of the city, had succeeded in vastly improving his squad's fitness.

Born in Birkenhead, and with a good dry measure of Scouse wit, Ron Saunders was underwhelmed by the overall quality of Norwich City's squad when he arrived.

"A mixed bunch," he described them, "some good players, some not so good; some good types of players, and some not so good types. Obviously, the problem was to sort them out."

So, as an Anglia TV reporter had asked, in September 1969, what was the first thing he did when he arrived at Carrow Road, as if the question even needed asking.

"Sorted them out," Saunders replied, with not even a hint of a smile on his face.

Ron Saunders' first sorting out was in Norwich City's attack. They'd been weak up front for most of the previous season. Only Kenny Foggo, with nine goals from 33 games, had scored more than four goals for the team, and he'd been voted their Player of the Season, as a result.

Saunders then signed Peter Silvester, Reading's top goal-scorer, and their Player of the Season, during the Summer of 69. Only twenty years old, Silvester had scored twenty-six goals, from 79 games, during his three seasons at Elm Park. He scored his first goal for Norwich, in his second match, the Canaries' 2-0 home win over Oxford.

In October 1969, just three months after his arrival, Ron Saunders then paid Coventry City £25,000 for one of the most brilliant and skilful midfield dynamos to ever play for Norwich.

Graham Paddon, Manchester-born, had signed for Noel Cantwell's progressive Coventry team, just a year earlier, as an eighteen year old, but he was unable to displace either Willie Carr or Ernie Hunt, in the Sky Blues' team.

Paddon's arrival launched the most successful period in Norwich City's history. They finished mid-table, again, at the end of 1969-70, but Duncan Forbes was voted the club's Player of the Season, after they'd conceded only 46 league goals, their second-best ever defensive record.

Three months into the following 1970-71 season, Saunders signed a fellow Scouser, twenty-two year old Liverpool midfielder Doug Livermore. With both Livermore and Foggo shelling the opposition penalty areas with bombardments of balls, Peter Silvester was City's joint-top scorer, along with Foggo, with fifteen goals.

Norwich City cruised to another mid-table finish, in 1970-71, but with a greater sense of balance, and a more youthful way of life, with Silvester, Paddon, Livermore, and another local midfield player, Trevor Howard, all under twenty-two years old.

There was much hope at Carrow Road for 1971-72.

That hope was not forlorn, as the Canaries went unbeaten during their opening thirteen matches, winning eight of them, to top the Second Division table, for the first time ever, three points ahead of Millwall.

On Saturday 23rd October, 22,763 packed the crumbling terraces of The Den, as Millwall welcomed Norwich, coldly, to Cold Blow Lane. Peter Silvester's first half header was levelled by an unfortunate own goal by David Stringer, the Canaries' longest-serving outfield player.

In the second half, though, Barry Kitchener, Millwall's greatest ever player, hit a ferocious drive to win the game 2-1, and also close the gap at the top to just one point.

It was merely a blip for the Canaries, though, as they immediately went on a seven match unbeaten run, beating Cardiff, Hull, Middlesbrough and Swindon, while drawing on three other occasions.

David Cross had also signed from his home town club, Rochdale, during October, for £40,000, a record transfer fee for both clubs. Cross had scored his first goal for Norwich, during their first match after that Millwall defeat, a 2-1 home win over Cardiff City. That defeat at The Den was indeed merely a blip for the Canaries, and they'd regained their three point lead over Millwall by mid-December.

As well as their rampant start to the league season, Norwich had also beaten Brighton, Carlisle and Grimsby to reach the League Cup Quarter-finals.

They hosted Chelsea, the European Cup Winners' Cup holders, on Wednesday 17th November, with 35,927 packed inside Carrow Road. Norwich were dearly missing Duncan Forbes, though, out of action for four weeks, and Peter Osgood, the King of Stamford Bridge, swivelled past Dave Stringer, and scored to send Chelsea into the last four.

Stan Bowles, another (future) West London legend, scored a hat-trick as Carlisle United stunned Norwich on Saturday 18th December, hammering the Canaries 3-0. It was only their second defeat of the season, but even so, they still held a two point lead over Millwall, at the top of the Second Division, on Christmas Day 1971.

Another massive crowd, 31,041, had packed Carrow Road on Boxing Day, as two Ken Foggo goals, and another from Peter Silvester, secured a 3-0 hammering of Charlton Athletic. Further wins over both Oxford and Fulham, early in the New Year, had extended Norwich's lead at the top to five points.

DIVISION TWO LEADERS, 8TH JANUARY 1972

	PL	W	D	L	F	A	PTS
NORWICH CITY	25	15	8	2	39	19	38
Millwall	25	11	11	3	42	31	33
QPR	25	12	8	5	37	19	32
Sunderland	25	9	11	5	37	38	29
Birmingham	25	8	12	5	36	25	28

An FA Cup Third round 0-3 home thrashing by Hull then triggered a sad, barren run of six league games without a win, though, and their strong lead at the top completely collapsed.

By the middle of March, Millwall were the new Second Division leaders, one point ahead of Norwich City. And Sunderland, Birmingham and Middlesbrough were all chasing like hounds, just three points further back, poised to pounce on second-placed Norwich, the shattered fox.

Their fans rescued them. On a great, floodlit Wednesday night, 15th March 1972, over Thirty Thousand again packed Carrow Road for the visit of lowly Hull City. Lifted by the sheer noise, the Canaries were bouncing, with a mixture of relief and joy.

Trevor Howard and Kenny Foggo scored on either side of half-time, giving Norwich a crucial 2-0 win, stopping their slide, and returning the Canaries to the top of the Division.

Portsmouth beat them 2-1 at Fratton Park on the following Saturday, though, despite Trevor Howard's late goal, and the pressure was very much back on the Canaries.

Jimmy Bone had been a prolific goal scorer for Partick Thistle, having scored fifty goals in just 107 Scottish League games, most of them First Division games.

On Tuesday 29th February, Ron Saunders had made a Leap Year swoop for the twenty-two year old striker, to give Norwich a leap on the chasing pack.

Only four months earlier, Jim Bone had scored Partick's fourth goal during their 4-1 Scottish League Cup Final win over Celtic, at Hampden Park, in front of 62,470, the biggest crowd of his career.

That Celtic side had included Jimmy Johnstone, Kenny Dalglish, Bobby Murdoch, Lou Macari, Tommy Gemmell and David Hay, and it had been an incredible shock, as well as an incredible coup for Ron Saunders. Bone was the fifth player, aged 22 years or younger, to have joined Norwich City since Saunders took charge.

Jimmy Bone scored just once during his first four Norwich City matches, though, as they suffered yet another mini-slump, winning only that home match against Hull, so only 23,605 had nervously attended the visit of Blackpool, on Saturday 25th March.

The pressure was on the Canaries.

NORWICH CITY		BLACKPOOL
Kevin Keelan	1	John Burridge
Clive Payne	2	Dave Hatton
Geoff Butler	3	Steve Harrison
Dave Stringer	4	Peter Suddaby
Duncan Forbes	5	Glyn James
Max Briggs	6	Chris Simpkin
Doug Livermore	7	Tommy Hutchison
Jimmy Bone	8	Alan Suddick
David Cross	9	Keith Dyson
Graham Paddon	10	Peter Hardcastle
Kenny Foggo	11	Micky Burns

There was no pressure on Norwich, that afternoon. First, a Simpkin nudge on David Cross, inside the area, was rightly penalised, and Graham Paddon smashed his left-footed penalty kick high into the top corner of John Burridge's goal.

Clive Payne's long forward pass was headed by Bone, out wide to Cross, on the right wing. Cross crossed for Foggo to stoop and head home for 2-0. Blackpool attacked, but Payne dispossessed Micky Burns, inside the Norwich penalty area, and he sent Paddon running free, racing away, on the threadbare pitch, towards the centre circle.

Graham Paddon, their bright, golden-haired, long-haired virtuoso, casually lofted a long, left-footed pass, over to Foggo, hugging the right wing. Kenny Foggo's cross to the far post was met by Cross, who rose beautifully to head past Burridge for their third.

Dave Stringer's long free-kick, from halfway, was then flicked on by Bone, over Burridge, with a mighty leap, before Micky Burns' goal, at the end of the first half, made it 4-1 at the break.

Norwich's fifth goal, though, during the second half, was the best goal of the game, and among the goals of the season. It was one of the Goals of the Decade, even?

Graham Paddon received the ball inside the centre circle and he raced past Simpkin. Blackpool were badly missing the presence of Terry Alcock. Paddon then sprayed a pass wide right to Foggo, who was given room to turn and return an inside pass to Paddon, well outside of the Blackpool penalty area.

With World class confidence, and from twenty-five yards out, Paddon just opened his body and he swung a left-footed strike, high into the roof of John Burridge's goal.

David Cross and Jimmy Bone both scored during Norwich's 2-0 win away at Charlton Athletic, and on Easter Monday, City then drew 0-0 away at fourth-placed QPR, with 25,257, the Hoops' largest crowd of the season, inside Loftus Road.

Norwich were still top, but by only one point, just ahead of Millwall.

Neither Norwich, nor Millwall had ever played First Division football before, while high-scoring Birmingham City were now at the front of the chasing pack, only four points below Millwall, with a game in hand, and with seven games still to play.

On the very next day, Tuesday 4th April, eighth-placed Bristol City visited Carrow Road, and 35,076, their second Thirty-five thousand home crowd of the season, went wild as David Cross headed in Graham Paddon's corner, giving the Canaries a 1-0 half-time lead. Jim Bone added a second after the break, but the Robins' legends Gerry Gow and Gerry Sweeney both scored to fully earn their surprise 2-2 away draw.

On the following Saturday, at home to Sheffield Wednesday, Phil Hubbard's right wing corner was thundered past Pearson by Duncan Forbes' towering header in front of Carrow Road's 27,244 crowd.

Norwich were now three points clear of Millwall, and also four points above Birmingham in third place. Two wins from their last four games would be enough to secure promotion to the First Division. After losing 1-0 away at Middlesbrough, 31,736 again packed Carrow Road for their final home match of the season, against Swindon Town, on Saturday 22nd April.

The Norwich defence was strong, while Graham Paddon's deep cross from the left was powered in, past Peter Downsborough, by the head of captain Duncan Forbes.

15,530 squeezed into Orient's Brisbane Road ground, two days later, on Bank Holiday Monday, for Norwich City's 2-1 win to secure their promotion to the First Division, for the first time.

Over half of that jubilant crowd were from East Anglia, as Kenny Foggo scored with a sweet strike, on the turn, from inside the penalty area.

Graham Paddon then stroked home his penalty kick, for a brilliant win.

Norwich were up, but not yet Champions. They needed one more point. Millwall had lost at Burnley on the previous Saturday, and they were actually in danger of losing their promotion place, having been in the top two all season, while Birmingham had won nine, and lost none, of their last fifteen games.

Both Millwall and Birmingham won on Tuesday 25th April, and on the final Saturday of the season, Millwall beat Preston 2-0, with over 19,000 inside The Den, to finish their season in second place. Birmingham had also won away at Sheffield Wednesday, though, but they had one more game to play, due to their FA Cup run.

Norwich City drew 1-1 away at Watford, with 22,421 packing Vicarage Road, over double the Hornets' average crowd. Dave Stringer's header, from just inside Watford's penalty area, was enough to earn their crucial point. And Birmingham City then beat Orient 1-0 on the following Tuesday to deprive Millwall of their much-deserved promotion place.

Two years later, the Football League's format changed to three up and three down, between the top two Divisions, but those three teams had all deserved to go up.

Kenny Foggo was City's top scorer in their first-ever Championship winning season, with fourteen goals, but Norwich's goals came from all along their front line, with Foggo, Silvester, Cross and Paddon all combining for forty league goals.

Dave Stringer was voted Player of the Season, having played in every game, but Kevin Keelan and Clive Payne were also ever-presents. Graham Paddon, who was Norwich City's genuine golden haired jewel, had missed only two games.

Norwich City's first-ever season in the First Division, in 1972-73, ended in a desperate fight for survival, but it contained several real highlights.

On Saturday 26th August, over 30,000 squashed into a warm Carrow Road, for the visit of reigning Champions Derby County. Graham Paddon's late, left-footed strike, from the edge of the penalty area, secured a great 1-0 home win.

Then, four days later, on the following Wednesday, another Thirty Thousand home crowd watched Paddon and Stringer both score to beat League Cup holders Stoke City 2-0, lifting Norwich up to seventh in Division One, after six games.

The Canaries hovered nicely around the top ten, for the next two months of their first season in the First Division, before they hosted Ipswich Town, their fierce local rivals, on Saturday 11th November. 34,739, their second-biggest home crowd of the season, were frustrated, though, as Town held on grimly for a goalless draw.

Norwich had also beaten Leicester, Hull and Stockport, to reach the League Cup Quarter-finals for the second successive season, but they were drawn away at Arsenal.

Graham Paddon enjoyed the game of his life, on Wednesday 21st November, putting in one of the best individual performances of the whole season, as he outplayed Arsenal's midfield of Alan Ball and Peter Storey, hitting a terrific hat-trick in City's 3-0 away win, and in front of a Highbury crowd of 37,671.

After beating West Bromwich Albion 2-0 on the previous Saturday, with Dave Stringer and Graham Paddon both scoring, Norwich had risen to Sixth place in the table, after eighteen First Division matches. They were only five points behind leaders Liverpool, and on level points with fifth-placed Ipswich, as well as reaching the final four of a major Cup competition for only the third time in their history.

They were looking like a top quality team.

Norwich lost their next four league games, though, and they'd dropped to fourteenth place, by Saturday 16th December 1972. They had travelled to Chelsea on the previous Wednesday, however, for their League Cup Semi-final, first leg match. Jimmy Bone and David Cross both scored early goals for the ebullient Canaries, and they returned to the Broads with a great 2-0 away win.

Three weeks later, 34,265 packed Carrow Road, and Steve Govier headed his second ever goal as Norwich secured a simple 1-0 win, and the Canaries were heading for Wembley for the first time in their history. After the New Year, five successive defeats, though, all closely-fought defeats, to Derby, Leeds, Sheffield United, West Ham and Newcastle, had dropped Norwich to just one point above Manchester United in second-bottom position.

Despite their unbelievable first three months of flowing, bright football, and the promise of European qualification, the Canaries were deep in a relegation battle by the end of February.

On Saturday 3rd March, though, 100,000 filled Wembley Stadium for the League Cup Final, as Norwich City faced Bill Nicholson's entertaining Tottenham side.

The match, sadly, was a flat affair, and not at all entertaining.

Mike England kept David Cross quiet, while Duncan Forbes and Dave Stringer outmuscled England stars Chivers and Peters; and Spurs' midfield dynamos John Pratt and Steve Perryman had clamped the heavy shackles on Graham Paddon's left foot. Pat Jennings was not troubled at all, but Spurs didn't play very well either, and Kevin Keelan also had hardly anything to do all afternoon.

It took one moment of genuine greatness from a truly great player to settle the match, late on, as substitute Ralph Coates hammered in a loose ball, from outside the area. Tottenham hung on for their 1-0 win, and lifted their third major trophy in three seasons.

Back in the league, Norwich were attempting to halt their slide down to the bottom. Kenny Foggo had been packed off to Portsmouth in January, sold for just £25,000 after scoring fifty-four league goals in 182 games. Ron Saunders had also exchanged Jim Bone for Sheffield United's bearded midfield schemer Trevor Hockey.

Hockey had played a career total of 443 Football League matches, for Bradford, Nottingham Forest, Newcastle and Birmingham, as well as the Blades.

On Friday 16th February, though, Saunders smashed the club's record transfer fee, by paying West Brom £75,000 for attacking midfielder Colin Suggett. Suggett had played a total of 214 First Division matches for West Brom and Sunderland, scoring 44 goals.

Then, on Thursday 8th March, just five days after their Wembley defeat, Ron Saunders also paid £65,000 to Manchester City for their left winger Ian Mellor, a deal that Malcolm Allison was very unhappy about.

The Maine Road board of directors wanted some money back, though, having paid so much for Rodney Marsh a year earlier. Mellor had started thirty-six league games for City, and those three new players brought some vastly needed First Division experience for their final twelve games of the season.

Norwich continued to struggle throughout March, and into April, however, gaining only three points from seven matches, and by Saturday 7th April, they were rock bottom of the First Division, level on twenty-six points with West Brom, but only a point below Crystal Palace.

One week later, nearly twenty-five thousand attended Carrow Road for Norwich's first win in fifteen league and cup matches, since they'd beaten Chelsea at home in the League Cup Semi-finals. They beat Chelsea at home, again, thanks to David Cross's second half close-range blast.

Cross finished off a superb passing move, that ran through Hockey, Paddon and Suggett, while Mellor had cleverly pulled Mickey Droy out of position, creating space in the area for Cross to fire home.

Then, Norwich won away at bottom club West Brom, after top scorer David Cross had scored his sixteenth goal of the season, but they lost star player Graham Paddon for the remainder of the season, after he'd suffered a pulled muscle.

Two days later, on Easter Monday, away at Molineux, Alan Sunderland hit two, and John Richards, the First Division's top scorer from open play, added a third, his twenty-fifth of the season, as Wolves hammered Norwich 3-0.

Despite this, the Canaries still held a two point lead over both Palace and West Brom, but with an inferior goal average to both teams. On the following evening, after their defeat at Wolves, Norwich City hosted Crystal Palace for their penultimate match of the season. Max Briggs replaced the injured Paddon in midfield, and a huge crowd, 36,922, their largest crowd since the early Sixties, swelled the banks of Carrow Road, next to the banks of the Wensum.

NORWICH CITY		CRYSTAL PALACE
Kevin Keelan	1	John Jackson
Clive Payne	2	Paddy Mulligan
Alan Black	3	Tony Taylor
Dave Stringer	4	Bill Roffey
Duncan Forbes	5	Mel Blyth
Trevor Hockey	6	Iain Phillip
Doug Livermore	7	Derek Possee
Colin Suggett	8	David Payne
David Cross	9	John Craven
Max Briggs	10	Charlie Cooke
Ian Mellor	11	Don Rogers
Trevor Howard	12	Alan Whittle

With the most skilful player on the pitch, Charlie Cooke, unable to find any time due to Briggs' tight marking, Livermore, Hockey, Suggett and Mellor all controlled the game, with Norwich playing a clever 4-5-1 formation, and Palace were simply run out of it. The talented Possee and Rogers looked like First Division lightweights, and Colin Suggett headed in Mellor's cross just before half-time, and then Dave Stringer smashed in a header from Suggett's corner kick, for a crucial 2-1 win, and certain First Division survival.

Kevin Keelan was the Canaries' only ever-present player, and he'd kept eight league clean sheets during the season, but how he won the club's Player of the Season award, above Graham Paddon, I'll never understand.

Paddon had scored twelve goals, from midfield, in 48 league and cup matches, but he'd held the worst of the Norwich City midfield together, with his cultured left foot, for much of the season.

In 1973, while out injured, Graham Paddon grew a great beard and moustache to complement his rugged, golden long hair. Paddon closely resembled The Eagles' slide guitarist Don Felder, and he produced the same effortless class.

Norwich City's average crowd of 28,420 had also made them the twelfth best supported team in England, but despite their resurgent end to the 1972-73 season, which promised stability, the new season began very badly.

First, in June 1973, Ron Saunders sold Trevor Hockey, who'd glued their team together, to Aston Villa, and as a result, Norwich won just two of their first sixteen First Division matches, and they failed to score in half of them.

Saunders' last activity in the transfer market, on Tuesday 13th November, was to sell striker David Cross to Coventry City, for a club record transfer fee of £150,000.

The bearded twenty-two year old had struck twenty-one league goals in 84 games, and he'd been a key player in both the Canaries' promotion to and subsequent survival in the First Division.

David Cross retired in 1986, having scored 194 Football League goals.

Nine days later, Ron Saunders, with military swiftness and hard-edged opportunism, left Carrow Road to become the new manager of Manchester City.

He left Norwich without a goal scorer, and in third-bottom position, above both West Ham and Birmingham, but in the relegation zone, under the League's new three-up and three-down rules for the top two divisions.

Norwich drew 0-0 at Manchester United two days later, in front of an Old Trafford crowd of just 36,000. Then, on Tuesday 27th November, after days of haggling, they finally persuaded John Bond, the highly-rated manager of AFC Bournemouth, to become their new manager.

HEAD FOR THE TOP WITH THE CHERRIES

John Bond had been appointed as manager of Bournemouth and Boscombe Athletic, back in May 1970. Boscombe, as they were called, had just been relegated from Division Three, for the first time in their forty-seven years' Football League history.

Boscombe had set an almost unbeatable record of forty-seven continuous years in the Third Division. In the forty-three years since 1970, no other club has even come close to equalling that record. It is, admittedly, an unwanted record.

Ted MacDougall was born in Inverness, about as far from Boscombe as you could get, in the British Isles. He had joined from York City, back in July 1969, for a new club record transfer fee of £10,000. He had been the Cherries' top goal-scorer, in their relegation season, with twenty-three league and cup goals from forty-nine matches.

Boscombe had been relegated in fourth-bottom position, having finished level on points with Gillingham, but they only had a 0.68 goal average, compared to the Gills' 0.81 goal average. John Bond realised, immediately, that Ted MacDougall's goals were not going to be enough to get the Cherries back up to the Third Division.

Bond first converted failed forward Tony Powell into a defender. The former Bath City striker had scored just one single goal from thirty-three league games during 1969-70, but his rugged, rough-nosed hardness seemed, to Mr Bond, a perfect start in solving his team's defensive weaknesses, having leaked over seventy goals during their relegation season.

On Saturday 29th August 1970, David Jones made his league debut for Boscombe. The six foot one inch tall former apprentice, from Bristol, played alongside Tony Powell in the Cherries' 2-0 win away at Newport County.

Boscombe won seven Fourth Division games in a row, up to late September, with Ted Mac-Dougall firing nine goals from his first eight matches.

In October, Bond again broke the club's record transfer fee by paying Torquay United £12,000, for their Arbroath-born midfield commander, John Benson.

Benson had played over 240 league games for the Gulls, and he made his Cherries debut against Chester, as Boscombe failed to win for the second successive game. After Benson's arrival, the Cherries won only three out of their next six matches.

An obvious pattern was developing, though. In spite of their improving football, Boscombe mostly won when Ted MacDougall scored, but when he failed to score, then usually they lost, and they began to slip away from the top of the Fourth Division.

At the beginning of December, Bond played an absolute blinder in the transfer market, paying Gillingham just £9,000 for Mel Machin. Machin had been the player, along with David Peach, who'd ran the Gills' midfield in their crunch relegation clash against Boscombe, back in April. He had played over 150 league games for Gillingham, either in midfield or defence.

Boscombe played just two games in December, due to the weather, and they lost both of them. Then, just before the New Year, John Bond smashed Boscombe's record transfer fee, by paying York City £20,000 for striker Phil Boyer. That was the signing that completed Bond's re-building, and Boyer, who'd scored 27 goals in 108 games for York, went straight into the team for their match at Barrow.

A prolific partnership, that lasted for nearly a decade, immediately clicked, as MacDougall scored twice in their 2-1 win to lift the Cherries back up to fifth place.

The twin strike-force of MacDougall and Boyer scored a combined thirty-four goals, in just 24 league games, between January and May. Overall, Ted MacDougall had smashed in forty-nine league and cup goals, from just 51 games, and Boscombe ended up as runners-up in Division Four, behind Jimmy Sirrel's Notts County.

It was not Third Division status, though, that was the end ambition for John Bond's Boscombe. With the team he'd built, it was time, he felt, finally, that they could just jump, straight up again, to Division Two.

Head for the top with the Cherries, proclaimed their wonderfully Art Deco designed red and black match-day programmes for the 1971-72 season.

John Bond had also changed the design of Boscombe's first team shirts to red and black stripes, based on AC Milan's colours.

Bournemouth and Boscombe were striving for the Second Division, for the first time in their history, but they even had ideas of First Division football at Dean Court.

A large crowd of 11,295, three thousand more than their 1971 average, attended the Cherries' first game of the 1971-72 season, the second highest Third Division crowd of the day, and Keith Miller, Phil Boyer and Ted MacDougall all scored to secure an excellent 3-1 win over Shrewsbury.

Boscombe won six of their first eight games, and they were top of Division Three, by late September. By October, however, Aston Villa had overtaken them at the top, following successive away draws at Notts County and Plymouth Argyle.

A 2-1 win over fourth-placed Swansea secured Boscombe's return to the top, though, and they remained top until Saturday 23rd October, when second-placed Aston Villa visited Dean Court.

20,305, Boscombe's biggest crowd since the Fifties, filled the ground. The home crowd noise could be heard all over Poole Bay, and their team, the greatest team to ever represent Bournemouth and Boscombe, was inspired.

BOURNEMOUTH AND BOSCOMBE		ASTON VILLA
Fred Davies	1	Tommy Hughes
Mel Machin	2	Keith Bradley
Bill Kitchener	3	Fred Turnbull
John Benson	4	Bruce Rioch
David Jones	5	George Curtis
Tony Powell	6	Brian Tiler
Micky Cave	7	Ray Graydon
Ted MacDougall	8	Geoff Vowden
Phil Boyer	9	Andy Lochhead
Keith Miller	10	Ian Hamilton
Tony Scott	11	Willie Anderson

Phil Boyer, and Ted MacDougall's fierce diving header had fired the Cherries into a 2-0 half-time lead, and then Tony Powell powered a mighty header in from Cave's corner, for a terrific 3-0 win, to go clear at the top.

Ted MacDougall hit a hat-trick during their 5-0 away win at Mansfield Town, and then the only goal of the game as they beat Torquay United 1-0, with nearly fourteen thousand inside Dean

Court. By the middle of November, the Cherries were two points clear at the top of Division Three, ahead of both Notts County and Aston Villa.

They'd won eleven, and lost just two, of their opening seventeen games, and Ted MacDougall had scored seventeen of their thirty-five goals.

In the FA Cup First round, Boscombe welcomed Southern Premier League side Margate, from the north Kent seaside, on Saturday 20th November.

12,079, the second largest crowd of the round, were treated to a moment of football history, as the Cherries beat Margate 11-0, and Ted MacDougall set an all-time individual FA Cup goal-scoring record, by firing in nine of their eleven goals.

Micky Cave and Mel Machin netted their other two goals.

On Saturday 11th December, another healthy 14,634 crowd packed Dean Court for the visit of Southend United, in their FA Cup Second round match. That was the largest FA Cup crowd of the round, and only two Second Division games had attracted more supporters. Boscombe's crowd was larger than those at Sunderland, Burnley, Hull City and Preston North End.

The Cherries won 2-0, after goals from Boyer and MacDougall, securing a plum, money-spinning Third round match against either Arsenal, Leeds United or Liverpool? No, they were drawn away at Walsall.

On Christmas Day 1971, having beaten Halifax Town 3-1 a week earlier, Boscombe were joint leaders of Division Three, with Notts County, having won thirty points from twenty matches.

A massive crowd of 30,600 then filled the Goldstone Ground on Boxing Day, for the South Coast derby between Brighton and Boscombe. Willie Irvine, formerly of Burnley, and Kit Napier both scored for the Seagulls, as Brighton won 2-1, lifting themselves up into the top five, while Boscombe dropped out of the top two, for the first time that season.

A superb Phil Boyer hat-trick then fired them back into the top two, though, on New Year's Day, after their 4-0 thrashing of Wrexham. Boscombe had only just risen above third-placed Villa through their superior goal average of just 0.06. Then, following a goalless draw away at sixth-placed Rotherham, on Saturday 8th January, things remained very tight at the top, with only six points separating the top six clubs.

DIVISION THREE LEADERS, SATURDAY 8TH JANUARY 1972

	PL	W	D	L	F	A	PTS
Notts County	23	15	5	3	41	16	35
BOSCOMBE	23	13	7	3	44	20	33
Aston Villa	23	15	2	6	45	22	32
Swansea City	23	13	5	5	31	18	31
Brighton	23	12	6	5	34	23	30
Rotherham	23	11	7	5	37	26	29
Shrewsbury	23	11	4	8	39	27	26

In the FA Cup, Walsall shocked Boscombe, beating them 1-0 at Fellows Park, on Saturday 15th January, but then a week later, the Cherries hosted league leaders Notts County. Once again, another First Division crowd had packed Dean Court.

Another heaving, horrent home crowd of 21,154 roared their heroes on to victory. Les Bradd and Tony Hateley, the former Liverpool superstar, had combined to score half of County's goals, and Don Masson, a future World Cup Finals midfielder for Scotland, had also contributed five from midfield.

That didn't matter. Boyer and MacDougall, the attacking partnership that *did* matter, both struck first half goals, and the Cherries' back four of Machin, Jones, Powell and Kitchener bolted up the shop, after the break.

THE BATTLE OF BRITAIN

That 2-0 win over County was followed by a 1-1 draw away at Port Vale, and a 1-0 home win over Plymouth Argyle. By Saturday 5th February, though, Aston Villa had overtaken both Boscombe and Notts County, having played more games. Brighton had also just stayed in the race, but the chasing pack were now well detached.

DIVISION THREE LEADERS, SATURDAY 5TH FEBRUARY 1972

	PL	W	D	L	F	A	PTS
Aston Villa	27	19	2	6	52	22	40
BOSCOMBE	26	15	8	3	48	21	38
Notts County	25	16	5	4	42	18	37
Brighton	27	15	7	5	43	28	37
Rotherham	25	12	8	5	39	26	32

Forty-eight Thousand packed into Villa Park on the following Saturday, for the Battle of Britain; Aston Villa versus Bournemouth and Boscombe Athletic.

Villa's crowd was 16,000 greater than their average attendance, and it was also larger than all but one of that day's First Division matches.

Only the 52,000 at Highbury, for Arsenal's 2-0 home win over Derby County, was greater than the 48,110 at Villa Park. Villa v Boscombe drew bigger crowds than Everton v Leeds United, Wolves v West Ham, and even Manchester United v Newcastle.

The game was terrific, too. The inevitable MacDougall flung himself at Tony Scott's right sided cross and he scored with a darting diving header, giving the Cherries a 1-0 half-time lead, and delighting their ten thousand away fans.

However, Geoff Vowden struck an equaliser after the break, but David Jones, Boscombe's battle-hardened defensive general, then limped off the pitch, injured.

Andy Lochhead rose highest to head Villa to a hard-earned, if undeserved, 2-1 win. The 27,000 home fans on the vast slopes of the Holte End exploded, and some invaded the pitch, as if they had won the European Cup, unaware that they'd have to wait ten years for that.

For Boscombe, it was hard to lift themselves up after such a shattering defeat. With such a huge crowd, at such a wonderful stadium as Villa Park, it had felt akin to losing a Cup Final in May. Their bodies ached, but their spirits also took some lifting.

A week later, Mel Machin rescued a desperate point for the Cherries, at home to Mansfield, before a drab goalless draw at home to Walsall on the following Wednesday. The Cherries had been overtaken by Notts County, on goal average, but the Magpies had also played two less games.

Boscombe's promotion hopes were fading, having taken only two points from their last three matches. Their defeat at Villa wasn't really as devastating a result as it had felt, but the two subsequent home draws were very, very damaging.

On the final Saturday in February, Boscombe visited Torquay United, adrift at the bottom of the table, and being a sort of South-west derby, nearly 10,000 packed onto the rusting, crumbling Plainmoor ground, almost double Torquay's average crowd.

Ted MacDougall found his touch again, scoring in each half, to give the Cherries a desperately needed 2-0 away win. That win on the English Riviera was followed by a 3-0 win over Bradford, and also a 2-0 win over Bristol Rovers, both at home, and then on Saturday 11th March, defender Bill Kitchener headed a crucial late winner at the Vetch Field, during their superb 2-1 come-back win away at Swansea.

That great run of four successive wins, bringing in the Spring, had sprung the Cherries right back up into second place, three points clear of third-placed Brighton and Hove Albion.

THIRD DIVISION LEADERS, 11TH MARCH 1972

	PL	W	D	L	F	A	PTS
Aston Villa	32	23	3	6	62	24	49
BOSCOMBE	33	19	10	4	59	25	48
Brighton	32	19	7	6	59	33	45
Notts County	30	17	8	5	47	25	42

As the middle of March arrived, though, they had also lost their no-nonsense, imperious, aerial ball-winner, *Knocker* Tony Powell, during that 2-0 win at Torquay.

He was ruled out for five weeks. And they missed him.

Boscombe were held to a 1-1 draw at Walsall, on Tuesday 14th March, and then they lost 2-1 at home to Bolton Wanderers on the following Saturday.

Oldham then beat them 3-1 at Boundary Park, before, on the final Saturday in March, they were held 1-1 away at Rochdale.

It was a disastrous run of results that had almost ruined all their good work.

Fortunately for the Cherries, Brighton had had a rough patch themselves, taking only five points from their last five games. Aston Villa remained top, with Bournemouth and Boscombe three points behind, and Brighton were a point behind them, although they'd played one less game.

On Saturday 1st April, Tony Powell returned to action for their home South Coast derby match against Brighton. 22,540 packed Dean Court, the Cherries' largest crowd of the season, and their biggest crowd since the Busby Babes were their visitors in the FA Cup Quarter-finals, back in 1957.

The roars could be heard on the Isle of Wight, when Ted MacDougall toe-poked the Cherries 1-0 up, during the first half, his forty-second goal of the season. Bertie Lutton headed the Seagulls level after the break, though, and Brighton hung on for a classic 1-1 draw.

Aston Villa had beaten seventh-placed Swansea to extend their lead to five points, with a game in hand, but Boscombe were literally clinging onto second place by their fingertips.

A goalless draw away in the Peak District, at Chesterfield, on the following Wednesday, was followed by a Friday night win on Merseyside. Ted MacDougall both of Boscombe's goals in their 2-1 win at Tranmere Rovers.

Another large crowd of 14,076 watched them slip up again, on Saturday 15th April, as Barnsley battled for a goalless draw to remain just above the bottom four.

Boscombe had dropped to fourth place, but they were only two points behind Brighton, with just a handful of games left.

They bounced back for a 2-1 win over Bristol Rovers, away at Eastville, on the following Tuesday, and then they won 2-0 away at York City on Saturday 22nd April. Ted MacDougall and Phil Boyer both scored either side of half-time, to close the gap on Brighton to just a point, but the Cherries had a huge goal average advantage over the Seagulls.s

	PL	W	D	L	F	A	PTS	G.A.
Aston Villa	43	30	5	8	78	30	65	2.60
Brighton	43	25	10	8	77	44	60	1.75
BOSCOMBE	43	22	15	6	70	35	59	2.00

Sadly, Brighton never slipped up, and they took five points from their last three games, while Boscombe lost 2-1 away at Blackburn on the following Wednesday.

After an irrelevant 2-0 home win over Oldham, over eleven thousand die-hard fans turned up at Dean Court, for their last game of the season, on Wednesday 3rd May.

If the game had meant anything at all, it would have been another crowd of over 22,000. Their goalless draw at home to Tranmere left Bournemouth and Boscombe in third place at the end of the season, though, three points behind promoted Brighton.

If it had been a three-up and three-down system, as it should have been, a system that was introduced a year later by the Football League, Boscombe would have been promoted to Division Two, and pushed on, *Heading For The Top*, towards Division One.

It seems a ridiculous system, looking back now, when four Third Division teams were relegated, but only two were promoted; a system designed to protect fading Second Division giants like Fulham, Preston and Sheffield Wednesday.

Ted MacDougall had scored forty-seven league and cup goals, while his partner in attack, Phil Boyer, had added another sixteen. It had been a long, long season, in a very tough Third Division, from which ten teams have since played in either the First Division or Premier League, and of which two, Villa and Blackburn, have actually become English Champions.

Ted MacDougall was loving life at Bournemouth and Boscombe. He'd even started up his own Sports Store on Christchurch Road, in Boscombe, Ted MacDougall Sports Ltd, advertising his new look short shorts on the back page of the Cherries matchday journals.

He scored seven goals in thirteen games at the start of the 1972-73 season, before, on Wednesday 27th September, Manchester United paid a club record transfer fee of £200,000 for Ted Mac-Dougall.

MacDougall had scored a fantastic 126 league and cup goals, in only 164 games, in his three and a third seasons at Dean Court. His value had multiplied by twenty times, since John Bond had paid just £10,000 to York City, back in 1969.

AFC BOURNEMOUTH

At the start of the 1972-73 season, John Bond had the club's name changed to AFC Bournemouth, a name change that wasn't popular with many Cherries fans, as it had eliminated the actual name of the very town in which they played their home games from the club's new name. The Dean Court stadium remains on the east side of the A338, in Boscombe, and many home fans continue to refer to the club as Boscombe, but from then on, in the media, they became known as Bournemouth.

Anyway, AFC Bournemouth became the top team in the Football League, in alphabetical order, but it is only their trade name. The club remains officially registered as Bournemouth and Boscombe Athletic Football Club.

After attracting crowds of more than 20,000 on three occasions in 1971-72, Bournemouth's largest home crowd of the season, in 1972-73, was the 18,344 that attended Dean Court for their top of the table clash against Bolton Wanderers, on Saturday 17th February 1973.

Harry Redknapp had had a lacklustre start to his South coast career, since signing from West Ham United, back in August. His corner-kicks were often weak, his crosses uncertain, and far too often he was caught in possession.

One thing you couldn't deny him, though, was that he had class.

After December, and particularly after Bournemouth had paid Cardiff City £70,000 for striker Brian Clark, Harry Redknapp became a key player in their team, being a vibrant force that had bounded Bournemouth back to the top of the table.

After a goalless first half, against a workmanlike Bolton team, Redknapp crossed for Phil Boyer to volley the Cherries into the lead, early in the second half. Micky Cave then secured their 2-0 win, with a header from Redknapp's left-sided corner kick.

Bournemouth returned to the top of Division Three, with just three points separating the top five teams.

THIRD DIVISION LEADERS, SATURDAY 17TH FEBRUARY 1973

	PL	W	D	L	F	A	PTS
BOURNEMOUTH	32	14	11	7	55	32	39
Bolton Wanderers	30	15	7	8	44	28	37
Oldham Athletic	31	14	9	8	57	41	37
Bristol Rovers	33	13	10	10	53	40	36
Notts County	32	15	6	11	41	39	36

Once again, though, the long run-in across the Melling Road, over the last two fences, and then the tiring chase towards the elbow, before the finish, had the beating of Bournemouth, just as Crisp's huge lead was overhauled by Red Rum at Aintree.

The Cherries took only eleven points from their last fourteen matches, winning only three, but they lost six of them. Bournemouth ended up in seventh place, and seven points below the two promoted clubs, Bolton Wanderers and Notts County.

The glory days were over.

On Saturday 15th August 1973, only 11,379 watched Bournemouth lose their first match of the season, 0-3 at home to Bristol Rovers. Despite winning six of their next nine matches, lifting them up to third place, many fans had become a little nauseated by their seaside rollercoaster adventure, every single season.

On Wednesday 14th November, with Bournemouth fourth-placed in Division Three, only 8,395 watched their 1-0 home win over Charlton Athletic, as centre half David Jones headed in the only goal of the game.

It was Bournemouth's last game at Dean Court with John Bond in charge.

THE SOUTH COAST INVASION

On Tuesday 27th November 1973, after days of haggling, Norwich City finally persuaded John Bond to become their new manager. Having agreed all of his personal terms, Bond immediately appointed Ken Brown, Bournemouth's chief coach, as his chief coach at Carrow Road, and then during the early part of December, Mel Machin, John Benson and Fred Taylor all followed their old boss up to Norfolk.

Machin and Benson had played a combined total of nearly 200 league games for Bournemouth, and both players went straight into the Canaries' team for their 1-1 draw with Liverpool, while Taylor was appointed as City's goalkeeping coach.

They were, however, certainly not the last ex-Bournemouth and Boscombe players to be signed by Norwich City boss John Bond.

Ted MacDougall had not enjoyed footballing life at all in the fourteen months since he'd left Bournemouth. He'd bitterly disliked living in the north, while at Manchester United, scoring only five goals in fifteen First Division games.

So, on Saturday 24th February 1973, Tommy Docherty sold him to West Ham United, for £170,000. Docherty had only been appointed as United manager two months earlier, following the sacking of Frank O'Farrell.

The luxurious style of play that MacDougall offered, a purely predatory type of striker that he was, did not fit in with Docherty's plans.

"Ted made it known that he wasn't happy at the club," Tommy Docherty remembered. "He wanted a move back down south. This made me happy as he didn't really feature in my plans."

MacDougall's arrival at Upton Park initially reinvigorated West Ham's season. With the Hammers seven points behind a UEFA Cup qualifying place, and down in ninth place, he then scored four goals in just six games, and West Ham won five of them to go level on points with fourth-placed Ipswich Town on Good Friday.

Town were ahead of West Ham on goal average, with a superiority of just 0.01 goals.

West Ham then failed to win any of their final three games, though, and MacDougall's East End struggles really started. His aloof and reputedly arrogant manner didn't mix at all well in West Ham's close-knit changing room.

In particular, Billy Bonds, their future team leader, became increasingly irritated.

"There was an immediate oil and water personality clash," Bonds admitted.

After winning only one of their first thirteen matches of the 1973-74 season, during which MacDougall failed to score a single goal, West Ham were second from bottom, when they visited Leeds United on Saturday 3rd November. The league leaders hammered West Ham 4-1, and MacDougall scored his first league goal of the season, but then he moaned about the service, and the lack of quality of service from his midfield, with Bonds, one of the Hammers' key midfield stars, well within earshot.

Billy Bonds responded that he was equally unhappy with the lack of quality of MacDougall's work-rate. Their heated exchange continued into the changing room, and then spiralled into a fight, with Ron Greenwood having to leap between the two players, with Bonds clambering out of the team bath, attempting to strangle MacDougall, and splashing filthy, dirty, soapy water all over his manager's grey suit.

So, on Wednesday 5th December, John Bond came to the rescue of his former Cherries striker, when he signed Ted MacDougall in an exchange deal that sent Graham Paddon down to Upton Park. Basically, on the same day, Norwich sold Paddon for £160,000, but then they also paid £145,000 for MacDougall, making a net profit of £15,000. Most Canaries fans believed that the loss of Graham Paddon was solely the cause of their relegation in 1974.

Paddon, who'd played 162 league games for Norwich, had arrived at Upton Park with West Ham United two points below Norwich, and in second-bottom position, but by the end of the season, they were just ten points below a UEFA Cup qualifying place. At Carrow Road, however, despite Ted MacDougall scoring eleven goals from twenty-five games, Norwich won only five out of twenty-six league games with John Bond as their manager.

Without Paddon pulling the strings in midfield, they were relegated in bottom position, and eight points below safety.

John Bond had actually strengthened his attack, back on Tuesday 5th February, paying his old team Bournemouth £150,000 for their centre forward, Phil Boyer, who'd scored forty-six goals during his four seasons at Dean Court.

Wolves had beaten Norwich, 2-1 on aggregate, with the Canaries' hands tied behind their backs, in the League Cup Semi-finals. It was Norwich City's second successive appearance in the last four of the League Cup, but without either Graham Paddon, or their trio of cup-tied ex-Bournemouth players, they didn't stand a chance.

Despite Norwich City's relegation, Bond believed his team could bounce straight back up to Division One, and on the eve of the new season, he signed his sixth player from his old club. He agreed an exchange deal that sent midfielder Trevor Howard down to Dean Court, and brought in his old centre-back *Knocker* Tony Powell.

Powell had played 219 league games for the Cherries, and the former amateur boxer became a key member of Norwich City's 1974-75 promotion-chasing team, either as a central defender, or as a defensive midfield player.

Bond also travelled down the A140, to Ipswich, and he signed their thirty-one year old midfield grafter Peter Morris. Morris had been an Ipswich Town regular during 1973-74, playing thirty-six First Division matches, as they'd finished in fourth place, and qualified for the UEFA Cup.

Bobby Robson had been keen to start his young midfielder Brian Talbot alongside Colin Viljoen, though, so he was very happy to allow Morris to move up to Norfolk.

Peter Morris had played 220 First Division matches at Portman Road, having started his career at his hometown team Mansfield Town. By the time he came to Norwich, Morris had already totalled over five hundred Football League matches.

John Bond also signed Colin Sullivan, who'd played 230 league games for Plymouth Argyle, since making his Pilgrims' debut away at Rotherham, back in March 1968.

A Saltash-born, twenty-four year old left back, Sullivan had missed only one out of fifty-six league and cup games during 1973-74, and he'd been very impressive in Plymouth's great run to the League Cup Semi-finals. They'd conceded only two goals in their five matches, en route to the last four, before Manchester City's superstars, Bell, Lee, Law, Summerbee and Marsh, etc, managed to just beat them, 3-1 on aggregate.

Powell, Morris and Sullivan all started City's first match of the new season, their 2-1 home win over Blackpool on Saturday 17th August 1974.

Tony Powell scored their first goal of the season, before Ted MacDougall made sure of the two points, but only 18,000 had watched their win, Norwich City's lowest crowd for an opening game for four years. Norwich lost just one of their first nine matches, though, and they were up in second place on Saturday 28th September, when leaders Manchester United visited Carrow Road.

Phil Boyer was tripped up in the United area by Arnie Sidebottom, after 23 minutes, as he'd rushed onto Colin Sullivan's through ball.

Ted MacDougall calmly stroked the ball low past Alex Stepney, from the penalty spot, and the 25,000 Canaries' fans went wild. Just three minutes later, though, Lou Macari nearly equalised, diving full length to head a Gerry Daly cross beyond Keelan.

Kevin Keelan, though, had managed to throw his arm back another few inches, and he brilliantly turned the ball round his post. Brian Greenhoff then headed just wide, from Jim McCalliog's cross, before Tony Powell's fantastic thirty yard drive flew past Stepney, but went just a couple of inches over United's crossbar.

Just before the hour mark, Ted MacDougall was fouled by Alex Forsyth, and Mel Machin's free-kick was chipped across the United area, for MacDougall to turn and volley an unstoppable rocket beyond Stepney, high into the far top corner of the Manchester United goal.

Phil Boyer then hit the post, after Stepney could only parry a Geoff Butler drive, and Martin Buchan just managed to clear the ball away, as MacDougall was about to bury the rebound for his hat-trick.

That famous 2-0 win was the first of five successive victories, through to the end of October, as Norwich beat United, Millwall, Nottingham Forest, Portsmouth, and then finally Orient, on Saturday 26th October, away at Brisbane Road.

That was John Miller's debut for the Canaries, after his £45,000 move from rivals Ipswich Town. He'd gone straight into their team, in place of Mel Machin who was suffering from pneumonia.

Phil Boyer and Ted MacDougall (from the penalty spot) had put Norwich 2-0 up, within the first half-hour, before, just a few minutes prior to half-time, John Miller made a match-winning impact.

Miller met a cross from right-back Geoff Butler, just outside the Orient area, and he volleyed the ball, perfectly and fiercely from twenty-five yards out. Keeper John Jackson did very well to get one hand to the shot, but he could only deflect it away, and straight to Phil Boyer, who slid in from close range.

After that 3-0 win, Norwich City's form collapsed after November, up to Christmas, though, and they won only once in seven matches.

By Christmas Day, Norwich were only just hanging onto the third promotion place, having fallen two points below Bob Stokoe's Sunderland.

The Canaries had reached their third successive League Cup Semi-final, though, in direct contrast to their disappointing run of league results. They'd disposed of Bolton Wanderers and West Brom, back in September and October, respectively, before finally beating First Division high flyers Sheffield United in November.

On Wednesday 4th December, they hosted East Anglian rivals Ipswich Town, in the Quarter-finals, with nearly 35,000 filling a heavily-policed Carrow Road.

Colin Suggett played a one-two with Phil Boyer, then he sprayed the ball out wide to John Miller, whose first-time low cross was met and finished well by the rampaging Suggett. A controversial moment occurred soon after, though.

Trevor Whymark headed Clive Woods' cross onto the inside of Keelan's far post.

The ball had appeared to bounce onto the goal-line, before Dave Stringer managed to get back and launch the ball away, to safety.

But, no!

Referee Jack Taylor, who'd reffed the World Cup Final just five months earlier, whistled and then pointed to the centre circle to signal that he'd given the goal.

The packed home crowd were infuriated, but Norwich could not score a second goal, and Ipswich Town, second-placed in the First Division, held on for their 1-1 away draw to take the Canaries back to Portman Road.

Over 29,000 attended the replay on the following Tuesday, and John Miller, who'd been sold by Ipswich Town, six weeks earlier, enjoyed the finest night of his career.

The brown-skinned Miller had been treated dismally at Portman Road, having started just 37 First Division matches over the previous four and a third seasons.

The home crowd booed him, chanted *"REJECT!!!"* taunts at him, and a small minority of the Ipswich home fans shouted *even worse things* at him, but the thick-skinned Miller just rolled his sleeves up, ignored it all, and got on with winning the game.

After 33 minutes, he glided in Ted MacDougall's left wing cross at Sivell's near post, before running and then just sitting down on the touchline, right under the Ipswich fans.

Miller sat there, smiling, as MacDougall, Machin, Morris and Powell all ran across to lift him up.

Two minutes into the second half, Phil Boyer's sublime through-ball beat the entire Ipswich back four of Burley, Hunter, Beattie and Mills.

John Miller raced onto the pass and he beat Laurie Sivell, before hammering his angled shot into the empty net. He raced away, jubilant, with his arms aloft in triumph.

Norwich City's 2-1 away win earned them a Semi-final against Second Division leaders Manchester United, the highest ranked team remaining in the tournament.

Over 58,000 were squashed into Old Trafford, the third biggest crowd in all of English football during the 1974-75 season, on Wednesday 15th January 1975, for the League Cup Semi-final, first leg match between Manchester United and Norwich City.

Tony Powell actually gave Norwich City a half-time lead with a thudding header, but Lou Macari scored a second half brace to give United a barely-deserved 2-1 lead.

With the final whistle just moments away, though, MacDougall made the most of a Manchester United defensive mess-up, and he drove his shot home to give the Canaries a brilliant away draw.

One week later, 31,672 packed Carrow Road, and the place just went crazy after Colin Suggett's towering header, twenty-nine minutes into the second half, proved enough to give Norwich a 3-2 aggregate win, and sent them to their second Wembley Cup Final in just three seasons.

Aston Villa had beaten Fourth Division Chester City in the other Semi-final.

Norwich City's league form picked up after darkest January, too, after their three successive defeats against Cardiff, York and Oxford following the New Year.

They took seven points from four matches during February, beating Bristol Rovers, West Bromwich Albion and Oldham. Their problem was that their League Cup Final opponents, Aston Villa, had also been rampant since Christmas, gaining eleven points from six matches. Villa were just one point below third-placed Norwich, and with a game in hand, as the two teams met at Wembley, on Saturday 1st March.

ASTON VILLA		NORWICH CITY
Jim Cumbes	1	Kevin Keelan
John Robson	2	Mel Machin
Charlie Aitken	3	Colin Sullivan
Ian Ross	4	Peter Morris
Chris Nicholl	5	Duncan Forbes
Bobby McDonald	6	Dave Stringer
Ray Graydon	7	John Miller
Brian Little	8	Ted MacDougall
Keith Leonard	9	Phil Boyer
Ian Hamilton	10	Colin Suggett
Frank Carrodus	11	Tony Powell

Norwich did themselves no justice in the Final. They were even worse than they'd been two years before. The Canaries' problem was that Miller was heavily shackled by the vastly experienced Aitken, leaving Suggett as their only creative outlet in midfield. The rest of their midfield was defensively structured. With the young, quick wingers Little and Carrodus rampaging forward, Machin was pre-occupied with defending duties, and he couldn't support the midfield as well as he normally did.

A drab, damp, dismal afternoon was heading for another dreary thirty minutes, when Chris Nicholl glanced a header towards the far left corner of Keelan's goal. Keelan was beaten, but Mel Machin dived and saved the shot, on the goal-line, with his hand.

Kevin Keelan saved Ray Graydon's penalty kick, but Graydon reacted quickest and he scored from the rebound, to win the Cup for Villa.

On Saturday 8th March, with nearly 30,000 packed into Carrow Road, Norwich were held to a goalless draw by second-placed Sunderland. Duncan Forbes fought a great battle with Sunderland's hairy, grizzled striker Vic Halom, and he was left with blood streaming down his face, after suffering a shocking eye injury.

Aston Villa had beaten Nottingham Forest, to move above the Canaries, leaving their promotion hopes in disarray. John Bond needed help.

He had an Ace up his sleeve, though.

Bond had been good friends with Tottenham's Martin Peters, since the early Sixties, when they were West Ham teammates. Peters had become disillusioned at White Hart Lane, since Bill Nicholson's resignation. The Spurs changing room had become filled with a "baleful atmosphere." So, when Bond made him an offer, Peters immediately accepted and he answered "the call of the country."

John Bond paid a bargain price of just £50,000 for the thirty-one year old World Cup winner.

Norwich had not even played First Division football until two and a half years previously. Now, they were signing World Cup winners. They'd come a long way.

Martin Peters' first match for Norwich was away at leaders Manchester United, with 56,202 filling Old Trafford. Ted MacDougall, captain for the day, for his return to Old Trafford, rifled home a second half goal, from close range, equalising Pearson's goal.

Kevin Keelan was the star of the show, though, denying Alex Forsyth twice, Coppell, McIlroy, Houston twice, Pearson and also Macari, with a string of superb saves throughout the match, and he earned the Canaries a great point.

That 1-1 draw, as well as Peters' arrival, had reinvigorated Norwich City, and also re-instilled their confidence, re-launching their promotion push, and at exactly the right time of the season. They then beat Hull City and Bristol City, both 1-0 wins, before losing 2-1 to FA Cup Semi-finalists Fulham.

Victories over Orient, and then bottom club Sheffield Wednesday, though, lifted them right back up into the top three, but their struggling 1-1 draw away at Millwall, after Geoff Butler's last-gasp equaliser, had dropped them back down to fourth.

On Saturday 19th April, 24,552 packed Carrow Road for the visit of Brian Clough's Nottingham Forest, and Norwich needed nothing less than two points to keep the pressure up on Sunderland. Dave Stringer was suspended for the first time in his twelve year career, so Tony Powell was moved back from midfield to partner captain Duncan Forbes.

The pair had few problems against John O'Hare and Barry Butlin.

Martin Peters gave John Middleton no chance with a beautifully-placed header, from Suggett's deep cross, for his first Norwich goal, one minute before half-time.

Peters then headed down Colin Suggett's free-kick, in the second half, for Phil Boyer to drive in a deflected shot. Boyer then thrashed in Suggett's right wing cross, with only six minutes remaining, to complete their 3-0 win.

With only two games remaining, Norwich were still in fourth place, but in a healthy position. Sunderland were level on points with the Canaries, and with a superior goal average, but they had only one game remaining, away at second-placed Aston Villa, while Norwich had two games left.

The Canaries hammered Portsmouth 3-0 (McGuire, Peters, Boyer), at Fratton Park, while Aston Villa had beaten Sunderland 2-0, on Saturday 26th April.

Norwich were promoted back to the First Division, at the first attempt, and from a tougher Second Division than when they went up in 1972. They then enjoyed a celebratory last match of the season, at home to Aston Villa, on the following Wednesday night.

35,999, Norwich City's second-biggest crowd of the decade, filled every inch of their ground, and their home fans enjoyed a memorable night. During the first half, Phil Boyer scored his nineteenth league and cup goal of the season, to completely explode Carrow Road.

It mattered little, on that night, that Villa had won 4-1.

Norwich were back in the First Division, and despite them not having Graham Paddon, they had a much stronger team this time around.

Ted MacDougall and Phil Boyer enjoyed a great partnership, scoring forty-one goals between them, while Kevin Keelan had kept twenty-three clean sheets.

Colin Suggett, Norwich City's Player of the Season, had missed only one game out of fifty-four, and he'd started the three hundredth Football League game of his career, on that final day of the season, at the age of just twenty-six.

Norwich started 1975-76 reasonably well. By late September, they'd won three matches, drawn three, and lost three, and they were bang in the middle of the table, where they remained for most of the season.

Then, on Thursday 25th September, John Bond paid just £40,000 to Brian Clough's Nottingham Forest for his former Bournemouth defender, David Jones.

Norwich City suffered a horrible November, though, losing four games in a row, and they were only two points above the relegation zone, on Saturday 29th November, the lowest point of their season, as they travelled up to Liverpool.

Tony Powell had suffered a knee injury during their 2-1 defeat at home to Newcastle, a week earlier, that kept him out of action for over three months, so Dave Stringer, their thirty-two year old veteran, returned for his first start of the season.

Nevertheless, there were still four survivors from Bournemouth's 1970-71 Fourth Division team playing at Anfield, in a First Division match.

LIVERPOOL		NORWICH CITY
Ray Clemence	1	Kevin Keelan
Tommy Smith	2	David Jones
Phil Neal	3	Colin Sullivan
Phil Thompson	4	Peter Morris
Ray Kennedy	5	Duncan Forbes
Emlyn Hughes	6	Dave Stringer
Kevin Keegan	7	Mel Machin
Brian Hall	8	Ted MacDougall
Steve Heighway	9	Phil Boyer
John Toshack	10	Colin Suggett
Ian Callaghan	11	Martin Peters

John Bond played a tactical masterstroke against the title challengers. He dropped Phil Boyer to midfield, to attack from deep, starting the match with Martin Peters and Ted MacDougall up front.

At half-time, though, he told them both to play out wide in the second half. Phil Thompson and Emlyn Hughes were surprised to see they had nobody to mark, and amidst the confusion, Suggett, Peters and MacDougall all scored. Emlyn Hughes replied, but Norwich City's 3-1 away win was one of the very best in their history, in front of an Anfield crowd of nearly 35,000.

Liverpool's team had included eight players who won the European Cup Final, against Borussia Moenchengladbach, eighteen months later.

On Saturday 31st January 1976, Norwich City showed that they really had arrived, and finally deserved their place in First Division football. They out-played Leeds United at Elland Road.

Leeds United had been European Cup Finalists just eight months earlier, and they were still second in Division One, just one point behind leaders Manchester United, and with a game in hand.

At this stage, they were no fading giants.

With Leeds' captain Billy Bremner missing because of a foot injury, though, the Canaries made the most of his absence. Mel Machin played as sweeper behind Forbes and Stringer, and he met every through-ball with class, that was intended for either Clarke and McKenzie. Allan Clarke did more defending than attacking, and he did very well to flick a dangerous ball back to his keeper, from Suggett's corner kick, after Boyer's cross had been turned behind by Madeley.

After ten minutes, Martin Peters stole the ball off his former England teammate Paul Madeley, on the left side of the Leeds penalty area. His cross deflected off Boyer, into the path of Ted MacDougall, who slid the ball in at the far post.

MacDougall punched the air, with delight, at the Elland Road end.

Duncan McKenzie then wriggled past McGuire, Stringer and Jones, but at the end of his great twenty yard run, Keelan came out to snatch the ball from under his feet, just as McKenzie was about to shoot, from twelve yards out.

Besides that, Norwich were mostly comfortable, and it was Leeds United who were holding on, with Boyer always running the home defence ragged.

LEEDS UNITED		NORWICH CITY
David Harvey	1	Kevin Keelan
Paul Reaney	2	David Jones
Frankie Gray	3	Colin Sullivan
Trevor Cherry	4	Mick McGuire
Paul Madeley	5	Duncan Forbes
Norman Hunter	6	Dave Stringer
Peter Lorimer	7	Mel Machin
Allan Clarke	8	Ted MacDougall
Duncan McKenzie	9	Phil Boyer
Terry Yorath	10	Colin Suggett
Eddie Gray	11	Martin Peters
Joe Jordan	12	Tony Powell

They held on until the 65th minute, when Mick McGuire caught Hunter in possession, on the edge of the Leeds penalty area, and he fired in a shot that deflected off Madeley, deceiving David Harvey on its way into the net.

Three minutes from the end, MacDougall rose to head in Phil Boyer's cross, and Norwich City had no more relegation worries following that superb 3-0 away win.

Norwich beat their local rivals Ipswich 1-0 on the Wednesday night of 31st March, and with over 31,000 inside Carrow Road, after Martin Peters' early goal, to lift themselves back up to mid-table.

Their biggest home crowd of that season though, 31,211, had watched their fourth great win of the season, against the Champions-elect, Queens Park Rangers.

QPR only had to avoid defeat at lowly Norwich, to be virtually assured of the First Division title, ahead of Liverpool. Norwich City won 3-2, though, on a warm, sunny afternoon, after goals from MacDougall, Peter Morris and Phil Boyer, and QPR subsequently lost the League Championship title by just one point.

Ted MacDougall was the top goal-scorer in the First Division, with twenty-three league goals, the first and only time that a Norwich City player has been the top striker in English football. Phil Boyer and Martin Peters also shared twenty-one goals between them, as the Canaries finished in tenth position, and Peters also won City's Player of the Season award.

Martin Peters, Ted MacDougall and Kevin Keelan were all ever-presents for Norwich during 1975-76, and Dave Stringer played his 498th league and cup game for the club, on the final day of that season, as they won 2-0 away at Stoke City.

Dave Stringer played at left-back for Norwich, away at Liverpool, on the opening day of 1976-77, but following their 1-0 defeat, he played no more.

After 499 games for the Canaries, he signed for Cambridge United in September. He returned to Carrow Road in 1980, as Norwich's Youth Team manager, under Ken Brown, and then he guided the Canaries to an FA Youth Cup Final win over Everton, in 1983, with both Louie Donowa and Jeremy Goss in his team.

After the controversial sacking of Ken Brown, in November 1987, that had reduced the Norwich manager to tears at a press conference, when he actually found out about his departure, Dave Stringer was appointed as their new manager.

Stringer was seen by many as the safe option, appointed only to attempt to quell the fans' anger, absolutely furious at their club chairman Robert Chase, but he did lead the Canaries to a tremendous, unbelievable league and cup double-chasing season, in 1988-89.

Norwich City were actually top of the First Division, on Boxing Day 1988, and they were still in second place during late March, only two points behind leaders Arsenal, and having also reached the FA Cup Semi-finals.

Ultimately, though, Norwich *only* finished fourth, and they also lost to Everton in their Villa Park Semi-final, on the day of the Hillsborough tragedy.

Dave Stringer led Norwich to another FA Cup Semi-final, three years later, when they were shocked by Second Division Sunderland. He'd also brought Chris Sutton, Ruel Fox, Jeremy Goss, Mark Bowen, Bryan Gunn, Ian Butterworth, Rob Newman and Robert Ullathorne into Norwich City's team. They became the nucleus of the great Canaries team that qualified for the UEFA Cup, for the very first time, in 1993.

Stringer had resigned back in May 1992, though, leaving new manager Mike Walker to take all the glory.

Ted MacDougall left Norwich City on 14th September 1976, joining Southampton for a fee of £50,000, just so he could be nearer to his Sportswear business in Boscombe.

He'd scored fifty-one league goals, from 112 games, at Carrow Road. He went on to score 42 league goals in two seasons for Southampton, and eventually helped the Saints back up to Division One.

John Bond responded by bringing in Viv Busby from Fulham, John Ryan from Luton, and also Jimmy Neighbour from Spurs, as Norwich went through a gentle period of transition, spending the first six weeks of the season inside the bottom three.

They slowly pulled themselves out of the relegation zone, though, and hovered dangerously above a tight and very competitive battle to stay up.

After Martin Peters' goal had given them a 1-0 win over West Ham, on Wednesday 10th November, Norwich had the clear fresh air of four points between them and the bottom three, Bristol City, Sunderland and West Ham.

On the very next day, Bond paid £110,000 to West Ham for their midfield star Graham Paddon. The Messiah had returned.

Graham Paddon had won an FA Cup winners' medal, and also played in a European Cup Winners' Cup Final, during his three great years at Upton Park.

Norwich travelled to Sunderland, on Saturday 18th December, with their new look team, but just one point above Tottenham in third-bottom position.

Sunderland looked a shadow of the team that had won a glorious, closely-fought Second Division Championship trophy, back in May, above Bristol City, West Brom and Bolton Wanderers.

Norwich City took full advantage. It was an absolute pleasure to see a midfield of Paddon, Peters, Suggett and Neighbour, but it was actually John Ryan's long ball that had missed them all out, and set the moustached Viv Busby up to bury the ball past Barry Siddall, from inside the area.

SUNDERLAND		NORWICH CITY
Barry Siddall	1	Kevin Keelan
Dick Malone	2	John Ryan
Joe Bolton	3	Colin Sullivan
Tony Towers	4	Colin Suggett
Jeff Clarke	5	David Jones
Jim Holton	6	Tony Powell
Bobby Kerr	7	Jimmy Neighbour
Billy Hughes	8	Viv Busby
Bob Lee	9	Phil Boyer
Alan Brown	10	Graham Paddon
Alan Foggon	11	Martin Peters

Norwich City ended up in sixteenth place, just three points above the bottom three, surviving the toughest-ever relegation fight, with just five points separating the bottom ten clubs.

Graham Paddon remained at Carrow Road until the end of 1980-81, after playing a career total of 340 games for Norwich, scoring thirty-seven mostly spectacular, left-footed goals. Paddon had become more of an anchor role, though, becoming a holding midfield player, during his second spell with the Canaries, rather than the attacking dynamo he was during the early Seventies.

He was always a popular player among his teammates, both at West Ham as well as Norwich, a gentleman as well as a class player, with the most fantastic left foot.

Graham Paddon died unexpectedly at his home, in his beloved County of Norfolk, on Monday 19th November 2007, at the age of just fifty-seven. Black armbands were worn by both teams during Norwich City's match against Coventry City, Paddon's first club, on the following Saturday. One minute's applause paid a moving tribute to one of Norwich City's greatest ever players.

Martin Peters won two Player of the Season awards, at Norwich City, and he played over two hundred league matches for the Canaries, until 1980. Over his five and a quarter seasons at Carrow Road, Peters missed only thirteen league games.

Alongside Duncan Forbes, Kevin Keelan and Dave Stringer, Peters was an inaugural member of the Norwich City Hall of Fame in 2002. Of the Canaries' team that won promotion back to Division One, in April 1975, only Colin Sullivan, Peter Morris and John Miller are not in their Hall of Fame.

Machin, MacDougall, Boyer, Suggett and Powell were all added later.

Duncan Forbes played 357 league and cup matches for Norwich, between 1968 and 1981. Despite his loud and aggressive manner, Forbes knew his limits, and he was never sent off, although he was booked many times. He even became a subject of jokes from referees, as to whether they should just book him in the changing room, to save time on the pitch later.

Forbes finally retired from football in 2001, having been Norwich City's Chief Scout for thirteen years.

Kevin Keelan retired from professional football after Norwich City's 3-5 home defeat to Liverpool, on Saturday 9th February 1980. It was the game when Justin Fashanu had fired in BBC TV's Goal of the Season, and also Keelan's 673rd competitive match for the Canaries, an all-time club record.

In 238 First Division matches, Keelan conceded an average of 1.49 goals per game, but during his 333 Second Division games, he'd only conceded 1.20 goals per game.

In 2008, he was voted into the all-time Norwich City eleven, in spite of thousands of votes cast for both Bryan Gunn and Robert Green, by fans too young to remember Kevin Keelan. He returned to Carrow Road in May 2008, from his Florida home, to accept his award.

Kevin Keelan was also awarded an MBE, back in 1980.

John Bond left Norwich City on 1st October 1980, to become Manchester City's new manager. He also took his long time coaching assistants John Benson and John Sainty with him to Maine Road, but his head coach Ken Brown remained at Carrow Road, to become the new Norwich manager.

Ken Brown developed a new-look Norwich City team for the Eighties.

They were relegated in 1981, after six years of First Division football, but they succeeded in bouncing straight back a year later, just as they did in 1975.

Ken Brown introduced Chris Woods, Steve Bruce, Dave Watson, Ian Culverhouse, Mike Phelan, Martin O'Neill, John Deehan, and also veterans Asa Hartford and Mike Channon, as he led the Canaries to their first ever Wembley Cup Final triumph in 1985, beating Sunderland 1-0 in the League Cup Final.

John Bond had led Manchester City to the 1981 FA Cup Final, one of the very best of all time, but they lost to Tottenham Hotspur, after a replay.

He'd also signed Tommy Hutchison, Gerry Gow, Steve McKenzie and Phil Boyer, paying £225,000 for the latter player.

Phil Boyer had been the First Division's top goal-scorer the previous season, with twenty-three goals for Southampton. Boyer's time at Maine Road was blighted by injuries, though, while also suffering the heartbreak of missing that 1981 Cup Final, and he was forced to retire from league football, having scored 159 goals in 523 league games, two hundred and sixty-seven of them for his boss John Bond.

Bond was sacked by Manchester City in February 1983, after they'd dropped from second down to tenth place, in just three months. He was replaced by his assistant John Benson, who couldn't arrest their slide down the table. With four games remaining, City were seven points ahead of Swansea in the relegation zone, but on the last day of the season, Saturday 14th May, they lost at home to Luton Town and were relegated down to Division Two for the first time in twenty years.

Benson re-joined John Bond at Burnley, after Man City had sacked him, but both were sacked, yet again, after a very unpopular period in charge at Turf Moor. In 1991-92, John Bond was manager of Shrewsbury Town, but he was advised by police not to attend their match at Burnley, so angry the Clarets' fans had remained towards him.

John Benson died on 30th October 2010, aged sixty-seven, after a short illness.

The seven years, between 1973 and 1980, when John Bond was the boss of Norwich, had transformed the tenet of the East Anglian club.

"It was like coming out of War-time when he took over from Ron Saunders," Robin Sainty, chairman of the Independent Norwich City Supporters Club, remembered.

"Saunders had made City very effective, but you couldn't accuse them of being exciting or creative. Then John Bond came in and it was a whole different thing."

Dave Stringer explained, "John Bond brought a lot more openness to the club and believed in more flair. It was difficult at first because he wanted players to express themselves more, but he brought in people like MacDougall, Boyer and Peters who could do that."

John Bond died on Wednesday 26th September 2012, aged seventy-nine.

Dozens of tributes from fans and his former players were written in the Eastern Daily Press, describing him as the greatest and best manager in Norwich City's history.

"He was more than just a manager," David Cuffley wrote. "He was a larger than life man who made the football world more colourful."

One minute's silence was observed in memory of him, before the Canaries' League Cup Third round match against Doncaster Rovers on that warm Wednesday night.

Under John Bond, Norwich became a club that was built for, both structurally and geographically, top flight football. The club proved itself to be discontent with some romantic idea of being a much-loved provincial, quaintly-rural outpost that had occasionally enjoyed, and illuminated, the High Life, like either Grimsby or Carlisle.

They converted the South Stand terrace to all-seating, and replaced the vast, crumbling River End bank with a new two-tiered stand, seating above a terraced area, that also included the club's own public house, the first ever to be built inside a Football League ground.

The foundations they'd laid, as well as the mostly family-type ownership of the club, had allowed Norwich City to thrive, long term, when other clubs, less well-built for the future, have struggled since the Seventies.

The board kept faith with staff already employed at the club, with Ken Brown and Dave Stringer taking them forward after 1980, instead of searching for big name managers, who could well have bankrupted City with big money signings for short term gains. Both Brown and Stringer placed an emphasis on development and youth promotion for the future.

That great nucleus of Keelan, Machin, Stringer, Forbes, Powell, Suggett, Paddon, Peters, MacDougall and Boyer launched the brightest of futures for the most beautiful of cities.

Norwich is indeed among the most beautiful of all cities, with its majestic, 96 metres tall Twelfth-century Cathedral, made of brightly gleaming Caen limestone, as well as its winding, medieval cobbled lanes of Elm Hill. The wherries, yachts and Kingfishers whizz quietly by, along the Wensum and Yare rivers, and the city also boasts countless great pubs, including the Adam and Eve from 1249 AD. Norwich boasts more public houses, per square metre, than any city in England.

The FA Premier League seems a much poorer place for the absence of Norwich City, these days, but that feeling was born with the teams of John Bond and Ron Saunders.

CARRY ON, CONSTABLE COUNTRY

A T THE BEGINNING OF THE SEVENTIES, Ipswich was just a picturesque Suffolk port, situated near the mouth of the River Orwell, and only a few miles to the north of Constable's Stour Valley. Entering Ipswich on the wonderfully leafy and tree-lined A1214, you could easily think you were entering Lyndhurst or Brockenhurst, down in the New Forest.

With a population of just over 130,000, Ipswich was about a sixth the size of Leeds, and smaller than Bedford, Bournemouth and Bury. Ipswich was a provincial town, no more, no less, the same as Watford, Northampton, or Reading.

Just as their East Anglian rivals Norwich had struggled to escape from the bottom divisions, for a long, long time, Ipswich Town had also spent nearly twenty years, after their election into the Football League in 1938, failing to get out of Division Three (South), and they were often at the lower end of that bottom division.

They finally won promotion to Division Two in 1954, but were immediately relegated again. Alf Ramsey then became their manager in 1955, and he took them back up in 1957, as Division Three (South) Champions, before they then gained promotion to the First Division in 1961, on the back of seventy league goals scored by the prolific attacking partnership of Ray Crawford and Ted Phillips.

In 1962, Ipswich Town made the most of the shallow waters of Division One, as nobody could stop Crawford and Phillips scoring, and they cruised to their first, and only League Championship title, with average home crowds of only 20,000. Portsmouth-born Crawford and the stern-faced, Suffolk-born Phillips were again the stars of the show, scoring sixty-one First Division goals between them, as Ipswich romped to 24 wins, scoring 93 goals, to finish three points above both Burnley and Spurs.

While Ray Crawford and Ted Phillips received most of the credit for Ipswich winning the title, Alf Ramsey was full of admiration for the dark-haired and diminutive, Edinburgh-born wing half Billy Baxter, who anchored the middle of the field, winning the ball, and driving his team forward.

Baxter was another of a rich, long-running tradition of small Scottish players who could handle themselves amidst the game's physical battles. Fearless, though only five feet eight, he was a ball winner in the air, as well as on the ground, and he could hold and pass a ball as well as Bobby Moore, the player who Alf Ramsey compared to Baxter, after he became England manager in May 1963.

Ipswich were relegated back to Division Two in 1964, after a disastrous season under Jackie Milburn's management had dropped them to the bottom of the table, only two years after they were Champions. It was the most dramatic turnaround in the history of the First Division. Milburn left

Portman Road in September 1964, with Ipswich bottom of the Second Division, and Billy Baxter then also handed in a transfer request, telling his chairman John Cobbold that "there was no future at Portman Road."

Ray Crawford and Ted Phillips had both gone by then, to Wolves and Orient, respectively.

John Cobbold, or **Mr John** as he was called by all at Portman Road, was grandson of the ninth Duke of Devonshire, and he'd been chairman of both Ipswich Town, and the Tolly Cobbold brewery since 1957.

Mr John worried deeply that his team was breaking up, and he subsequently blew the roof off the club's wages structure to keep Baxter.

"We are manager-less, almost pointless," Mr John proclaimed publicly, "but we cannot afford to be Baxter-less." Billy Baxter stayed, but with a feeling that he was more important to the club than any subsequent manager, and a new era of player power developed at Portman Road, which proved problematic for future managers.

Bill McGarry took charge at Ipswich, and after three seasons of upper mid-table mediocrity, he led the club to a tight promotion race, during 1967-68, against both QPR and Blackpool. At the beginning of that season, he'd signed Tommy Carroll, a Dublin-born right back, from non-league Cambridge City, and the Irishman played 38 games as Ipswich won the Second Division Championship trophy by a single point.

Billy Baxter had captained them to that title, at centre-half, but Bill McGarry had also built for the future, introducing Colin Viljoen, Clive Woods, Mick Mills and Peter Morris to first team action. In November 1968, though, McGarry left Portman Road to become manager at Wolves, who at that time, quite simply, had better players and fifteen thousand more fans than Ipswich Town.

Bobby Robson had been a good player, spending eleven years with Fulham, playing alongside Johnny Haynes, Alan Mullery and George Cohen, and then latterly, Allan Clarke and Les Barrett. He'd been in England's World Cup squad for both the 1958 and 1962 World Cup Finals tournaments, starting at inside-right in three of England's four games over in Sweden, in 1958.

Robson was then appointed manager of Fulham, early in 1968, but he couldn't prevent Fulham being relegated to Division Two, although he **was** the man who'd signed Malcolm MacDonald, from Tonbridge, for just one thousand pounds.

But with Fulham facing another relegation struggle in the Second Division, Bobby was shocked to see the news that he'd been sacked by Fulham, on an Evening Standard placard, under the street lights outside Putney Station, in November 1968.

In January 1969, he was summoned to Suffolk to meet John Cobbold, who offered Robson the job as Ipswich manager.

Both of the early favourites for the job, Frank O'Farrell and Billy Bingham, had declined Ipswich Town's offers. Mr John suggested that they preferred not to bother with such ugly formalities as a legal contract, but he gave Robson his assurance that he'd spend at least two years at Portman Road.

Bobby Robson liked Mr John so much, so gently affable, so gentlemanly, honest and charismatic he was, that he shook hands straight away, on an offer of £5,000 a year.

Ipswich were fifth from bottom of Division One in January 1969, but half a dozen points above relegation worries. Robson's arrival, though, brought about an instant improvement to their results, winning seven and losing only three of their last fifteen league matches, and they rose to twelfth in the table, just four points below Southampton, who'd qualified for the Fairs Cup.

Ipswich struggled to score goals throughout 1969-70, though, and they finished the season just five points above the relegation place, fifth from bottom of Division One.

For the first time in their Football League history, they'd scored less than a goal per game, and their leading scorer was Colin Viljoen with just six league goals.

By 1970, Billy Baxter had decided that he'd had enough of Bobby Robson, and it was time he got rid. He criticized Robson in the Sunday papers, and with Tommy Carroll as his ally, they started to conduct a series of confrontations, and instilled an atmosphere of conflict inside the Ipswich changing room. They contradicted the manager whenever possible, designed to destroy the confidence of Bobby Robson, who they'd never liked since he arrived.

Robson was only six years older than Baxter, and it was very possible that the Ipswich club legend fancied the job as his career drew to a close.

Robson was tougher than he looked, though. At the start of the following season, he stripped the captaincy from Baxter, and he made Mick Mills, his twenty-one year old full-back, Ipswich Town captain instead.

It didn't go down well.

Then he gave a league debut to Geoff Hammond, their twenty year-old youth team right back from Sudbury, at the end of September 1970, away at Cup winners Chelsea.

That did not go down at all well with Carroll, who then walked out after blasting Robson for his decision, and he returned home to Dublin.

Robson subsequently fined and suspended Tommy Carroll, but Billy Baxter continued to create an uncomfortable atmosphere in the Ipswich Town changing room. So, in January 1971, Bobby Robson then also dropped Baxter from the Ipswich team, for the first time in his entire career. He replaced Baxter with yet another twenty year old youth team graduate, Bobby Bell from Cambridge.

Ipswich won their next match, 2-1 at home to bottom club Blackpool, after Mick Lambert and Geoff Hammond both scored. Unfortunately for Robson, Town lost their next two away games, away at Arsenal, and also at relegation rivals Crystal Palace.

27,286, their second largest home crowd of the season, then packed into Portman Road for the visit of runaway leaders Leeds United. Colin Viljoen and Mick Hill both scored first half goals to give Ipswich a superb 2-1 half-time lead. Peter Lorimer had fired a rocket in, before half-time, to keep United in the match. After the break, though, Leeds came out and they were unbelievably good.

Allan Clarke turned and fired in, from just inside the area, to equalise. Bremner then fed Clarke with a delightful ball, to put Leeds 3-2 up, before Mick Jones was fouled inside the Ipswich area, and Johnny Giles smashed his penalty kick high into the top left corner of Laurie Sivell's goal.

After Leeds' superb come-back 4-2 win, Bobby Robson and his team slumped back to the changing room, absolutely shocked, shattered and inconsolable after they had been so outplayed by that greatest of teams, in the second half. They were all stunned then, to see Baxter and Carroll celebrating, both laughing and joking, and even ordering a bottle of Champagne to celebrate.

Perhaps the pair were happy that they now had to return to the Ipswich team? Both Mick McNeill and Bobby Bell had just been given a torrid time in the second half by that liveliest of all attacking partnerships, Clarke and Jones.

Bobby Robson was having none of it. He saw the Champagne drinking incident as disgraceful behaviour, worthy of gutter dwellers, apparently celebrating and rejoicing in their *younger* teammates' defeat. He froze both of them out of the next Ipswich team, at home to Manchester City. He put the team-sheet up on the notice-board, again without the names of either Billy Baxter and Tommy Carroll on it, so Carroll tore it off, and screwed it up into the face of Robson, telling him he "could stuff his fucking team up his fucking arse."

The pair started to throw punches at each other. So Billy Baxter jumped in as well, standing toe to toe with Robson, and joined in with his renegade teammate, fighting away. Cyril Lea, Ipswich's Wrexham-born coach, who'd been their caretaker manager during the two months between Bill McGarry and Bobby Robson, then joined in with the fight, in support of his boss.

"It was like a bad bar-room joke," Bobby Robson had described the incident. "An Englishman, a Scotsman, an Irishman and a Welshman swinging at each other.

No-one was knocked down, but it certainly was not handbags at ten paces. Punches were thrown."

It was Bobby Robson's young right-back, Geoff Hammond, who showed the maturity and bravery to jump in and break it all up.

Bobby Robson was furious. He knew this was the time when he knew he *had* to beat this out of the club permanently, or he would be beaten, and finished as a manager, forever.

It *had* been over two years since he took over as manager, so Mr John had kept his word. With an Ipswich club legend like Billy Baxter pushing him, he knew he was on thin ice. It should be noted, though, that Ipswich did beat Manchester City 2-0, after goals from Colin Viljoen and Frank Clarke.

Mr John and his board backed Bobby Robson completely, and also demanded that he should sell those two players at the earliest opportunity. Billy Baxter had not seen that coming, as he'd been dining out on Mr John's loyalty and admiration for him, for the previous seven years.

Baxter was sold to Hull City in March 1971, for just £12,500, despite him fully apologising, in all fairness, for his behaviour towards Robson.

The last player from their 1962 League Champions to leave Portman Road, Billy Baxter had played over 400 league games for Ipswich Town, and he remains one of their all-time greatest players.

Baxter just wasn't as great as Bobby Robson became.

If he'd seen that coming, perhaps he'd have been a little nicer to Bobby, and his future might well have been a little different?

Billy Baxter moved to Northampton Town, as their player-manager, a year after he joined Hull. Under his charge, though, the Cobblers had to apply for re-election to the Football League, for two years in succession, and only six years after they'd been a First Division club.

Baxter left Northampton in 1973, and then he retired completely from league football.

After reaching pension age, Billy Baxter fought one last fight, a losing battle, against cancer.

He very sadly lost one of his great legs, before dying in Dunfermline, aged seventy, on Monday 25th May 2009.

By the end of the season, Ipswich had lost just two out of their final eight matches, and they finished up fourth from bottom, seven points above the relegation zone.

Bobby Robson had even recalled Tommy Carroll for their last two games of the season, goalless draws against Wolves and Chelsea.

Colin Viljoen was again Ipswich Town's top scorer, with twelve league and cup goals, while Frank Clarke, Mick Hill and Jimmy Robertson shared twenty-four goals between them.

Laurie Sivell had played a successive run of twenty-nine matches in goal, while David Best was injured, keeping eleven clean sheets. Sivell, a twenty year old youth team graduate, from Lowestoft, had kept goal while Town pulled away from relegation worries, as well as helping Ipswich to the FA Cup Fifth round. They lost in a home replay to Stoke City, with a near-record crowd of 30,232 filling Portman Road.

David Best returned to the team in April, though, and he kept four clean sheets in seven games. Ipswich Town always had two great goalkeepers, under Bobby Robson's management. Captain Mick Mills was their only ever-present during a turbulent season, while Peter Morris had missed only one game, playing in Billy Baxter's old position, holding the midfield and protecting his back four.

Tommy Carroll played his last match for Ipswich on Monday 23rd August 1971, as they drew 0-0 away at West Ham. He joined Birmingham City in October, for £20,000, after playing 116 league games at Portman Road. Birmingham were involved in a tight promotion race after Christmas 1971, and Carroll missed just one of Blues' final twenty-eight matches. They kept fifteen clean sheets with Carroll playing at right back, and were promoted back to the First Division at the end of the season.

Ipswich Town had an unglamorous start to the new season, winning just once from their first seven games, and scoring only three goals. They did draw four of those games 0-0, however, so they sat very safely in mid-table with six points.

At the beginning of September, Bobby Robson paid £60,000 to Third Division side Blackburn Rovers, for Northern Ireland's international centre-back Allan Hunter.

The transfer saw the spirited, but limited Bobby Bell headed off up to Ewood Park.

With the introduction of Hunter, Ipswich's defence was becoming one of the tightest in England. After eighteen games, they had won as many games as they'd lost, but they became draw specialists, having drawn eight games, five of them goalless.

They were among just four First Division teams to have conceded less than a goal per game.

During 1971-72 though, the greatest First Division season ever, Ipswich were miserable at worst, usually boring, and just about mediocre at best.

They scored more than two goals in a game just three times out of forty-five league and cup matches, and it was only the introduction of Trevor Whymark, at the beginning of March, that gave Town's fans something to really scream about.

Trevor Whymark, twenty-one years old and from just over the East Anglian border, from near Diss in Norfolk, had scored four goals from twelve games towards the end of the season.

It appeared to the more hopeful supporters that Bobby Robson's problems in attack might be coming to an end? Indeed they were, and so were the years of mediocrity.

On Saturday 12th August 1972, Ipswich Town travelled to Manchester United, for their first game of the season, in front of a 51,429 Old Trafford crowd.

It was very appropriate that such a huge crowd was there to see the birth of a great team. This was a new look Ipswich team. Kevin Beattie had been found in Carlisle by one of Bobby Robson's scouts, John Carruthers, and he'd risen through the youth team to make his league debut against Manchester United, aged just nineteen. And while neither Bryan Hamilton or Mick Lambert were exactly making their debuts, both were starting their careers as Ipswich Town first team regulars.

Bryan Hamilton had been the top goal-scorer in the Irish League during 1971, with Linfield, winning both the Ulster Footballer of the Year and Northern Ireland Football Writers' Player of the Year awards.

Ipswich Town snapped him up, for a tiny fee of just a few hundred pounds, a real steal, and he'd started eight matches during the previous season.

Hamilton had already played eight games for Northern Ireland by the time 1972-73 began.

Mick Lambert had made his debut for Ipswich nearly four years earlier, under Bill McGarry, but he'd never been a first team regular, starting just forty-five league games over those four seasons.

Trevor Whymark had kept his place in attack, though, alongside the moderate forward Rod Belfitt.

MANCHESTER UNITED		IPSWICH TOWN
Alex Stepney	1	David Best
Tom O'Neil	2	Mick Mills
Tony Dunne	3	Kevin Beattie
Willie Morgan	4	Ian Collard
Steve James	5	Allan Hunter
Martin Buchan	6	Derek Jefferson
George Best	7	Bryan Hamilton
Brian Kidd	8	Colin Viljoen
Bobby Charlton	9	Rod Belfitt
Denis Law	10	Trevor Whymark
Ian Moore	11	Mick Lambert

Ipswich took the lead early on, after Kevin Beattie's epic, long ball, from ten yards inside his own half, had landed between Dunne and James, inside the United area, but neither defender took responsibility. So Trevor Whymark stole in to poke his shot past Stepney's dive.

Lambert's left sided corner was attacked, from outside the United area, by a fierce, towering header from Beattie. The ball stung Stepney's fingertips as he attempted to tip it over his bar, falling back into his own net, and then just watching as the ball landed back onto the angle of his goal, before bouncing away for another corner.

In the second half, Ian Moore ventured on a determined run from halfway, sailing past Hunter, before chipping a cross over Jefferson, towards the far post. Law headed the ball back for Kidd to head low inside the Ipswich goalpost, only for David Best to leap, off-balance, and brilliantly tip the ball away, before pouncing on it safely.

Ian Moore was the only United player who threatened Ipswich, that afternoon.

Dazzling, daring and difficult to contain, Moore was unfortunate that Bobby Charlton was anonymous, while George Best was flat-footed and disinterested, given the run-around all afternoon by Colin Viljoen, focused, fleet-footed and fast-witted.

With seven minutes remaining, Beattie's left-sided free-kick was only half-cleared by Dunne, and Ian Collard returned an up-and-under into the United area. Bryan Hamilton outwitted Dunne, cutting inside then volleying the ball beyond Stepney, inside the far post for a 2-0 lead.

With time running out, and the United crowd beginning to slow hand-clap, Moore attacked the Ipswich area again, running inside and outside substitute Geoff Hammond and also Mick Mills. He fired, left-footed, towards the near post of Best's goal. The keeper parried his shot, but Law scooped in the rebound, from close range.

There were no celebrations or congratulations.

That victory was seen, both by TV viewers and Town fans, that Ipswich had finally arrived on the big stage. They could still defend very well, but now they could also create chances, and they could attack in numbers. On the following Saturday, newly-promoted Birmingham City were the new seasons' first visitors to Portman Road.

This game allowed Tommy Carroll, Birmingham's right back a chance to say farewell to his old teammates, and shake the hand of his former manager. Carroll had done really well, helping the Blues to promotion, and he performed with dignity and professionalism that afternoon.

Ipswich won 2-0, though, after goals from John Miller, in for the injured Mick Lambert, and also Trevor Whymark. Tommy Carroll played his last game for Birmingham in a 0-0 draw on Saturday 28th October, before he was ruled out of action due to a bad knee injury. He was forced to retire from league football a year later, at the age of thirty-one, and returned to Ireland to manage Shelbourne.

By the middle of September, Ipswich Town were second in the First Division, after winning five of their opening nine games.

They were level on points with leaders Everton, but with an inferior goal average. A failure to win any of their next four matches, though, then dropped Town back down to mid-table.

On Wednesday 11th October 1972, Sir Alf Ramsey selected twenty-three year old Mick Mills to play at right back against Yugoslavia, at Wembley. England drew 1-1 in the first of Mills' forty-two full international appearances.

Belfitt, Beattie and Whymark ended Ipswich's barren run, on Saturday 21st October, all scoring in their 3-1 win over reigning Champions Derby County. They then faced four tough games from the end of October, through to the end of November.

They first visited Goodison Park on 28th October, where Mick Lambert and Rod Belfitt both scored to earn a 2-2 draw with Everton. Everton had led 2-0 at half-time, but with Kevin Beattie now partnering Allan Hunter in central defence, Town now had spirit as well as skill.

Rod Belfitt's goal against Everton was his last for Ipswich. On the following Monday, Bobby Robson had remained up on Merseyside, and he offered Everton a £50,000 transfer fee, plus Rod Belfitt, for their Liverpool-born striker David Johnson.

David Johnson had scored eleven First Division goals in fifty games for the Toffees, but he'd scored only once in ten starts for Everton, since the beginning of that current season, and he'd even been dropped from the first team, a week before their match with Ipswich.

Fans back in Suffolk were confused why they'd just given away their leading goal-scorer plus a cash payment of £50,000 for a reserve team player.

Bobby Robson had felt, though, that he'd found the final piece of his jigsaw.

David Johnson went straight into the team for their next game against Leeds United, at Portman Road. Nearly 28,000 filled the ground, on Saturday 4th November, and fireworks were launched that night. Trevor Whymark gave Ipswich a 2-1 half-time lead, after Paul Madeley's own goal, under pressure from new striker Johnson, had opened the scoring.

Peter Lorimer equalised for Leeds, late on, but their 2-2 draw against the mighty Whites had illustrated how much Ipswich had progressed in just one year.

A week later, Ipswich Town travelled the short journey north, up the A140 for their away match, their first ever First Division game, at East Anglian rivals Norwich City. Nearly 35,000 packed Carrow Road, but Ipswich earned a valuable point, after another hard-earned goalless draw.

Finally, on Saturday 18th November, Ipswich travelled to Wolves, UEFA Cup Finalists at the end of the previous season, and they won 1-0 (Whymark).

After a tough, and very tricky, quartet of matches, three of which were away from home, Ipswich had edged back up into the top five.

David Johnson scored his first goal for Ipswich during their 1-1 draw, away at Manchester City, on Saturday 2nd December, and eventually by 17th February, after a great run of five wins from six matches, they were proper First Division title contenders, with two games in hand over the league leaders Arsenal.

	PL	W	D	L	F	A	PTS
Arsenal	31	18	8	5	43	27	44
Liverpool	30	17	8	5	53	32	42
Leeds United	29	16	8	5	51	30	40
IPSWICH TOWN	29	14	10	5	43	29	38
Derby County	31	14	6	11	40	43	34

Steve Heighway and Kevin Keegan both netted typical Liverpool goals on the following Saturday, to beat Ipswich 2-1 at Anfield, after David Johnson replied with his fifth goal of the season. They bounced back, though, beating West Ham 1-0 away, with the prolific Johnson scoring his sixth goal from his last thirteen games.

That win at Upton Park kept Ipswich just four points behind the leaders, as they faced Arsenal at Portman Road, on Saturday 10th March. Both teams were desperate to win, with defeat probably ruling either team out of the title race.

IPSWICH TOWN		ARSENAL
Laurie Sivell	1	Bob Wilson
Mick Mills	2	Pat Rice
Colin Harper	3	Bob McNab
Peter Morris	4	Peter Storey
Allan Hunter	5	Frank McLintock
Kevin Beattie	6	Peter Simpson
Bryan Hamilton	7	George Armstrong
Colin Viljoen	8	Alan Ball
David Johnson	9	John Radford
Trevor Whymark	10	Ray Kennedy
Mick Lambert	11	Eddie Kelly

A record crowd of 34,636 filled Portman Road for the greatest Ipswich Town team, since their title-winning 1962 team. The average age of Ipswich's team was under twenty-four, though, and they danced around the much older Arsenal side for the opening half-hour. Viljoen's vision and poise was just too classy for Ball, and Trevor Whymark gave them the lead, flicking in Bryan Hamilton's cross, while Bob Wilson also made good saves from both Beattie and Johnson.

Just before half-time, though, John Radford seized upon a rare defensive mistake to score from close range, sending the teams in level at the break, after a one-sided half.

The experience of Arsenal had the bulk of possession in the second half, allowing the ball to do the work, while Ipswich did all the running. Harper was harshly adjudged to have fouled Armstrong, and Alan Ball clinically cracked his spot-kick high up into the top left corner of Sivell's goal.

Arsenal went on to finish runners-up behind Liverpool, while Ipswich Town slumped, winning only two of their final ten matches. They did, however, pick up just enough points to finish one point ahead of Wolves, and they qualified for the UEFA Cup, in fourth place.

This Ipswich team was built for the future, though, and while they competed very, very strongly for two more First Division titles over the following eight years, Arsenal did not seriously challenge for another title until 1989.

Trevor Whymark and Bryan Hamilton were joint top scorers, with eleven goals each, while David Johnson had scored seven goals. Ipswich Town scored goals from all over their team, though, with only captain Mick Mills failing to score a single goal during 1972-73, and Viljoen, Lambert and Beattie had also scored fifteen First Division goals between them. Kevin Beattie's aerial ability had also become a key attacking tactic in Bobby Robson's options.

Peter Taylor, Derby County's assistant manager, had observed that Kevin Beattie was "a marvellous athlete, of international class, and able to jump above the crossbar to head goals."

David Johnson, in spite of his devilish pace and clinical shooting, had been quiet during his first season at Portman Road, finding his feet in Suffolk, if you like. But he then began to Roar through the following season. After a 1-1 home draw with Leicester, Johnson scored twice, adding to Whymark's opener, for an exciting 3-3 draw with West Ham. Bonds, Brooking and Best all scored for the Hammers, but then Everton beat Ipswich 3-0. Newcastle had also beaten Ipswich 3-1, away at Portman Road, to leave Town in fifth-bottom position, and just two points off the bottom.

That wasn't as bad as it got.

Mick Lambert and David Johnson both scored to beat Manchester United 2-1, on Saturday 8th September 1973, but then, Newcastle United defeated Ipswich Town, again by three goals to one, at St James's Park, sending Town down to fourth-bottom position.

Only goal average was keeping Ipswich Town out of the relegation zone.

That was as bad as it got.

Ipswich then went on a fourteen match league and cup unbeaten run, winning six of their league games, beating Burnley, Birmingham, Chelsea, Wolves, Coventry, and also Dave Mackay's Derby County. They'd beaten Leeds United 2-0 in the League Cup Second round, with more than 26,000 at Portman Road, and then they beat Fulham after a replay.

In the UEFA Cup, Ipswich were given a terrific, terrifying draw against Real Madrid, for the start of their first European adventure for eleven years. Only 25,000 attended their home leg against the most successful club in European history, but Ipswich Town won 1-0, after Benito Rubinan's second-half own goal.

80,000 filled the Bernabau, a fortnight later, on Wednesday 3rd October, but despite heavy pressure, and nasty intimidation from both the home crowd and players, Ipswich's defence kept everything out. Since their home defeat to Arsenal, six months earlier, their young side had grown, and they'd developed a firm backbone, too.

In the Second round, on Tuesday 23rd October, Lazio, the current Italian Serie A leaders, arrived at Portman Road, en route to their first-ever Italian Championship.

Trevor Whymark made his mark on the European stage, smashing in four goals, two in each half, to give Ipswich a staggering 4-0 lead, but Lazio then reverted to dirty Italian tactics, that had rightly sullied the reputation of Italian clubs in Europe.

Giancarlo Oddi flew in with his right boot up, making no attempt to play the ball, and with some venom, stamping his studs into David Johnson's stomach.

Oddi just got up, and left Johnson lying in agony on the pitch.

That was a harsh awakening for the 26,000 Portman Road crowd. They just couldn't believe it as the stretcher-bearers sprinted out, and then hurried off with the bullet-wounded Johnson, who was ruled out of action for their next three matches.

Two weeks later, over in Rome, Johnson was back, but on the bench, as Lazio sailed into a 4-1 lead, after Giorgio Chinaglia's magnificent hat-trick. Chinaglia had actually been given a free transfer by Swansea City. Colin Viljoen's second half penalty kick had kept Ipswich just in it, but they really were on the rack.

Lazio kept up the pressure, but David Johnson then replaced Clive Woods, and he danced past the bastard Oddi to fire Ipswich to a 6-4 aggregate win, silencing 35,000 Romans.

By the following Saturday, 10th November, after Mick Lambert and Kevin Beattie had fired them to a 3-0 home win over Derby, Ipswich were up to sixth place, and only one point below second-placed Burnley.

There were five headed goals during their next game, a 4-2 defeat in the Anfield mud, away to Liverpool. Keegan headed two goals, and Cormack another, while David Johnson and Bryan Hamilton coolly headed Town back into the match. A Geoff Hammond tackle on John Toshack, though, ricocheted back off the Welsh striker, and out of play, so the referee awarded an Ipswich goal kick.

The linesman, however, flagged him over, having seen it as a foul by Hammond.

Well, it looked like the Welshman went down very easily, and without much of a touch, but the referee changed his mind and he awarded a penalty kick to Liverpool, much to the frustration and fury of the Ipswich players.

The ball was booted away, twice, off the penalty spot by blue shirted players, and the tall figure of David Best stood menacingly over Kevin Keegan, as he prepared to take the kick, before being ordered back to his line. Keegan just fired his kick high up into the top corner of the Ipswich goal.

Trevor Whymark scored twice, a week later, as Town beat Man City 2-1, but then runaway leaders Leeds United hammered them 3-0 at Portman Road. Beattie leapt highest, to head a long ball from Trevor Cherry back into his midfield, but the unmarked Terry Yorath looped a great long range shot into the roof of Best's goal.

Mick Jones headed in Yorath's left wing cross, and then Allan Clarke scored the best goal of the game. He collected a forward pass from Bremner, on the right wing, then waltzed past both Mills and Collard, and then swept behind Viljoen, before firing, left-footed, from twenty yards out, past the dive of Best at his near post.

Leeds United, in all-yellow, were jubilant, having equalled a First Division record with nineteen unbeaten league games, from the start of a season.

Mick Lambert hit two goals, and Geoff Hammond their other, as Ipswich hammered Birmingham City 3-0 on the Saturday before Christmas, and then on Boxing Day, David Johnson fired in a penalty during their 2-1 away win at Norwich City.

Mick Lambert had scored Town's second, as they won the East Anglian derby match, with over 30,000 inside Carrow Road.

Ipswich had also eliminated Twente Enschede, 3-1 on aggregate, in the UEFA Cup Third round, during December. Playing in midfield for Twente, though, was a twenty-one year old Franz Thijssen, a future Ipswich Town legend and Footballer of the Year during the early Eighties.

Ipswich then won only one of their next four league games, from the end of December until the end of February, that left them down in eighth position.

David Best had played the last of his 168 First Division matches for Ipswich Town, during their 1-1 draw with Stoke City, on Saturday 12th January. Best eventually moved to Portsmouth on Thursday 28th February, and he played fifty-three Second Division matches at Fratton Park, before retiring at the age of thirty-two.

Laurie Sivell played in goal for most of the remainder of that season, while George Burley had also made his debut for Ipswich, at right back, against Manchester United on the last Saturday of 1973.

The seventeen year old Scot had given such a sensational display, while deputising for the injured Geoff Hammond, that Burley partnered Mick Mills at full back positions for the next nine years at Portman Road.

On Saturday 2nd February, a crowd of just 20,053 were at Portman Road to watch eighth-placed Ipswich play tenth-placed Southampton.

The missing ten thousand home fans missed a treat.

IPSWICH TOWN		SOUTHAMPTON
Laurie Sivell	1	Eric Martin
George Burley	2	Bob McCarthy
Mick Mills	3	David Peach
Peter Morris	4	Hugh Fisher
Allan Hunter	5	Paul Bennett
Kevin Beattie	6	Jim Steele
Bryan Hamilton	7	Terry Paine
Colin Viljoen	8	Mike Channon
David Johnson	9	Bobby Stokes
Trevor Whymark	10	Tony Byrne
Mick Lambert	11	Gerry O'Brien

In the most wonderful mixture of possession football, impassable defence and imperious attacks, Ipswich slaughtered Southampton 7-0. Trevor Whymark and Bryan Hamilton both bagged braces, while Lambert, Beattie and Mills completed the scoring in Town's greatest ever First Division victory. Ipswich then gained only eight points from their next nine matches, up to late March, but they remained in a strong position to secure another UEFA Cup qualifying place, due to the declines in form of Burnley, Newcastle and also Leicester City.

March also saw the end of Ipswich Town's 1973-74 UEFA Cup dreams, in the Quarter-finals. Kevin Beattie's second half goal at Portman Road gave them a 1-0 first leg lead over Lokomotiv Leipzig, but the East Germans also won 1-0, two weeks later, at the Bruno-Plahe-Stadion.

And Lokomotiv won 4-3 on penalties, after extra-time.

They'd been without Colin Viljoen, though, who was out for the rest of the season, after suffering a knee injury during their 3-1 defeat at home to West Ham, on Tuesday 5th February, so Brian Talbot made his debut for Ipswich, four days later, during their 1-0 win at Burnley. On Saturday 30th March, Talbot scored twice, his first ever league goals, as Town beat Coventry 3-0, lifting themselves up to fourth in the table.

David Johnson, Bryan Hamilton and Peter Morris all scored at Maine Road, on Saturday 6th April, in their 3-1 win over Manchester City, and then Ipswich enjoyed a Good Friday, also beating QPR by 1-0 at Loftus Road, after Trevor Whymark scored his eleventh goal of the season.

Ipswich had risen to third place, and on the following day, Saturday 13th April, 33,285, their largest crowd of the season, packed Portman Road for the visit of second-placed Liverpool.

Trevor Whymark gave Ipswich a 1-0 lead, tucking the ball under Ray Clemence's dive, following some crisp passing between Brian Talbot and Peter Morris. After the break, though, the over-exuberant Emlyn Hughes levelled the scores, and Liverpool hung on for the point.

On Bank Holiday Monday, 15th April, Ipswich played their third game in four days, beating QPR 1-0 at home, after David Johnson's second half goal, and then they qualified for the UEFA Cup again, on the following Saturday, after Burnley lost to Norwich City.

Another twenty year-old debutant, Paul Cooper, had played his first game in goal for Ipswich at Elland Road, on that Saturday, 20th April, a game that Leeds United needed to win to secure their second First Division title.

With a huge crowd of over 44,000 roaring them on, Leeds United began brightly, with Lorimer and Bremner both blasting the ball past Cooper before half-time. Brian Talbot pulled one back, just before the break, though, and then Don Revie feared the worst, when Bryan Hamilton scored a deserved equaliser.

Allan Clarke poached a late winner to win the Championship, and send the vast home crowd wild. Ipswich Town lost their final game, 1-0 at home to Sheffield United, having nothing really to fight for, and they again finished fourth, one point behind Derby County.

Bryan Hamilton won the club's Player of the Season award, having scored sixteen First Division goals, from forty-one games, while David Johnson, Trevor Whymark and Mick Lambert combined to score thirty-three league goals between them.

Kevin Beattie was ever-present for Ipswich, alongside captain Mick Mills, and was the winner of the first-ever PFA Young Player of the Season award.

During the Summer of 1974, Bobby Robson made his rejuvenated Town even younger, after he sent Peter Morris, his thirty year-old midfield anchor, up to Norwich City, and subsequently promoted Brian Talbot to a regular starting place in midfield, next to the fit-again Colin Viljoen.

Peter Morris had played 220 league matches for Ipswich, 206 of them in the First Division. He became an unsung hero of Norwich City's promotion and League Cup Final team during 1974-75.

Ipswich won their first four matches of the new season, beating Spurs and Arsenal, both away, by 1-0, and then Burnley 2-0, at home, before they smashed Arsenal 3-0 at Portman Road, on Tuesday 27th August. Winger Mick Lambert fired in two goals, and Kevin Beattie scored a third before half-time. After the break, they just kept the ball, as Arsenal had done to them eighteen months earlier, and they simply outclassed a team including Brian Kidd, Charlie George, John Radford, and also a young Liam Brady.

David Johnson was kicked off the pitch by his old team Everton, at Portman Road, on Saturday 7th September, but substitute Clive Woods slipped in to fire Ipswich to a 1-0 half-time lead. For the fifth time in six matches, their water-tight back four of Burley, Hunter, Beattie and Mills, in front of Laurie Sivell, kept a clean sheet.

On the second Saturday in September, Ipswich made the short journey along the A12 and A120, to Luton Town, who were playing their first season in the First Division for fifteen years. With nearly 18,000 inside Kenilworth Road, Brian Talbot scored twice, the first a penalty kick, having displaced Colin Viljoen as Town's regular penalty taker.

Bryan Hamilton and Trevor Whymark both fired second half goals, as Town won 4-1 to top the First Division table for the first time since 1962.

As *Telstar,* the soundtrack for Ipswich's last title challenge, was replaced by *The Bay City Rollers,* the youngest First Division leaders since the Busby Babes, with an average age of a little over twenty-three, then defeated both Chelsea and Stoke to remain top for the next month.

An Autumn slump saw them knocked out of the UEFA Cup First round by Twente Enschede, 3-3 on aggregate, with Franz Thijssen's side winning on away goals, and they also won none of their six league games after Tuesday 24th September.

By the end of October, Ipswich had dropped to third place, but they did improve in November, beating Liverpool 1-0 (Talbot), Coventry City 4-0 (Johnson 3, Talbot), and finally, Carlisle United 3-1 (Hamilton, Johnson, Lambert).

They then beat Tottenham Hotspur 4-0 (Viljoen, Beattie, Lambert, Osborne), on Saturday 14th December, and then Leicester City 1-0, one week later, to return to the top of the league by Christmas. Trevor Whymark had scored that goal to take Ipswich back to the top, but it was a total team achievement, with nine different players responsible for their fourteen goals over the previous eight games.

Clive Woods had scored Town's goal, on 9th November, during their 2-1 defeat at Wolves.

Who did opponents mark? That was the big question.

Roger Osborne, who had made his debut against Wolves back in October 1973, scored three goals in six starts over the Festive period, in place of the injured Bryan Hamilton, as Ipswich cemented their Championship charge with a 2-0 win (Osborne, Johnson) over second-placed Middlesbrough, on Saturday 11th January.

There were, however, only three points separating the top eight teams.

FIRST DIVISION LEADERS, 11TH JANUARY 1975

	PL	W	D	L	F	A	PTS
IPSWICH TOWN	26	15	2	9	36	19	32
Everton	25	9	13	3	36	25	31
Middlesbrough	26	11	8	7	37	30	30
Stoke City	26	11	8	7	39	33	30
Burnley	26	12	6	8	46	40	30
Liverpool	24	12	5	7	34	22	29
Derby County	25	11	7	7	40	33	29
Man City	26	11	7	8	32	34	29

In the FA Cup, Ipswich won 2-1 away at Wolves, with Viljoen and Johnson both scoring, and then, in the Fourth round, and in front of a record 34,709 Portman Road crowd, Mick Mills' second half strike beat the might of Liverpool.

In the Fifth round, though, Ipswich were caught cold by a daring Aston Villa side, League Cup Finalists and Second Division promotion hopefuls.

A series of delightful one-two's between Bobby McDonald, Alun Evans and Keith Leonard sliced through Town's tight defence, with McDonald finishing sharply, in spite of Allan Hunter's strong challenge.

In the second half, Villa really stunned the 31,297 Portman Road crowd, by doubling their lead with their exuberant football. Ray Graydon drove over a right wing cross, following a great run by Frank Carrodus, and Leonard, beyond the far post, nodded back into Ipswich's six yard box. The blonde Alun Evans leapt in the mud, almost on the goal-line, and he headed into the open goal.

With Ipswich 0-2 down, Viljoen collected the ball in midfield, and he flicked a delightful sliding ball, with the outside of his right boot to Lambert, running into the Villa area. Lambert crossed for Johnson to score at the far post, from six yards, with just half an hour remaining.

John Robson then sent a long free-kick to the edge of the Ipswich area. George Burley leapt above Ian Hamilton, and he headed the ball down for Viljoen to turn and run, from five yards outside of his own area. Viljoen played the ball wide to Hamilton, who flicked forward to Whymark, inside the centre circle.

Whymark headed on for Johnson to loft a clever ball behind Villa's defence, for Talbot to chase. Brian Talbot beat Bruce Rioch to the ball, just outside the area, and took one touch to get past Cumbes. Then substitute Bryan Hamilton charged in from the left, and placed the loose ball inside the far side of the goal. It was a sublime move, starting from their own area, running through six players, with a total of just seven touches of the ball, their Goal of the Season, and it sent their home fans delirious.

With time running out, and Ipswich not terribly keen on a replay, Lambert drove over a right wing corner. Beattie leapt and flicked the ball towards the far post, where Hamilton nodded home for a terrific come-back win, bringing all the blue and white scarves out at the home end. It had easily been the tie of the round.

Drawn at home to European Cup Quarter-finalists Leeds United, in the Sixth round, on Saturday 8th March, Ipswich Town were still well in the race for a League and Cup Double, only four points behind leaders Everton with ten games remaining.

IPSWICH TOWN		LEEDS UNITED
Laurie Sivell	1	David Stewart
George Burley	2	Paul Madeley
Mick Mills	3	Frank Gray
Brian Talbot	4	Billy Bremner
Allan Hunter	5	Gordon McQueen
Kevin Beattie	6	Norman Hunter
Bryan Hamilton	7	Terry Yorath
Colin Viljoen	8	Allan Clarke
David Johnson	9	Joe Jordan
Trevor Whymark	10	Johnny Giles
Mick Lambert	11	Eddie Gray

A record Portman Road attendance of 38,010, **_never to be bettered,_** watched a classic match between Ipswich Town's best-ever team and a Leeds United side that was headed towards the European Cup Final, and to outplay Bayern Munich.

It was an unrestrained, relentless attacking exhibition of superior football, that eventually resulted in a goalless stalemate.

50,074, the biggest Elland Road crowd for nearly Five Years, attended the replay on the following Tuesday, and David Johnson finally broke the deadlock, giving Ipswich a 1-0 lead, but substitute Duncan McKenzie equalised for Leeds, late on.

The match finished 1-1, after extra-time.

Due to Leeds United's European Cup Quarter-final tie against Anderlecht, the second replay was played two weeks later, with 35,000 filling Filbert Street, Leicester.

That match was yet another stalemate, goalless just like the first game, so two nights later, on Thursday 27th March, again at Filbert Street, but in front of just 19,000 hard-core fans, there was a proper goal-fest. Top scorers Allan Clarke and Trevor Whymark both scored first half goals, and despite Johnny Giles' second half curler, Bryan Hamilton and Clive Woods both also netted to win the greatest FA Cup Quarter-final ever, sending Ipswich into the last four, and as hot favourites for the Cup.

Amidst all this epic Cup-tie football, Ipswich had beaten both Newcastle and Stoke, and also drawn 1-1 away at leaders Everton (Whymark), on Saturday 22nd March.

Just two days after their exhausting win over Leeds United, Ipswich entertained Leicester City, and they won 2-1 in front of nearly 29,000 at Portman Road.

Frank Worthington had made the most of Town's tiredness, giving City a half-time lead, but Clive Woods and Colin Viljoen both struck back after the break.

FIRST DIVISION LEADERS, SATURDAY 29TH MARCH 1975

	PL	W	D	L	F	A	PTS
Liverpool	37	17	11	9	53	35	45
Everton	36	14	16	6	49	35	44
IPSWICH TOWN	36	20	3	13	55	37	43
Middlesbrough	37	16	11	10	50	36	43
Stoke City	37	15	13	9	59	46	43
Derby County	35	17	8	10	57	45	42

It must be noted that Ipswich Town were the most aggressive and adventurous team in the First Division during 1974-75. They either went for victory, or they were beaten. They'd drawn thirteen fewer games than Everton, who were better placed to overtake Liverpool.

It must also be remembered that if it had been a three-points-for-a-win system in 1974-75, then Ipswich would have been top, and indeed, they would have gone on to lift that League Championship trophy.

Ipswich suffered from the loss of Talbot, Beattie, Hunter and Johnson, at various times, though, over the last month of that season, and they won only three of their remaining six matches, drawing two of them, but losing one crucial game, 2-1 away at Leeds United, on Saturday 19th April.

They ended up in third place, just two points behind Champions Derby County. Although they had qualified, once again, for the UEFA Cup, it was felt that a safe and sedate style of football had triumphed over Ipswich Town's fresh and free-flowing football. Derby County fans will no doubt see it differently.

Ipswich had lost the League, but they also lost the Cup. On Saturday 5th April, 58,000 filled Villa Park for their Semi-final against West Ham United.

It was easily the better quality of the two Semi-finals, and many had wished it was the Final, after Ipswich had finally beaten Leeds, while the Hammers had won away at Arsenal.

As a spectacle, though, their match was a non-event. Both teams concentrated on not losing, rather than winning, with few chances at either end. Ipswich's hopes suffered a big blow when Allan Hunter was forced off injured, and John Wark replaced him.

Wark had made his Ipswich debut during their famous 3-2 win over Leeds in that Quarter-final third replay, at Filbert Street. Aged just seventeen, he'd been captain of their FA Youth Cup winning team, beating West Ham in the Final.

Born and brought up in Glasgow, John Wark was another discovery of Town's Glasgow-based Scout, George Finlay, who'd already found George Burley, and then eventually also produced Alan Brazil.

John Wark started three games, in the space of five days, at the end of March, in place of Kevin Beattie, and Ipswich lost none of them.

Four days later, on Wednesday 9th April, over 45,000 Town and Hammers fans piled onto the open and vast terraces of Stamford Bridge, as a freezing and swirling snowstorm fell heavily onto them.

Alan Taylor, who'd scored twice in West Ham's 2-0 win at Arsenal, fired in a first half opener, but then, Billy Jennings' own goal had sent the teams back into their changing rooms, at half-time, on level terms. **BOVRIL** was definitely required.

After the break, there was a controversial moment that still infuriates Ipswich fans to this day. Bryan Hamilton scored a perfectly good goal, firing home from the edge of the West Ham area, which the linesman had signalled as a goal. The referee, though, Clive Thomas from Treorchy, who was behind play, decided to disallow the goal for an offside by another Ipswich player in the penalty area. The linesman hadn't signalled for either Woods or Whymark to have been offside, and as they hadn't received a pass, and neither player was interfering with Mervyn Day's sight of the ball, it shouldn't have mattered, but they weren't offside anyway.

Clive Thomas did disallow it, though, and Ipswich Town, who were the more accomplished team, felt robbed. Alan Taylor poached a late winner to give the football romantics their dream Final, as Fulham's Bobby Moore faced his old West Ham United mates at Wembley.

Ipswich Town would have been great Champions in 1975. They would have been deserved Double winners too, but it just didn't happen, due to both a refereeing mistake and the Football League's antiquated points system.

Under a three points-for-a-win system, Ipswich were Champions in 1974-75, beating Derby County on both Goal Average, and Goal Difference, whichever you choose. They had the best goal difference in the First Division, at plus twenty-two, and the second best goal average, too, only 0.04 behind Liverpool's goal average.

Ipswich were the most attacking team in English football, since Everton's innovative late-Sixties team, with every regular outfield player scoring goals, except for George Burley. Bryan Hamilton was their top scorer, with seventeen league and cup goals, but Johnson, Whymark and Talbot had combined for thirty-nine goals between them. Viljoen, Lambert, Woods and Beattie also contributed a further twenty-three goals.

Laurie Sivell kept twenty clean sheets in fifty-four matches, and their regular back four of Burley, Hunter, Beattie and Mills had equalled Ipswich Town's best-ever defensive record, conceding only forty-four goals in 42 First Division games.

Ipswich Town were a better team than Derby County's 1974-75 team. In truth, they were certainly even as good a team as Derby's 1972 title-winning team, but that epic four match FA Cup Quarter-final tie against Leeds United, as well as their Semi-final disappointment, had probably taken it out of them during those final seven days of the season, when they took just three points from their last three games.

Laurie Sivell played the opening game of the following season, a shock 0-3 home defeat to Newcastle United, and Paul Cooper then took over as first choice goalkeeper, for the next decade, at Portman Road. Sivell became the best long-term second choice goalkeeper in the history of English League football. He played a total of just thirty-eight more games for Ipswich, over the following nine seasons.

Sivell played the German goalkeeper Schmidt in Huston's 1981 film Escape to Victory, and after retiring, having played 141 First Division matches for Ipswich, he became a fishmonger, getting up at 2.30am and taking fresh fish from Lowestoft down to his mobile shop in London.

"Fish mongering was something I could do," Sivell admitted.

Ipswich Town started 1975-76 badly, and they were actually fighting a relegation battle by the start of September. Brian Talbot broke a leg during their goalless draw at Coventry, on Saturday 6th September, and he missed over half of that season.

Colin Viljoen also suffered a horrendous knee injury in late October, and he too missed the rest of the season.

Then, on Thursday 27th November, Everton paid Ipswich just £40,000 for top scoring midfield maestro Bryan Hamilton. Hamilton had scored forty-three goals in 142 First Division games, at Portman Road, and one day later, Derby County paid Burnley £300,000 for Leighton James. Bobby Robson had let a potential legend go, far too easily, and too cheaply.

No way was James worth ten times as much as Hamilton.

Hamilton played fifty games for Northern Ireland, and after becoming Tranmere Rovers' player-manager in the Eighties, for five years, he was appointed as manager of Northern Ireland in 1994. Under his watch, **Norn Iron** just missed out on a Euro 96 Finals Play-off place, finishing behind the Republic on goal difference.

He left in 1997, after his country failed to qualify for France 98.

With the inclusion of new talents like Roger Osborne, John Peddelty, Terry Austin and Pat Sharkey, Ipswich enjoyed a Spring Uprising in 1976, the highlight of which was their 3-0 home win over FA Cup Finalists Manchester United.

Mick Lambert, Trevor Whymark and David Johnson all scored, with nearly 35,000 inside Portman Road, their biggest home crowd of the season by a long way. It was that defeat that realistically ended the First Division title hopes of a young, resurgent United team.

Ipswich finished in sixth place, but they missed out on a UEFA Cup place, when Southampton beat Man Utd 1-0 at Wembley.

In August 1976, Bob Paisley paid Ipswich a club record transfer fee of £200,000 for their centre forward David Johnson. Tottenham Hotspur had also offered an equivalent bid, but Johnson refused to go to White Hart Lane, holding out instead for a move to his hometown team, who he supported as a boy.

David Johnson had scored thirty-five goals in 143 First Division starts for Ipswich, but it was his devilish, dastardly, and dark moustached hard running into dangerous channels, creating space, and goals, for Whymark, Hamilton, Viljoen, Talbot and Lambert, that was far more valuable to Town's attacking machine, than his own individual goals return.

Johnson helped the Reds to the European Cup Final that season, but he lost his place to Jimmy Case, in Rome. He missed out again, at Wembley in 1978, as Liverpool defeated Bruges, but then he enjoyed the highlight of his career, in May 1981, as he played the whole match, as Liverpool beat Real Madrid 1-0 in Paris.

A second, superior wave of young talent emerged in 1976-77, as John Wark finally found a regular first team place, in midfield alongside Brian Talbot.

Eric Gates also started to play more regularly, mostly as a substitute, but in October, Bobby Robson paid a club record transfer fee of £220,000 for Plymouth Argyle's prolific goal-scorer Paul Mariner. John Peddelty and Terry Austin were sent to Devon as part of the deal.

Colin Viljoen never really recovered from his knee injury, and although he returned in December 1977, he was only deputising for John Wark, playing just ten matches, and he was left out of Ipswich Town's 1978 FA Cup Final team, against Arsenal.

After 305 league games for Town, scoring forty-five goals, Viljoen moved to Manchester City in 1978, but he didn't settle well, and he moved again, two years later, to Second Division side Chelsea.

At the height of his influence on matches, during May 1975, after Ipswich Town's Double near-miss, he played twice for England, their goalless draw away to Northern Ireland, and then their 2-2 home draw with Wales.

On the following Saturday, he was replaced in the team by QPR's Gerry Francis, as England hammered Scotland 5-1, and he was not selected by Don Revie, again.

But that wasn't necessarily a bad thing.

George Burley, Mick Mills, Brian Talbot, Allan Hunter, Kevin Beattie, Clive Woods and Mick Lambert were all regulars from 1974-75, who'd also played in Ipswich's famous 1978 Cup Final win over Arsenal.

Mick Lambert left Portman Road a year later, after eleven years at Portman Road, joining Peterborough United, where he played only twenty-one matches, before retiring. Lambert had scored thirty-nine First Division goals, from the left wing, in 210 games for Ipswich Town. He regularly returns to Portman Road, as an Ipswich supporter, and is also a registered player in the Suffolk Bowls League.

Trevor Whymark played 261 First Division matches during his ten years at Ipswich, and he scored seventy-five goals. Unfortunately, he was replaced by David Geddis, for the 1978 FA Cup Final, and doesn't even get a mention in Bobby Robson's autobiography.

"Whymark was the best player I've ever seen head a ball," Talksport's Alan Brazil said of his Ipswich Town attacking partner. "I mean, crikey! the power he got in his headers!" Whymark joined NASL side Vancouver Whitecaps, in 1979 and 1980, scoring prolifically, twenty-five goals in 57 games, and then he played for Grimsby Town and Southend, before retiring in the mid-Eighties.

Brian Talbot left Ipswich Town in January 1979, for Arsenal, for a club record £450,000 transfer fee, and he won the FA Cup for a second successive year, following the Gunners' dramatic 3-2 win over Manchester United.

Talbot had played 227 league and cup games for Ipswich, and he then played 254 First Division matches at Highbury, before moving to Watford in 1985.

When he finally left Watford, Brian Talbot had totalled 479 First Division matches, after thirteen seasons. He was appointed as West Bromwich Albion's manager in 1988, but was sacked following their FA Cup Third round 2-4 home defeat to non-league Woking, in January 1991.

In 1997, Brian Talbot was appointed manager of non-league Rushden and Diamonds, and he took the small Northants club up into the Football League in 2001.

Allan Hunter, **BIG** Allan Hunter, became Ipswich Town's most-capped player, with fifty-three games for Northern Ireland. He left Portman Road in 1982, after playing 280 First Division games for Ipswich. He was the big, bearded, broad-chested, tough man alongside the total footballer of Kevin Beattie. They were the best central defensive partnership in the First Division, between 1972 and 1975, alongside Derby's Roy McFarland and Colin Todd. In 2007 Allan Hunter was inducted into Ipswich Town's inaugural Hall of Fame, along with Mick Mills, Kevin Beattie, George Burley, and John Wark, as well as Billy Baxter.

When Terry Butcher first began to appear for Ipswich, during the Spring of 1978, he was playing a reserve team match at Portman Road, while Allan Hunter was watching from the stands. Butcher crossed himself, against his chest, prior to kick-off, so after the game, Hunter grabbed hold of Butcher, and he asked him if he was a catholic.

"No," Butcher replied. He was an English Protestant.

Allan Hunter told him, Terry Butcher, that he was never to cross himself again, before any match, ever again. He said that he would "really sort him out," if he ever saw him doing it again.

Terry Butcher was among the hardest men in Eighties football, a no-nonsense centre back who was heroic for both Ipswich and England, helping England qualify for Italia 90, against Sweden in November 1989, with blood streaming down from his head and all over his white England shirt.

But he yielded before the menace of Allan Hunter, so Hard was Hunter.

Terry Butcher never crossed his chest, again, before any games, throughout his career.

Kevin Beattie, Hunter's superlative partner in defence, was the quickest defender that Bobby Robson ever saw. He could run 100 yards, on grass, and in football boots, in just ten seconds.

Bobby Robson described Kevin Beattie as "the best English player produced in my time," better than Gascoigne, Hoddle, Beardsley, Beckham or Scholes.

Peter Taylor was also a huge admirer, and would have loved him at Forest.

He hated Beattie's bad luck, though.

"Boiling chip pans spill over him," Taylor said of Beattie.

"We never saw the best of him, for long enough periods."

Kevin Beattie also appeared in John Huston's film Escape to Victory, as an action double for Michael Caine. While relaxing on set, Sylvester Stallone challenged him to an arm-wrestling match, which Beattie easily won.

Stallone was so upset, he wouldn't talk to Beattie again for the remainder of the filming.

Kevin Beattie played 228 First Division matches for Ipswich, but he should have played over five hundred, considering he'd made his debut at just eighteen.

He missed too many matches through injury, and he would have played more games for England, too, but for a crisis of confidence that had caused him to go missing before an England friendly match in 1975.

Nevertheless, his central defensive partnership with Allan Hunter was the best in Ipswich Town's history, just edging the partnership that produced their second golden age, in the early Eighties, with Terry Butcher and Russell Osman.

Mick Mills left Ipswich Town in November 1982, joining Southampton in a £40,000 deal. He'd played 591 First Division matches at Portman Road, and had also captained England during the 1982 World Cup Finals, in Spain.

He was awarded the MBE in 1984, and he played over a hundred First Division games for Southampton, including thirty-four during 1983-84, when the Saints finished the season as runners-up to Champions Liverpool, and also reached the FA Cup Semi-finals. They lost in extra-time, to Everton, after Adrian Heath's late goal.

Mick Mills and George Burley were the greatest ever full-back partnership in Ipswich Town's history. George Burley left Ipswich for Sunderland in 1985, after the Rokerites had been relegated to the Second Division. During his twelve years at Portman Road, Burley had played 394 First Division games, while also winning the FA Cup in 1978, but he was injured for the UEFA Cup Final, three years later.

In December 1994, Burley was appointed as manager of Ipswich, and he spent eight years in charge of the club. He led Town to four successive Premier League play-off places from 1997, losing three of them, to Sheffield United, Charlton Athletic and Bolton Wanderers, before they finally defeated Barnsley 4-2, on Bank Holiday Monday 29th May 2000, with 73,427 inside Wembley Stadium.

George Burley's Ipswich then finished fifth in their first season back in the Premier League, in 2001, missing out on a Champions League place by just two points to Leeds United. The following season was more difficult, though, despite their decent UEFA Cup run, and Ipswich were relegated again.

On Friday 11th October 2002, George Burley was sacked by Ipswich Town.

Of 413 matches with Burley in charge, Ipswich won 188, and lost just 129, with a winning percentage of 45%. He was the longest serving manager at Portman Road since Bobby Robson, and Ipswich have failed to really replace him, ever since.

Bobby Robson left Ipswich Town during the Summer of 1982, to become the new England boss. Robson oversaw a colourful reign as England manager, failing to qualify for the 1984 European Championships, before enjoying an eventful, but eventually bitter exit from the 1986 Mexico World Cup Finals. England produced a dreadful performance in the 1988 European Championships, before just scraping into the Italia 90 World Cup Finals.

Bobby Robson moulded the crème de la crème of his managerial career, while in Italy. He fielded the wonderful midfield unit of Trevor Steven, Paul Gascoigne, David Platt and Chris Waddle, behind their World class front two of Lineker and Beardsley.

At their best, they were as good as any of Sir Alf Ramsey's England teams, while at their worst, they were lucky. It was a terrific combination, and England really looked like World Cup winners, once again… until their luck ran out in their Semi-final penalty shoot-out, against the West Germans.

To this day, England have failed to field a team as good as that team in Turin.

At the end of his eight year reign, Bobby Robson was the best England manager since Sir Alf Ramsey, and he still is.

Paul Cooper played 550 league and cup games as Ipswich Town's goalkeeper, between 1974 and 1987. He is regarded as the greatest-ever goalkeeper in the club's history, even though Laurie Sivell was in goal during 1974-75, when Ipswich should have won the Double.

John Wark played 266 league matches for Ipswich, scoring 94 goals, before a big money move to Liverpool in 1984. He played at Anfield for four years, before returning to Ipswich Town in 1988, but then he left Portman Road again, two years later, for Middlesbrough.

Wark returned to Ipswich Town, for a second time, in 1991, and he was their captain when they became inaugural members of the English Premier League in 1992.

John Wark played his last-ever league game for Ipswich in November 1996, aged thirty-nine, nearly twenty-three years after his debut.

In 1981, Wark had also appeared in John Huston's film Escape to Victory, as well as several other Ipswich Town players, and he was given one famous line of dialogue, during the film.

"I'll take the top bunk," he said.

At the Premier showing of the film, the entire Ipswich team went along to watch, with John Wark, and he'd been telling them all of his one line in the film, alongside Michael Caine, Sylvester Stallone and Max von Sydow. They all found it, then, absolutely hilarious when they saw that his voice had been dubbed by a posh Scottish voice.

The film-makers had found Wark's hard accent just a little too Glaswegian to understand.

John Wark scored a total of 135 league goals for Ipswich, in 509 matches, over his three spells at Portman Road. He also scored seven goals for Scotland, in twenty-nine international appearances, including two goals during the 1982 World Cup Finals, against New Zealand.

Bobby Robson won two Dutch League titles with PSV Eindhoven, in 1991 and 1992, and then he won the European Cup Winners' Cup, with Barcelona, in 1997.

In September 1999, though, he returned to the hearts of English people, when he was appointed as Newcastle United's new manager, at sixty-six years of age.

Newcastle were a fading force after the wonderful Keegan years, but Ruud Gullit, in particular, had been a disastrous Newcastle manager. He'd refused to give Robert Lee a squad number, and he also dropped Alan Shearer.

Newcastle were bottom of the Premier League when Bobby Robson arrived.

Bobby Robson immediately gave Robert Lee a squad number, 37, and he reinstated Alan Shearer to the team. Newcastle United subsequently thrashed Sheffield Wednesday 8-0, their all-time record top flight victory, as Robson guided them to a safe mid-table position, while also winning the February 2000 Manager of the Month award, along the way.

Newcastle finished in eleventh place, but they'd scored sixty-three goals, the third-highest scoring team in the Premier League. The Magpies again finished eleventh, in 2000-01, before qualifying for a UEFA Champions League place at the end of the following 2001-02 season, after finishing fourth.

In the 2002-03 UEFA Champions League competition, the Toon Army were drawn in Group E, a tough draw for Bobby Robson's bottom-seeded Newcastle, against Juventus, Dynamo Kiev and Feyenoord, all former European Cup winners.

After losing away in Kiev and Turin, both 2-0 defeats, and 1-0 at home to Feyenoord, Newcastle were bottom of the group, four points beneath third-placed Feyenoord.

Gerry Boland said that Newcastle were "an embarrassment to all English teams in the Champions League."

Newcastle then beat Juventus 1-0 at St James's Park, on Tuesday 1st October. Full back Andy Griffin had scored with a sharp drive from the right, to only just keep alive their Champions League hopes, but then, they also beat Dynamo Kiev 2-1, on Tuesday 29th October.

Bobby Robson's Newcastle went to Rotterdam on Wednesday 13th November 2002, not only needing to beat Feyenoord, but they were also reliant on Juventus winning away in Ukraine.

Juve did win 2-1, but United, having stormed to a 2-0 lead during the second half, were then pegged back, and they were drawing 2-2 after ninety minutes.

Then, after a minute into stoppage time, Craig *Bellamy!* smashed home a great strike from a narrow angle, sending Newcastle United into the last sixteen of the UEFA Champions League. It was the most dramatic comeback in the history of the Champions' League group stages, and the most euphoric moment of Sir Bobby Robson's managerial career, since Italia 90.

Bobby Robson had been knighted during the Queen's Golden Jubilee celebrations, in June 2002, but he was also awarded the freedom of the city of Newcastle upon Tyne, that same year.

In 2002-03, Newcastle finished third in the Premier League, and again qualified for the Champions League. They failed to win their qualifying round match, however, and had to settle for a place in the UEFA Cup.

Sir Bobby Robson then guided his Newcastle side past NAC Breda, Basel, Valerenga, Real Mallorca, and then his old club PSV Eindhoven, to reach the UEFA Cup Semi-finals, United's best season in European competitions, since 1969.

Two goals from Didier Drogba helped Marseille past Newcastle, into the Final, and at the end of August 2004, after a disappointing start to the season, Sir Bobby Robson was sacked by Newcastle United. In 2003-04, they had finished fifth, again qualifying for the UEFA Cup.

Sir Bobby Robson died, aged seventy-six, on Friday 31st July 2009, after years of battling an aggressive form of cancer, and beating many of them.

It's one of those moments where you remember where you were, exactly, when you heard of major news events. I'm too young to remember Kennedy's death, but I do remember precisely where I was when I heard about Hillsborough in 1989, Elvis's death, and also the 9/11 attacks.

When I heard about Sir Bobby Robson's death, I was between Poplars Farm and Verney Farm Cottage, in Kimblewick, Bucks, delivering mail. I had to stop the van, on the lane, to shed some tears. In fact, I cried several times that day.

I'm crying again, as I write this.

On the following day, Saturday 1st August, during their pre-season friendly away at Celtic Park, Sunderland fans clapped, and sang vociferously, "there's only one Bobby Robson!" to the tune of Guantanamera, in a standing ovation and applause of the former manager of their fiercest, most-hated rivals.

The standards of either Newcastle or Sunderland fans have not sunk so low, that they will attempt to wreck a moment of respect for the legend of a rival team, as some other teams' fans have done recently, but to show such loud respect and love of a man who managed Newcastle, the Sunderland fans not only illustrated their absolute class, but the affection that fans, from all over Europe, had held for Sir Bobby.

On Tuesday 16th July 2002, Ipswich Town had unveiled a statue of Sir Bobby, outside the Cobbold Stand, at Portman Road. John Cobbold, Mr John, was the greatest-ever chairman of Ipswich, during their three greatest eras, before he died in the early Eighties. It was very appropriate that Bobby was situated there.

On Saturday 26th September 2009, the North Stand at Portman Road was named the Sir Bobby Robson Stand. He'd also been awarded the freedom of the town of Ipswich, a year before his death.

In the history of English football, Bobby Robson was right up there with the very best: Shankly, Busby, Clough, Ramsey, Revie and even Ferguson.

The one and only trouble with Sir Bobby was that he didn't give his Ipswich team from 1972-75 enough credit. His 1978 team had won the Cup, and his 1981 team had won the UEFA Cup, and they'd also finished second in the First Division, so he gave those teams all the praise in his autobiography.

In 1981, Ipswich won 23 league games, and they finished second, four points behind Aston Villa, but back in 1975, they also won 23 games, and finished third, just two points behind Derby County, and behind Liverpool on goal average.

Ipswich would have won the league back in 1975, under a three points-for-a-win system, but in 1981, under a three points-for-a-win system, they would have finished seven points behind Champions Aston Villa.

And during their 1978 FA Cup run, Ipswich scraped past Second Division relegation battlers Cardiff City, and then Fourth Division re-election candidates Hartlepool, and Second Division relegation strugglers Bristol Rovers, before hammering a very poor, second-from-bottom Second Division Millwall side, 6-1 in the Quarter-finals.

They finally faced a decent team, West Brom, in the Semi-finals, winning 3-1 at Highbury, before then hammering Arsenal 1-0 at Wembley.

Back in 1975, Ipswich won away, at mid-table First Division side Wolves, before beating the title favourites Liverpool 1-0, at Portman Road, in the Fourth round. They then completed their dramatic, and classic, comeback 3-2 win over League Cup Finalists Aston Villa, before their four game epic triumph over eventual European Cup Finalists Leeds United in the Quarter-finals.

After a replay, and also Bryan Hamilton's controversially disallowed goal, against West Ham United, they finally exited the FA Cup in the Semi-Finals, after nine tough, tough matches, having faced five teams who were all First Division teams during the following 1975-76 season.

Ipswich's 1975 team was a better team than their 1978 Cup-winning team, and they were definitely at least as good as their 1981 team, but **probably** better, in my opinion.

What Bobby Robson's 1972-75 Ipswich Town team brought to English football was a great team built entirely on youth, plus the odd bargain purchase, that laid the firmest foundations for longevity, and future major successes in rural Suffolk.

In the beautiful land of Constable Country, Bobby Robson had developed a masterpiece by 1974, that will, maybe, never be faked.

A TALE OF TWO UNITEDS, Part Three

ON WEDNESDAY 3RD JANUARY 1973, Manchester United's eighteen year old attacking midfield playmaker Sammy McIlroy sustained serious injuries in a car accident, and he missed the remainder of the season. In truth, he wouldn't have started too many matches, with Bobby Charlton, George Best, Ian Moore, Willie Morgan and Lou Macari filling all the attacking roles. But McIlroy was back, by the start of 1973-74, with both Charlton and Best gone, and Moore seriously injured.

After losing 3-0 away at Arsenal on the opening day of the season, during which McIlroy had replaced the young, long haired debutant Gerry Daly, he started, out on the left wing, for Manchester United's 1-0 home win over Stoke City.

Sammy McIlroy then scored the winner, during their 2-1 win over newly promoted QPR, on Saturday 1st September, after Jim Holton's header had equalised Gerry Francis' opening goal.

One week later, Brian Greenhoff, the younger brother of Stoke City's star player Jimmy Greenhoff, made his Manchester United debut, in central defence, after being promoted from their youth team.

Bobby Robson's young Ipswich Town team won 2-1, though, and Sammy McIlroy suffered a nasty leg injury, that kept him out of action until the middle of December.

Ian Moore returned to the team as Manchester United hosted Leicester City, on Wednesday 12th September, but the Foxes won 2-1, after Mike Stringfellow and Keith Weller had scored in each half. Moore kept his place for their home match against West Ham, three days later, and he'd scored the second goal in their 3-1 win, while Brian Kidd scored a brace.

Ian Moore suffered complications to his recurrent knee injury, though, and three months later, after receiving medical advice, Manchester United's most expensive-ever player was forced to retire from football at just twenty-eight years of age.

After his move from Nottingham Forest, Ian Moore had scored just eleven goals from 39 First Division games, for a mostly-struggling Manchester United team.

It could actually be whispered that perhaps Brian Clough was right, and he should have signed for Derby County.

More to the point, the loss of both Moore and McIlroy left Tommy Docherty short of creative talents. In fact, he felt he had no talent at all to supply the front runners Macari and Kidd. He met with his assistant Pat Crerand, as well as Sir Matt Busby, to discuss a real possibility of George Best returning to the club. Without any service from midfield, Manchester United faced another desperate relegation dog fight.

George Best and Tommy Docherty met in September 1973, with George admitting that he'd love to return to the club. The Doc was delighted, and welcomed him back, but he assured Best that this would be his one and only chance.

George Best returned to the Manchester United training ground, and he underwent a month of hard training, before a friendly match was finally arranged, away at Irish League side Shamrock Rovers, on Monday 15th October.

In front of a capacity crowd of 25,000 packing Glenmalure Park, on the Southside of Dublin, George Best was brilliant, *scintillating* even, scoring twice for a 2-1 United lead, before the game was abandoned with just ten minutes remaining, as thousands of kids just couldn't control themselves any longer, and they spontaneously invaded the pitch to congratulate him.

Bestie was back.

Leeds United were fined £3,000 in July 1973 by the FA, for their previous bad behaviour, and their general on-field misdemeanours. The fine was suspended for a year, though, to be revised after an assessment of their players' future conduct.

It was a slap in the face, after their behaviour towards opponents and referees had improved in 1972-73, and they'd only just been the victims of Milan's bullying tactics in the Cup Winners' Cup Final. Brian Clough, the manager of Derby County, had failed to see it like that, though.

Clough had a written rant published in the Sunday Express, with a huge headline spread across the back page, claiming that the FA had let Leeds United off, and that they should have been relegated.

It would be fair to assume that Brian Clough wouldn't be very welcome at Elland Road for a long while.

A NEW LEAF

Even so, the public pillorying of Leeds United, during that Summer of 1973, had left Don Revie conscience-stricken for three days. After their defeat to Sunderland, in the FA Cup Final, Revie promised he'd train them harder than ever, and he certainly did.

Leeds United organised practise matches, where coaches acted as referees, and they deliberately gave wrong decisions to provoke argument. At first, the players shouted back and went mad, but they kept being reminded that these were the sorts of decisions they'd face, and would have to accept all season.

These types of matches were repeated and repeated and repeated.

It was *Classic Pavlovian Conditioning* on a football pitch, and by the time pre-season training ended, Leeds United were fitter than they'd been for years, and they weren't bothered about refereeing decisions anymore. They just got on with their games.

Leeds United won their first seven First Division matches of 1973-74, scoring nineteen goals, and conceding just four.

Centre back Gordon McQueen, their £30,000 signing from St Mirren in September 1972, had played only six matches during 1972-73, but he became Norman Hunter's regular partner in central defence in August 1973.

On Saturday 22nd September, Leeds United hosted Manchester United, with over 47,000, Elland Road's biggest crowd of the season, roaring on the league leaders.

Manchester United bore an almost entirely different look to the team that lost their epic 1970 FA Cup Semi-final, just three and a half years before, while Leeds United had seven survivors, but Peter Lorimer and Terry Cooper were both out injured, while Mick Bates wasn't selected.

LEEDS UNITED		MANCHESTER UNITED
David Harvey	1	Alex Stepney
Trevor Cherry	2	Martin Buchan
Paul Madeley	3	Tony Young
Billy Bremner	4	Brian Greenhoff
Gordon McQueen	5	Jim Holton
Norman Hunter	6	Steve James
Joe Jordan	7	Willie Morgan
Allan Clarke	8	Trevor Anderson
Mick Jones	9	Lou Macari
Johnny Giles	10	Brian Kidd
Eddie Gray	11	George Graham

Despite their lowly position of fourteenth place, Manchester United had plenty of battlers, with Buchan, Greenhoff, Holton, Macari, Kidd, Morgan and George Graham, ready to raise themselves for big games like this, against their fierce, old rivals.

For the first time, and the only time, during their opening fourteen league games, Leeds United failed to score, as Manchester United hung on for a goalless draw.

On the following Wednesday, players from the two Uniteds, both old and new, united to help Scotland qualify for the 1974 World Cup Finals, their first major tournament for sixteen years.

Billy Bremner, Jim Holton, Willie Morgan, Denis Law and Joe Jordan, as well as Tommy Hutchison of Coventry, complemented an otherwise Scottish League composed team, as they beat Czechoslovakia 2-1, with 100,000 packed inside Hampden Park.

Manchester United's Jim Holton and Leeds United's Joe Jordan scored the goals that sent Scotland to Dortmund and Frankfurt.

Leeds United continued their unbeaten run, through October and November, and into darkest December. On Saturday 8th December, they faced a dangerous Ipswich Town side, at Portman Road, with the home team challenging for a UEFA Cup place.

A win, or a draw, for United, would equal the twenty-four year old record for an unbeaten nineteen match start to a First Division season. Wearing yellow, Leeds United took the lead when Terry Yorath lobbed in a long range shot that clipped the crossbar as it came down behind keeper Laurie Sivell.

Terry Yorath's left wing cross was powerfully headed in off the far post by Mick Jones, before, in the 88th minute, Allan Clarke scored the best goal of the match. Receiving the ball from Billy Bremner, he rode Mick Mills' heavy thump, then ran between both Viljoen and Hamilton, before firing inside Sivell's near post from outside of the penalty area.

A week later, nearly 41,000 filled Stamford Bridge, and Joe Jordan and Mick Jones both scored as Leeds United beat Chelsea 2-1 to set a new record of twenty games unbeaten from the start of a First Division season.

After beating Norwich City, on the Saturday before Christmas, Leeds United led the First Division by seven points on Christmas Day 1973, but with the reigning Champions Liverpool lurking behind in second place, and Leeds United had let slip similar leads over the past three seasons.

FIRST DIVISION LEADERS, SATURDAY 22ND DECEMBER 1973

	PL	W	D	L	F	A	PTS
LEEDS UNITED	21	15	6	0	40	11	36
Liverpool	21	12	5	4	27	16	29
Burnley	20	10	6	4	27	19	26
Derby County	21	9	6	6	24	20	24
Leicester City	21	8	7	6	26	22	23
QPR	21	7	9	5	33	28	23

On Saturday 20th October 1973, a heavily bearded George Best returned to Manchester United's team, for the first time in nearly eleven months, and a penalty kick taken by goalkeeper Alex Stepney secured a tight 1-0 win over Birmingham City, with 49,000 inside Old Trafford.

Manchester United rose a couple of places, up to eighteenth, but George Best's return was a mere placebo to placate their fans. He lacked the same deeply-ground degree of hunger for success, as before, and his contribution was lacking imagination. Nearly fifty thousand had turned up for his first game back, but by the end of the year, only 36,000 were bothering to show up to see his standard, run of the mill displays.

On Thursday 27th December 1973, Tommy Docherty paid Brentford £55,000 for Argyll-born defender Stewart Houston, continuing his Scottish influx at Old Trafford. A tall full-back, at nearly six foot, Houston made his Manchester United debut on New Year's Day, and he kept his place at left back for the rest of the season.

Alex Forsyth, who Docherty had bought over a year earlier, had a Glaswegian accent so hard, that neither Docherty, Houston, Holton, nor Buchan could ever understand. Forsyth, however, became Manchester United's regular right back, from mid-January.

Manchester United became the first team to field an entirely Scottish back four in the First Division.

On Friday 4th January 1974, George Best failed to turn up for training, yet again, and one week later, Manchester United suspended him for two weeks, and transfer-listed him for good. His Manchester United career was finally over.

Bestie had played his final match for the team during their 3-0 defeat away at QPR on New Year's Day. He'd scored 179 goals in 470 league and cup games for Manchester United, in over eleven years. Those statistics don't do him justice, though.

That defeat at QPR, George Best's final game for Manchester United, had dropped them into the bottom three, and triggered a terrible run of just one win in eleven First Division matches, that sunk them right down to the bottom of the table.

George Best's impact on the team, back in their greatest years, was electrically charged, when every match was a Best match; when he could draw rapturous applause from the Kop, after single-handedly beating Liverpool at Anfield, back in 1967. He scored six goals at Northampton Town, in a 1972 FA Cup match, after the Cobblers had taken the lead. His two headed goals, three right-footed strikes, and a left-footed finish had given him a golden, perfect, double hat-trick.

Sadly, many of the tapes, which contained some of his finest moments, were erased by both the BBC and ITV. That act of erasure remains, whatever the demands were, a crime against art.

George Best was, and always will be, Manchester United's greatest-ever player.

Duncan Edwards, before Best, had died too young, while Paul Scholes, Ryan Giggs, Wayne Rooney, Cristiano Ronaldo and Eric Cantona all received deserved acclaim during the Premier League era, but Best was still the best.

Tommy Docherty said of Bestie, "one of (his) problems was he was a light sleeper. When it got light, he went home and went to sleep." George Best made a comeback with Stockport County, in November 1975, and he even scored on his debut, their winning goal at home to Swansea City, with the 9,220 Edgeley Park crowd tripling County's average attendance.

Best scored two goals in three matches for Stockport, but then he was gone.

During the late Seventies, he also played for Fulham and Hibernian, but he felt more at home in the NASL, with the pace of the game, and the naïve standards of defending best illuminating his ageing talent. He played for six seasons in the United States, with Los Angeles, Fort Lauderdale and San Jose. George Best's alcoholism, though, caused him great embarrassment, and huge troubles, both physically and legally, throughout his life, after his football career.

At 1255 hours GMT, on Friday 25th November 2005, having spent eight weeks in London's Cromwell Hospital, George Best died, aged only fifty-nine, after multiple organ failure, caused by a kidney infection.

Manchester United unveiled a statue of *"the Holy Trinity,"* Best, Charlton and Law, outside their East Stand at Old Trafford, on Thursday 29th May 2008.

In the UEFA Cup, in November, Leeds United had scraped past a truly great Hibernian side, including such legends as Pat Stanton, Arthur Duncan, Alex Cropley, John Blackley, Eric Schaedler, Jim McArthur and Des Bremner. Bremner actually went on to win a European Cup winners' medal with Aston Villa, in 1982, but Pat Stanton was Hibs' greatest ever player, after their *Famous Five* of the Forties and Fifties.

Over 36,000 had totally packed Easter Road, on Wednesday 7th November, and watched their green and white army brilliantly hold the runaway English First Division leaders to a 0-0 aggregate draw, but Leeds United eventually went through to the Third round, after a 5-4 penalty shootout win.

Vitoria Setubal knocked Leeds United out of the UEFA Cup, 3-2 on aggregate, during December, but by playing Ellam, Hampton, Mann, Liddell, and a young Frankie Gray, in the away leg, Revie clearly demonstrated where his priorities laid.

In the FA Cup Third round, Leeds United eliminated Wolves, after a replay, and then they outclassed Peterborough United. Lorimer, Jordan (2), and Yorath all scored first half goals, sending Leeds towards an easy 4-0 half-time lead, and an eventual 4-1 away win, in front of a massive 28,000 London Road crowd.

Back in the First Division, Leeds United continued their unbeaten run, right through January 1974, drawing with Spurs and Everton, but then beating Southampton 2-1 (Mick Jones, Joe Jordan).

Trevor Cherry then rescued a point, at home to Chelsea, after Bill Garner had given the Blues a 1-0 half-time lead, on Saturday 2nd February.

Three days later, at home to Arsenal, Leeds United were again losing 1-0 at half-time, to Alan Ball's early goal. Joe Jordan headed in two more goals, though, after the break, as well as Peter Simpson's unfortunate own goal, and Leeds went on to win 3-1.

60,025, the biggest First Division crowd of the 1973-74, filled Old Trafford on Saturday 9th February, as the runaway leaders Leeds United visited second-bottom Manchester United, for their twenty-ninth game of the season.

MANCHESTER UNITED		LEEDS UNITED
Alex Stepney	1	David Harvey
Martin Buchan	2	Paul Reaney
Stewart Houston	3	Trevor Cherry
Brian Greenhoff	4	Billy Bremner
Jim Holton	5	Gordon McQueen
Steve James	6	Norman Hunter
Willie Morgan	7	Peter Lorimer
Lou Macari	8	Allan Clarke
Brian Kidd	9	Mick Jones
Tony Young	10	Terry Yorath
Alex Forsyth	11	Paul Madeley
Sammy McIlroy	12	Joe Jordan

By packing his midfield with defensive players, Greenhoff, Forsyth and Young, Tommy Docherty made it very tough for Leeds United, and it looked as if Manchester United would repeat the goalless draw that they'd battled for, back in September.

With the scores still goalless in the second half, Don Revie upped his formation, though, sending on Jordan for Reaney. With the opposition keeping eight men behind the ball, why would he need a back four? Leeds United immediately benefitted from the change. Mick Jones capitalised on a defensive error to score from the edge of the area, before Joe Jordan fired Yorath's pass beyond Stepney, to finish off their 2-0 win.

FIRST DIVISION LEADERS, 9TH FEBRUARY 1974

	PL	W	D	L	F	A	PTS
LEEDS UNITED	29	19	10	0	51	16	48
Liverpool	28	16	7	5	37	23	39
Ipswich Town	28	13	6	9	47	42	32
Derby County	28	11	9	8	33	26	31
Everton	28	11	9	8	30	27	31

Leeds United now led the First Division by nine points.

In the FA Cup Fifth round, 37,000 went wild at Bristol City's Ashton Gate, as Keith Fear flicked Gerry Gow's through-ball, from out of the mud, over David Harvey, to equalise Billy Bremner's early opener.

Three days later, on the afternoon of Tuesday 19th February, the Robins again played superbly in front of a 47,182 Elland Road crowd, Leeds United's biggest crowd of the season, and Don Gillies outpaced Terry Cooper, smashing home a shock late winner for City.

It was back to business as usual in the First Division, though, on the following Saturday, away at lowly Stoke City, as Billy Bremner and Allan Clarke gave Leeds United an early 2-0 lead.

In front of nearly 40,000, the Victoria Ground's biggest crowd of the season, however, Mike Pejic pulled a goal back, and then Alan Hudson equalised for Stoke, just before half-time. After

Leeds United lost Johnny Giles, again to injury, having only just started his first game since October, Denis Smith finished off a dramatic comeback, firing home for a 3-2 win over the leaders.

The defeat at home to Bristol City, followed by their first league defeat of the season, in their thirtieth match, as well as losing Johnny Giles for another five weeks, unsettled Leeds United, and their winning rhythm suddenly disappeared.

They could only draw at home to both Leicester City and Newcastle United, before Peter Lorimer's penalty kick secured a scrappy and edgy home 1-0 win over relegation strugglers Manchester City, on Saturday 9th March.

March 1974 was an awful month for Leeds United. In the crunch game of the year, the Match of the Season, Liverpool v Leeds United, Steve Heighway delighted the 56,003 Anfield crowd, with an elegant finish, for a 1-0 Liverpool victory.

The gap at the top of the First Division had been reduced to just six points, but Liverpool still had two games in hand over the leaders.

Even worse, a week later, Burnley totally thrashed Leeds United 4-1 at Elland Road, stunning their 39,335 home crowd, and then to really finish the month off terribly, Clyde Best, Pop Robson and Trevor Brooking all scored in West Ham United's 3-1 win over Leeds at Upton Park, on Saturday 30th March.

Their lead at the top was just four points by the end of March, but Liverpool had played three games less.

FIRST DIVISION LEADERS, 30TH MARCH 1974

	PL	W	D	L	F	A	PTS
LEEDS UNITED	36	20	12	4	58	29	52
Liverpool	33	20	8	5	41	23	48
Derby County	36	14	14	8	45	33	42
Ipswich Town	36	15	10	11	59	52	40
QPR	34	12	15	7	50	41	39

With Manchester United bottom of the league on Saturday 23rd March, and totally detached from safety, Tommy Docherty recalled Gerry Daly from the reserves. The nineteen year old playmaker had signed from League of Ireland club Bohemians a year earlier, but now was his time, and he became a key first team player thereafter.

Docherty had also signed former Scottish international midfielder Jim McCalliog from Wolves, for £60,000, on Thursday 14th March.

McCalliog was twenty-seven years old, and he'd been Wolves' captain in the 1972 UEFA Cup Final. With both Daly and McCalliog in their midfield, Manchester United began to play more like a team at the top of the league, for the following month.

Their main problem had been scoring goals. Manchester United had scored just twenty-five in thirty-three First Division matches, and by Christmas 1973, goalkeeper Alex Stepney was actually their joint top goal-scorer with two goals.

FIRST DIVISION BOTTOM FIVE, 23RD MARCH 1974

	PL	W	D	L	F	A	PTS
Southampton	35	10	11	14	40	56	31
West Ham	35	9	11	15	44	53	29
Birmingham	34	9	9	16	38	55	27
Norwich City	35	6	13	16	33	50	25
MAN UTD	33	6	10	17	25	40	22

On Saturday 30th March, Manchester United won 3-1 away at Chelsea. Willie Morgan, Gerry Daly and Sammy McIlroy had all scored to spark a mini-revival.

Four days later, on Wednesday 3rd April, McIlroy scored again, with defenders Alex Forsyth and Jim Holton adding second half goals in their thrilling 3-3 home draw against UEFA Cup hopefuls Burnley. On the following Saturday, Lou Macari and Brian Greenhoff both scored second half goals in a 2-0 away win at Norwich City.

A week later, on Saturday 13th April, Jim McCalliog scored his first goal for Manchester United, during their 1-0 win over FA Cup Finalists Newcastle United.

By Easter Bank Holiday Monday, Manchester United were only three points below safety, as Everton visited Old Trafford.

It was a bustling and classy performance, in front of their 48,424 home crowd. McCalliog's pedigree ran Everton's back four ragged, giving Darracott, particularly, a torrid time. McCalliog opened the scoring, in the first half, with a sharp strike from the edge of the penalty area, beating Lawson's dive, and sending the ball flying into the bottom right corner of the goal.

MANCHESTER UNITED		EVERTON
Alex Stepney	1	Dave Lawson
Tony Young	2	Terry Darracott
Stewart Houston	3	Steve Seargeant
Brian Greenhoff	4	David Clements
Jim Holton	5	Roger Kenyon
Martin Buchan	6	John Hurst
Willie Morgan	7	Mike Bernard
Lou Macari	8	Mick Buckley
Sammy McIlroy	9	Bob Latchford
Jim McCalliog	10	Mike Lyons
Gerry Daly	11	George Telfer

Full back Stewart Houston added a second before half-time, and then McCalliog made it three, before the end, 3-0 to United. The introduction of both McCalliog and Daly had transformed the previously goal-shy strugglers into a goal scoring machine. During their last five games, nine different players had scored a total of twelve goals for Manchester United, and they'd gained nine points.

With a game in hand over nineteenth-placed Southampton, and with a far superior goal average, Manchester United could actually touch safety, with just four games remaining.

FIRST DIVISION BOTTOM FOUR, 15TH APRIL 1974

	PL	W	D	L	F	A	PTS
Southampton	39	10	13	16	43	64	33
MAN UTD	38	10	11	17	37	44	31
Birmingham	38	10	11	17	43	60	31
Norwich City	38	6	14	18	34	56	26

On the following Saturday, away at Southampton, with nearly 31,000 inside The Dell, Jim McCalliog fired home his fourth goal in three games, from the penalty spot, before half-time, but Mike Channon, the First Division's top goal-scorer in 1973-74, equalised after the break, and United were held to a 1-1 draw.

A win would have been ideal, but an away draw wasn't such a bad result. Manchester United's unbeaten run had been extended to six matches, and they still had a game in hand on the Saints, with survival well in their own hands.

That changed on the following Tuesday, St George's Day, as Everton gained revenge for their hammering at Old Trafford, three weeks earlier. Mike Lyons headed a late goal for a 1-0 win, to greatly reduce Manchester United's survival hopes, especially after Birmingham City had thrashed QPR 4-0 on the same night.

United were now three points below safety. They still had a game in hand, but with only two games remaining, time was running out. Their penultimate game of the 1973-74 season, on the final Saturday of the season, was at home to neighbours Manchester City.

The mathematics were simple. Firstly, Manchester United had to win. Secondly, both Southampton and Birmingham had to draw, at best, although defeats for both teams would've been better. They then needed to beat Stoke City away, on the following Mayday Bank Holiday Monday, but their destiny was out of their hands.

Nearly 57,000 filled Old Trafford, on Saturday 27th April 1974, on a dramatic afternoon, but the game was heading for a goalless draw, with five minutes remaining. A right-side cross flashed into the United area, and Denis Law, in sky blue, back-heeled the ball with his back to goal.

The ball beat Alex Stepney, and rolled into the corner of the net. Law, who'd been released by Tommy Docherty only a year earlier, was swamped by his City teammates, but he was gutted and just walked back to his own half, close to tears, with his arms down by his sides, as each City player came to hug him and pat him on his back.

Hooligans then invaded the pitch, from the Scoreboard End, and the match was abandoned, but the result stood.

Denis Law thought that he had relegated his old team, but he hadn't.

Southampton had beaten Everton 3-0, but Birmingham City had also beaten Norwich City 2-1, thereby relegating both Southampton and Manchester United, along with Norwich, even if United had won.

On the following Monday, Stoke City beat Manchester United 1-0, and they were headed for Second Division football for the first time since 1936. Goal-scoring had been their problem for most of the season, recording less than a goal per game for the first and only time in their history. Sammy McIlroy was their top scorer with just six league goals, followed by Lou Macari on five.

Defensively, though, they were sound. They'd conceded just 48 goals, the lowest total of any relegated First Division team, ever, and they'd kept fourteen clean sheets. They had a settled back four by the end of the season, with Forsyth, Holton, Buchan and Houston, and also midfield youngsters McIlroy and Daly were emerging.

After their 1-4 home defeat to Burnley, Brian James wrote in The Sunday Times, "Leeds United were haunted by doubt, undermined by misunderstandings… their morale was on the verge of destruction." Going into April, Liverpool were the bookmakers' new favourites for the title, but sometimes, it requires the influence of outside forces to jolt a great team back to being good again.

On Saturday 6th April, third-placed Derby County arrived at Elland Road, in Leicester City dark blue shirts, sensing the blood of Leeds. They were mistaken.

Joe Jordan flicked the ball to Billy Bremner, and Bremner released Lorimer, on the run, into the Derby penalty area. Peter Lorimer outmuscled Peter Daniel, and chipped the ball over Colin Boulton, from twelve yards.

That was Lorimer's first league goal from open play since Saturday 8th September.

Billy Bremner then volleyed home, from the edge of the area, after Trevor Cherry's long free-kick, late on in the second half, for a crucial 2-0 win. Liverpool had also beaten QPR 2-1 at Anfield, though, to keep the pressure on Leeds United.

The pressure that had almost buried Leeds United, though, then twisted its weight towards Liverpool. First, Terry Nicholl scored his first, and only First Division goal for Sheffield United in his brief top flight career, as the Blades beat Liverpool 1-0 on Monday 8th April, with nearly 32,000 inside Bramall Lane.

On Good Friday, Liverpool blew another of their games in hand, when they drew 1-1 away at Manchester City, after Francis Lee equalised Peter Cormack's first half goal. On the following after-noon, Liverpool were held to another 1-1 draw by third-placed Ipswich Town, at Portman Road, just as Leeds United were held to a goalless draw at Coventry City.

Liverpool were three points behind Leeds United, but with only one game in hand.

On Easter Monday, 15th April, Sheffield United held Leeds to another goalless draw, provid-ing Liverpool with another great chance to catch the leaders. Liverpool were four points behind Leeds United, with two games in hand, but with a hugely inferior goal average.

On the following night, both Liverpool and Leeds United played, Liverpool at home to Man City, and Leeds away at Sheffield United. At half-time, Liverpool were thrashing Manchester City 4-0, while at Bramall Lane, Sheffield United were holding Leeds to a goalless draw, roared on by a forty thousand home crowd. Two second half goals from Peter Lorimer, though, rescued Leeds after the break, one from the penalty spot, and the other blasted in with Allan Clarke standing in an off-side position, but not interfering with play. Leeds United travelled home, back up the M1, as strong favourites for the First Division title, again.

FIRST DIVISION LEADERS, TUESDAY 16TH APRIL 1974

	PL	W	D	L	F	A	PTS
LEEDS UNITED	40	22	14	4	62	29	58
Liverpool	38	22	10	6	49	27	54

On the following Saturday, 20th April, Liverpool were held to a 0-0 draw by neighbours Ever-ton, with nearly 56,000 packed into Anfield, while Leeds United beat Ipswich Town 3-2, (Peter Lorimer's blast, and then an off-side Billy Bremner tap-in put them 2-0 up. But Ipswich came back fluently, drawing level after the break, before Allan Clarke's hand-balled shot past Sivell). After Snif-fer's fortuitous winner, there was a tremendous, euphoric buzz of anticipation amongst the 44,015 packed inside Elland Road, for their final home game of the season.

They actually won the title without even playing, on Wednesday 24th April. Ray Kennedy's second half strike was enough for Arsenal to beat Liverpool 1-0, away at Anfield, and Leeds United could no longer be caught.

Champions Leeds United visited QPR on the final Saturday of the season, and a home record crowd of 35,353 filled Loftus Road. After a goalless first half, Allan Clarke dashed onto Joe Jordan's through ball, and he scored his thirteenth league goal of the season.

Leeds United's 1-0 win secured a five point gap between them and Liverpool, a gap that belies how close it all really was before the end.

Leeds United had led the league from start to finish, and they'd kept twenty-one clean sheets. Mick Jones, playing his last season for Leeds United, before injury ended his career, was their top goal-scorer with seventeen league and cup goals, just ahead of Allan Clarke, on sixteen.

Scotland's World Cup trio, Billy Bremner, Peter Lorimer and Joe Jordan scored a combined total of thirty-four league and cup goals, in the greatest season that Leeds United had ever enjoyed.

THE FOUR SEASONS

So, after 174 First Division matches for Leeds United, Allan Clarke finally had a First Division Championship winners' medal, having joined the reigning English Champions during the summer of Sixty-nine. A new era of David Harvey, Trevor Cherry, Gordon McQueen, Terry Yorath and Joe Jordan had helped the club to their first title in five years.

What about those four seasons in between, from 1969 to 1973? What about that classic Leeds United team of Sprake, Reaney, Cooper, Bremner, Charlton, Hunter, Lorimer, Clarke, Jones, Giles, Gray and Madeley, the team that never won the title? When they were in their prime? Did their failure to win the title detract from their greatness?

Leeds United won the league in 1969, and in 1974, but in between, they finished as runners-up three times, and in third place once. They also reached five Cup Finals, winning just two of them, but exactly how dominant was their Greatest Team during the four seasons between 1969 and 1973, between the arrival of Allan Clarke, and the departure of Jack Charlton?

Leeds United had gained 231 total points, over those four seasons, at an average of nearly 58 points per season, twelve more points than the 219 points gained by Liverpool during the same period.

Leeds United won 93 First Division matches, during those four seasons, seven more victories than either Liverpool or Arsenal. They scored three hundred goals, at an average of 75 per season, fifty-five more goals than Derby County had scored during the same period, but they conceded only 155 goals, at an average of 38.75 per season, and 0.92 per match. Only Liverpool had conceded fewer goals, just 138, over those four seasons.

Leeds United lost only thirty First Division matches during the four seasons, five less than the 35 defeats suffered by Liverpool. Leeds United also played 240 league and cup matches, over those four seasons, at an average of sixty games a season. These were the days before squad rotation, remember, and in 98% of those matches, Don Revie fielded his best available eleven.

Did Leeds United's failure to win the title, during the four seasons, 1969-73, detract from their greatness? No, it definitely didn't.

A Mellor, of LUFC Talk's Fan Forum, wrote that it just didn't matter that Don Revie didn't win more trophies, given their dominance. "For the record, Revie who was a God and superior to Clough/Shanks etc had one glaring weakness - winning the one offs/the must-wins. Had us competing on every level at a time when no one else did but just fell short - maybe squad size, maybe psychological but it happened.

It hurt but in the end it's part of the reason why I love him. A flawed genius who turned the second city from rugby. No one else managed that. And no other club is like LUFC as a result."

Over those seven seasons 1967-73, Man Utd, Man City, Leeds, Everton, Arsenal, Derby and Liverpool all won the league. It was a feat that has never been repeated. If you ask anyone, though, who was the best team of them all, over those years, it would be Leeds United. They *were* the best.

I'm 49 now, but if I die at 99, the one team that affected me more than any other in my life was Leeds.

I absolutely loved Newcastle's "Entertainers", from 1992-95, they were the finest Newcastle United team I ever saw, and ever will see. But if I was asked how they'd do against that 69-73 Leeds team, *I'd-be-worried.*

Actually, deep in my heart, I'd know that Bremner and Giles would have Lee Clark and Paul Bracewell's numbers, they would control the game, with Leeds romping to a 2-0 win.

Despite not winning the First Division title, in either 1970, 1971, 1972 or 1973, Leeds United were the most successful, the most feared, and the greatest team in English football, over those four seasons, during which many First Division clubs had fielded their greatest teams.

1973-74 was merely the official crowning of the achievements of that 1969-73 Leeds United side.

For Manchester United, relegation proved to be a blessing, not a curse.

On Friday 3rd May 1974, Tommy Docherty made his only significant signing prior to the following season, paying £200,000 to Hull City for their centre forward Stuart Pearson.

Pearson was classy, skilful, quick and combative, and he'd scored 44 goals in 126 Second Division matches for the Tigers. He'd also been their leading goal-scorer over the previous three seasons.

Tommy Docherty recouped some of the cash by selling Brian Kidd to Arsenal, for £110,000. Kidd had played 203 First Division matches for Manchester United, scoring fifty-two goals, and he became the tenth member of their 1968 European Cup winning team to leave Old Trafford.

Martin Buchan, Jim Holton and Willie Morgan had all performed well at the 1974 World Cup Finals, in West Germany, alongside Leeds United's David Harvey, Billy Bremner, Peter Lorimer and Joe Jordan. The two Uniteds had provided seven of Scotland's eleven that drew with Brazil, but should have won, and then drew 1-1 with Yugoslavia.

Scotland were eliminated on goal difference, in third place in Group 2, having been unbeaten, and conceding just one goal from three games. In all probability, that was Scotland's best-ever team.

Manchester United stormed into the Second Division, in August 1974, winning all of their first four matches, against Orient, Millwall, Portsmouth and Cardiff City. By late September, they were unbeaten from their opening nine matches, winning seven of them, and they led the league by five points.

Their 2-0 defeat away at second-placed Norwich City, on the last Saturday in September, proved only to be a randomly placed dustbin lying in the middle of the road, as their bright, new, red Ford Cortina Mark III 2000E rampaged through the dusty, derelict City streets of Division Two.

By November, Manchester United had re-established their five point lead at the top of the Second Division. They were once again a free-scoring outfit, firing twenty-nine goals from their first sixteen matches, and conceding only seven.

In fact, Manchester United's lead at the top of the table was never under threat, as record attendances were set throughout the season, and on Saturday 30th November, nearly 61,000 bulged the walls of Old Trafford, for their game against Sunderland.

MANCHESTER UNITED		SUNDERLAND
Alex Stepney	1	Jim Montgomery
Alex Forsyth	2	Dick Malone
Stewart Houston	3	Ron Guthrie
Brian Greenhoff	4	Bobby Moncur
Jim Holton	5	Dave Watson
Martin Buchan	6	Ian Porterfield
Willie Morgan	7	Bobby Kerr
Sammy McIlroy	8	Billy Hughes
Stuart Pearson	9	Vic Halom
Lou Macari	10	Pop Robson
Gerry Daly	11	Tony Towers
Ron Davies	12	Tom Finney

Sunderland, the FA Cup winners just eighteen months previously, had replaced Norwich City in second place, and they'd brought over ten thousand fans down from Wearside.

Never again would over sixty thousand attend a second tier English Football League match.

The game, which was featured on BBC TV's Match of the Day, was a classic. Stuart Pearson had fired United into an early lead, but Sunderland's bustling, powerful striker Billy Hughes equalised.

Sammy McIlroy's superb left wing cross was volleyed in by captain Willie Morgan, just before half-time, for a 2-1 United lead. Alex Stepney made some great saves, after the break, from Porterfield, from Halom, from Moncur, and from Robson, but eventually, Sunderland's tremendous pressure proved fruitful.

Hughes slammed home his second goal of the match, from Vic Halom's through ball, with a quarter of an hour remaining, and the away fans made such a noise, you'd have thought Sunderland were at home.

As the game approached injury time, "the close dovetailing between Macari and Daly produced an opportunity for McIlroy," as Tommy Docherty recalled.

"McIlroy didn't disappoint the United fans and Old Trafford erupted."

Both Sunderland and Manchester United received a standing ovation from the 61,000 crowd. Not a single arrest was made at the match by Greater Manchester Police.

Jim Holton suffered a serious injury, though, and he had to be replaced by the former Southampton and Wales legend Ron Davies, for their next match away at Sheffield Wednesday. He never played again for Manchester United. Holton joined Sunderland for the 1976-77 season, and then played for Coventry City for three years, before retiring, and running a pub in Coventry.

Jim Holton died, aged just 42, on Tuesday 5th October 1993, after he suffered a heart attack at the wheel of his car.

In February 1975, Tommy Docherty sold Jim McCalliog to Southampton, for £40,000, after he'd been concerned about McCalliog's work-rate, and he signed winger Steve Coppell from Tranmere Rovers, for £50,000.

Coppell, only five feet and six inches tall, and weighing just ten stone, was swift and strong, he crossed the ball neatly and also shot at goal sharply. A University student from Liverpool, he was just the very man who Tommy Docherty needed for United's First Division future, having scored ten goals from 35 league games for Tranmere.

Nearly 59,000 packed into Old Trafford, on Saturday 26th April, as Manchester United celebrated their Second Division Championship title, by hammering Blackpool 4-0, with Stuart Pearson scoring twice, and Lou Macari and Brian Greenhoff both also scoring in the second half.

Pearson was his club's top league scorer for the fourth successive season, with seventeen goals for United, while Macari, McIlroy and Daly also combined for twenty-nine league goals between them. Their regular back four of Forsyth, Houston, Buchan and Holton, then latterly Brian Greenhoff, had helped Alex Stepney keep twenty-seven league and cup clean sheets.

Willie Morgan was transferred to Burnley, in June 1975. Morgan, who'd made his debut for United against Spurs in August 1968, just three months after their European Cup Final win, had played 238 league matches at Old Trafford, scoring only 23 goals.

Following Sir Alf Ramsey's sacking by the FA, on Wednesday 1st May 1974, Don Revie was appointed as England's new manager. Revie had been the best manager that Leeds United ever had, and probably will ever have, taking them to two Football League titles, five runners-up places, four Cup wins, and ten Cup Final appearances.

It was then, a little surprising, for both Leeds United's players and fans, when the club appointed Brian Clough as their new manager. It is probably more surprising, for the rest of us, that they had appointed him without a long term plan. It was, perhaps, surprising that they hadn't legislated for a bad start to the 1974-75 season, knowing the aversion that most Leeds players had held towards Mr Clough, after his HEADLINE heavily-critical comments about them, just a year earlier.

It was very surprising that time hadn't been allowed for both parties to settle down, for calm to arrive, for Bremner to return, as the club sacked Brian Clough after only six league matches, and only four points behind a UEFA Cup qualifying place.

Anyway, in contrast to Manchester United's unbeaten start in Division Two, Leeds United won only one of their first seven league and cup matches, losing four times, and they were just one point above the relegation zone, when Brian Clough was sacked, on Friday 13th September 1974.

England legend Jimmy Armfield was appointed as the new manager of Leeds United three weeks later, on Friday 4th October. Armfield had played his last-ever First Division match only three and a half years earlier, and he adopted a softer approach in managing the matured Leeds United squad.

Within a month, Leeds United were back to form, and they gained twenty-six points from just eighteen matches, winning ten of them, between the beginning of November and Saturday 15th March 1975.

By March, Leeds United were back in the title race again, thanks, in a large way, to the legacy of Brian Clough. Duncan McKenzie, Cloughie's star signing, had been bought for a club record transfer fee of £250,000, and the intelligent but unpredictable striker had endured a difficult start to the season, after scoring twenty-six Second Division goals for promotion battlers Nottingham Forest during 1973-74.

Duncan McKenzie scored eight First Division goals in just eleven games between early November 1974 and the end of January 1975, and after taking six points from four games in February, Leeds were up to sixth in the First Division, and only four points behind leaders Everton.

Leeds United gave up their defence of their First Division title in late March, following their epic FA Cup Quarter-final tie against Ipswich. The two teams had drawn 0-0, 1-1, and then 0-0, again, before a third replay at Filbert Street, on Thursday 27th March.

Ipswich finally overcame Leeds 3-2, to meet West Ham in the Semi-finals.

It was in the 1974-75 European Cup, however, that Leeds United would be best remembered.

After disposing of FC Zurich, just a couple of days prior to Jimmy Armfield's arrival, 5-3 on aggregate, Peter Lorimer and Gordon McQueen gave them a 2-1 away win over Ujpest Dozsa, on Wednesday 23rd October. Further goals from McQueen, Lorimer and Bremner, a fortnight later, secured their 5-1 aggregate win, and a Quarter-final place.

On Wednesday 5th March, over 43,000 packed into Elland Road for their European Cup Quarter-final first leg match against Anderlecht. Joe Jordan and Gordon McQueen headed first half goals, before Peter Lorimer hammered Leeds to a great 3-0 home win.

A week later, Terry Cooper joined his old teammate Jack Charlton at Middlesbrough. Voted the best left-back at the 1970 World Cup Finals, in Mexico, Cooper hadn't been a first team regular for Leeds since breaking his leg against Stoke City, in April 1972.

Terry Cooper had started only twelve First Division matches in nearly three full seasons at Elland Road, having found Trevor Cherry, and even Frankie Gray, impossible to dislodge.

After 250 league games for Leeds, Cooper joined Jack Charlton's finely-tuned, defensively disciplined Middlesbrough, and their greatest-ever back four of Craggs, Boam, Maddren and Cooper kept twenty-one clean sheets, in Boro's first thirty-six league and cup games following Cooper's arrival at Ayresome Park.

Leeds United won a place in the European Cup Semi-finals, in Brussels, on Wednesday 19th March, after a delightful chip from Billy Bremner had secured a 4-0 aggregate win over Anderlecht, and Van der Elst and Rensenbrink.

On Wednesday 9th April, one of the greatest ever nights in Leeds United's history, 50,393 literally filled Elland Road for their European Cup Semi-final first leg match against Barcelona. After ten minutes, Johnny Giles launched a long pass into the Barcelona area, from the centre circle, which Joe Jordan flicked into the path of Billy Bremner. Bremner hammered the ball, on the half-volley, over keeper Sadurni, into the top left corner of the goal. McQueen then headed just wide of Sadurni's goal, from Giles' free-kick.

Sadurni had to palm Eddie Gray's left wing cross over his own crossbar, and then Jordan had his shot tipped over by Sadurni, after another long pass from the influential Giles. Bremner argued that he should have been allowed to shoot after Jordan had stolen the ball out of his path.

LEEDS UNITED		BARCELONA
David Stewart	1	Salvador Sadurni
Paul Reaney	2	Enrique Costas
Frankie Gray	3	Marinho Peres
Billy Bremner	4	Gallego
Gordon McQueen	5	Antonio De La Cruz
Paul Madeley	6	Carles Rexach
Terry Yorath	7	Johan Neeskens
Allan Clarke	8	Migueli
Joe Jordan	9	Juan Asensi
Johnny Giles	10	Johan Cruyff
Eddie Gray	11	Juan Carlos Heredia

Johnny Giles' free-kick from the left was flicked on by the leaping Allan Clarke, and Bremner darted in to meet the ball inside the six yard box, but Sadurni punched the ball away, from off Bremner's toe. As Leeds waved forward again, Clarke's shot was blocked out, by Gallego, for another corner.

The Barcelona defence hadn't played that well, and Leeds should have punished them more with all the chances that they'd created. With Johan Cruyff, the best footballer in the World, though, and the equally influential Neeskens, there was always the danger that Barcelona could break, and they did.

Cruyff picked up the ball after the resultant Leeds United corner kick, and he sped away, tracked by Paul Madeley. From ten yards inside the Leeds United half, Cruyff played a beautifully weighted pass to Heredia, but Paul Reaney won the ball, with an equally beautiful tackle, just a foot outside the penalty area, and with Heredia poised to shoot.

The referee, though, chasing well behind, sixty yards back, penalised Reaney, who was astonished and perplexed. Allan Clarke ran back and pointed out the referee's error, to the referee, and he was subsequently booked.

You got away with nothing in Europe, unless you were from the Mediterranean.

Johan Cruyff played the free-kick to his left, and from twenty yards, Juan Asensi drove his shot past Stewart's dive, and just inside the left post, with twenty-five minutes remaining.

Paul Madeley fed Paul Reaney, out on the right wing. Reaney beat Asensi, before crossing from the right edge of the Barcelona penalty area. At the far post, Joe Jordan headed the ball back across goal, Yorath just eased it away from his two markers, and from the right hand edge of the six yard box, Allan Clarke slammed the ball high up into the goal.

A fortnight later, on Wednesday 23rd April, St George's Day, 110,000 filled the giant Nou Camp stadium in Barcelona, but Jimmy Armfield had a master-plan that might help protect their slender 2-1 first leg lead, switching Peter Lorimer from the left wing over to the right wing, after just ten minutes.

The switch caught Barcelona's defence cold, and Joe Jordan flicked on a huge David Stewart drop kick, for Lorimer to beat his marker, and bury the ball into the net. Allan Clarke almost scored shortly afterwards, as Barca's defence were totally rattled, but Cruyff and Neeskens then began to pile on the pressure.

Manuel Clares flicked in a header with just over twenty minutes remaining, and then Gordon McQueen was sent off following a goalmouth skirmish, but David Stewart was superb in Leeds United's goal.

Paul Madeley had also stood shoulder to shoulder with Johan Cruyff, the World's best footballer, and came out even. Leeds United hung on for a fantastic, surprising, and heroic 3-2 aggregate win over the most valuable team in the world.

On Wednesday 28th May 1975, Jimmy Armfield's Leeds United met Bayern Munich, the reigning European Champions, in Paris, but a couple of particularly outrageous decisions by the French referee Michel Kitabdijan cost United very dear.

BAYERN MUNICH		LEEDS UNITED
Sepp Maier	1	David Stewart
Bjorn Andersson2		Paul Reaney
Bernd Durnberger	3	Frank Gray
Hans-Georg Schwarzenbeck	4	Billy Bremner
Franz Beckenbauer	5	Paul Madeley
Franz Roth	6	Norman Hunter
Conny Torstensson	7	Peter Lorimer
Rainer Zobel	8	Allan Clarke
Gerd Muller	9	Joe Jordan
Uli Hoeness	10	Johnny Giles
Jupp Kappellmann	11	Terry Yorath

Four minutes into the match, Sweden's hardened World Cup defender Bjorn Andersson was injured after a hard tackle from Terry Yorath, and he was replaced by the young, inexperienced Sepp Weiss.

With five key players from West Germany's World Cup Final win, less than a year earlier, Bayern were mostly dominated by Leeds United, thereafter. Franz Beckenbauer was very lucky to get away with a handball, halfway into the first half, as the French ref ignored all penalty appeals.

Ten minutes before half-time, though, Beckenbauer, *Der Kaiser,* was guilty of a cynical trip on Allan Clarke, inside his own six yard box. With Teutonic authority, though, the World Cup winning captain got up and told Kitabdijan that it was a corner-kick for Leeds.

As Clarke knelt in astonishment, that was just where the referee pointed. Sepp Maier, with ball in hand, looked a little embarrassed. Three minutes before half-time, Uli Hoeness was also injured after a foul by Frank Gray, and he was replaced by German international striker Klaus Wunder.

After an hour, with Leeds United camped inside the Bayern half, Sepp Maier denied Billy Bremner with a brilliant reflex save from Bremner's close range snapshot, but he could do absolutely nothing about Peter Lorimer's hotshot half-volley, after Johnny Giles' free-kick had been headed into his path by Hunter, shortly afterwards.

The referee awarded a goal. Leeds were 1-0 up, with about twenty-five minutes remaining, but Franz Beckenbauer had other ideas. Despite protests from Billy Bremner, Beckenbauer began to boss the referee, claiming that Bremner had been in an offside position. The nearside linesman had not raised a flag for any offside, but Beckenbauer sent the referee over to him anyway, walking and talking with him as he went.

After a brief discussion with his linesman, who had offered no signal for any offside offence, Michel Kitabdijan ran back to the Bayern penalty area, waving his arms, signalling no goal.

With neither the referee, nor his linesman, signalling anything wrong with Lorimer's goal, as indeed there was nothing wrong with it, Bremner was ruled, ridiculously, to have been offside, which he wasn't anyway. He'd rushed back from an offside position, into which he'd been pushed by a German defender, and as Lorimer shot, he'd been played onside by Durnberger. In any case, Bremner hadn't received a pass, hadn't interfered with play, and he wasn't obstructing Maier's vision, at all.

Just as Jeff Astle's goal, back in April 1971, was correct, this goal was much, much more correct.

Leeds didn't go mad. ***Though They Had Every Justification To Go Mad.***

This was a European Cup Final, and they had to continue their football, which they did, and they kept pressing Bayern, though a little disheartened.

On the break, Swedish international Torstensson found Roth, who squeezed the ball across Stewart's body, into the far corner of the Leeds United goal, and then, Gerd Muller, ***Der Bomber,*** just beat Stewart's dive, at his near post, to finish Leeds off.

It was a cruel finish.

The travelling Leeds United supporters, many of whom had personally witnessed the travesty of the 1973 European Cup Winners' Cup Final, had been bitterly upset, and they showed their frustrations after Lorimer's great goal had been disallowed.

Unfortunately, the French police, geared up for trouble from the English football fans, after the disgraceful scenes involving Tottenham supporters at the 1974 UEFA Cup Final, in Rotterdam, just waded in with shields and batons.

The Leeds fans retaliated by breaking up seats, and hurling them back at the police, as missiles.

Back to the football, Jimmy Armfield had sent on Eddie Gray, for Yorath, with ten minutes remaining, after they'd gone 1-0 down, and he felt he might have sent on Duncan McKenzie, too, but for him, such was the mood, it felt like nothing could go right. McKenzie was NOT happy.

Leeds United had played such a perfect European Cup Final, up to that disallowed goal.

Jimmy Armfield just didn't see the point.

He did see a point in arguing, however, when UEFA imposed a four year ban on Leeds United from playing in all UEFA competitions. Almost single-handedly, Jimmy Armfield fought, without any support from the Leeds United board, against the severity of the ban.

In Jimmy Armfield's own private investigations, he discovered that Leeds United fans had arrived at the Parc des Princes, with bottles of duty free drinks to take back to Yorkshire, only to discover an alcohol ban inside the stadium, and all drinks would have to be confiscated, if they wanted to enter the stadium.

With both the police and stadium staff present, many of the Leeds supporters had drunk their bottles of alcohol, before entering the stadium. Armfield also made two trips to the UEFA headquarters in Geneva, paying his own air fare and hotel accommodation, with evidence that the Parisian police had initially ***over-reacted,*** when they'd waded in with batons and shields.

In response, UEFA reduced the ban to two years, and they thanked Jimmy Armfield for his decent efforts, while Michel Kitabdijan never again refereed a top class football match in European competition, although he was never officially, nor publicly, banned.

The Leeds United board reimbursed Armfield his personal expenses in fighting the ban, but he never received a "thank you" from any of them.

The 1975 European Cup Final marked the beginning of the end of an era for Leeds United. Mick Jones hadn't played all season, because of his knee injury, and he looked a despondent figure, sat behind the substitutes' bench, in Paris. Jones was finally forced to announce his retirement in October 1975, at just thirty years of age.

Mick Jones had scored one hundred and eleven league and cup goals in 312 games, but it was his partnership with Allan Clarke that Leeds United missed most of all. When they were on form, which was most of the time, Jones and Clarke were among the most feared, the most dangerous, and the most exciting attacking partnerships in English football history. Mick Jones and Allan Clarke had scored a combined 133 First Division goals in the five seasons between 1969 and 1974.

Allan Clarke said that Mick Jones "was the best striking partner I played with for either club or country."

Mick Jones was "the target man," Sniffer continued, "and chased any lost cause. He had terrific close control and used his strength to hold the ball up while I looked for space to support him. We were compared with Toshack and Keegan, Radford and Kennedy, Chivers and Gilzean, and Osgood and Baldwin."

"None of them touched us," Clarke concluded.

Johnny Giles, the second best midfield player to ever play for Leeds United, had also played his last game for the club. Having lost the European Cup Final, he needed a fresh challenge, and hungry for management, he joined West Bromwich Albion, on Wednesday 16th July 1975, as their player-manager.

Giles had played 380 First Division games for Leeds United, scoring eighty-six goals, but creating many, many more goals than that for his team. Sir Matt Busby had admitted that selling Giles to Leeds was his "greatest mistake," and Sir Alf Ramsey regretted that the Dublin-born midfield master "wasn't an Englishman."

More so, it was Sir Alf's "one regret."

"Johnny Giles could grab hold of a match, tuck it in his back pocket and carry it around with him. He didn't need to find space. It was as if space found him. (He had) a perception, a footballing brain and the wonderful natural instinct that separates great players from the rest. He could play a pass of the most delicate nature and perfect precision."

That most glowing, and accurate, appraisal of Giles, was said by the man who was reputed to have always called him "Irishman," Mr Brian Clough.

Cloughie was another manager who'd also had huge regrets about Giles, and he also suggested, "who knows what might have happened if we'd got on?"

Johnny Giles led West Brom back into the First Division in April 1976, and he played seventy-five matches for Albion, before resigning in 1977. As he departed from West Bromwich Albion, though, to manage Shamrock Rovers, Giles had turned them into a better team than Leeds United. He introduced Laurie Cunningham and Bryan Robson to First Division football, and he'd laid foundations upon which Ron Atkinson developed into exciting title challengers in 1978.

It was mostly Johnny Giles' West Brom side that led the First Division, on New Year's Day 1979.

1975 was a significant turning point for both Manchester United and Leeds United. Manchester United's inability to hold onto their young European Cup winning players, and being forced to totally re-build under Tommy Docherty, was finally beginning to bring rewards, while Leeds United had stuck together, for over a decade, but were now suffering the natural effects of ageing.

Gravity always wins, even against the most successful, the most feared, and the greatest team in English football. Transition, that had been frivolously ignored by the fiercely United team spirit of Leeds, now ground its unforgiving, deep, muddy tracks right through the club, regardless of their wishes.

Transition, that had adversely affected the fortunes of Manchester United, after 1970, was now their greatest friend, as their young, vibrant, fresh-faced team was ready to once again challenge Leeds United, and tear the First Division apart.

THE DEEP NORTH, Part Two

The Twin Towers

THE 1969-70 SEASON WAS NOT ONLY a disaster for Sunderland, it was a positive nightmare for Ian Porterfield.

Having committed the error of standing up to manager Alan Brown, during the Summer of 69, at Sunderland's pre-season training camp in Denmark, Porterfield was frozen out for their entire, miserable campaign. He wasn't even allowed to train with the first team, or even the reserves, at the worst of times, and twice he gave a written transfer request to the club, but twice he was refused. His only place of happiness was at home, with his wife and kids, but even there in the warmth, he was out in the cold.

Most of Sunderland's players simply suffered Alan Brown's sergeant-major attitude towards them. On one occasion, Brown brought a golf ball to training, and he ordered his defenders to head it, to toughen up the muscles in their foreheads. They then got blasted for messing it up, but nobody stood up to him, except for Porterfield.

The poor lad was greatly missed in Sunderland's battle to stay up, but in making an example of Porterfield, as a reminder to his team, as to who was in charge, Alan Brown probably cost Sunderland their place in Division One.

During that brilliant Mexico World Cup Summer, the two men must have shook hands and apologised, because Ian Porterfield was back in Sunderland's team for their first game of 1970-71.

Porterfield actually started thirty-nine league games that season, and only ever-presents Jim Montgomery and captain Martin Harvey had played more than him.

Jim Montgomery played his 300th league game for Sunderland, during their 3-3 home draw with Watford on Saturday 22nd August. Bobby Park, Billy Hughes and Bobby Kerr all scored, in Sunderland's first home match of the season in front of a poor crowd of just over sixteen thousand.

By late October, Sunderland had scored just nineteen league goals, from fourteen matches, winning only four of them, and they'd also been knocked out of the League Cup, by Fourth Division Lincoln City.

More importantly, Roker Park was still not attracting proper crowds, with 18,741 being Sunderland's largest attendance prior to Christmas, for their 0-1 home defeat to Hull City.

They won just enough games, though, to escape the worries of a second successive relegation battle, but they'd lost far too many to get anywhere near the promotion race.

In the middle of December, their top goal-scorer Joe Baker, with ten goals from just fifteen games, left Roker Park for Scottish First Division side Hibs. Immediately, Alan Brown then paid a club record transfer fee of £100,000 to Rotherham United for their twenty-four year old forward Dave Watson. Born in Nottingham, Watson wasn't actually a forward; he was a rugged, commanding, tough centre-back, but Brown played him as a centre-forward, directly replacing Baker.

Dave Watson scored on his debut, as well, a second half leveller during Sunderland's 1-1 draw away at Watford, before Middlesbrough arrived on Boxing Day, and Sunderland suddenly attracted a crowd.

Middlesbrough had enjoyed a much better first half to the season than their Wearside rivals. They'd won ten, and lost only seven, of their opening twenty-two games, while John Hickton had scored seventeen league and cup goals.

They'd been missing Willie Maddren, though, since late November, after he'd been injured during their 1-0 home win over Millwall, and the experienced Ferryhill-born Bill Gates deputised at centre-half, alongside Frank Spraggon, for Middlesbrough's Boxing Day visit to Roker Park.

A huge crowd of 42,617, the second largest Second Division crowd that season, packed Roker Park for a cracking mid-table encounter, in which both sides had little to gain, and nothing to lose.

SUNDERLAND		MIDDLESBROUGH
Jim Montgomery	1	Bill Whigham
Cecil Irwin	2	Alex Smith
Martin Harvey	3	Gordon Jones
Colin Todd	4	George Smith
Ritchie Pitt	5	Bill Gates
Ian Porterfield	6	Frank Spraggon
Brian Chambers	7	Derrick Downing
Bobby Kerr	8	Eric McMordie
Dave Watson	9	Hugh McIlmoyle
Gordon Harris	10	John Hickton
Billy Hughes	11	Joe Laidlaw
Bobby Park	12	David Mills

Ian Porterfield cut the ball across goal for Bobby Kerr to finish, and then Billy Hughes hammered home a loose ball from two yards out, to give Sunderland a 2-1 half-time lead. John Hickton had headed a first half goal beyond Montgomery, before firing in his nineteenth goal of the season, after the break. Joe Laidlaw had left the Sunderland defence for dead, running clear in acres of space, and he whipped in a vicious low cross. The ball went in off Hickton's shin, just beating Monty's dive. It was real Christmas defending, and the 2-2 draw did neither Sunderland nor Middlesbrough any good.

While Sunderland and Boro were enduring their struggles in the Second Division, Newcastle United were enjoying another European adventure. They were eighth in Division One, in late September, only a point behind fourth-placed Liverpool, as they flew out of Newcastle Airport, for the start of their 1970-71 Fairs Cup campaign.

Newcastle had been given possibly the toughest draw of all, in the First round, against Inter Milan, the European Champions from 1964 and 1965, and losing European Cup Finalists back in 1967. Just three months earlier, five Internazionale players had played against Brazil in the World Cup Final.

It was a star-studded who's who from Panini's 1970 World Cup sticker collection…

Giacinto Facchetti was the Italian national captain, and his Inter teammates included Tarcisio Burgnich, Mario Bertini, Sandro Mazzola and striker Roberto Boninsegna. Of all the draws that Newcastle were given, throughout their three-year participation in the Fairs Cup, between 1968 and 1971, this was easily their toughest.

On Wednesday 23rd September, a hostile San Siro greeted United, who sensed a chance, as Inter were without the injured Bertini, and the rested Boninsegna. Even so, Inter still had a formidable, World class defence, marshalled by Facchetti and the rugged, grizzled Burgnich, while the elegant and intelligent, moustached Mazzola ran the midfield with creative passes and clever touches. It was always an uphill battle.

Newcastle's brilliant back four of Craig, Burton, Moncur and Clark, though, with Arentoft and Gibb both providing disciplined protection, kept Inter out, and with the scores level, at 0-0, approaching half-time, the unthinkable happened.

Newcastle actually took the lead.

Pop Robson's floated free-kick was attacked by Wyn Davies, diving into an Italian ruck of boots and studs, and he powered his header past Vieri.

Newcastle United nearly hung on for the most unlikely of away wins, but in the dying minutes, Giancarlo Cella, who'd played for Italy in the 1960 Rome Olympic Games, squeezed in an equaliser.

United drew 0-0 at home with Coventry City, who had just brilliantly won 4-1 away at Trakia Plovdiv, in *their* first ever season in European football, before Internazionale arrived at St James's Park, a week later, on Wednesday 30th September.

An all-ticket sell-out crowd of 60,000 filled the ground for one of the most memorable matches, for all the wrong reasons, to have ever been played at Newcastle. It was appropriate that Newcastle wore their change strip of all red, to allow Inter to play in their black and royal blue stripes, because the Italians played all of the dirty tricks there were, even after they knew they'd lost.

Inter Milan badly missed their club legend Mazzola in midfield, and without his craft, they resorted to *a good deal of graft…*

…if you can call elbows in the ribs, kidney punches, ankle stamping, and spitting, *a good deal of graft.*

Burgnich, to his credit, was also missing, but Boninsegna, Italy's goal-scorer during the 1970 World Cup Final, returned to Inter's attack, not that he saw much of the ball.

The great, dignified and experienced captain Giacinto Facchetti was there, though, to drive his great Inter Milan team forward, from the back, like a Franz Beckenbauer or a Brian Labone, graceful and effortless.

Facchetti was nothing of the sort. He was the worst of the lot. You have to ignore his clean-cut, tall film star looks, vaguely resembling Steve McGarrett from Hawaii 5-0. His game plan was the ugliest ever seen, anywhere in the football fields of England's green and pleasant land. Facchetti was nothing but the ugly leader of the darkest forces of the *URUK-HAI* at *HELM'S DEEP.*

Bobby Moncur gave Newcastle the lead during the first half, heading into the goal, past a diabolically late leap for the ball, by the keeper Vieri.

Inter subsequently lost their heads.

A minute later, Wyn Davies cleverly appeared as if he was going to challenge Vieri, but he didn't. The Italians took this action personally, and a fracas followed, just a lot of shoving and a lot of shouting.

Inter's goalkeeper, Lido Vieri, who was amazingly in Italy's World Cup Finals squad in Mexico, then punched the Belgian referee, Joseph Minnoy, to his knees. As the Inter Milan players swarmed around the referee, pleading with him, obstructing him, poking at him, and basically bullying him, the Northumbrian police actually entered the penalty area to protect him.

Vieri was sent off, and Bordon replaced the forward Achilli, to go in goal, but from then on, the Italians, down to ten men, punched, kicked, stamped and spat on almost every Newcastle player, and in the thick of the action, with United playing whatever football there was allowed to be played.

Wyn Davies was, pretty much, *almost every Newcastle player.*

Wyn Davies might not have been the most prolific centre forward to ever play for Newcastle, and he might not have been the most-capped, or the most decorated, but after that Inter Milan game, he was certainly their bravest, without any question.

Iam McFaul didn't have to make a save, all game, and Frank Clark hit the bar, after he'd beaten two defenders, in a great run from halfway. But it was Wyn Davies, *the Mighty Wyn,* who fired United to a superb 2-0 lead, in the second half, right under the mighty Leazes End.

The place just went wild. The Leazes End, and all of St James's Park sang, loudly, *"Come On Without, Come On Within. You've not seen nothing like the Mighty Wyn!"*

You could have heard the song in Sunderland.

Back then, more so than today, Italian club sides appeared to try and bully, and effectively, cheat their way to success. Derby County were victims, two and a half years later, in their European Cup Semi-final in Turin, and Leeds United were also victims of a disgraceful refereeing performance, against AC Milan, in their European Cup Winners' Cup Final in Athens.

It was great to see, then, as it's always great to see, an English team come out on top, by just playing football, against an Italian team of legends employing the most disgraceful and undignified cheating tactics.

All that extraordinary effort, though, was for nothing. Newcastle were given a *gimme,* in the Second round, drawn against the little known Pecsi Dozsa.

They beat the Hungarians 2-0, on Wednesday 21st October, with over fifty thousand inside St James's Park. Wyn Davies headed a cracking double, one in each half, to take his league and cup tally to four goals.

A fortnight later, Newcastle travelled to the small, southern Hungarian town of Pecs, on the River Danube. The town was so small, there was no hotel large enough to accommodate the Newcastle United squad. Many United players had to share rooms with the travelling sports writers.

Pecsi's pitch was like a ploughed cow field, and control was improbable. Bobby Moncur deflected a cross into his own net, and then, big John McNamee was very harshly adjudged to have fouled Daka.

Janos Mate's penalty was superb, though, hitting the top right corner of McFaul's goal, even though the keeper had guessed the right way. With the aggregate scores level, and Newcastle unable to play football on that pitch, extra-time arrived, but made no difference to the momentum of the match.

Newcastle were by far the better team, but they couldn't force home their superiority. The pitch had beaten them.

The tie was decided by a penalty shoot-out, on the very same night as Everton defeated Borussia Moenchengladbach, on penalty kicks, in the European Cup.

These were the first ever penalty shoot-outs in European football.

Unfortunately, while all of Pecsi's kicks were as perfect as Janos Mate's, during the match, giving McFaul absolutely no chance, Newcastle had sadly practised their penalty shooting at their training ground, and not on the Town Moor, which might have been more useful.

Pecsi won 3-0 on penalties, after a 2-2 aggregate score draw.

Ben Arentoft, who missed one of Newcastle's three penalties, finally had his international exile ended in 1971, as the DBU abolished its strict rules of amateurism, and Arentoft played a further five games for Denmark, as a Newcastle player, at twenty-eight years of age.

As a result, Newcastle's Ben Arentoft was the first English league footballer to play for a continental European national team, before the mass introduction of foreign players following the 1978 World Cup Finals.

After leaving Newcastle in September 1971, for Blackburn Rovers, having played fifty-nine times for United, Arentoft became the head of child probation for Copenhagen's city council.

By Christmas 1970, Newcastle had won nine, lost seven, and drawn six of their opening 22 First Division matches, and were sitting handily in tenth position, but just two points behind Manchester City, in fifth place.

Middlesbrough beat Leicester City 1-0, at Ayresome Park, in front of their biggest home crowd of the season, 30,682, on Saturday 9th January, as John Hickton's second half goal defeated the Second Division leaders. Boro went on a great run of just one defeat in eleven league matches, from the end of October, to late February, with Hickton scoring ten goals in those eleven games. They rose to fifth place, as a result, only a single point behind second-placed Cardiff City.

On the Friday night of 26th February, though, Watford beat Middlesbrough 1-0 at Vicarage Road, and Boro dropped down to sixth. Eight days later, they responded with a 3-0 thrashing of eighth-placed Swindon Town, bouncing back up to fifth, above both Hull City and Carlisle United, and with just two points separating the top seven.

SECOND DIVISION LEADERS, 6TH MARCH 1971

	PL	W	D	L	F	A	PTS
Cardiff City	30	15	10	5	53	25	40
Sheffield United	30	15	9	6	50	33	39
Luton Town	29	14	10	5	44	20	38
Leicester City	29	15	8	6	44	26	38
MIDDLESBROUGH	31	16	6	9	49	31	38

As exciting as the promotion race was, at the top of the table, it was of no interest at all to the fallen giants, Sunderland.

Sunderland won only two of fourteen Second Division matches, from early December to the end of March, and during the two months of February and March 1971, they scored only one goal from eight games.

Colin Todd had been flogged to Derby County, for £170,000, to raise some cash, and only 10,827 had attended their goalless draw at Roker Park, against Portsmouth, on Saturday 13th March. These were really the darkest ever times on Wearside, and really couldn't get any darker?

Well, they could, really. They were still ten points clear of the relegation zone, but on Saturday 3rd April, only 8,596 attended their home game with Swindon Town, the lowest crowd at Roker Park for over two decades.

Billy Hughes and Bobby Kerr scored two goals apiece, mind, as Sunderland won 5-2. They ended the 1970-71 season in thirteenth position, twelve points above the relegation places, but fourteen points below the top two.

Middlesbrough also blew their promotion push, but in a much more disappointing manner than a year earlier. They won only one of their final eleven games, drawing all of their last eight matches, and they ended up in seventh place, six points above Sunderland, but eight points below Sheffield United, promoted in second place behind Champions Leicester City.

John Hickton had scored twenty-five league goals, from forty-one games, and he was also the Second Division's leading scorer. Ayresome Park's average crowd was 18,615, nearly three thousand higher than Sunderland's average attendance, despite Roker Park being a much larger ground by nearly twenty thousand.

Newcastle United won just one of their nine league matches after Christmas 1970, and by Saturday 13th March, they'd dropped to sixteenth position, nine points below a UEFA Cup qualifying place.

The wonderful European adventures were over, for a long time, for the Geordies. Newcastle won four, and lost just three of their final eleven games, and they finished bang in the middle of the table.

Joe Harvey had also said goodbye to Pop Robson, after falling out with their twenty-five year old Sunderland-born striker, following Robson's suggestions that Newcastle was being run unprofessionally.

He probably had a point, but in February 1971, Ron Greenwood paid £120,000, a record transfer fee for both clubs, to bring Pop Robson to West Ham United.

Robson scored the winning goal for Newcastle, in his final game for United, during their 1-0 win over Spurs, on Saturday 20th February, with nearly 32,000 inside St James's. He'd scored eighty-two First Division goals in 205 games for United, and went on to become the First Division's top goal-scorer, during the 1972-73 season, after scoring 28 goals for West Ham.

Pop Robson was the much more prolific striker in the Davies-Robson partnership, but he was never as much-loved as Wyn Davies. Davies' tremendous popularity, that survives strongly to this very day, was due to his tremendous bravery and presence, committing himself firmly to the United cause, as well as creating openings for Robson, Dyson and Foggon. The Wyn Davies-Pop Robson attacking partnership, though, was one of the greatest in Newcastle United's history, up to then.

United's fans had only just got used to being without Robson, when they also heard of the departure of their star player, the Mighty Wyn. Davies was sold to Manchester City, at twenty-nine years old, for just £60,000, on Tuesday 3rd August 1971.

By far the most popular player at St James's Park since Jackie Milburn, Wyn Davies had scored fifty-three goals in his 215 league and cup games for Newcastle, but he created far more, many more goals for his teammates.

Tough to mark, and impossible to beat in the air, Davies was also sublimely skilled with his feet, little flicks and chips for Robson, etc., to run onto. Many of Pop Robson's ninety league and cup goals for United were created by Wyn Davies, and against the very best opposition in Europe, as well.

Wyn Davies took his trade to Manchester City, and he provided the same service for superstars Francis Lee, Colin Bell and Mike Summerbee, as he'd provided for Robson, Foggon and Dyson. Man City were on course for a richly-deserved First Division title, topping the table by five points in late March 1972, with just eight games to play.

Malcolm Allison then decided to overcook his perfect soufflé, by paying a club record transfer fee for Rodney Marsh.

As a result Davies, who'd scored eight goals in forty First Division games, while also setting up many of Francis Lee's thirty-three goals, was deprived of a League Championship winners' medal.

Pop Robson's immediate replacement was Sheffield United's John Tudor, signed in part exchange for full back David Ford and Shildon-born goalkeeper John Hope, who kept goal for the Blades for all but four games during 1971-72, helping them to the top of the First Division by late September.

John Tudor had scored thirty league goals in sixty-four starts for the Blades, but he'd scored nine in just twenty-one, during Sheffield United's promotion-winning season of 1970-71. Manager John Harris had brought in Trevor Hockey to boost his midfield, though, and Tudor was offloaded after the New Year.

The signing of the heavily side-burned, blonde haired Tudor was a no-lose situation for Joe Harvey. If Tudor didn't work out, there was no loss, but if he was a success, then the £120,000 he'd received for Pop Robson was free cash.

John Tudor scored five First Division goals, in just sixteen games, during the final third of the season, proving not a tremendous success as a main striker, but neither was he a failure as a support striker.

Therefore, Joe Harvey used the £120,000 cash he received for Robson, plus the cash he'd received for Wyn Davies, and he paid Luton Town a massive, club record transfer fee of £180,000 for Malcolm MacDonald, a London-born flash geezer, who started as a full-back for Bobby Robson's Fulham, but had scored forty-nine league goals in just 88 games, as a striker at Kenilworth Road.

At a press conference, welcoming Newcastle's high profile new signing to St James's Park, Malcolm MacDonald announced that he would score thirty goals for Newcastle in his first season. The local and national press ridiculed his proudly, and loudly, announced boasts, printing huge headlines. "**SUPERMOUTH!**" they called him.

As Newcastle United lost 2-0 away at Crystal Palace, on the opening Saturday of the 1971-72 season, before drawing 0-0 away at Spurs, on the following Wednesday, **SUPERMOUTH!** must have felt the pressure growing on him, from all over, as Liverpool arrived in the North-east, on Saturday 21st August. With the Popular Side of St James's Park demolished, for the construction of the new East Stand, 39,720 absolutely packed the ground, and they witnessed a Superstar in the making.

"It was one of the most fabulous atmospheres that I have ever experienced in my time in football," Malcolm MacDonald claimed later.

NEWCASTLE UNITED		LIVERPOOL
Iam McFaul	1	Ray Clemence
David Craig	2	Chris Lawler
Frank Clark	3	Alec Lindsay
Tommy Gibb	4	Tommy Smith
Ollie Burton	5	Larry Lloyd
Bobby Moncur	6	Emlyn Hughes
Keith Dyson	7	Kevin Keegan
John Tudor	8	Peter Thompson
Malcolm MacDonald	9	Steve Heighway
David Young	10	John Toshack
Terry Hibbitt	11	Ian Callaghan

Terry Hibbitt, out on the Newcastle left wing, was a reject from Don Revie's Leeds United. Joe Harvey had paid a mere £30,000 for Hibbitt on Wednesday 12th August.

Frailly-built and skinny-legged, but sharp-thinking and hard-working, Hibbitt became one of the best five players to ever wear the Newcastle United number eleven shirt. He formed an almost telepathic understanding with Malcolm MacDonald, and his crosses resulted in many of MacDonald's goals over the following four seasons.

Liverpool arrived with one of their greatest teams for years, including over half of the eleven men that won the European Cup, six years later, but this was not their day.

David Young was fouled in the Liverpool penalty area, early in the second half, and Newcastle were awarded a penalty kick. MacDonald volunteered to take it, but he remembered, as he'd put the ball on the spot, *the roaring silence* that descended, deafeningly, as he walked back before turning to take the kick. **Supermouth**, as he'd been dubbed, could he handle the pressure? Here he was, just twenty-one years old, with great, thick black sideburns covering his cheeks, preparing to take a penalty kick against one of the best teams of the past decade, while Newcastle had Ollie Burton, their confident and proven First Division penalty taker, standing back to watch.

MacDonald just strode forward and he nonchalantly struck the ball, left-footed, smashing it, high up into the top left corner of Clemence's goal, right in front of the Gallowgate End.

Later on, during the first half, Malcolm MacDonald took a pass from Tommy Gibb, who was superb in midfield, and he side-stepped Chris Lawler, dragging the ball into the box, before firing an angled shot, from the left side of the penalty area, up into the roof of the Liverpool goal.

After half-time, John Tudor turned Hibbitt's forward ball into the path of MacDonald. MacDonald took on Alec Lindsay, and beat him, before firing a low shot beneath Ray Clemence's dive, right under the packed Leazes End, which exploded into black and white chaos, and crazed celebrations.

The newspapers had branded MacDonald **Supermouth!** The fans, though, were shouting and singing a new name about Malcolm MacDonald, that stuck, and was sung forever more.

"SUPERMAC! SUPERMAC! SUPERMAC! "

On that day, Saturday 21ˢᵗ August 1971, **Supermac!** was born. Of course, amidst all the joy and delirium, Emlyn Hughes and Kevin Keegan also scored for Liverpool, but Newcastle won 3-2, and the game and all of Tyneside belonged to Supermac.

Supermac scored another three goals, over their next twelve First Division matches, though, and after a club record run of six successive defeats during October, Newcastle United were rock bottom of Division One, by Saturday 30th October.

Stuart Boam had joined Middlesbrough, during June 1971, for a £50,000 fee, having played 175 league matches for Mansfield Town. Boam was a big, six foot one inch, rugged defender, who slotted straight into the Boro back line.

Three games into the new season, Stan Anderson also bought in John Craggs from Newcastle United. Craggs, who joined for £60,000, had played 52 First Division games for the Magpies, and he'd also played in Newcastle's Fairs Cup victories over both Vitoria Setubal and Rangers, back in 1969.

With both Boam and Craggs in their defence, Middlesbrough kept seventeen clean sheets during 1971-72, and they won ten of their opening fifteen Second Division matches, sitting in third place, level on points with second-placed Millwall, but only two points behind leaders Norwich City.

Irish goalkeeper Jim Platt had also joined Boro, back in the Spring of 1970, but he'd been kept out of the team for over a year by Bill Whigham. Signed from Northern Irish league club Ballymena

United, Platt finally made his Middlesbrough debut on Saturday 2nd October, for their 1-0 win over Blackpool, and he kept his place for the following twelve years.

Boro fell apart, once again though, losing five of their next nine matches up to early January, winning only once, and they had totally fallen away from the promotion race by the time just 13,117 had watched them beat Bristol City 1-0, at Ayresome Park.

Boro's fans were used to dramatic collapses.

After Dave Watson had scored his fourth goal of the season for Sunderland, still wearing the number nine shirt, during their 1-0 win over Burnley, on 2nd October, they were fourth in Division Two, and only two points behind Bristol City.

Sunderland then went on a run of fourteen dull matches, losing just twice, but they had drawn eight of them. On Boxing Day 1971, though, a day of monster crowds, over 26,000 packed Hull City's Boothferry Park, twice the Tigers' average home attendance, and Ritchie Pitt, Dennis Tueart and Billy Hughes all scored in a great 3-2 comeback win, after Ken Knighton and Stuart Pearson had both scored for Hull.

Sunderland moved up to fourth place, after they'd beaten Sheffield Wednesday 2-0, on New Year's Day, trailing second-placed Millwall by just three points. Disaster struck at Brisbane Road, a week later though, as Orient hammered them 5-0, and then they visited the fading force of Middlesbrough, on Saturday 22nd January.

34,846 packed Ayresome Park, Boro's highest attendance for four days, after 40,000 had filled the ground for their FA Cup Third round replay 1-0 win over Manchester City (Hickton), on the preceding Tuesday.

Both teams were desperate to win to keep in touch with both Norwich and Millwall.

MIDDLESBROUGH		SUNDERLAND
Jim Platt	1	Jim Montgomery
John Craggs	2	Dick Malone
Gordon Jones	3	Keith Coleman
Willie Maddren	4	Martin Harvey
Stuart Boam	5	Ritchie Pitt
Bill Gates	6	Brian Chambers
Nobby Stiles	7	Billy Hughes
Eric McMordie	8	Bobby Kerr
David Mills	9	Dave Watson
John Hickton	10	Ian Porterfield
Derrick Downing	11	Dennis Tueart
Joe Laidlaw	12	John Latham

Nobby Stiles had signed from Manchester United, for just £20,000, during the close season, as a short term solution to the lack of steel in Boro's midfield.

He and Maddren were immense in midfield, though, and John Hickton fired two first half goals, linking up nicely with the twenty year-old David Mills, who was enjoying a sustained run in Middlesbrough's attack, for the first time.

Stuart Boam had a bruising battle with Dave Watson, but he just came out on top, as Middlesbrough suddenly re-discovered their promotion form.

They won four of their next five league games, up to the middle of March, but only thirteen thousand fans bothered to watch their 2-1 home win over Oxford United, on Saturday 11th March, with David Mills scoring in each half. That was a win that lifted Boro up to fifth, only five points behind leaders Norwich, and with a game in hand.

It was as if the Middlesbrough fans almost expected another collapse, but it was sad to see such a poor home crowd, after 40,000 had watched them beat Man City in their FA Cup Third round replay, and then 36,489 watched them beat Millwall, before another home crowd of nearly forty thousand suffered a 0-3 defeat against Manchester United in their Fifth round replay.

It had been a brief, golden period in Boro's history.

Sunderland, too, had put their defeat at Ayresome Park to the backs of their minds, and they went on a seven match unbeaten run, up to the end of March, winning four times, including a 3-2 thriller over Portsmouth, back on Saturday 1st March, but with only 8,273 inside Roker Park.

After the arrival of Newcastle's reserve left back Ron Guthrie, Keith Coleman eventually became surplus to requirements at Sunderland, having made his debut for their 1-0 win over Swindon, back in September. Coleman, from Washington, played forty-nine games at Roker Park, before he moved to West Ham United in September 1973, for a small fee of just £20,000. Coleman eventually became a superb right back for the Hammers, and he started their 1976 European Cup Winners' Cup Final match.

By Saturday 11th March 1972, both North-eastern red and white teams were looking good for a late season promotion challenge.

DIVISION TWO LEADERS, 11TH MARCH 1972

	PL	W	D	L	F	A	PTS
Millwall	32	14	15	3	52	38	43
Norwich City	31	15	12	4	43	28	42
SUNDERLAND	32	13	13	6	50	45	39
Birmingham	31	12	14	5	47	26	38
MIDDLESBROUGH	31	17	4	10	41	35	38
QPR	31	13	10	8	42	26	36

Newcastle United manager Joe Harvey recognised that the lack of a creative midfield player was the cause of his team's tumble to the foot of the First Division, by late October. Jimmy Smith missed most of the 1971-72 season, due to a knee injury, and then Tommy Gibb was injured in the middle of October and ruled out until late February. There was one man who Harvey was after, and he was some player.

Tony Green was a slightly-built, five foot seven tall, fair-haired midfield creator, who'd been brilliant at Blackpool over the last few years, inspiring the Tangerines to a superb Anglo-Italian Cup win, with Alan Suddick alongside him.

He'd already played four times for Scotland, and during an era of great young creative Scottish midfield players, Hartford, Gemmill and Carr, Tony Green looked the jewel of them all, and ready to rule the World, with Billy Bremner next to him.

Blackpool were reluctant to let him go, but with Tony Green eager to move to Tyneside, and then Joe Harvey offering Keith Dyson as a makeweight in the deal, Blackpool eventually agreed to sell Tony Green, on 28th October 1971, in a club record transfer deal amounting to £140,000.

Mr Harvey was absolutely delighted. "I couldn't get another player as good as him, if I paid twice the money," he admitted. Tony Green even scored on his Newcastle debut, on Saturday 6th November, during United's 3-1 home win over Southampton.

Supermac scored the other two, one set up by Green, and the other by Terry Hibbitt.

Pat Howard and Stewart Barrowclough had also joined Newcastle from Barnsley, back in mid-September, for £30,000 apiece. Centre half Pat Howard was never as accomplished a player as Ollie Burton, and neither was he ever as feared as big John McNamee, nor ever as popular with United fans as either of them, but he was a tough tackler, and he adopted a no-nonsense attitude for the Newcastle United cause.

Barrowclough was only nineteen when he arrived, and due to the absence of Jimmy Smith, he played in most of United's remaining thirty-four games of the season. He had an accurate right foot, and he could also beat a man, but Stuart Barrowclough was safe and dependable, rather than dynamic or sensational.

After the arrival of the influential Tony Green, though, Newcastle United won six of their next twelve games, up to late January 1972, and they rose six places, up to sixteenth position, and well away from the relegation zone.

An all-time famous giant-killing occurred at Edgar Street, on Saturday 5th February, however, after Hereford United had beaten Newcastle 2-1, after extra-time, in their FA Cup Third round replay.

Ronnie Radford and Ricky George stunned the Magpies, after Supermac had put United 1-0 up late in the match.

"It was without doubt, the worst moment I have ever experienced in the game," Joe Harvey said afterwards. "I was sick when we lost that one."

In all fairness, that Hereford United team was no ordinary Southern League club. They really were a great club.

By the time that Joe Harvey was no longer the manager of Newcastle United, by 1975, Hereford were heading firmly towards the Second Division.

Sunderland won only four of their final ten matches, drawing three and losing three of them, and they finished the season down in fifth place, but only six points behind runners-up Birmingham City. Their average crowd, though, was again a shocking 15,905, over two thousand below Middlesbrough's average attendance.

Dave Watson and Dennis Tueart had scored a combined twenty-six league goals, while Bobby Kerr and Billy Hughes also chipped in with seventeen between them. Watson was Sunderland's only ever-present player, but Dick Malone, Ritchie Pitt and Bobby Kerr all missed just one game each.

In spite of being in a strong position, for the second time in three seasons, and with just six weeks remaining, Middlesbrough had also once again completely fell apart.

They won just two of their final eleven matches, but they lost five times.

By the final Saturday of the season, their fans had had enough.

Only 9,539 turned up to see Boro beat Hull 3-0 at Ayresome Park, just two months after Forty Thousand fans had been packing their ground, several times.

Middlesbrough finished the season way down in mid-table, with the promoted clubs out of sight and out of their league. John Hickton, their top scorer, had had his poorest season, scoring only twelve league goals.

A week after losing at Hereford United, Newcastle travelled to Manchester United, and in front of nearly 45,000, the Magpies, but particularly Tony Green, put on one of their finest ever performances, perfectly illustrating the rollercoaster life of a Newcastle United supporter.

Unfortunately, after partnering Pat Howard in central defence, a fortnight earlier, Ollie Burton suffered a bad knee injury during their goalless draw at Huddersfield.

Burton did not return to action throughout the following season, though, and he was forced to retire from professional football, during the Summer of 1973, having played 187 First Division games for Newcastle.

Saturday 12th February belonged completely to Tony Green. He had a style and a swagger all of his own, and he outplayed Best, Law and Charlton. He could shoot at goal from fully thirty yards out, with either foot, and he was so quick on the ball.

MANCHESTER UNITED		NEWCASTLE UNITED
Alex Stepney	1	Iam McFaul
Tom O'Neil	2	David Craig
Francis Burns	3	Frank Clark
Alan Gowling	4	Tommy Gibb
Steve James	5	Pat Howard
David Sadler	6	Bobby Moncur
Willie Morgan	7	Stuart Barrowclough
Brian Kidd	8	Tony Green
Bobby Charlton	9	Malcolm MacDonald
Denis Law	10	John Tudor
George Best	11	Terry Hibbitt
Sammy McIlroy	12	Irving Nattrass

Tony Green was the most complete footballer Newcastle United had ever had on their books. He's since been compared to a combination of Paul Gascoigne and Peter Beardsley, two of the greatest ever Newcastle talents. Green was central, on this day, against a Manchester United team that had led the First Division until three weeks before, and he created both of Newcastle's goals.

In the first half, Green chipped forward for John Tudor to finish past Stepney, and then he crossed from the left, after the break, for Barrowclough to steal in at the far right post, and drive the ball over Stepney, for a great 2-0 away win.

From then on, though, Newcastle won more than they lost, but they also drew as many games as they lost, in their final fourteen matches, and they finished up in eleventh place.

Malcolm MacDonald was their only ever-present player, and also, by a long, long way, their top goal-scorer, during his first season at St James's, with twenty-three First Division goals. Supermac had scored thirty league and cup goals for Newcastle, though, just as he'd predicted when he arrived.

Despite this, Tony Green was voted as United's Player of the Season, even though he'd played only twenty-seven league games. The impact of Tony Green's influence on United couldn't be recorded because many Newcastle games, during the early Seventies, weren't televised. So most of his games only live on in the fans' memories.

Sunderland endured another poor start to the 1972-73 season, winning only four and losing five of their opening fourteen games.

On Saturday 28th October, after drawing 0-0 at home to Fulham, and with just 11,618 inside Roker Park, their lowest crowd of the season up to then, Sunderland were down in fourteenth place, well behind the promotion places.

Crowds were now so poor, that the club began to do the unthinkable, and they actually advertised their home games on the back pages of the Sunderland Echo.

On Wednesday 1st November 1972, having been frustrated both by his team's performances, and by the Sunderland board's reluctance to extend his contract, Alan Brown finally resigned as manager, after 532 games in charge of Sunderland.

Alan Brown wasn't terribly well loved by some at the club, and supporters had stopped warming to him since their relegation season, but he did leave a vast amount of quality youth graduates to his successor.

Jim Montgomery, Ritchie Pitt, Bobby Kerr, Billy Hughes and Dennis Tueart had all became first team regulars, during his time as manager, and Micky Horswill had come in during the latter stages of the 1971-72 season, securing Sunderland's midfield.

He'd also signed the teenagers Dick Malone and Dave Watson. In spite of his managerial shortcomings at the top level, Alan Brown left a lasting legacy behind him on Wearside.

Sunderland had tried, unsuccessfully, to lure Brian Clough away from Champions Derby County, back to his native North-east. But Cloughie, despite being the Roker Park fans' favourite to take over, wasn't about to leave his beloved Derby, playing in the European Cup, for a lowly Second Division team.

Eventually, they moved for the former Newcastle United legend Bob Stokoe, who'd played nearly 300 matches for the Magpies, throughout their Cup-winning glory years during the Fifties.

Stokoe was manager of high-flying Second Division side Blackpool, and he'd developed a wonderful team, with its magnificent midfield of Tony Green (prior to his move to Newcastle), Tommy Hutchison, Alan Suddick and also Micky Burns.

On 23rd November, Bob Stokoe was appointed as the new manager, after two days of wrangling and negotiations regarding compensation to Blackpool. He was allowed to stay and oversee Blackpool's League Cup Quarter-final replay at home to Wolves.

Five days later, on Tuesday 28th November, nearly 20,000 filled Bloomfield Road to say farewell to Stokoe, but a late Derek Dougan goal put Wolves into the Semi-finals.

Once he was at Roker Park, Bob Stokoe made changes. He sharpened up the club.

He fixed the old clock at The Clock End, which had been broken for years, and he freshened up the red and white paintwork on the Roker Park stands; little things like that. He also changed the team strip, though, three and a half months into the season.

Sunderland's kit for the 1972-73 season made them look like a pub team in the Wearside Sunday League. It was the most basic red and white striped shirt you could ever find, with plain white shorts. Even school teams had better looking kits than that tired old rubbish. There wasn't even a club badge on the shirts' chests.

Bob fixed it.

Before Christmas, Sunderland emerged in a new, improved, sharper-looking, red and white striped shirt, with a stylish red collar and red cuffs, and with a club badge. SAFC was printed, diagonally, in heraldic lettering on the shirts, but that wasn't all.

Bob Stokoe knew the history of the club, being a Geordie, and he re-introduced Black shorts to Sunderland's kit, replacing the ineffectual white shorts previously worn.

Suddenly, the players had a dynamic new kit to feel proud and privileged to play in. Something had to lift them. Less fans turned up for Stokoe's first game in charge at Roker Park, though, than had bade him farewell back at Bloomfield Road.

By the start of January, Stokoe had converted Dave Watson to his preferred position of centre-back, alongside David Young, who'd signed from Newcastle for £35,000, after a horror show for

United, back on Saturday 23ʳᵈ September, at home to Leeds United, a game that pretty much finished his career on Tyneside.

Tony Green had scored Newcastle's first goal of the 1972-73 season, on the opening Saturday, as Newcastle beat UEFA Cup Finalists Wolves 2-1, with nearly 34,000 packed into St James's Park, that was still missing its Popular Side.

The new East Stand was well into its construction, by then, at a cost of half a million pounds, so Newcastle's ground capacity was still under 40,000.

Green and John Tudor both scored first half goals during that win, and a week later, Supermac and Tudor fired late second half goals, to secure their 2-1 away win at Sheffield United.

Supermac also scored during their 1-1 draw with West Brom, but Newcastle then lost twice, both at home, to Ipswich and Tottenham, in late August, before they finally travelled to Crystal Palace, on Saturday 2ⁿᵈ September.

Newcastle again lost, 2-1 in front of a Selhurst Park crowd of nearly 22,000, but on that Sunny, early Autumn afternoon, they lost much more than a game of football.

Tony Green went into a tackle with Mel Blyth, sticking his leg in, but the knee twisted. Everything went, his ligaments, his cartilage, the lot. Green was stretchered off the pitch, but at the time, nobody knew the extent of his injury, nor even that they'd seen the last of Tony Green, a true club legend, in a Newcastle United shirt.

After months of unsuccessful surgery, Tony Green was forced to announce his retirement, at the age of just 27, over a year later.

In the thirty-three First Division matches that Green had played since his arrival at St James's Park, Newcastle had won fifteen, double the amount of defeats they'd suffered. In contrast to their first fifteen games of the 1971-72 season, when Newcastle had won just twice and lost nine, Newcastle had been totally turned around by the presence of Tony Green.

Despite playing only thirty-five league and cup matches for United, Tony Green is still loved by supporters, to this day, as if he'd played over 350 matches.

With Tony Green "injured", *Jinky* Jimmy Smith made a timely return to Newcastle's midfield, having grown his dark hair long, very, very long during his absence from the game. Looking like The Sweet's guitarist, Andy Scott, Jimmy Smith had suddenly gained the ability to spray the ball all around the pitch, onto a sixpence, finding teammates with an ease that nobody anticipated.

Those two seasons 1972-73 and 1973-74 were the finest of *Jinky's* career. His passing was so subliminal, so extraordinary, there were times when he'd receive loud applause from one part of St James's Park, while the rest responded with groans of disappointment, before they also applauded, once they'd seen where the ball landed. Jimmy Smith would let fly with his right boot, but sometimes only those behind him could see the target of his passing, so abstract were the angles of his direction.

While Tony Green was the best midfield player to ever put on a Newcastle shirt, as well as Robert Lee, probably, Jimmy Smith was their single best passer of a ball, on his day, and possibly in the whole of the First Division, at that time.

Smith had come back a completely different player to the lacklustre lightweight prior to his injury, and thankfully, "his day" came more often than not, following his return to action in September 1972.

Newcastle beat Arsenal 2-1, on Saturday 9ᵗʰ September, with both Supermac and David Craig scoring, before then winning 3-0 away at Coventry City, a week later, thanks to Supermac's hat-trick.

"On their day," John Motson suggested, "MacDonald, Tudor and company could take on the best in the land and beat them."

Supermac supported this viewpoint. "There were games when we were awful," he admitted. "But then, the next game, we would be so good that we were virtually untouchable."

On Saturday 23rd September, at a still three-quarters built St James's Park, 38,962, their biggest home crowd of the season, watched a five goal thriller between Newcastle and the mighty Leeds United, favourites for virtually every trophy going.

Newcastle got straight off to a great start. David Craig fed the ball forward to Supermac. Supermac then laid the ball off, outside to Jimmy Smith, on the right side of the Leeds penalty area.

Smith fired a right-footed blast past Harvey, into the far left corner of the goal.

Leeds came straight back, as Mick Jones turned, twenty-five yards out, and threaded the ball through to Allan Clarke, just outside the Newcastle area. Surrounded by three Newcastle players, Hibbitt, Howard and Young, Clarke curled in a superb shot, from eighteen yards out. The ball swerved back to beat McFaul's dive at the far left post.

NEWCASTLE UNITED		LEEDS UNITED
Iam McFaul	1	David Harvey
David Craig	2	Paul Reaney
Frank Clark	3	Trevor Cherry
Tommy Gibb	4	Billy Bremner
Pat Howard	5	Jack Charlton
David Young	6	Norman Hunter
Stewart Barrowclough	7	Peter Lorimer
Jimmy Smith	8	Allan Clarke
Malcolm MacDonald	9	Mick Jones
John Tudor	10	Johnny Giles
Terry Hibbitt	11	Mick Bates
Gordon Hodgson	12	Joe Jordan

"That's in," Barry Davies cried, "oh, a fine goal too!"

Howard leapt and overpowered Jones in the air, heading Mick Bates' hopeful, forward ball thundering straight back into the Leeds half, where Smith beat Cherry to the ball, and then Barrowclough collected the loose ball, wide right, and he ran at the Leeds defence. He breezed past Norman Hunter, before crossing from the right side of the area, for John Tudor to glance a deft header past Harvey from six yards out.

David Young, playing his last game at St James's Park, though, before being sold to Sunderland, was put under a little pressure by Allan Clarke, and he played a diabolical square ball back inside, into his own area, but beyond his keeper McFaul.

Mick Jones poked the ball into the empty net for the equaliser. McFaul was livid.

Newcastle raised a gear, though, and went 3-2 up after the break. Jimmy Smith flicked a superb pass with the outside of his right boot, forward for Tudor to turn and beat Hunter. Tudor sprayed the ball out wide right for Gibb to sprint onto, out of midfield. Tommy Gibb's low cross was dummied by Barrowclough, six yards out, and Supermac!, on the far side of the six yard box, smashed a low shot back into the near right side of Leeds United's goal.

Newcastle held on for their brilliant 3-2 win over the title favourites, and they then lost only five games from their next twenty-three First Division games, up to the middle of March, while winning ten times.

Alan Kennedy made his Newcastle United debut, on Saturday 10th March, at left back, at home to Stoke City, after Frank Clark was moved over to cover the injured Bobby Moncur at centre back. Sunderland-born, and only eighteen years old, Alan Kennedy was a fearless, attacking fullback, whose youthful exuberance had suggested he might make it to the very top.

Supermac! scored his nineteenth goal of the season in that 1-0 win over Stoke, and the Geordies were getting ready for another European adventure, with Newcastle United in a UEFA Cup qualifying place.

FIRST DIVISION LEADERS, 10TH MARCH 1973

	PL	W	D	L	F	A	PTS
Liverpool	33	20	8	5	60	35	48
Arsenal	34	20	8	6	48	31	48
Leeds United	31	18	8	5	56	33	44
Ipswich Town	32	15	10	7	46	33	40
NEWCASTLE	33	15	9	9	52	39	39
Wolves	32	14	8	10	50	42	36
Derby County	34	14	7	13	42	48	35
Tottenham	31	13	7	11	43	34	33
West Ham Utd	33	12	9	12	51	43	33

Down at Middlesbrough, Durham-born David Armstrong had played in all of Boro's last five games of the 1971-72 season, and then he made his first start of the 1972-73 season on Saturday 16th September, at home to Preston North End.

The brightly fair haired product of Boro's excellent youth system became a regular on the left wing a month later, and they went on a four match unbeaten run during October and November, beating both Huddersfield and Preston, and drawing with leaders Burnley, as well as with third-placed Aston Villa.

By Saturday 11th November, Middlesbrough were fifth in the Second Division, after seventeen games, and only three points behind joint-leaders Burnley and QPR.

Back in the Summer of 1971, Newcastle United had sold Alan Foggon to Cardiff City, for just £25,000, after Joe Harvey had decided to move forwards with both Malcolm MacDonald and John Tudor in attack. Foggon was an exciting and electric attacker, but he'd been very erratic at St James's Park.

Alan Foggon had been bought by Cardiff to replace John Toshack, but he wasn't a great success at Ninian Park, and he longed for a return to the North-east.

So, on Thursday 26th October, Stan Anderson paid just £10,000 for the twenty-two year old, but he didn't play him, cleverly, except for a couple of sub appearances, until after Christmas.

Alan Foggon fired their winner during Boro's 1-0 win at home to Oxford United, on Saturday 30th December. Prior to that win, though, they'd won just one of their last seven league matches, and had sunk to mid-table. Only nine thousand home fans had watched that win over Oxford.

Graeme Souness then made his Middlesbrough debut during their 2-1 defeat away at Fulham, on Saturday 6th January, having signed from Tottenham Hotspur, just three days earlier, for a fee of just £30,000.

Souness had been advised to wait for his chance by Martin Peters, at White Hart Lane, but when Bill Nicholson had chosen to play John Pratt alongside Steve Perryman in the Spurs midfield, after Alan Mullery had moved to Fulham, Souness was fed up, so he moved to Ayresome Park.

Despite the additions of Souness and Foggon, though, Middlesbrough continued to lose as many as they won, after the New Year, in front of home crowds of well under 10,000, and on Saturday 13th January, Plymouth Argyle also knocked them out of the FA Cup, in the Third round.

Middlesbrough's morale had never been so low for seven years.

Sunderland had scraped through their FA Cup Third round tie, after a replay, beating Notts County 2-0, with over 30,000 inside Roker Park, after second half goals from both Dave Watson and Dennis Tueart.

Bob Stokoe then paid his old club Newcastle United just £15,000, for Ron Guthrie, their reserve team left-back. Guthrie wasn't ever going to displace Frank Clark, and with the young Alan Kennedy being praised in the Journal, as a future fixture in United's back four, it was unlikely that Guthrie would ever make it at St James's Park.

Ron Guthrie was a good, unflustered, and weathered twenty-eight year old blocker, with a stocky thirteen stone build, and he made his debut on Saturday 20th January, away at Swindon Town. Ian Porterfield gave Sunderland a 1-0 half-time lead, but Swindon equalised, through Butler, leaving Sunderland fifth from bottom, and only one point above the relegation places.

Sunderland had lost just three of their previous ten league games, but they'd also won only twice. They had risen only one place since their lowest point of the season, back in early December, just after Stokoe's arrival, when they were only two points above rock bottom.

Still, it seemed that the fans believed things were improving on Wearside, and on Saturday 27th January, 22,781 brought the Roker Roar back to Sunderland, for the visit of fourteenth-placed Millwall. It was a lower mid-table, almost meaningless game, but it attracted the second biggest Second Division crowd of that day, bigger than the crowd for the top two teams, QPR and Burnley, who'd met at Loftus Road.

It was also Sunderland's biggest home league crowd for over a year.

Dennis Tueart and Bobby Kerr both broke through Millwall's tough defensive outfit, marshalled by Barry Kitchener, scoring second half goals for a 2-0 win that moved Sunderland one place further away from relegation worries.

A week later, Sunderland were at home to Fourth Division Reading, in the FA Cup Fourth round. As FA Cup games went, this was barely mentioned, except on Wearside. For a team halfway down Division Four, it would have been more attractive if Reading had been drawn at home.

One of only two Fourth Division teams left in the competition, at home to one of the fallen giants of English football, slumped near the bottom of the Second Division? That would have been better. They might even have made Match of the Day? Sunderland at home to Reading was just terrible.

Only a few months earlier, Reading had tried to sign Ian Porterfield, and the two clubs had even agreed a fee of £20,000, but Porterfield didn't want to drop to the Fourth Division. In any case, Reading couldn't raise the cash to pay for him, so the deal was scrapped.

Charlie Hurley, Reading's manager, had played 358 league games for Sunderland, the last one as recently as 1969, and he'd even been a teammate with five players in Sunderland's line-up.

A huge crowd of 33,913 gave Hurley a great welcome back to Roker Park.

"CHARLIE! CHARLIE! CHARLIE!" they shouted from all over his old home ground.

The Roker Roar was silenced, soon after, when Les Chappell had headed Reading ahead after fifteen minutes, from Gordon Cumming's corner. Sunderland equalised, though, when Reading keeper Steve Death saved a shot from Billy Hughes, but he couldn't hold onto the ball, and Dennis Tueart was first to react, firing in the rebound.

After the break, Sunderland were well on top, but Death was superb, saving from Hughes, Porterfield and Kerr, while both Tueart and Malone also hit the crossbar.

Reading hung on to take Sunderland back to Berkshire for the replay, four days later.

A huge crowd of nearly 20,000, four times Reading's average attendance, filled their modest Elm Park ground, but Dave Watson put Sunderland 1-0 up after only ninety seconds. Then, after a quarter of an hour, Tueart chipped a shot over Steve Death, before captain Bobby Kerr slammed in a third before half-time.

Although Cumming scored from the penalty spot, during the second half, Sunderland's defence were never really bothered, and Jim Montgomery never had to make a proper save.

Sunderland's reward for their 3-1 away win was a trip to Manchester City, with their superstars Colin Bell, Francis Lee, Rodney Marsh and Mike Summerbee.

It didn't look a good draw.

Two days after Sunderland's win at Reading, Bob Stokoe paid just £10,000 for Luton Town's leading goal-scorer Vic Halom. Halom had already scored ten Second Division goals for the Hatters during 1972-73, from just twenty-five games, before he arrived at Roker Park, on Friday 9th February.

Vic Halom had a wild, unkempt look about him, with his long, thick dark hair, resembling the Sensational Alex Harvey.

Since Bob Stokoe had become their manager, many Sunderland players made the most of the freedom they now enjoyed, with regards to their appearance.

Slade, The Sweet and T-Rex were all huge, and it was no longer cool to look too neat, or short-haired. Most of the Sunderland players grew their hair long, for the first time. Captain Bobby Kerr even grew a great, thick moustache to complement his thick, shoulder-length hair.

Eight days later, on Saturday 17th February, Vic Halom scored his first goal for Sunderland, with nearly 26,000 inside Roker Park. Micky Horswill, Billy Hughes and Dennis Tueart scored the others, in their 4-0 thrashing of Middlesbrough.

Since their FA Cup defeat to Plymouth, Middlesbrough had improved their Second Division form, drawing twice and winning twice, in their next four games, rising to seventh in the table. That embarrassing 4-0 defeat at Roker Park, though, had killed any slight promotion hopes their fans might have possibly held onto.

Of their next seven matches, up to early April, Boro won two, lost two, and they drew three, to stay in the top ten. An end of season surge, however, drove Middlesbrough to win all of their last four matches, and to finish up in fourth place.

Boro won 3-1 away at Nottingham Forest, with Foggon hitting a brace, and Hickton one from the penalty spot, before they beat Sheffield Wednesday 3-0 at Ayresome Park. Foggon and Hickton each added another to their totals, while Bill Gates had headed his third of the season.

Willie Maddren scored a late winner away at Luton, on St George's Day, and then finally, John Hickton fired a superb second half hat-trick, on the final day of the season, to beat Orient 3-2 at Ayresome Park. Hickton was again Middlesbrough's top scorer, with fifteen league and cup goals, while Foggon and Mills scored fourteen between them. Alan Foggon had scored seven goals from just twelve games.

Middlesbrough's home crowd at that final game of the season was just 7,939, and although they'd finished fourth in the table, it again looked another false position. Boro were fourteen points behind second-placed QPR, but also only fourteen points above relegated Huddersfield Town.

Stan Anderson, who'd been Middlesbrough's manager since 1966, and he had led the club straight up from Division three, finally resigned at the end of the season, dejected after six seasons of failure to lift Boro back up into the First Division.

They had finished fourth-placed in three of those six seasons.

On Tuesday 8th May 1973, Middlesbrough appointed Jack Charlton as their new manager, on his 38th birthday. Charlton had only just retired from playing, after nearly eight hundred appearances for Leeds United.

Stan Anderson had left Jack Charlton with a great, competitive group of young players. David Armstrong was still only eighteen, while Graeme Souness had just turned twenty. Platt, Craggs, Spraggon, Boam, Maddren, Foggon and Mills were all still in their early twenties, while top scorer John Hickton, who'd scored 131 league goals in just 272 games, was the *old man* of the team, at twenty-eight years old.

Jack Charlton might have seen his job as similar to that of Brian Clough's, when he'd taken over at Derby County? The raw materials were all there, but he needed some experience. He needed some quality, international experience.

Jack Charlton effectively needed a **Dave Mackay,** to come into the team, and lift them up to greatness.

David Young had been clattered into by Sheffield Wednesday's Peter Rodrigues, on Saturday 10th February. It was a poor challenge for which the future Southampton captain was booked, but he really ought to have been sent off.

Young's ankle was badly damaged, though, and he was ruled out for two months.

Ritchie Pitt had lost his place in the team after Dave Watson was reverted to his natural centre back position, and he'd actually been loaned out to Arsenal. Without playing any games for the Gunners, Pitt was enjoying London life, and he was ready to face Leicester City in the First Division after an injury to Peter Simpson, when he was suddenly ordered back up to Roker Park.

Sunderland's end of season run-in looked like a meaningless, mid-table limp towards May, except for one big game, away at Manchester City, with Sunderland generally expected to be lambs to the slaughter.

Ritchie Pitt was far from happy at being pulled away from Highbury, and he failed to see any real reason for it.

On the morning of the FA Cup Fifth round, Saturday 24th February, Sunderland were the 250-1 outsiders of the sixteen remaining teams, while Manchester City were among the red-hot favourites to win the Cup, along with Leeds, Derby and Arsenal.

A huge crowd of 54,478 packed into Maine Road, twenty-two thousand more than City's average crowd, expectant of a straightforward, easy win over this little-heard-of and never-to-be-heard-of-ever-again Second Division team.

Indeed, City had attacked straight from the kick-off.

Jim Montgomery had to save well from Rodney Marsh, while Mike Summerbee was giving Ron Guthrie a terrible time out on the right wing.

After fifteen minutes, Summerbee sped past Guthrie, and then he crossed for Mike Doyle to head on for Tony Towers to ping a superb shot past Montgomery, from outside the area. Four minutes later, Francis Lee also missed a great chance to put City 2-0 up, from only ten yards.

Sunderland, though, grew more into the match. Guthrie calmed down and he began to cope more confidently with Summerbee's combative attacks. Dave Watson and Ritchie Pitt became unbothered by City's aerial balls, forcing a ground battle into the middle of the park, where Bobby Kerr, Ian Porterfield and Micky Horswill proved equal to Colin Bell, Tony Towers and

Derek Jeffries. This was one particular game when City had missed the class of Alan Oakes, out injured since September.

Ten minutes before half-time, Sunderland got the break that changed the shape of the game. Dennis Tueart went in hard on Joe Corrigan inside the City area, and a direct free-kick was awarded. Corrigan was ordered to re-take the kick, though, after he'd played a short pass to Willie Donachie, who then stepped back inside his own penalty area, under pressure from the energetic Horswill.

Joe Corrigan played a short ball, again, to the surprised Donachie, and Scotland's international full back was caught in possession by Horswill. Horswill beat Donachie, and then fired past Corrigan, from inside the area, to level the scores, with both Donachie and Corrigan glaring accusingly at each other.

Donachie had certainly been hesitant, but given the situation, Corrigan should have just banged the ball long, second time around.

Micky Horswill was still just nineteen years old, and the youngest of this Sunderland team, but his battling, hard running performance was probably the most important of any in their team. With a passion to compete that was as fiery as his long red hair, Horswill had turned Sunderland's fortunes with that opportune piece of fortune, and Sunderland's team spirit was lifted to that of Horswill's, thereafter.

Micky Horswill wouldn't give City's creative conductor, Colin Bell, even a second of freedom. He had the talent of doing the simplest things excellently, pressuring aggressively, and tackling sharply, but fairly.

He read interceptions quickly, and was relentless in his pestering of City's midfielders. It was a disgrace that no football card was ever made of Micky Horswill, by either A & BC or Topps.

After the break, with the scores level, Sunderland found themselves playing the better football. Dick Malone dispossessed Marsh with no-nonsense ease, and he passed forwards to Dennis Tueart. Tueart found Billy Hughes, out on the left wing, just inside the City half, and Hughes darted off, at great pace, away from Tony Book, towards the City area. Jeffries chased valiantly, and just caught up with the Sunderland forward, on the edge of his own area, but Hughes cut inside him, with Jeffries wrong-footed, and he smashed the ball, from fifteen yards, at goal.

Joe Corrigan dived full-length, and even got a touch to Hughes' shot, but the ball squeezed just inside his far post. Tommy Booth stood, open-mouthed, totally aghast.

"Hughesy was such a quick lad," Vic Halom recalled. "I was working as much as I could (without the ball) to get up with him."

It was "one of the most important goals I ever scored," admitted Billy Hughes.

Had the game been televised by the BBC, it would have been Goal of the Month, but Manchester City at home to lowly Sunderland was the last match of the day that the BBC had predicted that viewers would want to watch.

It was, in retrospect, just about the only match worth watching, in that Fifth round.

Four minutes later, Summerbee swung in a corner-kick, and Rodney Marsh jumped up, right in front of Jim Montgomery, literally pushing the Sunderland keeper backwards. Montgomery, who'd jumped to catch an easy ball, with Marsh making no effort to head it, could only get his palm to it. So unbalanced he was, as a result of Marsh's illegal challenge, playing only the man while pretending to go for the ball, that it landed at the back of Sunderland's goal.

Just as Sunderland waited for a whistle, for a foul on their keeper, all hell then broke loose as the ref actually signalled a goal to Manchester City. Marsh wheeled away, grinning, as if he'd levelled the scores, and Maine Road exploded with noise.

An own goal by Montgomery was officially recorded, to throw salt in the wounds.

Even then, Sunderland were the better side. Tueart crossed for Halom to head at goal, from close range, only for the great Joe Corrigan to brilliantly leap and tip the ball over his crossbar.

Billy Hughes broke through, late on, and he fired to Corrigan's right, but the City keeper flung himself to push the ball behind for another corner. Ritchie Pitt and Dave Watson were then absolutely immense as City pushed for a late, undeserved, winner, both defenders fully fired up by their tremendous away supporters.

At the end there was a significant confrontation between Mick Horswill and Tony Towers, who was sent off for violent conduct, while Horswill was booked for ungentlemanly conduct.

After that terrific 2-2 away draw, an all-ticket crowd of 51,782 packed into Roker Park for the replay, three days later, on Tuesday 27th February.

Many had felt there were many more than fifty-two thousand inside the ground, but even so, it was the first crowd of more than fifty thousand at Sunderland, since their Good Friday meeting against Newcastle, back in 1970.

Due to a peculiarity of the FA's rules, Tony Towers, who was sent off at Maine Road, was available to play, while Mike Summerbee, who was only booked but had subsequently exceeded his allowance of disciplinary points, was suspended.

This suited Sunderland, as Summerbee had been a much more potent threat during the first game. The replay was also a classic, and in front of one of the greatest atmospheres, in anyone's memory, ever experienced at Roker Park.

There was a stiff cold wind hitting Roker Park, that February night, from the North Sea, which both teams struggled to deal with, but Sunderland dealt with it better.

After fourteen minutes, Porterfield and Guthrie played a couple of one-two's down the left wing, before Guthrie passed forward to Hughes, who found Porterfield with a reverse pass inside. Porterfield played the ball square to Horswill, who split Jeffries and Book with a sublime angled pass to Bobby Kerr.

SUNDERLAND		MANCHESTER CITY
Jim Montgomery	1	Joe Corrigan
Dick Malone	2	Tony Book
Ron Guthrie	3	Willie Donachie
Micky Horswill	4	Mike Doyle
Dave Watson	5	Tommy Booth
Ritchie Pitt	6	Derek Jeffries
Bobby Kerr	7	Ian Mellor
Billy Hughes	8	Colin Bell
Vic Halom	9	Rodney Marsh
Ian Porterfield	10	Francis Lee
Dennis Tueart	11	Tony Towers

Kerr flicked the ball, confidently, to Halom, who smacked a spectacular goal, from thirty yards out, into the far corner of Corrigan's net, and right in front of the Fulwell End. Rodney Marsh almost equalised soon after, amidst the raucous Roker roar, but his overhead kick rebounded off Montgomery's far post.

Halfway into the first half, Sunderland then went 2-0 up. Kerr crossed for Hughes, inside the City area, and although his initial shot was blocked by Willie Donachie, Billy Hughes reacted quickest and found the gap between Donachie and Bell, smashing an unstoppable drive past Corrigan, high into City's net.

After the break, Francis Lee, the top goal-scorer in England, pulled a goal back, driving in past Montgomery, after Colin Bell had cushioned a header into his path.

Sunderland responded just minutes later though, as Porterfield, Malone and Halom all combined to play in Ian Porterfield, who shot at goal from inside the City area. Corrigan managed to get a hand to the ball, but Billy Hughes just beat his captain Kerr to the loose ball, and he tapped it into the net.

The Roker Roar of unbridled jubilation sent Sunderland into the Quarter-finals, and a home game against Luton.

"We didn't just beat Manchester City that night," Billy Hughes boasted, "we played them off the park." He was right, too.

Suddenly, Sunderland were playing like a First Division team, and not just any First Division team, but one of the top teams.

The transformation of almost the same team that were almost bottom of the Second Division, back in December, to FA Cup Quarter-finalists in February, was almost of comic book stuff.

After the match. Bob Stokoe had warm words for Ritchie Pitt, the player he'd pretty much fallen out with, and had tried to get rid of, before he lost David Young to injury.

"I might have sold him to Lincoln earlier this season for £15,000," Stokoe admitted, "but I couldn't have bought anyone for £50,000 as good as Pitt is now."

All was now happy in the Sunderland camp.

Ritchie Pitt had been re-born, in his "second career" at Roker Park. He forged a great partnership with Dave Watson, with his fearlessly aggressive style, allied to Watson's graceful, aerial dominance.

Sporting a thick afro hairstyle, as big as either Michael Jackson's or Diana Ross's, that added half a foot to his six feet and one inch of height, Pitt had become a pivotal part of a defence that became the third best in Division Two, behind Burnley and QPR, over the last three months of the season.

On Saturday 17th March, 53,151 filled Roker Park again, for their Quarter-final match against Luton Town. Sunderland's crowd was the largest of all the Sixth round matches, with Stamford Bridge, The Baseball Ground and Molineux all hosting the others that day. It was also the third-largest crowd of all the FA Cup matches that season, up to then.

BBC's Match of the Day cameras didn't make the mistake of missing *this* game.

Luton Town were flying high in Division Two, up in sixth place, but they'd been as high as third, back in late November. They'd already knocked Newcastle United out of the Cup, winning 2-0 at St James's Park, in the Fourth round. John Aston, who'd joined from Manchester United in July 1972, scored both goals to beat the Magpies, and he was Luton's best player. He had a tendency to blow hot or cold, though, and against Sunderland, he blew cold, as Derek Hales replaced him in the second half.

Luton were missing their club record signing, striker Barry Butlin, who'd scored five goals in fourteen matches since joining from Derby County, for £50,000, back in November. Butlin had been badly injured during their 3-2 defeat away at Millwall, on Monday 26th February, and he'd been ruled out of action for the rest of the season.

Luton worked hard, in any case, and they kept the scores level, goalless, at half-time. The home crowd began to really lift Sunderland after the break, with Luton a little distracted by the Roker

Roar. 53,000 never really turned up to watch Luton Town, anywhere, and the Hatters certainly became affected by the noise. Their tight, rugged and well-focussed defence was forced to make up for a lack of offensive power, with the vastly experienced Bobby Thomson, John Moore and John Ryan.

Twice, though, they went missing.

First, Bobby Kerr whipped in a fierce left wing corner to the far post, for Watson to head home, and then, shortly afterwards, another Bobby Kerr corner was nodded back into the six yard box by Ritchie Pitt, and Ron Guthrie swivelled and volleyed in from close range, for his first ever Sunderland goal.

Into the FA Cup Semi-finals, for the first time in thirty-six years, Sunderland were drawn against Arsenal, on the following Monday. Arsenal were in close second place, chasing Liverpool in Division One, and that night, Sunderland celebrated by winning 3-1 away at Preston North End.

Billy Hughes scored twice, with Vic Halom adding the other, and on the following Saturday, Sunderland beat Fulham 2-1 away, after Tueart and Halom scored.

39,930 then piled into Roker Park, on Tuesday 27th March, for the visit of Carlisle United. Former Boro forward Joe Laidlaw gave the Cumbrians a 1-0 half-time lead, but Billy Hughes and Dennis Tueart, from the penalty spot, both scored after the break, securing Sunderland's sixth win in seven games.

On the Saturday before their Cup Semi-final, Sunderland were up to thirteenth place in Division Two, after Bristol City had fought for a 2-2 draw at Roker Park.

In their ten games at Roker Park since the New Year, Sunderland had averaged crowds of 34,248, more than Newcastle United.

Having been fifth in Division One, on Saturday 10th March, and looking great for a fourth season in European competition, Newcastle United promptly self-destructed.

On Saturday 17th March, Kirby-born Terry McDermott came on, as a substitute, for his Newcastle debut, during their 2-1 defeat at Manchester United. McDermott, who'd just joined from Bury, for only £25,000, was a hard working midfield schemer who became a first team regular, one week later, as United drew 1-1 with Chelsea.

Newcastle drew 0-0 away at Leicester City, but then West Ham United overtook them in the table, after beating the Magpies 2-1 at St James's Park, thanks to goals in each half from their record signing Ted MacDougall. A draw at Southampton, and a defeat at Manchester City followed, and by the time Newcastle gained their first win in seven matches, on Saturday 21st April, after Tudor scored twice to beat Liverpool 2-1 at St James's, their European dream had died.

37,240 had packed the ground for that great win, but four days later, only 23,410 watched United's last home game of the season, a goalless draw with lowly Everton.

Newcastle finished the 1972-73 season with a 3-2 defeat away at Spurs, despite Tudor and McDermott giving them a 2-0 half-time lead. They had disastrously taken just six points from their final nine matches, and Supermac had failed to score in any of them, although he had missed their draws against both Chelsea and Leicester.

If they had taken just a point per match, they'd have qualified for the UEFA Cup, in fourth place, but this was Newcastle United's rollercoaster ride. They didn't do the simple things like just taking a point per match, when it really mattered.

After such an entertaining season, Newcastle finished, very disappointingly, down in ninth place, but just three points below fourth-placed Ipswich.

Their average crowd was nearly 28,000 during a season when St James's Park was only three-quarters built. Even with one arm tied behind their backs, Newcastle United were still the thirteenth best supported team in England.

Supermac was their top scorer, yet again, with nineteen league and cup goals, although John Tudor was United's top scorer in the First Division, with eighteen.

Tudor and Supermac had scored a combined thirty-five league goals.

An all-ticket 55,000 crowd packed Hillsborough for Sunderland's FA Cup Semi-final against Arsenal, on Saturday 7th April, as the Sunderland fans totally filled Sheffield Wednesday's massive Spion Kop End.

Micky Horswill had turned twenty in March, and he was given the honour of marking the talented, but tenacious Alan Ball. It was apt that Horswill should be tested against the World Cup winner, because Alan Ball was the player to whom Horswill was mostly compared.

On the whole, Horswill was compared favourably to Ball, throughout the match. Horswill got kicked by Ball, and he kicked Ball back.

He got right into Ball's face, and he stopped him playing.

Sunderland, wearing an all-white change strip, generally stopped Arsenal from playing. Pitt and Watson were again superb against both Charlie George and Ray Kennedy, while Dick Malone worked hard all afternoon to contain the lively George Armstrong.

Billy Hughes and Ian Porterfield looked after any attacking raids by Arsenal's full backs, McNab and Rice, but they were lively enough to break away from their markers, when on the attack themselves.

Alan Ball might have been impressed by Sunderland's all-attack or all-defence style of game, depending on whether they had the ball or not, as it was so similar to Everton's when they'd won the league, only three years before.

Horswill's left-footed shot, from the edge of the area, was well saved by Bob Wilson, after eighteen minutes. The Arsenal keeper crashed into his left post, as he fell, after tipping the ball over the crossbar.

Two minutes later, a Micky Horswill long ball up the middle was chased down by Halom, but Jeff Blockley got to the ball first. Blockley completely messed up his attempt to pass the ball back to Wilson though, and Vic Halom pounced, nipping in and getting a foot to the ball. He rounded the Arsenal keeper, but stumbled as he advanced on goal, inside the area. Halom just managed to regain his feet, though, and he rolled the ball into the empty net with his ankle.

Jim Montgomery blocked a George Armstrong shot with his feet, soon afterwards, from Pat Rice's free-kick, and then Armstrong hooked the ball back onto the post immediately afterwards.

Halom then brought out a superb diving save from Wilson, before flicking a Bobby Kerr cross past Wilson, but Bob McNab got back to clear the ball off the line.

Peter Storey was booked for fouling Hughes, after he'd galloped past McNab, and then Halom went close to scoring again, firing just wide from the edge of the area.

Jim Montgomery pulled off a brilliant reflex save, just before half-time, diving low to his right to turn a deflected George Armstrong shot around the foot of the post, for an Arsenal corner. Monty had initially been moving to his left, to cover the initial shot, but the deflection off Halom forced him to react quickly, and he brilliantly just got to the ball in time. Alan Ball hugged Montgomery in a show of complete respect.

The 1-0 half-time lead was crucial, if Sunderland wanted to get to Wembley.

John Radford came on for Blockley after the break, as Storey dropped back into defence, and Charlie George dropped into midfield, alongside Ball, to allow Radford and Kennedy, Arsenal's Double-winning double act, to get at Sunderland's defence.

Sunderland went 2-0 up, after sixty-four minutes, though. Dennis Tueart flicked on Bobby Kerr's long throw-in, at the edge of the six yard box, and Billy Hughes ballooned a second flicked header up and over the despairing Wilson, and the ball landed just inside the far post.

Jim Montgomery was resolute in goal, keeping Sunderland ahead with a series of superb saves under sustained pressure, as Arsenal had camped themselves in the Sunderland half. Charlie George fired a free-kick just wide of the left post, before he gave Arsenal hope, with only five minutes remaining, stabbing home a left-footed shot from Peter Simpson's low cross.

Charlie George wasted no time celebrating. He ran into the goal, picked up the ball, and ran back to place it on the centre spot, ignoring all congratulations. There was no more action, though, as Sunderland's two banks of five kept Arsenal out. They were finally at Wembley, to face Leeds United, who'd beaten Wolves 1-0 at Maine Road.

Bob Stokoe went to the Kop End, as Sunderland's players celebrated, and saluted the magnificent fans with his arms aloft, in his shirt and tie. Influenced by the new film, *Jesus Christ Superstar!*, which was on in the cinemas, the Sunderland fans chanted *"Messiah! Messiah! Messiah!"*, and thereafter, Stokoe would forever be remembered as the Messiah!, on Wearside.

After their Semi-final win, Sunderland won five of their next seven Second Division matches, and then drew 1-1 away at Orient, on Monday 30th April, their final match before the FA Cup Final. They'd conceded just six goals during their nine matches in that epic month of April 1973, scoring thirteen, and they kept four clean sheets.

On current form, since the New Year, Sunderland had been as good as both Burnley and QPR, who'd both been promoted to the First Division. At the end of the following season, Burnley finished sixth in Division One, and QPR were eighth.

Many people outside of the North-east didn't realise it, but Sunderland weren't the total minnows they were made out to be, by the time they'd reached Wembley. They were more of a First Division team, and far from cannon fodder for the giants of Leeds United, but not many believed it.

In spite of Bob Stokoe's insistence that they would win the FA Cup, Sunderland were vast underdogs, as they walked out onto the Wembley pitch, beneath those famous Twin Towers, alongside the mighty Leeds United, to the enormous roar of 100,000 fans, the likes of which has been heard in very few subsequent Finals.

Bob Stokoe wore a bright red and white tracksuit, that was so brightly coloured, it actually hurt your eyes if you tried to look at it for too long on your Colour Television.

He was the first manager in a Cup Final not to wear a formal suit and tie, but he purposely wore his tracksuit to make him look very different, the exact opposite to Don Revie, in fact.

Stokoe disliked Revie tremendously. And you really got that from television pictures, looking back years after. The Leeds manager had allegedly offered cash to the young Bob Stokoe, claims supported nor confirmed by any other person, during his early management days at Bury, back in 1962. An alleged cash amount had been offered, from Revie to Stokoe, if Stokoe told his Bury team to go easy on Leeds as they were fighting to stay in the Second Division.

Leeds have always refuted these unsubstantiated claims, but they were made, and Bob Stokoe remained evidently deeply bitter towards Don Revie.

This game, the FA Cup Final, was very personal for him, and he wanted to show it. It made for great TV pictures, and Revie looked nervous as they walked onto the pitch together, leading out their great teams behind them.

Leeds United wore their trademark blue and gold tags in their socks, and they all wore their full names on the backs of their white Admiral designed tracksuit tops.

Sunderland's players also had their names on the backs of their red and white tracksuit tops, for the occasion, but they didn't wear the sock tags.

They didn't salute the crowd from the centre circle before kick-off, either, something Leeds did at all their home games, and they did it here too, at Wembley Stadium.

They were roundly booed by the loud and rowdy Sunderland fans, and you could barely hear the Leeds fans.

At the coin toss, in the centre circle, Billy Bremner and Bobby Kerr became the two smallest captains in FA Cup Final history. Bremner was just five feet, four and a half inches, while Kerr was just five feet four.

While Leeds United's team had an average age of nearly 28, Sunderland were almost three years younger, per man, with an average age of just over 25. It showed too, not just in the enthusiasm, zest and energy of their entire team, but also in their hairstyles.

While Leeds United were not exactly a short back and sides team, they looked decidedly more middle management than Sunderland, looking like Rodney Bewes from Whatever Happened To The Likely Lads?, with their hair salon styled and finely coiffured.

Sunderland were a different bunch altogether. They were more rough and ready, wild and maverick, and they looked generally more exciting. Montgomery, Horswill, Watson, Pitt, Kerr, Hughes, Halom and Tueart all had hair down to their shoulders.

While Leeds mostly resembled middle managers, Sunderland looked like the serious rock stars, Glam Rock and pop stars they'd listened to at home.

Ian Porterfield looked more like Cliff Richard during his longer hair/***Power To All Our Friends*** period, a little more clean cut compared to teammates Vic Halom and Billy Hughes, but he still looked positively racy, against Johnny Giles, Eddie Gray and Mick Jones who still looked like the Beach Boys, singing ***Surfer Girl,*** ten years earlier.

LEEDS UNITED		SUNDERLAND
David Harvey	1	Jim Montgomery
Paul Reaney	2	Dick Malone
Trevor Cherry	3	Ron Guthrie
Billy Bremner	4	Micky Horswill
Paul Madeley	5	Dave Watson
Norman Hunter	6	Ritchie Pitt
Peter Lorimer	7	Bobby Kerr
Allan Clarke	8	Billy Hughes
Mick Jones	9	Vic Halom
Johnny Giles	10	Ian Porterfield
Eddie Gray	11	Dennis Tueart
Terry Yorath	12	David Young

In the very first minute, Mick Jones and Johnny Giles combined to play in Allan Clarke, thirty yards out, but as Clarke ran across the face of Sunderland's penalty area, for just a few yards, before the afro-haired Ritchie Pitt tripped him, cynically, and knee-high, sending Sniffer rolling, sprawling in agony

.It was a shocking challenge. You shouted "OUCH!" when you first see it, and it looked even worse on every subsequent replay.

It was a statement, though. Pitt should have been booked, but he wasn't.

He was turning Norman Hunter's admission, but particularly Leeds United's philosophy, on its head. "We never get booked for the first tackle," Hunter had said.

Pitt knew that, and so did Sniffer, lying on the pitch, writhing in the mud, for only about forty-five seconds, before getting back up, and without a single word of complaint.

Sniffer knew the game was on, and he wasn't going to waste time moaning about it, nor was Billy Bremner who said nothing to Pitt as he went to stand alongside him, waiting for the Leeds free-kick.

Peter Lorimer lashed his low shot wide of Montgomery's right hand post.

Billy Hughes was then sent five feet up into the air, after a crunching foul by Johnny Giles. Hughes just got up, and he also hobbled away without any complaint.

Eddie Gray sent Mick Jones into the Sunderland area, with a lofted pass, but Ritchie Pitt just had the legs to play the orange ball back to Montgomery.

Micky Horswill was ever present, blocking all forward balls into his own penalty area, as well as constantly harassing and chasing down the Leeds United back four, giving them little time on the ball.

Ian Porterfield advanced down the Sunderland left, after twelve minutes, and he played a square ball across to Hughes, twenty-five yards out.

Billy Hughes fired a direct, fierce drive just over David Harvey's crossbar.

Horswill then fired in a low shot, from just outside the Leeds area, after Guthrie's cross was headed out by Reaney. The orange ball glanced inches wide of the left post. Dave Watson slid in superbly to dispossess Clarke, just as Leeds' leading scorer was about to shoot from the penalty spot, after Cherry had driven in a low cross.

Watson's great tackle had saved a certain goal.

After twenty-one minutes, Allan Clarke was harshly booked, very harshly indeed, after helping his team defend Porterfield's free-kick. He became involved in a very physical tussle with big Vic Halom, and he just clipped Halom from behind as he slipped on the wet, fragile turf.

"Maybe that was a little tough?" suggested Brian Moore. Sniffer couldn't believe it.

Every Sunderland fan in the Stadium shouted "What a load of rubbish!" at Norman Hunter, after the hard man had fouled Dennis Tueart on halfway, leaving Tueart needing treatment.

Hunter was booed with his next touch by the vast red and white half of Wembley.

Lorimer crossed deep from the right of Sunderland's area, after half an hour, with Clarke poised to head in, at the far post. Dick Malone, though, flew in from nowhere with an excellent defensive header, virtually stealing the ball off of Clarke's forehead.

Bobby Kerr then lofted a long, high ball towards the Leeds goal, from thirty-five yards out, and David Harvey, under close pressure from Hughes, had to tip the ball away, over his crossbar for a Sunderland corner.

Billy Hughes took the kick from the left corner flag. His ball flew just over Watson's head, but Halom managed to play the ball back in, off his thigh. Ian Porterfield chipped it up and buried his shot into the back of the Leeds net.

After thirty-one minutes, the 250-1 outsiders, back in January, were leading 1-0.

"*We Shall Not, We Shall Not Be Moved,*" sang the rampant, bouncing Sunderland fans, with their red and white scarves aloft.

"And look at them!" exclaimed Brian Moore!

After two delightful back-heeled flicks from Tueart and Hughes down the Sunderland right, Kerr's cross into the Leeds area was headed out to Horswill, who volleyed high over Harvey's bar.

With just a couple of minutes to go before half-time, Allan Clarke controlled Reaney's long pass. He turned and shot, from just inside the Sunderland area, but Watson slid in and deflected the goal-bound shot just a yard wide of the right post.

Peter Lorimer's corner kick was punched away by Montgomery, back to Lorimer, but his second cross was weak, and scrambled away. Clarke managed to thread the ball back to Lorimer, though, who beat Dennis Tueart and he fired a hot shot at Sunderland's goal, from just twelve yards out. Montgomery sat up firmly, though, and he palmed the ball away, with both of his hands, textbook goalkeeping.

Leeds kept up the pressure in the fading moments of the first half, keeping Sunderland penned inside their own penalty area. A poor ball from Trevor Cherry, though, allowed Porterfield to drive forward, using up a valuable thirty seconds, as Hunter blocked Hughes' shot, and then Harvey leapt on the ball at Halom's feet.

Johnny Giles shot, from twenty yards, flew well wide of Montgomery's goal, but that was the last significant action of the first half.

Overall, Sunderland had been quicker and cleverer in midfield, and Dave Watson was the pick of a supreme Sunderland defence, eating up every long ball sent forward, and also giving Allan Clarke a torrid time in the process. They fully deserved their half-time lead.

Leeds looked anxious and frustrated.

As Sunderland ran onto the Wembley pitch, against the Twin Towers skyline, for the second half, Leeds United's players were walking, looking weary and anxious. Billy Bremner, though, had changed into a short-sleeved shirt. He, at least, meant business.

Bremner's twenty yard shot, just three minutes after the break, zipped on the wet turf, but it was parried by Montgomery, before Malone stuck the orange ball out for another corner kick to Leeds.

As they kept up the pressure, Leeds won a free-kick out on their right wing. Bremner's cross was planted into an empty net by Trevor Cherry, but Allan Clarke had already fouled Montgomery as he leapt to catch the ball.

After fifty-five minutes, Sunderland launched their first sustained attack of the second half. Madeley blocked Tueart's shot from the edge of the area, and Hunter blocked Porterfield's drive, on the rebound. The loose ball was collected by Guthrie on the edge of the Leeds penalty area, and he drove it high, clipping the outside of the left post, and rippling the side-netting of Harvey's goal.

Then, Paul Madeley's forward pass was volleyed first time, by Peter Lorimer, from the edge of the Sunderland area, into the side-netting of Montgomery's goal.

Twenty minutes into the second half, Mick Jones had the orange ball, on the edge of the *D*, but heavily marked by both Pitt and Porterfield. He steered the ball back to Reaney, thirty-five yards out, and Reaney clipped a great cross towards the left side of Sunderland's six yard box. Trevor Cherry dived full length to meet it, firing in a bullet header, which Jim Montgomery dived to his left to parry.

From just four yards out, Peter Lorimer drove the rebound goalwards.

"And a GOAL!" shouted Brian Moore….. "NO!"

Montgomery had stretched and leapt further to his left, getting his left hand to Lorimer's shot, and he sent the ball rocketing up towards his crossbar, and away to safety.

Dick Malone cleared the danger.

"My goodness, I thought Lorimer got that one!" exclaimed Brian Moore. Even Jimmy Hill had got it wrong. "It turns out to be an ***incredible*** miss," he'd originally opined.

"There it is, Lorimer coming in…. Oh, in fact, it wasn't. What a save! In fact, that was a fantastic save!!" Jimmy Hill doubly exclaimed!!

It was one of the greatest saves of all time, a World Class save, compared favourably with Gordon Banks' save against Brazil, during the 1970 World Cup Finals.

Jim Montgomery's double save was to be remembered as one of the greatest moments of footballing excellence, in FA Cup Final history.

After nearly seventy minutes, Lorimer crossed from the right, and Watson jumped high above Clarke, once again, but he headed only to Giles, on the left of the six yard box. Giles chested the ball down, and from about eight yards out, he drove the orange ball eight yards over Montgomery's bar.

"Is this the moment?" Brian Moore had cried. "No it's not!"

THE HAPPIEST CUP WIN OF THEM ALL

Horswill and Halom broke quickly down the right, after seventy-one minutes, and Halom drove in a shot from the right side of the Leeds United area, but Harvey safely caught it, at his near post.

Johnny Giles called for Harvey's quick throw, out on the right, and then he whipped a great ball forward, that Kerr could not stop. Clarke ran clear, with the through-ball, before shooting from just inside the Sunderland area, but Montgomery caught the faintest of touches to send the ball just wide of the far left post.

Micky Horswill had harassed and hustled Bremner, Giles, Madeley and Cherry, etc, all afternoon, and Bobby Kerr had effectively turned Eddie Gray into an anonymous figure, out on the left. This Eddie Gray was not the Eddie Gray of the 1970 Wembley Final, and with fifteen minutes left, he was replaced with Terry Yorath, adding more urgency and ferocity to Leeds' attacks.

Lorimer flicked on Giles' right wing cross, for Cherry to stoop and head into the turf, towards goal, but Montgomery dived low to clutch the ball, with both arms, on his goal-line. Jim Montgomery then caught Yorath's low shot from the right, with only twelve minutes remaining.

Four minutes later, Billy Hughes should have played a simple back pass to Montgomery, but the boos from the Leeds United fans in the crowd, expecting a simple back pass, had persuaded him not to do so. So Hughes tried to play himself out of trouble, being a forward, but Cherry dispossessed him. Hughes was then booked for the most innocuous foul on Cherry, pulling him back, as he prepared to run clear. His own sense of pride caused Billy Hughes to become the second player booked in the '73 Final.

With just five minutes remaining, Porterfield fouled Hunter just outside his own penalty area, but Lorimer's free-kick was blocked by the Sunderland wall. Halom's shot from the edge of the area, with only two minutes remaining, was well defended by the classy Paul Madeley.

Halom met the rebound, though, and he blasted the ball high towards the top right corner of the Leeds United goal. David Harvey dived, full length, to tip the ball round his post, for a Sunderland corner... "and a tremendous save by Harvey!"

Leeds United never had another shot at Montgomery, and Sunderland held out, easily, for the greatest post-war FA Cup Final upset. Stokoe, with a cream raincoat and trilby hat now covering his red tracksuit, galloped onto the pitch at the final whistle, to embrace his goalkeeper Jim Montgomery. Left back Ron Guthrie also joined in with the embrace, and captain Bobby Kerr, from the banks of Loch Lomond, ran in and he stole Bob Stokoe's trilby, sticking it on his own long haired head, with his comedy moustache and all, before dancing away to celebrate.

It was an iconic image, capturing the sheer romance of one of the greatest Cup Finals. Leeds United had certainly not played badly. They had certainly turned up for the match, but on the day, Sunderland, at their very, very best, were just a bit better.

"*HA'WAY THE LADS!*" *GOAL* magazine subsequently celebrated, with Bobby Kerr holding aloft the FA Cup, on its front cover of May 19th 1973. "*The happiest Cup win of them all.*"

Smiles have rarely been brighter, or more joyful, during Wembley Stadium's ninety year history.

The 1972-73 season was an absolute dream for Ian Porterfield, who was forever loved by everyone at Sunderland Football Club, for evermore.

BLACK COUNTRY BLUES

WITH A GOOD TWENTY-FIVE MINUTES still remaining, during the 1968 FA Cup Final, Albion's players were already shattered, having chased around after Everton's superior ball players for more than an hour, on a Wembley pitch that was little better than a ploughed potato field.

Bobby Hope hobbled up, quite literally, to take the left-sided corner, won by Clive Clark, off Tommy Wright.

Tony Brown, who was everywhere for Albion, throughout the match, had confessed afterwards, "legs just gave way near the end. Couldn't feel me legs at all, that last half-hour… just driving meself."

At the end of 1967-68, Everton and West Bromwich Albion were only six points apart, in fifth and eighth place, respectively, but they were really poles apart.

Everton had still been in the title race, with just a month to go, along with City, United, Leeds and Liverpool, but defeats away at Nottingham Forest and Manchester City, in late April, had finally killed their hopes.

They finished up only six points behind the Champions, Manchester City, in the end.

Albion could certainly score goals. With their fluent scoring front three of Astle, Brown and Clark hitting a combined total of sixty-three league and cup goals, that season, West Brom were the third highest scoring First Division team, with seventy-five goals. Their defence, though, was not so dominant.

While Everton had one of the top defensive records in the First Division, conceding only forty goals from forty-two games, West Brom had conceded sixty-two goals.

Everton had reached the FA Cup Final after conceding just one goal from their five games against Southport, Carlisle United, Tranmere Rovers, Leicester City and Leeds United. In contrast, West Brom had conceded seven goals in nine games, needing four replays en route to their Semifinal win over Birmingham City, at Villa Park.

Everton and West Bromwich Albion were indeed poles apart, and Everton were hot favourites to win the Cup. West Brom had Jeff Astle, though, who'd scored in every round, up to the Final, and he'd scored thirty-four league and cup goals in 49 games.

Astle had failed to score against Everton in either of Albion's two First Division games against the Toffeemen, though. During 1967-68, Everton had thrashed West Brom by an aggregate score of eight goals to three.

Albion had required replays against Colchester United and Southampton, in their Third and Fourth round ties, before travelling to Portsmouth in the Fifth round.

A massive 43,800 crowd packed Fratton Park, double Portsmouth's average Second Division attendances, on Saturday 9th March, but Portsmouth were frustrated by a dogged, dreary and dour display, and the Pompey manager responded, after the match, that the FA Cup would be devalued if Albion won the Cup.

No matter, West Brom's twin attack of Jeff Astle and Clive Clark had secured a great 2-1 away win.

43,503 filled The Hawthorns, after Albion were rewarded with a home tie against Liverpool in the Quarter-finals, on Saturday 30th March, but Liverpool fought hard for a goalless draw, without either Tony Hateley or Tommy Smith, to take West Brom back to Anfield.

Nine days later, on Monday 8th April, a huge crowd of 54,273, Anfield's second biggest home attendance of the season, welcomed the return of Tony Hateley.

Ian St John's free-kick was headed onto Osborne's crossbar by big Ron Yeats, but Hateley had returned to strike the rebound past Osborne from the edge of the area. And it was Tony Hateley who sent The Kop into a loud, crisp performance of "Ee-aye-addio, we're going to win the Cup!"

Liverpool's great defence only had to hold onto their fifteenth clean sheet of the season to reach the Semi-finals, but out of nowhere, Jeff Astle cracked in a sharp shot, from the edge of the box, past Tommy Lawrence's dive.

The Kop was silenced.

Albion's defence grew in stature, as the game went into extra-time, and Liverpool's front six of Ian Callaghan, Ian St John, Emlyn Hughes, Peter Thompson, Tony Hateley and Roger Hunt counter-attacked with a heavy, red onslaught, but Talbut, Kaye, Williams and Fraser were all excellent, blocking all that came their way, in thirty extra minutes of the most electric football ever played, as the Anfield crowd roared Liverpool on, and on.

West Brom held on, though, and ten days later, on Thursday 18th April, over fifty-six thousand packed Manchester City's Maine Road ground, for the second replay, with Tommy now back for Liverpool.

LIVERPOOL		WEST BROMWICH ALBION
Tommy Lawrence	1	John Osborne
Chris Lawler	2	Dennis Clarke
Geoff Strong	3	Graham Williams
Tommy Smith	4	Doug Fraser
Ron Yeats	5	John Talbut
Emlyn Hughes	6	John Kaye
Ian Callaghan	7	Tony Brown
Roger Hunt	8	Ian Collard
Tony Hateley	9	Jeff Astle
Ian St John	10	Bobby Hope
Peter Thompson	11	Clive Clark

Jeff Astle swept Albion into the lead, just over halfway into the first half. Ian Collard had collected a loose pass, then side-stepped St John, and he played a clever pass into Astle, on the edge of the area. With his first touch, Astle lofted the ball over Lawrence, into the roof of the net, to loud Black Country roars.

Shortly afterwards, John Kaye suffered a bad cut over his eye, so Tony Hateley took advantage, levelling the scores, just before half-time. Kaye emerged for the second half with his head heavily bandaged, as Liverpool, sensing victory, turned up the heat. John Osborne saved brilliantly, twice, from World Cup hero Roger Hunt, and John Talbut won a brilliant aerial battle with Hateley, as the crosses just reined in.

An excellent ten pass move led to the winning goal, though, running through Dennis Clarke, Hope, Collard, Brown and Astle, before Clive Clark buried the ball past Lawrence, to send Albion into the Semi-finals, where they faced their local rivals, Second Division Birmingham City, for a great chance to reach Wembley.

Leeds-born Clive Clark had made his league debut for QPR, ten years earlier, aged only seventeen. He was a skilful, incisive left winger, and then in 1960, he'd joined West Brom for just £17,000.

Clark had been Albion's top scorer on three occasions during the Sixties, and he'd helped maintain them as a winning First Division team that always scored more goals than they conceded.

Also joining Albion back in 1960 was Bobby Hope, a sixteen year old Glaswegian, who'd joined straight from school. A precocious teenager, Hope's ability to run a ball out of defence and midfield, picking his passes with pinpoint accuracy, made him one of the game's best goal-makers and inside forwards in the game, throughout the decade.

Bill Shankly didn't often praise players outside of his own Liverpool team, but he did say about Bobby Hope, "I like that boy. He can put a ball on a sixpence."

Hope had scored thirty-four goals in 225 First Division matches, during his first eight years at The Hawthorns.

With West Brom and Birmingham both from the West Midlands, Villa Park was the obvious choice for their FA Cup Semi-final, on Saturday 27th April.

A gigantic 60,831 crowd filled the place, as a result, from pitch-side all the way up to the top walls of the expansive Holte End, for the least glamorous of the two Semi-finals.

63,000 had filled Old Trafford for the other game, between Everton and Leeds United.

West Brom were red-hot favourites to win, but Birmingham were the better footballing team on the day, having already beaten Arsenal in the Fifth round, and then Dave Sexton's mighty, stylish Chelsea in the Quarter-finals.

John Osborne made a string of sharp saves from former England forward Fred Pickering, but eventually, Brown and Astle both scored to send Albion to Wembley, with a flattering 2-0 win.

There was no time to drink Champagne and celebrate.

Nearly 46,000 packed into The Hawthorns, just two days later, on Bank Holiday Monday 29th April, for the visit of the First Division leaders, and European Cup Semi-finalists, Manchester United, and Best, Law, Charlton, Crerand, Stiles, Kidd, Aston, et al.

At just seventeen, though, Asa Hartford made only his second ever start for West Brom, in for the injured Clive Clark, and he scored his first ever goal as Albion went crazy.

Jeff Astle was in particularly dazzling form, that Monday night, giving David Sadler a terrible time, scoring a brilliant hat-trick, and he was directly involved in all the other goals, as Albion were leading 6-1 after seventy minutes. Ronnie Rees, Tony Brown and Hartford had scored their other goals, while a Denis Law penalty kick was United's consolation.

Brian Kidd scored two late goals to make the score-line more "respectable", at 6-3, but even then, Law had three chances during the closing minutes, all from a yard out, and all of which he missed, which could have earned United the most unlikely and dramatic of score draws.

It wasn't to be, and that defeat swung the title race advantage towards Maine Road. Three years later, West Brom would wreck the title hopes of another great team…

On Saturday 18th May, Graham Williams led West Brom out for the FA Cup Final against Everton. Williams, from Rhyl, had originally joined Albion as a seventeen year old, during the mid-Fifties.

He had since played 279 First Division games, mainly at left back, and then became their club captain in 1965, leading Albion to victory over West Ham United, 5-3 on aggregate, in the 1966 League Cup Final.

Watched by the gorgeous HRH Princess Alexandra, probably the most stylish royal of her generation, the Princess Diana or Kate Middleton of her time, Joe Royle and Alan Ball kicked off the first ever FA Cup Final to be broadcast live on Colour Television.

WEST BROMWICH ALBION		EVERTON
John Osborne	1	Gordon West
Doug Fraser	2	Tommy Wright
Graham Williams	3	Ray Wilson
Tony Brown	4	Howard Kendall
John Talbut	5	Brian Labone
John Kaye	6	Colin Harvey
Graham Lovett	7	Jimmy Husband
Ian Collard	8	Alan Ball
Jeff Astle	9	Joe Royle
Bobby Hope	10	John Hurst
Clive Clark	11	Johnny Morrissey
Dennis Clarke	12	Roger Kenyon

Early on, Albion created the first attack of the game. John Hurst fouled Jeff Astle, and Astle's header, from Graham Williams' free-kick, was cleared over to the right wing, from where Doug Fraser crossed, and Tony Brown volleyed just over Gordon West's angle from six yards out.

On a sticky Wembley surface, play during the first quarter-hour was scrappy, and any promises of fluent passing displays were dispelled by wild, raging tackles, as well as players simply slipping on the mud.

Colin Harvey won a full-blooded, meaty challenge with Lovett, and he played wide to Morrissey, who rode Fraser's lunge, and then set off down the left, only for referee Leo Callaghan to blow for a foul. Fraser's knee was gashed, though, as he'd slid in on Morrissey, and he was carried off for a short time. Fraser came back on, but he was given three stitches on his knee during the half-time interval.

While Everton were running the game, with their triumvirate of Kendall, Harvey and Ball controlling the flow of the game, and the tenacity of ball-winner Hurst supplying the wide players Husband and Morrissey.

In contrast, West Brom were forced to feed on occasional breaks, but Everton's tight, well-oiled rear-guard of Merseybeat boy Tommy Wright, captain Brian Labone, Hurst, and their World Cup winner Ray Wilson had caught any loose runs from either Hope or Clark in offside positions.

John Osborne spilled Morrissey's superb cross, under pressure from Royle, and was grounded as he punched away. Jimmy Husband swivelled and scooped wide of the open net from twelve yards.

The first and best chance of the game was missed badly.

Osborne required medical attention for his shoulder injury for over a minute. Full back Fraser, with his bandaged leg, then hacked down Alan Ball, and John Kaye scythed down Colin Harvey, who stayed down.

"Wakey, wakey, ref!" shouted a Scouse voice in the crowd, while John Hurst looked aghast that Mr Callaghan had failed to book Kaye.

The Everton crowd chanted, "we want football! We want football!" After a couple of minutes of heat spray treatment, Harvey trotted back into Everton's attack.

Just five minutes before half-time, Ball won possession and he teed up Howard Kendall, twenty-five yards out. Kendall's first time blast just cleared the beaten Osborne's crossbar.

Everton, for all their possession, and in spite of West Brom's dogged defence, as well as the poor state of the pitch, looked the easy winners. Alan Ball was again pivotal in Everton's next attack, running from the centre circle, and passing wide left out to Morrissey. Morrissey cut inside and let fly a twenty yard rocket, at which Osborne flung himself and just tipped the ball over his bar.

Into the second half, Albion's captain Williams cynically tripped Jimmy Husband, after he'd been beaten on his outside, just outside the right hand angle of the eighteen yard box.

From a dangerous position, Tommy Wright's floated free-kick was claimed by the leaping Osborne. With those types of set-piece balls, Everton had no chance.

From Osborne's throw, Fraser ran from his own area to the edge of the Everton area, evading two challenges, and he played in Clive Clark, out on the left. Clark's driven cross was blocked by the retreating Wright on his own bye-line, thwarting the finest piece of football from West Brom, so far.

After Bobby Hope's corner had been cleared away, Tommy Wright attacked down the right, beating Williams, and forcing an Everton corner kick. The referee made a mistake, though, and he awarded a throw-in to Everton.

West Brom took advantage and they cleared the danger.

Jeff Astle headed Bobby Hope's left-sided cross just past West's right hand post, the first direct attack by Albion on Everton's goal, ten minutes into the second half.

Husband again beat Williams, down the right wing, but the Welsh left back physically pulled back Everton's leading FA Cup goal-scorer. Morrissey attacked from the Everton left, but Fraser stuck out his right leg, and he tripped Morrissey up, just outside the Albion area.

In today's game, both of Albion's full backs would have been sent off, by now, and Albion would have had to play the last twenty-five minutes with just nine men.

"Attack! Attack! Attack, attack, attack!", the Everton fans continued to shout loudly. "We want football! We want football!"

It would be true to say that Everton were also guilty of foul play, but West Brom, and Fraser and Williams particularly, were cynical when Everton were in dangerous attacking positions.

Tony Brown worked hard, but he was totally overran by Kendall, Ball and Harvey. Clark, Hope and Astle were all isolated figures, as Albion's side was continuously stretched by the superior Merseysiders.

Labone passed back to West, and the Everton keeper hoofed a huge kick up into the air. Jimmy Husband controlled the ball, with just one touch, inside the Albion area, and then he played it out wide right to Alan Ball. Ball teased Hope, before returning the pass to Husband, thirty yards out.

Husband sailed past Talbut's diving tackle and floated into the area, ready to shoot. Fraser, Brown and Kaye, though, had all swarmed around him, like wasps, and they broke down the attack, as Husband took one touch too many.

Astle headed Hope's centre into the arms of Gordon West, and then, Collard headed Bobby Hope's left-sided corner kick just over the bar, from eight yards.

West Brom, but Bobby Hope in particular, were beginning to find some confidence on that heavy surface. Harvey, Kendall, and even Ball were starting to misplace the odd pass.

Lovett hacked down Ray Wilson, the thirty-three year old left back, but again, John Osborne rose highest to catch Wilson's long free-kick, despite being under pressure from both Royle and Hurst.

Kendall carried the ball out of his area, and he released to Alan Ball, out on the left wing. The England star got the better of Fraser, before belting a twenty yard blast at Osborne's near post, which the Albion keeper dived at and held onto, gratefully.

Morrissey danced a delightful dummy past both Hope and Fraser, and then crossed from just inside the left side of the area.

Alan Ball glanced his header just a few feet wide, from the edge of the six yard box.

Kendall picked up a loose Albion clearance, and he crossed from the right for Morrissey, out on the bye-line to the left of the penalty area. Morrissey centred back for Alan Ball to nod home, from six yards out, but Husband leapt in ahead of him, and headed just over, just five minutes before the end.

After 86 minutes, Jeff Astle ran clear, from halfway, with just Labone to beat. Labone challenged Astle, just outside his own area, but Astle side-stepped the tackle, and steadied himself to shoot.

Colin Harvey had galloped back, though, lightning-quick, like *Sir Ivor,* to challenge Astle on the edge of the area, winning the ball, before Gordon West collected.

Dennis Clarke replaced John Kaye at the start of extra-time, to become the first ever substitute in an FA Cup Final. Bobby Hope linked passes with Tony Brown, in a wonderful move from halfway, and then fired just over the bar, from twenty yards.

Two minutes into extra-time, Jeff Astle rode a tackle from Kendall, ten yards inside the Everton half, and ran towards the Everton area. He fired weakly, right-footed, and wide. Brian Labone blocked his shot anyway, but Harvey was unable to meet the second ball, and clear it away, so Astle pounced on the rebound.

He fired high into West's goal-net from the edge of the area, with his left foot.

Tony Brown then had a half-chance to put Albion 2-0 up, firing just inches wide with a thirty yard daisy-cutter, through a crowd of players, with Gordon West struggling to scramble across.

Two minutes into the second period of extra-time, Everton should have levelled. Wright crossed from the right, and as Osborne came out to challenge, John Hurst was presented with an open goal to head into, but he sent his bullet header wide of the right hand post. He could have just scuffed his header in….

In the end, though, West Brom hung on for a famous 1-0 win.

It had been clear to all that Albion had not been the better team, on the day, and Everton could be proud of the way they had played, and of the dignity they showed to their opponents, in defeat. They never lost their heads, in spite of some dodgy tackling, and some soft refereeing, but they just persevered, very professionally, to win the game. West Brom could be congratulated for the way they battled, though, on a terrible pitch, that helped neither team in playing fluent football.

This was far from being *"The happiest Cup win of them all."*

John Talbut, though, had battled so honestly and admirably against the young nineteen year old Joe Royle, Everton's leading scorer, and he admitted that Everton had been the better team, possibly.

"I'm not saying Everton didn't have the pressure on us. We were under pressure 90% of the game," Talbut told David Coleman. "We were very fortunate on a few occasions, and there was some good goalkeeping, and a little bit of luck on our side. Everton could have had at least one, perhaps two," he continued, but he had no problems justifying West Brom's Cup win.

"I think we deserved that one goal in the later stages of the game, and of course, we went through." An articulate and calmly spoken man, and about the only Albion player who actually could talk, after such a physically and mentally draining game, John Talbut had signed from Burnley back in December 1966, for £30,000.

Two years later, though, Talbut was displaced in the team by the younger John Wile, and during the Summer of 1971, Talbut left The Hawthorns.

At the age of thirty, John Talbut was appointed as player-manager of Belgian side KV Mechelen, having played 144 First Division games for Albion.

On the evening of that fine, Spring Saturday evening, **ASTLE IS THE KING** was painted, **big** and **bold**, on the brickwork of the B4173 canal bridge in Primrose Hill, Netherton, near Dudley, and right in the heart of the Black Country.

The words were removed after a while, but they reappeared, and then were removed again. Every time they were removed, though, **ASTLE IS THE KING** reappeared in bright, white paint, almost immediately. The bridge became an icon for Albion fans, and an infamous, cult landmark in footballing history.

From then on, The King was born, and he would never, ever be replaced at The Hawthorns.

The 1968 FA Cup Final was the first to be broadcast live in colour, after the arrival of the exciting new age of Colour Television, that had a huge influence on the growing popularity of football.

Before Colour Television had made its debut, English league football was in a grainy world between Pathe News, and the colourful, exciting pictures from the 1970 Mexico World Cup Finals.

Match of the Day had a theme tune nobody could remember, *"Drum Majorette,"* written by Major Leslie Statham, bandleader of the Welsh Guards.

Presented by Kenneth Wolstenholme, the programme had a very dry look about it, not designed to send the excitement cells racing.

In August 1968, though, London Weekend Television began transmissions of The Big Match, on Sunday afternoons. The Big Match became the less formal, and more enjoyable of the two weekly football highlights shows.

Although the 1968 FA Cup Final was broadcast on Colour Television, colour transmissions were still virtually non-existent. Very few people even possessed a Colour Television set, as they were so expensive, and colour transmissions so rare.

In November 1969, though, as a new Glam Rock decade was about to dawn, BBC Television began its colour transmissions, and ITV also did likewise in four of its regions, Thames/London Weekend, ATV, Granada and Yorkshire.

On Saturday 15th November 1969, BBC TV broadcast the first ever colour episode of Match of the Day, with Liverpool 2-0 West Ham United as its showpiece match. These were the days when the BBC wouldn't advertise which games they were showing on Match of the Day, until after all of Saturday's league matches had finished. They had an agreement with football clubs, to help avoid attendances falling at grounds.

On the following day, Sunday 16th November, London Weekend TV broadcast the first ever colour broadcast of The Big Match. Chelsea 1-1 Everton was its showpiece game, and certainly the better game, in terms of pedigree.

By the end of 1969, over 200,000 Colour Television sets had been sold, or rented, in the United Kingdom.

For the start of 1970-71, after the glorious Summer of World Cup football, *Match of the Day* suddenly thumped out an exciting, brand new theme tune, written by Brian Stoller.

That new theme tune, one of the most famous in British TV history, if not the most famous, has been Saturday night's theme tune to Match of the Day ever since.

Over on ITV, unless you lived with Victorian grandparents and weren't allowed to watch the dirty filth, *The Big Match* began to spread its wings across the Independent Television Networks.

Presented by Brian Moore, who also commentated on many of the matches, it developed regional differences. So, if London Weekend was your local station, you'd see Chelsea v Spurs, but if you were in the Tyne-Tees region, you'd be shown highlights of Newcastle v Liverpool, from the previous day, with Brian Moore introducing, and then reflecting on each match.

In most areas, *The Big Match* was the only programme in which you could see your local team, in action, on Colour Television. Some regions had variations on the programme's title; for instance, ATV broadcast *Star Soccer,* from the Midlands, presented by Gary Newbon, with commentary by Hugh Jones. In the Tyne-Tees region, The Big Match was called *Shoot!*

The Big Match, unlike the more serious looking Match of the Day, had a more fun look to it. While Saturday night viewers enjoyed the passionate, but righteous reflections of David Coleman, and then Jimmy Hill, Sunday afternoon viewers laughed at special guest presenters Malcolm Allison, Brian Clough, Rodney Marsh, Terry Venables, and the bald-headed Terry Mancini wearing a queer assortment of wigs.

Then, for 1973-74, *The Big Match* unveiled the most exciting sporting theme tune ever, and one of British television's most brilliant theme tunes.

La Soiree by David Ordini was the theme tune to *The Big Match* for the remainder of the Seventies, blasting out of television sets with blaring brasses and a booming timpani, and a bloody wonderful sound it was too! If you'd ever scored a goal on a school football field, or any suburban area of grass, you imagined this joyful music accompanying your celebration.

On the first day of the 1968-69 season, Saturday 10th August, Asa Hartford started for West Brom, in place of Ian Collard, for their goalless draw with Sheffield Wednesday.

From Clydebank, Hartford went on to play 26 First Division matches during 1968-69, mostly in place of the injured Clive Clark, who missed well over half of the season.

Asa Hartford also started all of Albion's European Cup Winners' Cup matches, scoring twice in their 3-3 aggregate win over FC Bruges, during September and October. Hartford and Tony Brown both scored in their 2-0 second leg home win at The Hawthorns, with nearly 34,000 celebrating their away goals victory.

In November, having just turned eighteen, Hartford scored another crucial goal away in Romania, as Albion had held Dinamo Bucharest to a 1-1 draw, beneath a brutal barrage of bottles and bricks thrown by the home crowd.

Tony Brown and Jeff Astle shared the goals as Albion thrashed Dinamo 4-0, again in front of a home crowd of more than 33,000, winning 5-1 on aggregate.

Astle was missing from their 3-0 win over Norwich City, in the FA Cup Third round, on Saturday 4th January, but he returned eleven days later, as West Brom visited Dunfermline Athletic, Scotland's surprise team in the Cup Winners' Cup, for their Quarter-final first leg match.

A massive crowd of over 22,000 packed the modestly sized East End Park, making a gigantic racket, roaring for the blood of every Englishman. West Brom's central defensive partnership of John

Kaye and John Talbut kept out the Pars' rampant attack, led by Pat Gardner, taking a good 0-0 away draw back to The Hawthorns.

31,204 filled Craven Cottage, on Saturday 25th January, as Second Division Fulham hosted West Brom in the FA Cup Fourth round.

Asa Hartford and substitute Ronnie Rees both scored in Albion's 2-1 away win.

Then, on Wednesday 12th February, a massive crowd of 45,354 bulged the barriers at The Hawthorns, for Albion's Fifth round tie at home to Arsenal.

Without the suspended Bobby Hope, West Brom were huge underdogs and they fought hard, but they won 1-0, after Tony Brown had let fly a superb free-kick, from twenty yards out, just a couple of minutes before the end of the match.

Tony Brown and Jeff Astle were becoming one of the most feared attacking partnerships in England, scoring a combined thirty-eight First Division goals during 1968-69, to keep Albion up in the top ten.

A week later, on a frozen, icy pitch, West Brom went a goal down, early on, to Dunfermline, during their ECWC Quarter-final, second leg match.

Despite the Black Country roars of 32,000 home fans, Albion could not break through, and they went out, surprisingly, 0-1 on aggregate, after Pat Gardner's goal had proved decisive.

That devastating home defeat had denied them a very winnable Semi-final tie against Slovan Bratislava.

52,285 filled Stamford Bridge's vast terraces, on Saturday 1st March, for Albion's last hope for silverware, in their FA Cup Quarter-final match, away at Chelsea.

West Brom manager Alan Ashman had the wizard Charlie Cooke, Chelsea's star midfield player, double marked by both Dennis Martin and Graham *Shove* Lovett, throughout the game, to boos from the Shed End. Bobby Tambling's free-kick, from the right wing, after yet another foul on Cooke, was then headed past Osborne by the unmarked David Webb.

If Cooke broke free from his midfield markers, then John Talbut just stopped him every time, often unfairly, and usually punished with set-pieces that he, Kaye or Osborne just swallowed up.

Talbut had offended in such a *gentlemanly* and *apologetic* manner, though, time after time, that he'd always kept himself out of the referee's notebook.

John Dempsey headed just a yard wide of Osborne's goal, with an open goal to aim at, from Cooke's free-kick. That goal would have killed off West Brom's hopes, had it been scored.

Then, Fraser, Lovett and Kaye played a delightful triangular passing movement out of their own half, and the ball ended up at Bobby Hope's feet, out on the left.

Hope crossed into the Chelsea area, and Astle headed on for Tony Brown, running from deep. Brown swivelled past Hollins, and then Dempsey, twice, before firing beyond Peter Bonetti, into the top far corner of the goal.

Into the second half, the influential Bobby Hope again crossed deep from the left, and Dennis Martin's shot forced Bonetti to dive and make a good save at the foot of his left post. From Martin's right-side corner kick, though, Jeff Astle sent his bullet header flying past Bonetti's dive, but the referee had already blown his whistle for a penalty kick to West Brom, for an offence that nobody else had seen.

Tony Brown fired his penalty kick, hard, to Bonetti's left post, but *The Cat* superbly saved it, palming the ball away for another Albion corner.

On the break, after a sustained period of Chelsea pressure had broken down, Brown bombed away from halfway, leaving Webb trailing behind him, and he squared for Astle, inside Chelsea's penalty area. Astle shot past Dempsey, and although Bonetti got his hand to the ball, he couldn't prevent it from rolling over the goal-line.

With the game moving into injury-time, and with Chelsea desperate for an equaliser, Ron Harris's free-kick was flicked on for Peter Osgood, just six yards out, but Ossie's point blank volley was magnificently saved, and *caught*, just inside his right hand post, right on the goal-line, by John Osborne. As outstanding as Osborne had been in the Cup Final against Everton, that save from John Osgood was probably the best save of his career. It was Brilliant.

John Osborne had joined West Brom back in January 1967, having played over a hundred Fourth Division games for Chesterfield. He was also West Bromwich Albion's captain in BBC TV's sporting quiz show *Quiz Ball,* where he led them to the title, with his wealth of knowledge.

As good a goalkeeper as he was though, Osborne could do absolutely nothing about Allan Clarke's dipping shot that swerved beyond him, late on in their Semi-final against underdogs Leicester City, at Hillsborough, on Saturday 29th March.

Even the rain pouring down on the canal bridge in Netherton, on *ASTLE IS THE KING,* just pissed people off. The atmosphere at Albion was dampened so deeply, it took nearly a decade to get the good times back again.

Still, Alan Ashman wasn't to know that, and he persevered in trying to turn Albion into one of the top First Division teams.

Back on Wednesday 7th May 1969, Jeff Astle had made his England debut, against Wales at Wembley, playing alongside Francis Lee in attack. Less than two months later, on Saturday 2nd July, Ashman paid a club record transfer fee of £100,000 to Sunderland, for Colin Suggett, their leading goal-scorer for the previous two seasons.

Suggett was an attacking player with lightning speed and good positional sense, but he also had the ability to create as well as score goals.

Slimly built, just five feet eight inches tall and eleven stone, Colin Suggett went straight into Albion's team away at Southampton, for their first game of the 1969-70 season.

Sensationally, Suggett scored a superb second half brace, as West Brom won 2-0.

Albion had another underwhelming start to the season, thereafter, gaining just nine points from their first thirteen matches, and they were only a point above bottom club Sunderland. West Brom travelled to Arsenal on Tuesday 7th October, as Len Cantello made his first appearance of the season, having played a couple of matches towards the back end of the previous season. With Tony Brown out, Cantello anchored the midfield well, and following Astle's first half strike, Albion earned a good 1-1 draw.

On the following Saturday, the mighty Leeds United visited, and Jeff Astle again scored, just before the break. Mick Jones levelled, though, to earn a point for the reigning Champions. West Brom remained a side that, at their very best, could mix it with the very best, when the heat was on.

With 45,488 filling The Hawthorns, a fortnight later, Manchester United visited West Brom, on Saturday 25th October. This was a post-Busby United in transition, though, with Sartori in for Law, Ure in for Stiles, and Francis Burns in for Crerand.

Still, United still had Best, Charlton and Kidd, and Brian Kidd fired home George Best's pass, giving them a 1-0 half-time away lead.

Albion came out after the break inspired, though, as Suggett, Hope, Hartford and Astle terrorised the United defence. Tony Brown and Bobby Hope both scored, but it should have been a much more emphatic win, so superior were West Brom.

By Boxing Day 1969, Albion were up to fifteenth in Division One, but they faded to sixteenth place by the end of the season. On Saturday 8th April 1970, Manchester United had gained some vengeance by destroying West Brom by seven goals to nil.

A month earlier, Albion had lost a tough, tight battle in the League Cup Final at Wembley, losing 2-1 to Man City, after extra-time. They'd beaten Aston Villa, Ipswich Town, Bradford City, Leicester City and Carlisle United, all teams lower placed than themselves in the Football League, en route to their fourth major Cup Final in five seasons.

In spite of Albion's lowly First Division finish, Jeff Astle was Division One's leading goal-scorer, during 1969-70, with twenty-five goals from just 34 games. He was selected by Sir Alf Ramsey for the England World Cup squad to go to Mexico.

On Sunday 7th June, in Guadalajara, Astle came on as substitute for Francis Lee, against Brazil. From only twelve yards out, Jeff Astle shot wide, *incredibly,* with only Felix between himself and the goal. Had he scored, England were on the ascendancy and might only not have lost 1-0, but they might have beaten Brazil, and had an easier route of Peru and Uruguay during the knockout stages.

With just ten minutes remaining, Alan Ball also drove the ball onto the crossbar.

West Germany then awaited England in the Quarter-finals, after Allan Clarke's penalty kick had secured victory over Czechoslovakia.

Colin Suggett was West Brom's only ever-present player during 1969-70, and he and Tony Brown shared twenty-two First Division goals, in support of Jeff Astle.

Tony Brown was a stocky, five feet six-and-a-half inches tall, bustling type of forward. Brown hit the ball with the full force of his eleven and a half stone body, an explosive punch that earned him the nickname *Bomber,* and he rarely failed to score from the penalty spot.

During 1970-71, *Bomber* Brown had the best season of his career, becoming the First Division's top goal-scorer, as he blasted in twenty-eight First Division goals from 42 games.

Apart from their famous 2-1 away win at Elland Road, on 17th April, when Suggett, Hartford, Astle and Brown had outplayed the league leaders, and wrecked Leeds United's title hopes, West Brom had achieved several other memorable results against top teams, that kept them well clear of relegation worries, in a First Division that was a lot stronger than it had been, back in the Sixties.

One week after they'd shocked Leeds, they also held Champions-elect Arsenal to a 2-2 home draw, with Hartford and Brown both scoring, and in front of a huge crowd of over 37,000. But back in October, they'd also hammered the reigning Champions Everton 3-0, at home, after goals from Brown, Astle and George McVitie.

Tony Brown also blasted a hat-trick past Manchester United, during their 4-3 win, with over 41,000 inside The Hawthorns, Albion's biggest home crowd of the season, back on Saturday 6th March. John Wile had scored their other goal.

John Wile had replaced John Talbut as Albion's centre-half, alongside John Kaye, on Saturday 19th December 1970, for their 1-1 draw with Blackpool. Signed from Peterborough United for just £35,000, after he'd played 116 league games at London Road, Wile became the base of West Brom's spine for the remainder of the Seventies.

Born in Sherburn, up in the North-east, John Wile was a fearless, hardened defender, in the Jack Charlton or Roy McFarland mould, and he also presented himself as a dangerous threat at Albion's corner kicks and set-pieces.

West Brom had lost one of their Cup Final heroes, back in early January, when Nottingham Forest paid £35,000 for their Scottish full back Dougie Fraser. Fraser had played 257 First Division games for Albion, and then he played a further fifty-five top flight games for Forest, until they were relegated in May 1972.

Albion's best performance of the 1970-71 season, though, apart from their win away at Elland Road, was when they visited Anfield, on Saturday 2nd April, with Liverpool still in the hunt for a much-needed UEFA Cup place.

With 43,580 inside Anfield, the biggest crowd to watch Albion during 1970-71, both teams were missing key players. Liverpool were without John Toshack, their club record signing, who'd joined from Cardiff back in November, while West Brom missed the attacking influence of Colin Suggett, who'd been out since January.

LIVERPOOL		WEST BROMWICH ALBION
Ray Clemence	1	John Osborne
Chris Lawler	2	Lyndon Hughes
Alec Lindsay	3	Alan Merrick
Tommy Smith	4	Len Cantello
Larry Lloyd	5	John Wile
Emlyn Hughes	6	John Kaye
Ian Callaghan	7	George McVitie
Alun Evans	8	Tony Brown
Steve Heighway	9	Jeff Astle
Bobby Graham	10	Bobby Hope
Brian Hall	11	Asa Hartford

Defences reigned supreme for an hour, with Wile and Kaye eating up everything that came the way of either Evans or Graham, before Asa Hartford showed a piece of genuine class, turning Emlyn Hughes inside out with a swivel and a swerve, before delivering a beautifully weighted ball inside. Tony Brown bombed in and hammered home from just inside the Liverpool area, giving Ray Clemence no chance.

The uber-blonde haired Alun Evans poached a leveller, late on, and Albion were denied another famous win at Anfield, but they were applauded off the pitch by many home supporters. Even Bill Shankly knew that his team had been outplayed and, three months later, he rectified his *problem* by signing Kevin Keegan.

Asa Hartford, who had been in sparkling form for West Brom, was the subject of a British record transfer fee, in November 1971. With Eddie Gray's fitness having been inconsistent since 1970, after a series of injuries, Leeds manager Don Revie needed a quality reinforcement, and he saw Hartford as that man.

A Scotsman, Asa Hartford would have fitted in like a glove alongside Leeds United's Celtic midfield of Bremner, Giles and Lorimer, and on Wednesday 3rd November, he cleared out his locker at The Hawthorns, and joined Leeds United in a £170,000 deal.

Three days later, though, the football world was stunned when Leeds called off the deal, after medical examinations revealed a suspected *"hole in the heart"* condition.

Asa Hartford was warmly welcomed back to West Brom, and he went on to play First Division football for another fourteen years.

Leeds United failed to sign another player during Revie's three remaining years as manager, and it proved a huge mistake for Leeds to cancel the signing of Hartford.

Asa Hartford missed Albion's home defeat to Stoke City, but he played in all but one of their remaining matches of 1971-72, including another famous 2-1 win over Manchester United, on Saturday 29th January 1972.

A massive crowd, 47,012 again filled The Hawthorns, and they roared Albion to victory over Best, Charlton, Law and Kidd, after they'd trailed at half-time to Brian Kidd's header.

Bobby Gould and Jeff Astle both scored second half goals in a spectacular come back, sparking a run of five wins in seven games, into early March, that alleviated their relegation worries.

Alistair Robertson had become John Wile's regular partner in central defence, back on Saturday 9th October, for Albion's 2-0 win away at Crystal Palace. A Glaswegian, Robertson had joined the club back in 1969, as a seventeen year old, having already represented Scotland at schoolboy level.

The great John Kaye left The Hawthorns just a month later, having played 284 First Division matches for West Brom, and scoring 45 goals. He joined Hull City for just £25,000, at thirty-one years old, and then three years later, he was appointed as manager of the Tigers.

On Wednesday 8th March 1972, Albion boss Don Howe paid Leicester City £55,000 for Alistair Brown, who'd scored thirty-one league goals in 99 games at Filbert Street. Of the eleven games in which Ally Brown played, in midfield, to end the season, Albion lost only three times and they finished ten points above the relegation places.

They'd also recorded their best win of the season, on Thursday 27th April, over European Cup Winners' Cup holders Chelsea. This was the one and only game that Asa Hartford was forced to miss after his return to The Hawthorns, from Elland Road.

In Hartford's place, was Bobby Hope making only his sixteenth start of the season. Still only twenty-eight, Hope had become marginalised after the younger players' arrivals, and this home game against Chelsea was his penultimate game for Albion.

WEST BROMWICH ALBION		CHELSEA
John Osborne	1	Peter Bonetti
Gordon Nisbet	2	Paddy Mulligan
Alan Merrick	3	Ron Harris
Colin Suggett	4	John Hollins
John Wile	5	John Dempsey
Alistair Robertson	6	David Webb
Bobby Hope	7	Charlie Cooke
Bobby Gould	8	Steve Kember
Tony Brown	9	Tommy Baldwin
Alistair Brown	10	Alan Hudson
Len Cantello	11	Peter Houseman

Bobby Hope was class personified, spraying the long passes all around to Suggett, Cantello, and Ally Brown. Chelsea were missing their mercurial star, Peter Osgood, injured during their defeat at Tottenham, in early April, and they ended up simply chasing shadows all night long.

Tony Brown hammered Albion into a first half lead, delighting the 18,489 hard-core home crowd, that made the noise of a 35,000 packed house.

After the break, Bobby Gould, Ally Brown and Len Cantello all scored, as West Brom ended their home campaign with a 4-0 thrashing of a top six team.

Also missing from Albion's team was Jeff Astle, who'd suffered a terrible season, with various physical troubles, and he scored only two goals from 22 First Division games.

Astle was a shadow of the unstoppable force from the late Sixties, but he continued to be missing from action for a further ten months, as West Brom plunged towards relegation during 1972-73.

Bobby Hope left Albion, on 26th May 1972, joining newly-promoted Birmingham City for a fee of £60,000. Hope had played 346 First Division games for West Brom, and he was one of their finest ever creative talents. At Birmingham, though, he also eventually became surplus to requirements, unable to break into City's electric Blue front line of Francis, Latchford, Hatton, Campbell and Taylor.

In 1972-73, Albion went down in bottom position, with only Tony Brown reaching double figures in goals scored, with fourteen in both league and cups.

On Wednesday 4th December 1972, though, Don Howe had paid Glasgow Rangers a club record transfer fee of £135,000 for wide midfield attacker Willie Johnston.

Willie Johnston had been a key player for Rangers as they'd won the European Cup Winners' Cup in 1971-72, scoring two goals during their 3-2 Final victory over Dynamo Moscow, in Barcelona.

Two and a half months later, however, with relegation appearing inevitable, Albion cashed in on Colin Suggett, selling him to fellow First Division strugglers Norwich City, for just £80,000.

Suggett had played 128 Division One matches for West Brom, scoring just twenty goals. His goal for Norwich, though, against Crystal Palace on Tuesday 24th April, had helped keep the Canaries in the top flight.

For the following season, West Brom were in the promotion race for most of the season, up until March, but they were always behind Middlesbrough and Luton, and they even knocked Everton out of the FA Cup, after a Fourth round home replay.

On Saturday 16th February, 40,000 packed out The Hawthorns for the visit of Newcastle United, in their highly-anticipated Fifth round tie, with Albion strongly fancied to upset the Magpies, playing in away colours of yellow, green, and light blue.

Newcastle really did play like Brazil that day, though, and Malcolm MacDonald, Stuart Barrowclough and John Tudor buried Albion's Wembley hopes, winning 3-0 en route to the FA Cup Final.

Jeff Astle was again missing for most of that season, but he finally returned on Saturday 23rd February, for their home match against Bristol City, against whom he scored his 137th league goal during their 2-2 draw. Astle's season only lasted five games, though, after he limped off in two of the latter three.

He'd made his final appearance for Albion, as a substitute for Tony Brown, during their 2-2 draw at home to Cardiff City, on Saturday 30th March 1974.

His contract was cancelled at the end of the season, after 292 league games for Albion, 286 of which were First Division matches.

Jeff Astle was quite possibly the most popular player to have ever worn the West Bromwich Albion shirt. He will forever be regarded as The King at The Hawthorns, and the song *Astle is the King,* to the tune of *Camptown Races,* is still sung by Baggies fans today.

Astle ended his career playing for a variety of non-league clubs, including Dunstable Town, alongside George Best, and for whom he scored 25 goals during 1974-75.

He also played for Weymouth and Atherstone, before finally retiring in 1977.

He ran an industrial cleaning company, after football, with his company logo along the sides of his van, accompanied with the slogan, *"Astle Never Misses The Corners."*

In 1994, Jeff Astle became a regular star on the BBC TV football comedy show, Fantasy Football League, and he'd always close the shows, with his *Jeff Astle Sings* act, singing famous hit songs like Come On Eileen, Rhinestone Cowboy and The Locomotion, while the end credits rolled.

On Saturday 19th January 2002, Jeff Astle died, aged only fifty-nine years old, of a degenerative brain disease.

The coroner found that his disease had been caused by the repeated heading of footballs.

Jeff Astle had scored a total of 174 league and cup goals for West Brom, from 361 games, and his death was mourned by all football fans.

A series of special editions of Fantasy Football League were broadcast after his death.

The first show, of this short series, started very simply with two minutes' silence by presenters, guests and audience, in tribute.

Eighteen months after his death, The Astle Gates were unveiled at The Hawthorns, on Friday 11th July 2003, with a wonderful, colourful wrought-iron plaque, portraying Jeff Astle, in Albion colours, celebrating one of his 174 goals.

On Saturday 2nd March 1974, Albion were in the thick of the Second Division promotion race, having beaten local rivals Aston Villa 3-1, away at Villa Park. Tony Brown had scored twice, and John Wile the other, lifting West Brom up to fourth, level on points with third-placed Orient.

However, a run of just one win from their last eleven matches ruined their season, and they ended up in eighth place, only four points behind third-placed Carlisle United, who were managed by their former manager Alan Ashman. Ashman then claimed that getting Carlisle promoted to the First Division was a greater achievement than winning the FA Cup with Albion in 1968.

On Tuesday 13th August 1974, Manchester City paid a British record transfer fee of £250,000 for Asa Hartford. Hartford had played 214 league games for West Brom, and he'd been one of their very brightest ever talents.

It was sad for Hartford that he'd left West Brom languishing in lower league football, despite having the raw talent and core of a team that should have been much greater than it was, while Leeds United had just won a truly brilliant First Division title.

It was even sadder that, in April 1979, Hartford was languishing in sixteenth place, with Manchester City, while West Brom were strongly fighting Liverpool for the First Division title, only four points behind the mighty Reds, but with a game in hand, at a time when Hartford's spark and influence could have turned the title Albion's way.

Never mind, Asa Hartford went to City in August 1974.

In October 1974, John Osborne returned to West Brom, after initially retiring from football, back in the Summer of 1973. His return to goalkeeping duties inspired a great run for Albion, as they lost only three games from their next thirteen, winning six and drawing four of them.

On New Year's Day 1975, West Brom sat in a very healthy looking fourth place, in the Second Division.

	PL	W	D	L	F	A	PTS
Manchester United	25	16	5	4	41	19	37
Sunderland	24	13	7	4	41	17	33
Norwich City	24	11	9	4	33	20	31
WEST BROM	25	11	7	7	30	18	29
Bristol City	24	10	7	7	24	16	27
Oxford United	25	11	5	9	26	34	27

Once again, though, Albion fell apart, losing six of their ten matches from February onwards, and to rub salt in their wounds, they also lost 3-2 in the FA Cup Fourth round, to First Division Carlisle United, managed by Alan Ashman.

On Monday 7th April, Albion club legend Don Howe was told that his contact wouldn't be renewed for the 1975-76 season, so he decided to leave West Brom immediately. Assistant manager George Wright took over for the last three games of the season, and with neither promotion nor relegation to worry about, he started the Chester-le-Street born teenager Bryan Robson in all three of those games, in Albion's midfield. At just eighteen years old, Robson scored in both their 2-0 win over Cardiff, on Saturday 19th April, and also during their 2-1 defeat away at Nottingham Forest.

Five days before Don Howe left, though, Albion had attracted an all-time low crowd of just 7,651, for their 4-1 win at home to Notts County, and it was clear that some sort of soul and inspiration was needed at The Hawthorns.

On Tuesday 5th July 1975, during the bright hot Summer when the Bay City Rollers, 10cc, Mud, and Windsor Davies and Don Estelle topped the UK charts, Johnny Giles joined West Bromwich Albion as their player-manager.

Ever since Bobby Hope had left The Hawthorns, Albion had lacked a strong possession midfield player, calm and unhurried, who could pick out either the simple ball or the incisive, defence-splitting pass. Johnny Giles, the Republic of Ireland's greatest ever player, was that man to finally replace Hope. Giles subsequently brought England's World Cup hero Geoff Hurst from Stoke, to West Brom, but that was not a success.

After eleven Second Division games, at the start of the 1975-76 season, West Brom were struggling down in fifteenth place, nine points behind leaders Bristol City.

Giles then brought in fellow Irish Republic player Mick Martin, from Manchester United, and also former Chelsea defender Paddy Mulligan, from Crystal Palace.

On Saturday 1st November, though, only 12,595 die-hards had turned up for their home match against Notts County. West Brom could only draw 0-0.

They were in a mess.

So Giles decided to start playing Bryan Robson regularly, from the end of November. Robson started thirteen of Albion's next eighteen Second Division matches, and they won ten of them, launching West Brom up to fourth place by the end of March, just one point behind third-placed Bolton Wanderers, before Robson limped out of their goalless draw with Blackpool.

Despite the loss of Bryan Robson, however, the midfield talents of Giles, Willie Johnston, Ally Brown and Mick Martin, setting up goals for both Tony Brown and Joe Mayo, from the Black Country, combined with Bolton Wanderers' catastrophic slump in form during April, ensured that

Albion returned to the First Division, just a single point ahead of Bolton, who'd led the Second Division at the end of February.

It could be argued that it *was* Bolton's epic FA Cup Fifth round tie against League Cup Finalists Newcastle, that went to a second replay, at Elland Road, in front of a midweek crowd of 42,280, that had derailed Bolton's promotion hopes, just when it looked like they were a good First Division team.

On Saturday 10th March, Bolton Wanderers visited West Bromwich Albion, with 25,319 inside The Hawthorns.

WEST BROMWICH ALBION		BOLTON WANDERERS
John Osborne	1	Barry Siddall
Paddy Mulligan	2	Peter Nicholson
Bryan Robson	3	Tony Dunne
Tony Brown	4	Roy Greaves
John Wile	5	Paul Jones
Alistair Robertson	6	Sam Allardyce
Mick Martin	7	Willie Morgan
Len Cantello	8	Neil Whatmore
Joe Mayo	9	Garry Jones
Johnny Giles	10	Peter Reid
Willie Johnston	11	Peter Thompson
Ally Brown	12	Steven Taylor

It was a high quality Second Division match, in which the young Peter Reid battled superbly with the great Johnny Giles, en route to an illustrious career with Everton and England. The moustached Joe Mayo pounced on a loose ball before half-time, though, and then John Wile lost a young Sam Allardyce, for just a split second, at an Albion corner, and he headed his second goal inside a week, for a crucial 2-0 win.

Then, on Saturday 24th April 1976, fifteen thousand Albion fans travelled up the M6 motorway, a river of blue and white that day, up to Oldham Athletic, where they outnumbered the home supporters by two to one.

Wearing their away colours of green and yellow stripes, Albion had to win to secure promotion back to the First Division. Tony Brown scored a wonderful winning goal, his fourteenth of the season, in front of the Match of the Day cameras, showing a team well worthy of First Division football.

Mulligan had played the ball up the right wing to Mick Martin. Martin crossed for Ally Brown, who rose to nod the ball down for Tony Brown, who juggled it from his left foot onto his right, and then he fired into the top left corner of Chris Ogden's goal.

THE BLACK FLASH

I'm well aware that West Brom's team from 1978-79, the best team in West Bromwich Albion's history, is totally outside of the Glam Soccer era, but it has to be celebrated, in this book, because the spine of their early 70s team, Wile, Cantello and Tony Brown, formed the spine of the 78-79 team..

Johnny Giles' West Brom started 1976-77 very well, and after hammering the First Division leaders, Tommy Docherty's Manchester United, by four goals to nil, on Wednesday 6th October (Giles, Ally Brown, Cantello, Treacy), Albion sat high right up high in fifth position, after ten games.

They suffered a mid-season dip in form, though, and then dropped to mid-table. But then they went unbeaten in nine games, between 28th February 1976 and 5th April 1977, and they won seven of them, to rise back up to fifth place.

It was during that period, though, when Johnny Giles signed a player that transformed West Brom's future and made them legends.

There had been few black players in the First Division during the Glam Soccer era. Clyde Best had been the most prominent player, a huge character, but he was the only one, really. John Miller had played on and off for both Ipswich and Norwich, while West Ham also had Ade Coker and Johnny Charles, who played occasionally, and Arsenal had a young defender, Brendan Batson, who'd played a few games during the early Seventies.

There wasn't any movement, yet, regarding black footballers at the very top of English football. The Midlands was a multi-cultural region, though, and West Bromwich Albion, in particular, were ready for it.

On Thursday 6th March 1977, Johnny Giles paid £110,000 to Orient for Laurie Cunningham, who'd scored fifteen Second Division goals in 72 games.

Cunningham's pace and classy close-control reinvigorated Albion's attack.

Laurie Cunningham immediately became a favourite at The Hawthorns, rivalling Tony Brown and Willie Johnston. He was nicknamed *The Black Flash,* scoring six goals in thirteen First Division matches, as Albion ended up in seventh place, their best finish since 1966, but they were only four points below European qualification.

On Wednesday 20th April though, Johnny Giles announced that he would be resigning at the end of that season, on the day before his old teammate Jack Charlton also resigned as Middlesbrough boss. Giles claimed that his time as player-manager of Albion was the happiest of his career, in spite all the medals he won at Leeds.

The pressure of a managerial career, allied to the power of non-footballing club Directors, was too much for him, though, to pursue a career in management.

During the previous twelve months, he'd also seen Bertie Mee and Jimmy Adamson leave their clubs, after "intolerable pressures," but also Dave Mackay, Billy Bingham and Tony Waddington had all been ridiculously sacked by their clubs.

More and more often, the future of great managers lay in the hands of shareholders with absolutely no knowledge of football.

Later on, during the Summer of '77, even Tommy Docherty was sacked by Manchester United, despite them winning the FA Cup, and Eddie McCreadie and Jimmy Bloomfield were both also forced out at Chelsea and Leicester.

On June 21st 1977, West Brom legend Ronnie Allen was appointed as Albion's new manager. Allen had scored over 200 league goals for the club, back in the Fifties, and his first signing was another black player, and another future legend at The Hawthorns.

Built like Joe Frazier, but with the pace of Don Quarry, Cyrille Regis had ripped apart Isthmian League defences, scoring 24 goals for Hayes FC during 1976-77, and as West Brom's footballing Scout, Ronnie Allen had been monitoring him for Albion boss Johnny Giles.

The price for Regis was just £5,000, but the Albion board were reluctant to pay it. Allen was so confident that Cyrille Regis would be a First Division star, though, he offered to pay the fee himself, if Regis failed.

Albion had still not offered Ronnie Allen a long term contract by December 1977, however, so he was approached by the Saudi Arabian FA, who wanted him to coach their national team. Allen subsequently signed an eighteen month contract, worth about £100,000, with the Saudis.

After a very short spell under the player-management of John Wile, West Brom then appointed Ron Atkinson as their new manager on January 12th 1978.

One month later, Atkinson returned to his former team, Cambridge United, for their right back Brendan Batson. Born in Grenada, Batson had played 163 league games for Cambridge, and he'd helped lift them off the bottom of the Fourth Division, and into a promotion place in Division Three, having failed to gain a regular place at Arsenal.

Batson, Regis and Cunningham became the beating heart and Soul of West Bromwich Albion during the late Seventies, adding Colour, of a footballing variety, to a spine of Wile, Robertson, Cantello, Robson, Ally Brown and Tony Brown.

Just like Coventry had been in the late Sixties, West Brom became many fans' second team as Heatwave, Earth, Wind and Fire, and the Jacksons displaced Slade, T-Rex, and The Sweet at the top of the UK charts.

Ron Atkinson nicknamed his trio of black stars "*The Three Degrees*," as West Brom became the first ever First Division team to have three black players in their team.

I'm well aware that that West Brom team from 1978-79, the best team in West Bromwich Albion's history, is mostly from outside of the Glam Soccer era, but it has to be celebrated because Wile, Cantello, the two Browns, and also Robertson were survivors from their previous, mostly dour First Division existence, as mostly Cup specialists.

Of the West Brom team that had hammered Leeds away at Elland Road, back in 1971, Wile, Cantello and Tony Brown were the very spine of that West Brom side that also hammered Manchester United 5-3 at Old Trafford, in December 1978, and went top of the First Division, level with Liverpool.

They became the most attractive side in English football, playing with width, flair, drive and thrust. They lost 1-0 to Red Star Belgrade, in front of a massive Ninety-five Thousand crowd, in the UEFA Cup Quarter-finals, with bonfires burning on the vast terraces of the Crvena Zvezda.

Albion eventually saw their title challenge killed off by the harsh winter of 1978-79, and they tailed off to finish third, their best finish since 1954.

That 1954 West Brom side did not, though, have the reigning European Champions Liverpool, nor the forthcoming European Champions Nottingham Forest, standing in their way.

John Osborne finally left Albion in 1978, after 250 league games during his two spells at The Hawthorns. He had kept twenty-two clean sheets as Albion gained promotion from the Second Division in 1975-76, and he'll be remembered as the greatest goalkeeper West Brom ever had.

In 2004, Osborne was elected, following a 2004 fans' poll, as one of the Sixteen Greatest Ever Albion Players, to celebrate the West Brom's 125th anniversary.

After leaving Albion, he joined his old boss Johnny Giles, at Shamrock Rovers.

He became commercial manager of Worcestershire County Cricket Club, during their most successful period, between 1986 and 1995. John Osborne died, aged only fifty-seven, on Saturday 7th November 1998.

John Wile also made it into Albion's Sixteen Greatest Ever Players, having played 500 league games at The Hawthorns, before finally leaving in June 1983. His partnership with Alistair Robertson was the greatest central defensive partnership in West Brom's history. Alistair Robertson had himself played 506 league games, 403 of which were First Division matches by the time he joined Wolverhampton Wanderers in 1986.

Ally Brown played 228 First Division matches for Albion, over ten years, plus fifty Second Division games, while scoring a total of 72 league goals. The moustached, Musselburgh-born £55,000 steal from Leicester, Ally Brown was Albion's leading goal-scorer during their 1975-76 promotion season, with ten league goals, but he'd also top-scored in their great 1978-79 season, scoring eighteen First Division goals, as part of a thirty-three goal attacking partnership with Cyrille Regis.

In 1981, Ally Brown joined Portland Timbers of the NASL, scoring nine goals from 24 games, and he also had six assists as he helped the Oregon team into the Play-offs.

Former apprentice Len Cantello played 301 league games for Albion, including thirty-two during their great 1978-79 season, before he joined fellow First Division club Bolton Wanderers during the Summer of 1979. Cantello had played in every outfield position for West Brom, except for central defence.

Willie Johnston played only 207 league games for Albion, between 1973 and 1978, but such was his impact, in such a short spell, he was also voted into their Sixteen Greatest Ever Players.

Johnston would have played more games, but his twenty-one game Scotland career ended, at the age of thirty-one. After losing to Peru in their opening game of the 1978 World Cup Finals, he was found to have provided a positive test for the banned drug Reactivan.

Willie Johnston has always pleaded his innocence, despite embarrassing front page pictures of him being escorted home by police, following his expulsion from Argentina, and he was never the same player again. He started only three games for Albion during the 1978-79 season, before he moved to Vancouver, a broken man.

Willie Johnston will always be remembered, though, by Albion fans, as a real crowd pleaser, and a positive character in the changing room.

He might well have been the man to turn Albion into Champions of England in 1979.

Bryan Robson played 198 league games, most of them in the First Division, for Albion. He missed only one match during 1978-79, and he was then transferred to Manchester United, for a British record transfer fee of £1,500,000, in October 1981.

Robson's anticipation, sense of timing, hunger, and his eagerness to win, made him one of the all-time bargains, even in an era when One Million Pound transfers were flying about like crane flies during the Autumn of 1981. He played ninety games for his country, becoming England's sixth most-capped player, ever.

Bryan Robson also played in three World Cup Finals tournaments, the first England outfield player to do so, and he was selected for six PFA First Division Teams of the Year, between 1981 and 1989.

He was awarded an OBE, in 1990, and finally retired in 1994, after accepting Manchester United's second successive Premier League Trophy, jointly with Steve Bruce. Bryan Robson had played a total of 543 First Division/Premier League matches for both West Bromwich Albion and Manchester United.

If Jeff Astle was *The King* at West Brom, then Tony Brown was *Mr Albion*.

Tony Brown scored 262 domestic league and cup goals for Albion, from 681 games, becoming both West Brom's record goal-scorer, and their player with the most appearances, when he finally left The Hawthorns during the 1980-81 season.

Bomber was simply the heart and soul of Albion. Without Tony Brown, it was possible that Cunningham, Regis and Batson might have just been peripheral talents at West Brom. He held the whole team together, and he drove them forward, just as he'd done with Bobby Hope and Jeff Astle over a decade earlier.

During 1978-79, at the age of thirty-three, Tony Brown scored nine First Division goals in twenty-nine games, including two blasts in that 5-3 away win at Old Trafford.

Albion created the Astle Gates at The Hawthorns, but they'll unveil a statue to Tony Brown over the next ten to thirty years. He was simply the greatest player in West Brom's history, and the only player, a key player too, from their 1968 Cup winning team, all through the Seventies, to their wonderful 1978-79 team. These Were Albion's Greatest Post-war teams, and Tony Brown was the Heart and Soul of all of them.

On Sunday 22nd May 2011, West Bromwich Albion fans celebrated the great man, with a Tony Brown Day, at their final game of that season. Thousands of Baggies fans turned up at St James's Park, Newcastle, all wearing Tony Brown masks, portraying his famous dark, drooping moustache from the mid-Seventies.

It was strongly rumoured that Tony Brown, still a huge Albion fan himself, was actually amongst them, wearing his own mask.

Mr Albion, indeed.

OLD GOLD AND BLACK DOOG

I T ALWAYS AMAZED ME THAT Derek Dougan was such a legend, such a hero, and such a cult figure at Wolves. He spent just over eight years at Molineux, having signed from Leicester City, for £50,000.

He scored only 93 First Division goals, from just 258 games, and he was generally outscored by the slightly lesser-lauded John Richards during the early Seventies.

Doog was, though, the biggest character in their team, mercurial, influential and inspirational, driving Wolves upwards. "***PREPARE TO MEET THY DOOG***," their huge Banner proclaimed, on the much-missed North Bank at Molineux.

He, more than anyone, had a passion and a faith in Wolves' future, rather than in their past, and he became the protagonist of the last truly Great team in the history of that great Black Country club.

Two years after he'd joined Wolves, Derek Dougan wrote, "some people say that Wolves' best days are gone. I prefer to think that the best are yet to come."

Shortly after his arrival at Molineux, in 1967, Dougan had tried to persuade his manager Ronnie Allen to sign Leicester City's unsettled England keeper Gordon Banks. Allen decided to keep faith in his teenage keeper Phil Parkes, though, so Banks joined lowly Stoke City instead.

If Gordon Banks had gone to Wolves, things might have been very different.

Six years later, while playing in a League Cup match at Tranmere Rovers, Dougan was reunited with Allen, who then admitted his great mistake in not buying Banks.

Derek Dougan was Northern Ireland's centre-forward during their first ever World Cup Finals match, against Czechoslovakia, in Halmstad, on Sunday 8th June 1958. Doog was a Portsmouth player then, and only twenty years old, but despite their 1-0 victory, he didn't play again during the tournament, as the Irish had a quality team.

Spearheaded by Burnley's Jimmy McIlroy, and driven by Tottenham's Danny Blanchflower, Northern Ireland reached the Quarter-finals, when they were finally undone by Just Fontaine's France. Dougan left Portsmouth in 1959, and he travelled via Blackburn Rovers, Aston Villa, Peterborough United and Leicester City, totalling 288 league games, before joining Wolverhampton Wanderers in March 1967.

Dougan smashed a hat-trick on his home debut, against Hull City, in front of a 30,000 Molineux crowd. He forced in two from close range, but his third displayed the flair of a World Class player. He collected Dave Wagstaffe's pass and back-heeled the ball over his own head, before he turned, *just like Bergkamp,* and then volleyed the dropping ball high into the goal.

An instant hero was acclaimed, during that 4-0 thrashing of Hull City.

Doog had signed for Wolves, as a twenty-nine year old, and many Wolves fans had assumed that his stay would be as brief as at all of his previous clubs. He became an immediate hit, though, following a home debut never to be forgotten, as Hull City were **SUB-DOOGED.**

The masses of Wolves fans on the North Bank, as well as on the enormous South Bank, had crafted some wonderful songs for their Doog. They sung a really great one to the tune of Bing Crosby's 1945 hit, McNamara's Band.

> "His name is Derek Dougan and from Leicester he did come.
> To play for Ronnie Allen's Wolves, back in Division One.
> And if you come to Molineux,
> You'll always hear us cry,
> We are the Best Team in the land,
> As no-one can deny!"

The Wolves fans even touted Doog for the job of Prime Minister, demanding, *"WILSON OUT! DOUGAN IN! WILSON OUT! DOUGAN IN!"*

The upshot of this affection and adoration was that it became mutual. Promotion back to the First Division was ensured, literally with weeks to spare, so Wolves fans thought that Dougan's job was done, and he'd be off again as he was turning thirty, halfway into the new season.

But that was not to be. With the North Bank chanting his name behind him, and the mighty South Bank praising him to his face, Doog had finally found his spiritual home of Molineux. Already at Molineux, and playing regularly when Dougan had arrived, were three players who became key players of Wolves' great team over the following seven or eight seasons.

David Wagstaffe, *Waggy,* had played over 140 league games for his home town club Manchester City, over the first four years of the Sixties. A fast and tricky winger, Waggy then joined Wolves on Boxing Day 1964, for just £40,000, while still only twenty-one years old.

Fair haired and well balanced, Waggy became one of the best natural outside lefts in the First Division, and one of the most accurate crossers of a ball, but at a time when Sir Alf Ramsey was ignoring wingers for England's national team.

Mike Bailey joined Wolves in March 1966, one year before Doog joined. Bailey had played over a hundred and fifty games for Charlton Athletic, before arriving at Molineux in another £40,000 deal.

Bailey also had some international pedigree, having played two games for England back in 1964, their 10-0 thrashing of USA in New York, and their 2-1 home win over Wales, at Wembley Stadium. He was a tough-tackling right half, or midfield player, with a big barrel chest, and he tackled with his whole body, not just with his feet.

When Mike Bailey hit you, you knew you'd been hit.

Mike Bailey was the driving force behind the forward players, making many of their goals, and he was voted as the Midlands' Player of the Season after Wolves were promoted in 1967, behind Second Division Champions Coventry City.

Phil Parkes was a six foot, three and a half inch giant of a goalkeeper, born in the Black Country, in West Bromwich. *Lofty* had made his Wolves debut against Preston North End, during their promotion season, in November 1966, and he'd saved a penalty in their 3-2 win. Parkes kept his place as Ronnie Allen ignored the presence of Gordon Banks on the open market, after he'd been transfer-listed by Leicester City.

Derek Dougan was Wolves' top goal-scorer, during his first two full seasons at Molineux, with seventeen First Division goals in 1967-68, and then eleven in 1968-69.

During those seasons, he'd played in attack with either Peter Knowles or Hugh Curran, but Wolves were only a lowly First Division team, finding their feet, finishing down in seventeenth place in 1968, and then sixteenth in 1969.

Wolves had been further strengthened during their first season back in Division One, after Frank Munro had arrived from Aberdeen in January 1968, for £55,000.

The big, six foot tall, thirteen stone central defender had lost the Scottish Cup Final, back in May, following Celtic's 2-0 victory over Aberdeen in front of a massive 126,000 Hampden Park crowd.

Derek Parkin, *Parky,* was signed by Ronnie Allen one month later, from Huddersfield Town. Ronnie Allen had paid £80,000, a British record transfer fee for a full back, for Parky, who played his first Wolves game at home to Newcastle United, his ***home town club,*** on Saturday 24th February 1968.

That game, a 0-2 home defeat, was the first of 134 consecutive first team appearances for Parky, at the beginning of his Wolves career, still a club record.

During the following season, in November 1968, Kenny Hibbitt was signed by Ronnie Allen, for a giveaway price of £5,000, from Bradford Park Avenue, who were bottom of the Fourth Division. Bradford was Hibbitt's home town, but he hadn't played many games for the worst team in the Football League.

Some folk at Molineux were worried at the possible waste of money on a nobody who might actually have been released for free a few months later.

They need not have worried. Kenny Hibbitt was going to literally repay that small fee at least one hundred times over.

In spite of his modest roots, his skills were strictly First Division. Hibbitt was naturally skilled on the ground, but he was also combative, and good in the air too, while his right foot had more than a touch of Peter Lorimer about it, full of power and accuracy. Kenny Hibbitt was Allen's last signing for Wolves. They'd won only five of their first nineteen First Division matches of 1968-69, although they'd lost only seven.

Ronnie Allen was sacked by Wolves in late November 1968, and he was replaced by Bill McGarry. Allen's attacking philosophy was displaced by a grim, strict work ethic and fitness programme introduced by McGarry. Bill McGarry had played nearly 600 league games for Port Vale, Huddersfield and Boscombe.

Born in Stoke on Trent, McGarry was magnificently fit, even at the age of forty-one, and he was aggressive, competitive and enthusiastic when he arrived at Molineux. Fellow Stoke-on-Trenter, Freddie Steele, who played 250 league games in the Potteries, had said of McGarry, "he's a tough bugger.

He wasn't born, you know. He was cast at ***Shelton Bar.***"

Doog remembered the moment when Bill McGarry first arrived at Molineux, on Monday 25th November, very well. Every Wolves player was waiting in the home changing room, when in strolled "a small man wearing a tight-fitting, light blue tracksuit. In those days, tracksuits were rare, but the style of this one left not much room for leg movement."

When he attempted to lift his foot up onto the bench seating that ran all around the room, as they do in all changing rooms, Bill McGarry missed the bench and he fell over.

Attempting to look unbothered, McGarry rose and roared, "look, I'm the manager. I don't give two fucks if you don't like me. I don't want you to like me."

Most of those young Wolves players bought by Ronnie Allen were "impressed, even over-awed," according to Doog.

Doog was neither impressed nor overawed, though, and he thoroughly resented McGarry's military style, throughout the remaining seven years of his time at Wolves. Ironically, McGarry's management style and coaching techniques actually worked at Molineux. Wolves became one of the fittest teams in the First Division.

McGarry saw out the 1968-69 season, as Wolves lost just nine of his twenty-one First Division games in charge, but they had brilliantly hammered the reigning Champions Manchester City 3-1, on Tuesday 8th April. Doog, Peter Knowles and Frank Munro all scored to secure their First Division safety, with only 25,533 inside Molineux.

In July 1969, Bill McGarry paid £70,000 to Sheffield Wednesday for their Scottish international midfielder Jim McCalliog. McCalliog had played 150 First Division matches for the Owls, scoring nineteen goals from right midfield.

Jim McCalliog had scored a famous goal on his international debut for Scotland, at Wembley Stadium, on Saturday 15th April 1967. During their 1968 European Championship qualifying match against England, McCalliog had cut in from the left, and then driven a rasping shot past Gordon Banks, putting the Scots 3-1 up.

Then, in the impetuousness of youth, McCalliog stole the ball away, off the centre spot, from under the noses of Geoff Hurst and Bobby Charlton, waiting to kick off.

He danced a jig of joy with the ball, inside the centre circle, before flicking the ball back to the bewildered England legends with a cheeky back heel.

McCalliog made his Wolves debut on Saturday 9th August 1969, at home to Stoke City. In front of decent crowd of 32,260, Derek Dougan turned on the style against their illustrious opposition of Eastham, Greenhoff, Dobing and Ritchie.

Waggy played Doog in with a tremendous reverse pass, and Doog hit a perfectly-balanced shot just inside Gordon Banks' far post. Banks had got a slight touch, but not enough to keep the ball out.

Mike Bailey then threaded a through-ball between Eastham and Smith, and Peter Knowles planted the ball low into the bottom left corner of the goal, after beating Bloor's challenge, before Knowles, himself, chipped a lovely through-ball into Dougan's path, and Doog slammed his shot past Banks, from the edge of the box.

Dougan and Peter Knowles had been brilliant in attack, unplayable at times, so colourful and acute was their passing, as Wolves won 3-1.

Peter Knowles retired from football, though, at just twenty-four years of age, during the 1969-70 season, having played only eight games. Wolves had toured the United States during the Summer of 1969, and while he was in Kansas, Knowles joined the Jehovah's Witnesses. A religious force, a different kind of force, as opposed to injury, had cut his football career short.

Derek Dougan was certain that Knowles would have matured into an England international. Doog even "visualised him as a future England regular, but he was unable to reconcile what he took to be a religious calling, with his chosen profession. It was a sad day when he decided to quit and devote himself to his new faith.

But for a chance call at his house, by a Jehovah's Witness, Knowles might have gone on to become one of the most brilliant footballers in the game."

In spite of his retirement, Peter Knowles' contract was retained by the club for twelve years, something unheard of in modern football. He had scored sixty-one league goals for Wolves, from 174 games.

In 1982, thirteen years later, Wolves' manager Graham Hawkins finally came to the conclusion, that Peter Knowles wouldn't be returning to professional football, at thirty-six years old, and he had Knowles' contract cancelled

In 1991, inspired by Peter Knowles' story, unique among modern footballers, Billy Bragg wrote a beautiful song, God's Footballer, for his **Don't Try This At Home** album.

> "God's footballer turns on a sixpence,
> And brings the Great Crowd to their feet in praise of him.
> God's footballer quotes from the Gospels,
> While knocking on doors in the Black Country back streets.
> He scores goals on a Saturday,
> And saves Souls on a Sunday."

Bill McGarry was lucky enough to have had a ready-made replacement for Peter Knowles, left for him by his predecessor.

John Richards had first joined Wolves back in 1967, straight from his school in Warrington, at just sixteen years old. Sharp and brave, Richards finally made his Wolves debut away at West Brom, on Saturday 28th February 1970, amidst a fierce, frenzied Black Country atmosphere, with nearly 38,000 packed inside The Hawthorns.

Richards set up one of Hugh Curran's two goals in their 3-3 draw.

Hugh Curran had scored 110 career goals in just 210 games for Third Lanark, Corby Town, Millwall, and Norwich City, prior to arriving at Molineux in January 1969. Curran was Wolves' top scorer during 1969-70, with nineteen goals, as Wolves ended up in the heights of thirteenth place in Division One.

Derek Dougan and Jim McCalliog had also combined for sixteen goals between them. In June 1970, Bobby Gould, that journeyman of all journeymen, joined Wolves in a £55,000 deal from Arsenal. Gould had a remarkably prolific record of fifty-six league goals from just 135 starts, but he'd found it hard to settle anywhere.

1970-71 was a golden season for Wolves, though, and on Saturday 3rd October, a huge crowd of 38,629 piled into Molineux for the visit of the great Manchester United. United were suffering at the time, having won just three of their opening ten matches, and were missing Law, Crerand, Stiles and Stepney.

WOLVERHAMPTON WANDERERS		MANCHESTER UNITED
Phil Parkes	1	Jimmy Rimmer
Bernard Shaw	2	William Watson
Derek Parkin	3	Francis Burns
Mike Bailey	4	John Fitzpatrick
Frank Munro	5	Steve James
John McAlle	6	David Sadler
Jim McCalliog	7	Willie Morgan
Kenny Hibbitt	8	Alan Gowling
Bobby Gould	9	Bobby Charlton
Derek Dougan	10	Brian Kidd
David Wagstaffe	11	George Best
John Richards	12	Carlo Sartori

Bobby Gould had the game of his career, smashing a magnificent hat-trick, volleying beyond Rimmer, having been put through by John Richards for his third, holding his arms aloft beneath the vast South Bank, smiling delightedly, as he awaited the congratulations of his teammates.

Bobby Gould top-scored for Wolves, during 1970-71, with seventeen First Division goals from thirty-five games, as they finished up in fourth place, level on points with third placed Tottenham.

Wolves had scored sixty-four goals, more than any other teams, except Arsenal and Leeds, but they'd also conceded fifty-four, and they missed out on third place through goal average. Wolves had also won 22 of their 42 matches, but they lost only twelve games, their best record for ten years.

Hugh Curran also scored sixteen First Division goals, including a hat-trick against Nottingham Forest on Friday 2nd April, while Derek Dougan had combined with Jim McCalliog for nineteen goals, in support of their front two.

1970-71 had been a great season.

Wolves had qualified for the UEFA Cup, but the best was still to come.

John Richards had only made eight starts for Wolves, during the season and a half since he'd made his debut, scoring just the one goal, but in September 1971, following only one win from their first five games, Bill McGarry replaced Bobby Gould with John Richards, in attack alongside Doog.

On Wednesday 15th September, Bobby Gould was sold, yet again, in his career, for just £60,000, to West Bromwich Albion. He had scored eighteen First Division goals for Wolves, from only thirty-nine games, yet he failed to settle.

Also finding opportunities difficult to come by was Hugh Curran, who had scored an immense total of forty First Division goals from just 77 games, during his two seasons at Molineux, but he'd been frozen out of McGarry's new Richards/Dougan attacking partnership. Curran subsequently made only four league appearances during 1971-72, before he moved to Oxford United, for £50,000, on Friday 15th September 1972.

Wolves won 1-0 away at Stoke City on Saturday 4th September 1971, after Danny Hegan's second half goal, and one week later, Hegan scored again to earn a 1-1 draw at home to Everton.

Danny Hegan had also joined Wolves, from West Brom, back in May 1970, but he'd played only half a dozen, or so, games, during that 1970-71 season.

Doog observed of Hegan, "he had a football brain and he knew how to transmit his brainwaves to his feet. He wasn't among the quickest of players, but was better suited at going forward from a deep position.

The trouble was, Hegan was bought to play right midfield, and McCalliog had that number seven shirt, unless either of the front two were out, when McCalliog filled the centre forward position, as he'd done for Scotland, so Hegan's chances were limited.

By September 1971, at only twenty years old, John Richards was finally a first team regular, and he scored in Wolves' UEFA Cup First round first leg home match against Portuguese side Academica Coimbra. John McAlle and Doog hit the others during their great 3-0 win at Molineux.

Away in Portugal, Doog scored a hat-trick, and McAlle also scored again, as Wolves wound up a 7-1 aggregate win, on Wednesday 29th September. Just four days earlier, Doog had also fired a hat-trick against struggling Nottingham Forest, during Wolves' 4-2 home win.

Wolves visited Den Haag, in Holland, on Wednesday 20th October, and won 3-1. Doog, McCalliog and Hibbitt all scored to virtually secure their place in the Third round. Three Dutch own goals, a fortnight later, as well as Doog's sixth goal of the competition, completed another 7-1 aggregate win.

On Saturday 6th November, Wolves were fourteenth in the table, having lost more games than they'd won in the First Division, but from the following Saturday they went on a run of twelve league and cup games without defeat, winning nine of them.

On Saturday 13th November, Wolves beat title contenders Derby County 2-1, with nearly thirty-three thousand inside Molineux, after John Richards had scored in each half. A week later, the reigning Champions Arsenal visited Molineux, with 28,831 inside the ground.

The twenty-odd thousand fans, who'd stayed away, missed the greatest performance of Wolves' last great age, with Doog at his most majestic and magnificent. Richards was also at his unstoppable best, while Waggy and Hibbitt both outclassed Arsenal's top class midfield.

WOLVERHAMPTON WANDERERS		ARSENAL
Phil Parkes	1	Bob Wilson
Bernard Shaw	2	Pat Rice
Derek Parkin	3	Sammy Nelson
Mike Bailey	4	Peter Storey
Frank Munro	5	John Roberts
John McAlle	6	Frank McLintock
Jim McCalliog	7	George Armstrong
Kenny Hibbitt	8	Charlie George
John Richards	9	John Radford
Derek Dougan	10	Ray Kennedy
David Wagstaffe	11	George Graham

It was Arsenal, though, who'd opened the scoring. John Radford flicked on a long throw, and Ray Kennedy finished from close range, giving the Champions a half-time lead. Attacking their own North Bank End of the ground, after the break, though, Wolves were at their very, very best.

Wagstaffe cut in from the right wing, and he unleashed a missile from thirty-five yards out, straight into the top left corner of Bob Wilson's goal.

Wagstaffe then launched a huge pass out of defence, into the path of the galloping Hibbitt, ten yards inside Arsenal's half. Hibbitt teased and tormented Nelson, before Peter Storey slid in to tackle, very hard, just outside his own penalty area.

Hibbitt simply side-stepped him though, and then he *smashed* the ball, right-footed, beyond Wilson's dive, from twenty yards out.

Smash then sent Dougan rushing out, to the left side of the Arsenal area, pursued by both McLintock and Storey, sandwiching him and biting at his ankles.

From an almost impossible angle, Doog just guided the ball back inside, past the wrong-footed Wilson. The ball hit the far post of the Arsenal goal before bouncing in.

These were three great contenders for Goal of the Month, all in the same half of one game. The North Bank went wild, in a frenzy of noise and excitement.

Roberts was penalised for a foul on Richards, and a penalty-kick was awarded. Jim McCalliog just swept his kick past Wilson, low into the left corner of the Arsenal goal.

Hibbitt's corner kick was then met by Dougan, who shot past Wilson, from the edge of the area, to complete a 5-1 hammering of the Champions. Arms aloft and smothered by his jubilant teammates, Dougan stood beneath the crazy North Bank.

On days like these, Wolves were unbeatable by anyone.

Those days came thick and fast over the next two months. On the following Wednesday, 24th November, John Richards fired Wolves' winner, away in the DDR, beating Carl Zeiss Jena 1-0 in their UEFA Cup Third round, first leg tie.

Jim McCalliog and Dave Wagstaffe gave Wolves a 2-0 half-time lead away at local rivals West Brom, on Saturday 27th November, with over 36,000 packing The Hawthorns.

Ex-Wolves striker Bobby Gould and Tony Brown both pulled Albion back into it, after the break, but John Richards then fired in from the edge of the box, to make the two points safe. Doog and Richards scored to secure a scrappy 2-2 home draw with lowly Huddersfield, at the start of December, but then Doog scored another two during Wolves' 3-0 second leg win over Carl Zeiss Jena, of East Germany.

Kenny Hibbitt, *Smash,* drove in their other goal, as Wolves won 4-0 on aggregate. They were in the Quarter-finals, come March, and drawn against Juventus!

Wolves led 2-0 at half-time, away at the early season entertainers and runaway leaders Sheffield United, on Saturday 11th December. An Eddie Colquhoun own goal, and John Richards' seventh of the season had silenced the near 30,000 crowd inside Bramall Lane. Alan Woodward and Tony Currie, though, scored a couple of second half crackers, to hold Wolves to a second successive First Division 2-2 draw.

Wolves did return to winning ways, a week before Christmas, beating Stoke City 2-0 at Molineux, after Doog and an Alan Bloor own goal had given them the two points.

A massive crowd of nearly Thirty-eight Thousand completely packed Leicester City's Filbert Street ground on Boxing Day, and a goal in each half, a mighty header from Frank Munro, and then a crafty Doog chip, had earned Wolves a 2-1 win.

On New Year's Day 1972, Newcastle United, with their free-scoring double act of Supermac and John Tudor, and the creative talents of Tony Green and Terry Hibbitt, Kenny's brother, were walloped 2-0 by Wolves' gold and black machine.

Geordie full back Derek Parkin and John Richards had scored in each half.

On Saturday 8th January, Wolves visited the First Division leaders, Manchester United, and in front of a 46,781 crowd, they outclassed Charlton, Law and Kidd.

MANCHESTER UNITED		WOLVERHAMPTON WANDERERS
Alex Stepney	1	Phil Parkes
Tony Dunne	2	Bernard Shaw
Francis Burns	3	Derek Parkin
Alan Gowling	4	Mike Bailey
Paul Edwards	5	Frank Munro
David Sadler	6	John McAlle
Willie Morgan	7	Jim McCalliog
Brian Kidd	8	Kenny Hibbitt
Bobby Charlton	9	John Richards
Denis Law	10	Derek Dougan
Sammy McIlroy	11	David Wagstaffe
Carlo Sartori	12	Hugh Curran

Despite leading Division One, United hadn't won since Saturday 4th December, and without George Best, missing after a post-New Year break from football, they lacked the creative spark to undo a Wolves defence which had conceded just fourteen goals during their last fifteen league and cup matches.

Sammy McIlroy, in for Best, was impressive though, and eventually he'd become an influential match-winner for United, but not today.

McIlroy scored a great second half goal, collecting the ball, thirty yards out, and beating McCalliog, before driving a shot past Parkes, from the edge of the area.

It was a goal that sowed the seeds of suggestion of the legend that McIlroy would become at Old Trafford, but it was a mere consolation for United, as Wolves already had the game won.

Waggy's cross from the right was blocked by Morgan, but the ball ran free for Doog, who kept his cool and curled a magnificent shot into the right hand corner of Stepney's goal.

Hibbitt's left-sided corner kick was headed down by Doog, and Richards got the final touch as the ball bounced around the United six yard box.

Wolves went in 2-0 up at half-time, but after the break they never let up.

Paul Edwards was harshly ruled to have fouled Richards, on the edge of the box, and maybe it was just outside, but anyway, Jim McCalliog smashed his penalty kick high up into the top left corner of United's goal. Stepney had gone the right way, but he came nowhere near to saving that shot.

At five o'clock on that dark January night, Wolves were only four points behind the First Division leaders. Wolves have never come within a Light Year of such a Grand Position, in the Forty years since then.

This was probably the second greatest team to have ever represented Wolverhampton Wanderers Football Club.... But possibly Wolves' very Greatest-ever team?

FIRST DIVISION LEADERS. 8TH JANUARY 1972

	PL	W	D	L	F	A	PTS
Manchester Utd	25	14	7	4	50	33	35
Manchester City	25	13	8	4	48	25	34
Leeds United	25	14	6	5	38	20	34
Derby County	25	13	7	5	42	23	33
Sheffield United	25	13	6	6	45	33	32
WOLVES	25	12	7	6	45	35	31
Tottenham	25	10	9	6	40	28	29
Arsenal	25	12	5	8	35	27	29
Liverpool	25	11	6	8	30	26	28

On the following Saturday, Wolves drew 1-1 at home to Leicester City, in their FA Cup Third round game, their twelfth successive match without defeat, but they'd lost captain Mike Bailey to a bad leg injury, and he was unable to start any more games for the remainder of the season.

Leicester City won the replay 2-0, inflicting a defeat on Wolves for the first time in over two months. Bill McGarry had selected Alan Sunderland, for only his fourth game, in Mike Bailey's absence, but the eighteen year old was no substitute for Bailey's energy, his ball-winning ability, or his general influence on the team.

Liverpool visited Molineux on Saturday 22nd January, and 33,638 watched a 0-0 stalemate, but Wolves had extended their unbeaten run in the league to ten games.

They were still only four points behind the new leaders Leeds United, when they visited second-placed Manchester City at the end of January.

Despite John Richards scoring for Wolves, early on, City were absolutely rampant and they led 3-1 at half-time, after two goals from Francis Lee and a Tommy Booth thunderbolt. Lee completed his hat-trick, after the break, and Tony Towers then added a fifth, as City won 5-2 and overtook Leeds to go top of the First Division.

John Richards' second goal of the match was only a consolation for Wolves.

A fortnight later, away at West Ham United, John Richards scored his fifth league goal in five matches since the New Year. Still only twenty-one, Richards was developing into one of the very best strikers in the First Division, and *King John* totally outpaced Bobby Moore, in the second half, before firing a low shot past Bobby Ferguson, securing their 1-0 away win that just kept Wolves' title hopes alive.

Wolves were still only five points behind leaders Manchester City, with just fourteen games to play, and although a goalless draw at Coventry, and then a 2-2 draw at home to Ipswich, after Hibbitt and McCalliog had both scored, had prevented them from making up any ground on first place, they didn't lose any ground either.

With just twelve games remaining, Wolves were still in sixth place, going into March, and only five points behind Manchester City.

On Saturday 4th March, four days before their UEFA Cup Quarter-final, first leg match away in Turin, Wolves travelled to third-placed Derby County, who'd only gained two more points than their visitors.

With Bailey out, Danny Hegan was given a chance as Wolves' playmaker, in the middle of the park. Doog had reckoned that that particular number four position, the body that play ran through most frequently, controlling the pace of the game and maintaining possession, the Billy Bremner or Alan Mullery role in a team, was Danny Hegan's natural position.

Hegan played well, and he kept the Wolves number four shirt for the remainder of that season. Derby County had been going well, but they'd lost 2-0 at Arsenal, three weeks before, and nobody, except for the most fanatical Derby fan, or Brian Clough, really believed that they could win the league.

A big crowd of nearly 34,000 squeezed into The Baseball Ground, for a classic title eliminator. John Robson fouled Waggy, midway through the first half, and ten thousand travelling Wolves fans went wild when Jim McCalliog converted his fifth penalty kick of the season.

Wolves went in at half-time, on Saturday 4th March, with the live table showing Wolves in equal-third position, behind only Man City and Leeds, in the greatest ever First Division title race.

Derby came out and raised their game after the break, though. Roy McFarland levelled the scores with a powerful header, from Alan Durban's corner.

Then, a contentious and bitterly-disputed penalty kick was awarded to Derby, after an apparent foul by Jon McAlle.

Alan Hinton, who never missed from the spot, fired beyond Parkes' dive, high into the Wolves net. With Man City, Leeds, Derby and Liverpool all winning, the title race was maybe between just five clubs now, with Tottenham also, just, still in the race. That 1972 Spurs team was a great team, but their main problem was that Bill Nicholson didn't think they were good enough to be Champions, so they had no chance. Then he went and sent their best player, Alan Mullery, on loan to Fulham over the following week, which completely ruled them out of it.

At the end of the day, Wolves were nine points below Man City, who'd played an extra game in the week, but they ended the season disappointingly, badly missing Mike Bailey during a run of very winnable games against Everton, Leicester, Chelsea, Sheffield United and West Brom, winning none of them, and taking just one point.

Wolves ended the season down in ninth place, eleven points behind Champions Derby County.

On Tuesday 7th March 1972, Wolves visited Juventus, top of Serie A and destined to become Italian Champions of 1971-72. Juve were packed with Italian legends like Fabio Capello, Franco Causio, Pietro Anastasi, Francesco Morini and Luciano Spinosi. They also boasted, in attack, a West German World Cup legend, in Helmut Haller.

Wolves, though, were sensational. Every man, Parkes, Shaw, Taylor (Sunderland), Hegan, Munro, McAlle, McCalliog, Hibbitt, Richards, Dougan and Wagstaffe, had played the games of their lives. Although Anastasi scored, McCalliog's great strike from just inside the area, whilst surrounded by black and white defenders, earned a magnificent 1-1 draw to take back to the Black Country.

Fifteen days later, beneath a huge home crowd of 40,421, Danny Hegan's thirty yard rocket, and a headed goal by the gangling Doog, ensured that Wolves had beaten the best foreign team left in the tournament. Helmut Haller's penalty kick made it a nervous finale, as any mistake would give the tie to Juve on away goals, but Wolves defended superbly to hold on.

Their 3-2 aggregate victory over Juventus was one of the greatest wins by an English team over European opposition, in the history of European club competitions.

Just over a year later, Juventus reached the European Cup Final.

In the Semi-finals, Wolves were drawn against Ferencvaros, of Hungary.

It looked the kindest of draws, as Tottenham were drawn against AC Milan in the other tie of the round, but Wolves had earned it.

On the afternoon of Wednesday 5th April, a hostile, 45,000 crowd packed the Nepstadion, in Budapest, and the draw suddenly didn't seem so kind, as Ferencvaros tore into Wolves. Surprisingly, though, and totally against the run of play, Wolves took the lead, when John Richards beat Novak for pace, and he fired past Voros.

Bernard Shaw was penalised for a foul on the legendary Florian Albert, European Footballer of the Year in 1967, and joint top goal-scorer at the 1962 World Cup Finals. Szoke smashed his penalty kick past Parkes.

Albert had ran the midfield, and Wolves had to defend for almost all of the game. The Hungarians forced corner after corner, and pressure upon pressure. Phil Parkes made four or five great saves, including an excellent leg save from Szoke's second penalty kick of the game, but Ferencvaros continued to pile forward.

Albert scored what appeared to be a deserved winner to take to England, but Frank Munro dramatically and powerfully headed home a late, late leveller, his first ever Cup goal. Wolves had been comprehensively outplayed, but their strong backbone, team spirit and work ethic had served them brilliantly, and ultimately, their fitness had given them a 2-2 draw that they didn't expect, or even deserve.

Wolves, though, had become a proper European side, soaking up constant pressure from a superior team, and then punishing their opponents on their rare counter attacks. For years, superior teams like Leeds United, Manchester City, Liverpool and Everton had fallen victim to teams doing exactly this to them, and getting eliminated by inferior sides hitting them with a sucker punch.

Back at Molineux, two weeks later, Steve Daley, having just turned nineteen, four days earlier, made only his fourth start for Wolves, in place of the injured Wagstaffe. Daley sent the 37,000 home fans dancing deliriously, when he put Wolves 1-0 up in the very first minute, flicking in Sunderland's deep cross from the right.

In spite of the great Florian Albert marching majestically around the Molineux turf, it was Wolves who ran this particular show, and Munro's towering header, from McCalliog's centre, put them 2-0 up, although Ku's consolation goal gave the Magyars some hope.

But late on, the Greek referee awarded Ferencvaros a penalty kick.

Phil Parkes, though, brilliantly saved yet another Szoke penalty kick .

Wolves had reached their first major Cup Final for twelve years, after their tremendous tour around Europe, but they remained in England for the Final, as Tottenham had amazingly beaten AC Milan in their Semi-final, having recalled Alan Mullery from Fulham.

Molineux hosted the first leg of the 1972 UEFA Cup Final, on Wednesday 3rd May, in front of just 38,362, a smaller crowd than that who'd watched their Quarter-final win over Juventus.

In the absence of Mike Bailey, Jim McCalliog captained Wolves for the Final. Gerry Taylor, who'd played nearly one hundred league games since December 1966, had replaced Derek Parkin at left back, after Parky was struggling to recover from a heart complaint suffered back in February. He wouldn't permanently return until February 1973, having been missed for nearly a full year of football.

WOLVERHAMPTON WANDERERS		TOTTENHAM HOTSPUR
Phil Parkes	1	Pat Jennings
Bernard Shaw	2	Joe Kinnear
Gerry Taylor	3	Cyril Knowles
Danny Hegan	4	Alan Mullery
Frank Munro	5	Mike England
John McAlle	6	Phil Beal
Jim McCalliog	7	Alan Gilzean
Kenny Hibbitt	8	Steve Perryman
John Richards	9	Martin Chivers
Derek Dougan	10	Martin Peters
Dave Wagstaffe	11	Ralph Coates

The first half was goalless, but Danny Hegan chipped a superb shot from sixty yards, that had appeared to have beaten Pat Jennings, who was out of position. But Jennings managed to recover; he flew into the air and just tipped the ball over his crossbar.

Doog ranked that Hegan shot as great as Pele's long range shot against Czechoslovakia, during the 1970 World Cup Finals.

After 57 minutes, Mike England floated a free-kick into the Wolves area, and it was met by Martin Chivers, who launched himself like Prince Siegfried and propelled the ball past Parkes, into the far right corner of the goal.

Wolves equalised, though, with just about twenty minutes remaining. A contentious free-kick had been awarded to Wolves, just about twenty yards out, after Mullery was harshly ruled to have handled the ball. Danny Hegan took a quick one, square to McCalliog, who hammered the ball, left-footed, under Jennings, whose desperate leg save only diverted it inside his near post.

Doog then had the home fans in the North Bank in a frenzy, scoring from close range, but the referee, Tofik Bahramov, ruled the goal out for a foul on Joe Kinnear.

The decisive goal of the match was a classic. Phil Beal broke up a Wolves attack inside his own penalty area. Cyril Knowles collected the loose ball, and he carried it to near halfway, before playing a long pass up to Chivers' head. Chivers knocked the ball down to Perryman, who played a short pass, straight back to Chivers, out wide on the Spurs left wing. Chivers moved inside with three touches, and then he smashed a right-footed rocket past Parkes from over thirty yards out.

That was the best goal of Martin Chivers' career.

Wolves had been better in possession. Wagstaffe, Hibbitt, Hegan, Richards and McCalliog had all played the ball about confidently and intelligently. Mullery, England and Beal were an impenetrable barrier, though, on the night, with Peters and Perryman providing good support to their defence, getting their hands dirty.

Doog was simply smothered, and starved of any chances, except for his *goal.*

A fortnight later, 53,000 packed White Hart Lane, and despite Waggy's wonderful thirty-yard drive equalising Alan Mullery's headed goal, Spurs hung on to win the UEFA Cup, 3-2 on aggregate.

Wolves had beaten the very best teams, and some of the very greatest players in Europe, but in Tottenham Hotspur, they faced one of the very best Spurs teams in the club's history. Although an all-English UEFA Cup Final didn't very much interest much of the rest of Europe, the 1972 UEFA Cup Final, the very first UEFA Cup Final, had set the highest standards of footballing quality, a level of competition and passion, that very few subsequent UEFA Cup Finals have managed to equal.

For fifteen minutes after the Final, Bill Nicholson was apologising to the Wolves players in their changing room, claiming that he thought the better side had lost.

Derek Dougan, at thirty-four years of age, was again Wolves' top goal-scorer, during the 1971-72 season, with twenty-four league and cup goals. John Richards, playing only his first full season, had scored sixteen, while Jim McCalliog scored fifteen, and Kenny Hibbitt also chipped in with nine. Wolves were one of the most exciting teams of the era, and at their very best, they were the best team in England, but ultimately, that season of hope and excitement for Wolves had ended in dismay.

Despite Wolves starting 1972-73 reasonably well, winning four of their opening seven matches, and sitting just two points below the First Division leaders, Arsenal, on Saturday 2nd September, their league season quickly fell apart.

Derek Parkin had returned from his heart problems, but then they lost him to a broken leg, during their 3-2 home win over Spurs, on Saturday 19th August. Waggy , though, was also in and out, all season, playing in only half of Wolves' matches.

Following their 3-2 win over top flight new boys and entertainers Birmingham City, on Saturday 2nd September, Wolves won only three of their next thirteen league games, a run that dropped Wolves out of the title race, and down to thirteenth place.

Wolves enjoyed a good run in the League Cup, though, having been drawn against lower league opposition in every round, up to the Semi-finals.

Doog and Richards both scored on Tuesday 5th September, as Wolves scraped past Orient, 2-1 at Molineux, and then a month later, they hammered Sheffield Wednesday 3-1, again at home. On Hallowe'en, only 21,000 were inside Molineux, as Bristol Rovers, who'd shocked Manchester United in the Third round, were spanked 4-0 (Richards, McCalliog 2, Kindon).

In the Quarter-finals, Wolves managed to avoid any of the five First Division teams remaining in the competition, and they were given another home draw against Bob Stokoe's Blackpool. Again, another disappointing crowd of hard-core Wolves fans, just 17,312, attended such an important match.

It was the smallest crowd of the four Quarter-finals by far.

Former Newcastle forward Keith Dyson made the most of the lacklustre atmosphere, and fired the Tangerines into a 1-0 half-time lead. Jim McCalliog levelled after the break, though, to earn Wolves a replay at Bloomfield Road.

Two days later, Stokoe resigned as Blackpool manager and he was then appointed as Sunderland's new boss, but he was allowed to stay on to take charge of the Tangerines for one more game, their replay against Wolves.

On Tuesday 28th November, Blackpool's second biggest crowd of the season, 19,812, was stunned when Doog headed in a late winner to send Wolves into the Semi-finals, and to face the League Cup favourites Tottenham Hotspur.

Molineux finally attracted a decent crowd, on Wednesday night, 20th December, though not an awe-inspiring, spine-tingling crowd.

28,357 were stunned as Spurs, just as they'd done seven months earlier, again won 2-1 away from home. Martin Peters and John Pratt had both scored first half goals, in reply to Kenny Hibbitt's early penalty kick, but despite having the bulk of possession in the second half, Wolves were unable to beat Pat Jennings, who was rated as the World's best goalkeeper by this time.

The Football League had originally ruled that the second leg of their Semi-final had to be played on New Year's Day 1973, a decision that had outraged both Bill Nicholson and Bill McGarry. It was an incredible demand to expect players to play such an important match on the day after the New Year celebrations, not to mention creating travelling problems for Wolves fans on a Bank Holiday

On the Thursday after the Molineux first leg match, however, the League eventually agreed, and they allowed the second leg to be played on Saturday 30th December, with both Spurs' and Wolves' First Division matches being postponed and re-scheduled.

A massive crowd of nearly 42,000 packed White Hart Lane, the third biggest attendance of the competition that season, and with 10,000 Wolves fans present, loud and clear, the fever-pitch atmosphere inspired a classic match.

A Terry Naylor own goal gave Wolves a 1-0 half-time lead, and then John Richards, having been fed a great through-ball by Alan Sunderland, stole a yard on Mike England before firing past Pat Jennings to set Wolves up for a Wembley Final.

Martin Peters, though, levelled the aggregate scores before the end, with a classy touch and finish. The match, which was the main match on BBC TV's Match of the Day programme that night, then went into extra-time.

It was Martin Chivers, who'd been the cause of Wolves' downfall during the UEFA Cup Final, who brilliantly buried the ball beyond Parkes, from the edge of the area, to send Spurs to Wembley.

There was no let-up in the Cup dramas for Wolves. A fortnight after they'd been dramatically beaten by Spurs, they were drawn at home to Manchester United in the FA Cup Third round.

Finally, Molineux attracted a crowd almost worthy of its immense size, for the first time since the visit of Juventus, eight months earlier. 40,005 filled both huge Banks, North and South, for the visit of United, who were bottom of Division One.

This was a different United to the team that led the First Division, but lost at home to Wolves, one year earlier. Best was out, Law played only two more games for United, and Charlton was into the final months of his long career.

Captain Mike Bailey scored in only the second minute of the match, to win the game 1-0, but he was again forced off before the end with a broken bone in his foot, and ruled out until mid-April.

In the Fourth round, nearly 31,000 watched Wolves beat Second Division Bristol City 1-0, on Saturday 3rd February. John Richards showed a flash of genius, turning sharply inside the box, then dribbling past both Merrick and Drysdale, before finishing a fine individual goal, from close range, just before half-time.

A tough, tightly-knit Millwall were Wolves' visitors in the Fifth round, three weeks later. The Lions, who'd just failed to gain promotion to the First Division in 1971-72, and had won 2-0 at Everton in the Fourth round, made Wolves fight at the back for almost all of the match, as they attacked without fear.

In front of 31,668, Dougan's cushioned header was met by John Richards, inside the Millwall area, seven minutes into the game, and Richards' right-footed shot just beat Barry Kitchener's attempted block, six yards out. Wolves struggled thereafter, though, and they reached the Quarter-finals in spite of an unimpressive performance.

FIFTY THOUSAND CROWDS RETURN TO WOLVES

That win over Millwall inspired Wolves to their best First Division form of the season. On the following Tuesday, Doog fired a second half winner away at Birmingham, in front of a mammoth West Midlands derby crowd of nearly 44,000.

On Saturday 3rd March, Doog scored a hat-trick, and Richards hit two, as Wolves then hammered Manchester City 5-1, at Molineux. A week later, Wolves won 2-0 away at Chelsea, after Doog and Richards scored their fifteenth and twenty-third goals of the season, respectively.

Those three wins had lifted Wolves back up to sixth place in Division One, five points behind fourth-placed Ipswich, but then their rearranged midweek draw away at Crystal Palace reduced the deficit to four points, as they entertained Coventry City in the FA Cup Quarter-finals.

A massive, swarming crowd of 50,106, the first fifty thousand-plus attendance at Wolves since 1968, filled Molineux on Saturday 17th March 1973.

WOLVERHAMPTON WANDERERS		COVENTRY CITY
Phil Parkes	1	Bill Glazier
Gerry Taylor	2	Mick Coop
Derek Parkin	3	Chris Cattlin
Bernard Shaw	4	Wilf Smith
Frank Munro	5	Roy Barry
John McAlle	6	Bobby Parker
Jim McCalliog	7	Dennis Mortimer
Kenny Hibbitt	8	Brian Alderson
John Richards	9	Colin Stein
Derek Dougan	10	Willie Carr
Dave Wagstaffe	11	Tommy Hutchison

After six minutes, a mighty header from Frank Munro, from just outside his own penalty area, flew forty yards to a leaping Doog, ten yards inside Coventry's half. Doog flicked on for his partner John Richards to chase, with Parker tracking him. The sheer pace of Richards, the power of his acceleration, absolutely killed Bobby Parker, and he shot past Glazier, from just inside the Coventry City penalty area.

Dougan then flicked in a left-sided corner from Kenny Hibbitt, but the referee blew for an apparent foul, to Doog's disbelief. Kenny Hibbitt then headed a loose City clearance into the path of Richards, just inside Coventry's area, but Cattlin and Coop came in with a sandwich tackle, and sent him sprawling.

The referee blew for a penalty kick.

Kenny Hibbitt, *Smash,* simply smashed his kick low and hard, the ball beating Bill Glazier's great dive, hitting the far left bottom corner of the goal. Wolves had been totally dominant, vibrant even, and they fully deserved their 2-0 win, in contrast to their lacklustre, lumbering lug against the Lions.

On the following Tuesday, Hibbitt and Richards both scored again as Wolves beat West Brom 2-0, in the last Black Country derby match for four and a half years.

33,520, their second biggest league crowd of the season, watched Wolves move up to just one point below fifth-placed Newcastle United.

Wolves held title-chasing Leeds United to a 0-0 draw away at Elland Road, but they were then held to a 1-1 home draw by Sheffield United. Richards had scored his twenty-sixth goal of the season, ahead of their FA Cup Semi-final, but Wolves were still only a point behind Newcastle, and with a game in hand.

Wolves' reward for beating Coventry was a Semi-final tie against Leeds United, the Cup favourites, and 52,505 filled Maine Road on Saturday 7th April, as Wolves took a ten match unbeaten run into the match.

For Leeds, Hunter was missing, so Terry Yorath partnered Jack Charlton in central defence, and Madeley filled in for the injured Eddie Gray, in midfield. Barry Powell was selected ahead of Jim McCalliog, at right midfield, for Wolves, and Bernard Shaw kept his place in the centre, with the fit-again Mike Bailey back on the bench.

Other than that, both teams were at full-strength for a game in which defences were on top throughout.

Doog beat Big Jack at Leeds United corners, and Big Jack beat Doog at Wolves corners. Munro and McAlle, in dealing with Clarke and Jones, were as good as any central defensive partnership in England.

Peter Lorimer's twenty-five yard free-kick rocket was taken hard in the chest by Kenny Hibbitt, *Smash!,* heroic in the Wolves wall. Mike Bailey came on for Hibbitt, for his first game since early January, and the match looked set for a replay, following the second score-less stalemate between the teams, inside a fortnight.

All Wolves had lacked, though, was a player like Billy Bremner, who could do anything. Bremner smashed home the winner, just as he'd done against Manchester United, three years earlier, for Leeds, late, late on.

For the third time in eleven months, Wolves were inconsolable.

There had been two bright sides to the story, though. Wolves' FA Cup run had brought the big, big crowds back to Molineux. Over their five games during the competition, Wolves had averaged home crowds of over 41,000.

However, they only got big crowds in the Cup. Despite their resurgence after the New Year, and their strong campaign for another UEFA Cup place, Wolves' average league crowd in 1972-73 was just 24,418, the sixth lowest in the First Division.

The other bright side, though, was that if Leeds beat Sunderland in the FA Cup Final, which they surely would, Wolves would qualify for the UEFA Cup, even if they finished in sixth position. Wolves only had to stay ahead of Derby County, three points behind, to qualify for Europe.

As it happened, Newcastle totally fell apart in April, anyway, and Wolves actually rose to fifth place after beating Everton 4-2 (Richards 3, Hibbitt), Norwich City 3-0 (Sunderland 2, Richards), and then Coventry City 3-0 (Sunderland, Richards, Powell), before the end of April.

Alan Sunderland, still only nineteen, had become a first team regular, as McGarry was re-building for the future after Wolves' Semi-final defeat. Sunderland had scored four goals in Wolves' final five First Division games, including their second half equaliser as they drew 2-2 away at Tottenham on Monday 30th April. This time around, it was a happy draw at White Hart Lane, because it secured fifth place and the certainty of European football in 1973-74, regardless of the FA Cup Final result.

FIRST DIVISION LEADERS, 2ND MAY 1973

	PL	W	D	L	F	A	PTS
Liverpool	42	25	10	7	72	42	60
Arsenal	41	23	11	7	56	37	57
Leeds United	41	20	11	10	65	44	51
Ipswich Town	42	17	14	11	55	45	48
WOLVES	41	18	11	12	66	51	47
West Ham	42	17	12	13	67	53	46
Tottenham	42	16	13	13	58	48	45
Newcastle Utd	42	16	13	13	60	51	45
Derby County	41	18	8	15	53	54	44

On Friday 4th May 1973, the night before the FA Cup Final, Wolves visited Derby for their final game of the season, needing just a point to finish above Ipswich in fourth place.

Can you imagine that, today? Wolves battling Ipswich for the fourth Champions League place? Alternatively, Derby needed to win to rise above Newcastle to qualify for the UEFA Cup, should Leeds beat Sunderland the following day, as everyone expected them to do so; everyone except for Sunderland's fans; everyone except Sunderland fans and Derek Dougan.

Doog was heavily ridiculed by the highly amused Jack Charlton, during ITV's live coverage of the Cup Final, when he predicted that Sunderland would win, after he'd watched the Leeds players walking around the pitch, before getting changed for the match.

With a big crowd of nearly 32,000 inside The Baseball Ground, on that Friday night, Roy McFarland and a Roger Davies brace, all scored before half-time, won the match 3-0 for Derby County, and the Rams finished seventh. They would qualify for the UEFA Cup, ahead of second-placed Arsenal, if Leeds won the Cup, but they didn't.

John Richards was the top goal-scorer in English football during 1972-73, at just twenty-two years old, with thirty-three league and cup goals, and King John was also their only ever-present outfield player.

Goalkeeper Phil Parkes had also been an ever-present for fifth-placed Wolves.

John McAlle missed only one match, and 1972-73 was arguably his best season. Not especially known for their defensive dominance, Wolves kept eighteen clean sheets that season. Liverpool-born, McAlle had originally joined as an apprentice back in 1965, aged just fifteen, and the giant, six feet one inch defender made his first team debut three years later.

Known simply as *Scouse* at Molineux, John McAlle was half of Wolves' greatest central defensive partnership, alongside Frank Munro, after Billy Wright's era.

Scouse played a total of 508 league and cup games for Wolves, until he left in 1981, after the big money signing of Emlyn Hughes, as well as a series of injuries had side-lined him.

McAlle finished his career playing for amateur league Harrisons FC, of Great Wyrley, in the Wolverhampton League, before retiring to become a landscape gardener in South Staffordshire, just to the north of Wolverhampton.

Wolves won only four of their opening nineteen games of 1973-74, and they were only two points above the relegation zone on Saturday 8th December.

Most of their team had been out for at least half a dozen games each, over those first four months. Bailey had been out, Hibbitt had been out, Sunderland had been out, Hegan had been out, and Parkes had been out.

In the League Cup, Wolves had won 3-0 away at Third Division Halifax Town, with a big crowd of over 8,000 inside The Shay, on Tuesday 8th October. Sunderland, Doog and Richards all scored to secure a Third round tie away at Tranmere, where they were held to a 1-1 draw, before scraping through 2-1, after a replay at Molineux.

Back in the UEFA Cup, Wolves won 2-0 away at Belenenses, in Lisbon. Richards and Doog scored in front of 20,000, and then back at Molineux, Bill McGarry played an experimental side, with both Gary Pierce and Peter Eastoe, as well as playing Alan Sunderland in Mike Bailey's position. Wolves still won 2-1, after Eastoe and McCalliog had both scored, and they went through, 4-1 on aggregate.

In the League Cup Fourth round, a crowd of just 7,623, the smallest Molineux crowd for decades, saw Wolves hammer Exeter City 5-1. Hibbitt scored twice, Richards scored twice, and Doog added another, securing a Quarter-final tie with Liverpool.

Lokomotiv Leipzig then smashed Wolves 3-0, in the UEFA Cup Second round, in late October, before, in front of a dreadful and shameful 14,500 Molineux crowd, Wolves actually won the second leg 4-1, in early November. Kindon, Munro, Doog and Hibbitt all scored during a tremendous fight-back. The East Germans won 4-4 on the away goals rule, but Wolves' fans should've been ashamed of their turnout.

John Richards scored the only goal of the game, on Wednesday 19th December, in their League Cup Quarter-final 1-0 home win over Liverpool, to send Wolves into their fourth major Cup Semi-final inside twenty months, but in front of another poor Molineux crowd of just 15,000.

Richards also scored in both legs of their Semi-final, against Norwich, as Wolves drew 1-1 away at Carrow Road, on Wednesday 23rd January, and then on the following Saturday, 32,605 piled into Molineux for their vital 1-0 home win.

Back in the First Division, following their early season flirtation with the relegation zone, throughout September, October and November, Wolves recovered after Christmas, as all their stars returned, and they'd climbed up to mid-table by the Spring, finishing up in twelfth position, only five points below a UEFA Cup place, but also only five points above the relegation zone.

So, on Saturday 2nd March 1974, 100,000 filled Wembley Stadium for the League Cup Final between Wolves and Manchester City, who'd defeated Plymouth Argyle in their Semi-final. On league form, there was little to split the teams.

They were now both as mediocre as the other. City were in tenth position, with thirty points, while Wolves were five places below them, on twenty-eight points.

WOLVES		MANCHESTER CITY
" *Lofty*"	1	Keith MacRae
Palmer	2	Glyn Pardoe
Parky	3	Willie Donachie
Mike	4	Mike Doyle
Frank	5	Tommy Booth
Scouse	6	Tony Towers
Sunderland	7	Mike Summerbee
Smash	8	Colin Bell
King John	9	Francis Lee
Doog	10	Denis Law
Waggy	11	Rodney Marsh

It turned out, however, to be one of the most entertaining of all League Cup Finals. Late in the first half, the afro-haired Geoff Palmer crossed Alan Sunderland's pull-back long into the City area, and Kenny Hibbitt smashed a right-footed volley past MacRae, into the far right corner of City's goal.

Gary Pierce, who was deputising for the injured Lofty, Phil Parkes, then palmed Rodney Marsh's sublime free-kick around his left hand post, just before half-time. Immediately afterwards, Willie Donachie's left-sided free-kick was headed straight into Pierce's arms.

Rodney Marsh squeezed a left-wing cross past Mike Bailey, into the second half, and Colin Bell fired beyond Pierce, from six yards out. Bell then headed Summerbee's left-sided corner kick towards the top left corner of Wolves' goal, but Gary Pierce, having the game of his life being Lofty, flung himself up and he tipped the ball just over.

Mike Bailey, Wolves' captain, threaded a wonderful ball into Sunderland's path, on the right side of the City area. Sunderland's cross was diverted by Towers into the path of John Richards, King John, who buried his shot into the far left corner of the City goal.

Wolves could have won the UEFA Cup in 1972, they might have even won the title in 1972, had they not lost Mike Bailey, and perhaps, they should have won the FA Cup in 1973. Instead, they won the League Cup in 1974.

Gary Pierce, understudying for the injured first-choice keeper Phil Parkes, Lofty, was voted as the Man of the Match. Eventually, Pierce became Wolves' first choice keeper in his own right, playing nearly a hundred league games before leaving in 1979, and he was also an ever-present as Wolves won the Second Division title during 1976-77.

In 1974-75, the season when almost every other team, except for Wolves, had a decent chance of winning the league at some stage, the Age of Doog came to an end.

Derek Dougan started just three First Division games, as younger, lesser talents as Steve Kindon, John Farley and Barry Powell emerged. Wolves attracted an average home crowd of just 23,000, finished in an inconsequential twelfth position, yet again, and they were eliminated from the FA Cup and the League Cup at the earliest possible rounds.

They were beaten 5-4 on aggregate, by Porto, in the UEFA Cup First round, and they finished ten points below a UEFA Cup qualifying spot, but only six points above a relegation place.

That was prophetic.

On Saturday 26th April, Derek Dougan played his 307th and final match for Wolves, at thirty-seven years of age, coming on as a substitute for Steve Kindon, so he could, at least, end his career alongside his greatest attacking partner, John Richards.

Richards had scored during the first half of Wolves' 1-1 home draw with the European Cup Finalists Leeds United.

34,875, their greatest home crowd of that 1974-75 season, by a long way, were rapturous in their applause as Leeds United formed a guard of honour opposite the Wolves team, and Billy Bremner warmly shook the hand of his great adversary in both club and international football.

It was a touch of genuine class, and it brought a tear to many eyes.

It was a tribute to his extraordinary talents that Doog was Wolves leading First Division scorer during 1973-74, with ten goals, and fifteen in both league and cups, at the age of thirty-six, although John Richards had scored eighteen league and cup goals, despite scoring only nine league goals.

Derek Dougan begun his autobiography by discussing Voltaire. He was a special type of player, but he was also an eloquent PFA Chairman, and he fought for the rights of all professional footballers, beyond the boundaries of other PFA Chairmen. He fought passionately for the rights and conditions of professional footballers to control their destinies, and the many benefits afforded to modern elite footballers stand as a reflection of Doog's legacy as PFA Chairman.

Doog scored 123 league and cup goals for Wolves, a brilliant effort for a short term fix, while also playing 43 times for Northern Ireland, many of them alongside his much-loved friend George Best.

Derek Dougan died, aged sixty-nine, on Sunday 24th June 2007. His funeral was like an international State Funeral, with Pat Jennings, Johnny Giles, Denis Law, Martin O'Neill, Jim McCalliog, Dave Wagstaffe (who acted as a pall bearer), Mike Bailey, Gordon Taylor, and most of his Wolves teammates from between 1967 and 1975, all paying their respects, as well as most of the city of Wolverhampton.

Wolves were relegated back to Division Two during 1975-76, after winning only ten league games, in spite of John Richards' twenty-five league and cup goals.

Phil Parkes had played his 305th and final league match as Wolves' lost 3-1 away at Coventry City, on Saturday 17th April 1976, and although he remained as a member of their squad throughout their 1976-77 promotion season, he didn't play at all. Gary Pierce started all 42 of their Second Division matches.

For all he'd done for the club, it was shocking luck for Lofty, having played in every match during their 1973-74 League Cup run, conceding just four goals from seven games, that he'd been ruled out of the Wembley Final because of an injury.

Lofty left for the USA, and the NASL, where he helped Vancouver Whitecaps win the NASL Soccer Bowl in 1979, finally winning a major honour at the end of his career.

In the history of Wolverhampton Wanderers Football Club, only the great Bert Williams, keeper for Wolves' First Division Championship-winning team during the Fifties, had played more games in goal for Wolves than Phil Parkes.

Frank Munro had played 371 league and cup games for Wolves, before he left Molineux after the 1976-77 season, playing thirty-three games in helping his team win the 1977 Second Division Championship trophy, and returning to First Division football at the first attempt. He signed for Celtic, for £25,000, and he was made captain by Jock Stein, on his debut against St Mirren. 1977-78 was a poor season for Celtic, though, one of their worst ever, in fact, and Munro was released in April 1978.

Frank Munro, Wolves' greatest defender of the Seventies, their heroic, hardened centre-back, suffered a stroke during 1994, and he was wheelchair-bound thereafter, having lost the use of his legs. When hearing of the death of his great friend Doog, he affectionately saluted Derek Dougan for regularly visited him while he was ill.

Frank Munro died, aged sixty-three, on Tuesday 16th August 2011, after suffering a bout of pneumonia.

Kenny Hibbitt was Wolves' leading goal-scorer when they won the Second Division title in 1977, with sixteen goals. He was also one of only four surviving players from their 1974 League Cup winning team to also win the 1980 League Cup. Derek Parkin, Geoff Palmer and John Richards were the other players to have won Cup winners medals in both 1974 and 1980.

Hibbitt scored 114 league and cup goals from 574 games, between 1969 and 1984, and he was inducted into the Wolverhampton Wanderers' Hall of Fame, in November 2010, along with Derek Dougan, joining former teammates John Richards, Mike Bailey and Derek Parkin, who were already in there.

One day, Phil Parkes, Frank Munro, John McAlle, Mike Bailey and Dave Wagstaffe will all also join them there.

Mike Bailey also left Wolves during the Summer of 1977, having played little part during their title winning campaign, due to another injury. One of Wolves' greatest captains, Bailey played 436 league and cup games, in his eleven years at Molineux. He currently works as a Scout for Premier League side Everton.

Derek Parkin remained at Wolves until March 1982, before moving to Stoke City for just £40,000. He still holds the club's appearances record, to this day, having played 501 league games, and 609 league and cup matches.

Parky was a Wolves ever-present on five occasions, including during their 1976-77 season, when he lifted the Second Division trophy as captain.

He was awarded a Testimonial by Wolves in 1979, and then became a landscape gardener after retiring from football in the Spring of 1983, having been replaced in Stoke City's defence by a young Steve Bould.

Dave Wagstaffe was unhappily transferred to Blackburn Rovers for just £6,000 in Match 1976, having been one of the very finest wingers to have ever played for Wolves, playing 404 league and cup matches over twelve years. Waggy had scored 32 goals for Wolves, but he had set up at least two hundred.

"The encouraging roar when I got the ball was a tremendous fillip," he confessed, crediting the Molineux fans who'd inspired his performances.

He was disappointed that he wasn't able to help prevent Wolves' relegation to the Second Division, but at Blackburn he was afforded a certain respect, and given a new freedom on the pitch, by Jim Smith, in contrast to the strict regime stamped down by Bill McGarry.

"Play it as you see it," was Jim Smith's instruction to Waggy, which very much suited the thirty-two year old. Wagstaffe played a total of 125 league games at Ewood Park, and he helped Rovers finish as runners-up in the Third Division, behind Champions Grimsby Town, under Howard Kendall's player-management.

Alan Sunderland was a regular in the Wolves team when they returned to the First Division in 1977, and he'd been one of their key attacking players, scoring fifteen goals from midfield, at the age of just twenty-three.

Just three months into 1977-78 though, Sunderland was sold to Arsenal for a club record transfer fee of £220,000. He had scored thirty goals for Wolves, in one hundred and fifty-eight league games, but his last season was his best.

He was then Arsenal's top scorer for two seasons, at the start of the Eighties, and he even played one game for England, against Australia, in May 1980. Alan Sunderland will always be remembered, though, for his last minute winner at the end of Arsenal's 3-2 win over Manchester United, in the 1979 FA Cup Final.

If Doog was the inspiration and influence of Wolves' classic team from 1970 to 1974, and Frank Munro was the rock upon which the team flourished, and Mike Bailey was the True Grit leader, the beating heart of their team, and Waggy and Smash were the skilful schemers, unlocking opposing defences, then John Richards was The King, the pin-up poster star of Wolves, and one of the Premium strikers of the Seventies.

John Richards was Wolves' top goal-scorer on six occasions throughout the decade, and ought to have received more international recognition than he did, winning just the one England cap, against Northern Ireland in May 1973, after scoring thirty-three goals during 1972-73. Richards could never flourish, though, in Sir Alf Ramsey's wingless 4-3-3 formation, playing up top with Channon and Chivers, with no Waggy or Smash alongside him, providing the crosses.

Despite England winning 2-1, after Martin Chivers' brace, John Richards was never selected again.

In 1982, Richards was transferred out, at the age of just thirty-one, firstly on loan to Derby County, before he finally left for good for CS Maritimo, of the Portuguese League. It was a very unpopular decision by manager Graham Hawkins, with all Wolves fans, and Wolves subsequently slid quickly all the way down to the Fourth Division, by 1986, and to near extinction.

At CS Maritimo, on the beautiful island of Madeira, Richards scored twenty-three goals in just forty-four games, and he helped the Madeiran club gain promotion up to the *Primeira Divisao* in 1985.

John Richards had scored 194 league and cup goals for Wolves, in 461 games, and he was the club's all-time record goal-scorer when he left Molineux. He never wanted to leave Wolves, and he would easily have smashed the 200 goals total had he stayed.

During the Nineties, Richards' Wolves goal-scoring record was broken by Steve Bull, but it must be acknowledged that all of Steve Bull's goals were scored outside of the First Division, or Premier League, while John Richards scored 129 of his goals in the First Division, and also five goals in European competitions, to boot.

There really is no comparison between the two Wolves legends.

Wolves only won the 1974 League Cup, during their most colourful period, since the days of Pathe News and Jimmy Young's chart-topping hits, but at least they did win something. They should have won a lot more, but they didn't.

If, just if, Wolves had hung onto their lead at The Baseball Ground, back in March 1972, and if Mike Bailey had returned early, to lead them to wins over West Brom, Leicester, Chelsea and Sheffield United, as expected; if Wolves HAD gone on to beat Derby County to the title, how would they be remembered? How might we have remembered them, as First Division Champions, if all those "Ifs" had happened?

Wolves were certainly better than just a good team. Frank Munro and John McAlle, while lacking the consistent top class of Todd and McFarland, Charlton and Hunter, Doyle and Booth, McLintock and Simpson, and also Smith and Lloyd, they were the very best of the rest, and far more dominant than Manchester United's defence.

Waggy was up there with George Armstrong and Alan Hinton, with his superb production from the wings, and in the absence of Eddie Gray, through injury, for most of the early Seventies, he was the best left winger in the First Division.

Kenny Hibbitt was as electric, as influential, and as devastatingly dangerous, in midfield, as Colin Bell, on his day, which was 90% of the time.

The trouble was, Colin Bell was Colin Bell 100% of the time.

Mike Bailey was Wolves' greatest captain since the Fifties, firing up his team with dirt ground-in, organisational skills, probing the attacks with thoughtful passes, while breaking down opposing attacks with crunching, crashing tackles. He was not Billy Bremner, though, who was absolutely the ultimate footballer.

That was why Leeds United were just a bit better.

Doog and Richards were, though, for those three seasons 1971-74, as dangerous as Clarke and Jones, as prolific as Keegan and Toshack, as feared as Chivers and Gilzean, and better, much better than Hector and O'Hare. Doog and King John had combined for forty goals during 1971-72, fifty goals during 1972-73, and then thirty-five goals during 1973-74.

John Richards and Derek Dougan, for all the excellence that had backed them up in Wolves' team, were the two players that really made Wolves *shine*.

Doog and King John made Wolves a team that would have been great Champions, if they had become Champions. Wolves would have been regarded and remembered as great Champions. The trouble was, they were up against four or five other great Champions every season.

Wolves could have been Champions, but they did exceed themselves, in spite of Bill McGarry, their super-fit, fitness-obsessed, but tactically-limited coach.

McGarry succeeded with the majority of that team built by Ronnie Allen, but Wolves fell short of the uppermost honours due to his tactical inexperience.

If Brian Clough and Peter Taylor gone to Wolves, instead of Derby County, who knows what might have been?

Wolves had won only the League Cup in 1974, and then again in 1980, of course, but of all the teams that have only won the League Cup, since its introduction into the English game, back in 1962, that Wolves team was by far, by a long, long way, the very best of them all.

If they had, just by way of an active imagination, managed to win that First Division title between 1971 and 1974, nobody would have really minded.

FROM DARK SATANIC MILLS

B
Y 1967, BURNLEY HAD DEVELOPED into a lowly, mid-table First Division team, only five years after being league runners-up and FA Cup Finalists, and just seven years after being crowned as Champions of England.

They'd also finished third, back in 1963, behind Everton and Tottenham.

Brian O'Neil was one of six survivors from that 1962-63 season, as Burnley kicked off their 1967-68 season, with John Angus, Gordon Harris, Arthur Bellamy, Willie Irvine and Andy Lochhead their others. John Angus, though, was the sole survivor from Burnley's Championship-winning team of 1960.

O'Neil, the **Bedlington Terrier,** had made his Burnley debut in April 1963, and he became their ball-winner, the midfield engine much loved by the Turf Moor crowd. He was virtually ever-present over the following four seasons, and only missed matches when he was suspended, but he'd served quite a few suspensions.

Harry Potts had taken over as Burnley's manager, back in 1958, with the club having settled into a mostly comfortable mid-table position since gaining promotion back to Division One, back in 1947. Potts led them to the First Division title two years later, and that was followed by a fourth place finish in 1961, finishing fifteen points behind Bill Nicholson's Tottenham.

Burnley had scored 102 First Division goals, that season, while they'd conceded 77 goals; which was ridiculous. That's not football, it's a basketball score. Down in twelfth place were Chelsea, for whom the young Jimmy Greaves had scored forty-one goals from only forty league games.

Chelsea had scored 98 goals, but they'd conceded one hundred!

In the 1971-72 Rothmans Football Yearbook, there's an interesting essay by John Camkin, entitled **Achievements of Arsenal should not obscure football's problems.**

Camkin lamented that "fewer goals are being scored than ever before.

There must be a return to so called **Old-fashioned ideas,** when scoring was the fundamental object of the game."

The essay threw a load of stats at you, pointing out that in 1961, Spurs had scored 115 league goals, while Arsenal had scored only 71 goals, ten years later. He reminded us that Newcastle United had been relegated in 1961, after scoring 86 goals, fifteen more than the 1970-71 Champions.

Camkin never mentioned the 109 goals that Newcastle had conceded.

He concluded that "the game in 1970-71 was, by and large, dull and negative."

I totally disagreed with the essay. It was romantic, nostalgic nonsense, and it ignored entirely the footballing ideals that led to a more defensive game. It wouldn't have been any fun for Jimmy Greaves to score forty-one goals for a Chelsea team that couldn't defend, and finished twelfth.

Brian Clough had also scored countless hat-tricks for Middlesbrough in 6-6 draws, results that deprived him of the chance to play First Division football at his peak, although those games would have no doubt delighted idealists such as John Camkin.

The introduction of greater and sharper defences in football meant that the goals scored, although fewer, were better in technique because the degree of difficulty was tougher.

Francis Lee scored thirty-three First Division goals in 1971-72, when the top three clubs had conceded just 33, 31 and 30 goals, respectively, illustrating perfectly that goals could be scored fluently, even in a defensively tighter First Division.

Anyway, Burnley enjoyed four seasons of being a top four side, under Harry Potts, mainly because there wasn't much else around then. Any good team could have done well during the early Sixties, before all the really good modern teams, Man Utd, Leeds, Liverpool, Everton, Man City and Derby all emerged, and by the early Seventies, there were good teams all the way down the First Division. In the early Sixties, there weren't.

There were some very mediocre teams that just existed in Division One.

By 1964 Burnley were such a team. They'd all caught up. Tottenham were and remained a great team, but even they found it hard to win things with all the slicker, sharper 4-4-2 and 4-3-3 teams stopping Jimmy Greaves from scoring forty goals.

He had to make do with just thirty goals, instead.

So, by the mid-Sixties, Burnley had developed into a lowly, mid-table First Division team. They did win 24 games, however, during 1965-66, to finish a close third place behind Liverpool and Leeds United.

By then, Ralph Coates was Burnley's regular outside left. Coates had made his Clarets debut in December 1964, aged just eighteen. A wonderful, creative and naturally talented left-footed player, he scored five goals in thirty-five matches that season, but he was the architect of many more.

There were calls for Coates to be included in Alf Ramsey's World Cup squad, that Summer, but Alf didn't like wingers, and despite them finishing third in Division One, not a single Burnley player was selected for the 1966 England squad.

In June 1967, Harry Potts paid Rotherham United a club record transfer fee of £30,000 for centre forward Frank Casper. This shocked Burnley fans on the Longside at Turf Moor, not because of any opinions they may have had regarding Casper, but simply because Burnley didn't buy players.

Frank Casper was the *first* player for whom Burnley had paid an actual fee, in real cash, since back in 1959, when Potts had bought Alex Elder from Glentoran, for £5,000.

Casper went straight into Burnley's forward line, for their first game of the season, at home to newly-promoted Coventry City.

Frank Casper scored Burnley's first goal of the season, and Northern Ireland international striker Willie Irvine scored their second, as Burnley won 2-1 in front of only 21,483 home fans.

One month later, on Saturday 23rd September 1967, Martin Dobson made his Burnley debut, in attack, against Wolves at Molineux.

Only nineteen, but clever and highly-skilled, the Blackburn-born playmaker set up Gordon Harris's first goal, playing a wonderful wall pass back into Harris's path. Despite Gordon Harris scoring twice, though, Wolves won 3-2.

Just four months after their shock signing of Frank Casper, Harry Potts paid another £30,000 cash fee, on Tuesday 24th October 1967, to Chelsea this time, for their nineteen year old central defender Colin Waldron.

Colin Waldron had previously played at Bury, with Colin Bell, and he was given the choice of joining either Liverpool or Chelsea. He chose Tommy Docherty's Chelsea, but his short time at Stamford Bridge wasn't a happy time. He played only nine games, before joining Burnley. Waldron made his debut, at left back, in Burnley's 2-2 draw away at Southampton, on Saturday 28th October.

Dave Thomas had also made his Burnley debut during their final match of 1966-67, as a sixteen year old, becoming the Clarets' youngest-ever first team player. Two weeks after Colin Waldron's arrival at Turf Moor, the Nottinghamshire-born apprentice played his second game for Burnley, away at The Hawthorns, on Saturday 11th November.

There was no armistice for the Clarets on that bleak Black Country Saturday afternoon, as West Brom recorded a record post-war hammering of Burnley.

Frank Casper had been injured during their 1-1 draw with Chelsea, a week earlier, but Ralph Coates was also out, injured, and Martin Dobson had been dropped to the reserves. Apart from Waldron and Thomas, Burnley's team mostly resembled the 1963 Clarets line-up, and it was just no longer good enough, in this league.

Bobby Hope scored twice, as did Clive Clark. Both Jeff Astle and Tony Brown, obviously, also scored, while Colquhoun and Kaye completed the caning, as Albion won 8-1.

Dave Thomas was dropped, as Casper immediately returned for the following match, but the end was nigh for both Gordon Harris and Willie Irvine.

Frank Casper top scored for Burnley during 1967-68, with fourteen goals, as they won fourteen games, just enough to keep them half a dozen points above the bottom two.

The highlight of their season, though, was a cracking 2-1 win over reigning Champions Manchester United, Best, Law, Charlton, Crerand, Kidd, Aston and all, on Saturday 17th February, sending the fantastic 32,165 Turf Moor crowd into a frenzy.

Brian O'Neil levelled George Best's eighteenth goal of the season, and then Martin Dobson came on as a substitute for Andy Lochhead. Running onto Casper's headed flick-on, Dobson half-volleyed the ball past Alex Stepney from twenty yards out.

During the Summer of 1968, Harry Potts had a mini-clear-out of the old and the ordinary.

Willie Morgan had been their only ever-present in 1967-68, playing in all forty-eight league and cup matches, but he was sold to the new European Champions Manchester United.

Andy Lochhead also departed for Leicester City, after scoring 102 First Division goals in 225 games for the Clarets. At Leicester, the balding Lochhead partnered Allan Clarke in attack, and he scored twelve goals in forty First Division matches, helping the Foxes to the FA Cup Final, but Leicester City were relegated to Division Two.

Burnley suffered an erratic start to the 1968/69 season, earning eight points from their first ten games, but they were hammered 5-0 at West Ham, and also 7-0 at Tottenham, while beating European Champions Manchester United 1-0, after Brian O'Neil's ripper of a goal, in front of a massive Turf Moor crowd of nearly 33,000.

On Saturday 28th September, though, Doug Collins made his Burnley debut, as Chelsea visited Turf Moor. Calm-natured, and with a natural passing ability second to none, Collins became a regular in Burnley's midfield from then on.

Dave Thomas had taken the right midfield spot, following Morgan's departure, and with Ralph Coates out on the left wing, and Brian O'Neil commanding their middle, Burnley were beginning to look a promising, young 4-4-2 team for the future.

Thomas scored twice, as Burnley beat Chelsea 2-1, but then the following week, defender Jim Thomson left Chelsea for Burnley, for a club record transfer fee of £40,000.

Just as Dave Mackay had never heard of Derby, Thomson did not have any idea where Burnley was, but he couldn't wait to move, just because Harry Potts had told him that Burnley was a lot closer to Scotland than London was. A Glaswegian, Jimmy Thomson had played thirty-nine First Division matches for Chelsea, but he'd become desperately homesick for his Caledonian homeland, and he immediately agreed to move to Burnley.

Burnley was also surrounded by huge hills, just like Glasgow, settling beneath the imposing and beautiful Pendle Hill, the third highest mountain in Lancashire. These natural surroundings made Thomson feel at home, as opposed to London's high rise tower blocks.

Jim Thomson suffered a nightmare of a debut, though, at home to Liverpool, playing at right back, and charged with marking England's former winger Peter Thompson.

Time after time, Thompson committed Thomson to clumsy, ill-judged challenges, and then he sped away towards goal. He set up two goals for Roger Hunt, and also scored one himself, before substitute Geoff Strong completed the rout. After losing 0-4 at home, Thomson was immediately rested, and he started only six of Burnley's remaining First Division matches.

Their greatest performance of the season was on Saturday 19th October 1968, when the First Division leaders Leeds United visited Burnley, with 26,434 filling the wide Turf Moor terraces.

BURNLEY		LEEDS UNITED
Harry Thomson	1	Gary Sprake
Fred Smith	2	Paul Reaney
Les Latcham	3	Terry Cooper
Martin Dobson	4	Billy Bremner
Colin Waldron	5	Jack Charlton
Colin Blant	6	Norman Hunter
Dave Thomas	7	Mike O'Grady
John Murray	8	Johnny Giles
Frank Casper	9	Mick Jones
Ralph Coates	10	Paul Madeley
Steve Kindon	11	Eddie Gray
Doug Collins	12	Peter Lorimer

Ralph Coates and Dave Thomas tore Leeds apart with some dynamic wing play and inventive passing, from the very start. First, Coates fired in a curling shot from just outside the left corner of the Leeds penalty area, the ball dipping just inside the angle of Sprake's goal. Frank Casper headed in from Thomas's deep right wing cross, and then Dave Thomas sent over a corner that Murray flicked in at the near post.

Martin Dobson released Casper, with a wonderfully weighted pass, beating Leeds United's off-side trap, before Casper skipped round Sprake and side-footed into the empty net. Ralph Coates teased and tormented O'Grady, before he actually sat down, *on the ball*, out on the touchline.

He then played a one-two with Casper, before his angled pass was chipped up and over Sprake's sprawling dive by the hardworking Steve Kindon.

Billy Bremner had driven in a late consolation goal, during Burnley's 5-1 brilliant thrashing of the 1968-69 League Champions, but Leeds did get their revenge on the Saturday before Christmas, smashing Burnley 6-1 at Elland Road.

Burnley had also lost 7-0 away at Manchester City back in December, but again they managed to win one in three of their games and finished well above the relegation places, in fourteenth position. Frank Casper was again the Clarets' leading scorer with twenty league and cup goals.

With Martin Dobson now firmly a fixture in Burnley's midfield, alongside Brian O'Neil, and with Thomas and Coates both rampaging down their wings, Burnley began the 1969-70 season with a draw at newly-promoted Derby, and then, they hammered Sunderland 3-0 at home, (Casper 2, Kindon).

Spurs hammered Burnley twice, before Dave Thomas, Frank Casper and Martin Dobson all scored during their classic 3-3 draw away at Liverpool, in front of a stunned Anfield crowd of over fifty-one thousand.

Reigning Champions Leeds United were the visitors on Tuesday 26th August, as 28,000 filled Turf Moor. Colin Waldron had lost his place in the team, though, after he'd fallen out with manager Harry Potts, over his eagerness to jointly open a restaurant with Colin Bell, the Bell Waldron in Whitefield, just south of Bury.

Waldron played only fifteen First Division games during the 1969-70 season.

Against Leeds, Burnley played a brilliant match. John Angus, thirty years old, contained the threat of Eddie Gray, while Brian O'Neil battled boldly against the best midfield there was, and Martin Dobson showed glimpses of absolute class, sliding in a diagonal pass for O'Neil to blast past Sprake.

Leeds United's new attacking partnership, however, had Merrington and Sam Todd tied up in knots, as Allan Clarke dribbled into the Burnley area, and he deftly flicked the ball back for Mick Jones to side-foot in from ten yards out.

After the break, though, despite tremendous pressure by Burnley's rampant attack, they couldn't break through Leeds' World Class back four, and the 1-1 draw was a minor classic.

Mick Docherty, captain of Burnley's FA Youth Cup winning team, that had beaten Coventry City in the 1968 Final, made his first team debut against Newcastle at the beginning of November, but he'd eventually replace John Angus at right back, permanently, in March 1971.

In February 1970, though, after Burnley had smashed Nottingham Forest 5-0, Harry Potts decided he could no longer get along with his coach Jimmy Adamson.

Jimmy Adamson had played for Burnley from 1947 until 1964, and during their Championship winning season of 1959-60, he was their ever-present captain.

He then played 34 league games during 1961-62, at thirty-three years old, as Burnley finished second behind Ipswich Town.

Jimmy Adamson also captained Burnley to the 1962 FA Cup Final, losing 3-1 to Tottenham. He was voted as the Football Writers' Footballer of the Year in 1962, but he hung up his boots two years later, having played 486 games for Burnley.

Adamson had been a sublime right-half, but he could play any of the wing-half positions, even centre-half, so he knew the game well, and he immediately joined the Burnley coaching staff, but there was a personality clash with Harry Potts.

After the thrashing of Forest, Potts was moved upstairs to their General Manager position, and Burnley appointed Jimmy Adamson as their new manager. Once again, Burnley won just about one in three of their league games, and they finished up down in fourteenth place, again, but thirteen points above the relegation zone.

In May 1970, Jimmy Adamson sold Brian O'Neil to Southampton, for £75,000, a record transfer fee for both clubs.

O'Neil had played 277 league and cup matches for Burnley, in eight seasons, scoring 25 goals.

He was the bite in Burnley's team, much loved by the Turf Moor crowd, and most felt that if he hadn't been sold, then Burnley would never have been relegated.

Jimmy Adamson restored the classy Colin Waldron to the first team, though, and then he gave Geoff Nulty a regular place in Burnley's team, playing in various positions, including left back, centre back, centre forward and left wing.

Nulty eventually became a good box to box midfield ball winner, good in the air, and a smart tackler on the ground. Once settled, he was never as great as Brian O'Neil, though he did become a decent replacement, but too late to survive relegation.

1970-71 was a disappointing season. Despite the signing of striker Paul Fletcher, for £60,000, from his hometown club Bolton Wanderers, on Tuesday 2nd March, Burnley won only seven games and they went down with bottom club Blackpool, in April 1971.

If you were to look for a positive from Burnley's season, though, you could point to their last fourteen matches after late February. With Geoff Nulty converted to O'Neil's midfield position for the remainder of the season, next to Dobson, Burnley won five games and they earned thirteen points from those matches.

It wasn't enough to pull Burnley out of the bottom two, but they were at least displaying some mid-table sort of form.

Paul Fletcher was just twenty years old, quiet and reserved, but he held the ball up well, had great pace, and for a five foot nine inch lad, he was very strong in the air, too. Fletcher became the perfect partner for the more skilful Frank Casper.

Burnley were a balanced side, at least, and that offered some hope as they went down to the Second Division.

The hope didn't last long. Burnley were, after all, a selling club.

In May 1971, Burnley's England international midfield star, Ralph Coates, was sold to Tottenham Hotspur for a British record cash fee of £190,000, after 216 First Division games for the Clarets, scoring 26 goals.

Ralph Coates had finally made his England debut, prior to the World Cup Finals, back in April 1970. By then, because of the formation revolution, Coates had been transformed from a straightforward outside left, to a midfield role on the left side of a 4-4-2 formation, and he loved his new two-dimensional responsibilities.

As a result he'd been selected in Sir Alf Ramsey's 28 man provisional squad taken to Mexico, but he failed, against all predictions, to make the final 22, and he was sent back home.

Of all the great players that Burnley sold, between 1968 and 1976, it was the sale of Ralph Coates that Clarets fans found hardest to accept.

In August 1971, after Burnley had drawn with Cardiff City, and beaten Luton Town, John Angus was forced to retire, at thirty-two years of age, after 438 league matches at Turf Moor. He was the Clarets' greatest ever right back, and the last of Burnley's Championship winning team to retire.

On Saturday 11th September 1971, Fulham visited Turf Moor, and a club legend made his first regular, first team appearance for Burnley, although he had already given three fleeting glimpses of his talents back in December 1970.

Just over ten thousand were there to see the real beginning of Leighton James's glittering Burnley career.

BURNLEY		FULHAM
Peter Mellor	1	Malcolm Webster
Mick Docherty	2	Mike Pentecost
Eddie Cliff	3	Fred Callaghan
Arthur Bellamy	4	Dave Moreline
Colin Waldron	5	Reg Matthewson
Martin Dobson	6	Jimmy Dunne
Dave Thomas	7	John Conway
Alan West	8	Roger Cross
Paul Fletcher	9	Steve Earle
Frank Casper	10	Barry Lloyd
Leighton James	11	Les Barrett

Leighton James was electric, unstoppable and intensely focussed on winning, scoring a goal in each half, and displaying a distinct amount of arrogance as he breezed past Pentecost, supplying Fletcher and Casper with a regular supply of ball.

Already, Jimmy Adamson had found a replacement for Ralph Coates.

The trouble was, Burnley had missed the injured Geoff Nulty for most of that season, and with no ball winner, they finished down in seventh place, ten points behind the two promoted clubs, Norwich and Birmingham.

Frank Casper, though, benefitting from the supreme supply of crosses from Dave Thomas and Leighton James, had had his best season, scoring eighteen league goals from thirty-nine games, while Fletcher, Dobson and James also contributed twenty-seven goals between them.

SHOOT!

Alan Stevenson had signed for Burnley, back in January, from Chesterfield, after over a hundred league games for the Spireites. Jimmy Adamson had paid £50,000 for the Derbyshire-born goalkeeper, and Stevenson played in all of Burnley's last seventeen matches, but he'd conceded only two goals in Burnley's last six games, with the Clarets winning them all.

That run of wins had coincided with the recall of Jimmy Thomson into central defence, alongside Colin Waldron, on Tuesday 4th April. Since his debut against Liverpool, nearly four years earlier, Thomson had been out in the cold, starting an average of less than ten games per season, but he forged a legendary partnership with Waldron.

It was around this time that **SHOOT!** Magazine had a **Focus On** Colin Waldron, their weekly profile on a footballers' likes and dislikes, favourite other player, ambitions, and their favourite food?

Most players, during the Seventies, would usually reply "Steak and chips," to that last question. Colin Waldron, though, a food connoisseur who'd already opened his Bell Waldron restaurant with England's Colin Bell, replied "Steak au Poivre".

It was appropriate that he played in Claret.

SHOOT! was also another huge reason why football was so popular during the early Seventies. Prior to the late Sixties, there were only the brilliantly written, but old-fashioned and very Conservative **Charles Buchan's Football Monthly**, the World's first football magazine, and also the predominately black and white publication, **SOCCER STAR**.

Then, during the Summer of 1968, **GOAL** magazine made its debut, running against **SOCCER STAR** on a weekly basis. With more colourful pictures than **SOCCER STAR**, **GOAL** contained serious articles by Ken Jones, Clifford Webb, and also a Diary by Bobby Charlton, written over three pages.

GOAL also boasted a two-page article, "The Girl Behind the Man" profile, on a different player's wife, or girlfriend, every week, which was great for the Dads.

However, the bar was raised on 16th August 1969, just after Man had landed on the Moon, when *SHOOT!* shot onto the magazine racks. With less pages, just forty, against *GOAL's* forty-eight pages, but with far more pages than *SOCCER STAR's* twenty-eight, it also sold at a cheaper price, which was great for kids. *SHOOT!* was available for just one shilling, while both *GOAL* and *SOCCER STAR* were one and six.

SHOOT! also had more colour pictures than the other magazines, and they were of a sharper quality, with more action photos of players. They offered free gifts, too, like clip-out six inch cardboard stands of Bobby Moore, in his England strip. Those *IPC* stand-up figures became as popular as *A & BC* cards, or *FKS* stickers, and they go for ten pounds, apiece, on eBay these days.

Also, while *GOAL* had its Bobby Charlton diary, *SHOOT!* included articles written by Bobby Moore and George Best. There were less well-structured essays, but more fun articles about how Roy McFarland became a master defender, or who was better for England: Colin Harvey or Emlyn Hughes? It would compare and contrast the merits of both players, before finally deciding which player should go to Mexico.

Both players should go. That was usually the verdict. It was easy, and less demanding than its predecessors, but it was far more attractive, and that's why *IPC* had a winner with *SHOOT!*

SHOOT! did have a truly match-winning feature, though, compiled by Stan Lover, Chairman of the London Referees' Society, that lasted for decades.

YOU ARE THE REF presented a series of scenarios, via some comical illustrations, that a referee might have to deal with, and asked the reader what they would do? As a result, there was a whole generation of *SHOOT!* readers who knew the laws of the game better than most Twenty-first Century Premier League footballers.

SOCCER STAR sadly folded, soon after the introduction of *SHOOT!,* and *Charles Buchan's Football Monthly* ceased production in June 1974, after twenty-three years.

Neither magazine could really compete with either *SHOOT!* or *GOAL,* and by 1975, even *GOAL* had ceased its independent production, and it became incorporated by *SHOOT!* magazine, selling as a double-billed *SHOOT! and GOAL* magazine.

With more online information, though, and with club websites and fan-sites flooding the internet, even *SHOOT!* failed to survive, changing to a monthly publication in 2001, just like Charlie Buchan, but it permanently folded seven years later.

The *SHOOT ANNUAL!,* the ever-popular stocking filler, is still published, however, and it remains a best-seller, every Christmas.

It was the introduction of *SHOOT!* and *GOAL* that made football ever more popular, making the game, and its stars, more attractive and accessible to fans. You would actually go to sleep at night, the night before the new *SHOOT!* went on sale, hoping your letter was printed. Would it be Allan Clarke of Leeds United and England, At Home With The Stars? And Who Really Are The Greatest? Arsenal or Leeds?

SHOOT! was the magazine of the Seventies.

Who would be in the colour posters? Would it be Tony Currie, or Frank Worthington? Who will be across the huge centre pages?

It could be Newcastle United, or Burnley, or Colin Waldron?

Jimmy Adamson had predicted, when he was appointed as manager of Burnley in 1970, that the Clarets would be the "Team of the Seventies."

During the Summer of 1972, he snapped up Keith Newton, from former League Champions Everton, on a free transfer.

Newton had previously played 306 league games for arch rivals Blackburn Rovers, between 1960 and 1969. He'd played in the classic FA Youth Cup Final of 1959, alongside centre half Mike England, and behind centre forward Fred Pickering, as Blackburn beat West Ham United, including both Bobby Moore and Geoff Hurst.

In December 1969, Newton then signed for Everton, for £90,000, a World record fee for a full back, reinforcing the Toffees' defence as they succeeded in romping to the 1969-70 First Division title.

Keith Newton was selected, along with fellow Evertonians Brian Labone and Alan Ball, for the 1970 World Cup Finals in Mexico. Although he was a left back, Newton started as right back, in England's crucial Group stage wins over Romania and Czechoslovakia, and he played the entire, epic, one hundred and twenty minutes of their Quarter-final 3-2 defeat against West Germany, in Leon.

Newton had created both of England's goals, scored by Mullery and Peters, giving England a 2-0 lead, but they were unable to hold onto it.

After 1970-71, Keith Newton had fallen out with manager Harry Catterick, after he'd been asked to just smack the ball long out of defence, rather than skilfully manoeuvring his way out of difficulties.

The disagreement led to Newton's expulsion from the Everton first team, after October 1971, when he was replaced by John McLaughlin. Keith Newton was only thirty-three years old, when he signed for Burnley, but he still had the class and calibre to become, once again, one of the greatest First Division full backs.

After drawing at home to Carlisle United, and then away at Fulham, Burnley hosted newly-promoted Aston Villa, who'd romped to the Third Division title, ahead of Brighton and Boscombe, during the previous season.

With their balanced, attacking line-up of Stevenson, Docherty, Newton, Dobson, Waldron, Thomson, Thomas, Casper, Fletcher, Collins and James, Burnley simply outclassed Villa. Doug Collins, Paul Fletcher and Martin Dobson all netted in a fast-flowing, fluent first half, and then, Frank Casper hammered in a great volley, from Leighton James's square ball, late on, for a 4-1 victory. A week later, after 2-0 wins over both Preston and Portsmouth, Burnley rose to the top of the Second Division, where they stayed for most of the rest of the season.

Geoff Nulty returned from injury, on 30th September, replacing Dave Thomas during the second half of their 2-2 draw at Luton Town, after Leighton James had scored twice. From then on, Nulty played seventy-nine consecutive league games, holding the Burnley midfield together, before an injury, in August 1974, ended his run.

That was Dave Thomas's final game for Burnley, after playing 175 league and cup games at Turf Moor. On Thursday 19th October 1972, QPR paid £165,000 for Thomas to supply the crosses for Stan Bowles and Don Givens, and prepare for First Division football. Dave Thomas hadn't quite become a legend at Burnley, as Ralph Coates had been, but he did become one of QPR's greatest ever players, being the Hoops' creative jewel during the most exciting period of their history.

Eighteen months earlier, the very thought of being without both Ralph Coates and Dave Thomas would have been unthinkable for Burnley fans, but here they were, and things suddenly weren't so bad. They had turned into Wingless Wonders, relying more on midfield possession and creative passing moves, although the dynamic Leighton James offered brilliant wide support with his breath-taking ball control and electrifying dribbles, but he was no out and out winger.

After the departure of Dave Thomas, Jimmy Adamson didn't add to his squad. He used the versatile Billy Ingham, Burnley's very own Paul Madeley, sitting in at full-back, midfield or attack throughout the season, playing nearly half of the season just filling in, wherever he was needed.

Burnley's regular eleven of Stevenson, Docherty, Newton, Dobson, Waldron, Thomson, Nulty, Casper, Fletcher, Collins and James lost only once before the New Year, winning nine out of their fourteen matches following Dave Thomas's departure.

After the Festive period, Burnley's form continued through the first three and a half months of 1973. They won seven out of twelve games, and lost only three, prior to Easter Monday, 16th April, when FA Cup Finalists Sunderland arrived at Turf Moor.

Burnley needed just one point to secure promotion back to the First Division, and their largest home crowd of the season, 22,896, packed the Longside and Bee Hole terraces, for Burnley's finest performance of the season.

BURNLEY		SUNDERLAND
Alan Stevenson	1	Jim Montgomery
Billy Ingham	2	Dick Malone
Keith Newton	3	Ron Guthrie
Martin Dobson	4	Mick Horswill
Colin Waldron	5	Dave Watson
Jim Thomson	6	Ritchie Pitt
Geoff Nulty	7	Bobby Kerr
Frank Casper	8	Brian Chambers
Paul Fletcher	9	Dennis Tueart
Doug Collins	10	Ian Porterfield
Leighton James	11	David Young

The sheer class of Dobson, Collins, James and Casper sweetly played the ball through the aggressive and muscular Wearside rear-guard, that had defeated both Arsenal and Manchester City, so far that season. After Casper was fouled by Ritchie Pitt, Fletcher headed in Doug Collins' free-kick to give Burnley a 1-0 half-time lead.

Sunderland were missing both Billy Hughes and Vic Halom, their two key forwards, both knackered as they were playing nine matches in just over three weeks, within the month of April. Injuries continued to affect Sunderland's chances of promotion over the following two seasons, even though they were the classiest team in the Second Division, after Burnley and QPR both went up.

After the break, the Clarets stepped up a notch and all their players looked hungry for the ball. A slick passing move between Collins, Nulty and Newton led to Fletcher's second goal of the match, a simple side-footed shot slid beneath Montgomery from six yards, but Monty denied Fletcher a hat-trick with a brilliant save from his close range header, late on.

That 2-0 win over Sunderland was followed by a 2-0 win away at Oxford United (Casper, Ingham), and then 3-0 home wins over both Brighton (James, Casper, Dobson), and Luton Town (James, Thomson, Collins).

Colin Waldron's headed goal, away at Preston on Saturday 28th April, made sure Burnley won the Second Division Championship trophy, having won twenty-four games and finishing on 62 points, one point ahead of QPR. The two promoted teams were far and away the two best teams in Division Two, finishing eleven points clear of third placed Aston Villa.

Alan Stevenson had played in all 42 games, conceding only 35 goals, and he kept a club record eighteen clean sheets. Burnley had scored 72 Second Division goals, giving them a record goal difference of plus thirty-seven, and also a record goal average of 2.06.

Paul Fletcher was their top goal-scorer with fifteen goals, but captain Martin Dobson, Frank Casper and Leighton James had all combined to provide a further thirty-four goals between them.

Alan Stevenson, Keith Newton, Colin Waldron, Jim Thomson, Leighton James and Frank Casper were all ever-presents during their Championship winning season, while Martin Dobson had only missed their goalless draw with Middlesbrough, and Paul Fletcher missed just two games.

Burnley had a team fit for the First Division, but on Monday 4th June 1973, Jimmy Adamson further strengthened his squad by paying £35,000 to Swindon Town for twenty-eight year old midfield player Peter Noble. Noble had twice been Swindon's leading goal scorer during the late Sixties, having scored sixty-two league goals in 212 games. It was Noble's goal that had stunned Burnley, back in December 1968, knocking the Clarets out of the League Cup Semi-finals.

Peter Noble was Burnley's substitute for their first game back in the First Division, away at Sheffield United, on Saturday 25th August, but right back Mick Docherty suffered a cruciate ligament injury, and he was ruled out for the entire season.

Noble went on, and he played so well at full back, he remained there for Burnley's next fifty-four league and cup games.

Doug Collins and Martin Dobson both scored first half goals in Burnley's 2-0 win. Burnley beat Chelsea next, before drawing at home to Coventry, to go third in the table. On Wednesday 5th September, away at Tottenham, Frank Casper was in World Class form, twisting and turning young Michael Dillon, time and time again, teasing Cyril Knowles, and tormenting Ray Evans.

As dismal as their defence was that night, though, Tottenham's attacking five of Chivers, Peters, Gilzean, Perryman and Ralph Coates were brilliant. Spurs led 2-1 at half-time, against the run of play, after Knowles and Chivers had cancelled out Leighton James' rocket that swerved away and then back inside of Jennings' left post.

Referee Jack Taylor then awarded a penalty to Burnley, after Dillon had fouled Frank Casper, and Casper himself equalised from the spot.

He then laid the ball off for Doug Collins to curl in a classy shot from just inside the Spurs area, as Burnley rose to second in the table after coming back to win 3-2.

On the following Saturday, Burnley continued their magnificent start, as Casper scored his third goal in five games, but Geoff Nulty also struck late on, for a 2-0 win away at Wolves.

Over 25,000 filled Turf Moor on Tuesday 11th September, for the visit of Spurs, who'd been destroyed by Frank Casper only six days before. Casper was a marked man, straight from kick-off.

Casper was hammered, first by Perryman, and then, decisively, by Knowles. It was a diabolical tackle, and it put Frank Casper, Burnley's top goal-scorer, out of action for five and a half months. Despite that, Nulty and Waldron gave Burnley a 2-1 half-time lead, but the dignified Martin Peters levelled for Tottenham late on.

Ray Hankin, a lively and hungry seventeen year old, Wallsend-born striker, replaced Casper, and he scored on his debut, at home to Derby County, to earn a decent 1-1 draw, after the giant Roger Davies had given the Rams a half-time lead.

After losing their first game of the season, away at Ipswich, Burnley entertained Johnny Hart's Manchester City, at the end of September, with another big crowd of nearly 25,000 inside Turf Moor.

Paul Fletcher was excellent, dangerous at every attack, with the experienced and expertly Doyle and Booth both unable to hold him. Fletcher drove home a first half double, and then he set up his captain Martin Dobson to fire home from the edge of the area, for their biggest home win of the season, thrashing City 3-0.

A week later, Colin Waldron's scrambled goal during the second half, away at West Ham United, gave Burnley a 1-0 win, lifting them back up to second place. With their wonderful, flowing style of possession football, Burnley then beat QPR 2-1 at Turf Moor, and they were the only pursuers of runaway leaders Leeds United.

FIRST DIVISION LEADERS, 13TH OCTOBER 1973

	PL	W	D	L	F	A	PTS
Leeds United	11	8	3	0	23	7	19
BURNLEY	11	7	3	1	21	11	17
Derby County	12	6	3	3	16	10	15
Coventry City	12	6	3	3	14	9	15
Everton	11	5	4	2	13	9	14

After just eleven games, Burnley had already won as many games as they won during the whole of the 1970-71 season, but Everton beat them 1-0 on the following Saturday, and then Manchester United held them to a goalless draw, with nearly 32,000 packed inside Turf Moor.

Paul Fletcher and Ray Hankin both scored to earn a 2-2 draw away at eighth-placed Southampton, but without a win in three games, Burnley had dropped to fourth place, behind Leeds, Newcastle and Everton.

BURNLEY		LEEDS UNITED
Alan Stevenson	1	David Harvey
Peter Noble	2	Paul Reaney
Keith Newton	3	Trevor Cherry
Martin Dobson	4	Billy Bremner
Colin Waldron	5	Gordon McQueen
Jim Thomson	6	Norman Hunter
Geoff Nulty	7	Peter Lorimer
Ray Hankin	8	Allan Clarke
Paul Fletcher	9	Mick Jones
Doug Collins	10	Mick Bates
Leighton James	11	Paul Madeley

37,894, Burnley's largest crowd of the season, squeezed into Turf Moor, on Saturday 10th November, as Leeds United came to defend their unbeaten record.

Fans climbed the floodlight pylons, and they sat on rooftops, and indeed, Burnley haven't attracted a bigger crowd ever since. Missing both Johnny Giles and Eddie Gray, Leeds United defended at their very best, and they kept a clean sheet against Burnley's bombardment of their penalty area, roared on by an incredible home crowd. That goalless draw was the hardest match that Leeds had to play, throughout their twenty-nine game unbeaten run in the First Division that season.

	PL	W	D	L	F	A	PTS
Leeds United	15	11	4	0	29	8	26
BURNLEY	15	7	6	2	23	14	20
Newcastle	15	8	3	4	24	15	19
Liverpool	15	8	3	4	16	11	19
Everton	15	7	5	3	18	13	19
Ipswich	15	7	5	3	25	20	19

Burnley dropped down to fifth a week later, after losing 2-0 away at Leicester City, but they responded brilliantly by beating Stoke City 1-0 (Fletcher), Norwich City 1-0 (Ingham), and then Arsenal 2-1 (Hankin, Waldron), on Saturday 15th December, to move back up to third in the table.

Colin Bell and Mike Doyle both scored in Manchester City's 2-0 win over Burnley, on the Saturday before Christmas, and then on Boxing Day, Wednesday 26th December, they played their finest game of the season, at home to second placed Liverpool.

Because of the freezing, driving rain, their attendance was a disappointing 24,404. Even so, that crowd would have been the largest of the season at Turf Moor, when they'd won the Second Division title a season earlier.

From early on, Leighton James really worried Liverpool, with his astonishing ball control, and breathtaking runs, but when he stopped playing with them, and finally punished them, he looked World Class. Collecting the ball, just inside his own half, he sped up the left wing, roared on by the Longside, riding a heavy tackle by Tommy Smith. He just left the Liverpool hard man behind him, fallen on his hind, on the soaking wet pitch. James advanced and crossed perfectly for Fletcher to rise high above Lloyd, and guide his header beyond Clemence.

In the pouring Pendle rain, Burnley's midfield triangles, between James, Dobson and Newton, and between Collins, Dobson and Noble, with Nulty conducting their performance, literally tore Liverpool apart.

Liverpool, though, were famed for their ability to absorb heavy pressure, having won the UEFA Cup back in May, and as Keegan, Callaghan, Hughes and Cormack found their feet on the soaked turf, they equalised through Peter Cormack's sixth goal of the season. Kevin Keegan then missed a penalty, fluffing his kick, and blasting it well wide of Stevenson's goal.

Late on, Geoff Nulty released Leighton James with a defence-splitting pass, and James then drove over a deep cross for the fearless teenage striker Hankin to head home his seventh goal of the season, for a famous, deserved and loudly-celebrated win over the reigning Champions.

Halfway through the season, Burnley were the cleanest breath of fresh air to arrive in Division One, since Coventry City and Derby County during the late Sixties, and they looked good for a UEFA Cup place.

FIRST DIVISION LEADERS, 26TH DECEMBER 1973

	PL	W	D	L	F	A	PTS
Leeds United	22	16	6	0	41	11	38
Liverpool	22	12	5	5	28	18	29
BURNLEY	21	11	6	4	29	20	28
Everton	22	9	7	6	25	20	25
Derby County	22	9	7	6	24	20	25

That, though, was as good as it got for Burnley. The Clarets slumped badly over the first two and a half months of 1974, failing to win any of their next ten First Division games, and losing six of them. By mid-March, they had dropped to eighth place.

In the FA Cup, however, Burnley made some progress. After winning 2-0 away at Grimsby Town in the Third round (Newton, Hankin), they then hammered local rivals Oldham Athletic away, in the Fourth round. In front of a sell-out 26,000 Boundary Park crowd, and with former Burnley legend Andy Lochhead playing up front for Oldham, Martin Dobson scored twice to kill any fairy-tale hopes, while Fletcher and James completed their 4-1 away thrashing.

Burnley secured a workmanlike home win over Aston Villa, with over 29,000 packed into Turf Moor, on Saturday 16th February. Paul Fletcher's ninth goal of the season, during the first half, won their Fifth round tie 1-0, but it was a struggle.

On Saturday 9th March, Frank Casper was back in their team to face Wrexham, at home, in the Quarter-finals. Wrexham were also fighting a fierce Third Division promotion battle, and they'd knocked out Shrewsbury Town, Rotherham, Crystal Palace, Second Division leaders Middlesbrough, and then Southampton, during their long, long journey to the last eight.

Colin Waldron and Jim Thomson succeeded in keeping out Wrexham's attack that had scored fifty-four goals, and beneath a massive 35,500 crowd, bursting Turf Moor to capacity, Frank Casper turned in a Keith Newton cross, off his knee, and Burnley won 1-0. It wasn't the prettiest goal of Casper's career, but it was the most important, so far. That win rejuvenated the Clarets.

On Saturday 16th March, they beat Everton 3-1, after goals from Waldron, Nulty and James gave Burnley their first league win for eleven games, but then a week later, they visited the runaway leaders Leeds United.

After going a record 29 matches unbeaten from the start of the season, Leeds had lost twice in their last five league games, and Bristol City had knocked them out of the FA Cup. Liverpool were closing in on them, and a fading Burnley side, at home, was just what the doctor ordered.

Saturday 23rd March 1974 was, very possibly, the greatest day in the history of Burnley Football Club.

With nearly 40,000 packed inside Elland Road, Burnley set about Leeds United from the start. Doug Collins, calm and creative, commanded the centre, and constantly unlocked the Leeds defence with his shrewd passing.

LEEDS UNITED		BURNLEY
David Harvey	1	Alan Stevenson
Paul Reaney	2	Peter Noble
Trevor Cherry	3	Keith Newton
Billy Bremner	4	Martin Dobson
Gordon McQueen	5	Colin Waldron
Norman Hunter	6	Jim Thomson
Peter Lorimer	7	Geoff Nulty
Allan Clarke	8	Frank Casper
Joe Jordan	9	Paul Fletcher
Terry Yorath	10	Doug Collins
Paul Madeley	11	Leighton James
Mick Jones	12	Billy Ingham

The energetic Leighton James, with his blistering pace, made Paul Reaney, the league's best right back, work hard all day. Reaney fouled James, and Doug Collins' free-kick was then misjudged by Hunter, and Casper headed the ball back into Leeds' six yard box, where Fletcher scored with a sharp finish.

Leeds, with Bremner and Madeley taking control, upped the pressure, though, and had Burnley trapped inside their own half, but the Clarets defended superbly until just before half-time. Bremner's corner kick was hit by Clarke, and the ball squeezed through the crowded goal area, and into the net.

Leeds had pulled themselves back, right on the stroke of half-time.

But no! Noble advanced up the right, straight from kick-off, and crossed to Fletcher, facing away from goal, and closely marked by Hunter. Paul Fletcher executed a delightful, perfect bicycle kick shot, from ten yards out, that gave Harvey no chance.

2-1 up at half-time, Burnley then raised their game after the break. With half an hour left, Dobson tackled Madeley, and then Casper and Fletcher combined to set up the classy Collins, out on the right side of the Leeds area. Doug Collins' exquisite chip over David Harvey, with the outside of his right boot, made it three.

Ten minutes later, Waldron rose highest to head Collins' right-sided free-kick back into the danger area, for Nulty to force home from close range.

Jimmy Adamson sent on Billy Ingham for Man of the Match Doug Collins, to shut up shop, and their 4-1 away win was Burnley's greatest performance since 1960, and more than any other match, exhibited the true excellence of that team.

If you could bottle up all that was wonderful about that Clarets team, and pour it out, in one vintage serving, showing off all its qualities in one ninety minute presentation, it would be that great away win at Elland Road.

That was the one and only time that Leeds United were absolutely spanked, at home, under the management of Don Revie.

Unfortunately, late on, Frank Casper was given a parting gift, via the boot of Norman Hunter. He limped on to the end of the game, but he looked barely fit to even walk, and his leg was heavily strapped up for their FA Cup Semi-final against Newcastle United, a week later.

Many Burnley fans felt that Ray Hankin probably should have started up front, seeing how injured Casper actually was. It was a gamble that back-fired, especially how superior Burnley were throughout the match. It was Casper's last action of the season, and he wasn't fit to play again for another eighteen months, so badly injured was his leg. With 55,000 at Hillsborough, Malcolm MacDonald broke Burnley hearts with two second half goals.

Still, Burnley still had a UEFA Cup place to fight for. Ray Hankin was re-called, as he should have been in Sheffield, and he set up both goals scored by Martin Dobson and Geoff Nulty, during their 2-1 win away at Newcastle United, eleven days after their FA Cup defeat.

Ray Hankin then scored both goals on Good Friday, in Burnley's 2-1 home win over Birmingham. Draws against Leicester and Birmingham followed, before a disastrous defeat away at bottom club Norwich. Ted MacDougall's disputed penalty kick cost the Clarets dear.

However, Burnley responded well on Bank Holiday Monday, 22nd April, at home to Southampton. Fletcher, James and Nulty all scored in the Clarets' 3-0 win, that left Burnley clinging on to fifth place, with one game remaining, as rampant Stoke City were coming up late, on the back of a superb nine-match unbeaten run.

FIRST DIVISION LEADERS, 22ND APRIL 1974

	PL	W	D	L	F	A	PTS
Leeds United	41	23	14	4	65	31	60
Liverpool	39	22	11	6	50	28	55
Ipswich Town	41	18	11	12	67	57	47
Derby County	41	16	14	11	50	42	46
BURNLEY	41	16	13	12	55	52	45
Stoke City	40	13	16	11	52	42	42

On the final Saturday of the season, top scorer Paul Fletcher scored his fifteenth goal of the season, at home to Cup Finalists Newcastle, but Malcolm MacDonald scored again, his twenty-fifth goal of the season, and Burnley were held to their fourteenth draw of the season.

Stoke City had beaten Chelsea 1-0 away, and then on the following Monday, they also beat relegated Manchester United 1-0 at home, to overtake Burnley into fifth place, on goal average. When Liverpool hammered Newcastle 3-0 in the Cup Final, Stoke qualified for the UEFA Cup.

As well as Paul Fletcher's fifteen goals, Leighton James and Ray Hankin shared twenty-three goals, and Geoff Nulty, Burnley's only ever-present, had scored nine. Burnley kept nine clean sheets during their first twenty-one league games, but only two in the second half of the season.

Burnley averaged First Division home crowds of 20,634, the last time that Turf Moor averaged crowds of over 20,000 until the 2009-10 season, after they'd been promoted to the FA Premier League.

Burnley's 1974-75 season was disrupted drastically by injury, and might have been a disaster. That it wasn't, and that Burnley even dared to threaten the First Division title race, and as late as the middle of March, was purely down to the sheer team spirit of their seven survivors from 1973-74, and the quality of the reinforcements.

Firstly, Frank Casper didn't feature at all during the season. His injury suffered against Leeds, and aggravated in the FA Cup Semi-final, put him out of action until October 1975. Secondly, Jim Thomson also suffered an injury during Burnley's first match, a 1-2 home defeat to Wolves, that kept him out of action until the New Year.

Thirdly, Geoff Nulty, Burnley's calm midfield anchor upon which their success had been founded, was then injured after just three games, and he never started another match for the Clarets. He did return, as a substitute, during Burnley's 4-2 defeat at Wolves in the middle of December, but a week later he was sold to Newcastle.

Joe Harvey agreed to pay £120,000 for Nulty, on Saturday 21st December, and he was eventually appointed captain at St James's Park, leading the Magpies to the League Cup Final in 1976. Geoff Nulty had played 144 league and cup games, in four years at Burnley, scoring 24 goals.

Fourthly, and most disappointingly for Clarets' fans, captain Martin Dobson had also started his last game for Burnley, like Geoff Nulty, during their 2-0 defeat away at Ipswich Town, on Saturday 24th August.

Three days later, Everton paid £300,000 for *Dobbo*. Despite living in the high life again, Burnley could only attract average crowds half the size of the First Division giants, due to their geographical location. They just couldn't afford to turn down that sort of cash. Martin Dobson wasn't happy.

"I am just a pawn in this game," he claimed. "It is just like a cattle market."

The cultured attacking playmaker had scored fifty-one goals from 257 league and cup matches, during his seven seasons at Turf Moor. Dobson should have won a First Division Championship winners medal in 1975, but Everton choked when the title was in their hands, and they finished fourth, three points behind the Champions.

Martin Dobson returned to his beloved Burnley in 1979, but they were a lowly Second Division by then, and in spite of his presence, Burnley were relegated to the Third Division, at the end of 1979-80, for the first time in the club's history.

Playing as sweeper, though, Dobson captained Burnley to the Third Division title in 1982, finishing above Carlisle and Fulham. Under his captaincy, they also reached the FA Cup Quarter-finals, and the League Cup Semi-finals, in 1983.

Dobbo, one of Burnley's most beloved players in their history, left again in 1984, having played 233 matches in his second spell with the Clarets. In his two spells at Turf Moor, he totalled 494 league and cup appearances, and he scored 76 goals.

Martin Dobson returned to Burnley in September 2008, as Director of Youth Development. Eight months later, Burnley gained promotion back to the top flight of English football, the Premier League, for the first time in thirty-three years.

As a result of these set-backs, Jimmy Adamson promoted Ian Brennan, from the reserves, to the left back position, and then he switched Keith Newton over to his 1970 World Cup position of right back.

Peter Noble was moved forward, into Geoff Nulty's position. Billy Rodaway, from Liverpool, replaced Jim Thomson at centre back, beside Colin Waldron, and the muscular and hungry Ray Hankin retained his place up front, alongside Paul Fletcher.

In midfield, Jimmy Adamson introduced a tiny, young Welsh lad, to replace Martin Dobson. Only five feet and three inches tall, and weighing under nine stone, Brian Flynn had already made his debut in Burnley's 1-1 draw with Arsenal, back on Saturday 2nd February, but his enthusiasm and energy made him a cult legend at Turf Moor.

Flynn was rewarded with his first Welsh international cap, against Luxembourg, on Wednesday 20th November 1974, so well he was playing for Burnley.

After four matches, though, Burnley were down in the relegation zone, having taken just a single point from their 3-3 draw away at Chelsea on Wednesday 21st August (Hankin, Dobson,

Fletcher), but Burnley then won nine of their next eleven league and cup matches, reaching the League Cup Fourth round, and rising to sixth place in Division One, only two points behind leaders Liverpool.

With Billy Ingham having then replaced the injured Brian Flynn in late November, Burnley's rollercoaster rolled down and back up the table over the next four months, dropping as low as thirteenth, but then right back up again to third place, by late February.

It was indeed a rollercoaster ride. On Saturday 4th January 1975, Burnley were drawn at home to Southern League side Wimbledon, in the FA Cup Third round. All the memories of their 1974 Cup run were killed, as the big bearded Viking raiders Roger Connell and Kieron Somers, really a librarian, both tore Burnley's defence apart.

It was Mick Mahon, though, who'd created two of Colchester's goals during their shock FA Cup Fifth round 3-2 win over Leeds back in 1971, who swooped in from the left wing and swept home a sharp finish, after Alan Stevenson had parried Ian Cooke's initial shot, sending Wimbledon into a Fourth round tie with Leeds United.

Wimbledon became the first ever non-league team to eliminate a First Division team from the FA Cup, away from home.

In spite of that calamity, Burnley took seven points from their first four league matches of 1975. Burnley then beat Sheffield United 2-1, on Saturday 22nd February (Noble, Fletcher), and they also hammered Coventry City 3-0, on St David's Day. Welshman Leighton James had given the Clarets a 1-0 half-time lead, before Peter Noble and Paul Fletcher completed the rout, sending Burnley up to second.

With just ten matches remaining, it looked very much like a two-way battle between Everton's mighty defence and the First Division's top scorers Burnley, for the title.

You'll also observe that if it had been three points for a win back in 1974-75, Burnley would've been top of the league with fifty-five points.

FIRST DIVISION LEADERS, 1st MARCH 1975

	PL	W	D	L	F	A	PTS
Everton	31	13	14	4	46	28	40
BURNLEY	32	16	7	9	55	45	39
Stoke City	32	13	11	8	48	38	37
Ipswich Town	32	17	2	13	45	30	36
Liverpool	31	14	8	9	43	32	36
Leeds United	32	14	8	10	45	36	36
Derby County	31	14	8	9	47	42	36
Man City	31	14	8	9	44	43	36

One week later, on Saturday 8th March, Burnley hosted fifth-placed Liverpool, and 31,812 filled Turf Moor, their biggest crowd of the season, for their biggest match of the season.

Liverpool had topped the table until the New Year, but they'd been without a win for four matches.

BURNLEY		LIVERPOOL
Alan Stevenson	1	Ray Clemence
Billy Ingham	2	Tommy Smith
Keith Newton	3	Phil Neal
Brian Flynn	4	Phil Thompson
Colin Waldron	5	Terry McDermott
Jim Thomson	6	Emlyn Hughes
Peter Noble	7	Kevin Keegan
Ray Hankin	8	Brian Hall
Paul Fletcher	9	Steve Heighway
Doug Collins	10	Ray Kennedy
Leighton James	11	Ian Callaghan

With Liverpool including nine members of their European Cup winning team, two years later, needed a win themselves, to catch up with neighbours Everton. If this Burnley/Liverpool match was played today, it would be the 4.00 pm kick-off match on *Sky Sports Super Sunday.*

Ray Hankin headed Burnley into a half-time lead, after Emlyn Hughes had misjudged Peter Noble's deep cross, but Terry McDermott, Liverpool's recent signing from Newcastle, stepped inside Jimmy Thomson and he curled a shot into the far left corner of Stevenson's goal. The 1-1 draw did few favours to either team, but Burnley remained in second place, just two points behind Everton, and two points ahead of third-placed Derby County, with Liverpool and Stoke a point further back.

A week later, though, it began to go wrong.

Burnley led 1-0 at half-time, away at West Ham United, after Doug Collins had volleyed in from Brian Flynn's chipped pass.

Keith Robson and Alan Taylor both hit second half goals, though, to give the Hammers a 2-1 win, and to add insult to injury, striker Paul Fletcher had to go off injured, after substitute Rodaway had already replaced Brian Flynn.

West Ham had scored the winner while Burnley only had ten men on the field.

Paul Fletcher was ruled out for the rest of that season, and Burnley won only one more game, from their remaining eight games, and they dropped down to tenth position, eight points behind Champions Derby County.

Peter Noble and Leighton James were both ever-presents during a rollercoaster of a season, that rose sharply after a flat start, went up and down and then sharply up again, right in the middle.

It went right to the top, but then it did a complete loop with everyone upside down, and then zoomed, zoomed down to the finish.

1974-75 had included their most humiliating defeat, ever, but then they were also right in the thick of the First Division title race, with just ten games left.

It had nearly everything, but ultimately, nothing yet again. Nevertheless, Leighton James, Ray Hankin, Peter Noble and Paul Fletcher all combined to score fifty-six league and cup goals.

Burnley continued their patchy form into 1975-76. By the middle of October, the Clarets had won only three of their first thirteen games, and they'd slumped to seventeenth place, only three points above the bottom three.

Mick Docherty, though, had returned to Burnley's defence, at right back, after a two year absence.

Peter Noble was playing in a more attacking role, too, just as he'd done at Swindon, and he was their top scorer after scoring fourteen league and cup goals from just nineteen games, he looked set to become the first Burnley player to score twenty league goals in a season, since Willie Irvine in 1966.

November arrived, though, and eliminated any positive hopes for Burnley's season, as their situation was downgraded from disappointing to disastrous.

On Saturday 8th November, Peter Noble suffered an ankle injury while scoring a penalty, his fifteenth goal of the season, and he was ruled out for nearly two-thirds of the remainder of that season.

A week later, Leighton James played his last game for Burnley, during their 1-5 home defeat to Wolves. Derby County paid Burnley £300,000 for James, in an attempt to defend their title as League Champions.

"Taffy" had scored fifty-five league and cup goals in 214 matches, in five years at Turf Moor. He then scored fifteen First Division goals in his two seasons at Derby, and he helped the Rams to an FA Cup Semi-final, and fourth place in Division One.

In late 1977, Burnley chairman Bob Lord was asked which player he'd most like to bring back to Turf Moor. In a heartbeat, he answered, "Leighton James."

So in September 1978, he did just that, paying QPR £165,000 to bring him back. James had moved from Derby to QPR in October 1977.

He remained at Burnley for two further seasons, scoring eleven goals in 93 matches, before moving on again, joining John Toshack's Welsh revolution at Swansea City, in May 1980.

Leighton James helped the Swans gain promotion to Division One, for the first time in their history. He was a key player in establishing Swansea as the top team in Division One, by Christmas 1981.

James returned to Turf Moor, again, in 1986, after leaving Newport County. By then, Burnley were a Fourth Division club, and he wore their number nine shirt in one of Burnley's most famous matches, at the end of their most infamous 1986-87 season, when Burnley defeated Orient 2-1 in May 1987 to maintain their Football League status.

Leighton James played a total of 393 league and cup games during his three spells with Burnley, while he'd also played 54 times for Wales.

On Saturday 29th November, during Burnley's 2-1 defeat at Tottenham, Alan Stevenson and Doug Collins both also suffered injuries that kept them out of action for most of the rest of the season. By December, Burnley were in the relegation zone, having lost all five of their First Division matches in November.

November 1975 was possibly the worst month in the history of Burnley F. C.

On Tuesday 6th January, after Burnley had been knocked out of the FA Cup, by Blackpool, Jimmy Adamson was sacked by Burnley, after nearly thirty years at Turf Moor. Adamson was the one man who had Burnley in his heart, more than any other, and their only chance of making the best out of an awful situation, and escaping the drop. The players were unhappy. The fans were inconsolable.

That decision was unbelievable.

After a very brief spell in charge of Sparta Rotterdam, Jimmy Adamson was appointed as Sunderland's new manager, on Wednesday 1st December 1976, following the Bob Stokoe's resignation. Sunderland were second bottom when he arrived at Roker Park, and then they lost all of their first seven league games with Adamson in charge. By mid-January, they were bottom, and six points adrift of safety.

Adamson replaced Billy Hughes with the giant Mel Holden in attack; he gave two Tyneside youngsters Shaun Elliott and Kevin Arnott regular starting places, and he also recruited Burnley veterans Mick Docherty and Colin Waldron into their defence.

Sunderland won nine of their next sixteen games, after February, losing only twice, and by Saturday 7th May, they'd risen to sixteenth place, one point clear of the relegation places, but due to a stitch-up between Coventry City and Bristol City, on the last day of the season, Sunderland were relegated, a point beneath both clubs.

In 1978, Adamson went to Leeds United, but due to the pressure of being constantly compared unfavourably to Don Revie, and the fact he lost some of his drive, he left two years later, and he never worked in professional football again.

Jimmy Adamson died, at the age of 82, on Tuesday 8th November 2011.

Although Jimmy McIlroy is generally seen as Burnley's greatest ever player, and he even had the East Stand at Turf Moor named after him, Jimmy Adamson, for first captaining and then managing Burnley during the two greatest periods of their history, was their greatest servant.

It can't be long before Jimmy Adamson is also honoured, in some way, at Turf Moor?

After Burnley's 3-1 defeat at Norwich City, on Saturday 10th January, Mick Docherty broke down again, and he never played for Burnley again. After playing 174 league and cup games for the Clarets, Docherty's contract was cancelled, by mutual consent, and after a brief period playing for Manchester City, he joined his old manager Jimmy Adamson, at Sunderland, playing 73 league games at Roker Park, and he later managed the club.

From the beginning of November until the end of April, Burnley won only six matches, and lost eighteen. They were relegated at the end of 1975-76, in second bottom position, five points from safety. It took thirty-three more years before Burnley returned to the top division of English football, and they've never had another team to compare with Jimmy Adamson's Burnley from between 1972 and 1975.

In May 1976, Colin Waldron joined Manchester United on a free transfer, as cover for Martin Buchan and Brian Greenhoff. It wasn't a successful move, though.

He played only three matches for United, before moving to Sunderland, and then to the NASL, playing for various clubs. Burnley's club captain had played 356 league and cup games, during his nine years at Turf Moor.

Doug Collins, Burnley's pass master and playmaker, also left Burnley in 1976, moving to Plymouth Argyle, where he'd paired up with former Liverpool star Brian Hall in midfield, and he supplied passes for future England superstar Paul Mariner. He left Home Park, after only 22 games, though, joining Sunderland in March 1977, before leaving after starting just four games.

Collins had played 217 league and cup matches for Burnley, including 132 matches during their vintage Claret period of 1972-75. Elegant, calm and skilful, he became player-manager at Rochdale, before emigrating to Australia.

Brian Flynn scored his first goal for Wales during their 2-2 draw with Scotland, in May 1975, after his brilliant first full season with Burnley. After the departures of all the stars from Burnley, Flynn was their only remaining jewel. After 120 league games for the Clarets, he was sold to Leeds United in November 1977, for £175,000.

Keith Newton retired from football after playing his last game for Burnley, four months later, in their 2-1 defeat away at Brighton, on Saturday 11th February 1978. Appointed as Burnley's captain after Colin Waldron left, Newton played 253 league and cup games, having spent six seasons at Turf Moor.

Keith Newton's death, on Monday 15th June 1998, after battling lung cancer, shocked the football world. Newton was only fifty-six years old, and both Burnley and Blackburn Rovers supporters stood, side by side, united in grief at the passing of a real legend of both clubs, on the day of his funeral.

Paul Fletcher left Burnley in 1979, having scored 86 goals from 349 games. Fletcher had been their top goal scorer, though, during their two most glorious seasons of 1972-74.

Peter Noble left Turf Moor one year later, joining Blackpool in January 1980, for just £25,000. Despite playing as a right back for much of his Burnley career, he'd scored eighty goals from 299 league and cup games, a better goal scoring ratio than most midfield players.

After retiring from professional football at the end of the 1980-81 season, Jimmy Thomson joined Morecambe as their player-coach.

Thomson re-joined Burnley, though, at the beginning of their infamous 1986-87 season, as the club's Commercial Manager. This was the season when there was not only a strong possibility of relegation to non-league football, but also the probability of bankruptcy was huge.

The team photograph had to be delayed until new shirts could eventually be purchased, and there was one famous day when Jimmy Thomson was reputed to be locked inside his office, while the bailiffs hammered on his door.

By not opening the door, Thomson had kept the dogs away, and he probably bought enough time for the club to be saved. A real club legend after playing 341 league and cup games for Burnley, today he is a corporate host at Turf Moor.

Over forty-five years after joining Burnley, despite not having a clue where it was, but purely because it was closer to Scotland, Jimmy Thomson remains in the great town of Burnley, *His Town.*

Alan Stevenson remained at Burnley until 1983. He equalled his own club record of keeping eighteen clean sheets when they won the Third Division Championship title in 1981-82, and then, during the following season, he anchored the Clarets to the FA Cup Quarter-finals and also the League Cup Semi-finals.

Stevenson was an ever-present on four different occasions, and his 540 league and cup appearances, over eleven years, placed him in fourth place on Burnley's all-time appearances list, behind Jerry Dawson, Jimmy McIlroy and John Angus.

For a club without money, with moderate average crowds, and in a relatively rural location, compared to the big city teams that gained most success during the Sixties and Seventies, Burnley had punched well above their weight. They enjoyed an awakening between 1972 and 1975, soaring high, right at the top of English football, among the Leeds Uniteds, the Liverpools, and the Cities.

There was an organic style of football, natural and pastoral, to Burnley's success. Without finances to strengthen their squad, and needing to sell their star players, at an average rate of one per season, Burnley played upon their basic, rugged resources, their Team Spirit, and they very nearly achieved the success that was so much out of their reach, on paper.

From *Dark Satanic Mills,* Burnley had brightened up the First Division, with their vintage Claret brand of balanced football that brought them to the brink of the big time of Championships, Cup Finals, and European football.

WITH WORTHINGTON EASE

M ATT GILLIES, A GREAT SCOTTISH manager, and one of the greatest managers in the history of Leicester City Football Club, resigned at the end of November 1968.

Gillies had gradually developed Leicester's team since their promotion from Division Two back in 1957, while he'd also led them to two FA Cup Finals, in 1961 and then again in 1963.

Gillies then led them to a League Cup Final win in 1964, beating Stoke City 4-3 on aggregate over the two legs, but he took them back again to the League Cup Final, just a year later.

Leicester had hammered Jimmy Hill's Coventry City 8-1 away, in the Quarter-finals, but in the Final, Tommy Docherty's Chelsea won 3-2 on aggregate.

City had not only survived, under Matt Gillies, but they'd actually flourished in the First Division, throughout the Sixties.

Then, during the Summer of 1968, Gillies persuaded Allan Clarke, the best and most exciting young striker in England, to join Leicester.

It was a tremendous boost for the club.

Allan Clarke gave the fans some great moments early on, scoring nine league and cup goals during his first fourteen matches at Leicester. By far, though, the highlight was his hat-trick in their 3-0 win over reigning Champions Manchester City, Bell, Lee, Summerbee and everyone, in front of over 30,000 at Filbert Street. Great moments were unfortunately thin on the ground, and City gained only ten points from their first twenty-one First Division matches. At the end of November, following their 7-1 defeat away at Everton, they were bottom of the table.

Leicester City responded by sacking their assistant manager and coach Bert Johnson.

It was Johnson who'd first introduced the innovative initiative of switching numbers around in the team, interfering with the institutional order of the **traditional one to eleven** formation.

So Matt Gillies would make Graham Cross or Frank McLintock wear inside forward shirts, and while the opposition was told to closely watch their number eight, or their number ten, their "hidden" forwards were left free to attack.

"It confused the opposition," Gillies admitted. "Players hadn't got beyond thinking about numbers back then." Bill Shankly was particularly impressed by Bert Johnson's idea, and he introduced the innovation into Liverpool's line-ups too. And so did Don Revie at Leeds United.

Matt Gillies resigned in protest, and in support of Johnson, his right hand man.

Allan Clarke visited Gillies to try and change his mind, but the great Scot could not go back.

Clarke couldn't get on at all with Gillies' successor, Frank O'Farrell, who had been manager of Torquay United for three seasons, but he just on with the job of scoring goals to keep Leicester up.

Goals for Clarke were scarce, though, and nobody else was scoring either.

Allan Clarke scored only six goals during their last thirty First Division games, while Rodney Fern and Andy Lochhead scored just six goals each, over the entire season.

In the FA Cup, though, Leicester had knocked Barnsley out in the Third round, after a replay. Then in the Fourth round, on Saturday 25th January, a massive crowd of over 31,000 packed The Den's vast crumbling terraces, but Len Glover's goal was enough to beat Millwall.

Len Glover, an orthodox left winger from Kennington in South London, was bought by Matt Gillies back in November 1967. He'd played 177 Second Division matches for Charlton Athletic, and he had cost Leicester City a club record transfer fee of £80,000.

Leicester were drawn at home to Liverpool in the Fifth round, and a near-capacity crowd of over 42,000 filled Filbert Street, on Saturday 1st March 1969. Leicester failed to score, though, for the thirteenth time that season, and they travelled to Liverpool, just two days later, for the replay on Monday 3rd March.

Liverpool's biggest crowd of the season, nearly 55,000, was shocked when Len Glover's cross was headed in by the balding Andy Lochhead, and Leicester's back eight then dug in to frustrate Roger Hunt, Ian St John and Ian Callaghan.

Peter Shilton saved Tommy Smith's penalty kick, right in front of the Kop, and against an endless run of one way traffic, Leicester unbelievably held on to win 1-0.

Andy Lochhead, from Milngavie, just south-east of Loch Lomond, had scored over a hundred goals in just 226 First Division games for Burnley, and he was Matt Gillies' last ever signing, during the October of 1968.

Just like Allan Clarke, Lochhead didn't at all enjoy life under Frank O'Farrell.

He was deeply unhappy when the man who had persuaded him to join Leicester was sacked, only a month after his arrival. He left for Aston Villa in February 1970, after scoring only twelve league goals from 44 matches for Leicester City.

Five days later, in the FA Cup Quarter-finals, Leicester City travelled to Mansfield, right in the heart of Sherwood Forest, and the Stags' *second-biggest ever crowd*, 23,500, had totally filled their Field Mill Ground capacity, on Saturday 8th March.

Mansfield Town had already knocked West Ham United, Sheffield United and Tow Law Town out of the Cup. This was their best-ever FA Cup run, and with a home draw against the seemingly rudderless and hopeless second bottom First Division club, they sensed a great chance to reach the Semi-finals.

Rodney Fern had been rescued by Matt Gillies, from the North Leicestershire Windmills League, back in January 1968, and with his straggly long brown hair, just like his idol Mick Jagger, he'd made his First Division debut for Leicester City, against Leeds United back in February.

His professional ambition was to win an FA Cup winners' medal, and he subsequently scored their winning goal, a clinical left-footed strike from inside the penalty box.

Against all of Leicester City's superstars, Mansfield Town had been beaten by a player who had been playing a long way beneath even Tow Law Town just over a year earlier.

Unfortunately, Leicester's goal-scoring woes continued in the league, and they failed to score in either of their two First Division matches immediately prior to their Cup Semi-final at Hillsborough, against West Brom.

With over 53,000 at the match, West Brom had a much stronger team on paper, just as Everton had had a stronger team in the previous year's Cup Final, against West Brom.

Albion had beaten both Bruges and Dinamo Bucharest to reach the European Cup Winners' Cup Quarter-finals, and Jeff Astle and Tony Brown had scored thirty-seven league and cup goals between them, prior to their Semi-final against Leicester.

The entire Leicester City team had scored just thirty-nine league and cup goals, from forty games, prior to their game against Astle and Brown.

It was a total mismatch.

WEST BROMWICH ALBION		LEICESTER CITY
John Osborne	1	Peter Shilton
Doug Fraser	2	Peter Rodrigues
Ray Wilson	3	Alan Woollett
Tony Brown	4	David Nish
John Talbut	5	John Sjoberg
John Kaye	6	Graham Cross
Dennis Martin	7	Rodney Fern
Graham Lovett	8	Bobby Roberts
Jeff Astle	9	Andy Lochhead
Bobby Hope	10	Allan Clarke
Asa Hartford	11	Len Glover
Clive Clark	12	Malcolm Manley

Leicester battled as they knew they could. Despite failing to score in either of their previous two league matches, they'd conceded only five goals in their eleven league and cup matches since the New Year. Their defence was well protected by their twenty-one year old captain David Nish, while Peter Shilton was unbeatable in goal, just as he'd been at Anfield, but he was physically flattened, early on, by both Astle and Brown.

Three minutes before full-time, John Kaye carelessly ballooned a clearance out of his penalty area. Allan Clarke waited, twenty yards out, and just as the ball dropped, he volleyed it crisply and high up into the roof of the West Brom net, beyond John Osborne's desperate dive.

Leicester missed John Sjoberg for the last games of their season, including the FA Cup Final, and he was badly missed. Sjoberg and Graham Cross had played a combined total of more than four hundred and fifty First Division matches for Leicester, in central defence, and that understanding was greatly missed at Wembley.

Mike Summerbee pulled emergency centre back Alan Woollett out of position, as he escaped to the bye-line and then crossed for Neil Young to score from twelve yards, with Leicester's defence desperately dishevelled.

Leicester still had five games left, following their 1-0 Cup Final defeat to Man City, but they only won two of them.

Over 41,000 filled Filbert Street for their final home game against Everton, on Wednesday 14th May, and if they'd won, they might have stayed up, but Alan Ball denied Leicester both points, despite Graham Cross heading past Gordon West, and after losing away at Manchester United on the following Saturday, they were relegated in twenty-first position, a point below Coventry City.

They'd won only nine league games all season, though, so they deserved to go down. Allan Clarke was their best player from a very disappointing and stressful season, and also their top scorer with twelve First Division goals, but he had absolutely fallen out with Frank O'Farrell.

He left for the new League Champions Leeds United for a British record transfer fee of £165,000.

Leicester faced life in the Second Division for the first time in thirteen seasons, and most fans under twenty years old could only remember Leicester in the First Division. Without Allan Clarke, and the hopes they'd had when they signed him only a year earlier, they were a bit demoralised.

Leicester had missed key players like Len Glover, John Sjoberg and Mike Stringfellow for half of the season, though, and with both Glover and Sjoberg, particularly, back in their team, Leicester City did better during 1969-70 than many fans had feared.

They finished up in third place, and only two points behind runners-up Blackpool. The unshaven, and moustached Rodney Fern had filled Allan Clarke's place in attack, and he was City's top scorer with sixteen league goals.

Then, on Wednesday 2nd September 1970, a locally-born England youth team player, from Coalville in Leicestershire, made his debut against Bristol City.

Steve Whitworth, only eighteen, made an immediate impact at right back in Leicester's defence. They beat the Robins 4-0, and Leicester's regular defence of Whitworth, Sjoberg, Cross and Nish, in front of Shilton, kept twenty-three clean sheets during 1970-71, as they won a superb Second Division Championship title.

Ally Brown, Frank O'Farrell's first signing, had matured into a proper threat in City's attack, and he top scored with fifteen goals, but nobody else was scoring consistently.

It was Leicester's supreme defence that had set them head and shoulders above the rest of the Second Division, conceding only Thirty Goals from 42 games.

They'd scored only 57 goals, though, and nine other Second Division teams scored more than that, including Luton, Carlisle and even Swindon Town. With a decent striker, Frank O'Farrell's Leicester could surely do very well in the First Division.

A DOYEN OF FLAIR

In June 1971, Frank O'Farrell left Leicester City to become Manchester United's new manager, the biggest job in football. He certainly had some real strikers at Old Trafford, like Best, Law and Charlton, but he never had a defence as good as Leicester City's, and that cost him his job just eighteen months later.

Jimmy Bloomfield had led Orient to the Third Division Championship title, back in 1970, but he left Brisbane Road in June 1971, to become Leicester's new manager.

He was a thirty-seven year old London boy, from Notting Hill, a wide boy, a crafty geezer, and a "doyen of flair", as Frank Worthington called him. It didn't take long for him to sign his first player, and Bloomfield returned to his home town to get him.

At Arsenal, Jon Sammels had fallen out of favour with the First Division and FA Cup Double winners, after the emergence of Charlie George, and with Peter Storey having moved into midfield from full back, at Highbury. Even Eddie Kelly was above him in Bertie Mee's pecking order.

After playing 215 First Division games for Arsenal, Sammels handed in a transfer request, and in late July 1971, Jimmy Bloomfield ensured him that Leicester was the place to be, paying £100,000 to Arsenal for him.

It was Jon Sammels' First Division experience that Bloomfield needed, and that was what he got, as the skilful and intelligent Sammels became a key player supplying Leicester's attack. By paying £100,000, though, it was also a statement of intent by Bloomfield, a marquee signing unlike the mild signings that O'Farrell had made.

As decent as players that John Farrington, Bobby Kellard and Malcolm Partridge were, they weren't the type of players to replace Allan Clarke, like for like.

Despite the quality of Sammels, and with Ally Brown scoring in Leicester's first game of the season, after only forty-five seconds, away at Huddersfield, they had a very poor start to the new season. After their first ten matches of 1971-72, Leicester had gained only six points, and they'd failed to score in half of those matches.

As October arrived, Jimmy Bloomfield went back to London to pick up a couple of bargains.

First, he paid £80,000 to Crystal Palace for Alan Birchenall, their attacking midfielder, and a real dressing room personality. Born in East Ham, Birchenall had started his career by scoring thirty-one league goals in 107 matches for Sheffield United in the mid-Sixties, before he returned to London.

He first joined Chelsea, before moving to Palace at the start of the Seventies, scoring thirty-one goals in 115 games for both clubs. *Birch* made his Leicester City debut at home to Crystal Palace, of all teams, on Saturday 2nd October.

Also making his Leicester debut in that Palace match was Keith Weller, Chelsea's twenty-five year old midfield playmaker. Jimmy Bloomfield had also paid £100,000 to Dave Sexton for Weller, while he was down in London.

Bloomfield picked up two real bargains there. Islington-born Weller had scored forty goals for Millwall in 121 league games, before he signed for Chelsea in 1970, for £100,000. He was also Chelsea's top goal-scorer during 1970-71, having scored thirteen First Division goals from 32 games, and he'd won a European Cup Winners' Cup winners medal, having played in both games against Real Madrid in the Final.

Chelsea manager Dave Sexton later described his decision to sell Keith Weller as the worst he'd ever made.

As a result of the experience and strength, *and the fun,* that Weller brought to Leicester City, they lost only three of their next twelve matches before Christmas.

On Saturday 8th January 1972, Ally Brown scored an early goal at home to title contenders Liverpool, to secure Leicester their vital 1-0 win.

After that, relegation was never an issue, and Leicester maintained a mid-table position to the end of the season, finishing fourteen points above the relegation zone.

But that was the last goal Brown ever scored for Leicester City.

On Wednesday 8th March, West Bromwich Albion paid £55,000 for Ally Brown. He'd scored a brilliant 31 goals in only 93 league games for the Foxes, but he then became a significant part of West Brom's entertaining team from the mid to late-Seventies. Despite playing his final Leicester City match back in February, Ally Brown was still their leading goal-scorer with just seven goals.

Fortunately, Leicester's steady defence had conceded just fifteen goals in thirty of their First Division matches. With a defence as good as that, they were hard to beat in a lot of matches. Their colourful attacking combination of Jon Sammels, Keith Weller, Len Glover and Alan Birchenall had scored a total of nineteen useful league goals, ensuring enough 1-1 draws and 1-0 wins, and delighting their 28,536 average crowd.

Leicester began 1972-73 with a draw and two defeats, that left them just above the bottom two, so Jimmy Bloomfield pulled off a great little bit of business during late August.

What Leicester really needed was a flamboyant, frank and foxy forward: a centre forward who could score twenty goals a season.

Frank Worthington had scored nineteen goals as Huddersfield Town had won the Second Division Championship title back in 1970, but he'd struggled with the Terriers in Division One, and they were relegated in April 1972, having finished bottom.

Liverpool also had a firm interest in signing Worthington, and they outbid Leicester's initial offer, reportedly agreeing a club £150,000 record fee for him. However, after signing for Liverpool, Worthington failed two medicals. Tests showed a high blood pressure, and Bill Shankly told Worthington that he couldn't gamble a club record fee on "a player with a question mark hanging over his head."

So, on Monday 21st August, Huddersfield Town were forced to accept the initial £100,000 offered to them by Jimmy Bloomfield.

Frank Worthington was tall, dark-haired, with huge sideburns, and he strutted around with a confident swagger. A swashbuckling hero, with a huge presence on the field, Worthington looked like Errol Flynn having turned to the wild side.

Worthington's first match for Leicester was against Manchester United, at Old Trafford. Just 26 minutes into his Leicester City career, Weller and Birchenall combined to set Frank Worthington up, inside the area.

With one touch to kill the ball, Frank Worthington then guided the ball around Stepney's dive, high into the far corner of the United goal. George Best equalised from the penalty spot, and the game ended 1-1, but a Superstar was born.

On that same day, Saturday 23rd August, Jimmy Bloomfield got on the old dog and bone, and he agreed to pay £112,000 to his old club Orient for left back Dennis Rofe, a British record transfer fee for a full back.

Dennis Rofe had missed only one game under Jimmy Bloomfield during 1969-70, as Orient sailed to the Third Division title. Rofe had also played in all of Orient's FA Cup matches, as they reached the Quarter-finals in 1972, just five months earlier.

Orient had beaten Leicester 2-0 in the Fourth round, shocking a Filbert Street crowd of 31,402, but they then claimed their second First Division scalp in the Fifth round, with over 30,000 filling Brisbane Road, when they won 3-2 at home to Chelsea.

It took a goal by World Cup winner Alan Ball to finally conquer Orient, as Arsenal won 1-0 at Brisbane Road, in spite of a partisan 31,678 East London crowd making it an uncomfortable afternoon for the reigning Champions.

Jimmy Bloomfield had watched that match on television, and he felt totally assured that Dennis Rofe could mix it against the very best First Division attacks.

The day after Rofe signed, Derby manager Brian Clough then paid a new British record transfer fee of £225,000 for David Nish. Cloughie had long admired Leicester City's cultured captain, and he saw Nish as the final piece of his jigsaw to bring the European Cup back to England, and to The Baseball Ground.

David Nish had played 228 league matches for Leicester City, but he was still only twenty-four years old. He'd been an ever-present for the Foxes on three occasions.

The good thing about the sale of David Nish, from Jimmy Bloomfield's prospective, was that he'd nearly balanced the books. He'd paid over £490,000 on Sammels, Birchenall, Weller, Worthington and Rofe since taking over at Filbert Street, and he'd made sales totalling £325,000 (he'd also sold Rodney Fern to Luton Town during the Summer for £45,000), but with most of their £165,000 War chest just gathering interest, since the sale of Allan Clarke, the accounts were finally just about level.

More importantly, though, he had a better team than when he first took over, and a much better team than Leicester City's 1969 team too.

During Dennis Rofe's second match for Leicester, at home to Liverpool on Wednesday 30th August, and with nearly 29,000 inside Filbert Street, Keith Weller scored a magnificent hat-trick, for City's first win of the season, overturning two early goals by the mighty John Toshack.

That magnificent 3-2 victory was followed by three defeats, though, and when Leicester visited fourth-placed Ipswich Town on Saturday 30th September, they were right back down, deep in relegation troubles again.

IPSWICH TOWN		LEICESTER CITY
David Best	1	Peter Shilton
Mick Mills	2	Steve Whitworth
Colin Harper	3	Dennis Rofe
Peter Morris	4	Jon Sammels
Allan Hunter	5	John Sjoberg
Kevin Beattie	6	Graham Cross
Bryan Hamilton	7	John Farrington
Colin Viljoen	8	Alan Birchenall
Clive Woods	9	Keith Weller
Trevor Whymark	10	Frank Worthington
Mick Lambert	11	Len Glover

Eleven days before he became England's regular goalkeeper, under Sir Alf Ramsey, Peter Shilton had an excellent game, stopping everything that Ipswich's lively attack threw at him.

Leicester were much cleverer, and more colourful and creative. Their full backs gave much stronger support to the attacks, while Weller, Glover and Farrington gave much grittier support to their defence. Goals in each half, from Glover and Worthington lifted the Foxes away from the relegation zone, with a great 2-0 away win.

What was great about this team was that it merged the very, very best of Matt Gillies' Leicester City team, Shilton, Sjoberg, Cross and Glover, with Jimmy Bloomfield's new generation.

And it worked too.

On Saturday 18th November, though, Martin Chivers' late goal had given Tottenham Hotspur a 1-0 away win at Filbert Street, but John Sjoberg was also carried off badly injured, and he never played for Leicester City again.

"The Swede" had played 413 league and cup games, including 256 First Division matches, during his twelve years at Filbert Street. Sjoberg was born in Aberdeen, but everyone called him *The Swede.*

He moved to Fourth Division side Rotherham United, but he only played in their first six matches before he was forced to retire, to start his Leicester printing business.

John Sjoberg died, aged sixty-seven, on Thursday 2nd October 2008, after fighting cancer at the LOROS (Leicestershire and Rutland Organisation for the Relief of Suffering) hospice.

John Sjoberg remains the Leicester City player with the most medals in the club's history, and he was arguably their greatest ever centre-half. I say arguably, because Gerry Boland, the *aylesburyfox,* had argued that Matt Elliott and Steve Walsh were both actually better, which is an argument, admittedly, but it was wrong, and I wrote to him explaining why he was wrong.

Certainly, Sjoberg's partnership with Graham Cross was Leicester's finest ever central defensive partnership, and his tough but fair, brave, uncompromising and completely classy performances were badly missed by City.

The Foxes dropped back to the bottom of Division One before Christmas. A run of thirteen matches, though, after Boxing Day and up to the end of March, during which they lost just twice, but drew seven times, pulled them clear, and Leicester finished 1972-73 in sixteenth place, seven points above relegated Crystal Palace.

By August 1973, twenty year old Malcolm Munro finally became Graham Cross's regular central defensive partner, after Alan Woollett and Malcolm Manley had shared the role after Sjoberg's injury, conceding only six goals during Leicester's final fifteen matches of 1972-73. Munro, a local Melton Mowbray lad, as tough as the crust on traditional pork pies, had also played three matches during the previous season, but he'd proved to Jimmy Bloomfield during pre-season that he was the top man.

During 1972-73, Jimmy Bloomfield had introduced a modern-looking all-white strip, with blue collar and cuffs, in an attempt to give Leicester a more imposing look, but it hadn't been popular, so in August 1973, Leicester City had reverted to their traditional blue shirts, with white collar and cuffs.

1973-74 turned out to be quite a season. After a string of injuries that had kept the unlucky Mike Stringfellow out of first team action for all but twenty-two league games since 1969, he finally returned to Leicester City's midfield at the start of the new season. One of City's goal-scorers during their League Cup Final triumph ten years earlier, Stringfellow was warmly welcomed back to Filbert Street by a 29,347 home crowd for their 1-1 draw against reigning Champions Liverpool.

Crowds of 30,000 were regularly filling Filbert Street again, after their average attendances had dropped to just under 23,000 during 1972-73.

Leicester's subsequent performances were boosted, and they were unbeaten after eight games, and fifth-placed in the First Division, only one point below second-placed Derby County.

LEICESTER CITY		LEEDS UNITED
Peter Shilton	1	David Harvey
Steve Whitworth	2	Trevor Cherry
Dennis Rofe	3	Paul Madeley
Mike Stringfellow	4	Billy Bremner
Malcolm Munro	5	Gordon McQueen
Alan Woollett	6	Norman Hunter
Keith Weller	7	Peter Lorimer
Jon Sammels	8	Allan Clarke
Frank Worthington	9	Mick Jones
Alan Birchenall	10	Johnny Giles
Len Glover	11	Mick Bates

On Saturday 13th October, Leicester City hosted Leeds United, the First Division's runaway leaders, who'd won all but two of their opening ten matches, and they were still unbeaten.

36,562 filled every inch of Filbert Street, as Leicester were close to fielding the finest team they'd ever had, with Alan Woollett covering for the injured Cross, but Leeds, without the regularly injured Eddie Gray, as well as the suspended Paul Reaney, had been playing some illuminating and irresistible football.

The first half was frantic, with City going 2-0 up inside the first twenty minutes, through Worthington and Birchenall, but Leeds came back and equalised before half-time. Mick Jones and Billy Bremner pulled the leaders back into it, and Leeds' formidable attack then piled heavy pressure onto Leicester's penalty area after the break, but Leicester's defence played well above itself.

One of City's finest all-round performances, against one of the greatest ever British teams, earned a deserved 2-2 draw. Leicester were up in eighth place, but only four points separated them from Burnley, up in second place, with Derby, Coventry, Everton, Newcastle and Liverpool in between.

Unfortunately, Mike Stringfellow's comeback from injury had stalled before the end of November, and neither John Farrington nor Malcolm Partridge had impressed during his absence.

On 28th November 1973, Jimmy Bloomfield paid £100,000 to Fulham for the final piece of his ultimate attacking jigsaw. Steve Earle had scored over one hundred league and cup goals during his seven seasons at Craven Cottage, and he'd been the club's goal-scorer for three of the previous four seasons. A quick and unselfish forward from Feltham, Steve Earle became Bloomfield's fifth signing from the smoke.

Under Matt Gillies' management, there had been a Scottish revolution with Sjoberg, McLintock, Manley, Lochhead, Walsh, Gibson, King, McIlmoyle, Roberts and Hodgson all arriving at Filbert Street, during the reign of the great Scot.

By December 1974, under Londoner Jimmy Bloomfield, Rofe, Weller, Sammels, Birchenall, and now, Earle had all arrived from the Capital, to join South London motor-mouth Len Glover at Filbert Street. Chris Garland, Jeff Blockley and Steve Kember all subsequently also arrived from London clubs, in 1975, under Bloomfield's management.

The evolution of this "Cockney invasion" resulted in a loud mouthed group of undisciplined and disorderly strutters, an ill-behaved crowd of players; they were endearing and distinctive, though, and struck an illuminating camaraderie into Leicester's changing room.

They just had a good time at Leicester City.

After a defeat up in the North-east, Jimmy Bloomfield told his team not to return to the hotel after one in the morning. Well, the vast majority of the team found a nightclub, and staggered back to the hotel between three and four in the morning. After breakfast, Bloomfield confronted the entire team on the coach, and he asked all those who'd obeyed his orders to leave the coach.

Three or four players got off to wait inside the hotel lobby; Shilton, Cross, Sammels and Woollett.

The majority of players that had stayed on the coach, to face Bloomfield's wrath, were the nucleus of his team: Worthington, Weller, Birchenall, Glover, Rofe, Earle, Munro and Whitworth.

Bloomfield fined them all a week's wages, on the spot.

"What?" Len Glover replied, in astonished incredulity, "a faaaaacking week's wages?" It was a huge punishment, back then, as players' wages were too modest to just lose, especially as they'd just been out until the early hours, in an expensive club.

Jimmy Bloomfield knew the beneficial value of team spirit, though, and also appreciated the results of its presence. "Suspended for a year!" he immediately snapped back at them.

Even the older players, the family men, who took no part amongst Worthington's "wanderers", were cheered and amused at their outrageous antics. When Leicester City ran out onto First Division pitches during 1973 and 1974, their great team spirit raised their performances to greater levels.

Four wins during December, 3-0 over Spurs, 2-0 over QPR, 2-1 at Coventry, and 2-0 over Arsenal, with Worthington, Glover and Earle all scoring nine goals between them, lifted Leicester up to fourth in the First Division on New Year's Day.

Steve Earle's sharp finish, in the second half, won Leicester's FA Cup Third round match at home to Tottenham, with over 28,000 inside Filbert Street.

Two weeks later, on Saturday 19th January, Leicester hosted sixth-placed Ipswich Town at Filbert Street. Len Glover had picked up a knock during their 1-1 draw away at Liverpool on New Year's Day, and he was forced to miss a couple of matches, so twenty year old winger David Tomlin, from Nuneaton, took his place.

LEICESTER CITY		IPSWICH TOWN
Peter Shilton	1	Laurie Sivell
Steve Whitworth	2	George Burley
Dennis Rofe	3	Mick Mills
Steve Earle	4	Peter Morris
Malcolm Munro	5	Glen Keeley
Graham Cross	6	Kevin Beattie
Keith Weller	7	Bryan Hamilton
Jon Sammels	8	Colin Viljoen
Frank Worthington	9	David Johnson
Alan Birchenall	10	Trevor Whymark
David Tomlin	11	Mick Lambert

Ipswich, though, were without their formidable centre-back Allan Hunter, and so nineteen year old Glen Keeley played his fourth and final match for Ipswich, prior to moving to Newcastle.

Leicester were in World Class form, in any case. Tomlin ran Burley ragged all game, and it was a shame he couldn't consistently reproduce this form, or he'd have played more than 27 games during his six seasons at Filbert Street. Frank Worthington was so unplayable, he literally took the piss out of Keeley, flicking the ball over the beleaguered blocker's head, turning and leaving him looking a fool, before he side-footed the ball home. Worthington smashed in an easy hat-trick, while Munro headed in Tomlin's corner kick, and then Kevin Beattie's own goal completed City's 5-0 rout.

It shouldn't be forgotten that this was a *great* Ipswich team, one that should have won the league a year later, and they responded to this mauling by winning 1-0 at Manchester City, and then hammering Southampton 7-0 at the start of February.

Even so, Leicester rose back up to fourth place in Division One.

FIRST DIVISION LEADERS, 19TH JANUARY 1974

	PL	W	D	L	F	A	PTS
Leeds United	26	17	9	0	45	14	43
Liverpool	26	14	7	5	34	22	35
Burnley	25	11	8	6	33	29	30
LEICESTER	26	10	9	7	36	27	29
Derby County	26	10	9	7	32	25	29
QPR	26	9	11	6	40	34	29

On Saturday 26th January, Leicester visited Fulham in the FA Cup Fourth round. In front of a large Craven Cottage crowd of over 26,000, Alan Mullery volleyed Fulham into a 1-0 lead, from thirty-five yards out. It was a tremendous goal that won the Goal of the Season award on BBC TV's

Match of the Day, but Leicester came back after the break, and Len Glover glanced in a deserved equaliser.

37,130, Leicester City's biggest crowd of the season, then bulged Filbert Street, four days later, and Len Glover and Fulham's Les Barrett both scored second half goals, forcing extra-time.

Frank Worthington hit a crisp winner from the edge of the area to win a wonderful Cup-tie that credited the Second Division team, who came back a year later, and rode their luck that they'd lacked against Leicester. They reached the 1975 Cup Final.

After being held to a goalless draw away at QPR, and then losing 2-1 at home to West Ham, Leicester dropped to seventh place by the middle of February.

They then faced an awkward away match at Luton Town in the Fifth round of the Cup, on Saturday 16th February. Luton were a good side, heading for promotion from the Second Division, as runners-up behind runaway Champions Middlesbrough.

A capacity crowd of 25,712 over-filled Kenilworth Road, just 3,000 under their record attendance, and the loud roar of resurgence bellowed around the compact ground.

Luton's tight defence, well-marshalled by former England defender Bobby Thomson, had conceded just eleven goals in twelve league games since the start of December.

Leicester City, though, had arrived with the same kind of spirit and ebullience that they'd had when they hammered Ipswich Town. Their defence was rarely bothered by Luton's lightweight attack, that had scored just nine goals during those twelve games, yet the Hatters had risen from sixth to third in Division Two.

They'd won most of their games 1-0, but not today.

Len Glover had also returned to a full-strength City team, and from the start, Leicester, but particularly Keith Weller and Steve Earle, totally battered the Hatters.

Dennis Rofe sprinted down the left wing, and he then took on Jimmy Husband, beating the former Everton superstar's challenge. Rofe crossed the ball into the area, for Earle to flick a right-footed volley past Graham Horn, from six yards out.

After the break, Len Glover tricked and teased John Ryan as he approached the Luton area. With a burst of pace, though, he just skipped past Ryan and then whipped over a sharp cross which Earle headed just inside the far post.

Keith Weller cut out a Luton clearance, and he raced down the right wing, breezing past John Faulkner, before floating over a cross which Worthington nodded in from close range, despite being closely marked by both keeper Horn and Bobby Thomson.

Weller then scored the goal of the game, and also ITV's Goal of the Season. Collecting a forward pass from Whitworth, he spun on the spot, turning Jimmy Ryan inside out, and then darting goalwards, from thirty yards out. Faulkner gave him just enough space to race into the area, and he coolly rode a lunging, desperate tackle by Garner, before curling the ball, left-footed, around Horn, and just inside the far post.

Back in the First Division, Leicester took only eight points from their final eleven games. Tiredness affected their consistency, particularly away from home, and their slim squad resources proved inadequate when both Glover and Birchenall were forced to miss half of their games after the New Year, blighting Leicester's efforts at European qualification for the first time since the early Sixties.

They were drawn away at QPR in the FA Cup Quarter-finals, with Rangers themselves on an upward spiral. Gordon Jago was patiently building a team that would eventually strongly challenge for the First Division title.

A club record crowd of 34,078 filled Loftus Road, on Saturday 9th March, with thousands locked out. Alan Birchenall had suffered an injury against Sheffield United, though, back in February, that had kept him out of action for ten weeks.

So Joe Waters, a twenty year old forward from Limerick, was making his first team debut in attack alongside Frank Worthington.

QPR		LEICESTER CITY
Phil Parkes	1	Peter Shilton
Dave Clement	2	Steve Whitworth
Ian Gillard	3	Dennis Rofe
Terry Venables	4	Steve Earle
Terry Mancini	5	Malcolm Munro
Frank McLintock	6	Graham Cross
Dave Thomas	7	Keith Weller
Gerry Francis	8	Jon Sammels
Mick Leach	9	Frank Worthington
Stan Bowles	10	Joe Waters
Don Givens	11	Len Glover

It was a tight, but compelling game, with Phil Parkes and Peter Shilton, two of the best four English goalkeepers in the First Division, keeping out everything from Worthington, Bowles, Earle and Givens. Weller and Sammels had matched Francis and Venables with industry and artistry, and the terrific excitement of the wing battles between Thomas and Glover never let up.

Unbelievably, with all of that top talent, it was the raw and tiny terrier Joe Waters who completely turned the match during the second half. First, he picked up the ball, twenty yards out, and then struck a screamer past the flying figure of Parkes.

Then, to secure Leicester's place in the Semi-finals, Waters collected Steve Earle's pass, and he spun away swiftly from Frank McLintock, before guiding the ball over Parkes, with a composed right-footed strike from ten yards out.

Joe Waters was unable to reproduce that class in the league, scoring only once in eight First Division games towards the end of the 1973-74 season, but after his Sixth round heroics against QPR, he'd always be fondly remembered at Filbert Street.

Joe Waters kept his place in the team for the Semi-final against Liverpool, with over 60,000 inside Old Trafford, but Waters was mostly ineffective against the Reds' tough and merciless defence.

In contrast, Peter Shilton had a superb match, as Liverpool piled the pressure on Leicester's besieged penalty area, just as they did back in 1969.

Again, Leicester just hung on, but in the replay at Villa Park, four days later, Mike Stringfellow started the game, instead of Waters, and despite Len Glover equalising Brian Hall's opener, Liverpool totally outplayed Leicester. They won the match 3-1, through Keegan's superb eighteen yard volley and also Toshack's tenth goal of the season.

Joe Waters lived on scraps through the following season, as Leicester's regular front six of Earle, Weller, Sammels, Glover, Birchenall and Worthington was impenetrable.

In February 1976, Grimsby Town manager Tommy Casey paid just £10,000 for Waters, who'd only started fourteen league and cup matches for Leicester in two years.

Waters became a club legend at Blundell Park, though, winning the club's Player of the Year award in 1977, and again in 1979, as captain of Grimsby's promotion winning team, from the

Fourth Division. Joe Waters played 356 league games for the Mariners, including 226 consecutive league matches between 1976 and 1980, setting a club record that will probably never be broken.

During eleven glorious days in May 1974, three Leicester City players came together to play for England, amidst a wonderful awakening of attractive and adventurous international football under the caretaker management of Joe Mercer.

On Saturday 11th May, Keith Weller was given his first cap against Wales in Cardiff, playing in an energetic midfield alongside Colin Bell, Emlyn Hughes and Kevin Keegan, with Mike Channon and Stan Bowles up front. Peter Shilton continued his spell in goal, having made eleven successive international appearances between February and November 1973, and he also kept his fifth clean sheet. It was a great debut for Weller, as England won 2-0, following goals from Bowles and Keegan.

Against Northern Ireland, on the following Wednesday, Frank Worthington came on as a substitute for Bowles, for his first England cap, and he subsequently set up teammate Keith Weller to fire past Pat Jennings.

The impact that Worthington made on that game earned him all of the newspaper headlines on the following day, as England might have won by five or six, but for the excellent Pat Jennings. Peter Shilton also kept his sixth clean sheet for England, while Keith Weller's goal was enough for England's 1-0 home win.

On the following Saturday, 18th May, at Hampden Park, Frank Worthington started their match against World Cup qualifiers Scotland, in attack with Mike Channon.

With Shilton in goal, and Weller in midfield, it was the first and so far, the only time that three Leicester City players have ever started an England international. To really put the icing on the cake, though, David Nish was also starting at right back.

Unfortunately the Scottish title-winning combo of McGrain, Bremner, Lorimer, Dalglish and Jordan were no better than England on the day, but they were luckier.

Joe Jordan's shot deflected sharply off Mike Pejic, and wrong-footed Shilton, before a freak own goal by Colin Todd secured a 2-0 home win, and also the Home International Championship trophy for the Scots to take to West Germany.

Frank Worthington was replaced late on by Malcolm MacDonald, but he kept his place, as well as both Shilton and Weller, for England's home friendly against Argentina, on Wednesday 22nd May.

A partisan Wembley crowd of 68,000 were ecstatic when Channon finished off Colin Bell's great pass for a 1-0 half-time lead.

After the break, Bell shot against the Argentinian bar from Keegan's corner kick. Worthington turned and he hooked home the rebound, for his first international goal.

A misunderstanding between Peter Shilton and debutant Alec Lindsay then allowed Mario Kempes a simple finish to pull the score back to 2-1, but soon after that, Kempes just fell over after an Emlyn Hughes tackle. The Argentinian referee awarded a hotly disputed penalty kick, which Kempes himself scored for a 2-2 draw.

After four games during which none of the Leicester players ever played poorly, that was, sadly, the end of Keith Weller's England career.

Weller was rested for the final three games of Joe Mercer's refreshing reign, spread over a week at the beginning of June, a tour of Eastern Europe, in Leipzig, Sofia and Belgrade, all away games at World Cup Finals qualifying countries.

Burnley's Martin Dobson, who'd also enjoyed a similarly great season, took Keith Weller's place, and new England boss Don Revie simply ignored Keith Weller, thereafter.

Peter Shilton was also given an early Summer break, but Frank Worthington played in all three games. By the end of the Summer, Don Revie was England's new manager, and he clearly didn't like Shilton as, apart from England's 5-0 hammering of Cyprus in April 1975, he never picked him, and it wasn't until 1979 when Shilton would ever again play a competitive international for England.

100,000 East Germans gave a hostile welcome to England, but a direct free-kick from Southampton's Mike Channon, after Worthington was fouled, earned England a 1-1 draw. In Sofia, Frank Worthington was the star of the show, cracking in a left footed rocket from the edge of the area, one minute before the break, for England's 1-0 win.

Incidentally, Bulgaria were an awful waste of time at the 1974 World Cup Finals.

In Belgrade, against a quality Yugoslavian team, one of the best teams at the World Cup Finals, Frank Worthington started his fifth successive England game, with Channon and Keegan both scoring for a good 2-2 away draw, and Malcolm MacDonald replaced Worthington, late on.

It had been a good tour, but frustrating in that England were far better than at least two of the 1974 World Cup Finals qualifiers.

Leicester City finished 1973-74 in ninth position, only four points behind Stoke City in a UEFA Cup qualifying place. Frank Worthington scored twenty-four league and cup goals, and he was the First Division's second highest scorer with twenty goals.

Keith Weller, Len Glover and Steve Earle also scored thirty league and cup goals between them, while Leicester's excellent defence were one of only three First Division teams, as well as Leeds and Liverpool, to concede less than a goal per game.

And then by the Summer, Leicester City players made up over a quarter of the England team, with more on the way, as well. Things had never been as good as this.

AS GOOD AS IT WAS EVER GOING TO BE

Peter Shilton, though, had very itchy feet. He refused to sign a new contract, and consequently, Mark Wallington was chosen to play in goal at the start of the 1974-75 season. Signed from Walsall for just £30,000 back in March 1972, Wallington had played only six First Division matches in two and a half years.

After the Summer of 1974, however, Wallington became Leicester's goalkeeper for eleven years, playing 460 league and cup matches, ending up third-placed on City's all-time appearances records.

For Peter Shilton, the football at Leicester City was "as good as it was ever going to be," by 1974.

Both Derby County and Stoke City were strongly interested in signing Shilton, but Shilton had preferred Stoke, because of the dreadful state of The Baseball Ground pitch.

Tony Waddington paid £325,000, a World Record transfer fee for a goalkeeper, for Peter Shilton in November 1974. Shilton had played 286 league games for Leicester City between 1966 and 1974. He went on, after his international exile under Don Revie, to set a World Record of 125 international games for England, including a record ten clean sheets in World Cup Finals matches.

Then, in 1996, Peter Shilton set a new record of 1,005 Football League appearances.

Leicester City struggled, for the most part, during 1974-75.

They started steadily enough, sitting in twelfth position in September, and in fourteenth place in mid-November, but due to the closeness of the First Division that season, they were never very far, far away from the battle for UEFA Cup places.

By the New Year, however, they'd dropped to bottom of the table, having failed to score in seven out of eight games between November and January. The highlight of their season was their epic FA Cup Fifth round tie against Arsenal.

After breezing past Oxford United in the Third round, Leicester then struggled against Isthmian League team Leatherhead in the Fourth round.

Leatherhead had already knocked out Colchester United, as well as thrashing Brian Clough and Peter Taylor's Brighton and Hove Albion, en route to Leicester.

With 32,000 packed inside Filbert Street, McGullicuddy and Chris Kelly, the *Leatherhead Lip*, had both scored first half goals to send the BBC's Teleprinter, at a quarter to four, on Saturday 25th January 1975, wild with anticipation....

> ....LEEDS UNITED 0 WIMBLEDON 0...
> ....WALSALL 1 NEWCASTLE UNITED 0...
> ....WEST HAM UNITED 0 SWINDON TOWN 0...
> ...LEICESTER CITY 0 LEATHERHEAD 2...

...Jon Sammels, Steve Earle and Keith Weller rescued Leicester City's dignity, firing them to a 3-2 win during the second half, but Leeds United and Newcastle both failed to do likewise, as their scores remained exactly the same...

Jeff Blockley had joined Leicester City for £100,000, back in January, and he'd replaced local boy Malcolm Munro in central defence, alongside Graham Cross. Despite having played nearly two hundred First Division matches for both Coventry City and Arsenal, though, Jeff Blockley was born and bred in Leicester.

City travelled to North London, in the FA Cup Fifth round, where 43,841, the second-largest crowd of the season at Arsenal, packed Highbury's banks for a drab 0-0 draw. Leicester City, with their Classic team, except for Wallington in for Shilton and Blockley in for Munro, had fought like foxes.

Four days later, on Wednesday 19th February, over 35,000 packed Filbert Street for the replay, which again ended goalless, and thirty minutes of extra-time were played.

Alan Birchenall fired in after Frank Worthington had headed on a defensive clearance, but John Radford's classy strike, on the half-volley, had levelled the game, and the tie went to a second replay, which was again held at Filbert Street after the toss of a coin.

39,025, Leicester's largest home crowd of the Seventies, totally filled Filbert Street on Monday 24th February, and after yet another goalless draw, the young Liam Brady replaced the boring John Matthews during extra-time, and Brady eventually crossed for John Radford to snatch a late, late away winner.

It had been an epic Cup-tie, but it had exhausted Arsenal. In the Quarter-finals, West Ham youngster Alan Taylor scored twice at Highbury to end the Gunners' dreams.

Chris Garland signed from Chelsea on Thursday 13th March, for £100,000, from Chelsea. Garland had scored twenty-two First Division goals in 92 games at Stamford Bridge, and he went straight into the team in place of the injured Len Glover.

At the beginning of April, Leicester won three successive First Division matches, all at Filbert Street. They'd beaten West Ham 3-0 (Garland 2, Worthington (pen)), Newcastle United 4-0 (Garland 2, Lee, Worthington), and finally Middlesbrough 1-0 (the great Frank Worthington).

That trio of wins pulled them well away from any relegation worries, and lifted them up to the heights of fifteenth place, and a great chance of a mid-table finish.

Leicester gained only a single point from their final three games, though, and they ended up in eighteenth place, just three points above relegated Luton Town.

Frank Worthington was again their top scorer with nineteen league and cup goals, but it had been a disappointing season, after the moderate highs of 1973-74.

In May 1975, however, Steve Whitworth was again selected by England manager Don Revie having made his international debut back in March 1975, during the Alan Hudson Show, as England had beaten World Champions West Germany 2-0. Whitworth also played at right back as England beat Cyprus 1-0 in Limassol, with Kevin Keegan scoring, during their European Championship qualifier.

Whitworth kept his place for all three Home International Championship matches, later that month, including their famous 5-1 home thrashing of Scotland, on Saturday 24th May, with England parading their new Admiral strip, with red and blue stripes down their sleeves, and also on their collar and cuffs.

In September, Steve Whitworth retained his place for England's 2-1 away win over Switzerland, in Basle. He then played against Portugal, away in Lisbon, with England needing a win to stand a chance of beating Czechoslovakia to the European Championship Quarter-finals.

England could only draw 1-1, and Steve Whitworth never played for England again, despite them never losing a game, and winning four out of the seven games in which he'd played.

Don Revie just couldn't make up his mind from game to game, and he even began to play Trevor Cherry and Phil Thompson in midfield during 1976, as England became a much more boring and defensive team, the *Leicester City* of international football, if you like…

…In 1975-76, Leicester City became a much more boring and defensive team.

Brian Alderson, a dour Scottish forward arrived from Coventry City, and the vastly-experienced Croydon-born Steve Kember had also arrived from Chelsea. They were two rugged, tough attacking players, and they replaced Alan Birchenall and Steve Earle in City's team.

Graham Cross returned back to Filbert Street late, after the start of the season, having remained with Leicestershire Cricket Club as they'd successfully won the County Championship during the Summer of 1975. Cross was effectively sacked by the club, after playing a club record 599 league and cup games, including 415 First Division matches, which still remains a Leicester City club record for most appearances.

Towards the late Seventies, Graham Cross played at Chesterfield, Brighton and Preston, before finally ending his career at Lincoln City during 1978-79, after a total of 620 Football League matches.

Graham Cross had also scored over 2,000 First Class runs for Leicestershire CC, between 1961 and 1976. Despite not being in the same class as either Chris Balderstone or Ted Hemsley, Cross was a decent County Championship player, and he'd also taken nearly one hundred wickets as a bowler.

Attacking wingers Steve Earle and Len Glover were effectively shown the door during 1975-76. Leicester City followed Coventry City as a safe, hard to beat team, with their beefed up midfield, geared towards percentages rather than expression or personality.

Once again, Leicester were among three First Division teams, as well as Liverpool and QPR, to concede less than a goal a game. Unlike the 1973-74 team, though, their 1975-76 team only just scored one goal per game. Bob Lee was their top scorer, while Frank Worthington had suffered a miserable season, scoring only nine goals.

In 1976-77, Frank Worthington was Leicester's top scorer again, but with only fourteen goals from 41 games. Average crowds plummeted to 18,000 as Leicester drew eighteen of their 42 matches, finishing again in a safe mid-table place.

The excitement was all but gone from Filbert Street.

In May 1977, Jimmy Bloomfield resigned.

Jimmy Bloomfield returned to London during the Summer of 1977, to manage Orient, once again. And during the following 1977-78 season, he took his Second Division club past Norwich, Chelsea and Middlesbrough, to the FA Cup Semi-finals, where they were finally beaten 3-0 by Arsenal, at Stamford Bridge.

Jimmy Bloomfield died, just five years after that match, aged only forty-nine, on Sunday 3rd April 1983.

Len Glover had left Leicester City in 1976, joining Tampa Bay Rowdies, in the NASL. Glover scored thirty-eight goals in 252 league games between 1967 and 1976, but he created many more goals in an era when, frustratingly, assists weren't recorded.

The roar of anticipation, though, that greeted him down the Popular Side at Filbert Street, whenever he got the ball on the wing was a spine-tingling sound and it demoralised many opposing full backs.

Glover remains one of the greatest characters to ever play for the Foxes.

He had an infectious personality, with the ability to "sell sand to the Arabs", as Frank Worthington remembered. Len Glover was reputedly the person on whom writer John Sullivan based his character **Derek Trotter,** from Only Fools and Horses.

Alan Birchenall was released by Leicester City in 1977 after nearly six seasons at Filbert Street. Birch had played 183 league and cup matches, scoring just fourteen goals, but as the playmaking forward alongside Worthington, and with the rampaging Weller, Earle, Sammels and Glover coming from deep, he had a hand in nearly a half of Leicester's First Division goals.

He moved to Notts County in September 1977, having played five games on loan at Meadow Lane, eighteen months earlier. Under manager Jimmy Sirrel, he reverted to a more defensive role and helped the Magpies escape relegation to Division Three.

Alan Birchenall left Notts County in April 1978, and he went to Memphis to play one season in the NASL.

For such a big Elvis fan, Memphis was the perfect place for **Birch** to end his career.

Birch was always very fondly remembered at Leicester, though, and he returned to Filbert Street in 1983, after his retirement, to become their club ambassador, responsible for welcoming new players to the club, and organising charity events.

With his microphone in hand, he still hosts pre-match and half-time events and presentations on Leicester City's pitch, a role he has happily performed for thirty years. Also, at the final home match of every season, Alan Birchenall runs around the Leicester City pitch for the whole ninety minutes, raising money for charity.

He laments the breakdown of the culture of the off-field team spirit which so benefitted Jimmy Bloomfield's Leicester City team.

When he was a player, he could be walking down Haymarket or Humberstone Gate, in the city centre, and someone would stop and ask him about a goal he missed in the last match. But now "they're off in their 4 x 4s with blacked out windows, and away to the back of beyond."

Also to leave Leicester before the end of 1977 was Jon Sammels, who moved to Vancouver Whitecaps, where he played two seasons in the NASL, in 1978 and 1979.

Jon Sammels had played 271 league and cup games in six and a half seasons at Leicester, after rebuilding his career well, following his unhappy departure from Highbury. An artistic and subtly skilled schemer, he'd played a combined total of 448 First Division matches for both Arsenal and Leicester City, and he scored twenty-one First Division goals for City from midfield.

Steve Earle also played his last match for Leicester during their 1977-78 relegation season. He scored twenty First Division goals in 91 First Division games for the Foxes, before then playing two and a half seasons in the NASL, between 1978 and 1980, with Tulsa Roughnecks.

Earle brought experience, and an explosive energy and electricity that perfectly complemented Leicester's attack, making City one of the most entertaining teams in England for two seasons.

Keith Weller left Leicester City shortly after the New Year of 1979, with only Wallington, Whitworth and Rofe remaining from the great Jimmy Bloomfield years. Leicester endured a dreadful season in 1978-79, struggling just above the Second Division relegation zone, and Weller left for the NASL.

He played in the NASL for five years, with New England, and then Fort Lauderdale Strikers, with Gerd Muller, Teofilio Cubillas and Brian Kidd.

Alan Birchenall suggested that Keith was "one of the five greatest players to ever pull on a Leicester City shirt," and it was criminal that he didn't play more than four games for England.

Keith Weller remained in the United States, after he retired from football, and he bought a coffee shop in Seattle. It was quite possible that Frasier and Niles might have argued about *T H Houghton,* while drinking coffee in Weller's shop at some point?

Keith was diagnosed with LMS, in April 2002, a rare form of cancer that attacks smooth muscle. Leicester City fans raised £40,000 to help fund his treatment, nearly twenty-five years after he left their club, but Keith Weller eventually died, aged only fifty-eight, on Saturday 13th November 2004.

Steve Whitworth was sold to Sunderland, in March 1979, for £120,000. The Leicestershire-born full back had played 353 league games for City in his nine years at Filbert Street. Whitworth won promotion back to the First Division with Sunderland, after finishing the 1979-80 season as runners-up, behind Champions Leicester City.

A fantastic, fast-paced right back, attacking and overlapping, with his seven England caps, Steve Whitworth was, without any doubt, Leicester City's finest ever right back.

Dennis Rofe was an ever-present in the league, for Leicester, on four occasions, and he played 324 league and cup matches in eight seasons at Filbert Street, before being surprisingly sold to Chelsea during the latter part of City's Second Division Championship season.

Rofe was appointed as Chelsea's captain in 1980, but he was unable to help them regain their place in Division One, and after moving on to First Division high-flyers Southampton, he retired from football in the mid-Eighties.

Dennis Rofe lacked the international class and elegance of David Nish, but he more than compensated with his enthusiasm, strength and energy.

While Nish was a quiet, serious-minded professional, Dennis Rofe's joviality in the Leicester City changing room had made him a key protagonist of the team spirit that enlightened their performances.

Frank Worthington was the star player and top goal-scorer of Leicester City's golden age under Jimmy Bloomfield's management, scoring seventy-eight goals in 237 league and cup matches. He joined Bolton Wanderers in September 1977, winning his second Division Two Championship winners medal in 1977-78, eight years after his first.

That was a great Bolton team, with both Worthington and Neil Whatmore in attack, Peter Reid in midfield alongside former Carlisle United workhorse Ray Train, with Willie Morgan out wide, and the uncompromising duo of Sam Allardyce and Roy Greaves back in central defence. Alan Gowling then joined in April 1978, bolstering their attack in preparation for the First Division.

After years of near-misses, Bolton manager Ian Greaves had finally got his team right.

Frank Worthington became the First Division's top striker, for the first time, during 1978-79, after scoring 24 goals. Worthington and Alan Gowling were the best attacking partnership that season, scoring forty-two combined league and cup goals.

After Bolton, Worthington starred at Birmingham, Leeds and Tranmere Rovers, before retiring in the late Eighties, at Stockport County. He'd also played in a second FA Cup Semi-final in 1984, for Southampton against Everton.

Lawrie McMenemy played a half-fit Steve Williams at Highbury, but the gamble back-fired, and big Lawrie had even compounded his mistake by leaving Williams on for the whole match, including extra-time.

In the 119th minute, Adrian Heath headed Everton into the Final, to face Watford. Frank Worthington described that defeat as one of the lowest moments of his career, and he blamed Southampton's boss, entirely, for their loss.

But what a career Frank had? He'd scored 150 First Division goals in 466 games, and he also totalled a massive 266 league and cup goals from 883 matches, over his twenty-one years as a professional footballer.

Frank Worthington spearheaded the greatest Leicester City team in their history.

It is difficult to qualify that claim, as Leicester had won trophies both before then, and also since the Jimmy Bloomfield era.

The Leicester team of the early Sixties, though, had capitalised on a transitional period of English football when they achieved their glory.

Following the Munich tragedy, and the decline of all the great legends, Lofthouse, Matthews, Finney, Milburn, Haynes; Tottenham Hotspur, and maybe Ipswich Town and Burnley, were possibly the only truly great teams of the first few years of the Sixties.

It was only after 1965 when the First Division really started to get competitive again, but also, during the early years of its existence, not many teams had taken the League Cup very seriously.

During the late Nineties, Leicester City were famed for their hard approach to football, mainly dependent on defensive tactics.

In the 1997 League Cup Semi-final, they scrambled past a fading Wimbledon, on their way down from the Premier League, on the away goals rule, before beating Middlesbrough, after a replay, to lift the Cup.

Then, in 1999-2000, Leicester won penalty shootouts against both Leeds and Fulham, before beating Tranmere Rovers 2-1 in their Wembley Final.

So one team wins something, while the other team doesn't, so the team that won something has to be better than the team that didn't? That's the logic, yes?

I never agreed with that, and I still don't. Nobody could possibly ever suggest that the Greeks from 2004, or that dull Italian team from 2006, were better than either Holland in 1974, or those Brazilians from 1978-1986?

With all due respect to those Cup-winning Leicester teams, they weren't Jimmy Bloomfield's Leicester City, and they never had to contend with Bill Shankly's Liverpool, nor Gordon Jago's QPR, nor Bertie Mee's Arsenal, to win their pots and pans.

In the First Division, Jimmy Bloomfield's Leicester City had to contend with the greatest teams in the history of Leeds United, Liverpool*, Derby County, Ipswich Town, Stoke City, QPR, Burnley, Sheffield United, Manchester City*, Birmingham City and Middlesbrough.

(at that time in their history*)

Against these teams, Leicester City played fluent, flowing, attractive and attacking, Total Football. At their best, and in half of their games they were at their best, they played just like Brazil. Unbeatable.

Against Tottenham Hotspur in November 1974, Frank Worthington skipped around Mike England's sliding ground tackle, and then he spun on a sixpence with a little side-step to land the great Ralph Coates lumbering on his backside, before skipping up the left wing and taking on Mike England once again.

One of the two or three greatest defenders of the Glam Soccer era, Mike England showed Worthington the line, which Frank gladly accepted.

Worthington ran at the outside of England, at full tilt, before checking back, just as England lunged in with a firm, left-footed challenge. Worthington eased inside of Mike England, and then he crossed for Mike Stringfellow to shoot, as the Welshman just sat on his bum, watching, for the second time inside ten seconds.

In the space of just twenty seconds, Frank Worthington had laid two of the greatest and most respected Tottenham players, *ever*, down on their arses three times, without even breaking sweat, and with total ease; with Worthington ease.

MY FRIEND STAN
(Got A Funny Old Man, Oh Yeah)

QUEENS PARK RANGERS HAD WON the first ever Football League Cup Final at Wembley Stadium, while they were still an unfashionable, little-known Third Division club, on Saturday 4th March 1967.

Inspired by their great inside forward Rodney Marsh, QPR had come back to win 3-2 after goals from Roger Morgan, Marsh and Mark Lazarus, having been 0-2 down against First Division West Bromwich Albion to win their first, and only, major trophy.

It was a magnificent, magical triumph, but that's not the QPR that we're celebrating.

After winning promotion to Division Two, just a couple of months after their Wembley triumph, they went on to achieve their second successive promotion up to the First Division, in 1968, finishing as runners-up behind Champions Ipswich Town.

A team built upon their tight defence of England World Cup squad goalkeeper Ron Springett, Dave Clement and Tony Hazell, they'd kept eighteen clean sheets and conceded only 36 goals in 42 games, but they weren't a prolific goal-scoring team. Rodney Marsh scored fourteen goals from just 25 games, and Ian Morgan had hit ten, while Mick Leach also scored nine from only 21 games.

25,895 attended Loftus Road, for their 2-0 win over Birmingham City, with Mick Leach and Ian Morgan both scoring, that sealed their promotion on Saturday 4th May 1968.

Unfortunately, their 1968-69 Division One campaign was a total disaster. Ron Springett could only play nine league games in goal, while their star Rodney Marsh played only one First Division game, due to injury.

Reigning European Champions Manchester United hammered QPR 8-1 on Wednesday 19th March, and only 12,000 attended their final home game against Stoke.

They finished the season bottom of Division One, and a massive thirteen points adrift of third-bottom placed Coventry City.

Over the next two seasons, QPR settled comfortably into mid-table in the Second Division, replacing their Sixties' midfielders Lazarus and the two Morgans, with Terry Venables, bought from Tottenham for £70,000 in June 1969, and also Gerry Francis, a Hammersmith-born youth team graduate.

Gordon Jago then replaced Les Allen as QPR's manager in 1971, and at the end of the following 1971-72 season, they just failed to gain promotion back to the First Division, finishing only two points behind promoted Birmingham City.

QPR's main weapon was their sharp defence of Dave Clement, Terry Mancini, Tony Hazell and Ian Gillard, plus Phil Parkes, their moustached, twenty-one year old Sedgley-born goalkeeper (not the moustached, West Bromwich-born Wolves keeper) , who'd signed from Walsall back in June 1970, for just £15,000.

QPR had conceded an all-time record Second Division total of just twenty-eight goals in forty-two games, at only 0.66666667 goals per game.

QPR just hadn't scored enough goals, only fifty-seven, and their superstar Rodney Marsh was again their top scorer with seventeen goals, but they played their last twelve games without Marsh, after Manchester City manager Malcolm Allison had paid a club record transfer fee of £200,000 for him, back in March.

It wasn't during those final twelve games, though, that they'd lost out on promotion. In fact, they'd only dropped five points from those matches, winning seven and drawing five. It was actually during Rodney Marsh's final five matches with Rangers, when everyone knew he was leaving, and everyone knew that he *wanted* to leave, that had caused the distraction and baulked their rhythm.

Their promotion charge flopped during those final five games with Rodney Marsh in attack, at home to Blackpool, and also away at Luton, Portsmouth, Bristol City and Birmingham. QPR won none of them, scoring just one goal. They drew twice, lost thrice, and they let in five goals.

On Tuesday night, April 25th, QPR hosted Fulham in a must-win game, the first of three final games, all at home, an end of season blitz on the top two, as their promotion campaign was back on full steam, having beaten Sunderland away only three days earlier.

QPR's biggest home crowd of the season, just 20,605, had attended Loftus Road for a game QPR had to win, but they also had to hope Birmingham City lost at home to Hull City, to maintain their promotion hopes. Fulham also needed points themselves, though, to lift themselves out of the relegation zone, up above Charlton Athletic, and they fought hard for a goalless draw.

With Birmingham also beating Hull 2-0, the Hoops' faint hopes were dashed.

Rangers did recover their form to hammer Carlisle United 3-0 on the following Saturday, and they also Cardiff City 3-0 on Bank Holiday Monday, but only 7,616 and 8,430 had watched those home games, as Birmingham also won their final two games to finish in second place.

During the Summer of 1972, Gordon Jago went some way to spending some of the £200,000 they had received for Marsh. Don Givens was bought from Luton Town, for just £40,000, having scored eight Second Division goals the previous season.

Givens went straight into QPR's team for their first game of 1972-73, drawing 2-2 away at Swindon Town. Their new team for a new decade was finally beginning to take shape, though, with the combative and powerful Gerry Francis an influential ever-present, and the mercurial Terry Venables artfully balancing their midfield. Along with Burnley, Sunderland, Millwall, Aston Villa, Blackpool, Middlesbrough and Nottingham Forest, QPR were well-fancied for a real promotion fight.

As disciplined and well-structured as they were, QPR were again struggling to turn draws into wins and they were behind the promotion pack after five games.

They'd drawn four times, and had gained only six points.

To counter this problem, Jago then bought Stan Bowles from Carlisle United. Bowles had been Carlisle's joint top goal scorer in Division Two, during the previous season, and Jago had somehow imagined him as their natural successor to Rodney Marsh. And at just £110,000, he'd cost just over half the price of Marsh. Five weeks later, though, came the most audacious signing of all.

From their biggest promotion rivals Burnley, Gordon Jago paid a club record fee of £165,000 for Dave Thomas, one of the most exciting wingers in the country.

In his first game for QPR, a 3-2 home win over Sunderland (Givens, Bowles 2), on Saturday 21st October, Dave Thomas was excellent and lively, beating both full backs and crossing brilliantly from both wings with either foot.

By the New Year, the promotion race was between just three teams, Burnley, QPR and Aston Villa. On Saturday 27th January, 22,518 packed Loftus Road for the meeting of the top two clubs. QPR beat Burnley 2-0 (Mick Leach, Don Givens), in front of their largest home crowd of the season, and then Villa promptly fell away, taking just four points from seven games through February and March.

The run-in was a simple procession for the top two, and Burnley led the way right to the finish, except for March 10th, when they'd lost at home to Sheffield Wednesday and QPR had led the Division for just one week.

QPR hosted Fulham on April 28th, almost a year to the day since their 1972 promotion hopes had been ended, and another huge crowd of 22,187 packed the home terraces to give their team a great send-off. Dave Clements and Stan Bowles both scored to give QPR a 2-0 win. The next time QPR played at Loftus Road, they'd be hosting either Leeds United, Liverpool, Derby or Arsenal.

Actually, it was going to be Southampton.

On May 9th, QPR played their final Second Division game of the season, on a Wednesday night, in front of an enormous Roker Park crowd, 43,265, the largest Second Division crowd of the season.

Sunderland had just won the FA Cup, and they paraded their trophy.

Stan Bowles reputedly knocked the FA Cup off its pitch-side table with his first kick of the game, for a bet. It was a fierce atmosphere, and the Sunderland fans had come to acclaim their Wembley heroes, not to congratulate QPR on their promotion.

Mick Horswill was sent off and the match was interrupted due to crowd trouble.

QPR won 3-0 (Thomas, Bowles 2), and then left quickly. Don Givens and Stan Bowles had scored a combined total of 40 Second Division goals, while their superb defence had kept 43 combined clean sheets during the two previous seasons, 1971-73.

No new players were recruited during the Summer of 1973, and QPR played their opening First Division match with roughly the same team that had won promotion. They were, however, without Gerry Francis who missed their first two games, and also left-back Ian Gillard, who'd been absent for all but eight games for the past year, and he wouldn't play again before Christmas.

QPR began steadily, drawing four times, and losing just once from their first five games, leaving them just inside the bottom half of the table. They then beat West Ham United, 3-2 away (Givens 2, Ron Abbott), but they also lost at Everton.

They were 13th in the table and securing a safe First Division mediocrity.

It wasn't good enough. Gordon Jago delved again into the transfer funds, in late September, and he emerged with an legend. Arsenal's double-winning captain and centre-back, the Gunners' *True Grit*, 33-year-old Frank McLintock had signed for QPR, having inexplicably fallen behind Jeff Blockley as regular partner to Peter Simpson in Arsenal's defence. Bertie Mee apparently described his decision to release McLintock as "the biggest mistake of my career".

It was an incredible coup. Gordon Jago was evolving QPR into a First Division force that was resembling the progressive revolution that Brian Clough had developed at Derby County. Things immediately improved.

QPR won 3-2 away at Newcastle United (Thomas, Francis, Leach), and then they drew 1-1 at home to local rivals Chelsea, in front of a massive 31,009 home crowd.

In tenth place just after Christmas, QPR then went on a superb run from New Year's Day up to March 23rd 1974, winning five, drawing four but only losing one of their ten games, blooming in fourth place in the First Division on the outbreak of Spring, after thirty-three games, and heading for European football.

They'd also eliminated fellow First Division teams Chelsea, Birmingham and Coventry from the FA Cup, and then were drawn at home to Leicester City in the Quarter-finals. A club record crowd of 34,078 filled Loftus Road, on Saturday 9th March, but QPR lost 0-2 to what was possibly Leicester City's greatest-ever team. Ian Gillard later admitted it was the biggest disappointment of his career.

On April 3rd, Phil Parkes and Stan Bowles made their England debuts in Sir Alf Ramsay's last match as England manager, as they drew 0-0 with Portugal away in Lisbon. However, they'd peaked too soon this season, and QPR won only one of their last nine games, finishing the season down in eighth place, but only four points below fourth-placed Ipswich Town.

On Saturday 27th April, QPR hosted Division One Champions Leeds United, and a new club record crowd of 35,353 again filled Loftus Road. Leeds won 1-0 (Allan Clarke), but QPR had broken their record home attendance twice inside six weeks.

QPR's fluent forward line of Stan Bowles, Don Givens, Mick Leach, Gerry Francis and Dave Thomas had also scored 49 First Division goals between them.

During the Summer of 1974, Jago strengthened his team, and further enriched his squad, by paying Chelsea £150,000 for David Webb.

Despite starting the new season without Frank McLintock, Stan Bowles or Mick Leach, QPR began the 1974-75 season just as they had the previous one, winning five points from five games in August.

Two of those points had been achieved at Elland Road, where it was reputed Brian Clough had been asked by his players where their dossiers were. Don Revie had compiled detailed dossiers for his players on their next opponents. Cloughie infamously, and allegedly, responded that they were playing QPR. They didn't need dossiers. "You stop Stan Bowles, you stop QPR. That's all you need to know." Bowles didn't play, and QPR won 1-0 (Gerry Francis).

However, during September 1974, QPR suffered what was arguably their worst ever month. On the pitch, they lost four of their five games, and drew the other.

QPR were bottom of the First Division after ten games.

Off the pitch, things had also gone badly for Gordon Jago. Firstly, Terry Mancini went onto the transfer list at his own request, as he couldn't be guaranteed a first team place, following David Webb's arrival, joining Frank McLintock in central defence.

Two days later, on 14th September, Terry Venables joined Crystal Palace after 176 league games for QPR. The fee was £70,000, but the deal had also involved Ian Evans going to Palace, where he'd play 137 games over the next five years.

Terry Venables played only fourteen more league games at Crystal Palace, though, before retiring and then eventually succeeding Malcolm Allison as Palace manager, going on to build their "Team of the Eighties".

Then, on September 23rd 1974, Stan Bowles was suspended by the club for being absent from a training session. Gordon Jago began to feel that he was being gradually undermined in the way he managed the team, and furthermore, he'd been criticized in the National press by Jim Gregory.

He was ridiculed by Gregory for ordering a red and white quartered third-choice team kit.

Club chairman Gregory had also refused Jago permission to manage the England under-23 team back in the Summer for a three-match tour. He was also unbelievably questioned as to why he'd taken the team up to a Manchester hotel on the Friday night before their late September match at Maine Road, avoiding a long, Saturday morning journey. Jago had felt he was being reduced to the mere role of just picking the first eleven players on match days, rather than being the manager of his football club, as he felt he'd been since 1971. It was all getting very petty, and very reminiscent of the turbulent relationship that Brian Clough and Sam Longson had endured at Derby.

Immediately, on Friday 27th September, Gordon Jago offered his resignation as QPR manager, which was accepted by Jim Gregory.

"That was the most disappointing day of my whole football career," Gordon Jago later admitted, "It was just huge disappointment. I knew that the team was going to go on to more success. To have gone into European Cup football would have been great, but it wasn't to be."

Then, on 3rd October, only two miles away from QPR, Chelsea chairman Brian Mears relieved Dave Sexton of his managerial duties. Sexton had won both the FA Cup and the European Cup Winners' Cup while at Stamford Bridge.

So, on 16th October, Jim Gregory capitalised, and he appointed Dave Sexton as QPR's new manager, on the very same day that Jago had taken over as manager of Second Division Millwall.

Under the caretaker-management of Middlesbrough's former boss Stan Anderson, Rangers had beaten Ipswich 1-0 (Francis), and they then drew 2-2 away at Arsenal (Bowles 2), lifting themselves out of the bottom three.

The remainder of 1974-75 was lacking in consistency. QPR won 14, lost 11 and drew five.

A run of four straight wins during December had pulled them clear of relegation worries. On Saturday 5th April, QPR's 2-0 win over Wolves (Givens, Thomas), even lifted them up to the heady heights of eighth place.

In the end, though, QPR finished in eleventh place, bang in mid-table. Don Givens and Stan Bowles had scored 26 goals between them, while Gerry Francis and Dave Thomas both combined for fourteen goals from midfield. However, during a season when the Championship race was so wide open, and with so many teams able to snatch the title, QPR could feel aggrieved at never having been involved at any stage, particularly after the feats of their first season back in the First Division.

1975-76 would almost put paid to any such grievances. Back in December 1974, Dave Sexton had paid £100,000 for Notts County's midfield grafter Don Masson. Masson was Sexton's first signing for QPR, and he'd become an invaluable and near ever-present influence in Rangers' midfield over the following two seasons.

Don Masson had played 273 league games for County, scoring eighty-one goals. He had missed only nine games over the previous four and a half seasons, during which County had risen from the Fourth Division to the fringes of the promotion race up to the First Division.

Masson was a superlative replacement for Terry Venables, continuing his predecessor's prolific work-rate, playing in all of QPR's remaining 21 games of 1974-75, but then he played in all forty-two games of 1975-76.

On 4th July 1975, Dave Sexton then signed John Hollins, the final piece of the jigsaw, his former Chelsea captain and possession playmaker, for only £80,000.

The *classic* QPR team, their very best-ever eleven, ran out for the very first time on Saturday 16th August 1975, the first day of that season, at home to Liverpool, the First Division title favourites, and in front of a large 27,113 home crowd.

QUEENS PARK RANGERS		LIVERPOOL
Phil Parkes	1	Ray Clemence
Dave Clement	2	Phil Neal
Ian Gillard	3	Joey Jones
John Hollins	4	Phil Thompson
Frank McLintock	5	Peter Cormack
David Webb	6	Emlyn Hughes
Dave Thomas	7	Kevin Keegan
Gerry Francis	8	Terry McDermott
Don Masson	9	Steve Heighway
Stan Bowles	10	John Toshack
Don Givens	11	Ian Callaghan
Mick Leach	12	Brian Hall

Bob Paisley's Liverpool team were real powerhouse opponents, and they provided a proper test for Rangers' Championship credentials.

In the first half, on the halfway line, Stan Bowles met Don Masson's ball out of defence, and he turned Emlyn Hughes inside out with a sublime back heel.

Gerry Francis then played a perfect one-two with Don Givens to slice through both Neal and Thompson, before he finished sharply just inside the Liverpool penalty area.

That goal was voted as BBC TV Match of the Day's Goal of the Season, at the end of 1975-76.

Then, late on in the second half, after McLintock and Webb had both weathered a fierce Liverpool onslaught, Dave Thomas, totally shattered, and with his hooped socks rolled down over his ankles, inadvertently played in Francis, in space at the right corner of the 18 yard box.

Gerry Francis's cross was thumped into the Liverpool net by a firm diving header from substitute Mick Leach, flying in between McDermott and Neal.

Two-nil, it was a tremendous start for QPR, and one that not many neutrals expected.

A week later, they bettered even *that* performance.

At the Baseball Ground, away at reigning Champions Derby County, and in front of a massive 27,590 crowd, Rangers romped to a rampant 3-0 half-time lead.

In the second half, though, the rampaging impetus was barely impeded by the Rams' imperious defence of Thomas, McFarland, Todd and Nish.

QPR won 5-1 away (Thomas, Bowles 3, Clement), against real top class opposition.

Their 1-0 win over Newcastle (Leach), and then a terrific 5-0 home win over seventh-placed Everton (Givens, Masson, Francis 2, Thomas) on Saturday 11th October, had put QPR on top of the First Division after twelve games.

FIRST DIVISION LEADERS, 11TH OCTOBER 1975

	PL	W	D	L	F	A	PTS
QPR	12	6	5	1	21	8	17
Manchester Utd	12	7	3	2	20	10	17
West Ham Utd	11	7	3	1	18	11	17
Liverpool	11	6	3	2	18	10	15
Derby County	12	6	3	3	16	15	15
Leeds United	11	6	2	3	16	12	14

On Saturday 29th November, QPR played an epic match at home to Stoke City, having dropped down to second place behind a resurgent Derby County. They'd won just once and taken only seven points from six games after their thrashing of Everton. Stoke City were just below the UEFA Cup places themselves, after winning eight of their last twelve games.

In the first half, Alan Hudson sent Jimmy Greenhoff through with a delightful flick, but Phil Parkes managed to send him wide and Gillard conceded a corner-kick with a brilliant tackle. John Mahoney then headed Geoff Salmons' resultant corner just over the crossbar. Don Masson put QPR 1-0 up, after a Stoke defensive error, giving Peter Shilton no chance in the mud-ridden goalmouth, by firing high into the roof of the net, from a tight angle.

During the second half though, Stoke City came back. Mike Pejic's clearance down the left was collected on the edge of the area by Jimmy Robertson, who crossed with an ingenious bicycle kick over his own head, into the middle of Rangers' area.

An unmarked, and bearded Ian Moores headed into the far corner of the clambering Parkes' goal. Driven on by the craft of Hudson, Salmons and Greenhoff, Stoke began to pile on the pressure. Robertson's free-kick was met on the edge of the six yard box by the combined leap of Phil Parkes, Ian Gillard and City's centre-half Alan Bloor.

Bloor's pressure caused Parkes to drop his catch, though, and **Bluto** tapped in the loose ball to give Stoke a 2-1 lead. Don Masson found rare space inside the centre circle, and he sprayed out wide left to Dave Thomas, who galloped at, and then beat the challenge of stand-in right-back Lewis, before looping over a cross to the far post.

Dave Clement, attacking from right-back, collected the ball inside the six yard box, and left-footed, he hammered their equaliser past Shilton.

Late on, in injury-time, Bowles was unnecessarily fouled by Haslegrove out on the right side of the pitch, and David Webb then attacked Masson's clipped free-kick.

His initial shot was blocked, but at the second chance, he smashed the ball back across Shilton's diving body at the near post and into the centre of the goal.

Loftus Road's 22,328 crowd bounced deliriously, amidst the unforgettably electric and frantic atmosphere, in the deepening early winter darkness.

That 3-2 win, and the two draws that followed, against both Manchester City and Derby County, lifted QPR back to the top of the First Division during the week before Christmas. Over Christmas and New Year, QPR lost four out of six games, against Liverpool, Arsenal, Manchester United and West Ham, though, and they were back in fifth place by the end of January.

Five successive wins lifted them back up to second place, but their goalless draw away at bottom-placed Sheffield United on Saturday 28th February proved very costly, as it turned out.

Nevertheless, QPR continued their terrific Spring run, beating Coventry City 4-1 (Thomas, Francis, Givens, Masson) on Saturday 6th March. They then beat Everton 2-0 (Bowles, Leach), away, on Saturday 13th March; before defeating Stoke City 1-0 (Webb), again away from home, then Manchester City 1-0 (Webb, again), and Newcastle United 2-1 (McLintock, Bowles), before finally, Middlesbrough 4-2 (Francis 2, Givens, Bowles) on Saturday 10th April.

That golden run of eleven wins from twelve games had blasted QPR back to the top of Division One, and with only three games left, the title was theirs to lose.

They had also displayed some of the most fluent and flamboyant, explosive and exciting, irresistible and incisive football, not only of the decade, but of all time.

	PL	W	D	L	F	A	PTS
QPR	39	22	11	6	61	29	55
Liverpool	39	20	14	5	55	27	54
Manchester Utd	37	20	10	7	62	38	50
Derby County	38	20	10	8	66	50	50
Leeds United	38	20	9	9	62	40	49

QPR travelled to East Anglia on Saturday 17th April, to play mid-table Norwich City with high hopes, and also with over twelve thousand travelling supporters.

A massive crowd, 31,231, Carrow Road's biggest of that season, experienced a game that went down in footballing legend for decades to come.

QPR, on top of the whole Football League, were playing a team that not only included a World Cup winner, but also the First Division's leading goal-scorer.

Player for player, though, the game was a non-contest.

Colin Suggett crossed from the left, and two awful, blundering headers from QPR defenders then gifted Ted MacDougall his 22nd First Division goal of the season.

QPR wanted to win, but given their superior goal average, a draw wouldn't have been disastrous, and then they'd be ready to beat Arsenal and Leeds, in their last two home games, to secure the title. They came straight back.

Bowles steadied the ball thirty yards out, and he laid it off to Thomas inside the left edge of the Norwich area. Dave Thomas turned Powell inside out, and then weaved past three defenders before burying the ball from six yards out.

"Brilliant goal by Thomas, superb!" Barry Davies screamed. During the second half, Parkes powerfully punched a Norwich City corner out, well clear of his penalty area. Peter Morris, though, hammered the ball on the half-volley, straight past the flying Parkes into the top corner of the goal from thirty-five yards.

What a time that was for Morris to score his one and only Norwich goal during his sixty-six league games for the Canaries.

Billy Steele then crossed from the left, and the rampaging David Jones thumped the ball back into the six yard box. Phil Boyer, unmarked, headed past Parkes from just a few yards out. Boyer was level with Webb as Jones poked the ball in, and so he was actually offside at that time, but the goal was given. The 3-1 score line was a terrible misrepresentation of the balance of play.

NORWICH CITY   QUEENS PARK RANGERS

Norwich City		Queens Park Rangers
Kevin Keelan	1	Phil Parkes
David Jones	2	Dave Clement
Billy Steele	3	Ian Gillard
Peter Morris	4	John Hollins
Duncan Forbes	5	Frank McLintock
Tony Powell	6	David Webb
Mick McGuire	7	Dave Thomas
Ted MacDougall	8	Gerry Francis
Phil Boyer	9	Don Masson
Colin Suggett	10	Stan Bowles
Martin Peters	11	Don Givens

QPR had dominated Norwich, but nothing had gone right. Gerry Francis lobbed Keelan from 30 yards, when sent clear by Bowles, but the ball landed on the roof of the net. Webb then headed in from close range, with the ball hitting Keelan's legs and then bouncing away. The Norwich keeper was seen to have been laughing after that incident, and at his own good luck.

A Tony Powell own goal, late on, gave QPR no consolation, and the destiny of the title was suddenly back in Liverpool's hands.

QPR won both of their last two home games, beating Arsenal 2-1 (Frank McLintock, Gerry Francis penalty kick), and then Leeds United 2-0 (Dave Thomas, Stan Bowles), with a massive total of 61,262 home fans packing Loftus Road for those two games.

However, Liverpool had beaten Stoke 5-3 on the same day as QPR lost at Norwich, and then on Easter Monday, they also won 3-0 away at Manchester City.

Controversy reared its head, though, when Liverpool were allowed to play their crucial last match away to Wolves on 4th May, ten days after QPR's final game.

This decision was made to allow John Toshack to play for Wales in a European Championship Quarter-final against Yugoslavia in Zagreb.

The decision outraged everyone at Shepherds Bush.

FIRST DIVISION LEADERS, 24TH APRIL 1976

	PL	W	D	L	F	A	PTS
QPR42	24	11	7	67	33	59	
Liverpool	41	22	14	5	63	30	58
Manchester Utd	41	22	10	9	66	42	54
Derby County	42	21	11	10	75	58	54
Leeds United	42	21	9	12	65	46	51

QPR captain Gerry Francis had felt that Liverpool should have played under exactly the same pressure as Rangers.

Liverpool beat Wolves at Molineux, on Tuesday 4th May, ten days after the end of the season, coming back from 1-0 down at half-time to win 3-1, and all of their three goals came during the last thirteen minutes. QPR had been watching the game live on a big screen at Shepherds Bush studios.

By the time Liverpool scored their third, most of the team, Stan Bowles included, were down in the local pub, drowning their sorrows.

QPR lost the league title by just one point, and finished three points above third placed Manchester United. Don Givens, Stan Bowles, Gerry Francis and Dave Thomas had scored 44 league goals between them, while Don Masson contributed six goals.

QPR's defence kept nineteen clean sheets, and they conceded only 33 goals from their forty-two games. As well as Don Masson, Phil Parkes also played in all 42 First Division matches. It would be the very, very best that QPR would ever be.

The following season began with captain Gerry Francis out of action with a chronic Sciatic injury. Francis played only eleven First Division games during 1976-77, and QPR really missed him. They lost 0-4 at home to Everton on the opening day of the season. Francis' injury problems had also helped to derail England manager Don Revie's attempts at qualifying for the 1978 World Cup Finals.

Gerry Francis was also England's captain and they missed his influence, drive and presence, as they lost out on goal difference to Italy for a place at Argentina 78. It was particularly their mild-mannered 2-1 home win over group whipping boys Finland on October 13th 1976, when Revie had played four centre-backs, Todd, Beattie, Thompson and Brian Greenhoff, in his back four, that was the most costly in Don Revie's failure.

As gradually and patiently as Gordon Jago had built QPR, and then Dave Sexton had developed them, into a real power in English football, and probably the best-ever team that failed to win the First Division (or Premier League) title, QPR descended just as quickly.

From second place in 1976, and just one point behind the Champions, QPR finished in fourteenth place in 1976-77, and only four points above the relegation zone.

In the UEFA Cup, though, QPR beat Brann Bergen of Norway, Slovan Bratislava of Czechoslovakia, and then FC Cologne in the Third round, reaching the Quarter-finals. They then hammered AEK Athens 3-0 (Francis 2 pens, Bowles), before losing 3-0 away in Greece.

AEK won 7-6 on penalty kicks to reach the Semi-finals. Stan Bowles really enjoyed playing in Europe, though, scoring ten goals from his eight games, and he finished as top scorer in UEFA competitions during 1976-77. Don Givens had also scored six UEFA Cup goals.

Frank McLintock retired, and then David Webb and Dave Thomas both left QPR after 1976-77, as Dave Sexton also left Loftus Road, replacing Tommy Docherty as Manchester United's manager.

McLintock had played 127 First Division games for QPR in nearly four seasons. He'd been a legend at Leicester, and then he became one of Arsenal's greatest legends, but he also became a Loftus Road legend. He returned to Leicester during the 1977 close season as their manager, and then in September, he signed his old teammate David Webb for £50,000.

David Webb had played 116 league games for QPR during his three seasons at Loftus Road. Neither McLintock nor Webb, however, could prevent Leicester from being relegated to the Second Division in April 1978.

Dave Thomas played 182 league games for QPR, scoring 29 goals, but Everton's manager Gordon Lee had paid £200,000 for him on the Eve of the 1977-78 season.

Dave Thomas's accurate passes and crosses created more Everton goals than any other player, and Bob Latchford benefitted greatly from his arrival at Goodison Park, becoming the First Division's top scorer with thirty league goals. Everton also finished third behind Champions Nottingham Forest, and runners-up Liverpool.

As a QPR player, Dave Thomas had won eight England caps between October 1974 and November 1975, mostly used as an impact substitute.

Don Masson, Sexton's first signing at QPR, played for nearly three full seasons at Loftus Road, and he missed only one First Division match. In total, he had missed only ten Football League matches in seven and a half seasons.

Masson played 116 league games for QPR, before he was transferred to Derby County in October 1977, in exchange for Welsh international attacker Leighton James.

Don Masson was a pivotal player in Scotland's qualification for the 1978 World Cup. However, he missed a penalty kick during Scotland's opening match against Peru, with the scores at 1-1. At that stage, Scotland were still highly fancied for the World Cup. During the last twenty minutes, though, Scotland tired, and Peru, much more used to the climate and also inspired by Cubillas, went on to win 3-1. Masson did not feature again, in either of their remaining games against Peru or Holland.

In 1977-78, QPR finished nineteenth, and only one point above relegation.

Don Givens was then signed by Birmingham City after a poor season up front.

Givens' 62 goals from 164 league games, however, during the four seasons 1972-76, placed him as QPR's top goal-scorer during that period. He became QPR's most capped player, also, playing 56 times for the Republic of Ireland. Furthermore, he'd helped Ireland almost qualify for the Quarter-final stages of the 1976 European Championships.

On Wednesday 30th October 1974, Don Givens scored a great hat-trick as Ireland hammered the Soviet Union 3-0. He also scored during their 1-1 draw in Turkey, but a 1-0 defeat in Switzerland proved very costly. Givens then scored all four of Ireland's goals in their 4-0 thrashing of Turkey on Wednesday 29th October 1975, to give the Republic some slight hope, but the Soviets rolled over Switzerland 4-1 in Kiev, and they topped Group 2, just a point ahead of Ireland.

In all, Don Givens' seventy-six goals for QPR from 242 league games make him one of the all-time great bargains at just £40,000.

QPR were relegated in twentieth place at the end of 1978-79, six points below safety. Relegation brought about the departure of five more players from their great team.

John Hollins then signed for Arsenal, aged 33, during the Summer of 1979.

Hollins had played 151 league games for QPR in four years. He went on to play a further 127 games for Arsenal until 1983, when he returned to Chelsea. He then played 29 Second Division matches as the Blues gained promotion back to Division One, along with Sheffield Wednesday and Newcastle.

John Hollins played a total of 743 league games, and all of them, except for his last 29 games, were in the First Division.

Phil Parkes made 344 league appearances for QPR. England's 0-0 draw in Portugal, back in 1974, had turned out to be his only international match, fortunate as he was to be a goalkeeper in an era of some of the very greatest English keepers of all time.

Neither Peter Shilton, Ray Clemence nor Joe Corrigan were any better than Phil Parkes, but they were selected.

Dave Sexton, who'd become Manchester United manager in 1977, had put in several bids for Phil Parkes, but he was unsuccessful every time. It was John Lyall, manager of West Ham United, who had to break the world record transfer fee for a goalkeeper, and he captured Parkes for £565,000. Parkes won the FA Cup during his first season at Upton Park, as well as the Second Division Championship at the end of his second season. He played 344 league games for West Ham, also.

Gerry Francis joined Second Division Champions Crystal Palace, the *Team of the Eighties,* in 1979. He had played 295 league games for QPR, and he'd also been the most capped England player at Loftus Road, winning twelve caps between October 1974 and June 1976, while captaining his country eight times. But for injuries, he'd have won more, and England may have been more successful during the late Seventies.

Dave Clement played 406 league games for Rangers, he was QPR's greatest-ever full-back, while also winning five England caps between March 1976 and February 1977. Clement was sold to Bolton Wanderers for the 1979-80 season, but he suffered a second successive relegation season as Bolton went down. He then broke his leg after moving to Fulham during the early 80s, and he thought his career was over. Whilst suffering from severe depression, Dave Clement committed suicide, aged only thirty-four, on Wednesday 31st March 1982.

After QPR's relegation, Stan Bowles joined European Champions Nottingham Forest in 1979, but he didn't fit into Brian Clough's work ethic, playing only 19 games, and he was quickly sold to Orient.

Nor did he find much favour with Brian Clough's nemesis, Don Revie. He only played five games for England, and in Revie's rigid and restrictive team systems that worked against his strengths, instead of freeing his abilities.

Stan will always, always, be King at Loftus Road, though, the QPR fans' number one all-time favourite player, with his ninety-seven goals in 315 league games.

Ian Gillard played 408 league games for QPR, and 485 in all competitions.

Only two other players have played more games for Rangers in their club history. He was QPR's only player from their classic side to remain after their relegation back to the Second Division in 1979, and he remained for three more seasons.

Gillard played three times for England between March 1975 and 30th October 1975, against West Germany, Wales and Czechoslovakia. However, Ipswich Town's captain Mick Mills became Revie's preferred option at left back. Ian Gillard's final game for QPR was their 1982 FA Cup Final replay defeat against Tottenham Hotspur.

The following season, 1982-83, was the very first season that QPR had fielded no players at all from their classic 1975-76 team, since the late Sixties.

QPR romped to the Second Division Championship, though, managed by Terry Venables. They were a clean, close-knitted and clinical team; Hucker, Neill, Dawes, Waddock, Hazell, Fenwick, Wicks, Sealy, Stainrod, Flanagan, Gregory and substitute Fereday, that had their foundations properly laid upon youth development and secured QPR's place in top flight English League football for fourteen more years.

However, QPR's 1975-76 team will always be remembered as their very best.

Stan Bowles, in particular, was probably the iconic figure of the entertaining and innovative football from the Glam Soccer era, with his straggly long hair, his hooped shirt flamboyantly untucked, and his socks loosely rolled down, like Dave Thomas, while playing the game with a smile on his face.

Football supporters from all over England are united with QPR fans on that theory; Our Friend Stan.

"WE COULD HAVE PLAYED FOR A MONTH, AND NOT SCORED"
Wembley, October 17th 1973, England v Poland

O N SUNDAY 16TH JULY 1972, ENGLAND were drawn against Wales and Poland in Group 5 of the qualifying stages for the 1974 World Cup Finals, over in West Germany.

England had to qualify for the World Cup Finals for the first time since 1962, and they had never previously failed to qualify for the World Cup Finals.

Many felt that England's group didn't look such a difficult task. Spain had been drawn against Yugoslavia, while the Soviet Union had drawn France as well as Johnny Giles' Republic of Ireland, and the winner of that particular group still had to play off against a South American group winner, even if they won their group.

Most felt Wales were the biggest threat of the group. They had John Toshack, Alan Durban, Wyn Davies, Mike England, Terry Yorath, Gary Sprake and Terry Hennessey all playing for teams at the top end of the First Division. Southampton's Ron Davies was still one of football's most feared forwards, while Burnley's exciting young winger Leighton James was becoming very highly rated.

Poland had never beaten England, but they'd proved to be tough opposition in England's two warm-up friendly matches before the 1966 World Cup. England had been held to a 1-1 draw at Goodison Park, and then scraped a 1-0 win in Chorzow.

However, on 10th September 1972, Poland had won the Football Gold Medal at the Munich Olympic Games, beating Hungary 2-1 at the Olympic Stadium, in front of 80,000. Deyna scored twice, and Gorgon, Gadocha, Lubanski and Szymczak all starred for the Poles. Poland had also beaten the Soviet Union 2-1, including a young Oleg Blokhin, in the Semi-finals.

Sir Alf Ramsey's England kicked off their World Cup qualifying campaign on Wednesday 15th November, away in Cardiff. A defensive 4-5-1 line-up was fielded to combat the Welsh attack of John Toshack and Ron Davies, with the lively Leighton James out wide.

On Wednesday 2nd August, though, the Football Association had imposed two-year international bans on Derby County's First Division Championship winning defender Colin Todd, and also Chelsea's Alan Hudson, after both players pulled out of the England under-23 squad's tour of Eastern Europe.

It was a shocking decision, an absolute over-reaction, that only served to deprive Ramsey of the opportunity to play the tightest central defensive partnership in English League football for the remainder of his time as England manager.

Brian Clough was furious with the F.A. He condemned the ban, stating that Colin Todd had been open and honest long before the squad was due to be picked.

If the player had needed a medical certificate, he would have got one from the Derby County doctor stating damaged ankle ligaments.

Colin Todd didn't want him to do that, because he didn't want to cheat his country.

It really was a shocking decision by the F.A.

Therefore, Roy McFarland was partnered by Bobby Moore, while Norman Hunter protected the back four. Arsenal's midfield battler Peter Storey played at right back, with Emlyn Hughes at left back. Kevin Keegan, Colin Bell and Alan Ball completed England's midfield, with Martin Chivers and Rodney Marsh starting up front.

Colin Bell scored the only goal of the game, though, as England started their campaign with a great 1-0 away win.

On Wednesday 24th January 1973, Wembley Stadium hosted the rematch between England and Wales. 62,273 were probably expecting a more attacking team at home to Wales. **Wales** were probably expecting a more attacking England team, and they countered with Leeds United's Terry Yorath replacing Ron Davies, in a Welsh 4-5-1 formation.

But no, Sir Alf Ramsey picked exactly the same eleven players that played in Cardiff. Norman Hunter, a left-half in the old days of 2-3-5, but now a proper centre-back, was used again as a defensive midfield player in an England match at Wembley. It wasn't his fault. He was defensively superior to Bobby Moore at the back anyway, and Peter Storey was no longer a right back. If anyone should've played holding midfield, it should have been Storey.

It wasn't to be. England's 4-5-1 formation actually invited Wales onto them, and Toshack gave them the lead, while neither Chivers nor Marsh were allowed to breathe by Mike England and John Roberts in the Welsh defence. Norman Hunter did equalise for England, with a superb volley from twenty-five yards out, drilled into the top left corner of the Welsh goal. But no attacking substitutions were made, and all the good work done at Ninian Park was undone by a flat performance.

Sir Alf's system did not achieve the necessary result, and it proved to be costly.

On Wednesday 28th March, Wales beat Poland 2-0 in Cardiff, after Leighton James and the bearded Trevor Hockey had both scored. Wales stormed to the top of their World Cup qualifying group.

	P	W	D	L	F	A	PTS
WALES	3	1	1	1	3	2	3
England	2	1	1	0	2	1	3
Poland	1	0	0	1	0	2	0

On Wednesday 6th June, England travelled to Chorzow, scene of their 1-0 away win, seven years earlier, and with Moore, Ball and Peters still in their team.

For two of that legendary trio of players, it was going to be an inglorious night.

73,714 packed the Stadion Slaski on a deafening, hostile, banner waving night. Sir Alf again picked a defensive team, except Peter Storey held the midfield this time.

Paul Madeley started at right-back, and Allan Clarke rightly replaced Rodney Marsh. With Martin Peters also replacing Keegan, it wasn't a bad 4-4-2 line-up: Shilton; Madeley, McFarland, Moore, Hughes; Ball, Storey, Bell, Peters; Chivers, Clarke.

However, the match started awfully for England, wearing an away strip of bright yellow shirts and blue shorts. After just seven minutes, Libuda's free-kick from the left darted in, and was deflected in off the near post, after bouncing off Shilton, by Robert Gadocha, who had too easily lost his marker Bobby Moore, inside the six yard box.

Right at the start of the second half, Poland scored a second goal.

Bobby Moore displayed a diabolical first touch, after receiving a headed pass from Storey, while in yards of space, and then his second touch was even worse. He was dispossessed by Lubanski, and the Gornik forward ran clear and drove the ball inside Shilton's far post.

But it got worse than that. Alan Ball lost his temper after a foul by Leslaw Cmikiewicz, and he grabbed the Legia Warsaw midfielder by the throat. He became only the second England player to be sent off, after Alan Mullery's dismissal against Yugoslavia during England's European Championship Semi-final defeat in 1968.

Poland very classily closed out their 2-0 win, while England resorted to lofting desperate long balls up to Clarke and Chivers.

On September 26th 1973, Poland beat Wales 3-0, again in Chorzow. Gadocha, Lato and Domarski all scored for the Poles, eliminating Wales from the 1974 World Cup.

	P	W	D	L	F	A	PTS
POLAND	3	2	0	1	5	2	4
England	3	1	1	1	2	3	3
Wales	4	1	1	2	3	5	3

With just one game to play, everything now counted down to the Wednesday night of 17th October, and England v Poland at Wembley Stadium. And England needed to win.

However, on that same night as the Poles' 3-0 hammering of Wales, England had hosted Austria in a friendly match, and something completely remarkable happened.

Austria were certainly no whipping boys. They were in the midst of a three-way World Cup qualification battle with Sweden and Hungary, themselves, in Group 1. Sweden eventually had to beat Austria 2-1 in a play-off game to qualify for West Germany 1974, after both countries had finished level at the top of their group, both on points and goal difference.

Sir Alf picked an attacking 4-3-3 formation against Austria, and it worked wonders. On a really great night, Norman Hunter replaced the ageing Bobby Moore, and Martin Peters captained the team. Tony Currie replaced Alan Ball, who was suspended for the Poland match, while Southampton's leading scorer Mike Channon replaced Storey in their front six. The team, Shilton; Madeley, McFarland, Hunter, Hughes; Currie, Bell, Peters; Channon, Chivers and Clarke played superbly and they totally demolished Austria. With not a single defensive player in their front six, and with Paul Madeley and Emlyn Hughes both overlapping regularly, Colin Bell orchestrated as if he were the best player in the World, and England won 7-0.

Mike Channon and Allan Clarke scored two goals each, and Martin Chivers, Tony Currie and Colin Bell made up their seven goals. It really was a great, great night.

In an era when football matches were not shown live on television, except for the FA Cup Final and the World Cup Finals matches, and the occasional Home Internationals match, ITV paid £50,000 for the exclusive rights to show the crucial England v Poland match live on television.

On Thursday 11th October, Sir Alf Ramsey asked the Football League to postpone several First Division matches that were scheduled to be played on Saturday 13th October, among them Leicester

City v Leeds United, Southampton v Liverpool, Manchester United v Derby County and Tottenham Hotspur v Arsenal.

The Football League refused, citing a possible financial loss to the clubs as their reason. On BBC radio, Alan Hardaker, Secretary of the Football League, had said, "it is not a war. Let us keep our sense of perspective. If we do lose, the game is not going to die. It will be a terrible thing for six weeks and then everybody will forget about it."

It is true that nobody expected England to lose, in fact all expected England to win, and it is that great complacency that shouts loud from Alan Hardaker's words.

Nobody has ever forgotten about it.

The historic, brilliant, exhilarating, bristling, exciting, melodramatic, terrific, memorable, terrible night finally arrived on Wednesday 17th October. It was the only thing people were talking about, all day, all over, at schools, offices, shops and pubs all day.

It was all they were talking about the next day, too.

100,000 filled Wembley Stadium, a complete sell-out, not the two-thirds full stadium for the dreary Wales match back at the start of the year. The optimism was loud, and the noise was unforgettable.

The National Anthems were played. The crowd sang God Save The Queen deafeningly. Every England player stood to attention. Peters and Shilton stood attentively with their arms straight down their sides. Clarke and Channon stood more at ease, hands behind their backs. No players sung the National Anthem, in those days. They stood and respected the Anthem.

Anthems done, the players ran away to their positions. Sir Alf Ramsey had chosen exactly the same eleven that had smashed Austria. It was another attacking 4-3-3 team, with Clarke, Channon and Chivers taking turns to sit in midfield, when England were without the ball. That was not often, though, with Colin Bell, England's *Iniesta,* again superbly orchestrating the front six, and he received rich support from both Madeley and Hughes out on the wings.

The good thing about this England team was that all of them were good with the ball, were good on the ball. Martin Peters and Tony Currie were good on the ball, didn't panic, ever. Allan Clarke and Mike Channon were both good running with the ball, as was the elegant Martin Chivers. Paul Madeley, Leeds United's Rolls Royce, was good on the ball. Emlyn Hughes, as comfortable in midfield as he was in Liverpool's defence, was good on the ball.

Roy McFarland, Brian Clough's "best stopper in Europe," was also good on the ball.

Norman Hunter was a Hard Man, a bloody tough tackler and an excellent defender, one of Europe's very best.

Poland lined up: Tomaszewski, Szymanowski, Gorgon, Musial, Bulzacki, Kasperczak, Lato, Cmikiewicz, Deyna (captain), Domarski, Gadocha. The first quarter-hour went by without much proper action, with England generally getting hold of the ball and establishing their supremacy in possession.

After 17 minutes, Peters chipped a free-kick over the Polish wall, 20 yards out. McFarland darted in and kept the ball alive at the bye-line, squaring it inside. Channon's flick was kept out by Tomaszewski, and the Poles scrambled to safety.

On 22 minutes, Peter Shilton collected a cross from Lato, on the run from the left, with ease. It was his first meaningful touch of the ball.

Ten minutes later, Peters collected Bell's wonderful cross-field ball on the right side of the area, and he lofted a cross to the far post, where Channon charged in and volleyed the ball against the legs of Clarke, who was lunging backwards to head it. *"COMMUNICATE!"*

On 36 minutes, Madeley cut inside from the right wing, and he sent a lovely left footed floated cross which Chivers nodded down to Clarke in the six yard box, but Clarke just couldn't get clear of the lunging Gorgon to send the ball goalwards. Poland cleared away for a corner.

From Bell's resultant corner kick, Hunter headed the ball down, and his pass was half-cleared. It was half-cleared to Currie on the right side of the area. Currie smashed in a sharp, darting cross, met by Channon's head, and the ball only just whistled over the crossbar, with Tomaszewski well beaten.

A minute later, Hughes picked up a half-clearance on the left, then cut inside and laid off to Bell on the edge of the 'D'. Bell's first-time shot flashed just a foot over the crossbar. Pressure was starting to result in chances.

Then, Currie played a perfectly-weighted ball down the right for Channon to run onto, good vision, good movement, and Channon's first-time cross was headed down by Clarke to Chivers, seven yards out. Chivers' left-footed volley was blocked by Bulzacki in red. As Poland attempted to clear, Tony Currie put in a sliding tackle, clean and perfect, keeping the ball alive. He played to Bell inside the area.

Bell's right-footed blast beat his defender and darted goalwards, but was it just tipped around the left side post by Tomaszewski.

Bell's corner was then controlled by Currie, but his shot was deflected behind for another corner by Domarski.

Currie's corner was defended out for a fourth corner, before Tomaszewski, finally, felt the ball between both of his arms and chest, safely, in the 40th minute.

England had built up sustained pressure that really rattled Poland, producing four corners and six shots in just three minutes. Poland could not get the ball out of their own third, making repeated unforced errors and returning the ball to an England player, time after time.

One minute before half-time, Roy McFarland lofted a high ball into the area, met by Clarke, whose flicked header was scrambled around the foot of his left post by Tomaszewski.

As the minutes ticked into injury-time, Tomaszewski threw the ball to his captain, Deyna, in left back position. Colin Bell slid in and brilliantly dispossessed Deyna. His cross provided a chance for Paul Madeley, attacking the Polish goal.

Madeley's shot smacked off the back of Musial and out for another corner.

Bell fed Clarke on the right of the penalty area. Clarke chipped a left-footed cross for Channon, eight yards out. Channon's looping header was tipped over the bar by the flying Tomaszewski. The first half ended with Poland managing to clear two more corners.

During the final ten minutes of the first half, Poland had not touched the ball past the halfway line.

Five minutes into the second half, Domarski ran onto Hunter's defensive clearance, free of a marker for the first time, and he shot just over Shilton's bar from 35 yards.

For the very first time, Poland had shot at England's goal.

"All we are saying, is give us a goal," the loud Wembley support began to sing, to the tune of the Plastic Ono Band's 1969 hit song.

"All we are saying, is give us a goal."

There was something about those Poles at the start of that second half, though, something that gave them a calmer, and more composed appearance. They were beginning to take their time with free-kicks. They were beginning to win free-kicks, something they hadn't done at all during the first half. Nerves began to fray, the Poles were beginning to hassle, harry and pressure England.

Tomaszewski saved Currie's 25 yard shot, after good work by Hughes, parrying it only to the feet of Channon, whose snap volley hit the outside of the net.

On 57 minutes, Kasperczak caught Tony Currie in possession near to the Polish corner flag, and he drove a firm pass up the left wing for Lato to run onto. It was a little too firm for Lato, however, and Hunter came across to clear, just inside the England half. Hunter trod on the ball, unfortunately, instead of playing it.

Lato arrived with a sharp tackle, and off he went like a demon. He cut inside, where the back-pedalling McFarland was struggling to contain him. Emlyn Hughes had been tracking Gadocha, who'd ran behind McFarland, but Lato squared to Domarski, instead. Domarski had ran from midfield, in free space, and he met the ball just inside the area. In spite of Hughes' lunging tackle, as the Liverpool player desperately tried to regain his position, Domarski hit a daisy-cutter first-time.

His shot sneaked under the diving body of Peter Shilton.

Many put the goal down to Hunter's error, Hunter's missed tackle, his fluffed clearance. But Norman Hunter never missed any tackle. He had got to the ball first.

He would have quite easily, and naturally, hoofed the ball up to row Q of Wembley Stadium, normally. He could have done it 100 times out of 100. The score would have been 0-0, still, and Poland would have just had a throw-in on the halfway line.

England were playing a high-pressure game of football, though, it should be remembered. Hunter was not only trying to clear the ball, he was trying to keep the ball alive, keep it on the field of play and in England's possession.

It just went wrong, but on the halfway line. It was on the halfway line.

It was what Poland did after Hunter's error that really punished England. This Polish attack was brilliant. Lato's speed of break was devastating. Gadocha's diagonal run to pull England's defence out of shape was smart. And Domarski's release from the traps caught England cold.

Shilton could have done better, also. He should have saved Domarski's shot. He said that the Wembley Cumberland turf, on that wet night, had made the ball move quick and greasy. He said that he should have just put his body between ball and goal, and just blocked the shot. He said he should have parried the ball out for a corner. Instead, he tried to make the perfect save.

Shilton had made a mistake, but it was a well-executed goal, and scored by a fierce strike force. England had kept the Polish attack well tamed for nearly an hour, but now they needed two goals to qualify for West Germany.

One minute later, Chivers' long throw was flicked on by Peters inside the area, and collected by Clarke on the edge of the six yard box. Clarke played back to Channon, the First Division's top scorer of 1973-74.

Channon hit the ball right-footed into the net, just inside the right post.

The Belgian referee, Vital Loraux, had awarded a free-kick to Poland. I still can't see where any foul was committed, but the whistle had already gone as Channon lined up his shot.

After 63 minutes, Channon picked up a loose Polish pass inside the Polish half, but he was fouled by Gorgon, thirty yards from goal. Chivers then took a quick free-kick to Peters, who ran into the Polish area and he went down under Musial's tackle.

Monsieur Loraux blew his whistle. England were awarded a penalty. The Poles protested. It was a very harsh decision. It was, though, probably as much a penalty as it had been a Polish free-kick, a few minutes earlier.

Peter Shilton could not watch, crouching on his heels, with his back to the action, but Allan Clarke spanked the ball, right-footed, high into the top right corner of Tomaszewski's goal.

After 66 minutes, Currie beat Kasperczak down the right wing and he whipped over a sharp cross that dipped under the crossbar, and Tomaszewski had to palm it away for another corner.

By the 70th minute, Poland were time wasting at every opportunity. Peters, Clarke and Channon all pointed to their wrists in front of the referee.

On 74 minutes, Currie was fouled running into the Polish half. Play on, Bell seized the advantage, and hit Channon down the right. Channon beat Musial, and crossed for Clarke, inside the area. Clarke rose highest, but headed just over. Clarke was looking more and more frustrated.

On 78 minutes, Hughes cut in from the left, beat his man, and fed Currie, dead central. Currie's low shot was caught by the diving Tomaszewski. Tony Currie blasphemed live on prime-time ITV.

Every Polish free-kick, or set-piece, was now taking between twenty and thirty seconds to be taken.

With ten minutes to go, the first of two huge chances was created. Emlyn Hughes had been enjoying a personal battle with Jan Domarski, and he was in a forward position, up at the left wing corner. Hughes floated over a dangerous centre that was met by Colin Bell's jump in the six yard box. Bell beat Tomaszewski, and the ball fell to Clarke just behind.

Allan Clarke gathered, then fired the gun, his half-volleyed shot cracked goalwards.

Tomaszewski, on the floor, stretched desperately, and the ball somehow just caught a part of his hand or his elbow, and it ballooned away for another corner kick.

Allan Clarke had scored nearly 100 goals for Leeds at that time, and you could see, you couldn't fail to see, the stunned look and the shaken, disbelieving shape of his body. He knew when he hit it, *a goal-scorer's instinct, if you like,* that that was a goal all the way, the goal to send England to Munich, Hamburg, Stuttgart or Cologne the following Summer.

He'd even turned to really celebrate.

Instead, Sniffer just stood there, just stood still and he shook his head. He threw a piece of turf away, just stood there.

Martin Peters came over and he had a word. The game was still on.

After 81 minutes, the game was nearly up. Domarski flicked on Tomaszewski's throw, and Lato pushed the ball into space behind Roy McFarland, the best stopper in Europe. McFarland had a yard or two on Lato, but Lato was the quickest player on the pitch, and he flew past McFarland.

McFarland had to grab Lato and pull him back, and probably should have been sent off. Fortunately for England, Monsieur Loraux only booked the apologetic, lucky Derby County captain.

Wembley hissed with relief, but most of all, with anxiety.

All of Wembley was hissing like a meadow of alarmed crickets.

This was a nervous and careless couple of minutes as, after 83 minutes, England had yet another escape. Domarski slid the ball behind the England defence, and Lato spun clear again, totally onside, with Hunter standing nailed to the turf, with his hand in the air. Shilton saved the situation, coming out of his area to challenge, and sending Lato wide.

The brilliant Peters ran back to defend the goal line, so Lato was forced to play the ball across to Kasperczak, who hammered the ball hopeful, high and wide.

After 89 minutes, Kevin Hector came on for his England debut, in place of Martin Chivers.

One minute later came the defining moment of that match, the awful clarification that it wasn't England's night. Tony Currie drove in a left-sided corner that was met fully by Hector's diving header.

But the ball just bounced away off the right knee of Antoni Szymanowski. Szymanowski was supposed to have been on the post, as the coaching manuals say. If he'd been on the post, the ball would not have ballooned off his knee, and England would have jetted off to West Germany.

He had moved three yards away from his post, and for once, Tomaszewski was all over the shop, and well beaten. Hector had met the ball full-blooded; but if he'd just put a slight glance on it, or just scuffed it, there was no other obstacle on the line, it was a goal.

And England were off to play this Total Football against West Germany and Holland. Such slender, minute measurements sometimes make the smallest differences between the greatest successes and unforgettable failures.

Despite this, England just kept coming. In the 92nd minute, Currie crossed from the left. Tomaszewski punched out. Bell, on the edge of the area, drilled the ball back in.

His shot beat Kasperczak, Tomaszewski and Musial, but not Miroslaw Bulzacki. Bulzacki had remained on the goal-line, having backed up his keeper as he'd originally punched. Bulzacki just hoofed the ball wide left, away to safety.

That was it. Thirty seconds later, the full-time whistle was blown, and England were out of the 1974 World Cup.

Nobody could criticize this England performance, although some did. England had given everything from the start to the very end. Colin Bell and Tony Currie, particularly, had the England games of their lives, making over sixty accurate passes between them inside the Polish half. Also, highly productive were Emlyn Hughes, Martin Peters, Paul Madeley and Mike Channon on the night, while Allan Clarke and Martin Chivers had done absolutely nothing wrong.

On any other night, and against a less committed defence, the score might have been three, four, five, six or seven, as it had been against Austria.

The troubles lay, not at England's failure to beat Poland, but that home draw against Wales. It was no consolation for the England players who failed to qualify.

Alan Hardaker had said that everybody would forget about it.

He was wrong. Neither Emlyn Hughes, nor Paul Madeley, nor Roy McFarland, nor Tony Currie, nor Mike Channon, nor Martin Chivers, nor Kevin Hector ever played in a World Cup Finals tournament. But it hit every player hard, let alone us, the fans, and that match takes up many pages in the autobiographies of all of the players.

It took Allan Clarke "weeks to get the game out of his system. The only consolation was that they could not have done anymore. They were inconsolable in the dressing room afterwards."

"It was total heartbreak and sobbing in the dressing room, afterwards," Martin Chivers confessed. "Grown men were crying their eyes out. I still have nightmares now. They'll never leave me."

It is no consolation, whatsoever, that Poland totally warranted their place at the 1974 Finals. In five successive games, Poland beat every team they faced. Argentina and Italy were both beaten by the Poles during the group stages, while they'd also thrashed Haiti 7-0.

In the Second round, they then beat both Sweden and Yugoslavia, before facing home team West Germany in a Frankfurt rainstorm. 62,000 watched Gerd Muller score after 75 minutes to edge the scrappiest and tightest of games 1-0.

Poland then beat Brazil 1-0 to finish in Third Place.

Grzegorz Lato, England's chief tormentor at Wembley, won the FIFA Golden Boot with seven goals, while Szarmach, who hadn't even featured at Wembley, had scored five. Captain Deyna scored three, as Poland were the tournament's top scorers, outscoring both of the two Finalists, West Germany and Holland.

The 1974 World Cup Finals showed English football supporters just how good Olympic Champions Poland were, and how good a defensive performance they'd displayed at Wembley, as well as their excellent counter-attacking game, even if luck had favoured them, more than once.

However, Poland's Third Place finish should also serve as a reminder of how well England played; a corner count of 26-2, a possession share of 66-34, and a shot count of 35-3. Only their 1990 Turin Semi-final penalty shoot-out defeat against West Germany can beat the quality of play, the drama, and the ultimate pain that Wednesday 17th October 1973 had.

Other significant games since 1973 have maybe come close, but the sustained high quality and substance of England's play against Poland, puts that night above all others, except Turin.

Sir Alf Ramsey was sure in his own mind how good that England team was that October night. At a school football event in Southampton, several years later, he was with Martin Chivers, and he proclaimed, "you know, that Seventy-three team was the strongest that I ever had."

That was Sir Alf Ramsey's last competitive game as England manager. He managed the team for two further friendly matches, against Italy at Wembley a month after the Poland game, and then away to Portugal in Lisbon, the following April.

Sir Alf had given England debuts to six players in those two matches: Phil Parkes, Mike Pejic, Martin Dobson, Dave Watson, Stan Bowles and Trevor Brooking.

On 1st May 1974, though, the Football Association finally sacked Sir Alf Ramsey. Under Sir Alf, England had won 69 out of 113 matches, while losing only 17 times.

There is no consolation for the team's failure to qualify for the 1974 World Cup, especially given that Bulgaria qualified from a relatively easy group and were a waste of space in Dusseldorf, Hanover and Dortmund, and then the Soviet Union even refused to play their second leg play-off game against Chile in Santiago, having been held to a 0-0 draw in Moscow, and they should really have been banned from FIFA World Cups for ten years. England's group that included Wales and Poland, originally perceived as an easy group, had actually proved to be one of the toughest.

There is no consolation, but here's my attempt. Peter Shilton, Paul Madeley, Emlyn Hughes, Colin Bell, Roy McFarland, Norman Hunter, Tony Currie, Mike Channon, Martin Chivers, Allan Clarke, Martin Peters and Kevin Hector are the best team, the greatest team ever to have not qualified for the World Cup Finals.

It was my honour to have been inconsolable with all of you.

LAKES SHINING CLEAR
AMONG THE MOUNTAINS

FOR MOST OF THE YEARS BETWEEN 1967 and 1973, Carlisle United were a decent, stable, but unspectacular mid-table Second Division team.

Carlisle had won the Third Division Championship back in 1965, and they then finished third in the Second Division two seasons later, but six points behind second-placed Wolves.

Then in 1970, Carlisle beat Huddersfield Town, Blackburn Rovers and even Chelsea, en route to the League Cup Quarter-finals, where Chris Balderstone's penalty kick despatched fellow Second Division side Oxford United after a replay at Brunton Park.

A huge, 20,322 home crowd watched their Carlisle United team including Alan Ross, Winstanley, Ternent, McVitie, Chris Balderstone and also Bob Hatton beating West Brom 1-0 in their Semi-final first leg, after Frank Barton scored a late winner.

West Brom hammered Carlisle 4-1 in the second leg, though, to reach Wembley.

Into the New Year, Carlisle United then knocked Nottingham Forest and Aldershot out of the FA Cup, both after replays.

They were drawn at home to Middlesbrough in the Fifth round. A club record 27,500 crowd totally filled Brunton Park, but goals from both Hickton and Downing sent Carlisle out of the Cup.

Then, during 1970-71, Carlisle went on a great, late season run, gaining eleven points from their last six games, winning five and drawing once, but they finished fourth, and only three points behind promoted Sheffield United.

Bob Hatton was their top goal-scorer with eighteen goals from 41 games, while his partner Bobby Owen had scored eleven from 33. Dennis Martin and Chris Balderstone both chipped in with nineteen between them from midfield.

Stan Ternent, from Tyneside, played the hard football in midfield behind the Cumbrians' fluent scoring machine, and he was a gritty ever-present in their team for two successive seasons. He eventually retired in 1974, having played 188 league games for Carlisle, to become coach at Sunderland, under Bob Stokoe.

The 1971-72 season began disappointingly, considering their superb form towards the end of the previous season. They'd won just twice in their first seven games, and then only five times during their opening fourteen games.

Their fourteenth game of that season, a 2-0 win away at Luton Town (Hatton, Balderstone), was Bob Hatton's last game for Carlisle United.

Hatton left for promotion chasers Birmingham City for a fee of £80,000 at the end of October 1971, and he then became a key player as Birmingham finished second-placed behind

---

Champions Norwich City. Bob Hatton had scored 38 goals in 93 Second Division matches for Carlisle, but he'd scored nine in their first fourteen games of the 1971-72 season.

Manager Alan Ashman immediately replaced Hatton with a cheap replacement from Crewe Alexandra.

Stan Bowles went on to score eleven league goals from only 28 league games during 1971-72, and he was their equal top goal-scorer with Bobby Owen, who'd played forty matches. Again, Dennis Martin and Chris Balderstone had chipped in with eighteen goals between them. However, Carlisle finished down in tenth place, once again well behind the promotion zone.

Ray Train was brought in from Bradford to add some bite to Carlisle's midfield. The diminutive midfield engine became an ever-present from December 1971 until September 1973, when an injury suffered during a heavy defeat against Luton Town had put him out of action for two months.

Stan Bowles only played five games at the start of the 1972-73 season, though, before he was sold to QPR for a club record fee of £110,000. For the second successive season Carlisle United had sold their star player to a club destined for promotion.

He was replaced as Carlisle's top scorer by Joe Laidlaw, a Summer signing from Middlesbrough. Laidlaw, a Wallsend-born Geordie, was a combative midfield player who scored 14 goals from 41 games during 1972-73. Striker Bobby Owen scored twelve, while Balderstone and Martin again chipped in with twelve between them.

Carlisle ended up fifth from the bottom of Division Two, just a single point above relegated Huddersfield Town. Fortunately, though fluent scorers Carlisle United hadn't been, Laidlaw and Owen had both scored just enough solitary goals during 1-1 draws or 1-0 wins, to only just keep them up.

Alan Ashman needed an injection of attacking thrust to avoid another relegation battle, and so on 24th August, on the eve of the 1973-74 season, he paid £35,000 to Ipswich Town for striker Frank Clarke.

Frank Clarke, the brother of Leeds and England forward Allan Clarke, had been side-lined at Portman Road by their new-look strike-force of David Johnson, Bryan Hamilton and Trevor Whymark. He'd also been a Shrewsbury Town club legend, having scored 89 goals from 218 games at Gay Meadow during the Sixties.

With much First Division experience at both QPR and Ipswich between 1967 and 1973, though, Clarke immediately made an impact, scoring for Carlisle on his debut. The Cumbrians were held to a 1-1 home draw with Cardiff City on 25th August 1973.

Chris Balderstone had decided to play out his County Championship cricket season for Leicestershire, and so he was missing from Carlisle's line-up until 18th September.

Among the last players to combine cricket and football at a professional level, Chris was certainly the last ever to play First Division football, and also Test Match cricket for England. He was selected for two Test Matches during the Summer of 1976, against the West Indies' fast bowling attack of Holding and Roberts. He did score 35 in one innings, but he struggled for runs, as did England, who lost that Series 3-0. Chris Balderstone was a top county batsman, though, and he scored 1,000 runs in the County Championship in eight out of ten seasons between 1972 and 1982.

He also had a wonderful left foot, and was a great passer of the ball with either foot.

Intelligent, he could read the game quicker than most around him, which more than compensated for him not being the quickest player, or hardest tackler.

When Carlisle visited Luton Town on Saturday 1st September, Balderstone's control, composure, speed of thought, balance and skill were much missed. Carlisle were trounced. They were 6-0 down at half-time. The Hatters took their foot off the gas in the second half, though, and Bobby Owen scored a scant consolation goal.

Only losing 6-1 in the end, the Cumbrians certainly looked nothing like a promotion team.

Carlisle United had lost four of their opening six games, winning only three points, and they were in the Second Division relegation zone on Tuesday 18th September.

Chris Balderstone was back, although in and out of the team, due to injuries, but Carlisle, with both Les O'Neill and Joe Laidlaw in midfield, had scrapped and battled their way up to mid-table by 10th November.

Les O'Neill, born at Hartford Colliery near Blyth, had worked as a coalminer in his home town, during his teenage years. Only five feet and seven inches tall, he was an honest, hard-working dynamo, good at running with the ball, and ghosting past opponents. He'd won the FA Youth Cup with Newcastle United, back in 1962, in the same team as Bobby Moncur, Alan Suddick and David Craig.

O'Neill scored two vital goals during their Semi-final second leg 4-2 home win over Portsmouth, when Pompey were 2-1 up, and 3-1 up on aggregate, to help Newcastle win the tie, 4-3 on aggregate.

He only played one game for Newcastle's first team, though.

By New Year's Day, Carlisle had gone on a good run of five wins from their last eight games, and they'd risen up to seventh-place. They then entertained Luton Town, who'd humiliated the Cumbrians back in September.

9,255, their second largest home crowd of the season up to then, demanded revenge.

CARLISLE UNITED		LUTON TOWN
Alan Ross	1	Graham Horn
Graham Winstanley	2	Don Shanks
John Gorman	3	Bobby Thomson
Les O'Neill	4	Peter Anderson
Bill Green	5	John Faulkner
Brian Tiler	6	Alan Garner
Dennis Martin	7	Jimmy Ryan
Ray Train	8	Alan West
Bobby Owen	9	Barry Butlin
Frank Clarke	10	Jimmy Husband
Joe Laidlaw	11	John Aston
Chris Balderstone	12	John Ryan

Bill Green and Dennis Martin both scored during Carlisle's great 2-0 win, lifting them right up to fourth place, just behind third placed Luton on goal average, and only four points behind second placed Orient.

Just over one month later, on Saturday 2nd February, Carlisle hosted second-placed Orient and they won 3-0 (Clarke 2, Laidlaw), in front of 9,422, but they remained in fourth place. They suffered poor run gaining only one point from their next three matches, though, and dropped back down to seventh, as Nottingham Forest, Blackpool and West Brom all moved above them.

MALCOLM STARK

Frank Clarke got Carlisle back on track with the only goal during their 1-0 win over Malcolm Allison's Crystal Palace on Saturday 16th March.

Frank Clarke then hammered in four goals as they thrashed bottom club Swindon Town 5-1, with Joe Laidlaw hitting the fifth, a fortnight later.

By then, Luton Town had rediscovered their red-hot form and they'd overhauled Orient to move into second place behind runaway leaders Middlesbrough, so the one remaining promotion spot was now being chased by six teams.

A poor 2-0 defeat at Bristol City was followed by their Good Friday 2-1 loss away at late promotion runners Sunderland, in front of a large 34,179 Roker Park crowd, that had dropped Carlisle back to the tail end of the teams chasing promotion.

However, on the following day, Saturday 13th April, Carlisle came from behind after Duncan McKenzie's early goal, to beat Nottingham Forest 2-1 (Owen, Laidlaw).

The battle for that last promotion place was tight…

SECOND DIVISION LEADERS, 13TH APRIL 1974

	PL	W	D	L	F	A	PTS
Middlesbrough	39	25	11	3	64	26	61
Luton Town	38	18	11	9	57	45	47
Orient	38	14	15	9	50	38	43
CARLISLE UNITED	38	17	9	12	57	44	43
West Brom	39	14	14	11	57	44	42
Blackpool	38	14	13	11	49	37	41
Sunderland	38	16	9	13	50	38	41
Nottingham Forest	38	13	14	11	51	38	40

…very tight.

On the following Tuesday, 16th April 1974, a massive crowd of 19,692 packed into Brunton Park for their home game against form team Sunderland, the bookmakers' original favourites to go up, who'd gained nine points from their last six games.

It was an epic promotion battle.

Sunderland arrived with eight survivors from the team that had famously beaten Leeds United at Wembley eleven months earlier, and they came to attack.

CARLISLE UNITED		SUNDERLAND
Alan Ross	1	Jim Montgomery
Peter Carr	2	Dick Malone
John Gorman	3	Ron Guthrie
Les O'Neill	4	Dennis Longhorn
Bill Green	5	Dave Watson
Chris Balderstone	6	Rod Belfitt
Dennis Martin	7	Bobby Kerr
Ray Train	8	Billy Hughes
Bobby Owen	9	Vic Halom
Frank Clarke	10	Ian Porterfield
Joe Laidlaw	11	Jackie Ashurst

Alan Ross in goal, however, was brilliant, and Carlisle United, certainly the best-ever Carlisle United team, worked hard amidst the raucous atmosphere.

They were then awarded a penalty during the second half, which the great Chris Balderstone smashed past Montgomery. Rarely was there ever such an explosion of noise at Brunton Park.

Wearsiders were furious at the result; they knew they were the better side, but they hadn't been good enough on the night to prove it.

Poor early season form, when at one point their entire forward line had been ruled out, was the main reason their promotion bid was left until so late.

Carlisle didn't worry too much about Wear fury though, they just celebrated.

That result put four teams, Orient, West Brom, Carlisle and Blackpool, equal on forty-three points, all separated only by goal average, and all chasing one promotion spot. It was still tight.

On the following Saturday, though, Carlisle suffered an all-mighty hangover away at Blackpool, as Keith Dyson, Terry Alcock (2), and Alan Suddick's penalty kick put the Irish Sea wind up the Cumbrians, and the Tangerines stormed to a 4-0 win.

West Brom had taken just one point from their last two games, so the promotion race was now down to a three horse race. Blackpool were clinging onto the final promotion place with 47 points, but they had only one game left.

Orient were fourth-placed with 46 from forty games, while Carlisle had 45 points.

On Tuesday 23rd April, Bobby Owen celebrated St George's Day with their winner away at Oxford United, sending Carlisle up to third with just one final game to play.

That final game was at home to Aston Villa on Saturday 27th April.

The exact same team that had beaten Sunderland, except for Graham Winstanley coming in for Bill Green in central defence, simply had to win. But they also had to hope that Orient failed to win either of their two remaining games.

During the first half, Gorman's left wing cross was headed in by the leaping Laidlaw, and their 12,494 home fans exploded, making the noise and atmosphere of a crowd double its' size. They went absolutely delirious, and joyously invaded the pitch.

After the break, their top scorer Frank Clarke doubled the lead, finishing Villa off with a free header inside the penalty area from Dennis Martin's right wing cross.

Orient had been held to a 1-1 draw away at Cardiff City, and so they now only had to beat Aston Villa themselves in their final home game postponed to the Friday before FA Cup Final Day.

On Friday 3rd May 1974, Aston Villa hung on for a 1-1 draw, in front of a gigantic 29,766 Brisbane Road crowd, which had included most of Carlisle's players.

Orient had choked, on the very last day of that season, and so Carlisle United were promoted to the First Division for the first time in their history.

Les O'Neill was absolutely overjoyed to be going back to Newcastle.

Manager Alan Ashman had managed Carlisle during the mid-sixties for four years, before moving to West Brom, and leading Albion to their great FA Cup win in 1968.

He took them back to the Semi-finals the following year, as well as reaching the European Cup Winners' Cup Quarter-finals. He finally left The Hawthorns to manage in Greece for just one season, before returning to Carlisle in 1972.

He admitted, on Border TV, that lifting Carlisle United up to the First Division was probably his greatest-ever achievement.

Optimism in Ashman's mind was exactly the same as that in all Cumbrian fans; Carlisle United were good enough to survive in the First Division.

Frank Clarke was their leading goal scorer during their promotion season, with sixteen goals from 36 Second Division games; a bargain buy, indeed. Carlisle's fans had even devised their own song for Clarke, to the tune of *Has Anybody Seen My Gal?*

"Six foot two and Eyes of blue, Frankie Clarke is after you,
Na na-na na-na, na-na na-na..."

It was a great tribute from the Cumbrian fans to their star striker, who was only five feet eleven and a half inches tall.

Joe Laidlaw had scored twelve from 42 league games, while Bobby Owen was again consistent, hitting eleven from 36. Dennis Martin and Les O'Neill had also contributed thirteen goals between them, from midfield.

CHELSEA		CARLISLE UNITED
Peter Bonetti	1	Alan Ross
Gary Locke	2	Peter Carr
Peter Houseman	3	John Gorman
John Hollins	4	Les O'Neill
Micky Droy	5	Bill Green
Ron Harris	6	Bobby Parker
Steve Kember	7	Hugh McIlmoyle
David Hay	8	Ray Train
Chris Garland	9	Frank Clarke
Bill Garner	10	Chris Balderstone
John Sissons	11	Joe Laidlaw
Charlie Cooke	12	Dennis Martin

Carlisle United were strengthened in June, when Alan Ashman smashed the club's transfer fee record, by paying Coventry City £60,000 for centre-back Bobby Parker.

The Cumbrians were blindly hopeful, on Saturday 17th August 1974, as Carlisle travelled down to Chelsea for their first ever First Division match, with 31,268 inside Stamford Bridge.

Goals in each half from Bill Green and Les O'Neill, though, won the game 2-0 for Carlisle, a tremendous start to their season. Then, on the following Tuesday, Carlisle travelled over to Middlesbrough, runaway Champions of the Division that Carlisle had only just scraped themselves out of.

28,719, a huge crowd for Middlesbrough, bigger than any Ayresome Park crowd during Middlesbrough's 1973-74 season, apart from the Sunderland game, watched Carlisle beat Middlesbrough 2-0 (O'Neill 2). Three goals in their opening two games had Les O'Neill actually topping the First Division's goal-scoring charts.

On the following Saturday, 24th August, Carlisle hosted their first ever First Division game at Brunton Park. Tottenham Hotspur, Bill Nicholson's Tottenham Hotspur, the UEFA Cup Finalists only three months before, were their visitors, but only 18,426 attended the game.

Maybe those absent were saving their money for Newcastle?

After twenty minutes, Mike England's tackle on Laidlaw inside the area was adjudged to have been a foul, but Pat Jennings saved Balderstone's penalty. The referee, however, ruled that Jennings had moved, so Balderstone blasted his re-taken penalty past Jennings. Carlisle hung on for a 1-0 win over an off-colour and off-key Spurs. Ray Train also hit a great 35 yard shot that rebounded off Jennings' crossbar.

CARLISLE UNITED		TOTTENHAM HOTSPUR
Alan Ross	1	Pat Jennings
Peter Carr	2	Ray Evans
Graham Winstanley	3	Terry Naylor
Les O'Neill	4	Phil Beal
Bill Green	5	Mike England
Bobby Parker	6	Ralph Coates
Dennis Martin	7	John Pratt
Ray Train	8	Steve Perryman
Hugh McIlmoyle	9	Chris Jones
Chris Balderstone	10	Martin Peters
Joe Laidlaw	11	Jimmy Neighbour

Bill Nicholson, already disillusioned with modern football after crowd trouble by Spurs fans in Rotterdam, at the UEFA Cup Final, and an apparent *lack of respect* from *some* players at White Hart Lane, resigned five days later.

Carlisle had won their first three games and they were on top of the First Division.

FIRST DIVISION LEADERS, 24TH AUGUST 1974

	PL	W	D	L	F	A	PTS
CARLISLE UNITED	3	3	0	0	5	0	6
Ipswich Town	3	3	0	0	4	0	6
Liverpool	3	2	1	0	4	2	5
Wolves	3	2	1	0	6	3	5
Everton	3	2	1	0	5	3	5

Only 18,473 attended their home match with Middlesbrough, three days later, but David Armstrong's goal spoilt the party, and *Liverpool replaced Carlisle United at the top of the First Division*: eleven words that would never be repeated ever again.

On Saturday 31st August, Sixties' legend Hugh McIlmoyle had given Carlisle United a 1-0 half-time lead away at Leicester City, but Frank Worthington then scored from the penalty spot, after Green had fouled Sammels. Carlisle only drew 1-1, and they dropped to fifth place, below Liverpool, Ipswich, Everton and Manchester City.

Carlisle United were still in a UEFA Cup qualifying place after five games, but the good times ended there. Over their next thirty First Division games, they won six, but lost twenty-three times. They plummeted into the relegation zone by 16th November, where they remained for the rest of the season. They hit rock bottom in February.

25,000 had attended their Boxing Day home match against Newcastle United, their largest crowd of the season, and the largest attendance at Brunton Park since their 1970 FA Cup tie against Boro, although exactly how Carlisle United couldn't sell out for this match was inexplicable.

The Magpies' Malcolm MacDonald/John Tudor attacking combination eventually cancelled out Bobby Owen's early goal as Newcastle defeated Carlisle 2-1.

Carlisle enjoyed a very brief return to form during the Easter holidays, with a shock 3-0 win over Everton (Joe Laidlaw penalty, Dennis Martin, Frank Clarke), and then a 4-2 hammering of Burnley (Les O'Neill, Laidlaw 2 (1 pen), Ray Train).

Following their 0-0 home draw with Coventry, on Tuesday 1st April 1975, the Cumbrians even moved up to second bottom of Division One.

Bottom team Luton Town then found some form, though, winning seven points from their final four games and the Hatters very nearly survived. But they didn't.

Carlisle United ended the 1974-75 season bottom of Division One, only five points below safety, and they had won twelve First Division games.

Carlisle United certainly hadn't been a disastrous Division One team.

Their goal difference of minus sixteen from 42 league games had been bettered by only six other relegated First Division teams since the War.

Also, only two First Division teams had been relegated after conceding fewer than Carlisle's 59 goals against. Manchester United had only conceded 48 during 1973-74, and Crystal Palace had conceded only 58 goals the previous year.

It was Carlisle's lack of goals scored that had cost them points. Of their twenty-five league defeats, sixteen were by just one single goal.

Joe Laidlaw was Carlisle United's top goal-scorer with twelve goals, while Les O'Neill and Dennis Martin had combined for a good total of fifteen goals from midfield. The moustached Frank Clarke had had a very disappointing season, though, scoring just four goals from thirty league starts, while Bobby Owen scored only three from nineteen.

During the Summer of 1975, whilst winning the County Championship with Leicestershire, Chris Balderstone ended his ten years with Carlisle after moving to Fourth Division side Doncaster Rovers. Famously, on Monday 15th September 1975, he'd ended the day on 51 not out batting against Derbyshire, and then immediately raced up to Belle Vue to start Rovers' evening 1-1 draw with Brentford.

On the following day, Chris returned to complete his century for Leicestershire.

His runs helped Leicestershire win the County Championship during that Summer of 1975. Having also opened the batting, ten years later, as they won their 1985 Benson and Hedges Cup Final against Essex, at Lords, on Saturday 20th July, under David Gower's captaincy, JC Balderstone won his sixth major honour with Leicestershire.

Chris Balderstone remains the player with the most winners' medals in Leicestershire County Cricket Club's long history.

Without the classy elegance of Balderstone, Carlisle had a poor season in 1975-76, battling relegation until Christmas, before rising to mid-table in the New Year, and finally ending the season just one place above the drop zone, but four points clear.

Frank Clarke was again their top scorer with nine goals from thirty-six games.

Ray Train joined Second Division promotion chasers Sunderland for £90,000, in March 1976. The composed defensive midfield player, who was regularly highlighted as Carlisle's best footballer, their engine, by Match of the Day pundits during 1974-75, had made 173 league appearances for the Cumbrians in over four years.

By 1976, that great Carlisle United team began to fall apart. Defender Bill Green moved to West Ham United in June, for £90,000, after 119 league games for Carlisle.

The Geordie, who'd had played in all forty-two of Carlisle's First Division games, alongside Bobby Parker, had some good times at West Ham, but the Hammers began to slump towards the late Seventies, and they had to rebuild around Brooking, Bonds and Devonshire for the Eighties. Bill Green took a good deal of stick, undeserved stick, from the Upton Park fans for their defensive problems during this period, and he left after their relegation in 1978.

Also during June 1976, Joe Laidlaw signed for Doncaster Rovers after 151 games and scoring 44 goals in four seasons at Brunton Park. After Billy Bremner became Rovers' manager at the end of November 1978, he made Joe Laidlaw captain.

Portsmouth's manager Frank Burrows had held Joe Laidlaw in high esteem.

"Every team needs a Joe Laidlaw," he said, "a tough battler to win the ball all over the park and keep everyone up to their job."

Considering that tribute, it's probable that the great Scot, Billy Bremner, had seen maybe a little of himself in Laidlaw. Joe Laidlaw eventually signed for Burrows' Portsmouth and he helped them to promotion from the Fourth Division in 1980.

Bobby Owen played for Northampton, on loan, during October 1976, then he went to Bury, and then to Workington, before he finally left Brunton Park for Doncaster Rovers in 1977, after 194 league games and 51 goals for Carlisle United.

John Gorman signed for Tottenham Hotspur for £60,000 in November 1976, where the hard-tackling, strong and commanding, attacking left-back founded a lifelong personal and professional friendship with Glenn Hoddle, with whom the Scot coached England, Southampton, Tottenham and Swindon Town. Gorman had played 229 league games for Carlisle United.

After Gorman left Brunton Park, Carlisle were relegated to the Third Division, and many Cumbrian fans directly blamed the loss of Gorman as being the final nail in the coffin, as they plunged downwards thereafter.

Les O'Neill signed for Queen of the South before the 1977-78 season after playing 177 games in the Cumbrians' midfield. His sixteen goals in 85 league and cup games during the two seasons 1973-75, though, were of special significance in Carlisle's history. Eamon Dunphy said that O'Neill had a heart as big as the Den, and he kept Carlisle going when things had stopped working.

"He is a pest," Dunphy admitted. "You get the ball and his leg sneaks through and knocks it away. That's all right the first time. But after twenty minutes you cannot get on the ball. Every time you do, there is this pest pestering you.

Driving you mad."

Alan Ross had set the club record for most league appearances during the 1979-80 season, before retiring after 466 games in thirteen years at Carlisle. Their legendary goalkeeper died, aged only fifty-seven, on Tuesday 2nd November 1999.

Chris Balderstone is in second-place on Carlisle United's league appearances list, behind only Alan Ross, having played 376 games, and he scored 88 goals between 1965 and 1975. He won his sixth major cricket trophy with Leicestershire CCC in July 1985, as an opening batsman in the John Player Trophy Final, after Leicestershire had beaten Essex by five wickets, even with Graham Gooch, Derek Pringle, Neil Foster and John Lever playing for Essex.

Subsequently, Balderstone became the most successful player in LCCC's history, a record yet to be broken.

He settled in Leicestershire after retiring, but Balderstone returned to Cumbria in 1999. He became a regular supporter at Brunton Park, watching Carlisle's new stars, before being diagnosed with prostate cancer, not long after he returned to Lakeland.

Chris Balderstone, the greatest player in Carlisle United's history, died at his Carlisle home, aged only fifty-nine, on Monday 6th March 2000, just four months after Alan Ross's death .

It's easy to take Carlisle United for granted as a decent, stable, but unspectacular mid-table Second Division team, between 1967 and 1973.

So I'll try to put their achievements of those two seasons 1973-75, and their average home crowds of nearly fifteen thousand, into some context.

Since they were relegated from the First Division, thirty-nine seasons ago, Carlisle have spent just six seasons inside the Football League's top two divisions. They've also finished inside the bottom three of the bottom division on six occasions.

It's easy to take that Carlisle United team for granted.

Some of the football played by Carlisle United during the 1973-74 season was a delight to watch, in their unique blue, red and white penguin shirts, and they fully deserved their one season in the First Division, at the club described by Shankly as English football's most isolated outpost.

Temporarily, ***the Lakes were shining clear among the Mountains, the hoary mountains.***

YOU CAN DO MAGIC!
(including the 1974-75 Season)

IN 1971, THE ENGLISH FIRST DIVISION welcomed the return of Sheffield United, following three seasons in Division Two. Tony Currie and Alan Woodward, two survivors from their 1968 relegation season, had scored a combined total of 47 league goals along with fellow forwards Billy Dearden and John Tudor, as the Blades finished runners-up behind Leicester City. John Tudor had left for Newcastle United at the end of January, though, for just £60,000, as manager John Harris subsequently paid £40,000 to Birmingham City, strengthening his midfield with Blues' captain Trevor Hockey.

Hockey had played nearly 200 league games at St Andrew's, and after his arrival, the Blades lost just two out of their final seventeen Second Division matches, beating off the close challenge of Cardiff, Carlisle and Hull City. Short, just five feet and six inches tall, but a pocket powerhouse, Trevor Hockey was an aggressive midfield ball winner, with a thick, dark, bristling beard.

"Give the ball to Tony Currie," was the simple instruction that John Harris gave to Trevor Hockey.

Between March 23rd and April 23rd 1971, Sheffield United didn't concede a single goal in seven successive matches. Eddie Colquhoun had been so dominant in central defence, the fans made up a song for their Prestonpans-born centre half, who'd joined the Blades from West Brom, in 1968.

> *"We ain't no barrel of money,*
> *But we have got Woodward and Currie,*
> *And with Eddie Colquhoun,*
> *Promotion soon,*
> *United."*

Nearly 43,000 packed Bramall Lane for their promotion clincher at home to Cardiff City, on Saturday 27th April. Billy Dearden scored twice, and John Flynn, Gil Reece and Tony Currie hit the others in an emphatic 5-1 win. United conceded only nine goals during their last seventeen matches, with Trevor Hockey's rich presence in midfield protecting Colquhoun's back line, but also supplying Tony Currie.

Sheffield United made an unbelievable start to the following season, dropping just two points from their first ten First Division matches, and they were top of the table on Saturday 25th September, three points ahead of second-placed Manchester United.

Bramall Lane's average crowd for United's first seven matches of that 1971-72 season was nearly 38,000. On Saturday 27th November, Alan Woodward scored four goals, including a penalty kick, as the Blades slaughtered Bobby Robson's Ipswich Town 7-0 (Woodward 4, Reece, Badger, Dearden).

Alan Woodward, Sheffield-born, was a quick, hard shooting forward, and distinguished, his hair as steel-silver, and skills as sharp, as the knives made in his home city. Woodward was deadly from the penalty spot, and an effective corner taker, occasionally scoring direct from corner kicks with his dangerously hit, in-swinging rockets. He missed only three of the Blades' 168 league matches between 1968 and 1972.

Aside from that 7-0 smashing of Ipswich, though, Sheffield United then fell away, sharply, from the top of the table after October, leaving Manchester City, Leeds, Derby and Liverpool to ultimately fight out *the greatest ever title race.*

The Blades finished the season in a very decent tenth place, but a long way behind the top four. With an average crowd of over 33,000, United were the ninth best supported Football League club during 1971-72, and they repaid their terrific home support by scoring an average of nearly two goals in every game at Bramall Lane.

Alan Woodward, Billy Dearden and Tony Currie had scored a combined total of forty-one First Division goals, benefitting from a great supply of balls from winger Geoff Salmons, who started all 42 of their league games, along with right back Len Badger.

Sheffield-born Badger had joined United ten years earlier, and by the end of the 1971-72 season, had played over 300 league games for the Blades. He had formed a well-balanced full-back partnership with Ted Hemsley, after the swift tackling Hemsley had arrived at Bramall Lane in 1969, having played 235 league games for Shrewsbury Town.

Ted Hemsley had been a county cricketer, also, playing for Worcestershire in the County Championship since 1966. He was awarded his county cap in 1969, after Sheffield United had paid Shrewsbury £30,000 for the Stoke-born left back.

It had looked as though Trevor Hockey's career was over, though, after he had suffered a horrible leg break during United's 3-3 home draw with Manchester City on Saturday 12th February.

To great relief and unanimous applause from the 37,000 St Andrews crowd, Hockey did return on the opening day of the following season, away at former club Birmingham City. He even scored United's opening goal in the first half, and also started the move that ended with Alan Woodward scoring, to secure a 2-1 away win.

Billy Dearden was the third-highest goal-scorer in the First Division during 1972-73, with twenty league goals, behind only Pop Robson and John Richards, but the Blades hovered just above the relegation places for most of the season.

Dearden was a fearless, determined, hard running forward, and excellent in the air, qualities best illustrated by his virtuoso performance against Roy McFarland and Colin Todd on Saturday 24th March 1973, when he gave the reigning Champions the hardest of times, scoring twice in United's 3-1 win over Derby. Signed for a bargain fee of just £10,000 from Fourth Division Chester, back in April 1970, Dearden was a qualified plumber who was also a master at finding leaks in First Division defences.

Eddie Colquhoun was rewarded for his dominant performances in defence, by being recalled to the Scotland team on Wednesday 18th October 1972, for their World Cup qualifier against Denmark, in Copenhagen.

Scotland won 4-1, and a month later he kept his place for their home match against the Danes, at Hampden Park. Goals from Kenny Dalglish, making his international debut, and Peter

Lorimer won the game 2-0 for the Scots, setting them up strongly for a place at the 1974 World Cup Finals.

However, during his sixth and final game for his country, in February 1973, Colquhoun was torn ragged by a ferocious attacking trio of Allan Clarke, Martin Chivers and Mike Channon, as Scotland were hammered 5-0 by England in a St Valentine's Day friendly match, at Hampden Park. Manchester United's Jim Holton replaced Colquhoun, and he kept his place as Scotland qualified for West Germany.

Trevor Hockey finally left Sheffield United after playing sixty-eight league games, in February 1973, after a brief, but unforgettable time at Bramall Lane, joining Norwich City in exchange for Jim Bone.

Hockey, who was voted as United's Player of the Year in 1972, remains a cult figure for Blades fans, to this day, having driven the team upwards during their greatest ever three month period, between August and November 1971.

Following his participation in a five-a-side tournament in Yorkshire, Trevor Hockey died on Thursday 2nd April 1987, aged only forty-three, after suffering a heart attack.

Hockey's replacement in midfield was Watford's former captain Keith Eddy, who'd signed for United for just £35,000, back in August 1972, having played 240 league games at Vicarage Road. Eddy became a great midfield anchor for the Blades, calm and composed, his clever ball-playing skills regularly releasing the pressure from dangerous defensive situations. He also eventually succeeded Trevor Hockey as team captain, and became their regular penalty taker.

Keith Eddy played in all of United's final seventeen games of 1972-73, steering them away from the relegation zone, up to fourteenth place, and ten points above the bottom two clubs.

With Billy Dearden out injured for most of the 1973-74 season, United were stuck in mid-table, and ended up in twelfth place. Tony Currie was an England regular by the late Summer of 1973, but he also missed most of the remainder of the season after February, having suffered a knee cartilage injury.

Ken Furphy then replaced John Harris as the Blades' manager in December 1973, with Harris becoming the club's Chief Scout. Alan Woodward was their top goal scorer, with seventeen First Division goals, but the season was an exercise in mediocrity due to the combined losses of both Dearden and Currie.

Ted Hemsley did lift some silverware, though. During the Summer of 1974, he helped Worcestershire to the County Championship title, beating Hampshire by just two points. Hemsley scored 301 runs from eight matches, including a top-scoring 85 at The Oval, against Surrey, on Wednesday 22nd May.

United had announced a trading loss of £170,000, though, at the end of the season, so Ken Furphy was forced to sell his star winger Geoff Salmons to big-spending Stoke City, in July 1974, for a club record transfer fee of £200,000. Despite United becoming a stable First Division side, playing some good football, and with probably the most skilful player in England, Bramall Lane had attracted average crowds 11,000 fewer than in 1971-72.

THE 1974-75 TITLE RACE

Ken Furphy replaced Salmons with Tony Field, a £70,000 purchase from Blackburn Rovers. Field had scored forty-six goals in just 104 league games for Rovers, but they had all been Third Division goals. Field was skilful, but less of a team player than Geoff Salmons, and he brought a bit of an attitude which made him unpopular with senior players at United.

"He just didn't have the quality," claimed Len Badger.

One new recruit who did have the quality was Scottish goalkeeper Jim Brown, who'd signed for United from Chesterfield, for £60,000, in March 1974. Brown kept five First Division clean sheets during the final weeks of the season, conceding just seven goals in ten games.

Nevertheless, not many Blades fans expected United to be title contenders the following season, nor to finish just four points below the Champions. No, never in a million years did they expect that, particularly after Leeds United's dominant title-winning season of 1973-74, and Bill Shankly's Liverpool getting stronger and stronger.

With Don Revie appointed as the new England manager, and replaced at Leeds by Brian Clough, and then Bill Shankly also announcing his shock retirement from football in July 1974, the 1974-75 title race suddenly looked harder to call than in previous seasons. Even predicting a top two or three was difficult, so many top class First Division teams there were, but the Blades were never a consideration by anyone.

Stoke City were highly fancied, having stormed up the table during the last few months of the previous season, just beating Burnley to fifth, and winning a UEFA Cup place on the very last day of their season. As well as Geoff Salmons, Tony Waddington had also purchased Alan Hudson, a player as good as Tony Currie on his day, from Chelsea towards the back end of the 1973-74 season.

Bobby Robson's young Ipswich Town side were also highly rated, having finished fourth in 1973-74, and they had a terrific team spirit. Derby County had also returned to form, finishing in third place after taking only eight points from their eleven matches in November and December, following the resignations of Brian Clough and Peter Taylor. New manager, and their former captain, Dave Mackay had even strengthened his team, after buying Bruce Rioch from Aston Villa, and adventurously, he'd also paid £100,000 to Manchester City for Francis Lee.

Nobody could ever have predicted just how tight the 1974-75 title race would be, nor how many teams would have a go at it.

The season began with reigning Champions Leeds United visiting Stoke City, on Saturday 17th August, their first competitive match under Brian Clough.

33,534, the third largest crowd of the day, witnessed the beginning of a downfall, and the promise of a new dawn in English football. If Stoke City were not nailed-on genuine title contenders before the game, they certainly were after it.

Leeds had been forced to start the season without England stars Allan Clarke and Norman Hunter, both serving two match suspensions, but captain Billy Bremner was also awaiting the decision of the forthcoming FA Disciplinary Committee regarding his punishment for his dismissal in the Charity Shield, along with Kevin Keegan.

The first half was cagey. Leeds had never really turned up, but Stoke hadn't got out of second gear. After half-time, though, Stoke ran all over sluggish Leeds.

STOKE CITY		LEEDS UNITED
John Farmer	1	David Harvey
John Marsh	2	Paul Reaney
Mike Pejic	3	Terry Cooper
Alan Dodd	4	Billy Bremner
Denis Smith	5	Gordon McQueen
John Mahoney	6	Trevor Cherry
Sean Haslegrave	7	Peter Lorimer
Jimmy Greenhoff	8	Paul Madeley
John Ritchie	9	Joe Jordan
Alan Hudson	10	Johnny Giles
Geoff Salmons	11	Duncan McKenzie

Leeds had been forced to start the season without England stars Allan Clarke and Norman Hunter, both serving two match suspensions, but captain Billy Bremner was also awaiting the decision of the forthcoming FA Disciplinary Committee regarding his punishment for his dismissal in the Charity Shield, along with Kevin Keegan.

The first half was cagey. Leeds had never really turned up, but Stoke hadn't got out of second gear. After half-time, though, Stoke ran all over sluggish Leeds.

After fifty minutes, Alan Hudson won the ball in midfield, and he curved a pass around Giles to John Ritchie, twenty-five yards out and with his back to goal. Ritchie immediately played a square ball inside, to the edge of the D, where John Mahoney outmuscled Bremner's challenge, and then hammered a left-footed shot past Harvey, from twenty yards out.

Hudson, Salmons and Pejic played the ball calmly around Billy Bremner, as they slowly gained territorial advantage inside the Leeds half. Stoke's numbers swelled, as they pressed Leeds back into their own area, and Pejic's long, low hard cross into the Leeds box was flicked by Geoff Salmons, straight to the feet of Jimmy Greenhoff. Greenhoff turned Cherry inside out, before firing past Harvey. A deflection on the ball from Cherry's desperate lunge had actually beaten Harvey, who had dived right, as the ball ballooned over him, to his left.

Leeds were thoroughly under the cosh, totally unable to get the ball out of their own half, neither Giles, nor Cooper, nor Madeley, nor Jordan. Man of the Match Hudson dispossessed McKenzie inside his own half and broke through the Leeds midfield, feeding Ritchie, just to the right of the D.

John Ritchie strongly held off Cherry's challenge, before slotting the ball through Harvey's legs, from just inside the box, for a 3-0 thrashing.

Sheffield United started with a disappointing 1-1 home draw against QPR, in front of just 16,000 at Bramall Lane, while the biggest crowd of the opening day was at Goodison Park, where over 42,000 watched a tight, tough, goalless tussle between Everton and Derby County.

Liverpool were the season's strong starters, winning 2-1 away at newly-promoted Luton Town (Smith, Heighway), before drawing 0-0 at Wolves on the following Tuesday, and then beating Leicester City 2-1 (Lindsay (2pens)), in front of 49,398 at Anfield, to go third, one point behind both Carlisle United and Ipswich Town.

Surprise leaders of Division One, on the second Saturday of the season, though, were Carlisle United, who had beaten Chelsea, Middlesbrough and Tottenham Hotspur. They led Ipswich, on goal average, who'd won away at Spurs on the opening day, and then won at Arsenal on Tuesday.

On Saturday 24th August, Ipswich Town hosted Burnley, playing in their away kit of white shirts and claret shorts. Geoff Nulty upended Mick Lambert inside the area, in the first half, so Brian Talbot finished safely from the penalty spot.

Then, Talbot, Colin Viljoen, Lambert and Bryan Hamilton all strung together a fluent passing move, which ripped Burnley wide open at the back, and Trevor Whymark hammered the ball high up into the top right corner of Alan Stevenson's net.

On the following Wednesday, 28th August, Billy Bremner and Kevin Keegan were both banned for five weeks by the FA, a long period that covered ten competitive matches, for their bust up in the Charity Shield at Wembley. It was a staggering, astonishing, unprecedented decision, and also ripped the heart out of Leeds United's attempt at defending their title.

Bremner hadn't actually done so much wrong, except for responding to a sharp uppercut by an incensed Kevin Keegan, who'd been cynically chopped in the kidneys by Johnny Giles, from behind, only to turn around and see Bremner there.

For Liverpool, though, Phil Boersma played brilliantly during Keegan's absence, hitting six goals in his ten games wearing the number 7 shirt, including a hat-trick in their 5-2, finely tuned, disposal of Spurs on Saturday 7th September.

Sheffield United pulled themselves up into the title race with a 2-1 home win over Newcastle on Tuesday 27th August (Cammack, Field), and then they hosted second placed Ipswich Town on the following Saturday, with only 18,000 inside Bramall Lane, leaving two-thirds of their vast ground empty.

Alan Woodward's fierce shot, after 34 minutes, had smashed onto Laurie Sivell's post but the ball rebounded back off the Ipswich captain Mick Mills, and into the goal. Tony Field had probably the best game of his career against Ipswich, firing United 2-0 up before half-time, from Micky Speight's left wing cross, but he then scored one of the Goals of the Season, after the break.

Field ran from the halfway line, beating the rough challenge of Kevin Beattie, before turning George Burley inside out, just outside the penalty box, and then he skipped a desperate sliding tackle by Allan Hunter, inside the area. Tony Field then curled his shot beyond Sivell's dive, as the ball just dipped back inside the far post.

Nick Udall described the goal as "one of the greatest goals seen at Bramall Lane."

Mick Lambert took advantage of some absent-minded defending to convert Colin Viljoen's free-kick, ten minutes from the end, but United's scintillating performance, as well as the victory, had delighted their home crowd.

On the same day, Stoke City, who'd been mediocre since their opening day hammering of Leeds, hosted newly-promoted Middlesbrough, who had started steadily, and were up in the top ten. Halfway into the first half, though, Stoke broke Boro's tight barrier. Alan Hudson played a ball out wide to Salmons, then galloped on forward. Salmons passed back inside to Mahoney, and as Hudson advanced into the area, Mahoney lofted the ball up to him.

Hudson chested the ball, and he skipped around the outside of Boro captain Stuart Boam, who handled very deftly just as Hudson got behind him. John Ritchie hammered his penalty kick straight down the middle, as Jim Platt went right.

Before half-time, though, European Cup winner Bobby Murdoch guided a well-thought through-ball between two Stoke players, into the Stoke City penalty area, for their attacking right back John Craggs to poke back into the path of Graeme Souness.

From twenty yards out, Souness hit the ball sublimely, with the outside of his right boot, sending the ball spinning up into the top right corner of John Farmer's goal. It was a classic goal. Boro could defend for their lives, but they had quality players too.

	PL	W	D	L	F	A	PTS
Liverpool	5	4	1	0	9	2	9
Ipswich Town	5	4	0	1	8	3	8
Everton	5	3	2	0	8	5	8
Man City	5	4	0	1	9	6	8
Carlisle Utd	5	3	1	1	6	2	7
Stoke City	5	2	2	1	7	4	6
Middlesbrough	5	2	2	1	6	4	6
Wolves	5	2	2	1	7	6	6
SHEFF UTD	5	2	2	1	8	7	6

On Saturday 14th September, Manchester City ended Liverpool's unbeaten run, winning 2-0 in front of their biggest crowd of the season.

With 45,194 inside Maine Road, Colin Bell outfoxed Alec Lindsay, then drove a low right-footed cross into the area, and Rodney Marsh netted from inside the six yard box. In the second half, City broke again, with Bell galloping down the right wing, and crossing to Mike Summerbee on the left side of Liverpool's area.

Summerbee squared back inside for Dennis Tueart, in a central position, to tap in for their second.

Ipswich Town took over as the new First Division leaders after their 4-1 hammering of Luton Town (Talbot 2 (1 pen), Hamilton, Whymark), with only 17,500 inside Portman Road. Ipswich stayed at the top of the First Division for another month, after beating Chelsea 2-0 (Talbot, Johnson), on Saturday 21st September, and then hammering title rivals Stoke City 3-1 on the following Tuesday (Viljoen, Hamilton, Whymark), in front of a 24,470 home crowd.

Stoke responded to their Portman Road defeat by drawing 1-1 at home to Derby County on the final Saturday of September, after England World Cup teammates Geoff Hurst and Francis Lee had both scored. Middlesbrough also won, beating Spurs 2-1 (Armstrong, Mills), and Liverpool then lost their third game in four, 1-0 away at Sheffield United.

With a large 29,443 crowd inside Bramall Lane, Alan Woodward's second half goal had lifted the Blades up to fifth in the table.

Everton hosted manager-less Leeds United on that last Saturday of September.

Leeds had sacked Brian Clough on Thursday 12th September, after a reported "vote of no-confidence" from the players, and they were being caretaker-managed by chief coach Syd Owen and also Billy Bremner.

In front of nearly 42,000, Leeds illustrated that their problem had not been entirely the fault of Brian Clough, as Owen had frozen out the three new players who Clough had signed: Duncan McKenzie, John McGovern and John O'Hare.

John McGovern, in fact, would never again play for Leeds, but it might as well have still been 1971, when you considered Syd Owen's total loyalty to Don Revie's squad players in his team selection.

EVERTON		LEEDS UNITED
Dai Davies	1	David Harvey
Mike Bernard	2	Paul Reaney
Steve Seargeant	3	Trevor Cherry
Mick Lyons	4	Terry Yorath
Roger Kenyon	5	Paul Madeley
Dave Clements	6	Norman Hunter
Mick Buckley	7	Peter Lorimer
Martin Dobson	8	Allan Clarke
Jim Pearson	9	Joe Jordan
Bob Latchford	10	Mick Bates
John Connolly	11	Frank Gray

Early on, Everton's bearded left-back Steve Seargeant launched a fierce, left-footed, thirty-five yard rocket, that flew past the dive of Harvey and just inside the far post.

It was the first and the only league goal of his career, but what a goal!

Joe Jordan's flicked header, from Trevor Cherry's long ball, set up Allan Clarke's headed equaliser from six yards out, but then, Bob Latchford flicked on Connolly's left-sided corner, and Mike Lyons poached a goal from inside the six yard box.

In the second half, Connolly's looping cross had confused Harvey, and Dave Clements, the former Coventry City legend, clipped in from six yards for a 3-1 lead.

Yorath hit a late consolation, but Leeds were never doing anything more than making up the numbers, and Syd Owen's spell in charge resulted in as bad a record, if not worse, than Brian Clough's, especially considering he had Allan Clarke available for all of his games, while Clough missed him for a third of his games in charge.

On Friday 4th October, Leeds United appointed Bolton Wanderers' manager, and the former Blackpool and England legend, Jimmy Armfield as their new manager.

FIRST DIVISION LEADERS, 28TH SEPTEMBER 1974

	PL	W	D	L	F	A	PTS
Ipswich Town	10	8	0	2	18	6	16
Man City	10	6	2	2	14	11	14
Liverpool	10	6	1	3	17	8	13
Everton	10	4	5	1	14	11	13
SHEFF UTD	10	5	4	3	14	14	13

So what happened next at Elland Road? For the reigning Champions' first game with Jimmy Armfield in charge, Duncan McKenzie, their record signing, was selected to start alongside Allan Clarke and Joe Jordan, and he also scored twice as Leeds beat Arsenal 2-0, on Saturday 5th October.

Anyway, Liverpool overtook Ipswich Town at the top of the First Division, after Bobby Robson's team had earned just two points from five games in October 1974, badly missing right back George Burley for eight games, and their top scorer Bryan Hamilton for half of the month.

By the end of October, Liverpool led the league, just a point ahead of Manchester City, who were enjoying another great title-chasing season, their third in eight seasons. Rodney Marsh was having his best season at Maine Road alongside Dennis Tueart, and in front of their excellent, intelligent, and fluent passing midfield of Summerbee, Bell, Oakes and Asa Hartford.

Liverpool and City were just ahead of Ipswich, Middlesbrough, Everton, Stoke, Derby, Burnley and Sheffield United, but only five points separated those nine clubs.

On Saturday 2nd November, third-placed Ipswich Town hosted leaders Liverpool, with 30,564 tightly swaying inside Portman Road.

IPSWICH TOWN		LIVERPOOL
Laurie Sivell	1	Ray Clemence
Mick Mills	2	Tommy Smith
Colin Harper	3	Alec Lindsay
Brian Talbot	4	Chris Lawler
Allan Hunter	5	Phil Boersma
Kevin Beattie	6	Emlyn Hughes
Bryan Hamilton	7	Kevin Keegan
Colin Viljoen	8	Brian Hall
David Johnson	9	Steve Heighway
Trevor Whymark	10	Ray Kennedy
Clive Woods	11	Ian Callaghan
Mick Lambert	12	Peter Cormack

Late on in the match, very late in a match during which defences had been thoroughly dominant, and any subtle skills were irrelevant in a fast, frantic and physical fight, the game was won with a combination of route one football, aerial ability and controlled pace.

Steve Heighway, on tired legs, had taken a shot from just outside the Ipswich area, but it was muffled by the combined challenge of Mills and Harper.

Laurie Sivell gathered the ball and his long kick was flicked on by the leaping Whymark and then collected by Johnson, sprinting towards the Liverpool area. Johnson beat Hughes, and also outwitted Lawler, before squaring for Brian Talbot to slot home from six yards, simply, and win the match 1-0.

Two weeks later, David Johnson's second half hat-trick helped hammer hapless Coventry City 4-0, and then Ipswich Town returned to the top of the table.

On Saturday 23rd November, however, Derby County had beaten Ipswich Town 2-0 (Hector, Rioch), and Liverpool could only draw 1-1 at home to West Ham, so Manchester City could take full advantage with a home win against Leicester.

Playing only his third match for City, and his first of that season, was twenty-three year old forward Barney Daniels. Salford-born, Daniels was a former Manchester United youth team player who'd failed to ever break into United's first team.

He replaced the injured Mike Summerbee.

MANCHESTER CITY		LEICESTER CITY
Keith MacRae	1	Mark Wallington
Geoff Hammond	2	Steve Whitworth
Willie Donachie	3	Steve Yates
Colin Bell	4	Jon Sammels
Mike Doyle	5	Malcolm Munro
Alan Oakes	6	Graham Cross
Barney Daniels	7	Keith Weller
Phil Henson	8	Steve Earle
Rodney Marsh	9	Frank Worthington
Asa Hartford	10	Alan Birchenall
Dennis Tueart	11	Len Glover

Daniels scored twice, the only two goals in his nine starts for City, while Tueart and Bell scored the others in their 4-1 win over Leicester, to go top of the First Division.

At the top of the table, with City the new leaders, the title race was still wide open, with only four points separating the leading twelve teams.

Stoke City had dearly missed centre forward John Ritchie, though, who'd suffered a career-ending double leg break during their 3-1 defeat away at Ipswich on Tuesday 24th September.

Without their top scorer, Stoke's goals were mostly spread between Jimmy Greenhoff, Geoff Hurst and Geoff Salmons.

Stoke's problem, uncharacteristic considering their brutally tough defence, was that they'd conceded thirty-one goals from just twenty-four league and cup games.

So, on Thursday 23rd November, Tony Waddington paid a club record transfer fee of £325,000 to Leicester City for England's Peter Shilton, a World record fee for a goalkeeper.

FIRST DIVISION LEADERS, 23RD NOVEMBER 1974

	PL	W	D	L	F	A	PTS
Manchester City	19	10	4	5	27	23	24
Liverpool	18	10	3	5	24	13	23
Ipswich Town	19	10	2	7	25	14	22
Everton	18	5	12	1	23	18	22
Derby County	19	8	6	5	32	27	22
West Ham Utd	19	8	5	6	35	28	21
Stoke City	18	7	7	4	31	25	21
SHEFF UTD	18	8	5	5	27	29	21
Birmingham	19	8	4	7	30	25	20
Newcastle Utd	18	7	6	5	26	24	20
Burnley	19	8	4	7	32	30	20
Middlesbrough	18	7	6	5	25	24	20

The arrival of Peter Shilton at The Victoria Ground provided an immediate boost to Stoke's results. Over the following fortnight, they beat QPR 1-0 (Geoff Hurst), and then Leicester City 1-0 (Denis Smith), before they finally hammered Birmingham City 3-0 (Jimmy Greenhoff 2, Ian Moores) on Saturday 7th December.

Those three wins, all clean sheets for Peter Shilton, had lifted Stoke City to the top of the First Division for the first time in twenty-eight years.

Everton and Manchester City were just a point behind, with Liverpool and West Ham United in fourth and fifth place, and Ipswich, Burnley, Derby, Middlesbrough and Newcastle completed the top half of the table, all separated by just five points.

Derby County's title challenge looked a little weak, having been without captain Roy McFarland since his awful injury suffered back in May, while playing for England against Northern Ireland. By December, though, they were also without McFarland's England teammates David Nish and Kevin Hector, when second-placed Everton visited The Baseball Ground, on Saturday 14th December.

Late in the match, with a tight game headed for a goalless draw, and boring the 24,991 Baseball Ground crowd, Mike Bernard passed forward to Garry Jones on halfway. Jones strode forward, with Newton backing off, before halfway into the Derby half, he lofted a long high cross over to the left side of the Derby area.

The bearded Bob Latchford had made a perfectly-timed run, dividing Daniel and Webster, and he leapt to head the ball powerfully in off Boulton's far right post.

Now, Everton were the new leaders of the First Division.

DERBY COUNTY		EVERTON
Colin Boulton	1	Dai Davies
Ron Webster	2	Mike Bernard
Rod Thomas	3	Steve Seargeant
Bruce Rioch	4	Dave Clements
Peter Daniel	5	Roger Kenyon
Colin Todd	6	John Hurst
Henry Newton	7	Garry Jones
Archie Gemmill	8	George Telfer
Roger Davies	9	Mike Lyons
Jeff Bourne	10	Bob Latchford
Francis Lee	11	John Connolly
Alan Hinton	12	Jim Pearson

On the same day, Ipswich Town hammered Spurs 4-0 (Viljoen, Beattie, Lambert and Roger Osborne), and goals from Steve Heighway and John Toshack had also given Liverpool a 2-0 win over Luton Town.

High-flyers Manchester City, for whom Marsh, Bell and Tueart had scored twenty combined goals in their opening twenty-one games, were locked out by West Ham's back four of Coleman, Taylor, Lock and Lampard, and held to a tight, high-quality goalless draw at Upton Park.

Mervyn Day had saved superbly from Rodney Marsh during the last ten minutes of the match, after Hammond had headed Tueart's cross back into the six yard box.

The reigning Champions Leeds United, under Jimmy Armfield's thoughtful and calm management, were beginning to announce their presence back in the top half of the table, for the first time.

Duncan McKenzie, Brian Clough's star signing, had scored eight goals in the twelve games since he'd been reinstated to the team. Leeds hosted the league leaders Stoke City, on Saturday 14th December, and they won 3-1 (McQueen, Lorimer, Yorath).

	PL	W	D	L	F	A	PTS
Everton	21	8	12	1	30	19	28
Liverpool	21	11	5	5	31	16	27
Stoke City	22	10	7	5	37	28	27
Manchester City	22	11	5	6	29	27	27
Ipswich Town	22	12	2	8	32	18	26
West Ham Utd	22	10	6	6	39	29	26
Middlesbrough	22	10	6	6	34	26	26
Burnley	22	10	4	8	40	36	24
Derby County	21	8	7	5	34	30	23
Leeds United	22	9	4	9	31	25	22

On the Saturday before Christmas, Carlisle United sprung the biggest shock of the season by beating the leaders, 3-2 away at Goodison Park.

Joe Laidlaw scored twice, and then Les O'Neill completed the Cumbrians' brilliant win over Everton, lifting them up to twentieth in the table, and above Leicester City.

Ipswich had already beaten a beleaguered Leicester City 1-0 (Whymark), on the Friday night before Christmas, to lead the First Division on Christmas Day 1974.

Derby County's form had been patchy all season, and they were falling too far behind the more consistent teams to be seen as serious title contenders. The Rams visited Manchester City on Saturday 28th December 1974. City, themselves, had been slipping, from top to sixth, having failed to win any of their last three matches, and they needed a victory.

40,188 expectant fans filled Maine Road, but Roger Davies, Derby's tall and classy centre forward headed down Rioch's right wing cross. Francis Lee then touched back for Henry Newton, to strike a superb, right-footed, twenty yard shot beyond Joe Corrigan.

Asa Hartford carried the ball over the halfway line, and he found Marsh, just outside the area. Rodney Marsh laid the ball off, over to the right side of the area, *like Jairzinho to Carlos Alberto*, and Bell screamed in with a sharp, classy *Colin Bell* finish.

Then David Nish won the ball, just inside the City half, and he passed it forward to Francis Lee, out on the left wing, and closely marked by both Geoff Hammond and Colin Bell. Lee turned inside both of them, and then outran them to the corner of the penalty area. On the run, Lee fired the ball, right footed, high into the top far corner of Corrigan's net, and then he ran away, his arms aloft, punching the air, delighted.

Barry Davies's commentary became the stuff of legend, as Lee had created and converted the goal. "Interesting... very interesting! Oh! Look at his face, just look at *his* face!" Davies's voice found a fantastic falsetto note on that final *his* of his commentary, one of the greatest pieces of football commentary of all time.

"Interesting. Very Interesting" became the title of Barry Davies's interesting autobiography in 2007. Anyway, that 2-1 win had lifted Derby up to ninth place, just behind City, and only three points below leaders Ipswich Town, as 1975 arrived.

The big surprises of the season were Jack Charlton's Middlesbrough.

Runaway winners of the Second Division, back in April, and based upon a fundamental principle of defence in depth, and dynamic counter-attacks, with quality players to supply and execute those attacks. Boro rose to second place on Boxing Day, after blonde-haired left winger David Armstrong had scored the only goal in their 1-0 win over Sheffield United, with 31,879 filling all the Ayresome Park home stands.

On Saturday 28th December, Boro visited fourth-placed Everton at Goodison Park.

Craggs and Spraggon, Foggon and Hickton, Maddren and Boam.

Boro's players were like a Northern poet's dream come home!

And with quality players like Murdoch, Souness, Armstrong and Mills, they could play just as well as they could mix it.

41,105 Evertonians watched Boro fight back to draw 1-1, with Bob Latchford and Willie Maddren both scoring, and Middlesbrough became the sixth team to (jointly) top the First Division, that season, as the New Year beckoned.

As the Champagne corks were cleared up and the 1975 air had wafted into homes, only two points separated the top eight clubs, and five points were separating the top twelve. Newcastle United, with Malcolm MacDonald and John Tudor having scored seventeen goals between them, had two games in hand on the leaders, but so did Liverpool, who also had the best goal average.

FIRST DIVISION LEADERS, 28TH DECEMBER 1974

	PL	W	D	L	F	A	PTS
Ipswich Town	25	14	2	9	34	19	30
Middlesbrough	25	11	8	6	37	28	30
Liverpool	23	12	5	6	36	20	29
Everton	24	8	13	3	33	25	29
Stoke City	25	11	7	7	39	33	29
West Ham Utd	25	10	8	7	42	33	28
Burnley	25	11	6	8	45	40	28
Manchester City	25	11	6	8	31	33	28
Derby County	24	10	7	7	38	33	27
Newcastle Utd	23	10	6	7	33	31	26
Leeds United	25	10	5	10	35	30	25
SHEFFIELD UTD	24	9	7	8	31	35	25

It was the tightest title race of all time, with over half of the First Division still seriously striving for superiority. If you didn't know who won the title in 1975, you could not have confidently picked the winner from those dozen teams. But one of those dozen teams did eventually lift the 1974-75 Division One Championship trophy.

Due to the FA Cup, only two rounds of First Division matches were scheduled during the longest month. Newcastle United fared the worst in January, out of that top dozen, getting hammered by relegation battlers Tottenham, at St James's Park, on Saturday 11th January. A huge, expectant home crowd of 38,270 filled both of the Gallowgate and Leazes Ends, but Alfie Conn, Spurs' afro-haired forward, scored a first half hat-trick on his Tottenham debut, as they raced to a 0-4 half-time lead.

Spurs eventually beat Newcastle 5-2.

Manchester City then hammered Newcastle 5-1 at Maine Road (Geoff Hammond, Dennis Tueart hat-trick, Colin Bell), for their first win in seven matches, and the Magpies were the first of the dozen to be eliminated from the 1975 title race.

West Ham United also had a poor January, losing at Leeds, and then only drawing at home to QPR. The Hammers, despite the class of Graham Paddon and Trevor Brooking, and the rugged, toughness of Bonds, Taylor, Lock and Lampard, had lacked a truly top class forward. They also dropped out of the title race.

West Ham had beaten Southampton and Swindon Town, though, to reach the FA Cup Fifth round. They then beat QPR in the last sixteen, before the explosion of their young twenty-one year old striker Alan Taylor, a £45,000 signing from Rochdale, back in November. The Lancaster-born Taylor scored six goals for the Hammers during the Quarter-finals, the Semi-finals, and then in the Final against Fulham, as West Ham became the last-ever all-English team to win the FA Cup.

Of the remaining ten teams, Everton, Derby, Burnley and Leeds all took the maximum four points from their January games; Man City earned three points, while Ipswich, Liverpool and Stoke had gained only two points.

Sheffield United were held to a 1-1 home draw by Man City, before one week later, on Saturday 18th January, they visited White Hart Lane.

On a quagmire of a field after heavy rain before and during the match, and with puddles of water covering the pitch, exploding up around the players' boots as they simply tried just to stay upright. Sliding tackles just sent them gliding for several yards beyond the ball, which often just stopped in its track on a North London pond.

Both teams got used to it, though, and by the second half, Alfie Conn and John Duncan were both denied goals by the excellent Jim Brown, who handled the soaking, muddied ball very safely. Cyril Knowles, however, then crossed low from the left, and after the ball had got stuck in the penalty area mud, Duncan buried his gift of a goal past Brown's dive.

Tony Field flicked the ball beyond Pat Jennings seventeen minutes later, from David Bradford's cross, and Tony Currie whizzed in to force the grounded ball over the goal-line. As the game ticked over towards full-time, the Blades produced a superb team move from their own goal, across and up the pitch, and all the way to the back of Pat Jennings' goal.

Currie collected Brown's throw-out, and he passed wide to Badger. Len Badger advanced and played forward for Field, who lifted a forward pass up to Eddy, just inside the Tottenham box. Keith Eddy had ran late from midfield, but he'd met the ball perfectly, glancing it past Jennings for a 2-1 lead.

Just two minutes before the end, United secured a great 3-1 away win when Woodward raced forward onto Tony Currie's diagonal ground ball and then blasted his shot beyond Jennings.

Middlesbrough, in second place on New Year's Day, had lost 2-0 away at Ipswich, and they were then held to a goalless draw by lowly Arsenal on 18th January.

Jack Charlton's side subsequently dropped down to sixth place.

Everton returned to the top of the league on Saturday 18th January, after hammering Birmingham City 3-0 (Latchford 2, own goal). Ipswich, Burnley, Liverpool, Derby, Boro, Stoke, Man City, Leeds and Sheffield United were all close behind, though, with only five points separating them at the beginning of February.

Everton stayed at the top on Saturday 1st February, after their narrow 1-0 win over Spurs. Jim Pearson had scored his third goal of the season in the second half, with nearly 41,000 inside Goodison Park. Ipswich Town kept up the pressure in second place, though, with a 2-0 win over Wolves.

Kevin Beattie and the classy Colin Viljoen both scored first half goals, as Ipswich continued to battle for a League and Cup double, but Liverpool and Derby County had both lost, while Burnley were held to a 1-1 draw away at Birmingham.

32,007 warmed themselves up at The Victoria Ground, as seventh-placed Stoke hosted fifth-placed Manchester City. Victory for either team would have been crucial to their title hopes, but with both teams in such a precarious situation, defeat would make it very difficult for either side to sustain a serious Championship challenge.

In contrasting areas of their line-ups, both teams had had their troubles all season. Man City had struggled for defensive consistency, with Joe Corrigan, Tommy Booth and Colin Barrett all missing for lengthy periods, due to injury. Stoke, though, had also struggled without a top class goal-scorer, after John Ritchie's enforced retirement.

Jimmy Greenhoff was their top scorer with eight goals, but Geoff Hurst was just behind him, with seven goals.

However, with their stable, strong back four, in front of England's Peter Shilton, and the midfield craft and graft of Hudson, Salmons and Mahoney, Stoke City always had the ability to create chances, giving themselves that chance of winning matches.

Manchester City felt the full force of that ability on that cold afternoon.

After a tight first half, and just thirty seconds before the half-time whistle, Alan Hudson cleverly dinked the ball around the outside of Hammond, and then he left the City defender behind, with an explosive burst of pace. Hudson then crossed from the right edge of the City area, for the bearded, Stoke-born Ian Moores to head past MacRae, just inside the near post.

Into the second half, Hudson threw the muddy ball to Jimmy Greenhoff, who returned it. Hudson rode Donachie's desperate challenge, then he played a one-two with Moores, just inside the City area. From the edge of the area, and deep in mud, Alan Hudson guided the ball around Tommy Booth, and beyond MacRae's dive.

The ball crept just inside the far right post.

Eight minutes before the end, John Mahoney tackled Tueart on the edge of his own area, and Hudson picked the ball up, before playing it forward to Geoff Salmons. Salmons fed Geoff Hurst, out wide left. Hurst outfoxed his marker, Mike Summerbee, who slipped in the mud. Hurst crossed from the edge of the area for the diving Moores to head home from six yards.

Then Denis Smith won the ball inside his own half, inside the dying minutes, and he galloped, through the traffic, into the City half. Smith steered the ball to Moores right on the edge of the penalty area, who guided a wall pass out to Hurst on the left side of the City area. Geoff Hurst lifted the ball, first time, over MacRae for Stoke's fourth goal, to go third in the First Division.

On the following Saturday, after that 4-0 win, Stoke rose to second place, when goals from both Greenhoff and Hudson helped beat Spurs 2-0 away at White Hart Lane.

Everton remained top, though, despite losing 2-1 at ninth-placed Manchester City, after Bell and Tueart had both scored to keep City just in the title race.

Liverpool hammered fellow title favourites Ipswich 5-2, after John Toshack and Kevin Keegan absolutely terrorised Kevin Beattie and Allan Hunter all afternoon. Brian Hall, Toshack (twice), Alec Lindsay and Peter Cormack had all scored for the rampant Reds.

On Saturday 15th February, however, Malcolm MacDonald was in sensational form as Newcastle United thrashed Liverpool 4-1. This was the wild man MacDonald, hairier, heavily moustached and side-burned, and not the hair salon, *boutique-beautied* Supermac who'd boldly bragged about how many he'd bury past Ray Clemence, during the 1974 FA Cup Final, and then not touched the ball.

He was in an astonishing mood, terrifying the Liverpool defence, that had badly missed Tommy Smith. Supermac *was* Supermac that day, scoring twice and also setting up John Tudor's goal, while Stuart Barrowclough netted their fourth, thrilling over 38,000 Geordie home fans.

Stoke City should have capitalised at home to Wolves, but they were held to a 2-2 draw, after Terry Conroy's and Eric Skeels' goals were levelled by Kenny Hibbitt and Frank Munro. Even so, due to Liverpool's defeat, and with Everton and Ipswich involved in the FA Cup Fifth round, Stoke returned to the top of the First Division.

FIRST DIVISION LEADERS, 15TH FEBRUARY 1975

	PL	W	D	L	F	A	PTS
Stoke City	30	13	10	7	48	36	36
Everton	28	11	13	4	41	27	35
Burnley	30	14	7	9	50	44	35
Ipswich Town	29	16	2	11	41	26	34
Liverpool	28	14	5	9	42	31	33
Manchester City	29	13	7	9	39	40	33
West Ham Utd	29	11	10	8	47	37	32
Middlesbrough	29	11	10	8	38	32	32
Derby County	28	12	8	8	42	37	32
Newcastle Utd	29	13	6	10	45	44	32
SHEFFIELD UTD	29	12	8	9	39	40	32
Leeds United	29	12	7	10	39	31	31

Amazingly, the five point gap between first and twelfth places had remained steady during the six weeks since the New Year.

Burnley were the First Division's top scorers, and having another superb season following their surprising and refreshing successes of the previous season, after being the only serious pursuers of runaway leaders Leeds United, along with Liverpool, before Christmas.

Missing out on a UEFA Cup place only on goal average, on the very last day of the season, finishing sixth, Burnley had sold captain and midfield playmaker Martin Dobson to Everton, back in August, and then Geoff Nulty went to Newcastle.

There was no way that Burnley should have been in this title race. Their diminutive Welsh midfield dynamo Brian Flynn, and Geordie attacker Ray Hankin had, however, boosted Burnley's superlative team spirit and once again, the Clarets played well above themselves.

On the final Saturday of February, Burnley beat Sheffield United 2-1 at Turf Moor, as Peter Noble and Paul Fletcher both scored to lift the Clarets up to second place.

On Saturday 1st March, Burnley visited Coventry, having dropped to third place, following Everton's midweek 3-1 home win over Luton (Telfer, Dobson, Latchford).

COVENTRY CITY		BURNLEY
Neil Ramsbottom	1	Alan Stevenson
Graham Oakey	2	Bill Ingham
Chris Cattlin	3	Keith Newton
Les Cartwright	4	Brian Flynn
John Craven	5	Colin Waldron
Alan Dugdale	6	Jimmy Thomson
Brian Alderson	7	Peter Noble
Willie Carr	8	Ray Hankin
Mick Ferguson	9	Paul Fletcher
Alan Green	10	Doug Collins
Tommy Hutchison	11	Leighton James

Burnley outplayed and outperformed an apathetic Coventry side, winning 3-0, with the great Willie Carr playing his penultimate game for the Sky Blues, before he moved to Wolves.

On St David's Day, Welsh international forward Leighton James, Burnley's top scorer, had given the Clarets a 1-0 half-time lead, before Peter Noble and Paul Fletcher completed their rout after the break.

Everton had beaten Arsenal 2-0 (Dobson, Lyons) to stay top, at Highbury, though, while Middlesbrough beat Stoke City 2-0 in front of an Ayresome Park crowd of nearly 26,000, Hickton and Foggon winning a big 'un.

On the following Saturday, the day of the FA Cup Quarter-finals, in which Ipswich, Leeds, West Ham and Middlesbrough were all still competing, Everton beat QPR 2-1 (Lyons, Latchford), and they established a two point lead at the top.

Derby County had also won 2-1, away at Chelsea, with the recalled Alan Hinton scoring his second goal of the season, as the Rams rose to third place.

FIRST DIVISION LEADERS, 8TH MARCH 1975

	PL	W	D	L	F	A	PTS
Everton	32	14	14	4	48	29	42
Burnley	33	16	8	9	56	46	40
Derby County	32	15	8	9	49	43	38
Liverpool	32	14	9	9	44	33	37
Stoke City	32	13	11	8	48	38	37
Ipswich Town	32	17	2	13	45	30	36
Leeds United	32	14	8	10	45	34	36
Man City	32	14	8	10	44	44	36
SHEFF UTD	32	14	8	10	42	42	36
Middlesbrough	32	12	11	9	40	33	35

Leeds United had managed to pull themselves up into the unlikeliest of title races, after their dreadful start. Duncan McKenzie's frenzy of goals, hitting eleven in just eighteen First Division matches between October and February, had set them on their way, and Leeds had achieved a ten match unbeaten run since Christmas.

A succession of tough games took their toll on Jimmy Armfield's team, however. March saw their FA Cup Sixth round epic tie against Ipswich go to a THIRD replay, before losing 2-3 at Filbert Street.

Leeds' 4-0 aggregate victory over Anderlecht in the European Cup Quarter-finals, also in March, resulted in them being drawn against Barcelona's all-stars in the last four.

Leeds United had played eleven games in March, eleven tough games, and all but one were won or lost by just a single goal, or drawn.

Following their superb, high-quality 0-0 home draw against leaders Everton on Saturday 15th March, with over 50,000 overfilling their mighty Elland Road, Leeds took just three points from their next five league games.

They could have defended their title successfully, but Barcelona weighed heavily on Leeds United's memories. Most of their players remembered their great seasons of 1970, '71, '72 and '73, when they'd fought 100% on all fronts, but won just two Cups.

In the end, Leeds United were harshly treated, and certainly cheated, during the European Cup Final against Bayern Munich, in May, but they won nothing yet again.

Leaders Everton, who'd looked hot title favourites on that Saturday of 8th March, had a dreadful second half of the mad month. Following their superb draw away at Leeds, they were beaten 2-0 by Middlesbrough, before being held to a 1-1 home draw by title rivals Ipswich, and then hammered by their "bogey team" Carlisle United.

Joe Laidlaw, Dennis Martin and Frank Clarke all scored in the Cumbrians' 3-0 win over the league leaders, with over 16,000 inside Brunton Park.

To this day, Carlisle United are the only Football League club with a 100% winning league record over Everton.

Ipswich Town won a brilliant game on Saturday 15th March, at home to Newcastle United, coming back from 2-4 down, to win the Match of the Season by 5-4.

After two goals apiece for Malcolm MacDonald and John Tudor, Bryan Hamilton completed his hat-trick, while Allan Hunter and David Johnson finished off their team's magical comeback victory.

On the following Tuesday, Ipswich won 2-1 away at third-placed Stoke City. Trevor Whymark and Mick Mills both scored second half goals, as Town pulled themselves level with Everton at the top.

On Saturday 22nd March, 46,269 attended Goodison Park for the Clash of the Titans, Everton versus Ipswich Town.

EVERTON		IPSWICH TOWN
Dai Davies	1	Laurie Sivell
Peter Scott	2	George Burley
Steve Seargeant	3	Mick Mills
Dave Clements	4	Brian Talbot
Roger Kenyon	5	Allan Hunter
John Hurst	6	Kevin Beattie
Mick Buckley	7	Bryan Hamilton
Jim Pearson	8	Colin Viljoen
Mike Lyons	9	David Johnson
Bob Latchford	10	Trevor Whymark
Garry Jones	11	Mick Lambert

Today, Sky Sports HD1 would have the match broadcast live at 4.00pm on a Sunday, and they'd call the day Sky Super Sunday.

Trevor Whymark scored early on, from a wonderful Ipswich counter-attack, orchestrated by Viljoen's calmness and intelligence, as Ipswich fully imposed their clear on-field superiority.

It all fell apart after half-time, for Ipswich, though. Midfield anchor Brian Talbot was sent off, and their outstanding winger Mick Lambert was then injured, and he had to be replaced by Clive Woods.

Everton capitalised on their one-man advantage and Mike Lyons poached on a defensive mistake to level the scores.

Even so, that was still a great away point for Ipswich, and it was they, along with Stoke, rather than the two Merseyside giants, who were both warm favourites for the title.

Ipswich Town could also still win the League and Cup double, though, as they were red-hot favourites for the FA Cup.

Liverpool, though, wouldn't give up. After drawing 0-0 at home to Sheffield United, on 15th March, with nine of their eleven that started the European Cup Final, two years later, against Borussia Moenchengladbach.

Clemence, Smith, Neal, McDermott, Hughes, Keegan, Heighway, Kennedy and Callaghan became their European Cup-winning legends.

They then, also disappointingly, drew 1-1 away at Leicester City, before disposing of relegation fodder Tottenham 2-0, away at White Hart Lane, on Saturday 22nd March (Keegan, Cormack).

Ninth-placed Sheffield United hosted FA Cup Semi-finalists West Ham on the same day, with 25,527 inside Bramall Lane. The Blades had been plugging away, just a handful of points behind the leaders, and they'd won five of their nine First Division games since the New Year, losing only once.

Bobby Gould netted after Alan Taylor and John McDowell had both combined to set him up, ten yards out, but the Blades came straight back. Tony Currie crossed deep from the left. Alan Woodward killed the ball instantly inside the right side of the area, then he took on and beat Paddon. Woodward crossed low and hard over to the far post. Mervyn Day saved Colquhoun's initial snapshot, but the ball ricocheted to Currie on the left post, who finished calmly as the West Ham defence all appealed for offside.

Trevor Brooking's right-sided corner was headed back into the penalty area by Graham Paddon, and Billy Jennings' overhead bicycle kick from eighteen yards was completely misjudged by Jim Brown, though, as West Ham led 2-1 at half-time.

SHEFFIELD UNITED		WEST HAM UNITED
Jim Brown	1	Mervyn Day
Len Badger	2	Keith Coleman
David Bradford	3	Frank Lampard
Keith Eddy	4	John McDowell
Eddie Colquhoun	5	Tommy Taylor
John Flynn	6	Kevin Lock
Alan Woodward	7	Billy Jennings
Micky Speight	8	Graham Paddon
Steve Cammack	9	Alan Taylor
Tony Currie	10	Trevor Brooking
Tony Field	11	Bobby Gould

After the break, Brown's long throw was carried over halfway by Steve Cammack, who lofted a long, high pass up to Woodward on the left side of the area. Woodward skipped outside Coleman's challenge, and then inside Kevin Lock, before he finished low just inside Mervyn Day's near post.

Tony Currie won the ball inside his own half, and he played a one-two with Woodward, out on the right wing touchline, before advancing into West Ham's half.

Currie teased, tormented and turned Kevin Lock this way and that, looking both right and left, before he just placed the ball, left-footed, and so sweetly just inside Mervyn Day's far post.

"What about that?!" John Motson exclaimed squeakily.
"A quality goal by a quality player!"

The title race was down to only eight teams with only about eight games remaining, as Spring dawned. Everton remained two points ahead, but the pack had closed. Ipswich, Boro, Liverpool, Stoke, Burnley, Derby and Sheffield United were all still within five points of the leaders.

Liverpool then hit some great form, just at the right time. On Tuesday 25th March, they had their revenge on Newcastle United. Kevin Keegan opened the scoring, before John Toshack doubled their lead before half-time. Toshack, and former Newcastle midfield architect Terry McDermott then made it 4-0 after the break, but in truth, Liverpool were in terrifying form and they could have hit double figures, so demoralised were Newcastle.

On the following Saturday, a second half Kevin Keegan penalty kick was enough to scrape a more hard-worked win over FA Cup Semi-finalists Birmingham City. That win sent Liverpool back to the top of the First Division.

On Easter Monday, 31st March 1975, Liverpool visited title rivals Stoke City, with nearly 46,000 filling The Victoria Ground. Stoke were boosted by the return of Terry Conroy, following an injury that had kept him out of action for the last seven months. Since his return, Conroy had scored five league goals in three matches.

Stoke won 2-0, even without their leader and inspiration Denis Smith, who'd broken his leg earlier in the month. Terry Conroy scored in each half, giving him seven goals from their last four matches, as Everton overtook Liverpool, following their 1-0 home win over Coventry City (Martin Dobson), while Stoke City rose to third in the table, just a point behind the leaders.

STOKE CITY		LIVERPOOL
Peter Shilton	1	Ray Clemence
John Marsh	2	Tommy Smith
Alan Dodd	3	Phil Neal
Eric Skeels	4	Phil Thompson
Danny Bowers	5	Peter Cormack
John Mahoney	6	Emlyn Hughes
Terry Conroy	7	Kevin Keegan
Jimmy Greenhoff	8	Brian Hall
Geoff Hurst	9	Steve Heighway
Alan Hudson	10	Ray Kennedy
Geoff Salmons	11	Terry McDermott

	PL	W	D	L	F	A	PTS
Everton	37	15	16	6	50	35	46
Liverpool	38	17	11	10	53	37	45
Stoke City	38	16	13	9	61	46	45
Ipswich Town	37	20	4	13	55	37	44
Derby County	36	18	8	10	61	47	44
Middlesbrough	37	16	11	10	50	36	43
Burnley	37	16	9	12	62	58	41
Man City	37	16	8	13	48	40	40
SHEFF UTD	36	15	10	11	47	47	40

Derby County were in even greater form though, and they'd beaten Burnley 5-2 on Easter Monday (Rioch, Nish, Davies, Hector 2), but then on the following night, Tuesday 1st April, they also defeated Man City 2-1 (Bruce Rioch 2).

On Saturday 5th April, Kevin Hector gave the Rams a half-time 1-0 lead away at Middlesbrough, but David Mills equalised late on. Then, on the following Wednesday, at home to Wolves, Derby's second game in hand, their captain Roy McFarland finally returned from injury, after eleven months out of action, and Francis Lee's second half strike won the game 1-0.

Derby were the new and surprising title favourites. They'd become the seventh team to lead the First Division during 1974-75, but just at the right time.

Derby County led the league by two points, ahead of Liverpool, Stoke and Everton. Ipswich were three points behind, but they had a game in hand. Middlesbrough, Burnley, Sheffield United and Manchester City were now all out of the title race.

Derby remained two points clear at the top on Saturday 12th April, ahead of fellow winners Liverpool and Everton, after Bruce Rioch's second half header at home to FA Cup Finalists West Ham, with 31,336 inside The Baseball Ground.

Sheffield United then defeated Stoke City 2-0 (Eddy (pen), Field), with over 33,000 packed inside Bramall Lane, and Stoke were now also out of the title race, while Ipswich had rebounded from their FA Cup Semi-final replay defeat at Stamford Bridge by beating QPR 2-1 (Hamilton, Whymark).

Ipswich were still three points behind Derby, but with a game in hand. With just three games remaining, though, the margin for error was minimal, and on the penultimate Saturday of the season, Leeds took revenge on Ipswich for their FA Cup Sixth round epic defeat, winning 2-1 at Elland Road (Trevor Cherry, Carl Harris).

Middlesbrough then beat Liverpool 1-0 (Alan Foggon), with over 34,000 inside Ayresome Park, a defeat that eliminated the Reds from the title race, as Derby County drew 0-0 away at Leicester City. Third-placed Everton then hosted Sheffield United in a must-win match at Goodison Park.

Sheffield United had been quietly tracking the top six teams, sitting nicely at the foot of the top ten since November, but they were beginning to show some steel teeth. Their 1-0 defeat away at Arsenal at the end of March had been the only defeat from their last eight games, and they were on the very top of their game when they visited Everton on Saturday 19th April.

EVERTON		SHEFFIELD UNITED
Dai Davies	1	Jim Brown
Mike Bernard	2	Len Badger
Dave Clements	3	David Bradford
Mick Buckley	4	Keith Eddy
Roger Kenyon	5	Eddie Colquhoun
John Hurst	6	John Flynn
Garry Jones	7	Alan Woodward
Martin Dobson	8	Micky Speight
Bob Latchford	9	Billy Dearden
David Smallman	10	Tony Currie
Jim Pearson	11	Tony Field
George Telfer	12	Colin Franks

Since the beginning of April, the Blades had beaten Stoke City 2-0 and drawn with Leeds, but with a mere 38,000 filling just two-thirds of Goodison Park for Everton's final home game, a superb and pulsating match that saw the Toffeemen race away to a 2-0 half-time lead.

Keith Eddy had been given the Sheffield United captaincy at the end of January, taking some of the pressure off Tony Currie. "Keith Eddy is more than a good captain," Ken Furphy illuminated his captain's value.

"He is also a brilliant player and tactician. The trouble is, I want two Keith Eddy's in my side, one in the back four and another in midfield." That might have made the Blades a Great Team.

David Smallman, a £70,000 signing from Wrexham, was deputising for the suspended Mick Lyons, and starting only his third First Division game. Smallman put Everton 1-0 up with his first goal for the club, and then a Garry Jones penalty kick doubled their lead before half-time.

Following a surprise spell of sustained pressure from United, just a few minutes into the second half, Keith Eddy headed Alan Woodward's corner kick past Dai Davies. Then, with just over a quarter-hour remaining, Len Badger's right wing cross was challenged in the air by both Dai Davies and David Bradford. Bradford's pressure ensured that Davies couldn't cleanly catch the ball, and it dropped for Billy Dearden to pounce and place the ball into the net.

The Blades completed their storming 3-2 comeback win, when Tony Field was sent free down the right, and he crossed into Everton's area. Tony Currie slipped in, took a touch, and then fired the ball just inside Davies' right post.

The Blades had lifted themselves up to seventh, with two games in hand on most of the teams above them, and they'd given themselves a great chance, with three winnable games remaining, to qualify for Europe for the first time in their history.

On Wednesday night, 23rd April, Ipswich Town visited Manchester City, needing a win to maintain their slim hopes of catching Derby. Despite being third at Christmas, City were now even out of the race for UEFA Cup places, and a below-average crowd of just 29,000 watched the match.

Colin Bell opened the scoring, collecting a square pass from Tueart and belting the ball, with the outside of his right boot, past the flying Laurie Sivell's hand, into the top right corner of the goal.

Town's joint-top goal-scorer Johnson was injured, and replaced by Clive Woods, but even though Bryan Hamilton equalised for Ipswich in the second half, the draw was not good enough for them.

MANCHESTER CITY		IPSWICH TOWN
Joe Corrigan	1	Laurie Sivell
Geoff Hammond	2	George Burley
Willie Donachie	3	Mick Mills
Mike Doyle	4	Brian Talbot
Tommy Booth	5	Allan Hunter
Alan Oakes	6	Kevin Beattie
Asa Hartford	7	Bryan Hamilton
Colin Bell	8	Colin Viljoen
Rodney Marsh	9	David Johnson
Barney Daniels	10	Trevor Whymark
Dennis Tueart	11	Mick Lambert

For the second time in three years, without even playing, Derby County were crowned as League Champions.

FIRST DIVISION LEADERS, 19TH APRIL 1975

	PL	W	D	L	F	A	PTS
Derby County	41	21	10	10	67	48	52
Liverpool	41	19	11	11	57	38	49
Everton	41	16	17	8	55	41	49
Ipswich Town	40	22	4	14	61	42	48
Stoke City	41	17	14	10	64	48	48
Middlesbrough	41	17	12	12	52	40	46
SHEFFIELD UTD	39	17	11	11	53	50	45

On the final Saturday of the season, 38,000 filled The Baseball Ground for the visit of relegated Carlisle United. The Football League Championship Trophy was presented to Archie Gemmill, Derby's captain for almost the whole season, in Roy McFarland's absence. A carnival atmosphere weighed heavily on the actual match, which was a big disappointment. Carlisle came and fought for every ball, and every lost cause, just as they had done all season.

They wouldn't be playing in front of anymore 38,000 crowds for a few decades, at least.

Had it been three points for a win, back then, Carlisle would have earned forty points. They battled for a 0-0 draw against the Champions in their last match.

Colin Boulton, Rod Thomas, David Nish, Bruce Rioch, Roy McFarland, Colin Todd, Henry Newton, Archie Gemmill, Roger Davies, Kevin Hector and Francis Lee, the Champions of England, weren't able to win, but they did keep their fourth successive clean sheet at the end of the season, all achieved with McFarland back in the team.

Derby conceded only four goals in their last nine matches of that season. They'd hit form and, most importantly, consistency at the right time of the season. The injured Rod Thomas, Steve Powell and Peter Daniel all also received Championship medals, as did substitute Alan Hinton, who came on as a sub for Lee in their final match.

Peter Daniel, McFarland's replacement in central defence, was voted as Derby's Player of the Season, while Colin Todd, his defensive partner for most of the season, was presented with the PFA Player of the Year award.

Derby's top goal-scorer was Bruce Rioch, with fifteen goals from 42 matches. Colin Boulton also played in all forty-two league games, while Archie Gemmill had only missed one game. Rioch, Hector, Lee and Davies scored fifty-two goals between them.

At the end of the season, Sheffield United were held to a goalless draw away at Birmingham City, and they only missed out on a UEFA Cup place on goal average. Liverpool beat QPR 3-1, finishing the season as runner-up, two points behind Derby.

Liverpool's awful run of seven matches, from February and March, when they earned just six points, had cost them dearly, but they remained the most feared team in the First Division, and they went on to win the First Division Championship seven times over the following nine seasons, under Bob Paisley's management, as well as winning four European Cups.

Ipswich hammered FA Cup Finalists West Ham, gaining no consolation at all for their Semi-final defeat. Brian Talbot, Trevor Whymark, Kevin Beattie and Allan Hunter all scored in their 4-1 win, in front of a season high 31,592 First Division crowd packing out Portman Road.

It should be noted that, under a three points for a win system, as adopted by the Football League six years later, Ipswich Town would have won the title, finishing above Derby on either goal average or goal difference. Ipswich, though, had finished in third place, ahead of Everton, Stoke, Sheffield United and Middlesbrough.

The four point gap between Champions Derby and sixth-placed Sheffield United equalled the lowest ever gap between the top six from 1949-50, and the eight point gap between the top ten clubs was also a post-War First Division record.

Burnley were the First Division's top scoring team, with Leighton James, Ray Hankin, Peter Noble and Paul Fletcher scoring a combined total of fifty-two goals, but only two other teams, Newcastle and Chelsea, had conceded more goals.

For Newcastle United, Malcolm MacDonald was the First Division's leading goal-scorer, with twenty-one goals, and he and John Tudor combined for forty-two league and cup goals.

On Wednesday 16th April 1975, Supermac majestically crowned his season by scoring all five goals during England's 5-0 win over Cyprus, in their European Championship Group 1 Qualifying match.

FIRST DIVISION TOP TEN, FINAL TABLE 1974-75

	PL	W	D	L	F	A	PTS
Derby County	42	21	11	10	67	49	53
Liverpool	42	20	11	11	60	39	51
Ipswich Town	42	23	5	14	66	44	51
Everton	42	16	18	8	56	42	50
Stoke City	42	17	15	10	64	48	49
SHEFFIELD UTD	42	18	13	11	58	51	49
Middlesbrough	42	18	12	12	54	40	48
Manchester City	42	18	10	14	54	44	46
Leeds United	42	16	13	13	57	49	45
Burnley	42	17	11	14	68	67	45

Sheffield United had enjoyed their best-ever season. Sure enough, they had finished fifth back in 1962, nine points behind the Champions Ipswich Town, but *that* First Division did not have *this*

Ipswich Town, *this* Liverpool, *this* Derby County, *this* Leeds United, *this* Stoke City, *this* Everton, *this* West Ham, or even *this* Middlesbrough.

It was Sheffield United's best season, just missing out on the first and only European campaign in their history.

Alan Woodward was their top scorer with twelve goals, but Woodward, along with Tony Currie, Billy Dearden, Tony Field, and penalty King Keith Eddy, Sheffield United's *famous five*, combined for 47 of their 58 league goals.

For the fifth time in his career, Woodward had played in all forty-two of the Blades' league matches, as did Tony Currie, Jim Brown and Tony Field.

1975-76 promised progress, after United's on-field prosperity in 1974-75, but it promptly proved to be a huge problem. The Blades won just three points from their first eleven games, and they'd scored only five goals.

On Monday 6th October, manager Ken Furphy was sacked by Sheffield United, just four months after taking them to the tides of the English Channel, but a point short of Europe. The Blades remained in bottom place all season, and they were relegated to Division Two by Easter, finishing eleven points adrift of safety by the end of the season. Alan Woodward, who missed only one game all season, had top scored with just ten goals.

Their defence had been ripped apart, though, with Ted Hemsley restricted to only nine matches, due to a recurrent injury, while Len Badger had left Bramall Lane halfway into the season. Also, Eddie Colquhoun never had a regular defensive partner, while Keith Eddy was also injured for their final seventeen games, to really rub in the salt.

Len Badger, generally regarded as the Blades' greatest ever full back, left Bramall Lane for Chesterfield on New Year's Day 1976. He'd played 457 matches for Sheffield United, before then appearing more than fifty times for the Spireites prior to his retirement in 1977.

Ted Hemsley, Badger's full back partner, had played 247 league games for United before leaving for Doncaster Rovers in 1977. Hemsley played infrequently at the Belle Vue Ground for two seasons, before retiring from football in 1979, having made 514 Football League appearances for Sheffield United, Shrewsbury and Doncaster.

Hemsley continued to play for Worcestershire County Cricket Club, though, until 1982, eventually totalling 243 First Class matches while at New Road.

Ted Hemsley had scored 9,740 First Class runs, at an average of 29.33, including eight centuries and 53 fifties. He'd also taken 180 catches in First Class cricket, and scored over 4,000 runs in One Day games.

Billy Dearden left Sheffield United in July 1976, after scoring sixty-one goals from 175 league games. His career was blighted by injury after the 1974-75 season, and he last appeared in Blades' colours during their 1-4 home defeat against Tommy Docherty's youthful and resurgent Manchester United, in December 1975.

Dearden ended his playing career at Chester, and then Chesterfield, during the late Seventies. He made a welcome and much-heralded return to Bramall Lane in June 2011, however, after being appointed Chief Scout by United manager Danny Wilson.

Keith Eddy scored sixteen First Division goals, from midfield, from 114 matches, but he also left the Blades following their relegation in 1976.

He joined Pele, Franz Beckenbauer, Dave Clements and Tony Field at New York Cosmos, in the NASL. Eddy eventually became captain of the Cosmos, for whom he played thirty matches, and he was also a NASL All-Star in 1976.

Eddie Colquhoun finally left in 1978, after 363 league matches in ten years at Bramall Lane. He joined Detroit Express in the NASL, along with goalkeeper Jim Brown, for two years, playing alongside Trevor Francis at first, but then also Ted MacDougall, Steve Seargeant and Alan Brazil.

After the exits of most of their 1974-75 team, and without any money at all, Sheffield United sunk like a stone, dropping into the Third Division by May 1979, for the very first time in their eighty-seven year Football League history, but then they'd even continued falling, falling down to Division Four two years later.

Alan Woodward eventually became Sheffield United's leading post-war goal-scorer, scoring 158 goals in 536 league matches between 1964 and 1978.

He left Bramall Lane in 1978, moving to Tulsa Roughnecks of the NASL, and he played there for three Summers, from 1979 to 1981. Woodward played 47 NASL games for Tulsa, scoring fourteen goals, and he also recorded twenty-one assists.

In a 2004 BBC South Yorkshire poll, Blades fans voted Alan Woodward as Sheffield United's fourth-greatest ever player, just behind Jimmy Hagan in third place, and with Brian Deane in second place.

Clear at the top of that 2004 BBC South Yorkshire poll, though, Well Clear, *Twenty Lengths* clear, in fact, was Sheffield United's greatest ever player: their dashing, flamboyant, fair-haired, long-haired, and long-passing genius, whose vision, flair and skill has rarely been seen since.

Tony Currie had played only 313 league matches for Sheffield United between 1968 and 1976, 346 competitive games in total, before he left for Jimmy Armfield's Leeds United during June 1976 for a club record transfer fee of £240,000.

Born on New Year's Day in 1950, Tony Currie always brought something from the party with him. "One of the best long ball passers, probably I've ever seen," Trevor Brooking had said of his England teammate. Currie could take a ball in his own half, with his boots thick with mud, and place the ball at Billy Dearden's feet, running into the opposition's penalty area, just as he'd done against Man City in February 1972.

Currie also scored fifty-five league goals during his eight and a bit years at Bramall Lane, despite never being regarded as a prolific scorer, but more of a wonderfully creative goal-maker.

His goals were memorable, though, just like his famous winner against West Ham United in 1975, or his forty yard rocket launch against Liverpool in October 1971, but he was, amongst a decade of unconventional entertainers like Stan Bowles, Alan Hudson, Frank Worthington and Charlie George, the King of the Entertainers.

On Tuesday night, 4th September 1973, Currie famously sat on the ball against Arsenal. During the previous season, Alan Ball had sat on the ball, as Arsenal beat the Blades 3-2 at Highbury. It had merely been suggested that Tony Currie might repay the compliment as Arsenal visited Bramall Lane.

Currie needed absolutely no persuasion. Sheffield United were 4-0 up at half-time, after Currie had scored twice, and he then received the ball inside his own penalty area, when he just sat down on the ball, thrilling his 30,000 home fans.

Alan Ball, however, had been on the halfway line when he sat on his ball. Currie was in a much riskier, more dangerous position, and as he got up, he'd actually tripped over the ball, and Arsenal nearly scored. Len Badger was not at all happy.

Two months later, during a 3-0 home win over Derby County, Currie dribbled down the touchline, while waving to the John Street Stand supporters.

It was wonderful stuff.

What really annoyed Tony Currie, though, was the false accusation that he was a lazy player, that he didn't tackle, and that he wasn't a team player.

Currie certainly was a team player, and he cared deeply about the teams he played for, but particularly Sheffield United, who he loved, and he still loves to this day.

He did tackle. Sir Alf Ramsey would never have selected Currie for such an important game as that Poland game back in October 1973, if Tony Currie was lazy, didn't tackle, or if he was just an individual Maverick.

During their penultimate match of 1974-75, Sheffield United were hammering Leicester City 4-0 on 26th April. Currie had scored their third goal, before half-time, with a perfectly-placed shot from twenty-five yards out. After the break, though, Leicester improved.

Alan Birchenall broke out of his own half for Leicester, and the back-tracking Currie went to pursue him. Tony Currie put in a good tackle, and the pair collided after the ball had gone out. They just lay there on the warm weather-hardened pitch.

Birchenall then asked, "give us a kiss, TC," just for a laugh.

And so, Tony Currie did just that, and the pair of them laughed, then carried on with the match. The picture became an iconic image of the fun-filled football played during the Glam Soccer era.

That picture was also tabloid front page news, though, and it was even brought up in the House of Commons. The two players received letters from both right wing groups and gay rights publications, either threatening them, or offering awards.

The overreaction was ridiculous.

It was just a happy little football story.

Tony Currie lived and he loved the game, but after the Blades went down, he did feel that *the ship was sunk.*

After Jimmy Armfield had paid a Leeds United club record transfer fee for him, he called Currie, "potentially the greatest midfield player in Britain."

Don Howe compared him with the best midfield player he had ever seen, the player whose number ten shirt Currie would be wearing, Johnny Giles.

"Tony will rank alongside him one day," Howe had claimed.

Tony Currie played 124 league and cup matches at Leeds United, in three years, winning the club's Player of the Year award in 1978, before he moved to QPR in 1979.

Under a Terry Venables-managed renaissance at Loftus Road, Currie's experience and class was significant in the development of youngsters like Simon Stainrod, Gary Micklewhite, Gary Waddock, Terry Fenwick, Warren Neill and also Clive Allen, and then in 1982, QPR reached the FA Cup Final, Currie's first ever Wembley Final.

Currie faced one of the few players since *his time,* whose passing, skill, imagination and vision was truly comparable to his… Tottenham's Glenn Hoddle.

It could've been said, though, that Currie worked much harder than Hoddle. The Final went to a replay, and Hoddle won the Cup for Spurs with a penalty kick, after Tony Currie had tackled Graham Roberts from behind, inside his own area.

Tony Currie played his last match for QPR on Saturday 13th November 1982, before leaving after ninety-six league and cup games for the Hoops.

He retired in 1984, having played only a dozen matches at lowly Torquay United.

Currie had played a total of 528 Football League matches. I suppose that many players have played over 500 league games, but there aren't many for whom the majority of his 500 games were unforgettable.

Most of Tony Currie's games were probably, simply and totally unforgettable.
He was a total joy to watch.

You Can Do Magic, a 1973 UK top five hit single by Limmie and Family Cookin', was regularly played by Sheffield United's club DJ Ian Ramsay, and then adopted by Bramall Lane's home crowd and it was sung for their hero, Tony Currie.

> *"You can do magic, you took the raindrops that filled my eyes,*
> *And then put them back up in the skies,*
> *And then made the grey skies blue...*
> *You Can Do Magic, magic, magic. You can do magic, baby."*

The song became Tony Currie's signature tune.
It didn't matter that Currie was more of a Stevie Wonder fan, and he'd have preferred Music Of My Mind, Talking Book or Innervisions. It just didn't matter; "You Can Do Magic" was *his* song, and it's always played whenever he appears back at Bramall Lane.
If he'd been Dutch, Tony Currie would have played fifty or sixty international matches for one of the best teams in the World, but he was English, and he was subsequently ignored by Don Revie during the greatest years of his career.
He played only seventeen games for England, most of them for Sir Alf Ramsey, and then for Revie's successor, Ron Greenwood.

Frank Worthington put Tony Currie firmly in the same class of player as Thierry Henry, Dennis Bergkamp and Gianfranco Zola from more recent years.
Worthington, who was Currie's roommate at England internationals, also suggested that even though players had all called him TC, "TC really stood for Top Class."
Pele even signed and presented his Brazil shirt, "*TO TC, FROM PELE*", which is still exhibited at the Bramall Lane club museum today.

Tony Currie really was Top Class, probably not quite in the class of either Henry or Bergkamp, but it does give you a flavour as to how good he really was.
He was given few international accolades, both due to the teams he played for, and due to Don Revie's aversion to flair players. But he was certainly as good as Hoddle, Gascoigne and Scholes, after his time, and of English midfielders from his time, only Bell, Peters and Ball were as good.

BROOKING, BONDS AND BEST:
BLOWING BUBBLES

I N 1967, WEST HAM UNITED FANS were feeling pretty chirpy about themselves. They had won the European Cup Winners' Cup, just two years earlier, but also, as **West Ham fans claimed forever more**, West Ham had won the World Cup for England, just a year earlier, with their famous spine of Moore, Peters and Hurst.

Geoff Hurst had become the first player, and still the only player to score a hat-trick during a World Cup Final; Martin Peters, the best box to box midfield player in England, had also scored their other goal in their 4-2 win, while Bobby Moore was their captain.

Moore had found Hurst with a wonderful long pass for his third goal, and he famously wiped his hands on his shirt as he climbed the Wembley steps, so he got no mud on the Queen's white gloves, just before he lifted the Jules Rimet Trophy.

Moore, Peters and Hurst were three of the most valuable players in the World, at that time.

West Ham had also finished the 1966-67 season down in sixteenth position, in Division One, only seven points above relegated Aston Villa, but twenty-four points behind the Champions Manchester United.

The Hammers had scored eighty First Division goals, second in the goal-scoring charts behind Man Utd, but they'd also conceded eighty-four goals, the third worst defensive record in Division One.

West Ham's fans were still feeling pretty chirpy about themselves.

Manager Ron Greenwood had known, though, that time never stands still. Teams that stand around admiring past glories quickly go downwards, just as Man City, Bolton, Wolves, Ipswich, Blackpool, Aston Villa and Blackburn had all discovered during the previous five years.

Over the following three years, between 1967 and 1970, Greenwood introduced an extraordinary teenage explosion of local talent, that had exceeded all other youth developments between Busby's Babes back in the Fifties, and then Fergie's Fledglings in the Nineties.

Harry Redknapp had made his debut for West Ham, aged only eighteen, back in 1965, but then he became a first team regular in 1967, whilst still only nineteen years old.

Born in Poplar, East London, in March 1947, Redknapp was a good looking, golden haired young star, who had teenage girls galloping from the Upton Park terraces in their high-heeled boots, across the mud, to embrace Redknapp, before running back to their places, delighted, having avoided the approaching policemen.

Moreover, Redknapp was an elegantly skilled, hard working outside right, who was fast and direct with the ball, and he had a decent cross. After Harry, though, Ron Greenwood introduced Billy Bonds, Trevor Brooking, Tommy Taylor, Frank Lampard, Clyde Best, Pat Holland, Kevin Lock and John McDowell, most of them teenagers, over the five years between 1967 and 1972.

Just like Harry, four of them were all from either East London, or the London area, who already loved West Ham, or grew to love West Ham United as their only club.

Billy Bonds was born in Woolwich, and he started his league career at his local team, Charlton Athletic, when he was only eighteen.

He played ninety-five Second Division games at The Valley, before Ron Greenwood paid £50,000 for Bonds, in May 1967, when he was still only twenty years old.

Bonds made his league debut, at right back, on the opening day of the 1967-68 season, at home to Sheffield Wednesday, in front of a 29,606 Upton Park crowd.

West Ham lost 2-3, however, despite Geoff Hurst and Martin Peters both scoring.

Geoff Hurst was born in Ashton under Lyne, up in Lancashire, but he'd moved to Chelmsford in Essex, during the early Fifties, when he was still a boy.

He spent hours in his Avon Road council house back garden, and on the Chignall Estate streets, practising his football skills. Then at fifteen years old, and about to leave school, Hurst was offered a job at West Ham, painting their grandstand over the Summer months of 1957, with a place at West Ham juniors to follow.

After three years of hardworking, and with no guaranteed success at the end of it, Hurst finally made his West Ham debut, due to a critical injury crisis, against Nottingham Forest, in February 1960. His performance was mediocre, though, as Forest won 3-1, and he played only nine games over the following season and a half.

Hurst started to play more regularly after 1962, and in 1963-64, he'd scored seven goals in seven FA Cup matches, as West Ham won the Cup. Geoff Hurst also played in all 42 First Division matches during the following season, scoring seventeen goals, as well as winning a European Cup Winners' Cup winner's medal.

In 1965-66, Hurst scored forty league and cup goals in fifty-nine games, and then in February 1966, he played the first of his forty-nine games for England, a 1-0 win over West Germany, at Wembley. He played in five of England's seven pre-tournament friendlies, scoring one goal, but then lost his place behind Jimmy Greaves and Roger Hunt, for their opening match of the World Cup Finals, against Uruguay.

After England had won Group One, to reach the Quarter-finals, Jimmy Greaves suffered a gashed leg against France, and Hurst took his place in the team to face Argentina. After Rattin was sent off, and spent eight minutes arguing with the German referee about his dismissal, England gradually ground down the physical ten-men Argentines, and after 78 minutes, Geoff Hurst glanced in a header, from teammate Martin Peters' cross, past Antonio Roma. A star was born.

Despite Jimmy Greaves' leg having healed, he was not recalled for the Final against West Germany, despite having scored forty-three goals in fifty-four England matches, and the rest is history. They think it's all over?

It was for Jimmy Greaves. He played only three more matches for England, during the spring of 1967, scoring just one goal against Spain, but he wasn't picked again.

Including his World Cup Final hat-trick, Hurst had raised his total goals tally, for the 1965-66 season, to forty-five from sixty-four matches. He then scored forty-four from only fifty-five games the following season, including twenty-nine First Division goals, his best-ever total, and he was the second highest league scorer behind Ron Davies.

West Ham scored ten goals from their first four matches in 1967-68, but they'd conceded thirteen. In the fourth of those matches, a 3-3 draw away at Burnley, Trevor Brooking made his West Ham United debut.

Only sixteen years old, Brooking was born in Barking, and he'd graduated through the Upton Park youth system, before signing professional terms in May 1966, while still only fifteen.

An elegant forward, Trevor Brooking combined grace and delicacy with speed and excellent timing, with his goal attempts. He scored nine goals in just twenty-four games, during his first season. Hurst, Moore and Peters had scored the Hammers' three goals at Burnley, but it was Brooking who deftly passed the ball into Martin Peters' path for his third goal of the season, before West Ham's defence again collapsed, late on, and another deserved two points went amiss.

Martin Peters had made his debut back in April 1962, having been promoted from West Ham's youth system, aged just eighteen. Born in the East End back in 1943, in Plaistow, when East London, and the Docklands, were a premium target for the Luftwaffe, Peters had grown up *sparely built*, and he was fed cod liver oil to build him up. When he was still only sixteen, the slightly-built Peters was signed by West Ham manager Ted Fenton in 1960, the same manager who'd signed Geoff Hurst, and also Bobby Moore.

Fenton was an amiable, warm, old-style Eastender, always wearing a Trilby hat and smoking a pipe. However, he was replaced as manager by Ron Greenwood, after eleven years in charge of West Ham, just over a year after Peters had joined.

Greenwood was more scholarly than Fenton, innovative and introducing new skills, new tactics and training methods. He was also more detached, and much more private, than his more familiar and friendlier predecessor.

Martin Peters found Greenwood's ideas fresh and challenging, excited to learn new ideas. He credited Ron Greenwood for helping him develop into an international class footballer, "ten years ahead of his time," as Alf Ramsey eventually described him.

Peters became a first team regular during 1962-63, and he scored the first of his one hundred league and cup goals for West Ham in their 6-1 thrashing of Manchester City, on Saturday 8th September 1962. Peters missed only six matches in 1962-63, but the following season, he lost his place in the team, making just eight league starts after Christmas, and also played no part in West Ham's FA Cup winning campaign.

He came back from that disappointment, though, playing forty-seven matches during 1964-65, and helped the Hammers win the 1965 European Cup Winners Cup Final, at Wembley Stadium, the first ever floodlit football match with a 100,000 crowd.

In 1965-66, Martin Peters played 68 competitive matches, including eight England games. He made his England debut on Wednesday 4th May, during England's 2-0 over Yugoslavia at Wembley. The World Cup Final, on Sunday 30th July, during which Peters had volleyed England into a 2-1 lead, thirteen minutes before full-time, was his sixty-eighth match of that season.

On Saturday 18th November 1967, Frank Lampard made his league debut, replacing the suspended Billy Bonds at right back. West Ham lost 2-3 at home to eventual Champions Manchester City, and Lampard waited over a month for his second game.

On Saturday 23rd December, Lampard was selected in his preferred position of left back, despite him being right-footed, for their big pre-Christmas match at home to Tottenham. At just nineteen years old, Lampard was another of the many players who'd graduated from West Ham's junior sides, to become a club legend.

Born in West Ham, Frank Lampard became a quick, overlapping full back who relished supporting his attack. In front of a big crowd of 32,122, West Ham were fired up by the Upton Park roar, and Billy Bonds scored his first ever goal, before Brian Dear scored their second during the Hammers' great 2-1 win over a superb Spurs team.

Three days later, Brian Dear, *Stag*, scored a hat-trick in West Ham's 4-2 home win over Leicester City, with Brooking hitting their other goal.

Then, on Saturday 30th December, *Stag*, who was a member of the Hammers' ECWC winning team back in 1965, fired another brace, in another 4-2 win over Leicester City, but away at Filbert Street. Brooking and John Sissons scored their other goals.

Trevor Brooking scored two more goals in West Ham's 7-2 thrashing of Fulham, on Saturday 3rd February, but then he fired his first hat-trick in their 5-0 win over Newcastle, two months later. That win was only West Ham's seventh clean sheet of the season, from thirty-nine matches.

Ron Greenwood was seriously attempting to rectify West Ham's defensive fragilities. As well as introducing both Bonds and Lampard to his defence, playing either side of captain Bobby Moore, Greenwood had also paid £65,000 to Kilmarnock for goalkeeper Bobby Ferguson, during the Summer of 1967.

Ferguson had kept goal when Kilmarnock won their first, and only, Scottish League Championship title in 1965. He'd kept a brilliant clean sheet on the very last day of the 1964-65 season, away at free-scoring Hearts, as Killie won by the vital 2-0 score-line to snatch the title away from Hearts, on goal average.

As a result, he'd been picked to represent Scotland on seven occasions, during the following season, and the £65,000 that West Ham had paid for him was a World record transfer fee for a goalkeeper.

As a result, West Ham did improve, defensively, during 1967-68. They conceded *only* sixty-nine league goals, which was fifteen fewer than during the previous season, and there were seven First Division sides with a worse defensive record, while the Hammers continued to score freely, seventy-three goals, just seven less than in 1967.

In 1968-69, West Ham performed even better, conceding just fifty goals in forty-two games, despite the prolonged absence of Frank Lampard for almost the whole season, until the very last game of the season.

Johnny Charles, the first black player to represent West Ham, had deputised superbly.

One of the highlights of their season was an 8-0 hammering of Sunderland, on Saturday 19th October 1968, at Upton Park. Trevor Brooking and Bobby Moore both scored, but Geoff Hurst had scored six goals, and he scored a hat-trick in each half.

So dynamic was Hurst's supreme master class in attacking, Sir Matt Busby had offered a World record transfer fee of £200,000 to take him to Old Trafford, but Ron Greenwood declined immediately.

That clean sheet, though, was West Ham's sixth of fourteen kept by Bobby Ferguson during 1968-69. Overall, they conceded one goal or less in 28 First Division matches, two thirds of their season.

Things were improving, and West Ham finished in eighth position, their best finish for ten years. Hurst and Peters scored a combined total of fifty-five league and cup goals, while both players had also started all forty-eight of their matches that season. Bobby Moore, Billy Bonds and Harry Redknapp all missed just the one match.

Martin Peters, with a goal per game ratio of one in two, was turning into one of the most sought-after midfielders in the World.

His box-to-box work-rate, the timing of his runs into the opposing penalty area, and his unique ability to snatch "impossible goals" on the blind side of defences, had raised his value, at nearly twenty-six years old, to World record levels.

Peters did not last the entire 1969-70 season as a West Ham player, though, and he lamented his leaving of Upton Park. "Our one-touch passing game was based on flair and freedom of expression," he suggested, adding that the style of play that they'd embraced was unsustainable throughout a long, tough, First Division season.

"Our game was not designed to close space and grind out 1-0 victories," Peters confessed.

This was true. During the three seasons between 1967 and 1970, West Ham were involved in just thirty matches during which only one or less goals were scored by either West Ham or their opponents. In contrast, sixty-two matches had seen three or more goals scored by either West Ham or their opponents.

They were just as exciting going forwards as they were vulnerable at the back.

On Bank Holiday Monday, 25th August, one of their largest ever crowds, a massive crowd of 39,220, had filled Upton Park for the full league debut of eighteen year old Bermudan-born forward Clyde Best, for the visit of Arsenal.

WEST HAM UNITED		ARSENAL
Bobby Ferguson	1	Bob Wilson
Billy Bonds	2	Peter Storey
Frank Lampard	3	Bob McNab
Martin Peters	4	Frank McLintock
Alan Stephenson	5	Terry Neill
Bobby Moore	6	Peter Simpson
Clyde Best	7	Jimmy Robertson
Ronnie Boyce	8	Charlie George
Trevor Brooking	9	David Court
Geoff Hurst	10	George Graham
Roger Cross	11	John Radford

Due to the absence of both Harry Redknapp and John Sissons, Roger Cross also made his debut, and he cracked in a fierce strike from just inside the box, following a delightful reverse pass by Brooking, giving the Hammers a 1-0 half-time lead.

Late on, though, Charlie George's cross was diverted back into his own goal by Frank Lampard, and Upton Park was stunned. Roger Cross scored five goals in just five First Division starts for the Hammers, but he couldn't maintain a regular place, and he eventually moved to Fourth Division Brentford in the middle of March 1970.

That West Ham side, though, might well be the most honoured club side in Football League history. Six players were honoured by the Queen. Bobby Moore had been awarded the OBE back in 1967, having captained England to their World Cup triumph. Surprisingly, he was never, ever knighted.

Geoff Hurst was awarded an MBE in 1975, and then knighted in 1998. Martin Peters was awarded an MBE in 1978, while he was at Norwich City. Trevor Brooking was awarded an MBE in 1981, and then a CBE in 1999, before he was also knighted in 2004. Billy Bonds was awarded an MBE in 1988, and then finally, Clyde Best was awarded an MBE in 2006.

Harry Redknapp returned to the West Ham line-up on Saturday 20th September, alongside Moore, Hurst, Peters, Brooking and Bonds, and he scored West Ham's first goal in their 3-0 thrashing of Sheffield Wednesday. Geoff Hurst and an own goal completed the scoring. One day, Harry Redknapp will almost certainly be honoured by the Queen, for services to football, surely?

Over one month later, on Saturday 25th October 1969, 29,191 half-filled Roker Park, as West Ham's line-up of Ferguson, Bonds, Lampard, Howe, Stephenson, Moore, Redknapp, Peters, Brooking, Hurst and Best, gained another 1-1 draw after Peters' first half strike, and could eventually become the only team in Football League history with seven of their eleven players being honoured by Queen Elizabeth II? That septet of players played regularly through the Autumn of 1969, and also into the Winter of 1969-70, drawing at Southampton, beating Crystal Palace 2-1, losing at Liverpool, losing at Ipswich, hammering Derby County 3-0 (Hurst 2, Peters), before getting slaughtered 0-4 by Manchester City at Upton Park.

Pat Holland, born in Poplar, had made his league debut for West Ham back in April 1969, as an eighteen year old. Nearly 35,000 had filled the wonderfully and idiosyncratically terraced Upton Park ground to watch his debut, but Arsenal secured a fourth place finish with their 2-1 win.

On that very same day, Pat Holland signed a professional contract with West Ham, but he had to wait nearly nine months for his second appearance in claret and blue.

41,643, a club record attendance, squeezed into the tightly packed Upton Park on Saturday 17th January 1970, for the visit of Manchester United, a weakened United side that missed George Best, Denis Law and Alex Stepney.

West Ham, though, were themselves without Trevor Brooking, Harry Redknapp, Frank Lampard, John Sissons or Ronnie Boyce.

Peter Eustace had, however, recently joined West Ham for a club record transfer fee of £90,000, from his home city club of Sheffield Wednesday. Still only twenty-five, Eustace had played 192 league games for the Owls, at half-back, or midfield, while scoring twenty goals.

To have a club record home crowd turn up for your home debut must have been quite an experience, not to forget the nineteen year old Pat Holland, out on the right wing, who was playing only his second match.

Despite being under-strength, Manchester United still had five survivors from their European Cup Final triumph just two years earlier, Charlton, Crerand, Aston, Kidd and Sadler.

WEST HAM UNITED		MANCHESTER UNITED
Bobby Ferguson	1	Jimmy Rimmer
Billy Bonds	2	Paul Edwards
Bobby Howe	3	Francis Burns
Martin Peters	4	Paddy Crerand
Alan Stephenson	5	Ian Ure
Bobby Moore	6	David Sadler
Pat Holland	7	Willie Morgan
Jimmy Lindsay	8	Carlo Sartori
Geoff Hurst	9	Bobby Charlton
Peter Eustace	10	Brian Kidd
Clyde Best	11	John Aston

Despite roared on by Upton Park's largest ever crowd, West Ham's offensive instincts were strangled by a battling United performance and they were unable to score, but without the genius of George Best or the attacking menace of Denis Law, they weren't much troubled at the back, either.

The game ended 0-0.

The Hammers lost their next two matches, against Burnley and Coventry, though, and they were in slight relegation troubles by February, just seven points above the bottom two before their visit to second-bottom Sunderland on Saturday 21st February.

Geoff Hurst headed in Harry Redknapp's cross before half-time, and West Ham hung on for a tight 1-0 win, lifting themselves well away from relegation worries, and up to seventeenth place, where they remained…

…On Saturday 14th March 1970, Martin Peters played his 364th and final league and cup match for West Ham, during their goalless draw at home to Ipswich Town. Just under 21,000 attended Peters' last match, as another season to nothing wore on, before his £200,000 British record transfer to Tottenham. The deal, however, also included Jimmy Greaves, at thirty years old, moving from White Hart Lane to Upton Park.

One week later, on Saturday 21st March, West Ham travelled to Manchester City, for Jimmy Greaves' first game with the Hammers, having scored 342 First Division goals in just 478 games, for both Chelsea and Spurs, plus 44 goals in fifty-seven matches for England, and also nine Serie A goals for AC Milan in twelve matches.

After only ten minutes, Boyce released Pat Holland down the right wing. Holland crossed low across the wettest and muddiest of pitches, and Greaves danced inside Mike Doyle's desperate diving challenge, and as he side-stepped Joe Corrigan's lunge, he placed the ball into the empty net.

Jimmy Greaves had now scored on his debut for every team he'd played for.

Billy Bonds fired up a long, diagonal, dipping cross that Tommy Booth lost on the slippery mud. Holland's shot was parried by Corrigan, into the unfortunate path of Greaves, who finished again in front of an empty net.

Geoff Hurst then fired home from Peter Eustace's through-ball, before Francis Lee gave City some slight hope, smashing a long range shot, from thirty yards out, that slid in the mud beyond Peter Grotier's dive.

In the second half, Hurst headed in to secure a great win against the League Cup winners, and European Cup Winners' Cup Semi-finalists, before Ronnie Boyce then scored one of the greatest goals of all time.

Joe Corrigan hoofed a drop-kick, from the far right of his own penalty area, from where there was less mud, and a little bit of grass. From inside the centre circle, though, Ronnie Boyce volleyed the ball, first time, and it flew beyond Corrigan, who was returning to his goal area. The ball bounced once inside the six yard box, before burying itself in the bottom of the bewildered keeper's net.

All of the West Ham players went wild with delight at such *"An Unbelievable Goal!"*, as David Coleman exclaimed. Joe Corrigan said later, "just for a second, that day, I thought we were playing with two balls."

Ronnie Boyce had first played First Division football for West Ham back in October 1960, aged only seventeen, and he'd scored their winning goal in the 1964 FA Cup Final, against Preston. He also won a European Cup Winners' Cup winner's medal, the following year. Born in East Ham, Ronnie Boyce played 332 league and cup games for the Hammers, before leaving Upton Park after the 1972-73 season.

After that superb 5-1 away win, West Ham fans had thought that they'd actually had the better of the deal that took Martin Peters to Tottenham. They were wrong.

In October 1970, Tommy Taylor signed for West Ham, from Orient, for £78,000, having played 114 league games at Brisbane Road, and helping them up into Division Two, as Third Division Champions in 1969-70, after he'd played in all of their forty-six league matches. Taylor was still only nineteen, however, when he made his First Division debut alongside Bobby Moore, replacing Alan Stephenson at centre half.

Tommy Taylor was the first of a handful of teenage talent, Ron Greenwood's second phase of his youth revolution, *his Teenage Rampage,* between 1970 and 1973.

Taylor brought some seriousness, and some defensive command to the middle of the West Ham defence.

43,322 packed Upton Park for West Ham's great comeback 2-2 draw against Spurs, on Saturday 17th October. For the second time inside the same calendar year, West Ham had smashed their previous record home attendance, and their crowd that day remains West Ham's biggest ever.

Peter Eustace and Geoff Hurst both scored, after Mullery and England had given Tottenham an early lead.

Never was the Upton Park roar so loud as when Hurst broke clear to beat Pat Jennings for his second half equaliser.

On Hallowe'en 1970, John McDowell made his West Ham debut at home to Blackpool, at right back. Another local boy, nineteen years old, born in East Ham, McDowell had graduated from the Hammers' youth team, but more importantly, his introduction into West Ham's back four had released Billy Bonds to play a more protective, and also productive role in their midfield.

It was a transformation of the West Ham formation that was not dissimilar to that at Highbury, after Peter Storey had moved into Arsenal's midfield.

West Ham United beat Blackpool 2-1, through goals from both Jimmy Greaves and Peter Eustace, but things went badly wrong thereafter. Of their next ten league matches, West Ham lost eight, yet they won only once, a superb 4-2 away win at Derby County on Saturday 5th December, with nearly 31,000 inside The Baseball Ground, inspired by a virtuoso midfield performance from Trevor Brooking.

That game was also memorable for being Jimmy Greaves' 500th Football League game of his career, and after sixteen minutes, he celebrated in style, zipping past both Dave Mackay and Alan Durban, before dinking the ball beyond Les Green.

Alan Durban fired two superb long range shots in reply, but Trevor Brooking strolled through the Derby midfield, in the mud, before driving the ball into the far corner of the goal, levelling the scores just before half-time.

Bonds, Brooking and Eustace broke the ball out of defence, twenty minutes before the end, and Clyde Best blasted a twenty yard strike high into the Derby goal.

Derby were then awarded a penalty, after Peter Eustace was ruled to have fouled Archie Gemmill.

Bobby Ferguson dived to his right and brilliantly pushed Mackay's penalty kick away to safety, before Brooking found Clyde Best, just six yards out, and the big Bermudan slotted the ball home for a 4-2 away win.

By Saturday 6th February 1971, though, West Ham were twentieth in the First Division, and they'd already suffered a New Year's Day scandal that was splashed across the tabloids' front pages, while away in Blackpool, before their FA Cup Third round match.

Bobby Moore, Jimmy Greaves, Brian Dear, Clyde Best and club physio Rob Jenkins went out drinking in a Blackpool nightclub, until the early hours of the Saturday morning of their match at Bloomfield Road, on 2nd January.

Blackpool won 4-0, following a sublime, supreme performance by Tony Green.

Ron Greenwood had initially attributed the result to the poor state of the pitch, and also the excellence of Green, the best player on the field, but once the tabloid newspapers had published photos of his players drinking (Clyde Best had spent the whole night with just a single Coke, to be fair), Greenwood wanted to sack all of them, Bobby Moore included, he'd felt *that* betrayed.

The board persuaded him to just fine all four players, so he suspended them for two weeks.

Brian Dear left shortly afterwards, anyway, joining non-league Woodford Town on a free transfer, having scored thirty-nine goals in eighty-five games, while Jimmy Greaves retired at the end of the season, disillusioned with professional football, after scoring only thirteen goals in thirty-eight games at West Ham.

Clyde Best was only nineteen, and despite him remaining sober, he was complicit in the deception of his manager, and the incident shocked him, as he'd felt he'd let down his teammates. He'd learnt a big lesson about his responsibilities, and never made a mistake like it again.

The relationship between Ron Greenwood and his captain Bobby Moore, though, was never the same again. Moore was stripped of the club captaincy, which was then given to the twenty-four year old Billy Bonds. He was left out of the games with Arsenal and Leeds, before being named as a sub for their home game with Derby.

"I could talk for hours about Bobby Moore, the player," Greenwood admitted. "But ask me about Bobby Moore, the man, and I'll dry up in a minute."

With Jimmy Greaves on his way out, and with Clyde Best injured until the end of the season, after being carried off at Arsenal. Ron Greenwood needed goals, or West Ham would be going down with Blackpool.

So, in the middle of February, West Ham paid Newcastle United a club record transfer fee of £120,000 for Bryan "Pop" Robson, who'd scored eighty First Division goals in 205 games at St James's Park.

Pop Robson's presence immediately sparked West Ham back into life, and he also put some zest back into Geoff Hurst's game, who scored six goals in their last fourteen matches. West Ham lifted themselves out of the bottom two, and finished 1970-71 in third bottom position, but seven points above relegated Burnley.

With Jimmy Greaves gone, West Ham played the majority of the following season with Pop Robson attacking from a wide role, supporting their regular front two of Hurst and Clyde Best. But even more satisfying was their new defensive stability.

The Hammers kept nineteen clean sheets during 1971-72, and conceded only fifty-one First Division goals, a great feat for a defence that had previously been regarded as soft.

On Saturday 2nd October 1971, West Ham travelled to the mighty Leeds United in great form, having only lost once in their previous nine league and cup games, while winning five of them. Leeds were missing the suspended Billy Bremner, and also the injured Allan Clarke, Mick Jones and Eddie Gray. They'd suffered a mediocre start to the season, and they were there for the taking by the rampant Hammers.

As a result, Elland Road was only two thirds full, with the 30,942 crowd being five thousand below their average.

Billy Bonds handled the physical threat of Giles brilliantly, and Leeds' threadbare attack got no change from either Taylor or Moore. Leeds United's defence, though, majestically protected by Madeley and Yorath, were also unbeatable, and Gary Sprake saved well from both Robson and Bonds late in the second half.

LEEDS UNITED		WEST HAM UNITED
Gary Sprake	1	Bobby Ferguson
Paul Reaney	2	John McDowell
Terry Cooper	3	Frank Lampard
Terry Yorath	4	Billy Bonds
Jack Charlton	5	Tommy Taylor
Norman Hunter	6	Bobby Moore
Peter Lorimer	7	Harry Redknapp
Jimmy Mann	8	Clyde Best
Rod Belfitt	9	Geoff Hurst
Johnny Giles	10	Trevor Brooking
Paul Madeley	11	Pop Robson

This was a new, hard-centred West Ham that looked forward to the Seventies.

Eighteen days later, on Wednesday 20th October, West Ham did finally beat Leeds, a Leeds United team **with** Bremner, Clarke and Jones, in their League Cup Third round replay, away at Elland Road. Leeds had held the Hammers to a 0-0 draw at Upton Park, two weeks earlier.

Clyde Best fired a dramatic late winner, from six yards out, past Paul Reaney and David Harvey, deep into extra-time, for a terrific 1-0 win.

After over five hours of football in October 1971, against the most-feared team in English football, the Hammers hadn't conceded a single goal against Leeds United.

They had found a backbone.

West Ham then overcame Liverpool 2-1 in the Fourth round, before Pop Robson's hat-trick and Clyde Best's brace had helped hammer Sheffield United 5-0 in the Quarter-finals, with a huge crowd of nearly 39,000 inside Upton Park.

After just five minutes, Billy Bonds had crossed from the right for Robson to blast an unstoppable header past John Hope.

Pop Robson then finished, left-footed, from Geoff Hurst's wonderfully threaded through-ball, for his second goal, before finally, Brooking set Clyde Best free, out on the right wing. Best's cross, meant for Billy Bonds, had drifted over Hope and dipped just under the Blades' crossbar.

3-0 up at half-time, West Ham were relentless in the second half. John Hope kept out good shots from Bonds, Brooking, Hurst and Lampard, before about a quarter of an hour before the end.

Bobby Moore squared his free-kick, twenty-five yards out, to Clyde Best, who volleyed the ball goalwards. Hope got his hands to the ball, but he flapped at it, and couldn't stop it from bouncing over the goal-line.

Just before the end, Trevor Brooking crossed from the left, and Pop Robson headed the ball down, before smashing it home, right footed, with his second touch, for his perfect hat-trick.

West Ham had won 5-0, but it could have been ten, so dominant they were.

On Saturday 11th December, Southampton hosted West Ham, in what appeared to be a non-descript mid-table First Division battle. On the same day, Chelsea hosted Leeds, Liverpool hosted Derby, and Manchester United also visited Stoke City, but this was the Match of the Day.

Playing in their away kit of all sky blue, with two claret hoops around their shirts, West Ham attacked from the start.

A heavily side-burned Trevor Brooking teed up a free-kick for Billy Bonds, thirty yards out, and Bonds drove his right-footed shot over the wall of players, beyond Eric Martin's dive, and into the far right corner of the Saints' goal.

Bonds then floated in a cross, from the right, for the mighty Clyde Best to steam in and plant an unstoppable header past Martin, from six yards out. Terry Paine's weak clearance, from the edge of his own area, was collected by Lampard, who fed Brooking, twenty yards out. Brooking rode O'Neil's tackle, and strode back into the Southampton area, before driving a low, right-footed shot into the far right corner.

West Ham led 3-0, away from home. Another great victory was done and dusted…

McDowell's forward ball to Geoff Hurst, on the right of the Saints' penalty area presented yet more danger, but the ball was miscontrolled, and as McDowell slid in to regain possession, Southampton's quick footed left winger Tommy Jenkins sprinted away, with open space ahead of him. He turned inside, rode Bonds' covering tackle, and then went past Bobby Moore, inside the area, leaving the England captain on his backside, but Moore had just clipped Jenkins as he was about to shoot.

A penalty kick was awarded.

Jimmy Gabriel coolly struck his spot-kick inside Bobby Ferguson's left post.

Terry Paine then crossed from the right corner flag, after some lacklustre defending by Brook-ing, and Mike Channon rose above McDowell to head in at the near post.

Inside the last ten minutes of the first half, West Ham had allowed a total thrashing of First Division opponents to become just a one goal lead. It was like the West Ham of old, a classic West Ham type of match, 3-2 up at half-time, but this was *SOME* Southampton team, in fairness.

Late in the second half, after some outstanding defending by the Hammers, Terry Paine sent a forward ball up to Channon, out on the right side of the West Ham penalty area.

Mike Channon beat Bobby Moore's challenge, and then cut a diagonal pass back to the penalty spot, back to Paine, whose momentum took him past three players, Lampard, Taylor and substitute David Llewelyn, before driving his left-footed reverse shot back across Ferguson's body, into the far right corner of the goal.

The 20,506 Dell crowd went wild with joy, along with their legend Terry Paine, after such a thrilling comeback.

Prior to that thriller at The Dell, West Ham had beaten Stoke City 2-1, away at The Victoria Ground, in their League Cup Semi-final, first leg match.

Geoff Hurst had beaten England teammate Gordon Banks from the penalty spot, and Clyde Best had also finished neatly from Harry Redknapp's perfect cross.

On the following Wednesday, 15th December 1971, 38,771 expectant fans packed Upton Park, but John Ritchie scored with just fifteen minutes remaining, capitalizing on a rare Tommy Taylor defensive error, and he raced through to level the aggregate scores at 2-2.

With just a minute left to play, though, Gordon Banks upended Harry Redknapp, after Redknapp had beaten Mike Pejic. Geoff Hurst took the penalty kick, and he fired his well-hit shot towards the far right corner of Stoke's goal, but Gordon Banks dived left and got a strong fist to the ball. The ball ballooned up and over Banks's crossbar.

It was a wonderful save that was compared to Gordon Banks's save against Brazil, during the Mexico World Cup, eighteen months earlier.

After extra-time, Stoke held on to win 1-0, and so, with the full-time aggregate scores level at 2-2, West Ham and Stoke played a replay, at Sheffield Wednesday's Hillsborough ground, on Wednesday 5th January 1972.

46,196 had made the trip to South Yorkshire, from East London and the Potteries, on a Wednesday night, for what will probably be the best League Cup Semi-final to have ever been contested.

That game finished goalless, so a second replay was necessary. Old Trafford was chosen as the venue, three weeks later, six weeks after the original Semi-final second leg match at Upton Park.

STOKE CITY		WEST HAM UNITED
Gordon Banks	1	Bobby Ferguson
John Marsh	2	John McDowell
Mike Pejic	3	Frank Lampard
Mike Bernard	4	Billy Bonds
Denis Smith	5	Tommy Taylor
Alan Bloor	6	Bobby Moore
Terry Conroy	7	Harry Redknapp
Jimmy Greenhoff	8	Clyde Best
John Ritchie	9	Geoff Hurst
Peter Dobing	10	Trevor Brooking
George Eastham	11	Pop Robson
John Mahoney	12	Peter Eustace

49,247, the largest-ever crowd for any second replay Cup match in English football history, then witnessed a classic match, on a soaking wet and mud-soaked pitch, for a full-blooded (in more ways than one), proper Cup-tie.

Early on in the match, John Ritchie used his body strength, inside the mud-ridden penalty area, before laying the ball square for Conroy to run onto. Ferguson dived at the ball, but Terry Conroy was committed to the challenge, and his boot dealt a heavy kick to Bobby Ferguson's head.

The ball ran loose, and Jimmy Greenhoff swept the ball into the empty net.

The referee Pat Partridge had already blown, though, for a foul on the Hammers' goalkeeper.

The trouble was, Bobby Ferguson was in real pain, and he needed treatment for his head wound. He lay in the mud for over six minutes, receiving medical treatment.

Play re-started, with Ferguson back up again, and back between the posts, but it had to be stopped again, almost immediately, as Ferguson was falling about like a drunk, and he was helped off the pitch. Bobby Moore offered to go in goal, so West Ham could continue until half-time with just ten men, before they could properly assess the situation during the interval.

Almost immediately after Moore had gone in goal, though, Redknapp threw the ball back to McDowell, and McDowell's back pass to Moore ballooned up off a mud divot, before falling to John Ritchie, who'd appeared to have predicted that mistake, on the edge of the Hammers' area.

McDowell rushed back and desperately challenged the big Stoke forward. The two players slid down in the mud, and referee Pat Partridge immediately awarded a penalty kick to Stoke City.

West Ham protested, but after calm had finally descended, Mike Bernard's kick, high towards the top left corner of the goal, a superb penalty kick, was saved by Bobby Moore, who'd dived high and got both hands to the ball.

Unfortunately, instead of tipping the ball around his goalpost, for a corner, Moore sent the ball back onto the edge of his six yard box, and Bernard blasted home the rebound.

Bonds ran from deep, with the ball, over halfway, past Eastham's soft challenge, and then side-stepping Greenhoff's sliding tackle, before shooting from twenty-five yards. The ball deflected off Bloor, and up over the flying Gordon Banks, into the net.

Bonds then won the ball again, just outside Stoke's penalty area, after dispossessing Eastham. He drove a right-sided cross past Pejic and Bloor, to the far post, where Brooking volleyed the ball, left-footed, across Banks's body, and just inside the right post.

Conroy, out on the Stoke right, then played the ball inside for Eastham. George Eastham found space and he teed up captain Peter Dobing, twenty yards out. Dobing took one touch, and then cracked the ball high up into Bobby Moore's goal. It had been a tremendous half, as the mud had sapped both teams' energies, but particularly West Ham's ten men, as they'd done brilliantly to be drawing 2-2 at the interval.

As the teams reappeared for the second half, Bobby Ferguson was back in goal for West Ham, but with his head heavily bandaged. His vision was not perfect, though, and Stoke did their best to capitalise. They rose for every high ball, forcing him to withdraw to his line, in case he made a mistake, and allowed a simple shot on goal.

Full back John Marsh hoofed a high, long cross into West Ham's area, onto the penalty spot. With Ferguson not confident at coming out to climb and claim a routine high cross, Tommy Taylor headed away, under pressure from Ritchie.

The ball darted away to Conroy, with his huge ginger sideburn chops, just inside the edge of the area. He volleyed, right-footed, first time, and the ball flew past Ferguson's dive, into the right hand corner of his net.

Bobby Ferguson, playing the most important match of his career, since Kilmarnock's title-winning triumph at Hearts, seven years earlier, had been beaten by the very player who'd inflicted his injury upon him.

Clyde Best's shot, inside the last quarter-hour of the match, had beaten Banks, but the ball bounced back off the far post, and Alan Bloor's crude challenge on Hurst, inside his own area, was ruled okay by Mr Partridge, despite loud penalty appeals from West Ham's players and supporters, as well as worried gasps from Stoke's fans. They'd got away with it.

At the end, both teams were utterly drained, both emotionally and physically, and they both just collapsed onto each other, mutually embracing as the final whistle blew. It had been a wonderful battle, between two of the greatest teams in the history of those two great clubs, over four matches, and Stoke went on to deservedly win their Wembley Final, against Chelsea.

Three weeks after that soul-sapping loss, West Ham just beat non-league Hereford United 3-1, in their FA Cup Fourth round replay. Geoff Hurst scored a hat-trick, after a goalless draw away at Edgar Street.

A massive crowd, 42,271, the third-largest to ever attend Upton Park, enjoyed a virtuoso, devastating attacking performance by their World Cup winner, playing one of his last games for the Hammers.

Huddersfield beat West Ham 4-2 in the Fifth round, at Leeds Road, and West Ham's season was over again by the end of February. They limped to a fourteenth place finish, which totally belied their quality, but this *was* the greatest ever English First Division, with Everton, West Brom, Stoke City, Coventry City and Southampton all below them.

West Ham had also recorded one of their greatest ever defensive seasons, conceding fifty-one goals, as opposed to the eighty-four that they'd conceded during their 1966 "World Cup winning" season.

Clyde Best was their top scorer during 1971-72, with twenty-three league and cup goals, while Pop Robson and Geoff Hurst had shared thirty goals between them.

Kevin Lock had also made his league debut for West Ham on Saturday 22nd April, during their penultimate match of the season, replacing Bobby Moore as they lost 2-1 away at Arsenal. The eighteen year old Eastender, born in Plaistow, had also played for Essex schoolboys, before becoming an England youth international.

Kevin Lock made only twenty-three First Division starting appearances over the following two seasons, 1972-74, before he finally became Tommy Taylor's regular central defensive partner in August 1974, when still only twenty years old.

Geoff Hurst played his last game for West Ham United on Saturday 15th April 1972, as they lost 0-2 at home to Liverpool. Nearly 33,000 were packed inside Upton Park, oblivious that this was the last time they'd see Hurst in claret and blue. Stoke City then paid West Ham just £80,000 for the thirty year old England striker, on 27th June.

Hurst had scored 249 league and cup goals in just 502 games for West Ham.

At Stoke, he was no longer the main man up front, scoring goals freely, as he'd done throughout the Sixties, at Upton Park. His ball-holding ability, his heading and positional sense made him the ideal support forward for the main strike threats of John Ritchie and Jimmy Greenhoff. The three players scored a combined forty-seven league and cup goals for Stoke City during 1972-73.

During 1972-73, Pat Holland became a regular in West Ham's attack, forcing Harry Redknapp to move to Third Division Bournemouth, in August 1972.

Redknapp had played 150 First Division games for the Hammers, but he never truly fulfilled his potential, after his promising youthful energy had lit up the Sixties. He even found himself in and out of the Bournemouth team, eventually.

Pop Robson, in contrast, had the season of his career during 1972-73, scoring twenty-eight First Division goals, and he became the top goal-scorer in English football.

His goals were a huge reason for West Ham achieving one of their highest ever First Division finishes. They ended up in sixth position, having scored sixty-seven goals, and they'd conceded only fifty-three.

West Ham ended up just two points behind fourth-placed Ipswich Town, but even if they'd beaten Arsenal in their final match at Upton Park, they still wouldn't have qualified for the UEFA

Cup, because of the ridiculous rule where two teams from the same city couldn't qualify for that competition.

This rule was finally abolished in 1975 after an appeal, when Liverpool had finished second and Everton were fourth in the First Division.

Despite a huge crowd of over 37,000 roaring them on, inside Upton Park, this had an impact on the Hammers' motivation, as Arsenal were already guaranteed the runners-up spot, and they won 2-1 (Kennedy, Radford).

Having helped transformed West Ham's previously fragile defence into a more tactically alert and tight back four, left back Frank Lampard was awarded his first England cap for their 1-1 home draw with Yugoslavia, on Wednesday 11th October 1972, at Wembley Stadium. Playing alongside his teammate Bobby Moore, it was the only time that two West Ham defenders represented England in the same match.

With an average crowd of 30,174, West Ham United were also the ninth best supported team in England during 1972-73, in spite of their tightly built ground.

West Ham had paid a club record transfer fee of £170,000 for Manchester United's self-assured striker, Ted MacDougall, in March 1973. MacDougall had scored 142 league goals in only 248 games, and then he scored four in West Ham's final ten First Division matches of 1972-73. He also developed an increasingly hostile personality clash, however, with Hammers' midfield hard man and team leader Billy Bonds.

The 1973-74 season started poorly for both West Ham and MacDougall. They won only twice during their opening twenty-three league and cup matches, while MacDougall scored just twice in sixteen games.

Amid the turmoil, two more players had made their West Ham debuts. Mervyn Day was an eighteen year old youth team goalkeeper, born in Chelmsford, who'd represented Essex schools, and had preferred to join West Ham, ahead of both Ipswich and Tottenham, who had also been interested in signing him.

After being offered a professional contract in 1973, Mervyn Day replaced Bobby Ferguson, for one game, as West Ham drew 3-3 at home with Ipswich Town, on Bank Holiday Monday, 27th August 1973.

Brooking, Bonds and Best gave West Ham a 3-1 lead, but David Johnson and Trevor Whymark both scored late on to secure a share of the points.

Blowing bubbles? More like blowing leads, just like the old days.

On Saturday 6th October, Mervyn Day became the regular West Ham keeper for the remainder of the season, after Bobby Ferguson was ruled out with a knee injury.

That match, a 0-1 home defeat against the First Division new boys, high flyers Burnley, and their wonderful midfield of James, Dobson, Collins and Nulty, also saw the West Ham United debut of Keith Coleman.

Washington-born Keith Coleman was the third of four North-easterners brought into the team by Ron Greenwood, after Pop Robson and also Mick McGiven, who'd played twenty-one matches as central defensive cover that season.

Coleman had played 49 league games for Sunderland, but the twenty-one year old was unable to oust Ron Guthrie at Roker Park. Keith Coleman played in all but one of West Ham's last thirty-three league and cup matches of the 1973-74 season.

After a 1-0 defeat at Liverpool, on Saturday 1st December, it was all over for Ted MacDougall at West Ham. It had been an awful combination. It was the worst period of MacDougall's career, and also the worst spell that West Ham had ever had, even with good players filling their team, but leaving them deep in relegation troubles.

After that Anfield defeat, the Hammers were second from bottom in the table, but Ron Greenwood orchestrated a major transfer that not only transformed their own future, but also the future of Norwich City.

In an effective £170,000 swap deal, Ted MacDougall went to Carrow Road, and he helped Norwich gain promotion back to Division One , and also reach the League Cup Final in 1975. In 1975-76, he became the First Division's leading goal-scorer, with twenty-three goals, as Norwich City became a proper, respectable top flight team for the first time in their history.

In exchange, arriving at Upton Park was one of the most influential, skilful and intellectual midfield talents who have ever played for West Ham United.

Graham Paddon had played in over one hundred and sixty league games for Norwich City. Manchester-born and still only twenty-three, Paddon had been the brightest diamond in the Canaries' team, shining brightly with his sublime left foot, as Norwich had romped into the First Division back in 1972.

West Ham had also lost Pop Robson, their top scorer from the previous season, the top scorer in England, during their 1-3 home defeat to Arsenal at the end of November. Things didn't look good. After losing 1-3 at home to Birmingham City, on Saturday 15th December, and then 2-0 away at Stoke City a week later, West Ham were rock-bottom of the First Division on Christmas Day.

With the drive of Billy Bonds, the quality of Trevor Brooking, the class of Graham Paddon, the creativity of Pat Holland, and their massive presence of Clyde Best, though, West Ham scrambled to safety.

On Boxing Day, at Stamford Bridge, they were 2-0 down to Chelsea at half-time, after goals from Ian Britton and Alan Hudson, and they looked doomed yet again.

West Ham drove forward after the break, though, as two goals from Clyde Best, and one apiece from Frank Lampard and Bobby Gould, gave West Ham a superb 4-2 away win that finally sparked their season to life.

On Saturday 5th January 1974, Bobby Moore played his 641st and final league and cup match for West Ham, during their 1-1 home draw with Third Division Hereford United, in the FA Cup Third round. He was replaced, late in the second half, by Pat Holland. Then he was sold to Fulham for just £25,000.

Bobby Moore had been persuaded to join Fulham by his old England teammate Alan Mullery. Out of the frying pan, and into the fire, Moore made his debut for Fulham, his first ever league match outside of the First Division, on Tuesday 19th March, as Middlesbrough won 4-0 away at Craven Cottage.

Moore established a great understanding with John Lacy in central defence at the Cottage, however, and although Fulham were never ever a promotion threat, they did reach the FA Cup Final a year later, meeting West Ham at Wembley Stadium after playing twelve Cup ties, but never winning a game in London, while knocking out First Division sides Everton, Carlisle United and then Birmingham City, en route.

Bobby Moore played 124 Second Division games for Fulham, at the end of his Football League career, before moving to the NASL, en route to John Huston's Escape to Victory. He had played 545 First Division games for West Ham, and was capped 108 times for England, including ninety times as captain of his country.

Bobby Moore died on Wednesday 24th February 1993, aged only fifty-one, after suffering from bowel and liver cancer. Four months later, he became only the second sportsman to be honoured with a memorial service at Westminster Abbey, attended by all of his 1966 World Cup winning teammates.

He was the only Englishman voted into FIFA's Team of the Century, back in 2000, chosen at centre half, alongside Franz Beckenbauer, and behind such attacking legends as Pele, Johan Cruyff, Maradona, Di Stefano, Garrincha and Michel Platini.

West Ham lost only three of their nineteen First Division games after the New Year, winning twenty-four points, and they rose to eighteenth position by the end of the season, although they were only nine points behind a UEFA Cup qualifying place.

Over 36,000 packed Upton Park for their last game of the season, at home to FA Cup Finalists, and First Division runners-up Liverpool, on Saturday 27th April, with West Ham safe from relegation, barring miracles, but needing a point to definitely survive.

After half an hour, Frank Lampard smashed a superb, swerving, twenty-five yard shot, that Ray Clemence seemed to think was heading wide, but it bent inwards, and into the top left corner of the Liverpool net.

Mervyn Day then brilliantly saved Alec Lindsay's penalty kick, just before half-time. After the break, though, John Toshack equalised with a great chip over Day.

Trevor Brooking then volleyed the Hammers ahead again, from twenty-five yards out, with just over twenty minutes remaining, but Kevin Keegan headed Liverpool level inside the last minute.

For the only time in his career, captain Billy Bonds was West Ham's top goal-scorer, with thirteen First Division goals. Clyde Best had scored twelve, without a regular attacking partner for the majority of the season, while Mervyn Day conceded one or less goals in twenty-two of his thirty-five league and cup games, as an eighteen year old, and during his first season in the First Division.

On 24th July 1974, Pop Robson moved back to the North-east, after scoring forty-seven First Division goals in 120 games for West Ham, joining Second Division promotion chasers Sunderland for £145,000.

A month later, on Saturday 24th August, Ron Greenwood "moved upstairs", becoming West Ham's club manager, and Ilford-born John Lyall became their new first team manager, at just thirty-four years of age. It was agreed, though, that Ron Greenwood would remain responsible for buying players, while Lyall found his feet.

After title chasers Everton had won 3-2 away at Upton Park, as West Ham missed Trevor Brooking for the first month of the season, due to a broken nose, Ron Greenwood recruited fresh talent.

On Tuesday 3rd September, Greenwood paid Third Division Watford £110,000 for forward Billy Jennings.

Jennings, from Hackney, had scored thirty-three league goals for the Hornets in eighty-one games, and he'd been voted as Watford's Player of the Season in 1973-74.

Born in the East End, it was hoped that his heart would be worth the money, a record transfer fee for a Third Division player, and then, two days later, the change from the sale of Pop Robson was spent.

Keith Robson had never sent the Leazes End fans wild with excitement, during his fourteen First Division games for Newcastle, scoring only three goals. Greenwood, though, had spotted something special in the County Durham-born attacker, the fourth North-easterner signed by West

Ham during the early Seventies, bought for just £45,000. Robson subsequently scored ten First Division goals for West Ham, from the left wing, in just twenty-five games during their 1974-75 season.

The arrivals of Jennings and Robson had proved to be the end of Clyde Best at Upton Park. He did start twelve First Division games in 1974-75, scoring no goals, but then he started only five games for the Hammers during 1975-76, scoring his forty-seventh and final First Division goal during their 2-0 home win over Sheffield United, on Saturday 20th September 1975.

Clyde Best's contract was cancelled in February 1976, after 210 league and cup games for West Ham, and having scored fifty-eight goals in five years. He'd already moved to Tampa Bay Rowdies, in January 1976, and he scored six goals in 19 NASL games.

It isn't his goals per game ratio, though, for which Clyde Best will be most remembered. He had a natural sense of balance, and a quick turn of pace, lightning fast over the first ten yards. He was also a big man, six foot two inches, and twelve stone in weight, and very difficult to shake off the ball.

He was a two-footed attacker, difficult to defend against, and he could leap like a panther. But with his hugely powerful neck muscles, Best was one of the very best headers of the ball during the early Seventies.

Clyde Best was, simply, the first black British sporting superstar. He was racially taunted, initially, by opponents as well as spectators, but by the end, he was greatly respected by all in football, and in sport.

West Ham started 1974-75 very poorly, winning only one of their first seven league and cup games, scoring just six goals. However, they won nine of their next fourteen First Division matches, losing only once, and in early December, they were in fifth position, midway through the season, and only two points behind the league leaders.

They were also the top goal-scorers in Division One.

FIRST DIVISION LEADERS, 7TH DECEMBER 1974

	PL	W	D	L	F	A	PTS
Stoke City	21	10	7	4	36	25	27
Everton	20	7	12	1	29	19	26
Manchester City	21	11	4	6	29	27	26
Liverpool	20	10	4	6	27	16	25
WEST HAM	21	10	5	6	39	29	25
Ipswich Town	21	11	2	8	28	18	24
Burnley	21	10	4	7	38	32	24
Derby County	20	8	7	5	34	29	23

West Ham failed to win any of their next six league games, though, but they lost just twice, and after beating Carlisle United 2-0, on Saturday 1st February, after Jennings and Holland had both scored they were still up in sixth place, and only four points behind Everton, the league leaders.

They fell away, thereafter, winning only twice, but losing eight times during their final fourteen games, eventually finishing down in thirteenth position.

It was during the 1974-75 FA Cup, though, in which West Ham enjoyed their greatest success.

They won 2-1 away at Southampton, at the start of January, before then scraping past Third Division Swindon Town, after a replay, on Tuesday 28th January.

39,193 packed Upton Park in the Fifth round, and they roared the Hammers to a great 2-1 home win over fellow First Division side QPR (Pat Holland, Keith Robson), on Saturday 15th February.

Back in November, Ron Greenwood had told John Lyall about a twenty-one year old forward that he'd been watching at Rochdale.

He was raw, but quick, and Greenwood felt that he had talent that they could develop at Upton Park. On Tuesday 26th November, they paid just £45,000 to get him.

Alan Taylor was a skinny, sparrow-legged, long-haired cheeky looking lad, a former motor mechanic from Morecambe, who'd been playing non-league football in the Northern Premier League, before he joined Rochdale.

For the FA Cup Quarter-finals, West Ham were given a tough draw away at Arsenal. Arsenal had absolutely spanked the Hammers 3-0, at the end of October, but after watching Arsenal again, prior to their cup-tie, John Lyall figured that he should get West Ham attacking Arsenal's ageing defence with pace.

Known as *Sparrer*, because of his sparrow legs, Alan Taylor was selected to start the match, only his second start for West Ham, three and a half months after joining.

With a massive crowd of nearly 57,000 packed inside Highbury, Arsenal struggled against West Ham's quick counter attacks, as well as the appalling pitch, following days of heavy rain, throughout the match.

Billy Jennings' through-ball got stuck in a muddy puddle inside the Arsenal penalty area, but the ball was played out wide to Graham Paddon, who crossed for Alan Taylor to volley in from close range, right in front of the overflowing North Bank.

In the second half, Alan Taylor ran free of the Arsenal defence and he fired past Jimmy Rimmer, for a 2-0 away win, to send West Ham into the FA Cup Semi-finals for the first time in eleven years.

West Ham were drawn against the FA Cup favourites, after Ipswich Town had defeated European Cup Semi-finalists Leeds United in a classic FA Cup Quarter-final that required three replays. 58,000 watched their goalless draw at Villa Park, on Saturday 5th April, before an astonishing replay at Stamford Bridge, on the following Wednesday.

Just over 45,000 braved a freezing, swirling snowstorm, and Ipswich were disallowed a seemingly perfectly good goal by referee Clive Thomas, but West Ham made the most of their luck, and Alan Taylor fired yet another FA Cup brace.

So, as opposed to the Ipswich Town v Birmingham City Cup Final that everyone expected, the fairytale Cup Final of Fulham v West Ham United was what they got…

…only the second ever all-London Cup Final, and with Bobby Moore facing his old teammates.

Of the West Ham team that faced Fulham, on Saturday 3rd May 1975, eight had made their debuts as teenagers, and nine were born in either London or Essex.

Only Alan Taylor, born in Lancaster, and Graham Paddon, from Manchester, were foreigners to the East End. After such a truly great run to reach the Final, Fulham never really performed.

They weren't allowed to perform.

WEST HAM UNITED		FULHAM
Mervyn Day	1	Peter Mellor
John McDowell	2	John Cutbush
Frank Lampard	3	John Fraser
Billy Bonds	4	Alan Mullery
Tommy Taylor	5	John Lacy
Kevin Lock	6	Bobby Moore
Billy Jennings	7	John Mitchell
Graham Paddon	8	Jimmy Conway
Alan Taylor	9	Viv Busby
Trevor Brooking	10	Alan Slough
Pat Holland	11	Les Barrett

After an hour's play, Pat Holland dispossessed John Cutbush on the halfway line, and he left the Fulham left back behind. Holland cut back inside, and then laid the ball off to Billy Jennings, twenty yards from goal.

Jennings' first time shot flew like a rocket, and Peter Mellor dived low to save it, but he couldn't hold onto the ball, only succeeding in pushing it into Alan Taylor's path, six yards out. Taylor drove the ball back in, from an angle, through Mellor's legs.

West Ham's second goal, three minutes later, was a wonderful, seven man move that began with Mervyn Day's throw-out to Billy Bonds. Bonds broke into the Fulham half, and he played a one-two with Jennings, before laying the ball off, for Frank Lampard, thirty yards out. Lampard's shot was blocked, but Graham Paddon collected the loose ball and he played it out wide left to Holland.

Pat Holland returned the ball to Paddon, who blasted a vicious shot at goal from a narrow angle. Mellor again stopped the shot, but couldn't hold it, so Alan Taylor pounced again, hitting the ball up into the roof of the net, from a couple of yards out.

It was a wonderful performance by a West Ham team, built from youth since 1967. At an average age of just 23.45 years old, they were among the youngest ever teams to have won the Cup, with captain Billy Bonds their oldest player, at twenty-eight.

West Ham United's 1975 team was also the last ever all-English team to win the FA Cup, and that *is* a record that is likely to stand forever.

Billy Jennings had been West Ham's leading goal-scorer during 1974-75, with fourteen in both league and cups. Keith Robson had scored eleven, with Billy Bonds also on ten, and Alan Taylor on eight. Alan Taylor also remains the only player to have scored two goals in the FA Cup Quarter-finals, two goals in the Semi-finals, and then two goals in the FA Cup Final.

Bobby Gould had scored nine First Division goals, also, but after being an unused sub during the Cup Final, he was off again, after starting just four West Ham games during 1975-76, and he re-joined Wolves in December 1975.

Their nineteen year old goalkeeper Mervyn Day was also honoured by his fellow profession-als, after winning the PFA's Young Player of the Year award.

Inspired by their Wembley win, West Ham went off like a train in August 1975, winning nine of their opening fifteen First Division matches, losing only twice. After hammering Birmingham

City 5-1 away, on Saturday 1ˢᵗ November, West Ham United were the joint league leaders, and they remained top of Division One for a fortnight.

By December, they'd dropped to third place, but they were still only one point behind leaders Derby County, with QPR in second place, after eighteen games.

They then won only two of their remaining twenty-four league games, however, losing sixteen times, and West Ham dropped heavily down to fifth-bottom, finishing the season only six points above relegated Wolves.

It was in the 1975-76 European Cup Winners' Cup, however, where West Ham did themselves proud. In the First round, they beat Lahden Reipas, of Finland, 5-2 on aggregate (Brooking, Bonds, Robson, Holland, Jennings), before a tough Second round draw against Ararat Erevan, of the Soviet Union.

They travelled to Armenia, for their first leg match, near to Mount Ararat in the Caucasus Mountains, where Noah's Ark was supposed to have finally come to rest after the Great Flood.

Alan Taylor silenced the hostile 66,662 home crowd, after fifty-six minutes, driving his shot past Abramian to give the Hammers the lead.

Soon after, though, Erevan's striker Petrosian lunged at Mervyn Day, as he was about to throw the ball out. Petrosian headed the ball out of Day's hands, and then, as Day struggled to get the ball back, Petrosian slotted the loose ball in for the equaliser.

It had been a clear foul on the goalkeeper, but the German referee allowed the goal to stand. John Lyall couldn't believe it.

"If Noah had turned up at that moment," he admitted, "I'd have drowned him."

In the second leg at Upton Park, though, Graham Paddon, Keith Robson and Alan Taylor all delighted their 30,399 home crowd, as West Ham hammered Ararat 3-1, winning 4-2 on aggregate.

In the first half of their Quarter-final, first leg match, away at Den Haag of Holland, though, West Ham were thoroughly thrashed. They conceded two penalties, and also two more goals, as Den Haag led 4-0 at half-time, and were running away with it.

"Go back out there and get at them," John Lyall told his team, during the interval. "We'll beat them at Upton Park, no trouble, so if you can get a goal or two back, we'll still be in it."

Billy Jennings scored those two goals in the second half, the most important of his career. First, he drove in from six yards, following Graham Paddon's pull-back from the bye-line, and then he headed in the second from Paddon's perfect left wing cross.

Both goals had been scored during the opening quarter-hour of the second half, and Den Haag were rattled. Keith Robson and Alan Taylor had also had fierce shots well saved by Thie, the Dutch goalkeeper, and then Jennings missed his kick, late on, when he was poised to complete his hat-trick.

West Ham continued their footballing superiority back home at Upton Park, a fortnight later, winning 3-1, with 29,829 packed inside their ground. Alan Taylor, Frank Lampard, and Billy Bonds from the penalty spot, had all scored first half goals, stunning Den Haag, and securing the Hammers their Semi-final place, on the away goals rule.

On Wednesday 31ˢᵗ March, West Ham visited Eintracht Frankfurt, who'd already knocked out Atletico Madrid. Eintracht boasted two members of West Germany's 1974 World Cup winning side, Jurgen Grabowski and Bernd Holzenbein, but their star player was Bernd Nickel, a skilful attacking midfield player feared for his long distance straight shots, and his direct free-kicks that flew like torpedoes, earning him the nickname **Doktor Hammer.**

There was no doubt about it. This Eintracht side were better than the 1860 Munich team that West Ham had beaten back in the 1965 Cup Winners' Cup Final.

55,000 filled the Waldstadion in Frankfurt, but only nine minutes into the match, Graham Paddon fired a brilliant, left-footed twenty-five yard rocket past Dr Peter Kunter. While Billy Jennings had scored his two most important goals against Den Haag in the previous round, that had certainly been Paddon's most important goal during his 150 games for the Hammers.

Eintracht came back to win the match 2-1, after Neuberger and Kraus both scored, but West Ham had given themselves a great chance to reach the Final, in Brussels.

Two weeks later, 39,202 filled Upton Park for the second leg, but they were left nervous and frustrated after a goalless first half, during which West Ham had had ninety per cent of the play. Just one goal was enough to put them through, but they also needed to keep a clean sheet.

Trevor Brooking, particularly, had been at his very best, consistently beating and getting behind both Eintracht full backs Reichel and Neuberger, floating over cross after cross, for Holland, for Robson, and for McDowell.

"He mesmerised a very good German side. *Boog* (Brooking) ran the game," Billy Bonds remembered. It was fitting, then, that Brooking opened the scoring, jumping up from the muddy penalty spot to head beyond Dr Kunter's dive, from Frank Lampard's left-sided cross.

West Ham then cleared the ball off the line three times within the space of a few seconds, as Frankfurt launched a sustained attack on their penalty area.

But then, from nowhere, Keith Robson, having seemed to have got the ball stuck under his feet in the mud, then lifted the ball, left-footed over Dr Kunter, from twenty-five yards out.

With a more comfortable 2-0 lead, West Ham began to play with less fear. Paddon played the ball out wide left, to Tommy Taylor, just inside his own half.

Tommy Taylor launched a long pass to the brilliant Brooking, who turned his pursuer Neuberger, inside and outside, before then placing the ball, from just outside the penalty area, past Kunter, into the far right corner of the goal.

"Yes! Number three! Magnificent!" cried Brian Moore, on ITV's The Midweek Match. "What a smile, and what a goal!"

TV commentators always seemed to speak with exclamation marks!

With just about two minutes remaining, Beverungen headed in after West Ham had failed to deal with a routine cross from the full back, and suddenly, one goal for the Germans would put them through, despite West Ham's total superiority.

Billy Jennings then missed a great chance to make it 4-1, after slipping in the Eintracht penalty area mud, before Frankfurt forced a corner, deep in injury time.

The Germans literally packed the West Ham penalty area, as Grabowski fired over his centre. Frankfurt had the Hammers totally penned in, but Tommy Taylor cleared.

Eintracht tried to come back, but the Swiss referee blew for full-time, and West Ham had reached their second European Final.

The Heysel Stadium in Brussels provided effective home advantage for West Ham's Belgian opponents, RSC Anderlecht.

And this was a crack Anderlecht side that contained several stars of World football, both present and future. It would be West Ham's toughest-ever test.

Rob Rensenbrink and Arie Haan had both starred for Holland during the 1974 World Cup Finals, bringing Total Football to Colour TV screens all over the World, and both Dutch players started the Final against West Germany.

Francois Van Der Elst was one of Belgium's greatest ever footballers, and in 1980, he inspired Belgium to their finest hour, reaching the European Championship Final, against West Germany, in Rome. Substitute Franky Vercauteren, who came on against West Ham, after just half an hour, played in all six matches during the 1986 World Cup Finals, as Belgium reached the Semi-finals, before being undone by Diego Maradona.

THE 1976 EUROPEAN CUP WINNERS' CUP FINAL

RSC ANDERLECHT		WEST HAM UNITED
Jan Ruiter	1	Mervyn Day
Michel Lomme	2	Keith Coleman
Hugo Broos	3	Frank Lampard
Gilbert Van Binst	4	Billy Bonds
Jean Thissen	5	Tommy Taylor
Jean Dockx	6	John McDowell
Francois Van Der Elst	7	Pat Holland
Arie Haan	8	Graham Paddon
Peter Ressel	9	Billy Jennings
Ludo Coeck	10	Trevor Brooking
Rob Rensenbrink	11	Keith Robson
Franky Vercauteren	SUB	Alan Taylor
Jacky Munaron	SUB	Bobby Ferguson
Torsten Andersen	SUB	Kevin Lock
Michel De Groote	SUB	Alan Curbishley

Anderlecht had had a much easier route to the Final than West Ham, beating Rapid Bucharest 2-1 in the First round, and then FK Borac Banja Luka, of Yugoslavia, 3-1 in the Second round.

They were also given the easiest of draws in the Quarter-finals, scraping past Wrexham of the English Third Division, by just 2-1, before again being given the easiest draw in the Semi-finals.

While West Ham and Eintracht Frankfurt clashed in their two classic matches, Anderlecht were beating BSG Sachsenring Zwickau, of East Germany, both home and away, 3-0 and 2-0 respectively. They were certainly going to be fresher.

After just three minutes, Bonds ran the ball from halfway inside his own half, having dispossessed Ressel, before releasing Paddon on the left side of the Anderlecht area, with a sublime flick of the outside of his right boot. Paddon crossed for Jennings, whose lobbed shot was caught by Ruiter.

Apart from that, though, the first fifteen minutes of action were tight and cagey, with neither side forcing too much pressure on the opposing defence. Both sides were happy to sit back, and absorb their opponents' attempts to attack.

Trevor Brooking then went on a strong run from his own half, before being hacked down by Coeck, forty yards from goal. The Belgian midfielder hurt himself in making the challenge, and he eventually had to be replaced after thirty-two minutes, after Anderlecht had gone 1-0 down, by the nineteen year old Vercauteren.

Franky Vercauteren went on to play sixty-three times for Belgium, including two World Cup Finals tournaments.

Frank Lampard's lofted free-kick flew out, tamely, for an Anderlecht goal kick.

West Ham then began to impose some offensive superiority. McDowell crossed from the right wing, and Keith Robson, on the left side of the area, headed back inside. Trevor Brooking volleyed goalwards, but Ruiter parried his shot, diving at his left hand post. It was the first meaningful shot of the match, after seventeen minutes.

Lampard's twenty yard shot was then saved, low at his near post, by Ruiter.

The menacing Arie Haan then ran into the Hammers' area, breaking two challenges, before his shot was blocked by Bonds, and the ball ran free to safety.

Billy Jennings, sent away by Paddon's deft flick out on the right, blasted a shot just over, from the edge of the Belgian penalty area. Then, as *I'm Forever Blowing Bubbles* echoed around the 60,000-filled stadium, Brooking sent in a left wing cross, and Jennings's looping header was tipped over the crossbar by the leaping Ruiter.

From the corner kick, Paddon crossed from the right, and Bonds beat his marker to head the ball down into the Anderlecht area. From just six yards out, Pat Holland pounced to finish with a low shot under Ruiter's dive.

Fully deserved, West Ham were 1-0 up, after twenty-eight minutes.

The whistling home crowd were stunned. Anderlecht were rattled, and almost immediately, Broos was forced into a soft pass back to his keeper, that Ruiter just managed to hack clear, with Jennings about to shoot from inside the area.

Bonds went on another of his strong, marauding runs from his own defence, deep into Anderlecht territory. McDowell gathered the ball on the right and he crossed for Brooking, whose leaping header beat Ruiter, but drifted just wide of the far left post.

Ruiter then caught Jennings' header, from Holland's right wing cross, just beneath his crossbar.

Anderlecht just couldn't get out of their own half.

McDowell shot over from thirty yards out, with Keith Robson howling for the ball, free on the left side of the area. Brooking beat Thissen down the right, and his low cross was volleyed over the bar, by Billy Jennings, from the edge of the six yard box.

It should have been two.

Ruiter's poor goal kick rolled straight to Paddon, twenty-five yards out, but his chipped, left-footed attempt floated just over Anderlecht's bar.

Paddon and Brooking then worked the ball out to Lampard, whose hard-hit low shot was gathered by Ruiter.

After forty-two minutes, Frank Lampard was put under pressure by Ressel, over at his own corner flag. Lampard, with the ball at his feet, only had to turn and play the ball back up-field, or even try to hit the ball hard into Ressel to win either a West Ham throw-in or a goal kick. He gave a good glance over to his left, though, over towards Mervyn Day, which gave Ressel, who'd won a UEFA Cup winners' medal with Feyenoord back in 1974, a clue as to what was going to happen.

Lampard twisted, and he attempted to pass the ball back to Day, but his pass was soft, and Ressel intercepted. Ressel played a square ball inside to Rob Rensenbrink, who evaded Billy Bonds' challenge, before smashing the ball past Day's dive.

It was almost half-time, and that had been Anderlecht's first, and only, shot on goal during the first half. Frank Lampard tore a stomach muscle while making the pass, and had to be replaced by Alan Taylor at half-time. The goal flattened West Ham, who had deserved to be at least two goals up, following their total superiority in possession and chances, especially as it had been an unnecessary goal to concede.

The lively substitute Alan Taylor forced a West Ham corner, immediately after the second half had started. Paddon's corner was then headed goalwards by Bonds, but Ruiter, under pressure from Jennings, climbed high to catch the ball.

Two minutes after the break, Anderlecht broke out, through the lively Vercauteren, who played in Van Der Elst, on the edge of the West Ham area.

Francois Van Der Elst chipped the ball up and over Mervyn Day's leaping dive, and it just dipped back inside the far post.

It was the first piece of real class that Anderlecht had shown, and suddenly they were winning 2-1, after West Ham had had the Cup Winners' Cup safely in their control, just five minutes earlier.

West Ham were without a specialist left back, and so Graham Paddon had to fill in for the injured Lampard. As a result, their midfield creativity was weakened, after the hard-working Keith Robson had dropped to support Bonds, with Alan Taylor partnering Jennings up front.

Jean Thissen was booked for a petulant hack at Alan Taylor's legs, after 54 minutes, and from Tommy Taylor's free-kick, Bonds headed down for Alan Taylor, six yards out, but Van Binst slid in to block Taylor's shot, conceding a corner kick.

Graham Paddon's corner kick was half-cleared to Tommy Taylor, twenty-five yards out, and the big centre back bulldozed a shot towards the top left corner of goal, but Ruiter leapt and turned the ball around his upright.

Rensenbrink then fired narrowly wide of Mervyn Day's left hand post, from the edge of the West Ham area, as the game descended into a spell of niggling fouls by both teams. Alan Taylor was fortunate not to have been booked for a foul on Rensenbrink, and then Paddon forced Dockx to the turf. The Belgian gracefully accepted Paddon's apologetic handshake after he arose.

Tommy Taylor tripped up Arie Haan from behind, and Haan clattered into Holland.

Then, on the break, the increasingly free-running Ressel played a one-two with Rensenbrink, capitalising on the absence of a West Ham left back, outpacing McDowell, before he fired inches wide of Mervyn Day's near post.

Billy Jennings' header from Brooking's left wing cross was tipped over by Ruiter, for another corner to West Ham.

As Anderlecht failed to clear another fluent Hammers' attack, that had ran through Robson, Paddon, Brooking and Jennings, Brooking received the ball from Paddon, out on the left, and he crossed low for Keith Robson to stoop and guide his header past Ruiter, and in off the far right post.

West Ham and their ten thousand fans exploded into celebrations of high frenzy.

With just over twenty minutes remaining, the scores were level again, following a period of Belgian superiority just after half-time, as West Ham's rhythm and shape had been disjointed after the loss of Lampard. They were back in the match, playing the ball about again, with confidence and class.

Vercauteren brought out a magnificent save from Mervyn Day, as West Ham scrambled the ball away, and then Day dived at Ressel's feet, after Rensenbrink's superb through-ball.

Pat Holland then brought down Rensenbrink, unnecessarily and inexplicably, with the Dutchman going wide, going nowhere, away from goal.

Holland pleaded his innocence, but it was a clear foul, and the French referee, Robert Wurtz, awarded a penalty kick to Anderlecht.

Rob Rensenbrink blasted his kick past Mervyn Day, putting Anderlecht 3-2 up.

Arie Haan was then booked for a poor challenge on Keith Robson, but with West Ham's energy sapped after their wonderful first half performance, and their frustration of giving away two cheap goals, Anderlecht finally began to impose their footballing pedigree.

Van Der Elst, Rensenbrink, Vercauteren, Haan and Ressel kept the ball better, spreading it wide, left and right, stretching West Ham's threadbare defence, pulling their midfielders back.

Large purple and white flags were waved all over three-quarters of the Heysel Stadium. Every time West Ham broke forward, they ran into a deep defensive wall, well marshalled by Dockx, Van Binst and Thissen, just as Anderlecht had done against Coleman, Taylor, McDowell and Lampard, throughout the first half.

With just two minutes remaining, Trevor Brooking was dispossessed while attacking the Anderlecht penalty area, on the bye line. The ball broke swiftly, through Van Binst and Thissen, up to Rensenbrink on the halfway line, and the Dutch star passed a beautifully weighted ball up to the quick running Van Der Elst, thirty yards out, and pursued by McDowell.

Francois Van Der Elst turned McDowell, and then Day, both inside out, before slotting the ball calmly into the empty net. He then knelt down inside the West Ham area, arms aloft, and collapsed with joy and exhaustion.

The brilliant Rensenbrink was the first to congratulate him.

The 4-2 final score-line was an emphatic one that Anderlecht did not deserve, but they had their good fortune, and they were good enough to make the most of it.

West Ham had out-possessed, outshot, and outplayed the **home team** for most of the game, but they made errors at crucial points, while the Belgian side kept their discipline and then buried their chances.

This was, though, the best team that Anderlecht ever fielded in their long history, and it would be remembered as one of the most wonderful Cup Winners' Cup Finals, up there, equal with the very best.

After four full seasons as first choice goalkeeper, Mervyn Day was displaced by Bobby Ferguson, halfway into the 1977-78 season, as West Ham were staring relegation in the face.

After Phil Parkes joined the Hammers in 1979, for a World record fee, Mervyn Day moved to Orient, having played 194 league games for West Ham, 181 of which were in the First Division.

Bobby Ferguson was unable to keep West Ham in Division One, despite a great run of five wins in six games, from late March through to the middle of April, that had lifted them up to sixth bottom.

Defeats to Manchester United, and then European Champions Liverpool, dropped them back into it, though, and despite a 2-1 win over Middlesbrough, West Ham were relegated, just one point below QPR, in April 1978.

Ferguson left West Ham United in 1980, at the age of thirty-five, after playing 277 league and cup matches for West Ham. With superb judgement, both in the air and on the ground, Bobby Ferguson had played a major part in the transition from the Hammers' clean-cut Sixties' team into the rougher, wilder Seventies bunch.

Tommy Taylor was an ever-present in West Ham's first team, throughout their unfortunate 1977-78 season, but once they struggled to get out of Division Two, he lost his place to Alvin Martin, a teenage talent who then graced the Hammers' defence throughout the Eighties.

Just as Taylor had replaced Alan Stephenson back in 1970, he himself was replaced by younger talents, ten years later, such was the West Ham way, under Ron Greenwood, and then John Lyall.

Tommy Taylor was not as greatly respected a player as Bobby Moore, but he was a much better, tougher and sharper defender. He could also create goals, in crucial situations, as he'd done for Trevor Brooking during the Semi-final against Frankfurt. He played 396 league and cup matches for West Ham, before joining Orient in 1979.

John McDowell, Taylor's central defensive partner during that superb Final against Anderlecht, played 297 league and cup games for West Ham, before he joined Norwich City, for just £20,000, in August 1979.

More significantly, McDowell had played ninety-seven league and cup games during their two greatest seasons, 1974-76. East Ham born, and a Hammer at heart, John McDowell never gave less than his best, despite being very much an unsung hero for one of the very best West Ham teams.

Pat Holland, who was so important in their FA Cup Final win over Fulham, suffered a knee injury against Notts County, on Saturday 17th January 1981, during West Ham's emphatic Second Division Championship winning season.

At the age of thirty, and after 296 league and cup games for the Hammers, Holland never played first team football for any team ever again.

Alan Taylor, the fresh-faced, skinny-legged hero of West Ham's FA Cup triumph, was also their top goal-scorer in 1975-76, scoring seventeen league and cup goals.

He played his 98th and final league match for the club, on 20th January 1979, during their 1-0 away win at Bristol Rovers.

Unable to regain his place, he joined Norwich City in the Summer of 79, at the age of just twenty-five, having scored only twenty-five league goals for West Ham, but it will always be the six FA Cup goals that he scored against Arsenal, Ipswich and Fulham that made Alan Taylor an Upton Park legend.

Billy Jennings, who scored those crucial goals in Holland, against Den Haag, scored a total of thirty-nine goals in 108 league and cup matches, before moving to Orient in 1979, with his mates Mervyn Day and Tommy Taylor. Jennings had a part in both of Alan Taylor's goals against Fulham, and he could, **and should,** have killed off Anderlecht with his close range shot, during the first half of the 1976 Final, but it wasn't to be.

Graham Paddon, whose crucial, special away goal against Eintracht Frankfurt effectively sent West Ham on their way to the European Cup Winners' Cup Final, had already left West Ham before their relegation season, returning to Norwich City, in the county that he loved so much, for £110,000, in November 1976.

Paddon had played 115 First Division matches for West Ham, scoring eleven goals, but alongside Billy Bonds, Trevor Brooking and Pat Holland, he had been the left footed playmaker of West Ham's greatest-ever, and their hairiest midfield.

With Paddon, Bonds, Frank Lampard, Brooking and Holland, West Ham United had definitely resembled The Eagles during the mid-Seventies, from their *Hotel California* period; all beards, long hair and large afro hairstyles.

Trevor Brooking played his six hundred and twenty-seventh, and final league and cup game for West Ham United on Monday 14th May 1984, as Everton visited Upton Park, just five days before their FA Cup Final win over Watford.

25,452 had come to say farewell to one of their greatest ever players.

Brooking had scored 102 goals for the Hammers, and he'd also played forty-seven games for England, making his last international appearance against Spain during the Second round of the 1982 World Cup Finals.

Brian Clough had loved Brooking's ability, regretting that he never managed him. He was "stylish and honest, and could play a beautiful pass," Clough suggested.

Appointed as the FA's Director of Development of Football, during the Twenty-first century, Sir Trevor Brooking was knighted by the Queen in 2004.

He had headed in the Hammers' winning goal against Arsenal, during their 1980 FA Cup Final 1-0 win, and he became one of just three West Ham United players to win two FA Cup winners' medals, as well as both Billy Bonds and Frank Lampard.

Frank Lampard made 660 first team league and cup appearances for West Ham between 1967 and 1985. He remains the second-most played footballer in the history of the club, behind his captain Billy Bonds.

In 1985, Lampard joined Southend United, who were then managed by his other captain Bobby Moore, playing for the Shrimpers during the 1985-86 season before finally retiring. His son, Frank Lampard Jr., became one of the most influential and effective English midfield players during the first dozen or so years of the Twenty-first century, joining Chelsea in 2001, from his first club West Ham, and eventually overtaking Bobby Tambling to become their all-time record goal-scorer.

Lampard Jr. became so important a player that he was very quickly known as just Frank Lampard, and Frank Lampard became Frank Lampard Senior!

Billy Bonds, *Bonzo,* was the most played footballer in West Ham United's history, playing 793 league and cup matches for the club, and scoring fifty-nine goals. Then in February 1990, he was appointed as West Ham's manager, following John Lyall's resignation.

"He never held back," Alan Taylor warmly remembered his old captain. "He always went in fully committed. The boss (John Lyall) always used to partner him up with Patsy Holland in training, and you can still hear some of them tackles now!"

An iconic figure who embodied the spirit of West Ham more than any other player, Bonds pulled on an England shirt on just one occasion, before their vital World Cup qualifier against Italy, in November 1977.

Despite Billy Bonds' former West Ham manager Ron Greenwood being England's manager, he nevertheless never got onto the pitch, from the sub's bench, as England won 2-0 at Wembley, despite needing a four goal victory to qualify for Argentina.

That didn't deeply bother Bonds, despite his disappointment, because he thought that was just the start of his international career, and he would progress to the full England team for their 1980 European Championship qualifying campaign.

It didn't happen like that, though, as Ron Greenwood opted for Chelsea's younger midfielder Ray Wilkins to hold his England team together.

Billy Bonds was awarded the MBE in 1988, but having been appointed as West Ham manager two years later, he resigned in August 1994, and he was succeeded by his old teammate Harry Redknapp.

That West Ham United team learnt, for the very first time, how to defend and counter-attack with fluency, with style and with effect.

That West Ham United team, from 1970-76, introduced the first British black superstar, Clyde Best, with his love of The Four Tops and The Supremes, and they provided real colour, of a claret and blue variety, to the Glam Soccer era.

That West Ham United team beat some of the best teams in Europe, in adverse circumstances, and also featured in First Division title races, for the very first time in their club's history.

That West Ham team, from 1970-76, was one of the very best in their history, if not the very best. They didn't have Moore, Hurst and Peters, but they had much, much more.

THE GREAT WESTERN EXPRESS

F OR NEARLY TEN YEARS AFTER THEY'D gained promotion from Division Three back in 1965, Bristol City had mostly been a lowly to middling Second Division club.

They'd reached the League Cup Semi-finals back in 1971, with Brian Drysdale, Geoff Merrick, Gerry Gow and Chris Garland, losing 1-3 on aggregate to Tottenham Hotspur, who went on to win the Cup, but no Glam Soccer *Hot Love Dyna-mite* had landed at Bristol Temple Meads on the Great Western Railway during those years, aside from a rare Watney Cup triumph for city rivals Bristol Rovers, in August 1972.

On 14th December 1972, Robins' manager Alan Dicks paid a £70,000 club record transfer fee to West Bromwich Albion for journeyman centre forward Bobby Gould, and then three months later, he paid a bargain £30,000 to Morton for Don Gillies. The Glencoe-born striker had scored 23 Scottish League First Division goals from only 45 starts. Those two signings lifted City, and on Saturday 27th March, Gould and Gillies both combined with three goals between them, hammering promotion chasers Aston Villa 3-0, but with only 15,654 inside Ashton Gate.

Bristol City rose from mid-table up to fifth place by the end of the 1972-73 season, and Bobby Gould finished that season with eight goals from just nineteen games, City's second highest goalscorer, behind Gerry Gow on twelve.

Bobby Gould also started the following season well, scoring five from his first seven games, as Bristol City won five of those games to top the Second Division on Saturday 22nd September 1973.

However, Gould's form then collapsed, as indeed did City's league position. He scored only two more goals during his next nine matches, and City dropped back to mid-table. In November, he asked for a transfer, so West Ham signed him for £70,000.

Don Gillies was a ready-made replacement for Gould, scoring four goals in the six games immediately after Bobby Gould's departure. However, in spite of Gillies, Keith Fear, Tom Ritchie and Trevor Tainton scoring twenty-five league goals between them, no player hit double figures at Ashton Gate, and City finished way down in sixteenth place, for another completely forgettable Second Division season.

It was during the 1973-74 FA Cup competition where City hit the headlines, though, after playing in three unforgettable matches.

The Robins had quietly crept, almost undetected, into the Fifth round, after knocking out Hull City after a replay, and then Hereford United, who'd already upset West Ham United 2-1 in their Third round home replay, with 17,423 filling Edgar Street.

In front of another packed-to-capacity, completely bonkers 17,431 Edgar Street crowd, City's captain Geoff Merrick killed The Bulls' FA Cup hopes with a first half near post header from Trevor Tainton's cross.

In the Fifth round, Bristol City were drawn at home to First Division leaders, and league and cup Double hopefuls Leeds United. By the time Leeds arrived at Ashton Gate on 16th February, they'd played a record 29 First Division games without defeat, since the start of the season, and were nine points clear of second-placed Liverpool.

BRISTOL CITY		LEEDS UNITED
Ray Cashley	1	David Harvey
Gerry Sweeney	2	Terry Yorath
Brian Drysdale	3	Trevor Cherry
Gerry Gow	4	Billy Bremner
Gary Collier	5	Gordon McQueen
Geoff Merrick	6	Norman Hunter
Trevor Tainton	7	Peter Lorimer
Tom Ritchie	8	Joe Jordan
Keith Fear	9	Mick Jones
Don Gillies	10	Johnny Giles
Ernie Hunt	11	Paul Madeley
Paul Cheesley	12	Allan Clarke

After Billy Bremner had volleyed in Peter Lorimer's corner, 37,000 home fans feared that Leeds would go through, with their solid defence effortlessly controlling a grimly-geared, hard-fought away victory.

Late in the second half, though, in the thick mud, Gerry Gow carried the ball into the centre circle, tracked by Bremner. He lofted a perfect long pass over Hunter's head, and between both McQueen and Cherry, into Keith Fear's path. Fear lifted his first time shot over David Harvey's body, just as McQueen's challenge came snapping in.

Three days later, on a Tuesday afternoon, and with 47,182 packing Elland Road, Leeds United's biggest crowd of the season, during one of Leeds United's greatest-ever seasons, that same Bristol City team won 1-0.

After half-time, Don Gillies outpaced Terry Cooper to meet Keith Fear's through-ball, before shooting, left-footed, on the run, and beating Harvey at the far post.

Gillies' goal had not only knocked Leeds United out of the FA Cup, but it also knocked shock-waves right through the league leaders. On the following Saturday, Leeds sailed into a first half 2-0 lead away at Stoke, only to then lose 3-2, their first league defeat in their thirtieth game. But they won only once out of their next seven First Division matches following Bristol City's win.

They were almost caught by Liverpool, before rediscovering their form, just in time.

City's reward for their Cup heroics was a Quarter-final home tie with Liverpool.

37,671 totally filled Ashton Gate, on Saturday 9th March, as Clemence, Smith, Lindsay, Thompson, Cormack, Hughes, Keegan, Hall, Heighway, Toshack and Callaghan arrived, played and routinely won 1-0. That was the Liverpool way.

John Toshack's second-half goal maintained Liverpool's march towards an FA Cup Final hammering of Newcastle United at Wembley, on Saturday 4th May.

The following season, 1974-75, saw Bristol City right on the edge of the promotion race all season. Manchester United and Aston Villa ended up running away with the top two places, but Norwich City only just edged both Sunderland and Bristol City to the third promotion place during the last two weeks.

Bristol City's back four of Gerry Sweeney, Gary Collier, Geoff Merrick and Brian Drysdale, in front of keeper Ray Cashley, had conceded only 33 league goals during their 42 Second Division games, and they'd kept seventeen clean sheets.

Don Gillies and Keith Fear were City's joint-top scorers with just nine goals apiece.

With a back four as settled and well-drilled as City's was, fans wondered what they could do if only they had two strikers who could both score umpteen goals a season.

Paul Cheesley had joined cheaply from Norwich City near the end of the 1973-74 season, but he'd been out injured for the majority of the following season.

He entered the 1975-76 season fully fit, though.

Tom Ritchie, an Edinburgh-born centre-forward, had joined City as a twenty year old back in 1972, but he'd scored only fourteen goals from 103 league games, over the previous three seasons.

Nevertheless, Tom Ritchie partnered Paul Cheesley in Bristol City's attack for the whole of their 1975-76 season.

In 1975-76, the Second Division promotion race was closely fought between four or five teams, and first place changed hands on several occasions.

Bristol City began well, although their crowds weren't great. By October 18th, they were top of the Division after winning eight of their first thirteen games.

Paul Cheesley had started the season in electric form, scoring eleven goals, including a hat-trick during their 4-1 away win at York City.

Ashton Gate crowds had, however, varied between only ten and twelve thousand.

19,132 turned up for their match against lowly, fifteenth-placed West Bromwich Albion, though, on Saturday 25th October. The two Browns, Ally and Tony, both scored second half goals, securing a shock 2-0 away win for Albion, and Sunderland subsequently replaced the Robins as Second Division leaders.

A run of four games without a win followed, and with just two points earned, City were just hanging on inside the top three, but only because the teams below them were also faltering. Notts County were fifth, but they'd won just twice in eleven games, while unbeaten rivals Bristol Rovers had risen to fourth place, but they then won only one more game prior to Christmas.

On Saturday 22nd November, Bristol City again hammered York 4-1 with a superb Tom Ritchie hat-trick, this time. Geoff Merrick headed in their fourth, but only 11,228 had again watched the match. City continued steadily, nevertheless, earning five points from their next four games, cementing their place inside the top three, behind leaders Sunderland and second-placed Bolton Wanderers.

21,471 had attended City's 2-2 Boxing Day home draw with Plymouth Argyle (Merrick, Collier), and then on the following day, Saturday 27th December, Tom Ritchie's blast secured a 1-0 away win at Portsmouth.

Four points from their first three games of 1976 then lifted City above Bolton Wanderers, and into second place, although the Robins had played one extra game.

On Saturday 7th February, a very healthy 23,316 Ashton Gate crowd again went home disappointed, as Southampton's stars (Osgood, Channon, McCalliog, etc) earned a good 1-1 draw.

Tom Ritchie had scored his twelfth goal of the season, but yet again, City failed to win in front of a good home crowd. Fortunately, they continued to maintain their good away form, after winning 1-0 away at Orient (Ritchie), one week later.

Bristol City returned to the top of the Second Division on Saturday 6th March, after two goals from Tom Ritchie and another from Paul Cheesley had hammered Luton Town 3-0, but the Robins **had** played two more games than second-placed Sunderland.

The Second Division Summit Meeting took place on a Tuesday night, 23rd March.

A big crowd, 38,395, Sunderland's third largest home crowd of the season, filled Roker Park for a pulsating match, between two quality teams destined for First Division football.

SUNDERLAND		BRISTOL CITY
Jim Montgomery	1	Ray Cashley
Dick Malone	2	Don Gillies
Joe Bolton	3	Brian Drysdale
Ray Train	4	Gerry Gow
Jackie Ashurst	5	Gary Collier
Bobby Moncur	6	Geoff Merrick
Bobby Kerr	7	Trevor Tainton
Billy Hughes	8	Tom Ritchie
Mel Holden	9	Paul Cheesley
Pop Robson	10	Gerry Sweeney
Roy Greenwood	11	Clive Whitehead

Amidst a rampant atmosphere, under the floodlights, City shared the points with Sunderland, after Gerry Sweeney and Mel Holden had both hit second half goals.

It had been **that** performance, more than any other, that proved City as totally worthy of First Division football. Their defence kept nineteen clean sheets in 1975-76, brilliantly marshalled by the Bristolian central defensive partnership of Merrick and Collier, with Gillies temporarily converted to right back, whilst Sweeney had covered for their injured midfielder Jimmy Mann.

Ray Cashley, Gary Collier, Geoff Merrick, Trevor Tainton, Paul Cheesley and Keith Fear were all Bristolians, born and bred, and most of that City team had played more than 200 league and cup games together. Their team ethic was heavily important and evident in the spirit they'd shown on the pitch.

Their promotion campaign came to a climax on a Tuesday night, 20th April, the day after Sunderland had beaten Bolton 2-1 at Roker Park to pull promotion from out of Bolton's hands, as Johnny Giles' West Brom had charged through strongly on the rails to go third in the table. Bristol City only had to beat Portsmouth at home to secure promotion back to the First Division for the first time in seventy years.

27,300, the Robins' largest home crowd of the season, packed Ashton Gate, and then, just three minutes into the game, left winger Clive Whitehead cut inside before he drove the ball past Pompey's keeper Phil Figgins.

The remainder of the match was particularly uncomfortable watching for the home fans as an enthusiastic Portsmouth side, with nothing to play for, but that included young striker Chris Kamara and veteran midfielder George Graham, piled pressure after pressure on City's defence. The

Robins' defensive line was well protected, though, by Gillies, Gow, Tainton and Whitehead, and they dug in for victory.

At the final whistle, a mass pitch invasion took place jubilantly, and City's players, all heroes, were chaired off the pitch on supporters' shoulders and into the Williams Stand changing rooms.

Sunderland won the Second Division Championship title on the final Saturday of the season, but City went up in second place, and West Bromwich Albion just beat an unlucky, but brilliant Bolton Wanderers team to that third promotion place.

Tom Ritchie and Paul Cheesley had scored 33 Second Division goals between them, proving to be a formidable attacking partnership, while City's classy defence had conceded only 35 goals in 42 games.

On the opening day of the 1976-77 First Division season, Bristol City visited the mighty Arsenal. 41,082 attended Highbury, on a bright, sunny, mid-August Saturday afternoon, as Paul Cheesley tormented and tore Arsenal's defence to bits.

ARSENAL		BRISTOL CITY
Jimmy Rimmer	1	Ray Cashley
Pat Rice	2	Gerry Sweeney
Sammy Nelson	3	Brian Drysdale
Trevor Ross	4	Jimmy Mann
David O'Leary	5	Gary Collier
Peter Simpson	6	Geoff Merrick
Alan Ball	7	Trevor Tainton
George Armstrong	8	Tom Ritchie
Malcolm MacDonald	9	Don Gillies
John Radford	10	Paul Cheesley
Alex Cropley	11	Clive Whitehead
Peter Storey	12	Keith Fear

In the second half Paul Cheesley headed in Clive Whitehead's flicked cross to give City the lead, and their winning goal, but Cheesley's whole performance was a display to remember.

Earlier, he'd towered above O'Leary to head the influential Whitehead's right wing cross against the foot of Rimmer's post. Then, in the second half, Ritchie's left wing cross was attacked by Cheesley but tipped over the bar by Rimmer. Cheesley was unbeatable and unchallengeable in the air, and then he leapt high above O'Leary again, flicking a long ball on for Ritchie to run onto, but the Scot prodded just over.

Cheesley was applauded off the pitch by the Highbury crowd, and he also received plaudits from *The Big Match* pundits, suggesting an imminent England call-up.

Three days later, at home to Stoke City, Paul Cheesley jumped for an aerial challenge with Peter Shilton, beating the England keeper, but he headed just over the crossbar. However, Cheesley landed off-weight on the late Summer dry turf, ripping his cartilage, but he also suffered torn ligaments, as well as a broken bone in his knee.

At just twenty-three years old, Paul Cheesley's football career was finished. He'd scored 20 goals in 63 league starts for Bristol City. Cheesley still manages the Knowle Hotel in Leighton Road, Bristol, with quiz nights on every Tuesday night, and a music quiz on the first Thursday of every month, serving a lovely pint of Wadworth's.

Losing Paul Cheesley was a huge loss, and City never scored enough goals to really become the First Division sensation they'd threatened to be on that opening Saturday.

Norman Hunter was signed from Leeds United for just £40,000 during October 1976, and left-back Brian Drysdale subsequently left Bristol City after 282 league games for the Robins.

Brian Drysdale, County Durham-born, with his brilliant Edwardian *Dr Watson* moustache, moved to Reading in February 1977. Although he helped the Royals off the bottom of Division Three, and they also kept six clean sheets towards the end of that season, Reading could not escape relegation down to Division Four, finishing just one point below Portsmouth in fifth-bottom position, and safety.

Geoff Merrick moved over to left-back to make room for Hunter in central defence. Hunter was brought in to add bite to their defence, but he was also given extra responsibility at City, given his experience. At Leeds, he'd win the ball and then just pass it to a ball player like Bremner, Giles or Gray as soon as he could. At Bristol City, other players were winning the ball, before giving it to their playmaker Hunter.

Norman Hunter played 108 First Division games for City, between 1976 and 1979.

In November 1976, Alan Dicks then paid Liverpool £50,000 for another former First Division Championship winner, Peter Cormack. Cormack's place in Liverpool's midfield had been taken by both Ray Kennedy and Terry McDermott.

Although City didn't show the sparkle they'd promised when beating Arsenal back in August, they became a composed and well-organised First Division outfit, and very hard to beat. They won enough 1-0's to just survive on the last day of the season, as Sunderland unfortunately dropped back down to the Division of which they'd been Champions, just a year earlier.

Attendances were also finally good at Ashton Gate, averaging nearly 25,000 during their first Division One season, and a huge 38,688 crowd had watched their 2-1 home win over Liverpool (Chris Garland 2), on Monday 16th May 1977.

With their great back four of Sweeney, Collier, Hunter and Merrick, and a decent quality, protective midfield of Tainton, Cormack, Gow and Whitehead, City had also conceded only 48 First Division goals, fewer than Derby County's 1975 League Champions had conceded, but they also kept thirteen clean sheets, excellent for a team finishing only one point above the relegation zone.

However, they'd scored only 38 goals, and top scorer Tom Ritchie had scored only seven goals, clearly missing his inspired partner Cheesley, while his various partners Jimmy Mann, Don Gillies and Chris Garland all struggled against the tougher First Division defences. Paul Cheesley had indeed been very badly missed.

Bristol City survived in the First Division for four seasons, though, and they even finished as high as mid-table on one occasion. They were finally relegated in 1980, just as their great promotion team gradually fell apart, through age.

Keith Fear, scorer of that crucial equaliser against Leeds United, had left Ashton Gate back in 1978, after nine years at City, having played 151 league games and scoring thirty-two goals.

Gary Collier also left in 1979, after playing 193 games at central defence in seven seasons, before he moved to the NASL. There weren't many better centre-backs in Bristol City's long history than Collier, their hardened six foot, one inch tall Bristolian, who was strong in the air and a sharply-focussed close marker.

Don Gillies left for City's neighbours Bristol Rovers in 1980, after 200 league games for City, the best years of his career. That £30,000 had been very well spent.

Gerry Gow had played 375 league games, scoring 48 goals, before he left during October 1980, joining John Bond's revived Manchester City, for a club record transfer fee of £175,000, after eleven years at Ashton Gate. The drooping moustached Glaswegian, their driving midfielder, gliding, skilful and strong, was a key player in City's team that reached the epic, famous 1981 Cup Final against Tottenham.

Tom Ritchie left Bristol City for Sunderland in 1980, after playing 321 league games and scoring 77 goals, but he then returned to Ashton Gate in 1982.

Also in 1980, Birmingham-born Clive Whitehead had returned to the West Midlands, after eight seasons at Bristol City, signing for West Bromwich Albion for £100,000, having played 229 games out on the left wing at Ashton Gate.

Ray Cashley, the Robins' greatest-ever goalkeeper, had played 262 games for City, from 1970 until 1981, and he famously scored during Bristol City's 3-1 win over Hull City on 18th September 1973, from a clearance. After a loan spell at Hereford United, he moved back to Bristol, joining Rovers where he played for three more seasons.

The most poignant departures, though, came in early 1982, after what became known in footballing folklore as the **Ashton Gate Eight.**

Since their relegation from the First Division, Bristol City's financial troubles had spiralled, just as their fortunes on the field had plummeted.

During January 1982, to save the club from extinction, eight City players just tore up their contracts, sacrificing any pay-offs, and in most cases, they said goodbye to their professional football careers, just to save their club vital money, and allowing Bristol City to continue to exist.

Those eight players, Trevor Tainton, Geoff Merrick, Gerry Sweeney, Jimmy Mann, Chris Garland, David Rodgers, Julian Marshall and Peter Aitken, are rightly remembered as real football heroes.

Trevor Tainton had been granted a testimonial, over five years earlier, and he'd played 486 league games, and over 500 in all competitions for Bristol City.

Their classy five foot, eight inch midfielder played in all 42 games of their historic 1976 promotion season, and the powerfully-built right footer was probably the Robins' greatest ever footballer.

Gerry Sweeney, the club's greatest-ever right back, but who'd been equally comfortable holding their midfield together, had played over 400 league games during his eleven seasons at Ashton Gate.

Jimmy Mann, a squad player during City's greatest seasons, eventually went on to hold down a regular attacking role in the team, playing 231 league games during his eight seasons at Ashton Gate, and he scored thirty-one goals.

Geoff Merrick, a great sweeper, one of the very best in the league, before he moved over to left back, had played 434 competitive games during his fourteen seasons at Ashton Gate. Known as **Mr Consistent,** Merrick was a well-disciplined and stylish defender, and easily Bristol City's finest ever defensive player.

This Bristol City was a team that rivalled Leeds United and Manchester City, not in terms of their on-field success, but in terms of their loyalty to the club, and to each other.

Their classic 1976 team of Cashley, Sweeney, Drysdale, Gow, Collier, Merrick, Tainton, Ritchie, Cheesley, Mann, Whitehead, Gillies and Fear had played a total of over 3,600 league games for the club, at an average of nearly 280 games per player.

Bristol City were no team filled with big names. None of them were ever bought for big money, but they were a slow developing team made up of local lads, plus a few Scottish and North-eastern, low-profile imports.

Just by sticking together and patiently progressing, they slowly achieved top class football and they made themselves great.

Over the last one hundred and something-teen years, Bristol City have played top flight football for only four seasons; those four seasons between 1976 and 1980.

There is no doubt at all, that as slow and as late as their run came, because if this book had departed a year early, in 1975, then Bristol City would certainly have missed their connection and been signed off to the maintenance shed with Aston Villa, Orient, Hull City, Fulham, Millwall, Sheffield Wednesday, Luton Town, Nottingham Forest, Charlton Athletic and Bolton Wanderers.

That Bristol City team, as late running as their train finally arrived, fully deserved their place amongst the great teams of the Seventies.

They *made* themselves great; *self-made* greatness, Great Western greatness.

THE DEEP NORTH, Part Three

The Return of the North Kings

SUNDERLAND'S FA CUP WIN IN 1973 had appeared to lift the clouds and all the gloom from the North-east. Darlington, who'd finished rock bottom of the Football League in 1972-73, managed to succeed in avoiding re-election at the end of 1973-74.

Hartlepool, who had applied for re-election more times than any other Football League club, won thirteen out of nineteen games between mid-October and early April, and they'd even flirted with a promotion battle with just seven games remaining.

Unfortunately, they lost four of those games, and dropped back down to mid-table.

Blyth Spartans had beaten Netherton, and then Alfreton, to reach the FA Cup Second round, where they'd held Third Division Grimsby Town to a 1-1 away draw, in front of a Blundell Park crowd of nearly 6,000.

Blyth were then promised a home draw against First Division Burnley if they'd won their replay, but the Mariners won 2-0 away, with 2,500 inside Blyth's Croft Park.

Even Northumberland's Berwick Rangers had won nine of their opening fourteen Scottish Second Division games, beating Kilmarnock twice, Airdrieonians and also Hamilton Accies. Kilmarnock had been the Scottish League Champions only eight years earlier; Airdrie topped the table for the whole season; and Hamilton were in second place when Berwick hammered them 4-0 away at Douglas Park.

Berwick were second in the Second Division on Saturday 3rd November, just one point behind Airdrie, in a promotion battle for top flight football for the first and only time in their fifty-eight year Scottish League history; looking set for league visits to Parkhead, Ibrox, Pittodrie, Easter Road and Tynecastle.

They continued to do well, losing just once in their next eleven games, and by the beginning of February, Berwick were still strong promotion hopefuls, just a single point behind second-placed Hamilton with a dozen games remaining.

They collapsed, though, winning only three of those twelve games, drawing six of them, and never again were Berwick even 500 miles from thoughts of promotion to the top division in Scottish football.

They finished sixth, some way behind the two promoted clubs, Airdrie and Kilmarnock, but due to the sunny skies over the Northumberland and County Durham coast, after Sunderland's FA Cup win, *the happiest Cup win of them all,* even Berwick Rangers were dreaming, instead of simply enduring.

Sunderland began their 1973-74 season just as they'd finished the previous season. Billy Hughes, their top scorer from 1972-73, scored their first of the new season to scrape a 1-1 draw at home to Orient.

That seemed like a disappointing result, but *that* Orient side enjoyed a sensational season during 1973-74, their second best since the War, with the weathered Mickey Bullock scoring most of their goals, alongside the lively and heavily bearded Barrie Fairbrother, his quick running partner in attack. Gerry Queen, Orient's fearless Glaswegian midfield menace, won the ball for their frailly-built, but gifted wing wizard Ricky Heppolette, who created many of Orient's fifty-five league goals.

With their rugged defence of Phil Hoadley, Tom Walley, Bill Roffey and Derrick Downing, Orient conceded only 42 goals, the third best defensive record in Division Two, and the third best defensive record of their entire history, as they eventually missed out on promotion to the First Division by just one point.

Sunderland then hammered Notts County 4-1 away. Vic Halom scored in each half, while Billy Hughes scored his second of the season, and Dennis Tueart, their second-highest scorer in 1972-73, scored their fourth.

After 1-1 draws at home to Cardiff City, and then away at Portsmouth, Dennis Tueart's first half goal was enough to beat Oxford United 1-0, away at The Manor Ground. After five games, Sunderland were in third place in Division Two, and level on seven points with the top two teams, Aston Villa and Bolton Wanderers.

Middlesbrough were one place below Sunderland, due to their lesser goal average, having beaten Portsmouth, Crystal Palace and Carlisle United. They'd lost 0-2 at home to Fulham, though, on Saturday 1st September, and were then held to a goalless draw at home to leaders Aston Villa a fortnight later.

It appeared to most that Middlesbrough would bravely fight another close promotion battle, before once again fading away. Less than 17,000 had attended Ayresome Park for their 1-0 home win over Carlisle. After two further goalless draws, away at both Orient and Blackpool, Boro remained just two points behind the new leaders Bristol City after seven games.

That draw away at Blackpool, on Saturday 22nd September, was Bobby Murdoch's league debut for Middlesbrough, though, after he'd signed on a free transfer from the Scottish League Champions Celtic.

Bobby Murdoch had won eight Scottish League titles and four Scottish Cups with Celtic, but best of all, he was one of the *Lisbon Lions,* the famous Celtic team that won the 1967 European Cup Final, in Lisbon, beating Inter Milan 2-1. He'd also won the Scottish Player of the Year Award in 1968-69.

Murdoch had put on a bit of weight, having turned to drink during several absences due to previous injuries, but he had the experience, he had the brains, and most of all he had the influence and the authority in midfield, as well as the skill, to push Boro onwards.

"Bob had the kind of gait which suggested that even when fit, he was always overweight," Boro manager Jack Charlton observed. "He admitted he had to diet to keep his weight down. He also told me he was working hard to get it under control. Thus, we had three of the best passers of the ball in England at the time in Murdoch, Souness and Armstrong."

Jack Charlton had needed a Dave Mackay type of player to take his young Boro team forward. Well, Mackay was thirty-three when he had signed for Derby County in 1968, but Murdoch was only twenty-nine when He moved to Teesside, after playing 290 Scottish First Division games for Celtic. The signing of Bobby Murdoch was possibly, *just possibly,* better than Brian Clough and Peter Taylor's signing of Mackay.

Murdoch scored his first goal for Middlesbrough in only his second game, their 2-0 home win over Bristol City, on Saturday 29th September.

He was the oldest player in the team, but their youngest player, David Armstrong, had scored the second, as only 17,049 had seen Boro rise to the top of Division Two, for the first time in forty-five years.

Three days later, on the Tuesday night, John Hickton scored twice, including a penalty kick, and Alan Foggon had hit the third, as Boro beat Orient 3-2 after an entertaining topsy-turvy promotion clash, in front of 22,164, the first Ayresome Park crowd of more than twenty thousand for fourteen months.

Middlesbrough's average home crowd, during 1972-73, had been a little over ten thousand long-suffering fans, who had very little hope for the future.

Hope had arrived, at last, though. Bobby Murdoch's second half goal beat Swindon Town 1-0 away, on Saturday 6th October. Those were the sorts of game that Boro had lost during the previous few seasons. Another big crowd of 22,135 attended their North Yorkshire derby match at home to Hull City, who boasted a top quality forward line of Ken Wagstaff and Stuart Pearson.

A late goal from reserve team striker Malcolm Smith, deputising for the injured David Mills, had secured their seventh league win of the season, and Middlesbrough were two points clear at the top of the Second Division.

Newcastle United, with a mostly settled eleven of McFaul, Nattrass, Clark, McDermott, Howard, Moncur, Smith, Cassidy, Supermac, Tudor and Hibbitt, began the season decently, winning four of their opening seven games, while losing only once, and they were third in the First Division by mid-September.

A draw away at Coventry was followed by defeats at home to QPR, and then away at Liverpool, and United dropped down to eighth in the table.

Newcastle then won four on the bounce, though.

Supermac's first half goal had secured a 1-0 win over Manchester City, on Saturday 13th October, and a week later, Supermac hit two second half goals, one from the penalty spot after John Tudor had been fouled, during their 2-0 win over Chelsea.

Two unsung moustached heroes, Stewart Barrowclough and Tommy Gibb, both scored in United's 2-0 win away at Tottenham, on Saturday 27th October. Gibb scored again, one week later, as well as Terry McDermott, during their 2-1 home win over Stoke City. United returned to second position in the First Division, behind runaway leaders Leeds United, but Keith Weller put paid to Newcastle's winning run, scoring in Leicester City's 1-0 win at Filbert Street, on the following Saturday.

Sunderland, third-placed in Division Two, played their first ever game in European football, on Wednesday 19th September, away in Budapest, the scene of Newcastle's magnificent Fairs Cup triumph, four years earlier.

In front of a fiery 35,000 Magyar crowd, inside the Nepstadion, the same Sunderland eleven that had beaten Leeds in the FA Cup Final won 2-0 away at Vasas Budapest. Billy Hughes and Dennis Tueart both scored second half goals in their historic win in the European Cup Winners' Cup.

Sunderland were, by a long way, the Bookies' favourites to be Second Division Champions, so good they'd been to go away to Eastern Europe, and outplay one of the very top Hungarian teams, who'd won two Hungarian League Championships during the previous ten years.

Frankly, Sunderland's ascent to the First Division couldn't possibly be stopped, especially under the brand new system of three up and three down, between the top two Divisions.

A big crowd of 27, 582 attended Roker Park for their third home game, against tenth placed Luton Town. A home win was a formality, on paper. On grass, though, it was different, and Luton actually scraped a 1-0 away win, after Barry Butlin scored the second of his seventeen league goals of the season, early in the game, for the Hatters.

The **big** story of that match, though, wasn't a huge story at that time. Ritchie Pitt had been carried off the pitch during the second half, after hurting his knee, but Micky Horswill had already been replaced by substitute David Young, so Sunderland had to battle with ten men for the last half hour, to try and earn some kind of point.

Against Luton's well-drilled defence, though, Sunderland couldn't do that, but Ritchie Pitt's knee injury, initially believed to have been minor, actually proved to be terminal. He'd got his studs caught in the turf as John Ryan had pushed him from behind. It was an innocuous, petulant foul that occurs in every single game, and it was punished with just a free-kick, and with not even a booking from the referee.

Ritchie Pitt had damaged medial ligaments in his right knee, though, and he was left lying on a stretcher in the hospital, for hours without treatment.

He never played another game for Sunderland ever again.

Sports medical intelligence has improved a great deal since 1973, and today, Pitt would be immediately treated. He played twenty-six games for Sunderland's reserves, before having his contract terminated in 1975. That was the life of a footballer, back then.

Just get on with your life now, and thanks for playing.

For Sunderland, the problem was that they'd lost a player who was now worth at least £100,000, and that was a huge loss for a club like Sunderland.

They couldn't just go and buy a £100,000 centre half, back then, to replace Ritchie Pitt.

David Young, who took Pitt's place in the team, was decent, but he was nowhere near the player that Pitt was, not as mean nor as tactically sharp, and Sunderland dropped crucial points, as a result.

Just two wins from their next six league games had left Sunderland down in the bottom half of the table by early November.

Sunderland did beat Vasas Budapest 1-0 in their European Cup Winners' Cup First round, second leg match, winning 3-0 on aggregate after Dennis Tueart scored from the penalty spot. In the Second round, they were drawn at home to Sporting Lisbon, who Newcastle had beaten en route to their 1969 Fairs Cup win.

Sporting were the second-most successful Portuguese club, behind Benfica, in both domestic and European football, and they boasted four members of the current Portugal national team, that had been fighting a tight battle with Bulgaria in their 1974 World Cup Finals qualifying group.

They also included Hector Yazalde, the Argentinian international striker, the *Lionel Messi* of his day, who scored forty-six league goals during 1973-74, winning the UEFA Golden Boot award.

On Wednesday 24th October, 31,568, the fourth largest Roker Park crowd of that season, enjoyed a display of true brilliance, against brilliance, amidst a truly rotten run of miserable mediocrity in the Second Division.

Just over half an hour into the game, Bobby Kerr fired Sunderland ahead, and then he crossed for Mick Horswill to head them into a two goal lead, with just twenty-five minutes remaining. Dennis Tueart appeared to have given Sunderland a 3-0 lead, but he was flagged for a disputed offside decision.

As time ticked towards full-time, the prolific Yazalde, who'd been well patrolled throughout the match by Dave Watson, headed a crucial away goal, after Sporting had broken against the run of play.

Even so, their 2-1 win was a decent result, after a dominant performance against one of the best teams in Europe, and the twenty-odd thousand fans that had stayed away deserved to miss the match.

A fortnight later, with fifty thousand packing the Estadio Jose Alvalade, as they should have done back at Roker, Yazalde and Fragulto scored in each half for a 2-0 victory, and Sporting went through, 3-2 on aggregate.

Sporting reached the Semi-finals of the Cup Winners' Cup, before being beaten by the eventual winners, Magdeburg of East Germany. Hector Yazalde went on to score 104 goals in 104 games for Sporting Lisbon, and he also scored twice for Argentina during the 1974 World Cup Finals.

Back in the Second Division, Sunderland continued to stumble.

They started November okay, though, losing away at Hull, before Dennis Tueart then scored a hat-trick, and Vic Halom also hit his eighth goal of the season, in Sunderland's 4-1 win over Swindon Town, on Saturday 10th November.

Halom, Tueart and Porterfield all then scored in their 3-0 hammering of Bolton Wanderers at Roker Park. They subsequently moved up to eighth place, after those wins, and they were only three points below the promotion zone in mid-November.

Sunderland won only two of their following twelve games, though, losing seven times, to drop straight back down, way down into the bottom half of the table, and eight points behind the promotion places by late January.

Manchester United travelled up to Newcastle, on Saturday 17th November, to face the third-placed Magpies, with just under 42,000 packed into St James's Park, and Tommy Cassidy had one of the games of his life.

Bought for just £25,000 from Glentoran, back in October 1970, Cassidy had failed to secure a regular starting place at Newcastle, playing just twenty-two First Division games during his first three years at the club.

Sometimes nicknamed *Hop-a-long,* due to his lazy, leisurely appearance, Cassidy had a quick brain, and he could thread a low through-ball into the tightest of gaps.

In the absence of the inconsistent Stewart Barrowclough, he finally enjoyed a good run in the team, right from the start of the season.

With the artful Terry McDermott in the middle, alongside Cassidy, and the lively Terry Hibbitt opposite the lethargic, but ingenious Jimmy Smith out on the wings, Newcastle enjoyed their best spell in League and Cups combined, during the 1973-74 season.

Tommy Cassidy scored twice against Manchester United, as they came back from two goals down, scored by George Graham and Lou Macari, and then he fed substitute Georgie Hope for the winner. Newcastle returned to second place in the league, but a long way behind the still unbeaten leaders Leeds.

FIRST DIVISION LEADERS, 17TH NOVEMBER 1973

	PL	W	D	L	F	A	PTS
Leeds United	16	12	4	0	32	8	28
NEWCASTLE UTD	16	9	3	4	27	17	21
Liverpool	16	9	3	4	20	13	21
Everton	16	8	5	3	21	14	21
Burnley	16	7	6	3	23	16	20
Ipswich Town	16	7	5	4	27	24	19

Of course, Newcastle United collapsed.

They won none of their next five games, and lost four successive games in December, including a frenzied battle against Leeds on Boxing Day. In front of a 54,474 St James's Park crowd, Newcastle were excellent, with Tommy Gibb, in for one of his fifteen games of that season, superlative in cutting out Billy Bremner, Leeds's best player.

Supermac went close to scoring, and John Tudor had a header wonderfully cleared off the line by Trevor Cherry, but United eventually went down 1-0, after Paul Madeley's early goal, scoring his second of the season.

John Tudor scored to beat his old team Sheffield United 1-0, just before New Year, and then Terry Hibbitt curled in a wonderful goal against Arsenal, away at Highbury, on New Year's Day, lifting Newcastle back up to seventh place, and only one point below the UEFA Cup places.

From the New Year onwards, though, Newcastle won just twice out of nineteen league games, losing nine times. They ended that 1973-74 season eighth from bottom, and only two points above Southampton, who were relegated.

After the New Year, there was only the FA Cup to play for, for Newcastle United.

With Bobby Murdoch and Graeme Souness running their midfield, and Alan Foggon, up front with John Hickton, finally achieving his potential, Middlesbrough won sixteen of their opening twenty-six matches. Stuart Boam had formed a telepathic understanding with Willie Maddren at the back, and with John Craggs and Frank Spraggon as full backs, Boro boasted the safest defence in the Football League. Goalkeeper Jim Platt had conceded only fifteen goals prior to the end of January.

37,038, the biggest Middlesbrough home crowd since Alan Peacock was knocking them in, had filled Ayresome Park on Boxing Day 1973 for the local red and white North-east derby match. Both teams were a little under-strength for a bruising battle, played at a fast, First Division pace, as Middlesbrough's John Craggs missed only his second game of the season, and he was replaced by local boy Peter Creamer.

For Bob Stokoe's side, Jim Montgomery missed his only game of the season, for *this* game of all games, and Trevor Swinburne played his second league game in goal. Swinburne had won the 1969 FA Youth Cup with Sunderland, at just fifteen years old, following their 6-3 aggregate win over West Brom.

He failed to break through to the first team, though, making only eight league starts during his nine years at Roker Park. Trevor Swinburne finally left Sunderland in 1977, for Carlisle United, where he played 280 games.

Also absent from Sunderland's team, but more significantly, was their midfield enforcer Micky Horswill. He'd limped off, injured, during their 1-1 home draw with West Brom, four days before, and Rod Belfitt, Leeds United's former utility forward, who'd signed for £70,000 from Everton, back in October, started in midfield.

Initially bought as cover for either Billy Hughes or Ian Porterfield, the money spent on Belfitt would prove to be money well spent, in the short term.

MIDDLESBROUGH		SUNDERLAND
Jim Platt	1	Trevor Swinburne
Peter Creamer	2	Dick Malone
Frank Spraggon	3	Ron Guthrie
Graeme Souness	4	Rod Belfitt
Stuart Boam	5	Dave Watson
Willie Maddren	6	David Young
Bobby Murdoch	7	Bobby Kerr
David Mills	8	Billy Hughes
John Hickton	9	Vic Halom
Alan Foggon	10	Ian Porterfield
David Armstrong	11	Dennis Tueart

Alan Foggon galloped clear of Young, running onto Bobby Murdoch's perfectly weighted ball, over the top of Sunderland's defence, before firing low past Swinburne.

Stuart Boam was then harshly adjudged to have fouled Porterfield, just inside the box. The challenge looked very soft, but Dennis Tueart fired his penalty kick high into the top right corner of Jim Platt's goal, only the fourteenth league goal he'd conceded in twenty-two games.

After the break, though, David Armstrong sent a right sided free-kick curling towards the far side of the Sunderland area. Stuart Boam, brilliant in the air, had beaten Guthrie and he powered in his header, beyond Swinburne's desperate dive.

Sunderland lost all three of their games during the Festive period, without Horswill, and on Wednesday 9th January, they were also knocked out of their FA Cup, in the Third round, after a replay, at home to Carlisle United, with just under 26,000 inside Roker Park.

When Horswill returned on the following Saturday, for their 0-0 draw at home to Oxford United, he was never right again, playing the full ninety minutes in just two of Sunderland's next six matches.

In spite of this, Sunderland started to win again, from the beginning of February. They hammered Millwall 4-0 (Halom 2, Hughes 2), and then Rod Belfitt scored his third goal for the club during their 2-1 home win against Bobby Charlton's Preston. Vic Halom's second half goal secured a hard-earned win that had lifted them back into the top ten. Vic Halom then scored his fourth goal in three games as Sunderland won 1-0 away at Sheffield Wednesday, on the last Saturday of February.

On Saturday 2nd March, 41,658 filled Roker Park's terraces, and their largest home crowd of the season watched runaway leaders Middlesbrough outclass a flat-footed Sunderland team, winning 2-0 after goals in each half from David Mills and Alan Foggon. When Dennis Longhorn replaced Micky Horswill during the second half, the home supporters had also seen their wonderful red-headed midfield warrior wave his goodbyes to Roker Park.

Three days later, on Saturday 9th March, Dennis Tueart scored his forty-fifth and forty-sixth league goals for Sunderland, as they returned to winning ways, beating Portsmouth 3-0, in front of a tiny, disheartened Roker Park crowd of only 8,142.

Bobby Kerr scored their third goal, but both Tueart and Horswill then missed Sunderland's 3-0 defeat away at Crystal Palace.

On the following Saturday, having already lost Ritchie Pitt to injury, Sunderland lost two more of their Cup Final heroes, when Manchester City paid a club record transfer fee of £275,000 for Dennis Tueart, but they also paid £100,000 for Micky Horswill.

Dennis Tueart had played 182 league games for Sunderland, but he went on to win the League Cup with City, as well as competing for the First Division title, while at Maine Road.

That move was certainly understandable for both clubs, and also for Tueart, who won England caps while he was at City, but the decision to let go their twenty-one year old warrior Horswill still baffles.

In return, Sunderland had paid a club record transfer fee of £125,000 for Tony Towers, who'd been so dependable for City during their First Division title charge in 1972, before losing his place to Rodney Marsh.

Apart from covering injuries at Maine Road, Micky Horswill was never likely to break into the midfield stronghold of Bell and Oakes, especially with their old teammate Tony Book managing the club after April.

In all, Horswill started just eleven First Division games for Man City, in fifteen months, and the moved badly harmed his stature in the game.

Micky Horswill lost confidence, and he eventually left Maine Road, during July 1975, for Plymouth Argyle.

Plymouth Argyle? This was a player who'd outplayed Colin Bell, Alan Ball and Billy Bremner during Sunderland's run to FA Cup glory. What a waste!

There are many, many wonderful football stories within the Glam Soccer era, but against that, there were many terrible moments. The career-ending injuries to Colin Bell, Tony Green, John Ritchie, Paul Cheesley and Glyn Pardoe all rank highest, but the waste of the talent of Micky Horswill moving to City ranks not far behind.

It resulted in the slow destruction of a great player who had self-constructed himself into a hyperactive, super midfielder in the same mould as Dennis Wise, David Batty and Michael Essien.

Mick Horswill played 102 league games for Plymouth, but the experience must have mildly tormented him to the end of his career, as he watched the fortunes of his beloved Sunderland both rise and fall.

He became the forgotten hero of their wonderful FA Cup win.

Micky Horswill deserved much better than that.

Newcastle began their 1973-74 FA Cup campaign at home to Isthmian League team Hendon, in front of a 31,606 St James's Park crowd. Centre back Pat Howard headed United ahead in the first half, but St James's Park and Joe Harvey had feared the worst after Rod Haider, an insurance broker, equalised for Hendon, after firing emphatically past Iam McFaul with twenty minutes remaining.

Hendon, rather than hosting the replay at their tiny Claremont Road ground, decided to switch the match to Watford's Vicarage Road.

Hendon's biggest-ever crowd of over fifteen thousand provided a huge cash bonus for the tiny London club, and the BBC TV cameras were also there, just as they'd been at Edgar Street, two years earlier, hoping for another potential giant-killing.

Cut to the parka-wearing fans running amok, with arms aloft, in celebration?

No. Supermac, Hibbitt, Tudor and McDermott (from the penalty spot) all scored as Newcastle hammered their non-league opposition 4-0, very professionally.

Again, in the Fourth round, Newcastle made it tough for themselves.

Drawn at home against Scunthorpe, ninth from bottom of the Fourth Division, Nolan Keeley had fired the Irons ahead before half-time, but Terry McDermott's thirty yard screamer, after the break, secured United an away replay at The Old Show Ground.

Scunthorpe's near record home crowd of over 19,000, again expecting another FA Cup shock win, were flattened after Supermac scored twice, and then Stewart Barrowclough slotted in another, as Newcastle won 3-0.

In the Fifth round, Newcastle were drawn away at West Bromwich Albion. Second Division West Brom weren't quite the team they were when they'd won the Cup six years earlier, but they still had quality players like Tony Brown, Asa Hartford, Willie Johnston and Len Cantello. West Brom were also very much in the Second Division promotion race, battling Orient, Blackpool, Luton, Carlisle and Nottingham Forest for the last two available places behind runaway leaders Middlesbrough.

A massive crowd of over 40,000 packed The Hawthorns, on Saturday 16th February, although nearly half of that crowd had made the long journey from the North.

West Brom had already knocked Everton out of the Cup, and once again the BBC TV cameras were at the game, ready to capture another giant-killing.

Newcastle United, wearing a new Brazilian-look away strip of yellow and green shirts, with light blue shorts, were many pundits' favourites to fall in a match that had Cup Upset written all over it.

Substitute Jimmy Smith, who'd replaced Terry Hibbitt early on, crossed from the right, and it was a good deep cross to Supermac at the far post. Supermac leapt and he headed the ball back across Peter Latchford's body, into the far right corner of West Brom's goal, to the frustration of his marker, John Wile.

"Jinky" Jimmy Smith had one of his most commanding games for Newcastle, and into the second half, a lovely passing move between Smith, Barrowclough, Supermac and Tudor, in the Hawthorns' mud, led to Stewart Barrowclough firing United into a 2-0 lead, from six yards out.

Frank Clark then lofted a ball down the left, for Barrowclough to cross, first time, and John Tudor placed his header just inside Latchford's near post.

"*BRAZIL! BRAZIL! BRAZIL!*" the Newcastle fans sang, in an ironic reference to their team's colours, from then on, every time either Smith, Supermac, Cassidy, McDermott or Tudor touched the ball.

Newcastle's reward for their superb 3-0 away win, was a Quarter-final tie at home to Nottingham Forest. Forest were a decent Second Division team, just like Sunderland were a year earlier, wearing a very flash red and white strip, just like Sunderland, and who'd absolutely hammered Manchester City, Bell, Lee, Summerbee, Marsh and all, in the previous round, just as Sunderland had done.....

Down in the Second Division, on Saturday 2nd February, Nottingham Forest had hammered Middlesbrough 5-1. That had only been Boro's second league defeat of the season, and they responded by going on an eleven match unbeaten run up to mid-April, winning nine in a row, scoring twenty-three goals, but conceding only three.

On Saturday 30th March, Middlesbrough beat second-placed Luton Town 1-0, away at Kenilworth Road, in front of a near sell-out 19,812 crowd. David Mills forced in a close range second half goal, securing the Second Division title, with six games left.

One week earlier, they'd assured promotion with a 1-0 home win over Oxford United, in front of an Ayresome Park crowd of nearly 27,000. Oxford's chairman, Bob Kearsey, had even previously accused Jack Charlton of promoting "anti-football."

"I'm sick and tired of the negative tactics employed by teams like Middlesbrough," he ranted. "They stink. They are traitors to the game."

It was a silly rant. Mr Kearsey clearly had little tactical grasp of the game. By **teams like Middlesbrough, did** he also mean Derby County, Leeds United and Liverpool, who built from the back, just like Boro did? As strong as Middlesbrough were at the back, and as much as the team could dig in to defend a lead, they did have quality midfield players, as well as exciting attacking talents, and you could never seriously describe them as anything like *anti-football.*

After they'd won the title, Boro beat Notts County 4-0 on Saturday 6th April, before easing off a little, resting Jim Platt, Bobby Murdoch, John Hickton, Alan Foggon and Frank Spraggon.

As a result of taking their foot off the pedal, Middlesbrough were held to a goalless draw by Bolton Wanderers, at Ayresome Park, before they lost at both Cardiff and Bolton during the Easter weekend.

On Saturday 20th April, though, Jack Charlton fielded his full strength first team for Boro's final home game, against Sheffield Wednesday, who were battling against relegation to Division Three.

The Owls were indeed battling, and they'd lost just two of their previous eight matches, winning four of them.

On Easter Monday, they'd beaten Preston North End 1-0, to effectively relegate Bobby Charlton's team, after a header by Tommy Craig, a future Newcastle star.

Sheffield Wednesday had arrived at Ayresome Park in a bit of good form.

Stuart Boam lifted the Second Division Championship trophy, in front of 25,287 home fans, but then Boro set about their work. Wednesday didn't have a bad side, with former Wolves defenders Shaw, who'd played in the 1972 UEFA Cup Final, and Holsgrove, plus future FA Cup winning captain Rodrigues.

MIDDLESBROUGH		SHEFFIELD WEDNESDAY
Jim Platt	1	Peter Springett
John Craggs	2	Peter Rodrigues
Frank Spraggon	3	Bernard Shaw
Graeme Souness	4	James Mullen
Stuart Boam	5	John Holsgrove
Willie Maddren	6	Roy Coyle
Bobby Murdoch	7	Eric Potts
Alan Foggon	8	Tommy Craig
David Mills	9	Brian Joicey
John Hickton	10	Eddie Prudham
David Armstrong	11	Danny Cameron
Harry Charlton	12	Peter Eustace

Brian Joicey had been a major influence in Coventry City's innovative and irresistible 1970 team, while Tommy Craig would become Newcastle United's Scottish international midfield general one year later.

Wednesday didn't have a bad side at all, but this Middlesbrough side was a positive Work of Art, and on this day they displayed it to all at Ayresome Park.

John Hickton flicked in a header from David Mills' cross, and then Mills fired home from the edge of the area, after Souness had beaten two players down the right, before cutting back a diagonal low cross inside.

Bobby Murdoch then rocketed a twenty yard shot into the top right corner of Springett's goal, to make the score 3-0.

At half-time.

Wednesday boss Steve Burtenshaw responded by replacing the ineffective Coyle with Peter Eustace, who should really have started the game.

Eustace had been West Ham's rock in midfield during the early Seventies, playing with Moore, Bonds, Hurst, Greaves and Brooking.

Peter Eustace was the very man to shore up the gaps in the Owls' midfield.

Boro just got better and better, though. You could have put both Bremner and Giles into this Wednesday team, and it would have made no difference.

Souness headed in his fourth goal for Middlesbrough, from Armstrong's corner, and then he fired in another, having been put through by Willie Maddren's long pass.

Alan Foggon made it six, skipping inside Holsgrove, before smashing the ball in, off Peter Springett's crossbar.

Graeme Souness completed his hat-trick, chipping in a direct free-kick from twenty-five yards out, before Alan Foggon played a one-two with Hickton, and then smashed home from six yards.

It really was like watching Brazil play in red and white. The 8-0 final score was just one goal short of Middlesbrough's record victory, and also just two goals short of Sheffield Wednesday's record defeat.

It was hardly a miracle, but what *was* a miracle was Wednesday picking themselves up a week later, to beat Bolton 1-0, and ensuring their ill-deserved survival in Division Two, while sending Malcolm Allison's Crystal Palace down to the Third Division.

Middlesbrough then won 4-2 away at relegated Preston North End, to end their 1973-74 season. Reserve team striker Peter Brine scored twice, while Foggon and Hickton both completed the scoring, but the Deepdale crowd of just over 16,000 witnessed the last competitive moment between two great brothers.

Jack Charlton and his brother Bobby, manager of Preston, two World Cup winners, warmly embraced at the end of the match, with one going up and the other going down, and eventually out of football management altogether, into media work and an executive post at Old Trafford.

Bobby had been, by far, the better footballer, but Jack became a World Class manager. He'd won the 1974 Manager of the Year award, ahead of both Don Revie and Bill Shankly, after leading Boro to the most emphatic title winning performance in Football League history.

Middlesbrough cruised to the Second Division title, in the end, finishing fifteen points clear of runners-up Luton Town. No other team has ever won any Division, in the history of the Football League, by such a margin, before or since.

Under a three points for a win system, Boro would have finished twenty-three points clear. After so many seasons, under the dignified management of North-east legend Stan Anderson, of disappointing late-season failures, they'd finally made mincemeat of Division Two, losing just four games out of forty-two, and winning twenty-seven.

Middlesbrough had kept twenty-seven clean sheets during 1973-74, and their regular defence of Platt, Craggs, Boam, Maddren and Spraggon missed only eight games, combined, out of a possible two hundred and ten Second Division matches.

In attack, Alan Foggon had had his greatest season, scoring twenty league and cup goals, with John Hickton and David Mills also sharing twenty-three between them. Graeme Souness had scored seven, during his first full season in league football, and Bobby Murdoch and David Armstrong contributed ten combined goals, but they'd created three times that amount with assists.

Prior to them losing 0-2 at home to Middlesbrough in early March, Sunderland had hammered Millwall 4-0 at Roker Park, on Saturday 2nd February, with Halom scoring twice, and Hughes the other two. That win, in front of only 17,486, less than nine months after Sunderland had won the Cup, was the start of a great run of just two defeats in eleven games, up to Easter.

Rod Belfitt had replaced the injured and inconsistent David Young throughout this period, providing proper experience and defensive expertise alongside Dave Watson.

Dave Watson, himself, had become an England player during their great run of eight league wins from eleven, making his international debut against Portugal, in Lisbon, Sir Alf Ramsey's last game as England manager.

England drew 0-0, and Watson then went on to play 63 times for England, thirteen of which were as a Sunderland player. Dave Watson became the first Sunderland player to play for England since Colin Grainger, back in 1957.

England lost none of their games during which Sunderland's Dave Watson started. Among those games were their 3-0 hammering of Czechoslovakia in a European Championship qualifying match, on 30th October 1974, and also their 2-0 spanking of West Germany, in a friendly match at Wembley, on 12th March 1975.

Dave Watson's last game for England, as a Sunderland player, was their 5-1 thrashing of Scotland at Wembley, in a Home International Championship match, on Saturday 24th May 1975.

On Good Friday, Sunderland hosted Carlisle United, in their biggest game of the season, so far. They'd won seven out of their last ten matches, but Carlisle, in fifth place, were cold. The Cumbrians had won only four out of their last twelve league matches.

SECOND DIVISION LEADERS, FRIDAY 12TH APRIL 1974

	PL	W	D	L	F	A	PTS
Middlesbrough	38	25	11	2	62	23	61
Luton Town	37	18	10	9	55	43	46
Orient	37	14	15	8	50	37	43
Blackpool	37	14	13	10	49	36	41
SUNDERLAND	37	16	9	12	49	36	41
Carlisle United	37	16	9	12	55	43	41
Nott'm Forest	37	13	14	10	50	36	40
West Brom	38	13	14	11	45	42	40

Roker Park's attendance of 34,179 was over four times the size of the crowd that had watched their 3-0 win over Portsmouth, just over a month earlier. Sunderland, undaunted by the apparent fickleness of many of their fans, were lifted by the passion of the majority.

Vic Halom and Billy Hughes both scored second half goals to secure a great 2-1 win, lifting Sunderland up into the meat of the promotion race, behind Middlesbrough and Luton.

Any one of six clubs could realistically claim the final promotion place, at the end of the first ever season of three up and three down, between the top two divisions.

Newcastle United welcomed Nottingham Forest, deeply involved in that Second Division promotion race, to St James's Park, on Saturday 9th March, for their FA Cup Quarter-final match. Over

54,000 totally filled their ground, the biggest crowd of the 1974 FA Cup competition, prior to the Semi-finals.

It was one of the most dramatic games ever played at Newcastle, but it also contained some of the most shameful scenes of crowd misbehaviour ever seen there.

Just ninety seconds into the match, Martin O'Neill hoisted a long, high ball, from just outside the centre circle, that bounced near the United six yard box. Ian Bowyer beat Bobby Moncur's shoulder challenge, and he leapt to head the ball over McFaul, and into the back of the net.

After twenty-five minutes, Newcastle equalised. Terry Hibbitt's right wing corner kick was only half-cleared by George Lyall, and so David Craig steamed into the area, and he smashed a rocket into the Forest net.

NEWCASTLE UNITED		NOTTINGHAM FOREST
Ian McFaul	1	Jim Barron
David Craig	2	Liam O'Kane
Frank Clark	3	John Winfield
Terry McDermott	4	Bob Chapman
Pat Howard	5	Dave Serella
Bobby Moncur	6	John Robertson
Stewart Barrowclough	7	Duncan McKenzie
Jimmy Smith	8	George Lyall
Supermac	9	Neil Martin
John Tudor	10	Martin O'Neill
Terry Hibbitt	11	Ian Bowyer
Alan Kennedy	12	John Galley

George Lyall's left-wing corner kick, from beneath the massed bank of Newcastle fans in the Leazes End, was flicked on at the near post by Duncan McKenzie, and the ball flew across the face of goal. The United defence were in a tangle, and they failed to clear. Liam O'Kane advanced and he slammed his shot into the roof of McFaul's net, from six yards out, sending Forest 2-1 up, going into the break.

Just about fifteen minutes into the second half, Forest put another good move together. McKenzie tackled Hibbitt, just inside the Newcastle half, and then he passed short to O'Neill. Martin O'Neill played back to John Robertson, and Robertson sprayed a beautiful ball up the left wing, for Bowyer to nod into the United area. Moncur went to clear, but he got a terrible touch, and McKenzie ran out to the loose ball, on the left side of the area. David Craig knocked him down from behind, and referee Gordon Kew, from Amersham, awarded a penalty kick to Forest.

It was a clear penalty, but for nearly a minute, Pat Howard argued, and complained, and he ranted at Mr Kew about his decision, right into the referee's face, and he stupidly got himself sent off.

George Lyall fired his penalty kick straight into the right corner of the Newcastle net, beating Iam McFaul's dive, and with just over half an hour to play, Newcastle United were 1-3 down, and also down to ten men.

The FA Cup dream that seemed so bright after their win at West Brom, was now just a sick nightmare.

The Newcastle fans in the Leazes End, behind the Nottingham Forest goal, then began to surge forward, against a thin line of police officers. The fans were almost on the bye-line as Bob Chapman blocked a John Tudor shot, deflecting it behind for another United corner.

Forest cleared Stewart Barrowclough's corner, and a minute later, several hundred Newcastle fans erupted out of the Leazes End, breaking the police lines, and they ran onto the pitch towards the east corner of the Gallowgate End, where the Nottingham Forest fans were.

There was no fighting. It was just a **handbags at twenty paces** type of stand-off.

Gordon Kew ordered both teams off the pitch, back to the changing rooms, for their safety, while the stand-off continued and more fans joined in, in the fun.

For eight minutes, both teams sat in their changing rooms, while police restored order on the pitch, arresting both old men and young kids. Referee Gordon Kew went to ask the Forest team if they wanted to go for a replay.

At 3-1 up, and playing against ten men, with just over twenty minutes remaining, and with a foot firmly in the Semis, Forest's players said "no", they'd finish the match.

After the re-start, though, ten-man Newcastle were a different animal, just as Forest were a bit flat, as well as flat-footed. From Terry McDermott's left-sided corner, Moncur's towering header was tipped over the bar by Jim Barron, after sixty-eight minutes.

Terry Hibbitt took the resultant corner from the right wing, and although Jim Barron jumped to claim the ball, Mr Kew awarded a penalty kick to Newcastle, after he'd spotted Barron pushing Supermac to the floor.

McDermott drilled the ball into the left corner of the Forest goal.

Terry Hibbitt then killed a long, towering Barron goal kick, dead, with just one touch, and he then set off, past O'Kane and Lyall, up the left wing.

He ran over half the length of the pitch, and nobody could stay with him.

Just a few yards from the Forest bye-line, Hibbitt crossed to the far post, where John Tudor threw himself at the ball, and powered a diving header past Jim Barron, as the Leazes End, and all of St James's Park went crazy.

With just seconds remaining, Jimmy Smith back-heeled a pass to John Tudor, on the Newcastle right. Tudor then crossed long into Forest's penalty area, to the far post, where Supermac cushioned a header back inside for captain Bobby Moncur to fire home, totally unmarked, from the edge of the six yard box.

With just ten men, what was the Newcastle captain, their only remaining centre half, doing attacking the Forest six yard box with such little time left on the clock?

It was tactical suicide, but that was the way Joe Harvey's Newcastle played, and it won the game, one of the most sensational FA Cup ties to have ever been played at St James's Park, and one of the greatest comebacks in FA Cup history.

Nottingham Forest's red shirted players just stood around the pitch, stunned, as all of Newcastle went to celebrate with Moncur. The black and white scarves all came out in the Leazes End, as **You'll Never Walk Alone** was sung as loudly as it could ever be sung.

Nineteen year-old full back Alan Kennedy had replaced the injured David Craig before the final whistle, so there were six future European Cup winning players on the pitch before the match ended.

On the following Monday, though, Nottingham Forest asked the FA to annul the match, arguing that the pitch invasion had caused the change of course of the game.

The Semi-final draw, made at lunch-time, drew Newcastle to play Burnley, the season's surprise high-flyers, and still fighting for a UEFA Cup place in Division One.

On Thursday 14th March, the FA annulled the result of Newcastle's Quarter-final win, declaring the match null and void due to the home crowd's misbehaviour.

The reaction from Newcastle was angry. Joe Harvey called the decision, "diabolical!"

"If the result doesn't stand," he queried, "how can the sending-off still stand?"

Supermac himself came out with an enigmatic statement. "My reaction is one of disgust, but not surprise," he declared. "I half expected a ridiculous solution, and they came up with one. The FA have taken all integrity away from referee Gordon Kew."

That last point was a good one. Although nobody can justify or commend the Newcastle fans for their pitch invasion, Gordon Kew refereed the game brilliantly, immediately taking both teams off the pitch, and he offered Forest the opportunity not to go back out, with a replay at their City Ground the result of the abandoned game. If Forest had been drawing 1-1, and still playing eleven men, there's little doubt they'd have taken the replay. They fancied their chances but they blew them.

Instead, Forest took a chance at a second bite of the cherry, and they came up lucky. Mindful of them declining Mr Kew's offer to replay at Nottingham, the FA also ruled that the replay would be played at Everton's Goodison Park.

It was a compromise, but still a very messy decision, and it did undermine the referee's authority. He had spoken to both teams, he'd assessed the ground situation, and then he declared the game good to continue.

On the Monday night of 18th March 1974, a massive crowd of 40,685 attended Nottingham Forest's "home" replay against Newcastle, played at Everton's Goodison Park.

The majority of the *neutral* crowd were Geordies, and although the game was end to end, and thoroughly exciting, broadcast live on BBC Radio's Evening Sports show, as Newcastle hit the woodwork on three occasions, and both keepers made several good saves, the game ended goalless after a scintillating period of extra-time.

Three nights later, on Thursday 21st March, again at Everton's Goodison Park, the two teams met in the second replay. Nottingham Forest were upset that they couldn't have the game at their City Ground, but it appeared that the FA were determined to keep the venue neutral, as in normal second replay situations, when there was a dispute of opinion between the two teams. Forest had had their chance to go back to Nottingham and win there.

A lesser crowd of 31,373 attended, but it was still a tremendous crowd for a second neutrally-staged FA Cup match within just a few days, between two teams, two sleeping giants, 213 miles apart.

After 30 minutes, Jimmy Smith leapt and headed a Jim Barron goal-kick back towards Forest's goal. Supermac set off fast after the ball, with only the moustached Dave Serella chasing him, hanging around his neck, and trying to bring him down.

Supermac was too strong, though, and he ran on to fire a low shot under Barron's body to send the majority of the crowd into celebration. Forest did score a late equaliser when Ian Bowyer hit a free-kick past McFaul, but the referee, David Smith of Stonehouse, harshly ordered the kick to be re-taken as Newcastle's wall wasn't ready.

"*HOWAY THE LADS! HOWAY THE LADS! HOWAY THE LADS!*" echoed around Liverpool that night, and on the long overnight train journey back to Newcastle, via various sleeping stops, on railway benches at Leeds and York, awaiting connections.

They were a different breed of fan, back then.

Just imagine, over 72,000 Newcastle and Nottingham Forest fans making two round trips of a combined 850 miles from their homes, within four days, and on weekday nights? Now Burnley awaited Newcastle United, in the Semi-finals, at Hillsborough.

On the day after Good Friday, Saturday 13th April, Sunderland hosted Bristol City, who'd just beaten Nottingham Forest 1-0 themselves at Ashton Gate, the day before. City had nothing to play for, though, while Sunderland had everything to play for.

With the pressure on, and with another half-decent Roker Park crowd of 28,884 roaring them on, Sunderland seemed to be more affected by playing an important match less than 24 hours after their win over Carlisle than the Robins were. Tom Ritchie gave City a first half lead, but Dennis Longhorn equalised just before half-time, firing past Ray Cashley after playing a one-two with Tony Towers.

After the break, though, Sunderland were leaden-footed and lacklustre, and Welsh international winger John Emanuel scored to secured a shock 2-1 away win for City.

On the following Tuesday, Sunderland visited Carlisle United, with nearly 20,000 packing the *hencoop*, as Bill Shankly described Brunton Park, a "glorified hencoop," guarded only by sheep.

A contentious penalty kick was awarded to Carlisle, and then converted by Chris Balderstone, during the second half, and Sunderland now needed a miracle to go up.

Blackpool hammered Carlisle 4-0 on the following Saturday, which gave Sunderland some hope, just as they'd won 2-1 away at Aston Villa (Towers, Kerr), to stay four points behind Blackpool, who were now third in the table.

On the final Saturday of the season, Tony Towers and Bobby Kerr both scored second half goals to beat Blackpool, with only 22,331 inside Roker Park.

Carlisle United had beaten Aston Villa 2-0, though, to rise to third, so Sunderland were doomed to another season in the Second Division.

Nevertheless, they ended the season by brilliantly winning a classic Mayday midweek match, away at second placed Luton Town.

In front of 20,285, Kenilworth Road's biggest crowd of the season, Billy Hughes, Jackie Ashurst, Tony Towers and Vic Halom all scored during Sunderland's excellent 4-3 away win.

Sunderland finished the 1973-74 season in sixth place, just two points below Carlisle United, who'd beaten Orient to the third promotion place by a single point.

Too many soft defeats in December and January had proved costly, and their excellent, resurgent run of eleven wins from sixteen games between February and May, scoring twenty-eight goals and conceding seventeen, had come just too late.

It could be said that if they'd just shut up shop during their two matches with both Bristol City and Carlisle, during mid-April, and drawn 0-0 in both games, they'd have been going up with Boro.

Too many ifs, but it would be Carlisle United enjoying *a Season in the Sun*, in 1974.

Newcastle United faced Burnley, on Saturday 30th March, at Hillsborough.

Burnley were flying high, up in seventh place, and just two points below a UEFA Cup place. They'd outplayed and outclassed the league leaders Leeds United, on the previous Saturday, winning 4-1 away at Elland Road.

Their top scorer Paul Fletcher had scored twice, but it was his strike partner, Frank Casper, who was Man of the Match, after pulling McQueen and Hunter all over the place. Late on in the match, though, Casper was heavily clobbered by Norman Hunter, and his leg was heavily strapped for their Semi-final match against Newcastle.

In comparison, Newcastle had been dropping fast into the bottom half of the table, having won none of their previous six league matches. With 55,000 packed inside Hillsborough, Burnley absolutely murdered Newcastle in the first half.

United were simply penned inside their own penalty area, and unable to break out, as Burnley, backed up by their two outstanding ball-playing full backs, Newton and Noble, piled pressure upon pressure on Newcastle's goal.

BURNLEY		NEWCASTLE UNITED
Alan Stevenson	1	Iam McFaul
Peter Noble	2	David Craig
Keith Newton	3	Frank Clark
Martin Dobson	4	Terry McDermott
Colin Waldron	5	Pat Howard
Jimmy Thomson	6	Bobby Moncur
Geoff Nulty	7	Tommy Cassidy
Frank Casper	8	Jimmy Smith
Paul Fletcher	9	Supermac
Doug Collins	10	John Tudor
Leighton James	11	Terry Hibbitt
Ray Hankin	12	Alan Kennedy

Burnley hit the woodwork twice, and Iam McFaul was at his sharpest, keeping out shots from both Fletcher and Waldron with great saves.

The massed black and white bank that piled high up onto Hillsborough's open Spion Kop end, a huge swarm of Newcastle fans that rose up, almost into the clouds, began to really get behind their team, during the second half, from behind their own goal.

Terry Hibbitt launched a long ball out of defence, and Supermac chased it, halfway into the Burnley half, battling with Colin Waldron.

He out-muscled the Clarets' captain, who attempted to pull Supermac down, just outside the area, but he wasn't strong enough.

Supermac kept his feet, and his head, and he poked a left-footed shot right at Alan Stevenson, which the Burnley keeper stopped, but couldn't hold. Supermac touched the ball away from Noble and Waldron, and then side-kicked the ball, right-footed, into the far left of Burnley's goal.

Burnley attempted to keep up the pressure on United's goal area, but with Casper barely walking wounded, the extra man was beginning to tell. Jimmy Adamson probably should have started the match with the big Geordie Ray Hankin in attack.

Keith Newton lofted a high cross into Newcastle's area, which Moncur headed out, and Tudor hooked the ball away, out wide, to the left touchline. Terry Hibbitt galloped onto the ball, and hit a first-time, half-volleyed through-ball that totally beat the covering Jimmy Thomson. Supermac absolutely flew past him, and placed the ball beneath Stevenson's dive, with a left-footed dink, from just inside Burnley's area.

Burnley had been the better footballing team, on the day, but they'd been outdone by the majestic combination of Hibbitt's unerring left foot, and Supermac's power, pace and presence.

Newcastle limped towards the end of the season, winning just one of their eight First Division matches played in April, after Supermac's brace had beaten Everton 2-1 on Saturday 6th April, in front of over 44,000 at St James's Park.

They also drew twice with Norwich City, and with both Birmingham and Burnley.

Those points were enough to keep them clear of relegation, just two points clear in fact, but they'd lost the rest of their remaining games, away at Stoke, at home to Spurs, and of course, at home to Burnley.

Martin Dobson and Geoff Nulty both scored during Burnley's 2-1 win at St James's Park, on Wednesday 10th April. Joe Harvey liked the look of Burnley's Geoff Nulty, and he paid Burnley £120,000 for the Clarets' midfield destroyer, eight months later.

The less said about the FA Cup Final, the better. Newcastle were poor in the first half at Wembley, as were Liverpool, and the scores were 0-0 at half-time on that warm, sunny Saturday afternoon of May 4th 1974.

After the break, though, Newcastle United were even worse, as Liverpool romped to a 3-0 hammering that totally flattered Newcastle, following two goals from Kevin Keegan and another from Steve Heighway. United's two full backs, Frank Clark and young Alan Kennedy, had done okay. They did little wrong, but Jackie Milburn had admitted he was ashamed of the rest of the Newcastle team.

What happened next, though, was one of the most amazing and moving experiences in English football history. In spite of their thoroughly pathetic display, Newcastle's players journeyed from Newcastle Central Station to St James's Park, in an open topped bus, to apologise to the city.

Thousands upon thousands of fans and ordinary, normal people had packed the streets, singing the name of the team, and at St James's Park, they packed both the Leazes End, and the whole pitch, with black and white scarves aloft, as far and wide as you could see. It was a truly remarkable sight.

Many of the players were in tears, literally overcome by the passion and devotion of their supporters. They had been awful, and they wished they could play it again, for the fans.

The FA Cup Final was the 342nd and final game that Bobby Moncur played for Newcastle United. A true gentleman, he was dignified both on and off the pitch, and one of United's most popular captains in their history.

Quite how Joe Harvey thought that Glen Keeley, who'd played four league games for Ipswich, was an improvement on the twenty-nine year old Bobby Moncur, I'll never know, but on Saturday 22nd June, Bob Stokoe paid just £30,000 for Moncur, to partner Dave Watson in the heart of Sunderland's defence.

It was a deal agreed live on air during ITV's coverage of the 1974 World Cup Finals in West Germany.

That wasn't the big story of the Summer, though, up in the North-east, Newcastle United's captain actually joining Sunderland.

What could possibly top that?

How about Pop Robson returning to the North-east, joining his hometown team Sunderland in a £145,000 deal? This was a massively huge deal for Sunderland who had never spent so big before.

Pop Robson had scored forty-seven First Division goals in 120 games for West Ham, and just one year earlier, he'd been the First Division's top goal-scorer, with twenty-eight goals from forty-two games.

It was a tremendous lift for the fans, after the discouraging disappointment of missing out on promotion so late in the previous season.

After they'd hammered Millwall 4-1 on the opening Saturday, away at The Den, over 34,000 packed into Roker Park for Sunderland's first home match of the season, against Southampton, to welcome home their local superstar.

They were not disappointed, despite being a little worried after Mike Channon's penalty kick had given the Saints a 1-0 half-time lead. Dave Watson headed an equaliser from Bobby Kerr's corner after the break, and when Pop Robson slotted home Billy Hughes' pass, you could have heard the Roker Roar all over Wearside. Hughes then converted Tony Towers' through-ball for an emphatic 3-1 win, and despite a 1-0 defeat away at West Brom, a Billy Hughes hat-trick led them to a 5-1 thrashing of Bristol Rovers, one week later.

Vic Halom's second half goal then gave them a 1-0 win away at York City, with nearly 15,000 packed inside Bootham Crescent, and Sunderland were third in the table by mid-September, behind Manchester United and Norwich City.

Newcastle United conceded ten goals during their first four First Division games of 1974-75, with Glen Keeley, their surprise signing of the Summer of 74, a former England youth international, partnering Pat Howard.

It was certainly not a central defensive partnership to worry First Division strikers.

35,938 had packed their home terraces, though, as Newcastle beat Coventry City on Saturday 17th August, the opening day of the season. Alan Kennedy scored his first ever goal, and then Supermac and Pat Howard finished off the Sky Blues, but United were then held to a 2-2 draw, at home to Sheffield United.

Micky Burns and Supermac both scored as Newcastle came back, after Eddy and Speight had put the Blades 2-0 up early in the second half.

Micky Burns had signed from Blackpool during the Summer, having scored fifty-three league goals for the Tangerines, and he'd been their top goal-scorer in four of the previous five seasons. Joe Harvey paid £170,000 for Burns, in July, to replace the regularly ineffective Stewart Barrowclough on the right wing. After a 4-2 defeat away at Wolves, and a 2-1 defeat at Sheffield United, though, Newcastle dropped into the bottom half of the First Division by the end of August.

United rallied, though, over the next two and a half months, enjoying one of their greatest league runs of the Seventies, losing only twice during their next thirteen matches, while winning six times. On Saturday 28th September, Pat Howard headed Newcastle to a 1-0 win over league leaders Ipswich Town.

In front of 43,520, their biggest home crowd of the season, Newcastle rose ten places up the First Division, moving into the top six, and only four points behind the leaders.

At the end of October, Terry McDermott played his last game for Newcastle, in the Seventies, after Liverpool manager Bob Paisley had paid £175,000 for the slightly built, hard running midfield star, who'd played fifty-three First Division games for United.

McDermott went on to play 328 league and cup games for Liverpool, winning three European Cup Finals, and four First Division titles, at Anfield, and he was also voted as the PFA Player of the Year in 1980.

He returned to Newcastle in 1982, aged thirty, and Terry McDermott was a key player in Arthur Cox's United team, alongside Kevin Keegan, Peter Beardsley and Chris Waddle, that won promotion back to the First Division, in May 1984.

On Saturday 9th November, Newcastle visited Middlesbrough, for United's first North-east derby match for five years. With both teams in the First Division's top ten, it was expected to be a cracker, in front of a massive Ayresome Park crowd of 39,000.

The game was a dull, goalless draw, though, and there were plenty of them during that closely-fought 1974-75 season, but on a positive note, if you admired the defensive art of the game, and also enjoyed a good twelve horse race in the league, then this was perhaps the best of all seasons.

MIDDLESBROUGH		NEWCASTLE UNITED
Jim Platt	1	Iam McFaul
John Craggs	2	Irving Nattrass
Frank Spraggon	3	Frank Clark
Graeme Souness	4	Tommy Cassidy
Stuart Boam	5	Glen Keeley
Willie Maddren	6	Pat Howard
Bobby Murdoch	7	Stewart Barrowclough
David Mills	8	Alan Kennedy
John Hickton	9	Supermac
Alan Foggon	10	John Tudor
David Armstrong	11	Terry Hibbitt

A week later, with nearly 34,000 inside St James's Park, Newcastle slaughtered Chelsea 5-0, with a young darkly moustached Geordie, Paul Cannell, playing up front with Supermac, in place of the suspended John Tudor.

By half-time, Chelsea's experienced and exalted defence of Gary Locke, Micky Droy, John Dempsey and Ron *Chopper* Harris had held Newcastle to another blank, with Peter Bonetti, England's World Cup keeper, not having one difficult save to make.

After the break, however, Newcastle opened the ***Black Gate of Mordor,*** and the giant Droy, the grim-witted Hay, and the sinister *Chopper* were all toppled by a fantastic, ferocious attack from the good guys.

Paul Cannell headed in Terry Hibbitt's left-footed right wing cross, at the far post, before Alan Kennedy won the ball from Steve Kember, deep inside his own half, and then ran at Chelsea.

The nineteen year old breezed past Dempsey, and then *Chopper,* before he fired past Bonetti from the edge of Chelsea's penalty area. Supermac ran onto Tommy Cassidy's wonderfully placed forward pass, and he walloped the ball past Bonetti.

Jimmy Smith sprayed the ball across to Nattrass, out on the right, who advanced inside, then played a reverse pass back out wide to Stewart Barrowclough, just outside the right hand edge of the Chelsea area.

Barrowclough teased *Chopper,* before side-stepping, then shooting low, from just inside the penalty area, with the ball just beating Peter Bonetti at his near post.

Supermac controlled Cassidy's long forward pass, and he rode a scything challenge from Dempsey, before driving beyond Bonetti into the top far corner. 5-0.

The match was broadcast on ***Shoot!,*** Tyne Tees Television's edition of The Big Match, and Alan Kennedy's excellent goal was highlighted as the Goal of the Weekend. The end credits and theme tune ran over his great run, finish and celebration, all in slow motion, with his unforgettable youthful exuberance and wild haired appearance.

As a result of that 5-0 win, Newcastle United rose to their best league position, at this stage of the season, between the 1920's and the 1990's, sitting just two points behind the First Division leaders, with a game in hand, after seventeen games.

	PL	W	D	L	F	A	PTS
Ipswich Town	18	10	2	6	25	12	22
Liverpool	17	10	2	5	23	12	22
Everton	18	5	12	1	23	18	22
Manchester City	18	9	4	5	21	22	22
Sheffield United	18	8	5	5	27	29	21
Stoke City	17	7	6	4	29	23	20
West Ham Utd	18	8	4	6	34	27	20
NEWCASTLE	17	7	6	4	25	20	20
Middlesbrough	17	7	6	4	24	21	20

After a great start to their season, Middlesbrough had endured an inconsistent first month of the season. John Hickton and Alan Foggon scored Boro's first goals in Division One for over two decades, in their 2-0 away win at Birmingham City, on the opening Saturday of the season, with over 32,000 inside St Andrews.

They were then stunned by Carlisle United, losing 0-2 at home, before being held to a 1-1 draw by Luton, also at Ayresome Park. On Tuesday 27th August, though, David Armstrong's early goal secured revenge on Carlisle, in their 1-0 win at Brunton Park.

They then drew 1-1 at Stoke City, and were held to a 1-1 home draw by Chelsea. Keith Eddy's penalty kick was enough for Sheffield United to beat Boro at Bramall Lane, on Saturday 14th September, and after seven games, Middlesbrough had won twice, lost twice, and drawn three games, to sit agitatedly in mid-table.

Third-placed Manchester City visited Middlesbrough, one week later, with all their superstars, Bell, Summerbee, Tueart, Hartford, Marsh and Oakes, as more than thirty thousand piled into Ayresome Park.

David Mills gave Boro a half-time lead, and Foggon then fired a second half brace, in their emphatic 3-0 hammering of City, before Armstrong and Mills then gave Boro a 2-1 away win at Spurs, at the end of September. After beating Wolves 2-1 (Hickton, Willey), on Saturday 5th October, Middlesbrough became a top five club.

A tough period followed in the late Autumn, as Boro lost David Mills to injury for half a dozen games, on November 9th, and they won only twice in nine matches, losing four of them, to drop back into the bottom half of the table.

One of their three draws, though, was an uncharacteristic 4-4 home draw with Coventry City, on Saturday 19th October.

Graeme Souness scored his first two goals of the season, with Mills and Foggon also netting in a ding dong battle, that was the second highest scoring First Division match of that season. Souness also made his Scotland debut in their 3-0 win over East Germany, at Hampden Park, on Wednesday 30th October.

Souness went on to play fifty-four competitive matches for Scotland, in an international career that included six matches in the World Cup Finals tournaments in Argentina '78, Spain '82, and then Mexico '86. He captained Scotland in 1982 and in 1986, but in 1978 he was left out of the team that performed shockingly against Peru and Iran. Ally McLeod included him for their final group 4 match against Holland.

Driven on by a midfield of Souness, Gemmill, Hartford and Rioch, Scotland finally began to play like World Champions, and they flew into a 3-1 lead halfway into the second half, needing a three goal win to progress into the last eight, before Johnny Rep's twenty-yard rocket killed their chances.

Graeme Souness hit his second brace of the season during Boro's 3-0 win over second-placed Ipswich Town, at Ayresome Park, on Saturday 7th December. Alan Foggon also scored in their first league victory for six weeks, watched by just 23,735.

Amazingly, even fewer turned up on the following Tuesday, for the visit of Leicester City, with only 22,699 watching their second 3-0 win in three days. Alan Foggon scored twice, his eleventh and twelfth goals of the season, while reserve striker Alan Willey fired in their third.

Bobby Moore had asked Jack Charlton how he'd managed to turn Foggon into a good player. "What have you done to that Foggon, then?" he'd said to his old teammate. Charlton himself hadn't been overly impressed by Foggon as a Newcastle player, and he'd inherited the forward when he was appointed as Boro's manager.

"Foggon wasn't a good player in the sense that he was tricky or clever with the ball at his feet," Jack Charlton suggested, "but Jesus, could he run! At school he'd been a 220 yards champion, and once I'd convinced him that this was the strong point of his game, he was a different player."

Charlton utilised Foggon as a key to unlock opposing teams' offside traps, playing the ball forward as the opposition's defence was charging out. He fined players for passing the ball to Foggon's feet in training so they became naturally conditioned to playing it just ahead of him, for him to chase.

"With his pace, Foggy was capable of latching on to it before the goalkeeper could react," Charlton told his team. "The timing had to be right, of course. If the ball was struck a split-second too late, he was liable to be caught offside."

Jack Charlton introduced an attacking system where Foggon was used as a loose midfield cannon, and the two forwards Hickton and Mills moved out with the opposing defenders, before the gun was fired.

"John Hickton was pretty alert, but David's basic instinct was to turn and chase in after the ball," Charlton concluded. "Mills must have been caught offside a hundred times in our first six games, but gradually he got the message."

On the penultimate Saturday before Christmas, Middlesbrough hosted their third successive home match, and they secured a third successive 3-0 win, over Birmingham City. Alan Foggon, John Hickton, and an own goal sent Boro back up to seventh place, before David Armstrong's second half goal earned a 1-1 away draw at fellow title chasers Burnley.

On Boxing Day, 31,879, Middlesbrough's biggest home crowd of the season, filled every inch of Ayresome Park's terracing for the visit of Sheffield United.

MIDDLESBROUGH		SHEFFIELD UNITED
Jim Platt	1	Jim Brown
John Craggs	2	Len Badger
Frank Spraggon	3	Ted Hemsley
Graeme Souness	4	Keith Eddy
Stuart Boam	5	Colin Franks
Willie Maddren	6	John Flynn
Bobby Murdoch	7	Alan Woodward
David Mills	8	David Bradford
John Hickton	9	Steve Cammack
Alan Foggon	10	Tony Currie
David Armstrong	11	Tony Field

The Blades were missing both their captain Eddie Colquhoun and star striker Billy Dearden, as well as their combative midfielder Micky Speight, and as a result, they were on the back foot throughout the whole game.

Boro had fielded their perfect eleven, in contrast, and they played the perfect game, getting ten men behind the ball when the Blades attacked, double marking their playmaker Tony Currie, but when they broke, they broke swiftly, sharply and deadly.

David Armstrong drove in from the wing, past Badger, and he wrong-footed Flynn, before blasting the ball high into the roof of United's goal.

FIRST DIVISION LEADERS, BOXING DAY 1974

	PL	W	D	L	F	A	PTS
Liverpool	23	12	5	6	34	20	29
MIDDLESBROUGH	24	11	7	6	36	27	29
Ipswich Town	24	13	2	9	33	19	28
Everton	23	8	12	3	32	24	28
West Ham United	24	10	8	6	41	31	28
Manchester City	24	11	6	7	30	31	28
Stoke City	24	10	7	7	37	32	27
Burnley	24	10	6	8	43	39	26
Newcastle United	23	10	6	7	33	31	26
Derby County	23	9	7	7	36	32	25

After the break, Jim Brown was brilliant in goal, though, keeping out great chances for Souness, Foggon, Mills and Boam. Boro's 1-0 win sent them up to second place, behind Liverpool only on goal average, but only four points separated the top eleven teams. Anyone could win it that season.

Sunderland had dropped back to fourth place, after drawing three successive games during the last week of September, before six wins from ten games lifted them back into second place by late November, behind leaders Manchester United.

On Saturday 30th November 1974, a massive 60,585 crowd, the largest crowd of the season in all of England, completely packed Old Trafford for the battle of the Second Division giants. Never since then has a crowd of more than Sixty Thousand ever attended any game in the second tier of English football.

Bobby Kerr dashed in to hit two first half goals, as Sunderland led 2-1 at half-time, with Stuart Pearson scoring United's goal. Willie Morgan equalised after the break, though, and then Sammy McIlroy curled in a late winner, in the Second Division's best game of the season.

Undaunted, Sunderland continued to win games. They hammered Portsmouth 4-1 (Halom, Hughes, Malone, Robson), on Saturday 7th December, at Roker Park, and then Pop Robson and Bobby Kerr scored in each half, a week later, as they beat Millwall 2-0 at home.

Sunderland drew 0-0 away at Oldham Athletic, the previous season's Third Division Champions, on the Saturday before Christmas, and then they beat York City 2-0 on Boxing Day, in front of their biggest home crowd of the season, up to then.

Bobby Kerr scored in each half, with 33,397 inside Roker Park, to keep Sunderland well clear in second place, and five points ahead of fourth placed West Brom.

SECOND DIVISION LEADERS, BOXING DAY 1974

	PL	W	D	L	F	A	PTS
Manchester United	24	16	5	3	41	18	37
SUNDERLAND	23	13	6	4	40	16	32
Norwich City	23	10	9	4	32	20	29
West Brom	24	10	7	7	28	18	27
Oxford United	24	11	5	8	26	33	27
Aston Villa	23	10	6	7	33	18	26
Blackpool	24	9	8	7	24	18	26

Billy Hughes scored as Sunderland drew 1-1 at Orient, on Saturday 28th December, before they then beat Chesterfield 2-0 in the FA Cup Third round, with 34,268 squeezed inside Roker Park. Joe Bolton and Pop Robson had scored in each half, setting up a jaw-dropping Fourth round tie away at First Division Middlesbrough. On the following Saturday, Pop Robson set Sunderland on the way to victory, giving them a 1-0 half-time lead away at struggling Portsmouth.

Inspired by former Gunners George Graham and Peter Marinello, though, Pompey stormed back to hammer Sunderland 4-2. Vic Halom's fifth goal of the season was only a consolation as they suffered their first defeat in seven games.

After their 1-1 draw away at Southampton, Sunderland hosted Second Division leaders Manchester United, on Saturday 18th January 1975.

45,976, the biggest Roker Park crowd since their 1973 FA Cup run, filled their ground for the greatest Second Division match-up of the Seventies.

SUNDERLAND		MANCHESTER UNITED
Trevor Swinburne	1	Alex Stepney
Dick Malone	2	Alex Forsyth
Joe Bolton	3	Stewart Houston
Bobby Moncur	4	Brian Greenhoff
Dave Watson	5	Steve James
Tony Towers	6	Martin Buchan
Bobby Kerr	7	Willie Morgan
Billy Hughes	8	Sammy McIlroy
Vic Halom	9	Tommy Baldwin
Pop Robson	10	Lou Macari
Tom Finney	11	Jim McCalliog

Tommy Docherty had lost United's leading scorer, Stuart Pearson, for a whole month, so he'd loaned in Tommy Baldwin, from Chelsea.

Also, Gerry Daly was missing from Manchester United's midfield, so the versatile Brian Greenhoff played alongside the wonderfully skilled Sammy McIlroy.

The match certainly wasn't the ding dong battle enjoyed by Match of the Day viewers, just two months earlier, it was very defensively played, with neither United nor Sunderland wanting to lose. Chances were scarce, but Stepney saved well from Pop Robson's reflex shot from only six yards out, and Swinburne, playing the second of his two matches that season, had kept out both Macari and Morgan, and then he dived full length to send Alex Forsyth's stinging drive behind for a corner.

At the end of the day, after their goalless draw, Sunderland remained five points behind Manchester United, but five points above fourth-placed Aston Villa, with just fifteen matches to play.

Promotion was in their own hands.

After their brilliant 5-0 demolition of Chelsea, Newcastle United were thrashed 4-1, themselves, by Burnley at Turf Moor. The Clarets had again avenged their Semi-final defeat, eight months before, after Peter Noble had hit a hat-trick, and Leighton James also scored from the penalty spot. That win over United sparked a great run of nine wins from their next fourteen for Burnley, losing only twice, to rise from the bottom half of the table up to second place by the beginning of March.

On the final Saturday of November, Newcastle reacted well by beating Manchester City, the First Division leaders, 2-1 at St James's Park, and in front of 37,000.

Pat Howard and Supermac had scored in each half to lift United back up to eighth place, only three points below the new leaders Stoke City, going into December.

Lowly Spurs and Coventry both hammered United, 3-0 and 2-0 respectively, during the first two weeks of December, before Newcastle rediscovered their form over Christmas. On Saturday 21st December, Alan Kennedy, John Tudor and Pat Howard all scored as they thrashed reigning Champions Leeds 3-0, with a modest crowd of just 32,535 inside St James's Park.

On Boxing Day, United travelled along the A69 to Carlisle, and 25,000 filled Brunton Park for the Cumbrians' most eagerly-awaited game of the season.

John Tudor gave Newcastle a 1-0 half-time lead, and despite Bobby Owen's second half goal for Carlisle, Supermac drove his fifteen yard shot past Alan Ross for their hard-fought, but well-earned 2-1 away win.

As 1975 arrived, Newcastle were down in ninth place, but still only four points behind the joint leaders Ipswich Town and Middlesbrough.

Middlesbrough totally blew their title chances after Boxing Day. After their 1-0 home win over Sheffield United (Armstrong), they drew 1-1 away at Everton, on Saturday 28th December, to remain in equal first place with new leaders Ipswich, but they then won none of their following six league games, and they lost three times.

By the end of February, Boro had slipped back down to tenth position, five points behind leaders Everton. A particular low point was their 0-1 home defeat to Leeds. Allan Clarke's goal had silenced a massive 39,500 crowd, the biggest Ayresome Park crowd since the early Sixties.

Failing to win the First Division title that season, with Middlesbrough, was the biggest disappointment of Jack Charlton's career, he later confessed.

In the FA Cup, though, Boro had enjoyed the best run in their history, up to then, although it hadn't started off so well. They'd struggled to hold Isthmian League side Wycombe Wanderers to a goalless draw, away at Wycombe's sloping Loakes Park ground, packed to capacity with a 12,000 crowd.

Back at Ayresome Park, three days later, in front of 30,000, Middlesbrough again struggled to beat their non-league opposition, but a lovely run and curled shot by David Armstrong, during the second half, was enough to secure a 1-0 win, and a home game against Sunderland in the Fourth round.

MIDDLESBROUGH		SUNDERLAND
Jim Platt	1	Trevor Swinburne
John Craggs	2	Dick Malone
Frank Spraggon	3	Joe Bolton
Graeme Souness	4	Bobby Moncur
Stuart Boam	5	Dave Watson
Willie Maddren	6	Jackie Ashurst
Bobby Murdoch	7	Bobby Kerr
David Mills	8	Billy Hughes
John Hickton	9	Vic Halom
Alan Foggon	10	Pop Robson
David Armstrong	11	Tony Towers

On Saturday 25th January, 39,400 packed into Ayresome Park to watch another Classic in the Mud.

Rarely have Sunderland and Middlesbrough, during their long history, faced each other with such settled, high quality teams, and it was a pulsating match, end to end stuff, amidst a fever-pitch atmosphere.

And after ten minutes, it was the Second Division high flyers who took the lead.

Graeme Souness's sloppy diagonal pass, on the edge of his area, had allowed Bobby Kerr a shot in the mud, that Jim Platt saved, but couldn't hold onto, and Pop Robson fired in the rebound to put Sunderland 1-0 up.

John Craggs performed a bit of **Clodoaldo** type dribbling and drag-backing against both Tony Towers and Billy Hughes, before he sprayed a pass the full width of the muddy, cow field surface of Ayresome Park, over to Frank Spraggon.

Spraggon advanced into the Sunderland half, and he fed David Mills on the edge of the Sunderland area. The ball was laid off by Mills for Souness, twenty-five yards out. Graeme Souness played a delightful through ball between both Ashurst and Moncur, and Bobby Murdoch read the pass brilliantly, galloping in to fire past Swinburne, from just inside the penalty area.

Into the second half, Spraggon clipped a pass inside for Craggs, who'd ventured inside into the Boro midfield. Craggs ran along the edge of the Sunderland box, before switching a reverse pass back into the feet of Mills, who'd broken the offside trap.

He was tripped by Trevor Swinburne, and a penalty was awarded.

John Hickton's penalty kick, hit low towards the left post, was almost saved by Swinburne, but the force of his shot, after his twenty yard run-up, had forced the ball over the goal-line.

Bobby Murdoch then played a World Class right-footed pass from the edge of his own penalty area, with Sunderland pressing in full numbers, and the ball landed five yards inside the mud of the Sunderland half, for David Mills to race onto, clear of any marker, from the centre circle to the edge of the penalty area, before Malone flew in with a desperate, diving tackle, but he did catch the player before the ball.

Referee Bob Matthewson, of Bolton, awarded a second penalty kick to Middlesbrough. This time, Hickton gave Swinburne no chance, running up and driving the ball high into the roof of the net, to the keeper's right.

John Hickton went and celebrated beneath the eruption of the massed home fans packed into the East End, along with Mills, Foggon and Spraggon.

In the Fifth round, on Saturday 15th February, with 28,000 packed inside their London Road ground, just a couple of thousand below their record attendance, Peterborough United held Middlesbrough to a 1-1 draw (Mills).

Back at Ayresome Park, three days later, in front of 34,303, Alan Foggon scored goals in each half, earning Boro a Quarter-final place for the first time in five years. They'd been drawn away at Birmingham, who they'd already beaten twice that season. In front of a passionate, raucous 47,260 St Andrews crowd, though, Birmingham City, even without their wonder kid Trevor Francis, were untouchable, and one solitary moment of genius by Bob Hatton broke Boro's cast iron defence.

After the break, as hard as Hickton, Mills, Armstrong, Foggon, Murdoch, Souness and Boam pounded against the normally Victoria sponge-soft Blues' defence, but keeper Dave Latchford was unbeaten.

After the New Year, Newcastle's form was just too erratic to sustain any title challenge. They were hammered twice in January, 5-2 and 5-1, by Spurs and Man City respectively, but then they beat Middlesbrough 2-1 on Saturday 1st February, with a 42,741 crowd packed inside St James's Park. Supermac and Micky Burns both scored second half goals to win the match, after Hickton had given Boro a 1-0 half-time lead.

Bottom club Luton also beat United 1-0 one week later, but then, on Wednesday night, 12th February 1975, Newcastle hammered title favourites Liverpool 4-1 at St James's Park. United took the Reds apart during the first half, with Tudor, Supermac and Barrowclough giving them an amazing 3-0 half-time lead, in front of 38,000.

Supermac then scored a fourth goal, after the break, before Liverpool grabbed a barely deserved consolation, so comprehensively they'd been beaten.

On the following Saturday, with over 40,000 again inside St James's, Newcastle completely slaughtered third placed Burnley 3-0 (Supermac 2, Barrowclough).

United rose back up to tenth place, and they were again only four points below leaders Stoke City. A 3-2 defeat at Chelsea was followed by their 1-0 win away at West Ham United, after Supermac had scored his twenty-second league and cup goal of the season. By the end of February, Newcastle United were still only four points behind the new league leaders Everton, with just eleven games remaining.

They lost seven of those remaining games, though, winning only once, and the home fans eventually began to turn their frustrations onto manager Joe Harvey.

At the end of the season, with United eighth from bottom, yet again, and just six points above relegated Luton Town, Newcastle sacked Joe Harvey and also his coach, Keith Burkinshaw. Harvey was moved "upstairs" to the role of General Manager, but the players couldn't believe he'd been replaced, especially by the young, little known Blackburn manager, Gordon Lee, who'd just led Rovers to the Third Division title.

Malcolm MacDonald loved playing for Joe Harvey as much as he disliked the way he was regarded by Gordon Lee. "Joe's philosophy was to put as many bloody good players in the eleven as you can," Supermac summed up. "You might not win things, but you're going to create a very entertaining time for the fans, and for football."

1974-75 was definitely Supermac's greatest season. For the second time in his career, he scored over thirty goals in competitive matches, but six of his thirty-three goals were scored for England, in just four international matches.

His twenty-one league goals had made him the top goal-scorer in the First Division, but under Gordon Lee, 99% effort from him was not good enough, to his immense frustration, and it would eventually lead to a parting of the ways.

After *their* collapse into mid-table, in January and February, and that heart-breaking home defeat to Leeds United, Middlesbrough then won four games in a row during March.

On Saturday 1st March, they beat leaders Stoke City 2-0 at Ayresome Park, Hickton and Foggon both scoring first half goals in front of 25,766.

Another 25,000 home crowd watched their 3-0 hammering of Spurs, a fortnight later, with Souness hitting two, after Hickton had given Boro a 1-0 half-time lead.

Three days later, on Tuesday 18th March, the new league leaders Everton came to Middlesbrough, and goals from Mills and Armstrong had given them a tremendous 2-0 win, with 32,813 squeezed into Ayresome Park.

Finally, on Saturday 22nd March, Boro went to Chelsea and they led 2-0 at half-time, after Willey and Craggs had both scored. Chelsea pulled one back, after the break, but Middlesbrough's 2-1 win lifted them back up into third place, and into strong title contention again, with just over half a dozen games remaining.

FIRST DIVISION LEADERS, 22ND MARCH 1975

	PL	W	D	L	F	A	PTS
Everton	35	14	16	5	49	32	44
Ipswich Town	35	19	3	13	53	36	41
MIDDLESBROUGH	35	15	11	9	47	34	41
Liverpool	35	15	11	9	48	35	41
Stoke City	35	15	11	9	56	43	41
Burnley	35	16	9	10	60	51	41
Derby County	34	16	8	10	52	45	40
Sheffield United	34	15	9	10	45	44	39

Boro won only once of their next five games, though, and they also lost three times, to drop back down to sixth, and out of contention.

Despite beating Liverpool 1-0 (Alan Foggon), with over 34,000 inside Ayresome Park, on Saturday 19th April, and then winning 2-0 away at Coventry City, a week later, Foggon and Hickton scoring in each half on the last day of the season, Middlesbrough made up no ground on the leaders. They finished in seventh place, two points behind a UEFA Cup qualifying place, and just three points behind runners-up Liverpool.

That was as close as Middlesbrough would ever come to winning the English First Division Championship trophy.

During March, Jack Charlton had paid £50,000 to bring his old teammate Terry Cooper from Leeds United to Middlesbrough. Once regarded as the finest left back in Europe, Cooper was now a thirty year old veteran, but he went straight into Boro's back four, for their final ten games of the season.

Cooper was sent off, however, for the first time in over 250 First Division matches, away at Chelsea, for making a sarcastic comment to a linesman.

"I thought the referee was pointing to a plane in the sky," Terry Cooper admitted, before he finally realised he'd been sent off.

That allowed Frank Spraggon, however, to play his 269th and final league game for Boro, at the age of twenty-nine, for their 2-0 win at home to Burnley (Murdoch, Foggon), at the end of March. Frank Spraggon had been a part of the greatest defence to ever play for Middlesbrough. If they'd been the defence behind Brian Clough, then Boro might have been League Champions during the late Fifties.

Middlesbrough kept twenty-five league and cup clean sheets during 1974-75, including eighteen in the First Division. With Frank Spraggon replaced by Terry Cooper during March, Jim Platt, John Craggs, Stuart Boam and Willie Maddren had missed only one league game between them all season.

Alan Foggon was Boro's top scorer with eighteen league and cup goals, while John Hickton and David Mills had shared twenty-two goals between them. Graeme Souness also chipped in with seven, as did David Armstrong. Middlesbrough's average home attendance of just under 30,000 was the eighth largest in England.

Including their goalless home draw with Manchester United, Sunderland won only two Second Division matches between Boxing Day and Easter, taking just eleven points out of a possible twenty-six, and their eleven point advantage over the third and fourth placed teams, Aston Villa and Norwich City, eventually disappeared.

Good Friday and Easter Monday, though, had brought treats back to Roker Park.

30,908 saw Sunderland romp to a 3-0 win over Orient (Watson, Hughes, Bolton), on Friday 28th March. Then on the following Easter Monday, Sunderland won 2-0 away at Bolton Wanderers, after Hughes and Towers both scored second half goals.

On Saturday 5th April, FA Cup Semi-final day, Vic Halom had scored a late winner to beat Hull City, in front of just under 30,000 at Roker Park. Their 1-0 away defeat at Oxford, though, seven days later, was a very poor result, and Sunderland no longer had promotion in their own hands, even after Joe Bolton, Pop Robson and Rod Belfitt had all scored in their 3-0 thrashing of Bristol City, on Saturday 19th April, in front of a 30,530 Roker Park crowd.

SECOND DIVISION LEADERS, 19TH APRIL 1975

	PL	W	D	L	F	A	PTS
Manchester United	41	25	9	7	62	30	59
Aston Villa	39	22	8	9	69	31	52
SUNDERLAND	41	19	13	9	65	33	51
Norwich City	40	19	13	8	54	33	51

It all came down to D-Day, Saturday 26th April, away at second-placed Aston Villa, who were already promoted, having hammered Sheffield Wednesday 4-0 during midweek. Sunderland needed to win, while also hoping Norwich didn't take three points from their last two games at Carrow Road, against Portsmouth and Villa.

A massive 57,266 crowd were packed inside Villa Park's vast spaces, with half of them from Wearside, for their biggest game since the 1973 FA Cup Final. Sunderland fans groaned, though, when they realised that Vic Halom, who'd limped off injured at Oxford, was still missing, and Belfitt was in for only his sixth game of that season.

This was also Ron Guthrie's seventy-sixth and final league and cup match for Sunderland. He was retired at the end of the season, having been refused a new contract, at the age of just thirty-one.

He signed on the dole, and then joined Ashington, of the Northern League.

Guthrie was also a member of Blyth Spartans' team that reached the FA Cup Fifth round in 1978, knocking out Enfield, Chesterfield and Stoke City, before losing after a replay to Wrexham, with over 42,000 inside St James's Park. Ron Guthrie, the fourth 1973 FA Cup hero to leave Sunderland, had real quality, but he was shabbily treated.

ASTON VILLA SUNDERLAND

Jim Cumbes	1	Jim Montgomery
John Robson	2	Dick Malone
Charlie Aitken	3	Ron Guthrie
Ian Ross	4	Bobby Moncur
Chris Nicholl	5	Dave Watson
Leighton Phillips	6	Joe Bolton
Bobby McDonald	7	Bobby Kerr
Brian Little	8	Billy Hughes
Keith Leonard	9	Rod Belfitt
Steve Hunt	10	Pop Robson
Frank Carrodus	11	Tony Towers
John Gidman	12	Dennis Longhorn

That Aston Villa side, though, had lacked real quality in most areas, and Sunderland really ought to have beaten them. But they didn't.

They lost 2-0, after second half goals from Ian Ross, from the penalty spot, and Brian Little, by far their most talented player, and probably their only player, other than John Robson and Leighton Phillips, that could've made it into that Sunderland team.

After their defeat, not since 1314 has an army of 20,000 Englishmen headed north so flat-spirited and demoralised as those Sunderland fans on that bright, Spring evening.

Norwich City had beaten Portsmouth anyway, and so Sunderland remained in Division Two for yet another season.

From 14th September 1974, when Sunderland first moved up into the top three, until the very end of the 1974-75 season, the Wearsiders had spent 202 of those 227 days in the Second Division promotion zone. Sadly, one of those twenty-five days spent down in fourth place had just happened to be on the last day of the season.

Pop Robson was Sunderland's top goal-scorer, hitting twenty-one league and cup goals. Billy Hughes had fired fifteen, while Vic Halom and Bobby Kerr also scored a combined fifteen league goals.

Bobby Kerr, Bobby Moncur, Pop Robson and Dick Malone were all ever-presents, while the ever-dependable and increasingly invaluable Tony Towers had missed only one match.

On Wednesday 18th June 1975, Dave Watson joined Manchester City for a club record transfer fee of £275,000, after playing 177 league games for Sunderland.

Jeff Clarke, City's twenty-one year old reserve team centre back, had moved to Roker Park, in return, as part of the deal. Clarke was a six foot tall, powerful, hairy monster who took no prisoners.

He'd maybe lacked Dave Watson's skill and presence, but Jeff Clarke was a good, honest, and hard to beat, hard back-boned back.

Mel Holden also joined Sunderland during that Summer of 1975. A black haired, moustached giant, at six feet and one inch tall, Holden had scored twenty-two league goals for Preston North End, from just sixty-nine starts.

Bob Stokoe paid Bobby Charlton £100,000 for his highly-rated twenty year old centre forward.

Newcastle's new boss Gordon Lee also brought new blood into St James's Park. Frank Clark was freed from the club, at thirty-one years old, so Brian Clough subsequently snapped him up at Nottingham Forest, during May 1975.

Frank Clark had played 456 league and cup games for Newcastle, including 345 First Division matches, making him one of their greatest ever full backs.

"When Newcastle gave me the sack, which was virtually what it was," admitted Frank Clark, "I nearly went somewhere like Northampton or Doncaster."

At Derby County, Brian Clough had been renowned for resurrecting Dave Mackay's career, after he'd been regarded as surplus to requirements at Tottenham. Frank Clark had the experience, professionalism and ability to help develop Forest's young defence of Viv Anderson and Kenny Burns, lifting the Reds back into the First Division, and he was eventually rewarded with a First Division Championship medal.

Twelve months later, in 1979, he completed one of the finest ever twilight careers in footballing history, when at the age of thirty-five, he won a European Cup Winners' medal, after Forest's 1-0 win over Malmo in Munich.

In August 1976, Frank Clark had been awarded a testimonial match by Newcastle, when the Magpies had beaten Sunderland 6-3, in a superb match at St James's Park.

Newcastle United, under Gordon Lee, were supposedly geared for the future, with their 22 year old County Durham-born full back Irving Nattrass permanently replacing David Craig, and Alan Gowling also replacing John Tudor in attack.

Alan Gowling was totally different to John Tudor. Gordon Lee had paid Huddersfield just £60,000 for Gowling, just ten days before the start of the 1975-76 season.

Tall and gangly, the Stockport-born six footer was an economics graduate from Manchester University, and he was one of the last of the Busby Babes, making his Manchester United debut, aged nineteen, scoring in their 4-2 win over Stoke City, back in March 1968.

Frank O'Farrell sold Gowling to Huddersfield Town, for £65,000, in June 1972, after he'd played seventy-one First Division matches at Old Trafford. Alan Gowling then scored fifty-eight league goals for Huddersfield, in just 128 games, having been converted from midfield to attack.

Gowling's goals couldn't prevent them from dropping from the Second Division down to the Fourth Division, though, inside just three seasons.

Tommy Craig had also joined Newcastle from Sheffield Wednesday, just prior to Christmas 1974, on the same day as Geoff Nulty, and for the same price, £120,000.

Nulty and Craig were Joe Harvey's last signings as Newcastle manager, but Gordon Lee adopted both players as the heart and soul of his footballing ethic of hard work, and a star-less Newcastle side. Gordon Lee also appointed Geoff Nulty as Newcastle's captain, following the departure of Frank Clark.

Tommy Craig replaced the silky skilled Terry Hibbitt in Newcastle's midfield. Hibbitt, just like Jimmy Smith, had found no regular place in Gordon Lee's more pragmatic team, and he was sold to Birmingham City at the end of August 1975, for £100,000.

One of the premium left-footed wingers in Newcastle United's history, Terry Hibbitt had played 138 First Division matches for the club. He was also hugely influential in driving Newcastle to the FA Cup Final, but Gordon Lee preferred the less dynamic and less dazzling Tommy Craig, more rugged, more of a ball winner, and more of a short passer than a great crosser of the ball, making United's midfield more compact and more absorbent.

The twenty-four year old Glaswegian midfield general was a very different player to Terry Hibbitt.

It wasn't as attractive to watch, but it was more functional, which was the way forward as football departed from the Glam Soccer era, and that was the way that Gordon Lee had wanted his United team to go.

Terry Hibbitt re-joined Newcastle in April 1978, after their relegation to the Second Division. Suffering from a persistent knee injury, though, he was never the same player, and Hibbitt was forced to quit after United's dreadful 1980-81 season, having made 257 league and cup appearances, over his two spells at St James's Park.

He died after losing his battle with cancer, aged only forty-six, on Friday 5th August 1994.

Newcastle United began the 1975-76 season brilliantly, sporting a brand new look.

In place of their classic shirts with the black and white round necked and cuffed shirts, they wore Umbro-designed new shirts with stylish black collars and cuffs, a new strip for a new era, for a new type of football at St James's Park.

Supermac fired two goals, and Tommy Craig another, from the penalty spot, as United hammered Ipswich Town 3-0, away at Portman Road.

Supermac equalised during the second half of Newcastle's midweek home match against Middlesbrough, with over 41,000 packed into St James's Park, after Alan Gowling's own goal had given Boro a 1-0 half-time lead, on his home debut.

Newcastle followed that hard-fought 1-1 draw with a 3-0 hammering of Leicester City, on Saturday 23rd August. Supermac had put Newcastle 1-0 up in the first half, before he scored his greatest ever goal, four minutes before half-time.

Supermac won the ball inside his own penalty area, and then he played out wide to Irving Nattrass, who broke free up the right wing, before chipping the ball back to Supermac, inside the centre circle.

Supermac took a couple of strides out of the centre circle, before, left-footed, he hit an out of this world strike, off the ground, from nearly forty yards out.

The ball flew past Mark Wallington, and it bulged the top of the Leicester City net, right in front of the Leazes End.

There was silence for a couple of seconds, before the noise erupted and the whole United team raced towards MacDonald.

"I've never struck the ball so perfectly in all my life," claimed Supermac.

"I got right over the top of it and hit it sweetly. Football's all about such moments."

Even Gordon Lee was taken aback by the quality of the strike. "It was a World Class goal. That takes some beating," he cried. "It was pure magic!"

Micky Burns added a third goal after half-time, for their second 3-0 win of the season, and Newcastle were in second place after three games.

Effective football under Gordon Lee, or cavalier, swashbuckling football under Joe Harvey, it didn't matter, Newcastle still suffered their obligatory collapse.

They lost three of their next four games, including a 4-0 thrashing away at Manchester City, and then dropped down to mid-table, which was where they remained for the rest of the season.

There were some highlights, though: Alan Gowling scored his first league goals for United on Saturday 20th September, with a hat-trick during their 5-1 win over Wolves.

Then Gowling and Supermac demonstrated their partnership at its best, hitting two goals apiece during their 5-2 win over Norwich City, on Saturday 18th October.

Gowling fired another hat-trick against Everton, on Saturday 10th January, as United won 5-0 in front of over 32,000 at St James's Park, before United won an absolute cracker against reigning Champions Derby County, in front of their biggest home crowd of the season, with 44,488 packing St James's Park.

Colin Todd's own goal had given Newcastle a 1-0 half-time lead, but the floodgates opened really opened before the break. Geoff Nulty headed Newcastle's second, but Steve Powell pulled one back, driving in a header from Leighton James's excellent reverse cross.

Tommy Craig slotted an un-saveable penalty kick beyond Moseley, after he himself had been up-ended by Powell, but again, Charlie George pulled the Rams back into it, heading in from close range. With the scores 3-2 at half-time, Bruce Rioch flicked home Gemmill's left wing cross to equalise, with only six minutes left. Tommy Craig then swung over a late corner kick, but Derby only succeeded in clearing the ball back to him. Craig ran at Derby's defence, and curled a direct pass at Supermac's head. Supermac scored his sixteenth goal of the season, re-directing the ball just inside the near post, right underneath the Leazes End. In the very last minute, Mahoney saved Charlie George's close range shot, and then Keeley headed Leighton James's effort off the line, from the rebound. The atmosphere at the final whistle was as if Newcastle had won the league.

That tremendous 4-3 win, on Saturday 7th February 1976, had lifted United up to ninth in Division One, their highest placing since September, in fact, but then Newcastle went and lost all of their next three matches.

The soft centre of Newcastle's team, their centre of defence had conceded far too many soft goals. United finished in fifteenth place at the end of the 1975-76 season, but they'd scored more goals at home (fifty-one) than any other First Division team.

In contrast, only three other teams conceded more goals at home than the twenty-six conceded by Newcastle, and furthermore, United won only four league games away from St James's Park.

Supermac was again United's top league goal-scorer, with nineteen, while Alan Gowling had had a great first season at Newcastle United, the best of his career, with sixteen goals. Again, it was the Black and White Army that were the stars at St James's Park, Newcastle's average home crowd of 33,059 making them the fifth best supported club in England.

Sunderland started 1975-76 like a train, winning three of their opening five games to rise to second in the table, just as they'd done the previous season. Their 1-0 defeat away at Plymouth dropped them out of the top three, but their 2-0 home win over West Brom (Halom, Hughes), on Saturday 13th September, lifted them back into the promotion zone, *and they never dropped below third place thereafter.*

During sixteen Second Division matches between late August and the end of November, Sunderland scored thirty-one goals, while they'd conceded only eight, and they kept nine clean sheets.

On Saturday 8th November, on a bright, golden afternoon, they hammered Cloughie's Nottingham Forest 3-0 (Pop Robson, Vic Halom 2), and they even had a goal disallowed.

By the beginning of December, Sunderland were running away with the title, just as Middlesbrough had done two years before, sitting four points clear of second-placed Bristol City. They won only five of their next fifteen league games, though, which saw them drop back to second place by the twenty-third of March, after their league progress had partly been distracted by a good FA Cup run.

Mel Holden and Pop Robson had scored a goal in each half, as they'd beaten Oldham 2-0 in the Third round, in front of a Roker Park crowd of nearly 30,000. Bad weather then forced a delay of their Fourth round home tie against Hull City by nine days, until Monday 2nd February, when Irish youngster Tom Finney hit an early goal to win the match, with over 32,000 inside Roker Park, to earn an away tie at Stoke.

It was just like 1973 all over again, as 41,176 totally packed The Victoria Ground, and over ten thousand Wearsiders had travelled south to roar on the Second Division leaders, against one of the best teams in England. It was one hell of an atmosphere.

Sunderland were still missing Billy Hughes, who'd been injured at Charlton Athletic back on Saturday 15th November, and he started only four more games that season.

Also, Vic Halom had suffered a season-ending injury in their 2-0 defeat away at Fulham, a week earlier, but Sunderland were well-disciplined and strongly-led by both Bobby Moncur and Bobby Kerr, and absolute equals to Stoke, and it took a superb save by Shilton to prevent Pop Robson from giving them a great away win.

STOKE CITY		SUNDERLAND
Peter Shilton	1	Jim Montgomery
John Marsh	2	Dick Malone
Alan Dodd	3	Joe Bolton
John Mahoney	4	Tony Towers
Denis Smith	5	Jeff Clarke
Alan Bloor	6	Bobby Moncur
Jimmy Robertson	7	Bobby Kerr
Jimmy Greenhoff	8	Jackie Ashurst
Ian Moores	9	Mel Holden
Alan Hudson	10	Pop Robson
Geoff Salmons	11	Tom Finney

With 47,583 packed inside Roker Park, three days later, Mel Holden and Pop Robson scored second half goals to send Sunderland into the Quarter-finals, with a great 2-1 win. Third Division Crystal Palace, managed by Malcolm Allison, who'd already won away at both Leeds United and Chelsea, were all that separated Sunderland from their second FA Cup Semi-final in just three years.

The fans were up for it, but the team were slumping a little in the league, having won only five of their last sixteen league games since the start of December.

Nearly 51,000 filled Roker Park on Saturday 6th March, but they were stunned when Alan Whittle turned in Peter Taylor's pass, after the break, and Palace held on to become the first Third Division team to reach the FA Cup Semi-finals for twenty-one years.

As FA Cup romances went, though, Crystal Palace's epic cup run, winning away in every single round from the Third round onwards, had actually rivalled Sunderland's great run, just three years earlier. Every neutral had wanted them to reach the Final.

Sunderland's Cup exit was a blessing in disguise, in any case. After their home defeat to Crystal Palace, they lost only twice in their last twelve matches.

At Ayresome Park, Middlesbrough began the season just as they'd ended the previous season: unspectacularly.

Of their opening eight matches, they won three, lost three and drew twice, scoring eight but conceding ten goals. Bobby Murdoch, thirty-two years old by then, was beginning to suffer from niggling little injuries, and he missed half of the season.

He'd helped taken the young underachieving Boro team of 1973 to almost the highest levels of league and cup football, just as Jack Charlton had envisioned.

Murdoch's absence from the team proved costly, and Boro's hopes of UEFA Cup qualification were severely affected.

On a positive note, though, with Terry Cooper well settled into their back four, the thirty-two year old former World Cup defender had brought valuable experience just as much as Murdoch had done.

Middlesbrough's brilliant back four of Craggs, Boam, Maddren and Cooper, in front of Jim Platt, then kept seven consecutive league and cup clean sheets between Saturday 20th September and 18th October, and Boro had risen up to sixth-place in the First Division, and just three points behind the leaders Liverpool.

In the League Cup, Boro also had a great run. First, John Hickton and David Mills had both scored during their 2-1 away win at Bury, on Tuesday 9th September, with the 9,121 Gigg Lane crowd doubling Bury's average home attendance.

A month later, in the Third round, Alan Foggon fired a second half winner to beat the reigning League Champions Derby County 1-0, with nearly 27,000 inside Ayresome Park. On Tuesday 11th November, Stuart Boam, John Hickton, from the penalty spot, and David Armstrong all scored in their emphatic 3-0 win over Peterborough United, in the Fourth round, to send Boro into their second successive Cup Quarter-final.

Middlesbrough were drawn away at Burnley, who weren't the team they'd been between 1972 and 1975. Without Martin Dobson, Geoff Nulty, Frank Casper, Paul Fletcher, and now Leighton James, who'd joined Derby County in a club record £300,000 transfer deal at the end of November, Burnley were deep inside the relegation zone and doomed to the Second Division.

So David Mills and Willie Maddren scored in each half, as Boro easily won 2-0 away, on Wednesday 3rd December, with only 15,000 inside Turf Moor, by a long way the smallest crowd of the League Cup Quarter-finals.

Middlesbrough were drawn against fellow UEFA Cup chasers Manchester City, in the Semi-finals, and 35,000, their biggest home crowd of the season, crammed into Ayresome Park for the first leg game, on Tuesday 13th January 1976.

MIDDLESBROUGH		MANCHESTER CITY
Jim Platt	1	Joe Corrigan
John Craggs	2	Colin Barrett
Ian Bailey	3	Willie Donachie
Graeme Souness	4	Mike Doyle
Stuart Boam	5	Tommy Booth
Willie Maddren	6	Alan Oakes
Bobby Murdoch	7	Peter Barnes
David Mills	8	Paul Power
John Hickton	9	Joe Royle
Terry Cooper	10	Asa Hartford
David Armstrong	11	Dennis Tueart
Alan Foggon	12	Gerard Keegan

Against a dynamic, lively attack of Royle, Hartford, Tueart, Barnes and Oakes, Terry Cooper was deployed as extra defensive cover by Jack Charlton, just as Paul Madeley often used to be at Leeds United, and their game plan worked.

John Hickton turned in David Armstrong's pass, after the break, and Middlesbrough held on for their fourth clean sheet in five League Cup matches.

By now, Graeme Souness had a full-blown perm on top of his head. If you thought this dreaded permed hairstyle had been born in Liverpool, forget it.

It was indeed a Middlesbrough player who boasted the first ever perm in First Division football.

Having conceded just a single goal in the tournament, thus far, Boro looked well set for their first ever visit to Wembley. They only had to score at Maine Road, and then City would've needed to score three. Middlesbrough had conceded three goals in a single league or cup match on just ten occasions during the previous three seasons, and they were favourites to reach the Final.

Eight days later, though, on Wednesday 21st January, Bobby Murdoch broke down again, and he was replaced by Tony McAndrew, and with Peter Brine playing up front in place of Alan Foggon, Boro just collapsed.

Gerard Keegan's header and Alan Oakes' sharply hit shot fired City to a 2-0 half-time lead, in front of a Maine Road crowd of over 44,000. As Boro still pressed for their vital away goal, City broke, against the run of play, and Peter Barnes skipped in before placing the ball inside Platt's right hand post.

Joe Royle added a fourth before the end for an emphatic 4-0 win, and City went to Wembley after an aggregate 4-1 victory.

After that defeat, Middlesbrough's season fell apart, far more dramatically than during the previous season. In twenty-six league and cup games between the middle of September, and the middle of January, Boro had conceded only sixteen goals. They'd scored just twenty-nine goals in those games, however, and it was that lack of offensive bite that bit Boro hard.

Once teams found a way to defend against Boro's Alan Foggon slingshot counter attack tactics, they found more time to attack their highly-rated defence, and they did just that.

Middlesbrough struggled to adjust, and for the first time since their promotion, they conceded more goals than they scored. Despite still riding high in sixth place, in early March, Boro lost seven of their last nine games, winning just twice, and they dropped down to a lowly thirteenth place by the end of the 1975-76 season.

David Mills and John Hickton were tied as their top league and cup goal-scorers, with just twelve goals each. Middlesbrough had conceded just five more goals than they'd conceded in 1974-75, but they'd scored eight goals fewer.

Only two other First Division teams, relegated clubs Sheffield United and Burnley, had scored fewer goals than Boro.

Middlesbrough's defence kept nineteen First Division clean sheets during 1975-76, and twenty-four in all competitive matches, which was a record for a bottom half of the table team, but they'd become known as an inherently defensive side.

Deflated by the criticism of his team, and despondent of their form, reflecting on their exciting counter-attacking style of 1974, Jack Charlton resigned as manager of Middlesbrough in April 1977, near to the end of the following season.

"We are on the crest of a slump," he'd enigmatically predicted just five days prior to his resignation.

Jack Charlton's Middlesbrough team remains, to this day, their most complete, and greatest ever team.

Bobby Murdoch retired at the end of the 1975-76 season, and he was most greatly missed by the team, just as they'd struggled without him prior to his arrival. They were mostly all better players by the time he left, but it wasn't the same without him.

He'd be remembered as one of the most influential and skilful players to ever represent Middlesbrough. Bobby Murdoch died in his home city of Glasgow, after suffering a stroke, aged only fifty-six, on Tuesday 15th May 2001. He is regarded as much of a club legend at Middlesbrough as he was at his beloved Celtic.

Alan Foggon scored forty-five league goals for Boro, in just 105 league starts, but he disagreed with Jack Charlton over the limitations of his abilities, so he left Ayresome Park for Old Trafford, in July 1976, but he played only three games for Manchester United, before Tommy Docherty sold him on to Sunderland, for just £25,000, on Friday 24th September. Foggon failed to score in eight First Division games, at Roker Park, before he finished his playing career starring at Northern League clubs, Consett and Whitley Bay.

It was in both of the domestic Cup competitions in which Newcastle United made the headlines during the 1975-76 season.

A club record crowd of 23,352 over-filled Southport's Haig Avenue ground, on Wednesday 10th September 1975. They'd climbed the floodlight stanchions, sat on top of fences, and also clambered over the advertising boards, for Southport's League Cup Second round tie at home to Newcastle United.

Alan Gowling scored his first ever goals for United, and he fired in four of them, while Paul Cannell, in place of the rested Supermac, added another two, during Newcastle's tremendous 6-0 away win.

After drawing 1-1 away at Bristol Rovers, on Wednesday 7th October, with more than 17,000 filling Eastville, Newcastle won 2-0 back at St James's, eight days later.

Tommy Craig scored from the penalty spot, before Irving Nattrass blasted in a late goal to settle it, and United were headed to QPR in the Fourth round.

Micky Burns, Supermac and Geoff Nulty all scored in a stylish away win at QPR, Newcastle winning 3-1 in front of a small Loftus Road crowd of just over 21,000, on Tuesday 11th November.

Only 29,123 attended Newcastle's Quarter-final home match against Notts County, on Wednesday 3rd December, and the oldest Magpies in the World worked very hard to nearly keep out their First Division hosts.

Supermac made their one goal, hurling in one of his long throw-ins, and under pressure from Gowling, Eric McManus, the County keeper, had flapped at the ball and knocked it into his own net.

Newcastle held on to their 1-0 lead, and they then were drawn against Spurs in the Semi-finals.

John Pratt's first half blast gave Tottenham Hotspur a 1-0 home win in the first leg, on Wednesday 14th January, in front of a big 40,215 White Hart Lane crowd. John Duncan's initial goal-bound header was stopped by Geoff Nulty's arm, but referee Clive Thomas had played the advantage, and Platt fiercely cracked home the loose ball.

Newcastle pressed for an equaliser, but they couldn't beat the World's best goalkeeper. Pat Jennings had pulled off a particularly stunning save, late on, as Tommy Craig drove the ball high towards the top of the Spurs' net. The ball had first appeared to have beaten the keeper, but Jennings arched backwards to clip the ball behind for a Newcastle corner.

NEWCASTLE UNITED		TOTTENHAM HOTSPUR
Mick Mahoney	1	Pat Jennings
Irving Nattrass	2	Terry Naylor
Alan Kennedy	3	Don McAllister
Geoff Nulty	4	John Pratt
Glen Keeley	5	Willie Young
Pat Howard	6	Keith Osgood
Micky Burns	7	Ralph Coates
Tommy Cassidy	8	Steve Perryman
Supermac	9	Martin Chivers
Alan Gowling	10	John Duncan
Tommy Craig	11	Jimmy Neighbour
Stewart Barrowclough	12	Chris Jones

A whole week later, a long, long, long time for a young Newcastle United fan, a massive crowd of over 51,000 filled St James's Park, on Wednesday 21st January 1976, for a real night to remember for all of Tyneside.

After just three minutes, Newcastle levelled the aggregate scores, as Supermac played a perfect pass for Gowling to run onto in the Spurs penalty area. Alan Gowling rounded Pat Jennings, and finished sharply.

A minute into the second half, Tommy Craig's corner kick was met by Glen Keeley, who'd leapt high above the Spurs' defence to head the ball powerfully down and away from Pat Jennings.

Ten minutes later, Tommy Cassidy beat McAllister, then drove in a low cross. Gowling dummied the ball, and captain Geoff Nulty steamed in and finished clinically just inside the far post.

Don McAllister scored a consolation goal with just about twenty minutes remaining, but this United side was not going to be divided, and they easily controlled the rest of the match, for a 3-2 Semi-final win on aggregate.

Newcastle United's players went on an heroic lap of honour around St James's Park, amidst the most electric of atmospheres, such as which have rarely been experienced. Few atmospheres at Newcastle, since then, have even come close to that late night.

All night and all through the following day, the whole of Tyneside celebrated. Grandmothers knitted black and white Cup Final scarves for school-kids, and huge black and white flags were paraded all over the great city.

This time, though, United weren't going to be embarrassed. They weren't going to be out-classed. Malcolm MacDonald had said, "if I see anyone looking around at Wembley, to find their wives or kids, then I will be having a word with them.

We've got work to do before we can start celebrating."

Lessons had been learned since 1974.

Words had been said, publicly, before that Final against Liverpool.

This time, no words were said, at all, regarding the match, prior to the Cup Final.

Newcastle United had learnt their lesson, and they would play a proper game of football on Saturday 28th February 1976.

The trouble was, Manchester City also had the same fans, the same feelings of hurt over the previous six years, and their team also played the Final at 100% of effort and capability.

Tommy Booth played superbly in Colin Bell's playmaking position, unhurried, unflustered, and imaginative in his passing. Asa Hartford, Dennis Tueart and Peter Barnes were buzzing all over the pitch, chasing and hustling, passing and crossing.

Joe Royle used all of his experience to constantly trouble both Keeley and Howard, at the centre of Newcastle's defence, and when Peter Barnes hooked in Mike Doyle's headed knock-down, from six yards out, after just eleven minutes, Newcastle's fans feared the worst.

Straight from the off, Newcastle showed they were here to play. Supermac galloped down the right, evading Doyle's tackle, and then he stepped inside Asa Hartford, before firing just wide of Joe Corrigan's left hand post, from the edge of the area.

Then, after thirty-five minutes, Alan Kennedy dashed up the left wing, across the halfway line, and he played an infield pass to Tommy Craig.

Tommy Craig played the ball on for Tommy Cassidy, who threaded a low pass past Mike Doyle, to Supermac on the left side of the City penalty area.

Supermac slipped a right footed pass, back inside, along the grass, for Alan Gowling to poke beyond Dave Watson and Joe Corrigan at the near post.

Newcastle had simply cut through City's tough defence, just as *Liverpool had undressed* them two years before, and they were absolutely delighted. All of United's players ran and leapt on top of Gowling.

Corrigan then dived bravely at Supermac's feet, when the United number 9 was in full flight, having broken through City's tight defence, just before half-time.

A minute after the break, though, Willie Donachie's left wing cross was headed back inside by Booth, and Dennis Tueart executed the most wonderful bicycle kick ever seen, from the penalty spot, as he buried the ball past Mick Mahoney.

Supermac then ran to the City bye-line and he crossed from the left. Micky Burns collected the ball on the edge of his six yard box, turned and curled his shot beyond Corrigan, but just inches wide of the far post.

Alan Kennedy's cross was headed on by Cassidy, and Corrigan dived low to save Micky Burns's header. Irving Nattrass threaded a pass through to Gowling inside the area, who fired high towards the top right corner of City's goal, but Corrigan leapt to tip the ball of the angle for a Newcastle corner.

It was a tremendous save, and Alan Gowling smiled ruefully. This wasn't ever going to be New-castle's day, no matter how well they played.

As time ran out, City scrambled clear Micky Burns' corner, while Newcastle had every outfield player inside City's area, and referee Jack Taylor blew for full-time.

It had taken one of the greatest goals to have ever been scored at Wembley Stadium to beat Newcastle United, and although spirits were downbeat, they weren't beaten. The embarrassment of 1974 had been blown away by United's brave performance, against a much superior City side, in truth, and Newcastle's fans had totally out-sung their sky blue opponents throughout the weekend.

That Newcastle team, technically inferior to their 1974 team, had done the city proud. Both teams had been adventurous and played good football, and Gordon Lee was full of praise: "We are going back to Newcastle with our heads up. We were very disappointed to lose, but the big fact was that we got there."

"Here in my heart," Gordon Lee also confessed, "I knew we weren't quite ready to be success-ful. We were a couple of players short.

(It was) a great experience for us all, though."

United had also reached the Quarter-finals of the FA Cup, following a fantastic Fifth round battle with the Second Division leaders, Bolton Wanderers. Supermac had scored another contender for *Goal of the Season,* chesting up a long throw-in, before turning and volleying the ball, from twenty yards out, into the far top corner of Barry Siddall's goal, during Newcastle's 3-3 away draw at Burnden Park.

Bolton Wanderers' home crowd of nearly 47,000 for that game was their biggest in decades. Bolton then went and battled for a goalless draw, four days later, on Wednesday 18th February, in front of a St James's Park crowd of over 50,000.

On the following Monday night, over 42,000 United and Wanderers fans packed Elland Road for their second replay, and Burns and Gowling scored in each half, securing a Quarter-final trip to The Baseball Ground, following their 2-1 win.

RETURN OF THE KINGS

After the break, Jim Brown was brilliant in goal, though, keeping out great chances for Souness, Foggon, Mills and Boam. Boro's 1-0 win sent them up to second place, behind Liverpool only on goal average, but only four points separated the top eleven teams. Anyone could win it that season.

After the break, Jim Brown was brilliant in goal, though, keeping out great chances for Souness, Foggon, Mills and Boam. Boro's 1-0 win sent them up to second place, behind Liverpool only on goal average, but only four points separated the top eleven teams. Anyone could win it that season.

Newcastle barely managed to field half of their first team players, on the Saturday after their League Cup Final defeat, following a flu epidemic at the club. Gowling scored twice, but Derby ran out 4-2 winners. Alan Gowling's fourteen goals in both of the domestic Cups, however, meant that he'd emulated Supermac's record of scoring thirty goals during his first season at St James's Park.

After they'd lost at home to Crystal Palace, on Saturday 6th March, Sunderland recovered to beat Orient 2-0 (Kerr 2), before losing 2-1 away at eighth-placed Nottingham Forest, on Wednes-day 17th March. They then drew 1-1 away at Oldham (Hughes), and also at home to leaders Bris-tol City (Holden).

FA Cup Semi-finalists Southampton then visited Roker Park on Saturday 27th March.

Roy Greenwood, a bargain basement signing from Hull City, back in January, scored twice in front of their 34,946 home crowd, with a goal in each half, and then Mel Holden fired his thirteenth goal of the season to seal a much-needed 3-0 win.

On the following Tuesday, Bobby Kerr's second half winner beat York City 1-0, with over 33,000 inside Roker Park, before Sunderland drew 0-0 away at Notts County on the first Saturday in April.

Sunderland returned to the top of the Second Division on Saturday 10th April, after their 3-0 thrashing of Gordon Lee's former team Blackburn Rovers (Holden, Robson, own goal), in front of another decent home crowd, with 33,523 inside Roker Park.

A week later, Sunderland then hammered Hull City 4-1, away at Boothferry Park (Robson, Rowell, Holden, own goal), increasing their lead at the top, after Bristol City had dropped a crucial point in a bone-crunching Good Friday goalless draw, away at fierce city rivals Bristol Rovers, with more than 26,000 filling Eastville. On the following Monday, Easter Monday, Sunderland hosted fourth-placed Bolton Wanderers, who'd also been in the promotion zone on every day since the middle of October, until just three weeks before.

A massive crowd of 51,983 filled Roker Park for the Second Division's game of the season. Apart from league games played at either Old Trafford or Anfield, that was the largest crowd in all of England, during 1975-76. If Sunderland could win, they were certain of First Division football next season, with two games still to play.

Bob Stokoe had paid £80,000 to Carlisle United for Ray Train, five weeks earlier, to boost Sunderland's ball-winning game. Ray Train had been Carlisle's best player, by far, in the First Division during the previous season, and his arrival at Roker Park had directly coincided with Sunderland's resurgence in the promotion race.

SUNDERLAND		BOLTON WANDERERS
Jim Montgomery	1	Barry Siddall
Dick Malone	2	Michael Walsh
Joe Bolton	3	Peter Nicholson
Tony Towers	4	Roy Greaves
Jackie Ashurst	5	Paul Jones
Bobby Moncur	6	Sam Allardyce
Bobby Kerr	7	Willie Morgan
Ray Train	8	Neil Whatmore
Mel Holden	9	Garry Jones
Pop Robson	10	Peter Reid
Roy Greenwood	11	Peter Thompson
Billy Hughes	12	Chris Jones

Tony Towers scored from the penalty spot, before half-time, after Walsh had handled the ball, and then Pop Robson hit his fifteenth goal of the season, running in and burying Mel Holden's knock-down, just as he'd previously done alongside Wyn Davies at Newcastle, and also Clyde Best at West Ham.

Bolton desperately tried to come back, and big Sam Allardyce's towering header brought them right back into the game, but Ray Train had restricted Peter Reid's freedom to pick his passes, and Sunderland held on for a famous 2-1 win.

After two dramatic near misses, Sunderland had finally secured promotion, three years after their Cup win, and with two games to spare.

Bolton went on to win their last two matches, but they finished one point behind Johnny Giles' West Brom, who'd come through like a train at the end, to grab that third crucial promotion place.

Sunderland lost 1-0 at Blackpool, on Tuesday 20th April, one day after their crucial win over Bolton, but on the final Saturday of the season, Joe Bolton and Billy Hughes both scored first half goals for a 2-0 home win over Portsmouth.

A 40,515 Roker Park crowd had watched Sunderland secure the Second Division Championship trophy, beating Bristol City by three points.

Two weeks later, Sunderland's Tony Towers made his England debut, in their 1-0 away win over Wales, at Ninian Park, Cardiff, on Saturday 8th May 1976.

Tony Towers had scored nine league goals during Sunderland's title-winning season, while Pop Robson and Mel Holden both scored fifteen league and cup goals. Billy Hughes and Bobby Kerr shared fourteen goals, while Sunderland's defence, superbly marshalled by the imperious Bobby Moncur, had kept twenty clean sheets.

<u>For the first time since 1954, all three North east teams would be together in the First Division.</u> ***The North Kings had returned.***

They had returned, but Middlesbrough and Sunderland had both returned to the very best of English football, as Champions of Division Two, and within two years of each other, after a combined total absence of twenty-six years away from the First Division, for the very season during which an English team were crowned as European Champions for only the second time.

Sunderland were held to a goalless draw away at Stoke City, in their first Division One game for more than six years, before a crowd of almost 37,000 warmly welcomed First Division football back to Roker Park, on Tuesday 24th August 1976, for their goalless draw at home to Leicester City.

Then, on Saturday 28th August, 41,211 packed Roker Park for Sunderland's 2-2 home draw with Arsenal. Pop Robson and Mel Holden had levelled the scores, following first half goals by Arsenal's Trevor Ross and also Malcolm MacDonald.

Back on July 29th 1976, following weeks of speculation, and a very public fall-out between Newcastle boss Gordon Lee and Supermac, Newcastle United sold Malcolm MacDonald to Arsenal for a British record transfer fee of £333,333 and 34 pence.

At first, furious fans had blamed Supermac for leaving Newcastle, and dozens of giant Malcolm MacDonald billboard posters, advertising Younger's Tartan Bitter, all over the city, were defaced. Later on, they'd change their mind, of course, but many just felt immediately bitter towards the arrogant, brilliant spearhead of their joyous football in the Seventies, who'd scored 121 league and cup goals in 227 games for the club, including ninety-five First Division goals.

Malcolm MacDonald was ***Supermac,*** no more.

On Saturday 4th December 1976, seventh-placed Arsenal hosted Newcastle United, with Malcolm MacDonald facing his old club for the first time, in front of a Highbury crowd of 34,053.

Micky Burns gave Newcastle an early lead, firing past Jimmy Rimmer from the edge of the area, but Trevor Ross then squeezed a shot through a crowd of players, and in off the left post of Mahoney's goal, to equalise.

From Alan Ball's left wing cross, MacDonald leapt and headed past Mahoney, and then Frank Stapleton's shot from a narrow angle, after MacDonald's headed flick-on, just crossed the line before Geoff Nulty could clear it away.

After the break, George Armstrong crossed low from the right, Stapleton flicked on, and Mac-Donald drove the ball in at the far post. Alan Gowling then turned in Tommy Cassidy's right wing cross, before Burns beat Arsenal's defence, and converted Cassidy's low through ball, from the edge of the area, to bring the scores back to 4-3.

In the closing minutes, though, Malcolm MacDonald rose high above Irving Nattrass, to head in Ross's right wing cross, for a superb hat-trick, and a classic 5-3 win over United.

If *Tiger and Scorcher* had published the story, you'd have said it was too far-fetched.

Newcastle lost 2-1 away at Aston Villa, but then 48,400 filled St James's Park for their first Tyne-Wear derby match for almost seven years; Newcastle United versus Sunderland, on Boxing Day 1976.

Sunderland had unfortunately, by this time, endured several casualties from their title–winning squad.

Firstly, Vic Halom had been sold to Oldham Athletic, during July 1976, having scored thirty-five league goals for Sunderland in 113 games.

One of the wild men of that great 1973 team, along with Hughes, Pitt and Horswill, Vic Halom then scored 43 Second Division goals for Oldham, in three seasons at Boundary Park, before he retired from professional football.

Halom stood for election as an MP, at the age of forty-three, in the 1992 General Election, as a Liberal Democrat, for the Sunderland North constituency. He received only 5,000 votes, though, and finished third, behind Labour and the Tories.

Bobby Moncur played only a handful of First Division matches for Sunderland, at the start of the 1976-77 season, before he moved to Carlisle United during November, as their new player-manager.

Moncur was badly missed in Sunderland's defence, being still only thirty-one years old, and having played eighty-six league games at Roker Park. He became almost as much of a hero at Sunderland as he'd been at Newcastle, an extremely rare feat.

Moncur played less than a dozen games for the Cumbrians, before retiring to become Carlisle's full-time manager.

Even the great Jim Montgomery failed to last beyond the first two months of the season.

On Saturday 2nd October 1976, the hero of the 1973 FA Cup Final played his 627th and last-ever game for Sunderland, an all-time club record.

He was replaced by Barry Siddall for their home game against Aston Villa, two weeks later.

Barry Siddall had been signed from Bolton Wanderers, on 29th September, for £80,000, and then, one day later, Bob Stokoe also forked out a club record transfer fee of £200,000 for Leicester City's centre forward Bob Lee, who'd only scored seventeen First Division goals for the Foxes, in sixty-three matches.

Jim Montgomery was then loaned out to Southampton in late October, where he conceded ten goals in five games, and didn't stay. So Monty was instead loaned out to Birmingham City, during February 1977, and after a goalless draw away at Derby, he was permanently signed by Blues' boss Willie Bell, for just £25,000, at thirty-three years old. After Birmingham City's relegation to Division Two in 1979, Monty became a goalkeeping coach at St Andrews.

Two weeks later, Pop Robson was sold back to West Ham, who were just one place above Sunderland, for a ridiculous fee of just £80,000. With Pop Robson's exit, however, went Sunderland's chances of survival. They lost 0-1 at home to Villa, in front of a 31,578 Roker Park crowd, and then Bob Stokoe offered his resignation to the Sunderland board of directors after the match.

"I don't think I can go any further with the club," he told them. "I think I have gone as far as I can."

He was asked to think about it overnight, but in the morning he hadn't changed his mind, and so on Monday 18th October, **BOB STOKOE RESIGNS** as manager of Sunderland made headline news.

After four years in charge, the fizz was disappearing at Roker Park, and it was both significant and symbolic that, <u>for the every first time,</u> ***not one single member of Sunderland's 1973 Cup-winning team*** was included in their team for Sunderland's tenth league game of 1976-77, a 2-0 defeat away at QPR, with Kerr, Hughes, Porterfield and Malone all injured.

On Wednesday 1st December 1976, Jimmy Adamson was appointed as Sunderland's new manager. Adamson, who'd turned Burnley into one of the best teams in England by the mid-Seventies, took over a team that was rock bottom of Division One.

It was a completely different Sunderland team that faced high-flying Newcastle United, on Boxing Day, to that which had won the Second Division title. What you'd have paid to watch the 1973 Newcastle team, with Tony Green, Supermac and Terry Hibbitt, play Sunderland's 1973 team in a proper match like this, and in front of a great 48,400 crowd like this?

NEWCASTLE UNITED		SUNDERLAND
Mick Mahoney	1	Barry Siddall
Irving Nattrass	2	Dick Malone
Alan Kennedy	3	Joe Bolton
Tommy Cassidy	4	Tony Towers
Aiden McCaffrey	5	Jeff Clarke
Geoff Nulty	6	Jim Holton
Stewart Barrowclough	7	Bobby Kerr
Paul Cannell	8	Billy Hughes
Micky Burns	9	Bob Lee
Alan Gowling	10	Alan Brown
Tommy Craig	11	Gary Rowell

Paul Cannell and Alan Kennedy scored in each half to win 2-0, against a severely weakened Sunderland team compared to that that had beaten Bolton, back in April.

Jim Holton had been brought in by caretaker boss Ian McFarlane, back in late October, from Manchester United. The Scottish defender, who'd played in all three of Scotland's World Cup Finals matches in 1974, against Zaire, Brazil and Yugoslavia, simply plugged the gap left by Bobby Moncur at the back.

Their 2-0 defeat, though, was Dick Malone's 236th and final league game for Sunderland.

Malone eventually left Sunderland in the Summer of 1977, having been displaced by Burnley's Mick Docherty.

He joined Hartlepool, before signing for his former boss Bob Stokoe, at Blackpool, two years later. When Alan Ball arrived at Bloomfield Road in 1980, though, as player-manager, he immediately cancelled Malone's contract.

At thirty-two years old, Malone then moved north, up to Queen of the South, and he helped the Doonhamers up to the Scottish First Division, whilst becoming regarded and remembered as one of the most skilful players to have ever played for Queens.

Dick Malone finally retired from football in 1982, at the age of thirty-four.

Billy Hughes played his final match for Sunderland as a substitute, during their 0-1 home defeat to Coventry City, on Monday 3rd January 1977, a result that firmly planted the Wearsiders at the bottom of Division One.

After scoring eighty-two league and cup goals from 332 games, Hughes, the last of the Wild Bunch, left Sunderland in September 1977, joining Derby County for £30,000.

He scored eight First Division goals in just nineteen games, at The Baseball Ground, but was then surprisingly sold to Leicester City, just three months later, for £45,000.

Billy Hughes ended his glorious career, un-enjoyably, as bottom club Leicester plummeted down to Division Two, scoring just two goals in eighteen games.

Why?

A terrifying sight for defenders when bombing forward, Hughes could shoot with either foot, running straight at the opposition, and it was a crying shame to see such a great attacking player finish his career so sadly and ingloriously.

He was "the most exciting player in Britain," Tommy Docherty had once described Billy Hughes, following Manchester United's superb 3-2 victory over Sunderland in that classic Old Trafford match, in November 1974.

The fizz *was* disappearing.

Amazingly, Jimmy Adamson's Sunderland nearly pulled off the greatest of escapes.

On Saturday 22nd January, Sunderland were seven points adrift of safety and well adrift at the bottom of Division One. Between February 11th and May 14th, though, they won nine, and lost just two out of sixteen First Division matches, including their 4-0 battering of Boro, a 6-1 walloping of West Brom, and also a 6-0 hammering of West Ham, all within fifteen glorious days between late February and early March.

That Spring uprising, driven by nine goals from Bob Lee, eight from Mel Holden, and five from Gary Rowell, lifted the Wearsiders up to sixteenth place, with just one game to play, but with five teams tied on thirty-four points. Tottenham and Stoke were down, and West Ham and QPR both saved themselves with their games in hand, so it was all down the last games of the season, played on Thursday 19th May.

Sunderland were fifth from bottom, and on the same points total as both Bristol City and Coventry City, immediately beneath them, knowing that an away draw at mid-table Everton would secure their safety. Even a defeat would be okay, as long as either Coventry or Bristol City, who were meeting at Highfield Road, won.

It was a day of controversy, as with just 36,903 attending the match at Coventry, and with Highfield Road having a capacity of 48,000, the kick-off was delayed by fifteen minutes due to crowd congestion. There was no such "congestion" over at Everton, where more than 36,000 also watched their match against Sunderland.

Everton won 2-0, after second half goals by Martin Dobson and Duncan McKenzie.

At Highfield Road, Tommy Hutchison scored a goal in each half for the Sky Blues, whilst Gerry Gow and Don Gillies equalised for the Robins in the second half.

With ten minutes remaining, plus stoppage time, Jimmy Hill, Coventry's Managing Director, had the **EVERTON 2-0 SUNDERLAND** final score flashed up on their electronic scoreboard. Subsequently, for the remainder of the match, both teams just passed the ball along their defences, and back to their keepers, knowing that the draw would keep them both up.

Whether it was planned, or not planned, by the avant-garde Mr Hill, it was certainly a shameful display of terrible sportsmanship, and Robins' defender Norman Hunter was not proud of it. "It was the most bizarre situation I have ever experienced in football," Hunter admitted, having felt trapped in that situation.

Sunderland were absolutely stitched up, but Jimmy Hill didn't see it quite like that. On his decision to broadcast the Everton result to the whole stadium, he suggested, "since it was such vital and welcome news for almost everyone at the ground, the sooner it was conveyed the sooner the relief and joy would be felt- *what theatre, what drama, what entertainment!"*

Whatever?.....

Anyway, under a three points for a win system, for which Jimmy Hill had long campaigned, Sunderland would have been very safe, and Coventry would have gone down with Stoke and Tottenham.

It certainly wasn't fair game, and the Football League should have delayed the start of the second half at Goodison Park, in order to maintain fairness, and to avoid such a *theatrical, dramatic and entertaining* disgrace.

For Sunderland, Bob Lee had scored thirteen First Division goals, while Mel Holden scored just nine. It was interesting that Pop Robson had once again been West Ham's top scorer with fourteen First Division goals, from just thirty games.

West Ham had finished just two points above Sunderland, so it seemed clear that selling their top scorer for just £80,000 had cost Sunderland their First Division status.

Pop Robson did return to Roker Park, in June 1979, for just £45,000, at thirty-three years old. He scored twenty Second Division goals in forty games, as Sunderland succeeded in gaining promotion back to the First Division, finishing second behind Leicester City in 1980.

Bryan "Pop" Robson finally retired, at thirty-nine years old, while at Carlisle United in 1985, after a superb Football League career, scoring two hundred and sixty-five goals in 674 games.

With the dour Tony McAndrew replacing the classy, innovative Bobby Murdoch, and the lively, free-running Alan Foggon gone, and replaced by the more conservative, former Liverpool reserve team player, Phil Boersma, in their attack, Middlesbrough did become an anti-football team, just as Bob Kearsey had described them, three years earlier.

After their 1-0 win over Newcastle, in front of an Ayresome Park crowd of 26,000, and then a 2-1 home win over Sunderland, in front of just 29,000, on the first two Saturdays of September, Middlesbrough were second in the table, after five games, and level on points with leaders Liverpool.

Then, after a couple of 1-0 wins, over both Leeds and Norwich, and a goalless draw away at Liverpool, Middlesbrough defeated West Brom 1-0, on Saturday 23rd October, following David Mills' second goal of the season. An Ayresome Park crowd of just 23,000 saw Boro go top of the First Division for the first time since the two World Wars.

They'd scored just eight goals in eleven games, but had conceded only six.

FIRST DIVISION LEADERS, 23RD OCTOBER 1976

	PL	W	D	L	F	A	PTS
MIDDLESBROUGH	11	6	3	2	8	6	15
Aston Villa	11	7	0	4	24	11	14
Liverpool	10	6	2	2	15	8	14
Everton	11	5	3	3	19	14	13
Ipswich Town	10	5	3	2	17	13	13
Newcastle United	11	4	5	2	17	13	13
Manchester City	11	4	5	2	15	11	13

After that *high point* in the club's history, Middlesbrough lost four in a row, to plummet back to mid-table, where they remained for most of the rest of the season.

By December, Boro were in tenth place, having scored only ten goals during their opening seventeen matches, while they'd conceded just fourteen goals.

They had become, quite simply, boring to watch, and by Saturday 16th April 1977, despite still being in tenth place, and just six points behind a UEFA Cup qualifying place, only 14,500 attended their 0-2 home defeat to QPR.

Middlesbrough's defence was still as strong as ever. John Craggs, Stuart Boam, Willie Maddren and Terry Cooper missed just seven games between them, out of a total of 168, and they conceded one or less goals in twenty-eight out of their forty-two First Division matches. But that was all they had, with no disrespect to midfield general Graeme Souness, nor top scorer David Mills, who'd scored fifteen goals, nor David Armstrong who hit eight from midfield.

For the first time since 1925, Middlesbrough had scored less than a goal per game, and, fearing the worst, Jack Charlton had resigned by the end of the season.

Middlesbrough had passed their peak, and they were on a downward cultural curve, just as Slade, T-Rex, Roxy Music and Pan's People were being replaced on *Top of the Pops* by Smokey, The Real Thing, Manhattan Transfer and Ruby Flipper.

After leaving Boro, Jack Charlton went to Sheffield Wednesday, and then Newcastle United, where he helped turn Chris Waddle and Peter Beardsley into international class forwards, but he also unearthed such Newcastle "legends" as Pat Heard, Gary Megson and Tony Cunningham.

He resigned as Newcastle manager in 1985, and was then appointed as manager of the Republic of Ireland a year later.

He led Ireland to two World Cup Finals tournaments, as well as the 1988 European Championship Finals. At one point, Ireland were ranked as high as sixth in the FIFA World Rankings, during his ten years in charge.

Willie Maddren played his last game for Middlesbrough, on Saturday 3rd September 1977, after he'd been run ragged by Cyrille Regis, during Boro's 2-1 defeat away at West Brom. His troublesome knee had seized up again, after weeks of playing in pain, and after an unsuccessful operation, he was forced to retire the following year, at just twenty-seven years old.

Maddren became Middlesbrough's club physiotherapist in 1982, but he was then promoted to first team manager at the end of the 1983-84 season, after helping the team survive relegation to the Third Division for only the second time in their history.

Willie Maddren's Middlesbrough also successfully, though scarcely survived relegation on the final day of the 1984-85 season, but throughout his time in charge, the club had been crippled by financial difficulties, and he was finally sacked after just thirteen matches of the 1985-86 season, with Boro rocketing down to Division Three, and also, towards liquidation.

Willie Maddren was finished with football, and he opened a sports shop business on Teesside. He'd played 351 league and cup games for the club, and had been awarded a Testimonial in 1978.

During 1995, he was diagnosed with Motor Neurone Disease, and after a long five year battle, he died on Tuesday 29th August 2000, aged only forty-nine years old.

He'd been given a standing ovation by the Middlesbrough fans, and most of his old teammates, as he made a guest appearance at The Riverside Stadium, before the end of the 1999-2000 season.

"This is one game I cannot win, but I will go down fighting," Willie Maddren told them.

There wasn't a dry eye in the Stadium.

Stuart Boam said of Maddren, "not only was he my playing partner, and a very good one, he was also a good friend."

Stuart Boam and Willie Maddren's telepathic understanding was possibly the very best defensive partnership in the First Division, between 1974 and 1976, and certainly the greatest in Boro's history. Willie Maddren had reminded Les Cocker of a young Norman Hunter, but Stuart Boam played 322 league games for Middlesbrough, before joining Newcastle United in August 1979, for £140,000.

Stuart Boam's arrival at St James's Park inspired Newcastle to run away at the top of the Second Division by the early weeks of 1980, but they collapsed in the last three months, and he left United in 1981, during the very darkest days in the Magpies' history. He rejoined his home town club Mansfield Town, who would certainly have been a better team than Newcastle United were in 1981.

Terry Cooper played 105 First Division games for Boro, of which forty-three were clean sheets, before he rejoined his old Leeds United teammate Norman Hunter, at Bristol City in 1978, and then his career finally ended at thirty-four years of age.

Graeme Souness joined Liverpool in January 1978, for £350,000, after an unhappy end to his 186 game league career at Middlesbrough.

He'd badly missed the presence and drive of his Scottish teammate Bobby Murdoch, in the Boro midfield, and even the arrival of Welsh international John Mahoney, from Stoke, couldn't persuade him to stay at Ayresome Park.

At Anfield, Graeme Souness finally found his heartland, alongside Kenny Dalglish and Terry McDermott, winning five First Division titles between 1978 and 1984, three European Cups, and also four League Cups.

After leaving Liverpool in 1984, Souness then won a Coppa Italia with Sampdoria in 1985, before winning three Scottish League titles with Rangers, in the late Eighties.

Souness was voted as the Number One Greatest Hard Man by The Daily Mail, in January 2009, ahead of Billy Bremner, Dave Mackay, Tommy Smith, Ron Harris, Stuart Pearce, Vinnie

Jones and Roy Keane. After retirement, he managed almost every Premier League club in England, except for Arsenal and Manchester United, as well as Torino and Benfica, overseas, and Rangers.

Graeme Souness was one of the greatest and most successful Scottish footballers ever, and he's right up there, equal with those legends, Baxter, Bremner and Mackay.

John Hickton started just seven games, out of eighty-four, during his last two seasons at Ayresome Park, while making thirteen appearances from the bench, and his contract was finally cancelled in April 1978.

He is still third on the club's all-time goal-scorers' list with 159 goals from 393 league starts.

John Hickton was the most prolific Middlesbrough centre forward of the last fifty years, though, and in his mid-thirties, he ended his playing days at Whitby Town.

David Mills was transferred to West Bromwich Albion on 5th January 1979, for a British record transfer fee of £482,222, having scored seventy-five goals in 295 league games for Middlesbrough.

Ron Atkinson switched Mills, then twenty-seven, back to midfield, reluctant to break up his prolific attacking partnership of Cyrille Regis and Ally Brown. *So why then did he spend a British record transfer fee on a forward?* The change of position resulted in a loss of form and numerous injuries, throughout his three years at West Brom, and David Mills endured a miserable time, scoring only six goals in fifty-nine games.

David Armstrong played three hundred and fifty-nine league games for Middlesbrough, scoring fifty-nine goals, and he played his first game for England, against Australia, in May 1980, becoming the first Boro player to play for England since Alan Peacock.

In August 1981, Southampton manager Lawrie McMenemy paid £600,000 for David Armstrong, and in 1983-84, he scored fifteen goals as the Saints finished in second place, only three points behind Champions Liverpool, but they also lost their FA Cup Semi-final against Everton, after extra-time, at Highbury.

David Armstrong was voted as Southampton's Player of the Season that season.

John Craggs played 409 league games for Boro, before returning to Newcastle United in 1982, aged thirty-three. Voted the best right back in Division Two back in 1973-74, by the PFA, Craggs played just a dozen games while at St James's Park, before he finished his five hundred game league career at Darlington.

Jim Platt left Middlesbrough in 1983, having made four hundred and eighty-one league appearances for the club, while also playing 23 times for Northern Ireland. He'd have played three times that amount for his country if it hadn't been for Pat Jennings, one of the two or three greatest-ever goalkeepers in Football League history.

Jim Platt was in Northern Ireland's World Cup Finals squads for both Spain 1982 and Mexico 1986. He played in their 2-2 draw with Austria, in the Second round, in Madrid, on Thursday 1st July 1982, and he remains the best-ever goalkeeper in Middlesbrough's history.

After Sunderland's relegation, Ian Porterfield moved to Sheffield Wednesday, after playing 231 league games for the Rokerites. Their 1973 goal-scoring hero didn't play a single First Division match during 1976-77, and he was actually loaned out to Reading back in November 1976.

Porterfield played over one hundred Third Division games for Wednesday, until his retirement in 1979, at the age of thirty-three. He went on to manage both Chelsea and Sheffield United, and also Aberdeen, but it was on the international stage where he was most celebrated as a coach.

He managed the national teams of Zimbabwe, Oman, Armenia, and Trinidad and Tobago, but his greatest achievement, probably of his entire football career, was as manager of the Zambian national team between 1993 and 1994.

In 1993, eighteen players of the Zambian team, as well as their coach, were all killed in an air crash over the Atlantic, en route to a match against Senegal.

Having been subsequently appointed as manager of Zambia, following the tragedy, Ian Porterfield led them to the African Nations Cup Final, in Tunis, on April 10th 1994.

Nigeria beat Zambia 2-1 in that Final, but that remains one of the greatest stories in World Soccer history, and back in Lusaka, Ian Porterfield was awarded the Freedom of Zambia.

He was a hero there, as well as in all of the countries where he'd coached.

At Sunderland, he was frozen out twice.

Ian Porterfield died of cancer, aged only sixty-one, on Tuesday 11th September 2007.

Prior to Sunderland's first Premier League game after his death, in their home match against Reading on the following Saturday, ten survivors from their 1973 FA Cup winning team were reunited on the pitch to pay their respects and fondly remember their great teammate and friend.

Bobby Kerr, the Little General, was voted as captain of the 1975-76 Second Division Team of the Year, by the PFA, and he missed only twenty-nine out of three hundred and fifty-two league games for Sunderland, between February 1970 and August 1978.

He was certainly the most fondly remembered of all the 1973 FA Cup team.

Bobby Kerr was also the last of the gang to leave, joining his old boss Bob Stokoe at Blackpool, in November 1978. After playing 427 league and cup games for Sunderland, having already overcome two broken legs, Bobby Kerr became landlord of the Hastings Hill pub, on the Chester Road in Sunderland, and then the Oddfellows Arms in Millfield, also on Wearside.

Back on Tyneside, Gordon Lee resigned as Newcastle United's manager in late January 1977, with eighteen months still remaining on his contract, and with his Newcastle side in a very strong position for UEFA Cup qualification.

He decided that "it would be beneficial to move nearer to his children who were educated in Lancashire."

Why then, did he leave Blackburn Rovers, only eighteen months earlier?

Just as moving to Newcastle United, away from his children, was a career move, so too was Gordon Lee's move to Everton, pure and simple. He had eliminated many of the fans' favourite players from the club, and moulded his type of team that played a direct style that could, in fairness, be as exciting on its day, as it could be dreadful on others; just like Joe Harvey's all-football team.

So why did the fans have to see so many favourite players leave, for a more functional type of football that brought no more consistency than before?

Quite simply, Gordon Lee left Newcastle with his job half-done, and although acting manager Richard Dinnis then guided United to a fifth-place finish in Division One, and qualification for their first ever UEFA Cup campaign, the actual cracks at the club had simply been papered over.

During the 1977-78 UEFA Cup, there were no repeats of any 1968-70 Fairs Cup heroics, and little known Bastia, from France, thrashed Newcastle in the Second round. Richard Dinnis was sacked, and Bill McGarry was then appointed, but even worse than that, United's famous and much-loved Leazes End was demolished towards the end of the 1977-78 season, as Newcastle sunk to the bottom of the First Division before Christmas, and were eventually relegated, eleven points adrift of safety.

For all three North-eastern clubs, the turning of 1976 into 1977 had brought three manager resignations, and the effective end of their Glam Soccer years.

Alan Kennedy, United's bright young hope, even left Newcastle in August 1978, following their relegation to the Second Division, joining European Champions Liverpool for £300,000. He never looked the same after moving down to Anfield.

He'd always looked young and full of passion in a Black and White shirt.

At Liverpool, he had his hair permed, but he also grew a silly moustache.

He did win First Division Championships, that has to be said, and he also scored two European Cup-winning penalty kicks, during Liverpool's 1-0 win over Real Madrid in 1981, and also their dramatic penalty-kicks win away at Roma in 1984, but with a perm and a silly moustache.

Alan Kennedy played 194 games for Newcastle, and only John Beresford has really surpassed him as United's second-greatest ever left back, after Frank Clark.

Tommy Cassidy spent nearly ten years at St James's Park, and he was the only member of their 1974 FA Cup Final team to remain with Newcastle after their relegation to Division Two. *Hopalong* played 212 games for United, and was an underrated influence in their midfield, who'd had a superb game against City in the 1976 League Cup Final, but he rarely got many plaudits.

He finally left Newcastle after the team's self-destruction towards the end of the 1979-80 season, with promotion firmly in their hands. Tommy Cassidy moved to Burnley in July 1980, for just £30,000.

Irving Nattrass also stayed, following Newcastle's relegation, after playing 275 games, before joining Boro in July 1979, for a club record transfer fee of £375,000.

There's not been an out and out better right back at St James's Park, since Nattrass.

David Craig, though, was Newcastle's greatest ever right back, but he suffered from persistent knee ligament troubles from the 1974-75 season until his eventual retirement in November 1978, at thirty-four years of age.

He missed the 1974 FA Cup Final due to his knee problems, but he'll be best remembered for his superb displays in the Fairs Cup, keeping out many of Europe's greatest forwards. David Craig had played over 400 games for Newcastle, and he and Frank Clark will always be the greatest full back partnership in United's history.

Under Joe Harvey, Bob Stokoe and Jack Charlton, the three big teams from the Deep North, together, had never had such a wonderful period, at the same time, and with such a spirit about the place, that buzzed so loudly and vibrantly.

Kids would decide on Friday afternoons, or even on the mornings before matches to just pay the 5p bus fare into town, and then pay their 35p pocket money to get into the ground without their parents.

Supporting your team with a passion was so much simpler then.

All three clubs used to fill their terraces with home fans. It was just the grandstands that had the empty seats, and there was a spontaneity about atmospheres back then, with real songs, and at all grounds, not just in the North-east, but certainly in the North-east. The kids would get there at about half-past, so they could get to, or nearer the front to see their superstars kicking the balls about prior to their changing room team talks, singing their names, and then, at bang on kick-off, the adults would arrive at the back, from the pubs, and the real fun would then start, with all the rude songs.

Roker Park and Ayresome Park were magnificent, distinguished grounds, but times changed, very sadly, and both clubs had to move to new all-seated stadiums.

Newcastle managed to remain at St James's Park, and although it regularly holds 58,000 in their fantastic, gigantic arena, the atmosphere isn't a quarter as good as when the old St James's Park, with its roofed Leazes End, had 40,000 packed inside.

All three teams have experienced good times since the Glam Soccer years.

In fact, Middlesbrough have won a major trophy, the League Cup, and they even magnificently reached a UEFA Cup Final, just as Newcastle have competed in several UEFA Champions Leagues, having finished as Premier League runners-up on three occasions, as well as reaching two FA Cup Finals, and a UEFA Cup Semi-final.

Sunderland also reached an FA Cup Final, and returned to European competition, and they've had new heroes to worship, Quinn, Phillips, and Sessignon.

They are, of course, not a patch on Kerr, Hughes, Porterfield, Tueart or Montgomery.

The football played by all three North-east teams between 1973 and 1976, though, was glorious, *magical* even. The *magic* was back.

The Kings had returned.

"I didn't bring the *magic.* It's always been here," Sunderland FC had written on the back of the plinth that holds the statue of Bob Stokoe, just outside the Stadium of Light.

"I just came back to find it."

The magic will always be there, in the North-east, in the Deep North, for the three sleeping giants, the Fellowship of the withering.

Often it'll be so well hidden that you'll only occasionally glimpse it, but then every so often it'll shine brilliantly again, through Waddle, Beardsley, Keegan, Asprilla, Ravanelli, Juninho, Viduka, Quinn, Phillips, and even Asamoah Gyan.

Never before or since, though, has the magic been so vivid for all three teams, and all at the same time, as for Newcastle United, Sunderland and Middlesbrough between 1973 and 1976.

A TALE OF TWO UNITEDS, Part Four

MANCHESTER UNITED CONTINUED THEIR free-flowing form, from the previous season, into their return to the First Division in August 1975.

Having acquired Tommy Jackson, on a free transfer, from Nottingham Forest, to replace the departed, bitter Willie Morgan, they won 2-0 away at Wolves, on Saturday 16th August, and then 2-0 away at Birmingham City, three days later. Lou Macari had scored twice at Molineux, and Sammy McIlroy did likewise at St Andrews.

Stuart Pearson also then scored twice, at home to Sheffield United, on the second Saturday of the season, as Manchester United won 5-1 to top the First Division, for the first time in four years. Gerry Daly, Sammy McIlroy and a Len Badger own goal completed their blasting of the Blades.

Manchester United lost only once during their opening eight First Division matches, and they remained at the top of Division One in late September. A defeat away at Derby, followed by draws with Manchester City and Leicester City, had reduced their lead over QPR at the top to virtually nothing, but then they faced Leeds United, away at Elland Road, on Saturday 11th October.

Leeds United manager Jimmy Armfield had signed no new players to replace either Johnny Giles or Mick Jones, prior to the 1975-76 season. In fact, he signed no new players at all during the whole season, taking time instead to calmly assess his squad.

While Leeds United were no longer a team of title-winning strength, neither were they mid-table fodder, and Jimmy Armfield afforded them that respect. They won six of their opening eleven league games, while losing just twice. Their fifteen league goals were mostly shared between Allan Clarke, Peter Lorimer and Duncan McKenzie. Joe Jordan had suffered a bad pre-season injury which kept him out until February.

LEEDS UNITED		MANCHESTER UNITED
David Stewart	1	Alex Stepney
Paul Reaney	2	Jimmy Nicholl
Frank Gray	3	Stewart Houston
Billy Bremner	4	Tommy Jackson
Paul Madeley	5	Brian Greenhoff
Norman Hunter	6	Martin Jackson
Trevor Cherry	7	Steve Coppell
Allan Clarke	8	Sammy McIlroy
Duncan McKenzie	9	Stuart Pearson
Terry Yorath	10	Lou Macari
Eddie Gray	11	Gerry Daly

Nevertheless, Leeds United were fourth in the table when league leaders Manchester United visited Elland Road.

40,264 packed their ground as Leeds could return to the top of the league, if they won.

Just as in 1972, however, when the transition-hit and ageing Manchester United had met the tightly-knit and well-oiled Leeds United machine. They had then been made to look a complete mess, but this Leeds United side were now a mess against Manchester's newly-United work of art.

Cherry, Yorath and McKenzie were out of position, or out of their depth, and the Red Devils fully capitalised on their weaknesses. Sammy McIlroy scored a goal in each half, to crown an imperious performance that Johnny Giles, at his peak, would've been very happy with.

European Cup Final goalkeeper David Stewart was brilliant, after keeping out close range shots from Greenhoff, Pearson (twice) and also Coppell, while Allan Clarke's late goal merely flattered the score for Leeds United.

Manchester United had been so dominant in possession, pressure and panache, but ironically, they dropped down to second place, on goal average, after QPR had hammered Everton 5-0. Leeds United dropped to sixth, but they were still only three points behind the new leaders.

After losing to both West Ham United and Liverpool, however, Manchester United dropped to fifth place, and Tommy Docherty, partly due to the injury Tommy Jackson had suffered, following Tommy Smith's tackle, but also due to the fact that Jackson, alone, was a little out of his depth in this team, then decided to strengthen his hand.

Gordon Hill had scored twenty goals for Millwall, during the previous two seasons. "He was incredible," his Millwall teammate Eamon Dunphy had admitted. "He was going out and turning those big burly full backs inside out. They're all trying to kick him, but they can't, and he hasn't got a care in the world."

Gordon Hill was just what Manchester United needed, and he was the final piece in the jigsaw for Docherty, who paid Millwall just £70,000 for him.

Hill slotted in perfectly, on the left side of their midfield, with Coppell on the right, and with McIlroy and Daly in the middle.

Their season significantly improved following Hill's arrival, winning six of their next nine games, and they returned to the top of the First Division by early January 1976.

As suggested in a previous chapter, West Ham United had greatly resembled The Eagles, with their big beards, long unkempt hair and generally rough-shod appearances.

With an average age of just twenty-one years old, though, Manchester United's new midfield, "a potential gold mine", as Bill Shankly had described them, Steve Coppell, Gerry Daly, Sammy McIlroy and Gordon Hill, looked more like The Bay City Rollers, with their fresh-faced boyish good looks.

Martin Buchan, at the back, might have been their older, and slightly uglier drummer Derek Longmuir.

Against Arsenal on Saturday 18th October, with nearly 53,000 inside Old Trafford, Steve Coppell hammered a left-footed, thirty-five yard shot beyond Jimmy Rimmer, and then Stuart Pearson chested down Greenhoff's long ball, and he buried the ball beneath Rimmer's body, from just inside the area.

Manchester United then scored the best goal of the match. Sammy McIlroy ran along the edge of the Arsenal penalty area, riding two tackles, before he released the ball to Coppell, who volleyed home from twenty-five yards out.

After that dazzling 3-1 win, Manchester United were the new flamboyant leaders of the First Division.

In the FA Cup, two goals from Gerry Daly had knocked Oxford United out in the Third round, before Manchester United then beat Peterborough United 3-1 in the Fourth round (Forsyth, McIlroy, Hill), with 56,352 packed inside Old Trafford.

Back in the First Division, Manchester United hosted Birmingham City on Saturday 31st January, and Alex Forsyth and Lou Macari gave them a 2-0 half-time lead, before Sammy McIlroy scored his eleventh goal of the season to complete another 3-1 win.

As February arrived, Manchester United were in with a really great chance of their first ever league and cup double.

FIRST DIVISION LEADERS, 31ST JANUARY 1976

	PL	W	D	L	F	A	PTS
MANCHESTER UNITED	27	16	6	5	44	25	38
Liverpool	27	13	11	3	44	23	37
Derby County	27	15	6	6	43	34	36
LEEDS UNITED	26	15	5	6	45	26	35
QPR	28	12	10	6	36	22	34

While Leeds United were losing 3-2 at Derby County, on Saturday 1st November, Norman Hunter and Francis Lee were both sent off for fighting. Lee insisted that he never threw a punch, on the muddy Baseball Ground pitch, but he was given a split lip by a thump from Hunter.

As both players walked off the pitch, though, following some verbal exchanges between the two, Lee did start throwing good, hard punches.

It appeared to be an eruption of pent-up emotion built up over all the years, and the two legends fought a very personal fist-fight while both sets of players, and also the referee, ran over to try and break it up.

One month later, both players were charged for bringing the game into disrepute.

Hunter was cleared, even though he had thrown the only punch during the initial incident for which both players were sent off. For continuing the battle, though, after they'd both been dismissed, Francis Lee was banned for four matches.

What did they really feel about the other player, both Hunter and Lee were asked by reporters outside FA headquarters?

"I have no comment," they replied.

One significant, but positive outcome from this incident was that Paul Madeley, for the first time in his twelve years at Elland Road, was finally given a regular shirt in the Leeds United team.

Rarely a substitute, Madeley was almost always in the team, covering for injury or suspension, playing everywhere, and he was the best player in football history for versatility.

For many seasons, despite not being a first-choice player in any position, Paul Madeley was often Leeds United's most-played player.

So, on Saturday 1st November, Madeley was chosen to play at centre-back, alongside Norman Hunter, in place of the injured Gordon McQueen.

Paul Madeley had been majestic in central defence against both Barcelona and Bayern Munich, in their European Cup games during the previous season, and so, Jimmy Armfield finally rewarded him with his regular place.

Trevor Cherry covered for Norman Hunter, during his suspension, with McQueen out for the remainder of the season, before Hunter returned to partner Paul Madeley, but Madeley, finally, was the man at the back for Leeds.

Also, Jimmy Armfield had brought Eddie Gray back to the first team. After late September, as a result of a more sensitive training programme, Eddie Gray missed only seven out of 34 First Division matches, his most consistent season since 1969.

Between Saturday 22nd November and Saturday 10th January 1976, Leeds United won seven out of eight league games, scoring nineteen goals and conceding just five. They rose from sixth up to second place, only one point behind leaders Manchester United.

With just eighteen games remaining, 1975-76 was threatening to truly become *A Tale of Two Uniteds.*

However, on Saturday 24th January, during their FA Cup Fourth round home match against Crystal Palace, Leeds United lost their captain Billy Bremner to injury, for two months. Dave Swindlehurst then scored a late winner, as Third Division Palace sprung the shock of the round, en route to the Semi-finals.

Leeds United then lost three successive league games, and they dropped out of the title race. Between mid-January and mid-March, while Bremner was missing, they gained only five points from seven matches.

On Saturday 14th February, 34,000 filled Filbert Street, for Leicester City's home match against Manchester United, in the FA Cup Fifth round. Lou Macari and Gerry Daly both scored first half goals, during a classy Reds' performance, and despite a hopeful strike by Bob Lee, very late on, they held on for a 2-1 away win.

As QPR were storming into form, though, Manchester United began to slump in the First Division. They failed to win four successive league matches, during the first three and a half weeks in February, and eventually dropped to third place.

Their 4-0 home win over European Cup Winners' Cup Quarter-finalists West Ham United (Forsyth, Macari, McCreery, Pearson), on Saturday 28th February, finally halted their slump.

The Bay City Rollers had steamrollered The Eagles.

The Eagles, though, were more of an Albums Band, and they came back to reach the European Cup Winners' Cup Final, in Brussels, where they outplayed Anderlecht for much of the game.

	PL	W	D	L	F	A	PTS
Liverpool	32	15	13	4	49	25	43
QPR	33	16	11	6	47	25	43
MANCHESTER UNITED	32	17	9	6	51	29	43
Derby County	32	17	8	7	52	41	42
LEEDS UNITED	30	16	6	8	47	31	38

Liverpool, QPR and Manchester United were all locked together at the top of the First Division, and only goal average separated them, with just ten games to go, and with reigning Champions Derby only a point behind.

On Saturday 6th March, 59,433 just about filled Old Trafford for Manchester United's FA Cup Quarter-final match at home to Wolves. John Richards scored his fifteenth goal of the season, to put Wolves 1-0 up, and then, Manchester United laid siege to Phil Parkes' goal, but Parkes pulled off a series of heroic saves, and it looked like Wolves were going through to the Semi-finals.

A late, late, deflected shot by Gerry Daly, though, earned United a deserved replay.

Three days later, on the Tuesday night, 44,373 packed the vast South Bank and the massed North Bank, Molineux's biggest crowd of the season, and Steve Kindon and John Richards delighted them by putting Wolves 2-0 up, early in the first half.

Then, to compound United's worries, top scorer Lou Macari limped off, and was replaced by Jimmy Nicholl.

Ten minutes before half-time, Steve Coppell's corner was headed in by Stuart Pearson, giving the joint-league leaders some hope.

In the second half, with Brian Greenhoff pushed forward into midfield, and Coppell, Hill, McIlroy and Daly literally squeezed Wolves into their own eighteen yard area. The pressure finally paid off a quarter-hour before the end.

Coppell burst past Derek Parkin and he crossed low for McIlroy to flick on for Greenhoff, who'd arrived from out of the shadows, to volley home for the equaliser.

At 2-2, the replay went into extra-time, and five minutes in, Daly and Pearson produced a sublime series of crisp passing, beautifully cutting through the Wolves midfield and defence. McIlroy latched onto the eventual through-ball, and he finished coolly. United held on for their brilliant comeback 3-2 win.

On the following Saturday, 13th March 1976, Manchester United hosted Leeds United with another 59,429 sell-out crowd filling Old Trafford. Leeds were missing Paul Madeley, but they had Billy Bremner back for his last-ever match against Manchester United, and David McCreery replaced the injured Lou Macari, in an otherwise full strength home team.

A win for Manchester United could've seen them back at the top of Division One, as well as in the FA Cup Semi-finals, with QPR facing a tough away trip to tenth-placed Everton, and Liverpool, having just lost at home to Middlesbrough, and without a win during their last three matches, visiting Birmingham City.

MANCHESTER UNITED		LEEDS UNITED
Alex Stepney	1	David Harvey
Alex Forsyth	2	Trevor Cherry
Stewart Houston	3	Frankie Gray
Gerry Daly	4	Billy Bremner
Brian Greenhoff	5	Terry Yorath
Martin Buchan	6	Norman Hunter
Steve Coppell	7	Duncan McKenzie
Sammy McIlroy	8	Allan Clarke
Stuart Pearson	9	Joe Jordan
David McCreery	10	Peter Lorimer
Gordon Hill	11	Eddie Gray

Stewart Houston headed in Gordon Hill's corner kick, before Stuart Pearson then dummied and side-stepped Norman Hunter, in classic Allan Clarke fashion, before rifling home a fierce drive, from just inside the area, putting Manchester United 2-0 up at half-time.

Trevor Cherry pulled back a scrappy goal for Leeds United, but in the end, the zippy, youthful class of Hill, Coppell, McIlroy and Daly really told, against the ageing legs of Bremner, Hunter and Lorimer. Gerry Daly placed a twenty yard curler past David Harvey's dive, for the two points. Billy Bremner drove in a late consolation to make the final score 3-2, a result that flattered his team, but it was the first time that Manchester United had ever done the double over Leeds United.

Unfortunately, QPR had beaten Everton 2-0, and Phil Neal's contentious penalty kick had also ended Liverpool's barren spell, so Manchester United remained down in third place, but they still had two games in hand on the leaders.

FIRST DIVISION LEADERS, 13TH MARCH 1976

	PL	W	D	L	F	A	PTS
Queens Park Rangers	35	18	11	6	53	26	47
Liverpool	34	16	13	5	50	27	45
MANCHESTER UNITED	33	18	9	6	54	31	45
Derby County	34	18	9	7	56	43	45
LEEDS UNITED	33	16	8	9	51	36	40

Despite their defeat at Old Trafford, the return of Billy Bremner inspired Leeds United to a brilliant run of four wins from their next four games.

Just as they'd probably lost their defence of their title during Bremner's ten game suspension back in August and September of 1974, Leeds United had possibly fallen too far behind the First Division leaders during Bremner's absence through injury over those first two months of 1976.

Billy Bremner, Joe Jordan, and debutant Carl Harris all scored in their 3-1 away win at Everton, on Saturday 20th March. Allan Clarke then scored twice, and Bremner netted his third goal in three games since he returned, as Leeds United then beat relegation candidates Arsenal a week later.

Their 3-2 away win at Newcastle United (own goal, Trevor Cherry, Carl Harris), on Wednesday 31st March, was followed by a 2-1 home win over Burnley (Duncan McKenzie, Peter Hampton) on Saturday 3rd April, FA Cup Semi-finals' day.

Only 25,384, their third-lowest home crowd of the season, had watched Leeds United move to just five points behind leaders QPR, but with a game in hand.

The 1975-76 title race was turning into a compelling five-way battle.

With the great sides of Liverpool and QPR's greatest-ever teams (up to then) setting the pace, and with Manchester United also short-priced to win the league, due to their games in hand, Derby County had similarly looked very nicely placed to successfully defend their title, as well as also winning the Double with their new-look team.

They *had* finished the previous season brilliantly, after all, to snatch the title away from Ipswich, Liverpool, Everton and Stoke.

Dave Mackay had also signed the great Leighton James from Burnley, back in December, and the Rams had a wonderfully balanced midfield with James, Powell, Gemmill and Rioch supporting their top scorer Charlie George, alongside either Francis Lee, Kevin Hector or Roger Davies up front.

And with their well-tested, regular defence of Thomas, McFarland, Todd and Nish, this was quite possibly Derby's best team of the Seventies.

Any of the top four could take the title with a good run during their last four or five matches.

FIRST DIVISION LEADERS, 3RD APRIL 1976

	PL	W	D	L	F	A	PTS
Queens Park Rangers	38	21	11	6	57	27	53
Liverpool	37	19	13	5	54	27	51
MANCHESTER UNITED	36	20	10	6	62	35	50
Derby County	37	20	10	7	63	46	50
LEEDS UNITED	37	20	8	9	62	40	48

Although their four successive wins had put them back into contention, Leeds United still had too much to do, given the form that the teams above them were in, given their run-ins, also, and given the fact that they had the worst of the top five teams.

Considering the fact that this was the worst Leeds United team for over a decade, and yet they were still title contenders, that was testament and a tribute to the quality and pedigree of their ageing players like Bremner, Clarke, Lorimer, Eddie Gray, Reaney, Madeley and Hunter.

Leeds drew 0-0 away at Tottenham, on Saturday 10th April, with over 40,000 inside White Hart Lane, but on the following Wednesday, they were stunned at home, losing 0-1 against bottom-placed Sheffield United. And that was the end of that.

An Elland Road crowd of under 23,000 had witnessed Alan Woodward's second half goal finally ending Leeds United's very faint hopes of Billy Bremner lifting a third Football League Championship trophy.

Leeds United won 2-1 at home to Manchester City, on the penultimate Saturday of the 1975-76 season, with a new generation of Carl Harris and David McNiven scoring their goals. Top goal-scorer Duncan McKenzie then fired in his seventeenth goal of the season during their 2-1 defeat away at Leicester City, on the following Tuesday, before they lost 2-0 away at league leaders QPR on the final Saturday of the season, to finish fifth in the First Division.

On Saturday 3rd April, with both Manchester United and Derby County so close to a league and cup double, and with Third Division Crystal Palace facing Second Division Southampton at Stamford Bridge, they faced each other at Hillsborough in their FA Cup Semi-final.

55,000 filled the ground, and many United fans were perched in the upper branches of tall trees, behind the Spion Kop End. Tommy Docherty had regretted the fact that this was only a Semi-final, and not the Final.

They were the two top scoring teams in the First Division, and both teams were playing some of the most exciting and attacking football in their clubs' history.

The other Semi-final was sky-high in its degrees of Romance, but nowhere near the high quality of football of this game.

Derby County had lost their top scorer Charlie George, who'd hit his twenty-fourth goal of the season, away at Stoke City, ten days earlier, and he was replaced by Roger Davies, with Francis Lee on the bench. Manchester United still missed Lou Macari, and the eighteen year old midfield worker David McCreery continued in his place.

MANCHESTER UNITED		DERBY COUNTY
Alex Stepney	1	Graham Moseley
Alex Forsyth	2	Rod Thomas
Stewart Houston	3	David Nish
Gerry Daly	4	Bruce Rioch
Brian Greenhoff	5	Roy McFarland
Martin Buchan	6	Colin Todd
Steve Coppell	7	Steve Powell
Sammy McIlroy	8	Archie Gemmill
Stuart Pearson	9	Kevin Hector
David McCreery	10	Roger Davies
Gordon Hill	11	Leighton James
Jimmy Nicholl	12	Francis Lee

Steve Coppell stabbed the ball just over the bar, from Gordon Hill's left-sided corner kick, before Brian Greenhoff tackled Colin Todd, just outside his own area, and he lofted a forward pass for Hill to bring the ball down, ten yards inside the Derby half.

Hill laid the ball outside for Gerry Daly, who ran at David Nish, before, just outside the penalty area, and as Nish slid in to challenge, Daly returned the ball back inside for Hill, just on the edge of the *D*.

Gordon Hill took a touch with his right foot, before left-footed, he curled the ball beyond Moseley's dive, into the top left corner from twenty yards.

Bruce Rioch then played in Roger Davies, inside the United area, but Stepney advanced to parry Davies's shot around his post for a corner.

Into the second half, Rioch linked up well with Leighton James, out on the Derby left, then he crossed from the bye-line. The tall Davies, on the edge of the six yard box, rose and headed the ball goalwards, but straight into Stepney's arms.

Coppell intercepted a defensive clearance by Derby, and he sped away back towards the penalty area, but Steve Powell brought him down, twenty-five yards from goal.

Gordon Hill stood calmly over the ball, and then he drove his left-footed, long range direct free-kick just inside the right post of Moseley's goal.

Gordon Hill was overjoyed, and the whole United team celebrated with him.

Derby could not get the ball off United during the final ten minutes of the match, so confident and controlled was their possession game.

Brian Greenhoff won the ball, just outside his own area, and he fed Stuart Pearson, on the halfway line, before racing forward for the return pass.

Greenhoff teased and turned Rod Thomas, before firing past Moseley, but the ball just shaved the far post, missing the goal by a whisker. It was counter attacking football at its best, and with centre-back Greenhoff both making, and executing the chance, running the full length of the pitch to do so.

That move perfectly emphasized Tommy Docherty's doctrine that United didn't have attackers and defenders, they had eleven attackers with the ball, and eleven defenders without it.

Rioch went blazing in on McIlroy, just before the end, as United played keep-ball by the Derby penalty area, taking him down by his knees. There were angry scenes afterwards, and Rioch should have been sent off, but he wasn't.

As Sammy McIlroy lay on the pitch, hurt, it was a sad end to a great game, but he was all right for their next match.

One week after their wonderful Semi-final win, with Wembley welcoming Manchester United back, after eight years away, the roof fell in on their title hopes.

Mick Lambert, Trevor Whymark and David Johnson all scored, as Ipswich Town had hammered them 3-0 at Portman Road, in front of nearly 35,000.

That result left United five points behind leaders QPR, with only five games remaining, and although they then defeated Everton 2-1 (own goal, McCreery), and also Burnley 1-0 (Macari), over the Easter weekend, they lost twice at the end of April, to both Stoke City and Leicester City.

Manchester United finished the season in third place, only four points behind Champions Liverpool. Despite their disappointment, though, they'd had a superb first season back in Division One.

Manchester United had qualified for Europe, for the first time in eight years, and they'd done so playing the most refreshing, flowing and fair football Old Trafford had seen for nearly a decade. Over their forty-two First Division games, they had had no players sent off, and they'd only incurred seven yellow cards all season.

Furthermore, United's regular first team had an average age of just twenty-four years old, and it was this youthful, ambitious football that was widely expected to roll over the Second Division makeweights, Southampton, at Wembley.

Lou Macari was back to full fitness, and Manchester United were the hottest odds-on favourites to win the FA Cup, since Leeds United back in 1973!

The problem for Manchester United, on Saturday 1st May, the hottest day of 1976, thus far!, Southampton not only had quality of the highest calibre in Channon, Osgood and McCalliog, they had far superior experience.

Southampton's outfield players had played nearly 3,000 combined league matches, while Manchester United's team had played a total of just over 1500. While Manchester United went at Southampton, right from the start, hitting the woodwork on two occasions, while Ian Turner also made three crucial saves, the Saints settled in, and paced themselves in the heat, before Channon and McCalliog both combined in the middle of the park to send Bobby Stokes clear, ten minutes from the end.

Stokes' excellent finish, across the diving body of Alex Stepney, and just inside the far post, won the FA Cup for Southampton, the first, and to date, the only major honour in their club's history.

The massed ranks of Manchester United fans, filling their huge terraced end of Wembley Stadium, stood, still, stunned, silent.

On 24th June 1976, Jimmy Armfield sold his top scorer Duncan McKenzie to Belgian League runners-up, and also European Cup Winners' Cup winners Anderlecht, for a club record transfer fee of £200,000.

That deal balanced out the £240,000 that Armfield had paid to Sheffield United, two weeks earlier, for the greatest player in the Blades' history.

Tony Currie had scored fifty-five goals in 313 league games at Bramall Lane, and he became an instant hero at Elland Road.

Leeds United drew their first game of 1976-77, at home to newly-promoted West Brom, with over 40,000 warmly welcoming Albion's new player-manager Johnny Giles back to Elland Road. Giles was his old superior self, commanding the midfield, with Bremner missing for the home team, and goals from Ally Brown and Tony Brown had given West Brom a 2-0 lead, before substitute Carl Harris and Allan Clarke both then scored to scrape a barely-deserved point for Leeds.

Billy Bremner returned, on Saturday 28th August, at Highfield Road. However, their 4-2 thrashing by Coventry left Leeds United just above the relegation zone, with only two points from three matches. Bremner's influence was more evident a week later, at home to Derby County.

Eddie Gray and Trevor Cherry both scored to give Leeds a good 2-0 win, but after their 1-0 defeat away at Tottenham, Leeds United hosted Newcastle United on Saturday 18th September 1976. Only 35,089 attended the match, totally unaware of its significance in the history of Leeds United Football Club.

LEEDS UNITED		NEWCASTLE UNITED
David Harvey	1	Mick Mahoney
Paul Reaney	2	Irving Nattrass
Frankie Gray	3	Alan Kennedy
Billy Bremner	4	Tommy Cassidy
Paul Madeley	5	Aiden McCaffrey
Norman Hunter	6	Geoff Nulty
Trevor Cherry	7	Stewart Barrowclough
Allan Clarke	8	Graham Oates
David McNiven	9	Micky Burns
Tony Currie	10	Paul Cannell
Eddie Gray	11	Tommy Craig
Carl Harris	12	Ray Blackhall

After Cassidy and Cannell had set Newcastle up for an unlikely 2-0 away win, Leeds came back, and goals from McNiven and substitute Harris secured a home point.

This was Billy Bremner's last ever match for Leeds United. After 586 Football League appearances, and ninety-two goals, he left Elland Road on Thursday 23rd September, for Second Division side Hull City.

Billy Bremner was the greatest player to ever play for Leeds United, and he will never be bettered.

"Although he played in midfield, the ground he covered was phenomenal," Allan Clarke said of his captain. "His determination and enthusiasm were second to none, and many of his goals were crucial, four of them winning Cup Semi-finals."

If you need a televisual example of Bremner's class and excellence, watch for Bremner's equalising goal against Celtic, in the 1970 European Cup Semi-final, in front of over 136,000.

The distance, about twenty-five yards; the ball, heavy as a cannon; the pitch, as heavy as a cow-field; but the pace of the shot was as devastating as a Cristiano Ronaldo free-kick.

He was, possibly, the best British footballer ever.

John Arlott, the greatest-ever BBC Radio Test Match Special commentator, alongside Brian Johnston, once said of Bremner, "if all First Division managers were allowed one player in their team, the idealists would choose George Best; but the realists, they would all choose Billy Bremner."

If I could attempt to adequately equate the skills and presence of Billy Bremner, in my own words, he was a combination of Roy Keane, Roberto Donadoni and Paul Gascoigne, but better than all three at their best.

Bremner was seen as the final piece of the jigsaw at Boothferry Park, to propel Hull City up into the First Division, for the very first time, but Hull were a shadow of the team they were, back in the early Seventies.

As an old footballer, Billy Bremner found the classless scuffles of Second Division football tougher than the top flight class, and Hull City slumped to fourteenth in the table, in spite of his presence.

He managed Doncaster during the late Seventies, and then led them to promotion up to the Third Division in 1981, after Rovers had been re-election candidates just two years earlier. Billy Bremner returned to Elland Road in the mid-Eighties, but like many of their greatest players, it didn't really work out for him in management.

Phil Rostron wrote of Bremner, "to witness Billy Bremner in action was to see combat, tenacity, confrontation, pragmatism, determination, dexterity, flair, athleticism and leadership all rolled into a diminutive frame that once gave birth to a headline, *TEN STONE OF BARBED WIRE.*"

That was possibly the finest ever sentence written about Bremner, and Rostron concluded that "as a footballer, Bremner was simply brilliant."

If I was forced to pick a team from all the players celebrated in this book, Billy Bremner would be the first name on my team-sheet, and my captain.

Billy Bremner scored a total of 115 league and cup goals for Leeds United, from 771 games, second on their all-time appearances list, behind only Jack Charlton.

He died on Sunday 7th December 1997, aged fifty-four, of a heart attack. Less than two years later, a statue of Bremner was unveiled outside the West Stand at Elland Road, on Saturday 7th August 1999, portraying the great man celebrating another Leeds United triumph.

A month after Billy Bremner had left Leeds United, another club legend then departed. Bristol City had paid £40,000 for their defender and ball winner, Norman Hunter. Hunter had played 543 Football League games, and he'd also earned twenty-eight England caps, while at Leeds United.

The Robins had lost their pivotal striker Paul Cheesley, following a career-ending injury against Stoke City, back in August, and subsequently, goals had been scarce.

Despite being involved in a relegation fight, all season, and finishing only one point above the relegation zone, though, Bristol City had kept eleven clean sheets, and conceded only thirty-four goals in the thirty-one First Division matches during which Norman Hunter partnered Gary Collier at the centre of City's defence.

Most First Division Champions in the history of the Football League have conceded more goals than that. Bristol City, with Norman Hunter, finished only seven points behind Leeds United at the end of the 1976-77 season.

Manchester United, for all their top class style of football, back in 1975-76, were in the bottom half of the table by the third week of November 1976, having won only four of their first fourteen First Division games.

A terrible storm that had ripped Stoke City's main stand to the ground, though, provided a fortuitous opportunity for Tommy Docherty. He paid Stoke just £100,000 for their star player Jimmy Greenhoff, who'd scored seventy-six goals in 274 league games at The Victoria Ground.

United's fortunes did not improve, however, and they dropped down to seventeenth place in December, before on Monday night, 27th December 1976, they hosted Everton. With a massive 56,786 crowd inside Old Trafford, Manchester United began their charge back to the top.

MANCHESTER UNITED		EVERTON
Alex Stepney	1	Dave Lawson
Jimmy Nicholl	2	Terry Darracott
Stewart Houston	3	Dave Jones
Sammy McIlroy	4	Mick Lyons
Brian Greenhoff	5	Ken McNaught
Martin Buchan	6	Bruce Rioch
Steve Coppell	7	Andy King
Jimmy Greenhoff	8	Martin Dobson
Stuart Pearson	9	Bob Latchford
Lou Macari	10	Duncan McKenzie
Gordon Hill	11	Ronnie Goodlass

Oh yes, that is *the* Duncan McKenzie who had joined Anderlecht, only six months earlier. It had been a disastrous move, though, and he joined Everton, on Monday 6th December, for £200,000.

After a goalless first half, Stuart Pearson gave Manchester United the lead, with his tenth goal of the season, before Jimmy Greenhoff scored his first goal for the club, sprinting away from Rioch, and then firing past Lawson, from just inside the Everton area. Gordon Hill and Lou Macari completed their brilliant 4-0 win.

Manchester United won fourteen of their next seventeen league and cup matches, rising to fourth in the First Division, and just seven points behind leaders Liverpool, by the middle of March. They also reached the FA Cup Semi-finals, as Lou Macari, Stuart Pearson, Gordon Hill and Jimmy Greenhoff shared twenty-five goals between them, over that dynamic two and a half months.

Gerry Daly had been the first of Docherty's Babes to leave Old Trafford, joining Derby County on Thursday 7th March 1977.

Derby were, amazingly, bottom of the First Division when Daly arrived. He scored seven goals in only seventeen games, though, and finished the season as the Rams' second top scorer, behind Leighton James. As a result of his calm and controlled midfield displays, Derby County rose to fifteenth place by the end of the season, and they'd lost only two of their seventeen matches, following Daly's arrival.

In the UEFA Cup, Manchester United had been given a superb draw in the First round, against Ajax of Amsterdam. Rudi Krol had given Ajax a 1-0 lead from the first leg, but with 59,000 rocking Old Trafford, goals in each half from Macari and McIlroy had brought United storming back to a 2-1 aggregate win.

Another massive crowd of 59,000 then filled Old Trafford for the visit of Juventus, in the Second round. Filled with legends Zoff, Bettega, Tardelli, Causio, Morini, Boninsegna, Gentile, Benetti, Cuccureddu and Scirea, Juventus came and they just hacked away at Manchester United.

The tall Pearson was particularly and nastily targeted by both Scirea and Gentile, but Gordon Hill's excellent explosive volley, from outside Juve's area, won the match 1-0 for United.

Juventus were delighted, though, to have come and absorbed all of United's sustained pressure, yet conceded just the one, solitary, World Class goal.

In the Turin rain, in the second leg, with 65,000 hostile Italians jeering every United touch, Juventus won 3-0, for a 3-1 aggregate victory.

Even so, Manchester United's young team had done themselves proud, back in Europe, but suffering the bad luck of the draw. While QPR and Derby had drawn Brann Bergen, Slovan Bratislava, Finn Harps and AEK Athens, respectively, during the first two rounds, United had drawn two of the greatest ever European clubs.

Leeds United settled for mid-table mediocrity, with centre-back Gordon McQueen even topping their goal-scoring charts, during early April, with just seven league goals. Joe Jordan scored three goals in April, though, to overtake him and finish top with ten goals.

In the FA Cup, however, they'd beaten fellow First Division clubs, Norwich, Birmingham and Manchester City, before winning 1-0 away at Wolves (Eddie Gray), in the Quarter-finals. Then in the Semi-finals, Leeds United faced, yes you know it, Manchester United, a repeat of their epic 1970 Semi-final.

This time, though, at Hillsborough, Manchester United were the much stronger team, and Jimmy Greenhoff and Steve Coppell gave the Reds a 2-0 half-time lead. Allan Clarke's second half penalty gave Leeds United some hope, but Manchester United held on for their 2-1 win, before then beating Liverpool 2-1 (Stuart Pearson, Jimmy Greenhoff), on Saturday 21st May, denying the Reds their historic treble of the First Division Championship, the European Cup, and the FA Cup.

In July 1977, after having an extramarital affair with the wife of Manchester United physiotherapist Laurie Brown, Tommy Docherty was sacked by the club. He had fallen in love with Mary Brown, and they intended to marry, which they did, and they're still very happily married, over thirty-five years later.

Only that Manchester United board could have fired their best manager since Sir Matt, who had won them their first silverware for nine years, and also taken the club back into Europe for the first time in eight years. They were short-priced second favourites for the 1977-78 First Division title.

Tommy Docherty had built this team up from an initial indifferent and inharmonic bunch, that was simply ageing, relegation fodder. Absolute madness! Instead, United had to wait a further sixteen years before winning the league title again. They were absolutely stark raving mad!!

At Leeds United, Jimmy Armfield was steadily managing the club through the transition from Don Revie's ageing team towards a new era. He'd followed up his signing of Tony Currie, by bringing in Arthur Graham from Aberdeen, and then he paid Burnley £175,000 for their diminutive Welsh midfield class act, Brian Flynn.

However, both Gordon McQueen and Joe Jordan left Leeds United, just after Christmas 1977, for a British record combined fee of nearly £850,000. Joe Jordan then became the first British player to score in three World Cup Finals tournaments, for Scotland in 1974, 1978 and 1982.

Jimmy Armfield had replaced the Scot McQueen with Manchester-born Paul Hart, paying Blackpool £300,000 for their six foot two, hardened defender. Despite all these changes, Armfield still managed to keep Leeds United in the top half of the First Division, and only six points behind a UEFA Cup qualifying place.

He'd lost seven big name OLD players, over just two years, and had provided the club with a hell of a lot of money in their bank account.

Leeds United's response was to sack Jimmy Armfield, on Monday 3rd July 1978.

Four years later, they were relegated to Division Two. If you put two and two together, you'll probably make four…

They were all absolutely stark raving mad!!

Jimmy Armfield has now been one of the finest, most knowledgeable, and most respected broadcasters on BBC Radio, for nearly thirty years. He never managed again, though, after his sacking by Leeds United.

Of the Two Uniteds, following the departures of both Tommy Docherty and Jimmy Armfield, the first to leave his club was Paul Reaney.

Reaney had played his 557th and final Football League match for Leeds United, during their 1-2 home defeat to West Ham, on Saturday 8th April 1978.

Paul Reaney was awarded a Testimonial match against Newcastle United, back in May 1976, and he is in third place on Leeds United's all-time appearances list, behind Jack Charlton and Billy Bremner.

He was regarded as the only player who could successfully mark George Best, at his very best, and but for a broken leg suffered near the end of the 1969-70 season, he would have played in the 1970 Mexico World Cup.

Reaney's quality, fitness and pace might have possibly helped England beyond the Quarter-final stage, and he should have become England's regular right back for years to come, under Sir Alf Ramsey.

That he didn't, is an astonishing fact.

Paul Reaney joined Bradford City, for the 1978-79 season, and he played thirty-three Fourth Division matches at Valley Parade, alongside former Leeds United teammates Mick Bates and David McNiven.

Gordon Hill was then sold by Manchester United's Dave Sexton, to Derby County, for £250,000 on Friday 13th April 1978.

He re-joined his former manager Tommy Docherty, and teammate Gerry Daly. Gordon Hill had started exactly one hundred First Division matches for Manchester United, scoring thirty-nine goals. While Sammy McIlroy had been the most accomplished United player since 1975, Hill was certainly their most dynamic.

Allan Clarke played his last match for Leeds United on Saturday 29th April 1978, a goalless draw away at QPR. He had scored one hundred and ten First Division goals in just 270 starting appearances for Leeds. Not the most awe-inspiring stats, I'd agree, that really don't adequately express how great he was, so I'll try a little harder.

Allan Clarke had scored a career total of 167 First Division goals, in 391 games, with Leeds, Leicester and also Fulham, and during the six seasons between 1969 and 1975, when he and Leeds United were both at their very best, he scored 128 league and cup goals from 286 games.

Sniffer was much more than a goal-scorer, though, creating as many goals for his team as he'd scored. He and Mick Jones are right up there amongst the very greatest of all attacking partnerships in the history of football, and he set up dozens of goals for Jones, Lorimer and Bremner, while helping Leeds United to reach six Cup Finals, three First Division runners-up places, and, of course, one League Championship winning season, within those six seasons, while other, more prolific strikers had won nothing. He'd also scored ten goals during his nineteen games for England.

Allan Clarke was, in my eyes, the greatest centre forward of the Seventies. He had the pedigree, the passion and the panache. He had the pace, the power and the presence. He had the agility, balance and grace of a ballet dancer, and yet he had the strength and tenacity of a street fighter.

His final season at Elland Road was virtually written off, due to injury, and he scored only three goals in eight First Division games. Clarke then joined Fourth Division Barnsley, during the Summer of 1978, but even at the age of thirty-two, he was Barnsley's second highest goal-scorer, with twelve goals from 34 games, as the Tykes gained promotion up to the Third Division, *for the first time in twenty years.*

Allan Clarke rejoined Leeds United, in September 1980, as their new manager, following Jimmy Adamson's resignation, but he was sacked in June 1982, having been unsuccessful in preventing Leeds from being relegated down to the Second Division.

Alex Stepney was the last member of Manchester United's 1968 European Cup Final team to leave Old Trafford. He played his 433rd and final First Division match, for United, during their 2-1 away defeat at Wolves, on the last day of the 1977-78 season.

His contract was cancelled in February 1979, having dropped behind Paddy Roche, and then Gary Bailey, as Dave Sexton's first-choice goalkeeper for United.

Behind Peter Schmeichel, Alex Stepney is the most successful goalkeeper in Manchester United's history.

Stuart Pearson missed all of the 1978-79 season, due to injury, and having fallen behind Joe Jordan as Manchester United's spearhead centre forward, in any case, he then signed for Second Division West Ham United in 1979.

Pearson had scored fifty-five goals in 139 league games, in his four full seasons at Old Trafford, but just like Allan Clarke, he was much more of a team player than a selfish striker, and he'd laid off as many goals for Hill, Coppell, McIlroy, Greenhoff, Macari and Daly, as he scored himself.

Pancho played in West Ham's 1980 FA Cup Final 1-0 victory over Arsenal, setting up Trevor Brooking's winning goal. He then struggled for a place, with youngsters like Paul Goddard emerging in the Hammers' attack, though, and only occasionally played during West Ham's 1980-81 Second Division title winning season, although he did come on as a substitute as they lost the 1981 League Cup Final to Liverpool.

Stuart Pearson eventually retired, aged just thirty-two, one year later, in 1982.

Peter Lorimer played his 450th and final First Division match for Leeds United, during their 3-0 home win over Birmingham City, on Saturday 30th September 1978.

His contract was cancelled in March 1979, and he joined Fourth Division York City for the 1979-80 season, scoring eight goals in 29 games.

Lorimer returned to Leeds United during the early Eighties, at thirty-seven years of age, when he was actually older than their present manager, Eddie Gray. His *hot shot* class still shone in the Second Division, though, and he played for nearly three more years at Elland Road, before he finally retired in 1986, just before his 40th birthday.

Peter Lorimer scored a total of 238 goals from 676 league and cup matches for Leeds United, a club goal-scoring record that still stands today, and always will.

It should have been 239 goals, though, after his perfectly-good eighteen yard strike should have been the goal that finally won Leeds United their European Cup in 1975.

David Harvey left Leeds United in 1980, moving to the NASL, having played 276 First Division matches. He also returned to Elland Road, though, during the 1982-83 season, when Leeds United were in the Second Division, and he played a further seventy-three league games over the next two seasons.

Paul Madeley finally played his last ever game for Leeds United against Arsenal, on Saturday 8th November 1980. But Arsenal won 5-0.

For a player who, for the first eleven years of his Leeds United career, was never a first-choice player in any outfield position, Madeley had played 711 league and cup matches, and he was a substitute on only thirteen occasions.

Furthermore, all but four of his 528 league starts were First Division games, and he'd also scored thirty-four goals. Although Paul Madeley is famous for playing in every position in the team, for me, he was always best as a defender.

Despite not being his club's first choice right back, he was often picked as England's right back, even when Paul Reaney was available, because Sir Alf Ramsey liked his all-round footballing abilities.

His performance against Poland, in October 1973, was of a highly polished international standard. He was faultless at the back, supporting the front six regularly, and he never gave the ball away.

Paul Madeley was one of the four best centre backs to ever play for Leeds United. He was also one of the two best right backs to ever play for Leeds United, and he was one of the two best left backs to ever play for Leeds United. He was also a very dignified, disciplined and elegant player, who was, as part of a defence renowned for being "dirty", rarely suspended or injured.

Trevor Cherry was "the new boy" in Leeds United's classic team. He was appointed club captain, by Jimmy Armfield, following Billy Bremner's departure in 1976.

He became one of Leeds United's most consistent and superior players, as the team went into a comparative decline, during the late Seventies. He played 399 First Division matches for Leeds, between 1972 and 1982, and, including his time at Leeds Road, he played a career total of 476 First Division matches.

Cherry also played twenty-seven games for England, between 1976 and 1980, and eventually he captained his country on one occasion, under Ron Greenwood. He also managed Bradford City, between 1982 and 1987, giving the club their best-ever on-field season in 1984-85, as they romped to the Third Division title.

On the final day of that season, however, during a supposedly celebratory match against Lincoln City, Bradford City suffered one of the worst-ever footballing tragedies.

Valley Parade's Main Stand was destroyed by fire, during the game, and 56 fans died terrible deaths.

Bradford's manager Trevor Cherry attended the funeral of every one of them.

Sammy McIlroy had played 342 league games for Manchester United, between 1971 and 1982, scoring fifty-seven goals, but after Ron Atkinson brought in Bryan Robson and Ray Wilkins, he was surplus to requirements, and he was transferred to Stoke.

McIlroy went on to play a further 133 First Division matches for Stoke City, before leaving them after they were relegated in 1985. After his retirement, he managed Macclesfield Town for seven years, before being appointed as manager of his native Northern Ireland. He led Northern Ireland from 2000 to 2003, but this wasn't the Northern Ireland of Jennings, Rice, Cassidy, McIlroy, Dougan or George Best, and he left after they'd finished bottom of their 2004 European Championship qualifying group, having failed to win a single match, and also losing 0-1 at home to Armenia.

Sammy McIlroy became manager of Morecambe in 2005-06, though, and he led the Shrimpers to promotion into The Football League, after his first full season in charge.

Eddie Gray was a player who was very much a part of that great Leeds United team of the late Sixties. Skill-wise, at his very best, he was as good as George Best, he really was that good. After their superb, but ill-fated 1969-70 season, though, he had some heartbreaking bad luck with injuries.

Even so, due to Jimmy Armfield's faith in his ability, after he'd effectively been put out to grass by the club, Eddie Gray played 454 league games for Leeds United, scoring fifty-two goals, and 429 of those games were First Division matches.

However, just like Trevor Cherry, Gray also became a more influential and consistent performer as Leeds turned into a less-feared team.

During his first ten years at Elland Road, Eddie Gray had played only 209 First Division games, between 1965 and 1975, and before his twenty-seventh birthday.

However, during the seven years after his twenty-seventh birthday, between 1975 and 1982, Eddie Gray played 220 First Division games. Furthermore, he'd played 143 First Division games after his thirtieth birthday.

And amongst a Leeds United team that was renowned for their dirty tackling, and also harassing and intimidating referees, a reputation that was totally exaggerated, Eddie Gray was *never* booked.

Steve Coppell's wing partnership with Gordon Hill, between 1975 and 1977, was the most exciting of the whole decade, for any First Division team. With the wonderfully skilled Sammy McIlroy and Gerry Daly, and then Jimmy Greenhoff, in their attack, that was a brief golden period of Manchester United's history, and often unjustly overlooked, before they embarked on fifteen years of head tennis, until Giggs, Cantona, Kanchelskis and Scholes finally appeared during the early Nineties.

He remained at Old Trafford, after all of their "potential gold mine" had either moved on, or been moved on, eventually playing 322 First Division games for Manchester United, and scoring fifty-three goals. He was the best of the bunch, and he also played forty-two games for England, as a United player, but it was playing for his country that eventually brought about a premature end to his career.

Coppell was the victim of an atrocious high tackle from Hungary's thug-defender, Jozsef Toth, that completely shattered his knee during England's World Cup qualifying match against Hungary, in November 1981.

With Steve Coppell at his best in Spain '82, England might well have won that World Cup, which they weren't far short of doing, anyway, and he would have been up there with Best, Charlton, Law, Cantona and Giggs, at the very, very top of Manchester United's Hall of Fame.

Coppell made a brief comeback, and he even started United's 1983 League Cup Final defeat to Liverpool, but his knee yet failed again. After another operation, though, he was finally forced to retire, in October 1983, at just twenty-eight years old.

Lou Macari moved to Swindon Town, in July 1984, as their new player-manager, having played 329 league games for Manchester United, and scoring 79 goals.

By 1981, though, Macari had become a peripheral figure at Old Trafford, playing just twenty-five First Division games over three seasons up to 1984.

He stuck in, though, for the love of his club, and he'd even showed up occasionally at right back, playing the pass of the match to win one game.

Alongside Martin Buchan, Lou Macari was the other link between United's 1968 European Cup winners and their 1993 Premier League Champions, having played with both George Best and Bryan *Captain Marvel* Robson.

Leeds United and Manchester United had always had a rivalry.

To suggest that it had increased, during the Glam Soccer period of 1967 to 1976, would be naïve folly. During the mid-Sixties, though, when Denis Law came off the pitch at the end of a particularly physical match against Leeds, with his tough, red cotton shirt ripped to shreds and hanging off his body by a thread, there was an innocent equality that had fired up both teams.

With the Charlton brothers, Bobby and Jack, the two players with the most appearances for their respective teams, there was also a family connection, very rare these days, that ran strongly through the blood of both clubs. Even when Manchester United were relegated to Division Two, in the very same season as when Leeds United won the title, it was simply a footballing matter. Football fans all over England were dismayed after Manchester United, who they'd adopted as their second team following the Munich disaster, were going to be playing Second Division football.

By 1977, though, things had changed. It could be that Leeds United, after their dominance of the English game for seven or eight years, had rubbed up too many clubs the wrong way. Manchester United, though, after their youthful revolution, and their subsequent ascendancy over their Yorkshire rivals, may have attained some kind of subliminal superiority complex, as an initial defence mechanism.

Not once, though, since Leeds United's promotion to the First Division back in 1964, had they ever assumed any natural superiority over any other First Division team.

They were certainly bitter at losing certain matches, but as a team, they treated Liverpool with exactly the same respectful rivalry as they'd treated Manchester City, Derby County, Arsenal, and Manchester United.

Games were still won on the football pitch, and titles were won and lost on games, and of course, they were dirty at times. Leeds United had pushed the line, regarding the laws of the game, but it was the same for every opponent, until 1973-74, when they suddenly became angels.

There was, however, something about the transfers of Joe Jordan, and then Gordon McQueen, from Leeds United to Manchester United, at the end of 1977, that suggested attitudes between the two teams had become influenced by something more than just football results.

When Gordon McQueen felt that Leeds United were "a club going nowhere", and that "99% of players want to play for Manchester United, and the rest are liars," and he'd implied that he was just moving to "a bigger club," then something had changed.

What exactly did Gordon McQueen win at Manchester United, anyway?

First, it rubbed Leeds United supporters up the wrong way, in the very same way that their team had often done, albeit on the pitch, under Don Revie's management. Secondly, it gave Manchester United an arrogance, that many of their supporters eventually adopted, and have never lost.

As their arrogance, and their sense of superiority over Leeds United, then continued over Everton, over Manchester City, and over Arsenal, then over Newcastle United, over Nottingham Forest, before finally, they assumed an unpalatable, arrogant superiority over Liverpool, five times Champions of Europe.

Back in the day of long shorts and rugby-style shirts, Arsenal supporters never exhibited banners or flags proclaiming the number of titles that their team had won, nor taunting rivals Aston Villa on the number of years since they'd last won the title, or even the number of titles they'd won.

While many, many fans still hate Leeds United for their slightly unfair "dirty Leeds" image, most fans now hate Manchester United for the apparent arrogance of some of their supporters, a sometimes bitter arrogance that's a million miles away from the warm support, for which their fans were originally, and internationally famed.

While Coventry City, because of their flamboyant and care-free attacking style of pure football in the late Sixties, had became many fans' *second team*, Manchester United, likewise, with their joyous, fresh-faced and exciting twenty-one year old midfield quartet, became many fans' *second team*, during the mid-Seventies.

That has never been the case, since.

John Charles aside, that Leeds United team of 1969-73, each and every one of them, was the best outfield player, in their position, above any other Leeds United player.

Paul Reaney was the club's greatest-ever right back. Jack Charlton and Norman Hunter were their greatest-ever central defensive partnership, and Terry Cooper was their greatest-ever left back. Eddie Gray was their greatest-ever left winger, while Billy Bremner and Johnny Giles were not only Leeds United's greatest-ever midfield partnership, but also, quite possibly, the greatest midfield partnership in the long history of the Football League.

Peter Lorimer was their greatest-ever player to wear the number seven shirt, while Allan Clarke and Mick Jones were their greatest-ever attacking partnership. Paul Madeley was also, likewise, a better footballer than any Leeds United player since then, and if either Reaney, Hunter or Cooper had not been around, then he'd have also been the greatest-ever player in their respective positions.

Trevor Cherry was also not very far behind, and while both Gary Sprake and David Harvey were often ridiculed by purists for their lack of class at the very highest level, they were never outside of the top six or seven First Division goalkeepers.

I always said that if Leeds United could have signed Lev Yashin, or even Dino Zoff, as they could today, their first team would have been an artwork worthy of hanging on the National Gallery walls.

Manchester United were a different story, even if part of the same story.

While there is no doubt that George Best, Denis Law and Bobby Charlton would all make an all-time United eleven, it's probable that Paul Scholes and Roy Keane would keep out both Pat Crerand and Nobby Stiles.

Also, Peter Schmeichel would just nose in front of Alex Stepney. And Ryan Giggs, Gary Neville, Denis Irwin, Steve Bruce, Gary Pallister, Rio Ferdinand and Nemanja Vidic have all left greater legacies than the remainder of Manchester United's players from between 1967 and 1974.

Of Tommy Docherty's team, Martin Buchan was the one defender who wouldn't look out of place in Alex Ferguson's mean, ruthless back fours.

Gordon Hill, though, in spite of his total dynamic equality to Ryan Giggs, had lacked the longevity of the Welsh wing wizard's career, while Steve Coppell, speedy and sparkling out on the right wing, and possessing the pinpoint accuracy of David Beckham's crosses, lacked both Becks' bending, match-winning twenty-five yard free-kicks, and his media profile that extended Beckham's superstardom far beyond football.

Despite Brian Greenhoff, Martin Buchan, Sammy McIlroy, Gerry Daly, Stuart Pearson and Lou Macari all being completely excellent for United, their club board's idiocy in sacking their greatest manager, between Sir Matt and Sir Alex, over a purely personal matter, had deprived them of the real success they might, and probably would have achieved, after 1977.

What Tommy Docherty's Manchester United team did, though, during those three seasons from 1974-77, was very, very special. They put gladness back in the hearts and smiles on the faces of football fans, not only at Old Trafford, but in the living rooms, and on the school fields, all over the country.

That Leeds United team from between 1968 and 1975, though, was the greatest Leeds United team in their club's history. Moreover, it was one of the greatest ever teams in English First Division or Premier League history. A Tale of Two Uniteds should really be a tale of how two great English teams became loved, and really loved, by English football fans, forever.

Instead though, and due to no fault of those teams that played the football, both United clubs remain the most disliked, and the most hated in the English game, by a vast majority of opposing fans.

It was *the worst of times, but it was also the best of times* for those two great clubs. They did win only three league titles between them during the Glam Soccer years, but they finished in the top three on seven other occasions during those seasons, when twenty-two other teams had fielded their greatest teams playing at the very peaks of their powers.

Many books have been written and about the Greatness of Leeds United, Manchester United, George Best, Billy Bremner, Allan Clarke, Jack Charlton and Denis Law. But they were only so great because of the greatness of their opponents.

Bestie was so great because he regularly scored against Roy McFarland, Colin Todd, Tommy Smith, Emlyn Hughes, Bobby Moore, Frank McLintock, Peter Simpson, and John McGrath.

It didn't really matter to him.

Bremner and Giles were so great because they commanded midfields and matches in almost every game, against Colin Bell, Tony Currie, Martin Peters, Alan Ball, Alan Mullery, Ian Callaghan, John Hollins, Peter Storey, Keith Weller and Archie Gemmill.

But they never, ever got the better of Micky Horswill.

Allan Clarke and Mick Jones were so great because they were the very best against Dave Mackay, Mike England, Brian Labone, Allan Hunter, Kevin Beattie, George Curtis, Mike Doyle, Tommy Booth, and even West Brom's fouling full backs Williams and Fraser.

Jack Charlton and Norman Hunter were among the greatest-ever central defensive partnerships because they kept out Denis Law, Greavsie, Geoff Hurst, Big Chiv, Ossie, Doog, King John, Supermac, Mike Channon, the Golden Boy Trevor, Worthington, Jimmy Greenhoff and even the King of Highbury Charlie George.

Books have been written about all of them, because they were the best.

But they were only the best because of the very best.

It was the worst of times, sometimes; but mostly *it was the best of times.*

BIBLIOGRAPHY:

After Extra Time (Dirty Leeds' Uncut) by Robert Endeacott (2012)
Alan Mullery: The Autobiography by Alan Mullery with Tony Norman (2006)
Arsenal; The Official Illustrated History 1886-2009 by Phil Soar and Martin Tyler (2009)
An Autobiography by Denis Law (1979)
An Autobiography by Bob Paisley (1983)
An Autobiography by Peter Shilton (2004)
Association Football Know the Game, in collaboration with The Football Association
(E.P. PUBLISHING 1970)

Best and Edwards: Football, Fame and Oblivion by Gordon Burn (2006)
Bestie; The authorized biography of George Best by Joe Lovejoy (1998)
Big Chiv: My Goals In Life by Martin Chivers with Paolo Hewitt (2009)
Bill Nicholson; Football's Perfectionist by Brian Scovell (2010)
Biting Talk: Norman Hunter my autobiography by Norman Hunter with Don Warters (2004)
Bonzo: An Autobiography by Billy Bonds (1988)
Both Sides of the Border; My Autobiography by Archie Gemmill (2006)
Burnley Football Club; The Complete A to Z by Dean Hayes (1999)

Cloughie: Walking On Water by Brian Clough with John Sadler (2002)
Colin Bell: Reluctant Hero by Colin Bell with Ian Cheeseman (2005)
A Complete Who's Who of Newcastle United compiled by Paul Joannou (1983)

The Damned Utd by David Peace (2006)
Derby County: Champions Of England 1971-72 & 1974-75 by Edward Giles (2005)
The Doc; Hallowed Be Thy Game. My Story by Tommy Docherty (2006)
Doog by Derek Dougan (1980)

Everton Greats by Ken Rogers (1989)
Everton; The People's Club by David Prentice (2007)

Fanthology Edited by Robert Endeacott and Graeme Garvey (2004)
The Football Grounds of Great Britain by Simon Inglis (1987)
The Football League Match By Match 1962/63 Edited by Tony Brown (2010)
The Football League Match By Match 1966/67 Edited by Tony Brown (2011)

The Football League Match By Match 1967/68 Edited by Tony Brown (2010)
The Football League Match By Match 1968/69 Edited by Tony Brown (2010)

The Ghost of '66: Martin Peters the Autobiography by Martin Peters with Michael Hart (2006)
The Glory Years: Manchester City 1966-70 by David Clayton and Simon Thorley (2004)
Goodison Maestros; The 50 Greatest Everton players since 1945 by Dean Hayes (2003)
Got, Not Got by Derek Hammond and Gary Silke (2011)
Greavsie: The Autobiography by Jimmy Greaves (2003)
Interesting, Very Interesting by Barry Davies (2007)
Jack Charlton: The Autobiography by Jack Charlton with Peter Byrne (1996)
The Jimmy Hill Story; My Autobiography by Jimmy Hill (1998)
Just Like My Dreams; My Life With West Ham by John Lyall (1989)

The King; My Autobiography by Denis Law (2003)

Leeds United's 'Rolls-Royce': The Paul Madeley Story with David Saffer (2003)
Liverpool: My Team by Steve Heighway (1977)

Matches of the Day 1958-83 by Derek Dougan and Patrick Murphy (1984)
The Mavericks: English Football When Flair Wore Flares by Rob Steen (1994)
Mick Channon; The Authorised Biography by Peter Batt (2004)
Mike Summerbee: The Autobiography by Mike Summerbee with Jim Holden (2008)
My Autobiography by Bobby Robson (1999)
My Autobiography by Kevin Keegan (1997)

Newcastle United: Fifty Years Of Hurt by Ged Clarke (2007)
1966 And All That; My Autobiography by Geoff Hurst (2001)
No Glossing Over It: How Football Cheated Leeds United by Gary Edwards (2011)

Of Fossils & Foxes: The official definitive history of Leicester City Football Club
By Dave Smith and Paul Taylor (2001)
One Hump or Two? : The Frank Worthington Story by Frank Worthington
with Steve Wells & Nick Cooper (1994)
Only A Game by Eamon Dunphy (1976)
Only The Best Is Good Enough; The Howard Kendall Story by Howard Kendall and Ian Ross
    (1991)

A Photographic History of English Football by Tim Hill (2005)
The Pride and Glory; Official 120 Year History of Burnley Football Club by
Edward Lee and Phil Whalley (2002)
A Quality Player- The Life and Career of Tony Currie by Elliot J. Huntley (2007)

Red Or Dead by David Peace (2013)
Right Back to the Beginning: Jimmy Armfield The Autobiography by
Jimmy Armfield with Andrew Collomosse (2004)
Rothmans Football Year Book 1970-71
Rothmans Football Year Book 1971-72
Rothmans Football Year Book 1972-73

Rothmans Football Year Book 1973-74
Rothmans Football Year Book 1974-75
Rothmans Football Year Book 1975-76
Rothmans Football Year Book 1976-77
Rothmans Football Year Book 1977-78
Rothmans Football Year Book 1978-79
Rothmans Football Year Book 1979-80

Sheffield United: Thirty Memorable Games from the Seventies by Nick Udall (2011)
Sniffer: The Life And Times of Allan Clarke with David Saffer (2001)
Stokoe, Sunderland And '73 by Lance Hardy (2009)

Trevor Francis: anatomy of a £1 million player by Rob Hughes with Trevor Francis (1980)
United; The First 100 Years... and more; The Official History of
Newcastle United 1882 to 2000 by Paul Joannou (2000)

Waggy's Tales: Dave Wagstaffe's Four Decades at Molineux by Dave Wagstaffe (2008)
We Are The Damned United: The Real Story of Brian Clough at Leeds United by Phil Rostron
    (2009)
West Bromwich Albion; The First Hundred Years by G. A. Willmore (1979)
West Ham United; 101 Beautiful Games by Martin Godleman (2008)
With Clough By Taylor by Peter Taylor (with Mike Langley) (1980)

Thank you also to Charles Dickens' *A Tale Of Two Cities*, The Poems of Wilfred Owen, Siegfried Sassoon's *War Poems*, William Wordsworth's *The Prelude*, JRR Tolkien's *The Lord of the Rings*, Noddy Holder and Jim Lea's *My Friend Stan*, Sandy Linzer's *You Can Do Magic*, Billy Bragg's *God's Footballer*, and Freddie Mercury's *Bohemian Rhapsody*, from which very small references or quotes were used to greatly enhance this book.

Lovingly dedicated to Gordon West, Geoff Strong, Brian Labone, Mike Doyle, Brian Greenhoff, Frank Munro, Ernie Machin, Ralph Coates, Dave Wagstaffe, Neil Young and Ron Davies, all of whom very sadly died while I was writing this book.

Max will have some great men, and a superb football team to join to help him towards becoming a truly great player.

http://glamsoccer.co.uk/
Also find GLAMSOCCER on twitter and facebook.

Produced with generous help and assistance from Jonathan Young (especially), and Paul Town (Stadium Portraits Paul Town) for all his great help in finding a cover for the book. Nigel Spicer (Nigel's Web-space), Gary Silke (GOT, NOT GOT), Darren Iley, Richard Grace, Dave Bissmire, Gerry Boland, Derek Marlow, Stuart Randall, Matt Addison, Mark Hardie, Paul Linnell, Jane Furphy, all at LUFCTALK, Janet Henshaw, Phil Rogers, Gordon Ballantyne, Andy and Angie Ledger, Steve Iley, Dave Walker, Richard Tunstall, Gerald Casey, Dave Iley, Neil Cooper, Neil Hance and Logan Iley.

Lightning Source UK Ltd.
Milton Keynes UK
UKOW02n1549110314

227956UK00001B/27/P